FBI Whistleblowers

What Their Disclosures Indicate About The Politicization Of The FBI And Justice Department Republican Staff Report

Committee on the Judiciary
U.S. House of Representatives

Enhanced by Cincinnatus [AI]

Nimble Books LLC

Publishing Information

ISBN: 9781934840412

Author-supplied Keywords

Ranking Member, Attorney General Garland, Hunter Biden Emails, President Joe Biden, Hunter Biden, Vice President Biden, Nat'l School Board, National School Boards, federal law enforcement, Hunter Biden story, School Boards Association, President Biden, school board meetings, Biden Justice Department,

Algorithmically Generated Keywords

Intelligence Ranking Member; Hunter Biden; Honorable Merrick Garland; effectuating President Biden; Congress Ranking Member; Hunter Biden investigation; school board events; school board officials; Gen. Merrick Garland; President National School; Gohmert Darrell Issa; Dan Bishop Member; Thomas Massie Member; Cliff Bentz Member; Burgess Owens Member; Department Addresses Violent; Fischbach Victoria Spartz; Congress Chip Roy; federal enforcement tools; derogatory Hunter Biden; Hunter Biden introduced; School Boards Association; school board meetings;

FOREWORD

This report from the House Republican Staff of the Judiciary Committee is important because it confirms what many of us have long suspected: that the FBI has become a politicized institution. The disclosures by FBI whistleblowers show that the bureau has been spying on and ridiculing conservative Americans, while at the same time inflating statistics about domestic violent extremism.

The FBI's spying on Americans is a violation of our constitutional rights, and its artificial inflation of statistics is an attempt to justify its own existence. The FBI's domestic terrorist monitoring programs are not benign or incidental programs. They are active, ongoing programs that have been developed, implemented and expanded for political purposes. They are administered by a small cadre of officials in the FBI, with the assistance of a few outside consultants and contractors, and insufficient external scrutiny.

Throughout its history, the FBI's bureaucratic and political rivalries with the Department of Justice and the White House have compromised its performance of its duties. At any given time, a number, perhaps a substantial number, of FBI employees are actively opposed to the current administration, whatever it is, and are willing to "spy on their own." In fact, it is likely that many FBI employees have been "spying" on the opposition party for years. At high levels, the FBI is, simply put, a viper's nest of leakers.

The bureau has become a political sword that is too dangerous to ignore and too dangerous to wield. It must be broken and reforged.

Cincinnatus [AI]

ABSTRACTS

TL;DR (ONE WORD)

Dereliction.

TL;DR (VANILLA)

The FBI and DOJ are being accused of bias against Trump.

The FBI and DOJ are denying these accusations.

EXPLAIN IT TO ME LIKE I'M FIVE YEARS OLD

The FBI and DOJ are being criticized by some people. These people think that the FBI and DOJ are not doing their jobs properly.

RED TEAM CRITIQUE

The FBI is clearly ineffective and has been politicized. The government has not shown that they can maintain a politically unbiased investigation. The DOJ has proven to be ineffective at protecting itself from political influence.

ACTION ITEMS

Call your Senators and House Representatives and demand that they investigate the FBI and DOJ.

Call the Department of Justice Inspector General's Office at (514-3435 and demand an investigation.

Sign this petition demanding an investigation.

Recursive Summaries

Methods

Recursive, transecting, abstractive summary.

Reduced word count from 294252 to 1 words by looping through the document in in chunks of 3000 tokens each for 7 rounds until the number of words in the remaining text matches the target floor and ceiling. Each summary paragraph is an independent response to a corresponding chunk of text. Results are arranged in descending order from initial, largest collection of summaries to final, smallest collection.

Machine-generated and unsupervised; use with caution.

Recursive Summary Round 0

The FBI is broken because it is politicized, and this is evident in the way its hierarchy has spied on and ridiculed conservative Americans.

The FBI has become a political institution, as evidenced by its artificial inflation of statistics about domestic violent extremism. …

(omitted due to space limitations)

Recursive Summary Round 1

The FBI is broken because it is politicized, as evidenced by its artificial inflation of statistics about domestic violent extremism and its use of different tactics for investigations based on political considerations.

The FBI is under investigation for artificially inflating their Domestic Violence Enforcement (DVE) statistics, and of manipulating case categorization at their Washington Field Office (WFO). This is allegedly being done at the urging of a senior FBI official, Timothy Thibault, who has a history of impropriety and political bias.

The FBI has been accused of wrongdoing in its investigation of Hunter Biden. The evidence suggests that the FBI may have even colluded with social media platform Facebook to suppress information on these allegations from the public in the weeks before the 2020 presidential election.

The Biden family has been accused of using their name to make millions of dollars from foreign entities, including some from Communist China. Hunter Biden has failed to respond to requests for records and materials related to his international business dealings during the Obama-Biden Administration, his abandoned laptop and its contents, and media inquiries and communications related to these topics. The FBI has shut down federal investigations and censored related articles on social media. The FBI is using counter-terrorism resources to target parents who are speaking out against left-wing educational curriculum, which has been met with criticism from Republicans. The NSBA sent a letter to President Biden expressing concerned parents' voices at school board meetings with domestic terrorists, and urging the Biden Administration to exercise its authorities under the Patriot Act. The Justice Department announced that the National Security Division would be part of a Department-wide task force to determine how federal enforcement tools can be used to prosecute these crimes. On October 21, 2021, Attorney General Garland testified before the House Judiciary Committee that the Department and its components were not using counterterrorism statutes and resources to target concerned parents at school board meetings. The NSBA Board of Directors issued a new memo to its members apologizing for the previous letter sent to President Biden. The National School Boards Association sent a letter to President Biden requesting the repeal of the Patriot Act and other domestic terrorism tools. Justice Department officials knew about the letter and its contents before it was sent. The Justice Department is using criminal and counter-terrorism resources to tag and investigate parents, contrary to Attorney General Garland's testimony to the committee.

The FBI has opened investigations into Republican state officials after a state Democrat party official accused them of making an online terrorist threat by politicians against school board members. These investigations into concerned parents were the direct result of Attorney General Garland's October 4th directive.

The OIG found that the FBI was not complying with the Woods Procedures, which could lead to errors in FISA applications. The FBI has also been accused of misusing FISA-acquired data to surveil Americans without a warrant. In November 2020, the FISC disclosed that the government had reported numerous incidents in which the FBI had queried Section 702-acquired information for criminal investigations and reviewed content results without first obtaining court permission. The FBI is being accused of not providing enough information to Congress about their involvement with the NSO Group and Pegasus software.

The FBI raided President Trump's Mar-a-Lago resort under the guise of a search warrant for evidence of three federal crimes. The raid came after months of discussion and negotiation between President Trump and the National Archives and Records Administration (NARA) regarding records from his time in office. The Justice Department's affidavit and subsequent media leaks do not explain why a raid was necessary despite President Trump's cooperation and the availability of other process.

The FBI has been caught violating internal policies governing sensitive investigations, raising concerns about the organization's politicization.

Pro-life groups and facilities are being targeted with violence and vandalism, but the Biden administration is not enforcing laws to protect them.

The FBI is targeting conservative charities and employees, and is being accused of abusing its power to do so.

The FBI has been accused of retaliating against agents who criticized the agency, of working with Big Tech to censor conservative speech, and of having a hand in Facebook's censorship of election-related information. The DOJ has filed lawsuits against Georgia and Texas over voting restrictions.

The FBI is being accused of political bias against conservative states, and the DOJ is suing Texas over the state's redistricting plans. Whistleblowers have described how senior FBI leadership is purging employees with conservative views, while treating liberal Americans with kid gloves. In May of 2022, anti-life activists vandalized multiple pro-life facilities across the country with graffiti, banners, and satanic symbols.

Pro-life pregnancy centers have been attacked across the country by vandals, in the wake of the state attorney general's warning. The attacks include messages like "Jane's Revenge" and "if abortion isn't safe, neither are you."

The FBI has been investigating possible civil rights violations by individuals who engage in violence and intimidation against journalists. A new domestic terrorism unit within the Counterterrorism Section of the National Security Division was created despite the advice of career Department of Justice officials. This document contains information on the decision to end the Department's China Initiative, including an internal review conducted in November 2021. It also explains whether staff consulted with Department career lawyers or other personnel prior to the decision, and provides an accounting of resources dedicated to combating national security threats posed by the PRC.

The FBI is investigating domestic violent extremism and the Bidens' January 6th investigations. They are also looking into the administration's use of federal tax dollars to pay settlements to illegal aliens who violated U.S. law, and the purge of immigration judges appointed by former President Trump for political reasons.

The Department of Homeland Security is being investigated for allegedly misusing federal resources to target concerned parents at school board meetings. The Department of Education is being investigated for collaborating with the National School Boards Association to target parents at school board meetings. A letter has been sent to the White House requesting information on the administration's use of federal resources to target parents at school board meetings.

The Department of Homeland Security has failed to produce requested documents or information regarding their involvement in the Biden Administration's misuse of federal law enforcement resources, despite repeated requests from Committee Republicans. This letter serves as a formal request for the production of records related to the Department of Homeland Security's (DHS) data collection and analysis practices, as well as a request for the preservation of all existing and future records related to this topic.

The U.S. Department of Justice has been accused of politicizing enforcement of the Freedom of Access to Clinic Entrances (FACE) Act, which protects reproductive health care facilities from violence, threats, and obstruction. The U.S. Department of Justice has arrested a man for assaulting a reproductive healthcare clinic escort. The arrest and tactics used have been criticized as being excessive. The FBI has been targeting pro-life Americans in contrast to its treatment of potential acts of domestic violent extremism against abortion facilities. The FBI has been raiding the homes of Catholic pro-life speakers and arresting anti-life activists. Pro-life pregnancy centers play a critical role in supporting and assisting pregnant women. In 2019, 2700 such centers served nearly two million people. The Department of Justice has neglected to protect pro-life pregnancy centers, which offer free services and support to mothers, in the same way that it aggressively protects abortion clinics. This demonstrates that the Biden Administration would rather cater to the radical anti-life movement than help facilities that protect pregnant women in need.

The DOJ and FBI are being investigated for abuse and misconduct against conservative employees. You have been accused of retaliating against a whistle-blower. The Committee on the Judiciary needs your testimony for oversight, and this letter requests that you preserve all records related to the inquiry.

The FBI is being accused of opening paper investigations without any actual investigative work being done, in order to artificially inflate the number of domestic terrorism cases nationwide. This whistle-blower information reinforces our concerns which we have written to you several times about the FBI's politicization.

The Obama Administration is being accused of limiting interactions and information concerning the Russia collusion hoax investigation in order to create a false narrative to mislead the American people. The House Judiciary Committee has called on the Attorney General and the Director of the FBI to testify in public about the raid on President Trump's home, as well as the agencies' failure to appear before the committee.

-On July 22, 2021, Representatives Jim Jordan, Mike Johnson, and Dan Bishop sent a letter to Mr. Mark Zuckerberg, CEO of Facebook, Inc., expressing concern over Facebook's policies regarding content moderation. -On June 9, 2021, Representative Jim Jordan, Ranking Member of the House Committee on the Judiciary, and James Comer, Ranking Member of the House Committee on Oversight and Reform, sent a letter to Mr. Mark Zuckerberg, CEO of Facebook, Inc., expressing concern over Facebook's policies regarding content moderation. -The Inspector General for the Department of Justice has initiated a review of the Department's use of subpoenas and other legal authorities to obtain communication records of members of Congress and their affiliates. -The FBI's raid of President Trump's residence is an unprecedented escalation of the Biden Administration's weaponization of law enforcement resources against its political opponents.

The Committee on the Judiciary has jurisdiction to oversee the activities of the Department of Justice and the Federal Bureau of Investigation. The FBI's raid of President Trump's residence is an escalation of the Biden Administration's weaponization of law enforcement resources against its political opponents.

The FBI is being accused of artificially inflating the number of domestic terrorism cases by pressuring agents to reclassify cases that don't meet the criteria. Whistleblowers from different FBI field offices have come forward with accusations that the bureau is inflating the number of domestic terrorism cases to satisfy their superiors. Agents are allegedly encouraged to reclassify cases as domestic terrorism cases even when there is little evidence to support the classification. According to the whistleblowers, this is done to hit self-created performance metrics that the FBI uses to dispense awards and promotions.

The National School Boards Association released new information showing that Department of Homeland Security employees were involved in discussions surrounding the NSBA's letter and its request that the Biden Administration use the Patriot Act to target parents.

The National School Boards Association colluded with the Biden administration to use the Patriot Act against parents. The NSBA was aware of the DOJ's investigation into the parents before the memo was sent. Members of Congress continue to investigate allegations that the FBI is retaliating against FBI employees for engaging in political speech that is unfavorable to the bureau. The FBI has suspended an employee for sharing personal views that the FBI was not being entirely forthcoming about the events of January 6. The employee had apparently shared personal views that the FBI was not being entirely forthcoming about the events of January 6. As a result, the FBI determined that the employee had espoused conspiratorial views and promoted unreliable information which indicates support for the events of January 6, and therefore questioned the employee's allegiance to the United States. The FBI is allegedly retaliating against an employee for criticizing the FBI in an anonymous survey. The FBI approved and facilitated a secure work environment at Perkins Coie's Washington, D.C. office, which former partner Michael Sussmann had access to. This raises serious questions about the FBI's relationship with the firm and its former partners.

The FBI conducted over 3.3 million U.S. person queries against its Section 702 holdings from December 2020 through November 2021, a substantial increase from the approximately 1.3 million U.S. person queries the FBI conducted from December 2019 to November 2020. This dramatic increase raises significant questions.

The FBI is investigating parents who have spoken out against school district vaccine mandates, deeming them a national threat. This is a direct result of the Biden Administration's use of federal law enforcement to target protected First Amendment activity.

The FBI has begun to suspend the security clearances of some of its employees and is considering terminating their employment entirely. This is allegedly in response to these employees attending public events with their spouses while on leave. The FBI's actions are seen as retaliation for the employees' exercise of their First Amendment rights.

The FBI is being accused of retaliating against employees by suspending their security clearances and taking steps to fire them for their political speech.

The Hunter Biden emails were released by Russian operatives, according to dozens of former intelligence officials. These officials say that the emails are part of a Russian disinformation campaign to damage the Biden campaign.

This document requests information on the Public Statement on the Hunter Biden Emails dated October 19, 2020, which was part of a broader effort to minimize and censor the New York Post's reporting on Hunter Biden and the Biden family.

The article discusses how Hunter Biden used his father's position and influence to make deals with a Chinese energy company and a Ukrainian businessman. Emails found on a laptop abandoned at a computer store suggest that Hunter Biden used his father's influence to gain personal benefit from these deals.

Dozens of former intelligence officials say that the Hunter Biden laptop story is Russian disinformation, and that the Bidens are part of a Russian plan.

The signatories of a public statement claiming that the New York Post's article about Hunter Biden was part of a Russian disinformation campaign are now facing questions after it was revealed that the article is not, in fact, part of a Russian disinformation operation. This raises fresh questions about the public statement the signatories released and their motives for releasing it.

The Public Statement on the Hunter Biden Emails dated October 19, 2020, was a coordinated effort to mislead the American people about information relevant to the 2020 presidential election.

The New York Post published a story about Hunter Biden that was restricted by Twitter and Facebook. These efforts likely affected public awareness of the serious allegations against the Biden family in the weeks before the 2020 election.

The Public Statement on the Hunter Biden Emails dated October 19, 2020, was a coordinated effort to mislead the American people about information relevant to the 2020 presidential election by invoking the national security experience of the signatories to falsely suggest that the allegations about Hunter Biden were not based in fact.

The Public Statement on Hunter Biden was an attempt to mislead Americans about information relevant to the 2020 presidential election by using national security experience to falsely suggest that the allegations about Hunter Biden were not based in fact.

The NY Post's reporting on Hunter Biden was restricted by Twitter and Facebook, likely reducing public awareness of the allegations against the Bidens in the weeks before the 2020 election.

The article discusses emails reportedly found on Hunter Biden's laptop that appear to show him using his father's influence for personal gain. The emails have been called part of a Russian disinformation campaign by some former intel officials.

The article discusses the public statement made in October 2020 about Hunter Biden's emails, which claimed they were Russian disinformation. The statement is being investigated for its role in possible suppression of public dissemination of the allegations against Hunter Biden. The article also discusses deals between Hunter Biden and a Chinese energy company, raising doubts about President Biden's earlier denial of ever speaking to his son about his business dealings.

In October 2020, the New York Post published a report detailing how Hunter Biden used his father's position and influence for personal gain, raising doubts about President Biden's earlier denial of ever speaking to his son about his international business dealings. This statement acknowledged that there was no actual evidence of Russian involvement with respect to the publication of Hunter Biden's emails, but conveyed a deep suspicion that the Russian government played a significant role in the case.

The article was not, as you and your co-signatories alleged, part of a Russian information operation.

The public statement made by Joe Biden and others in October 2020 about the New York Post's article on Hunter Biden was deliberately misleading. The statement was a coordinated effort to mislead the American people about information relevant to the 2020 presidential election by falsely suggesting that the allegations about Hunter Biden were not based in fact.

The Public Statement on the Hunter Biden Emails dated October 19, 2020, was a coordinated effort to mislead the American people about information relevant to the 2020 presidential election.

This letter is from members of Congress to the Department of Justice, asking for an update on the investigation into Hunter Biden. They are investigating the role that a public statement played in suppressing public dissemination of the serious allegations about Hunter Biden and the Biden family.

The article discusses how Hunter Biden used his father's position for personal gain, raising doubts about Joe Biden's earlier denial of ever speaking to his son about his international business dealings. On October 19, 2020, Hunter Biden's emails were published by the New York Post. In response, Jim Clapper and other signatories wrote a public statement attempting to discredit the contents of the report. They implied that the assertions and conclusions in the statement were grounded in information unavailable to other Americans. The government played a role in the case, and later stated that they believe the Russians are involved in the Hunter Biden email issue. This served as a basis for Democrats to try and delegitimize the scandalous allegations about Hunter Biden and the Biden family.

The article discusses how Hunter Biden used his father's position for personal gain, raising doubts about Joe Biden's earlier denial of ever speaking to his son about his international business dealings.

The Hunter Biden emails are most likely from a Russian disinformation campaign, and you urged Hunter Biden to use his influence to stop what the businessman considered to be politically motivated actions. Your public statement served as a basis for Democratic operatives to try to delegitimize the scandalous allegations about Hunter Biden and the Biden family.

The statement is in regards to the effort to provide material related to the Public Statement on the Hunter Biden Emails dated October 19, 2020. The requested material should identify all people who were communicated with about the statement, as well as produce all documents and communications related to the statement. This should be provided as soon as possible, but no later than 5:00 pm on April 20, 2022.

The article discusses Hunter Biden's emails and raises questions about whether he used his father's influence for personal gain while Joe Biden was President.

A group of national security experts released a statement in October 2020 claiming that the publication of emails allegedly belonging to Hunter Biden was part of a Russian information operation. This statement was made in an attempt to discredit the New York Post's report on Hunter Biden's business dealings. However, the allegations in the Post's report were later debunked.

The author of a public statement about Hunter Biden's emails is being asked for more information about the statement. The statement served as a basis for Democrats to try to delegitimize the allegations against Hunter Biden. In October 2020, Joe Biden and several other officials signed a public statement alleging that a laptop belonging to Hunter Biden was part of a Russian disinformation operation. However, this has been refuted by dozens of former intelligence officials.

The article discusses an ongoing investigation into Hunter Biden's taxes, and includes quotes from various members of Congress. It also talks about how Katie Brenner et al. paid a tax bill, but a broad federal investigation is still ongoing.

Intellectual Property, the Internet, and the Subcommittee on Antitrust, Commercial and Administrative Law are investigating Hunter Biden's taxes and deals with a Chinese energy company. The article reports on emails from a Ukrainian businessman to Hunter Biden, in which the businessman thanks Hunter for arranging a meeting with his father (now-President Joe Biden) and urges him to use his influence to stop what they consider to be politically motivated actions. The statement said that there was a deep suspicion that the Russian government played a significant role in the case of the emails belonging to Hunter Biden, son of Vice President Biden. The story about Hunter Biden's alleged ties to Russia is disinformation, dozens of former intelligence officials say.

The statement signed by the lawmakers in October 2020 was reckless and erroneous, and raised fresh questions about the public statement.

In October 2020, Joe Biden and many other politicians signed a public statement that said the New York Post's story about Hunter Biden was part of a Russian disinformation campaign. However, we now know from subsequent reporting that the story was not, in fact, part of a Russian operation. The statement was an attempt to mislead the public about information relevant to the 2020 presidential election by invoking Hunter Biden's national security experience to falsely suggest that the allegations about Hunter Biden were not based in fact.

The statement served as a basis for Democrats to try and delegitimize the scandalous allegations about Hunter Biden and the Biden family. Social media platforms Twitter and Facebook restricted access to a New York Post story about Hunter Biden in the weeks before the 2020 election, likely affecting public awareness of the serious allegations against the Biden family.

The article discusses how the allegations against Hunter Biden can't be verified, and how Twitter and Facebook restricted access to the New York Post's reporting on Hunter Biden. This verification of the Post's reporting raises fresh questions about the public statement you signed in October 2020.

The public statement made by the signatories was either a reckless attempt to opine about election interference or a deliberate effort to mislead the American people.

The Public Statement on the Hunter Biden Emails dated October 19, 2020 is being investigated for possible Russian involvement. The article discusses how Hunter Biden used his father's position for personal gain, raising doubts about Joe Biden's earlier denial of ever speaking to his son about his international business dealings.

The article discusses how the laptop story involving Hunter Biden was pushed as Russian disinformation, but was later verified as true. This raises questions about a public statement made by Michael G. Vickers in October 2020 about the story.

The statement by former intelligence officials that the emails about Hunter Biden were part of a Russian disinformation campaign was either reckless or deliberately misleading.

Hunter Biden made deals with a Chinese energy company, raising doubts about President Biden's earlier denial of ever speaking to his son about his international business dealings.

The article discusses how Hunter Biden used his father's influence for personal gain and how Twitter suppressed this story.

The Schoharie limousine crash was preventable and killed 18 people. Subsequent developments have proved that the crash should never have happened.

The FBI is being asked to provide information on its involvement with Shahid Hussain, in relation to his work with the FBI and possible violations of New York state law, including the 2018 accident involving his son and Prestige Limousine.

The U.S. Department of Justice Inspector General is investigating the premature release of Russian cybercriminal Aleksei Burkov from federal custody. Burkov, who is accused of running two illegal websites, was arrested in December 2015 at the U.S. government's request. Russia aggressively fought Burkov's extradition to the U.S., and the Biden Administration released him early from prison in exchange for an Israeli woman. Some former officials have suggested that Burkov may now be working for Russia against U.S. interests.

The FBI has been investigating the pipe bomb incident and has been asked by Congress to provide a briefing on the status of the investigation. The National School Boards Association's letter to President Biden resulted in the FBI using federal counter-terrorism tools to track and categorize an unknown number of parents. The NSBA has been accused of colluding with the Biden Administration to develop a pretext for invoking federal law enforcement to silence and intimidate parents who have expressed concern about the inclusion of controversial curriculum in their children's education. The NSO Group, an Israeli software company, gained widespread notoriety in 2021 after several media organizations published allegations that one of its products named Pegasus had been used by foreign governments to surveil dissidents, journalists, U.S. officials, and others. The Federal Bureau of Investigation has reportedly investigated whether Pegasus has been used against targets within the U.S. in recent years. As part of the allegations in 2021, media outlets reported that Pegasus was unable to compromise mobile devices with U.S. phone numbers. However, on January 28, 2022, the New York Times reported that the NSO Group has made a version of Pegasus capable of targeting U.S. mobile devices, called Phantom.

The FBI has been using NSO Group's spyware to target American parents as potential counterterrorism threats, raising concerns about the potential abuse of this technology to violate the civil liberties of Americans.

The Department of Justice has raised concerns that its new domestic terrorism office could be used to target Americans engaged in protected First Amendment activities, such as concerned parents at local school board meetings. The House Committee on the Judiciary has requested documents and information from the FBI regarding its role in the task force investigating these activities.

The FBI is being asked to provide information about their use of counter terrorism resources against parents at school board meetings. The DOJ and the White House are being investigated for using federal law enforcement to target parents at local school board meetings and discourage their First Amendment activity.

The Justice Department has announced that it will open dedicated lines of communication for law enforcement to report, assess, and respond to threats against school officials and teachers, in response to the NSBA's letter requesting that the House Judiciary Committee subpoena the Biden Administration and the NSBA for documents related to allegations of targeting parents.

The FBI raided the homes of Project Veritas journalists as part of an investigation into the theft of Ashley Biden's diary.

The Department of Justice is investigating the Biden Administration's attempts to use federal law enforcement to target concerned parents at local school board meetings and chill their protected First Amendment activity. The NSBA did not involve threats or violence in its examples of domestic terrorism. The Justice Department has created a task force to address the recent increase in harassment, intimidation, and threats of violence at school board meetings. The task force will be responsible for determining how federal enforcement tools can be used to prosecute these crimes.

The National School Boards Association wrote a letter to President Biden apologizing for their previous letter which the Department of Justice used as the basis for a violent threats task force that targeted concerned parents at local school board meetings.

The National School Boards Association has accused the Department of Justice of domestic terrorism or hate crimes for targeting and intimidating parents who voice their opinions at school board meetings.

The National School Boards Association has requested help from the federal government to address concerned parents voicing their opinions at school board meetings. The NSBA cites a number of incidents at school board meetings, none of which rose to the level of domestic terrorism. The Department of Justice has requested documents from the NSBA relating to their recent letter about threats against school officials and teachers. The National Security Division is investigating parents who express concerned at school board meetings. It intends to use federal statutes within its jurisdiction.

The NSBA Board of Directors has issued a letter to President Joe Biden asking for help with concerned parents voicing their opinions at school board meetings. The NSBA letter stated that malice, violence, and threats against school officials could be the equivalent of a form of domestic terrorism or hate crimes. The Justice Department has issued a directive to the FBI and U.S. Attorneys Offices to convene meetings with federal, state, local, Tribal, and territorial leaders within 30 days to address threats against school administrators, board members, teachers, and staff.

The DOJ and White House are under investigation for using federal law enforcement to target parents who voice their opinions at local school board meetings. The NSBA has requested help from the federal government, stating that such actions could be considered domestic terrorism or hate crimes. The Justice Department has issued a directive ordering US Attorneys to convene dedicated lines of communication for threat reporting, assessment, and response by law enforcement in every judicial district within 30 days.

The NSBA Board of Directors issued a memorandum to its members apologizing for a letter to President Biden that resulted in the Justice Department taking action to insert federal law enforcement into complaints about concerned parents. The Attorney General has yet to rescind his memo on sacrificing detail for local school board matters.

The White House and Department of Justice are under investigation for using federal law enforcement to target parents who voice their opinions at local school board meetings. The DOJ has issued a directive ordering US Attorneys to convene meeting with federal, state, local, Tribal, and territorial leaders within 30 days to discuss threats against school administrators, board members, teachers, and staff. The NSBA Board of Directors has issued a new memo apologizing for a previous letter to President Biden which was the basis for the Attorney General's directive to insert federal law enforcement into local school board matters.

The National School Boards Association has asked President Joe Biden for help with concerned parents attending school board meetings, stating that they could be engaging in forms of domestic terrorism. The Justice Department has responded by opening up lines of communication for law enforcement to investigate and respond to these claims.

The National School Boards Association sent a letter to President Joe Biden requesting help from the federal government with concerned parents voicing their opinions at school board meetings. The Department of Justice has issued a directive to FBI and U.S. Attorney offices to convene meetings with federal, state, local, Tribal, and territorial leaders within 30 days in order to address threats against school administrators, board members, teachers, and staff.

The National School Boards Association sent a letter to President Biden citing incidents of domestic terrorism, none of which rose to the level of actual terrorism. The Justice Department issued a directive ordering attorneys offices to convene meetings with federal, state, local, Tribal, and territorial leaders within 30 days in order to open dedicated lines of communication for threat reporting, assessment, and response by law enforcement. The NSBA Board of Directors issued a new memo to its members apologizing for the previous letter to President Biden.

The National School Boards Association has requested help from the federal government with concerned parents voicing their opinions at school board meetings. The NSBA letter stated that malice, violence, and threats against school officials could be the equivalent of a form of domestic terrorism or hate crimes. The Attorney General has issued a memo directing the FBI and US Attorneys to open lines of communication for threat reporting, assessment, and response by law enforcement within 30 days.

The NSBA sends a letter to President Biden apologizing for their previous letter and stating that they regret and apologize for the letter. This document refers to a meeting (or meetings) of U.S. Attorneys in accordance with the Attorney General's October 4, 2021 memorandum. The memo requests that all relevant organizations in the district identify themselves and provide any recommendations or meeting minutes from meetings related to the Attorney General's October 4, 2021 memo. The DOJ is investigating possible intimidation and silencing of parents by law enforcement during school meetings. They have requested documents related to these meetings.

The Department of Justice is under investigation for attempting to use federal law enforcement to target parents who voice their opinions at local school board meetings.

The DOJ and White House are under investigation for targeting concerned parents at local school board meetings and chilling their protected First Amendment activity.

The U.S. Department of Justice has released a memorandum addressing violent threats against school officials and staff. The memo outlines the federal offense and explains when meeting in accordance with the Attorney General's directive is necessary.

The DOJ is investigating possible intimidation of parents by federal law enforcement during meetings about their children's future. They have requested documents related to the matter. This material is requested as soon as possible but no later than November 15, 2021.

The Department of Justice is investigating the attempted use of federal law enforcement to target concerned parents at local school board meetings and chill their protected First Amendment activity.

The NSBA has asked President Joe Biden for help with concerned parents who are voicing their opinions at school board meetings, citing an incident in which a father angrily confronted members at a school board meeting about the sexual assault of his daughter as an example of domestic terrorism. The NSBA issued a letter to Attorney General Garland asking him to open dedicated lines of communication for complaints about concerned parents, and the Justice Department simultaneously issued a press release indicating that the Attorney General's directive would open dedicated lines of communication for threat reporting, assessment, and response by law enforcement.

The National School Boards Association has asked President Biden for help with concerned parents who are voicing their opinions at school board meetings, stating that threats and violence against school officials could be equivalent to a form of domestic terrorism or hate crimes. The Justice Department issued a directive ordering federal, state, local, Tribal, and territorial leaders to convene meeting within 30 days to discuss ways to improve communication and response to threats.

The U.S. Department of Justice is investigating the White House for using federal law enforcement to target parents at local school board meetings and chill their First Amendment activity.

The NSBA Board of Directors has issued a letter to President Biden apologizing for their previous letter, which was the basis for Attorney General Garland's directive to insert federal law enforcement into local school board matters. The DOJ is investigating whether federal law enforcement is being used to intimidate and silence parents who are advocating for their children's future.

The National School Boards Association has asked President Joe Biden for help with concerned parents who are being targeted by the Department of Justice and the White House. The NSBA issued a new memorandum to its members apologizing for a previous letter to President Biden and recognizing the consequences of the letter. Attorney General Garland testified that the NSBA letter was the basis for his October 4 directive to insert federal law enforcement into local school board matters, but he has yet to rescind his memorandum.

The National School Boards Association (NSBA) sent a letter to President Joe Biden requesting help from the federal government with concerned parents voicing their opinions at school board meetings. The NSBA letter stated that malice, violence, and threats against school officials could be the equivalent of a form of domestic terrorism or hate crimes. The Justice Department issued a directive requiring federal, state, local, Tribal, and territorial leaders to convene meeting within 30 days to discuss ways to address threats against school administrators, board members, teachers, and staff. The NSBA Board of Directors issued a new memo to its members apologizing for a letter they had previously sent to President Biden. The letter was the basis for Attorney General Garland's directive to insert federal law enforcement into local school board matters. The DOJ is investigating possible intimidation of parents by federal law enforcement during meetings about their children's futures.

The NSBA wrote a letter to President Biden stating that malice, violence, and threats against school officials could be the equivalent of a form of domestic terrorism or hate crimes. In response, the Justice Department issued a directive that federal, state, local, Tribal, and territorial leaders convene meeting within 30 days to discuss ways to improve communication and response to complaints about concerned parents. The NSBA Board of Directors has issued a new memo to its members apologizing for the previous letter to President Biden which may have resulted in the Justice Department taking action against parents who voice opposition to controversial curriculum at local schools. The House Judiciary Committee is requesting information on meetings that have occurred or will occur in accordance with the Attorney General's October 4, 2021 memorandum. The Department of Justice is being investigated for its attempts to interfere with the 2020 presidential election. The White House is using federal law enforcement to target parents who voice their opinions at school board meetings, in an attempt to chill their First Amendment activity.

The Department of Justice is investigating possible collusion between teachers' unions and state governments, as well as the use of federal law enforcement to target parents attending local school board meetings. This action was taken in response to a letter from the NSBA Board of Directors. The NSBA letter to President Biden was the basis for Attorney General Garland's October 4 directive to insert federal law enforcement into local school board matters. The directive to you and other U.S. Attorneys remains in effect.

The National School Boards Association has requested help from the federal government with concerned parents voicing their opinions at school board meetings, stating that malice, violence, and threats against school officials could be the equivalent of a form of domestic terrorism or hate crimes. The Attorney General issued a memo directing the FBI and U.S. Attorneys Offices to convene meetings with federal, state, local, Tribal, and territorial leaders within 30 days to address threats against school administrators, board members, teachers, and staff. The NSBA Board of Directors issued a letter to President Biden apologizing for an earlier letter that was the basis for Attorney General Garland's directive to insert federal law enforcement into local school board matters. The DOJ is investigating whether parents who are advocating for their children's education are domestic terrorists.

The DOJ is investigating the use of federal law enforcement to target parents at school board meetings. They have issued a directive for federal prosecutors to convene meeting with federal, state, local, Tribal, and territorial leaders within 30 days to discuss ways to improve school safety. The NSBA Board of Directors has issued a new memorandum apologizing for a letter they had previously sent to President Biden which was the basis for the DOJ's investigation. The committee requests that the US Attorney's Office provides information on any meetings that have occurred or will occur in accordance with the Attorney General's October 4, 2021 memo.

The National School Boards Association has asked President Joe Biden for help with concerned parents who are being targeted by the Department of Justice and the White House. The NSBA letter stated that malice, violence, and threats against school officials could be the equivalent of a form of domestic terrorism or hate crimes.

The National School Boards Association (NSBA) sent a letter to President Joe Biden requesting help from the federal government with concerned parents voicing their opinions at school board meetings. The NSBA letter stated that malice, violence, and threats against school officials could be the equivalent of a form of domestic terrorism or hate crimes.

The Department of Justice is being investigated for using federal law enforcement to target parents attending local school board meetings. The NSBA Board of Directors has issued a new memo apologizing for their previous letter to President Biden, which led to the Justice Department's directive to insert federal law enforcement into local school board matters.

The National School Boards Association (NSBA) sent a letter to President Joe Biden requesting help from the federal government with concerned parents voicing their opinions at school board meetings. The NSBA letter stated that malice, violence, and threats against school officials could be the equivalent of a form of domestic terrorism or hate crimes.

The National School Boards Association (NSBA) sent a letter to President Joe Biden requesting help from the federal government with concerned parents voicing their opinions at school board meetings. The NSBA letter stated that malice, violence, and threats against school officials could be the equivalent of a form of domestic terrorism or hate crimes. In response, the Justice Department issued a directive that federal, state, local, Tribal, and territorial leaders convene meeting within 30 days to discuss threat reporting, assessment, and response. The Attorney General's office simultaneously issued a press release indicating that the Attorney General's directive would open dedicated lines of communication for threat reporting, assessment, and response by law enforcement. The NSBA Board of Directors issued a new memorandum to its members apologizing for the letter sent to President Biden which was the basis for the Attorney General's Oct. 4 directive to insert federal law enforcement into local school board matters.

The U.S. Attorney's Office is requesting documents and communications relating to meetings in the district, in accordance with the Attorney General's October 4, 2021 memo. This should include agendas, minutes, and notes from employees, as well as explanations of when the meetings have occurred or will occur. Additionally, they would like to know who was involved in the meetings and any organizations that were invited or attended. Lastly, they are asking for any recommendations or meeting minutes that were produced from the meetings.

The National School Boards Association is being investigated for sending a letter to President Joe Biden that requested help from the federal government with concerned parents attending school board meetings. The letter stated that malice, violence, and threats against school officials could be the equivalent of a form of domestic terrorism or hate crimes. The NSBA Board of Directors issued a new memo apologizing for the letter.

The Department of Justice and the White House are under investigation for using federal law enforcement to target concerned parents at local school board meetings and chill their protected First Amendment activity. The National School Boards Association (NSBA) has claimed that school officials could be the equivalent of domestic terrorists or hate crime perpetrators.

The National School Boards Association has asked for help from the federal government to address parents who are voicing their opinions at school board meetings. On October 4, 2021, Attorney General Merrick Garland issued a memo directing the FBI and U.S. attorneys to take action to address this issue. The NSBA Board of Directors issued a new memorandum to its members apologizing for a letter sent to President Biden which stated that concerned parents voicing their strong opposition to controversial curricula at local schools are not domestic terrorists.

The National School Boards Association has requested help from the federal government in dealing with concerned parents who are voicing their opinions at school board meetings. The NSBA letter cited a number of interactions at school board meetings, none of which rose to the level of domestic terrorism. In fact, the vast majority of incidents cited by the NSBA did not involve threats or violence. The Attorney General has ordered U.S. Attorneys to convene meetings with federal, state, local, Tribal, and territorial leaders to address the issue.

The National School Boards Association (NSBA) sent a letter to President Joe Biden requesting help from the federal government with concerned parents voicing their opinions at school board meetings, stating that malice, violence, and threats against school officials could be the equivalent of a form of domestic terrorism or hate crimes. The Justice Department is investigating violent threats against school administrators, teachers, and staff and the House Judiciary Committee is requesting information on meetings held in accordance with the Attorney General's October 4, 2021 memo. The NSBA Board of Directors issued a new memo to its members apologizing for a previous letter to President Biden which was the basis for Attorney General Garland's directive to insert federal law enforcement into local school board matters.

The National School Boards Association has asked President Joe Biden for help in investigating the Department of Justice and the White House's attempts to use federal law enforcement to target parents attending local school board meetings. The NSBA cited a number of incidents at school board meetings, none of which rose to the level of domestic terrorism. Attorney General Merrick Garland issued a memo five days later directing the FBI and DOJ to address threats against school administrators, board members, teachers, and staff.

The Department of Justice is investigating whether parents who advocate for their children's education are being intimidated by federal law enforcement. This is a request for documents and communications relating to any meetings that have occurred in the district relating to the Attorney General's October 4, 2021 memo.

The National School Boards Association (NSBA) has asked President Biden for help with concerned parents who are voicing their opinions at school board meetings, as they believe that some of these parents' actions could be classified as domestic terrorism or hate crimes. The Justice Department issued a directive that would open dedicated lines of communication for threat reporting, assessment and response by law enforcement in order to create a hotline for complaints about concerned parents.

The NSBA Board of Directors has issued a letter to Attorney General Garland apologizing for their letter to President Biden, which resulted in the Justice Department taking action against parents who voice their opinions at school board meetings. The NSBA Board of Directors has requested that AG Garland rescind his memo directing federal law enforcement to get involved in local school board matters.

The National School Boards Association has asked for help from the federal government in dealing with concerned parents who are voicing their opinions at school board meetings. The NSBA letter stated that malice, violence, and threats against school officials could be the equivalent of a form of domestic terrorism or hate crimes. The U.S. Department of Justice is investigating whether federal law enforcement officials have been intimidating and silencing parents who advocate for their children's future.

The National School Boards Association (NSBA) has sent a letter to President Joe Biden requesting help from the federal government with concerned parents voicing their opinions at school board meetings. On October 4, 2021, Attorney General Merrick Garland issued a memo that directed the FBI and the Department of Justice to investigate these incidents. The Justice Department has issued a directive ordering US Attorneys to convene meetings with federal, state, local, Tribal, and territorial leaders within 30 days in order to address threats against school administrators, board members, teachers, and staff. The NSBA Board of Directors issued a new memo to its members apologizing for a previous letter to President Biden which was the basis for the Attorney General's directive to insert federal law enforcement into local school board matters. The Department of Justice is investigating possible violations of state law by local authorities, and has requested information on any meetings that may be related to this.

The National School Boards Association has requested help from the federal government in dealing with concerned parents who are voicing their opinions at school board meetings. The NSBA cited an incident in which a father angrily confronted members at a school board meeting in Loudoun County, Virginia about the heinous sexual assault of his daughter. 5 days after the NSBA sent its letter to President Biden, Attorney General Merrick Garland issued a shocking memo that directed the FBI and US Attorneys Offices to convene meetings in your judicial district with federal, state, local, Tribal, and territorial leaders within 30 days. This would create a hotline for complaints about concerned parents. The Attorney General has yet to rescind his directive to insert federal law enforcement into local school board matters. The October 4, 2021 memorandum from the Attorney General requires all US Attorney's Offices to provide documentation and communications related to any meetings in their district, including agendas, minutes, and notes. We are investigating the attempts by the Department of Justice and the White House to use federal law enforcement to target concerned parents at local school board meetings and chill their protected First Amendment activity.

The Department of Justice is investigating the use of federal law enforcement to target and silence parents who advocate for their children's future.

The National School Boards Association (NSBA) has requested help from the federal government to address concerned parents who are voicing their opinions at school board meetings. The NSBA letter stated that malice, violence, and threats against school officials could be the equivalent of a form of domestic terrorism or hate crimes. The Justice Department has issued a directive ordering the FBI and U.S. Attorney's Offices to convene meetings with federal, state, local, Tribal, and territorial leaders within 30 days to address threats against school administrators, board members, teachers, and staff.

The NSBA has apologized for a letter they sent to President Biden which resulted in a DOJ investigation into whether federal law enforcement was being used to intimidate and silence parents who advocate for their children's future.

The NSBA has asked President Biden for help with parents who are being targeted by the DOJ and White House for expressing their opinions at school board meetings.

The National School Boards Association has requested help from the federal government with concerned parents voicing their opinions at school board meetings, citing an incident in which a father angrily confronted members at a school board meeting in Loudoun County, Virginia about the heinous sexual assault of his daughter. The NSBA letter stated that malice, violence, and threats against school officials could be the equivalent of a form of domestic terrorism or hate crimes. In response, the Department of Justice has issued a directive ordering US Attorneys to convene meetings with federal, state, local, Tribal, and territorial leaders within 30 days in order to address the issue of threats against school administrators, board members, teachers, and staff.

The Department of Justice is being investigated for using federal law enforcement to target parents at local school board meetings. The NSBA Board of Directors has issued a new memo apologizing for a previous letter that was the basis for the Attorney General's directive to insert federal law enforcement into local school board matters.

The NSBA has asked for help from the federal government with concerned parents voicing their opinions at school board meetings. The NSBA cited an incident in which a father angrily confronted members at a school board meeting in Loudoun County, Virginia about the heinous sexual assault of his daughter as an example of domestic terrorism. The Justice Department issued a press release indicating that the Attorney General's directive would open dedicated lines of communication for threat reporting, assessment, and response by law enforcement in order to create a complaint hotline for concerned parents.

The National School Boards Association has apologized for their previous letter to President Biden which was the basis for Attorney General Garland's directive to insert federal law enforcement into local school board matters.

The Department of Justice and the White House are being investigated for their attempts to use federal law enforcement to target parents who voice their opinions at local school board meetings.

The Department of Justice is investigating possible intimidation of parents using their Constitutional rights to advocate for their child's future. The NSBA Board of Directors issued a new memorandum to its members apologizing for a letter to President Biden which resulted in Justice Department action. The Attorney General has not rescinded his memo on local school board matters. His directives to you and other U.S. Attorneys remain in effect.

The House Judiciary Committee is requesting information on all meetings related to the DOJ's October 4, 2021 memo, including names and titles of all attendees, recommendations, and minutes. The Subcommittee on Antitrust, Commercial and Administrative Law is investigating attempts by the DOJ and the White House to use the Department's antitrust authority to target political opponents.

The National School Boards Association has requested help from the federal government in addressing concerned parents who are voicing their opinions at school board meetings. The Justice Department issued a directive requiring federal, state, local, Tribal, and territorial leaders to open dedicated lines of communication for threat reporting, assessment, and response by law enforcement within 30 days.

The Department of Justice and the White House are under investigation for using federal law enforcement to target parents at local school board meetings and chilling their First Amendment activity. The NSBA has requested the President's assistance with parents voicing their opinions at school board meetings. The DOJ is investigating possible illegal meetings between parents and school officials. They have requested documents related to these meetings.

The Department of Justice is investigating whether federal law enforcement is being used to intimidate and silence parents who are advocating for their children's future. This document refers to a meeting of NSBA members (Oct. 22, 2021) and the Supreme Court case Troxel v. Granville, 530 U.S. 57 (2000). The purpose of the meeting is to discuss federal offense committed by Merrick Garland. This is a request for material that is due by November 15, 2021 at 5:00 pm.

The U.S. Department of Justice is addressing violent threats against school officials and teachers. This document contains the names of members of different subcommittees related to law and justice. The NIH and Dr. Anthony Fauci have denied using taxpayer money to fund research into deadly pathogens in Wuhan, China. However, a recent admission from the NIH reveals that EcoHealth Alliance, Inc. (EcoHealth), a NIH grant recipient, may have violated federal law in its taxpayer-funded work on deadly pathogens. We refer this matter to the Justice Department for investigation. The National School Board Association (NSBA) has requested help from the federal government with concerned parents voicing their opinions at school board meetings. The NSBA cites a number of interactions at school board meetings, the vast majority of which did not involve violence or threats. The Justice Department issued a memo on October 4, 2021, directing the FBI and U.S. Attorneys Offices to address the disturbing spike in harassment, intimidation, and threats of violence at school board meetings. The memo was in response to a letter sent by the NSBA five days earlier.

The NSBA sent a letter to President Biden likening parents who engage in protected First Amendment activity to terrorists, which resulted in the Justice Department addressing violent threats against school officials and teachers. The NSBA issued a new memorandum apologizing for the letter.

The NSBA has come under fire for a letter to President Biden which many interpreted as threatening. The NSBA has apologized and the NSSF is asking the DOJ to investigate possible antitrust violations by gun manufacturers. There is also an accusation that President Biden's son-in-law has a financial stake in a company that sells Critical Race Theory materials to schools, which has led to calls for the federal government to intervene against individuals or hate groups targeting schools and educators.

The Department of Justice has dropped cases against Chinese researchers accused of hiding military ties and committing visa fraud, which will encourage spying, according to the Director of the Federal Bureau of Investigation. The House Judiciary Committee has asked for information on the resources assigned to the China Initiative, including any classified information.

The Department of Justice is suing Georgia over GOP voting restrictions, and has been asked to provide information on the assessment of Concerned Women for America and the number of terrorists, criminals, and gang members apprehended at the southern border.

The OIG released an investigative summary with findings of misconduct by a former senior FBI official. The summary states that the senior FBI official had unauthorized contacts with the media from 2014 through 2016, in violation of FBI policy. In addition to substantive communications with reporters, this media contact included unauthorized social engagements outside of FBI Headquarters involving drinks, lunches, and dinners. The senior official also violated federal regulations and FBI policy when the senior official accepted tickets from members of the media to two black tie dinner events, one valued at $225 and the other valued at $300, and received transportation to one event from a reporter, all without prior authorization.

The Justice Department is requested to provide information on its efforts to identify and prosecute individuals involved in the assaults of Mr. Ngo and other journalists, in violation of federal statutes securing their civil rights. We write to request information about the recent appointment of Susan Hennessy to a senior position in the Justice Department's National Security Division (NSD). Ms. Hennessy's appointment raises serious concerns about potential political bias and perceived conflicts of interest due to her past work.

The FBI has been violating privacy rules with its warrantless surveillance power and has been accused of abusing the FISA process to illegally surveil an American citizen associated with President Trump's campaign. The DOJ's Inspector General found that the FBI had been providing unsupported, uncorroborated, or inconsistent information in its surveillance applications on US persons. The recent FISC opinion raises more questions about the FBI's respect for the constitutional and statutory parameters of FISA. Rioters in Portland have vandalized multiple businesses, museums, and places of worship. The DOJ has designated Portland as a jurisdiction that has permitted violence and destruction of property to persist. Left-wing anarchists in Portland have developed a riot apparatus that includes streams of funding for accommodation, travel, riot gear, and weapons, which has resulted in murder, hundreds of arson cases, and damage to federal property.

The Department of Justice is prosecuting individuals who attack federal property, and working to prevent further damage in New York City, Portland, and Seattle.

Recursive Summary Round 2

The FBI is being accused of artificially inflating their Domestic Violence Enforcement statistics, and of manipulating case categorization at their Washington Field Office. This is allegedly being done at the urging of a senior FBI official, Timothy Thibault, who has a history of impropriety and political bias.

The FBI has been accused of political bias and of violating internal policies. The DOJ has filed lawsuits against Georgia and Texas over voting restrictions. Whistleblowers have described how senior FBI leadership is purging employees with conservative views. In May of 2022, anti-life activists vandalized multiple pro-life facilities across the country.

The FBI has been investigating possible civil rights violations by individuals who engage in violence and intimidation against journalists, and has created a new domestic terrorism unit within the Counterterrorism Section of the National Security Division. The Department of Homeland Security is being investigated for allegedly misusing federal resources to target concerned parents at school board meetings. The U.S. Department of Justice has been accused of politicizing enforcement of the Freedom of Access to Clinic Entrances (FACE) Act, and has arrested a man for assaulting a reproductive healthcare clinic escort.

The Department of Justice is being investigated for abuse and misconduct against conservative employees, and the FBI is being accused of opening paper investigations without any actual investigative work being done. This letter requests that you preserve all records related to the inquiry.

The FBI is being accused of artificially inflating the number of domestic terrorism cases by pressuring agents to reclassify cases that don't meet the criteria.

The FBI is being accused of retaliating against employees by suspending their security clearances and taking steps to fire them for their political speech. The Hunter Biden emails were released by Russian operatives, according to dozens of former intelligence officials. These officials say that the emails are part of a Russian disinformation campaign to damage the Biden campaign. The signatories of a public statement claiming that the New York Post's article about Hunter Biden was part of a Russian disinformation campaign are now facing questions after it was revealed that the article is not, in fact, part of a Russian disinformation operation.

The article discusses the public statement made in October 2020 about Hunter Biden's emails, which claimed they were Russian disinformation. The statement is being investigated for its role in possible suppression of public dissemination of the allegations against Hunter Biden.

In October 2020, Joe Biden and several other officials signed a public statement alleging that a laptop belonging to Hunter Biden was part of a Russian disinformation operation. However, this has been refuted by dozens of former intelligence officials.

The Public Statement on the Hunter Biden Emails dated October 19, 2020 is being investigated for possible Russian involvement.

Hunter Biden used his father's influence for personal gain, raising doubts about Joe Biden's earlier denial of ever speaking to his son about his international business dealings. The article discusses how the laptop story involving Hunter Biden was pushed as Russian disinformation, but was later verified as true. This raises questions about a public statement made by Michael G. Vickers in October 2020 about the story.

The FBI and DOJ are under investigation for targeting parents at local school board meetings and discouraging their First Amendment activity. The NSBA wrote a letter to President Biden apologizing for their previous letter which the Department of Justice used as the basis for a violent threats task force that targeted concerned parents at local school board meetings.

The National School Boards Association has accused the Department of Justice of domestic terrorism or hate crimes for targeting and intimidating parents who voice their opinions at school board meetings. The NSBA has requested help from the federal government to address this issue. The Justice Department has issued a directive ordering US Attorneys to convene meeting with federal, state, local, Tribal, and territorial leaders within 30 days to discuss threats against school administrators, board members, teachers, and staff.

The National School Boards Association has asked President Joe Biden for help with concerned parents attending school board meetings. The Justice Department has responded by opening up lines of communication for law enforcement to investigate and respond to these claims.

The DOJ is investigating the possible use of federal law enforcement to target and intimidate parents at local school board meetings.

The National School Boards Association has asked President Joe Biden for help with concerned parents who are being targeted by the Department of Justice and the White House. The NSBA issued a new memorandum to its members apologizing for a previous letter to President Biden and recognizing the consequences of the letter. Attorney General Garland testified that the NSBA letter was the basis for his October 4 directive to insert federal law enforcement into local school board matters, but he has yet to rescind his memorandum.

The National School Boards Association has asked President Joe Biden for help with concerned parents who are being targeted by the Department of Justice and the White House. The NSBA letter stated that malice, violence, and threats against school officials could be the equivalent of a form of domestic terrorism or hate crimes.

The National School Boards Association is being investigated for sending a letter to President Joe Biden that requested help from the federal government with concerned parents attending school board meetings. The letter stated that malice, violence, and threats against school officials could be the equivalent of a form of domestic terrorism or hate crimes.

The National School Boards Association has asked President Joe Biden for help in investigating the Department of Justice and the White House's attempts to use federal law enforcement to target parents attending local school board meetings.

The NSBA has asked for help from the federal government in dealing with concerned parents who are voicing their opinions at school board meetings, stating that some of these parents' actions could be classified as domestic terrorism or hate crimes. On October 4, 2021, Attorney General Merrick Garland issued a memo that directed the FBI and the Department of Justice to investigate these incidents.

The National School Boards Association (NSBA) has requested help from the federal government to address concerned parents who are voicing their opinions at school board meetings. The NSBA letter stated that malice, violence, and threats against school officials could be the equivalent of a form of domestic terrorism or hate crimes. The Justice Department has issued a directive ordering the FBI and U.S. Attorney's Offices to convene meetings with federal, state, local, Tribal, and territorial leaders within 30 days to address threats against school administrators, board members, teachers, and staff.

The National School Boards Association has requested help from the federal government with concerned parents voicing their opinions at school board meetings, citing an incident in which a father angrily confronted members at a school board meeting. The NSBA has apologized for their previous letter to President Biden which was the basis for Attorney General Garland's directive to insert federal law enforcement into local school board matters. The Department of Justice and the White House are being investigated for their attempts to use federal law enforcement to target parents who voice their opinions at local school board meetings.

The DOJ is investigating possible illegal meetings between parents and school officials, and has requested documents related to these meetings.

The NSBA has come under fire for a letter to President Biden which many interpreted as threatening, and has apologized. The OIG released an investigative summary with findings of misconduct by a former senior FBI official. The Justice Department is requested to provide information on its efforts to identify and prosecute individuals involved in the assaults of Mr. Ngo and other journalists, in violation of federal statutes securing their civil rights.

The FBI has been accused of violating privacy rules and abusing the FISA process, while left-wing anarchists in Portland have developed a riot apparatus that has resulted in murder and damage to federal property. The DOJ is prosecuting individuals who attack federal property and working to prevent further damage in affected cities.

RECURSIVE SUMMARY ROUND 3

FBI being accused of artificially inflating Domestic Violence Enforcement statistics and manipulating case categorization at Washington Field Office. This is allegedly being done at the urging of a senior FBI official, Timothy Thibault, who has a history of impropriety and political bias.

The National School Boards Association has asked President Joe Biden for help with concerned parents who are being targeted by the Department of Justice and the White House.

The National School Boards Association has asked President Joe Biden for help with concerned parents who are being targeted by the Department of Justice and the White House. The NSBA letter stated that malice, violence, and threats against school officials could be the equivalent of a form of domestic terrorism or hate crimes.

The Justice Department is investigating possible illegal meetings between parents and school officials, has come under fire for a letter to President Biden which many interpreted as threatening, and has released an investigative summary with findings of misconduct by a former senior FBI official. The department is also requested to provide information on its efforts to identify and prosecute individuals involved in the assaults of Mr. Ngo and other journalists, in violation of federal statutes securing their civil rights. Furthermore, the FBI has been accused of violating privacy rules and abusing the FISA process, while left-wing anarchists in Portland have developed a riot apparatus that has resulted in murder and damage to federal property. The DOJ is prosecuting individuals who attack federal property and working to prevent further damage in affected cities.

Recursive Summary Round 4

The FBI is accused of inflating Domestic Violence Enforcement statistics and manipulating case categorization at Washington Field Office. This is allegedly being done at the urging of a senior FBI official, Timothy Thibault, who has a history of impropriety and political bias. The National School Boards Association has asked President Joe Biden for help with concerned parents who are being targeted by the Department of Justice and the White House. The Justice Department is investigating possible illegal meetings between parents and school officials, has come under fire for a letter to President Biden which many interpreted as threatening, and has released an investigative summary with findings of misconduct by a former senior FBI official. Furthermore, the FBI has been accused of violating privacy rules and abusing the FISA process, while left-wing anarchists in Portland have developed a riot apparatus that has resulted in murder and damage to federal property. The DOJ is prosecuting individuals who attack federal property and working to prevent further damage in affected cities.

Recursive Summary Round 5

The FBI is being accused of inflating statistics, manipulating case categorization, and violating privacy rules. Meanwhile, the DOJ is being criticized for its handling of an investigation into possible illegal meetings between parents and school officials, and left-wing anarchists in Portland have developed a riot apparatus that has resulted in murder and damage to federal property.

Recursive Summary Round 6

The FBI and DOJ are under fire from various groups.

EDITORIAL CARTOONS

House Republican investigation of the Biden Administration; hostile cartoon; sketch; grayscale; herblock style (Nimble Books, using Stable Diffusion). The white male vibe is authentic, and the Newspeak slogan on the wall is all too appropriate.

FBI WHISTLEBLOWERS: WHAT THEIR DISCLOSURES INDICATE ABOUT THE POLITICIZATION OF THE FBI AND JUSTICE DEPARTMENT

Republican Staff Report
Committee on the Judiciary
U.S. House of Representatives

November 4, 2022

Executive Summary

The Federal Bureau of Investigation, under the stewardship of Director Christopher Wray and Attorney General Merrick Garland, is broken. The problem lies not with the majority of front-line agents who serve our country, but with the FBI's politicized bureaucracy. The problem lies, for example, with the FBI hierarchy that spied on President Trump's campaign and ridiculed conservative Americans. The problem lies with FBI bureaucrats who altered and mischaracterized evidence to federal courts, circumvented safeguards, and exploited weaknesses in policies governing investigations and informants to target politically disfavored subjects and to protect favored ones. The problem lies with the FBI structure that centralizes high-profile cases in D.C., in the hands of politicized actors with politicized incentives. Quite simply, the problem—the rot within the FBI—festers in and proceeds from Washington.

Over the last year, a multitude of whistleblowers have approached Judiciary Committee Republicans with allegations of political bias by the FBI's senior leadership and misuses of the agency's federal law-enforcement powers. These whistleblowers have risked their careers out of fidelity to principle and a commitment to restoring public trust in the FBI. This report begins to tell their stories. Even at this early stage, one startling conclusion is clear: the FBI and its parent agency, the Justice Department, have become political institutions.

This report details the problems, as recounted in whistleblower disclosures and other forms, that undermine the FBI's fundamental law-enforcement mission. Whistleblowers describe the FBI's Washington hierarchy as **"rotted at its core,"** maintaining a **"systemic culture of unaccountability,"** and full of **"rampant corruption, manipulation, and abuse."** Whistleblowers describe how the FBI has abused its law-enforcement authorities for political purposes, and how actions by FBI leadership show a political bias against conservatives. For example:

- **The FBI is artificially inflating statistics about domestic violent extremism in the nation.** Whistleblowers have described how FBI leadership is pressuring line agents to reclassify cases as domestic violent extremism even if the matter does not meet the criteria. They also explained how the FBI is misrepresenting the scale of domestic violent extremism nationwide by categorizing January 6th-related investigations as organic cases stemming from local field offices, instead of all related to one single incident. In both ways, the FBI is fueling the Biden Administration's narrative that domestic violent extremism is the biggest threat to our nation.

- **The FBI is abusing its counterterrorism authorities to investigate parents who spoke at school board meetings.** Whistleblowers disclosed how, shortly after the National School Boards Association urged President Biden to use the Patriot Act against American parents, the FBI Counterterrorism Division set up a special "threat tag" to track school board-related cases. Whistleblowers provided evidence of how the FBI opened investigations into one mom for allegedly telling a local school board "we are coming for you" and a dad simply because he "rails against the government" and "has a lot of guns."

- **The FBI has abused its foreign intelligence authorities to spy on American citizens, including people associated with the campaign of President Trump in 2016.** These facts have been documented in Inspector General reports and Foreign Intelligence Surveillance Court opinions, but there is little indication the FBI has changed—or is willing to change—course.

- **The FBI is clearing the Bureau of employees who dissent from its woke, leftist agenda.** The FBI is actively seeking to "purge" FBI employees holding conservative views—or, in President Biden's view, those who are a "threat to American democracy"[1]— because they hold conservative views. The FBI has even taken retaliatory actions against at least one whistleblower who has spoken out.

- **Whistleblowers have explained how the FBI's "political meddling" "is dragging the criminal side [of the Bureau] down" as resources are "pulled away" from real law-enforcement duties.** As a prime example, one whistleblower described how he was "told that child sexual abuse material investigations were no longer an FBI priority and should be referred to local law enforcement agencies" so that he could work a Washington-directed politically charged case instead. Such a mis-prioritization is not only a dereliction of duty, but it is a grave disservice to the victims of crimes that do not advance the FBI's political agenda.

The examples outlined in this report concern FBI abuses and misconduct primarily, due to the experiences of the whistleblowers and the conduct to which they are exposed. But because the FBI is a component of the Justice Department, it is virtually impossible to examine the FBI's actions without also examining those of the Justice Department. For example, in creating a threat tag to track investigations into concerned parents, the FBI was executing on a directive from Attorney General Garland and the Justice Department. In addition, the recent examples of misconduct must properly be examined in the context of years of serious abuses from the FBI and Justice Department. As such, where necessary for context and explanation, this report includes a discussion of misconduct and abuses apparent in the Justice Department in addition to the FBI.

The FBI has a troubling history of using its authorities to advance political goals. Under J. Edgar Hoover, the Bureau surveilled Dr. Martin Luther King, Jr., engaging in "an intense campaign" to discredit the civil rights leader.[2] Following the September 11, 2001, terrorist attacks, then-FBI Director Robert Mueller sought to change the FBI's "culture" to produce a "centraliz[ed]" and "intelligence driven" organization.[3] With its new centralized structure, FBI leadership began running investigations out of headquarters rather than the originating field offices—something that had been standard practice for nearly a century.[4] Mueller started the trend of filling leadership positions with Washington bureaucrats "who lacked the institutional

---

[1] Remarks, The White House, Remarks by President Biden on the Continued Battle for the Soul of the Nation (Sept. 1, 2022).

[2] Sam Briger, *Documentary exposes how the FBI tried to destroy MLK with wiretaps, blackmail,* NPR (Jan. 18, 2021).

[3] Thomas J. Baker, *How Robert Mueller shredded the FBI's credibility,* WALL ST. J. (Sept. 14, 2022).

[4] *Id.*

knowledge of career agents."[5] From information provided by whistleblowers, these cultural and structural problems continue to this day.

Director Wray began at the FBI in the wake of James Comey's disastrous tenure, when the Bureau's Washington leadership used the power of federal law enforcement to attack President Donald Trump and his campaign. Wray had an opportunity to clean up the leadership culture at the FBI, to end the politicization, and to restore trust and integrity in the FBI's mission. By any objective measure, Wray has failed.

Americans deserve to have confidence that the enormous power and reach of federal law enforcement will be used fairly and free of any indication of politicization. The FBI has the power, quite literally, to ruin a person's life—to invade their residence, to take their property, and even to deprive them of their liberty. The potential abuse of this power, or even the appearance of abuse, erodes the fundamental principle of equality under the law and confidence in the rule of law. The FBI's tremendous power is precisely why the people's elected representatives in Congress must conduct vigorous oversight, particularly in light of allegations of abuse and misconduct made to date. This issue transcends partisan politics, and the information contained in this report should concern all policymakers.

This report presents what is known so far about the extent of problems festering within the FBI's Washington bureaucracy. There is likely much more to be uncovered in the months ahead. But from what is known, it is clear the FBI needs repair. Too many whistleblowers have said that they are "saddened" by what they see happening at the Bureau. Too much is at stake to sacrifice the trust and accountability in our federal law-enforcement apparatus. The necessary first step in fixing the FBI's broken culture and out-of-control hierarchy is to identify and understand the problem. This report begins to do just that.

---

[5] *Id.*

ATTENTION:

All Justice Department and FBI Employees

You have a right to speak with Congress

Every federal employee of the Department of Justice and FBI has an unfettered right to communicate with Congress, without the approval, consent, or awareness of the Department or the FBI. Federal law protects these disclosures.

Whistleblowers are an invaluable source for Congress in identifying, understanding, and remedying waste, fraud, abuse, and mismanagement. The Committee on the Judiciary is charged with conducting constitutional oversight of the Department of Justice and FBI.

Any Justice Department or FBI personnel with information are encouraged to contact the Republican staff of the Judiciary Committee at (202) 225-6906.

Table of Contents

I. FBI Leadership Is Abusing its Law-Enforcement Authorities for Political Reasons

The law-enforcement authorities of the FBI are extensive and powerful. Justice—and the exertion of this law-enforcement power—should be blind to and unaffected by politics. Under the malevolent leadership of Merrick Garland, however, the FBI and Justice Department has been a willing participant of the Biden Administration's weaponization of law enforcement.

President Biden has shown no problem in labeling his political opponents as racists, fascists, and domestic terrorists. The FBI under Director Wray has been willing to exert its law-enforcement tools in a manner guided by political calculations. Whistleblowers allege that the FBI is manipulating data about domestic violent extremism to support the Biden Administration's political agenda. Other information suggests the FBI prioritizes investigations and uses differing tactics based on political considerations—using aggressive tactics against political opponents of the Biden Administration while going softer on, or outright ignoring, allegations against the Administration's political allies. Perhaps the best case study of the FBI's and Justice Department's abuse of authorities for political purposes is the FBI's use of counterterrorism resources to target moms and dads who spoke out at school board meetings in the fall of 2021.

As a result, there emerges an apparent double standard in the enforcement of federal law. On the one hand, for example, the FBI has aggressively and rapidly exercised its vast powers to enforce federal law to protect pro-abortion facilities while failing to enforce the same law to protect pro-life centers. The same selective enforcement of federal law is evident in how the Justice Department has aggressively pursued prosecutions related to January 6, 2021, while virtually ignoring federal crimes stemming from left-wing riots in the summer of 2020. Similarly, the FBI and Justice Department has used aggressive tactics in matters concerning conservative elected officials while giving kid-glove treatment to prominent left-wing officials.

This section highlights several ways in which the FBI—and by extension, the Justice Department—has abused its law-enforcement authorities for apparently political purposes. These examples, garnered from whistleblowers' disclosures and other sources, are not exhaustive. But they provide a current assessment of the "rot" that has festered within the FBI's Washington leadership.

A. The FBI is artificially inflating and manipulating domestic violent extremism statistics for political purposes.

Whistleblowers have disclosed to the Committee that the FBI is pressuring agents to reclassify cases as domestic violent extremism (DVE), but it appears the FBI is also manufacturing DVE cases where they may not otherwise exist and even manipulating its case categorization system to feign a national problem. At a time when the Biden Administration maintains that DVE is the "greatest threat" facing the United States, the FBI appears to be complicit in artificially creating the Administration's political narrative.[6]

---

[6] *The Way Forward on Homeland Security: Hearing Before the H. Comm. on Homeland Sec.*, 117th Cong. (2021) (statement of Hon. Alejandro Mayorkas, Sec'y, U.S. Dep't of Homeland Sec.).

i. The FBI is artificially padding domestic violent extremism statistics by pressuring agents to reclassify investigations.

The FBI defines a domestic violent extremist as "an individual based and operating primarily within the United States or its territories without direction or inspiration from a foreign terrorist group or other foreign power who seeks to further political or social goals wholly or in part through unlawful acts of force or violence."[7] According to the Biden Administration, investigations into DVEs have increased "significantly."[8] In June 2021, FBI Director Wray testified before the House Judiciary Committee that the FBI has a "very, very active domestic terrorism investigation program" and that the FBI had "doubled the amount of domestic terrorism investigations."[9] Attorney General Garland has repeated this talking point, publicly stating that "[t]he number of open FBI domestic terrorism investigations this year has increased significantly."[10]

Whistleblower disclosures made by multiple FBI employees from different field offices indicate that the Biden Administration's narrative is misleading. On July 27, 2022, Committee Republicans wrote to Director Wray in response to whistleblower disclosures that FBI agents are pressured to bolster the number of cases of DVEs to satisfy their superiors.[11] One whistleblower explained that because agents are not finding enough DVE cases, they are encouraged and incentivized to reclassify matters as DVE cases even though there is minimal, circumstantial evidence to support the reclassification. Another whistleblower, who led at least one high profile domestic terrorism investigation, stated that Washington Field Office's Assistant Special Agent in Charge (ASAC) Timothy Thibault and the FBI's former Assistant Director of the Counterterrorism Division Jill Sanborn pressured agents to move cases into the DVE category to hit self-created performance metrics.[12] According to whistleblowers, the FBI uses these metrics to dispense awards and promotions. Whistleblowers have described this scheme as an environment of "pressure" within the FBI. Recently, Sanborn, through her attorneys, agreed to appear for a transcribed interview with the Committee on December 2, 2022.[13]

---

[7] FED. BUREAU OF INVESTIGATION AND DEP'T OF HOMELAND SEC., STRATEGIC INTELLIGENCE ASSESSMENT ON DATA AND DOMESTIC TERRORISM AT 2, NOTE 3 (MAY 2021).

[8] *Threats to the Homeland: Evaluating the Landscape 20 Years After 9/11: Hearing Before the S. Comm. on Homeland Sec. & Governmental Affairs*, 117th Cong. (2021) (testimony of Hon. Christopher A. Wray, Dir., Fed. Bureau of Investigation); Hon. Merrick B. Garland, Atty Gen., Domestic Terrorism Policy Address at U.S. Dep't of Justice (Jun. 15, 2021).

[9] *Oversight of the Federal Bureau of Investigation, Hearing Before H. Comm. on the Judiciary,* 117th Cong. at 154 (2021) (statement of Hon. Christopher A. Wray, Dir., Fed. Bureau of Investigation).

[10] Hon. Merrick B. Garland, Atty Gen., Domestic Terrorism Policy Address at U.S. Dep't of Justice (Jun. 15, 2021).

[11] Letter from Rep. Jim Jordan, Ranking Member, H. Comm. on the Judiciary, to Hon. Christopher A. Wray, Dir., Fed. Bureau of Investigation (Jul. 27, 2022).

[12] *Id.; see also* Letter from Reps. Jim Jordan & Mike Johnson, H. Comm. on the Judiciary, to Ms. Jill Sanborn, Senior Dir. Of Geopolitical Strategy & Risk Analysis, Roku Inc. (Aug. 10, 2022).

[13] Letter from Reps. Jim Jordan & Mike Johnson, H. Comm. on the Judiciary, to Ms. Jill Sanborn, Senior Dir. Of Geopolitical Strategy & Risk Analysis, Roku Inc. (Oct. 18, 2022).

ii. The Washington Field Office is manipulating its case filing system to feign a nationwide rise in domestic terrorism.

Following Committee Republicans' July 27, 2022 letter to Director Wray,[14] new whistleblowers came forward with information about how the FBI manipulated the manner in which it categorized January 6-related investigations to create a misleading narrative that domestic terrorism is organically surging around the country. These new whistleblower disclosures indicate that the Washington Field Office's (WFO) handling of DVE investigations relating to January 6 "diverge[s]" from established practice in a way that overstates the national DVE threat.

One whistleblower described how FBI agents ordinarily characterize and label cases according to the originating field office, with leads "cut" to other field offices for specific assistance in that geographic location.[15] The whistleblower alleged that "the FBI has not followed regular procedure" with respect to January 6 cases, which should all be officially led by the WFO and categorized as WFO cases. The whistleblower explained:

> Instead, task force members in Washington D.C. identify "potential subjects" and possible locations where these individuals reside. The task force disseminates information packets with instructions to open full investigations to [local] Field Offices around the country. As such, if a subject lives in Dallas, the Dallas Field Office is expected to open the case . . . .

Although the local field offices therefore appear to be running the cases on paper, the WFO is directing the field office special agents to just "open the case" in their geographic area and the WFO is performing and approving "all of the investigative work and paperwork for the casefile." The whistleblower described how "there are active criminal investigations of January 6th subjects in which I am listed as the 'Case Agent,' but have not done any investigative work" and the whistleblower's supervisor "has not approved any paperwork within" those investigative files. This scheme gives the FBI a pretense to support Director Wray's assertion that "[t]he FBI is a field-based law enforcement organization, and the vast majority of our investigations should continue to be worked by our field offices," while actually running the investigation from Washington.[16]

The whistleblower explained how the WFO's deviation from established practice misrepresents the DVE threat nationwide:

> The manipulative casefile practice creates false and misleading crime statistics. Instead of hundreds of investigations stemming

[14] Letter from Rep. Jim Jordan, Ranking Member, H. Comm. on the Judiciary, to Hon. Christopher A. Wray, Dir., Fed. Bureau of Investigation (Jul. 27, 2022).
[15] Letter from Rep. Jim Jordan, Ranking Member, H. Comm. on the Judiciary, to Hon. Christopher A. Wray, Dir., Fed. Bureau of Investigation (Sept. 19, 2022).
[16] Letter from Hon. Christopher A. Wray, Dir., Fed. Bureau of Investigation, to Hon. Michael Horowitz, Inspector Gen., U.S. Dep't of Justice (Dec. 6, 2019).

from a single, black swan incident at the Capitol, FBI and DOJ officials point to significant increases in domestic violent extremism and terrorism around the United States.

In other words, the FBI's case categorization creates the illusion that FBI field offices around the country are investigating a groundswell of domestic terrorism cases, giving the impression that the threat of DVE is present in jurisdictions across the nation. In reality, however, the cases all stem from the same related investigation concerning the actions at the Capitol on January 6. Such an artificial case categorization scheme allows FBI leadership to misleadingly point to "significant" increases in DVE threats nationwide.[17]

In addition, the whistleblower disclosed that the FBI is sacrificing its other important federal law-enforcement duties to pursue these January 6 investigations. The whistleblower recalled, for example, being "told that child sexual abuse material investigations were no longer an FBI priority and should be referred to local law enforcement agencies." This decision to ignore such serious crimes is a dereliction of the FBI's mission to investigate violations of federal laws and a disservice to the victims of child sexual abuse crimes.

iii. A senior FBI official responsible for pushing DVE investigations has an alleged history of impropriety and political bias.

Not only have Committee Republicans learned that the FBI is artificially padding DVE statistics and manipulating case categorization at the WFO, but the official responsible for pressuring agents to reclassify cases as DVE cases at the WFO has a history of impropriety and political bias. This official, Timothy Thibault, worked as an ASAC in the FBI's WFO, which has traditionally handled the nation's "most politically charged investigations."[18] According to whistleblowers and other information, Thibault has allowed his political bias to infect and steer his decision-making at the FBI.

In a letter to Director Wray, Senate Judiciary Ranking Member Chuck Grassley revealed how Thibault had made partisan social media posts that suggest a bias against conservatives.[19] Thibault allegedly used his official title in these posts. According to Senator Grassley, "Thibault's social media postings, comments, and 'likes' demonstrate a pattern of improper commentary related to, for example, ongoing FBI investigations including those under his

---

[17] *See, e.g.*, *Threats to the Homeland: Evaluating the Landscape 20 Years After 9/11: Hearing Before the S. Comm. on Homeland Sec. & Governmental Affairs*, 117th Cong. (2021) (testimony of Hon. Christopher A. Wray, Dir., Fed. Bureau of Investigation)*; see also Oversight of the Federal Bureau of Investigation: Hearing Before H. Comm. on the Judiciary*, 117th Cong. (2021) (statement of Hon. Christopher A. Wray, Dir., Fed. Bureau of Investigation); Hon. Merrick B. Garland, Atty Gen., Domestic Terrorism Policy Address at U.S. Dep't of Justice (Jun. 15, 2021). ("The number of open FBI domestic terrorism investigations this year has increased significantly.").

[18] Andrew C. McCarthy, *What the hell has happened to the FBI? Chapter 342,872,* NAT'L REV. (Jun. 1, 2022).

[19] Letter from Sen. Chuck Grassley, Ranking Member, S. Comm. on the Judiciary, to Hon. Merrick B. Garland, Atty Gen., U.S. Dep't of Justice, and Hon. Christopher A. Wray, Dir., Fed. Bureau of Investigation (May 31, 2022).

purview."[20] Following a letter from Senator Grassley, Thibault "suppressed" his accounts from public view.[21]

In addition, Thibault has apparently allowed partisanship to affect his decisions to open and pursue public corruption investigations, including an investigation involving electors and the Trump campaign.[22] FBI whistleblowers disclosed to Senator Grassley that there is a "double standard in the application of Justice Department and FBI policies [that] has resulted in investigations opened in a manner appearing to benefit the political aims and objectives of a select few Justice Department and FBI officials."[23] Whistleblowers disclosed that Thibault, along with Richard Pilger of the Justice Department's Election Crimes Branch, "were deeply involved in the decisions to open and pursue" an investigation into the Trump campaign and individuals linked to 2020 electors.[24] Contrary to FBI protocol, the predicating document—used to get approvals for opening a full investigation from the FBI Director and Attorney General—contained "selective assertions created in large part by Thibault" and from liberal organizations"[25]

According to whistleblowers, Thibault and Pilger "did not support" and "marginalized" FBI agents seeking to uniformly apply Department and FBI policies on approving and opening election crime investigations.[26] Thibault and Pilger allegedly fostered an environment in which political bias infects "the process and procedure to open and pursue investigations."[27]

Pilger, too, has a sordid history of using federal law-enforcement powers to target conservatives. In 2010, responding to a public appeal from Senator Sheldon Whitehouse about so-called "dark money" in politics, Pilger pushed the idea to notorious Internal Revenue Service official Lois Lerner that the Obama Justice Department could criminally prosecute conservative nonprofit groups.[28] This pressure campaign ultimately resulted in the IRS targeting scandal, in which the IRS systematically delayed and overly scrutinized the tax-exempt applications filed by conservative groups. Pilger quit the Justice Department following the 2020 election because he believed that he—not the Attorney General—had authority to dictate investigative steps relating to election fraud.[29] Pilger quickly rejoined the Justice Department in his former role at the outset of the Biden Administration.

---

[20] *Id.*
[21] Letter from Sen. Chuck Grassley, Ranking Member, S. Comm. on the Judiciary, to Hon. Merrick B. Garland, Atty Gen., U.S. Dep't of Justice, and Hon. Christopher A. Wray, Dir., Fed. Bureau of Investigation (Jul. 18, 2022).
[22] *Id.*
[23] *Id.*
[24] *Id.*
[25] *Id.*
[26] *Id.*
[27] *Id.*
[28] Staff Report, H. Comm. on Oversight & Gov't Reform, The Internal Revenue Service's Targeting of Conservative Tax-Exempt Applicants: Report of Findings for the 113th Congress at 173-176, 113th Cong. (2014); *see also* John Solomon, *DOJ official named in FBI politicization also played role in Lois Lerner IRS scandal,* JUST THE NEWS (Jul. 31, 2022).
[29] Evan Perez, *Top prosecutor quits after Barr election fraud order*, CNN (Nov. 10, 2020); Staff Report, S. Comm. on the Judiciary, In Their Own Words: A Factual Summary of Testimony from Senior Justice Department Officials Relating to Events from December 14, 2020 to January 3, 2021, 117th Cong. (2021).

Thibault was also allegedly part of the effort to suppress evidence damaging to the Biden family in the weeks before the 2020 presidential election. Senator Grassley revealed how Thibault was part of a "scheme" to discredit derogatory Hunter Biden information and how he ordered the closure of an additional avenue for reporting damaging information about Hunter Biden.[30] Whistleblowers who contacted Senator Grassley alleged that "there was a scheme in place among certain FBI officials to undermine derogatory information connected to Hunter Biden by falsely suggesting it was disinformation."[31]

In August 2020, FBI Supervisory Intelligence Analyst Brian Auten created an assessment that caused "derogatory information on Hunter Biden" to be "falsely labeled as disinformation."[32] Additionally, whistleblowers disclosed that investigators from FBI Headquarters "placed their findings" regarding whether Hunter Biden information was disinformation "in a restricted access sub-file reviewable only by the particular agents responsible for uncovering the specific information," closing the door to proper oversight of the investigation.[33] In October 2020, Thibault ordered the closure of another avenue for additional derogatory Hunter Biden reporting "without providing a valid reason as required by FBI guidelines." Thibault "attempted to improperly mark the matter in FBI systems so that it could not be opened in the future."[34]

At an August 2022 hearing before the Senate Judiciary Committee, Director Wray disclosed that "until relatively recently" Thibault was an ASAC at the WFO. When pressed about Thibault's impropriety, Director Wray declined to answer, alluding to "specific ongoing personnel matters."[35] In late August 2022, Thibault reportedly resigned and "was walked out of the FBI."[36]

On September 23, 2022, Committee Republicans wrote to Thibault noting that "whistleblowers have come to Congress alleging that you were part of a scheme to undermine and discredit allegations of criminal wrongdoing by members of the Biden family."[37] The letter requested that Thibault submit to a transcribed interview before the House Committee on the Judiciary and preserve all records related to the matter.[38] On October 7, 2022, Thibault, through

---

[30] Letter from Sen. Chuck Grassley, Ranking Member, S. Comm. on the Judiciary, to Hon. Merrick B. Garland, Attorney Gen., U.S. Dep't of Justice, and Hon. Christopher A. Wray, Dir., Fed. Bureau of Investigation (Jul. 25, 2022).

[31] *Id.*

[32] *Id.*

[33] *Id.*

[34] Letter from Sen. Chuck Grassley, Ranking Member, S. Comm. on the Judiciary, to Hon. Merrick B. Garland, Atty Gen., U.S. Dep't of Justice, and Hon. Christopher A. Wray, Dir., Fed. Bureau of Investigation (Jul. 18, 2022).

[35] *Oversight of the Federal Bureau of Investigation: Hearing Before the S. Comm. on the Judiciary,* 117th Cong. (2022).

[36] Andres Triay & Catherine Herridge, *Top-level FBI agent under fire for role in Hunter Biden investigation resigns,* CBS NEWS (Aug. 31, 2022).

[37] Letter from Reps. Jim Jordan, Darrell Issa, & Mike Johnson, H. Comm. on the Judiciary, to Mr. Timothy Thibault (Sept. 23, 2022).

[38] *Id.*

his attorney, declined to appear for a transcribed interview.[39] Thibault's refusal to testify contravened his earlier public statement that he "welcome[d] any investigation" into these matters.[40] Committee Republicans reiterated the request for a transcribed interview in a second letter on October 14, 2022, noting that Thibault's baseless assertion that "sensitive law enforcement information and/or pending investigations"[41] prevents his cooperation with the inquiry ignores the importance of congressional oversight, as well as the Committee's past practice in examining allegations of misconduct at the FBI.[42]

iv. The FBI appears to have manufactured at least one DVE case: the attempted kidnapping of Governor Gretchen Whitmer.

Not only is the FBI apparently exaggerating the number of actual DVE cases, it appears to have manufactured at least one DVE case. Weeks before the November 2020 presidential election, the Justice Department filed a criminal complaint against six men for allegedly conspiring to kidnap Michigan Governor Gretchen Whitmer. Evidence presented at trial suggests that FBI assets were directly involved in the kidnapping plot.

Defense attorneys argued that the FBI set up their clients. Evidence presented in the trial revealed an extravagant taxpayer-funded FBI entrapment scheme that involved at least twelve confidential human sources (CHS) and undercover agents who assembled a group of men over a half-year period "with unstable personal histories (that left them extraordinarily susceptible to persuasion) and injected into the mix the kind of father-figure, military-hero role models the men craved in their lives."[43] At the time of their recruitment by FBI assets, multiple defendants were allegedly destitute.[44]

The FBI's involvement in the scheme was substantial. According to defense attorneys, "[t]he government's agents actively planned and coordinated its efforts to induce the defendants to engage in incriminating behavior and statements, even going so far as designing the objective and structural components of the conspiracy alleged in the indictment."[45] Court documents detailed text communications between FBI CHSs and their FBI handlers that show the FBI pushed for the defendants' alleged criminal behavior. For instance, "surveillance trips were planned and orchestrated entirely by FBI agents supporting undercover informants."[46] Text

---

[39] Letter from Mr. Charles E. Duross, Partner, Morrison & Foerster LLP, to Reps. Jim Jordan, Darrell Issa, & Mike Johnson, H. Comm. on the Judiciary (Oct. 7, 2022); *see also* Letter from Reps. Jim Jordan, Darrell Issa, & Mike Johnson, H. Comm. on the Judiciary, to Mr. Timothy Thibault (Sept. 23, 2022).

[40] *See* Catherine Herridge (@CBS_Herridge), TWITTER (Aug. 30, 2022, 8:21 PM); Tom Winter, *Lawyer says FBI agent's retirement had nothing to do with Hunter Biden investigation*, NBC NEWS (Aug. 31, 2022).

[41] Letter from Mr. Charles E. Duross, Partner, Morrison & Foerster LLP, to Reps. Jim Jordan, Darrell Issa, & Mike Johnson, H. Comm. on the Judiciary (Oct. 7, 2022).

[42] Letter from Reps. Jim Jordan, Darrell Issa, & Mike Johnson, H. Comm. on the Judiciary, to Mr. Timothy Thibault (Oct. 14, 2022).

[43] Appeal of Magistrate Judge's Order Denying Motion to Compel, *United States v. Franks*, No. 1:20-CR-183 at 7 (W.D. Mich. Sept. 16, 2021).

[44] Tresa Baldas & Arpan Lobo, *'You guys are our last chance': Adam Fox's lawyer urges Whitmer kidnap plot jury to acquit*, DETROIT FREE PRESS (Apr. 5, 2022).

[45] Defendants' Joint Supplement to Motions to Compel, *United States v. Fox et al.*, No. 1:20-CR-183 at 3 (W.D. Mich. Aug. 27, 2021).

[46] *Id.*

messages revealed that someone called "Big Dan," an FBI CHS revealed to be Dan Chappel, "suggested the recons, invited the participants, provided transportation, gas, food, and direction, and largely determined where [the group] went and when and how they got there."[47] According to one court document, "Big Dan" was paid "in cash for his expenses and time, including purchasing a phone, a smart watch, and a $4,307.00 laptop computer."[48] In total, the FBI paid "Big Dan" over $54,000 between March 2020 to October 2020.[49]

Text messages produced to the defense also revealed that "Big Dan" allegedly suggested a separate plot targeting former Virginia Governor Ralph Northam. In a text message, "Big Dan" told FBI Special Agent Jayson Chambers, his FBI handler, that he intended to contact his target, a man named "Frank" in Virginia. Chambers, an FBI Special Agent, directed Big Dan: "The mission is to kill the governor specifically."[50] According to defense attorneys, "[t]he objective of the [alleged Virginia] plot is clearly being derived and advanced by Special Agent Chambers. By issuing this edict, 'Big Dan' has been charged to develop that [Virginia] plot specifically. The plot in this case shared the same objective: the governor."[51]

The FBI also used a longtime CHS and convicted felon, Stephen Robeson, to assist in the alleged Michigan plot. Robeson worked as a CHS since the early 2000s.[52] According to one court document, between the end of 2019 and May 2020, Robeson worked as a CHS with the Milwaukee, Norfolk, Baltimore, and Detroit FBI field offices.[53] Working for the FBI, Robeson organized field and "training" exercises drawing the defendants into the alleged plot.[54] According to a court document, Robeson's actions "ranged from arranging meetings and providing conference rooms to coordinate FTXs [Field Training Exercises] for the defendants to attend and transporting weapons, defendants and explosives across the country."[55] Defense lawyers asserted that Robeson's "handling [FBI] agents knew of his role within the group and acquiesced in his actions under the guise of maintaining access and credibility within the group."[56]

On July 28, 2022, Representative Dan Bishop questioned Assistant Attorney General Matthew Olsen about the case during a Judiciary Committee oversight hearing of the Justice Department's National Security Division.[57] Olsen refused to answer any questions about the

---

[47] *Id.*

[48] Defendants' Adam Dean Fox's Brief in Support of Motion in Limine to Allow the Admission of CHS Dan's Out of Court Statements, *United States v. Fox et al.*, No. 1:20-CR-183 at 5 (W.D. Mich. July 12, 2022).

[49] *Id.*

[50] Defendants' Joint Supplement to Motions to Compel, *United States v. Fox et al.*, No. 1:20-CR-183 at 5 (W.D. Mich. Aug. 27, 2021).

[51] *Id.*

[52] Joint Motion to Compel Testimony, *United States v. Fox et al.*, No. 1:20-CR-183 at 1 (W.D. Mich. Mar. 23, 2022).

[53] *Id.*

[54] Ken Bensinger & Jessica Garrison, *The FBI Investigation Into The Alleged Plot To Kidnap Michigan Gov. Gretchen Whitmer Has Gotten Very Complicated*, BUZZFEED NEWS (Dec. 16, 2021).

[55] Joint Motion to Compel Testimony, *United States v. Fox et al.*, No. 1:20-CR-183 (W.D. Mich. Mar. 23, 2022).

[56] *Id.* at 2.

[57] *Oversight of the Department of Justice National Security Division, Hearing Before the H. Comm. on the Judiciary*, 117th Cong. at 119 (July 28, 2022) (statement of Hon. Matthew Olsen, Assistant Atty Gen., U.S. Dep't of Justice).

FBI's involvement in the kidnapping plot. Similarly, on August 4, 2022, Senate Judiciary Committee Member Senator Ted Cruz asked FBI Director Wray about the case. Wray also refused to answer most questions.[58]

B. The FBI downplayed and sought to reduce the spread of the serious allegations of wrongdoing leveled against Hunter Biden.

Mounting evidence from the last two years shows that Hunter Biden, son of President Biden, has received preferential treatment from federal law enforcement, who seem to have turned a blind eye to the potential national security threats presented by his business dealings with Chinese, Russian, and other foreign nationals. Other evidence suggests that the FBI may have even colluded with social media platform Facebook to suppress information on these allegations from the public in the weeks before the 2020 presidential election.[59] The way the FBI has approached the allegations concerning Hunter Biden and the Biden family is especially striking when considered alongside public information about how the FBI leadership has aggressively used law-enforcement authorities against conservatives.

In September 2020, then-Senate Chairmen Ron Johnson and Chuck Grassley released an explosive report detailing "potential criminal activity relating to transactions among and between Hunter Biden, his family, and his associates with Ukrainian, Russian, Kazakh, and Chinese nationals."[60] The Chairmen detailed how Hunter Biden allegedly received $3.5 million from the wife of the former mayor of Moscow[61] and paid "thousands of dollars" to individuals involved in human trafficking and organized prostitution.[62] In addition, the report detailed Hunter Biden's questionable associations with people affiliated with the Chinese communist regime:

> Hunter Biden and his family, to include James Biden and Sara Biden, associated with other Chinese nationals such as Gongwen Dong. In one case, the three of them went on a $100,000 global spending spree after Gongwen Dong and Hunter Biden opened a joint account. In addition, Hunter Biden received millions of dollars over a period of years from Gongwen Dong's companies. According to records acquired by the Committees, many of these transactions involved potential criminal financial activity.[63]

---

[58] *Oversight of the Federal Bureau of Investigation, Hearing Before the S. Comm. on the Judiciary*, 117th Cong. (Aug. 4, 2022) (statements of Hon. Christopher A. Wray, Dir., Fed. Bureau of Investigation).

[59] *See* Letter from Sen. Chuck Grassley, Ranking Member, S. Comm. on the Judiciary, and Sen. Ron Johnson, Ranking Member, Permanent Subcomm. on Investigations, to the Hon. Merrick B. Garland, Atty Gen., U.S. Dep't of Justice, and Hon. Christopher A. Wray, Dir., Fed. Bureau of Investigation (Aug. 29, 2022); Letter from Sen. Chuck Grassley, Ranking Member, S. Comm. on the Judiciary, and Sen. Ron Johnson, Ranking Member, Permanent Subcomm. on Investigations, to Mr. Mark Zuckerberg, Chairman & Chief Exec. Officer, Meta Platforms, Inc. (Aug. 29, 2022); Letter from Rep. Jim Jordan, Ranking Member, H. Comm. on the Judiciary, and Rep. James Comer, Ranking Member, H. Comm. on Oversight and Reform, *et al.*, to Mr. Mark Zuckerberg, Chief Exec. Officer, Meta Platforms, Inc. (Sept. 1, 2022).

[60] Staff Report, S. Comm. on Homeland Security & Governmental Affairs & S. Comm. on Finance, Hunter Biden, Burisma, and Corruption: The Impact on U.S. Government Policy and Related Concerns, 116th Cong. at 65 (2020).

[61] *Id.* at 69.

[62] *Id.* at 65 & n. 267.

[63] *Id.* at 84.

The report demonstrated that the FBI had been aware of aspects of the alleged misconduct for years. The report detailed widespread concern within the Obama-Biden Administration about Hunter Biden's role on the board of Burisma Holdings, a Ukrainian company founded by oligarch Mykola Zlochevsky.[64] Then-U.S. Special Envoy and Coordinator for International Energy Affairs, Amos Hochstein, personally raised concerns to then-Vice President Biden and, after Vice President Biden spoke to Hunter, to Hunter Biden himself.[65] In addition, State Department official George Kent raised concerns to the FBI about a $7 million bribe paid by Zlochevsky to Ukraine's prosecutor general just seven months after Hunter Biden joined Burisma's board.[66] Chairmen Johnson and Grassley noted that they had asked the FBI about its actions in response to these allegations, but received no answers.[67]

On September 24, 2020, House Judiciary Committee Republicans followed up with a letter to FBI Director Wray to ask what investigative steps—if any—the FBI had taken in response to the information in the Senate report.[68] The FBI stonewalled the Committee, sending a nonresponsive letter stating that "the FBI can neither confirm nor deny the existence of any ongoing investigation or persons or entities under investigation."[69]

Then, beginning on October 14, 2020, the *New York Post* published a series of articles detailing how Hunter Biden used the influence of his father for personal gain—with then-Vice President Biden's awareness and apparent participation.[70] In particular, the *Post* reported on one email from May 2017 about "expectations" for "renumeration packages" with a Chinese firm that included "20 H"—apparently referring to Hunter Biden—and "10 held by H for the big guy."[71] A former business partner of Hunter Biden's released a public statement at the time in which he asserted that he was a recipient of this email, that the email was "genuine," and that the email's reference to "the Big Guy" referred to then-Vice President Biden.[72]

---

[64] *Id.* at 13-18.

[65] *Id.* at 16-18.

[66] *Id.* at 29.

[67] *Id.* at 30.

[68] Letter from Rep. Jim Jordan, Ranking Member, H. Comm. on the Judiciary, to the Hon. Christopher A. Wray, Dir., Fed. Bureau of Investigation (Sept. 24, 2020).

[69] Letter from Ms. Jill C. Tyson, Assistant Dir., Office of Cong. Affairs, Fed. Bureau of Investigation, to Rep. Jim Jordan, Ranking Member, H. Comm. on the Judiciary (Oct. 7, 2020).

[70] Emma-Jo Morris & Gabrielle Fonrouge, *Smoking-gun email reveals how Hunter Biden introduced Ukrainian businessman to VP dad,* N.Y. POST (Oct. 14, 2020).

[71] Emma-Jo Morris & Gabrielle Fonrouge, *Emails reveal how Hunter Biden tried to cash in big on behalf of family with Chinese firm,* N.Y. POST (Oct. 15, 2020).

[72] Statement of Anthony R. Bobulinski (Oct. 22, 2020) ("What I am outlining is fact. I know it is fact because I lived it. I am the CEO of Sinohawk Holdings which was a partnership between the Chinese operating through CEFC/Chairman Ye and the Biden family. I was brought into the company to be the CEO by James Gilliar and Hunter Biden. The reference to 'the Big Guy' in the much-publicized May 13, 2017 email is in fact a reference to Joe Biden. The other 'JB' referenced in that email is Jim Biden, Joe's brother. Hunter Biden called his dad 'the Big Guy' or 'my Chairman' and frequently referenced asking him for his sign-off or advice on various potential deals that we were discussing. I've seen Vice President Biden saying he never talked to Hunter Biden about his business. I've seen firsthand that that's not true, because it wasn't just Hunter's business, they said they were putting the Biden family name and its legacy on the line. . . . I don't have a political ax to grind; I just saw behind the Biden curtain and I grew concerned with what I saw. The Biden family aggressively leveraged the Biden family name to make millions of dollars from foreign entities even though some were from communist controlled China.").

In an August 2017 email obtained by the *Post*, Hunter Biden explained how Ye Jianming changed the terms of Biden's three-year consulting agreement with CEFC China Energy, a company that is essentially an arm of the Chinese government, to a "much more lasting and lucrative arrangement" that was "much more interesting to me and my family."[73] Under the terms of the agreement, Hunter Biden wrote that he would receive $10 million a year "for introductions alone."[74] The *Post*'s reports cast doubts on now-President Biden's denial of ever speaking to Hunter Biden about his international business dealings.[75]

On April 5, 2022, Committee Republicans sent a letter to Hunter Biden requesting that he immediately preserve all records and materials relating to his international business dealings during the Obama-Biden Administration, his abandoned laptop and its contents, and media inquiries and communications related to these topics.[76] Hunter Biden and his attorneys have failed to respond to the Committee.

Whistleblower information suggests that FBI leadership in Washington may be the reason why the FBI seems to have provided Hunter Biden with special treatment. In July 2022, Senator Grassley sent a letter to Director Wray reporting allegations that FBI ASAC Thibault of the WFO shut down the investigation into Hunter Biden.[77] Ranking Member Grassley wrote:

> My office has been made aware that FBI agents responsible for this information were interviewed by the FBI HQ team . . . . It's been alleged that the FBI HQ team suggested to the FBI agents that the information was at risk of disinformation; however, according to allegations, all of the reporting was either verified or verifiable via criminal search warrants. In addition, ASAC Thibault allegedly ordered the matter closed without providing a valid reason as required by FBI guidelines. Despite the matter being closed in such a way that the investigative avenue might be opened later, it's alleged that FBI officials, including ASAC Thibault, subsequently attempted to improperly mark the matter in FBI systems so that it could not be opened in the future.[78]

In addition to shutting down federal investigations into criminal wrongdoing by Hunter Biden, FBI leadership may have similarly prevented the widespread dissemination of the allegations. On August 25, 2022, while speaking on a podcast with Joe Rogan, Meta CEO Mark

---

[73] Emma-Jo Morris & Gabrielle Fonrouge, *Emails reveal how Hunter Biden tried to cash in big on behalf of family with Chinese firm*, N.Y. POST (Oct. 15, 2020); *see also* Jenni Marsh, *The rise of and fall of a Belt and Road billionaire*, CNN (Dec. 2018) ("But one thing is clear: at its height, Ye [Jianming]'s company, CEFC China Energy, aligned itself so closely with the Chinese government that it was often hard to distinguish between the two.").

[74] *Id.*

[75] *See e.g.*, Nick Givas, *Joe Biden again denies speaking to son about Ukrainian business dealings*, FOX NEWS (Oct. 10, 2019).

[76] Letter from U.S. House Judiciary Republicans to Hunter Biden (Apr. 5, 2022).

[77] Letter from Sen. Chuck Grassley, Ranking Member, S. Comm. on the Judiciary, to the Hon. Merrick B. Garland, Atty Gen., U.S. Dep't of Justice, and Hon. Christopher A. Wray, Dir., Fed. Bureau of Investigation (July 25, 2022).

[78] *Id.*

Zuckerberg admitted that Facebook took "meaningful" steps to censor articles related to Hunter Biden's laptop on the social media platform following a warning by the FBI.[79] Zuckerberg said:

> Basically the background here is the FBI, I think basically came to us—some folks on our team—and was like, 'Hey, just so you know, you should be on high alert. We thought that there was a lot of Russian propaganda in the 2016 election. We have it on notice that basically there's about to be some kind of dump that's similar to that. So just be vigilant.'[80]

Congress is continuing to investigate the role the FBI may be playing in protecting Hunter Biden.[81]

C. The Justice Department and FBI is using counterterrorism resources to target parents resisting a far-left educational curriculum.

As the radical left continued to push a woke agenda on America's children, parents across the country started to speak out at school board meetings against critical race theory, mask mandates, and controversial curricula. As more parents spoke out, the National School Boards Association (NSBA) and the Biden Administration colluded to create a justification, articulated in an October 4 memorandum from Attorney General Garland, to use federal law-enforcement tools to silence parents. Committee Republicans have repeatedly called on Attorney General Garland to rescind his ill-conceived memorandum that brought the heavy hand of federal law enforcement down upon America's parents. It is unacceptable for the Biden Administration to use federal domestic terrorism resources to target American parents. The use of these resources chills protected First Amendment activity as parents rightfully fear that their passionate advocacy for their children could result in a visit from federal law enforcement.

i. Attorney General Garland issued a memorandum that inserted federal law enforcement into local school board meetings.

---

[79] The Joe Rogan Experience Podcast, *Episode #1863 – Mark Zuckerberg*, SPOTIFY (Aug. 25, 2022); *see also* Letter from Sen. Chuck Grassley, Ranking Member, S. Comm. on the Judiciary, and Sen. Ron Johnson, Ranking Member, Permanent Subcomm. on Investigations, to the Hon. Merrick B. Garland, Atty Gen., U.S. Dep't of Justice, and Hon. Christopher A. Wray, Dir., Fed. Bureau of Investigation (Aug. 29, 2022); Letter from Sen. Chuck Grassley, Ranking Member, S. Comm. on the Judiciary, and Sen. Ron Johnson, Ranking Member, Permanent Subcomm. on Investigations, to Mr. Mark Zuckerberg, Chairman & Chief Exec. Officer, Meta Platforms, Inc. (Aug. 29, 2022); Letter from Rep. Jim Jordan, Ranking Member, H. Comm. on the Judiciary, & Rep. James Comer, Ranking Member, H. Comm. on Oversight & Reform, *et al.*, to Mr. Mark Zuckerberg, Chief Exec. Officer, Meta Platforms, Inc. (Sept. 1, 2022).

[80] *Id.*

[81] *See* Letter from Sen. Chuck Grassley, Ranking Member, S. Comm. on the Judiciary, and Sen. Ron Johnson, Ranking Member, Permanent Subcomm. on Investigations, to the Hon. Merrick B. Garland, Atty Gen., U.S. Dep't of Justice, and Hon. Christopher A. Wray, Dir., Fed. Bureau of Investigation (Aug. 29, 2022); Letter from Sen. Chuck Grassley, Ranking Member, S. Comm. on the Judiciary, and Sen. Ron Johnson, Ranking Member, Permanent Subcomm. on Investigations, to Mr. Mark Zuckerberg, Chairman & Chief Exec. Officer, Meta Platforms, Inc. (Aug. 29, 2022); Letter from Rep. Jim Jordan, Ranking Member, H. Comm. on the Judiciary, & Rep. James Comer, Ranking Member, H. Comm. on Oversight & Reform, *et al.*, to Mr. Mark Zuckerberg, Chief Exec. Officer, Meta Platforms, Inc. (Sept. 1, 2022); Letter from Reps. Jim Jordan, Darrell Issa, & Mike Johnson, H. Comm. on the Judiciary, to Mr. Timothy Thibault (Sept. 23, 2022).

On September 29, 2021, the NSBA sent a letter to President Biden equating concerned parents voicing their opinion at school board meetings with domestic terrorists and urging the Biden Administration to exercise its authorities under the Patriot Act.[82] The NSBA letter stated that "malice, violence, and threats" against school officials "could be the equivalent of a form of domestic terrorism and hate crimes."[83] The letter cited a number of interactions at school board meetings, the vast majority of which did not involve violence or threats.[84] Notably, as one "example" of alleged domestic terrorism, the NSBA cited an instance in Loudoun County, Virginia, where a father angrily confronted members at a school board meeting about the heinous sexual assault of his daughter.[85]

On October 4, 2021, just five days after the NSBA letter, Attorney General Garland issued a memorandum that directed the FBI and U.S. Attorneys' Offices to address a purported "disturbing spike in harassment, intimidation, and threats of violence" at school board meetings.[86] The memorandum explained that the Department would be "using its authority and resources to discourage these threats, identify them when they occur, and prosecute them when appropriate."[87] In a press release announcing the Attorney General's memorandum, the Justice Department announced that the National Security Division would be part of a Department-wide task force "to determine how federal enforcement tools can be used to prosecute these crimes."[88] The press release also announced the existence of "open dedicated lines of communication for threat reporting, assessment and response by law enforcement"—in other words, a snitch line for complaints about concerned parents.[89]

On October 21, 2021, Attorney General Garland testified before the House Judiciary Committee that the Department and its components were not using counterterrorism statutes and resources to target concerned parents at school board meetings.[90] Specifically, he testified that he could not "imagine any circumstance in which the Patriot Act would be used in the circumstances of parents complaining about their children, nor . . . a circumstance where they would be labeled as domestic terrorists."[91] He also testified: "I do not think that parents getting angry at school boards for whatever reason constitute domestic terrorism. It's not even a close question."[92]

---

[82] Letter from Dr. Viola M. Garcia, President, Nat'l School Boards Assoc. & Mr. Chip Slaven, Chief Exec. Officer, Nat'l School Boards Assoc., to President Joseph R. Biden, White House (Sept. 29, 2021).

[83] *Id.*

[84] *Id.*; *see also* Caroline Downey, *Vast majority of incidents cited by school-board group to justify federal intervention didn't involve threats,* NAT'L REV. (Oct. 2, 2021).

[85] *Id.*; *see also* Jessica Chasmar, *Loudoun County father arrested at school board events says school tried to cover up daughter's bathroom assault*, FOX NEWS (Oct. 12, 2021).

[86] Memorandum from Hon. Merrick Garland, Atty Gen., U.S. Dep't of Justice, Partnership Among Federal, State, Local, Tribal, And Territorial Law Enforcement to Address Threats Against School Administrators, Board Members, Teachers, and Staff (Oct. 4, 2021).

[87] *Id.*

[88] Press Release, U.S. Dep't of Justice, Justice Department Addresses Violent Threats Against School Officials and Teachers (Oct. 4, 2021).

[89] *Id.*

[90] *Oversight of the United States Department of Justice: Hearing Before the H. Comm. on the Judiciary,* 117th Cong. at 32 (Oct. 21, 2021) (testimony from Hon. Merrick Garland, Attorney General, U.S. Dep't of Justice).

[91] *Id.*

[92] *Id.* at 76.

Following the Attorney General's testimony, the NSBA Board of Directors issued a new memorandum to its members apologizing for the letter, stating: "On behalf of NSBA, we regret and apologize for the letter."[93] (emphasis in original). Although Attorney General Garland testified that the NSBA letter was the basis for his October 4 directive to insert federal law enforcement into local school board matters, the Attorney General has yet to rescind his memorandum.

ii. The Biden Administration colluded with the NSBA to create a justification to use federal law enforcement against parents.

The NSBA letter and ensuing Biden Administration action was the product of weeks of discussions between the Justice Department, the White House, and the NSBA. On May 20, 2022, the NSBA released a report it had commissioned to examine the events surrounding its September 29 letter to President Biden.[94] This report offered new evidence of how the Justice Department coordinated with the White House to target parents. The report found that the first communications between the NSBA and the White House occurred on September 9, and that the Biden White House closely coordinated with the NSBA on its letter to President Biden.[95]

On September 21—eight days before the NSBA letter—Mary Wall, a Senior Policy Advisor to President Biden, emailed NSBA's Interim CEO and Executive Director Chip Slaven, asking:

> Is there any way we can take a look at the letter in advance of release? In specific, I'm meeting w colleagues from other WH offices and DOJ tomorrow morning to see if there might be any options we can pursue here, so **if you have concrete recommendations in your letter** (e.g., the threat assessment you mentioned), would be good to know so I can include in discussions.[96]

In response, Slaven emailed Wall a detailed summary of the contents of the letter, which included specific language about the Patriot Act and the use of domestic terrorism tools.[97]

The NSBA-commissioned report concluded that "White House officials discussed the existence of the [NSBA] Letter, its requests, and the contents of the Letter with Department of Justice officials more than a week before the Letter was finalized and sent to President Biden."[98] In other words, Justice Department officials knew that the NSBA would encourage President

---

[93] Memorandum from NSBA Board of Directors, Message to NSBA Members (Oct. 22, 2021).

[94] *Final Report on the Events Surrounding the National School Boards Association's September 29, 2021, Letter to the President*, NATIONAL SCHOOL BOARDS ASSOCIATION (May 20, 2022) [hereinafter NSBA Final Report].

[95] *Id.* at 3.

[96] E-mail from Ms. Mary Wall, Senior Policy Advisor to the Pres., Exec. Office of the Pres., to Mr. Chip Slaven, Interim CEO & Exec. Dir., Nat'l School Boards Assoc. (Sept. 21, 2021 10:10 PM) (emphasis added).

[97] E-mail from Mr. Chip Slaven, Interim CEO & Exec. Dir., Nat'l School Boards Assoc., to Ms. Mary Wall, Senior Policy Advisor to the Pres., Exec. Office of the Pres. (Sept. 21, 2021 11:26 PM).

[98] NSBA Final Report at 2.

Biden to invoke the Patriot Act and domestic terrorism resources against parents, and the Justice Department apparently raised no concern about this effort. The report also noted how President Biden telephoned the then-NSBA president to say he was "appreciative" of the September 29 letter and to invite her to the Oval Office.[99]

The NSBA-commissioned report also uncovered communications between Justice Department employees and NSBA staff prior to the release of the Attorney General's October 4 memorandum. The report found that on October 4, a Justice Department employee contacted Slaven "about steps the Department could take to address the threats referenced in Letter."[100] Justice Department officials and Slaven had a call that afternoon, after which Alivia Roberts, Special Assistant to the Director of Public Affairs, followed up with an email to Slaven that included an advance copy of Garland's memorandum.[101]

iii. The Justice Department is using criminal and counterterrorism resources to tag and investigate parents.

Contrary to Attorney General Garland's testimony to the Committee, whistleblower information shows that the Justice Department and the FBI quickly operationalized Attorney General Garland's directive. On October 20, 2021—the day before Attorney General Garland's testimony to the House Judiciary Committee—the FBI's Assistant Director for the Counterterrorism Division and the Assistant Director for the Criminal Division sent an email referencing Garland's October 4 directive and notifying FBI personnel about a new "threat tag" created to apply to school board investigations.[102] The email directed FBI personnel to apply this new EDUOFFICIALS threat tag to all "investigations and assessments of threats specifically directed against school board administrators, board members, teachers, and staff."[103] The email articulated the purpose as "scop[ing] this threat on a national level and provid[ing] an opportunity for comprehensive analysis of the threat picture for effective engagement with law enforcement partners at all levels."[104]

Information from whistleblowers show that the FBI has opened investigations with the EDUOFFICIALS threat tag in almost every region of the country and relating to all types of educational settings. The information received shows how, as a direct result of Attorney General Garland's October 4 directive, federal law enforcement is using counterterrorism resources to investigate protected First Amendment activity. For example:

- In one investigation, an FBI Field Office interviewed a mom for allegedly telling a local school board "we are coming for you." The complaint, which came into the FBI through the National Threat Operations Center snitch-line, alleged that the mom was a threat because she belonged to a "right wing mom's group" known as "Moms for Liberty" and

---

[99] NSBA Final Report at 23.

[100] *Id.* at 46.

[101] E-mail from Ms. Alivia Roberts, Special Assistant to the Dir. of Public Affairs, U.S. Dep't of Justice, to Mr. Chip Slaven, Interim CEO & Exec. Dir., Nat'l School Boards Assoc. (Oct. 4, 2021 4:59 PM).

[102] E-mail from Mr. Carlton Peeples, Deputy Assistant Dir., Criminal Investigative Div., Fed. Bureau of Investigation, to FBI_SACS (Oct. 20, 2021).

[103] *Id.*

[104] *Id.*

because she "is a gun owner." When an FBI agent interviewed the mom, she told the agent that she was upset about the school board's mask mandates and that her statement was a warning that her organization would seek to replace the school board with new members through the electoral process.

- An FBI Field Office opened an investigation into a dad opposed to mask mandates. The complaint came in through the National Threat Operations Center snitch-line and alleged that the dad "fit the profile of an insurrectionist" because he "rails against the government," "believes all conspiracy theories," and "has a lot of guns and threatens to use them." When an FBI agent interviewed the complainant, the complainant admitted they had "no specific information or observations of . . . any crimes or threats," but they contacted the FBI after learning the Justice Department had a website "to submit tips to the FBI in regards to any concerning behavior directed toward school boards."

- In another case, an FBI Field Office opened an investigation into Republican state elected officials after a state Democrat party official accused them of making an "online terroristic threat by politicians against school board members." This complaint also came into the FBI through the National Threat Operations Center snitch-line. It alleged that one Republican official "incited violence" against school board members by expressing displeasure with school districts' vaccine mandates.

These investigations into concerned parents were the direct result of Attorney General Garland's October 4 directive. Each of the cases was initiated following the directive, the complaints came into the FBI through the same snitch-line—the National Threat Operations Center—highlighted in the press release accompanying the October 4 memorandum. One complainant even told an FBI agent that they reported the tip to the FBI because of the snitch-line, despite having "no specific information" about any actual threat. The Justice Department has subjected these moms and dads to the opening of an FBI investigation about them, the establishment of an FBI case file that includes their political views, and the application of a "threat tag" to their names as a direct result of their exercise of their fundamental constitutional right to speak and advocate for their children. This information is just more evidence of how the FBI is a willing partner of the Biden Administration's use of federal law enforcement, including counterterrorism resources, to investigate concerned parents for protected First Amendment activity.

Committee Republicans have repeatedly called on Attorney General Garland to rescind his memorandum and have sought information and documents in over 100 letters to Departmental components.[105] To date, the Justice Department and FBI have only responded with

---

[105] *See* Letter from Rep. Mike Johnson et al, to Hon. Merrick B. Garland, Atty Gen., U.S. Dep't of Justice (Oct. 13, 2021); Letter from Rep. Jim Jordan et al, Ranking Member, H. Comm. on the Judiciary, to Hon. Merrick B. Garland, Atty Gen., U.S. Dep't of Justice (Oct. 25, 2021); Letter from Rep. Jim Jordan et al, Ranking Member, H. Comm. on the Judiciary, to Mr. E. Bryan Wilson et al, Acting U.S. Atty, District of Alaska (Nov. 1, 2021); Letter from Rep. Jim Jordan et al, Ranking Member, H. Comm. on the Judiciary, to Mr. Mark Lesko, Acting Assistant Atty Gen., Nat'l Sec. Division, U.S. Dep't of Justice (Nov. 2, 2021); Letter from Rep. Jim Jordan et al, Ranking Member, H. Comm. on the Judiciary, to Hon. Christopher Wray, Dir., Fed. Bureau of Investigation (Nov. 3, 2021); Letter from Rep. Jim Jordan, Ranking Member, H. Comm. on the Judiciary, to Hon. Merrick B. Garland, Atty Gen., U.S.

two dismissive half-page letters, and with no requested documents or substantive information. Every day that passes while the Garland memorandum remains in effect, the Biden Administration and the FBI continue to use criminal and counterterrorism resources against America's moms and dads.

D. The FBI is abusing its foreign surveillance authorities.

The FBI has continually violated its Foreign Intelligence Surveillance Act (FISA) authorities,[106] a pattern of abuses that have been well-documented by the Justice Department Office of Inspector General (OIG) and the FISA Court. Evidence available to the Committee shows the FBI's leadership has failed to implement meaningful reforms to prevent the abuse of such an awesome power.

Over the years, the OIG has issued numerous reports where it has critiqued the FBI's handling of surveillance authorities. In December 2019, the OIG issued a 478-page report finding the FBI had abused the FISA authority to illegally surveil former Trump campaign associate Carter Page.[107] That report found 17 significant "errors or omissions" and 51 wrong or unsupported factual assertions in the applications to surveil Page.[108] The OIG found that the FBI downplayed the significance of the Democrat National Committee-financed opposition research document prepared by Christopher Steele (so-called "Steele dossier") in the applications, intentionally misstated Steele's reliability as a source, and failed to disclose Steele's biases.[109] The OIG also noted how the FBI cherry-picked facts to support its applications—ignoring exculpatory evidence—and how one FBI lawyer even doctored evidence presented to a judge to support surveillance against Page.[110] The FBI's misconduct was so bad that the Justice Department was later forced to admit that "there was insufficient predication to establish probable cause to believe that [Carter] Page was acting as an agent of a foreign power."[111]

Despite these troubling OIG findings, FBI leadership sought to peddle a narrative that the FISA abuses were not too serious. In the 116th Congress, on February 5, 2020, Director Wray testified before the Committee. During the hearing, Director Wray indicated that the FBI was

---

Dep't of Justice (Nov. 16, 2021); Letter from Rep. Jim Jordan, Ranking Member, H. Comm. on the Judiciary, to Hon. Christopher Wray, Dir., Fed. Bureau of Investigation (Nov. 18, 2021); Letter from Rep. Jim Jordan, Ranking Member, H. Comm. On the Judiciary, to Hon. Christopher Wray, Dir., Fed. Bureau of Investigation (Feb. 10, 2022); Rep. Jim Jordan, Ranking Member, H. Comm. on the Judiciary, to Hon. Merrick B. Garland, Atty Gen., U.S. Dep't of Justice (May 11, 2021); Letter from Rep. Jim Jordan et al, Ranking Member, H. Comm. on the Judiciary, to Hon. Merrick B. Garland, Atty Gen., U.S. Dep't of Justice (Jun. 14, 2022).

[106] *See generally*, 50 U.S.C. §§ 1801-1808; 1822-1826; 1841-1846; 1861-1862; S. Rep. No. 94-755 (1976) (Book II, Intelligence Activities and the Rights of Americans). In 1978, Congress enacted FISA in response to revelations that the federal government had seriously abused warrantless surveillance, resulting in rampant privacy violations. FISA provided a statutory framework for government agencies to conduct surveillance for foreign intelligence purposes through electronic surveillance (*e.g.*, wiretapping), physical searches, pen registers and trap and trace devices, or the production of certain business records.

[107] U.S. DEP'T. OF JUSTICE, OFFICE OF INSPECTOR GEN., REVIEW OF FOUR FISA APPLICATIONS AND OTHER ASPECTS OF THE FBI'S CROSSFIRE HURRICANE INVESTIGATION (2019).

[108] *Id.* at viii & xiii.

[109] *Id.* at vi.

[110] *Id.* at xi.

[111] *In re Carter W. Page*, Nos. 16-1182, 17-52, 17-375, 17-679 (FISC Jan. 7, 2020).

taking the FISA abuses seriously and working to address them.[112] At that hearing, Director Wray testified that Americans should not "lose any sleep over" the "vast majority" of FISA applications.[113] Similarly, during a transcribed interview with the Committee in December 2018, former FBI Director Comey heralded the FBI's FISA operations as a "labor-intensive and supervision heavy" process with an emphasis on high standards.[114] Comey labeled it a "top tier" FBI program.[115]

Only a month after Wray's assurances, the OIG again disclosed serious problems with the FBI's FISA processes in a March 2020 management advisory. This management advisory noted extensive noncompliance with Woods Procedures—an internal FBI process to minimize factual inaccuracies in FISA applications by requiring the FBI to maintain supporting documentation for each factual assertion in the application.[116] The OIG wrote that it "do[es] not have confidence that the FBI has executed its Woods Procedures in compliance with FBI policy, or that the process is working as it was intended to help achieve the 'scrupulously accurate' standard for FISA applications."[117]

In its management advisory, the OIG alerted Director Wray to unsupported, uncorroborated, or inconsistent information in the Woods Files of all 25 surveillance applications on U.S. persons examined by the OIG.[118] The FBI was unable to even locate the Woods Files for four additional files that the OIG requested—meaning the OIG could not review those applications.[119] The OIG "identified an average of about 20 issues per application reviewed," with 65 issues found in one FISA application alone.[120] These OIG findings undercut the FBI leaderships' stated confidence in the FISA process.

This March 2020 management advisory was only an early warning notice that alerted Director Wray to extensive noncompliance with Woods Procedures. In September 2021, the OIG issued a more detailed report that confirmed its initial finding of widespread non-compliance with the Woods Procedures.[121] This report revealed that there "were over 400 instances of non-compliance with the Woods Procedures in connection with those 29 FISA applications" (four of which were not located).[122] The OIG identified instances where Woods Files did not include

---

[112] *Oversight of the Federal Bureau of Investigation, Hearing Before the H. Comm. on Judiciary,* 116th Cong. (Feb. 5, 2020).

[113] *Id.*

[114] Transcribed Interview of James Comey, in Wash., D.C. at 145 & 147 (Dec. 17, 2018).

[115] *Id.*

[116] U.S. DEP'T. OF JUSTICE, OFFICE OF INSPECTOR GEN., MANAGEMENT ADVISORY MEMORANDUM FOR DIRECTOR OF THE FEDERAL BUREAU OF INVESTIGATION REGARDING THE EXECUTION OF WOODS PROCEDURES FOR APPLICATIONS FILED WITH THE FOREIGN INTELLIGENCE SURVEILLANCE COURT RELATING TO U.S. PERSONS (2020).

[117] *Id.* at 8.

[118] *Id.* at 7.

[119] *Id.*

[120] *Id.*

[121] U.S. DEP'T. OF JUSTICE, OFFICE OF INSPECTOR GEN., AUDIT OF THE FEDERAL BUREAU OF INVESTIGATION'S EXECUTION OF ITS WOODS PROCEDURES FOR THE APPLICATIONS FILED WITH THE FOREIGN INTELLIGENCE SURVEILLANCE COURT RELATING TO U.S. PERSONS (2021).

[122] *Id.* at 7.

sufficient supporting documentation for statements in the application.[123] The OIG found four errors that the DOJ and the FBI admitted were "material"—that could have possibly altered the FISA court's determination of "probable cause" to grant a warrant.[124] The OIG stated there is a "need for the FBI and DOJ to ensure rigorous supervisory review and robust oversight to help reduce the risk of erroneous information being included in FISA applications."[125]

Additionally, according to information from the Office of the Director for National Intelligence (ODNI), the FBI has misused FISA-collected information to surveil Americans without a warrant.[126] Under existing law, the FBI receives a portion of the information the government collects under Section 702 of FISA, and is authorized to conduct queries of this information that are reasonably likely to return foreign intelligence information, or evidence of a crime. [127] Queries that involve U.S. persons should raise oversight sensitivities to ensure rights are protected. However, ODNI data revealed that the FBI conducted an estimated 3,394,053 U.S. person queries in 2021 compared to approximately 1,324,057 U.S. person queries in 2020.[128] ODNI stated that more than half of the queries, or about 1.9 million, were related to attempts to compromise U.S. critical infrastructure by foreign cyber actors, which the Biden Administration has attributed to Russian hackers.[129] The ODNI report also noted that, on at least four occasions, the FBI failed to obtain an order from the FISC before accessing the contents of Section 702-acquired information.[130]

The FISC has also raised alarm about the FBI's actions in using FISA-acquired data for domestic criminal and other non-intelligence purposes. In November 2020, the FISC disclosed that "the government ha[d] reported numerous incidents" in which the FBI queried Section 702-acquired information for criminal investigations and reviewed content results without first obtaining court permission.[131] The FISC noted the discovery of 40 queries in which the FBI accessed information for investigations involving "health-care fraud, transnational organized crime, violent gangs, domestic terrorism involving racially motivated violent extremists, as well as investigations relating to public corruption and bribery," all of which were unrelated to foreign surveillance.[132] According to the FISC, "[n]one of these queries was related to national security, and they returned numerous Section 702-acquired products in response."[133] Judge

---

[123] *Id.* (The OIG also found that out of over 7,000 FISA applications approved between January 2015 and March 2020, there were 183 FISA applications for which the Woods File was missing in whole or in part.)

[124] *Id.* at 10-11.

[125] Press Release, U.S. Dep't. of Justice, Office of the Inspector Gen., DOJ OIG Releases Audit Report on the FBI's Execution of its Woods Procedures for Applications Filed with the Foreign Intelligence Surveillance Court Relating to U.S. Persons (Sept. 30, 2021).

[126] *See generally* OFFICE OF THE DIR. OF NAT'L INTELLIGENCE, ANNUAL STATISTICAL TRANSPARENCY REPORT, CALENDAR YEAR 2021 (2022).

[127] *See* 50 U.S.C. § 1801(a—f).

[128] OFFICE OF THE DIR. OF NAT'L INTELLIGENCE, ANNUAL STATISTICAL TRANSPARENCY REPORT, CALENDAR YEAR 2021 AT 4, 21 (2022).

[129] *Id.* at 20; Dustin Volz, *FBI Conducted Potentially Millions of Searches of Americans' Data Last Year, Report Says*, WALL ST. J. (May 5, 2022).

[130] OFFICE OF THE DIR. OF NAT'L INTELLIGENCE, ANNUAL STATISTICAL TRANSPARENCY REPORT, CALENDAR YEAR 2021 AT 22 (2022).

[131] Memorandum Opinion and Order, *Document re Section 702 Certification* at 38-43 (FISA Ct. Nov. 18, 2020).

[132] *Id.* at 42.

[133] *Id.*

James E. Boasberg, the then-presiding judge of the FISC, concluded that "the Court is concerned about the apparent widespread violations . . . ."[134] The FISC ultimately issued an order expanding the FBI's FISA reporting requirements to include "the number of U.S.-Person queries run by the FBI against Section-702 acquired information."[135]

This incident was not the first time that the FISC reported about the FBI's "apparent widespread violations" of privacy rules in conducting surveillance under Section 702 of FISA.[136] In October 2018, Judge Boasberg disclosed that "the FBI, against the advice of its general counsel, queried the Section 702 data using more than 70,000 email addresses or phone numbers."[137] Similarly, in December 2019, Judge Boasberg "found that the FBI again transgressed the privacy rules by searching for information on a job candidate, potential sources and a crime victim."[138] These are just a few examples of the FBI's compliance failures, which both the OIG and the FISC have substantiated in other reports.[139]

Committee Republicans have conducted oversight of the FBI's rampant abuses of FISA authorities and its associated provisions.[140] To date, the FBI has not provided data or information to fully satisfy oversight requests or even to begin to alleviate concerns. The FBI's misuse of its FISA authorities is a prominent example of how the FBI is abusing the existing authorities under federal law.

Separately, Committee Republicans have examined the FBI's acquisition and testing of software that allows it to infiltrate private cellphones. The NSO Group, an Israeli software company, gained widespread notoriety in 2021 after several media organizations published allegations that one of its products—named "Pegasus"—had been used by foreign governments

---

[134] *Id.* at 44.

[135] *Id.* at 63.

[136] Memorandum Opinion and Order, *Document re Section 702 Certification* (FISA Ct. Nov. 18, 2020); Ellen Nakashima, *Federal court approved FBI's continued use of warrantless surveillance power despite repeated violations of privacy rules*, WASH. POST (Apr. 26, 2021).

[137] Ellen Nakashima, *Federal court approved FBI's continued use of warrantless surveillance power despite repeated violations of privacy rules*, WASH. POST (Apr. 26, 2021).

[138] *Id.*

[139] *See* U.S. DEP'T OF JUSTICE, OFFICE OF INSPECTOR GEN., REVIEW OF FOUR FISA APPLICATIONS AND OTHER ASPECTS OF THE FBI'S CROSSFIRE HURRICANE INVESTIGATION (2019); U.S. DEP'T OF JUSTICE, OFFICE OF INSPECTOR GEN., MANAGEMENT ADVISORY MEMORANDUM FOR THE DIRECTOR OF THE FEDERAL BUREAU OF INVESTIGATION REGARDING THE EXECUTION OF WOODS PROCEDURES FOR APPLICATIONS FILED WITH THE FOREIGN INTELLIGENCE SURVEILLANCE COURT RELATING TO U.S. PERSONS (2020); Memorandum Opinion and Order, *Document Regarding the Section 702 2018 Certification* at 66 (FISC Oct. 2018); Memorandum Opinion and Order, *Document re Section 702 Certification* (FISA Ct. Nov. 18, 2020); U.S. DEP'T OF JUSTICE, OFFICE OF INSPECTOR GEN., AUDIT OF THE FEDERAL BUREAU OF INVESTIGATION'S EXECUTION OF ITS WOODS PROCEDURES FOR THE APPLICATIONS FILED WITH THE FOREIGN INTELLIGENCE SURVEILLANCE COURT RELATING TO U.S. PERSONS (2021).

[140] *See* Letter from Rep. Jim Jordan, Ranking Member, H. Comm. on the Judiciary, to Hon. Michael E. Horowitz, Inspector Gen., U.S. Dep't of Justice (May 1, 2020); Letter from Rep. Jim Jordan *et al.*, Ranking Member, H. Comm. on the Judiciary, to Hon. Christopher A. Wray, Dir., Fed. Bureau of Investigation (June 30, 2020); Letter from Rep. Jim Jordan *et al.*, Ranking Member, H. Comm. on the Judiciary, to Hon. Christopher A. Wray, Dir., Fed. Bureau of Investigation (May 4, 2021); Letter from Rep. Jim Jordan *et al.*, Ranking Member, H. Comm. on the Judiciary, to Hon. Christopher A. Wray, Dir., Fed. Bureau of Investigation (Jan. 27, 2022); Letter from Rep. Jim Jordan, et al., Ranking Member, H. Comm. on the Judiciary, to Hon. Christopher A. Wray, Dir., Fed. Bureau of Investigation (May 24, 2022).

to surveil dissidents, journalists, U.S. officials, and others.[141] Pegasus is a spyware tool that allows an operator to compromise a target's mobile device without requiring any input from the target.[142] After compromising a device, the operator can retrieve data on the device, track the device's location, and commandeer the device's camera and microphone.[143] The FBI has reportedly investigated whether Pegasus has been used against targets within the U.S. in recent years.[144]

As part of the allegations, media outlets reported that Pegasus was incapable of compromising mobile devices with U.S. phone numbers.[145] However, on January 28, 2022, the *New York Times* reported that the NSO Group has made a version of Pegasus capable of targeting U.S. mobile devices, called "Phantom."[146] This same report alleged that the FBI had acquired access to NSO Group spyware in 2019, tested it, and retains the hardware necessary to use it.[147] The FBI has since acknowledged that it acquired and tested NSO Group spyware.[148]

On March 3, 2022, Committee Republicans wrote to FBI Director Wray seeking documents and information relating to the FBI's acquisition, testing, and any other uses of NSO Group's spyware.[149] Committee Members on both sides of the aisle similarly raised this issue with FBI Assistant Director Bryan Vorndran in a March 29, 2022 hearing.[150] Although the FBI provided a classified briefing on June 16, and offered limited written responses to three questions posed at the briefing,[151] Committee Republicans have received none of the requested documents or communications, or sufficient information to evaluate the FBI's involvement with the NSO Group or Pegasus software. Subsequent reporting about the possible purchase of NSO Group by

---

[141] *See, e.g.*, Drew Harwell & Craig Timberg, *NSO Group vows to investigation potential spyware abuse following Pegasus Project Investigation*, WASH. POST (Jul. 20, 2021); *see also* Craig Timberg et al., *Pegasus spyware used to hack U.S. diplomats working abroad*, WASH. POST (Dec. 3, 2021).

[142] Craig Timberg *et al., Pegasus spyware used to hack U.S. diplomats working abroad*, WASH. POST (Dec. 3, 2021).

[143] *Id.*

[144] *See* Joseph Menn & Jack Stubbs, *Exclusive: FBI proves use of Israeli firm's spyware in personal and government hacks – sources*, REUTERS (Jan. 30, 2020).

[145] *See* Craig Timberg *et al., Pegasus spyware used to hack U.S. diplomats working abroad*, WASH. POST (Dec. 3, 2021).

[146] Ronen Bergman & Mark Mazzetti, *The Battle for the World's Most Powerful Cyberweapon*, N.Y. TIMES (Jan. 28, 2022).

[147] *Id.*

[148] Ellen Nakashima, *FBI acknowledges it tested NSO Group's spyware*, WASH. POST (Feb. 2, 2022).

[149] Letter from Rep. Jim Jordan, Ranking Member, H. Comm. on the Judiciary, and Rep. Mike Johnson, Ranking Member, Subcomm. on the Constitution, Civil Rights, and Civil Liberties of the H. Comm. on the Judiciary, to Hon. Christopher A. Wray, Director, Fed. Bureau of Investigation (Mar. 3, 2022).

[150] *Oversight of the Federal Bureau of Investigation, Hearing before the H. Comm. on the Judiciary*, 117th Cong. (Mar. 29, 2022) (Rep. Thomas Massie: "Have you detected the use of this software domestically? . . . Mr. Bryan Vorndran: "Sir, there is reporting in the media about Apple filing a lawsuit against NSO, and there is a lot of information in that article. I can't comment further on your question truly due to classification. But if that is of interest to you, we could consider a background briefing." . . . Rep. Ted Lieu: "Previously, Congressman Massie asked you about a briefing. And I just want to make sure, will you commit to a bipartisan briefing classified on Pegasus, the NSO Group, and the SS7 issue?" Mr. Bryan Vorndran: "Sir, yes, and if I can expand, I mean, it is very important for me personally, as a representative for the cyber program at the FBI, to keep that as an open invitation in both directions between all of you and me, and from me to all of you, that whatever information that you would want access to, we would try to facilitate that.").

[151] Email from FBI to H. Comm. on the Judiciary (Aug. 4, 2022) (on file with Committee staff).

an American defense contractor also raises additional questions about the FBI's actions and plans to acquire a sophisticated spyware tool that could be used against American citizens.[152] The June 16, 2022 briefing did not touch on the FBI's reported involvement in the contemplated sale of NSO Group to the American defense contractor.

E. The Justice Department and FBI conducted an unprecedented raid on a former president's home.

On August 8, 2022, the FBI raided President Trump's Mar-a-Lago residence in Palm Beach, Florida, purportedly to seize government and presidential records.[153] In the process, the FBI seized numerous other materials such as books, magazines, newspapers, clothing, gifts, and privileged documents.[154] This unprecedented raid comes after months of ongoing discussions and negotiations between President Trump and the National Archives and Records Administration (NARA) regarding records from his time in office.[155] The FBI's use of such aggressive law-enforcement tactics against a political opponent of the Biden Administration is another indication of how the FBI is guided by political considerations. Former Justice Department and White House officials David Rivkin and Lee Casey criticized the FBI's aggressive tactics, explaining that the FBI "could and should have sought a less intrusive judicial remedy than a search warrant—a restraining order allowing the materials to be moved to a location with the proper storage facilities, but also ensuring Mr. Trump continuing access."[156]

The Biden Justice Department has provided limited justification for this unprecedented action through a heavily redacted warrant affidavit and selective leaks to favored media outlets. The affidavit alleged probable cause to suspect three federal crimes relating to federal records—misuse of national defense information; obstruction of justice by destroying, altering, or falsifying records related to a federal probe; and concealing, removing, or destroying protected federal documents.[157] The affidavit also alleged probable cause to suspect evidence of obstruction.[158] However, the unredacted portions of the affidavit provide little support for these allegations and the unprecedented action.

The Biden Justice Department has hidden behind a formal policy of not commenting on the investigation, while it engaged in selective leaks of salacious accusations without context. On August 11, 2022, Attorney General Garland publicly addressed the search for the first time,

---

[152] Mark Mazzetti & Ronen Bergman, *Defense Firm Said U.S. Spies Backed Its Bid for Pegasus Spyware Maker*, N.Y. TIMES (Jul. 10, 2022).

[153] Stephanie Pagones *et al.*, *FBI raids Trump's Mar-a-Lago: 'Unprecedented' for agency to execute search warrant against former president*, FOX NEWS (AUG. 8, 2022); Deepa Shivram, *Trump says FBI agents searched his Mar-a-Lago home in Florida*, NPR (Aug. 8, 2022).

[154] Sadie Gurman *et al.*, *Court Releases Detailed FBI Inventory of Material Seized at Trump's Mar-a-Lago*, WALL ST. J. (Sept. 2, 2022).

[155] Order, *Donald J. Trump v. U.S.*, No. 22-81294-CIV-CANNON at 2 (S.D. Fla. Sept. 5, 2022); Motion for Judicial Oversight and Additional Relief, *In the Matter of the Search of Mar-a-Lago*, No. 22-cv-81294-AMC (S.D. Fla. Aug. 22, 2022).

[156] David B. Rivkin Jr. & Lee A. Casey, *The Trump warrant had no legal basis*, WALL ST. J. (Aug. 22, 2022).

[157] Affidavit in support of an application under Rule 41 for a warrant to search and seize, *In the Matter of the Search of: Locations Within the Premises to be Searched in Attachment A*, p. 7-8 (S.D. Fla.) (unsealed Aug. 26, 2022); *see also* 18 U.S.C. §§ 793, 2071, and 1519.

[158] *Id.*; *see also* Editorial Board, *The Mar-a-Lago Affidavit: Is That All There Is?,* WALL ST. J. (Sept. 12, 2022).

stating, "I have made clear that the Department of Justice will speak through its court filings and its work."[159] On the same day as Attorney General Garland's promise, however, the *Washington Post* reported that FBI agents were seeking "classified documents relating to nuclear weapons" according to leaks from "people familiar with the investigation."[160] The *New York Times* later reported details about the material seized, citing leaks from "people briefed on the matter."[161]

The Justice Department's affidavit and subsequent media leaks do not explain why a raid was necessary despite President Trump's cooperation and the availability of other process. In January 2022, President Trump transferred 15 boxes of documents from Mar-a-Lago to NARA.[162] In February 2022, NARA issued a public statement noting the cooperation of President Trump in the identification and submission of certain records.[163] In fact, his submission of records was over-inclusive. According to NARA, this submission included personal and post-presidential records, along with presidential correspondence and documents with classification markings.[164]

Subsequently, in May 2022, President Trump voluntarily accepted service of a grand jury subpoena that sought documents bearing classification markings.[165] Throughout June 2022, the Department and President Trump's lawyers engaged in discussions about the matter.[166] On June 3, the FBI visited Mar-a-largo and President Trump allowed them to inspect his storage room.[167] President Trump also provided responsive documents during the visit.[168] On June 8, the FBI requested that President Trump further secure the storage room, which he did.[169] President Trump also made staff available for voluntary interviews.[170] On June 22, the FBI subpoenaed surveillance footage from cameras at Mar-a-Largo.[171] The Trump Organization voluntarily accepted the subpoena and provided the footage.[172] On September 13, a federal judge unsealed additional portions of the affidavit—although still largely redacted—that showed President Trump had returned even more documents to the Department than previously known.[173]

---

[159] Press Release, U.S. Dep't of Justice, Attorney General Merrick Garland Delivers Remarks, (Aug. 11, 2022).

[160] Devlin Barrett, Josh Dawsey, Perry Stein, & Shane Harris, *FBI searched Trump's home to look for nuclear documents and other items, sources say*, WASH. POST (Aug. 11, 2022).

[161] Maggie Haberman, Jodi Kantor, Adam Goldman, & Ben Protess, *Trump Had More Than 300 Classified Documents at Mar-a-Lago*, N.Y. TIMES (Aug. 22, 2022).

[162] *Id.*

[163] Press Release, National Archives, Press Statements in Response to Media Queries About Presidential Records (Feb. 8, 2022).

[164] *Id.*; *see also* Letter from David S. Ferriero, Archivist of the United States, to Carolyn B. Maloney, Chair, H. Comm. on Oversight & Reform (Feb. 18, 2022); Letter from Debra S. Wall, Acting Archivist of the United States, to Evan Corcoran (May 10, 2022).

[165] Motion for Judicial Oversight and Additional Relief at 5, *In the Matter of the Search of Mar-a-Lago*, No. 22-cv-81294-AMC (S.D. Fla. Aug. 22, 2022).

[166] *See generally*, *id.*

[167] *Id.* at 5.

[168] *Id.*

[169] *Id.* at 6.

[170] *Id.*

[171] *Id.*

[172] *Id.*

[173] Affidavit in support of an application under Rule 41 for a warrant to search and seize, *In the Matter of the Search of: Locations Within the Premises to be Searched in Attachment A*, p. 7-8 (S.D. Fla.) (unsealed Aug. 26, 2022, Sept.

Despite the publicly available evidence of cooperation, Attorney General Garland personally approved the decision to seek a warrant for excessive and unprecedented access to President Trump's private residence.[174] FBI agents spent approximately nine hours rummaging through President Trump's personal belongings.[175] They collected more than 11,000 documents, more than 1,600 press articles and printed materials, 19 items of clothing or gifts, and 33 books.[176] They also collected about 100 documents with classification markings.[177]

The way that the FBI and Justice Department used their law-enforcement authorities to raid President Trump's residence differed drastically from the kid-glove treatment it gave former Secretary Hillary Clinton. Unlike President Trump, Secretary Clinton was not commander-in-chief and therefore the ultimate arbiter of national security information. The FBI never raided her private residence to recover classified information on her personal server, executed a search warrant or served a subpoena. Instead, the Justice Department allowed her lawyers to sort through Secretary Clinton's emails and determine which emails to preserve and which to delete. In fact, during the Clinton investigation, the FBI granted her senior aides blanket immunity and even allowed one—Cheryl Mills—to sit in on Clinton's interview as her attorney, even though Mills was a fact witness herself.[178]

Despite Secretary Clinton's mishandling of classified information on her private server,[179] then-Director Comey exonerated her conduct.[180] Director Comey read into the "gross negligence" standard of 18 U.S.C. § 793(f) an intent element and he concluded that Secretary Clinton lacked the intent to mishandle classified information.[181]

Director Comey did so even though the FBI found that 110 emails in 52 separate email chains on Clinton's server contained classified information at the time the emails were transmitted or received.[182] Eight email chains contained Top Secret information, 36 email chains

---

13, 2022 ("Since the fifteen boxes were provided to [National Archives], documents bearing classifications markings, which appear to contain [national defense information] and were stored at the premises in an unauthorized location, have been produced to the government in response to a grand jury subpoena. . . ." On July 6, 2022, in response to the subpoena [served on June 24, 2022], representatives of the Trump Organization provided a hard drive to FBI agents.").

[174] Press Release, U.S. Dep't of Justice, Attorney General Merrick Garland Delivers Remarks (Aug. 11, 2022).

[175] Motion for Judicial Oversight and Additional Relief, *In the Matter of the Search of Mar-a-Lago*, No. 22-cv-81294-AMC at 8 (S.D. Fla. Aug. 22, 2022).

[176] Samuel Chamberlain & Emily Crane, *Detailed inventory of Trump Mar-a-Lago FBI raid released*, N.Y. POST (Sept. 2, 2022).

[177] Phillip Bump, *Trump's classified Mar-a-Lago documents, catalogued*, WASH. POST (Sept. 2, 2022).

[178] Dep't Off. of Inspector Gen., A Review of Various Actions by the Federal Bureau of Investigation and Department of Justice in Advance of the 2016 Election at ii, 161 (June 2018).

[179] State Dep't Off. of Inspector Gen., Office of the Secretary: Evaluation of Email Records Management and Cybersecurity Requirements, ESP-16-03 (May 2016).

[180] Early drafts of the FBI Director's statement on the matter described Clinton's behavior as "grossly negligent," which is the legal standard under 18 U.S.C. § 793(f). The description of Clinton's handling of classified information was subsequently changed from "grossly negligent" to "extremely careless" in the final statement.

[181] Fed. Bureau of Investigation, Statement by FBI Director James B. Comey on the Investigation of Secretary Hillary Clinton's Use of a Personal E-Mail System (July 5, 2016).

[182] *Id.*

contained Secret information, and eight email chains contained Confidential information.[183] Moreover, another 2,000 emails were later found to contain classified information.[184] According to the FBI, Clinton "used her personal e-mail extensively while outside the United States, including sending and receiving work-related emails in the territory of sophisticated adversaries."[185] The FBI initially determined it was "reasonably likely" that hostile actors gained access to [former] Secretary Clinton's private email account, but it later changed this determination to "possible."[186] Moreover, after discovery of her misuse of classified emails, Clinton allowed her representatives to use "BleachBit" to permanently wipe her emails.[187] According to Clinton, her lawyers deleted over 30,000 emails that she determined to be unrelated to her official duties, without any review of the records by government lawyers.[188]

According to Constitutional professor Jonathan Turley, "the FBI's handling of her [Hillary Clinton's] case will cast a long shadow over any potential prosecution of the former president [Trump], including the recent focus on an obstruction charge. There likely would be an assortment of 'but her emails' objections to a charge that could have been made as readily against Clinton or her associates."[189] Professor Turley further noted that "the transfer of top-secret and other classified documents to her private server, Clinton and her staff did not fully cooperate with investigators. During the investigations of her conduct, some of us marveled at the temerity of the Clinton staff in refusing to turn over her laptop and other evidence to State Department and DOJ investigators. The FBI had to cut deals with her aides to secure their cooperation."[190]

On August 15, 2022, Committee Republicans wrote Attorney General Garland, FBI Director Wray, and White House Chief of Staff Ronald Klain requesting documents and communications related to the FBI's raid of President Trump's residence.[191] The Department and FBI have failed to sufficiently comply with this request to date. The White House has not responded at all. Additionally, on September 14, 2022, the Committee considered a resolution, H. Res. 1325, which requests that President Biden—and directs Attorney General Garland to—provide an unredacted copy of the affidavit to the House of Representatives related to the extraordinary and unprecedented FBI raid of a former president's private residence. Democrats declined to join Republicans in the Committee's constitutional duty to conduct oversight of the

---

[183] *Id.*

[184] *Id.*

[185] Fed. Bureau of Investigation, Statement by FBI Director James B. Comey on the Investigation of Secretary Hillary Clinton's Use of a Personal E-Mail System (July 5, 2016).

[186] Dep't Off. of Inspector Gen., A Review of Various Actions by the Federal Bureau of Investigation and Department of Justice in Advance of the 2016 Election at iv (June 2018).

[187] *Id.* at 38.

[188] *Id.*; *see also*, Amy Chozick & Michael S. Schmidt, *Hillary Clinton tried to quell controversy over private email*, N.Y. TIMES, Mar. 10, 2015.

[189] Jonathan Turley, *Hats off to Hillary: Prosecuting Trump in the shadow of Clinton's emails*, THE HILL (Sept. 3, 2022).

[190] *Id.*

[191] *See* Letter from Rep. Jim Jordan, *et al.*, Ranking Member, H. Comm. on the Judiciary, to Hon. Merrick B. Garland, Atty Gen., U.S. Dep't of Justice (Aug. 15, 2022); Letter from Rep. Jim Jordan, *et al.*, Ranking Member, H. Comm. on the Judiciary, to Hon. Christopher A. Wray, Dir., Fed. Bureau of Investigation (Aug. 15, 2022); Letter from Rep. Jim Jordan, *et al.*, Ranking Member, H. Comm. on the Judiciary, to Mr. Ronald Klain, Chief of Staff, White House (Aug. 15, 2022).

Executive Branch and obtain access to the unredacted affidavit. Chairman Nadler misleadingly argued that "the affidavit has now been made public,"[192] ignoring that the publicly available version of the affidavit remains heavily redacted. Rather than receive more facts and information about the FBI's unprecedented raid of President Trump's former residence, Democrats voted to report H. Res. 1325 unfavorably to the House of Representatives. Committee Republicans disagreed with that action.

F. The FBI stalked a Republican Congressman while on a family vacation to seize his personal cell phone.

On the morning of August 10, 2022, FBI agents seized the cell phone of Representative Scott Perry while he was traveling with his family.[193] Reports indicate that the FBI's action is related to a joint investigation conducted by the Office of Inspector General (OIG) and the Justice Department.[194] Here, too, like the FBI's raid of President Trump's residence, the use of such an aggressive law-enforcement tactic against a prominent political opponent of the Biden Administration raises grave concerns about the FBI's politicization.

Relatedly, reports revealed the existence of a secret FBI audit detailing rampant violations of internal policies governing FBI investigations concerning "politicians, candidates, religious groups, news media and others."[195] The FBI conducted this internal review in 2019 to gauge compliance with FBI rules for handling high-profile and delicate cases—known as sensitive investigative matters (SIMs)—that generally involve the activities of a domestic public official, political candidate, or religious organization.[196] The FBI's audit of 353 cases found a total of 747 compliance errors in violation of internal FBI rules.[197] This internal audit and the staggering number of errors it found suggest a pattern of misconduct and mismanagement within the FBI in failing to uphold internal rules for its most sensitive cases.

The systematic policy violations disclosed included that FBI personnel failed to procure supervisory approval to open a sensitive investigation, failed to ensure appropriate legal review prior to opening a SIM, and failed to give timely written notice to the appropriate United States

---

[192] *H. Res. 1238 et al., Business Meeting of the H. Comm. on Judiciary,* 117th Cong. (Sept. 14, 2022) (statement of the Hon. Jerrold Nadler, Chairman, H. Comm. on the Judiciary).

[193] Michael Balsamo, *Rep. Scott Perry says FBI agents seized his cellphone*, ASSOC PRESS (Aug. 10, 2022). According to Congressman Perry, the FBI agents "made no attempt to contact my lawyer, who would have made arrangements for them to have my phone if that was their wish. I'm outraged – though not surprised - that the FBI under the direction of Merrick Garland's DOJ, would seize the phone of a sitting Member of Congress. My phone contains info about my legislative and political activities, and personal/private discussions with my wife, family, constituents, and friends. None of this is the government's business."

[194] Sarah Murray *et al.*, *Republican congressman says FBI seized his cell phone*, CNN (Aug. 10, 2022). According to reports, the Justice Department OIG used its laboratory in Northern Virginia to assist the FBI in conducting a forensic review of Representative Perry's phone. Reports indicate that Representative Perry's phone "was imaged after the search," creating a forensic copy of the device's contents—including communications protected by common-law privileges as well as the Constitution's Speech or Debate Clause.

[195] Ryan Lovelace, *Exclusive: Audit Reveals FBI rule-breaking in probes involving politicians, religious groups, media*, WASH. TIMES (Mar. 11, 2022) (reporting the existence of the FBI's secret 2020 audit).

[196] FED. BUREAU OF INVESTIGATION, INSPECTIONS DIVISION, EXTERNAL AUDIT AND COMPLIANCE SECTION, 2019 DOMESTIC INVESTIGATIONS AND OPERATIONS GUIDE AUDIT AT 3 (2020).

[197] *Id.*

Attorney's Office.[198] Of the 353 SIMs examined, the audit noted that more than half concerned a "domestic public official."[199] The audit found 74 cases "had a lack of investigative activity for periods of 90 days or longer," suggesting that these cases lingered for longer than necessary.[200] It also noted 33 cases in which the FBI headquarters failed to notify the Justice Department about "all known SIMs."[201] Portions of the internal audit, including sections concerning search warrants and investigative methods, are redacted in the publicly available version, suggesting there could be additional misconduct that the FBI continues to shield from public scrutiny.

Last year, during Director Wray's testimony before the Judiciary Committee, he claimed that the FBI "investigate[s] individuals with proper predication" and does not "investigate First Amendment groups . . . [or] people for speech, for association, for assembly, [or] for membership in domestic First Amendment groups."[202] However, the FBI's internal review—which the FBI never disclosed and which shows fundamental errors with FBI investigations touching on sensitive political and constitutional matters—is inconsistent with Director Wray's unqualified assurances.

On March 21, 2022, Committee Republicans sent a letter to Wray requesting documents and information related to the FBI's compliance with its own rules intended to protect American civil liberties.[203] Although the FBI provided a response to the March 21 letter simply asserting that it "takes especially seriously compliance regarding sensitive investigative matters,"[204] it did not produce any of the requested documents or communications like an unredacted copy of the 2019 audit.

G. The Justice Department and the FBI continue to allow attacks on pro-life facilities and churches to go unabated, while pushing an anti-life agenda.

The FBI's aggressive law-enforcement tactics against political opponents of the Biden Administration is striking in light of how the FBI has declined to use its law-enforcement tools against radical activists. This disparity is particularly noticeable in the context of anti-life violence and threats perpetrated by the far left.

On May 2, 2022, news outlets reported on and published a copy of an initial draft of an opinion in *Dobbs v. Jackson Women's Health Organization*, a then-pending case before the Supreme Court considering Mississippi's pro-life law.[205] On June 24, 2022, the Supreme Court issued its *Dobbs* opinion.[206] The majority opinion, authored by Justice Samuel Alito, upheld

---

[198] *Id.* at 4-6.

[199] *Id.* at 7.

[200] *Id.* at 6.

[201] *Id.* at 4.

[202] *Oversight of the Federal Bureau of Investigation: Hearing Before the H. Comm. on the Judiciary*, 117th Cong. at 63-64 (Jun. 10, 2021).

[203] Letter from Rep. Jim Jordan *et al.*, Ranking Member, H. Comm. on the Judiciary, to Hon. Christopher A. Wray, Dir., Fed. Bureau of Investigation (Mar. 21, 2022).

[204] Letter from Ms. Jill C. Tyson, Assistant Dir., Office of Cong. Affairs, Fed. Bureau of Investigation, to Rep. Jim Jordan, Ranking Member, H. Comm. on the Judiciary (May 13, 2022).

[205] Josh Gerstein & Alexander Ward, *Supreme Court has voted to overturn abortion rights, draft opinion shows*, POLITICO (May 2, 2022).

[206] *Dobbs v. Jackson Women's Health Org.*, 597 U.S. ____(2022).

Mississippi's pro-life law and overturned *Roe v. Wade* and *Planned Parenthood of Southeastern Pennsylvania v. Casey.*[207] The leak of the *Dobbs* draft and issuance of the final opinion prompted the left to propagate an intimidation and outrage campaign against Supreme Court justices at their private residences and pro-life facilities. Despite this harassment and violence aimed at the Court and pro-life facilities, the Biden Administration has declined to enforce the law to protect Supreme Court justices and their families.

Section 1507 of title 18 of the U.S. Code prohibits "pickets or parades . . . in or near a building or residence" of a judge when done with the intent to interfere, obstruct, or impede "the administration of justice" or "with the intent of influencing any judge . . . in the discharge of his duty."[208] While protesting is a protected and fundamental First Amendment activity, courts have distinguished conduct that is intended to obstruct or pervert the course of justice and does not retain such protections.[209]

According to an unclassified memorandum from the Department of Homeland Security dated May 13, 2022, violence against and targeting of Supreme Court justices, public officials, healthcare providers, and clergy is "likely to persist and may increase leading up to and following the issuing of the Court's official ruling."[210] Shortly after the leak of the draft opinion, Virginia Governor Glenn Youngkin and Maryland Governor Larry Hogan wrote to Attorney General Garland, urging him to "provide appropriate resources to safeguard the justices and enforce the law as it is written."[211]

One left-wing group, Ruth Sent Us, published the home addresses of the Court's six conservative justices and stirred up organized harassment at those residences.[212] Public footage of these events shows agitators loudly chanting, "abort the Court" and, "if we don't get it, shut it down," seeming to threaten consequences for the justices if they did not uphold *Roe v. Wade.*[213] The same group published the name of Justice Amy Coney Barrett's church and the school that her children attend, encouraging protestors to "voice your anger."[214]

On June 8, 2022, police officers arrested a California resident, Nicholas John Roske, near Justice Brett Kavanaugh's home.[215] Upon arrest, officers found a knife, a Glock 17 pistol, ammunition, two magazines, zip ties, pepper spray, hammer, crowbar, duct tape, boots with pads

---

[207] *Id.*

[208] 18 U.S.C. § 1507 (1994).

[209] *See, e.g., United States v. Gregg*, 226 F.3d 253, 267-268 (3d Cir. 2000) ("Activities that injure, threaten, or obstruct are not protected by the First Amendment, whether or not such conduct communicates a message.").

[210] Sophia Cai & Stef W. Kight, *DHS preparing for violence following abortion ruling,* AXIOS (May 18, 2022).

[211] Yael Halon, *Youngkin, Hogan send letter to Garland urging him to prosecute demonstrators outside Supreme justices' homes*, FOX NEWS (May 11, 2022).

[212] Anders Hagstrom, *Liberal group calls for protests at conservative Supreme Court justices' homes*, FOX NEWS (May 5, 2022).

[213] *See Abortion rights supports chant outside Supreme Court Justices' homes,* CNN (May 9, 2022); Patrick Reilly, *Abortion rights activities hold protests outside of Justice Alito's home,* N.Y. POST (May 10, 2022); *Protesters march to Justice Alito's home, hold 'vigil for abortion rights',* FOX NEWS (May 10, 2022); *America's Newsroom* (Fox News television broadcast May 10, 2022).

[214] Ruth Sent Us (@RuthSentUs), TWITTER (Jun. 8, 2022, 9:37 AM).

[215] Affidavit in Support of Criminal Complaint, *United States v. Roske*, No. 22-mj-1848-TJS at 1-2 (D. M.D. Jun. 8, 2022).

on the outside soles, and other items among Roske's possessions.[216] Roske told detectives that he was "upset about the leak of a recent Supreme Court draft decision regarding the right to abortion" and the Uvalde shooting.[217] Further, Roske told detectives that "he began thinking about how to give his life a purpose and decided that he would kill the Supreme Court Justice after finding the Justice's Montgomery County address on the Internet."[218] Additionally, Roske "indicated that he had purchased the Glock pistol and other items for the purpose of breaking into the Justice's residence and killing the Justice as well as himself."[219] Federal prosecutors charged Roske with attempted murder.[220]

Following the June 24, 2022, release of the *Dobbs* opinion, harassment against the justices continued. On July 1, 2022, Supreme Court Marshal Gail Curley wrote to Maryland and Virginia state officials, noting that "protest activity at justices' homes, as well as threatening activity, has only increased."[221] Given the intimidating protests, Curley requested that the state officials enforce certain state picketing and protesting statutes.[222] In response to Curley's request, Montgomery County Executive Marc Elrich insinuated that the letter was "not about security," and that the request "seemed to me to be just basically, you know, kind of like theater, maybe a little bit of a response to the fact that we reacted pretty negatively to what the Court decision was."[223]

Further, on July 7, 2022, protestors disrupted Justice Kavanaugh's dinner at a Washington, D.C. restaurant, which led to the justice escaping the restaurant through a back door.[224] Additionally, the left-wing group ShutDownDC offered "bounties" to D.C. industry workers for reporting confirmed sightings of conservative justices and additional money if the justices are still at the establishment thirty minutes after the initial report.[225]

All these actions appear to be attempts to intimidate and influence the justices' rulings in violation of section 1507. However, in the face of ongoing threats to the justices and their families, the DOJ has, without any public explanation, neglected to institute a single prosecution for those acting in apparent violation and even brazen defiance of the law. One commentator noted the "bigger picture [] that the attorney general is operating according to a partisan compass rather than an objective commitment to the law."[226]

In addition to anti-life extremists targeting Supreme Court justices, anti-life fanatics have targeted, destroyed, or vandalized nearly 70 pro-life facilities, groups, and churches to further

---

[216] *Id.* at 2.
[217] *Id.* at 2-3.
[218] *Id.* at 3.
[219] *Id.*
[220] Criminal Complaint, *United States v. Roske,* No. 22-mj-1848-TJS (D. M.D. Jun. 8, 2022).
[221] *Still No Peace at the Justices' Houses*, WALL ST. J. (Jul. 5, 2022).
[222] *Id.*
[223] *Why Marc Elrich Won't Protect Supreme Court Justices*, WALL ST. J. (Jul. 6, 2022).
[224] Chloe Folmar, *Morton's condemns abortion rights protestors for disrupting Kavanaugh's freedom to 'eat dinner,'* THE HILL (Jul. 8, 2022).
[225] Thomas Catenacci, *ShutDownDC group offers bounties on Twitter for public sightings of conservative Supreme court justices,* FOX NEWS (Jul. 8, 2022).
[226] Carrie Campbell Severino, *The People Want Attorney General Garland to Enforce the Law*, NAT'L REV. (Aug. 11, 2022).

their political cause. A list of these violent incidents is included as Appendix A. These actions appear to violate federal law. The Freedom of Access to Clinic Entrances (FACE) Act "prohibits threats of force, obstruction and property damage intended to interfere with reproductive health care services."[227] The statute creates criminal and civil penalties for violators. However, as the Justice Department acknowledges, "[t]he FACE Act is not about abortions."[228] The law also protects "pro-life pregnancy counseling services and any other pregnancy support facility providing reproductive health care."[229]

Pro-life pregnancy centers nationwide play a critical and important role in supporting and assisting pregnant women. In 2019, 2,700 such centers served nearly 2 million people, and continue to serve millions of women annually.[230] Pro-life pregnancy centers "exist to serve and support mothers in the courageous decision to give their children life, even under the most difficult circumstance."[231] Services and resources provided virtually free of charge include, but are not limited to: ultrasounds, pregnancy testing, STI/STD testing, parenting and prenatal education programs, diapers, baby outfits.[232]

Although federal law protects pro-life services and facilities, the Biden Administration has not enforced the law to protect these entities. For example, on June 10, 2022—in the same federal judicial district as Houck—vandals smashed the windows and graffitied the walls of HOPE Pregnancy Center.[233] There has been no press release from the Department regarding an investigation or charges in that case. Additionally, since the leak of the draft *Dobbs* opinion, Jane's Revenge, a radical anti-life group, "has claimed responsibility for at least 18 arson and vandalism attacks" on pro-life clinics and organizations.[234] While the FBI claims that it is investigating a "series of attacks and threats targeting pregnancy resource centers, faith-based organizations, and reproductive health clinics" the FBI has not executed any SWAT team "dawn" raids to make arrests in these cases.[235]

While the Administration has looked the other way on violence targeting pro-life groups and facilities, its enforcement of the FACE Act for the protection of anti-life activists borders on thuggish. On September 23, 2022, an FBI SWAT team raided the home of Pennsylvania resident Mark Houck to arrest him on an indictment charging FACE Act violations punishable by up to eleven years in prison, based on simple shoving incidents. The warrant alleged that on October 13, 2021, Houck shoved a Planned Parenthood volunteer escort outside a clinic.[236] Houck's wife,

---

[227] P.L. 103-259 (1994); U.S. Dep't of Justice, Nat'l Task Force on Violence Against Reproductive Health Care Providers, Protecting Patients and Health Care Providers, https://www.justice.gov/crt/protecting-patients-and-health-care-providers (last visited Sept. 27, 2022).

[228] *Id.*

[229] *Id.*

[230] *Pro-life Pregnancy Centers Served 2 Million People with Essential Medical, Education and Support Services in 2019*, CHARLOTTE LOZIER INSTITUTE (Oct. 21, 2020).

[231] *Id.*

[232] *Id.*

[233] Jenice Armstrong, *Angry about Roe? Then vote, don't vandalize,* PHILADELPHIA INQUIRER (Jun. 29, 2022).

[234] Jessica Chasmar, *Zero arrests in at least 17 Jane's Revenge attacks on pro-life organizations,* FOX NEWS (Sept. 14, 2022).

[235] *Id.*

[236] Press Release, U.S. Dep't of Justice, U.S. Atty's Office E.D. of Penn., Bucks County Man Indicated on Federal Charges for Assaulting a Reproductive Healthcare Clinic Escort (Sept. 23, 2022).

however, explained that Houck was provoked by the Planned Parenthood activist repeatedly making "crude . . . inappropriate and disgusting" comments to Houck's 12-year-old son and getting "into the personal space" of the child.[237] She said that a local court in Philadelphia had already thrown out a civil suit against Houck filed by the activist.[238]

The aggressive tactics taken by the FBI to arrest Houck are troubling. Houck's wife, who was present at the time of his arrest, stated that an FBI "SWAT team of about 25 came to my house with about 15 vehicles" and "they had about five guns pointed at my husband, myself and basically at my kids."[239] An anonymous FBI source denied to the media that the 25 agents were present, but did admit that authorities sent up to 20 agents to effectuate the arrest.[240] In addition, Houck's attorney indicated that the "dawn" raid was unnecessary as Houck offered to "appear voluntarily" and the FBI targeted him "solely to intimidate people of faith and prolife Americans."[241]

On October 5, 2022, the Justice Department announced charges, against eleven pro-life individuals for FACE Act violations stemming from a single event from over a year prior—on March 5, 2021—in Mount Juliet, Tennessee.[242] Among those charged was Eva Edl, a 87-year-old "long time" pro-life advocate who came to the United States after surviving a "communist concentration camp in Yugoslavia after World War II."[243] According to one report, the pro-life advocates arrested in March 2021 sang and prayed in a "hallway of a shared general medical office building" featuring an abortion clinic.[244] Several individuals were reportedly arrested at the time and posted bail for misdemeanor charges before the Justice Department charged them 17 months later.[245]

The double standard in enforcing the FACE Act to protect pro-abortion facilities while ignoring attacks on these pro-life facilities suggests that the Justice Department would rather cater to the anti-life movement then aid facilities that protect pregnant women in need. There is no indication this double standard is an aberration. In fact, in July 2022, the Department established a "Reproductive Rights Task Force."[246] Chaired by Associate Attorney General Vanita Gupta, the Task Force will "monitor and evaluate all state and local legislation and

---

[237] Patrick Delaney, *FBI raids home of Catholic pro-life speaker, author with guns drawn as his terrified kids watch*, LIFESITE (Sept. 23, 2022); *see also* Diana Glebova, *Lawyer for pro-life protester arrested by FBI says client offered to surrender, claims DOJ trying to 'intimidate people of faith,'* NAT'L REV. (Sept. 26, 2022).

[238] *Id.*

[239] Bradford Betz, Jon Brown, & Jake Gibson, *Pennsylvania pro-life activist arrested by FBI, charged with assaulting clinic escort,* FOX NEWS (Sept. 26, 2022).

[240] *Id.*

[241] Diana Glebova, *Lawyer for pro-life protester arrested by FBI says client offered to surrender, claims DOJ trying to 'intimidate people of faith,'* NAT'L REV. (Sept. 26, 2022).

[242] Press Release, U.S. Atty's Office M.D. of Tenn., U.S. Dep't of Justice, Eleven Charged with FACE Act Violations Stemming From 2021 Blockade of Mount Juliet Reproductive Health Clinic (Oct. 5, 2022).

[243] Peter D'Abrosca, *DOJ charges 15, including 87-year-old woman, for allegedly blocking door to Tennessee abortion clinic*, TENN. STAR (Oct. 7, 2022).

[244] Nancy Flanders, *87-year-old concentration camp survivor is one of 11 pro-lifers recently arrested by FBI*, LIVE ACTION (Oct. 10, 2022).

[245] *Id.*

[246] Press Release, U.S. Dep't of Justice, Justice Department Announces Reproductive Rights Task Force (Jul. 12, 2022).

enforcement actions that threaten" access to abortions where legal, coordinate "appropriate" federal responses, collaborate with stakeholders, and provide "technical assistance to Congress in connection with federal legislation to codify reproductive rights."[247] The Department's announcement included no mention that it would support state or federal laws protecting the sanctity of life.

H. The FBI conducted an "intelligence" assessment of a conservative charity under the guise of investigating unrelated alleged crimes.

Committee Republicans have discovered that the FBI is likely abusing its authorities to conduct wide-ranging assessments based on tenuous allegations. An FBI "assessment" is like an investigation, but requires less factual justification to undertake and the FBI may use only limited law-enforcement methods.[248] However, the FBI may still use methods such as observational surveillance; certain kinds of subpoenas; human sources; and federal, state, local, and tribal databases when conducting an assessment.[249] In 2016, the FBI conducted an assessment of Concerned Women of America (CWA), a domestic organization that advocates for certain policies at the federal, state, and local levels.[250] The FBI's assessment of CWA was ostensibly to look for financial crimes, although one document made public through a Freedom of Information Act request showed that there was an "Intelligence" component to the FBI's assessment.[251] The same document suggested that the reason the FBI suspected CWA of committing financial crimes is because a third-party charity rating service gave CWA an "underperform[ing]" rating.[252]

On August 11, 2021, Committee Republicans wrote a letter to the FBI seeking documents and information about the CWA assessment and the FBI's use of assessments generally.[253] Committee staff engaged with the FBI over a period of weeks to accommodate purported concerns from FBI legislative affairs personnel about sharing certain nonpublic documents as well as purported technological limitations that would prevent the FBI from providing the requested information. Ultimately, the FBI offered only public documents already in the Committee's possession, an unredacted version of a CWA assessment document that the Committee had in redacted form, and a document unrelated to the CWA assessment. The FBI refused to provide even generalized information about how many assessments it conducts, the rate at which those assessments lead to a formal investigation, and the identity of assessment targets. On October 22, 2021, the FBI sent a response letter that referred only to publicly available documents and the FBI's policy of not sharing documents and information pertaining

---

[247] *Id.*

[248] *See* THE ATTORNEY GENERAL'S GUIDELINES FOR DOMESTIC FBI OPERATIONS, U.S. DEPT. OF JUSTICE 16-20 (on file with the Committee).

[249] *Id.* at 20.

[250] *See* Patrick G. Eddington, *The FBI's Unjustified Targeting of Concerned Women for America*, CATO INSTITUTE (Jul. 14, 2021); *see also* Charity Assessment: Concerned Women for America, Fed. Bureau of Investigation (Jul. 5, 2016) (on file with the Committee); *see also What We Do*, CONCERNED WOMEN FOR AMERICA, https://concernedwomen.org/what-we-do-2.

[251] *See* Charity Assessment: Concerned Women for America, Fed. Bureau of Investigation (Jul. 5, 2016).

[252] *Id.*

[253] *See* Letter from Rep. Jim Jordan, Ranking Member, H. Comm. on the Judiciary, to Hon. Christopher A. Wray, Dir., Fed. Bureau of Investigation (Aug. 11, 2021).

to criminal subjects and victims.[254] The FBI's response letter did not satisfy the oversight request.

I. The FBI appears to not be aggressively investigating pipe bombs placed by political party headquarters on January 6, 2021, while prioritizing other January 6, 2021-related investigations.

On March 9, 2022, Committee Republicans sent a letter to Director Wray detailing a senior FBI special agent's whistleblower disclosure concerning the FBI's lackluster investigation into the pipe bombs placed near the headquarters of the Democratic National Committee and Republican National Committee on January 5, 2021.[255] According to the whistleblower, on February 7, 2022—over a year after the placement of the bombs—the FBI's Washington Field Office asked FBI field offices to canvass all confidential human sources nationwide for information about the individual and the crime.[256] In part, the message asked that the canvass "include sources reporting on all [types of] threats" because the suspect's "motive and ideology remain unknown."[257]

The whistleblower explained that the WFO request was "unusual" because it was transmitted more than a year after the FBI began its investigation, and it raises questions about the progress and extent of the FBI's investigation.

The slow pace of the pipe bombs investigation stands in contrast to other Department investigations and prosecutions related to the events of January 6, 2021. According to the U.S. Attorney's Office for the District of Columbia, as of October 6, 2022, it had arrested 880 people for January 6-related offenses, filed criminal charges against 272 defendants, and secured sentences for 280 defendants.[258] There are also serious concerns about the pre-trial detention of January 6 defendants. Julie Kelly, a journalist who has covered the events of January 6, explained in January 2022:

> The Justice Department has sought pretrial detention for at least 100 January 6 protestors . . . . [T]hese defendants have not been convicted of any crime. Most have no criminal record and some do not face violent charges related to their conduct on January 6. Many detainees don't even have a court date yet. . . . Detainees at the D.C. jail have reported numerous human rights and Constitutional violations. . . . Living conditions are also utterly unacceptable. Detainees do not have access to religious services, a law library, or even personal hygiene services. Some have not seen their families in nearly a year. Detainees have reported instances of racially and

---

[254] Letter from Ms. Jill C. Tyson, Assistant Director, Fed. Bureau of Investigation, to Rep. Jim Jordan, Ranking Member, H. Comm. on the Judiciary (Oct. 22, 2021).

[255] Letter from Rep. Jim Jordan, Ranking Member, H. Comm. on the Judiciary, to Hon. Christopher A. Wray, Dir., Fed. Bureau of Investigation (Mar. 9, 2022).

[256] Fed. Bureau of Investigation E-mail (Feb. 7, 2022) (on file with Committee staff).

[257] *Id.*

[258] U.S. Atty Office, D.C., 21 Months Since the Jan. 6 Attack on the Capitol, https://www.justice.gov/usao-dc/21-months-jan-6-attack-capitol.

> politically motivated verbal abuse. . . . Again, these men have not been convicted of any crime.[259]

Three appears to be a disparity in how the FBI and Justice Department are pursuing January 6-related matters. Compounding this appearance is how the FBI has failed to fully respond to inquiries from Congressional Republicans on this matter while providing information to the partisan Democrat-led Select Committee investigating the events of January 6, 2021.[260] The FBI's decision to provide information on a partisan basis is inconsistent with the FBI's purported impartiality and further erodes public confidence in the FBI's leadership.

* * *

The American people entrust the FBI with enormous power to fairly and evenhandedly enforce federal laws. As this report documents, the FBI has abused its law-enforcement authority in several ways—violating the fundamental civil rights of American citizens and chilling their participation in the political process. The examples and incidents highlighted in this report are not exhaustive, but they are indicative of the degree to which the FBI—and by extension the Justice Department—have strayed from their apolitical law-enforcement mission. Attorney General Garland and FBI Director Wray have weaponized federal law enforcement to target the Administration's political opponents and protect political allies. Instead of using their enormous law-enforcement capabilities to make America safer, the FBI is investing its limited time and resources to further a leftist political agenda. The American people deserve better, as do the many patriotic Americans who joined the Bureau to make America a better place.

---

[259] *"The First Step Act, the Pandemic, and Compassionate Release: What Are the Next Steps for the Federal Bureau of Prisons?": Hearing before the Subcomm. on Crime, Terrorism, and Homeland Sec. of the Comm. on the Judiciary*, 117th Cong. (2022) (testimony of Julie Kelly).

II. The FBI Is Purging Conservative Employees and Helping to Censor Conservative Viewpoints Online

President Biden has openly demagogued conservative viewpoints, even calling them a "threat to democracy."[261] From information available to Committee Republicans, the FBI is effectuating President Biden's vision within its ranks by actively "purg[ing]" FBI employees holding conservative views. These episodes are part and parcel of the larger plan to use federal law-enforcement actions and litigation to coerce the American public to submit to the Biden Administration's radical agenda. This section describes allegations received from whistleblowers and otherwise publicly available about the FBI's bias against conservative viewpoints.

A. The FBI is purging employees who refuse to align themselves with the leadership's political ideology.

Several FBI whistleblowers have disclosed that the FBI is taking steps toward terminating the employment of FBI employees who were engaged in protected First Amendment activity on January 6, 2021. According to several whistleblowers, the FBI is suspending the security clearances of FBI employees for their participation in protected First Amendment activity on January 6, 2021, questioning these employees' "Allegiance to the United States." Because a security clearance is required for FBI positions, these actions mean the FBI has suspended these employees indefinitely.

Two examples include veteran FBI employees who while on leave, attended public events in Washington, D.C., with their spouses. Republicans on the Committee were told that these employees did not enter the United States Capitol, have not been charged with any crime, and have not been contacted by law enforcement about their actions. Given these facts, it is deeply concerning that the FBI would question the allegiance of these employees and move to suspend their security clearances.

In another instance, the FBI suspended an agent's security clearance and eventually indefinitely suspended the agent from duty and pay. The FBI's predicate for the personnel action was that the agent apparently shared his personal views that the FBI was not being entirely forthcoming about the events of January 6. As a result, the FBI determined that agent had "espoused conspiratorial views" and "promoted unreliable information which indicates support for the events of January 6," and therefore the FBI questioned the agent's allegiance to the United States.

This agent had honorably served in the United States military for several years—including deployments in Kuwait and Iraq—valiantly earning multiple military commendation medals. While employed with the FBI, the agent has consistently been rated as "Exceeds Fully Successful" in performance evaluations, has received several awards, and has never been disciplined or reprimanded until this instance. In a letter sent to the FBI, the agent's lawyers explained that the FBI's accusations are a "monumental leap from objective fact" and a "distortion" of the agent's actions. They argue the security clearance suspension is a "gross

---

261 Remarks, The White House, Remarks by President Biden on the Continued Battle for the Soul of the Nation (Sept. 1, 2022).

injustice and clear constitutional violation[]"because the FBI is "punish[ing]" the agent for "run[ning] afoul of prevailing agency orthodoxy" while "exercising his First Amendment right of free speech."

This has been an ongoing trend. Another whistleblower, who has since left the FBI, informed Committee Republicans that the whistleblower faced retaliation for criticizing the FBI in an anonymous survey circulated by the Washington Field Office to employees following January 6. FBI leadership allegedly escalated an adverse personnel action against this employee after the employee had commented on the survey, which sought feedback about the Washington Field Office's actions "during the recent crisis/command post" event. The employee was never disciplined or reprimanded until after criticizing the FBI.

Although the Hatch Act prohibits FBI employees from engaging in partisan political campaigns or political management,[262] FBI employees do not give up their fundamental rights to participate in political speech activity or "hold personal political views."[263] The FBI's personnel actions against these employees therefore raise concerns that the Bureau may be taking steps toward firing these employees as retaliation for disfavored political speech. In fact, as documented in a letter received by an FBI employee who had their security clearance summarily suspended, FBI leadership has not even specifically informed the employee about the factual predicate for the suspension. FBI leadership advised the employee there was no right of review or even the opportunity to appeal the decision.

FBI whistleblowers told Committee Republicans that the same human resources official, Jennifer Moore, has been involved with the security clearance revocations for those employees targeted for their conservative views.[264] In addition, Moore has suspended at least one employee after the employee had made a protected whistleblower disclosure to Congress. In fact, Committee Republicans have received several disclosures about Moore herself, recounting allegations about her bias and mismanagement. Whistleblowers have disclosed that even when FBI leadership was made aware of Moore's impropriety, leadership continued to promote her.

Committee Republicans have sent several letters to Director Wray and DOJ Inspector General Horowitz seeking to ensure that FBI leadership is not retaliating against FBI employees for exercising their First Amendment rights.[265] Multiple whistleblowers have disclosed how the FBI leadership is conducting a "purge" of FBI employees holding conservative views. This perception is buttressed by previous, documented examples of political bias ingrained in the FBI's leadership culture—for example, when a senior FBI official wrote derisively to a colleague that he "could SMELL the Trump support" at a Walmart in southern Virginia, or when an FBI

---

[262] 5 U.S.C. § 7323 (2008).

[263] Letter from Hon. Michael Horowitz, Inspector Gen., U.S. Dep't of Justice, to Rep. Jim Jordan, Ranking Member, H. Comm. on the Judiciary (May 4, 2022).

[264] Letter from Rep. Jim Jordan, Ranking Member, H. Comm. on the Judiciary, to Ms. Jennifer Leigh Moore, Exec. Assistant Dir., Human Resources Branch, Fed. Bureau of Investigation (Sept. 29, 2022).

[265] *See* Letter from Rep. Jim Jordan, Ranking Member, H. Comm. on the Judiciary, to Hon. Michael Horowitz, Inspector Gen., U.S. Dep't of Justice (Apr. 26, 2022); Letter from Rep. Jim Jordan, Ranking Member, H. Comm. on the Judiciary, to Hon. Christopher A. Wray, Dir., Fed. Bureau of Investigation (May 6, 2022); Letter from Rep. Jim Jordan, Ranking Member, H. Comm. on the Judiciary, to Hon. Christopher A. Wray, Dir., Fed. Bureau of Investigation (Jun. 7, 2022).

attorney altered evidence in support of the FBI's warrantless surveillance of a Trump campaign associate.[266] The FBI has responded to these concerns with a hollow assertion that "FBI personnel must maintain objectivity and rigor in their work."[267] While the FBI may well be holding line agents to this standard, FBI leadership and supervisors are actively purging those who dare to hold a differing opinion.

B. The FBI is helping Big Tech to censor Americans' political speech.

In addition to purging conservative employees, evidence available to the Committee shows that the FBI is helping to censor conservative viewpoints. For example, Mark Zuckerberg's recent statements on Joe Rogan's podcast show that guidance from FBI leadership shaped some of Facebook's content-moderation decisions in the weeks preceding the 2020 presidential election. Relatedly, recent whistleblower allegations suggest that the FBI's "special relationship" includes Facebook voluntarily sending information to the FBI that may relate to citizens' private political speech.[268] Given the significant role large social media companies play—functioning as the modern public square, and as significant networks for private speech—the FBI leadership's apparent willingness to use its relationship with Big Tech to obtain user content raises significant concerns.

i. The FBI's guidance to Facebook about potential "misinformation" triggered content moderation related to the 2020 presidential election.

Shortly before the 2020 presidential election, Facebook suppressed an explosive *New York Post* article detailing how Hunter Biden used the position and influence of his father, now-President Biden, for personal gain, with the apparent awareness of President Biden. Committee Republicans wrote Facebook at that time asking about Facebook's knowing suppression of First Amendment-protected activity.[269] In March 2022, after other outlets had acknowledged the veracity of the Biden family's influence-peddling scheme, Committee Republicans wrote again with more questions about Facebook's actions to suppress critical election-related information.[270] Facebook never provided complete responses to these letters and, in the months since, has avoided any real accountability for its actions in interfering with election-related public discourse.

At the time of its publication, the *Post* article likely would have had significant implications for the presidential election. It detailed how Hunter Biden leveraged his father's influence as then-Vice President for personal gain. When Hunter Biden served on the board of Burisma, a Ukrainian company, a company executive asked him to "use [his] influence" to stop a

---

[266] *See* Press Release, U.S. Dep't of Justice, FBI Attorney Admits Altering Email Used for FISA Application During "Crossfire Hurricane" Investigation (Aug. 19, 2020).

[267] Letter from Ms. Jill Tyson, Assistant Dir., Office of Cong. Affairs, Fed. Bureau of Investigation, to Rep. Jim Jordan, Ranking Member, H. Comm. on the Judiciary (Sept. 2, 2022).

[268] Miranda Devine, *Facebook spied on private messages of Americans who questioned 2020 election*, N.Y. POST (Sept. 14, 2022).

[269] Letter from Rep. Jim Jordan, Ranking Member, H. Comm. on the Judiciary, to Mr. Mark Zuckerberg, CEO, Facebook, Inc. (Oct. 14, 2020).

[270] Letter from Rep. Jim Jordan, Ranking Member, H. Comm. on the Judiciary *et al.*, to Mr. Mark Zuckerberg, CEO, Facebook, Inc. (March 31, 2022).

domestic Ukrainian investigation into Burisma.[271] Another time, the same executive thanked Hunter Biden for arranging a meeting with then-Vice President Biden.[272] Eight months after that, Vice President Biden pressured the Ukrainian government to fire a prosecutor who was investigating Burisma, a firing about which Vice President Biden later bragged.[273] The *Post* article challenged President Biden's claim that he had "never spoken to [his] son about his overseas business dealings."[274] It appears that Facebook knowingly and deliberately used its platform to control election-related information accessible to the American people shortly before the 2020 election, and that Facebook did so to the primary benefit of then-Vice President Biden.

It now appears that Facebook took these steps following some form of guidance from the FBI. Meta CEO Mark Zuckerberg recently described how Facebook's censorship of the allegations about the Biden family before the 2020 election followed a message from the FBI that Facebook "should be on high alert" for "Russian propaganda."[275] Zuckerberg acknowledged that this official alert from the FBI is what led to Facebook reducing the circulation of the *Post*'s reporting on its platform, preventing Americans from fully understanding highly relevant allegations about President Biden's awareness of and involvement in his family's influence-peddling scheme.[276] An FBI directive that interferes in free and fair election-related public discourse raises significant risk of First Amendment violations through private-sector censorship at the government's behest.[277] Accordingly, the FBI's interface with Facebook, and its approach to disinformation and content moderation, raises significant concern about violations of Americans' First Amendment rights.

ii. Whistleblower suggests the FBI has a "special relationship" with Facebook in which it accepts private user information without any consent or legal process.

Other whistleblower information provided to Committee Republicans suggests that the FBI and Facebook have a so-called "special relationship" that may threaten constitutional protections and lead to partisan efforts. As part of a program likely codenamed "Operation Bronze Griffin," the FBI allegedly accepts private user information from Facebook, but without the user's consent or the legal process the FBI would otherwise need to independently pursue such user-related information. Furthermore, according to whistleblower information, the types of user content that Facebook provides have a partisan focus, tending only to concern users from one side of the political spectrum. The FBI's willingness to accept this political speech information from Facebook—outside of routine investigative pathways—further threatens

[271] Emma-Jo Morris & Gabrielle Fonrouge, *Smoking-gun email reveals how Hunter Biden introduced Ukrainian businessman to VP dad*, N.Y. POST (Oct. 14, 2020).

[272] *Id.*

[273] *Id.*; *see also* Council on Foreign Relations, Foreign Affairs Issue Launch with Former Vice President Joe Biden (Jan. 23, 2018), https://www.cfr.org/event/foreign-affairs-issue-launch-former-vice-president-joe-biden.

[274] Emma-Jo Morris & Gabrielle Fonrouge, *Smoking-gun email reveals how Hunter Biden introduced Ukrainian businessman to VP dad*, N.Y. POST (Oct. 14, 2020) (internal quotation marks omitted).

[275] *See, e.g.*, Victor Morton, *Mark Zuckerberg: Facebook suppressed Hunter Biden laptop story per FBI general request*, WASH. TIMES (Aug. 25, 2022).

[276] *Id.*

[277] *See, e.g.*, *Biden v. Knight First Amend. Inst. At Columbia Univ.*, 141 S. Ct. 1220, 1226 (2021) (Thomas, J., concurring) ("For example, although a private entity is not ordinarily constrained by the First Amendment, it is if the government coerces or induces it to take action the government itself would not be permitted to do, such as censor expression of a lawful viewpoint." (internal quotation marks and citation omitted)).

Americans' constitutional rights. In response to reporting on these allegations, the FBI "neither confirmed nor denied the allegations," but stated that relationships with social media providers ensure a "quick exchange of threat information" and an "ongoing dialogue."[278]

C. These episodes are all part of a larger effort within the Biden Administration to use law-enforcement resources to punish conservative views.

The FBI's attacks on conservative voices—both within its ranks and in the broader population—appear to be part of a broader effort by the Biden Administration to use the heavy hand of the federal government against conservative views.

Under Attorney General Garland, the Justice Department has politicized enforcement of and weaponized the Voting Rights Act (VRA) against Republican states that have enacted commonsense election integrity reforms, like Georgia and Texas. On July 28, 2021, the Department issued new guidance regarding state efforts to remove temporary, emergency voting procedures implemented during the unprecedented COVID-19 pandemic.[279] The Biden Administration's guidance bizarrely suggested states may not return to voting laws and procedures that existed prior to the pandemic, saying those laws and procedures may not be "presumptively lawful."[280] With the new guidance, the Department instead takes the position that these temporary, emergency measures are the new baseline from which to judge compliance with the VRA—contrary to Congress's intention in passing the legislation.[281]

The guidance and recent litigation undertaken by the Justice Department has made clear the Biden Administration intends to join with Congressional Democrats in attempting to undermine state election integrity laws by politicizing federal voting rights laws.

Georgia S.B. 202. On March 25, 2021, Georgia Governor Brian Kemp signed S.B. 202 into law.[282] The bill strengthened ballot box protections and enhanced the state's election integrity.[283] Following S.B. 202's enactment, in June 2021, Attorney General Garland announced that the Justice Department had filed suit against Georgia, alleging several S.B. 202 provisions "discriminate[] against Black voters" in violation of Section 2 of the VRA.[284] In response to the suit, Georgia Secretary of State Brad Raffensperger stated: "The Biden Administration continues to do the bidding of Stacy Abrams and spreads more lies about Georgia's election law . . . . It is no surprise that they would operationalize their lies with the full force of the federal government."[285] The suit is pending in the U.S. District Court for the Northern District of

---

278 Miranda Devine, *Facebook spied on private messages of Americans who questioned 2020 election,* N.Y. POST (Sept. 14, 2022).

279 Press Release, U.S. Dep't of Justice, Justice Department Issues Guidance on Federal Statutes Regarding Voting Methods and Post-election "Audits" (Jul. 28, 2021).

280 U.S. DEP'T OF JUSTICE, Guidance Concerning Federal Statutes Affecting Methods of Voting 1 (2021).

281 *See generally*, S. REP. NO. 109-295, at 2 (2006).

282 *Governor Kemp on Georgia Voting and Election Law,* C-SPAN (Mar. 25, 2021).

283 *Id.*

284 Erin Doherty, *Justice Department sues Georgia over GOP voting restrictions,* AXIOS (Jun. 25, 2021).

285 Claire Helm, *Gov. Kemp, Raffensperger responds to DOJ's suit over Georgia voting law,* WGXA NEWS (Jun. 25, 2021).

Georgia and has been consolidated with related litigation regarding S.B. 202.[286] However, on September 30, 2022, in a suit brought by a liberal activist group backed by gubernatorial candidate Stacy Abrams, a federal court upheld Georgia's voter integrity law.[287] The court found that "the challenged practices violate neither the constitution nor the VRA" and that the "burden on voters" to comply with the integrity measures "is relatively low."[288]

Democrats, including President Biden himself, have falsely alleged that the new Georgia voting law constitutes "Jim Crow 2.0" and "voter suppression." In reality, S.B. 202 strengthens ballot box protections and enhances the state's election integrity. One commentator stated the Justice Department's complaint "reads more like a press release from the Democratic National Committee than a serious lawsuit by an apolitical Justice Department."[289] The Heritage Foundation's Election Law fellow, Hans von Spakovsky, noted some of the flaws in the Biden Administration's lawsuit. For example, Georgia already has a voter identification requirement for in-person voting, which has been in place since 2008 and never ruled to be racially discriminatory—which makes it unclear how the new absentee voter identification requirements could be racially discriminatory.[290] In addition, the Eleventh Circuit Court of Appeals already "threw out a lawsuit filed against Alabama that made the same arguments" the Department is using in the Georgia lawsuit to contest the absentee voter identification requirement.[291] Similarly, Georgia's new ban on non-poll workers handing out food and water to voters waiting in line is "virtually identical" to a New York election law that prohibits giving voters refreshments unless the value is less than one dollar.[292] The Justice Department has never contested New York's ban.[293]

Democrat fearmongering about S.B. 202 has been unfounded. Georgia saw record turnout during its May 2022 primary election under its new voter integrity law, and more than 850,000 Georgians cast ballots in the primary, which represented a 168 percent increase in voter turnout compared to the last gubernatorial primary in 2018 and a 212 percent increase from the presidential primary in 2020.[294] After casting her ballot, one elderly, minority Georgia voter stated, "I had heard that they were going to try to deter us in any way possible. To go in there and vote as easily as I did and to be treated with the respect that I knew I deserved as an American citizen—I was really thrown back."[295]

Texas's Senate Bill 1. On September 7, 2021, Texas Governor Greg Abbott signed Senate Bill 1, an election integrity and security bill, into law.[296] The Governor's signature ended

---

[286] Order, The New Georgia Project, *et al.*, v. Raffensperger, No. 1:21-cv-2575 (N.D. Ga. Dec. 23, 2021).

[287] Order, Fair Fight Action, Inc., et al. v. Raffensperger, No. 1:18-CV-5391-SCJ (N.D. Ga. Sept. 30, 2021).

[288] *Id.* at 202 & 287.

[289] Hans A. von Spakovsky & Zack Smith, *In the Feds versus Georgia's voting law, bet on Georgia,* HERITAGE FOUND. (Jul. 6, 2021).

[290] *Id.*

[291] *Id.*

[292] *Id.*

[293] *Id.*

[294] Press Release, Georgia Secretary of State, Georgia Election Law Results in Records Early-Voting Turnout (May 21, 2022).

[295] Marc A. Thiessen, *Georgia's primary turnout shows Biden's falsehoods,* WASH. POST (May 27, 2022).

[296] Alexa Ura, *Gov. Greg Abbott signs Texas voting bill into law, overcoming Democratic quorum breaks,* TEXAS TRIBUNE (Sept. 7, 2021).

months of Democrat obstruction that included state Democrats fleeing to Washington, D.C., to deny the state house a quorum to conduct business.[297] The new reforms were in effect during the March 2022 primary elections.[298]

On November 4, 2021, the Justice Department filed a lawsuit against Texas, alleging that S.B. 1's provisions "deny eligible voters meaningful assistance in the voting booth and require rejection of mail ballot materials for immaterial errors or omissions" in violation of both Section 208 of the VRA and section 101 of the Civil Rights Act of 1964.[299] According to the Department, S.B. 1 unlawfully "restricts[s] what assistance in the polling booth voters who have a disability or are unable to read or write can receive" and unlawfully rejects "mail ballots and mail ballot request forms because of certain paperwork errors or omissions that are not material to establishing a voter's eligibility to cast a ballot."[300]

In response to the lawsuit, Texas Governor Greg Abbot tweeted: "Bring it. The Texas election integrity law is legal . . . . In Texas it is easier to vote but harder to cheat."[301] According to some legal commentators, the Department's lawsuit "wants to make illegal assistance easier to get away with" and "want[s] to make it easy to cheat using absentee ballots."[302] The case has been consolidated with similar litigation challenging S.B. 1, and the litigation remains ongoing in the U.S. District Court for the Western District of Texas.[303]

On December 6, 2021, Attorney General Garland announced another lawsuit against Texas for its newly drawn Congressional and state House districts. The Justice Department alleges that the new map denies "Black and Latino voters an equal opportunity to participate in the voting process and to elect representatives of their choice" in violation of the VRA.[304] According to the Department, "Decade after decade, Texas has enacted redistricting plans to violate the Voting Rights Act."[305] The complaint described how Texas added two new congressional seats largely as a result of population growth in minority communities, however the Texas legislature allegedly "designed the two new seats to have Anglo voting majorities."[306] The Department also alleged that in another congressional district, the legislature "surgically excised minority communities."[307]

In response to the complaint, Texas Attorney General Ken Paxton stated, "The Department of Justice's absurd lawsuit against our state is the Biden Administration's latest ploy

---

[297] *Id.*

[298] *Id.*

[299] Complaint, *U.S. v. Texas*, No. 5:21-cv-108 (W.D. Tex. Nov. 4, 2021).

[300] Press Release, U.S. Dep't of Justice, Justice Dep't Files Lawsuit Against the State of Texas to Protect Voting Rights, (Nov. 4, 2021).

[301] Governor Greg Abbott (@GregAbbott_TX), TWITTER (Nov. 4, 2021, 5:54 PM), https://twitter.com/GregAbbott_TX/status/1456379338920759298?s=20.

[302] Hans von Spakovsky & Zack Smith, *Garland's Lawsuit Against Texas Election Integrity Law is Partisan and Political*, THE HERITAGE FOUND. (Nov. 22, 2021).

[303] Order, *U.S. v. Texas*, No. 5:21-cv-844 (W.D. Tex. May 24, 2022).

[304] *See* Complaint, *U.S. v. Texas*, No. 3:21-cv-299 (W.D. Tex. Dec. 6, 2021); Ryan Lucas, *The Justice Department is suing Texas over the state's redistricting plans,* NPR (Dec. 6, 2021).

[305] Complaint, *U.S. v. Texas*, No. 3:21-cv-299 at 2(W.D. Tex. Dec. 6, 2021)

[306] *Id.* at 1.

[307] *Id.* at 2.

to control Texas voters. I am confident that our legislature's redistricting decisions will be proven lawful, and this preposterous attempt to sway democracy will fail."[308] The lawsuit was later consolidated with related litigation,[309] and litigation continues in the U.S. District Court for the Western District of Texas.[310]

While Attorney General Garland's Department has selectively decided to sue Texas for its redistricting map, the DOJ has declined to take similar action against redistricting plans from states with Democrat-controlled legislatures, such as Maryland. The *Washington Post* called Maryland the "most-gerrymandered state" in 2014, before the recent redistricting made it worse.[311] In a *Wall Street Journal* opinion piece, Maryland Governor Larry Hogan called out the Department for its hypocrisy, noting that the Maryland state legislature's decision to override his veto of the state's new Congressional map has made the "nation's most gerrymandered map even worse and create[ed] far more egregious civil-rights violations than in Texas."[312] A Maryland state court judge later threw out the Congressional map for gerrymandering, writing, "All of the testimony in this case supports the notions that the voice of Republican voters was diluted and their right to vote and be heard with the efficacy of a Democratic voter was diminished."[313] Attorney General Garland's political decisions to only sue conservative states is further evidence of the Biden Administration's use of the Justice Department to push its political agenda across the finish line.

* * *

Equal justice under the law is a cornerstone of American rule of law. By "purg[ing]" its ranks of conservative employees, shaping big tech's censorship of conservative viewpoints, and uneven law-enforcement actions and litigation targeted against conservative states, the FBI is failing to live up to this standard. In doing so, the FBI is carrying out the Biden Administration's plan to suppress dissent to its woke, leftist agenda.

---

[308] Texas Attorney General (@TXAG), TWITTER (Dec. 6, 2021, 2:16 PM), https://twitter.com/TXAG/status/1467935906309054474.

[309] Order Consolidating Case, *U.S. v. Texas et al.*, No. 3:21-cv-299 (W.D. Tex. Dec. 10, 2021).

[310] Mem. Opinion and Order Granting in Part and Denying in Part Defendants' Motion to Dismiss, *U.S. v. Texas et al.*, No. 3:21-cv-259 (W.D. Tex. May 23, 2022).

[311] Christopher Ingraham, *America's most gerrymandered congressional districts*, WASH. POST (May 15, 2014).

[312] *Gov. Larry Hogan: Mr. Garland, Please Sue My State*, WALL ST. J. (Dec. 17, 2021).

[313] Nick Corasaniti, *Judge Throws Out Maryland Congressional Map, in Blow to Democrats*, N.Y. TIMES (Mar. 25, 2022).

CONCLUSION

FBI Director Christopher Wray and Attorney General Merrick Garland have injected politics into the FBI, so much so that it is now fundamentally broken. Instead of serving justice and protecting the American public, FBI leadership has weaponized the agency's law-enforcement capabilities against half the American public. There is no place for politics within the FBI and now is the time to fix the nation's preeminent law-enforcement entity.

This report begins to accumulate the details of what is publicly known and what multiple whistleblowers have disclosed to Committee Republicans about the ills facing the FBI and its senior leadership. Whistleblowers have seen how "political meddling" is distracting and "pull[ing] away" resources from the FBI's traditional functions. They have described how senior FBI leadership is "purging" employees with conservative views. They talk about how the FBI leadership targets conservative Americans with aggressive law-enforcement tactics while treating liberal Americans with kid gloves. These whistleblowers want the FBI restored to the agency they "came into." These whistleblowers—and the brave men and women along whose side they serve—are assets to our nation. It is now time for FBI leadership to live up to the example of these agents in upholding the Constitution and the rule of law.

Ensuring an effective and even-handed federal law-enforcement authority should be a noncontroversial priority. Instead, Director Wray has indicated a belief that the FBI is immune to oversight or accountability.[314] Nothing could be further from the truth. It is time for Congress to begin the hard work of restoring integrity at the Department of Justice and Federal Bureau of Investigation.

[314] Email from the Hon. Christopher A Wray, Dir., Fed. Bureau of Investigation (Aug. 11, 2022 2:26 PM). ("There has been a lot of commentary about the FBI this week questioning our work and motives. Much of it is from critics and pundits on the outside who don't know what we know and don't see what we see.").

- **May 3, 2022:** Activists vandalized the Care Net Pregnancy Center in Frederick, Maryland with anti-life graffiti including, "not real clinic," "end forced motherhood," and "go to PP instead."[315]

- **May 3, 2022:** Anti-life activists protested outside of the Trotter House, a pro-life center in Austin, Texas and reportedly tore down the center's banner, and reportedly replaced it with signs including, "I am not property."[316]

- **May 3, 2022:** Colorado Church vandalized with messages of "my body, my choice" and You don't speak 4 God."[317]

- **May 4, 2022:** The sheriff's office in Boulder, Colorado investigated vandalism at the Sacred Heart of Mary Church. Vandals spray-painted "messages that support the right to an abortion" on the church's façade.[318]

- **May 5, 2022:** In Portland, Oregon, vandals smashed numerous windows and spray-painted graffiti on the Southeast Portland Pregnancy Resource Center.[319]

- **May 5, 2022:** Saint Joseph's Church & Academy in Armada, Michigan was vandalized with satanic symbols and messages.[320]

- **May 7, 2022:** Activists vandalized two pregnancy resource centers in Denton, Texas. On one of the centers, vandals wrote radical anti-life messages, including "not a clinic" and "forced birth is murder."[321]

- **May 7, 2022:** In Fort Collins, Colorado, activists painted "my body my choice" on the doors of a Catholic parish.[322]

- **May 7, 2022:** A known anti-life activist vandalized and urinated on the Alexandria, Virginia office of the pro-life group Concerned Women for America.[323]

---

[315] Jessica Chasmar, *At least 5 pro-life pregnancy centers vandalized within a week of SCOTUS opinion leak,* FOX NEWS (May 11, 2022).

[316] *Id.*

[317] Brittany Bernstein, *Colorado Church Vandalized with Pro-Abortion Graffiti in Wake of SCOTUS Leak,* NAT'L REV. (May 6, 2022).

[318] Janet Oravetz, *FBI investigates church vandalisms in Boulder, Fort Collins,* KUSA (May 13, 2022).

[319] *Id.*

[320] Micaiah Bilger, *Abortion Activists Vandalize Catholic Church With Satanic Symbols,* LIFENEWS (May 12, 2022).

[321] *Id.*

[322] Sandy Swanson, *West Fort Collins Catholic church vandalized with pro-abortion rights message Saturday,* COLORADOAN (May 9, 2022).

[323] Kyle Morris, Andrew Murray, & Jayme Chandler, *Concerned Women for America speak out after office vandalized,* FOX NEWS (May 10, 2022).

- **May 8, 2022:** On Mother's Day, vandals attempted to break into the Oregon Right to Life office in Keizer, Oregon. Suspects reportedly ignited and threw two Molotov cocktails at the building.[324]

- **May 8, 2022:** Vandals spray-painted anti-life messages such as "Abortion is a right," "Fake clinic," and "Liars" on the side of a pro-life pregnancy center in Manassas, Virginia.[325]

- **May 8, 2022:** Activists targeted a pro-life nonprofit center in Madison, Wisconsin, setting it ablaze and vandalizing it with the words: "If abortions aren't safe, then you aren't either."[326]

- **May 9, 2022:** Anti-life activists vandalized 3 Catholic churches in Texas.[327]

- **May 9, 2022:** Notre Dame de Lourdes Swarthmore, Pennsylvania vandalized with pro-choice graffiti: "You do not have the right to decide what people can do, #ProChoice."[328]

- **May 13, 2022:** Activists wrote "threatening messages" on the front of the Alpha Pregnancy Center in Reisterstown, Maryland, including the following: "if abortions aren't safe, neither are you," "you're anti choice not pro life," "not a clinic," and were signed "Jane's revenge."[329]

- **May 14, 2022:** Far-left vandals spray-painted graffiti on the Birthright pregnancy resource center in Frederick, Maryland.[330]

- **May 17, 2022:** Our Lady of Sorrows Church on the Lower East Side was vandalized, with multiple statues being broken and stolen.[331]

- **May 18, 2022:** Vandals targeted a "women's faith-based medical clinic" in Auburn, Alabama using keys to scratch the clinic's sign and staff members' vehicles.[332]

---

324 Danielle Wallace, *Oregon pro-life group struck by Molotov cocktails in failed Mother's Day break-in*, FOX NEWS (May 10, 2022); *see also* Kristine de Leon, *Molotov Cocktails thrown at Oregon Right to Life building; Keizer police investigating*, THE OREGONIAN (May 9, 2022).

325 Alexandra Desanctis, *Vandalism at a Northern Virginia pro-life resource center,* NAT'L REV. (May 9, 2022).

326 *Fire at Wisconsin anti-abortion office investigated as arson, police say*, CBS NEWS (May 9, 2022).

327 Emmett Jones, *3 Texas Catholic churches vandalized with pro-choice messages,* FOX NEWS (May 11, 2022).

328 Sam Wood, *Roman Catholic church in Swarthmore vandalized with pro-choice slogan,* PHILADELPHIA INQUIRER (May 19, 2022).

329 Lowell Melser, *Vandals spray-painted threatening messages onto pregnancy center in Reisterstown,* WBALTV (May 16, 2022).

330 Andy Ngo (@MrAndyNgo), TWITTER (May 15, 2022, 4:50 PM), https://twitter.com/mrandyngo/status/1525941738396913666

331 Sonia Rincon, *Cardinal Dolan, parishioners cling to faith after Catholic church in Manhattan vandalized*, ABC 7 (May 31, 2022).

332 Ansley Franco, *'The thing you can't compromise on as a Catholic': Vicar, parishioners respond to vandalism at women's clinic in Auburn,* OPELIKA-AUBURN NEWS (May 20, 2022).

- **May 21-22, 2022:** Self-proclaimed Puget Sound Anarchists took credit for damaging and leaving anti-life messages at 4 churches in Olympia, Washington. The group referred to the churches as "patriarchal sex abuse cults" that further the "violence of forced birth."[333]

- **May 23, 2022:** Vandals spray-painted crude messages on Mt. Avery Missionary Baptist church in Columbus, Mississippi.[334]

- **May 25, 2022:** In Lynnwood, Washington, anti-life activists smashed windows and vandalized the Next Step Pregnancy Center with the threat "if abortion isn't safe you aren't either."[335]

- **May 27, 2022:** Individuals associated with Jane's Revenge vandalized the Dove Medical pregnancy center in Eugene, Oregon.[336]

- **May 28, 2022:** The Archdiocese of Miami, Florida reported that Jane's Revenge left anti-life, misspelled messages on the Respect Life Office in Hollywood including, "If abortions aren't SAFE Then neither are you."[337]

- **June 2, 2022:** Jane's Revenge claimed credit for an attack in which its members broke windows and scrawled messages, including "god loves abortion" at Agape Pregnancy Resource Center in Des Moines, Iowa.[338]

- **June 2, 2022:** Anti-life activists targeted the Community Pregnancy Center in Anchorage, Alaska with graffiti, broken glass, and nails pointed upright in the parking lot.[339]

- **June 3, 2022:** Left-wing abortion activists targeted the Capitol Hill Crisis Pregnancy Center, throwing red paint on the door, eggs at the window, and spray-painting the building with "Jane Says Revenge."[340]

- **June 6, 2022:** In Asheville, North Carolina, vandals broke windows and left graffiti on the Mountain Area Pregnancy Services building. The threatening messages included: "If

---

333 John Christianson, *Anarchists take credit for vandalizing four pro-life churches in Washington state,* WASH. FREE BEACON (May 25, 2022).

334 Stephen Pimpo, *Graffiti reading 'rape' and 'incest' written on small church vandalized in Lowndes County,* WCBI (May 24, 2022).

335 *Lynnwood's Next Step Pregnancy Center vandalized,* LYNNWOOD TODAY (May 27, 2022).

336 Andy Ngo (@MrAndyNgo), TWITTER (May 30, 2022, 8:08 PM), https://twitter.com/MrAndyNgo/status/1531427308669702145.

337 Press Release, Archdiocese of Miami, Respect Life Office Vandalized (Jun. 1, 2022).

338 Katie Akin, *Jane's Revenge group claims responsibility for Des Moines pregnancy center vandalism,* DES MOINES REGISTER (Jun. 13, 2022).

339 Joel Davidson, *Anchorage pro-life center vandalized with graffiti, broken glass and nails,* ALASKA WATCHMAN (Jun. 9, 2022).

340 Julia Johnson, *See it: DC anti-abortion pregnancy center vandalized 'Jane Says Revenge,'* WASH. EXAMINER (Jun. 3, 2022).

abortions aren't safe, neither are you," "no forced birth," and an anarchist symbol.[341]

- **June 7, 2022:** "[A]bortion terrorist group Jane's Revenge" allegedly firebombed the CompassCare pro-life pregnancy center in Amherst, New York.[342]
- **June 10, 2022:** In Philadelphia, Pennsylvania, vandals smashed the windows and graffitied the walls of HOPE Pregnancy Center.[343]
- **June 10, 2022:** Federal law enforcement investigated a "suspicious" fire at the First Image Pregnancy Resource Center in Gresham, Oregon.[344]
- **June 15, 2022:** In Minneapolis, Minnesota, activists graffitied and smashed the windows of Minnesota Citizens Concerned for Life's office.[345]
- **June 19, 2022:** In Redford Township and Dearborn Heights, Michigan, activists smashed the windows of two pro-life pregnancy centers and left anti-life messages on the buildings.[346]
- **June 22, 2022:** In Jackson, Michigan, vandals graffitied and smashed the windows of the office of Jackson Right to Life.[347]
- **June 24, 2022:** Vandals targeted the North Carolina Republican Party's offices in Raleigh, North Carolina with threats of violence left on the building.[348]
- **June 25, 2022:** In Lynchburg, Virginia, anti-life activists vandalized the Blue Ridge Pregnancy Center.[349]
- **June 25, 2022:** In Paso Robles, California, vandals broke the windows and spray-painted the walls of Tree of Life Pregnancy Support center.[350]
- **June 25, 2022:** A statue memorializing children who died of abortion at the Holy

---

341 Kristy Kepley-Steward, *Investigation underway after vandals target a pregnancy services clinic,* ABC 13 NEWS (Jun. 7, 2022).

342 David Propper, *Anti-abortion Buffalo pregnancy center allegedly 'firebombed,'* N.Y. POST (Jun. 7, 2022).

343 Jenice Armstrong, *Angry about Roe? Then vote, don't vandalize,* THE PHILADELPHIA INQUIRER (Jun. 29, 2022).

344 *Probe into fire at Gresham anti-abortion center underway,* ASSOC. PRESS (Jun. 12, 2022).

345 Nick Longworth, *Minnesota pro-life organization vandalized, perpetrator takes credit online,* FOX 9 (Jun. 16, 2022).

346 Valerie Richardson, *Two Michigan pro-life centers vandalized as attacks spike ahead of Supreme Court ruling,* WASH. TIMES (Jun. 22, 2022).

347 Houston Keene, *Pro-life org, congressman's campaign office vandalized in Jane's Revenge-linked attack,* FOX NEWS (Jun. 22, 2022).

348 Press Release, North Carolina GOP, NCGOP Statement on Office Vandalism and Threats of Violence (Jun. 26, 2022).

349 Douglas Blair, *Her pro-life center was attacked by pro-abortion thugs. She fears it's 'going to get worse.',* THE DAILY SIGNAL (Jun. 29, 2022).

350 *Paso Robles pregnancy center vandalized, police say,* KSBY (Jun. 26, 2022).

Name of Mary Catholic Church in New Orleans, Louisiana was defaced.[351]

- **June 25, 2022:** Radical leftist rioters breached the Arizona Capitol, rioting against the *Dobbs* decision overturning *Roe*. The rioters forced Arizona State Senators to evacuate the building.[352]

- **June 25, 2022**: Individuals toppled over a statue of the Virgin Mary and stole two other statues at St. Anthony's Catholic Church in Harlingen, Texas in response to the *Dobbs* decision.[353]

- **June 25, 2022:** Anti-life activists defaced the Vermont State House in Montpelier, Vermont with the message, "If abortions aren't safe you aren't either."[354]

- **June 25, 2022:** In Cortez, Colorado, activists defaced the Heart To Heart Pregnancy Center with pro-abortion graffiti.[355]

- **June 25, 2022:** In Longmont, Colorado, vandals graffitied and set fire to the Life Choices Free Pregnancy Services.[356]

- **June 25, 2022:** In Renton, Washington, vandals spray-painted anti-life messages on St. Anthony's Catholic Church.[357]

- **June 25, 2022:** A church and a road were vandalized with pro-abortion graffiti in Fort Leon County, Florida.[358]

- **June 26, 2022:** Fairfax County Police investigated graffiti "related to the recent Supreme Court Roe v. Wade ruling," and "smoldering mulch" left on the St. John Neumann Catholic Community Church in Reston, Virginia.[359]

- **June 26, 2022:** In Winter Haven, Florida, anti-life activists destroyed security cameras and spray-painted the LifeChoice Pregnancy Center with threatening

---

[351] Josh Roberson, *Catholic statute vandalized in Algiers after Roe v. Wade decision,* FOX 8 (Jun. 25, 2022).

[352] Daniel Chaitin, *Rioting over Roe threatened Arizona Senate, caused 'criminal damage': Authorities,* WASH. EXAMINER (Jun. 25, 2022).

[353] Iris Karami, *Harlingen church vandalized, parishioner steps up,* VALLEY CENTRAL (Jun. 27, 2022).

[354] Danielle Wallace, *Pro-choice vandals scrawl threat on Vermont State House after Roe v. Wade decision: Police,* FOX NEWS (Jun. 26, 2022).

[355] Bill Donohue, *Nothing peaceful about these pro-abortion protests,* NEWSMAX (Jul. 5, 2022).

[356] Caroline Downey, *Pro-Abortion Extremists Set Colorado Pregnancy Center on Fire following Roe Reversal,* NAT'L REV. (Jun. 26, 2022).

[357] Jake Chapman, *Church in Renton vandalized with smashed windows and spray painted anti-Catholic messages,* KIRO 7 (Jun. 30, 2022).

[358] Christopher Cann, *Abortion-related graffiti spray-painted on Leon County church entrance sign and roadway,* TALLAHASSEE DEMOCRAT (June 28, 2022).

[359] Ivy Lyons, *'Particularly vigilant'—Reston church damaged, Arlington diocese says parishes are 'alert,'* WTOP (Jun. 26, 2022).

messages, including "we're coming for U," and "Jane's revenge."[360]

- **June 27, 2022:** In Yuba City, California, individuals threw rocks through the windows of A Woman's Friend pro-life clinic.[361]

- **June 28, 2022:** The Pathways Pregnancy Care Center in Littleton, New Hampshire reported graffiti on its building, and the messages "urged funding for abortion and disparaged God."[362]

- **June 29, 2022:** The St. Louise Catholic Church in Bellevue, Washington was vandalized with messages like "religion of hate" and "woman hater."[363]

- **June 30, 2022:** Jane's Revenge activists reportedly smashed windows and threw a Molotov cocktail device into the Hope Clinic for Women in Nashville, Tennessee. Federal law enforcement investigated the crime as an attempted arson and for vandalism charges.[364]

- **July 1, 2022:** In Madison, Wisconsin, vandals spray-painted anti-life graffiti on St. Bernard Catholic Church's signs and front door.[365]

- **July 1, 2022:** Multiple Catholic churches in Chippewa Falls, Wisconsin reported incidents of vandalism.[366]

- **July 2, 2022**: In Hialeah, Florida, individuals vandalized the Pregnancy Medical Clinic with spray-paint, writing "If abortions aren't safe neither are you," on the walls.[367]

- **July 3, 2022:** Holy Family Catholic Church was vandalized with pro-abortion messages, such as "I love abortion."[368]

- **July 4, 2022:** In St. Paul, Minnesota, activists spray-painted "Abort America," "Blood on your hands," and "Janes Revenge" on the Birthright crisis pregnancy center.[369]

---

360 Gary White, *'We're coming for U': Winter Haven pregnancy center vandalized with graffiti,* THE LEDGER (Jun. 27, 2022).

361 Lucy Hodgman, *'It felt targeted': Yuba City pregnancy resource clinic vandalized, window broken overnight,* SACRAMENTO BEE (Jul. 1, 2022).

362 Thea DiGiammerino, *Vandalism at NH pregnancy center being investigated as possible hate crime,* NBC BOSTON (Jul. 5, 2022).

363 Stephen Sorace, *Washington state catholic church vandalized with graffiti in suspected hate crime: 'woman haters,'* FOX NEWS (June 29, 2022).

364 Mary Alice Royse, *FBI, MNPD investigate attempted arson and vandalism at Nashville clinic,* WSMV 4 (Jun. 30, 2022).

365 *Vandals spray Madison church with abortion graffiti,* ASSOC. PRESS (Jul. 3, 2022).

366 *4 churches vandalized in Chippewa County,* WEAU (Jul. 1, 2022).

367 Marisela Burgos & Samantha Sosa, *Pro-life clinic vandalized in Hialeah,* WSVN 7 (Jul. 5, 2022).

368 David Larson, *Hillsborough Catholic parish vandalized,* THE CAROLINA J. (July 3, 2022).

369 Sam Stroozas, *'Crisis pregnancy center' vandalized in St. Paul,* MPR NEWS (Jul. 5, 2022).

- **July 7, 2022**: Activists vandalized two pro-life pregnancy centers in Worcester, Massachusetts hours after the state's attorney general issued a consumer advisory warning residents about such centers. Activists smashed glass in two doors and three windows in one facility (Clearway Clinic); two miles away, activists spray-painted Problem Pregnancy with blue and gold paint.[370]

- **July 7, 2022:** A pregnancy center in Moab, Ohio was vandalized with blue and black paint splattering the exterior walls and windows of the center.[371]

- **July 8, 2022**: Right to Life of Northeast Ohio Akron's office was vandalized with "if abortion isn't safe, neither r u".[372]

- **July 8-9, 2022:** In Bethesda, Maryland, individuals either vandalized or set fire to three churches, causing physical damage to the churches and their properties.[373] One church faces approximately $50,000 in damages because of the vandalism.[374]

- **July 10, 2022:** Vandals spray-painted the Church of the Ascension in Overland Park, Kansas with anti-life messages such as "My body my choice," and dumped red paint over the Virgin Mary statue.[375]

- **July 12, 2022:** A pro-life medical clinic was vandalized in Baton Rouge, Louisiana with red graffiti spray painted on the clinic.[376]

- **August 1, 2022**: In St. Paul, Minnesota, vandals broke doors and graffitied a pregnancy center, leaving messages such as "if abortions aren't safe, neither are you."[377]

- **August 1, 2022:** A Douglas County Church in Kansas City was vandalized with messages such as "protect choice."[378]

- **August 1, 2022:** In Lawrence, Kansas, two churches were vandalized with spray painted messages such as "vote no," "protect choice," and "no forced birth" on their properties.[379]

---

[370] Matthew McDonald, *Mass. Pro-Life Pregnancy Centers Attacked Hours After State Attorney General's Warning*, NAT'L CATHOLIC REGISTER (Jul. 9, 2022).

[371] Rachel Fixsen, *Pregnancy center vandalized*, MOAB SUN NEWS (July 7, 2022).

[372] Shannon Coan, *Right to Life of Northeast Ohio's Office vandalized in Akron*, AKRON BEACON J. (July 13, 2022).

[373] Allison Hageman & Derrick Ward, *Authorities Investigate Arson, Vandalism at 3 Bethesda Churches Over the Weekend*, NBC WASH. 4 (Jul. 10, 2022).

[374] *Id.*

[375] Stephen Sorace, *Kansas police investigating vandalism at church: 'My body my choice,'* FOX NEWS (Jul. 11, 2022).

[376] WAFB Staff, *Pro-life women's clinic vandalized, police say*, WAFB 9 (July 12, 2022).

[377] Marah H. Gottfried, *Doors broke, graffiti left behind at pregnancy center in St. Paul*, TWINCITIES PIONEER PRESS (Aug. 1, 2022)

[378] Sean McDowell, *Lawrence church vandalized over anti-abortion stance*, FOX 4 (Aug. 1, 2022)

[379] Chansi Long, *Two Lawrence churches vandalized ahead of Aug. 2 vote*, THE LAWRENCE TIMES (Aug. 1, 2022).

- **August 9, 2022:** In Pocatello, Idaho, the Compassion and Hope Pregnancy Center was vandalized with messages including, "forced birth center," "God is a woman," and "beware."[380]

- **August 15, 2022:** In Cuyahoga Falls, Ohio, a woman was accused of assault after throwing eggs and a dead raccoon at the Northeast Ohio Women's Center.[381]

- **August 18, 2022:** Anti-life extremists vandalized a pregnancy center in western Massachusetts with messages including "Jane's Revenge" and "if abortion isn't safe neither are you."[382]

- **September 16, 2022:** In Southfield, Michigan, vandals broke a window and left graffitied messages including, "Jane was here" and "if abortions aren't safe, neither are you" on a pregnancy counseling center.[383]

- **October 8, 2022:** Security camera footage showed anti-life activists spray-painting the sidewalk of the Church of the Resurrection in Lansing, Michigan with "abort the court" and "death to Christian nationalism."[384]

---

[380] Candice Spector, *Pocatello pregnancy center vandalized*, IDAHO STATE J. (Aug. 11, 2022).

[381] Abbey Marshall, *Woman accused of assaulting police and throwing eggs, dead raccoon at abortion clinic*, AKRON BEACON J. (Sept. 8, 2022); *see also* Andrea Blanco, *Woman arrested for attacking police after throwing dead raccoon at abortion clinic*, YAHOO (Sep. 8, 2022)

[382] Caroline Downey, *Pro-Abortion Extremists Vandalize Massachusetts Pregnancy Center*, NAT'L REV. (Aug. 19, 2022)

[383] Mara MacDonald, *Anti-abortion counseling center in Southfield vandalized*, WDIV LOCAL 4 (Sept. 22, 2022).

[384] Timothy H.J. Nerozzi, *Pro-choice vandals in Michigan caught on video spray-painting church,* FOX NEWS (Oct. 15, 2022).

Appendix B – Republican Letters on Politicization at the DOJ and FBI

1. November 2, 2022: Rep. Jim Jordan, Ranking Member, H. Comm. on the Judiciary, to the Hon. Merrick B. Garland, Atty Gen., U.S. Dep't of Justice
2. November 2, 2022: Rep. Jim Jordan, Ranking Member, H. Comm. on the Judiciary, to the Hon. Christopher A. Wray, Dir., Fed. Bureau of Investigation
3. October 28, 2022: Reps. Jim Jordan & Tom McClintock, H. Comm. on the Judiciary, to the Hon. Merrick B. Garland, Atty Gen., U.S. Dep't of Justice
4. October 18, 2022: Reps. Jim Jordan & Mike Johnson, H. Comm. on the Judiciary, to Jill Sanborn
5. October 17, 2022: Rep. Jim Jordan, Ranking Member, H. Comm. on the Judiciary, to Ronald A. Klain, Assistant to the President and Chief of Staff, The White House
6. October 17, 2022: Rep. Jim Jordan, Ranking Member, H. Comm. on the Judiciary, to the Hon. Miguel A. Cardona, EdD, Sec'y, U.S. Dep't of Education
7. October 17, 2022: Rep. Jim Jordan, Ranking Member, H. Comm. on the Judiciary, to the Hon. Alejandro Mayorkas, Sec'y, U.S. Dep't of Homeland Security
8. October 14, 2022: Rep. Jim Jordan, Ranking Member, H. Comm. on the Judiciary *et al.*, to Timothy Thibault
9. October 11, 2022: Reps. Jim Jordan & Mike Johnson, H. Comm. on the Judiciary, to the Hon. Merrick B. Garland, Atty Gen., U.S. Dep't of Justice
10. October 7, 2022: Reps. Jim Jordan & Mike Johnson, H. Comm. on the Judiciary, to the Hon. Jacqueline C. Romero, U.S. Atty, E.D. of Penn.
11. September 29, 2022: Rep. Jim Jordan, Ranking Member, H. Comm. on the Judiciary *et al.*, to Jennifer Leigh Moore, Exec. Dir., Human Res. Branch, Fed. Bureau of Investigation
12. September 23, 2022: Rep. Jim Jordan, Ranking Member, H. Comm. on the Judiciary *et al.*, to Timothy Thibault
13. September 19, 2022: Rep. Jim Jordan, Ranking Member, H. Comm. on the Judiciary, to the Hon. Christopher A. Wray, Dir., Fed. Bureau of Investigation
14. September 14, 2022: Rep. Jim Jordan, Ranking Member, H. Comm. on the Judiciary, to the Hon. Christopher A. Wray, Dir., Fed. Bureau of Investigation

15. September 2, 2022: Rep. Jim Jordan, Ranking Member, H. Comm. on the Judiciary *et al.*, to the Hon. Merrick B. Garland, Atty Gen., U.S. Dep't of Justice

16. September 1, 2022: H. Judiciary Comm. and H. Oversight & Reform Comm. Republicans to Mark Zuckerberg, Chief Exec. Officer, Meta Platforms, Inc.

17. August 29, 2022: Rep. Jim Jordan, Ranking Member, H. Comm. on the Judiciary, to the Hon. Michael E. Horowitz, Inspector Gen., U.S. Dep't of Justice

18. August 15, 2022: H. Comm. on the Judiciary Republicans to the Hon. Christopher A. Wray, Fed. Bureau of Investigation

19. August 15, 2022: H. Comm. on the Judiciary Republicans to Ronald A. Klain, Assistant to the President and Chief of Staff, the White House

20. August 15, 2022: H. Comm. on the Judiciary Republicans to the Hon. Merrick B. Garland, Atty Gen., U.S. Dep't of Justice

21. August 10, 2022: Reps. Jim Jordan & Mike Johnson, H. Comm. on the Judiciary, to Jill Sanborn

22. July 27, 2022: Rep. Jim Jordan, Ranking Member, H. Comm. on the Judiciary, to the Hon. Christopher A. Wray, Dir., Fed. Bureau of Investigation

23. June 14, 2022: H. Comm. on the Judiciary Republicans to Ronald A. Klain, Assistant to the President and Chief of Staff, The White House

24. June 14, 2022: H. Comm. on the Judiciary Republicans to the Hon. Alejandro Mayorkas, Sec'y, U.S. Dep't of Homeland Security

25. June 14, 2022: H. Comm. on the Judiciary Republicans to the Hon. Merrick B. Garland, Atty Gen., U.S. Dep't of Justice

26. June 7, 2022: Rep. Jim Jordan, Ranking Member, H. Comm. on the Judiciary, to the Hon. Christopher A. Wray, Dir., Fed. Bureau of Investigation – REDACTED

27. June 1, 2022: Reps. Jim Jordan and Matt Gaetz, H. Comm. on the Judiciary, to the Hon. Christopher A. Wray, Dir., Fed. Bureau of Investigation

28. May 24, 2022: Rep. Jim Jordan, Ranking Member, H. Comm. on the Judiciary, and Rep. Mike Turner, Ranking Member, H. Permanent Select Comm. on Intelligence, to the Hon. Christopher A. Wray, Dir., Fed. Bureau of Investigation

29. May 19, 2022: Rep. Jim Jordan, Ranking Member, H. Comm. on the Judiciary, to the Hon. Michael E. Horowitz, Inspector Gen., U.S. Dep't of Justice

30. May 11, 2022: Reps. Jim Jordan & Mike Johnson, H. Comm. on the Judiciary, to the Hon. Merrick B. Garland, Atty Gen., U.S. Dep't of Justice – REDACTED

31. May 6, 2022: Rep. Jim Jordan, Ranking Member, H. Comm. on the Judiciary, to the Hon. Christopher A. Wray, Dir., Fed. Bureau of Investigation – REDACTED

32. May 3, 2022: Reps. Jim Jordan and Matt Gaetz, H. Comm. on the Judiciary, to William G. Malley, Managing Partner, Perkins Coie LLP

33. April 27, 2022: Rep. Jim Jordan, Ranking Member, H. Comm. on the Judiciary, to the Hon. Merrick B. Garland, Atty Gen., U.S. Dep't of Justice

34. April 26, 2022: Rep. Jim Jordan, Ranking Member, H. Comm. on the Judiciary, to the Hon. Michael E. Horowitz, Inspector Gen., U.S. Dep't of Justice – REDACTED

35. April 6, 2022: H. Judiciary Republicans to 51 Former Intelligence Community Officers
    i. Bakos
    ii. Bash
    iii. Brandmaier
    iv. Brennan
    v. Bruce
    vi. Buckley
    vii. Clapper
    viii. Corsell
    ix. David Cariens
    x. Davis
    xi. Fingar
    xii. George
    xiii. Gerstell
    xiv. Hall
    xv. Harrington
    xvi. Hayden
    xvii. Hepburn
    xviii. Janice Cariens
    xix. Kilbourn
    xx. Kolbe
    xxi. Ledgett
    xxii. Liepman
    xxiii. Marks
    xxiv. McLaughlin
    xxv. Mendez
    xxvi. Morell
    xxvii. Moseman
    xxviii. Nakhleh
    xxix. O'Shea
    xxx. Panetta

xxxi. Pfeiffer
xxxii. Polymeropoulos
xxxiii. Priess
xxxiv. Purcilly
xxxv. Rasmussen
xxxvi. Savos
xxxvii. Shapiro
xxxviii. Sipher
xxxix. Slick
xl. Snyder
xli. Strand
xlii. Tarbell
xliii. Terry
xliv. Travers
xlv. Treverton
xlvi. Tullius
xlvii. Vanell
xlviii. Vickers
xlix. Wiley
l. Wise
li. Wood

36. April 5, 2022: H. Comm. on the Judiciary Republicans to Hunter Biden

37. March 31, 2022: H. Comm. on the Judiciary Republicans to Parag Agrawal, Chief Exec. Officer, Twitter, Inc.

38. March 31, 2022: H. Comm. on the Judiciary Republicans to Mark Zuckerberg, Chief Exec. Officer, Facebook, Inc.

39. March 29, 2022: Rep. Jim Jordan, Ranking Member, H. Comm. on the Judiciary *et al.,* to the Hon. Christopher A. Wray, Dir., Fed. Bureau of Investigation

40. March 21, 2022: Rep. Jim Jordan, Ranking Member, H. Comm. on the Judiciary *et al.,* to the Hon. Christopher A. Wray, Dir., Fed. Bureau of Investigation

41. March 14, 2022: Rep. Jim Jordan, Ranking Member, H. Comm. on the Judiciary *et al.,* to Jacob Sullivan, National Security Advisor, The White House

42. March 9, 2022: Rep. Jim Jordan, Ranking Member, H. Comm. on the Judiciary, to the Hon. Christopher A. Wray, Dir., Fed. Bureau of Investigation

43. March 9, 2022: Rep. Jim Jordan, Ranking Member, H. Comm. on the Judiciary, to the National School Boards Association

44. March 3, 2022: Reps. Jim Jordan & Mike Johnson, H. Comm. on the Judiciary, to the Hon. Christopher A. Wray, Dir., Fed. Bureau of Investigation

45. March 3, 2022: Reps. Jim Jordan & Mike Johnson, H. Comm. on the Judiciary, to Tim Cook, Chief Exec. Officer, Apple Inc.

46. February 28, 2022: H. Comm. on the Judiciary Republicans to the Hon. Merrick B. Garland, Atty Gen., U.S. Dep't of Justice

47. February 17, 2022: Rep. Jim Jordan, Ranking Member, H. Comm. on the Judiciary *et al.,* to the Hon. Matthew G. Olsen, Assistant Atty Gen., Nat'l Sec. Div., U.S. Dep't of Justice

48. February 10, 2022: H. Comm. on the Judiciary Republicans to the Hon. Christopher A. Wray, Fed. Bureau of Investigation

49. January 27, 2022: Reps. Jim Jordan & Mike Johnson, H. Comm. on the Judiciary, to the Hon. Christopher A. Wray, Dir., Fed. Bureau of Investigation

50. Dec. 2, 2021: Rep. Jim Jordan, Ranking Member, H. Comm. on the Judiciary, to Rep. Jerrold Nadler, Chairman, H. Comm. on the Judiciary

51. November 24, 2021: Rep. Jim Jordan, Ranking Member, H. Comm. on the Judiciary *et al.,* to Timothy Langan, Assistant Dir., Counterterrorism Div., Fed. Bureau of Investigation

52. November 18, 2021: Rep. Jim Jordan, Ranking Member, H. Comm. on the Judiciary, to the Hon. Christopher A. Wray, Dir., Fed. Bureau of Investigation

53. November 18, 2021: Rep. Jim Jordan, Ranking Member, H. Comm. on the Judiciary *et al.*, to the Hon. Merrick B. Garland, Atty Gen., U.S. Dep't of Justice

54. November 16, 2021: Rep. Jim Jordan, Ranking Member, H. Comm. on the Judiciary, and Virginia Foxx, Ranking Member, H. Comm. on Education and Labor, to the Hon. Miguel A. Cardona, EdD, Sec'y, U.S. Dep't of Education

55. November 16, 2021: Rep. Jim Jordan, Ranking Member, H. Comm. on the Judiciary, to the Hon. Merrick B. Garland, Atty Gen., U.S. Dep't of Justice

56. November 12, 2021: Rep. Jim Jordan, Ranking Member, H. Comm. on the Judiciary, to Chip Slaven, Interim Executive Director & CEO, National School Boards Association

57. November 12, 2021: Rep. Jim Jordan, Ranking Member, H. Comm. on the Judiciary, to Dr. Viola M. Garcia, President, National School Boards Association

58. November 3, 2021: H. Comm. on the Judiciary Republicans to the Hon. Christopher A. Wray, Dir., Fed. Bureau of Investigation

59. November 2, 2021: H. Comm. on the Judiciary Republicans to Mark Lesko, Acting Assistant Atty Gen., Nat'l Sec. Div., U.S. Dep't of Justice

60. November 1, 2021: H. Comm. on the Judiciary Republicans to 93 U.S. Attorneys
    i. Wilson (AK)
    ii. Costello (AL)
    iii. Escalona (AL)
    iv. Stewart (AL)
    v. Fowlkes (AR)
    vi. Ross (AR)
    vii. McCormick (AZ)
    viii. Grossman (CA)
    ix. Hinds (CA)
    x. Talbert (CA)
    xi. Wilkison (CA)
    xii. Kirsch (CO)
    xiii. Boyle (CT)
    xiv. Phillips (DC)
    xv. Weiss (DE)
    xvi. Coody (FL)
    xvii. Gonzales (FL)
    xviii. Hoppmann (FL)
    xix. Erskine (GA)
    xx. Estes (GA)
    xxi. Leary (GA)
    xxii. Anderson (GU and NMI)
    xxiii. Philips (HI)
    xxiv. Berry (IA)
    xxv. Westphal (IA)
    xxvi. Gonzales (ID)
    xxvii. Lausch (IL)
    xxviii. Quivey (IL)
    xxix. Weinhoeft (IL)
    xxx. Childress (IN)
    xxxi. Johnson (IN)
    xxxii. Slinkard (KS)
    xxxiii. Bennett (KY)
    xxxiv. Shier (KY)
    xxxv. Evans (LA)
    xxxvi. Travis (LA)
    xxxvii. Van Hook (LA)
    xxxviii. Mendell (MA)
    xxxix. Barron (MD)
    xl. McElwee (ME)
    xli. Birge (MI)

xlii. Mohsin (MI)
xliii. Folk (MN)
xliv. Fleming (MO)
xlv. Moore (MO)
xlvi. Joyner (MS)
xlvii. LaMarca (MS)
xlviii. Johnson (MT)
xlix. Acker (NC)
l. Hairston (NC)
li. Stetzer (NC)
lii. Chase (ND)
liii. Sharp (NE)
liv. Farley (NH)
lv. Honig (NJ)
lvi. Federici (NM)
lvii. Chiou (NV)
lviii. Freedman (NY)
lix. Peace (NY)
lx. Ross (NY)
lxi. Williams (NY)
lxii. Brennan (OH)
lxiii. Patel (OH)
lxiv. Johnson (OK)
lxv. Troester (OK)
lxvi. Wilson (OK)
lxvii. Asphaug (OR)
lxviii. Brandler (PA)
lxix. Kaufman (PA)
lxx. Williams (PA)
lxxi. Muldrow (PR)
lxxii. Myrus (RI)
lxxiii. DeHart (SC)
lxxiv. Holmes (SD)
lxxv. Hamilton (TN)
lxxvi. Murphy (TN)
lxxvii. Stewart (TN)
lxxviii. Ganjei (TX)
lxxix. Hoff (TX)
lxxx. Lowery (TX)
lxxxi. Meacham (TX)
lxxxii. Martinez (UT)
lxxxiii. Aber (VA)
lxxxiv. Kavanaugh (VA)
lxxxv. Shappert (VI)
lxxxvi. Ophardt (VT)
lxxxvii. Brown (WA)

lxxxviii. Waldref (WA)
lxxxix. Frohling (WI)
xc. O'Shea (WI)
xci. Ihlenfeld (WV)
xcii. Thompson (WV)
xciii. Murray (WY)

61. October 28, 2021: H. Comm. on the Judiciary Republicans to the Hon. Jerrold Nadler, Chairman, H. Comm. on the Judiciary

62. October 27, 2021: Rep. Jim Jordan, Ranking Member, H. Comm. on the Judiciary, and Rep. James Comer, Ranking Member, H. Comm. on Oversight and Reform, to the Hon. Merrick B. Garland, Atty Gen., U.S. Dep't of Justice

63. October 27, 2021: H. Comm. on the Judiciary Republicans to the National School Boards Association

64. October 25, 2021: H. Comm. on the Judiciary Republicans to the Hon. Merrick B. Garland, Atty Gen., U.S. Dep't of Justice

65. October 13, 2021: H. Comm. on the Judiciary Republicans to the Hon. Merrick B. Garland, Atty Gen., U.S. Dep't of Justice

66. September 27, 2021: Reps. Jim Jordan and Andy Biggs, H. Comm. on the Judiciary, to the Hon. Merrick B. Garland, Atty Gen., U.S. Dep't of Justice

67. August 12, 2021: Reps. Jim Jordan & Mike Johnson, H. Comm. on the Judiciary, to the Hon. Merrick B. Garland, Atty Gen., U.S. Dep't of Justice

68. August 11, 2021: Rep. Jim Jordan, Ranking Member, H. Comm. on the Judiciary, to the Hon. Christopher A. Wray, Dir., Fed. Bureau of Investigation

69. July 26, 2021: Rep. Jim Jordan, Ranking Member, H. Comm. on the Judiciary, to the Hon. Christopher A. Wray, Dir., Fed. Bureau of Investigation

70. July 21, 2021: Rep. Jim Jordan, Ranking Member, H. Comm. on the Judiciary, to the Hon. Michael E. Horowitz, Inspector Gen., U.S. Dep't of Justice

71. June 11, 2021: Rep. Kevin McCarthy, Republican Leader, and Rep. Jim Jordan, Ranking Member, H. Comm. on the Judiciary, to the Hon. Merrick B. Garland, Atty Gen., U.S. Dep't of Justice

72. June 10, 2021: Rep. Jim Jordan, Ranking Member, H. Comm. on the Judiciary *et al.*, to the Hon. Merrick B. Garland, Atty Gen., U.S. Dep't of Justice

73. June 8, 2021: Rep. Jim Jordan, Ranking Member, H. Comm. on the Judiciary *et al.*, to the Hon. Merrick B. Garland, Atty Gen., U.S. Dep't of Justice

74. June 3, 2021: Rep. Jim Jordan, Ranking Member, H. Comm. on the Judiciary *et al.*, to the Hon. Merrick B. Garland, Atty Gen., U.S. Dep't of Justice

75. May 4, 2021: Reps. Jim Jordan and Andy Biggs, H. Comm. the Judiciary, to the Hon. Christopher A. Wray, Dir., Fed. Bureau of Investigation

76. April 27, 2021: Rep. Jim Jordan, Ranking Member, H. Comm. on the Judiciary, to the Hon. Merrick B. Garland, Atty Gen., U.S. Dep't of Justice

77. March 29, 2021: Rep. Jim Jordan, Ranking Member, H. Comm. on the Judiciary, to the Hon. Merrick B. Garland, Atty Gen., U.S. Dep't of Justice

JERROLD NADLER, New York
CHAIRMAN

JIM JORDAN, Ohio
RANKING MEMBER

ONE HUNDRED SEVENTEENTH CONGRESS

Congress of the United States

House of Representatives

COMMITTEE ON THE JUDICIARY

2138 RAYBURN HOUSE OFFICE BUILDING

WASHINGTON, DC 20515-6216

(202) 225-3951
judiciary.house.gov

November 2, 2022

The Honorable Merrick B. Garland
Attorney General
U.S. Department of Justice
950 Pennsylvania Avenue, N.W.
Washington, DC 20530

Dear Attorney General Garland:

We are conducting oversight of the Department of Justice's operations and actions concerning various matters. As a part of this oversight, Committee Republicans have sent letters to Departmental components requesting documents and information on several issues,[1] including but not limited to the Department's targeting of journalists with Project Veritas, the shuttering of the Department's China Initiative, the Department's one-sided enforcement of the FACE Act, and the Department's unprecedented raid on President Trump's residence. Our requests to you or your subordinates remain outstanding.

The American people deserve transparency and accountability from our most senior law-enforcement official in the executive branch. Committee Republicans intend to continue to examine these matters, including into the 118th Congress if necessary. We reiterate our requests, which are itemized in the attached appendix and incorporated herein, and ask that you, as the custodian of all Department records, produce the entirety of the requested material as soon as possible but no later than November 16, 2022.

Furthermore, this letter serves as a formal request to preserve all existing and future

[1] Letter from Rep. Jim Jordan, *et al.,* Ranking Member, H. Comm. on the Judiciary, to Hon. Merrick Garland, Atty Gen., U.S. Dep't of Justice (June 8, 2021); Letter from Rep. Jim Jordan, *et al.,* Ranking Member, H. Comm. on the Judiciary, to Hon. Merrick Garland, Atty Gen., U.S. Dep't of Justice (Nov. 18, 2021); Letter from Rep. Jim Jordan, *et al.,* Ranking Member, H. Comm. on the Judiciary, to Hon. Matthew G. Olsen, Assistant Atty Gen., U.S. Dep't of Justice (Feb. 17, 2022); Letter from Rep. Andy Biggs, *et al.,* Ranking Member, Subcomm. on Crime, Terrorism, and Homeland Security of the H. Comm. on the Judiciary, to Hon. Matthew G. Olsen, Assistant Atty Gen., U.S. Dep't of Justice (Mar. 30, 2022); Letter from Rep. Jim Jordan, *et al.,* Ranking Member, H. Comm. on the Judiciary, to Hon. Merrick Garland, Atty Gen., U.S. Dep't of Justice (Apr. 27, 2022); Letter from Rep. Jim Jordan, *et al.,* Ranking Member, H. Comm. on the Judiciary, to Hon. Merrick Garland, Atty Gen., U.S. Dep't of Justice (June 23, 2022); Letter from Rep. Jim Jordan, *et al.,* Ranking Member, H. Comm. on the Judiciary, to Hon. Merrick Garland, Atty Gen., U.S. Dep't of Justice (Aug. 15, 2022); Letter from Rep. Jim Jordan, *et al.,* Ranking Member, H. Comm. on the Judiciary, to Hon. Jacqueline C. Romero, Atty Gen., U.S. Atty, U.S. Dep't of Justice, Eastern District of PA (Oct. 7, 2022).

records and materials in your possession relating to the topics addressed in this letter. You should construe this preservation notice as an instruction to take all reasonable steps to prevent the destruction or alteration, whether intentionally or negligently, of all documents, communications, and other information, including electronic information and metadata, that are or may be responsive to this congressional inquiry. This instruction includes all electronic messages sent using your official and personal accounts or devices, including records created using text messages, phone-based message applications, or encryption software.

Sincerely,

Jim Jordan
Ranking Member

cc: The Honorable Jerrold L. Nadler
Chairman

Enclosure

Appendix: Outstanding Oversight Requests

June 8, 2021

1. Explain the Justice Department's current efforts to identify and prosecute individuals involved in the assaults of Mr. Andy Ngo and other journalists in violation of federal statutes securing their civil rights; and

2. Explain how the Justice Department, in coordination with other relevant federal and state law enforcement agencies, is working to prevent individuals from engaging in violence and intimidation designed to impair the free exercise and enjoyment of rights and privileges that Mr. Andy Ngo and other journalists possess under the Constitution and laws of the United States.

November 18, 2021

3. Explain when and how the FBI became aware of the diary purportedly belonging to President Biden's daughter and describe when and why it opened an investigation into the matter;

4. Provide copies of the search warrants, affidavits, and all other supporting documents related to the FBI's search of residences of James O'Keefe and other current or former journalists or employees of Project Veritas;

5. Explain the factual and legal predicate for the FBI to conduct raids at the homes of James O'Keefe and other current or former journalists or employees of Project Veritas;

6. Describe the process the Department followed when obtaining subpoenas for the FBI to obtain information from, or records of, James O'Keefe and other current or former journalists or employees of Project Veritas, including whether you and/or any other Department officials approved the decision to obtain such subpoenas;

7. Explain what steps, if any, the Department has taken or will take to investigate the leaking of Project Veritas' information to the *New York Times*; and

8. Explain whether any official or employee of the Executive Office of the President communicated with the Department and/or the FBI about investigating or searching the residences of James O'Keefe and other current or former employees of Project Veritas.

February 17, 2022

1. All documents and communications referring or relating to the creation of the Department of Justice's new domestic terrorism unit within the Counterterrorism Section of the National Security Division;

2. All documents and communications between or among officials or employees of the Executive Office of the President and the Department or National Security Division about the creation of the new domestic terrorism office within the Counterterrorism Section of the National Security Division;

3. An explanation as to why you decided to establish a new domestic terrorism office within the Counterterrorism Section of the National Security Division, in contravention of prior advice of career Department of Justice officials;

4. An explanation as to whether you or your staff consulted with the Department's career lawyers in the Counterterrorism Section or elsewhere in the Department prior to the establishment of this new office. If so, provide all recommendations and advice, both formal and informal, that was made to the National Security Division about the newly-formed office;

5. An explanation whether the resources and personnel of this new domestic terrorism office is being used or will be used to target concerned parents at local school board meetings;

6. Quantify the number of personnel assigned to the newly-formed domestic terrorism office within the Counterterrorism Section of the National Security Division; and

7. Quantify the number of active domestic terrorism investigations, including by type of case, for the period of January 1, 2021, to the present.

March 30, 2022:

1. All documents and communications referring or relating to the decision to end the Department's China Initiative, to include an unredacted copy of the Department's three-month internal review initiated by you in November 2021;

2. An explanation as to whether you or your staff consulted with the Department's career lawyers or other personnel in the Department prior to the decision to end the Department's China Initiative. If so, provide all recommendations and advice, both formal and informal, that was provided to you or your staff; and

3. An accounting of the Department's resources dedicated to combating national security threats posed by the People's Republic of China.

April 27, 2022:

1. Preserve all records relating to the Department's disciplinary and personnel actions against Deputy U.S. Marshals who defended federal property in Portland, Oregon from far-left rioters in the summer of 2020.

June 23, 2022:

1. All documents and communications between or among the Department of Justice and the Executive Office of the President referring or relating to the harassment and intimidation campaign outside justices' homes; and

2. All documents and communications between or among employees of the Department of Justice referring or relating to the harassment and intimidation campaign outside justices' homes, including those sent or received by employees of the United States Attorney's Office for the District of Maryland and the United States Attorney's Office for the Eastern District of Virginia.

August 15, 2022:

1. All documents and communications referring or relating to the execution of a search warrant on President Trump's residence;

2. All documents and communications referring or relating to the decision to seek a search warrant for President Trump's residence;

3. All documents and communications referring or relating to the use of confidential human source(s) in connection with the search of President Trump's residence;

4. All documents and communications between or among the Department of Justice, Federal Bureau of Investigation, or the Executive Office of the President about a search of President Trump's residence;

5. All documents and communications between or among the Department of Justice, Federal Bureau of Investigation, or the United States Secret Service about a search of President Trump's residence; and

6. All documents and communications between or among the Department of Justice, the Federal Bureau of Investigation, or the National Archives and Records Administration about a potential search of President Trump's residence.

October 7, 2022:

1. All documents and communications between the U.S. Attorney's Office for the Eastern District of Pennsylvania and other components of the Department of Justice referring or

relating to enforcement of the Freedom of Access to Clinic Entrances Act between May 2, 2022, and present;

2. All documents and communications between the U.S. Attorney's Office for the Eastern District of Pennsylvania, the Department of Justice, or the Executive Office of the President referring or relating to the Department's Reproductive Rights Task Force;

3. All documents and communications between the U.S. Attorney's Office for the Eastern District of Pennsylvania and the Department of Justice referring or relating to investigations of attacks on pregnancy resource centers between May 2, 2022, and the present;

4. All documents and communications referring or relating to the attack on the HOPE Pregnancy Center in Philadelphia, Pennsylvania, that occurred on June 10, 2022; and

5. All documents and communications between the U.S. Attorney's Office for the Eastern District of Pennsylvania and the Federal Bureau of Investigation referring or relating to the arrest of Mark Houck.

JERROLD NADLER, New York
CHAIRMAN

JIM JORDAN, Ohio
RANKING MEMBER

ONE HUNDRED SEVENTEENTH CONGRESS

Congress of the United States
House of Representatives
COMMITTEE ON THE JUDICIARY
2138 Rayburn House Office Building
Washington, DC 20515-6216
(202) 225-3951
judiciary.house.gov

November 2, 2022

The Honorable Christopher A. Wray
Director
Federal Bureau of Investigation
935 Pennsylvania Avenue, N.W.
Washington, DC 20535

Dear Director Wray:

We are investigating allegations of politicization and bias at the Federal Bureau of Investigation. As a part of this oversight, Committee Republicans have sent you letters requesting documents and information on several matters,[1] including but not limited to whistleblower disclosures alleging the FBI's improper use of law-enforcement resources for political purposes and the FBI's "purging" of employees with disfavored viewpoints. To date, the FBI has not sufficiently responded to any of our specific requests for documents or information. Our various requests to you, accordingly, remain outstanding.

The FBI is not immune from transparency or above accountability for its actions. Committee Republicans intend to continue to examine the politicization and bias at the FBI, including into the 118th Congress if necessary. We reiterate our requests, which are itemized in the attached appendix and incorporated herein, and ask that you, as the custodian of all FBI records, produce the entirety of the requested material as soon as possible but no later than November 16, 2022.

Furthermore, this letter serves as a formal request to preserve all existing and future records and materials in your possession relating to the topics addressed in this letter. You should

---

[1] Letter from Jim Jordan, Ranking Member, H. Comm. on the Judiciary, to Christopher A. Wray, Dir. Fed. Bureau of Investigation (Mar. 9, 2022); Letter from Rep. Jim Jordan, *et al.*, Ranking Member, H. Comm. on the Judiciary, to Hon. Christopher A. Wray, Dir., Fed. Bureau of Investigation (Mar. 21, 2022). Letter from Rep. Jim Jordan, *et al.*, Ranking Member, H. Comm. on the Judiciary, to Hon. Christopher A. Wray, Dir., Fed. Bureau of Investigation (May 24, 2022); Letter from Rep. Jim Jordan, *et al.*, Ranking Member, H. Comm. on the Judiciary, to Hon. Christopher A. Wray, Dir., Fed. Bureau of Investigation (June 1, 2022); Letter from Jim Jordan, Ranking Member, H. Comm. on the Judiciary, to Christopher A. Wray, Dir. Fed. Bureau of Investigation (July 27, 2022); Letter from Rep. Jim Jordan, *et al.*, Ranking Member, H. Comm. on the Judiciary, to Hon. Christopher A. Wray, Dir., Fed. Bureau of Investigation (Aug. 15, 2022); Letter from Jim Jordan, Ranking Member, H. Comm. on the Judiciary, to Christopher A. Wray, Dir. Fed. Bureau of Investigation (Sept. 14, 2022); Letter from Jim Jordan, Ranking Member, H. Comm. on the Judiciary, to Christopher A. Wray, Dir. Fed. Bureau of Investigation (Sept. 19, 2022).

construe this preservation notice as an instruction to take all reasonable steps to prevent the destruction or alteration, whether intentionally or negligently, of all documents, communications, and other information, including electronic information and metadata, that are or may be responsive to this congressional inquiry. This instruction includes all electronic messages sent using your official and personal accounts or devices, including records created using text messages, phone-based message applications, or encryption software.

Sincerely,

Jim Jordan
Ranking Member

cc: The Honorable Jerrold L. Nadler
Chairman

Enclosure

Appendix: Outstanding Oversight Requests

March 9, 2022:

1. A staff briefing about the status and extent of the FBI's pipe bomb investigation.

March 21, 2022:

1. An unredacted copy of the FBI Inspection Division's audit titled "2019 Domestic Investigations and Operations Guide Audit" dated January 10, 2020;

2. All documents and communications referring or relating to the FBI Inspection Division's 2019 Domestic Investigations and Operations Guide Audit dated January 10, 2020;

3. A description of the FBI's predicate to open sensitive investigative matters of politicians, candidates, religious groups, and others, as documented in the FBI Inspection Division's 2019 Domestic Investigations and Operations Guide Audit dated January 10, 2020;

4. An explanation of whether the FBI has resolved compliance issues related to sensitive investigative matters identified in the secret audit; and

5. Unredacted copies of all internal reviews conducted by the FBI's Inspection Division between November 1, 2019, and the present.

May 24, 2022:

1. A full accounting of the approximately 3,394,053 U.S. person queries conducted by the FBI in calendar year (CY) 2021, including:

    a. The total number of unique query terms that are a U.S. citizen, an alien lawfully admitted for permanent residence, an unincorporated association, or a corporation which is incorporated in the United States. If the FBI does not have the capability to identify the number of unique query terms, provide an explanation as to why;

    b. The Section 702-derived contents reviewed in each query, if any; and

    c. The number of preliminary or full investigations into any U.S. citizens the FBI has initiated as a result of information obtained through any of these U.S. person queries, and the nature of the predication for each such investigation.

2. An explanation of the facts and circumstances of the approximately 1.9 million U.S person queries that are apparently the result of an FBI investigation into alleged Russian hackers who sought to compromise U.S. critical infrastructure, including:

a. The rationale for why these queries were found to be compliant with the FBI's Section 702 querying procedures;

b. The total number of U.S. citizens the FBI identified as victims of these compromises(s) pursuant to these queries;

c. The total number of U.S. victims the FBI notified about the compromises(s) pursuant to the Crime Victims' Rights and Restitution Act, 34 U.S.C. § 20141, or the Crime Victims' Rights Act, 18 U.S.C. § 3771; and

d. A detailed statement about the FBI's investigation, including the status of the investigation and any information uncovered about the identity of the Russian actors and their involvement with or connection to the Russian government, if any.

3. Provide the total number of FBI U.S. person queries of Section 702-derived information, by year, for CY 2015 through CY 2019.

4. An explanation for why the FBI failed to comply with the statutory requirement to obtain an order from the Foreign Intelligence Surveillance Court before accessing the contents of Section 702-acquired information on at least four instances in 2021, including:

    a. The basis for each query;

    b. A description of the contents accessed, and a statement about whether the query was conducted in order to retrieve such contents; and

    c. The date on which the FBI discovered each violation and the date on which the FISC was alerted to each violation.

5. Provide a detailed accounting of every instance since December 2019 in which the FBI has queried, accessed, otherwise used information obtained pursuant to Section 702 for evidence of a crime unrelated to national security;

6. Identify the frequency of batch queries of FISA-acquired data for 99 or fewer queries, and explain why users must only obtain attorney approval before conducting a batch search of 100 or more queries;

7. Explain whether the FBI has located all of the missing Woods Files identified in the Department of Justice's Office of Inspector General September 2021 report, and provide the reason(s) why the FBI cannot locate all missing Woods Files;

8. Quantify the number of FBI employees who have access to Section 702 FISA-acquired data; and

9. Produce all guidance documents and training materials currently issued to FBI personnel with access to FISA-acquired data.

June 1, 2022:

1. All documents and communications referring or relating to the establishment, maintenance, and accreditation of the Secure Work Environment at Perkins Coie's Washington, D.C. office location, for the period of January 1, 2016, to December 1, 2021;

2. All documents and communications between or among the FBI for the period of January 1, 2016, to December 1, 2021, referring or relating to Michael Sussmann;

3. An explanation as to why the FBI approved a Secure Work Environment at Perkins Coie's Washington, D.C. office location;

4. An explanation as to the FBI's relationship with Michael Sussmann, for the period of January 1, 2016, to December 1, 2021, including:

    a. When did the FBI provide Michael Sussmann an FBI badge with special access to its headquarters;

    b. Why did the FBI provide Michael Sussmann an FBI badge to access its headquarters;

    c. A list of all FBI employees who met with Michael Sussmann, for the period January 1, 2016, to December 1, 2021, at FBI headquarters, including dates and times;

    d. Whether the FBI provided Michael Sussmann access to any of its Sensitive Compartmented Information Facilities to review any classified information and sensitive law-enforcement information; and

5. Since the September 2021 federal indictment of Michael Sussmann, and his subsequent resignation from Perkins Coie, whether the FBI continues its arrangement of this Secure Work Environment at Perkins Coie's Washington, D.C. office location.

July 27, 2022:

1. All documents and communications referring or relating to eGuardians, preliminary investigations, and full investigations classified as domestic violent extremism, including by type of case, for the period of January 1, 2020, to the present;

2. All documents and communications between or among employees of the Federal Bureau of Investigation, the Department of Justice, and the Executive Office of the President

referring or relating to classifying or reclassifying domestic violent extremism cases, for the period of January 1, 2020, to the present;

3. The total number of preliminary investigations and full investigations of domestic violent extremism, including by type of case, for the period of January 1, 2020, to the present; and

4. The total number of Confidential Human Sources that contributed to any reports of domestic violent extremism cases, for the period of January 1, 2020, to the present.

August 15, 2022:

1. All documents and communications referring or relating to the execution of a search warrant on President Trump's residence;

2. All documents and communications referring or relating to the decision to seek a search warrant for President Trump's residence;

3. All documents and communications referring or relating to the use of confidential human source(s) in connection with the search of President Trump's residence;

4. All documents and communications between or among the Department of Justice, Federal Bureau of Investigation, or the Executive Office of the President about a search of President Trump's residence;

5. All documents and communications between or among the Department of Justice, Federal Bureau of Investigation, or the United States Secret Service about a search of President Trump's residence; and

6. All documents and communications between or among the Department of Justice, the Federal Bureau of Investigation, or the National Archives and Records Administration about a potential search of President Trump's residence.

September 14, 2022:

1. All documents and communications referring or relating to the FBI's Domestic Terrorism Symbols Guide on Militia Violent Extremism, for the period of January 1, 2020, to the present; and

2. A full and complete explanation as to why the FBI's Domestic Terrorism Strategic Unit did not include symbols, images, phrases, events, and individuals about left-wing violent extremists' group in the FBI's Domestic Terrorism Symbols Guide.

September 19, 2022:

1. All documents and communications referring or relating to the Washington Field Office's policies and procedures for opening investigations into potential subjects of the events occurring on January 6, 2021;

2. All documents and communications referring or relating to eGuardians, preliminary investigations, and full investigations regarding January 6 investigations for which the FBI's WFO is initiating, conducting, approving investigative work even if the WFO is not listed in the casefile as the responsible field office;

3. All documents and communications sent or received by WFO employees instructing agents in other FBI Field Offices to open full investigations into potential subjects of January 6 investigations;

4. A complete accounting of all DVE cases opened since January 6, 2021, in which the WFO has identified subjects or directed other field offices to execute search or arrest warrants, to include the following information:

    a. The case identifier;

    b. The responsible field office;

    c. The date opened; and

    d. The current disposition of the matter;

5. The number of arrest and search warrants sworn out by agents from the WFO, but executed in the geographic area of another FBI field office; and

6. The number of all FBI agents involved in January 6 investigations, identified by FBI field office.

JERROLD NADLER, New York
CHAIRMAN

JIM JORDAN, Ohio
RANKING MEMBER

ONE HUNDRED SEVENTEENTH CONGRESS

Congress of the United States

House of Representatives

COMMITTEE ON THE JUDICIARY

2138 RAYBURN HOUSE OFFICE BUILDING
WASHINGTON, DC 20515-6216
(202) 225-3951
judiciary.house.gov

October 28, 2022

The Honorable Merrick B. Garland
Attorney General
U.S. Department of Justice
950 Pennsylvania Avenue, N.W.
Washington, DC 20530

Dear Attorney General Garland:

We are investigating the Biden Administration's callous disregard for the safety and security of our southern border, including the Justice Department's abuse of U.S. immigration law and policy to advance the Biden Administration's political interests. Since your confirmation we have written to you requesting information about the Administration's use of federal taxpayer dollars to pay settlements to illegal aliens who violated U.S. law, and your purge of immigration judges appointed by former President Trump for political reasons. Our letters have gone unanswered. The American people deserve better than to be ignored by an Administration intent on undermining the rule of law and erasing our national borders.

Committee Republicans will continue to pursue these matters, including into the 118th Congress if necessary. Accordingly, we reiterate our outstanding requests, which are itemized in the attached appendix and incorporated herein, and ask that you, as the custodian of all Departmental records, produce the entirety of the requested material as soon as possible but no later than November 11, 2022.

Furthermore, this letter serves as a formal request to preserve all existing and future records and materials in your possession relating to the topics addressed in this letter. You should construe this preservation notice as an instruction to take all reasonable steps to prevent the destruction or alteration, whether intentionally or negligently, of all documents, communications, and other information, including electronic information and metadata, that are or may be responsive to this congressional inquiry. This instruction includes all electronic messages sent using your official and personal accounts or devices, including records created using text messages, phone-based message applications, or encryption software.

Sincerely,

Jim Jordan
Ranking Member

Tom McClintock
Ranking Member
Subcommittee on Immigration and Citizenship

cc: The Honorable Jerrold L. Nadler
Chairman

Enclosure

Appendix: Outstanding Immigration-Related Documents and Information Requests to the Department of Justice

---

November 5, 2021:

1. All documents and communications referring or relating to the decision(s) to make payments to illegal aliens encountered at the southern border in 2017 and 2018, including the authorization of any payments, between or among Attorney General Merrick Garland, Deputy Attorney General Lisa Monaco, Principal Deputy Assistant Attorney General Brian Boynton, or Director of the Office of Immigration Litigation William Peachey.

2. All documents and communications referring or relating to the decision(s) to make payments to illegal aliens encountered at the southern border in 2017 and 2018 between or among employees of the Department of Justice and employees of the Executive Office of the President.

3. All documents and communications referring or relating to the decision(s) to make payments to illegal aliens encountered at the southern border in 2017 and 2018 between or among employees of the Department of Justice and employees of the Department of Homeland Security.

4. All documents and communications referring or relating to the decision(s) to make payments to illegal aliens encountered at the southern border in 2017 and 2018 between or among employees of the Department of Justice and employees of the Department of Health and Human Services.

5. Is the Department considering payments to alien parents or legal guardians whose child was removed from their custody after a determination by U.S. Customs and Border Protection that the parent or legal guardian presented a danger to the child?

6. Is the Department considering payments to alien parents or legal guardians whose child was removed from their custody after a determination by U.S. Customs and Border Protection that the parent or legal guardian had a conviction for an offense relating to child abuse or neglect?

7. Is the Department considering payments to alien parents or legal guardians whose child was removed from their custody after a determination by U.S. Customs and Border Protection that the parent or legal guardian had a conviction for an offense relating to sexual abuse of a minor?

8. Is the Department considering payments for aliens who do not meet the requirements of the class certified in the Ms. L. v. U.S. Immigration and Customs Enforcement, et. al litigation?

9. Is the Department considering payments to alien parents or legal guardians who, after being provided the chance to take their child with them when returning to their home country, chose instead to leave their child in U.S. government custody or in the care and custody of another individual inside the United States?

10. Out of what fund(s) will the payments to aliens be paid?

11. For how many aliens who are outside the United States is the Department considering payments pursuant to the litigation described above?

12. For how many aliens inside the United States is the Department considering payments pursuant to the litigation described above?

July 20, 2022:

1. The number of immigration judges whose employment was terminated during or at the end of their probationary period between January 20, 2021, and the present.

2. The number of immigration judges who resigned during or at the end of their probationary period between January 20, 2021, and the present.

3. The number of immigration judges whose employment was terminated during or at the end of their probationary period, each fiscal year for FY 2007 through to-date FY 2022.

4. The termination letter provided to each immigration judge whose employment was terminated during or at the end of their probationary period between January 20, 2021, and the present.

5. The termination letter provided to each immigration judge whose employment was terminated during or at the end of their probationary period between October 1, 2006, and January 20, 2021.

6. All documents and communications referring or relating to the decision(s) to terminate the employment of each immigration judge whose employment was terminated during or at the end of their probationary period, between January 20, 2021, and the present, sent or received by the following individuals:

    a. Attorney General Merrick Garland;
    b. Deputy Attorney General Lisa Monaco;
    c. Principal Deputy Assistant Attorney General Brian Boynton;
    d. Director of the Executive Office for Immigration Review David Neal;
    e. Deputy Director of Executive Office for Immigration Review Mary Cheng;
    f. Chief Immigration Judge Tracy Short;
    g. Principal Deputy Chief Immigration Judge Daniel Weiss;

h. Senior Counsel to the Deputy Attorney General Margy O'Herron;
i. Assistant Chief Immigration Judge Rebecca Walters;
j. Assistant Chief Immigration Judge David Cheng; and
k. Former Acting Deputy Director of the Executive Office for Immigration Review Charles Adkins-Blanch.

7. All documents and communications referring or relating to the decision(s) to terminate the employment of each immigration judge whose employment was terminated during or at the end of their probationary period, between January 20, 2021, and the present, sent or received by the then-Assistant Chief Immigration Judge for the immigration court at which the terminated immigration judge worked.

8. All documents and communications referring or relating to the decision(s) to terminate the employment of each immigration judge whose employment was terminated during or at the end of their probationary period, between January 20, 2021, and the present, between or among Department employees and immigration-related non-governmental groups, including but not limited to the American Immigration Lawyers Association, the Capital Area Immigrants' Rights (CAIR) Coalition, Ayuda, and the Immigration and Human Rights Clinic at the University of the District of Columbia.

9. All documents and communications referring or relating to the decision(s) to terminate the employment of each immigration judge whose employment was terminated during or at the end of their probationary period, between January 20, 2021, and the present, between or among Department employees and any private bar immigration attorney, immigration law professor (full-time or adjunct), immigration author, and immigration blogger.

JERROLD NADLER, New York
CHAIRMAN

JIM JORDAN, Ohio
RANKING MEMBER

ONE HUNDRED SEVENTEENTH CONGRESS
Congress of the United States
House of Representatives
COMMITTEE ON THE JUDICIARY
2138 Rayburn House Office Building
Washington, DC 20515-6216
(202) 225-3951
judiciary.house.gov

October 18, 2022

Ms. Jill Sanborn
c/o Mr. Carter Burwell
Debevoise & Plimpton
801 Pennsylvania Avenue N.W.
Washington, DC 20004

Dear Ms. Sanborn:

On August 10, 2022, we wrote to you requesting that you appear for a transcribed interview concerning your actions while employed at the Federal Bureau of Investigation. Although your attorneys claimed you "want[] to be responsive" to our request, you failed to take any meaningful steps to arrange your transcribed interview for over two months. Only late last Friday did your attorneys offer a specific date for a transcribed interview—December 2, 2022—a date six weeks in the future and nearly four months since our initial request.

Your attorneys have maintained that a forthcoming letter from the FBI will fully respond to our request and obviate the need for your testimony. You should know, however, that we do not agree with this assertion. As Committee staff has informed your attorneys, our request to you for a transcribed interview is separate and distinct from the requests for documents and information we have made to the FBI and the Justice Department.

Your attorneys have also suggested that the FBI must approve your appearance for a transcribed interview. You should be aware that, here too, we do not share your attorneys' view. Every federal employee, and former employee, has a right to speak with Congress without interference, intimidation, or obstruction from his or her employing agency. To the extent that the FBI is or has been preventing your ability to respond to our request in a timely and comprehensive manner, we will be interested in examining these facts during your transcribed interview.

You have had over two months to complete your requested due diligence on our request for a transcribed interview. We have been patient and accommodating in attempting to work in good faith with your attorneys. Your testimony remains essential to our inquiry, and as such, we welcome your appearance for a transcribed interview on December 2, 2022, at 10:00 a.m. Because you are represented by personal counsel in this matter, agency counsel will not be permitted to attend the interview. If you have any questions about these proceedings, please ask your attorneys to contact Committee staff on your behalf.

Thank you for your attention to this matter.

Sincerely,

Jim Jordan
Ranking Member

Mike Johnson
Ranking Member
Subcommittee on the Constitution, Civil Rights and Civil Liberties

cc: The Honorable Jerrold L. Nadler, Chairman

JERROLD NADLER, New York
CHAIRMAN

JIM JORDAN, Ohio
RANKING MEMBER

ONE HUNDRED SEVENTEENTH CONGRESS

Congress of the United States
House of Representatives
COMMITTEE ON THE JUDICIARY

2138 RAYBURN HOUSE OFFICE BUILDING
WASHINGTON, DC 20515–6216
(202) 225–3951
judiciary.house.gov

October 17, 2022

Mr. Ronald A. Klain
Assistant to the President and Chief of Staff
The White House
Washington, DC 20500

Dear Mr. Klain:

We are investigating the Biden Administration's misuse of federal criminal and counterterrorism resources to target concerned parents at school board meetings. We know from publicly available information that employees of the Executive Office of the President were involved in discussions surrounding the National School Boards Association's (NSBA) September 29, 2021, letter to President Biden and the letter's specific request that the Biden Administration use the Patriot Act to target parents. We also know that President Biden called the NSBA head to tell her he was "appreciative" of the letter and to invite her to the Oval Office. The American people, however, deserve much more accountability and transparency about the Biden Administration's anti-parent directives.

On June 14, 2022, Committee Republicans wrote to you requesting documents and information regarding the White House's collusion with the NSBA and its involvement in effectuating the misuse of federal criminal and counterterrorism resources against parents.[1] Now over four months later, you have failed to produce any of the requested documents or information. This is unacceptable.

Parents voicing their concerns at school board meetings are not domestic terrorists. Yet, the Attorney General's anti-parent directive of October 4, 2021, remains in effect, and as a result, the threat of federal law enforcement continues to chill the First Amendment rights of American parents. Committee Republicans intend to continue to pursue this serious misuse of federal law-enforcement resources, including if necessary into the 118th Congress. We reiterate our requests, which are itemized in the attached appendix and incorporated herein, and ask that you produce the entirety of the requested material as soon as possible but no later than October 31, 2022.

Furthermore, this letter serves as a formal request to preserve all existing and future records and materials in your possession relating to the topics addressed in this letter. You should construe this preservation notice as an instruction to take all reasonable steps to prevent the

[1] Letter from Rep. Jim Jordan et al., Ranking Member, H. Comm. on the Judiciary, to Mr. Ronald A. Klain, Assistant to the President and Chief of Staff, The White House (Jun. 14, 2022).

destruction or alteration, whether intentionally or negligently, of all documents, communications, and other information, including electronic information and metadata, that are or may be responsive to this congressional inquiry. This instruction includes all electronic messages sent using your official and personal accounts or devices, including records created using text messages, phone-based message applications, or encryption software.

Sincerely,

Jim Jordan
Ranking Member

cc: The Honorable Jerrold L. Nadler
Chairman

Enclosure

Appendix: Document Requests to the White House

June 14, 2022:

1. All documents and communications between or among employees or officials of the Executive Office of the President referring or relating to the NSBA;

2. All documents and communications between or among employees or officials of the Executive Office of the President and employees or officials of the Department of Justice, Department of Homeland Security, Department of Education, and any executive branch department or agency referring or relating to the NSBA or school board-related threats;

3. All documents and communications between or among employees or officials of the Executive Office of the President and employees or officials of the Department of Justice referring or relating to the Attorney General's memorandum dated October 4, 2021; and

4. All documents and communications between or among employees or officials of the Executive Office of the President and employees of the NSBA referring or relating to the NSBA's September 29, 2021, letter to President Biden.

JERROLD NADLER, New York
CHAIRMAN

JIM JORDAN, Ohio
RANKING MEMBER

ONE HUNDRED SEVENTEENTH CONGRESS

Congress of the United States
House of Representatives
COMMITTEE ON THE JUDICIARY
2138 RAYBURN HOUSE OFFICE BUILDING
WASHINGTON, DC 20515-6216
(202) 225-3951
judiciary.house.gov

October 17, 2022

The Honorable Miguel A. Cardona, EdD
Secretary
U.S. Department of Education
400 Maryland Avenue, S.W.
Washington, DC 20202

Dear Secretary Cardona:

We are investigating the Biden Administration's misuse of federal criminal and counterterrorism resources to target concerned parents at school board meetings. We know from publicly available information that the Biden Administration, including the Education Department, colluded with the National School Boards Association to manufacture a pretext for the use of federal law-enforcement authorities against parents.[1] The American people, however, deserve much more accountability and transparency.

On November 16, 2021, we wrote to you requesting documents and information regarding your Department's interactions with the NSBA and the subsequent appointment of then-NSBA President Dr. Viola Garcia to the National Assessment Governing Board.[2] To date, over eleven months later, the Department has only responded with a generic, hollow response letter, and has not produced any of the requested documents or information. [3] This letter did not sufficiently respond to our reasonable requests or alleviate our concerns.

Parents voicing their concerns at school board meetings are not domestic terrorists. Yet, the Attorney General's anti-parent directive of October 4, 2021, remains in effect, and as a result, the threat of federal law enforcement continues to chill the First Amendment rights of American parents. Committee Republicans intend to continue to pursue this serious misuse of federal law-enforcement resources, including if necessary into the 118th Congress. We reiterate our requests, which are itemized in the attached appendix and incorporated herein, and ask that you, as the custodian of all Departmental records, produce the entirety of the requested material as soon as

---

[1] *See* E-mail from Dr. Viola Garcia, President, Nat'l School Boards Assoc. (Oct. 2, 2021, 6:59 AM); *Final Report On the Events Surrounding the National School Boards Association's September 29, 2021, Letter to the President*, NATIONAL SCHOOL BOARDS ASSOCIATION at 38 (May 20, 2022).
[2] Letter from Rep. Jim Jordan, Ranking Member, H. Comm on the Judiciary & Rep. Virginia Foxx, Ranking Member, H. Comm. on Edu. & Labor, to Hon. Miguel A. Cardona, Sec'y, U.S. Dep't of Edu. (Nov. 16, 2021).
[3] Letter from Ms. Gwen Graham, Assistant Sec'y, Leg. & Cong. Affairs, U.S. Dep't of Edu., to Rep. Jim Jordan, Ranking Member, H. Comm. on the Judiciary (Apr. 1, 2022).

possible but no later than October 31, 2022.

Furthermore, this letter serves as a formal request to preserve all existing and future records and materials in your possession relating to the topics addressed in this letter. You should construe this preservation notice as an instruction to take all reasonable steps to prevent the destruction or alteration, whether intentionally or negligently, of all documents, communications, and other information, including electronic information and metadata, that are or may be responsive to this congressional inquiry. This instruction includes all electronic messages sent using your official and personal accounts or devices, including records created using text messages, phone-based message applications, or encryption software.

Sincerely,

Jim Jordan
Ranking Member

cc: The Honorable Jerrold L. Nadler
Chairman

Enclosure

Appendix: Document Requests to the Department of Education

November 16, 2021:

1. All documents and communications for the period January 20, 2021, to the present referring or relating to the NSBA;

2. All documents and communications for the period January 20, 2021, to the present between or among Department of Education employees or staff and any NSBA officer, Board member, delegate, or staff referring or relating to the September 29, 2021 letter to President Biden or the October 4, 2021, memorandum from Attorney General Garland;

3. All documents and communications for the period January 20, 2021, to the present between or among Department of Education employees or staff and Executive Office of the President employees or staff referring or relating to the September 29, 2021 letter to President Biden or the October 4, 2021, memorandum from Attorney General Garland;

4. All documents and communications for the period January 20, 2021, to the present between or among Department of Education employees or staff and Department of Justice employees or staff referring or relating to the September 29, 2021 letter to President Biden or the October 4, 2021, memorandum from Attorney General Garland;

5. All documents and communications for the period January 20, 2021, to the present regarding Dr. Viola Garcia's appointment to the National Assessment Governing Board; and

6. All documents and communications for the period January 20, 2021, to the present between or among Department of Education employees or staff and White House employees or staff regarding Dr. Viola Garcia's appointment to the National Assessment Governing Board.

JERROLD NADLER, New York
CHAIRMAN

JIM JORDAN, Ohio
RANKING MEMBER

ONE HUNDRED SEVENTEENTH CONGRESS

Congress of the United States
House of Representatives

COMMITTEE ON THE JUDICIARY

2138 RAYBURN HOUSE OFFICE BUILDING

WASHINGTON, DC 20515-6216

(202) 225-3951
judiciary.house.gov

October 17, 2022

The Honorable Alejandro Mayorkas
Secretary
U.S. Department of Homeland Security
301 7th Street SW
Washington, DC 20528

Dear Secretary Mayorkas:

We are investigating the Biden Administration's misuse of federal criminal and counterterrorism resources to target concerned parents at school board meetings. We know from publicly available information that Department of Homeland Security (DHS) employees were involved in discussions surrounding the National School Boards Association's September 29, 2021, letter to President Biden and its request that the Biden Administration use the Patriot Act to target parents.[1] The American people, however, deserve much more accountability and transparency.

On June 14, 2022, Committee Republicans wrote to you requesting documents and information regarding DHS's involvement in the Biden Administration's misuse of federal law-enforcement resources.[2] The Department responded to this request—over three months later—on September 16, 2022, stating that it was "working to identify responsive records."[3] As of today, over four months since our initial request and a month since your initial response, the Department has failed to produce any of the requested documents or information.

Parents voicing their concerns at school board meetings are not domestic terrorists. Yet, the Attorney General's anti-parent directive of October 4, 2021, remains in effect, and as a result, the threat of federal law enforcement continues to chill the First Amendment rights of American parents. Committee Republicans intend to continue to pursue this serious misuse of federal law-enforcement resources, including if necessary into the 118th Congress. We reiterate our requests,

---

[1] *Final Report On the Events Surrounding the National School Boards Association's September 29, 2021, Letter to the President*, NATIONAL SCHOOL BOARDS ASSOCIATION at 5 & 45 (May 20, 2022).
[2] Letter from Rep. Jim Jordan et al., Ranking Member, H. Comm. on the Judiciary, to Hon. Alejandro Mayorkas, Sec'y, U.S. Dep't of Homeland Sec. (Jun. 14, 2022).
[3] Letter from Ms. Alice Lugo, Assistant Sec'y for Legislative Affairs, U.S. Dep't of Homeland Sec., to Rep. Jim Jordan, Ranking Member, H. Comm. on the Judiciary (Sept. 16, 2022).

which are itemized in the attached appendix and incorporated herein, and ask that you, as the custodian of all Departmental records, produce the entirety of the requested material as soon as possible but no later than October 31, 2022.

Furthermore, this letter serves as a formal request to preserve all existing and future records and materials in your possession relating to the topics addressed in this letter. You should construe this preservation notice as an instruction to take all reasonable steps to prevent the destruction or alteration, whether intentionally or negligently, of all documents, communications, and other information, including electronic information and metadata, that are or may be responsive to this congressional inquiry. This instruction includes all electronic messages sent using your official and personal accounts or devices, including records created using text messages, phone-based message applications, or encryption software.

Sincerely,

Jim Jordan
Ranking Member

cc: The Honorable Jerrold L. Nadler
Chairman

Enclosure

Appendix: Document Requests to the Department of Homeland Security

June 14, 2022:

1. All documents and communications referring or relating to the National School Boards Association's September 29, 2021, letter to President Biden or the Attorney General's October 4, 2021, memorandum;

2. All documents and communications between or among Department of Homeland Security employees and National School Boards Association staff, officers, and/or executive board members, including but not limited to the communications of Julia Treanor, for the period January 20, 2021, to the present; and

3. Please explain whether you consider the Attorney General's October 4, 2021, memorandum to be lawful and whether you, or any Department of Homeland Security officials raised concerns about its enforcement.

JERROLD NADLER, New York
CHAIRMAN

JIM JORDAN, Ohio
RANKING MEMBER

ONE HUNDRED SEVENTEENTH CONGRESS

Congress of the United States

House of Representatives

COMMITTEE ON THE JUDICIARY

2138 RAYBURN HOUSE OFFICE BUILDING

WASHINGTON, DC 20515–6216

(202) 225–3951
judiciary.house.gov

October 14, 2022

Mr. Timothy Thibault
c/o Mr. Charles E. Duross
Morrison & Foerster LLP
2100 L Street, N.W., Suite 900
Washington, DC 20037

Dear Mr. Thibault:

We are in receipt of your attorney's letter, dated October 7, 2022, in which you declined to appear for a transcribed interview concerning allegations of abuse and misconduct within the Federal Bureau of Investigation.[1] Your refusal to testify is curious in light of your earlier public statement that you "welcome any investigation" into these matters.[2] As we previously informed you, whistleblowers have come forward with allegations that you took certain official actions for political reasons. As we continue to investigate the politicization of the Justice Department and FBI, your testimony remains crucial to our inquiry.

Your baseless assertion that "sensitive law enforcement information and/or pending investigations"[3] prevents your cooperation with our inquiry ignores the importance of congressional oversight as well as the Committee's past practice in examining misconduct at the FBI. The Supreme Court has repeatedly explained that the congressional oversight power is "broad and indispensable," "encompass[ing] inquiries into the administration of existing laws, studies of proposed law, and surveys of defects in our societal, economic, or political system for the purpose of enabling the Congress to remedy them."[4] The Judiciary Committee, authorized to conduct such oversight pursuant to the Rules of the House of Representatives, has exercised this authority on several recent occasions to examine allegations of misconduct at the Department and FBI. There is no rationale or legal basis for your refusal to cooperate with our inquiry for the reasons articulated in your attorney's October 7 letter.

---

[1] Letter from Mr. Charles E. Duross, Partner, Morrison & Foerster LLP, to Reps. Jim Jordan, Darrell Issa, & Mike Johnson, H. Comm. on the Judiciary (Oct. 7, 2022). *See also* Letter from Reps. Jim Jordan, Darrell Issa, & Mike Johnson, H. Comm. on the Judiciary, to Mr. Timothy Thibault (Sept. 23, 2022).

[2] *See* Tweet by Catherine Herridge, Twitter.com (Aug. 30, 2022, 8:21 p.m.) ("Media Statement on Behalf of Timothy R. Thibault"); Tom Winter, *Lawyer says FBI agent's retirement had nothing to do with Hunter Biden investigation*, NBC NEWS (Aug. 31, 2022).

[3] Letter from Mr. Charles E. Duross, Partner, Morrison & Foerster LLP, to Reps. Jim Jordan, Darrell Issa, & Mike Johnson, H. Comm. on the Judiciary (Oct. 7, 2022).

[4] *See, e.g.*, *Trump v. Mazars LLP*, No. 19-715 at 11 (U.S. slip op. July 9, 2020) (internal quotation marks and citations omitted).

In addition, your attorney asserts that you cannot comply with our document-preservation notice because you have left federal service. Notably, this assertion ignores that our notice includes both official *and* personal records that may be responsive to the topics we are investigating. To the extent that you possess any personal records—or copies of official records in your personal possession—that may be responsive to our inquiry, we ask that your attorney confirm to us on your behalf that you are taking all necessary steps to preserve these records. Alternatively, if you possess no personal records about the topics addressed in our letters to you, or any copies of official records in your personal possession, we ask that your attorney make such a representation to us on your behalf.

Our request that you appear for a transcribed interview remains outstanding. Your testimony is necessary for our oversight, and you can be assured that Committee Republicans will continue to pursue this matter into the 118th Congress. We again reiterate our request that you appear promptly for a transcribed interview. Please direct your attorney to contact Committee staff to schedule this transcribed interview without undue delay.

Thank you for your attention to this matter.

Sincerely,

Jim Jordan
Ranking Member

Darrell Issa
Ranking Member
Subcommittee on Courts, Intellectual Property and the Internet

Mike Johnson
Ranking Member
Subcommittee on the Constitution, Civil Rights and Civil Liberties

cc: The Honorable Jerrold L. Nadler, Chairman

JERROLD NADLER, New York
CHAIRMAN

JIM JORDAN, Ohio
RANKING MEMBER

ONE HUNDRED SEVENTEENTH CONGRESS

Congress of the United States

House of Representatives

COMMITTEE ON THE JUDICIARY

2138 RAYBURN HOUSE OFFICE BUILDING
WASHINGTON, DC 20515–6216
(202) 225–3951
judiciary.house.gov

October 11, 2022

The Honorable Merrick B. Garland
Attorney General
U.S. Department of Justice
950 Pennsylvania Avenue, N.W.
Washington, DC 20530

Dear Attorney General Garland:

We are investigating the Biden Administration's misuse of federal criminal and counterterrorism resources to target concerned parents at school board meetings. We know from whistleblowers and publicly available information that the Biden White House colluded with the National School Boards Association to manufacture a pretext for the use of federal law-enforcement authorities against parents, which you operationalized via a memorandum dated October 4, 2021. The American people, however, deserve much more accountability and transparency.

Since October 2021, we have sent over 100 letters to Departmental components requesting documents and information regarding the Biden Administration's misuse of law-enforcement resources.[1] To date, the Department has responded to these requests with only two half-page letters, and has not produced any of the requested documents or information. These letters do not sufficiently respond to our reasonable requests or alleviate our concerns.

---

[1] *See* Letter from Rep. Mike Johnson et al, to Hon. Merrick Garland, Atty Gen., U.S. Dep't of Justice (Oct. 13, 2021); Letter from Rep. Jim Jordan et al, Ranking Member, H. Comm. on the Judiciary, to Hon. Merrick Garland, Atty Gen., U.S. Dep't of Justice (Oct. 25, 2021); Letter from Rep. Jim Jordan et al, Ranking Member, H. Comm. on the Judiciary, to Mr. E. Bryan Wilson et al, Acting U.S. Atty, District of Alaska (Nov. 1, 2021); Letter from Rep. Jim Jordan et al, Ranking Member, H. Comm. on the Judiciary, to Mr. Mark Lesko, Acting Assistant Atty Gen., Nat'l Sec. Division, U.S. Dep't of Justice (Nov. 2, 2021); Letter from Rep. Jim Jordan et al, Ranking Member, H. Comm. on the Judiciary, to Hon. Christopher Wray, Dir., Fed. Bureau of Investigation (Nov. 3, 2021); Letter from Rep. Jim Jordan, Ranking Member, H. Comm. on the Judiciary, to Hon. Merrick Garland, Atty Gen., U.S. Dep't of Justice (Nov. 16, 2021); Letter from Rep. Jim Jordan, Ranking Member, H. Comm. on the Judiciary, to Hon. Christopher Wray, Dir., Fed. Bureau of Investigation (Nov. 18, 2021); Letter from Rep. Jim Jordan, Ranking Member, H. Comm. On the Judiciary, to Hon. Christopher Wray, Dir., Fed. Bureau of Investigation (Feb. 10, 2022); Rep. Jim Jordan, Ranking Member, H. Comm. on the Judiciary, to Hon. Merrick Garland, Atty Gen., U.S. Dep't of Justice (May 11, 2021); Letter from Rep. Jim Jordan et al, Ranking Member, H. Comm. on the Judiciary, to Hon. Merrick Garland, Atty Gen., U.S. Dep't of Justice (Jun. 14, 2022).

Parents voicing their concerns at school board meetings are not domestic terrorists. Yet, your anti-parent directive remains in effect, and as a result, the threat of federal law enforcement continues to chill the First Amendment rights of American parents. We intend to continue to pursue this serious misuse of federal law-enforcement resources. We reiterate our requests, which are itemized in the attached appendix and incorporated herein, and ask that you, as the custodian of all Departmental records, produce the entirety of the requested material as soon as possible but no later than October 25, 2022.

Furthermore, this letter serves as a formal request to preserve all existing and future records and materials in your possession relating to the topics addressed in this letter. You should construe this preservation notice as an instruction to take all reasonable steps to prevent the destruction or alteration, whether intentionally or negligently, of all documents, communications, and other information, including electronic information and metadata, that are or may be responsive to this congressional inquiry. This instruction includes all electronic messages sent using your official and personal accounts or devices, including records created using text messages, phone-based message applications, or encryption software.

Sincerely,

Jim Jordan
Ranking Member

Mike Johnson
Ranking Member
Subcommittee on the Constitution,
Civil Rights and Civil Liberties

cc: The Honorable Jerrold L. Nadler
Chairman

Enclosure

Appendix: Document Requests to Departmental Components

Attorney General Merrick Garland

May 11, 2022:

1. All documents and materials identified in our letters to Departmental components dated November 1, 2021, November 2, 2021, November 3, 2021, and November 18, 2021, immediately; and

June 14, 2022:

1. All documents and communications between Mary Wall, Senior Policy Advisor to the President, and any Department of Justice employees referring or relating to the National School Boards Association's letter dated September 29, 2021; the Attorney General's memorandum dated October 4, 2021; or alleged threats or violence at school board meetings; and

2. All documents and communications between Department of Justice employees and National School Boards Association staff, officers, and/or executive board members, including but not limited to the communications sent or received by Anthony Coley, Senior Advisor to the Attorney General, and Alivia Roberts, Special Assistant to the Director of Public Affairs.

February 28, 2022:

1. All documents requested from various Departmental components regarding the Department's misuse of federal counterterrorism resources to target parents.

FBI Director Christopher Wray

November 3, 2021:

1. All documents and communications referring or relating to convening meeting(s) with U.S. Attorneys' Offices in accordance with the Attorney General's October 4, 2021 memorandum, the establishment of the Department's task force, or the FBI's role as a member of the task force;

2. All agendas, minutes, and notes created or relied upon by FBI employees referring or relating to meeting(s) in each judicial district in accordance with the Attorney General's October 4, 2021 memorandum or the FBI's role as a member of the task force;

3. Please explain whether you consider the Attorney General's October 4, 2021 memorandum to be lawful and whether you intend to direct FBI agents and employees to enforce the Attorney General's directives;

4. Please explain whether you have issued any internal guidance to FBI field offices or special agents in charge referring or relating to the Attorney General's October 4, 2021 memorandum;

5. Please explain the FBI's role in convening meetings as directed by the Attorney General's October 4, 2021 memorandum;

6. Please explain the FBI's role in the Department's task force, including what federal statutes the FBI intends to use in investigating concerned parents at school board meetings;

7. Please identify by name, title, and field office each FBI employee involved in the meeting(s) and task force referenced in the Attorney General's October 4, 2021 memorandum;

8. Please identify all federal, state, local, Tribal, and territorial organizations invited to or that have attended the meetings convened in accordance with the October 4, 2021 memorandum;

9. Please provide all recommendations, both formal and informal, and any meeting minutes produced at the meeting(s) in accordance with the Attorney General's October 4, 2021 memorandum; and

10. Please provide all recommendations, both formal and informal, that the FBI has made to the Department's task force.

November 18, 2021:

1. Provide the number of parents who have been tagged by FBI with the EDUOFFICIALS threat tag;

2. All documents and communications referring or relating to the EDUOFFICIALS threat tag;

3. All documents and communications referring or relating to investigations identified and labeled with the EDUOFFICIALS threat tag; and

4. All documents and communications referring or relating to FBI investigations of school board threats sent or received by the following individuals:

    a. Carlton L. Peeples, Deputy Assistant Director, Criminal Investigative Division;

    b. Jay Greenberg, Deputy Assistant Director, Criminal Investigative Division;

c. Calvin A. Shivers, Assistant Director, Criminal Division;

d. Brian M. Cohen, Criminal Division;

e. Timothy R. Langan Jr., Assistant Director, Counterterrorism Division; and

f. Kevin Vorndran, Deputy Assistant Director, Counterterrorism Division.

February 10, 2022:

1. All documents and materials requested in the November 3 and November 18, 2021 letters.

<u>All 93 U.S. Attorneys' Offices</u>

November 1, 2021:

1. All documents and communications referring or relating to convening meeting(s) in your judicial district in accordance with the Attorney General's October 4, 2021 memorandum;

2. All agendas, minutes, and notes created or relied upon by U.S. Attorney's Office employees referring or relating to meeting(s) in your judicial district in accordance with the Attorney General's October 4, 2021 memorandum;

3. Please explain when meeting(s) in your judicial district in accordance with the Attorney General's October 4, 2021 memorandum have occurred or will occur;

4. Please identify by name and title of all U.S. Attorney's Office employees involved in the meeting(s) in your judicial district in accordance with the Attorney General's October 4, 2021 memorandum ;

5. Please identify all federal, state, local, Tribal, and territorial organizations invited to or that have attended the meetings convened in your judicial district in accordance with the October 4, 2021 memorandum; and

6. Please provide all recommendations, both formal and informal, and any meeting minutes produced at the meeting(s) in your judicial district in accordance with the Attorney General's October 4, 2021 memorandum.

<u>Assistant Attorney General of the National Security Division</u>

November 2, 2021:

1. All documents and communications referring or relating to the establishment of the Department's task force and the National Security Division's role as a member of the task force;

2. All documents and communications between employees of the Department of Justice and U.S. intelligence agencies referring or relating to alleged threats posed by concerned parents at local school board meetings, the NSBA's letter dated September 29, 2021, or the Attorney General's memo dated October 4, 2021;

3. All agendas, minutes, and notes created by or relied upon by National Security Division employees referring or relating to the Department's task force;

4. Please explain the National Security Division's role in the Department's task force, including what federal statutes within the Division's jurisdiction it intends to use in investigating concerned parents at school board meetings;

5. Please identity by name and title all National Security Division employees involved in the Department's task force; and

6. Please provide all recommendations, both formal and informal, that the National Security Division has made to the Department's task force.

JERROLD NADLER, New York
CHAIRMAN

JIM JORDAN, Ohio
RANKING MEMBER

ONE HUNDRED SEVENTEENTH CONGRESS

Congress of the United States

House of Representatives

COMMITTEE ON THE JUDICIARY

2138 RAYBURN HOUSE OFFICE BUILDING

WASHINGTON, DC 20515–6216

(202) 225–3951
judiciary.house.gov

October 7, 2022

The Honorable Jacqueline C. Romero
U.S. Attorney
Eastern District of Pennsylvania
615 Chestnut Street, Suite 1250
Philadelphia, PA 19106

Dear Ms. Romero:

We continue to investigate politicization at the Biden-Garland Department of Justice and Federal Bureau of Investigation. Several recent actions by the Department reinforce the conclusion that the Justice Department is using its federal law-enforcement authority as a weapon against the Administration's political opponents. Since the unprecedented leak of a draft Supreme Court opinion in *Dobbs v. Jackson Women's Health Organization*, the Justice Department has politicized enforcement of the Freedom of Access to Clinic Entrances (FACE) Act. We write to conduct oversight of your authorization of a dawn raid of the home of a pro-life leader, in front of his wife and seven children, when he had offered to voluntarily cooperate with authorities.

The FACE Act "prohibits threats of force, obstruction and property damage intended to interfere with reproductive health care services."[1] According to the Justice Department, the Act also protects "pro-life pregnancy counseling services and any other pregnancy support facility providing reproductive health care."[2] Since the leak of the *Dobbs* opinion, however, the Department has almost exclusively enforced the FACE Act to protect anti-life activists while failing to prosecute harassment and intimidation of pro-life supporters.[3]

On September 23, 2022, the FBI raided the home of Mark Houck, a pro-life leader residing within your judicial district, to execute an arrest warrant for allegedly violating the FACE Act. You alleged in a press release that Houck had shoved a Planned Parenthood volunteer outside a clinic almost a year earlier, on October 13, 2021.[4] Houck's wife, Ryan-

---

[1] Pub. L. 103-259 (1994); U.S. Dep't of Justice, Nat'l Task Force on Violence Against Reproductive Health Care Providers, Protecting Patients and Health Care Providers, https://www.justice.gov/crt/protecting-patients-and-health-care-providers (last visited Sept. 27, 2022).

[2] *Id.*

[3] Hans A. von Spakovsky & Charles Stimson, *FBI, Justice Department twist federal law to arrest, charge pro-life activist,* HERITAGE FOUND. (Sept. 28, 2022).

[4] Press Release, U.S. Dep't of Justice, U.S. Atty's Office E.D. of Penn., Bucks County Man Indicated on Federal Charges for Assaulting a Reproductive Healthcare Clinic Escort (Sept. 23, 2022).

Marie, however, explained that the Planned Parenthood activist had repeatedly made "crude . . . inappropriate and disgusting" comments about Houck in the presence of their 12-year-old son and "had gotten into the personal space" of the child.[5] She said that a local court in Philadelphia had already thrown out a civil suit against Houck filed by the activist.[6]

The Department's decision to arrest Houck, as well as the tactics used to effectuate the arrest, are troubling. Ryan-Marie Houck recounted how an FBI "SWAT team of about 25 came to my house with about 15 vehicles" and "they had about five guns pointed at my husband, myself and basically at my kids."[7] An anonymous FBI source denied to the media that the 25 agents were present, but did admit that authorities sent up to 20 agents to effectuate the arrest.[8] Houck's attorney subsequently disclosed that the dawn raid was unnecessary because Houck had offered to appear voluntarily and the FBI targeted Houck "solely to intimidate people of faith and prolife Americans."[9]

The Department's treatment of Houck stands in stark contrast to its treatment of "potential acts of domestic violent extremism" against pro-life facilities.[10] For example, on June 10, 2022, vandals smashed the windows and graffitied the walls of HOPE Pregnancy Center, a pro-life pregnancy center in your judicial district.[11] There was no press release from your office regarding an investigation or charges in that case. Just last week, an 83-year-old pro-life volunteer in Lake Odessa, Michigan was shot while canvassing a local neighborhood about an abortion ballot proposal.[12] There has been no outcry or press conference from the Justice Department in response to this crime. Since the leak of the draft *Dobbs* opinion, Jane's Revenge, a radical anti-life group, "has claimed responsibility for at least 18 arson and vandalism attacks" on pro-life clinics and organizations.[13] While the FBI says that it is investigating a "series of attacks and threats targeting pregnancy resource centers, faith-based organizations, and reproductive health clinics," to our knowledge, the Department and FBI have not executed any SWAT team dawn raids to make arrests of anti-life activists.[14]

Pro-life pregnancy centers nationwide play a critical and important role in supporting and assisting pregnant women. In 2019, 2,700 such centers served nearly two million people, and

---

[5] Patrick Delaney, *FBI raids home of Catholic pro-life speaker, author with guns drawn as his terrified kids watch*, LIFESITE (Sept. 23, 2022); *see also* Diana Glebova, *Lawyer for pro-life protester arrested by FBI says client offered to surrender, claims DOJ trying to 'intimidate people of faith,'* NAT'L REV. (Sept. 26, 2022).
[6] *Id.*
[7] Bradford Betz, Jon Brown, & Jake Gibson, *Pennsylvania pro-life activist arrested by FBI, charged with assaulting clinic escort,* FOX NEWS (Sept. 26, 2022).
[8] *Id.*
[9] Diana Glebova, *Lawyer for pro-life protester arrested by FBI says client offered to surrender, claims DOJ trying to 'intimidate people of faith,'* NAT'L REV. (Sept. 26, 2022).
[10] Jessica Chasmar, *Zero arrests in at least 17 Jane's Revenge attacks on pro-life organizations,* FOX NEWS (Sept. 14, 2022).
[11] Jenice Armstrong, *Angry about Roe? Then vote, don't vandalize,* THE PHILADELPHIA INQUIRER (Jun. 29, 2022).
[12] Emma Colton, *Elderly pro-life volunteer in Michigan shot after 'heated conversation,' pro-life group says*, FOX NEWS (Sept. 24, 2022).
[13] Jessica Chasmar, *Zero arrests in at least 17 Jane's Revenge attacks on pro-life organizations,* FOX NEWS (Sept. 14, 2022).
[14] *Id.*

continue to serve millions of women annually.[15] Pro-life pregnancy centers "exist to serve and support mothers in the courageous decision to give their children life, even under the most difficult circumstance."[16] Services and resources provided virtually free of charge include, but are not limited to: ultrasounds, pregnancy testing, STI/STD testing, parenting and prenatal education programs, diapers, and baby outfits.[17] Pro-life pregnancy centers deserve the same protections that the Department aggressively provides abortion clinics.

The Department's lackluster response to the attacks against pro-life facilities demonstrates that the Biden Administration would rather cater to the radical anti-life movement than help facilities that protect pregnant women in need. So that we can better understand why you have declined to evenly enforce federal law in your judicial district, please provide the following documents and information:

1. All documents and communications between the U.S. Attorney's Office for the Eastern District of Pennsylvania and other components of the Department of Justice referring or relating to enforcement of the Freedom of Access to Clinic Entrances Act between May 2, 2022, and present;

2. All documents and communications between the U.S. Attorney's Office for the Eastern District of Pennsylvania, the Department of Justice, or the Executive Office of the President referring or relating to the Department's Reproductive Rights Task Force;

3. All documents and communications between the U.S. Attorney's Office for the Eastern District of Pennsylvania and the Department of Justice referring or relating to investigations of attacks on pregnancy resource centers between May 2, 2022, and the present;

4. All documents and communications referring or relating to the attack on the HOPE Pregnancy Center in Philadelphia, Pennsylvania, that occurred on June 10, 2022; and

5. All documents and communications between the U.S. Attorney's Office for the Eastern District of Pennsylvania and the Federal Bureau of Investigation referring or relating to the arrest of Mark Houck.

Please provide this information as soon as possible but no later than 5:00 p.m. on October 21, 2022. Furthermore, this letter serves as a formal request to preserve all existing and future records and materials in your possession relating to the topics addressed in this letter. You should construe this preservation notice as an instruction to take all reasonable steps to prevent the destruction or alteration, whether intentionally or negligently, of all documents, communications, and other information, including electronic information and metadata, that are or may be responsive to this congressional inquiry. This instruction includes all electronic messages sent

---

[15] *Pro-life Pregnancy Centers Served 2 Million People with Essential Medical, Education and Support Services in 2019*, CHARLOTTE LOZIER INSTITUTE (Oct. 21, 2020).
[16] *Id.*
[17] *Id.*

using your official and personal accounts or devices, including records created using text messages, phone-based message applications, or encryption software.

Thank you for your prompt attention to this matter.

Sincerely,

Jim Jordan
Ranking Member

Mike Johnson
Ranking Member
Subcommittee on the Constitution,
Civil Rights and Civil Liberties

cc: The Honorable Merrick Garland, U.S. Attorney General
The Honorable Jerrold L. Nadler, Chairman

JERROLD NADLER, New York
CHAIRMAN

JIM JORDAN, Ohio
RANKING MEMBER

ONE HUNDRED SEVENTEENTH CONGRESS

Congress of the United States

House of Representatives

COMMITTEE ON THE JUDICIARY

2138 RAYBURN HOUSE OFFICE BUILDING

WASHINGTON, DC 20515-6216

(202) 225-3951
judiciary.house.gov

September 29, 2022

Ms. Jennifer Leigh Moore
Executive Assistant Director
Human Resources Branch
Federal Bureau of Investigation
935 Pennsylvania Avenue, N.W.
Washington, DC 20535

Dear Ms. Moore:

We are investigating serious allegations of abuse and misconduct within the senior leadership of the Department of Justice and the Federal Bureau of Investigation. During the course of this investigation, we have received protected whistleblower disclosures that the FBI is engaging in a "purge" of employees with conservative views by revoking their security clearances and indefinitely suspending these employees. Many of the formal notices for these adverse personnel actions have been signed by you. Recently, we received information suggesting you have retaliated against at least one whistleblower who has made protected disclosures to Congress. As we informed Director Christopher Wray, we take whistleblower retaliation seriously and we therefore require that you appear for a transcribed interview as soon as possible.

FBI whistleblowers have told the Committee that you have been involved with the security clearance revocations for those employees targeted for their conservative views. In addition, we understand that you have engaged in whistleblower retaliation and prohibited personnel practices. Under Title 5 of the United States Code, once a whistleblower makes a protected disclosure, an agency is prohibited from retaliating against the employee for that disclosure by taking or failing to take a personnel action.[1] We have advised Director Wray, as well as Attorney General Merrick Garland, that whistleblower disclosures to Congress are protected by law.[2] Your efforts to interfere with FBI employees who seek to expose the Bureau's misconduct by communicating directly with Congress cannot be condoned.

---

[1] 5 U.S.C. § 2302 (2021).

[2] *See e.g.* Letter from Rep. Jim Jordan, Ranking Member, H. Comm. on the Judiciary, to Hon. Christopher A. Wray, Dir., Fed. Bureau of Investigation (Mar. 9, 2022); Reps. Jim Jordan & Mike Johnson, H. Comm. on the Judiciary, to Hon. Merrick Garland, Atty Gen., U.S. Dep't of Justice (May 11, 2022); Letter from Rep. Jim Jordan, Ranking Member, H. Comm. on the Judiciary, to Hon. Christopher A. Wray, Dir., Fed. Bureau of Investigation (Sept. 19, 2022).

The Committee on the Judiciary has legislative and oversight jurisdiction over the Department of Justice and the FBI pursuant to Rule X of the Rules of the House of Representatives. Your testimony is necessary for our oversight. Please contact Committee staff at (202) 225-6906 by October 4, 2022, to schedule your transcribed interview. If you are represented by private counsel, we look forward to communicating with them shortly.

Furthermore, this letter serves as a formal request to preserve all existing and future records and materials in your possession relating to the topics addressed in this letter. You should construe this preservation notice as an instruction to take all reasonable steps to prevent the destruction or alteration, whether intentionally or negligently, of all documents, communications, and other information, including electronic information and metadata, that are or may be responsive to this congressional inquiry. This instruction includes all electronic messages sent using your official and personal accounts or devices, including records created using text messages, phone-based message applications, or encryption software.

Thank you for your attention to this matter.

Sincerely,

Jim Jordan
Ranking Member

Darrell Issa
Ranking Member
Subcommittee on Courts, Intellectual Property and the Internet

Mike Johnson
Ranking Member
Subcommittee on the Constitution, Civil Rights and Civil Liberties

cc: The Honorable Christopher A. Wray, Director, Federal of Bureau of Investigation
The Honorable Jerrold L. Nadler, Chairman

JERROLD NADLER, New York
CHAIRMAN

JIM JORDAN, Ohio
RANKING MEMBER

ONE HUNDRED SEVENTEENTH CONGRESS

Congress of the United States

House of Representatives

COMMITTEE ON THE JUDICIARY

2138 RAYBURN HOUSE OFFICE BUILDING

WASHINGTON, DC 20515–6216

(202) 225–3951
judiciary.house.gov

September 23, 2022

Mr. Timothy Thibault
c/o Morrison & Foerster LLP
2100 L Street, N.W.
Washington, DC 20037

Dear Mr. Thibault:

We have been investigating serious allegations of abuse and misconduct within the senior leadership of the Department of Justice and the Federal Bureau of Investigation. Brave whistleblowers have informed us that as an Assistant Special Agent in Charge at the Washington Field Office, you pressured line agents to reclassify cases as "domestic violent extremism" even though there was minimal, circumstantial evidence to support a reclassification.[1] Other whistleblowers have come to Congress alleging that you were part of a scheme to undermine and discredit allegations of criminal wrongdoing by members of the Biden family.[2] Accordingly, we believe that you possess information relating to our investigation and we request your assistance with our inquiry.

The Committee on the Judiciary has legislative and oversight jurisdiction over the Department of Justice and the FBI pursuant to Rule X of the Rules of the House of Representatives. We are investigating several allegations concerning the politicization of the Department and the FBI. Your testimony is necessary to advance our oversight. We ask that you please contact Committee staff to schedule a transcribed interview as soon as possible, but no later than 5:00 p.m. on October 7, 2022. Your attorney may contact Committee staff at (202) 225-6906 to schedule a transcribed interview without undue delay.

Furthermore, this letter serves as a formal request to preserve all existing and future records and materials in your possession relating to the topics addressed in this letter. You should construe this preservation notice as an instruction to take all reasonable steps to prevent the destruction or alteration, whether intentionally or negligently, of all documents, communications, and other information, including electronic information and metadata, that are or may be

[1] Letter from Rep. Jim Jordan, Ranking Member, H. Comm. on the Judiciary, to Hon. Christopher Wray, Dir., Fed. Bureau of Investigation (Jul. 27, 2022); Ashley Oliver, *Exclusive – Whistleblower: Same FBI boss who shut down Hunter Biden dirt also pressured agents to juice domestic violent extremism stats*, BREITBART (Jul. 27, 2022).

[2] Letter from Sen. Chuck Grassley, Ranking Member, S. Comm. on the Judiciary, to Hon. Merrick Garland, Atty Gen., U.S. Dep't of Justice & Hon. Christopher Wray, Dir., Fed. Bureau of Investigation (Jul. 25, 2022) ("ASAC Thibault allegedly ordered the [Hunter Biden inquiry] closed without providing a valid reason as required by FBI guidelines. . . . [I]t's alleged that FBI official, including ASAC Thibault, subsequently attempted to improperly mark the matter in FBI systems so that it could not be opened in the future.").

responsive to this congressional inquiry. This instruction includes all electronic messages sent using your official and personal accounts or devices, including records created using text messages, phone-based message applications, or encryption software.

Thank you for your attention to this matter.

Sincerely,

Jim Jordan
Ranking Member

Darrell Issa
Ranking Member
Subcommittee on Courts, Intellectual Property and the Internet

Mike Johnson
Ranking Member
Subcommittee on the Constitution, Civil Rights and Civil Liberties

cc: The Honorable Jerrold L. Nadler, Chairman

JERROLD NADLER, New York
CHAIRMAN

JIM JORDAN, Ohio
RANKING MEMBER

ONE HUNDRED SEVENTEENTH CONGRESS

Congress of the United States
House of Representatives
COMMITTEE ON THE JUDICIARY

2138 RAYBURN HOUSE OFFICE BUILDING
WASHINGTON, DC 20515-6216
(202) 225-3951
judiciary.house.gov

September 19, 2022

The Honorable Christopher A. Wray
Director
Federal Bureau of Investigation
935 Pennsylvania Avenue, N.W.
Washington, DC 20535

Dear Director Wray:

We continue to hear from brave whistleblowers about disturbing conduct at the Federal Bureau of Investigation, including politicization within the Washington Field Office (WFO). On July 27, 2022, we wrote to you about protected whistleblower disclosures that FBI officials—including an Assistant Special Agent in Charge from the WFO—were pressuring agents to reclassify cases as "domestic violent extremism" (DVEs) even if the cases do not meet the criteria for such a classification.[1] Since then, new whistleblowers have come forward with concerning information about how the FBI is deliberately manipulating the way case files related to January 6 investigations are maintained in order to create a false and misleading narrative that domestic violent extremism is increasing around the country.

New whistleblower disclosures indicate that the WFO's handling of DVE investigations relating to January 6 "diverge[s]" from established practice in a way that overstates the national DVE threat. One whistleblower has described how cases are ordinarily characterized and labeled by the originating field office, with leads "cut" to other field offices for specific assistance in that geographic location. The whistleblower alleged "the FBI has not followed regular procedure" with respect to January 6 cases, which should all be officially led by the WFO and categorized as WFO cases, explaining:

> Instead, task force members in Washington D.C. identify "potential subjects" and possible locations where these individuals reside. The task force disseminates information packets with instructions to open full investigations to [local] Field Offices around the country. As such, if a subject lives in Dallas, the Dallas Field Office is expected to open the case . . . .

Although the local field offices therefore appear to be running the cases on paper, the WFO is directing the field office special agents to just "open the case" in their geographic area

[1] Letter from Jim Jordan, Ranking Member, H. Comm. on the Judiciary, to Christopher A. Wray, Dir. Fed. Bureau of Investigation (July 27, 2022).

and the WFO is performing and approving "all of the investigative work and paperwork for the casefile." The whistleblower described how "there are active criminal investigations of January 6th subjects in which I am listed as the 'Case Agent,' but have not done any investigative work" and the whistleblower's supervisor "has not approved any paperwork within" those investigative files. This scheme allows you to continue to support on paper your assertion that "[t]he FBI is a field-based law enforcement organization, and the vast majority of our investigations should continue to be worked by our field offices," while actually running the investigation from Washington.[2]

The whistleblower explained how the WFO's deviation from established practice misrepresents the DVE threat nationwide:

> The manipulative casefile practice creates false and misleading crime statistics. Instead of hundreds of investigations stemming from a single, black swan incident at the Capitol, FBI and DOJ officials point to significant increases in domestic violent extremism and terrorism around the United States.

In other words, the FBI's case categorization creates the illusion that threats from DVE are present in jurisdictions across the nation, when in reality they all stem from the same related investigation concerning the actions at the Capitol on January 6. Such an artificial case categorization scheme allows FBI leadership to misleadingly point to "significant" increases in DVE threats nationwide.[3] These allegations are consistent with disclosures we have received from other whistleblowers that high-ranking FBI officials—including a senior WFO official—are pressing front-line agents to categorize cases as DVE matters to fit a political narrative.

In addition, the whistleblower disclosed that the FBI is sacrificing its other important federal law-enforcement duties to pursue January 6 investigations. The whistleblower recalled, for example, being "told that child sexual abuse material investigations were no longer an FBI priority and should be referred to local law enforcement agencies." Such a posture is not only a dereliction of the FBI's mission to investigate violations of federal laws, but it is a grave disservice to the victims of child sexual abuse and other crimes that do not advance the FBI leadership's political agenda.

The overwhelming majority of front-line FBI special agents and employees are dedicated law-enforcement officers committed to protecting the American people and upholding the

---

[2] Letter from Hon. Christopher A. Wray, Dir., Fed. Bureau of Investigation, to Hon. Michael Horowitz, Inspector Gen., U.S. Dep't of Justice (Dec. 6, 2019).

[3] *See, e.g., "Threats to the Homeland: Evaluating the Landscape 20 Years After 9/11": Hearing before the S. Comm. on Homeland Sec. & Governmental Affairs*, 117th Cong. (2021) (testimony of FBI Director Christopher Wray). *See also Oversight of the Federal Bureau of Investigation, Hearing Before H. Comm. on the Judiciary*, 117th Cong. at 154 (2021) (statement of FBI Director Christopher Wray); Remarks, U.S. Dep't of Justice, Attorney General Merrick B. Garland Remarks: Domestic Terrorism Policy Address (Jun. 15, 2021). In June 2021, you testified that the FBI has a "very, very active domestic terrorism investigation program" and that the FBI had "doubled the amount of domestic terrorism investigations." Attorney General Merrick Garland has also repeated this talking point, stating that "[t]he number of open FBI domestic terrorism investigations this year has increased significantly."

Constitution. But we have consistently heard whistleblowers describe a "rotted" culture within the FBI's senior leadership in Washington. Contrary to your belief, the FBI is not immune to oversight or accountability. To inform our ongoing oversight of the politicization at the FBI, please provide the following documents and information:

1. All documents and communications referring or relating to the Washington Field Office's policies and procedures for opening investigations into potential subjects of the events occurring on January 6, 2021;

2. All documents and communications referring or relating to eGuardians, preliminary investigations, and full investigations regarding January 6 investigations for which the FBI's WFO is initiating, conducting, approving investigative work even if the WFO is not listed in the casefile as the responsible field office;

3. All documents and communications sent or received by WFO employees instructing agents in other FBI Field Offices to open full investigations into potential subjects of January 6 investigations;

4. A complete accounting of all DVE cases opened since January 6, 2021, in which the WFO has identified subjects or directed other field offices to execute search or arrest warrants, to include the following information:
    a. The case identifier;
    b. The responsible field office;
    c. The date opened; and
    d. The current disposition of the matter;

5. The number of arrest and search warrants sworn out by agents from the WFO, but executed in the geographic area of another FBI field office; and

6. The number of all FBI agents involved in January 6 investigations, identified by FBI field office.

Please provide this information as soon as possible, but no later than 5:00 p.m. on October 3, 2022. We remind you that whistleblower disclosures to Congress are protected by law and that we will not tolerate any effort to retaliate against whistleblowers for their disclosures.

Sincerely,

Jim Jordan
Ranking Member

cc: The Honorable Jerrold L. Nadler, Chairman

JERROLD NADLER, New York
CHAIRMAN

JIM JORDAN, Ohio
RANKING MEMBER

ONE HUNDRED SEVENTEENTH CONGRESS

Congress of the United States

House of Representatives

COMMITTEE ON THE JUDICIARY

2138 RAYBURN HOUSE OFFICE BUILDING

WASHINGTON, DC 20515-6216

(202) 225-3951
judiciary.house.gov

September 14, 2022

The Honorable Christopher A. Wray
Director
Federal Bureau of Investigation
935 Pennsylvania Avenue, N.W.
Washington, DC 20535

Dear Director Wray:

On July 27, 2022, we wrote to you about whistleblower disclosures that FBI officials were pressuring agents to reclassify cases as "domestic violent extremism" (DVEs) even if the cases do not meet the criteria for such a classification.[1] You have failed to acknowledge our letter or even begin to respond substantively. Since our letter, new publicly available information and additional protected whistleblower disclosures suggest the FBI's actions are far more pervasive than previously known.

On August 2, 2022, a media organization obtained a copy, which new whistleblower disclosures have authenticated, of the FBI's "Domestic Terrorism Symbols Guide" on "Militia Violent Extremists" (MVEs).[2] The FBI's document included symbols like "2A" and states that "MVEs justify their existence with the Second Amendment, due to the mention of a 'well regulated Militia,' as well as the right to bear arms."[3] The document also includes "commonly referenced historical imagery or quotes," like the "Betsy Ross Flag" and the "Gadsden Flag," as symbols of so-called terrorists.[4] Additionally, the FBI document includes a section labeled "symbols of militia networks some MVEs may self-identify with," and describes one group, called American Contingency, as "[m]ainstream media, nationwide, mostly online activity, low history of violence."[5] American Contingency is a company founded by former U.S. servicemember Mike Glover, who has publicly rejected the FBI's accusations that he is a

---

[1] Letter from Jim Jordan, Ranking Member, H. Comm. on the Judiciary, to Christopher A. Wray, Dir., Fed. Bureau of Investigation (July 27, 2022).
[2] Press Release, *FBI Whistleblower LEAKS Bureau's 'Domestic Terrorism Symbols Guide' on 'Militia Violent Extremists' Citing Ashli Babbitt as MVE Martyr*, PROJECT VERITAS (Aug. 2, 2022). The FBI document states "[t]he use or sharing of these symbols should not independently be considered evidence of MVE presence or affiliation or serve as an indicator of illegal activity, as many individuals use these symbols for their original, historic meaning, or other non-violent purposes." *Id.*
[3] *Id.*
[4] *Id.*
[5] *Id.*

terrorist and has described American Contingency's charitable work on behalf of communities devastated by natural disasters.[6]

The FBI's recent characterization of American Contingency as a DVE organization is striking in light of new whistleblower disclosures that show that the FBI had concluded as recently as 2020 that the group was not a threat. According to whistleblower information, in July 2020, an FBI employee in northern Virginia flagged American Contingency as a "domestic terrorist group" because Glover "appears to be rallying individuals to 'take action'" and "speaks about his distaste for how the government is handling the current situations in the US and encourages people to 'join' his cause." Notes made in the FBI's e-Guardian incident reporting system, reflected below, show how the FBI rifled through Glover's life—obtaining his military records, his veteran's disability rating, and even his monthly disability benefit—before concluding that American Contingency "desires to assist Americans in preparing themselves for catastrophic events and not to overthrow the United States Government. A background investigation and review of Glover's social media failed to support the allegation that Glover is a threat to the United States or its citizens."

Authorized Method:	Administrative note for informational purposes.
Description:	Glover is a decorated Veteran of the United States. His videos posted on Youtube.com and his military record attest to his patriotism for the United States. Glover desires to assist Americans in preparing themselves for catastrophic events and not to overthrow the United States Government. A background investigation and review of Glover's social media failed to support the allegation that Glover is a threat to the United States or its citizens. Therefore, it is requested captioned lead be closed for information only.
Status:	Completed
History:	
08/26/2020 12:09:42 PM	Created Note: Request lead be closed for information only [redacted]

This whistleblower information suggests that the FBI opened an investigation into an American citizen—and deemed him a potential "threat"—simply because he exercised his First Amendment right to speak out in protest of the government. As the whistleblower commented:

> It doesn't take a First Amendment scholar to realize what is protected speech and what isn't . . . . It seems clear that this is an instance where an FBI employee reported something because it didn't align with their own woke ideology. . . . I think this is a primary example of how woke and corrupt the FBI has become.

Even after the FBI determined in 2020 that American Contingency was not a threat, the FBI still labeled the group as a violent extremist group in an official FBI alert. This disclosure comports with other whistleblowers who have described how the FBI is pressuring its employees to

---

[6] American Contingency, https://www.americancontingency.com/ (last accessed Aug. 18, 2022). The FieldCraft Survival Channel, I am NOT a terrorist, YouTube (Aug. 4, 2022), https://www.youtube.com/watch?v=p4JBDcN7YFo. *See also* American Contingency, How We Got Here, https://www.americancontingency.com/how-we-got-here/ (last visited Aug. 18, 2022).

recharacterize cases as DVE cases to artificially pad its data and advance a misleading political narrative.

This whistleblower information further reinforces our concerns—about which we have written to you several times—about the FBI's politicization. One whistleblower described the level of politicization within the FBI's leadership as "rotted at its core." As we have detailed, multiple whistleblowers have disclosed how the Biden FBI is conducting a "purge" of FBI employees holding conservative views. You have ignored these concerns and instead suggested the FBI is above any criticism or accountability.[7] The front-line men and women of the FBI—many of whom have come forward as whistleblowers—deserve our respect and gratitude. But the FBI leadership in Washington is in desperate need of accountability and reform.

To inform our ongoing oversight of the FBI, please provide the following documents and information:

1. All documents and communications referring or relating to the FBI's Domestic Terrorism Symbols Guide on Militia Violent Extremism, for the period of January 1, 2020, to the present; and

2. A full and complete explanation as to why the FBI's Domestic Terrorism Strategic Unit did not include symbols, images, phrases, events, and individuals about left-wing violent extremists' group in the FBI's Domestic Terrorism Symbols Guide.

Please provide this information as soon as possible, but no later than 5:00 p.m. on September 28, 2022. In addition, our earlier requests made in the July 27 letter remain outstanding, and we once more reiterate these requests. We remind you that whistleblower disclosures to Congress are protected by law and that we will not tolerate any effort to retaliate against whistleblowers for their disclosures.

Sincerely,

Jim Jordan
Ranking Member

cc: The Honorable Jerrold L. Nadler, Chairman

[7] Email from the Hon. Christopher A Wray, Dir., Fed. Bureau of Investigation (Aug. 11, 2022 2:26 PM). ("There has been a lot of commentary about the FBI this week questioning our work and motives. Much of it is from critics and pundits on the outside who don't know what we know and don't see what we see.").

Congress of the United States
Washington, DC 20515

September 2, 2022

The Honorable Merrick B. Garland
Attorney General
U.S. Department of Justice
950 Pennsylvania Avenue, NW
Washington, D.C. 20530-0001

Dear Mr. Attorney General:

As you know, on August 8, 2022, the Federal Bureau of Investigation (FBI) raided former President Donald J. Trump's home in Palm Beach, Florida. This unprecedented and shocking act should have necessitated timely and meaningful engagement with Congress. However, rather than choosing transparency, the Department of Justice (DOJ) waited almost three weeks to offer a briefing. Unfortunately, DOJ's request made no mention of appearing before the Members of Congress who conduct primary Article I oversight over the DOJ and the FBI—namely, those on the House and Senate Judiciary committees.

In these extraordinary circumstances, the DOJ is proceeding in a manner that is eroding public trust and confidence. Indeed, during remarks on August 11, 2022 about the raid, you stated that "the Department of Justice will speak through its court filings and its work." Continuing, you stated that "standing department rules and our ethical obligations prevent me from providing further details as to the basis of the search at this time." Yet just hours later, on that very same day, "people familiar with the investigation" began planting stories in the press, purporting to leak selected information, and framing up their self-serving framing of the issues. This conduct—claiming publicly that the DOJ cannot provide transparency, while allowing anonymous leaks to create a one-sided narrative—eliminates the DOJ's claim to continue with this shroud of secrecy. You stated: "More information will be made available in the appropriate way and at the appropriate time." The appropriate time is now, and the appropriate way is to publicly appear before and answer these important questions to the congressional committees of jurisdiction that oversee your department.

Yet rather than appearing before the relevant committees of jurisdiction, the DOJ appears to want to limit interactions on this matter to a narrow group of Members. Concerningly, this request mimics initial engagements by the Obama Administration during the Russia collusion hoax investigation, in which senior Obama Administration officials attempted to limit interactions with Congress and shroud their politically motivated investigation into the Trump Campaign under the guise of national security. This secrecy allowed bad actors to leak cherry-picked information about alleged Russian collusion to create false public narratives and mislead the American people. After several years and through the efforts of Republicans on the House Permanent Select Committee on Intelligence and the House Judiciary Committee, the American people discovered the Obama Administration's abuse and politicization of our national security apparatus. We refuse to let you or senior officials in the DOJ or the FBI attempt to repeat history and hide facts regarding this matter from congressional oversight.

The unprecedented nature of the FBI's search of President Trump's home and the broad public interest surrounding the raid require more than just a private briefing with the congressional and intelligence committee leadership. The Biden Administration cannot ignore its obligation to submit to public hearings in the House Judiciary Committee, which is charged with broad oversight of the operations and functions of the DOJ and the FBI. Republicans on the House Judiciary Committee have called on you to testify in public; the Administration's failure to appear before the Judiciary Committee only willfully illustrates a desire by the DOJ and the FBI to avoid oversight by their committee of primary jurisdiction. As elected representatives of the American people, we will not abide by any attempt from unelected administration bureaucrats to limit access to information and impede their constitutional oversight responsibilities by appropriate congressional committees.

Further, you have ignored Republican requests for documents relating to the unprecedented raid on President Trump's home. To ensure effective oversight, you must produce all requested materials immediately without redactions or withholdings. During previous congressional investigations into actions taken by the DOJ and the FBI, those agencies attempted to shield documents from congressional review, often arguing classification or citing ambiguous national security concerns as reasons to limit congressional oversight. We will not accept any unlawful attempts to limit congressional access to documents. In summation, we request the following:

1. Your appearance, along with FBI Director Christopher Wray, in public hearings before the House Judiciary Committee concerning the raid on President Trump's home; and

2. The provision of all communications and documents requested by Republicans relating to the raid on President Trump's home.

A cornerstone of our democracy is the equal application of the law. Unfortunately, our country has seen rampant politicization of the DOJ and the FBI during the past year and a half. The American people deserve and demand better, and you can start to remedy these ills by appearing publicly and answering all questions from the congressional committees of jurisdiction, as well as the immediate production of all requested materials to Congress.

Sincerely,

Kevin McCarthy

KEVIN McCARTHY
House Republican Leader

Mike Turner
Ranking Member
House Permanent Select Committee on Intelligence

Jim Jordan
Ranking Member
House Judiciary Committee

James Comer
Ranking Member
House Oversight Committee

Congress of the United States

Washington, DC 20515

September 1, 2022

Mr. Mark Zuckerberg
Chief Executive Officer
Meta Platforms, Inc.
1 Hacker Way
Menlo Park, CA 94025

Dear Mr. Zuckerberg:

Shortly before the 2020 presidential election, Facebook suppressed an explosive *New York Post* article detailing how Hunter Biden used the position and influence of his father, now-President Biden, for personal gain, with the apparent awareness of President Biden. We wrote to Facebook at the time with important questions about Facebook's knowing suppression of First Amendment-protected activity.[1] In March 2022, after other outlets finally acknowledged the veracity of the Biden family's influence-peddling scheme, we wrote again with additional questions about Facebook's actions to suppress critical election-related information.[2] Facebook has never provided complete responses to these letters and, in the months since, has avoided any real accountability for its actions in interfering with election-related public discourse.

Recently, you described how Facebook's censorship of the allegations about the Biden family before the 2020 election followed a message from the Federal Bureau of Investigation that Facebook "should be on high alert" for "Russian propaganda."[3] You acknowledged that this official alert from the FBI is what led to Facebook reducing the circulation of the *Post*'s reporting on its platform, preventing Americans from fully understanding highly relevant allegations about President Biden's awareness of and involvement in his family's influence-peddling scheme.[4] Accordingly, we write to request additional information about Facebook's actions to interfere in free and fair election-related public discourse.

---

[1] Letter from Rep. Jim Jordan, Ranking Member, H. Comm. on the Judiciary, to Mr. Mark Zuckerberg, CEO, Facebook, Inc. (Oct. 14, 2020).
[2] Letter from from Rep. Jim Jordan, Ranking Member, H. Comm. on the Judiciary, et al., to Mr. Mark Zuckerberg, CEO, Facebook, Inc. (March 31, 2022).
[3] *See, e.g.*, Victor Morton, *Mark Zuckerberg: Facebook suppressed Hunter Biden laptop story per FBI general request*, WASH. TIMES (Aug. 25, 2022).
[4] *Id.*

We have seen in recent months how some in government have sought to use Big Tech to censor divergent viewpoints and silence opposing political speech.[5] Government-driven and Big Tech-implemented censorship suppresses freedom of speech and free thought online in ways that harm public discourse. Facebook's suppression of the *Post* article—and allegations of Biden family corruption highly relevant to the 2020 presidential election—following guidance from the FBI is highly troubling.

For these reasons, we request—in addition to responses to all outstanding requests from our October 14, 2020, and March 31, 2022, letters—that you produce the following documents and information:

1. All documents and communications between October 1, 2020, and the present, between or among any employee or contractor of Facebook and any individual affiliated with the FBI referring or relating to the *New York Post*'s reporting about the Biden family.

2. All documents and communications between October 1, 2020, and the present, between or among any employee or contractor of Facebook and any individual affiliated with the Biden for President campaign or the Democratic National Committee referring or relating to the *New York Post*'s reporting about the Biden family.

3. All documents and communications between October 1, 2020, and the present, between or among any employee or contractor of Facebook and any individual affiliated with the FBI referring or relating to purported election misinformation in the 2020 presidential election.

4. All documents and communications between October 1, 2020, and the present, referring or relating to Facebook's plans to implement, or its actions based on, the FBI's message to be "on high alert" for election misinformation.

Please produce all documents and information requested above as soon as possible but no later than 5:00 p.m. on September 15, 2022. Furthermore, this letter serves as a formal request to preserve all existing and future records and materials relating to the topics addressed in this letter. You should construe this preservation notice as an instruction to take all reasonable steps to prevent the destruction or alteration, whether intentionally or negligently, of all documents, communications, and other information, including electronic information and metadata, that are or may be responsive to this congressional inquiry. This instruction includes all electronic messages sent using your official and personal accounts or devices, including records created using text messages, phone-based message applications, or encryption software.

---

[5] *See, e.g.*, Letter from Representatives Jim Jordan, Mike Johnson, & Dan Bishop, to Mr. Mark Zuckerberg, CEO, Facebook, Inc. (July 22, 2021); Letter from Rep. Jim Jordan, Ranking Member, H. Comm. on the Judiciary, & James Comer, Ranking Member, H. Comm. on Oversight and Reform, to Mr. Mark Zuckerberg, CEO, Facebook, Inc. (June 9, 2021); Vivek Ramaswamy & Jed Rubenfeld, *Twitter Becomes a Tool of Government Censorship*, WALL ST. J. (Aug. 17, 2022).

Thank you for your prompt attention to this matter.

Sincerely,

Jim Jordan
Ranking Member
Committee on the Judiciary

James Comer
Ranking Member
Committee on Oversight and Reform

Steve Chabot
Member of Congress

Louie Gohmert
Member of Congress

Darrell Issa
Member of Congress

Ken Buck
Member of Congress

Matt Gaetz
Member of Congress

Mike Johnson
Member of Congress

Andy Biggs
Member of Congress

Tom McClintock
Member of Congress

W. Gregory Steube
Member of Congress

Tom Tiffany
Member of Congress

Thomas Massie
Member of Congress

Chip Roy
Member of Congress

Dan Bishop
Member of Congress

Michelle Fischbach
Member of Congress

Scott Fitzgerald
Member of Congress

Cliff Bentz
Member of Congress

Jody Hice
Member of Congress

Glenn S. Grothman
Member of Congress

Michael Cloud
Member of Congress

Nancy Mace
Member of Congress

Yvette Herrell
Member of Congress

Virginia Foxx
Member of Congress

Bob Gibbs
Member of Congress

Clay Higgins
Member of Congress

Ralph Norman
Member of Congress

Pete Sessions
Member of Congress

Fred Keller
Member of Congress

Andrew S. Clyde
Member of Congress

C. Scott Franklin
Member of Congress

Jake LaTurner
Member of Congress

Pat Fallon
Member of Congress

Byron Donalds
Member of Congress

Mike Flood
Member of Congress

cc: The Honorable Jerrold L. Nadler, Chairman, Committee on the Judiciary
The Honorable Carolyn B. Maloney, Chairwoman, Committee on Oversight and Reform

JERROLD NADLER, New York
CHAIRMAN

JIM JORDAN, Ohio
RANKING MINORITY MEMBER

U.S. House of Representatives
Committee on the Judiciary

Washington, DC 20515–6216
One Hundred Sixteenth Congress

August 29, 2022

The Honorable Michael E. Horowitz
Inspector General
U.S. Department of Justice
950 Pennsylvania Avenue N.W., Suite 4706
Washington, DC 20530

Dear Inspector General Horowitz:

On the morning of August 10, 2022, Federal Bureau of Investigation agents seized the cell phone of Representative Scott Perry while he was traveling with his family.[1] Recent reports indicate that the FBI's action is related to a joint investigation conducted by the Office of Inspector General (OIG) and the Justice Department.[2] The OIG's role relating to the seizure of Representative Perry's phone is inconsistent with your responsibility to conduct independent oversight of the Department and extremely troubling in light of your statutory reporting requirements to Congress.[3] We have been vocal and consistent supporters of the OIG over many years, but your decision to assist the FBI in this politically charged matter demands a full and complete explanation about your unusual actions.

According to reports, the Justice Department OIG used its laboratory in Northern Virginia to assist the FBI in conducting a forensic review of Representative Perry's phone.[4] Reports indicate that Representative Perry's phone "was imaged after the search," creating a forensic copy of the device's contents—including communications protected by common-law privileges as well as the Constitution's Speech or Debate Clause.[5] The OIG's assistance to the FBI in imaging Representative Perry's phone—in addition to posing questions about why the nation's top law-enforcement agency cannot perform this task itself—raises serious concerns about why you would be willing to sacrifice the OIG's independence to assist the FBI in advancing such a politically charged matter.

---

[1] Michael Balsamo, *Rep. Scott Perry says FBI agents seized his cellphone*, AP NEWS (Aug. 10, 2022). According to Congressman Perry, the FBI agents "made no attempt to contact my lawyer, who would have made arrangements for them to have my phone if that was their wish. I'm outraged – though not surprised - that the FBI under the direction of Merrick Garland's DOJ, would seize the phone of a sitting Member of Congress. My phone contains info about my legislative and political activities, and personal/private discussions with my wife, family, constituents, and friends. None of this is the government's business." *Id.*

[2] Sarah Murray, et al., *Republican congressman says FBI seized his cell phone*, CNN (Aug. 10, 2022).

[3] *See* generally P.L. 95-452 (1978).

[4] Sarah Murray, et al., *Republican congressman says FBI seized his cell phone*, CNN (Aug. 10, 2022).

[5] *Id*; U.S. Const. art. I, § 6, cl. 1.

Your decision to assist the FBI relating to the seizure of a Member of Congress's phone creates a serious conflict of interest for the OIG in reviewing the Department's actions. In June 2021, the OIG initiated a review of the Department's use of subpoenas and other legal authorities to obtain communication records of Members of Congress, other individuals, and journalists.[6] On the one hand, the OIG is reviewing whether the Department's actions in those cases were based upon any improper considerations; however, because of your decision, the OIG appears to be directly involved with seizing and imaging the phone of a Member of Congress. The OIG is now conflicted from reviewing the basis and propriety of the FBI's controversial decision to seize Representative Perry's phone.

Congress and the American people cannot afford to lose faith in the OIG, especially as the Biden Administration continues to weaponize federal law-enforcement resources against its political opponents and so many FBI whistleblowers continue to come forward with shocking allegations. You, as the former chair of the Council of the Inspectors General on Integrity and Efficiency, should not be so reckless as to risk the independence of your office to carry out the investigative work of an agency you oversee. Pursuant to the Committee's constitutional oversight authority and the Inspector General Act, we are examining your decision to assist the FBI relating to the seizure of Representative Perry's phone and the OIG's actions in this matter. Accordingly, please provide the following documents and information:

1. All documents and communications between or among employees of the Department of Justice Office of Inspector General, the Department of Justice, and the Federal Bureau of Investigation referring or relating to the seizure of a cell phone belonging to Representative Perry or to any matter concerning a Member of Congress for the period of January 2021 to the present;

2. All documents and communications between or among employees of the Department of Justice Office of Inspector General referring or relating to the seizure of a cell phone belonging to Representative Perry for the period of January 2021 to the present;

3. A complete and detailed timeline of all OIG communications with Justice Department entities/employees and all OIG actions relating to the seizure and/or imaging of Representative Perry's phone;

4. A complete and detailed explanation of the decision of the Department of Justice Office of Inspector General to assist the FBI with the seizure and/or imaging of Representative Perry's phone, including whether the FBI or Office of Inspector General considered other, less intrusive, means of pursuing its inquiry;

5. A complete and detailed explanation of the Department of Justice Office of Inspector General's forensic examination of the phone belonging to Representative Perry, including

---

[6] INSPECTOR GEN., DEP'T OF JUSTICE, *DOJ OIG Initiates a Review of the Department of Justice's Use of Subpoenas and Other Legal Authorities to Obtain Communication Records of Members of Congress and Affiliated Persons, and the News Media* (June. 11, 2021).

but not limited to all actions taken, whether any OIG employee has reviewed any of the phone's contents, and whether the OIG retains any data from the phone; and

6. A complete and detailed explanation of whether any Department of Justice Office of Inspector General employees suggested to the FBI or the Justice Department that the seizure of a Member of Congress's cell phone raises Constitutional concerns, and that the OIG should not participate in such unnecessary and aggressive actions.

Please produce this material as soon as possible but no later than 5:00 p.m. on September 12, 2022. If you have any questions about this request, please contact Committee staff at (202) 225-6906. We expect your complete and unfettered cooperation with our inquiry.

Sincerely,

Jim Jordan
Ranking Member

JERROLD NADLER, New York
CHAIRMAN

JIM JORDAN, Ohio
RANKING MEMBER

ONE HUNDRED SEVENTEENTH CONGRESS

Congress of the United States

House of Representatives

COMMITTEE ON THE JUDICIARY

2138 RAYBURN HOUSE OFFICE BUILDING

WASHINGTON, DC 20515-6216

(202) 225-3951
judiciary.house.gov

August 15, 2022

The Honorable Christopher A. Wray
Director
Federal Bureau of Investigation
Washington, DC 20535

Dear Director Wray:

The FBI's unprecedented raid of President Trump's residence is a shocking escalation of the Biden Administration's weaponization of law-enforcement resources against its political opponents. The American people deserve transparency and accountability from our most senior law-enforcement officials in the executive branch. We will settle for nothing but your complete cooperation with our inquiry.

Under the Biden Administration, the Justice Department has shattered public confidence in the equal application of justice. The Department has filed politically motivated lawsuits against Republican-led states on policies disfavored by the Biden Administration, artificially inflated domestic violent extremism statistics to advance the Biden Administration's political narrative, used counterterrorism resources to target parents at school board meetings opposed to policies supported by the Biden Administration, and selectively prosecuted and investigated political opponents of the Biden Administration. These actions not only undermine the stated mission of the Department, they violate the most fundamental tenets of our country.

The American people deserve answers for the Biden Administration's continued misuse of law-enforcement resources against its political opponents. Accordingly, please produce the following material:

1. All documents and communications referring or relating to the execution of a search warrant on President Trump's residence;

2. All documents and communications referring or relating to the decision to seek a search warrant for President Trump's residence;

3. All documents and communications referring or relating to the use of confidential human source(s) in connection with the search of President Trump's residence;

4. All documents and communications between or among the Department of Justice, Federal Bureau of Investigation, or the Executive Office of the President about a search of President Trump's residence;

5. All documents and communications between or among the Department of Justice, Federal Bureau of Investigation, or the United States Secret Service about a search of President Trump's residence; and

6. All documents and communications between or among the Department of Justice, the Federal Bureau of Investigation, or the National Archives and Records Administration about a potential search of President Trump's residence.

Please provide this material as soon as possible, but no later than 5:00 p.m. on August 29, 2022. In addition, please preserve all responsive documents in your possession, custody, or control. You should construe this communication as an instruction to preserve all documents, communications, and other information, including electronic information and metadata, that are or may be potentially responsive to this inquiry. This instruction includes all electronic messages sent using official and personal accounts or devices, including records created using text messages, phone-based message applications, or encryption software. For purposes of this request, "preserve" includes taking reasonable steps to prevent the partial or full destruction, alteration, testing, deletion, shredding, incineration, wiping, relocation, migration, theft, mutation, or negligent or reckless handling that could render the information incomplete or inaccessible. These steps include preserving all compilations of documents that have already been gathered in response to other government or litigation requests, even if copies of individual documents or materials may still exist elsewhere in the organization.

The Committee on the Judiciary has jurisdiction to oversee the activities of the Department of Justice and the Federal Bureau of Investigation pursuant to Rule X of the Rules of the House of Representatives. Please contact Committee staff at (202) 225-6906 if you have any questions about this matter.

Sincerely,

Jim Jordan
Ranking Member

Steve Chabot
Member of Congress

Louie Gohmert
Member of Congress

Darrell Issa
Ranking Member
Subcommittee on Courts, Intellectual Property, and the Internet

Matt Gaetz
Member of Congress

Mike Johnson
Ranking Member
Subcommittee on the Constitution, Civil Rights and Civil Liberties

Andy Biggs
Ranking Member
Subcommittee on Crime, Terrorism, and Homeland Security

Tom McClintock
Ranking Member
Subcommittee on Immigration and Citizenship

W. Gregory Steube
Member of Congress

Tom Tiffany
Member of Congress

Thomas Massie
Member of Congress

Chip Roy
Member of Congress

Dan Bishop
Member of Congress

Michelle Fischbach
Member of Congress

Victoria Spartz
Member of Congress

Scott Fitzgerald
Member of Congress

Cliff Bentz
Member of Congress

Burgess Owens
Member of Congress

cc: The Honorable Jerrold L. Nadler, Chairman

JERROLD NADLER, New York
CHAIRMAN

JIM JORDAN, Ohio
RANKING MEMBER

ONE HUNDRED SEVENTEENTH CONGRESS

Congress of the United States
House of Representatives
COMMITTEE ON THE JUDICIARY

2138 RAYBURN HOUSE OFFICE BUILDING

WASHINGTON, DC 20515-6216

(202) 225-3951
judiciary.house.gov

August 15, 2022

Mr. Ronald A. Klain
Assistant to the President and White House Chief of Staff
The White House
Washington, DC 20500

Dear Mr. Klain:

The FBI's unprecedented raid of President Trump's residence is a shocking escalation of the Biden Administration's weaponization of law-enforcement resources against its political opponents. The American people deserve transparency and accountability from our most senior law-enforcement officials in the executive branch. We will settle for nothing but your complete cooperation with our inquiry.

During the Biden Administration, the Justice Department has shattered public confidence in the equal application of justice. The Department has filed politically motivated lawsuits against Republican-led states on policies disfavored by the Biden Administration, artificially inflated domestic violent extremism statistics to advance the Biden Administration's political narrative, used counterterrorism resources to target parents at school board meetings opposed to policies supported by the Biden Administration, and selectively prosecuted and investigated political opponents of the Biden Administration. These actions not only undermine the stated mission of the Department, they violate the most fundamental tenets of our country.

The American people deserve answers for the Biden Administration's continued misuse of law-enforcement resources against its political opponents. Accordingly, please produce the following material:

1. All documents and communications referring or relating to the execution of a search warrant on President Trump's residence;

2. All documents and communications referring or relating to the decision to seek a search warrant for President Trump's residence;

3. All documents and communications referring or relating to the use of confidential human source(s) in connection with the search of President Trump's residence;

4. All documents and communications between or among the Department of Justice, Federal Bureau of Investigation, or the Executive Office of the President about a search of President Trump's residence; and

5. All documents and communications between or among the Executive Office of the President and the National Archives and Records Administration about the Trump Administration's presidential records.

Please provide this material as soon as possible, but no later than 5:00 p.m. on August 29, 2022. In addition, please preserve all responsive documents in your possession, custody, or control. You should construe this communication as an instruction to preserve all documents, communications, and other information, including electronic information and metadata, that are or may be potentially responsive to this inquiry. This instruction includes all electronic messages sent using official and personal accounts or devices, including records created using text messages, phone-based message applications, or encryption software. For purposes of this request, "preserve" includes taking reasonable steps to prevent the partial or full destruction, alteration, testing, deletion, shredding, incineration, wiping, relocation, migration, theft, mutation, or negligent or reckless handling that could render the information incomplete or inaccessible. These steps include preserving all compilations of documents that have already been gathered in response to other government or litigation requests, even if copies of individual documents or materials may still exist elsewhere in the organization.

The Committee on the Judiciary has jurisdiction to oversee the activities of the Department of Justice and the Federal Bureau of Investigation pursuant to Rule X of the Rules of the House of Representatives. Please contact Committee staff at (202) 225-6906 if you have any questions about this matter.

Sincerely,

Jim Jordan
Ranking Member

Steve Chabot
Member of Congress

Louie Gohmert
Member of Congress

Darrell Issa
Ranking Member
Subcommittee on Courts, Intellectual Property, and the Internet

Matt Gaetz
Member of Congress

Mike Johnson
Ranking Member
Subcommittee on the Constitution,
Civil Rights and Civil Liberties

Andy Biggs
Ranking Member
Subcommittee on Crime, Terrorism,
and Homeland Security

Tom McClintock
Ranking Member
Subcommittee on Immigration
and Citizenship

W. Gregory Steube
Member of Congress

Tom Tiffany
Member of Congress

Thomas Massie
Member of Congress

Chip Roy
Member of Congress

Dan Bishop
Member of Congress

Michelle Fischbach
Member of Congress

Victoria Spartz
Member of Congress

Scott Fitzgerald
Member of Congress

Cliff Bentz
Member of Congress

Burgess Owens
Member of Congress

cc: The Honorable Jerrold L. Nadler, Chairman

JERROLD NADLER, New York
CHAIRMAN

JIM JORDAN, Ohio
RANKING MEMBER

ONE HUNDRED SEVENTEENTH CONGRESS

Congress of the United States

House of Representatives

COMMITTEE ON THE JUDICIARY
2138 RAYBURN HOUSE OFFICE BUILDING
WASHINGTON, DC 20515-6216
(202) 225-3951
judiciary.house.gov

August 15, 2022

The Honorable Merrick B. Garland
Attorney General
U.S. Department of Justice
Washington, DC 20530

Dear Attorney General Garland:

The FBI's unprecedented raid of President Trump's residence is a shocking escalation of the Biden Administration's weaponization of law-enforcement resources against its political opponents. The American people deserve transparency and accountability from our most senior law-enforcement officials in the executive branch. We will settle for nothing but your complete cooperation with our inquiry.

Under your tenure, the Justice Department continues to shatter public confidence in the equal application of justice. The Department has filed politically motivated lawsuits against Republican-led states on policies disfavored by the Biden Administration, artificially inflated domestic violent extremism statistics to advance the Biden Administration's political narrative, used counterterrorism resources to target parents at school board meetings opposed to policies supported by the Biden Administration, and selectively prosecuted and investigated political opponents of the Biden Administration. These actions not only undermine the stated mission of the Department, they violate the most fundamental tenets of our country.

The American people deserve answers for the Biden Administration's continued misuse of law-enforcement resources against its political opponents. Accordingly, please produce the following material:

1. All documents and communications referring or relating to the execution of a search warrant on President Trump's residence;

2. All documents and communications referring or relating to the decision to seek a search warrant for President Trump's residence;

3. All documents and communications referring or relating to the use of confidential human source(s) in connection with the search of President Trump's residence;

4. All documents and communications between or among the Department of Justice, Federal Bureau of Investigation, or the Executive Office of the President about a search of President Trump's residence;

5. All documents and communications between or among the Department of Justice, Federal Bureau of Investigation, or the United States Secret Service about a search of President Trump's residence; and

6. All documents and communications between or among the Department of Justice, the Federal Bureau of Investigation, or the National Archives and Records Administration about a potential search of President Trump's residence.

Please provide this material as soon as possible, but no later than 5:00 p.m. on August 29, 2022. In addition, please preserve all responsive documents in your possession, custody, or control. You should construe this communication as an instruction to preserve all documents, communications, and other information, including electronic information and metadata, that are or may be potentially responsive to this inquiry. This instruction includes all electronic messages sent using official and personal accounts or devices, including records created using text messages, phone-based message applications, or encryption software. For purposes of this request, "preserve" includes taking reasonable steps to prevent the partial or full destruction, alteration, testing, deletion, shredding, incineration, wiping, relocation, migration, theft, mutation, or negligent or reckless handling that could render the information incomplete or inaccessible. These steps include preserving all compilations of documents that have already been gathered in response to other government or litigation requests, even if copies of individual documents or materials may still exist elsewhere in the organization.

The Committee on the Judiciary has jurisdiction to oversee the activities of the Department of Justice and the Federal Bureau of Investigation pursuant to Rule X of the Rules of the House of Representatives. Please contact Committee staff at (202) 225-6906 if you have any questions about this matter.

Sincerely,

Jim Jordan
Ranking Member

Steve Chabot
Member of Congress

Louie Gohmert
Member of Congress

Darrell Issa
Ranking Member
Subcommittee on Courts, Intellectual Property, and the Internet

Matt Gaetz
Member of Congress

Mike Johnson
Ranking Member
Subcommittee on the Constitution,
Civil Rights and Civil Liberties

Andy Biggs
Ranking Member
Subcommittee on Crime, Terrorism,
and Homeland Security

Tom McClintock
Ranking Member
Subcommittee on Immigration
and Citizenship

W. Gregory Steube
Member of Congress

Tom Tiffany
Member of Congress

Thomas Massie
Member of Congress

Chip Roy
Member of Congress

Dan Bishop
Member of Congress

Michelle Fischbach
Member of Congress

Victoria Spartz
Member of Congress

Scott Fitzgerald
Member of Congress

Cliff Bentz
Member of Congress

Burgess Owens
Member of Congress

cc: The Honorable Jerrold L. Nadler, Chairman

JERROLD NADLER, New York
CHAIRMAN

JIM JORDAN, Ohio
RANKING MEMBER

ONE HUNDRED SEVENTEENTH CONGRESS

Congress of the United States

House of Representatives

COMMITTEE ON THE JUDICIARY

2138 RAYBURN HOUSE OFFICE BUILDING

WASHINGTON, DC 20515-6216

(202) 225-3951
judiciary.house.gov

August 10, 2022

Ms. Jill Sanborn
Senior Director Geopolitical Strategy & Risk Analysis
Roku Inc.
1701 Junction Court, Suite 100
San Jose, CA 95112

Dear Ms. Sanborn:

On July 27, 2022, we wrote to FBI Director Christopher Wray about whistleblower disclosures that FBI officials were pressuring agents to reclassify cases as "domestic violent extremism" (DVEs) even if the cases do not meet the criteria for such a classification.[1] Between January 2020 and April 2021, according to public information, you served as the Assistant Director of the FBI Counterterrorism Division, and then as Executive Assistant Director of the National Security Branch until you left federal service.[2] Accordingly, we believe that you may possess information relating to this matter and we request your assistance with our inquiry.

Whistleblower disclosures made by multiple FBI employees from different field offices suggest that FBI agents are bolstering the number of cases of DVEs to satisfy their supervisors. For example, one whistleblower explained that because agents are not finding enough DVE cases, they are encouraged and incentivized to reclassify cases as DVE cases even though there is minimal, circumstantial evidence to support the reclassification. Another whistleblower stated that a field office Counterterrorism Assistant Special Agent in Charge and the FBI's then-Assistant Director of the Counterterrorism Division pressured agents to move cases into the DVE category to hit self-created performance metrics. This whistleblower identified you as one official who exerted pressure on agents to reclassify cases as DVE matters.

The Committee on the Judiciary has legislative and oversight jurisdiction over the Department of Justice and the FBI pursuant to Rule X of the Rules of the House of Representatives. We are investigating several allegations concerning the politicization of the FBI, including allegations that the FBI is padding its DVE data. Your testimony is necessary to

---

[1] Letter from Jim Jordan, Ranking Member, H. Comm. on the Judiciary, to Christopher A. Wray, Dir. Fed. Bureau of Investigation (July 27, 2022).

[2] @Jill Sanborn, LINKEDIN, https://www.linkedin.com/in/jill-sanborn-74a402190; Press Release, Fed. Bureau of Investigation, *Jill Sanborn Named Assistant Director of the Counterterrorism Division* (Jan. 8, 2020); Press Release, Fed. Bureau of Investigation, *Jill Sanborn Named Executive Assistant Director of the National Security Branch*, (May 7, 2021).

advance our oversight. We therefore ask that you please contact Committee staff to schedule a transcribed interview as soon as possible, but no later than 5:00 p.m. on August 24, 2022. You may contact Committee staff at (202) 225-6906.

Thank you for your attention to this matter.

Sincerely,

Jim Jordan
Ranking Member

Mike Johnson
Ranking Member
Subcommittee on the Constitution, Civil Rights and Civil Liberties

JERROLD NADLER, New York
CHAIRMAN

JIM JORDAN, Ohio
RANKING MEMBER

ONE HUNDRED SEVENTEENTH CONGRESS

Congress of the United States
House of Representatives
COMMITTEE ON THE JUDICIARY

2138 RAYBURN HOUSE OFFICE BUILDING
WASHINGTON, DC 20515–6216
(202) 225–3951
judiciary.house.gov

July 27, 2022

The Honorable Christopher A. Wray
Director
Federal Bureau of Investigation
935 Pennsylvania Avenue, N.W.
Washington, DC 20535

Dear Director Wray:

We continue to hear from brave whistleblowers about disturbing conduct at the Federal Bureau of Investigation. From recent protected disclosures, we have learned that FBI officials are pressuring agents to reclassify cases as "domestic violent extremism" even if the cases do not meet the criteria for such a classification. Given the narrative pushed by the Biden Administration that domestic violent extremism is the "greatest threat" facing our country,[1] the revelation that the FBI may be artificially padding domestic terrorism data is scandalous.

The FBI defines a domestic violent extremist (DVE) as "an individual based and operating primarily within the United States or its territories without direction or inspiration from a foreign terrorist group or other foreign power who seeks to further political or social goals wholly or in part through unlawful acts of force or violence."[2] According to you and other Biden Administration officials, investigations into DVEs have increased "significantly."[3] In June 2021, you testified that the FBI has a "very, very active domestic terrorism investigation program" and that you had "doubled the amount of domestic terrorism investigations."[4] Attorney General Merrick Garland has repeated this talking point, stating that "[t]he number of open FBI domestic terrorism investigations this year has increased significantly."[5]

---

[1] *"The Way Forward on Homeland Security": Hearing of the H. Comm. on Homeland Sec.*, 117th Cong. (2021) (statement of Homeland Security Secretary Alejandro Mayorkas).

[2] FED. BUREAU OF INVESTIGATION AND DEP'T OF HOMELAND SECURITY, STRATEGIC INTELLIGENCE ASSESSMENT ON DATA AND DOMESTIC TERRORISM at 2, note 3 (May 2021).

[3] *"Threats to the Homeland: Evaluating the Landscape 20 Years After 9/11": Hearing before the S. Comm. on Homeland Sec. & Governmental Affairs*, 117th Cong. (2021) (testimony of FBI Director Christopher Wray); Remarks, U.S. Dep't of Justice, Attorney General Merrick B. Garland Remarks: Domestic Terrorism Policy Address (Jun. 15, 2021).

[4] *Oversight of the Federal Bureau of Investigation, Hearing Before H. Comm. on the Judiciary,* 117th Cong. at 154 (2021) (statement of Director Christopher Wray).

[5] Remarks, U.S. Dep't of Justice, Attorney General Merrick B. Garland Remarks: Domestic Terrorism Policy Address (Jun. 15, 2021).

New whistleblower disclosures made by multiple FBI employees from different field offices indicate that the Biden Administration's narrative may be misleading. We have received accusations that FBI agents are bolstering the number of cases of DVEs to satisfy their superiors. For example, one whistleblower explained that because agents are not finding enough DVE cases, they are encouraged and incentivized to reclassify cases as DVE cases even though there is minimal, circumstantial evidence to support the reclassification. Another whistleblower—who led at least one high profile domestic terrorism investigation—stated that a field office Counterterrorism Assistant Special Agent in Charge and the FBI's Director of the Counterterrorism Division have pressured agents to move cases into the DVE category to hit self-created performance metrics. According to whistleblowers, the FBI uses these metrics to dispense awards and promotions. Every whistleblower has called it an environment of "pressure" within the FBI.

These whistleblower allegations that the FBI is padding its domestic violent extremist data cheapens actual examples of violent extremism. This information also reinforces our concerns—about which we have written to you several times—regarding the FBI's politicization under your leadership. As we have detailed, multiple whistleblowers have disclosed how the Biden FBI is conducting a "purge" of FBI employees holding conservative views. You have ignored these concerns. It appears instead that the FBI is more focused on classifying investigations to meet a woke left-wing agenda.

To inform our ongoing oversight of the politicization at the FBI, please provide the following documents and information:

1. All documents and communications referring or relating to eGuardians, preliminary investigations, and full investigations classified as domestic violent extremism, including by type of case, for the period of January 1, 2020, to the present;

2. All documents and communications between or among employees of the Federal Bureau of Investigation, the Department of Justice, and the Executive Office of the President referring or relating to classifying or reclassifying domestic violent extremism cases, for the period of January 1, 2020, to the present;

3. The total number of preliminary investigations and full investigations of domestic violent extremism, including by type of case, for the period of January 1, 2020, to the present; and

4. The total number of Confidential Human Sources that contributed to any reports of domestic violent extremism cases, for the period of January 1, 2020, to the present.

Please provide this information as soon as possible, but no later than 5:00 p.m. on August 10, 2022. In addition, we ask for a briefing about this topic, including the FBI's Threat Review Prioritization process to review and prioritize threats to inform its strategies.

If a full response requires the disclosure of classified information, please provide such information under separate cover. We remind you that whistleblower disclosures to Congress are protected by law and that we will not tolerate any effort to retaliate against whistleblowers for their disclosures.

Thank you for your prompt attention to this matter.

Sincerely,

Jim Jordan
Ranking Member

cc: The Honorable Jerrold L. Nadler
Chairman

The Honorable Michael E. Horowitz
Inspector General, U.S. Department of Justice

JERROLD NADLER, New York
CHAIRMAN

JIM JORDAN, Ohio
RANKING MEMBER

ONE HUNDRED SEVENTEENTH CONGRESS
Congress of the United States
House of Representatives
COMMITTEE ON THE JUDICIARY
2138 RAYBURN HOUSE OFFICE BUILDING
WASHINGTON, DC 20515–6216
(202) 225–3951
judiciary.house.gov

June 14, 2022

Mr. Ronald A. Klain
Assistant to the President and Chief of Staff
The White House
Washington, DC 20500

Dear Mr. Klain:

We continue to investigate the Biden Administration's misuse of federal counterterrorism resources to target concerned parents. On May 20, 2022, the National School Boards Association (NSBA) released a third-party report into the development of its September 29, 2021, letter to President Biden that urged federal law-enforcement intervention at school board meetings.[1] The review concluded that the White House not only colluded with the NSBA to craft the substance of the letter, but that following the letter President Biden called the then-NSBA President to say he was "appreciative" of the letter and to invite her to the Oval Office.[2] Based on this new information, we write to request documents within the possession of the Executive Office of the President.

The NSBA letter to President Biden alleged that "malice, violence, and threats" against school officials "could be the equivalent of a form of domestic terrorism or hate crimes."[3] The letter urged the President to use federal counterterrorism tools, including the Patriot Act, to target parents speaking out at school board meetings on behalf of their children.[4] Five days after the NSBA letter, on October 4, 2021, Attorney General Merrick Garland directed the Federal Bureau of Investigation (FBI) and U.S. Attorneys' Offices to take action.[5] The Justice Department issued a press release announcing "open dedicated lines of communication for threat reporting, assessment and response by law enforcement"—in other words, create a snitch line for complaints about concerned parents.[6] The release announced that the FBI would be part of a

---

[1] *Final Report on the Events Surrounding the National School Boards Association's September 29, 2021, Letter to the President*, NATIONAL SCHOOL BOARDS ASSOCIATION (May 20, 2022) [hereinafter NSBA Final Report].
[2] *Id.* at 5-6, 23.
[3] Letter from Dr. Viola M. Garcia, President, Nat'l School Board Assoc. & Mr. Chip Slaven, Chief Exec. Officer, Nat'l School Board Assoc., to President Joseph R. Biden, White House (Sept. 29, 2021).
[4] *Id.*
[5] Memorandum from Atty Gen. Merrick Garland, U.S. Dep't of Justice, Partnership Among Federal, State, Local, Tribal, And Territorial Law Enforcement to Address Threats Against School Administrators, Board Members, Teachers, and Staff (Oct. 4, 2021).
[6] Press Release, U.S. Dep't of Justice, Justice Department Addresses Violent Threats Against School Officials and Teachers (Oct. 4, 2021).

Department-wide task force "to determine how federal enforcement can be used to prosecute these crimes."[7] We know from brave whistleblowers that the FBI had operationalized the Attorney General's directive by creating a unique threat tag—EDUOFFICIALS—which agents used to label dozens of parents as potential threats.[8]

The NSBA-commissioned review uncovered troubling collusion between the White House and the NSBA in the development of the September 29 letter. The review concluded that:

> The Letter was the result of twenty days of research and drafting by the NSBA under the direction of Mr. [Chip] Slaven [then-Interim CEO and Executive Director of the NSBA]. While directing NSBA staff in drafting the letter, Mr. Slaven was simultaneously discussing his efforts with Ms. [Mary] Wall, a White House official, and providing the White House, through Ms. Wall, with advance information regarding the contents of the Letter. Evidence indicates that Ms. Wall used advance information from Mr. Slaven regarding the planned Letter and its specific content to "include in discussions" with "other [White House] offices" and Department of Justice before the Letter was finalized and sent to President Biden.[9]

Evidence shows that Mr. Slaven worked especially close with Ms. Wall, Senior Policy Advisor to the President. The report details how Ms. Wall "conferred" with Mr. Slaven on a call before the letter was sent, during which she requested NSBA's list of "egregious examples" of parents at local school board meetings.[10] The report also notes that "pursuant to Ms. Wall's requests"—just eight days before the letter was finalized and sent to the President—Mr. Slaven "provided the White House with an advance summary of the Letter's contents and its list of requests for federal intervention"—including reference to the Patriot Act—"so White House officials could 'include' the planned contents of the Letter in discussions with Department of Justice officials on September 22, 2021."[11] It also appears other White House officials and offices may have been involved.[12]

---

[7] *Id.*
[8] Email from Carlton Peeples, Deputy Assistant Director, Criminal Investigative Div., Fed. Bureau of Investigation, to FBI_SACS (Oct. 20, 2021); Letter from Rep. Jim Jordan & Rep. Mike Johnson to Merrick B. Garland, Att'y Gen. (May 11, 2022).
[9] NSBA Final Report at 5-6.
[10] *Id.* at 3.
[11] *Id.*; *see also* NSBA Final Report, Appendix Exhibits at 371, E-mail from Ms. Mary Wall, Senior Policy Advisor to the Pres., Exec. Office of the Pres., to Mr. Chip Slaven, Interim CEO & Exec. Dir., Nat'l School Boards Assoc. (Sept. 21, 2021 10:10 PM) ("Is there any way we can take a look at the letter in advance of release? In specific, I'm meeting w colleagues from other WH offices and DOJ tomorrow morning to see if there might be any options we can pursue here, so if you have concrete recommendations in your letter (e.g. the threat assessment you mentioned), would be good to know so I can include in discussions.).
[12] *Id.* at 4-5.

The collaboration between the White House, Justice Department, and NSBA to develop the justification for the NSBA's September 29 letter brought down the heavy hand of the federal law enforcement apparatus upon America's parents. We know from the NSBA-commissioned report that the White House did not object to or otherwise discourage the NSBA from asking the President to use the Patriot Act and domestic terrorism statutes against America's parents—a request of which the President said he was "appreciative." We also know from whistleblowers that federal counterterrorism resources were, in fact, used against parents as the direct result of the NSBA letter to President Biden and Attorney General Garland's directive. This information only strengthens our concerns that the Biden Administration is chilling protected First Amendment activity as parents rightfully fear that their passionate advocacy for their children could result in a visit from federal law enforcement.

Therefore, to assist in our oversight of the Biden Administration's use of federal law enforcement—including counterterrorism resources—with respect to school board-related threats, we ask that you produce the following material for the period January 20, 2021, to the present:

1. All documents and communications between or among employees or officials of the Executive Office of the President referring or relating to the NSBA;

2. All documents and communications between or among employees or officials of the Executive Office of the President and employees or officials of the Department of Justice, Department of Homeland Security, Department of Education, and any executive branch department or agency referring or relating to the NSBA or school board-related threats;

3. All documents and communications between or among employees or officials of the Executive Office of the President and employees or officials of the Department of Justice referring or relating to the Attorney General's memorandum dated October 4, 2021; and

4. All documents and communications between or among employees or officials of the Executive Office of the President and employees of the NSBA referring or relating to the NSBA's September 29, 2021, letter to President Biden.

Please provide this information as soon as possible but no later than 5:00 p.m. on June 28, 2022.

Thank you for your attention to this matter.

Sincerely,

Jim Jordan
Ranking Member

Steve Chabot
Member of Congress

Louie Gohmert
Member of Congress

Darrell Issa
Ranking Member
Subcommittee on Courts, Intellectual Property, and the Internet

Ken Buck
Ranking Member
Subcommittee on Antitrust, Commercial and Administrative Law

Matt Gaetz
Member of Congress

Mike Johnson
Ranking Member
Subcommittee on the Constitution, Civil Rights and Civil Liberties

Andy Biggs
Ranking Member
Subcommittee on Crime, Terrorism and Homeland Security

Tom McClintock
Ranking Member
Subcommittee on Immigration and Citizenship

W. Gregory Steube
Member of Congress

Tom Tiffany
Member of Congress

Thomas Massie
Member of Congress

Chip Roy
Member of Congress

Dan Bishop
Member of Congress

Michelle Fischbach
Member of Congress

Victoria Spartz
Member of Congress

Scott Fitzgerald
Member of Congress

Cliff Bentz
Member of Congress

Burgess Owens
Member of Congress

cc: The Honorable Jerrold L. Nadler, Chairman

JERROLD NADLER, New York
CHAIRMAN

JIM JORDAN, Ohio
RANKING MEMBER

ONE HUNDRED SEVENTEENTH CONGRESS

Congress of the United States

House of Representatives

COMMITTEE ON THE JUDICIARY

2138 RAYBURN HOUSE OFFICE BUILDING

WASHINGTON, DC 20515-6216

(202) 225-3951
judiciary.house.gov

June 14, 2022

The Honorable Alejandro Mayorkas
Secretary
U.S. Department of Homeland Security
301 7th Street SW
Washington, DC 20528

Dear Secretary Mayorkas:

We continue to investigate the Biden Administration's misuse of federal law-enforcement resources to target concerned parents. New information from the National School Boards Association (NSBA) shows that Department of Homeland Security (DHS) employees were involved in discussions surrounding the NSBA's letter and its request that the Biden Administration use the Patriot Act to target parents. On top of your effort to establish a so-called Disinformation Board, this new information raises questions about whether DHS believes counterterrorism resources should appropriately be used to target American parents.

On May 20, 2022, the NSBA released a third-party report it commissioned to examine the events surrounding its September 29, 2021, letter to President Biden.[1] This review offered new evidence of DHS's involvement in the Biden Administration's response to the NSBA letter. On October 1—two days after the NSBA letter—Julia Treanor, a senior official of DHS's School Safety Task Force, within Cybersecurity and Infrastructure Security Agency, requested a meeting with NSBA staff to discuss the letter and NSBA's request for federal assistance.[2] The meeting was scheduled to occur on October 21, 2021, but without explanation it was cancelled.[3] The NSBA-commissioned report does not offer any details as to why the meeting was later cancelled.

Additionally, on September 8, 2021, the NSBA's then-Interim Chief Executive Officer and Executive Director, Chip Slaven, received several emails from NSBA's then-immediate past President, Charlie Wilson, concerning alleged threats surrounding school boards. In response, Slaven indicated he would consider making a request to DHS for a threat assessment. Slaven wrote:

---

[1] *Final Report On the Events Surrounding the National School Boards Association's September 29, 2021, Letter to the President*, NATIONAL SCHOOL BOARDS ASSOCIATION (May 20, 2022) [hereinafter NSBA Final Report].
[2] NSBA Final Report, at 5, 22.
[3] *Id.* at 5.

> I have been very concerned over these issues for several weeks. This rhetoric is troubling and reminds me of similar language during the 1990's after Waco and Ruby Ridge. I have been exploring several options to try and address these issues including contacting the Department of Justice and/or Department of Homeland Security and asking for threat assessment for school boards and public schools.[4]

The NSBA-commissioned report does not specify whether Mr. Slaven ever approached DHS about these matters.

The report shows serious collusion between the Biden Administration and the NSBA to create the justification to use the heavy hand of federal law enforcement against concerned moms and dads advocating for their children's future. Committee Republicans will not let this matter rest. We are committed to fully examining the Biden Administration's use of counterterrorism resources in relation to school board meetings.

To assist in our oversight of the Biden Administration's use of federal law enforcement, including counterterrorism resources, with respect to school board-related threats, and to fully understand DHS's involvement in this matter, we ask that you produce the following documents and information:

1. All documents and communications referring or relating to the National School Boards Association's September 29, 2021, letter to President Biden or the Attorney General's October 4, 2021, memorandum;

2. All documents and communications between or among Department of Homeland Security employees and National School Boards Association staff, officers, and/or executive board members, including but not limited to the communications of Julia Treanor, for the period January 20, 2021, to the present; and

3. Please explain whether you consider the Attorney General's October 4, 2021, memorandum to be lawful and whether you, or any Department of Homeland Security officials raised concerns about its enforcement.

[4] E-mail from Mr. Chip Slaven, Interim CEO & Exec. Dir., Nat'l School Boards Assoc., to Mr. Charlie Wilson, Immediate Past Pres., Nat'l School Boards Assoc., (Sept. 8, 2021 5:08 PM).

Please provide this information as soon as possible but no later than 5:00 p.m. on June 28, 2022. Thank you for your attention to this matter.

Sincerely,

Jim Jordan
Ranking Member

Steve Chabot
Member of Congress

Louie Gohmert
Member of Congress

Darrell Issa
Ranking Member
Subcommittee on Courts, Intellectual Property, and the Internet

Ken Buck
Ranking Member
Subcommittee on Antitrust, Commercial and Administrative Law

Matt Gaetz
Member of Congress

Mike Johnson
Ranking Member
Subcommittee on the Constitution, Civil Rights and Civil Liberties

Andy Biggs
Ranking Member
Subcommittee on Crime, Terrorism and Homeland Security

Tom McClintock
Ranking Member
Subcommittee on Immigration and Citizenship

W. Gregory Steube
Member of Congress

Tom Tiffany
Member of Congress

Thomas Massie
Member of Congress

Chip Roy
Member of Congress

Dan Bishop
Member of Congress

Michelle Fischbach
Member of Congress

Victoria Spartz
Member of Congress

Scott Fitzgerald
Member of Congress

Cliff Bentz
Member of Congress

Burgess Owens
Member of Congress

cc: The Honorable Jerrold L. Nadler
Chairman

JERROLD NADLER, New York
CHAIRMAN

JIM JORDAN, Ohio
RANKING MEMBER

ONE HUNDRED SEVENTEENTH CONGRESS

Congress of the United States

House of Representatives

COMMITTEE ON THE JUDICIARY

2138 RAYBURN HOUSE OFFICE BUILDING

WASHINGTON, DC 20515-6216

(202) 225-3951
judiciary.house.gov

June 14, 2022

The Honorable Merrick B. Garland
Attorney General
U.S. Department of Justice
950 Pennsylvania Avenue, N.W.
Washington, DC 20530

Dear Attorney General Garland:

We continue to investigate the Biden Administration's misuse of federal law-enforcement resources to target concerned parents. Since October 2021, we have sent nearly 100 letters to Departmental components requesting documents and information related to this investigation.[1] To date, we have received only two half-page responses from your Department, and none of the requested documents or substantive information. New information from the National School Boards Association (NSBA) shows that Justice Department employees coordinated with the White House well in advance of the NSBA's letter and likely knew—and raised no concerns—that the NSBA letter would urge the use of the Patriot Act to target parents.

On May 20, 2022, the NSBA released a third-party report it commissioned to examine the events surrounding its September 29, 2021, letter to President Biden.[2] This review offered startling new evidence of how the Justice Department coordinated with the White House to target concerned parents. On September 21—eight days before the NSBA letter—Mary Wall, a Senior Policy Advisor to President Biden, emailed NSBA's Interim CEO and Executive Director Chip Slaven asking:

---

[1] *See* Letter from Rep. Mike Johnson et al, to Hon. Merrick Garland, Atty Gen., U.S. Dep't of Justice (Oct. 13, 2021); Letter from Rep. Jim Jordan et al, Ranking Member, H. Comm. on the Judiciary, to Hon. Merrick Garland, Atty Gen., U.S. Dep't of Justice (Oct. 25, 2021); Letter from Rep. Jim Jordan et al, Ranking Member, H. Comm. on the Judiciary, to Mr. E. Bryan Wilson et al, Acting U.S. Atty, District of Alaska (Nov. 1, 2021); Letter from Rep. Jim Jordan et al, Ranking Member, H. Comm. on the Judiciary, to Mr. Mark Lesko, Acting Assistant Atty Gen., Nat'l Sec. Division, U.S. Dep't of Justice (Nov. 2, 2021); Letter from Rep. Jim Jordan et al, Ranking Member, H. Comm. on the Judiciary, to Hon. Christopher Wray, Dir., Fed. Bureau of Investigation (Nov. 3, 2021); Letter from Rep. Jim Jordan, Ranking Member, H. Comm. on the Judiciary, to Hon. Merrick Garland, Atty Gen., U.S. Dep't of Justice (Nov. 16, 2021); Letter from Rep. Jim Jordan, Ranking Member, H. Comm. on the Judiciary, to Hon. Christopher Wray, Dir., Fed. Bureau of Investigation (Nov. 18, 2021); Letter from Jim Jordan, Ranking Member, H. Comm. on the Judiciary, to Hon. Christopher Wray, Dir., Fed. Bureau of Investigation (Feb. 10, 2022); Jim Jordan, Ranking Member, H. Comm. on the Judiciary, to Hon. Merrick Garland, Atty Gen., U.S. Dep't of Justice (May 11, 2021).

[2] *Final Report On the Events Surrounding the National School Boards Association's September 29, 2021, Letter to the President*, NATIONAL SCHOOL BOARDS ASSOCIATION (May 20, 2022) [hereinafter NSBA Final Report].

> Is there any way we can take a look at the letter in advance of release? In specific, I'm meeting w colleagues from other WH offices and DOJ tomorrow morning to see if there might be any options we can pursue here, so if **you have concrete recommendations in your letter** (e.g. the threat assessment you mentioned), would be good to know so I can include in discussions.[3]

In response, Slaven emailed Wall a detailed summary of the contents of the letter, which included specific language about the Patriot Act and the use of domestic terrorism tools.[4] The NSBA-commissioned report concluded that "White House officials discussed the existence of the [NSBA] Letter, its requests, and the contents of the Letter with Department of Justice officials more than a week before the Letter was finalized and sent to President Biden."[5] In other words, Justice Department officials knew that the NSBA would encourage President Biden to invoke the Patriot Act and domestic terrorism resources against parents, and the Justice Department apparently raised no concern about this effort.

The NSBA-commissioned report also uncovered communications between Justice Department employees and NSBA staff prior to the release of your October 4 memorandum that directed federal law enforcement to target America's parents. The report found that on October 4 a Department employee contacted Slaven "about steps the Department could take to address the threats referenced in the letter."[6] Justice Department officials and Slaven had a call that afternoon, after which Alivia Roberts, Special Assistant to the Director of Public Affairs, followed up with an email to Slaven that included an advance copy of your memorandum as an attachment.[7]

During your sworn testimony before the Committee in October, you testified that you had no awareness of whether your employees communicated with the White House or the NSBA in advance of your memorandum.[8] It is now abundantly clear from the NSBA-commissioned review that your memorandum was the product of weeks of discussions between the Justice Department, the White House, and the NSBA. Your failure to correct the Committee's record over the past six months calls in to question your commitment to candor before the Committee, especially in light of our repeated inquiries to you and the evidence showing that the FBI targeted parents despite your statement otherwise.

---

[3] E-mail from Ms. Mary Wall, Senior Policy Advisor to the Pres., Exec. Office of the Pres., to Mr. Chip Slaven, Interim CEO & Exec. Dir., Nat'l School Boards Assoc. (Sept. 21, 2021 10:10 PM) (emphasis added).
[4] E-mail from Mr. Chip Slaven, Interim CEO & Exec. Dir., Nat'l School Boards Assoc., to Ms. Mary Wall, Senior Policy Advisor to the Pres., Exec. Office of the Pres. (Sept. 21, 2021 11:26 PM).
[5] NSBA Final Report at 2.
[6] *Id.* at 46.
[7] E-mail from Ms. Alivia Roberts, Special Assistant to the Dir. of Public Affairs, U.S. Dep't of Justice, to Mr. Chip Slaven, Interim CEO & Exec. Dir., Nat'l School Boards Assoc. (Oct. 4, 2021 4:59 PM).
[8] *Oversight of the United States Department of Justice: Hearing Before the H. Comm. on the Judiciary,* 117th Cong. at 92 (2021) (testimony from Hon. Merrick Garland, Atty Gen., U.S. Dep't of Justice).

The NSBA-commissioned report shows serious collusion between the Biden Administration and the NSBA to create the justification to use the heavy hand of federal law enforcement against concerned moms and dads advocating for their children's future. Committee Republicans will not let this matter rest. We are committed to fully examining the Biden Administration's use of counterterrorism resources in relation to school board meetings. We therefore again reiterate our outstanding document requests to the various Departmental components and ask that you produce this material immediately. In addition, we request:

1. All documents and communications between Mary Wall, Senior Policy Advisor to the President, and any Department of Justice employees referring or relating to the National School Boards Association's letter dated September 29, 2021; the Attorney General's memorandum dated October 4, 2021; or alleged threats or violence at school board meetings; and

2. All documents and communications between Department of Justice employees and National School Boards Association staff, officers, and/or executive board members, including but not limited to the communications sent or received by Anthony Coley, Senior Advisor to the Attorney General, and Alivia Roberts, Special Assistant to the Director of Public Affairs.

Because you are still months-delinquent in fulfilling our earlier oversight requests, please provide this information immediately.

Thank you for your attention to this matter.

Sincerely,

Jim Jordan
Ranking Member

Steve Chabot
Member of Congress

Louie Gohmert
Member of Congress

Darrell Issa
Ranking Member
Subcommittee on Courts, Intellectual Property, and the Internet

Ken Buck
Ranking Member
Subcommittee on Antitrust, Commercial and Administrative Law

Matt Gaetz
Member of Congress

Mike Johnson
Ranking Member
Subcommittee on the Constitution, Civil Rights and Civil Liberties

Andy Biggs
Ranking Member
Subcommittee on Crime, Terrorism and Homeland Security

Tom McClintock
Ranking Member
Subcommittee on Immigration and Citizenship

W. Gregory Steube
Member of Congress

Tom Tiffany
Member of Congress

Thomas Massie
Member of Congress

Chip Roy
Member of Congress

Dan Bishop
Member of Congress

Michelle Fischbach
Member of Congress

Victoria Spartz
Member of Congress

Scott Fitzgerald
Member of Congress

Cliff Bentz
Member of Congress

Burgess Owens
Member of Congress

cc: The Honorable Jerrold L. Nadler
Chairman

JERROLD NADLER, New York
CHAIRMAN

JIM JORDAN, Ohio
RANKING MEMBER

ONE HUNDRED SEVENTEENTH CONGRESS

Congress of the United States

House of Representatives

COMMITTEE ON THE JUDICIARY

2138 RAYBURN HOUSE OFFICE BUILDING

WASHINGTON, DC 20515-6216

(202) 225-3951
judiciary.house.gov

June 7, 2022

The Honorable Christopher A. Wray
Director
Federal Bureau of Investigation
935 Pennsylvania Avenue, N.W.
Washington, DC 20535

Dear Director Wray:

We continue to investigate allegations that the Federal Bureau of Investigation is retaliating against FBI employees for engaging in disfavored political speech. On May 6, 2022, we sent you a letter that detailed examples of the FBI suspending the security clearances of FBI employees for their participation in protected First Amendment activity.[1] To date, you have failed to acknowledge our letter or begin to arrange for the requested briefing. Since our May 6 letter, we have received new protected whistleblower disclosures that suggest the FBI's actions are far more pervasive than previously known. Multiple whistleblowers have called it a "purge" of FBI employees holding conservative views.

As one example, the FBI targeted [redacted], who works in the FBI's [redacted] by suspending [redacted] security clearance and eventually indefinitely suspending [redacted] from duty and pay. [redacted] had apparently shared [redacted] personal views that the FBI was not being entirely forthcoming about the events of January 6. As a result, the FBI determined that [redacted] had "espoused conspiratorial views" and "promoted unreliable information which indicates support for the events of January 6," and therefore the FBI questioned [redacted] allegiance to the United States.

[redacted] honorably served in the United States military for several years—including deployments in Kuwait and Iraq—valiantly earning multiple military commendation medals. While employed with the FBI, [redacted] has been rated as "Exceeds Fully Successful" in performance evaluations, has received several awards, and has never been disciplined or reprimanded until this instance. In a letter sent to the FBI, [redacted] lawyers explained that the FBI's accusations are a "monumental leap from objective fact" and a "distortion" of [redacted] actions. They argue the security clearance suspension is a "gross injustice and clear constitutional violation[]"because the FBI is "punish[ing]" [redacted] for "run[ning] afoul of prevailing agency orthodoxy" while "exercising [redacted] First Amendment right of free speech."

---

[1] Letter from Jim Jordan, Ranking Member, H. Comm. on the Judiciary, to Christopher A. Wray, Dir., Federal Bureau of Investigation (May 6, 2022) (on file with committee).

In addition, another whistleblower, who has since left the FBI, has informed us that ■ faced retaliation for criticizing the FBI in an anonymous survey circulated by the ■■■■ ■■■■ to employees following January 6. The FBI allegedly escalated an adverse personnel action against this employee after ■ commented on the survey, which sought feedback about the ■■■■ actions "during the recent crisis/command post" event. The employee, too, was never disciplined or reprimanded until after ■ criticized the FBI.

We are conducting oversight to ensure the FBI is not retaliating against FBI employees for exercising their First Amendment rights and engaging in disfavored political speech. We reiterate our earlier requests for your personal assurance that the FBI will cooperate fully with the Department of Justice's Office of Inspector General's examination of these matters and for a briefing on the FBI's purge of employees holding disfavored viewpoints.

We remind you that whistleblower disclosures to Congress are protected by law and that we will not tolerate any effort to retaliate against whistleblowers for their disclosures. Thank you for your prompt attention to this matter.

Sincerely,

Jim Jordan
Ranking Member

cc: The Honorable Jerrold L. Nadler
Chairman

The Honorable Michael E. Horowitz
Inspector General, U.S. Department of Justice

JERROLD NADLER, New York
CHAIRMAN

JIM JORDAN, Ohio
RANKING MEMBER

ONE HUNDRED SEVENTEENTH CONGRESS

Congress of the United States

House of Representatives

COMMITTEE ON THE JUDICIARY

2138 RAYBURN HOUSE OFFICE BUILDING

WASHINGTON, DC 20515-6216

(202) 225-3951
judiciary.house.gov

June 1, 2022

The Honorable Christopher A. Wray
Director
Federal Bureau of Investigation
935 Pennsylvania Avenue, N.W.
Washington, DC 20535

Dear Director Wray:

We write to request information to assist the Committee's continued oversight of the Federal Bureau of Investigation's (FBI) actions and decision-making related to the handling of debunked claims about President Trump, his campaign, and presidential transition. We have learned that since March 2012, the FBI approved and facilitated a Secure Work Environment at Perkins Coie's Washington, D.C. office, which continues to be operational. In a letter dated May 25, 2022, the law firm confirmed and acknowledged the arrangement.[1]

We have been informed that former Perkins Coie partner Michael Sussmann had access to this Secure Work Environment, and during the course of his recent trial it was disclosed he had special badge access to FBI headquarters.[2] Given the allegations related to Sussmann and Perkins Coie's partner Marc Elias and their roles with the presidential campaign of Secretary Hillary Clinton, this information raises serious questions about the FBI and Perkins Coie's arrangement of a Secure Work Environment as well as the FBI's close relationship with the firm's former partners. We have learned that Sussmann had access to this Secure Work Environment until some point in 2021, with limited supervised access thereafter. Within a General Services Administration-approved security container and key locker, the Secure Work Environment has an FBI-owned secure telephone, a fax machine, and a security token card.

---

[1] Letter from Michael D. Bopp, Counsel for Perkins Coie LLP, to Reps. Jim Jordan and Matt Gaetz, H. Jud. Comm (May 25, 2022).

[2] *See* Post Editorial Board, *How FBI bigwig aided and abetted Hillary Clinton plot*, N.Y. POST (May 19, 2022); Jerry Dunleavy, *FBI opened Alfa-Bank inquiry based on 'referral' from DOJ — but it came from Sussmann*, WASH. EXAMINER (May 23, 2022); Andrew C. McCarthy, *In the Sussmann Trial, What a Difference a Text Makes*, NAT'L. REVIEW (May 19, 2022). (Text messages between Michael Sussmann and then-general counsel James Baker on September 18, 2016: Mr. Sussmann "Jim [Baker] – It's Michael Sussmann. I have something time-sensitive (and sensitive) I need to discuss. Do you have availability for a short meeting tomorrow? I'm coming on behalf of a client or company – want to help the Bureau. Thanks." Mr. Baker. "Ok. I will find a time. What might work for you?" Mr. Sussmann. "Any time but lunchtime – you name it." Mr. Baker. "200pm at my office? Do you have a badge or do you need help getting into the building?" Mr. Sussmann. "I have a badge. Please remind me of your room #?").

To assist us with our continued oversight work, please provide the following documents and information:

1. All documents and communications referring or relating to the establishment, maintenance, and accreditation of the Secure Work Environment at Perkins Coie's Washington, D.C. office location, for the period of January 1, 2016, to December 1, 2021;

2. All documents and communications between or among the FBI for the period of January 1, 2016, to December 1, 2021, referring or relating to Michael Sussmann;

3. An explanation as to why the FBI approved a Secure Work Environment at Perkins Coie's Washington, D.C. office location;

4. An explanation as to the FBI's relationship with Michael Sussmann, for the period of January 1, 2016, to December 1, 2021, including:

    a. When did the FBI provide Michael Sussmann an FBI badge with special access to its headquarters;

    b. Why did the FBI provide Michael Sussmann an FBI badge to access its headquarters;

    c. A list of all FBI employees who met with Michael Sussmann, for the period January 1, 2016, to December 1, 2021, at FBI headquarters, including dates and times;

    d. Whether the FBI provided Michael Sussmann access to any of its Sensitive Compartmented Information Facilities to review any classified information and sensitive law-enforcement information; and

5. Since the September 2021 federal indictment of Michael Sussmann, and his subsequent resignation from Perkins Coie, whether the FBI continues its arrangement of this Secure Work Environment at Perkins Coie's Washington, D.C. office location.

Please provide this information as soon as possible but no later than 5:00 p.m. on June 15, 2022. If you have any questions about this request, please contact Judiciary Committee staff at (202) 225-6906. Thank you for your attention to this matter.

Sincerely,

Jim Jordan
Ranking Member

Matt Gaetz
Member of Congress

cc: The Honorable Jerrold L. Nadler
Chairman

Congress of the United States
Washington, DC 20515

May 24, 2022

The Honorable Christopher A. Wray
Director
Federal Bureau of Investigation
935 Pennsylvania Avenue, N.W.
Washington, DC 20535

Dear Director Wray:

The House Committee on the Judiciary and the House Permanent Select Committee on Intelligence continue to conduct oversight of the executive branch's use of Foreign Intelligence Surveillance Act (FISA) authorities, which is of particular importance as Congress considers reauthorization of FISA Section 702. In November 2020, the Foreign Intelligence Surveillance Court (FISC) issued an order expanding the FBI's FISA reporting requirements to include "the number of U.S. person queries run by the FBI against Section 702-acquired information."[1] As a result, ODNI's recently released *Annual Statistical Transparency Report* included this information for the first time. The report revealed that from December 2020 through November 2021 the FBI conducted over 3.3 million U.S. person queries against its Section 702 holdings.[2] This was a substantial increase from the number of U.S. person queries the FBI conducted from December 2019 to November 2020, which the report stated was approximately 1.3 million.[3] This dramatic increase raises significant questions. We therefore write to request your full and prompt cooperation with our oversight efforts as we seek to understand why the number of U.S. person queries more than doubled from the prior year.

As you know, under Section 702, the Attorney General (AG) and the Director of National Intelligence (DNI) may jointly authorize the targeting of (i) non-U.S. persons (ii) who are reasonably believed to be outside of the United States (iii) to acquire foreign intelligence information.[4] Section 702 requires the AG, in consultation with the DNI, to adopt targeting, minimization, and querying procedures that meet the requirements of Section 702 and are consistent with the Fourth Amendment.[5] These procedures must be reviewed and approved by the FISC on an annual basis.[6]

The FBI receives a portion of the information the government collects under Section 702, and is authorized to conduct queries of this information that are reasonably likely to return

[1] Memorandum Opinion and Order, *Document re Section 702 Certification* at 63 (FISA Ct. Nov. 18, 2020).
[2] Off. of the Director of National Intelligence, Annual Statistical Transparency Report, Calendar Year 2021 at 21 (Apr. 2022).
[3] *Id.*
[4] *See* 50 U.S.C. § 1881(a).
[5] 50 U.S.C. § 1881(d)-(f)(2).
[6] 50 U.S.C. § 1881(h)-(j).

foreign intelligence information or evidence of a crime. Queries that involve U.S. persons raise particular oversight sensitivities to ensure rights are protected. As noted above, according to ODNI, the FBI's U.S. person queries dramatically increased in 2021.[7] Specifically, ODNI estimated that the FBI conducted 3,394,053 U.S. person queries in 2021 compared to about 1,324,057 U.S. person queries in 2020,[8] representing over a 250 percent increase in a single year. ODNI stated that more than half of the queries, or about 1.9 million, were related to attempts to compromise U.S. critical infrastructure by foreign cyber actors, which the Biden Administration has attributed to Russian hackers.[9] The ODNI report also noted that, on at least four occasions, the FBI failed to obtain an order from the FISC before accessing the contents of Section 702-acquired information.[10]

Rigorous Congressional oversight of the FBI's Section 702-related activities is essential given FBI's track record utilizing its FISA authorities. In November 2020, the FISC disclosed that "the government ha[d] reported numerous incidents" in which the FBI queried Section 702-acquired information for criminal investigations and reviewed unminimized content results without first obtaining court permission.[11] The FISC noted the discovery of 40 queries in which the FBI accessed information for investigations involving "healthcare fraud, transnational organized crime, violent gangs, domestic terrorism involving racially motivated violent extremists, as well as investigations relating to public corruption and bribery," all of which were unrelated to foreign surveillance.[12] According to the FISC, "[n]one of these queries was related to national security, and they returned numerous Section 702-acquired products in response."[13] This is just one example of FBI's habitual compliance failures, which both the Department of Justice Office of Inspector General and the FISC have substantiated in other reports.[14]

As Congress continues to evaluate the potential reauthorization of Section 702, we must have all necessary information to assess the executive branch's use of the existing authorities. To inform our ongoing oversight, please provide the following documents and information:

1. A full accounting of the approximately 3,394,053 U.S. person queries conducted by the FBI in calendar year (CY) 2021, including:

---

[7] ODNI report, *supra* note 2.
[8] *Id.* at 4, 21.
[9] *Id.* at 20; Dustin Volz, *FBI Conducted Potentially Millions of Searches of Americans' Data Last Year*, Report Says, WALL ST. J. (May 5, 2022). The Administration declined to disclose additional details on the alleged cyber threats like whether the Russian government was involved. Volz, *supra.*
[10] ODNI report, *supra* note 2, at 22.
[11] Memorandum Opinion and Order, *Document re Section 702 Certification*, at 38-43 (FISA Ct. Nov. 18, 2020).
[12] *Id.* at 42.
[13] *Id.*
[14] *See* Dep't of Justice Off. of Inspector Gen., Review of Four FISA Applications and Other Aspects of the FBI's Crossfire Hurricane Investigation (Dec. 2019); Dep't of Justice Off. of Inspector Gen., Management Advisory Memorandum for the Director of the Federal Bureau of Investigation Regarding the Execution of Woods Procedures for Applications Filed with the Foreign Intelligence Surveillance Court Relating to U.S. Persons (Mar. 2020); Memorandum Opinion and Order, Document regarding the Section 702 2018 Certification at 66 (FISC Oct. 2018); Memorandum Opinion and Order, Document re Section 702 Certification (FISA Ct. Nov. 18, 2020); Dep't of Justice Off. of Inspector Gen., Audit of the Federal Bureau of Investigation's Execution of Its Woods Procedures for the Applications Filed with the Foreign Intelligence Surveillance Court Relating to U.S. Persons (Sept. 2021).

   a. The total number of unique query terms that are a U.S. citizen, an alien lawfully admitted for permanent residence, an unincorporated association, or a corporation which is incorporated in the United States. If the FBI does not have the capability to identify the number of unique query terms, provide an explanation as to why;

   b. The Section 702-derived contents reviewed in each query, if any; and

   c. The number of preliminary or full investigations into any U.S. citizens the FBI has initiated as a result of information obtained through any of these U.S. person queries, and the nature of the predication for each such investigation.

2. An explanation of the facts and circumstances of the approximately 1.9 million U.S person queries that are apparently the result of an FBI investigation into alleged Russian hackers who sought to compromise U.S. critical infrastructure, including:

   a. The rationale for why these queries were found to be compliant with the FBI's Section 702 querying procedures;

   b. The total number of U.S. citizens the FBI identified as victims of these compromises(s) pursuant to these queries;

   c. The total number of U.S. victims the FBI notified about the compromises(s) pursuant to the Crime Victims' Rights and Restitution Act, 34 U.S.C. § 20141, or the Crime Victims' Rights Act, 18 U.S.C. § 3771; and

   d. A detailed statement about the FBI's investigation, including the status of the investigation and any information uncovered about the identity of the Russian actors and their involvement with or connection to the Russian government, if any.

3. Provide the total number of FBI U.S. person queries of Section 702-derived information, by year, for CY 2015 through CY 2019.

4. An explanation for why the FBI failed to comply with the statutory requirement to obtain an order from the Foreign Intelligence Surveillance Court before accessing the contents of Section 702-acquired information on at least four instances in 2021, including:

   a. The basis for each query;

   b. A description of the contents accessed, and a statement about whether the query was conducted in order to retrieve such contents; and

   c. The date on which the FBI discovered each violation and the date on which the FISC was alerted to each violation.

Additionally, Republicans on the Judiciary Committee have sent multiple letters requesting information about the FBI's use of FISA authorities that have not been sufficiently answered, and this information is relevant to Committees' ongoing oversight. Therefore, please provide the following documents and information:

1. Provide a detailed accounting of every instance since December 2019 in which the FBI has queried, accessed, otherwise used information obtained pursuant to Section 702 for evidence of a crime unrelated to national security;

2. Identify the frequency of batch queries of FISA-acquired data for 99 or fewer queries, and explain why users must only obtain attorney approval before conducting a batch search of 100 or more queries;

3. Explain whether the FBI has located all of the missing Woods Files identified in the Department of Justice's Office of Inspector General September 2021 report, and provide the reason(s) why the FBI cannot locate all missing Woods Files;

4. Quantify the number of FBI employees who have access to Section 702 FISA-acquired data; and

5. Produce all guidance documents and training materials currently issued to FBI personnel with access to FISA-acquired data.

Please provide this information as soon as possible, but no later than 5:00 p.m. on June 7, 2022. If a full response requires the disclosure of classified information, please provide such information under separate cover. After you have provided this information in writing, we ask that you arrange for the FBI to provide a staff-level briefing.

Thank you for your prompt attention to this important matter.

Sincerely,

Jim Jordan Ranking Member House Committee on the Judiciary	Michael R. Turner Ranking Member House Permanent Select Committee on Intelligence

cc: The Honorable Jerrold Nadler, Chairman, House Committee on the Judiciary
The Honorable Adam Schiff, Chairman, House Permanent Select Committee on Intelligence

JERROLD NADLER, New York
CHAIRMAN

JIM JORDAN, Ohio
RANKING MEMBER

ONE HUNDRED SEVENTEENTH CONGRESS
Congress of the United States
House of Representatives
COMMITTEE ON THE JUDICIARY
2138 RAYBURN HOUSE OFFICE BUILDING
WASHINGTON, DC 20515-6216
(202) 225-3951
judiciary.house.gov

May 19, 2022

The Honorable Michael E. Horowitz
Inspector General
U.S. Department of Justice
950 Pennsylvania Avenue NW, Suite 4706
Washington, D.C. 20530

Dear Inspector General Horowitz:

Committee Republicans received your notification that an employee of the Department of Justice Office of the Inspector General (OIG) leaked nonpublic information, including a draft copy, of the Department of Justice OIG's review of the Trump Administration's immigration enforcement policies.[1] For more than two years, this employee, who has since left your office, used his personal phone to make nearly 350 phone calls to numbers belonging to journalists from three media outlets. Those news outlets then published articles with nonpublic information about the Trump Administration's zero tolerance policy.[2] This former employee "abruptly resigned" from your office in December 2020 and rejected requests for interviews about the unauthorized disclosures of nonpublic information to the media.[3]

This matter raises serious concerns about the politicization of the Department of Justice OIG, which could lead to a lack of confidence and trust in your work. Although the former employee's motivations are unknown, one could reasonably assume that he leaked this information out of partisan animus toward the policies of the Trump Administration. Such a conclusion is a potential crisis for your office.

To allow us to better understand details about these leaks, determine the extent of this serious misconduct, and evaluate your handling of the matter, Committee Republicans ask that you please provide the following documents and information:

---

[1] Letter from Michael E. Horowitz, Inspector Gen., Dep't of Justice, to Jim Jordan, Ranking Member, H. Comm. on the Judiciary, et al., (May 11, 2022); Dep't of Justice Off. of Inspector Gen., Review of the Department of Justice's Planning and Implementation of Its Zero Tolerance Policy and Its Coordination with the Departments of Homeland Security and Health and Human Services (Jan. 2021).
[2] Letter from Michael E. Horowitz, Inspector Gen., Dep't of Justice, to Jim Jordan, Ranking Member, H. Comm. on the Judiciary, et al., at 3 (May 11, 2022).
[3] *Id.* at 5.

1. The complete unredacted case file of the Department of Justice OIG's review of the Trump Administration's immigration enforcement policies, including but not limited to all emails sent and received by the former Department of Justice OIG employee;

2. The complete unredacted case file of the investigation into the leaks of unauthorized information involving the former Department of Justice OIG employee, to include all documents, communications, and other evidence related to the review in your office's possession;

3. The complete unredacted personnel file for the former Department of Justice OIG employee, including but not limited to his resume and application for employment, employee performance reviews, references, trainings, and other similar material;

4. Explain the former Department of Justice OIG employee's role and responsibilities during his employment with the Department of Justice OIG;

5. Identify with specificity all investigations, audits, examinations, or other Department of Justice OIG work performed by the former employee during his employment; and

6. Explain whether the former employee's apparent political bias contributed to or affected the Department of Justice OIG's work in any other matter.

Please provide this information as soon as possible but no later than 5:00 p.m. on June 2, 2022. After you have provided this information in writing, we ask that your staff provide a staff-level briefing on this matter. Thank you for your attention to this important matter.

Sincerely,

Jim Jordan
Ranking Member

cc: The Honorable Jerrold Nadler, Chairman

JERROLD NADLER, New York
CHAIRMAN

JIM JORDAN, Ohio
RANKING MEMBER

ONE HUNDRED SEVENTEENTH CONGRESS

Congress of the United States

House of Representatives

COMMITTEE ON THE JUDICIARY

2138 RAYBURN HOUSE OFFICE BUILDING

WASHINGTON, DC 20515-6216

(202) 225-3951
judiciary.house.gov

May 11, 2022

The Honorable Merrick B. Garland
Attorney General
Department of Justice
950 Pennsylvania Avenue, N.W.
Washington, DC 20535

Dear Attorney General Garland:

In sworn testimony before this Committee, you denied that the Department of Justice or its components were using counterterrorism statutes and resources to target parents at school board meetings.[1] We now have evidence that contrary to your testimony, the Federal Bureau of Investigation has labeled at least dozens of investigations into parents with a threat tag created by the FBI's Counterterrorism Division to assess and track investigations related to school boards. These cases include investigations into parents upset about mask mandates and state elected officials who publicly voiced opposition to vaccine mandates. These investigations into concerned parents are the direct result of, and would not have occurred but for, your directive to federal law enforcement to target these categories of people.

On October 4, 2021, in response to a request from the National School Boards Association that the federal government use counterterrorism tools, including the Patriot Act, to target parents at school board meetings, you issued a memorandum directing the FBI to address these threats.[2] The press release accompanying your memorandum highlighted the FBI's National Threat Operations Center to serve as a snitch-line for tips about parents at school board meetings.[3] By October 20, the FBI had operationalized your directive. In an FBI-wide email, the FBI's Counterterrorism Division and Criminal Division announced the creation of a new threat tag—EDUOFFICIALS—and directed all FBI personnel to apply it to school board-related threats.[4]

---

[1] *Oversight of the United States Department of Justice: Hearing Before the H. comm. on the Judiciary,* 117th Cong. (2021) (testimony from Hon. Merrick Garland, Atty Gen., U.S. Dep't of Justice).
[2] Memorandum from Atty Gen. Merrick Garland, U.S. Dep't of Justice, Partnership Among Federal, State, Local, Tribal, And Territorial Law Enforcement to Address Threats Against School Administrators, Board Members, Teachers, and Staff (Oct. 4, 2021).
[3] Press Release, U.S. Dep't of Justice, Justice Department Addresses Violent Threats Against School Officials and Teachers (Oct. 4, 2021).
[4] Email from Carlton Peeples, Deputy Assistant Director, Criminal Investigative Div., Fed. Bureau of Investigation, to FBI_SACS (Oct. 20, 2021).

We have learned from brave whistleblowers that the FBI has opened investigations with the EDUOFFICIALS threat tag in almost every region of the country and relating to all types of educational settings. The information we have received shows how, as a direct result of your directive, federal law enforcement is using counterterrorism resources to investigate protected First Amendment activity. For example:

- In one investigation begun following your directive, the FBI's [redacted] Field Office interviewed a mom for allegedly telling a local school board "we are coming for you." The complaint, which came into the FBI through the National Threat Operations Center snitch-line, alleged that the mom was a threat because she belonged to a "right wing mom's group" known as "Moms for Liberty" and because she "is a gun owner." When an FBI agent interviewed the mom, she told the agent that she was upset about the school board's mask mandates and that her statement was a warning that her organization would seek to replace the school board with new members through the electoral process.

- The FBI's [redacted] Field Office opened an investigation, subsequent to your directive, into a dad opposed to mask mandates. The complaint came in through the National Threat Operations Center snitch-line and alleged that the dad "fit the profile of an insurrectionist" because he "rails against the government," "believes all conspiracy theories," and "has a lot of guns and threatens to use them." When an FBI agent interviewed the complainant, the complainant admitted they had "no specific information or observations of . . . any crimes or threats," but they contacted the FBI after learning the Justice Department had a website "to submit tips to the FBI in regards to any concerning behavior directed toward school boards."

- In another case initiated after your directive, the FBI's [redacted] Field Office opened an investigation into Republican state elected officials over allegations from a state Democratic party official that the Republicans "incited violence" by expressing public displeasure with school districts' vaccine mandates. This complaint also came into the FBI through the National Threat Operations Center snitch-line.

This whistleblower information is startling. You have subjected these moms and dads to the opening of an FBI investigation about them, the establishment of an FBI case file that includes their political views, and the application of a "threat tag" to their names as a direct result of their exercise of their fundamental constitutional right to speak and advocate for their children. This information is evidence of how the Biden Administration is using federal law enforcement, including counterterrorism resources, to investigate concerned parents for protected First Amendment activity. Although FBI agents ultimately—and rightly—determined that these cases did not implicate federal criminal statutes, the agents still exerted their limited time and resources investigating these complaints. This valuable law-enforcement time and resources could have been expended on real and pressing threats.

These investigations into concerned parents were the direct result of your October 4 directive to the FBI. Each of the cases was initiated following your directive. Each of the complaints came into the FBI through the same snitch-line—the National Threat Operations Center—highlighted in the press release accompanying your October 4 memorandum. One complainant even told an FBI agent that they reported the tip to the FBI because of the snitch-line, despite having "no specific information" about any actual threat. These facts lead us to conclude that these investigations into concerned parents, and likely many more like them, would not have occurred but for your directive.

Parents have an undisputed right to direct the upbringing and education of their children,[5] which includes voicing their strong opposition to controversial curricula at local schools. This whistleblower information raises serious concerns that your October 4 memorandum will chill protected First Amendment activity as parents will rightfully fear that their passionate advocacy for their children could result in a visit from federal law enforcement. You have refused to rescind your October 4 memorandum and its anti-parent directives. In light of this new whistleblower information, we again call on you to rescind your October 4 memorandum.

Committee Republicans have been investigating the Biden Administration's misuse of law-enforcement resources to target concerned parents since last fall.[6] You have failed to substantively respond to our requests for documents and your sworn testimony to the Committee is now contradicted by whistleblower information. Please be assured that Committee Republicans will not let this matter drop. Accordingly, we request the following information:

1. Produce all documents and materials identified in our letters to Departmental components dated November 1, 2021, November 2, 2021, November 3, 2021, and November 18, 2021, immediately; and

2. Take all reasonable steps immediately to preserve all records responsive to our letters to Department components.

In addition, we remind you that whistleblower disclosures to Congress are protected by law and that we will not tolerate any effort to retaliate against whistleblowers for their disclosures.

Sincerely,

Jim Jordan
Ranking Member

Mike Johnson
Ranking Member
Subcommittee on the Constitution, Civil Rights and Civil Liberties

[5] *Troxel v. Granville,* 530 U.S. 57, 65 (2000) (citing *Meyer v. Nebraska,* 262 U.S. 390, 399 (1923)).
[6] Letter from House Judiciary Committee Republicans to Hon. Christopher A. Wray, Dir., Fed. Bureau of Investigation (Nov. 3, 2021).

cc: The Honorable Jerrold L. Nadler
Chairman

JERROLD NADLER, New York
CHAIRMAN

JIM JORDAN, Ohio
RANKING MEMBER

ONE HUNDRED SEVENTEENTH CONGRESS

Congress of the United States
House of Representatives

COMMITTEE ON THE JUDICIARY
2138 RAYBURN HOUSE OFFICE BUILDING
WASHINGTON, DC 20515–6216
(202) 225–3951
judiciary.house.gov

May 6, 2022

The Honorable Christopher A. Wray
Director
Federal Bureau of Investigation
935 Pennsylvania Avenue, N.W.
Washington, DC 20535

Dear Director Wray:

We have been alerted that the Federal Bureau of Investigation appears to be attempting to terminate the employment of FBI employees who were engaged in protected First Amendment activity on January 6, 2021. The Department of Justice Office of Inspector General is now examining whether the FBI's actions violate federal civil service laws.[1] While FBI employees may not participate in partisan political campaigns,[2] FBI employees do not give up their rights to engage in political speech activity. We have serious concerns that the FBI appears to be retaliating against employees for engaging in political speech disfavored by FBI leadership.

According to several whistleblowers, the FBI is suspending the security clearances of FBI employees for their participation in protected First Amendment activity on January 6, 2021. Among the justifications for the suspensions, the FBI cited "Adjudicative Guideline A — Allegiance to the United States," implying that the FBI believes the employees who attended protests on January 6 are no longer loyal to the United States. Because a security clearance is required for FBI positions, the suspension of the security clearance means the FBI has suspended these employees from work indefinitely. Such a suspension is likely to be the first step in terminating employment.

One such targeted employee is [redacted] working in the FBI's [redacted] who also honorably served in the United States military for over 20 years. [redacted] has been working for the FBI for more than a decade. According to whistleblowers, while on leave, these FBI employees attended public events in Washington, D.C., with their spouses. We have been told that [redacted] and the other FBI employees did not enter the United States Capitol, have not been charged with any crime, and have not been contacted by law enforcement about their actions.

---

[1] *See* letter from Michael E. Horowitz, Inspector Gen., Dep't of Justice, to Jim Jordan, Ranking Member, H. Comm. on the Judic. (May 4, 2022).
[2] 5 U.S.C. § 7323.

Given these facts, it is extremely concerning that the FBI would seek to suspend the security clearances of these employees and begin the process to potentially terminate their employment altogether. Even more insulting is that the FBI would openly question the patriotism of long-time FBI employees, including at least one veteran, because they exercised their First Amendment rights on their personal time without breaking any laws. The totality of the FBI's actions as relayed to us present the appearance that the FBI may be retaliating against these employees for disfavored political speech. This perception is buttressed by documented examples of political bias ingrained the FBI's leadership culture—for example, when a senior FBI official wrote derisively to a colleague that he "could SMELL the Trump support" at a Walmart in southern Virginia,[3] or when an FBI attorney altered evidence in support of the FBI's warrantless surveillance of a Trump campaign associate.[4]

We are conducting oversight to ensure the FBI is not retaliating against FBI employees for exercising their First Amendment rights. We ask for your personal assurance that the FBI will cooperate fully with the Inspector General's examination. In addition, because we continue to see repeated abuses by the FBI under your leadership—including most recently the FBI's misuse of counterterrorism resources to target concerned parents and its rampant abuse of FISA authorities to spy on Americans—we ask that you arrange a staff-level briefing concerning the FBI's personnel actions against employees involved in First Amendment protected activity on January 6. Please schedule this briefing as soon as possible, but no later than 5:00 p.m. on May 20, 2022.

Finally, we remind you that whistleblower disclosures to Congress are protected by law and that we will not tolerate any effort to retaliate against whistleblowers for their disclosures. We look forward to receiving your prompt cooperation with this inquiry.

Sincerely,

Jim Jordan
Ranking Member

cc: The Honorable Jerrold L. Nadler
Chairman

---

[3] Text message from Peter Strzok (Aug. 26, 2016). During congressional testimony, Inspector General Horowitz explained that he did not rule out political bias as a basis for the FBI's misconduct. *See "Examining the Inspector General's Report on Alleged Abuses of the Foreign Intelligence Surveillance Act": Hearing before the S. Comm. on the Judic.*, 116th Cong. (2019).

[4] *See* Press Release, Dep't of Justice, FBI Attorney Admits Altering Email Used for FISA Application During "Crossfire Hurricane" Investigation (Aug. 19, 2020).

JERROLD NADLER, New York
CHAIRMAN

JIM JORDAN, Ohio
RANKING MEMBER

ONE HUNDRED SEVENTEENTH CONGRESS

Congress of the United States

House of Representatives

COMMITTEE ON THE JUDICIARY

2138 RAYBURN HOUSE OFFICE BUILDING

WASHINGTON, DC 20515-6216

(202) 225-3951
judiciary.house.gov

May 3, 2022

Mr. William G. Malley
Managing Partner
Perkins Coie LLP
700 13th Street, N.W.
Washington, DC 20005

Dear Mr. Malley:

We write to request information to assist the Committee's continued oversight of the Department of Justice's (DOJ) actions and decision-making related to the handling of debunked claims about President Trump, his campaign, and presidential transition.[1] This oversight includes the Federal Bureau of Investigation's use of the Foreign Intelligence Surveillance Act (FISA) as a mechanism to improperly target the Trump campaign.[2] We have learned that starting in 2009, the Justice Department installed and maintained a Secure Work Environment at Perkins Coie's Washington, D.C. office. In light of the allegations related to former Perkins Coie partners Michael Sussmann and Marc Elias and their roles with the presidential campaign of Secretary Hillary Clinton, this information raises questions about the firm's arrangement with DOJ as well as the administration and management of this Secure Work Environment.

In particular, we have been informed that Mr. Sussmann oversaw this Secure Work Environment until late 2021. In September 2021, the DOJ indicted Sussmann for making false statements to the FBI in September 2016 in connection with alleged communications between the Trump Organization and a Russian bank.[3] We understand that Sussmann continued to manage this Secure Work Environment even after his federal indictment.

---

[1] *See* Letter from Rep. Jim Jordan & Rep. Andy Biggs, H. Comm. on the Judiciary, to Christopher A. Wray, Fed. Bureau of Investigation (May 4, 2021); Letter from Rep. Jim Jordan & Rep. Mike Johnson, H. Comm. on the Judiciary, to Christopher A. Wray, Fed. Bureau of Investigation (Jan. 27, 2022); Letter from Rep. Jim Jordan, et al., H. Comm. on the Judiciary, to Christopher A. Wray, Fed. Bureau of Investigation (Mar. 21, 2022).

[2] *See* Dep't of Justice Off. of Inspector Gen., Review of Four FISA Applications and Other Aspects of the FBI's Crossfire Hurricane Investigation (Dec. 2019); Dep't of Justice Off. of Inspector Gen., Management Advisory Memorandum for the Director of the Federal Bureau of Investigation Regarding the Execution of Woods Procedures for Applications Filed with the Foreign Intelligence Surveillance Court Relating to U.S. Persons (Mar. 2020); Memorandum Opinion and Order, Document re Section 702 Certification (FISA Ct. Nov. 18, 2020); Dep't of Justice Off. of Inspector Gen., Audit of the Federal Bureau of Investigation's Execution of Its Woods Procedures for the Applications Filed with the Foreign Intelligence Surveillance Court Relating to U.S. Persons (Sept. 2021).

[3] United States v. Sussman, No. 1:21-cr-00582-CRC (D.D.C.) (Indictment of Michael Sussman) (filed Sept. 16, 2021).

To assist the Committee with its continued oversight work, please provide the following information:

1. A full accounting of Perkins Coie's arrangement with the Justice Department to install a Secure Work Environment at its Washington, D.C. office location, to include:

    a. Who paid for its installation and maintenance, and at what cost;

    b. The dates it has been in operation;

    c. Whether Michael Sussmann still has access to this Secure Work Environment and if not, when was his access terminated; and

    d. Did this Secure Work Environment include a General Services Administration-approved security container, and any other federal government products.

2. Please explain whether this Secure Work Environment is operating under the control of Perkins Coie or the Department of Justice.

3. Since the September 2021 federal indictment of Michael Sussmann, and his subsequent resignation from Perkins Coie, has the Department of Justice continued its arrangement of this Secure Work Environment at Perkins Coie's Washington, D.C. office.

Please provide this information as soon as possible but no later than 5:00 p.m. on May 17, 2022. If you have any questions about this request, please contact Judiciary Committee staff at (202) 225-6906. Thank you for your attention to this matter.

Sincerely,

Jim Jordan
Ranking Member

Matt Gaetz
Member of Congress

cc: The Honorable Jerrold L. Nadler
Chairman

JERROLD NADLER, New York
CHAIRMAN

JIM JORDAN, Ohio
RANKING MEMBER

ONE HUNDRED SEVENTEENTH CONGRESS

Congress of the United States

House of Representatives

COMMITTEE ON THE JUDICIARY

2138 RAYBURN HOUSE OFFICE BUILDING
WASHINGTON, DC 20515-6216
(202) 225-3951
judiciary.house.gov

April 27, 2022

The Honorable Merrick B. Garland
Attorney General
Department of Justice
Washington, DC 20530

Dear Attorney General Garland:

We write to request that the Department of Justice preserve all records relating to the Department's disciplinary and personnel actions against Deputy U.S. Marshals (DUSMs) who defended federal property in Portland, Oregon, from left-wing rioters in summer 2020. According to news reports, the Department has declined to pay for legal counsel as these DUSMs defend themselves in civil suits related to Antifa attacks on the federal courthouse in Portland.[1] After Congress expressed concern about the Department's decision, several Senators led by Senator Cotton say that the Department is retaliating against three of the DUSMs, placing them on limited duty and informing them—for the first time—that they are under investigation for their actions in Portland.[2] The Senators note that these personnel actions come almost two years after the Antifa riots, and despite the DUSMs receiving Department recognition and positive performance reviews for their defense of federal property in Portland.[3]

The Committee on the Judiciary has jurisdiction over the Department of Justice and federal law-enforcement matters. These allegations about retaliation against federal law-enforcement personnel are concerning. You should construe this preservation notice as an instruction to take all reasonable steps to prevent the destruction or alteration, whether intentionally or negligently, of all documents, communications, and other information, including electronic information and metadata, that is or may be potentially responsive to this congressional inquiry. This instruction includes all electronic messages sent using official and personal accounts or devices, including records created using text messages, phone-based message applications, or encryption software.

Thank you for your prompt attention to this matter.

Sincerely,

Jim Jordan
Ranking Member

cc: The Honorable Jerrold L. Nadler, Chairman

[1] *See, e.g.*, Aishah *Cotton threatens to block DOJ nominees over refusal to defend US Marshals in 2020 Portland Antifa riots*, Fox News, Jan. 31, 2022.

[2] *See* Letter from Sen. Tom Cotton et al. to Merrick Garland, Att'y Gen. (Apr. 26, 2022).

[3] *Id.*

JERROLD NADLER, New York
CHAIRMAN

JIM JORDAN, Ohio
RANKING MEMBER

ONE HUNDRED SEVENTEENTH CONGRESS

Congress of the United States
House of Representatives

COMMITTEE ON THE JUDICIARY
2138 Rayburn House Office Building
Washington, DC 20515–6216
(202) 225–3951
judiciary.house.gov

April 26, 2022

The Honorable Michael E. Horowitz
Inspector General
U.S. Department of Justice
950 Pennsylvania Avenue N.W., Suite 4706
Washington, DC 20530

Dear Inspector General Horowitz:

We have been contacted by whistleblowers who have made protected disclosures about disturbing and potentially unlawful personnel actions at the Federal Bureau of Investigation. In light of these disclosures, we write to request that the Department of Justice Office of Inspector General (OIG) review whether the FBI has circumvented or violated any applicable policies, procedures, or basic due process protections in taking substantial steps toward terminating the employment of FBI employees who were engaged in protected First Amendment activity on January 6, 2021.

According to several whistleblowers, the FBI is suspending the security clearances of FBI employees for their participation in protected First Amendment activity on January 6, 2021. Among the reasons cited for these actions, the FBI cites "Adjudicative Guideline A — Allegiance to the United States." Because a security clearance is required for FBI positions, these actions mean the FBI has suspended these employees indefinitely. One such employee is [redacted] working in the FBI's [redacted] who also honorably served in the United States military for over 20 years. [redacted] has been working for the FBI for more than a decade. The FBI's formal notice of suspension to [redacted] is enclosed. According to whistleblowers, while on leave, these FBI employees attended public events in Washington, D.C., with their spouses. We have been told that these employees did not enter the United States Capitol, have not been charged with any crime, and have not been contacted by law enforcement about their actions. Given these facts, it is deeply concerning that the FBI would question the allegiance of these employees to the United States as a reason for suspending their security clearances.

Although the Hatch Act prohibits FBI employees from engaging in partisan political campaigns or political management,[1] FBI employees do not give up their fundamental rights to participate in political speech activity. The FBI's personnel actions against these employees therefore raise concerns that the Bureau may be taking significant steps toward firing these

---

[1] 5 U.S.C. § 7323.

employees as retaliation for disfavored political speech. In fact, as documented in a letter received by a second FBI employee who had their security clearance summarily suspended, the FBI has not even specifically informed the employee about the factual predicate for the suspension. The FBI advised the employee there was no right of review or even the opportunity to appeal the decision. Effectively terminating highly trained and experienced personnel without the slightest modicum of due process is unnecessary and unwise. As the OIG has extensively documented through several investigative actions, the FBI is an error-prone agency with a record of mismanagement and pervasive political bias.

We urge you to evaluate the FBI's actions in these matters to determine whether the FBI has circumvented or violated any applicable policies, procedures, or basic due process considerations by taking substantial steps toward terminating the employment of FBI employees on the basis of constitutionally protected speech. We ask that the OIG provide an unclassified report, to the extent possible with a classified appendix where necessary, regarding the findings and conclusions from its review.

Thank you for your attention to this important and pressing matter.

Sincerely,

Jim Jordan
Ranking Member

Enclosure

JERROLD NADLER, New York
CHAIRMAN

JIM JORDAN, Ohio
RANKING MEMBER

ONE HUNDRED SEVENTEENTH CONGRESS

Congress of the United States

House of Representatives

COMMITTEE ON THE JUDICIARY

2138 RAYBURN HOUSE OFFICE BUILDING

WASHINGTON, DC 20515–6216

(202) 225–3951
judiciary.house.gov

April 6, 2022

Ms. Nada Bakos
c/o Central Intelligence Agency
via e-mail

Dear Ms. Bakos:

On October 14, 2020, the *New York Post* published a report detailing how Hunter Biden used the position and influence of his father, now-President Joe Biden, for personal gain with the apparent awareness of President Biden.[1] This article raised doubts about President Biden's earlier denial of ever speaking to his son about his international business dealings.[2] The *Post* reported on an email in which a Ukrainian businessman urged Hunter Biden to "use [his] influence to convey a message / signal, etc. to stop what we consider to be politically motivated actions."[3] In another email, the same businessman thanked Hunter Biden for arranging a meeting with his father, calling it "an honor and pleasure."[4] The *Post* reported that these emails came from a laptop belonging to Hunter Biden that he had abandoned in a Delaware computer shop.[5]

On October 19, 2020, you signed a public statement attempting to discredit the contents of the *New York Post*'s reporting about Hunter Biden.[6] This statement emphasized the national security credentials of you and the other signatories, implying that the assertions and conclusions in the statement were grounded in information unavailable to other Americans. Referencing this unique experience, you wrote:

> It is for all these reasons that we write to say that the arrival on the US political scene of emails purportedly belonging to Vice President Biden's son Hunter, much of it related to his time serving on the Board of the Ukrainian gas company Burisma, has all the classic earmarks of a Russian information operation.[7]

---

[1] Emma-Jo Morris & Gabrielle Fonrouge, *Smoking-gun email reveals how Hunter Biden introduced Ukrainian businessman to VP dad*, N.Y. Post, Oct. 14, 2020.
[2] *E.g.* Nick Givas, *Joe Biden again denies speaking to son about Ukrainian business dealings*, Fox News, Oct. 10, 2019.
[3] Morris & Fonrouge, *supra* note 1.
[4] *Id.*
[5] *Id.*
[6] Jim Clapper et al., Public Statement on the Hunter Biden Emails (Oct. 19, 2020).
[7] *Id.*

Although this statement acknowledged that you had seen no actual "evidence" of Russian involvement with respect to the publication of Hunter Biden's emails, you nonetheless conveyed a "deep[] suspicio[n] that the Russian government played a significant role in the case."[8] Later in the statement, you went further to state a "view"—not merely a suspicion anymore—"that the Russians are involved in the Hunter Biden email issue . . . ."[9]

Your public statement served as a basis for Democrat operatives to try to delegitimize the scandalous allegations about Hunter Biden and the Biden family. On the same day as your statement, *Politico* published a story about the statement, with the conclusive headline, "Hunter Biden story is Russian disinfo, dozens of former intel officials say."[10] Departing from the statement's careful wording, the *Politico* story quoted one signatory to the letter as being confident that "once again the Russians are interfering" in our elections.[11] Fifteen minutes after *Politico* published its story, Jen Psaki, who now serves as Press Secretary to the President, tweeted a link to the *Politico* story.[12] The Biden campaign repeatedly cited your statement to dismiss the allegations against Hunter Biden.[13] During the final presidential debate, Vice President Biden also dismissed concerns about Hunter Biden's international business dealings as part of a "Russian plan."[14]

Your public statement was consistent with a broader effort to minimize and censor the *New York Post*'s reporting about Hunter Biden and the Biden family. National news organizations called the allegations about Hunter Biden "dubious" and a "non-scandal"; CBS News reporter Leslie Stahl said the allegations "can't be verified"; and NPR called it a "waste . . . of time" and a "pure distraction."[15] Separately, Twitter and Facebook restricted access to the *New York Post*'s reporting about Hunter Biden, with Twitter locking the *Post*'s account and Facebook deferring to a so-called independent fact-check that never occurred.[16] These efforts likely affected public awareness of the serious allegations surrounding the Biden family in the crucial weeks before the 2020 election.

We now know from subsequent reporting that the *New York Post*'s article about Hunter Biden was not, as you and your co-signatories alleged, part of a "Russian information

---

[8] *Id.*
[9] *Id.*
[10] Natasha Bertrand, *Hunter Biden story is Russian disinfo, dozens of former intel officials say*, Politico, Oct. 19, 2020.
[11] *Id.*
[12] Tweet by Jen Psaki, Twitter.com (Oct. 19, 2020, 10:45 p.m.), https://twitter.com/jrpsaki/status/1318382779659411458.
[13] *E.g.* Houston Keene, *Flashback: Biden officials pushed angle that Hunter laptop was 'Russian disinfo,'* Fox News, Mar. 17, 2022.
[14] Deirdre Shesgreen, *"Nothing was unethical": Joe Biden defends Hunter Biden under pressure from Trump in debate*, USA Today, Oct. 22, 2020.
[15] Joe Concha, *Media's pre-election burial of Hunter Biden story proves dereliction of duty*, The Hill, Dec. 11, 2020.
[16] *E.g.* Elizabeth Dwoskin, *Facebook and Twitter take unusual steps to limit spread of New York Post story*, Wash. Post, Oct. 15, 2020.

operation."[17] This belated verification of the *Post*'s reporting raises fresh questions about the public statement you signed in October 2020. At best, the public statement was a reckless attempt by you and your co-signatories to erroneously opine about purported election interference. At worse—and more likely—the public statement was a deliberate and coordinated effort to mislead the American people about information relevant to the 2020 presidential election by invoking your national security experience to falsely suggest that the allegations about Hunter Biden were not based in fact.

The concerted effort to suppress public dissemination of the serious allegations about Hunter Biden and the Biden family, as first reported in October 2020 by the *New York Post*, was a grave disservice to American citizens' informed participation in our democracy. We are investigating the role that the public statement played in this effort. Accordingly, please provide the following material:

1. Identify all people with whom you communicated about the inception, drafting, editing, signing, publishing, or promotion of the "Public Statement on the Hunter Biden Emails" dated October 19, 2020; and

2. Produce all documents and communications referring or relating to the "Public Statement on the Hunter Biden Emails" dated October 19, 2020.

Please produce this material as soon as possible but no later than 5:00 p.m. on April 20, 2022. In addition, we request that you take all reasonable steps to preserve records that may be potentially responsive to this inquiry.

Thank you for your attention to this matter.

Sincerely,

Jim Jordan
Ranking Member

Steve Chabot
Member of Congress

Louie Gohmert
Member of Congress

Darrell Issa
Ranking Member
Subcommittee on Courts, Intellectual Property, and the Internet

---

[17] *E.g.* Katie Brenner et al., *Hunter Biden paid tax bill, but broad federal investigation continues*, N.Y. Times, Mar. 16, 2022; Matt Viser et al., *Inside Hunter Biden's multimillion-dollar deals with a Chinese energy company*, Wash. Post, Mar. 30, 2022.

Ken Buck
Ranking Member
Subcommittee on Antitrust, Commercial and Administrative Law

Matt Gaetz
Member of Congress

Mike Johnson
Ranking Member
Subcommittee on the Constitution, Civil Rights and Civil Liberties

Andy Biggs
Ranking Member
Subcommittee on Crime, Terrorism and Homeland Security

Tom McClintock
Ranking Member
Subcommittee on Immigration and Citizenship

W. Gregory Steube
Member of Congress

Tom Tiffany
Member of Congress

Thomas Massie
Member of Congress

Chip Roy
Member of Congress

Dan Bishop
Member of Congress

Michelle Fischbach
Member of Congress

Victoria Spartz
Member of Congress

Scott Fitzgerald
Member of Congress

Cliff Bentz
Member of Congress

Burgess Owens
Member of Congress

JERROLD NADLER, New York
CHAIRMAN

JIM JORDAN, Ohio
RANKING MEMBER

ONE HUNDRED SEVENTEENTH CONGRESS

Congress of the United States
House of Representatives

COMMITTEE ON THE JUDICIARY

2138 RAYBURN HOUSE OFFICE BUILDING

WASHINGTON, DC 20515–6216

(202) 225–3951
judiciary.house.gov

April 6, 2022

Mr. Jeremy Bash
via e-mail

Dear Mr. Bash:

On October 14, 2020, the *New York Post* published a report detailing how Hunter Biden used the position and influence of his father, now-President Joe Biden, for personal gain with the apparent awareness of President Biden.[1] This article raised doubts about President Biden's earlier denial of ever speaking to his son about his international business dealings.[2] The *Post* reported on an email in which a Ukrainian businessman urged Hunter Biden to "use [his] influence to convey a message / signal, etc. to stop what we consider to be politically motivated actions."[3] In another email, the same businessman thanked Hunter Biden for arranging a meeting with his father, calling it "an honor and pleasure."[4] The *Post* reported that these emails came from a laptop belonging to Hunter Biden that he had abandoned in a Delaware computer shop.[5]

On October 19, 2020, you signed a public statement attempting to discredit the contents of the *New York Post*'s reporting about Hunter Biden.[6] This statement emphasized the national security credentials of you and the other signatories, implying that the assertions and conclusions in the statement were grounded in information unavailable to other Americans. Referencing this unique experience, you wrote:

> It is for all these reasons that we write to say that the arrival on the US political scene of emails purportedly belonging to Vice President Biden's son Hunter, much of it related to his time serving on the Board of the Ukrainian gas company Burisma, has all the classic earmarks of a Russian information operation.[7]

---

[1] Emma-Jo Morris & Gabrielle Fonrouge, *Smoking-gun email reveals how Hunter Biden introduced Ukrainian businessman to VP dad*, N.Y. Post, Oct. 14, 2020.
[2] *E.g.* Nick Givas, *Joe Biden again denies speaking to son about Ukrainian business dealings*, Fox News, Oct. 10, 2019.
[3] Morris & Fonrouge, *supra* note 1.
[4] *Id.*
[5] *Id.*
[6] Jim Clapper et al., Public Statement on the Hunter Biden Emails (Oct. 19, 2020).
[7] *Id.*

Although this statement acknowledged that you had seen no actual "evidence" of Russian involvement with respect to the publication of Hunter Biden's emails, you nonetheless conveyed a "deep[] suspicio[n] that the Russian government played a significant role in the case."[8] Later in the statement, you went further to state a "view"—not merely a suspicion anymore—"that the Russians are involved in the Hunter Biden email issue . . . ."[9]

Your public statement served as a basis for Democrat operatives to try to delegitimize the scandalous allegations about Hunter Biden and the Biden family. On the same day as your statement, *Politico* published a story about the statement, with the conclusive headline, "Hunter Biden story is Russian disinfo, dozens of former intel officials say."[10] Departing from the statement's careful wording, the *Politico* story quoted one signatory to the letter as being confident that "once again the Russians are interfering" in our elections.[11] Fifteen minutes after *Politico* published its story, Jen Psaki, who now serves as Press Secretary to the President, tweeted a link to the *Politico* story.[12] The Biden campaign repeatedly cited your statement to dismiss the allegations against Hunter Biden.[13] During the final presidential debate, Vice President Biden also dismissed concerns about Hunter Biden's international business dealings as part of a "Russian plan."[14]

Your public statement was consistent with a broader effort to minimize and censor the *New York Post*'s reporting about Hunter Biden and the Biden family. National news organizations called the allegations about Hunter Biden "dubious" and a "non-scandal"; CBS News reporter Leslie Stahl said the allegations "can't be verified"; and NPR called it a "waste . . . of time" and a "pure distraction."[15] Separately, Twitter and Facebook restricted access to the *New York Post*'s reporting about Hunter Biden, with Twitter locking the *Post*'s account and Facebook deferring to a so-called independent fact-check that never occurred.[16] These efforts likely affected public awareness of the serious allegations surrounding the Biden family in the crucial weeks before the 2020 election.

We now know from subsequent reporting that the *New York Post*'s article about Hunter Biden was not, as you and your co-signatories alleged, part of a "Russian information

---

[8] *Id.*
[9] *Id.*
[10] Natasha Bertrand, *Hunter Biden story is Russian disinfo, dozens of former intel officials say*, Politico, Oct. 19, 2020.
[11] *Id.*
[12] Tweet by Jen Psaki, Twitter.com (Oct. 19, 2020, 10:45 p.m.), https://twitter.com/jrpsaki/status/1318382779659411458.
[13] *E.g.* Houston Keene, *Flashback: Biden officials pushed angle that Hunter laptop was 'Russian disinfo,'* Fox News, Mar. 17, 2022.
[14] Deirdre Shesgreen, *"Nothing was unethical": Joe Biden defends Hunter Biden under pressure from Trump in debate*, USA Today, Oct. 22, 2020.
[15] Joe Concha, *Media's pre-election burial of Hunter Biden story proves dereliction of duty*, The Hill, Dec. 11, 2020.
[16] *E.g.* Elizabeth Dwoskin, *Facebook and Twitter take unusual steps to limit spread of New York Post story*, Wash. Post, Oct. 15, 2020.

operation."[17] This belated verification of the *Post*'s reporting raises fresh questions about the public statement you signed in October 2020. At best, the public statement was a reckless attempt by you and your co-signatories to erroneously opine about purported election interference. At worse—and more likely—the public statement was a deliberate and coordinated effort to mislead the American people about information relevant to the 2020 presidential election by invoking your national security experience to falsely suggest that the allegations about Hunter Biden were not based in fact.

The concerted effort to suppress public dissemination of the serious allegations about Hunter Biden and the Biden family, as first reported in October 2020 by the *New York Post*, was a grave disservice to American citizens' informed participation in our democracy. We are investigating the role that the public statement played in this effort. Accordingly, please provide the following material:

1. Identify all people with whom you communicated about the inception, drafting, editing, signing, publishing, or promotion of the "Public Statement on the Hunter Biden Emails" dated October 19, 2020; and

2. Produce all documents and communications referring or relating to the "Public Statement on the Hunter Biden Emails" dated October 19, 2020.

Please produce this material as soon as possible but no later than 5:00 p.m. on April 20, 2022. In addition, we request that you take all reasonable steps to preserve records that may be potentially responsive to this inquiry.

Thank you for your attention to this matter.

Sincerely,

Jim Jordan
Ranking Member

Steve Chabot
Member of Congress

Louie Gohmert
Member of Congress

Darrell Issa
Ranking Member
Subcommittee on Courts, Intellectual Property, and the Internet

---

[17] *E.g.* Katie Brenner et al., *Hunter Biden paid tax bill, but broad federal investigation continues*, N.Y. Times, Mar. 16, 2022; Matt Viser et al., *Inside Hunter Biden's multimillion-dollar deals with a Chinese energy company*, Wash. Post, Mar. 30, 2022.

Ken Buck
Ranking Member
Subcommittee on Antitrust, Commercial and Administrative Law

Matt Gaetz
Member of Congress

Mike Johnson
Ranking Member
Subcommittee on the Constitution, Civil Rights and Civil Liberties

Andy Biggs
Ranking Member
Subcommittee on Crime, Terrorism and Homeland Security

Tom McClintock
Ranking Member
Subcommittee on Immigration and Citizenship

W. Gregory Steube
Member of Congress

Tom Tiffany
Member of Congress

Thomas Massie
Member of Congress

Chip Roy
Member of Congress

Dan Bishop
Member of Congress

Michelle Fischbach
Member of Congress

Victoria Spartz
Member of Congress

Scott Fitzgerald
Member of Congress

Cliff Bentz
Member of Congress

Burgess Owens
Member of Congress

JERROLD NADLER, New York
CHAIRMAN

JIM JORDAN, Ohio
RANKING MEMBER

ONE HUNDRED SEVENTEENTH CONGRESS

Congress of the United States
House of Representatives

COMMITTEE ON THE JUDICIARY
2138 RAYBURN HOUSE OFFICE BUILDING
WASHINGTON, DC 20515-6216
(202) 225-3951
judiciary.house.gov

April 6, 2022

Ms. Patty Brandmaier
via e-mail

Dear Ms. Brandmaier:

On October 14, 2020, the *New York Post* published a report detailing how Hunter Biden used the position and influence of his father, now-President Joe Biden, for personal gain with the apparent awareness of President Biden.[1] This article raised doubts about President Biden's earlier denial of ever speaking to his son about his international business dealings.[2] The *Post* reported on an email in which a Ukrainian businessman urged Hunter Biden to "use [his] influence to convey a message / signal, etc. to stop what we consider to be politically motivated actions."[3] In another email, the same businessman thanked Hunter Biden for arranging a meeting with his father, calling it "an honor and pleasure."[4] The *Post* reported that these emails came from a laptop belonging to Hunter Biden that he had abandoned in a Delaware computer shop.[5]

On October 19, 2020, you signed a public statement attempting to discredit the contents of the *New York Post*'s reporting about Hunter Biden.[6] This statement emphasized the national security credentials of you and the other signatories, implying that the assertions and conclusions in the statement were grounded in information unavailable to other Americans. Referencing this unique experience, you wrote:

> It is for all these reasons that we write to say that the arrival on the US political scene of emails purportedly belonging to Vice President Biden's son Hunter, much of it related to his time serving on the Board of the Ukrainian gas company Burisma, has all the classic earmarks of a Russian information operation.[7]

---

[1] Emma-Jo Morris & Gabrielle Fonrouge, *Smoking-gun email reveals how Hunter Biden introduced Ukrainian businessman to VP dad*, N.Y. Post, Oct. 14, 2020.
[2] *E.g.* Nick Givas, *Joe Biden again denies speaking to son about Ukrainian business dealings*, Fox News, Oct. 10, 2019.
[3] Morris & Fonrouge, *supra* note 1.
[4] *Id.*
[5] *Id.*
[6] Jim Clapper et al., Public Statement on the Hunter Biden Emails (Oct. 19, 2020).
[7] *Id.*

Although this statement acknowledged that you had seen no actual "evidence" of Russian involvement with respect to the publication of Hunter Biden's emails, you nonetheless conveyed a "deep[] suspicio[n] that the Russian government played a significant role in the case."[8] Later in the statement, you went further to state a "view"—not merely a suspicion anymore—"that the Russians are involved in the Hunter Biden email issue . . . ."[9]

Your public statement served as a basis for Democrat operatives to try to delegitimize the scandalous allegations about Hunter Biden and the Biden family. On the same day as your statement, *Politico* published a story about the statement, with the conclusive headline, "Hunter Biden story is Russian disinfo, dozens of former intel officials say."[10] Departing from the statement's careful wording, the *Politico* story quoted one signatory to the letter as being confident that "once again the Russians are interfering" in our elections.[11] Fifteen minutes after *Politico* published its story, Jen Psaki, who now serves as Press Secretary to the President, tweeted a link to the *Politico* story.[12] The Biden campaign repeatedly cited your statement to dismiss the allegations against Hunter Biden.[13] During the final presidential debate, Vice President Biden also dismissed concerns about Hunter Biden's international business dealings as part of a "Russian plan."[14]

Your public statement was consistent with a broader effort to minimize and censor the *New York Post*'s reporting about Hunter Biden and the Biden family. National news organizations called the allegations about Hunter Biden "dubious" and a "non-scandal"; CBS News reporter Leslie Stahl said the allegations "can't be verified"; and NPR called it a "waste . . . of time" and a "pure distraction."[15] Separately, Twitter and Facebook restricted access to the *New York Post*'s reporting about Hunter Biden, with Twitter locking the *Post*'s account and Facebook deferring to a so-called independent fact-check that never occurred.[16] These efforts likely affected public awareness of the serious allegations surrounding the Biden family in the crucial weeks before the 2020 election.

We now know from subsequent reporting that the *New York Post*'s article about Hunter Biden was not, as you and your co-signatories alleged, part of a "Russian information

---

[8] *Id.*
[9] *Id.*
[10] Natasha Bertrand, *Hunter Biden story is Russian disinfo, dozens of former intel officials say*, Politico, Oct. 19, 2020.
[11] *Id.*
[12] Tweet by Jen Psaki, Twitter.com (Oct. 19, 2020, 10:45 p.m.), https://twitter.com/jrpsaki/status/1318382779659411458.
[13] *E.g.* Houston Keene, *Flashback: Biden officials pushed angle that Hunter laptop was 'Russian disinfo,'* Fox News, Mar. 17, 2022.
[14] Deirdre Shesgreen, *"Nothing was unethical": Joe Biden defends Hunter Biden under pressure from Trump in debate*, USA Today, Oct. 22, 2020.
[15] Joe Concha, *Media's pre-election burial of Hunter Biden story proves dereliction of duty*, The Hill, Dec. 11, 2020.
[16] *E.g.* Elizabeth Dwoskin, *Facebook and Twitter take unusual steps to limit spread of New York Post story*, Wash. Post, Oct. 15, 2020.

operation."[17] This belated verification of the *Post*'s reporting raises fresh questions about the public statement you signed in October 2020. At best, the public statement was a reckless attempt by you and your co-signatories to erroneously opine about purported election interference. At worse—and more likely—the public statement was a deliberate and coordinated effort to mislead the American people about information relevant to the 2020 presidential election by invoking your national security experience to falsely suggest that the allegations about Hunter Biden were not based in fact.

The concerted effort to suppress public dissemination of the serious allegations about Hunter Biden and the Biden family, as first reported in October 2020 by the *New York Post*, was a grave disservice to American citizens' informed participation in our democracy. We are investigating the role that the public statement played in this effort. Accordingly, please provide the following material:

1. Identify all people with whom you communicated about the inception, drafting, editing, signing, publishing, or promotion of the "Public Statement on the Hunter Biden Emails" dated October 19, 2020; and

2. Produce all documents and communications referring or relating to the "Public Statement on the Hunter Biden Emails" dated October 19, 2020.

Please produce this material as soon as possible but no later than 5:00 p.m. on April 20, 2022. In addition, we request that you take all reasonable steps to preserve records that may be potentially responsive to this inquiry.

Thank you for your attention to this matter.

Sincerely,

Jim Jordan
Ranking Member

Steve Chabot
Member of Congress

Louie Gohmert
Member of Congress

Darrell Issa
Ranking Member
Subcommittee on Courts, Intellectual Property, and the Internet

---

[17] *E.g.* Katie Brenner et al., *Hunter Biden paid tax bill, but broad federal investigation continues*, N.Y. Times, Mar. 16, 2022; Matt Viser et al., *Inside Hunter Biden's multimillion-dollar deals with a Chinese energy company*, Wash. Post, Mar. 30, 2022.

Ken Buck
Ranking Member
Subcommittee on Antitrust, Commercial and Administrative Law

Matt Gaetz
Member of Congress

Mike Johnson
Ranking Member
Subcommittee on the Constitution, Civil Rights and Civil Liberties

Andy Biggs
Ranking Member
Subcommittee on Crime, Terrorism and Homeland Security

Tom McClintock
Ranking Member
Subcommittee on Immigration and Citizenship

W. Gregory Steube
Member of Congress

Tom Tiffany
Member of Congress

Thomas Massie
Member of Congress

Chip Roy
Member of Congress

Dan Bishop
Member of Congress

Michelle Fischbach
Member of Congress

Victoria Spartz
Member of Congress

Scott Fitzgerald
Member of Congress

Cliff Bentz
Member of Congress

Burgess Owens
Member of Congress

JERROLD NADLER, New York
CHAIRMAN

JIM JORDAN, Ohio
RANKING MEMBER

ONE HUNDRED SEVENTEENTH CONGRESS
Congress of the United States
House of Representatives
COMMITTEE ON THE JUDICIARY
2138 RAYBURN HOUSE OFFICE BUILDING
WASHINGTON, DC 20515-6216
(202) 225-3951
judiciary.house.gov

April 6, 2022

The Honorable John Brennan
Strauss Center
2315 Red River Street
Austin, Texas 78712

Dear Mr. Brennan:

On October 14, 2020, the *New York Post* published a report detailing how Hunter Biden used the position and influence of his father, now-President Joe Biden, for personal gain with the apparent awareness of President Biden.[1] This article raised doubts about President Biden's earlier denial of ever speaking to his son about his international business dealings.[2] The *Post* reported on an email in which a Ukrainian businessman urged Hunter Biden to "use [his] influence to convey a message / signal, etc. to stop what we consider to be politically motivated actions."[3] In another email, the same businessman thanked Hunter Biden for arranging a meeting with his father, calling it "an honor and pleasure."[4] The *Post* reported that these emails came from a laptop belonging to Hunter Biden that he had abandoned in a Delaware computer shop.[5]

On October 19, 2020, you signed a public statement attempting to discredit the contents of the *New York Post*'s reporting about Hunter Biden.[6] This statement emphasized the national security credentials of you and the other signatories, implying that the assertions and conclusions in the statement were grounded in information unavailable to other Americans. Referencing this unique experience, you wrote:

> It is for all these reasons that we write to say that the arrival on the US political scene of emails purportedly belonging to Vice President Biden's son Hunter, much of it related to his time serving on the Board of the Ukrainian gas company Burisma, has all the classic earmarks of a Russian information operation.[7]

---

[1] Emma-Jo Morris & Gabrielle Fonrouge, *Smoking-gun email reveals how Hunter Biden introduced Ukrainian businessman to VP dad*, N.Y. Post, Oct. 14, 2020.
[2] *E.g.* Nick Givas, *Joe Biden again denies speaking to son about Ukrainian business dealings*, Fox News, Oct. 10, 2019.
[3] Morris & Fonrouge, *supra* note 1.
[4] *Id.*
[5] *Id.*
[6] Jim Clapper et al., Public Statement on the Hunter Biden Emails (Oct. 19, 2020).
[7] *Id.*

Although this statement acknowledged that you had seen no actual "evidence" of Russian involvement with respect to the publication of Hunter Biden's emails, you nonetheless conveyed a "deep[] suspicio[n] that the Russian government played a significant role in the case."[8] Later in the statement, you went further to state a "view"—not merely a suspicion anymore—"that the Russians are involved in the Hunter Biden email issue . . . ."[9]

Your public statement served as a basis for Democrat operatives to try to delegitimize the scandalous allegations about Hunter Biden and the Biden family. On the same day as your statement, *Politico* published a story about the statement, with the conclusive headline, "Hunter Biden story is Russian disinfo, dozens of former intel officials say."[10] Departing from the statement's careful wording, the *Politico* story quoted one signatory to the letter as being confident that "once again the Russians are interfering" in our elections.[11] Fifteen minutes after *Politico* published its story, Jen Psaki, who now serves as Press Secretary to the President, tweeted a link to the *Politico* story.[12] The Biden campaign repeatedly cited your statement to dismiss the allegations against Hunter Biden.[13] During the final presidential debate, Vice President Biden also dismissed concerns about Hunter Biden's international business dealings as part of a "Russian plan."[14]

Your public statement was consistent with a broader effort to minimize and censor the *New York Post*'s reporting about Hunter Biden and the Biden family. National news organizations called the allegations about Hunter Biden "dubious" and a "non-scandal"; CBS News reporter Leslie Stahl said the allegations "can't be verified"; and NPR called it a "waste . . . of time" and a "pure distraction."[15] Separately, Twitter and Facebook restricted access to the *New York Post*'s reporting about Hunter Biden, with Twitter locking the *Post*'s account and Facebook deferring to a so-called independent fact-check that never occurred.[16] These efforts likely affected public awareness of the serious allegations surrounding the Biden family in the crucial weeks before the 2020 election.

We now know from subsequent reporting that the *New York Post*'s article about Hunter Biden was not, as you and your co-signatories alleged, part of a "Russian information

---

[8] *Id.*
[9] *Id.*
[10] Natasha Bertrand, *Hunter Biden story is Russian disinfo, dozens of former intel officials say*, Politico, Oct. 19, 2020.
[11] *Id.*
[12] Tweet by Jen Psaki, Twitter.com (Oct. 19, 2020, 10:45 p.m.), https://twitter.com/jrpsaki/status/1318382779659411458.
[13] *E.g.* Houston Keene, *Flashback: Biden officials pushed angle that Hunter laptop was 'Russian disinfo,'* Fox News, Mar. 17, 2022.
[14] Deirdre Shesgreen, *"Nothing was unethical": Joe Biden defends Hunter Biden under pressure from Trump in debate*, USA Today, Oct. 22, 2020.
[15] Joe Concha, *Media's pre-election burial of Hunter Biden story proves dereliction of duty*, The Hill, Dec. 11, 2020.
[16] *E.g.* Elizabeth Dwoskin, *Facebook and Twitter take unusual steps to limit spread of New York Post story*, Wash. Post, Oct. 15, 2020.

operation."[17] This belated verification of the *Post*'s reporting raises fresh questions about the public statement you signed in October 2020. At best, the public statement was a reckless attempt by you and your co-signatories to erroneously opine about purported election interference. At worse—and more likely—the public statement was a deliberate and coordinated effort to mislead the American people about information relevant to the 2020 presidential election by invoking your national security experience to falsely suggest that the allegations about Hunter Biden were not based in fact.

The concerted effort to suppress public dissemination of the serious allegations about Hunter Biden and the Biden family, as first reported in October 2020 by the *New York Post*, was a grave disservice to American citizens' informed participation in our democracy. We are investigating the role that the public statement played in this effort. Accordingly, please provide the following material:

1. Identify all people with whom you communicated about the inception, drafting, editing, signing, publishing, or promotion of the "Public Statement on the Hunter Biden Emails" dated October 19, 2020; and

2. Produce all documents and communications referring or relating to the "Public Statement on the Hunter Biden Emails" dated October 19, 2020.

Please produce this material as soon as possible but no later than 5:00 p.m. on April 20, 2022. In addition, we request that you take all reasonable steps to preserve records that may be potentially responsive to this inquiry.

Thank you for your attention to this matter.

Sincerely,

Jim Jordan
Ranking Member

Steve Chabot
Member of Congress

Louie Gohmert
Member of Congress

Darrell Issa
Ranking Member
Subcommittee on Courts, Intellectual Property, and the Internet

[17] *E.g.* Katie Brenner et al., *Hunter Biden paid tax bill, but broad federal investigation continues*, N.Y. Times, Mar. 16, 2022; Matt Viser et al., *Inside Hunter Biden's multimillion-dollar deals with a Chinese energy company*, Wash. Post, Mar. 30, 2022.

Ken Buck
Ranking Member
Subcommittee on Antitrust, Commercial and Administrative Law

Matt Gaetz
Member of Congress

Mike Johnson
Ranking Member
Subcommittee on the Constitution, Civil Rights and Civil Liberties

Andy Biggs
Ranking Member
Subcommittee on Crime, Terrorism and Homeland Security

Tom McClintock
Ranking Member
Subcommittee on Immigration and Citizenship

W. Gregory Steube
Member of Congress

Tom Tiffany
Member of Congress

Thomas Massie
Member of Congress

Chip Roy
Member of Congress

Dan Bishop
Member of Congress

Michelle Fischbach
Member of Congress

Victoria Spartz
Member of Congress

Scott Fitzgerald
Member of Congress

Cliff Bentz
Member of Congress

Burgess Owens
Member of Congress

JERROLD NADLER, New York
CHAIRMAN

JIM JORDAN, Ohio
RANKING MEMBER

ONE HUNDRED SEVENTEENTH CONGRESS

Congress of the United States
House of Representatives
COMMITTEE ON THE JUDICIARY
2138 RAYBURN HOUSE OFFICE BUILDING
WASHINGTON, DC 20515-6216
(202) 225-3951
judiciary.house.gov

April 6, 2022

Dr. James B. Bruce
via e-mail

Dear Dr. Bruce:

On October 14, 2020, the *New York Post* published a report detailing how Hunter Biden used the position and influence of his father, now-President Joe Biden, for personal gain with the apparent awareness of President Biden.[1] This article raised doubts about President Biden's earlier denial of ever speaking to his son about his international business dealings.[2] The *Post* reported on an email in which a Ukrainian businessman urged Hunter Biden to "use [his] influence to convey a message / signal, etc. to stop what we consider to be politically motivated actions."[3] In another email, the same businessman thanked Hunter Biden for arranging a meeting with his father, calling it "an honor and pleasure."[4] The *Post* reported that these emails came from a laptop belonging to Hunter Biden that he had abandoned in a Delaware computer shop.[5]

On October 19, 2020, you signed a public statement attempting to discredit the contents of the *New York Post*'s reporting about Hunter Biden.[6] This statement emphasized the national security credentials of you and the other signatories, implying that the assertions and conclusions in the statement were grounded in information unavailable to other Americans. Referencing this unique experience, you wrote:

> It is for all these reasons that we write to say that the arrival on the US political scene of emails purportedly belonging to Vice President Biden's son Hunter, much of it related to his time serving on the Board of the Ukrainian gas company Burisma, has all the classic earmarks of a Russian information operation.[7]

---

[1] Emma-Jo Morris & Gabrielle Fonrouge, *Smoking-gun email reveals how Hunter Biden introduced Ukrainian businessman to VP dad*, N.Y. Post, Oct. 14, 2020.
[2] *E.g.* Nick Givas, *Joe Biden again denies speaking to son about Ukrainian business dealings*, Fox News, Oct. 10, 2019.
[3] Morris & Fonrouge, *supra* note 1.
[4] *Id.*
[5] *Id.*
[6] Jim Clapper et al., Public Statement on the Hunter Biden Emails (Oct. 19, 2020).
[7] *Id.*

Although this statement acknowledged that you had seen no actual "evidence" of Russian involvement with respect to the publication of Hunter Biden's emails, you nonetheless conveyed a "deep[] suspicio[n] that the Russian government played a significant role in the case."[8] Later in the statement, you went further to state a "view"—not merely a suspicion anymore—"that the Russians are involved in the Hunter Biden email issue . . . ."[9]

Your public statement served as a basis for Democrat operatives to try to delegitimize the scandalous allegations about Hunter Biden and the Biden family. On the same day as your statement, *Politico* published a story about the statement, with the conclusive headline, "Hunter Biden story is Russian disinfo, dozens of former intel officials say."[10] Departing from the statement's careful wording, the *Politico* story quoted one signatory to the letter as being confident that "once again the Russians are interfering" in our elections.[11] Fifteen minutes after *Politico* published its story, Jen Psaki, who now serves as Press Secretary to the President, tweeted a link to the *Politico* story.[12] The Biden campaign repeatedly cited your statement to dismiss the allegations against Hunter Biden.[13] During the final presidential debate, Vice President Biden also dismissed concerns about Hunter Biden's international business dealings as part of a "Russian plan."[14]

Your public statement was consistent with a broader effort to minimize and censor the *New York Post*'s reporting about Hunter Biden and the Biden family. National news organizations called the allegations about Hunter Biden "dubious" and a "non-scandal"; CBS News reporter Leslie Stahl said the allegations "can't be verified"; and NPR called it a "waste . . . of time" and a "pure distraction."[15] Separately, Twitter and Facebook restricted access to the *New York Post*'s reporting about Hunter Biden, with Twitter locking the *Post*'s account and Facebook deferring to a so-called independent fact-check that never occurred.[16] These efforts likely affected public awareness of the serious allegations surrounding the Biden family in the crucial weeks before the 2020 election.

We now know from subsequent reporting that the *New York Post*'s article about Hunter Biden was not, as you and your co-signatories alleged, part of a "Russian information

---

[8] *Id.*
[9] *Id.*
[10] Natasha Bertrand, *Hunter Biden story is Russian disinfo, dozens of former intel officials say*, Politico, Oct. 19, 2020.
[11] *Id.*
[12] Tweet by Jen Psaki, Twitter.com (Oct. 19, 2020, 10:45 p.m.), https://twitter.com/jrpsaki/status/1318382779659411458.
[13] *E.g.* Houston Keene, *Flashback: Biden officials pushed angle that Hunter laptop was 'Russian disinfo,'* Fox News, Mar. 17, 2022.
[14] Deirdre Shesgreen, *"Nothing was unethical": Joe Biden defends Hunter Biden under pressure from Trump in debate*, USA Today, Oct. 22, 2020.
[15] Joe Concha, *Media's pre-election burial of Hunter Biden story proves dereliction of duty*, The Hill, Dec. 11, 2020.
[16] *E.g.* Elizabeth Dwoskin, *Facebook and Twitter take unusual steps to limit spread of New York Post story*, Wash. Post, Oct. 15, 2020.

operation."[17] This belated verification of the *Post*'s reporting raises fresh questions about the public statement you signed in October 2020. At best, the public statement was a reckless attempt by you and your co-signatories to erroneously opine about purported election interference. At worse—and more likely—the public statement was a deliberate and coordinated effort to mislead the American people about information relevant to the 2020 presidential election by invoking your national security experience to falsely suggest that the allegations about Hunter Biden were not based in fact.

The concerted effort to suppress public dissemination of the serious allegations about Hunter Biden and the Biden family, as first reported in October 2020 by the *New York Post*, was a grave disservice to American citizens' informed participation in our democracy. We are investigating the role that the public statement played in this effort. Accordingly, please provide the following material:

1. Identify all people with whom you communicated about the inception, drafting, editing, signing, publishing, or promotion of the "Public Statement on the Hunter Biden Emails" dated October 19, 2020; and

2. Produce all documents and communications referring or relating to the "Public Statement on the Hunter Biden Emails" dated October 19, 2020.

Please produce this material as soon as possible but no later than 5:00 p.m. on April 20, 2022. In addition, we request that you take all reasonable steps to preserve records that may be potentially responsive to this inquiry.

Thank you for your attention to this matter.

Sincerely,

Jim Jordan
Ranking Member

Steve Chabot
Member of Congress

Louie Gohmert
Member of Congress

Darrell Issa
Ranking Member
Subcommittee on Courts, Intellectual Property, and the Internet

---

[17] *E.g.* Katie Brenner et al., *Hunter Biden paid tax bill, but broad federal investigation continues*, N.Y. Times, Mar. 16, 2022; Matt Viser et al., *Inside Hunter Biden's multimillion-dollar deals with a Chinese energy company*, Wash. Post, Mar. 30, 2022.

Ken Buck
Ranking Member
Subcommittee on Antitrust, Commercial and Administrative Law

Matt Gaetz
Member of Congress

Mike Johnson
Ranking Member
Subcommittee on the Constitution, Civil Rights and Civil Liberties

Andy Biggs
Ranking Member
Subcommittee on Crime, Terrorism and Homeland Security

Tom McClintock
Ranking Member
Subcommittee on Immigration and Citizenship

W. Gregory Steube
Member of Congress

Tom Tiffany
Member of Congress

Thomas Massie
Member of Congress

Chip Roy
Member of Congress

Dan Bishop
Member of Congress

Michelle Fischbach
Member of Congress

Victoria Spartz
Member of Congress

Scott Fitzgerald
Member of Congress

Cliff Bentz
Member of Congress

Burgess Owens
Member of Congress

JERROLD NADLER, New York
CHAIRMAN

JIM JORDAN, Ohio
RANKING MEMBER

ONE HUNDRED SEVENTEENTH CONGRESS

Congress of the United States
House of Representatives

COMMITTEE ON THE JUDICIARY
2138 RAYBURN HOUSE OFFICE BUILDING
WASHINGTON, DC 20515-6216
(202) 225-3951
judiciary.house.gov

April 6, 2022

The Honorable David B. Buckley
via e-mail

Dear Mr. Buckley:

On October 14, 2020, the *New York Post* published a report detailing how Hunter Biden used the position and influence of his father, now-President Joe Biden, for personal gain with the apparent awareness of President Biden.[1] This article raised doubts about President Biden's earlier denial of ever speaking to his son about his international business dealings.[2] The *Post* reported on an email in which a Ukrainian businessman urged Hunter Biden to "use [his] influence to convey a message / signal, etc. to stop what we consider to be politically motivated actions."[3] In another email, the same businessman thanked Hunter Biden for arranging a meeting with his father, calling it "an honor and pleasure."[4] The *Post* reported that these emails came from a laptop belonging to Hunter Biden that he had abandoned in a Delaware computer shop.[5]

On October 19, 2020, you signed a public statement attempting to discredit the contents of the *New York Post*'s reporting about Hunter Biden.[6] This statement emphasized the national security credentials of you and the other signatories, implying that the assertions and conclusions in the statement were grounded in information unavailable to other Americans. Referencing this unique experience, you wrote:

> It is for all these reasons that we write to say that the arrival on the US political scene of emails purportedly belonging to Vice President Biden's son Hunter, much of it related to his time serving on the Board of the Ukrainian gas company Burisma, has all the classic earmarks of a Russian information operation.[7]

---

[1] Emma-Jo Morris & Gabrielle Fonrouge, *Smoking-gun email reveals how Hunter Biden introduced Ukrainian businessman to VP dad*, N.Y. Post, Oct. 14, 2020.
[2] *E.g.* Nick Givas, *Joe Biden again denies speaking to son about Ukrainian business dealings*, Fox News, Oct. 10, 2019.
[3] Morris & Fonrouge, *supra* note 1.
[4] *Id.*
[5] *Id.*
[6] Jim Clapper et al., Public Statement on the Hunter Biden Emails (Oct. 19, 2020).
[7] *Id.*

Although this statement acknowledged that you had seen no actual "evidence" of Russian involvement with respect to the publication of Hunter Biden's emails, you nonetheless conveyed a "deep[] suspicio[n] that the Russian government played a significant role in the case."[8] Later in the statement, you went further to state a "view"—not merely a suspicion anymore—"that the Russians are involved in the Hunter Biden email issue . . . ."[9]

Your public statement served as a basis for Democrat operatives to try to delegitimize the scandalous allegations about Hunter Biden and the Biden family. On the same day as your statement, *Politico* published a story about the statement, with the conclusive headline, "Hunter Biden story is Russian disinfo, dozens of former intel officials say."[10] Departing from the statement's careful wording, the *Politico* story quoted one signatory to the letter as being confident that "once again the Russians are interfering" in our elections.[11] Fifteen minutes after *Politico* published its story, Jen Psaki, who now serves as Press Secretary to the President, tweeted a link to the *Politico* story.[12] The Biden campaign repeatedly cited your statement to dismiss the allegations against Hunter Biden.[13] During the final presidential debate, Vice President Biden also dismissed concerns about Hunter Biden's international business dealings as part of a "Russian plan."[14]

Your public statement was consistent with a broader effort to minimize and censor the *New York Post*'s reporting about Hunter Biden and the Biden family. National news organizations called the allegations about Hunter Biden "dubious" and a "non-scandal"; CBS News reporter Leslie Stahl said the allegations "can't be verified"; and NPR called it a "waste . . . of time" and a "pure distraction."[15] Separately, Twitter and Facebook restricted access to the *New York Post*'s reporting about Hunter Biden, with Twitter locking the *Post*'s account and Facebook deferring to a so-called independent fact-check that never occurred.[16] These efforts likely affected public awareness of the serious allegations surrounding the Biden family in the crucial weeks before the 2020 election.

We now know from subsequent reporting that the *New York Post*'s article about Hunter Biden was not, as you and your co-signatories alleged, part of a "Russian information

---

[8] *Id.*
[9] *Id.*
[10] Natasha Bertrand, *Hunter Biden story is Russian disinfo, dozens of former intel officials say*, Politico, Oct. 19, 2020.
[11] *Id.*
[12] Tweet by Jen Psaki, Twitter.com (Oct. 19, 2020, 10:45 p.m.), https://twitter.com/jrpsaki/status/1318382779659411458.
[13] *E.g.* Houston Keene, *Flashback: Biden officials pushed angle that Hunter laptop was 'Russian disinfo,'* Fox News, Mar. 17, 2022.
[14] Deirdre Shesgreen, *"Nothing was unethical": Joe Biden defends Hunter Biden under pressure from Trump in debate*, USA Today, Oct. 22, 2020.
[15] Joe Concha, *Media's pre-election burial of Hunter Biden story proves dereliction of duty*, The Hill, Dec. 11, 2020.
[16] *E.g.* Elizabeth Dwoskin, *Facebook and Twitter take unusual steps to limit spread of New York Post story*, Wash. Post, Oct. 15, 2020.

operation."[17] This belated verification of the *Post*'s reporting raises fresh questions about the public statement you signed in October 2020. At best, the public statement was a reckless attempt by you and your co-signatories to erroneously opine about purported election interference. At worse—and more likely—the public statement was a deliberate and coordinated effort to mislead the American people about information relevant to the 2020 presidential election by invoking your national security experience to falsely suggest that the allegations about Hunter Biden were not based in fact.

The concerted effort to suppress public dissemination of the serious allegations about Hunter Biden and the Biden family, as first reported in October 2020 by the *New York Post*, was a grave disservice to American citizens' informed participation in our democracy. We are investigating the role that the public statement played in this effort. Accordingly, please provide the following material:

1. Identify all people with whom you communicated about the inception, drafting, editing, signing, publishing, or promotion of the "Public Statement on the Hunter Biden Emails" dated October 19, 2020; and

2. Produce all documents and communications referring or relating to the "Public Statement on the Hunter Biden Emails" dated October 19, 2020.

Please produce this material as soon as possible but no later than 5:00 p.m. on April 20, 2022. In addition, we request that you take all reasonable steps to preserve records that may be potentially responsive to this inquiry.

Thank you for your attention to this matter.

Sincerely,

Jim Jordan
Ranking Member

Steve Chabot
Member of Congress

Louie Gohmert
Member of Congress

Darrell Issa
Ranking Member
Subcommittee on Courts, Intellectual Property, and the Internet

---

[17] *E.g.* Katie Brenner et al., *Hunter Biden paid tax bill, but broad federal investigation continues*, N.Y. Times, Mar. 16, 2022; Matt Viser et al., *Inside Hunter Biden's multimillion-dollar deals with a Chinese energy company*, Wash. Post, Mar. 30, 2022.

Ken Buck
Ranking Member
Subcommittee on Antitrust, Commercial and Administrative Law

Matt Gaetz
Member of Congress

Mike Johnson
Ranking Member
Subcommittee on the Constitution, Civil Rights and Civil Liberties

Andy Biggs
Ranking Member
Subcommittee on Crime, Terrorism and Homeland Security

Tom McClintock
Ranking Member
Subcommittee on Immigration and Citizenship

W. Gregory Steube
Member of Congress

Tom Tiffany
Member of Congress

Thomas Massie
Member of Congress

Chip Roy
Member of Congress

Dan Bishop
Member of Congress

Michelle Fischbach
Member of Congress

Victoria Spartz
Member of Congress

Scott Fitzgerald
Member of Congress

Cliff Bentz
Member of Congress

Burgess Owens
Member of Congress

JERROLD NADLER, New York
CHAIRMAN

JIM JORDAN, Ohio
RANKING MEMBER

ONE HUNDRED SEVENTEENTH CONGRESS

Congress of the United States

House of Representatives

COMMITTEE ON THE JUDICIARY

2138 RAYBURN HOUSE OFFICE BUILDING

WASHINGTON, DC 20515–6216

(202) 225–3951
judiciary.house.gov

April 6, 2022

The Honorable James R. Clapper
Belfer Center, Harvard Kennedy School
79 John F. Kennedy Street
Cambridge, MA 02138

Dear Mr. Clapper:

On October 14, 2020, the *New York Post* published a report detailing how Hunter Biden used the position and influence of his father, now-President Joe Biden, for personal gain with the apparent awareness of President Biden.[1] This article raised doubts about President Biden's earlier denial of ever speaking to his son about his international business dealings.[2] The *Post* reported on an email in which a Ukrainian businessman urged Hunter Biden to "use [his] influence to convey a message / signal, etc. to stop what we consider to be politically motivated actions."[3] In another email, the same businessman thanked Hunter Biden for arranging a meeting with his father, calling it "an honor and pleasure."[4] The *Post* reported that these emails came from a laptop belonging to Hunter Biden that he had abandoned in a Delaware computer shop.[5]

On October 19, 2020, you signed a public statement attempting to discredit the contents of the *New York Post*'s reporting about Hunter Biden.[6] This statement emphasized the national security credentials of you and the other signatories, implying that the assertions and conclusions in the statement were grounded in information unavailable to other Americans. Referencing this unique experience, you wrote:

> It is for all these reasons that we write to say that the arrival on the US political scene of emails purportedly belonging to Vice President Biden's son Hunter, much of it related to his time serving on the Board of the Ukrainian gas company Burisma, has all the classic earmarks of a Russian information operation.[7]

---

[1] Emma-Jo Morris & Gabrielle Fonrouge, *Smoking-gun email reveals how Hunter Biden introduced Ukrainian businessman to VP dad*, N.Y. Post, Oct. 14, 2020.
[2] *E.g.* Nick Givas, *Joe Biden again denies speaking to son about Ukrainian business dealings*, Fox News, Oct. 10, 2019.
[3] Morris & Fonrouge, *supra* note 1.
[4] *Id.*
[5] *Id.*
[6] Jim Clapper et al., Public Statement on the Hunter Biden Emails (Oct. 19, 2020).
[7] *Id.*

Although this statement acknowledged that you had seen no actual "evidence" of Russian involvement with respect to the publication of Hunter Biden's emails, you nonetheless conveyed a "deep[] suspicio[n] that the Russian government played a significant role in the case."[8] Later in the statement, you went further to state a "view"—not merely a suspicion anymore—"that the Russians are involved in the Hunter Biden email issue . . . ."[9]

Your public statement served as a basis for Democrat operatives to try to delegitimize the scandalous allegations about Hunter Biden and the Biden family. On the same day as your statement, *Politico* published a story about the statement, with the conclusive headline, "Hunter Biden story is Russian disinfo, dozens of former intel officials say."[10] Departing from the statement's careful wording, the *Politico* story quoted one signatory to the letter as being confident that "once again the Russians are interfering" in our elections.[11] Fifteen minutes after *Politico* published its story, Jen Psaki, who now serves as Press Secretary to the President, tweeted a link to the *Politico* story.[12] The Biden campaign repeatedly cited your statement to dismiss the allegations against Hunter Biden.[13] During the final presidential debate, Vice President Biden also dismissed concerns about Hunter Biden's international business dealings as part of a "Russian plan."[14]

Your public statement was consistent with a broader effort to minimize and censor the *New York Post*'s reporting about Hunter Biden and the Biden family. National news organizations called the allegations about Hunter Biden "dubious" and a "non-scandal"; CBS News reporter Leslie Stahl said the allegations "can't be verified"; and NPR called it a "waste . . . of time" and a "pure distraction."[15] Separately, Twitter and Facebook restricted access to the *New York Post*'s reporting about Hunter Biden, with Twitter locking the *Post*'s account and Facebook deferring to a so-called independent fact-check that never occurred.[16] These efforts likely affected public awareness of the serious allegations surrounding the Biden family in the crucial weeks before the 2020 election.

We now know from subsequent reporting that the *New York Post*'s article about Hunter Biden was not, as you and your co-signatories alleged, part of a "Russian information

---

[8] *Id.*
[9] *Id.*
[10] Natasha Bertrand, *Hunter Biden story is Russian disinfo, dozens of former intel officials say*, Politico, Oct. 19, 2020.
[11] *Id.*
[12] Tweet by Jen Psaki, Twitter.com (Oct. 19, 2020, 10:45 p.m.), https://twitter.com/jrpsaki/status/1318382779659411458.
[13] *E.g.* Houston Keene, *Flashback: Biden officials pushed angle that Hunter laptop was 'Russian disinfo,'* Fox News, Mar. 17, 2022.
[14] Deirdre Shesgreen, *"Nothing was unethical": Joe Biden defends Hunter Biden under pressure from Trump in debate*, USA Today, Oct. 22, 2020.
[15] Joe Concha, *Media's pre-election burial of Hunter Biden story proves dereliction of duty*, The Hill, Dec. 11, 2020.
[16] *E.g.* Elizabeth Dwoskin, *Facebook and Twitter take unusual steps to limit spread of New York Post story*, Wash. Post, Oct. 15, 2020.

operation."[17] This belated verification of the *Post*'s reporting raises fresh questions about the public statement you signed in October 2020. At best, the public statement was a reckless attempt by you and your co-signatories to erroneously opine about purported election interference. At worse—and more likely—the public statement was a deliberate and coordinated effort to mislead the American people about information relevant to the 2020 presidential election by invoking your national security experience to falsely suggest that the allegations about Hunter Biden were not based in fact.

The concerted effort to suppress public dissemination of the serious allegations about Hunter Biden and the Biden family, as first reported in October 2020 by the *New York Post*, was a grave disservice to American citizens' informed participation in our democracy. We are investigating the role that the public statement played in this effort. Accordingly, please provide the following material:

1. Identify all people with whom you communicated about the inception, drafting, editing, signing, publishing, or promotion of the "Public Statement on the Hunter Biden Emails" dated October 19, 2020; and

2. Produce all documents and communications referring or relating to the "Public Statement on the Hunter Biden Emails" dated October 19, 2020.

Please produce this material as soon as possible but no later than 5:00 p.m. on April 20, 2022. In addition, we request that you take all reasonable steps to preserve records that may be potentially responsive to this inquiry.

Thank you for your attention to this matter.

Sincerely,

Jim Jordan
Ranking Member

Steve Chabot
Member of Congress

Louie Gohmert
Member of Congress

Darrell Issa
Ranking Member
Subcommittee on Courts, Intellectual Property, and the Internet

---

[17] *E.g.* Katie Brenner et al., *Hunter Biden paid tax bill, but broad federal investigation continues*, N.Y. Times, Mar. 16, 2022; Matt Viser et al., *Inside Hunter Biden's multimillion-dollar deals with a Chinese energy company*, Wash. Post, Mar. 30, 2022.

The Honorable James R. Clapper
April 6, 2022
Page 4

Ken Buck
Ranking Member
Subcommittee on Antitrust, Commercial and Administrative Law

Matt Gaetz
Member of Congress

Mike Johnson
Ranking Member
Subcommittee on the Constitution, Civil Rights and Civil Liberties

Andy Biggs
Ranking Member
Subcommittee on Crime, Terrorism and Homeland Security

Tom McClintock
Ranking Member
Subcommittee on Immigration and Citizenship

W. Gregory Steube
Member of Congress

Tom Tiffany
Member of Congress

Thomas Massie
Member of Congress

Chip Roy
Member of Congress

Dan Bishop
Member of Congress

Michelle Fischbach
Member of Congress

Victoria Spartz
Member of Congress

Scott Fitzgerald
Member of Congress

Cliff Bentz
Member of Congress

Burgess Owens
Member of Congress

JERROLD NADLER, New York
CHAIRMAN

JIM JORDAN, Ohio
RANKING MEMBER

ONE HUNDRED SEVENTEENTH CONGRESS

Congress of the United States

House of Representatives

COMMITTEE ON THE JUDICIARY

2138 RAYBURN HOUSE OFFICE BUILDING

WASHINGTON, DC 20515–6216

(202) 225–3951
judiciary.house.gov

April 6, 2022

Mr. Peter Corsell
via e-mail

Dear Mr. Corsell:

On October 14, 2020, the *New York Post* published a report detailing how Hunter Biden used the position and influence of his father, now-President Joe Biden, for personal gain with the apparent awareness of President Biden.[1] This article raised doubts about President Biden's earlier denial of ever speaking to his son about his international business dealings.[2] The *Post* reported on an email in which a Ukrainian businessman urged Hunter Biden to "use [his] influence to convey a message / signal, etc. to stop what we consider to be politically motivated actions."[3] In another email, the same businessman thanked Hunter Biden for arranging a meeting with his father, calling it "an honor and pleasure."[4] The *Post* reported that these emails came from a laptop belonging to Hunter Biden that he had abandoned in a Delaware computer shop.[5]

On October 19, 2020, you signed a public statement attempting to discredit the contents of the *New York Post*'s reporting about Hunter Biden.[6] This statement emphasized the national security credentials of you and the other signatories, implying that the assertions and conclusions in the statement were grounded in information unavailable to other Americans. Referencing this unique experience, you wrote:

> It is for all these reasons that we write to say that the arrival on the US political scene of emails purportedly belonging to Vice President Biden's son Hunter, much of it related to his time serving on the Board of the Ukrainian gas company Burisma, has all the classic earmarks of a Russian information operation.[7]

---

[1] Emma-Jo Morris & Gabrielle Fonrouge, *Smoking-gun email reveals how Hunter Biden introduced Ukrainian businessman to VP dad*, N.Y. Post, Oct. 14, 2020.
[2] *E.g.* Nick Givas, *Joe Biden again denies speaking to son about Ukrainian business dealings*, Fox News, Oct. 10, 2019.
[3] Morris & Fonrouge, *supra* note 1.
[4] *Id.*
[5] *Id.*
[6] Jim Clapper et al., Public Statement on the Hunter Biden Emails (Oct. 19, 2020).
[7] *Id.*

Although this statement acknowledged that you had seen no actual "evidence" of Russian involvement with respect to the publication of Hunter Biden's emails, you nonetheless conveyed a "deep[] suspicio[n] that the Russian government played a significant role in the case."[8] Later in the statement, you went further to state a "view"—not merely a suspicion anymore—"that the Russians are involved in the Hunter Biden email issue . . . ."[9]

Your public statement served as a basis for Democrat operatives to try to delegitimize the scandalous allegations about Hunter Biden and the Biden family. On the same day as your statement, *Politico* published a story about the statement, with the conclusive headline, "Hunter Biden story is Russian disinfo, dozens of former intel officials say."[10] Departing from the statement's careful wording, the *Politico* story quoted one signatory to the letter as being confident that "once again the Russians are interfering" in our elections.[11] Fifteen minutes after *Politico* published its story, Jen Psaki, who now serves as Press Secretary to the President, tweeted a link to the *Politico* story.[12] The Biden campaign repeatedly cited your statement to dismiss the allegations against Hunter Biden.[13] During the final presidential debate, Vice President Biden also dismissed concerns about Hunter Biden's international business dealings as part of a "Russian plan."[14]

Your public statement was consistent with a broader effort to minimize and censor the *New York Post*'s reporting about Hunter Biden and the Biden family. National news organizations called the allegations about Hunter Biden "dubious" and a "non-scandal"; CBS News reporter Leslie Stahl said the allegations "can't be verified"; and NPR called it a "waste . . . of time" and a "pure distraction."[15] Separately, Twitter and Facebook restricted access to the *New York Post*'s reporting about Hunter Biden, with Twitter locking the *Post*'s account and Facebook deferring to a so-called independent fact-check that never occurred.[16] These efforts likely affected public awareness of the serious allegations surrounding the Biden family in the crucial weeks before the 2020 election.

We now know from subsequent reporting that the *New York Post*'s article about Hunter Biden was not, as you and your co-signatories alleged, part of a "Russian information

---

[8] *Id.*
[9] *Id.*
[10] Natasha Bertrand, *Hunter Biden story is Russian disinfo, dozens of former intel officials say*, Politico, Oct. 19, 2020.
[11] *Id.*
[12] Tweet by Jen Psaki, Twitter.com (Oct. 19, 2020, 10:45 p.m.), https://twitter.com/jrpsaki/status/1318382779659411458.
[13] *E.g.* Houston Keene, *Flashback: Biden officials pushed angle that Hunter laptop was 'Russian disinfo,'* Fox News, Mar. 17, 2022.
[14] Deirdre Shesgreen, *"Nothing was unethical": Joe Biden defends Hunter Biden under pressure from Trump in debate*, USA Today, Oct. 22, 2020.
[15] Joe Concha, *Media's pre-election burial of Hunter Biden story proves dereliction of duty*, The Hill, Dec. 11, 2020.
[16] *E.g.* Elizabeth Dwoskin, *Facebook and Twitter take unusual steps to limit spread of New York Post story*, Wash. Post, Oct. 15, 2020.

operation."[17] This belated verification of the *Post*'s reporting raises fresh questions about the public statement you signed in October 2020. At best, the public statement was a reckless attempt by you and your co-signatories to erroneously opine about purported election interference. At worse—and more likely—the public statement was a deliberate and coordinated effort to mislead the American people about information relevant to the 2020 presidential election by invoking your national security experience to falsely suggest that the allegations about Hunter Biden were not based in fact.

The concerted effort to suppress public dissemination of the serious allegations about Hunter Biden and the Biden family, as first reported in October 2020 by the *New York Post*, was a grave disservice to American citizens' informed participation in our democracy. We are investigating the role that the public statement played in this effort. Accordingly, please provide the following material:

1. Identify all people with whom you communicated about the inception, drafting, editing, signing, publishing, or promotion of the "Public Statement on the Hunter Biden Emails" dated October 19, 2020; and

2. Produce all documents and communications referring or relating to the "Public Statement on the Hunter Biden Emails" dated October 19, 2020.

Please produce this material as soon as possible but no later than 5:00 p.m. on April 20, 2022. In addition, we request that you take all reasonable steps to preserve records that may be potentially responsive to this inquiry.

Thank you for your attention to this matter.

Sincerely,

Jim Jordan
Ranking Member

Steve Chabot
Member of Congress

Louie Gohmert
Member of Congress

Darrell Issa
Ranking Member
Subcommittee on Courts, Intellectual Property, and the Internet

---

[17] *E.g.* Katie Brenner et al., *Hunter Biden paid tax bill, but broad federal investigation continues*, N.Y. Times, Mar. 16, 2022; Matt Viser et al., *Inside Hunter Biden's multimillion-dollar deals with a Chinese energy company*, Wash. Post, Mar. 30, 2022.

Ken Buck
Ranking Member
Subcommittee on Antitrust, Commercial and Administrative Law

Matt Gaetz
Member of Congress

Mike Johnson
Ranking Member
Subcommittee on the Constitution, Civil Rights and Civil Liberties

Andy Biggs
Ranking Member
Subcommittee on Crime, Terrorism and Homeland Security

Tom McClintock
Ranking Member
Subcommittee on Immigration and Citizenship

W. Gregory Steube
Member of Congress

Tom Tiffany
Member of Congress

Thomas Massie
Member of Congress

Chip Roy
Member of Congress

Dan Bishop
Member of Congress

Michelle Fischbach
Member of Congress

Victoria Spartz
Member of Congress

Scott Fitzgerald
Member of Congress

Cliff Bentz
Member of Congress

Burgess Owens
Member of Congress

JERROLD NADLER, New York
CHAIRMAN

JIM JORDAN, Ohio
RANKING MEMBER

ONE HUNDRED SEVENTEENTH CONGRESS

Congress of the United States

House of Representatives

COMMITTEE ON THE JUDICIARY

2138 RAYBURN HOUSE OFFICE BUILDING

WASHINGTON, DC 20515-6216

(202) 225-3951
judiciary.house.gov

April 6, 2022

Mr. David Cariens
c/o Central Intelligence Agency
via e-mail

Dear Mr. Cariens:

On October 14, 2020, the *New York Post* published a report detailing how Hunter Biden used the position and influence of his father, now-President Joe Biden, for personal gain with the apparent awareness of President Biden.[1] This article raised doubts about President Biden's earlier denial of ever speaking to his son about his international business dealings.[2] The *Post* reported on an email in which a Ukrainian businessman urged Hunter Biden to "use [his] influence to convey a message / signal, etc. to stop what we consider to be politically motivated actions."[3] In another email, the same businessman thanked Hunter Biden for arranging a meeting with his father, calling it "an honor and pleasure."[4] The *Post* reported that these emails came from a laptop belonging to Hunter Biden that he had abandoned in a Delaware computer shop.[5]

On October 19, 2020, you signed a public statement attempting to discredit the contents of the *New York Post*'s reporting about Hunter Biden.[6] This statement emphasized the national security credentials of you and the other signatories, implying that the assertions and conclusions in the statement were grounded in information unavailable to other Americans. Referencing this unique experience, you wrote:

> It is for all these reasons that we write to say that the arrival on the US political scene of emails purportedly belonging to Vice President Biden's son Hunter, much of it related to his time serving on the Board of the Ukrainian gas company Burisma, has all the classic earmarks of a Russian information operation.[7]

---

[1] Emma-Jo Morris & Gabrielle Fonrouge, *Smoking-gun email reveals how Hunter Biden introduced Ukrainian businessman to VP dad*, N.Y. Post, Oct. 14, 2020.
[2] *E.g.* Nick Givas, *Joe Biden again denies speaking to son about Ukrainian business dealings*, Fox News, Oct. 10, 2019.
[3] Morris & Fonrouge, *supra* note 1.
[4] *Id.*
[5] *Id.*
[6] Jim Clapper et al., Public Statement on the Hunter Biden Emails (Oct. 19, 2020).
[7] *Id.*

Although this statement acknowledged that you had seen no actual "evidence" of Russian involvement with respect to the publication of Hunter Biden's emails, you nonetheless conveyed a "deep[] suspicio[n] that the Russian government played a significant role in the case."[8] Later in the statement, you went further to state a "view"—not merely a suspicion anymore—"that the Russians are involved in the Hunter Biden email issue . . . ."[9]

Your public statement served as a basis for Democrat operatives to try to delegitimize the scandalous allegations about Hunter Biden and the Biden family. On the same day as your statement, *Politico* published a story about the statement, with the conclusive headline, "Hunter Biden story is Russian disinfo, dozens of former intel officials say."[10] Departing from the statement's careful wording, the *Politico* story quoted one signatory to the letter as being confident that "once again the Russians are interfering" in our elections.[11] Fifteen minutes after *Politico* published its story, Jen Psaki, who now serves as Press Secretary to the President, tweeted a link to the *Politico* story.[12] The Biden campaign repeatedly cited your statement to dismiss the allegations against Hunter Biden.[13] During the final presidential debate, Vice President Biden also dismissed concerns about Hunter Biden's international business dealings as part of a "Russian plan."[14]

Your public statement was consistent with a broader effort to minimize and censor the *New York Post*'s reporting about Hunter Biden and the Biden family. National news organizations called the allegations about Hunter Biden "dubious" and a "non-scandal"; CBS News reporter Leslie Stahl said the allegations "can't be verified"; and NPR called it a "waste . . . of time" and a "pure distraction."[15] Separately, Twitter and Facebook restricted access to the *New York Post*'s reporting about Hunter Biden, with Twitter locking the *Post*'s account and Facebook deferring to a so-called independent fact-check that never occurred.[16] These efforts likely affected public awareness of the serious allegations surrounding the Biden family in the crucial weeks before the 2020 election.

We now know from subsequent reporting that the *New York Post*'s article about Hunter Biden was not, as you and your co-signatories alleged, part of a "Russian information

---

[8] *Id.*
[9] *Id.*
[10] Natasha Bertrand, *Hunter Biden story is Russian disinfo, dozens of former intel officials say*, Politico, Oct. 19, 2020.
[11] *Id.*
[12] Tweet by Jen Psaki, Twitter.com (Oct. 19, 2020, 10:45 p.m.), https://twitter.com/jrpsaki/status/1318382779659411458.
[13] *E.g.* Houston Keene, *Flashback: Biden officials pushed angle that Hunter laptop was 'Russian disinfo,'* Fox News, Mar. 17, 2022.
[14] Deirdre Shesgreen, *"Nothing was unethical": Joe Biden defends Hunter Biden under pressure from Trump in debate*, USA Today, Oct. 22, 2020.
[15] Joe Concha, *Media's pre-election burial of Hunter Biden story proves dereliction of duty*, The Hill, Dec. 11, 2020.
[16] *E.g.* Elizabeth Dwoskin, *Facebook and Twitter take unusual steps to limit spread of New York Post story*, Wash. Post, Oct. 15, 2020.

operation."[17] This belated verification of the *Post*'s reporting raises fresh questions about the public statement you signed in October 2020. At best, the public statement was a reckless attempt by you and your co-signatories to erroneously opine about purported election interference. At worse—and more likely—the public statement was a deliberate and coordinated effort to mislead the American people about information relevant to the 2020 presidential election by invoking your national security experience to falsely suggest that the allegations about Hunter Biden were not based in fact.

The concerted effort to suppress public dissemination of the serious allegations about Hunter Biden and the Biden family, as first reported in October 2020 by the *New York Post*, was a grave disservice to American citizens' informed participation in our democracy. We are investigating the role that the public statement played in this effort. Accordingly, please provide the following material:

1. Identify all people with whom you communicated about the inception, drafting, editing, signing, publishing, or promotion of the "Public Statement on the Hunter Biden Emails" dated October 19, 2020; and

2. Produce all documents and communications referring or relating to the "Public Statement on the Hunter Biden Emails" dated October 19, 2020.

Please produce this material as soon as possible but no later than 5:00 p.m. on April 20, 2022. In addition, we request that you take all reasonable steps to preserve records that may be potentially responsive to this inquiry.

Thank you for your attention to this matter.

Sincerely,

Jim Jordan
Ranking Member

Steve Chabot
Member of Congress

Louie Gohmert
Member of Congress

Darrell Issa
Ranking Member
Subcommittee on Courts, Intellectual Property, and the Internet

[17] *E.g.* Katie Brenner et al., *Hunter Biden paid tax bill, but broad federal investigation continues*, N.Y. Times, Mar. 16, 2022; Matt Viser et al., *Inside Hunter Biden's multimillion-dollar deals with a Chinese energy company*, Wash. Post, Mar. 30, 2022.

Ken Buck
Ranking Member
Subcommittee on Antitrust, Commercial and Administrative Law

Matt Gaetz
Member of Congress

Mike Johnson
Ranking Member
Subcommittee on the Constitution, Civil Rights and Civil Liberties

Andy Biggs
Ranking Member
Subcommittee on Crime, Terrorism and Homeland Security

Tom McClintock
Ranking Member
Subcommittee on Immigration and Citizenship

W. Gregory Steube
Member of Congress

Tom Tiffany
Member of Congress

Thomas Massie
Member of Congress

Chip Roy
Member of Congress

Dan Bishop
Member of Congress

Michelle Fischbach
Member of Congress

Victoria Spartz
Member of Congress

Scott Fitzgerald
Member of Congress

Cliff Bentz
Member of Congress

Burgess Owens
Member of Congress

JERROLD NADLER, New York
CHAIRMAN

JIM JORDAN, Ohio
RANKING MEMBER

ONE HUNDRED SEVENTEENTH CONGRESS

Congress of the United States

House of Representatives

COMMITTEE ON THE JUDICIARY

2138 RAYBURN HOUSE OFFICE BUILDING

WASHINGTON, DC 20515-6216

(202) 225-3951
judiciary.house.gov

April 6, 2022

Mr. Brett Davis
c/o Central Intelligence Agency
via e-mail

Dear Mr. Davis:

On October 14, 2020, the *New York Post* published a report detailing how Hunter Biden used the position and influence of his father, now-President Joe Biden, for personal gain with the apparent awareness of President Biden.[1] This article raised doubts about President Biden's earlier denial of ever speaking to his son about his international business dealings.[2] The *Post* reported on an email in which a Ukrainian businessman urged Hunter Biden to "use [his] influence to convey a message / signal, etc. to stop what we consider to be politically motivated actions."[3] In another email, the same businessman thanked Hunter Biden for arranging a meeting with his father, calling it "an honor and pleasure."[4] The *Post* reported that these emails came from a laptop belonging to Hunter Biden that he had abandoned in a Delaware computer shop.[5]

On October 19, 2020, you signed a public statement attempting to discredit the contents of the *New York Post*'s reporting about Hunter Biden.[6] This statement emphasized the national security credentials of you and the other signatories, implying that the assertions and conclusions in the statement were grounded in information unavailable to other Americans. Referencing this unique experience, you wrote:

> It is for all these reasons that we write to say that the arrival on the US political scene of emails purportedly belonging to Vice President Biden's son Hunter, much of it related to his time serving on the Board of the Ukrainian gas company Burisma, has all the classic earmarks of a Russian information operation.[7]

---

[1] Emma-Jo Morris & Gabrielle Fonrouge, *Smoking-gun email reveals how Hunter Biden introduced Ukrainian businessman to VP dad*, N.Y. Post, Oct. 14, 2020.
[2] *E.g.* Nick Givas, *Joe Biden again denies speaking to son about Ukrainian business dealings*, Fox News, Oct. 10, 2019.
[3] Morris & Fonrouge, *supra* note 1.
[4] *Id.*
[5] *Id.*
[6] Jim Clapper et al., Public Statement on the Hunter Biden Emails (Oct. 19, 2020).
[7] *Id.*

Although this statement acknowledged that you had seen no actual "evidence" of Russian involvement with respect to the publication of Hunter Biden's emails, you nonetheless conveyed a "deep[] suspicio[n] that the Russian government played a significant role in the case."[8] Later in the statement, you went further to state a "view"—not merely a suspicion anymore—"that the Russians are involved in the Hunter Biden email issue . . . ."[9]

Your public statement served as a basis for Democrat operatives to try to delegitimize the scandalous allegations about Hunter Biden and the Biden family. On the same day as your statement, *Politico* published a story about the statement, with the conclusive headline, "Hunter Biden story is Russian disinfo, dozens of former intel officials say."[10] Departing from the statement's careful wording, the *Politico* story quoted one signatory to the letter as being confident that "once again the Russians are interfering" in our elections.[11] Fifteen minutes after *Politico* published its story, Jen Psaki, who now serves as Press Secretary to the President, tweeted a link to the *Politico* story.[12] The Biden campaign repeatedly cited your statement to dismiss the allegations against Hunter Biden.[13] During the final presidential debate, Vice President Biden also dismissed concerns about Hunter Biden's international business dealings as part of a "Russian plan."[14]

Your public statement was consistent with a broader effort to minimize and censor the *New York Post*'s reporting about Hunter Biden and the Biden family. National news organizations called the allegations about Hunter Biden "dubious" and a "non-scandal"; CBS News reporter Leslie Stahl said the allegations "can't be verified"; and NPR called it a "waste . . . of time" and a "pure distraction."[15] Separately, Twitter and Facebook restricted access to the *New York Post*'s reporting about Hunter Biden, with Twitter locking the *Post*'s account and Facebook deferring to a so-called independent fact-check that never occurred.[16] These efforts likely affected public awareness of the serious allegations surrounding the Biden family in the crucial weeks before the 2020 election.

We now know from subsequent reporting that the *New York Post*'s article about Hunter Biden was not, as you and your co-signatories alleged, part of a "Russian information

---

[8] *Id.*
[9] *Id.*
[10] Natasha Bertrand, *Hunter Biden story is Russian disinfo, dozens of former intel officials say*, Politico, Oct. 19, 2020.
[11] *Id.*
[12] Tweet by Jen Psaki, Twitter.com (Oct. 19, 2020, 10:45 p.m.), https://twitter.com/jrpsaki/status/1318382779659411458.
[13] *E.g.* Houston Keene, *Flashback: Biden officials pushed angle that Hunter laptop was 'Russian disinfo,'* Fox News, Mar. 17, 2022.
[14] Deirdre Shesgreen, *"Nothing was unethical": Joe Biden defends Hunter Biden under pressure from Trump in debate*, USA Today, Oct. 22, 2020.
[15] Joe Concha, *Media's pre-election burial of Hunter Biden story proves dereliction of duty*, The Hill, Dec. 11, 2020.
[16] *E.g.* Elizabeth Dwoskin, *Facebook and Twitter take unusual steps to limit spread of New York Post story*, Wash. Post, Oct. 15, 2020.

operation."[17] This belated verification of the *Post*'s reporting raises fresh questions about the public statement you signed in October 2020. At best, the public statement was a reckless attempt by you and your co-signatories to erroneously opine about purported election interference. At worse—and more likely—the public statement was a deliberate and coordinated effort to mislead the American people about information relevant to the 2020 presidential election by invoking your national security experience to falsely suggest that the allegations about Hunter Biden were not based in fact.

The concerted effort to suppress public dissemination of the serious allegations about Hunter Biden and the Biden family, as first reported in October 2020 by the *New York Post*, was a grave disservice to American citizens' informed participation in our democracy. We are investigating the role that the public statement played in this effort. Accordingly, please provide the following material:

1. Identify all people with whom you communicated about the inception, drafting, editing, signing, publishing, or promotion of the "Public Statement on the Hunter Biden Emails" dated October 19, 2020; and

2. Produce all documents and communications referring or relating to the "Public Statement on the Hunter Biden Emails" dated October 19, 2020.

Please produce this material as soon as possible but no later than 5:00 p.m. on April 20, 2022. In addition, we request that you take all reasonable steps to preserve records that may be potentially responsive to this inquiry.

Thank you for your attention to this matter.

Sincerely,

Jim Jordan
Ranking Member

Steve Chabot
Member of Congress

Louie Gohmert
Member of Congress

Darrell Issa
Ranking Member
Subcommittee on Courts, Intellectual Property, and the Internet

[17] *E.g.* Katie Brenner et al., *Hunter Biden paid tax bill, but broad federal investigation continues*, N.Y. Times, Mar. 16, 2022; Matt Viser et al., *Inside Hunter Biden's multimillion-dollar deals with a Chinese energy company*, Wash. Post, Mar. 30, 2022.

Ken Buck
Ranking Member
Subcommittee on Antitrust, Commercial and Administrative Law

Matt Gaetz
Member of Congress

Mike Johnson
Ranking Member
Subcommittee on the Constitution, Civil Rights and Civil Liberties

Andy Biggs
Ranking Member
Subcommittee on Crime, Terrorism and Homeland Security

Tom McClintock
Ranking Member
Subcommittee on Immigration and Citizenship

W. Gregory Steube
Member of Congress

Tom Tiffany
Member of Congress

Thomas Massie
Member of Congress

Chip Roy
Member of Congress

Dan Bishop
Member of Congress

Michelle Fischbach
Member of Congress

Victoria Spartz
Member of Congress

Scott Fitzgerald
Member of Congress

Cliff Bentz
Member of Congress

Burgess Owens
Member of Congress

JERROLD NADLER, New York
CHAIRMAN

JIM JORDAN, Ohio
RANKING MEMBER

ONE HUNDRED SEVENTEENTH CONGRESS

Congress of the United States
House of Representatives

COMMITTEE ON THE JUDICIARY
2138 RAYBURN HOUSE OFFICE BUILDING
WASHINGTON, DC 20515-6216
(202) 225-3951
judiciary.house.gov

April 6, 2022

Dr. Thomas Fingar
via e-mail

Dear Dr. Fingar:

On October 14, 2020, the *New York Post* published a report detailing how Hunter Biden used the position and influence of his father, now-President Joe Biden, for personal gain with the apparent awareness of President Biden.[1] This article raised doubts about President Biden's earlier denial of ever speaking to his son about his international business dealings.[2] The *Post* reported on an email in which a Ukrainian businessman urged Hunter Biden to "use [his] influence to convey a message / signal, etc. to stop what we consider to be politically motivated actions."[3] In another email, the same businessman thanked Hunter Biden for arranging a meeting with his father, calling it "an honor and pleasure."[4] The *Post* reported that these emails came from a laptop belonging to Hunter Biden that he had abandoned in a Delaware computer shop.[5]

On October 19, 2020, you signed a public statement attempting to discredit the contents of the *New York Post*'s reporting about Hunter Biden.[6] This statement emphasized the national security credentials of you and the other signatories, implying that the assertions and conclusions in the statement were grounded in information unavailable to other Americans. Referencing this unique experience, you wrote:

> It is for all these reasons that we write to say that the arrival on the US political scene of emails purportedly belonging to Vice President Biden's son Hunter, much of it related to his time serving on the Board of the Ukrainian gas company Burisma, has all the classic earmarks of a Russian information operation.[7]

---

[1] Emma-Jo Morris & Gabrielle Fonrouge, *Smoking-gun email reveals how Hunter Biden introduced Ukrainian businessman to VP dad*, N.Y. Post, Oct. 14, 2020.
[2] *E.g.* Nick Givas, *Joe Biden again denies speaking to son about Ukrainian business dealings*, Fox News, Oct. 10, 2019.
[3] Morris & Fonrouge, *supra* note 1.
[4] *Id.*
[5] *Id.*
[6] Jim Clapper et al., Public Statement on the Hunter Biden Emails (Oct. 19, 2020).
[7] *Id.*

Although this statement acknowledged that you had seen no actual "evidence" of Russian involvement with respect to the publication of Hunter Biden's emails, you nonetheless conveyed a "deep[] suspicio[n] that the Russian government played a significant role in the case."[8] Later in the statement, you went further to state a "view"—not merely a suspicion anymore—"that the Russians are involved in the Hunter Biden email issue . . . ."[9]

Your public statement served as a basis for Democrat operatives to try to delegitimize the scandalous allegations about Hunter Biden and the Biden family. On the same day as your statement, *Politico* published a story about the statement, with the conclusive headline, "Hunter Biden story is Russian disinfo, dozens of former intel officials say."[10] Departing from the statement's careful wording, the *Politico* story quoted one signatory to the letter as being confident that "once again the Russians are interfering" in our elections.[11] Fifteen minutes after *Politico* published its story, Jen Psaki, who now serves as Press Secretary to the President, tweeted a link to the *Politico* story.[12] The Biden campaign repeatedly cited your statement to dismiss the allegations against Hunter Biden.[13] During the final presidential debate, Vice President Biden also dismissed concerns about Hunter Biden's international business dealings as part of a "Russian plan."[14]

Your public statement was consistent with a broader effort to minimize and censor the *New York Post*'s reporting about Hunter Biden and the Biden family. National news organizations called the allegations about Hunter Biden "dubious" and a "non-scandal"; CBS News reporter Leslie Stahl said the allegations "can't be verified"; and NPR called it a "waste . . . of time" and a "pure distraction."[15] Separately, Twitter and Facebook restricted access to the *New York Post*'s reporting about Hunter Biden, with Twitter locking the *Post*'s account and Facebook deferring to a so-called independent fact-check that never occurred.[16] These efforts likely affected public awareness of the serious allegations surrounding the Biden family in the crucial weeks before the 2020 election.

We now know from subsequent reporting that the *New York Post*'s article about Hunter Biden was not, as you and your co-signatories alleged, part of a "Russian information

---

[8] *Id.*
[9] *Id.*
[10] Natasha Bertrand, *Hunter Biden story is Russian disinfo, dozens of former intel officials say*, Politico, Oct. 19, 2020.
[11] *Id.*
[12] Tweet by Jen Psaki, Twitter.com (Oct. 19, 2020, 10:45 p.m.), https://twitter.com/jrpsaki/status/1318382779659411458.
[13] *E.g.* Houston Keene, *Flashback: Biden officials pushed angle that Hunter laptop was 'Russian disinfo,'* Fox News, Mar. 17, 2022.
[14] Deirdre Shesgreen, *"Nothing was unethical": Joe Biden defends Hunter Biden under pressure from Trump in debate*, USA Today, Oct. 22, 2020.
[15] Joe Concha, *Media's pre-election burial of Hunter Biden story proves dereliction of duty*, The Hill, Dec. 11, 2020.
[16] *E.g.* Elizabeth Dwoskin, *Facebook and Twitter take unusual steps to limit spread of New York Post story*, Wash. Post, Oct. 15, 2020.

operation."[17] This belated verification of the *Post*'s reporting raises fresh questions about the public statement you signed in October 2020. At best, the public statement was a reckless attempt by you and your co-signatories to erroneously opine about purported election interference. At worse—and more likely—the public statement was a deliberate and coordinated effort to mislead the American people about information relevant to the 2020 presidential election by invoking your national security experience to falsely suggest that the allegations about Hunter Biden were not based in fact.

The concerted effort to suppress public dissemination of the serious allegations about Hunter Biden and the Biden family, as first reported in October 2020 by the *New York Post*, was a grave disservice to American citizens' informed participation in our democracy. We are investigating the role that the public statement played in this effort. Accordingly, please provide the following material:

1. Identify all people with whom you communicated about the inception, drafting, editing, signing, publishing, or promotion of the "Public Statement on the Hunter Biden Emails" dated October 19, 2020; and

2. Produce all documents and communications referring or relating to the "Public Statement on the Hunter Biden Emails" dated October 19, 2020.

Please produce this material as soon as possible but no later than 5:00 p.m. on April 20, 2022. In addition, we request that you take all reasonable steps to preserve records that may be potentially responsive to this inquiry.

Thank you for your attention to this matter.

Sincerely,

Jim Jordan
Ranking Member

Steve Chabot
Member of Congress

Louie Gohmert
Member of Congress

Darrell Issa
Ranking Member
Subcommittee on Courts, Intellectual Property, and the Internet

[17] *E.g.* Katie Brenner et al., *Hunter Biden paid tax bill, but broad federal investigation continues*, N.Y. Times, Mar. 16, 2022; Matt Viser et al., *Inside Hunter Biden's multimillion-dollar deals with a Chinese energy company*, Wash. Post, Mar. 30, 2022.

Ken Buck
Ranking Member
Subcommittee on Antitrust, Commercial and Administrative Law

Matt Gaetz
Member of Congress

Mike Johnson
Ranking Member
Subcommittee on the Constitution, Civil Rights and Civil Liberties

Andy Biggs
Ranking Member
Subcommittee on Crime, Terrorism and Homeland Security

Tom McClintock
Ranking Member
Subcommittee on Immigration and Citizenship

W. Gregory Steube
Member of Congress

Tom Tiffany
Member of Congress

Thomas Massie
Member of Congress

Chip Roy
Member of Congress

Dan Bishop
Member of Congress

Michelle Fischbach
Member of Congress

Victoria Spartz
Member of Congress

Scott Fitzgerald
Member of Congress

Cliff Bentz
Member of Congress

Burgess Owens
Member of Congress

JERROLD NADLER, New York
CHAIRMAN

JIM JORDAN, Ohio
RANKING MEMBER

ONE HUNDRED SEVENTEENTH CONGRESS
Congress of the United States
House of Representatives
COMMITTEE ON THE JUDICIARY
2138 RAYBURN HOUSE OFFICE BUILDING
WASHINGTON, DC 20515-6216
(202) 225-3951
judiciary.house.gov

April 6, 2022

Mr. Roger Zane George
via e-mail

Dear Mr. George:

On October 14, 2020, the *New York Post* published a report detailing how Hunter Biden used the position and influence of his father, now-President Joe Biden, for personal gain with the apparent awareness of President Biden.[1] This article raised doubts about President Biden's earlier denial of ever speaking to his son about his international business dealings.[2] The *Post* reported on an email in which a Ukrainian businessman urged Hunter Biden to "use [his] influence to convey a message / signal, etc. to stop what we consider to be politically motivated actions."[3] In another email, the same businessman thanked Hunter Biden for arranging a meeting with his father, calling it "an honor and pleasure."[4] The *Post* reported that these emails came from a laptop belonging to Hunter Biden that he had abandoned in a Delaware computer shop.[5]

On October 19, 2020, you signed a public statement attempting to discredit the contents of the *New York Post*'s reporting about Hunter Biden.[6] This statement emphasized the national security credentials of you and the other signatories, implying that the assertions and conclusions in the statement were grounded in information unavailable to other Americans. Referencing this unique experience, you wrote:

> It is for all these reasons that we write to say that the arrival on the US political scene of emails purportedly belonging to Vice President Biden's son Hunter, much of it related to his time serving on the Board of the Ukrainian gas company Burisma, has all the classic earmarks of a Russian information operation.[7]

---

[1] Emma-Jo Morris & Gabrielle Fonrouge, *Smoking-gun email reveals how Hunter Biden introduced Ukrainian businessman to VP dad*, N.Y. Post, Oct. 14, 2020.
[2] *E.g.* Nick Givas, *Joe Biden again denies speaking to son about Ukrainian business dealings*, Fox News, Oct. 10, 2019.
[3] Morris & Fonrouge, *supra* note 1.
[4] *Id.*
[5] *Id.*
[6] Jim Clapper et al., Public Statement on the Hunter Biden Emails (Oct. 19, 2020).
[7] *Id.*

Although this statement acknowledged that you had seen no actual "evidence" of Russian involvement with respect to the publication of Hunter Biden's emails, you nonetheless conveyed a "deep[] suspicio[n] that the Russian government played a significant role in the case."[8] Later in the statement, you went further to state a "view"—not merely a suspicion anymore—"that the Russians are involved in the Hunter Biden email issue . . . ."[9]

Your public statement served as a basis for Democrat operatives to try to delegitimize the scandalous allegations about Hunter Biden and the Biden family. On the same day as your statement, *Politico* published a story about the statement, with the conclusive headline, "Hunter Biden story is Russian disinfo, dozens of former intel officials say."[10] Departing from the statement's careful wording, the *Politico* story quoted one signatory to the letter as being confident that "once again the Russians are interfering" in our elections.[11] Fifteen minutes after *Politico* published its story, Jen Psaki, who now serves as Press Secretary to the President, tweeted a link to the *Politico* story.[12] The Biden campaign repeatedly cited your statement to dismiss the allegations against Hunter Biden.[13] During the final presidential debate, Vice President Biden also dismissed concerns about Hunter Biden's international business dealings as part of a "Russian plan."[14]

Your public statement was consistent with a broader effort to minimize and censor the *New York Post*'s reporting about Hunter Biden and the Biden family. National news organizations called the allegations about Hunter Biden "dubious" and a "non-scandal"; CBS News reporter Leslie Stahl said the allegations "can't be verified"; and NPR called it a "waste . . . of time" and a "pure distraction."[15] Separately, Twitter and Facebook restricted access to the *New York Post*'s reporting about Hunter Biden, with Twitter locking the *Post*'s account and Facebook deferring to a so-called independent fact-check that never occurred.[16] These efforts likely affected public awareness of the serious allegations surrounding the Biden family in the crucial weeks before the 2020 election.

We now know from subsequent reporting that the *New York Post*'s article about Hunter Biden was not, as you and your co-signatories alleged, part of a "Russian information

---

[8] *Id.*
[9] *Id.*
[10] Natasha Bertrand, *Hunter Biden story is Russian disinfo, dozens of former intel officials say*, Politico, Oct. 19, 2020.
[11] *Id.*
[12] Tweet by Jen Psaki, Twitter.com (Oct. 19, 2020, 10:45 p.m.), https://twitter.com/jrpsaki/status/1318382779659411458.
[13] *E.g.* Houston Keene, *Flashback: Biden officials pushed angle that Hunter laptop was 'Russian disinfo,'* Fox News, Mar. 17, 2022.
[14] Deirdre Shesgreen, *"Nothing was unethical": Joe Biden defends Hunter Biden under pressure from Trump in debate*, USA Today, Oct. 22, 2020.
[15] Joe Concha, *Media's pre-election burial of Hunter Biden story proves dereliction of duty*, The Hill, Dec. 11, 2020.
[16] *E.g.* Elizabeth Dwoskin, *Facebook and Twitter take unusual steps to limit spread of New York Post story*, Wash. Post, Oct. 15, 2020.

operation."[17] This belated verification of the *Post*'s reporting raises fresh questions about the public statement you signed in October 2020. At best, the public statement was a reckless attempt by you and your co-signatories to erroneously opine about purported election interference. At worse—and more likely—the public statement was a deliberate and coordinated effort to mislead the American people about information relevant to the 2020 presidential election by invoking your national security experience to falsely suggest that the allegations about Hunter Biden were not based in fact.

The concerted effort to suppress public dissemination of the serious allegations about Hunter Biden and the Biden family, as first reported in October 2020 by the *New York Post*, was a grave disservice to American citizens' informed participation in our democracy. We are investigating the role that the public statement played in this effort. Accordingly, please provide the following material:

1. Identify all people with whom you communicated about the inception, drafting, editing, signing, publishing, or promotion of the "Public Statement on the Hunter Biden Emails" dated October 19, 2020; and

2. Produce all documents and communications referring or relating to the "Public Statement on the Hunter Biden Emails" dated October 19, 2020.

Please produce this material as soon as possible but no later than 5:00 p.m. on April 20, 2022. In addition, we request that you take all reasonable steps to preserve records that may be potentially responsive to this inquiry.

Thank you for your attention to this matter.

Sincerely,

Jim Jordan
Ranking Member

Steve Chabot
Member of Congress

Louie Gohmert
Member of Congress

Darrell Issa
Ranking Member
Subcommittee on Courts, Intellectual Property, and the Internet

---

[17] *E.g.* Katie Brenner et al., *Hunter Biden paid tax bill, but broad federal investigation continues*, N.Y. Times, Mar. 16, 2022; Matt Viser et al., *Inside Hunter Biden's multimillion-dollar deals with a Chinese energy company*, Wash. Post, Mar. 30, 2022.

Ken Buck
Ranking Member
Subcommittee on Antitrust, Commercial and Administrative Law

Matt Gaetz
Member of Congress

Mike Johnson
Ranking Member
Subcommittee on the Constitution, Civil Rights and Civil Liberties

Andy Biggs
Ranking Member
Subcommittee on Crime, Terrorism and Homeland Security

Tom McClintock
Ranking Member
Subcommittee on Immigration and Citizenship

W. Gregory Steube
Member of Congress

Tom Tiffany
Member of Congress

Thomas Massie
Member of Congress

Chip Roy
Member of Congress

Dan Bishop
Member of Congress

Michelle Fischbach
Member of Congress

Victoria Spartz
Member of Congress

Scott Fitzgerald
Member of Congress

Cliff Bentz
Member of Congress

Burgess Owens
Member of Congress

JERROLD NADLER, New York
CHAIRMAN

JIM JORDAN, Ohio
RANKING MEMBER

ONE HUNDRED SEVENTEENTH CONGRESS

Congress of the United States

House of Representatives

COMMITTEE ON THE JUDICIARY

2138 RAYBURN HOUSE OFFICE BUILDING

WASHINGTON, DC 20515–6216

(202) 225–3951
judiciary.house.gov

April 6, 2022

Mr. Glenn Gerstell
c/o National Security Agency
via e-mail

Dear Mr. Gerstell:

On October 14, 2020, the *New York Post* published a report detailing how Hunter Biden used the position and influence of his father, now-President Joe Biden, for personal gain with the apparent awareness of President Biden.[1] This article raised doubts about President Biden's earlier denial of ever speaking to his son about his international business dealings.[2] The *Post* reported on an email in which a Ukrainian businessman urged Hunter Biden to "use [his] influence to convey a message / signal, etc. to stop what we consider to be politically motivated actions."[3] In another email, the same businessman thanked Hunter Biden for arranging a meeting with his father, calling it "an honor and pleasure."[4] The *Post* reported that these emails came from a laptop belonging to Hunter Biden that he had abandoned in a Delaware computer shop.[5]

On October 19, 2020, you signed a public statement attempting to discredit the contents of the *New York Post*'s reporting about Hunter Biden.[6] This statement emphasized the national security credentials of you and the other signatories, implying that the assertions and conclusions in the statement were grounded in information unavailable to other Americans. Referencing this unique experience, you wrote:

> It is for all these reasons that we write to say that the arrival on the US political scene of emails purportedly belonging to Vice President Biden's son Hunter, much of it related to his time serving on the Board of the Ukrainian gas company Burisma, has all the classic earmarks of a Russian information operation.[7]

---

[1] Emma-Jo Morris & Gabrielle Fonrouge, *Smoking-gun email reveals how Hunter Biden introduced Ukrainian businessman to VP dad*, N.Y. Post, Oct. 14, 2020.
[2] *E.g.* Nick Givas, *Joe Biden again denies speaking to son about Ukrainian business dealings*, Fox News, Oct. 10, 2019.
[3] Morris & Fonrouge, *supra* note 1.
[4] *Id.*
[5] *Id.*
[6] Jim Clapper et al., Public Statement on the Hunter Biden Emails (Oct. 19, 2020).
[7] *Id.*

Although this statement acknowledged that you had seen no actual "evidence" of Russian involvement with respect to the publication of Hunter Biden's emails, you nonetheless conveyed a "deep[] suspicio[n] that the Russian government played a significant role in the case."[8] Later in the statement, you went further to state a "view"—not merely a suspicion anymore—"that the Russians are involved in the Hunter Biden email issue . . . ."[9]

Your public statement served as a basis for Democrat operatives to try to delegitimize the scandalous allegations about Hunter Biden and the Biden family. On the same day as your statement, *Politico* published a story about the statement, with the conclusive headline, "Hunter Biden story is Russian disinfo, dozens of former intel officials say."[10] Departing from the statement's careful wording, the *Politico* story quoted one signatory to the letter as being confident that "once again the Russians are interfering" in our elections.[11] Fifteen minutes after *Politico* published its story, Jen Psaki, who now serves as Press Secretary to the President, tweeted a link to the *Politico* story.[12] The Biden campaign repeatedly cited your statement to dismiss the allegations against Hunter Biden.[13] During the final presidential debate, Vice President Biden also dismissed concerns about Hunter Biden's international business dealings as part of a "Russian plan."[14]

Your public statement was consistent with a broader effort to minimize and censor the *New York Post*'s reporting about Hunter Biden and the Biden family. National news organizations called the allegations about Hunter Biden "dubious" and a "non-scandal"; CBS News reporter Leslie Stahl said the allegations "can't be verified"; and NPR called it a "waste . . . of time" and a "pure distraction."[15] Separately, Twitter and Facebook restricted access to the *New York Post*'s reporting about Hunter Biden, with Twitter locking the *Post*'s account and Facebook deferring to a so-called independent fact-check that never occurred.[16] These efforts likely affected public awareness of the serious allegations surrounding the Biden family in the crucial weeks before the 2020 election.

We now know from subsequent reporting that the *New York Post*'s article about Hunter Biden was not, as you and your co-signatories alleged, part of a "Russian information

---

[8] *Id.*
[9] *Id.*
[10] Natasha Bertrand, *Hunter Biden story is Russian disinfo, dozens of former intel officials say*, Politico, Oct. 19, 2020.
[11] *Id.*
[12] Tweet by Jen Psaki, Twitter.com (Oct. 19, 2020, 10:45 p.m.), https://twitter.com/jrpsaki/status/1318382779659411458.
[13] *E.g.* Houston Keene, *Flashback: Biden officials pushed angle that Hunter laptop was 'Russian disinfo,'* Fox News, Mar. 17, 2022.
[14] Deirdre Shesgreen, *"Nothing was unethical": Joe Biden defends Hunter Biden under pressure from Trump in debate*, USA Today, Oct. 22, 2020.
[15] Joe Concha, *Media's pre-election burial of Hunter Biden story proves dereliction of duty*, The Hill, Dec. 11, 2020.
[16] *E.g.* Elizabeth Dwoskin, *Facebook and Twitter take unusual steps to limit spread of New York Post story*, Wash. Post, Oct. 15, 2020.

operation."[17] This belated verification of the *Post*'s reporting raises fresh questions about the public statement you signed in October 2020. At best, the public statement was a reckless attempt by you and your co-signatories to erroneously opine about purported election interference. At worse—and more likely—the public statement was a deliberate and coordinated effort to mislead the American people about information relevant to the 2020 presidential election by invoking your national security experience to falsely suggest that the allegations about Hunter Biden were not based in fact.

The concerted effort to suppress public dissemination of the serious allegations about Hunter Biden and the Biden family, as first reported in October 2020 by the *New York Post*, was a grave disservice to American citizens' informed participation in our democracy. We are investigating the role that the public statement played in this effort. Accordingly, please provide the following material:

1. Identify all people with whom you communicated about the inception, drafting, editing, signing, publishing, or promotion of the "Public Statement on the Hunter Biden Emails" dated October 19, 2020; and

2. Produce all documents and communications referring or relating to the "Public Statement on the Hunter Biden Emails" dated October 19, 2020.

Please produce this material as soon as possible but no later than 5:00 p.m. on April 20, 2022. In addition, we request that you take all reasonable steps to preserve records that may be potentially responsive to this inquiry.

Thank you for your attention to this matter.

Sincerely,

Jim Jordan
Ranking Member

Steve Chabot
Member of Congress

Louie Gohmert
Member of Congress

Darrell Issa
Ranking Member
Subcommittee on Courts, Intellectual Property, and the Internet

---

[17] *E.g.* Katie Brenner et al., *Hunter Biden paid tax bill, but broad federal investigation continues*, N.Y. Times, Mar. 16, 2022; Matt Viser et al., *Inside Hunter Biden's multimillion-dollar deals with a Chinese energy company*, Wash. Post, Mar. 30, 2022.

Ken Buck
Ranking Member
Subcommittee on Antitrust, Commercial and Administrative Law

Matt Gaetz
Member of Congress

Mike Johnson
Ranking Member
Subcommittee on the Constitution, Civil Rights and Civil Liberties

Andy Biggs
Ranking Member
Subcommittee on Crime, Terrorism and Homeland Security

Tom McClintock
Ranking Member
Subcommittee on Immigration and Citizenship

W. Gregory Steube
Member of Congress

Tom Tiffany
Member of Congress

Thomas Massie
Member of Congress

Chip Roy
Member of Congress

Dan Bishop
Member of Congress

Michelle Fischbach
Member of Congress

Victoria Spartz
Member of Congress

Scott Fitzgerald
Member of Congress

Cliff Bentz
Member of Congress

Burgess Owens
Member of Congress

JERROLD NADLER, New York
CHAIRMAN

JIM JORDAN, Ohio
RANKING MEMBER

ONE HUNDRED SEVENTEENTH CONGRESS

Congress of the United States

House of Representatives

COMMITTEE ON THE JUDICIARY

2138 RAYBURN HOUSE OFFICE BUILDING

WASHINGTON, DC 20515–6216

(202) 225–3951
judiciary.house.gov

April 6, 2022

Mr. Steven L. Hall
c/o Central Intelligence Agency
via e-mail

Dear Mr. Hall:

On October 14, 2020, the *New York Post* published a report detailing how Hunter Biden used the position and influence of his father, now-President Joe Biden, for personal gain with the apparent awareness of President Biden.[1] This article raised doubts about President Biden's earlier denial of ever speaking to his son about his international business dealings.[2] The *Post* reported on an email in which a Ukrainian businessman urged Hunter Biden to "use [his] influence to convey a message / signal, etc. to stop what we consider to be politically motivated actions."[3] In another email, the same businessman thanked Hunter Biden for arranging a meeting with his father, calling it "an honor and pleasure."[4] The *Post* reported that these emails came from a laptop belonging to Hunter Biden that he had abandoned in a Delaware computer shop.[5]

On October 19, 2020, you signed a public statement attempting to discredit the contents of the *New York Post*'s reporting about Hunter Biden.[6] This statement emphasized the national security credentials of you and the other signatories, implying that the assertions and conclusions in the statement were grounded in information unavailable to other Americans. Referencing this unique experience, you wrote:

> It is for all these reasons that we write to say that the arrival on the US political scene of emails purportedly belonging to Vice President Biden's son Hunter, much of it related to his time serving on the Board of the Ukrainian gas company Burisma, has all the classic earmarks of a Russian information operation.[7]

---

[1] Emma-Jo Morris & Gabrielle Fonrouge, *Smoking-gun email reveals how Hunter Biden introduced Ukrainian businessman to VP dad*, N.Y. Post, Oct. 14, 2020.
[2] *E.g.* Nick Givas, *Joe Biden again denies speaking to son about Ukrainian business dealings*, Fox News, Oct. 10, 2019.
[3] Morris & Fonrouge, *supra* note 1.
[4] *Id.*
[5] *Id.*
[6] Jim Clapper et al., Public Statement on the Hunter Biden Emails (Oct. 19, 2020).
[7] *Id.*

Although this statement acknowledged that you had seen no actual "evidence" of Russian involvement with respect to the publication of Hunter Biden's emails, you nonetheless conveyed a "deep[] suspicio[n] that the Russian government played a significant role in the case."[8] Later in the statement, you went further to state a "view"—not merely a suspicion anymore—"that the Russians are involved in the Hunter Biden email issue . . . ."[9]

Your public statement served as a basis for Democrat operatives to try to delegitimize the scandalous allegations about Hunter Biden and the Biden family. On the same day as your statement, *Politico* published a story about the statement, with the conclusive headline, "Hunter Biden story is Russian disinfo, dozens of former intel officials say."[10] Departing from the statement's careful wording, the *Politico* story quoted one signatory to the letter as being confident that "once again the Russians are interfering" in our elections.[11] Fifteen minutes after *Politico* published its story, Jen Psaki, who now serves as Press Secretary to the President, tweeted a link to the *Politico* story.[12] The Biden campaign repeatedly cited your statement to dismiss the allegations against Hunter Biden.[13] During the final presidential debate, Vice President Biden also dismissed concerns about Hunter Biden's international business dealings as part of a "Russian plan."[14]

Your public statement was consistent with a broader effort to minimize and censor the *New York Post*'s reporting about Hunter Biden and the Biden family. National news organizations called the allegations about Hunter Biden "dubious" and a "non-scandal"; CBS News reporter Leslie Stahl said the allegations "can't be verified"; and NPR called it a "waste . . . of time" and a "pure distraction."[15] Separately, Twitter and Facebook restricted access to the *New York Post*'s reporting about Hunter Biden, with Twitter locking the *Post*'s account and Facebook deferring to a so-called independent fact-check that never occurred.[16] These efforts likely affected public awareness of the serious allegations surrounding the Biden family in the crucial weeks before the 2020 election.

We now know from subsequent reporting that the *New York Post*'s article about Hunter Biden was not, as you and your co-signatories alleged, part of a "Russian information

---

[8] *Id.*

[9] *Id.*

[10] Natasha Bertrand, *Hunter Biden story is Russian disinfo, dozens of former intel officials say*, Politico, Oct. 19, 2020.

[11] *Id.*

[12] Tweet by Jen Psaki, Twitter.com (Oct. 19, 2020, 10:45 p.m.), https://twitter.com/jrpsaki/status/1318382779659411458.

[13] *E.g.* Houston Keene, *Flashback: Biden officials pushed angle that Hunter laptop was 'Russian disinfo,'* Fox News, Mar. 17, 2022.

[14] Deirdre Shesgreen, *"Nothing was unethical": Joe Biden defends Hunter Biden under pressure from Trump in debate*, USA Today, Oct. 22, 2020.

[15] Joe Concha, *Media's pre-election burial of Hunter Biden story proves dereliction of duty*, The Hill, Dec. 11, 2020.

[16] *E.g.* Elizabeth Dwoskin, *Facebook and Twitter take unusual steps to limit spread of New York Post story*, Wash. Post, Oct. 15, 2020.

operation."[17] This belated verification of the *Post*'s reporting raises fresh questions about the public statement you signed in October 2020. At best, the public statement was a reckless attempt by you and your co-signatories to erroneously opine about purported election interference. At worse—and more likely—the public statement was a deliberate and coordinated effort to mislead the American people about information relevant to the 2020 presidential election by invoking your national security experience to falsely suggest that the allegations about Hunter Biden were not based in fact.

The concerted effort to suppress public dissemination of the serious allegations about Hunter Biden and the Biden family, as first reported in October 2020 by the *New York Post*, was a grave disservice to American citizens' informed participation in our democracy. We are investigating the role that the public statement played in this effort. Accordingly, please provide the following material:

1. Identify all people with whom you communicated about the inception, drafting, editing, signing, publishing, or promotion of the "Public Statement on the Hunter Biden Emails" dated October 19, 2020; and

2. Produce all documents and communications referring or relating to the "Public Statement on the Hunter Biden Emails" dated October 19, 2020.

Please produce this material as soon as possible but no later than 5:00 p.m. on April 20, 2022. In addition, we request that you take all reasonable steps to preserve records that may be potentially responsive to this inquiry.

Thank you for your attention to this matter.

Sincerely,

Jim Jordan
Ranking Member

Steve Chabot
Member of Congress

Louie Gohmert
Member of Congress

Darrell Issa
Ranking Member
Subcommittee on Courts, Intellectual Property, and the Internet

---

[17] *E.g.* Katie Brenner et al., *Hunter Biden paid tax bill, but broad federal investigation continues*, N.Y. Times, Mar. 16, 2022; Matt Viser et al., *Inside Hunter Biden's multimillion-dollar deals with a Chinese energy company*, Wash. Post, Mar. 30, 2022.

Ken Buck
Ranking Member
Subcommittee on Antitrust, Commercial and Administrative Law

Matt Gaetz
Member of Congress

Mike Johnson
Ranking Member
Subcommittee on the Constitution, Civil Rights and Civil Liberties

Andy Biggs
Ranking Member
Subcommittee on Crime, Terrorism and Homeland Security

Tom McClintock
Ranking Member
Subcommittee on Immigration and Citizenship

W. Gregory Steube
Member of Congress

Tom Tiffany
Member of Congress

Thomas Massie
Member of Congress

Chip Roy
Member of Congress

Dan Bishop
Member of Congress

Michelle Fischbach
Member of Congress

Victoria Spartz
Member of Congress

Scott Fitzgerald
Member of Congress

Cliff Bentz
Member of Congress

Burgess Owens
Member of Congress

JERROLD NADLER, New York
CHAIRMAN

JIM JORDAN, Ohio
RANKING MEMBER

ONE HUNDRED SEVENTEENTH CONGRESS

Congress of the United States

House of Representatives

COMMITTEE ON THE JUDICIARY

2138 RAYBURN HOUSE OFFICE BUILDING

WASHINGTON, DC 20515-6216

(202) 225-3951
judiciary.house.gov

April 6, 2022

Mr. Kent Harrington
via e-mail

Dear Mr. Harrington:

On October 14, 2020, the *New York Post* published a report detailing how Hunter Biden used the position and influence of his father, now-President Joe Biden, for personal gain with the apparent awareness of President Biden.[1] This article raised doubts about President Biden's earlier denial of ever speaking to his son about his international business dealings.[2] The *Post* reported on an email in which a Ukrainian businessman urged Hunter Biden to "use [his] influence to convey a message / signal, etc. to stop what we consider to be politically motivated actions."[3] In another email, the same businessman thanked Hunter Biden for arranging a meeting with his father, calling it "an honor and pleasure."[4] The *Post* reported that these emails came from a laptop belonging to Hunter Biden that he had abandoned in a Delaware computer shop.[5]

On October 19, 2020, you signed a public statement attempting to discredit the contents of the *New York Post*'s reporting about Hunter Biden.[6] This statement emphasized the national security credentials of you and the other signatories, implying that the assertions and conclusions in the statement were grounded in information unavailable to other Americans. Referencing this unique experience, you wrote:

> It is for all these reasons that we write to say that the arrival on the US political scene of emails purportedly belonging to Vice President Biden's son Hunter, much of it related to his time serving on the Board of the Ukrainian gas company Burisma, has all the classic earmarks of a Russian information operation.[7]

---

[1] Emma-Jo Morris & Gabrielle Fonrouge, *Smoking-gun email reveals how Hunter Biden introduced Ukrainian businessman to VP dad*, N.Y. Post, Oct. 14, 2020.
[2] *E.g.* Nick Givas, *Joe Biden again denies speaking to son about Ukrainian business dealings*, Fox News, Oct. 10, 2019.
[3] Morris & Fonrouge, *supra* note 1.
[4] *Id.*
[5] *Id.*
[6] Jim Clapper et al., Public Statement on the Hunter Biden Emails (Oct. 19, 2020).
[7] *Id.*

Although this statement acknowledged that you had seen no actual "evidence" of Russian involvement with respect to the publication of Hunter Biden's emails, you nonetheless conveyed a "deep[] suspicio[n] that the Russian government played a significant role in the case."[8] Later in the statement, you went further to state a "view"—not merely a suspicion anymore—"that the Russians are involved in the Hunter Biden email issue . . . ."[9]

Your public statement served as a basis for Democrat operatives to try to delegitimize the scandalous allegations about Hunter Biden and the Biden family. On the same day as your statement, *Politico* published a story about the statement, with the conclusive headline, "Hunter Biden story is Russian disinfo, dozens of former intel officials say."[10] Departing from the statement's careful wording, the *Politico* story quoted one signatory to the letter as being confident that "once again the Russians are interfering" in our elections.[11] Fifteen minutes after *Politico* published its story, Jen Psaki, who now serves as Press Secretary to the President, tweeted a link to the *Politico* story.[12] The Biden campaign repeatedly cited your statement to dismiss the allegations against Hunter Biden.[13] During the final presidential debate, Vice President Biden also dismissed concerns about Hunter Biden's international business dealings as part of a "Russian plan."[14]

Your public statement was consistent with a broader effort to minimize and censor the *New York Post*'s reporting about Hunter Biden and the Biden family. National news organizations called the allegations about Hunter Biden "dubious" and a "non-scandal"; CBS News reporter Leslie Stahl said the allegations "can't be verified"; and NPR called it a "waste . . . of time" and a "pure distraction."[15] Separately, Twitter and Facebook restricted access to the *New York Post*'s reporting about Hunter Biden, with Twitter locking the *Post*'s account and Facebook deferring to a so-called independent fact-check that never occurred.[16] These efforts likely affected public awareness of the serious allegations surrounding the Biden family in the crucial weeks before the 2020 election.

We now know from subsequent reporting that the *New York Post*'s article about Hunter Biden was not, as you and your co-signatories alleged, part of a "Russian information

---

[8] *Id.*
[9] *Id.*
[10] Natasha Bertrand, *Hunter Biden story is Russian disinfo, dozens of former intel officials say*, Politico, Oct. 19, 2020.
[11] *Id.*
[12] Tweet by Jen Psaki, Twitter.com (Oct. 19, 2020, 10:45 p.m.), https://twitter.com/jrpsaki/status/1318382779659411458.
[13] *E.g.* Houston Keene, *Flashback: Biden officials pushed angle that Hunter laptop was 'Russian disinfo,'* Fox News, Mar. 17, 2022.
[14] Deirdre Shesgreen, *"Nothing was unethical": Joe Biden defends Hunter Biden under pressure from Trump in debate*, USA Today, Oct. 22, 2020.
[15] Joe Concha, *Media's pre-election burial of Hunter Biden story proves dereliction of duty*, The Hill, Dec. 11, 2020.
[16] *E.g.* Elizabeth Dwoskin, *Facebook and Twitter take unusual steps to limit spread of New York Post story*, Wash. Post, Oct. 15, 2020.

operation."[17] This belated verification of the *Post*'s reporting raises fresh questions about the public statement you signed in October 2020. At best, the public statement was a reckless attempt by you and your co-signatories to erroneously opine about purported election interference. At worse—and more likely—the public statement was a deliberate and coordinated effort to mislead the American people about information relevant to the 2020 presidential election by invoking your national security experience to falsely suggest that the allegations about Hunter Biden were not based in fact.

The concerted effort to suppress public dissemination of the serious allegations about Hunter Biden and the Biden family, as first reported in October 2020 by the *New York Post*, was a grave disservice to American citizens' informed participation in our democracy. We are investigating the role that the public statement played in this effort. Accordingly, please provide the following material:

1. Identify all people with whom you communicated about the inception, drafting, editing, signing, publishing, or promotion of the "Public Statement on the Hunter Biden Emails" dated October 19, 2020; and

2. Produce all documents and communications referring or relating to the "Public Statement on the Hunter Biden Emails" dated October 19, 2020.

Please produce this material as soon as possible but no later than 5:00 p.m. on April 20, 2022. In addition, we request that you take all reasonable steps to preserve records that may be potentially responsive to this inquiry.

Thank you for your attention to this matter.

Sincerely,

Jim Jordan
Ranking Member

Steve Chabot
Member of Congress

Louie Gohmert
Member of Congress

Darrell Issa
Ranking Member
Subcommittee on Courts, Intellectual Property, and the Internet

---

[17] *E.g.* Katie Brenner et al., *Hunter Biden paid tax bill, but broad federal investigation continues*, N.Y. Times, Mar. 16, 2022; Matt Viser et al., *Inside Hunter Biden's multimillion-dollar deals with a Chinese energy company*, Wash. Post, Mar. 30, 2022.

Ken Buck
Ranking Member
Subcommittee on Antitrust, Commercial and Administrative Law

Matt Gaetz
Member of Congress

Mike Johnson
Ranking Member
Subcommittee on the Constitution, Civil Rights and Civil Liberties

Andy Biggs
Ranking Member
Subcommittee on Crime, Terrorism and Homeland Security

Tom McClintock
Ranking Member
Subcommittee on Immigration and Citizenship

W. Gregory Steube
Member of Congress

Tom Tiffany
Member of Congress

Thomas Massie
Member of Congress

Chip Roy
Member of Congress

Dan Bishop
Member of Congress

Michelle Fischbach
Member of Congress

Victoria Spartz
Member of Congress

Scott Fitzgerald
Member of Congress

Cliff Bentz
Member of Congress

Burgess Owens
Member of Congress

JERROLD NADLER, New York
CHAIRMAN

JIM JORDAN, Ohio
RANKING MEMBER

ONE HUNDRED SEVENTEENTH CONGRESS

Congress of the United States
House of Representatives
COMMITTEE ON THE JUDICIARY
2138 RAYBURN HOUSE OFFICE BUILDING
WASHINGTON, DC 20515-6216
(202) 225-3951
judiciary.house.gov

April 6, 2022

The Honorable Michael V. Hayden
via e-mail

Dear General Hayden:

On October 14, 2020, the *New York Post* published a report detailing how Hunter Biden used the position and influence of his father, now-President Joe Biden, for personal gain with the apparent awareness of President Biden.[1] This article raised doubts about President Biden's earlier denial of ever speaking to his son about his international business dealings.[2] The *Post* reported on an email in which a Ukrainian businessman urged Hunter Biden to "use [his] influence to convey a message / signal, etc. to stop what we consider to be politically motivated actions."[3] In another email, the same businessman thanked Hunter Biden for arranging a meeting with his father, calling it "an honor and pleasure."[4] The *Post* reported that these emails came from a laptop belonging to Hunter Biden that he had abandoned in a Delaware computer shop.[5]

On October 19, 2020, you signed a public statement attempting to discredit the contents of the *New York Post*'s reporting about Hunter Biden.[6] This statement emphasized the national security credentials of you and the other signatories, implying that the assertions and conclusions in the statement were grounded in information unavailable to other Americans. Referencing this unique experience, you wrote:

> It is for all these reasons that we write to say that the arrival on the US political scene of emails purportedly belonging to Vice President Biden's son Hunter, much of it related to his time serving on the Board of the Ukrainian gas company Burisma, has all the classic earmarks of a Russian information operation.[7]

---

[1] Emma-Jo Morris & Gabrielle Fonrouge, *Smoking-gun email reveals how Hunter Biden introduced Ukrainian businessman to VP dad*, N.Y. Post, Oct. 14, 2020.
[2] *E.g.* Nick Givas, *Joe Biden again denies speaking to son about Ukrainian business dealings*, Fox News, Oct. 10, 2019.
[3] Morris & Fonrouge, *supra* note 1.
[4] *Id.*
[5] *Id.*
[6] Jim Clapper et al., Public Statement on the Hunter Biden Emails (Oct. 19, 2020).
[7] *Id.*

Although this statement acknowledged that you had seen no actual "evidence" of Russian involvement with respect to the publication of Hunter Biden's emails, you nonetheless conveyed a "deep[] suspicio[n] that the Russian government played a significant role in the case."[8] Later in the statement, you went further to state a "view"—not merely a suspicion anymore—"that the Russians are involved in the Hunter Biden email issue . . . ."[9]

Your public statement served as a basis for Democrat operatives to try to delegitimize the scandalous allegations about Hunter Biden and the Biden family. On the same day as your statement, *Politico* published a story about the statement, with the conclusive headline, "Hunter Biden story is Russian disinfo, dozens of former intel officials say."[10] Departing from the statement's careful wording, the *Politico* story quoted one signatory to the letter as being confident that "once again the Russians are interfering" in our elections.[11] Fifteen minutes after *Politico* published its story, Jen Psaki, who now serves as Press Secretary to the President, tweeted a link to the *Politico* story.[12] The Biden campaign repeatedly cited your statement to dismiss the allegations against Hunter Biden.[13] During the final presidential debate, Vice President Biden also dismissed concerns about Hunter Biden's international business dealings as part of a "Russian plan."[14]

Your public statement was consistent with a broader effort to minimize and censor the *New York Post*'s reporting about Hunter Biden and the Biden family. National news organizations called the allegations about Hunter Biden "dubious" and a "non-scandal"; CBS News reporter Leslie Stahl said the allegations "can't be verified"; and NPR called it a "waste . . . of time" and a "pure distraction."[15] Separately, Twitter and Facebook restricted access to the *New York Post*'s reporting about Hunter Biden, with Twitter locking the *Post*'s account and Facebook deferring to a so-called independent fact-check that never occurred.[16] These efforts likely affected public awareness of the serious allegations surrounding the Biden family in the crucial weeks before the 2020 election.

We now know from subsequent reporting that the *New York Post*'s article about Hunter Biden was not, as you and your co-signatories alleged, part of a "Russian information

---

[8] *Id.*
[9] *Id.*
[10] Natasha Bertrand, *Hunter Biden story is Russian disinfo, dozens of former intel officials say*, Politico, Oct. 19, 2020.
[11] *Id.*
[12] Tweet by Jen Psaki, Twitter.com (Oct. 19, 2020, 10:45 p.m.), https://twitter.com/jrpsaki/status/1318382779659411458.
[13] *E.g.* Houston Keene, *Flashback: Biden officials pushed angle that Hunter laptop was 'Russian disinfo,'* Fox News, Mar. 17, 2022.
[14] Deirdre Shesgreen, *"Nothing was unethical": Joe Biden defends Hunter Biden under pressure from Trump in debate*, USA Today, Oct. 22, 2020.
[15] Joe Concha, *Media's pre-election burial of Hunter Biden story proves dereliction of duty*, The Hill, Dec. 11, 2020.
[16] *E.g.* Elizabeth Dwoskin, *Facebook and Twitter take unusual steps to limit spread of New York Post story*, Wash. Post, Oct. 15, 2020.

operation."[17] This belated verification of the *Post*'s reporting raises fresh questions about the public statement you signed in October 2020. At best, the public statement was a reckless attempt by you and your co-signatories to erroneously opine about purported election interference. At worse—and more likely—the public statement was a deliberate and coordinated effort to mislead the American people about information relevant to the 2020 presidential election by invoking your national security experience to falsely suggest that the allegations about Hunter Biden were not based in fact.

The concerted effort to suppress public dissemination of the serious allegations about Hunter Biden and the Biden family, as first reported in October 2020 by the *New York Post*, was a grave disservice to American citizens' informed participation in our democracy. We are investigating the role that the public statement played in this effort. Accordingly, please provide the following material:

1. Identify all people with whom you communicated about the inception, drafting, editing, signing, publishing, or promotion of the "Public Statement on the Hunter Biden Emails" dated October 19, 2020; and

2. Produce all documents and communications referring or relating to the "Public Statement on the Hunter Biden Emails" dated October 19, 2020.

Please produce this material as soon as possible but no later than 5:00 p.m. on April 20, 2022. In addition, we request that you take all reasonable steps to preserve records that may be potentially responsive to this inquiry.

Thank you for your attention to this matter.

Sincerely,

Jim Jordan
Ranking Member

Steve Chabot
Member of Congress

Louie Gohmert
Member of Congress

Darrell Issa
Ranking Member
Subcommittee on Courts, Intellectual Property, and the Internet

---

[17] *E.g.* Katie Brenner et al., *Hunter Biden paid tax bill, but broad federal investigation continues*, N.Y. Times, Mar. 16, 2022; Matt Viser et al., *Inside Hunter Biden's multimillion-dollar deals with a Chinese energy company*, Wash. Post, Mar. 30, 2022.

Ken Buck
Ranking Member
Subcommittee on Antitrust, Commercial and Administrative Law

Matt Gaetz
Member of Congress

Mike Johnson
Ranking Member
Subcommittee on the Constitution, Civil Rights and Civil Liberties

Andy Biggs
Ranking Member
Subcommittee on Crime, Terrorism and Homeland Security

Tom McClintock
Ranking Member
Subcommittee on Immigration and Citizenship

W. Gregory Steube
Member of Congress

Tom Tiffany
Member of Congress

Thomas Massie
Member of Congress

Chip Roy
Member of Congress

Dan Bishop
Member of Congress

Michelle Fischbach
Member of Congress

Victoria Spartz
Member of Congress

Scott Fitzgerald
Member of Congress

Cliff Bentz
Member of Congress

Burgess Owens
Member of Congress

JERROLD NADLER, New York
CHAIRMAN

JIM JORDAN, Ohio
RANKING MEMBER

ONE HUNDRED SEVENTEENTH CONGRESS

Congress of the United States

House of Representatives

COMMITTEE ON THE JUDICIARY

2138 RAYBURN HOUSE OFFICE BUILDING

WASHINGTON, DC 20515-6216

(202) 225-3951
judiciary.house.gov

April 6, 2022

Mr. Don Hepburn
c/o Central Intelligence Agency
via e-mail

Dear Mr. Hepburn:

On October 14, 2020, the *New York Post* published a report detailing how Hunter Biden used the position and influence of his father, now-President Joe Biden, for personal gain with the apparent awareness of President Biden.[1] This article raised doubts about President Biden's earlier denial of ever speaking to his son about his international business dealings.[2] The *Post* reported on an email in which a Ukrainian businessman urged Hunter Biden to "use [his] influence to convey a message / signal, etc. to stop what we consider to be politically motivated actions."[3] In another email, the same businessman thanked Hunter Biden for arranging a meeting with his father, calling it "an honor and pleasure."[4] The *Post* reported that these emails came from a laptop belonging to Hunter Biden that he had abandoned in a Delaware computer shop.[5]

On October 19, 2020, you signed a public statement attempting to discredit the contents of the *New York Post*'s reporting about Hunter Biden.[6] This statement emphasized the national security credentials of you and the other signatories, implying that the assertions and conclusions in the statement were grounded in information unavailable to other Americans. Referencing this unique experience, you wrote:

> It is for all these reasons that we write to say that the arrival on the US political scene of emails purportedly belonging to Vice President Biden's son Hunter, much of it related to his time serving on the Board of the Ukrainian gas company Burisma, has all the classic earmarks of a Russian information operation.[7]

---

[1] Emma-Jo Morris & Gabrielle Fonrouge, *Smoking-gun email reveals how Hunter Biden introduced Ukrainian businessman to VP dad*, N.Y. Post, Oct. 14, 2020.
[2] *E.g.* Nick Givas, *Joe Biden again denies speaking to son about Ukrainian business dealings*, Fox News, Oct. 10, 2019.
[3] Morris & Fonrouge, *supra* note 1.
[4] *Id.*
[5] *Id.*
[6] Jim Clapper et al., Public Statement on the Hunter Biden Emails (Oct. 19, 2020).
[7] *Id.*

Although this statement acknowledged that you had seen no actual "evidence" of Russian involvement with respect to the publication of Hunter Biden's emails, you nonetheless conveyed a "deep[] suspicio[n] that the Russian government played a significant role in the case."[8] Later in the statement, you went further to state a "view"—not merely a suspicion anymore—"that the Russians are involved in the Hunter Biden email issue . . . ."[9]

Your public statement served as a basis for Democrat operatives to try to delegitimize the scandalous allegations about Hunter Biden and the Biden family. On the same day as your statement, *Politico* published a story about the statement, with the conclusive headline, "Hunter Biden story is Russian disinfo, dozens of former intel officials say."[10] Departing from the statement's careful wording, the *Politico* story quoted one signatory to the letter as being confident that "once again the Russians are interfering" in our elections.[11] Fifteen minutes after *Politico* published its story, Jen Psaki, who now serves as Press Secretary to the President, tweeted a link to the *Politico* story.[12] The Biden campaign repeatedly cited your statement to dismiss the allegations against Hunter Biden.[13] During the final presidential debate, Vice President Biden also dismissed concerns about Hunter Biden's international business dealings as part of a "Russian plan."[14]

Your public statement was consistent with a broader effort to minimize and censor the *New York Post*'s reporting about Hunter Biden and the Biden family. National news organizations called the allegations about Hunter Biden "dubious" and a "non-scandal"; CBS News reporter Leslie Stahl said the allegations "can't be verified"; and NPR called it a "waste . . . of time" and a "pure distraction."[15] Separately, Twitter and Facebook restricted access to the *New York Post*'s reporting about Hunter Biden, with Twitter locking the *Post*'s account and Facebook deferring to a so-called independent fact-check that never occurred.[16] These efforts likely affected public awareness of the serious allegations surrounding the Biden family in the crucial weeks before the 2020 election.

We now know from subsequent reporting that the *New York Post*'s article about Hunter Biden was not, as you and your co-signatories alleged, part of a "Russian information

---

[8] *Id.*
[9] *Id.*
[10] Natasha Bertrand, *Hunter Biden story is Russian disinfo, dozens of former intel officials say*, Politico, Oct. 19, 2020.
[11] *Id.*
[12] Tweet by Jen Psaki, Twitter.com (Oct. 19, 2020, 10:45 p.m.), https://twitter.com/jrpsaki/status/1318382779659411458.
[13] *E.g.* Houston Keene, *Flashback: Biden officials pushed angle that Hunter laptop was 'Russian disinfo,'* Fox News, Mar. 17, 2022.
[14] Deirdre Shesgreen, *"Nothing was unethical": Joe Biden defends Hunter Biden under pressure from Trump in debate*, USA Today, Oct. 22, 2020.
[15] Joe Concha, *Media's pre-election burial of Hunter Biden story proves dereliction of duty*, The Hill, Dec. 11, 2020.
[16] *E.g.* Elizabeth Dwoskin, *Facebook and Twitter take unusual steps to limit spread of New York Post story*, Wash. Post, Oct. 15, 2020.

operation."[17] This belated verification of the *Post*'s reporting raises fresh questions about the public statement you signed in October 2020. At best, the public statement was a reckless attempt by you and your co-signatories to erroneously opine about purported election interference. At worse—and more likely—the public statement was a deliberate and coordinated effort to mislead the American people about information relevant to the 2020 presidential election by invoking your national security experience to falsely suggest that the allegations about Hunter Biden were not based in fact.

The concerted effort to suppress public dissemination of the serious allegations about Hunter Biden and the Biden family, as first reported in October 2020 by the *New York Post*, was a grave disservice to American citizens' informed participation in our democracy. We are investigating the role that the public statement played in this effort. Accordingly, please provide the following material:

1. Identify all people with whom you communicated about the inception, drafting, editing, signing, publishing, or promotion of the "Public Statement on the Hunter Biden Emails" dated October 19, 2020; and

2. Produce all documents and communications referring or relating to the "Public Statement on the Hunter Biden Emails" dated October 19, 2020.

Please produce this material as soon as possible but no later than 5:00 p.m. on April 20, 2022. In addition, we request that you take all reasonable steps to preserve records that may be potentially responsive to this inquiry.

Thank you for your attention to this matter.

Sincerely,

Jim Jordan
Ranking Member

Steve Chabot
Member of Congress

Louie Gohmert
Member of Congress

Darrell Issa
Ranking Member
Subcommittee on Courts, Intellectual Property, and the Internet

---

[17] *E.g.* Katie Brenner et al., *Hunter Biden paid tax bill, but broad federal investigation continues*, N.Y. Times, Mar. 16, 2022; Matt Viser et al., *Inside Hunter Biden's multimillion-dollar deals with a Chinese energy company*, Wash. Post, Mar. 30, 2022.

Ken Buck
Ranking Member
Subcommittee on Antitrust, Commercial
and Administrative Law

Matt Gaetz
Member of Congress

Mike Johnson
Ranking Member
Subcommittee on the Constitution,
Civil Rights and Civil Liberties

Andy Biggs
Ranking Member
Subcommittee on Crime, Terrorism
and Homeland Security

Tom McClintock
Ranking Member
Subcommittee on Immigration
and Citizenship

W. Gregory Steube
Member of Congress

Tom Tiffany
Member of Congress

Thomas Massie
Member of Congress

Chip Roy
Member of Congress

Dan Bishop
Member of Congress

Michelle Fischbach
Member of Congress

Victoria Spartz
Member of Congress

Scott Fitzgerald
Member of Congress

Cliff Bentz
Member of Congress

Burgess Owens
Member of Congress

JERROLD NADLER, New York
CHAIRMAN

JIM JORDAN, Ohio
RANKING MEMBER

ONE HUNDRED SEVENTEENTH CONGRESS

Congress of the United States

House of Representatives

COMMITTEE ON THE JUDICIARY

2138 RAYBURN HOUSE OFFICE BUILDING

WASHINGTON, DC 20515–6216

(202) 225–3951
judiciary.house.gov

April 6, 2022

Ms. Janice Cariens
c/o Central Intelligence Agency
via e-mail

Dear Ms. Cariens:

On October 14, 2020, the *New York Post* published a report detailing how Hunter Biden used the position and influence of his father, now-President Joe Biden, for personal gain with the apparent awareness of President Biden.[1] This article raised doubts about President Biden's earlier denial of ever speaking to his son about his international business dealings.[2] The *Post* reported on an email in which a Ukrainian businessman urged Hunter Biden to "use [his] influence to convey a message / signal, etc. to stop what we consider to be politically motivated actions."[3] In another email, the same businessman thanked Hunter Biden for arranging a meeting with his father, calling it "an honor and pleasure."[4] The *Post* reported that these emails came from a laptop belonging to Hunter Biden that he had abandoned in a Delaware computer shop.[5]

On October 19, 2020, you signed a public statement attempting to discredit the contents of the *New York Post*'s reporting about Hunter Biden.[6] This statement emphasized the national security credentials of you and the other signatories, implying that the assertions and conclusions in the statement were grounded in information unavailable to other Americans. Referencing this unique experience, you wrote:

> It is for all these reasons that we write to say that the arrival on the US political scene of emails purportedly belonging to Vice President Biden's son Hunter, much of it related to his time serving on the Board of the Ukrainian gas company Burisma, has all the classic earmarks of a Russian information operation.[7]

---

[1] Emma-Jo Morris & Gabrielle Fonrouge, *Smoking-gun email reveals how Hunter Biden introduced Ukrainian businessman to VP dad*, N.Y. Post, Oct. 14, 2020.
[2] *E.g.* Nick Givas, *Joe Biden again denies speaking to son about Ukrainian business dealings*, Fox News, Oct. 10, 2019.
[3] Morris & Fonrouge, *supra* note 1.
[4] *Id.*
[5] *Id.*
[6] Jim Clapper et al., Public Statement on the Hunter Biden Emails (Oct. 19, 2020).
[7] *Id.*

Although this statement acknowledged that you had seen no actual "evidence" of Russian involvement with respect to the publication of Hunter Biden's emails, you nonetheless conveyed a "deep[] suspicio[n] that the Russian government played a significant role in the case."[8] Later in the statement, you went further to state a "view"—not merely a suspicion anymore—"that the Russians are involved in the Hunter Biden email issue . . . ."[9]

Your public statement served as a basis for Democrat operatives to try to delegitimize the scandalous allegations about Hunter Biden and the Biden family. On the same day as your statement, *Politico* published a story about the statement, with the conclusive headline, "Hunter Biden story is Russian disinfo, dozens of former intel officials say."[10] Departing from the statement's careful wording, the *Politico* story quoted one signatory to the letter as being confident that "once again the Russians are interfering" in our elections.[11] Fifteen minutes after *Politico* published its story, Jen Psaki, who now serves as Press Secretary to the President, tweeted a link to the *Politico* story.[12] The Biden campaign repeatedly cited your statement to dismiss the allegations against Hunter Biden.[13] During the final presidential debate, Vice President Biden also dismissed concerns about Hunter Biden's international business dealings as part of a "Russian plan."[14]

Your public statement was consistent with a broader effort to minimize and censor the *New York Post*'s reporting about Hunter Biden and the Biden family. National news organizations called the allegations about Hunter Biden "dubious" and a "non-scandal"; CBS News reporter Leslie Stahl said the allegations "can't be verified"; and NPR called it a "waste . . . of time" and a "pure distraction."[15] Separately, Twitter and Facebook restricted access to the *New York Post*'s reporting about Hunter Biden, with Twitter locking the *Post*'s account and Facebook deferring to a so-called independent fact-check that never occurred.[16] These efforts likely affected public awareness of the serious allegations surrounding the Biden family in the crucial weeks before the 2020 election.

We now know from subsequent reporting that the *New York Post*'s article about Hunter Biden was not, as you and your co-signatories alleged, part of a "Russian information

---

[8] *Id.*
[9] *Id.*
[10] Natasha Bertrand, *Hunter Biden story is Russian disinfo, dozens of former intel officials say*, Politico, Oct. 19, 2020.
[11] *Id.*
[12] Tweet by Jen Psaki, Twitter.com (Oct. 19, 2020, 10:45 p.m.), https://twitter.com/jrpsaki/status/1318382779659411458.
[13] *E.g.* Houston Keene, *Flashback: Biden officials pushed angle that Hunter laptop was 'Russian disinfo,'* Fox News, Mar. 17, 2022.
[14] Deirdre Shesgreen, *"Nothing was unethical": Joe Biden defends Hunter Biden under pressure from Trump in debate*, USA Today, Oct. 22, 2020.
[15] Joe Concha, *Media's pre-election burial of Hunter Biden story proves dereliction of duty*, The Hill, Dec. 11, 2020.
[16] *E.g.* Elizabeth Dwoskin, *Facebook and Twitter take unusual steps to limit spread of New York Post story*, Wash. Post, Oct. 15, 2020.

operation."[17] This belated verification of the *Post*'s reporting raises fresh questions about the public statement you signed in October 2020. At best, the public statement was a reckless attempt by you and your co-signatories to erroneously opine about purported election interference. At worse—and more likely—the public statement was a deliberate and coordinated effort to mislead the American people about information relevant to the 2020 presidential election by invoking your national security experience to falsely suggest that the allegations about Hunter Biden were not based in fact.

The concerted effort to suppress public dissemination of the serious allegations about Hunter Biden and the Biden family, as first reported in October 2020 by the *New York Post*, was a grave disservice to American citizens' informed participation in our democracy. We are investigating the role that the public statement played in this effort. Accordingly, please provide the following material:

1. Identify all people with whom you communicated about the inception, drafting, editing, signing, publishing, or promotion of the "Public Statement on the Hunter Biden Emails" dated October 19, 2020; and

2. Produce all documents and communications referring or relating to the "Public Statement on the Hunter Biden Emails" dated October 19, 2020.

Please produce this material as soon as possible but no later than 5:00 p.m. on April 20, 2022. In addition, we request that you take all reasonable steps to preserve records that may be potentially responsive to this inquiry.

Thank you for your attention to this matter.

Sincerely,

Jim Jordan
Ranking Member

Steve Chabot
Member of Congress

Louie Gohmert
Member of Congress

Darrell Issa
Ranking Member
Subcommittee on Courts, Intellectual Property, and the Internet

[17] *E.g.* Katie Brenner et al., *Hunter Biden paid tax bill, but broad federal investigation continues*, N.Y. Times, Mar. 16, 2022; Matt Viser et al., *Inside Hunter Biden's multimillion-dollar deals with a Chinese energy company*, Wash. Post, Mar. 30, 2022.

Ken Buck
Ranking Member
Subcommittee on Antitrust, Commercial and Administrative Law

Matt Gaetz
Member of Congress

Mike Johnson
Ranking Member
Subcommittee on the Constitution, Civil Rights and Civil Liberties

Andy Biggs
Ranking Member
Subcommittee on Crime, Terrorism and Homeland Security

Tom McClintock
Ranking Member
Subcommittee on Immigration and Citizenship

W. Gregory Steube
Member of Congress

Tom Tiffany
Member of Congress

Thomas Massie
Member of Congress

Chip Roy
Member of Congress

Dan Bishop
Member of Congress

Michelle Fischbach
Member of Congress

Victoria Spartz
Member of Congress

Scott Fitzgerald
Member of Congress

Cliff Bentz
Member of Congress

Burgess Owens
Member of Congress

JERROLD NADLER, New York
CHAIRMAN

JIM JORDAN, Ohio
RANKING MEMBER

ONE HUNDRED SEVENTEENTH CONGRESS

Congress of the United States
House of Representatives
COMMITTEE ON THE JUDICIARY

2138 RAYBURN HOUSE OFFICE BUILDING
WASHINGTON, DC 20515-6216
(202) 225-3951
judiciary.house.gov

April 6, 2022

Mr. Timothy D. Kilbourn
c/o Central Intelligence Agency
via e-mail

Dear Mr. Kilbourn:

On October 14, 2020, the *New York Post* published a report detailing how Hunter Biden used the position and influence of his father, now-President Joe Biden, for personal gain with the apparent awareness of President Biden.[1] This article raised doubts about President Biden's earlier denial of ever speaking to his son about his international business dealings.[2] The *Post* reported on an email in which a Ukrainian businessman urged Hunter Biden to "use [his] influence to convey a message / signal, etc. to stop what we consider to be politically motivated actions."[3] In another email, the same businessman thanked Hunter Biden for arranging a meeting with his father, calling it "an honor and pleasure."[4] The *Post* reported that these emails came from a laptop belonging to Hunter Biden that he had abandoned in a Delaware computer shop.[5]

On October 19, 2020, you signed a public statement attempting to discredit the contents of the *New York Post*'s reporting about Hunter Biden.[6] This statement emphasized the national security credentials of you and the other signatories, implying that the assertions and conclusions in the statement were grounded in information unavailable to other Americans. Referencing this unique experience, you wrote:

> It is for all these reasons that we write to say that the arrival on the US political scene of emails purportedly belonging to Vice President Biden's son Hunter, much of it related to his time serving on the Board of the Ukrainian gas company Burisma, has all the classic earmarks of a Russian information operation.[7]

---

[1] Emma-Jo Morris & Gabrielle Fonrouge, *Smoking-gun email reveals how Hunter Biden introduced Ukrainian businessman to VP dad*, N.Y. Post, Oct. 14, 2020.
[2] *E.g.* Nick Givas, *Joe Biden again denies speaking to son about Ukrainian business dealings*, Fox News, Oct. 10, 2019.
[3] Morris & Fonrouge, *supra* note 1.
[4] *Id.*
[5] *Id.*
[6] Jim Clapper et al., Public Statement on the Hunter Biden Emails (Oct. 19, 2020).
[7] *Id.*

Although this statement acknowledged that you had seen no actual "evidence" of Russian involvement with respect to the publication of Hunter Biden's emails, you nonetheless conveyed a "deep[] suspicio[n] that the Russian government played a significant role in the case."[8] Later in the statement, you went further to state a "view"—not merely a suspicion anymore—"that the Russians are involved in the Hunter Biden email issue . . . ."[9]

Your public statement served as a basis for Democrat operatives to try to delegitimize the scandalous allegations about Hunter Biden and the Biden family. On the same day as your statement, *Politico* published a story about the statement, with the conclusive headline, "Hunter Biden story is Russian disinfo, dozens of former intel officials say."[10] Departing from the statement's careful wording, the *Politico* story quoted one signatory to the letter as being confident that "once again the Russians are interfering" in our elections.[11] Fifteen minutes after *Politico* published its story, Jen Psaki, who now serves as Press Secretary to the President, tweeted a link to the *Politico* story.[12] The Biden campaign repeatedly cited your statement to dismiss the allegations against Hunter Biden.[13] During the final presidential debate, Vice President Biden also dismissed concerns about Hunter Biden's international business dealings as part of a "Russian plan."[14]

Your public statement was consistent with a broader effort to minimize and censor the *New York Post*'s reporting about Hunter Biden and the Biden family. National news organizations called the allegations about Hunter Biden "dubious" and a "non-scandal"; CBS News reporter Leslie Stahl said the allegations "can't be verified"; and NPR called it a "waste . . . of time" and a "pure distraction."[15] Separately, Twitter and Facebook restricted access to the *New York Post*'s reporting about Hunter Biden, with Twitter locking the *Post*'s account and Facebook deferring to a so-called independent fact-check that never occurred.[16] These efforts likely affected public awareness of the serious allegations surrounding the Biden family in the crucial weeks before the 2020 election.

We now know from subsequent reporting that the *New York Post*'s article about Hunter Biden was not, as you and your co-signatories alleged, part of a "Russian information

---

[8] *Id.*
[9] *Id.*
[10] Natasha Bertrand, *Hunter Biden story is Russian disinfo, dozens of former intel officials say*, Politico, Oct. 19, 2020.
[11] *Id.*
[12] Tweet by Jen Psaki, Twitter.com (Oct. 19, 2020, 10:45 p.m.), https://twitter.com/jrpsaki/status/1318382779659411458.
[13] *E.g.* Houston Keene, *Flashback: Biden officials pushed angle that Hunter laptop was 'Russian disinfo,'* Fox News, Mar. 17, 2022.
[14] Deirdre Shesgreen, *"Nothing was unethical": Joe Biden defends Hunter Biden under pressure from Trump in debate*, USA Today, Oct. 22, 2020.
[15] Joe Concha, *Media's pre-election burial of Hunter Biden story proves dereliction of duty*, The Hill, Dec. 11, 2020.
[16] *E.g.* Elizabeth Dwoskin, *Facebook and Twitter take unusual steps to limit spread of New York Post story*, Wash. Post, Oct. 15, 2020.

operation."[17] This belated verification of the *Post*'s reporting raises fresh questions about the public statement you signed in October 2020. At best, the public statement was a reckless attempt by you and your co-signatories to erroneously opine about purported election interference. At worse—and more likely—the public statement was a deliberate and coordinated effort to mislead the American people about information relevant to the 2020 presidential election by invoking your national security experience to falsely suggest that the allegations about Hunter Biden were not based in fact.

The concerted effort to suppress public dissemination of the serious allegations about Hunter Biden and the Biden family, as first reported in October 2020 by the *New York Post*, was a grave disservice to American citizens' informed participation in our democracy. We are investigating the role that the public statement played in this effort. Accordingly, please provide the following material:

1. Identify all people with whom you communicated about the inception, drafting, editing, signing, publishing, or promotion of the "Public Statement on the Hunter Biden Emails" dated October 19, 2020; and

2. Produce all documents and communications referring or relating to the "Public Statement on the Hunter Biden Emails" dated October 19, 2020.

Please produce this material as soon as possible but no later than 5:00 p.m. on April 20, 2022. In addition, we request that you take all reasonable steps to preserve records that may be potentially responsive to this inquiry.

Thank you for your attention to this matter.

Sincerely,

Jim Jordan
Ranking Member

Steve Chabot
Member of Congress

Louie Gohmert
Member of Congress

Darrell Issa
Ranking Member
Subcommittee on Courts, Intellectual Property, and the Internet

---

[17] *E.g.* Katie Brenner et al., *Hunter Biden paid tax bill, but broad federal investigation continues*, N.Y. Times, Mar. 16, 2022; Matt Viser et al., *Inside Hunter Biden's multimillion-dollar deals with a Chinese energy company*, Wash. Post, Mar. 30, 2022.

Ken Buck
Ranking Member
Subcommittee on Antitrust, Commercial and Administrative Law

Matt Gaetz
Member of Congress

Mike Johnson
Ranking Member
Subcommittee on the Constitution, Civil Rights and Civil Liberties

Andy Biggs
Ranking Member
Subcommittee on Crime, Terrorism and Homeland Security

Tom McClintock
Ranking Member
Subcommittee on Immigration and Citizenship

W. Gregory Steube
Member of Congress

Tom Tiffany
Member of Congress

Thomas Massie
Member of Congress

Chip Roy
Member of Congress

Dan Bishop
Member of Congress

Michelle Fischbach
Member of Congress

Victoria Spartz
Member of Congress

Scott Fitzgerald
Member of Congress

Cliff Bentz
Member of Congress

Burgess Owens
Member of Congress

JERROLD NADLER, New York
CHAIRMAN

JIM JORDAN, Ohio
RANKING MEMBER

ONE HUNDRED SEVENTEENTH CONGRESS

Congress of the United States

House of Representatives

COMMITTEE ON THE JUDICIARY

2138 RAYBURN HOUSE OFFICE BUILDING

WASHINGTON, DC 20515-6216

(202) 225-3951
judiciary.house.gov

April 6, 2022

Mr. Paul Kolbe
via e-mail

Dear Mr. Kolbe:

On October 14, 2020, the *New York Post* published a report detailing how Hunter Biden used the position and influence of his father, now-President Joe Biden, for personal gain with the apparent awareness of President Biden.[1] This article raised doubts about President Biden's earlier denial of ever speaking to his son about his international business dealings.[2] The *Post* reported on an email in which a Ukrainian businessman urged Hunter Biden to "use [his] influence to convey a message / signal, etc. to stop what we consider to be politically motivated actions."[3] In another email, the same businessman thanked Hunter Biden for arranging a meeting with his father, calling it "an honor and pleasure."[4] The *Post* reported that these emails came from a laptop belonging to Hunter Biden that he had abandoned in a Delaware computer shop.[5]

On October 19, 2020, you signed a public statement attempting to discredit the contents of the *New York Post*'s reporting about Hunter Biden.[6] This statement emphasized the national security credentials of you and the other signatories, implying that the assertions and conclusions in the statement were grounded in information unavailable to other Americans. Referencing this unique experience, you wrote:

> It is for all these reasons that we write to say that the arrival on the US political scene of emails purportedly belonging to Vice President Biden's son Hunter, much of it related to his time serving on the Board of the Ukrainian gas company Burisma, has all the classic earmarks of a Russian information operation.[7]

---

[1] Emma-Jo Morris & Gabrielle Fonrouge, *Smoking-gun email reveals how Hunter Biden introduced Ukrainian businessman to VP dad*, N.Y. Post, Oct. 14, 2020.
[2] *E.g.* Nick Givas, *Joe Biden again denies speaking to son about Ukrainian business dealings*, Fox News, Oct. 10, 2019.
[3] Morris & Fonrouge, *supra* note 1.
[4] *Id.*
[5] *Id.*
[6] Jim Clapper et al., Public Statement on the Hunter Biden Emails (Oct. 19, 2020).
[7] *Id.*

Although this statement acknowledged that you had seen no actual "evidence" of Russian involvement with respect to the publication of Hunter Biden's emails, you nonetheless conveyed a "deep[] suspicio[n] that the Russian government played a significant role in the case."[8] Later in the statement, you went further to state a "view"—not merely a suspicion anymore—"that the Russians are involved in the Hunter Biden email issue . . . ."[9]

Your public statement served as a basis for Democrat operatives to try to delegitimize the scandalous allegations about Hunter Biden and the Biden family. On the same day as your statement, *Politico* published a story about the statement, with the conclusive headline, "Hunter Biden story is Russian disinfo, dozens of former intel officials say."[10] Departing from the statement's careful wording, the *Politico* story quoted one signatory to the letter as being confident that "once again the Russians are interfering" in our elections.[11] Fifteen minutes after *Politico* published its story, Jen Psaki, who now serves as Press Secretary to the President, tweeted a link to the *Politico* story.[12] The Biden campaign repeatedly cited your statement to dismiss the allegations against Hunter Biden.[13] During the final presidential debate, Vice President Biden also dismissed concerns about Hunter Biden's international business dealings as part of a "Russian plan."[14]

Your public statement was consistent with a broader effort to minimize and censor the *New York Post*'s reporting about Hunter Biden and the Biden family. National news organizations called the allegations about Hunter Biden "dubious" and a "non-scandal"; CBS News reporter Leslie Stahl said the allegations "can't be verified"; and NPR called it a "waste . . . of time" and a "pure distraction."[15] Separately, Twitter and Facebook restricted access to the *New York Post*'s reporting about Hunter Biden, with Twitter locking the *Post*'s account and Facebook deferring to a so-called independent fact-check that never occurred.[16] These efforts likely affected public awareness of the serious allegations surrounding the Biden family in the crucial weeks before the 2020 election.

We now know from subsequent reporting that the *New York Post*'s article about Hunter Biden was not, as you and your co-signatories alleged, part of a "Russian information

---

[8] *Id.*
[9] *Id.*
[10] Natasha Bertrand, *Hunter Biden story is Russian disinfo, dozens of former intel officials say*, Politico, Oct. 19, 2020.
[11] *Id.*
[12] Tweet by Jen Psaki, Twitter.com (Oct. 19, 2020, 10:45 p.m.), https://twitter.com/jrpsaki/status/1318382779659411458.
[13] *E.g.* Houston Keene, *Flashback: Biden officials pushed angle that Hunter laptop was 'Russian disinfo,'* Fox News, Mar. 17, 2022.
[14] Deirdre Shesgreen, *"Nothing was unethical": Joe Biden defends Hunter Biden under pressure from Trump in debate*, USA Today, Oct. 22, 2020.
[15] Joe Concha, *Media's pre-election burial of Hunter Biden story proves dereliction of duty*, The Hill, Dec. 11, 2020.
[16] *E.g.* Elizabeth Dwoskin, *Facebook and Twitter take unusual steps to limit spread of New York Post story*, Wash. Post, Oct. 15, 2020.

operation."[17] This belated verification of the *Post*'s reporting raises fresh questions about the public statement you signed in October 2020. At best, the public statement was a reckless attempt by you and your co-signatories to erroneously opine about purported election interference. At worse—and more likely—the public statement was a deliberate and coordinated effort to mislead the American people about information relevant to the 2020 presidential election by invoking your national security experience to falsely suggest that the allegations about Hunter Biden were not based in fact.

The concerted effort to suppress public dissemination of the serious allegations about Hunter Biden and the Biden family, as first reported in October 2020 by the *New York Post*, was a grave disservice to American citizens' informed participation in our democracy. We are investigating the role that the public statement played in this effort. Accordingly, please provide the following material:

1. Identify all people with whom you communicated about the inception, drafting, editing, signing, publishing, or promotion of the "Public Statement on the Hunter Biden Emails" dated October 19, 2020; and

2. Produce all documents and communications referring or relating to the "Public Statement on the Hunter Biden Emails" dated October 19, 2020.

Please produce this material as soon as possible but no later than 5:00 p.m. on April 20, 2022. In addition, we request that you take all reasonable steps to preserve records that may be potentially responsive to this inquiry.

Thank you for your attention to this matter.

Sincerely,

Jim Jordan
Ranking Member

Steve Chabot
Member of Congress

Louie Gohmert
Member of Congress

Darrell Issa
Ranking Member
Subcommittee on Courts, Intellectual Property, and the Internet

[17] *E.g.* Katie Brenner et al., *Hunter Biden paid tax bill, but broad federal investigation continues*, N.Y. Times, Mar. 16, 2022; Matt Viser et al., *Inside Hunter Biden's multimillion-dollar deals with a Chinese energy company*, Wash. Post, Mar. 30, 2022.

Ken Buck
Ranking Member
Subcommittee on Antitrust, Commercial and Administrative Law

Matt Gaetz
Member of Congress

Mike Johnson
Ranking Member
Subcommittee on the Constitution, Civil Rights and Civil Liberties

Andy Biggs
Ranking Member
Subcommittee on Crime, Terrorism and Homeland Security

Tom McClintock
Ranking Member
Subcommittee on Immigration and Citizenship

W. Gregory Steube
Member of Congress

Tom Tiffany
Member of Congress

Thomas Massie
Member of Congress

Chip Roy
Member of Congress

Dan Bishop
Member of Congress

Michelle Fischbach
Member of Congress

Victoria Spartz
Member of Congress

Scott Fitzgerald
Member of Congress

Cliff Bentz
Member of Congress

Burgess Owens
Member of Congress

JERROLD NADLER, New York
CHAIRMAN

JIM JORDAN, Ohio
RANKING MEMBER

ONE HUNDRED SEVENTEENTH CONGRESS
Congress of the United States
House of Representatives
COMMITTEE ON THE JUDICIARY
2138 RAYBURN HOUSE OFFICE BUILDING
WASHINGTON, DC 20515–6216
(202) 225–3951
judiciary.house.gov

April 6, 2022

Mr. Richard Ledgett
via e-mail

Dear Mr. Ledgett:

On October 14, 2020, the *New York Post* published a report detailing how Hunter Biden used the position and influence of his father, now-President Joe Biden, for personal gain with the apparent awareness of President Biden.[1] This article raised doubts about President Biden's earlier denial of ever speaking to his son about his international business dealings.[2] The *Post* reported on an email in which a Ukrainian businessman urged Hunter Biden to "use [his] influence to convey a message / signal, etc. to stop what we consider to be politically motivated actions."[3] In another email, the same businessman thanked Hunter Biden for arranging a meeting with his father, calling it "an honor and pleasure."[4] The *Post* reported that these emails came from a laptop belonging to Hunter Biden that he had abandoned in a Delaware computer shop.[5]

On October 19, 2020, you signed a public statement attempting to discredit the contents of the *New York Post*'s reporting about Hunter Biden.[6] This statement emphasized the national security credentials of you and the other signatories, implying that the assertions and conclusions in the statement were grounded in information unavailable to other Americans. Referencing this unique experience, you wrote:

> It is for all these reasons that we write to say that the arrival on the US political scene of emails purportedly belonging to Vice President Biden's son Hunter, much of it related to his time serving on the Board of the Ukrainian gas company Burisma, has all the classic earmarks of a Russian information operation.[7]

---

[1] Emma-Jo Morris & Gabrielle Fonrouge, *Smoking-gun email reveals how Hunter Biden introduced Ukrainian businessman to VP dad*, N.Y. Post, Oct. 14, 2020.
[2] *E.g.* Nick Givas, *Joe Biden again denies speaking to son about Ukrainian business dealings*, Fox News, Oct. 10, 2019.
[3] Morris & Fonrouge, *supra* note 1.
[4] *Id.*
[5] *Id.*
[6] Jim Clapper et al., Public Statement on the Hunter Biden Emails (Oct. 19, 2020).
[7] *Id.*

Although this statement acknowledged that you had seen no actual "evidence" of Russian involvement with respect to the publication of Hunter Biden's emails, you nonetheless conveyed a "deep[] suspicio[n] that the Russian government played a significant role in the case."[8] Later in the statement, you went further to state a "view"—not merely a suspicion anymore—"that the Russians are involved in the Hunter Biden email issue . . . ."[9]

Your public statement served as a basis for Democrat operatives to try to delegitimize the scandalous allegations about Hunter Biden and the Biden family. On the same day as your statement, *Politico* published a story about the statement, with the conclusive headline, "Hunter Biden story is Russian disinfo, dozens of former intel officials say."[10] Departing from the statement's careful wording, the *Politico* story quoted one signatory to the letter as being confident that "once again the Russians are interfering" in our elections.[11] Fifteen minutes after *Politico* published its story, Jen Psaki, who now serves as Press Secretary to the President, tweeted a link to the *Politico* story.[12] The Biden campaign repeatedly cited your statement to dismiss the allegations against Hunter Biden.[13] During the final presidential debate, Vice President Biden also dismissed concerns about Hunter Biden's international business dealings as part of a "Russian plan."[14]

Your public statement was consistent with a broader effort to minimize and censor the *New York Post*'s reporting about Hunter Biden and the Biden family. National news organizations called the allegations about Hunter Biden "dubious" and a "non-scandal"; CBS News reporter Leslie Stahl said the allegations "can't be verified"; and NPR called it a "waste . . . of time" and a "pure distraction."[15] Separately, Twitter and Facebook restricted access to the *New York Post*'s reporting about Hunter Biden, with Twitter locking the *Post*'s account and Facebook deferring to a so-called independent fact-check that never occurred.[16] These efforts likely affected public awareness of the serious allegations surrounding the Biden family in the crucial weeks before the 2020 election.

We now know from subsequent reporting that the *New York Post*'s article about Hunter Biden was not, as you and your co-signatories alleged, part of a "Russian information

---

[8] *Id.*
[9] *Id.*
[10] Natasha Bertrand, *Hunter Biden story is Russian disinfo, dozens of former intel officials say*, Politico, Oct. 19, 2020.
[11] *Id.*
[12] Tweet by Jen Psaki, Twitter.com (Oct. 19, 2020, 10:45 p.m.), https://twitter.com/jrpsaki/status/1318382779659411458.
[13] *E.g.* Houston Keene, *Flashback: Biden officials pushed angle that Hunter laptop was 'Russian disinfo,'* Fox News, Mar. 17, 2022.
[14] Deirdre Shesgreen, *"Nothing was unethical": Joe Biden defends Hunter Biden under pressure from Trump in debate*, USA Today, Oct. 22, 2020.
[15] Joe Concha, *Media's pre-election burial of Hunter Biden story proves dereliction of duty*, The Hill, Dec. 11, 2020.
[16] *E.g.* Elizabeth Dwoskin, *Facebook and Twitter take unusual steps to limit spread of New York Post story*, Wash. Post, Oct. 15, 2020.

operation."[17] This belated verification of the *Post*'s reporting raises fresh questions about the public statement you signed in October 2020. At best, the public statement was a reckless attempt by you and your co-signatories to erroneously opine about purported election interference. At worse—and more likely—the public statement was a deliberate and coordinated effort to mislead the American people about information relevant to the 2020 presidential election by invoking your national security experience to falsely suggest that the allegations about Hunter Biden were not based in fact.

The concerted effort to suppress public dissemination of the serious allegations about Hunter Biden and the Biden family, as first reported in October 2020 by the *New York Post*, was a grave disservice to American citizens' informed participation in our democracy. We are investigating the role that the public statement played in this effort. Accordingly, please provide the following material:

1. Identify all people with whom you communicated about the inception, drafting, editing, signing, publishing, or promotion of the "Public Statement on the Hunter Biden Emails" dated October 19, 2020; and

2. Produce all documents and communications referring or relating to the "Public Statement on the Hunter Biden Emails" dated October 19, 2020.

Please produce this material as soon as possible but no later than 5:00 p.m. on April 20, 2022. In addition, we request that you take all reasonable steps to preserve records that may be potentially responsive to this inquiry.

Thank you for your attention to this matter.

Sincerely,

Jim Jordan
Ranking Member

Steve Chabot
Member of Congress

Louie Gohmert
Member of Congress

Darrell Issa
Ranking Member
Subcommittee on Courts, Intellectual Property, and the Internet

---

[17] *E.g.* Katie Brenner et al., *Hunter Biden paid tax bill, but broad federal investigation continues*, N.Y. Times, Mar. 16, 2022; Matt Viser et al., *Inside Hunter Biden's multimillion-dollar deals with a Chinese energy company*, Wash. Post, Mar. 30, 2022.

Ken Buck
Ranking Member
Subcommittee on Antitrust, Commercial and Administrative Law

Matt Gaetz
Member of Congress

Mike Johnson
Ranking Member
Subcommittee on the Constitution, Civil Rights and Civil Liberties

Andy Biggs
Ranking Member
Subcommittee on Crime, Terrorism and Homeland Security

Tom McClintock
Ranking Member
Subcommittee on Immigration and Citizenship

W. Gregory Steube
Member of Congress

Tom Tiffany
Member of Congress

Thomas Massie
Member of Congress

Chip Roy
Member of Congress

Dan Bishop
Member of Congress

Michelle Fischbach
Member of Congress

Victoria Spartz
Member of Congress

Scott Fitzgerald
Member of Congress

Cliff Bentz
Member of Congress

Burgess Owens
Member of Congress

JERROLD NADLER, New York
CHAIRMAN

JIM JORDAN, Ohio
RANKING MEMBER

ONE HUNDRED SEVENTEENTH CONGRESS

Congress of the United States

House of Representatives

COMMITTEE ON THE JUDICIARY

2138 RAYBURN HOUSE OFFICE BUILDING

WASHINGTON, DC 20515–6216

(202) 225–3951
judiciary.house.gov

April 6, 2022

Mr. Andrew Liepman
via e-mail

Dear Mr. Liepman:

On October 14, 2020, the *New York Post* published a report detailing how Hunter Biden used the position and influence of his father, now-President Joe Biden, for personal gain with the apparent awareness of President Biden.[1] This article raised doubts about President Biden's earlier denial of ever speaking to his son about his international business dealings.[2] The *Post* reported on an email in which a Ukrainian businessman urged Hunter Biden to "use [his] influence to convey a message / signal, etc. to stop what we consider to be politically motivated actions."[3] In another email, the same businessman thanked Hunter Biden for arranging a meeting with his father, calling it "an honor and pleasure."[4] The *Post* reported that these emails came from a laptop belonging to Hunter Biden that he had abandoned in a Delaware computer shop.[5]

On October 19, 2020, you signed a public statement attempting to discredit the contents of thc *New York Post*'s reporting about Hunter Biden.[6] This statement emphasized the national security credentials of you and the other signatories, implying that the assertions and conclusions in the statement were grounded in information unavailable to other Americans. Referencing this unique experience, you wrote:

> It is for all these reasons that we write to say that the arrival on the US political scene of emails purportedly belonging to Vice President Biden's son Hunter, much of it related to his time serving on the Board of the Ukrainian gas company Burisma, has all the classic earmarks of a Russian information operation.[7]

---

[1] Emma-Jo Morris & Gabrielle Fonrouge, *Smoking-gun email reveals how Hunter Biden introduced Ukrainian businessman to VP dad*, N.Y. Post, Oct. 14, 2020.
[2] *E.g.* Nick Givas, *Joe Biden again denies speaking to son about Ukrainian business dealings*, Fox News, Oct. 10, 2019.
[3] Morris & Fonrouge, *supra* note 1.
[4] *Id.*
[5] *Id.*
[6] Jim Clapper et al., Public Statement on the Hunter Biden Emails (Oct. 19, 2020).
[7] *Id.*

Although this statement acknowledged that you had seen no actual "evidence" of Russian involvement with respect to the publication of Hunter Biden's emails, you nonetheless conveyed a "deep[] suspicio[n] that the Russian government played a significant role in the case."[8] Later in the statement, you went further to state a "view"—not merely a suspicion anymore—"that the Russians are involved in the Hunter Biden email issue . . . ."[9]

Your public statement served as a basis for Democrat operatives to try to delegitimize the scandalous allegations about Hunter Biden and the Biden family. On the same day as your statement, *Politico* published a story about the statement, with the conclusive headline, "Hunter Biden story is Russian disinfo, dozens of former intel officials say."[10] Departing from the statement's careful wording, the *Politico* story quoted one signatory to the letter as being confident that "once again the Russians are interfering" in our elections.[11] Fifteen minutes after *Politico* published its story, Jen Psaki, who now serves as Press Secretary to the President, tweeted a link to the *Politico* story.[12] The Biden campaign repeatedly cited your statement to dismiss the allegations against Hunter Biden.[13] During the final presidential debate, Vice President Biden also dismissed concerns about Hunter Biden's international business dealings as part of a "Russian plan."[14]

Your public statement was consistent with a broader effort to minimize and censor the *New York Post*'s reporting about Hunter Biden and the Biden family. National news organizations called the allegations about Hunter Biden "dubious" and a "non-scandal"; CBS News reporter Leslie Stahl said the allegations "can't be verified"; and NPR called it a "waste . . . of time" and a "pure distraction."[15] Separately, Twitter and Facebook restricted access to the *New York Post*'s reporting about Hunter Biden, with Twitter locking the *Post*'s account and Facebook deferring to a so-called independent fact-check that never occurred.[16] These efforts likely affected public awareness of the serious allegations surrounding the Biden family in the crucial weeks before the 2020 election.

We now know from subsequent reporting that the *New York Post*'s article about Hunter Biden was not, as you and your co-signatories alleged, part of a "Russian information

---

[8] *Id.*
[9] *Id.*
[10] Natasha Bertrand, *Hunter Biden story is Russian disinfo, dozens of former intel officials say*, Politico, Oct. 19, 2020.
[11] *Id.*
[12] Tweet by Jen Psaki, Twitter.com (Oct. 19, 2020, 10:45 p.m.), https://twitter.com/jrpsaki/status/1318382779659411458.
[13] *E.g.* Houston Keene, *Flashback: Biden officials pushed angle that Hunter laptop was 'Russian disinfo,'* Fox News, Mar. 17, 2022.
[14] Deirdre Shesgreen, *"Nothing was unethical": Joe Biden defends Hunter Biden under pressure from Trump in debate*, USA Today, Oct. 22, 2020.
[15] Joe Concha, *Media's pre-election burial of Hunter Biden story proves dereliction of duty*, The Hill, Dec. 11, 2020.
[16] *E.g.* Elizabeth Dwoskin, *Facebook and Twitter take unusual steps to limit spread of New York Post story*, Wash. Post, Oct. 15, 2020.

operation."[17] This belated verification of the *Post*'s reporting raises fresh questions about the public statement you signed in October 2020. At best, the public statement was a reckless attempt by you and your co-signatories to erroneously opine about purported election interference. At worse—and more likely—the public statement was a deliberate and coordinated effort to mislead the American people about information relevant to the 2020 presidential election by invoking your national security experience to falsely suggest that the allegations about Hunter Biden were not based in fact.

The concerted effort to suppress public dissemination of the serious allegations about Hunter Biden and the Biden family, as first reported in October 2020 by the *New York Post*, was a grave disservice to American citizens' informed participation in our democracy. We are investigating the role that the public statement played in this effort. Accordingly, please provide the following material:

1. Identify all people with whom you communicated about the inception, drafting, editing, signing, publishing, or promotion of the "Public Statement on the Hunter Biden Emails" dated October 19, 2020; and

2. Produce all documents and communications referring or relating to the "Public Statement on the Hunter Biden Emails" dated October 19, 2020.

Please produce this material as soon as possible but no later than 5:00 p.m. on April 20, 2022. In addition, we request that you take all reasonable steps to preserve records that may be potentially responsive to this inquiry.

Thank you for your attention to this matter.

Sincerely,

Jim Jordan
Ranking Member

Steve Chabot
Member of Congress

Louie Gohmert
Member of Congress

Darrell Issa
Ranking Member
Subcommittee on Courts, Intellectual Property, and the Internet

[17] *E.g.* Katie Brenner et al., *Hunter Biden paid tax bill, but broad federal investigation continues*, N.Y. Times, Mar. 16, 2022; Matt Viser et al., *Inside Hunter Biden's multimillion-dollar deals with a Chinese energy company*, Wash. Post, Mar. 30, 2022.

Ken Buck
Ranking Member
Subcommittee on Antitrust, Commercial and Administrative Law

Matt Gaetz
Member of Congress

Mike Johnson
Ranking Member
Subcommittee on the Constitution, Civil Rights and Civil Liberties

Andy Biggs
Ranking Member
Subcommittee on Crime, Terrorism and Homeland Security

Tom McClintock
Ranking Member
Subcommittee on Immigration and Citizenship

W. Gregory Steube
Member of Congress

Tom Tiffany
Member of Congress

Thomas Massie
Member of Congress

Chip Roy
Member of Congress

Dan Bishop
Member of Congress

Michelle Fischbach
Member of Congress

Victoria Spartz
Member of Congress

Scott Fitzgerald
Member of Congress

Cliff Bentz
Member of Congress

Burgess Owens
Member of Congress

JERROLD NADLER, New York
CHAIRMAN

JIM JORDAN, Ohio
RANKING MEMBER

ONE HUNDRED SEVENTEENTH CONGRESS

Congress of the United States

House of Representatives

COMMITTEE ON THE JUDICIARY

2138 RAYBURN HOUSE OFFICE BUILDING

WASHINGTON, DC 20515-6216

(202) 225-3951
judiciary.house.gov

April 6, 2022

Mr. Ronald Marks
via e-mail

Dear Mr. Marks:

On October 14, 2020, the *New York Post* published a report detailing how Hunter Biden used the position and influence of his father, now-President Joe Biden, for personal gain with the apparent awareness of President Biden.[1] This article raised doubts about President Biden's earlier denial of ever speaking to his son about his international business dealings.[2] The *Post* reported on an email in which a Ukrainian businessman urged Hunter Biden to "use [his] influence to convey a message / signal, etc. to stop what we consider to be politically motivated actions."[3] In another email, the same businessman thanked Hunter Biden for arranging a meeting with his father, calling it "an honor and pleasure."[4] The *Post* reported that these emails came from a laptop belonging to Hunter Biden that he had abandoned in a Delaware computer shop.[5]

On October 19, 2020, you signed a public statement attempting to discredit the contents of the *New York Post*'s reporting about Hunter Biden.[6] This statement emphasized the national security credentials of you and the other signatories, implying that the assertions and conclusions in the statement were grounded in information unavailable to other Americans. Referencing this unique experience, you wrote:

> It is for all these reasons that we write to say that the arrival on the US political scene of emails purportedly belonging to Vice President Biden's son Hunter, much of it related to his time serving on the Board of the Ukrainian gas company Burisma, has all the classic earmarks of a Russian information operation.[7]

---

[1] Emma-Jo Morris & Gabrielle Fonrouge, *Smoking-gun email reveals how Hunter Biden introduced Ukrainian businessman to VP dad*, N.Y. Post, Oct. 14, 2020.
[2] *E.g.* Nick Givas, *Joe Biden again denies speaking to son about Ukrainian business dealings*, Fox News, Oct. 10, 2019.
[3] Morris & Fonrouge, *supra* note 1.
[4] *Id.*
[5] *Id.*
[6] Jim Clapper et al., Public Statement on the Hunter Biden Emails (Oct. 19, 2020).
[7] *Id.*

Although this statement acknowledged that you had seen no actual "evidence" of Russian involvement with respect to the publication of Hunter Biden's emails, you nonetheless conveyed a "deep[] suspicio[n] that the Russian government played a significant role in the case."[8] Later in the statement, you went further to state a "view"—not merely a suspicion anymore—"that the Russians are involved in the Hunter Biden email issue . . . ."[9]

Your public statement served as a basis for Democrat operatives to try to delegitimize the scandalous allegations about Hunter Biden and the Biden family. On the same day as your statement, *Politico* published a story about the statement, with the conclusive headline, "Hunter Biden story is Russian disinfo, dozens of former intel officials say."[10] Departing from the statement's careful wording, the *Politico* story quoted one signatory to the letter as being confident that "once again the Russians are interfering" in our elections.[11] Fifteen minutes after *Politico* published its story, Jen Psaki, who now serves as Press Secretary to the President, tweeted a link to the *Politico* story.[12] The Biden campaign repeatedly cited your statement to dismiss the allegations against Hunter Biden.[13] During the final presidential debate, Vice President Biden also dismissed concerns about Hunter Biden's international business dealings as part of a "Russian plan."[14]

Your public statement was consistent with a broader effort to minimize and censor the *New York Post*'s reporting about Hunter Biden and the Biden family. National news organizations called the allegations about Hunter Biden "dubious" and a "non-scandal"; CBS News reporter Leslie Stahl said the allegations "can't be verified"; and NPR called it a "waste . . . of time" and a "pure distraction."[15] Separately, Twitter and Facebook restricted access to the *New York Post*'s reporting about Hunter Biden, with Twitter locking the *Post*'s account and Facebook deferring to a so-called independent fact-check that never occurred.[16] These efforts likely affected public awareness of the serious allegations surrounding the Biden family in the crucial weeks before the 2020 election.

We now know from subsequent reporting that the *New York Post*'s article about Hunter Biden was not, as you and your co-signatories alleged, part of a "Russian information

---

[8] *Id.*
[9] *Id.*
[10] Natasha Bertrand, *Hunter Biden story is Russian disinfo, dozens of former intel officials say*, Politico, Oct. 19, 2020.
[11] *Id.*
[12] Tweet by Jen Psaki, Twitter.com (Oct. 19, 2020, 10:45 p.m.), https://twitter.com/jrpsaki/status/1318382779659411458.
[13] *E.g.* Houston Keene, *Flashback: Biden officials pushed angle that Hunter laptop was 'Russian disinfo,'* Fox News, Mar. 17, 2022.
[14] Deirdre Shesgreen, *"Nothing was unethical": Joe Biden defends Hunter Biden under pressure from Trump in debate*, USA Today, Oct. 22, 2020.
[15] Joe Concha, *Media's pre-election burial of Hunter Biden story proves dereliction of duty*, The Hill, Dec. 11, 2020.
[16] *E.g.* Elizabeth Dwoskin, *Facebook and Twitter take unusual steps to limit spread of New York Post story*, Wash. Post, Oct. 15, 2020.

operation."[17] This belated verification of the *Post*'s reporting raises fresh questions about the public statement you signed in October 2020. At best, the public statement was a reckless attempt by you and your co-signatories to erroneously opine about purported election interference. At worse—and more likely—the public statement was a deliberate and coordinated effort to mislead the American people about information relevant to the 2020 presidential election by invoking your national security experience to falsely suggest that the allegations about Hunter Biden were not based in fact.

The concerted effort to suppress public dissemination of the serious allegations about Hunter Biden and the Biden family, as first reported in October 2020 by the *New York Post*, was a grave disservice to American citizens' informed participation in our democracy. We are investigating the role that the public statement played in this effort. Accordingly, please provide the following material:

1. Identify all people with whom you communicated about the inception, drafting, editing, signing, publishing, or promotion of the "Public Statement on the Hunter Biden Emails" dated October 19, 2020; and

2. Produce all documents and communications referring or relating to the "Public Statement on the Hunter Biden Emails" dated October 19, 2020.

Please produce this material as soon as possible but no later than 5:00 p.m. on April 20, 2022. In addition, we request that you take all reasonable steps to preserve records that may be potentially responsive to this inquiry.

Thank you for your attention to this matter.

Sincerely,

Jim Jordan
Ranking Member

Steve Chabot
Member of Congress

Louie Gohmert
Member of Congress

Darrell Issa
Ranking Member
Subcommittee on Courts, Intellectual Property, and the Internet

---

[17] *E.g.* Katie Brenner et al., *Hunter Biden paid tax bill, but broad federal investigation continues*, N.Y. Times, Mar. 16, 2022; Matt Viser et al., *Inside Hunter Biden's multimillion-dollar deals with a Chinese energy company*, Wash. Post, Mar. 30, 2022.

Mr. Ronald Marks
April 6, 2022
Page 4

Ken Buck
Ranking Member
Subcommittee on Antitrust, Commercial and Administrative Law

Matt Gaetz
Member of Congress

Mike Johnson
Ranking Member
Subcommittee on the Constitution, Civil Rights and Civil Liberties

Andy Biggs
Ranking Member
Subcommittee on Crime, Terrorism and Homeland Security

Tom McClintock
Ranking Member
Subcommittee on Immigration and Citizenship

W. Gregory Steube
Member of Congress

Tom Tiffany
Member of Congress

Thomas Massie
Member of Congress

Chip Roy
Member of Congress

Dan Bishop
Member of Congress

Michelle Fischbach
Member of Congress

Victoria Spartz
Member of Congress

Scott Fitzgerald
Member of Congress

Cliff Bentz
Member of Congress

Burgess Owens
Member of Congress

JERROLD NADLER, New York
CHAIRMAN

JIM JORDAN, Ohio
RANKING MEMBER

ONE HUNDRED SEVENTEENTH CONGRESS

Congress of the United States

House of Representatives

COMMITTEE ON THE JUDICIARY

2138 RAYBURN HOUSE OFFICE BUILDING

WASHINGTON, DC 20515-6216

(202) 225-3951
judiciary.house.gov

April 6, 2022

Mr. John McLaughlin
via e-mail

Dear Mr. McLaughlin:

On October 14, 2020, the *New York Post* published a report detailing how Hunter Biden used the position and influence of his father, now-President Joe Biden, for personal gain with the apparent awareness of President Biden.[1] This article raised doubts about President Biden's earlier denial of ever speaking to his son about his international business dealings.[2] The *Post* reported on an email in which a Ukrainian businessman urged Hunter Biden to "use [his] influence to convey a message / signal, etc. to stop what we consider to be politically motivated actions."[3] In another email, the same businessman thanked Hunter Biden for arranging a meeting with his father, calling it "an honor and pleasure."[4] The *Post* reported that these emails came from a laptop belonging to Hunter Biden that he had abandoned in a Delaware computer shop.[5]

On October 19, 2020, you signed a public statement attempting to discredit the contents of the *New York Post*'s reporting about Hunter Biden.[6] This statement emphasized the national security credentials of you and the other signatories, implying that the assertions and conclusions in the statement were grounded in information unavailable to other Americans. Referencing this unique experience, you wrote:

> It is for all these reasons that we write to say that the arrival on the US political scene of emails purportedly belonging to Vice President Biden's son Hunter, much of it related to his time serving on the Board of the Ukrainian gas company Burisma, has all the classic earmarks of a Russian information operation.[7]

---

[1] Emma-Jo Morris & Gabrielle Fonrouge, *Smoking-gun email reveals how Hunter Biden introduced Ukrainian businessman to VP dad*, N.Y. Post, Oct. 14, 2020.
[2] *E.g.* Nick Givas, *Joe Biden again denies speaking to son about Ukrainian business dealings*, Fox News, Oct. 10, 2019.
[3] Morris & Fonrouge, *supra* note 1.
[4] *Id.*
[5] *Id.*
[6] Jim Clapper et al., Public Statement on the Hunter Biden Emails (Oct. 19, 2020).
[7] *Id.*

Although this statement acknowledged that you had seen no actual "evidence" of Russian involvement with respect to the publication of Hunter Biden's emails, you nonetheless conveyed a "deep[] suspicio[n] that the Russian government played a significant role in the case."[8] Later in the statement, you went further to state a "view"—not merely a suspicion anymore—"that the Russians are involved in the Hunter Biden email issue . . . ."[9]

Your public statement served as a basis for Democrat operatives to try to delegitimize the scandalous allegations about Hunter Biden and the Biden family. On the same day as your statement, *Politico* published a story about the statement, with the conclusive headline, "Hunter Biden story is Russian disinfo, dozens of former intel officials say."[10] Departing from the statement's careful wording, the *Politico* story quoted one signatory to the letter as being confident that "once again the Russians are interfering" in our elections.[11] Fifteen minutes after *Politico* published its story, Jen Psaki, who now serves as Press Secretary to the President, tweeted a link to the *Politico* story.[12] The Biden campaign repeatedly cited your statement to dismiss the allegations against Hunter Biden.[13] During the final presidential debate, Vice President Biden also dismissed concerns about Hunter Biden's international business dealings as part of a "Russian plan."[14]

Your public statement was consistent with a broader effort to minimize and censor the *New York Post*'s reporting about Hunter Biden and the Biden family. National news organizations called the allegations about Hunter Biden "dubious" and a "non-scandal"; CBS News reporter Leslie Stahl said the allegations "can't be verified"; and NPR called it a "waste . . . of time" and a "pure distraction."[15] Separately, Twitter and Facebook restricted access to the *New York Post*'s reporting about Hunter Biden, with Twitter locking the *Post*'s account and Facebook deferring to a so-called independent fact-check that never occurred.[16] These efforts likely affected public awareness of the serious allegations surrounding the Biden family in the crucial weeks before the 2020 election.

We now know from subsequent reporting that the *New York Post*'s article about Hunter Biden was not, as you and your co-signatories alleged, part of a "Russian information

---

[8] *Id.*
[9] *Id.*
[10] Natasha Bertrand, *Hunter Biden story is Russian disinfo, dozens of former intel officials say*, Politico, Oct. 19, 2020.
[11] *Id.*
[12] Tweet by Jen Psaki, Twitter.com (Oct. 19, 2020, 10:45 p.m.), https://twitter.com/jrpsaki/status/1318382779659411458.
[13] *E.g.* Houston Keene, *Flashback: Biden officials pushed angle that Hunter laptop was 'Russian disinfo,'* Fox News, Mar. 17, 2022.
[14] Deirdre Shesgreen, *"Nothing was unethical": Joe Biden defends Hunter Biden under pressure from Trump in debate*, USA Today, Oct. 22, 2020.
[15] Joe Concha, *Media's pre-election burial of Hunter Biden story proves dereliction of duty*, The Hill, Dec. 11, 2020.
[16] *E.g.* Elizabeth Dwoskin, *Facebook and Twitter take unusual steps to limit spread of New York Post story*, Wash. Post, Oct. 15, 2020.

operation."[17] This belated verification of the *Post*'s reporting raises fresh questions about the public statement you signed in October 2020. At best, the public statement was a reckless attempt by you and your co-signatories to erroneously opine about purported election interference. At worse—and more likely—the public statement was a deliberate and coordinated effort to mislead the American people about information relevant to the 2020 presidential election by invoking your national security experience to falsely suggest that the allegations about Hunter Biden were not based in fact.

The concerted effort to suppress public dissemination of the serious allegations about Hunter Biden and the Biden family, as first reported in October 2020 by the *New York Post*, was a grave disservice to American citizens' informed participation in our democracy. We are investigating the role that the public statement played in this effort. Accordingly, please provide the following material:

1. Identify all people with whom you communicated about the inception, drafting, editing, signing, publishing, or promotion of the "Public Statement on the Hunter Biden Emails" dated October 19, 2020; and

2. Produce all documents and communications referring or relating to the "Public Statement on the Hunter Biden Emails" dated October 19, 2020.

Please produce this material as soon as possible but no later than 5:00 p.m. on April 20, 2022. In addition, we request that you take all reasonable steps to preserve records that may be potentially responsive to this inquiry.

Thank you for your attention to this matter.

Sincerely,

Jim Jordan
Ranking Member

Steve Chabot
Member of Congress

Louie Gohmert
Member of Congress

Darrell Issa
Ranking Member
Subcommittee on Courts, Intellectual Property, and the Internet

[17] *E.g.* Katie Brenner et al., *Hunter Biden paid tax bill, but broad federal investigation continues*, N.Y. Times, Mar. 16, 2022; Matt Viser et al., *Inside Hunter Biden's multimillion-dollar deals with a Chinese energy company*, Wash. Post, Mar. 30, 2022.

Ken Buck
Ranking Member
Subcommittee on Antitrust, Commercial and Administrative Law

Matt Gaetz
Member of Congress

Mike Johnson
Ranking Member
Subcommittee on the Constitution, Civil Rights and Civil Liberties

Andy Biggs
Ranking Member
Subcommittee on Crime, Terrorism and Homeland Security

Tom McClintock
Ranking Member
Subcommittee on Immigration and Citizenship

W. Gregory Steube
Member of Congress

Tom Tiffany
Member of Congress

Thomas Massie
Member of Congress

Chip Roy
Member of Congress

Dan Bishop
Member of Congress

Michelle Fischbach
Member of Congress

Victoria Spartz
Member of Congress

Scott Fitzgerald
Member of Congress

Cliff Bentz
Member of Congress

Burgess Owens
Member of Congress

JERROLD NADLER, New York
CHAIRMAN

JIM JORDAN, Ohio
RANKING MEMBER

ONE HUNDRED SEVENTEENTH CONGRESS
Congress of the United States
House of Representatives
COMMITTEE ON THE JUDICIARY
2138 RAYBURN HOUSE OFFICE BUILDING
WASHINGTON, DC 20515-6216
(202) 225-3951
judiciary.house.gov

April 6, 2022

Ms. Jonna Hiestand Mendez
c/o Central Intelligence Agency
via e-mail

Dear Ms. Mendez:

On October 14, 2020, the *New York Post* published a report detailing how Hunter Biden used the position and influence of his father, now-President Joe Biden, for personal gain with the apparent awareness of President Biden.[1] This article raised doubts about President Biden's earlier denial of ever speaking to his son about his international business dealings.[2] The *Post* reported on an email in which a Ukrainian businessman urged Hunter Biden to "use [his] influence to convey a message / signal, etc. to stop what we consider to be politically motivated actions."[3] In another email, the same businessman thanked Hunter Biden for arranging a meeting with his father, calling it "an honor and pleasure."[4] The *Post* reported that these emails came from a laptop belonging to Hunter Biden that he had abandoned in a Delaware computer shop.[5]

On October 19, 2020, you signed a public statement attempting to discredit the contents of the *New York Post*'s reporting about Hunter Biden.[6] This statement emphasized the national security credentials of you and the other signatories, implying that the assertions and conclusions in the statement were grounded in information unavailable to other Americans. Referencing this unique experience, you wrote:

> It is for all these reasons that we write to say that the arrival on the US political scene of emails purportedly belonging to Vice President Biden's son Hunter, much of it related to his time serving on the Board of the Ukrainian gas company Burisma, has all the classic earmarks of a Russian information operation.[7]

---

[1] Emma-Jo Morris & Gabrielle Fonrouge, *Smoking-gun email reveals how Hunter Biden introduced Ukrainian businessman to VP dad*, N.Y. Post, Oct. 14, 2020.
[2] *E.g.* Nick Givas, *Joe Biden again denies speaking to son about Ukrainian business dealings*, Fox News, Oct. 10, 2019.
[3] Morris & Fonrouge, *supra* note 1.
[4] *Id.*
[5] *Id.*
[6] Jim Clapper et al., Public Statement on the Hunter Biden Emails (Oct. 19, 2020).
[7] *Id.*

Although this statement acknowledged that you had seen no actual "evidence" of Russian involvement with respect to the publication of Hunter Biden's emails, you nonetheless conveyed a "deep[] suspicio[n] that the Russian government played a significant role in the case."[8] Later in the statement, you went further to state a "view"—not merely a suspicion anymore—"that the Russians are involved in the Hunter Biden email issue . . . ."[9]

Your public statement served as a basis for Democrat operatives to try to delegitimize the scandalous allegations about Hunter Biden and the Biden family. On the same day as your statement, *Politico* published a story about the statement, with the conclusive headline, "Hunter Biden story is Russian disinfo, dozens of former intel officials say."[10] Departing from the statement's careful wording, the *Politico* story quoted one signatory to the letter as being confident that "once again the Russians are interfering" in our elections.[11] Fifteen minutes after *Politico* published its story, Jen Psaki, who now serves as Press Secretary to the President, tweeted a link to the *Politico* story.[12] The Biden campaign repeatedly cited your statement to dismiss the allegations against Hunter Biden.[13] During the final presidential debate, Vice President Biden also dismissed concerns about Hunter Biden's international business dealings as part of a "Russian plan."[14]

Your public statement was consistent with a broader effort to minimize and censor the *New York Post*'s reporting about Hunter Biden and the Biden family. National news organizations called the allegations about Hunter Biden "dubious" and a "non-scandal"; CBS News reporter Leslie Stahl said the allegations "can't be verified"; and NPR called it a "waste . . . of time" and a "pure distraction."[15] Separately, Twitter and Facebook restricted access to the *New York Post*'s reporting about Hunter Biden, with Twitter locking the *Post*'s account and Facebook deferring to a so-called independent fact-check that never occurred.[16] These efforts likely affected public awareness of the serious allegations surrounding the Biden family in the crucial weeks before the 2020 election.

We now know from subsequent reporting that the *New York Post*'s article about Hunter Biden was not, as you and your co-signatories alleged, part of a "Russian information

---

[8] *Id.*
[9] *Id.*
[10] Natasha Bertrand, *Hunter Biden story is Russian disinfo, dozens of former intel officials say*, Politico, Oct. 19, 2020.
[11] *Id.*
[12] Tweet by Jen Psaki, Twitter.com (Oct. 19, 2020, 10:45 p.m.), https://twitter.com/jrpsaki/status/1318382779659411458.
[13] *E.g.* Houston Keene, *Flashback: Biden officials pushed angle that Hunter laptop was 'Russian disinfo,'* Fox News, Mar. 17, 2022.
[14] Deirdre Shesgreen, *"Nothing was unethical": Joe Biden defends Hunter Biden under pressure from Trump in debate*, USA Today, Oct. 22, 2020.
[15] Joe Concha, *Media's pre-election burial of Hunter Biden story proves dereliction of duty*, The Hill, Dec. 11, 2020.
[16] *E.g.* Elizabeth Dwoskin, *Facebook and Twitter take unusual steps to limit spread of New York Post story*, Wash. Post, Oct. 15, 2020.

operation."[17] This belated verification of the *Post*'s reporting raises fresh questions about the public statement you signed in October 2020. At best, the public statement was a reckless attempt by you and your co-signatories to erroneously opine about purported election interference. At worse—and more likely—the public statement was a deliberate and coordinated effort to mislead the American people about information relevant to the 2020 presidential election by invoking your national security experience to falsely suggest that the allegations about Hunter Biden were not based in fact.

The concerted effort to suppress public dissemination of the serious allegations about Hunter Biden and the Biden family, as first reported in October 2020 by the *New York Post*, was a grave disservice to American citizens' informed participation in our democracy. We are investigating the role that the public statement played in this effort. Accordingly, please provide the following material:

1. Identify all people with whom you communicated about the inception, drafting, editing, signing, publishing, or promotion of the "Public Statement on the Hunter Biden Emails" dated October 19, 2020; and

2. Produce all documents and communications referring or relating to the "Public Statement on the Hunter Biden Emails" dated October 19, 2020.

Please produce this material as soon as possible but no later than 5:00 p.m. on April 20, 2022. In addition, we request that you take all reasonable steps to preserve records that may be potentially responsive to this inquiry.

Thank you for your attention to this matter.

Sincerely,

Jim Jordan
Ranking Member

Steve Chabot
Member of Congress

Louie Gohmert
Member of Congress

Darrell Issa
Ranking Member
Subcommittee on Courts, Intellectual Property, and the Internet

[17] *E.g.* Katie Brenner et al., *Hunter Biden paid tax bill, but broad federal investigation continues*, N.Y. Times, Mar. 16, 2022; Matt Viser et al., *Inside Hunter Biden's multimillion-dollar deals with a Chinese energy company*, Wash. Post, Mar. 30, 2022.

Ken Buck
Ranking Member
Subcommittee on Antitrust, Commercial and Administrative Law

Matt Gaetz
Member of Congress

Mike Johnson
Ranking Member
Subcommittee on the Constitution, Civil Rights and Civil Liberties

Andy Biggs
Ranking Member
Subcommittee on Crime, Terrorism and Homeland Security

Tom McClintock
Ranking Member
Subcommittee on Immigration and Citizenship

W. Gregory Steube
Member of Congress

Tom Tiffany
Member of Congress

Thomas Massie
Member of Congress

Chip Roy
Member of Congress

Dan Bishop
Member of Congress

Michelle Fischbach
Member of Congress

Victoria Spartz
Member of Congress

Scott Fitzgerald
Member of Congress

Cliff Bentz
Member of Congress

Burgess Owens
Member of Congress

JERROLD NADLER, New York
CHAIRMAN

JIM JORDAN, Ohio
RANKING MEMBER

ONE HUNDRED SEVENTEENTH CONGRESS

Congress of the United States
House of Representatives
COMMITTEE ON THE JUDICIARY

2138 RAYBURN HOUSE OFFICE BUILDING

WASHINGTON, DC 20515-6216

(202) 225-3951
judiciary.house.gov

April 6, 2022

Mr. Michael Morell
via e-mail

Dear Mr. Morell:

On October 14, 2020, the *New York Post* published a report detailing how Hunter Biden used the position and influence of his father, now-President Joe Biden, for personal gain with the apparent awareness of President Biden.[1] This article raised doubts about President Biden's earlier denial of ever speaking to his son about his international business dealings.[2] The *Post* reported on an email in which a Ukrainian businessman urged Hunter Biden to "use [his] influence to convey a message / signal, etc. to stop what we consider to be politically motivated actions."[3] In another email, the same businessman thanked Hunter Biden for arranging a meeting with his father, calling it "an honor and pleasure."[4] The *Post* reported that these emails came from a laptop belonging to Hunter Biden that he had abandoned in a Delaware computer shop.[5]

On October 19, 2020, you signed a public statement attempting to discredit the contents of the *New York Post*'s reporting about Hunter Biden.[6] This statement emphasized the national security credentials of you and the other signatories, implying that the assertions and conclusions in the statement were grounded in information unavailable to other Americans. Referencing this unique experience, you wrote:

> It is for all these reasons that we write to say that the arrival on the US political scene of emails purportedly belonging to Vice President Biden's son Hunter, much of it related to his time serving on the Board of the Ukrainian gas company Burisma, has all the classic earmarks of a Russian information operation.[7]

---

[1] Emma-Jo Morris & Gabrielle Fonrouge, *Smoking-gun email reveals how Hunter Biden introduced Ukrainian businessman to VP dad*, N.Y. Post, Oct. 14, 2020.
[2] *E.g.* Nick Givas, *Joe Biden again denies speaking to son about Ukrainian business dealings*, Fox News, Oct. 10, 2019.
[3] Morris & Fonrouge, *supra* note 1.
[4] *Id.*
[5] *Id.*
[6] Jim Clapper et al., Public Statement on the Hunter Biden Emails (Oct. 19, 2020).
[7] *Id.*

Although this statement acknowledged that you had seen no actual "evidence" of Russian involvement with respect to the publication of Hunter Biden's emails, you nonetheless conveyed a "deep[] suspicio[n] that the Russian government played a significant role in the case."[8] Later in the statement, you went further to state a "view"—not merely a suspicion anymore—"that the Russians are involved in the Hunter Biden email issue . . . ."[9]

Your public statement served as a basis for Democrat operatives to try to delegitimize the scandalous allegations about Hunter Biden and the Biden family. On the same day as your statement, *Politico* published a story about the statement, with the conclusive headline, "Hunter Biden story is Russian disinfo, dozens of former intel officials say."[10] Departing from the statement's careful wording, the *Politico* story quoted one signatory to the letter as being confident that "once again the Russians are interfering" in our elections.[11] Fifteen minutes after *Politico* published its story, Jen Psaki, who now serves as Press Secretary to the President, tweeted a link to the *Politico* story.[12] The Biden campaign repeatedly cited your statement to dismiss the allegations against Hunter Biden.[13] During the final presidential debate, Vice President Biden also dismissed concerns about Hunter Biden's international business dealings as part of a "Russian plan."[14]

Your public statement was consistent with a broader effort to minimize and censor the *New York Post*'s reporting about Hunter Biden and the Biden family. National news organizations called the allegations about Hunter Biden "dubious" and a "non-scandal"; CBS News reporter Leslie Stahl said the allegations "can't be verified"; and NPR called it a "waste . . . of time" and a "pure distraction."[15] Separately, Twitter and Facebook restricted access to the *New York Post*'s reporting about Hunter Biden, with Twitter locking the *Post*'s account and Facebook deferring to a so-called independent fact-check that never occurred.[16] These efforts likely affected public awareness of the serious allegations surrounding the Biden family in the crucial weeks before the 2020 election.

We now know from subsequent reporting that the *New York Post*'s article about Hunter Biden was not, as you and your co-signatories alleged, part of a "Russian information

---

[8] *Id.*
[9] *Id.*
[10] Natasha Bertrand, *Hunter Biden story is Russian disinfo, dozens of former intel officials say*, Politico, Oct. 19, 2020.
[11] *Id.*
[12] Tweet by Jen Psaki, Twitter.com (Oct. 19, 2020, 10:45 p.m.), https://twitter.com/jrpsaki/status/1318382779659411458.
[13] *E.g.* Houston Keene, *Flashback: Biden officials pushed angle that Hunter laptop was 'Russian disinfo,'* Fox News, Mar. 17, 2022.
[14] Deirdre Shesgreen, *"Nothing was unethical": Joe Biden defends Hunter Biden under pressure from Trump in debate*, USA Today, Oct. 22, 2020.
[15] Joe Concha, *Media's pre-election burial of Hunter Biden story proves dereliction of duty*, The Hill, Dec. 11, 2020.
[16] *E.g.* Elizabeth Dwoskin, *Facebook and Twitter take unusual steps to limit spread of New York Post story*, Wash. Post, Oct. 15, 2020.

operation."[17] This belated verification of the *Post*'s reporting raises fresh questions about the public statement you signed in October 2020. At best, the public statement was a reckless attempt by you and your co-signatories to erroneously opine about purported election interference. At worse—and more likely—the public statement was a deliberate and coordinated effort to mislead the American people about information relevant to the 2020 presidential election by invoking your national security experience to falsely suggest that the allegations about Hunter Biden were not based in fact.

The concerted effort to suppress public dissemination of the serious allegations about Hunter Biden and the Biden family, as first reported in October 2020 by the *New York Post*, was a grave disservice to American citizens' informed participation in our democracy. We are investigating the role that the public statement played in this effort. Accordingly, please provide the following material:

1. Identify all people with whom you communicated about the inception, drafting, editing, signing, publishing, or promotion of the "Public Statement on the Hunter Biden Emails" dated October 19, 2020; and

2. Produce all documents and communications referring or relating to the "Public Statement on the Hunter Biden Emails" dated October 19, 2020.

Please produce this material as soon as possible but no later than 5:00 p.m. on April 20, 2022. In addition, we request that you take all reasonable steps to preserve records that may be potentially responsive to this inquiry.

Thank you for your attention to this matter.

Sincerely,

Jim Jordan
Ranking Member

Steve Chabot
Member of Congress

Louie Gohmert
Member of Congress

Darrell Issa
Ranking Member
Subcommittee on Courts, Intellectual Property, and the Internet

---

[17] *E.g.* Katie Brenner et al., *Hunter Biden paid tax bill, but broad federal investigation continues*, N.Y. Times, Mar. 16, 2022; Matt Viser et al., *Inside Hunter Biden's multimillion-dollar deals with a Chinese energy company*, Wash. Post, Mar. 30, 2022.

Ken Buck
Ranking Member
Subcommittee on Antitrust, Commercial and Administrative Law

Matt Gaetz
Member of Congress

Mike Johnson
Ranking Member
Subcommittee on the Constitution, Civil Rights and Civil Liberties

Andy Biggs
Ranking Member
Subcommittee on Crime, Terrorism and Homeland Security

Tom McClintock
Ranking Member
Subcommittee on Immigration and Citizenship

W. Gregory Steube
Member of Congress

Tom Tiffany
Member of Congress

Thomas Massie
Member of Congress

Chip Roy
Member of Congress

Dan Bishop
Member of Congress

Michelle Fischbach
Member of Congress

Victoria Spartz
Member of Congress

Scott Fitzgerald
Member of Congress

Cliff Bentz
Member of Congress

Burgess Owens
Member of Congress

JERROLD NADLER, New York
CHAIRMAN

JIM JORDAN, Ohio
RANKING MEMBER

ONE HUNDRED SEVENTEENTH CONGRESS

Congress of the United States

House of Representatives

COMMITTEE ON THE JUDICIARY

2138 RAYBURN HOUSE OFFICE BUILDING

WASHINGTON, DC 20515–6216

(202) 225–3951
judiciary.house.gov

April 6, 2022

Mr. John Moseman
c/o Central Intelligence Agency
via e-mail

Dear Mr. Moseman:

On October 14, 2020, the *New York Post* published a report detailing how Hunter Biden used the position and influence of his father, now-President Joe Biden, for personal gain with the apparent awareness of President Biden.[1] This article raised doubts about President Biden's earlier denial of ever speaking to his son about his international business dealings.[2] The *Post* reported on an email in which a Ukrainian businessman urged Hunter Biden to "use [his] influence to convey a message / signal, etc. to stop what we consider to be politically motivated actions."[3] In another email, the same businessman thanked Hunter Biden for arranging a meeting with his father, calling it "an honor and pleasure."[4] The *Post* reported that these emails came from a laptop belonging to Hunter Biden that he had abandoned in a Delaware computer shop.[5]

On October 19, 2020, you signed a public statement attempting to discredit the contents of the *New York Post*'s reporting about Hunter Biden.[6] This statement emphasized the national security credentials of you and the other signatories, implying that the assertions and conclusions in the statement were grounded in information unavailable to other Americans. Referencing this unique experience, you wrote:

> It is for all these reasons that we write to say that the arrival on the US political scene of emails purportedly belonging to Vice President Biden's son Hunter, much of it related to his time serving on the Board of the Ukrainian gas company Burisma, has all the classic earmarks of a Russian information operation.[7]

---

[1] Emma-Jo Morris & Gabrielle Fonrouge, *Smoking-gun email reveals how Hunter Biden introduced Ukrainian businessman to VP dad*, N.Y. Post, Oct. 14, 2020.
[2] *E.g.* Nick Givas, *Joe Biden again denies speaking to son about Ukrainian business dealings*, Fox News, Oct. 10, 2019.
[3] Morris & Fonrouge, *supra* note 1.
[4] *Id.*
[5] *Id.*
[6] Jim Clapper et al., Public Statement on the Hunter Biden Emails (Oct. 19, 2020).
[7] *Id.*

Although this statement acknowledged that you had seen no actual "evidence" of Russian involvement with respect to the publication of Hunter Biden's emails, you nonetheless conveyed a "deep[] suspicio[n] that the Russian government played a significant role in the case."[8] Later in the statement, you went further to state a "view"—not merely a suspicion anymore—"that the Russians are involved in the Hunter Biden email issue . . . ."[9]

Your public statement served as a basis for Democrat operatives to try to delegitimize the scandalous allegations about Hunter Biden and the Biden family. On the same day as your statement, *Politico* published a story about the statement, with the conclusive headline, "Hunter Biden story is Russian disinfo, dozens of former intel officials say."[10] Departing from the statement's careful wording, the *Politico* story quoted one signatory to the letter as being confident that "once again the Russians are interfering" in our elections.[11] Fifteen minutes after *Politico* published its story, Jen Psaki, who now serves as Press Secretary to the President, tweeted a link to the *Politico* story.[12] The Biden campaign repeatedly cited your statement to dismiss the allegations against Hunter Biden.[13] During the final presidential debate, Vice President Biden also dismissed concerns about Hunter Biden's international business dealings as part of a "Russian plan."[14]

Your public statement was consistent with a broader effort to minimize and censor the *New York Post*'s reporting about Hunter Biden and the Biden family. National news organizations called the allegations about Hunter Biden "dubious" and a "non-scandal"; CBS News reporter Leslie Stahl said the allegations "can't be verified"; and NPR called it a "waste . . . of time" and a "pure distraction."[15] Separately, Twitter and Facebook restricted access to the *New York Post*'s reporting about Hunter Biden, with Twitter locking the *Post*'s account and Facebook deferring to a so-called independent fact-check that never occurred.[16] These efforts likely affected public awareness of the serious allegations surrounding the Biden family in the crucial weeks before the 2020 election.

We now know from subsequent reporting that the *New York Post*'s article about Hunter Biden was not, as you and your co-signatories alleged, part of a "Russian information

---

[8] *Id.*
[9] *Id.*
[10] Natasha Bertrand, *Hunter Biden story is Russian disinfo, dozens of former intel officials say*, Politico, Oct. 19, 2020.
[11] *Id.*
[12] Tweet by Jen Psaki, Twitter.com (Oct. 19, 2020, 10:45 p.m.), https://twitter.com/jrpsaki/status/1318382779659411458.
[13] *E.g.* Houston Keene, *Flashback: Biden officials pushed angle that Hunter laptop was 'Russian disinfo,'* Fox News, Mar. 17, 2022.
[14] Deirdre Shesgreen, *"Nothing was unethical": Joe Biden defends Hunter Biden under pressure from Trump in debate*, USA Today, Oct. 22, 2020.
[15] Joe Concha, *Media's pre-election burial of Hunter Biden story proves dereliction of duty*, The Hill, Dec. 11, 2020.
[16] *E.g.* Elizabeth Dwoskin, *Facebook and Twitter take unusual steps to limit spread of New York Post story*, Wash. Post, Oct. 15, 2020.

operation."[17] This belated verification of the *Post*'s reporting raises fresh questions about the public statement you signed in October 2020. At best, the public statement was a reckless attempt by you and your co-signatories to erroneously opine about purported election interference. At worse—and more likely—the public statement was a deliberate and coordinated effort to mislead the American people about information relevant to the 2020 presidential election by invoking your national security experience to falsely suggest that the allegations about Hunter Biden were not based in fact.

The concerted effort to suppress public dissemination of the serious allegations about Hunter Biden and the Biden family, as first reported in October 2020 by the *New York Post*, was a grave disservice to American citizens' informed participation in our democracy. We are investigating the role that the public statement played in this effort. Accordingly, please provide the following material:

1. Identify all people with whom you communicated about the inception, drafting, editing, signing, publishing, or promotion of the "Public Statement on the Hunter Biden Emails" dated October 19, 2020; and

2. Produce all documents and communications referring or relating to the "Public Statement on the Hunter Biden Emails" dated October 19, 2020.

Please produce this material as soon as possible but no later than 5:00 p.m. on April 20, 2022. In addition, we request that you take all reasonable steps to preserve records that may be potentially responsive to this inquiry.

Thank you for your attention to this matter.

Sincerely,

Jim Jordan
Ranking Member

Steve Chabot
Member of Congress

Louie Gohmert
Member of Congress

Darrell Issa
Ranking Member
Subcommittee on Courts, Intellectual Property, and the Internet

---

[17] *E.g.* Katie Brenner et al., *Hunter Biden paid tax bill, but broad federal investigation continues*, N.Y. Times, Mar. 16, 2022; Matt Viser et al., *Inside Hunter Biden's multimillion-dollar deals with a Chinese energy company*, Wash. Post, Mar. 30, 2022.

Ken Buck
Ranking Member
Subcommittee on Antitrust, Commercial
and Administrative Law

Matt Gaetz
Member of Congress

Mike Johnson
Ranking Member
Subcommittee on the Constitution,
Civil Rights and Civil Liberties

Andy Biggs
Ranking Member
Subcommittee on Crime, Terrorism
and Homeland Security

Tom McClintock
Ranking Member
Subcommittee on Immigration
and Citizenship

W. Gregory Steube
Member of Congress

Tom Tiffany
Member of Congress

Thomas Massie
Member of Congress

Chip Roy
Member of Congress

Dan Bishop
Member of Congress

Michelle Fischbach
Member of Congress

Victoria Spartz
Member of Congress

Scott Fitzgerald
Member of Congress

Cliff Bentz
Member of Congress

Burgess Owens
Member of Congress

JERROLD NADLER, New York
CHAIRMAN

JIM JORDAN, Ohio
RANKING MEMBER

ONE HUNDRED SEVENTEENTH CONGRESS

Congress of the United States

House of Representatives

COMMITTEE ON THE JUDICIARY

2138 RAYBURN HOUSE OFFICE BUILDING

WASHINGTON, DC 20515-6216

(202) 225-3951
judiciary.house.gov

April 6, 2022

Mr. Emile Nakhleh
via e-mail

Dear Mr. Nakhleh:

On October 14, 2020, the *New York Post* published a report detailing how Hunter Biden used the position and influence of his father, now-President Joe Biden, for personal gain with the apparent awareness of President Biden.[1] This article raised doubts about President Biden's earlier denial of ever speaking to his son about his international business dealings.[2] The *Post* reported on an email in which a Ukrainian businessman urged Hunter Biden to "use [his] influence to convey a message / signal, etc. to stop what we consider to be politically motivated actions."[3] In another email, the same businessman thanked Hunter Biden for arranging a meeting with his father, calling it "an honor and pleasure."[4] The *Post* reported that these emails came from a laptop belonging to Hunter Biden that he had abandoned in a Delaware computer shop.[5]

On October 19, 2020, you signed a public statement attempting to discredit the contents of the *New York Post*'s reporting about Hunter Biden.[6] This statement emphasized the national security credentials of you and the other signatories, implying that the assertions and conclusions in the statement were grounded in information unavailable to other Americans. Referencing this unique experience, you wrote:

> It is for all these reasons that we write to say that the arrival on the US political scene of emails purportedly belonging to Vice President Biden's son Hunter, much of it related to his time serving on the Board of the Ukrainian gas company Burisma, has all the classic earmarks of a Russian information operation.[7]

---

[1] Emma-Jo Morris & Gabrielle Fonrouge, *Smoking-gun email reveals how Hunter Biden introduced Ukrainian businessman to VP dad*, N.Y. Post, Oct. 14, 2020.
[2] *E.g.* Nick Givas, *Joe Biden again denies speaking to son about Ukrainian business dealings*, Fox News, Oct. 10, 2019.
[3] Morris & Fonrouge, *supra* note 1.
[4] *Id.*
[5] *Id.*
[6] Jim Clapper et al., Public Statement on the Hunter Biden Emails (Oct. 19, 2020).
[7] *Id.*

Although this statement acknowledged that you had seen no actual "evidence" of Russian involvement with respect to the publication of Hunter Biden's emails, you nonetheless conveyed a "deep[] suspicio[n] that the Russian government played a significant role in the case."[8] Later in the statement, you went further to state a "view"—not merely a suspicion anymore—"that the Russians are involved in the Hunter Biden email issue . . . ."[9]

Your public statement served as a basis for Democrat operatives to try to delegitimize the scandalous allegations about Hunter Biden and the Biden family. On the same day as your statement, *Politico* published a story about the statement, with the conclusive headline, "Hunter Biden story is Russian disinfo, dozens of former intel officials say."[10] Departing from the statement's careful wording, the *Politico* story quoted one signatory to the letter as being confident that "once again the Russians are interfering" in our elections.[11] Fifteen minutes after *Politico* published its story, Jen Psaki, who now serves as Press Secretary to the President, tweeted a link to the *Politico* story.[12] The Biden campaign repeatedly cited your statement to dismiss the allegations against Hunter Biden.[13] During the final presidential debate, Vice President Biden also dismissed concerns about Hunter Biden's international business dealings as part of a "Russian plan."[14]

Your public statement was consistent with a broader effort to minimize and censor the *New York Post*'s reporting about Hunter Biden and the Biden family. National news organizations called the allegations about Hunter Biden "dubious" and a "non-scandal"; CBS News reporter Leslie Stahl said the allegations "can't be verified"; and NPR called it a "waste . . . of time" and a "pure distraction."[15] Separately, Twitter and Facebook restricted access to the *New York Post*'s reporting about Hunter Biden, with Twitter locking the *Post*'s account and Facebook deferring to a so-called independent fact-check that never occurred.[16] These efforts likely affected public awareness of the serious allegations surrounding the Biden family in the crucial weeks before the 2020 election.

We now know from subsequent reporting that the *New York Post*'s article about Hunter Biden was not, as you and your co-signatories alleged, part of a "Russian information

---

[8] *Id.*
[9] *Id.*
[10] Natasha Bertrand, *Hunter Biden story is Russian disinfo, dozens of former intel officials say*, Politico, Oct. 19, 2020.
[11] *Id.*
[12] Tweet by Jen Psaki, Twitter.com (Oct. 19, 2020, 10:45 p.m.), https://twitter.com/jrpsaki/status/1318382779659411458.
[13] *E.g.* Houston Keene, *Flashback: Biden officials pushed angle that Hunter laptop was 'Russian disinfo,'* Fox News, Mar. 17, 2022.
[14] Deirdre Shesgreen, *"Nothing was unethical": Joe Biden defends Hunter Biden under pressure from Trump in debate*, USA Today, Oct. 22, 2020.
[15] Joe Concha, *Media's pre-election burial of Hunter Biden story proves dereliction of duty*, The Hill, Dec. 11, 2020.
[16] *E.g.* Elizabeth Dwoskin, *Facebook and Twitter take unusual steps to limit spread of New York Post story*, Wash. Post, Oct. 15, 2020.

operation."[17] This belated verification of the *Post*'s reporting raises fresh questions about the public statement you signed in October 2020. At best, the public statement was a reckless attempt by you and your co-signatories to erroneously opine about purported election interference. At worse—and more likely—the public statement was a deliberate and coordinated effort to mislead the American people about information relevant to the 2020 presidential election by invoking your national security experience to falsely suggest that the allegations about Hunter Biden were not based in fact.

The concerted effort to suppress public dissemination of the serious allegations about Hunter Biden and the Biden family, as first reported in October 2020 by the *New York Post*, was a grave disservice to American citizens' informed participation in our democracy. We are investigating the role that the public statement played in this effort. Accordingly, please provide the following material:

1. Identify all people with whom you communicated about the inception, drafting, editing, signing, publishing, or promotion of the "Public Statement on the Hunter Biden Emails" dated October 19, 2020; and

2. Produce all documents and communications referring or relating to the "Public Statement on the Hunter Biden Emails" dated October 19, 2020.

Please produce this material as soon as possible but no later than 5:00 p.m. on April 20, 2022. In addition, we request that you take all reasonable steps to preserve records that may be potentially responsive to this inquiry.

Thank you for your attention to this matter.

Sincerely,

Jim Jordan
Ranking Member

Steve Chabot
Member of Congress

Louie Gohmert
Member of Congress

Darrell Issa
Ranking Member
Subcommittee on Courts, Intellectual Property, and the Internet

---

[17] *E.g.* Katie Brenner et al., *Hunter Biden paid tax bill, but broad federal investigation continues*, N.Y. Times, Mar. 16, 2022; Matt Viser et al., *Inside Hunter Biden's multimillion-dollar deals with a Chinese energy company*, Wash. Post, Mar. 30, 2022.

Ken Buck
Ranking Member
Subcommittee on Antitrust, Commercial and Administrative Law

Matt Gaetz
Member of Congress

Mike Johnson
Ranking Member
Subcommittee on the Constitution, Civil Rights and Civil Liberties

Andy Biggs
Ranking Member
Subcommittee on Crime, Terrorism and Homeland Security

Tom McClintock
Ranking Member
Subcommittee on Immigration and Citizenship

W. Gregory Steube
Member of Congress

Tom Tiffany
Member of Congress

Thomas Massie
Member of Congress

Chip Roy
Member of Congress

Dan Bishop
Member of Congress

Michelle Fischbach
Member of Congress

Victoria Spartz
Member of Congress

Scott Fitzgerald
Member of Congress

Cliff Bentz
Member of Congress

Burgess Owens
Member of Congress

JERROLD NADLER, New York
CHAIRMAN

JIM JORDAN, Ohio
RANKING MEMBER

ONE HUNDRED SEVENTEENTH CONGRESS
Congress of the United States
House of Representatives
COMMITTEE ON THE JUDICIARY
2138 RAYBURN HOUSE OFFICE BUILDING
WASHINGTON, DC 20515-6216
(202) 225-3951
judiciary.house.gov

April 6, 2022

Mr. Gerald A. O'Shea
c/o Central Intelligence Agency
via e-mail

Dear Mr. O'Shea:

On October 14, 2020, the *New York Post* published a report detailing how Hunter Biden used the position and influence of his father, now-President Joe Biden, for personal gain with the apparent awareness of President Biden.[1] This article raised doubts about President Biden's earlier denial of ever speaking to his son about his international business dealings.[2] The *Post* reported on an email in which a Ukrainian businessman urged Hunter Biden to "use [his] influence to convey a message / signal, etc. to stop what we consider to be politically motivated actions."[3] In another email, the same businessman thanked Hunter Biden for arranging a meeting with his father, calling it "an honor and pleasure."[4] The *Post* reported that these emails came from a laptop belonging to Hunter Biden that he had abandoned in a Delaware computer shop.[5]

On October 19, 2020, you signed a public statement attempting to discredit the contents of the *New York Post*'s reporting about Hunter Biden.[6] This statement emphasized the national security credentials of you and the other signatories, implying that the assertions and conclusions in the statement were grounded in information unavailable to other Americans. Referencing this unique experience, you wrote:

> It is for all these reasons that we write to say that the arrival on the US political scene of emails purportedly belonging to Vice President Biden's son Hunter, much of it related to his time serving on the Board of the Ukrainian gas company Burisma, has all the classic earmarks of a Russian information operation.[7]

---

[1] Emma-Jo Morris & Gabrielle Fonrouge, *Smoking-gun email reveals how Hunter Biden introduced Ukrainian businessman to VP dad*, N.Y. Post, Oct. 14, 2020.
[2] *E.g.* Nick Givas, *Joe Biden again denies speaking to son about Ukrainian business dealings*, Fox News, Oct. 10, 2019.
[3] Morris & Fonrouge, *supra* note 1.
[4] *Id.*
[5] *Id.*
[6] Jim Clapper et al., Public Statement on the Hunter Biden Emails (Oct. 19, 2020).
[7] *Id.*

Although this statement acknowledged that you had seen no actual "evidence" of Russian involvement with respect to the publication of Hunter Biden's emails, you nonetheless conveyed a "deep[] suspicio[n] that the Russian government played a significant role in the case."[8] Later in the statement, you went further to state a "view"—not merely a suspicion anymore—"that the Russians are involved in the Hunter Biden email issue . . . ."[9]

Your public statement served as a basis for Democrat operatives to try to delegitimize the scandalous allegations about Hunter Biden and the Biden family. On the same day as your statement, *Politico* published a story about the statement, with the conclusive headline, "Hunter Biden story is Russian disinfo, dozens of former intel officials say."[10] Departing from the statement's careful wording, the *Politico* story quoted one signatory to the letter as being confident that "once again the Russians are interfering" in our elections.[11] Fifteen minutes after *Politico* published its story, Jen Psaki, who now serves as Press Secretary to the President, tweeted a link to the *Politico* story.[12] The Biden campaign repeatedly cited your statement to dismiss the allegations against Hunter Biden.[13] During the final presidential debate, Vice President Biden also dismissed concerns about Hunter Biden's international business dealings as part of a "Russian plan."[14]

Your public statement was consistent with a broader effort to minimize and censor the *New York Post*'s reporting about Hunter Biden and the Biden family. National news organizations called the allegations about Hunter Biden "dubious" and a "non-scandal"; CBS News reporter Leslie Stahl said the allegations "can't be verified"; and NPR called it a "waste . . . of time" and a "pure distraction."[15] Separately, Twitter and Facebook restricted access to the *New York Post*'s reporting about Hunter Biden, with Twitter locking the *Post*'s account and Facebook deferring to a so-called independent fact-check that never occurred.[16] These efforts likely affected public awareness of the serious allegations surrounding the Biden family in the crucial weeks before the 2020 election.

We now know from subsequent reporting that the *New York Post*'s article about Hunter Biden was not, as you and your co-signatories alleged, part of a "Russian information

[8] *Id.*
[9] *Id.*
[10] Natasha Bertrand, *Hunter Biden story is Russian disinfo, dozens of former intel officials say*, Politico, Oct. 19, 2020.
[11] *Id.*
[12] Tweet by Jen Psaki, Twitter.com (Oct. 19, 2020, 10:45 p.m.), https://twitter.com/jrpsaki/status/1318382779659411458.
[13] *E.g.* Houston Keene, *Flashback: Biden officials pushed angle that Hunter laptop was 'Russian disinfo,'* Fox News, Mar. 17, 2022.
[14] Deirdre Shesgreen, *"Nothing was unethical": Joe Biden defends Hunter Biden under pressure from Trump in debate*, USA Today, Oct. 22, 2020.
[15] Joe Concha, *Media's pre-election burial of Hunter Biden story proves dereliction of duty*, The Hill, Dec. 11, 2020.
[16] *E.g.* Elizabeth Dwoskin, *Facebook and Twitter take unusual steps to limit spread of New York Post story*, Wash. Post, Oct. 15, 2020.

operation."[17] This belated verification of the *Post*'s reporting raises fresh questions about the public statement you signed in October 2020. At best, the public statement was a reckless attempt by you and your co-signatories to erroneously opine about purported election interference. At worse—and more likely—the public statement was a deliberate and coordinated effort to mislead the American people about information relevant to the 2020 presidential election by invoking your national security experience to falsely suggest that the allegations about Hunter Biden were not based in fact.

The concerted effort to suppress public dissemination of the serious allegations about Hunter Biden and the Biden family, as first reported in October 2020 by the *New York Post*, was a grave disservice to American citizens' informed participation in our democracy. We are investigating the role that the public statement played in this effort. Accordingly, please provide the following material:

1. Identify all people with whom you communicated about the inception, drafting, editing, signing, publishing, or promotion of the "Public Statement on the Hunter Biden Emails" dated October 19, 2020; and

2. Produce all documents and communications referring or relating to the "Public Statement on the Hunter Biden Emails" dated October 19, 2020.

Please produce this material as soon as possible but no later than 5:00 p.m. on April 20, 2022. In addition, we request that you take all reasonable steps to preserve records that may be potentially responsive to this inquiry.

Thank you for your attention to this matter.

Sincerely,

Jim Jordan
Ranking Member

Steve Chabot
Member of Congress

Louie Gohmert
Member of Congress

Darrell Issa
Ranking Member
Subcommittee on Courts, Intellectual Property, and the Internet

---

[17] *E.g.* Katie Brenner et al., *Hunter Biden paid tax bill, but broad federal investigation continues*, N.Y. Times, Mar. 16, 2022; Matt Viser et al., *Inside Hunter Biden's multimillion-dollar deals with a Chinese energy company*, Wash. Post, Mar. 30, 2022.

Ken Buck
Ranking Member
Subcommittee on Antitrust, Commercial and Administrative Law

Matt Gaetz
Member of Congress

Mike Johnson
Ranking Member
Subcommittee on the Constitution, Civil Rights and Civil Liberties

Andy Biggs
Ranking Member
Subcommittee on Crime, Terrorism and Homeland Security

Tom McClintock
Ranking Member
Subcommittee on Immigration and Citizenship

W. Gregory Steube
Member of Congress

Tom Tiffany
Member of Congress

Thomas Massie
Member of Congress

Chip Roy
Member of Congress

Dan Bishop
Member of Congress

Michelle Fischbach
Member of Congress

Victoria Spartz
Member of Congress

Scott Fitzgerald
Member of Congress

Cliff Bentz
Member of Congress

Burgess Owens
Member of Congress

JERROLD NADLER, New York
CHAIRMAN

JIM JORDAN, Ohio
RANKING MEMBER

ONE HUNDRED SEVENTEENTH CONGRESS

Congress of the United States
House of Representatives

COMMITTEE ON THE JUDICIARY
2138 RAYBURN HOUSE OFFICE BUILDING
WASHINGTON, DC 20515–6216
(202) 225–3951
judiciary.house.gov

April 6, 2022

The Honorable Leon Panetta
via e-mail

Dear Secretary Panetta:

On October 14, 2020, the *New York Post* published a report detailing how Hunter Biden used the position and influence of his father, now-President Joe Biden, for personal gain with the apparent awareness of President Biden.[1] This article raised doubts about President Biden's earlier denial of ever speaking to his son about his international business dealings.[2] The *Post* reported on an email in which a Ukrainian businessman urged Hunter Biden to "use [his] influence to convey a message / signal, etc. to stop what we consider to be politically motivated actions."[3] In another email, the same businessman thanked Hunter Biden for arranging a meeting with his father, calling it "an honor and pleasure."[4] The *Post* reported that these emails came from a laptop belonging to Hunter Biden that he had abandoned in a Delaware computer shop.[5]

On October 19, 2020, you signed a public statement attempting to discredit the contents of the *New York Post*'s reporting about Hunter Biden.[6] This statement emphasized the national security credentials of you and the other signatories, implying that the assertions and conclusions in the statement were grounded in information unavailable to other Americans. Referencing this unique experience, you wrote:

> It is for all these reasons that we write to say that the arrival on the US political scene of emails purportedly belonging to Vice President Biden's son Hunter, much of it related to his time serving on the Board of the Ukrainian gas company Burisma, has all the classic earmarks of a Russian information operation.[7]

---

[1] Emma-Jo Morris & Gabrielle Fonrouge, *Smoking-gun email reveals how Hunter Biden introduced Ukrainian businessman to VP dad*, N.Y. Post, Oct. 14, 2020.
[2] *E.g.* Nick Givas, *Joe Biden again denies speaking to son about Ukrainian business dealings*, Fox News, Oct. 10, 2019.
[3] Morris & Fonrouge, *supra* note 1.
[4] *Id.*
[5] *Id.*
[6] Jim Clapper et al., Public Statement on the Hunter Biden Emails (Oct. 19, 2020).
[7] *Id.*

Although this statement acknowledged that you had seen no actual "evidence" of Russian involvement with respect to the publication of Hunter Biden's emails, you nonetheless conveyed a "deep[] suspicio[n] that the Russian government played a significant role in the case."[8] Later in the statement, you went further to state a "view"—not merely a suspicion anymore—"that the Russians are involved in the Hunter Biden email issue . . . ."[9]

Your public statement served as a basis for Democrat operatives to try to delegitimize the scandalous allegations about Hunter Biden and the Biden family. On the same day as your statement, *Politico* published a story about the statement, with the conclusive headline, "Hunter Biden story is Russian disinfo, dozens of former intel officials say."[10] Departing from the statement's careful wording, the *Politico* story quoted one signatory to the letter as being confident that "once again the Russians are interfering" in our elections.[11] Fifteen minutes after *Politico* published its story, Jen Psaki, who now serves as Press Secretary to the President, tweeted a link to the *Politico* story.[12] The Biden campaign repeatedly cited your statement to dismiss the allegations against Hunter Biden.[13] During the final presidential debate, Vice President Biden also dismissed concerns about Hunter Biden's international business dealings as part of a "Russian plan."[14]

Your public statement was consistent with a broader effort to minimize and censor the *New York Post*'s reporting about Hunter Biden and the Biden family. National news organizations called the allegations about Hunter Biden "dubious" and a "non-scandal"; CBS News reporter Leslie Stahl said the allegations "can't be verified"; and NPR called it a "waste . . . of time" and a "pure distraction."[15] Separately, Twitter and Facebook restricted access to the *New York Post*'s reporting about Hunter Biden, with Twitter locking the *Post*'s account and Facebook deferring to a so-called independent fact-check that never occurred.[16] These efforts likely affected public awareness of the serious allegations surrounding the Biden family in the crucial weeks before the 2020 election.

We now know from subsequent reporting that the *New York Post*'s article about Hunter Biden was not, as you and your co-signatories alleged, part of a "Russian information

[8] *Id.*
[9] *Id.*
[10] Natasha Bertrand, *Hunter Biden story is Russian disinfo, dozens of former intel officials say*, Politico, Oct. 19, 2020.
[11] *Id.*
[12] Tweet by Jen Psaki, Twitter.com (Oct. 19, 2020, 10:45 p.m.), https://twitter.com/jrpsaki/status/1318382779659411458.
[13] *E.g.* Houston Keene, *Flashback: Biden officials pushed angle that Hunter laptop was 'Russian disinfo,'* Fox News, Mar. 17, 2022.
[14] Deirdre Shesgreen, *"Nothing was unethical": Joe Biden defends Hunter Biden under pressure from Trump in debate*, USA Today, Oct. 22, 2020.
[15] Joe Concha, *Media's pre-election burial of Hunter Biden story proves dereliction of duty*, The Hill, Dec. 11, 2020.
[16] *E.g.* Elizabeth Dwoskin, *Facebook and Twitter take unusual steps to limit spread of New York Post story*, Wash. Post, Oct. 15, 2020.

operation."[17] This belated verification of the *Post*'s reporting raises fresh questions about the public statement you signed in October 2020. At best, the public statement was a reckless attempt by you and your co-signatories to erroneously opine about purported election interference. At worse—and more likely—the public statement was a deliberate and coordinated effort to mislead the American people about information relevant to the 2020 presidential election by invoking your national security experience to falsely suggest that the allegations about Hunter Biden were not based in fact.

The concerted effort to suppress public dissemination of the serious allegations about Hunter Biden and the Biden family, as first reported in October 2020 by the *New York Post*, was a grave disservice to American citizens' informed participation in our democracy. We are investigating the role that the public statement played in this effort. Accordingly, please provide the following material:

1. Identify all people with whom you communicated about the inception, drafting, editing, signing, publishing, or promotion of the "Public Statement on the Hunter Biden Emails" dated October 19, 2020; and

2. Produce all documents and communications referring or relating to the "Public Statement on the Hunter Biden Emails" dated October 19, 2020.

Please produce this material as soon as possible but no later than 5:00 p.m. on April 20, 2022. In addition, we request that you take all reasonable steps to preserve records that may be potentially responsive to this inquiry.

Thank you for your attention to this matter.

Sincerely,

Jim Jordan
Ranking Member

Steve Chabot
Member of Congress

Louie Gohmert
Member of Congress

Darrell Issa
Ranking Member
Subcommittee on Courts, Intellectual Property, and the Internet

---

[17] *E.g.* Katie Brenner et al., *Hunter Biden paid tax bill, but broad federal investigation continues*, N.Y. Times, Mar. 16, 2022; Matt Viser et al., *Inside Hunter Biden's multimillion-dollar deals with a Chinese energy company*, Wash. Post, Mar. 30, 2022.

Ken Buck
Ranking Member
Subcommittee on Antitrust, Commercial and Administrative Law

Matt Gaetz
Member of Congress

Mike Johnson
Ranking Member
Subcommittee on the Constitution, Civil Rights and Civil Liberties

Andy Biggs
Ranking Member
Subcommittee on Crime, Terrorism and Homeland Security

Tom McClintock
Ranking Member
Subcommittee on Immigration and Citizenship

W. Gregory Steube
Member of Congress

Tom Tiffany
Member of Congress

Thomas Massie
Member of Congress

Chip Roy
Member of Congress

Dan Bishop
Member of Congress

Michelle Fischbach
Member of Congress

Victoria Spartz
Member of Congress

Scott Fitzgerald
Member of Congress

Cliff Bentz
Member of Congress

Burgess Owens
Member of Congress

JERROLD NADLER, New York
CHAIRMAN

JIM JORDAN, Ohio
RANKING MEMBER

ONE HUNDRED SEVENTEENTH CONGRESS

Congress of the United States
House of Representatives

COMMITTEE ON THE JUDICIARY
2138 RAYBURN HOUSE OFFICE BUILDING
WASHINGTON, DC 20515–6216
(202) 225–3951
judiciary.house.gov

April 6, 2022

Mr. Larry Pfeiffer
via e-mail

Dear Mr. Pfeiffer:

On October 14, 2020, the *New York Post* published a report detailing how Hunter Biden used the position and influence of his father, now-President Joe Biden, for personal gain with the apparent awareness of President Biden.[1] This article raised doubts about President Biden's earlier denial of ever speaking to his son about his international business dealings.[2] The *Post* reported on an email in which a Ukrainian businessman urged Hunter Biden to "use [his] influence to convey a message / signal, etc. to stop what we consider to be politically motivated actions."[3] In another email, the same businessman thanked Hunter Biden for arranging a meeting with his father, calling it "an honor and pleasure."[4] The *Post* reported that these emails came from a laptop belonging to Hunter Biden that he had abandoned in a Delaware computer shop.[5]

On October 19, 2020, you signed a public statement attempting to discredit the contents of the *New York Post*'s reporting about Hunter Biden.[6] This statement emphasized the national security credentials of you and the other signatories, implying that the assertions and conclusions in the statement were grounded in information unavailable to other Americans. Referencing this unique experience, you wrote:

> It is for all these reasons that we write to say that the arrival on the US political scene of emails purportedly belonging to Vice President Biden's son Hunter, much of it related to his time serving on the Board of the Ukrainian gas company Burisma, has all the classic earmarks of a Russian information operation.[7]

---

[1] Emma-Jo Morris & Gabrielle Fonrouge, *Smoking-gun email reveals how Hunter Biden introduced Ukrainian businessman to VP dad*, N.Y. Post, Oct. 14, 2020.
[2] *E.g.* Nick Givas, *Joe Biden again denies speaking to son about Ukrainian business dealings*, Fox News, Oct. 10, 2019.
[3] Morris & Fonrouge, *supra* note 1.
[4] *Id.*
[5] *Id.*
[6] Jim Clapper et al., Public Statement on the Hunter Biden Emails (Oct. 19, 2020).
[7] *Id.*

Although this statement acknowledged that you had seen no actual "evidence" of Russian involvement with respect to the publication of Hunter Biden's emails, you nonetheless conveyed a "deep[] suspicio[n] that the Russian government played a significant role in the case."[8] Later in the statement, you went further to state a "view"—not merely a suspicion anymore—"that the Russians are involved in the Hunter Biden email issue . . . ."[9]

Your public statement served as a basis for Democrat operatives to try to delegitimize the scandalous allegations about Hunter Biden and the Biden family. On the same day as your statement, *Politico* published a story about the statement, with the conclusive headline, "Hunter Biden story is Russian disinfo, dozens of former intel officials say."[10] Departing from the statement's careful wording, the *Politico* story quoted one signatory to the letter as being confident that "once again the Russians are interfering" in our elections.[11] Fifteen minutes after *Politico* published its story, Jen Psaki, who now serves as Press Secretary to the President, tweeted a link to the *Politico* story.[12] The Biden campaign repeatedly cited your statement to dismiss the allegations against Hunter Biden.[13] During the final presidential debate, Vice President Biden also dismissed concerns about Hunter Biden's international business dealings as part of a "Russian plan."[14]

Your public statement was consistent with a broader effort to minimize and censor the *New York Post*'s reporting about Hunter Biden and the Biden family. National news organizations called the allegations about Hunter Biden "dubious" and a "non-scandal"; CBS News reporter Leslie Stahl said the allegations "can't be verified"; and NPR called it a "waste . . . of time" and a "pure distraction."[15] Separately, Twitter and Facebook restricted access to the *New York Post*'s reporting about Hunter Biden, with Twitter locking the *Post*'s account and Facebook deferring to a so-called independent fact-check that never occurred.[16] These efforts likely affected public awareness of the serious allegations surrounding the Biden family in the crucial weeks before the 2020 election.

We now know from subsequent reporting that the *New York Post*'s article about Hunter Biden was not, as you and your co-signatories alleged, part of a "Russian information

---

[8] *Id.*
[9] *Id.*
[10] Natasha Bertrand, *Hunter Biden story is Russian disinfo, dozens of former intel officials say*, Politico, Oct. 19, 2020.
[11] *Id.*
[12] Tweet by Jen Psaki, Twitter.com (Oct. 19, 2020, 10:45 p.m.), https://twitter.com/jrpsaki/status/1318382779659411458.
[13] *E.g.* Houston Keene, *Flashback: Biden officials pushed angle that Hunter laptop was 'Russian disinfo,'* Fox News, Mar. 17, 2022.
[14] Deirdre Shesgreen, *"Nothing was unethical": Joe Biden defends Hunter Biden under pressure from Trump in debate*, USA Today, Oct. 22, 2020.
[15] Joe Concha, *Media's pre-election burial of Hunter Biden story proves dereliction of duty*, The Hill, Dec. 11, 2020.
[16] *E.g.* Elizabeth Dwoskin, *Facebook and Twitter take unusual steps to limit spread of New York Post story*, Wash. Post, Oct. 15, 2020.

operation."[17] This belated verification of the *Post*'s reporting raises fresh questions about the public statement you signed in October 2020. At best, the public statement was a reckless attempt by you and your co-signatories to erroneously opine about purported election interference. At worse—and more likely—the public statement was a deliberate and coordinated effort to mislead the American people about information relevant to the 2020 presidential election by invoking your national security experience to falsely suggest that the allegations about Hunter Biden were not based in fact.

The concerted effort to suppress public dissemination of the serious allegations about Hunter Biden and the Biden family, as first reported in October 2020 by the *New York Post*, was a grave disservice to American citizens' informed participation in our democracy. We are investigating the role that the public statement played in this effort. Accordingly, please provide the following material:

1. Identify all people with whom you communicated about the inception, drafting, editing, signing, publishing, or promotion of the "Public Statement on the Hunter Biden Emails" dated October 19, 2020; and

2. Produce all documents and communications referring or relating to the "Public Statement on the Hunter Biden Emails" dated October 19, 2020.

Please produce this material as soon as possible but no later than 5:00 p.m. on April 20, 2022. In addition, we request that you take all reasonable steps to preserve records that may be potentially responsive to this inquiry.

Thank you for your attention to this matter.

Sincerely,

Jim Jordan
Ranking Member

Steve Chabot
Member of Congress

Louie Gohmert
Member of Congress

Darrell Issa
Ranking Member
Subcommittee on Courts, Intellectual Property, and the Internet

---

[17] *E.g.* Katie Brenner et al., *Hunter Biden paid tax bill, but broad federal investigation continues*, N.Y. Times, Mar. 16, 2022; Matt Viser et al., *Inside Hunter Biden's multimillion-dollar deals with a Chinese energy company*, Wash. Post, Mar. 30, 2022.

Ken Buck
Ranking Member
Subcommittee on Antitrust, Commercial and Administrative Law

Mike Johnson
Ranking Member
Subcommittee on the Constitution, Civil Rights and Civil Liberties

Tom McClintock
Ranking Member
Subcommittee on Immigration and Citizenship

Tom Tiffany
Member of Congress

Chip Roy
Member of Congress

Michelle Fischbach
Member of Congress

Matt Gaetz
Member of Congress

Andy Biggs
Ranking Member
Subcommittee on Crime, Terrorism and Homeland Security

W. Gregory Steube
Member of Congress

Thomas Massie
Member of Congress

Dan Bishop
Member of Congress

Victoria Spartz
Member of Congress

Scott Fitzgerald
Member of Congress

Cliff Bentz
Member of Congress

Burgess Owens
Member of Congress

JERROLD NADLER, New York
CHAIRMAN

JIM JORDAN, Ohio
RANKING MEMBER

ONE HUNDRED SEVENTEENTH CONGRESS

Congress of the United States

House of Representatives

COMMITTEE ON THE JUDICIARY

2138 RAYBURN HOUSE OFFICE BUILDING

WASHINGTON, DC 20515–6216

(202) 225–3951
judiciary.house.gov

April 6, 2022

Mr. Marc Polymeropoulos
via e-mail

Dear Mr. Polymeropoulos:

On October 14, 2020, the *New York Post* published a report detailing how Hunter Biden used the position and influence of his father, now-President Joe Biden, for personal gain with the apparent awareness of President Biden.[1] This article raised doubts about President Biden's earlier denial of ever speaking to his son about his international business dealings.[2] The *Post* reported on an email in which a Ukrainian businessman urged Hunter Biden to "use [his] influence to convey a message / signal, etc. to stop what we consider to be politically motivated actions."[3] In another email, the same businessman thanked Hunter Biden for arranging a meeting with his father, calling it "an honor and pleasure."[4] The *Post* reported that these emails came from a laptop belonging to Hunter Biden that he had abandoned in a Delaware computer shop.[5]

On October 19, 2020, you signed a public statement attempting to discredit the contents of the *New York Post*'s reporting about Hunter Biden.[6] This statement emphasized the national security credentials of you and the other signatories, implying that the assertions and conclusions in the statement were grounded in information unavailable to other Americans. Referencing this unique experience, you wrote:

> It is for all these reasons that we write to say that the arrival on the US political scene of emails purportedly belonging to Vice President Biden's son Hunter, much of it related to his time serving on the Board of the Ukrainian gas company Burisma, has all the classic earmarks of a Russian information operation.[7]

---

[1] Emma-Jo Morris & Gabrielle Fonrouge, *Smoking-gun email reveals how Hunter Biden introduced Ukrainian businessman to VP dad*, N.Y. Post, Oct. 14, 2020.
[2] *E.g.* Nick Givas, *Joe Biden again denies speaking to son about Ukrainian business dealings*, Fox News, Oct. 10, 2019.
[3] Morris & Fonrouge, *supra* note 1.
[4] *Id.*
[5] *Id.*
[6] Jim Clapper et al., Public Statement on the Hunter Biden Emails (Oct. 19, 2020).
[7] *Id.*

Although this statement acknowledged that you had seen no actual "evidence" of Russian involvement with respect to the publication of Hunter Biden's emails, you nonetheless conveyed a "deep[] suspicio[n] that the Russian government played a significant role in the case."[8] Later in the statement, you went further to state a "view"—not merely a suspicion anymore—"that the Russians are involved in the Hunter Biden email issue . . . ."[9]

Your public statement served as a basis for Democrat operatives to try to delegitimize the scandalous allegations about Hunter Biden and the Biden family. On the same day as your statement, *Politico* published a story about the statement, with the conclusive headline, "Hunter Biden story is Russian disinfo, dozens of former intel officials say."[10] Departing from the statement's careful wording, the *Politico* story quoted one signatory to the letter as being confident that "once again the Russians are interfering" in our elections.[11] Fifteen minutes after *Politico* published its story, Jen Psaki, who now serves as Press Secretary to the President, tweeted a link to the *Politico* story.[12] The Biden campaign repeatedly cited your statement to dismiss the allegations against Hunter Biden.[13] During the final presidential debate, Vice President Biden also dismissed concerns about Hunter Biden's international business dealings as part of a "Russian plan."[14]

Your public statement was consistent with a broader effort to minimize and censor the *New York Post*'s reporting about Hunter Biden and the Biden family. National news organizations called the allegations about Hunter Biden "dubious" and a "non-scandal"; CBS News reporter Leslie Stahl said the allegations "can't be verified"; and NPR called it a "waste . . . of time" and a "pure distraction."[15] Separately, Twitter and Facebook restricted access to the *New York Post*'s reporting about Hunter Biden, with Twitter locking the *Post*'s account and Facebook deferring to a so-called independent fact-check that never occurred.[16] These efforts likely affected public awareness of the serious allegations surrounding the Biden family in the crucial weeks before the 2020 election.

We now know from subsequent reporting that the *New York Post*'s article about Hunter Biden was not, as you and your co-signatories alleged, part of a "Russian information

---

[8] *Id.*
[9] *Id.*
[10] Natasha Bertrand, *Hunter Biden story is Russian disinfo, dozens of former intel officials say*, Politico, Oct. 19, 2020.
[11] *Id.*
[12] Tweet by Jen Psaki, Twitter.com (Oct. 19, 2020, 10:45 p.m.), https://twitter.com/jrpsaki/status/1318382779659411458.
[13] *E.g.* Houston Keene, *Flashback: Biden officials pushed angle that Hunter laptop was 'Russian disinfo,'* Fox News, Mar. 17, 2022.
[14] Deirdre Shesgreen, *"Nothing was unethical": Joe Biden defends Hunter Biden under pressure from Trump in debate*, USA Today, Oct. 22, 2020.
[15] Joe Concha, *Media's pre-election burial of Hunter Biden story proves dereliction of duty*, The Hill, Dec. 11, 2020.
[16] *E.g.* Elizabeth Dwoskin, *Facebook and Twitter take unusual steps to limit spread of New York Post story*, Wash. Post, Oct. 15, 2020.

operation."[17] This belated verification of the *Post*'s reporting raises fresh questions about the public statement you signed in October 2020. At best, the public statement was a reckless attempt by you and your co-signatories to erroneously opine about purported election interference. At worse—and more likely—the public statement was a deliberate and coordinated effort to mislead the American people about information relevant to the 2020 presidential election by invoking your national security experience to falsely suggest that the allegations about Hunter Biden were not based in fact.

The concerted effort to suppress public dissemination of the serious allegations about Hunter Biden and the Biden family, as first reported in October 2020 by the *New York Post*, was a grave disservice to American citizens' informed participation in our democracy. We are investigating the role that the public statement played in this effort. Accordingly, please provide the following material:

1. Identify all people with whom you communicated about the inception, drafting, editing, signing, publishing, or promotion of the "Public Statement on the Hunter Biden Emails" dated October 19, 2020; and

2. Produce all documents and communications referring or relating to the "Public Statement on the Hunter Biden Emails" dated October 19, 2020.

Please produce this material as soon as possible but no later than 5:00 p.m. on April 20, 2022. In addition, we request that you take all reasonable steps to preserve records that may be potentially responsive to this inquiry.

Thank you for your attention to this matter.

Sincerely,

Jim Jordan
Ranking Member

Steve Chabot
Member of Congress

Louie Gohmert
Member of Congress

Darrell Issa
Ranking Member
Subcommittee on Courts, Intellectual Property, and the Internet

---

[17] *E.g.* Katie Brenner et al., *Hunter Biden paid tax bill, but broad federal investigation continues*, N.Y. Times, Mar. 16, 2022; Matt Viser et al., *Inside Hunter Biden's multimillion-dollar deals with a Chinese energy company*, Wash. Post, Mar. 30, 2022.

Ken Buck
Ranking Member
Subcommittee on Antitrust, Commercial and Administrative Law

Mike Johnson
Ranking Member
Subcommittee on the Constitution, Civil Rights and Civil Liberties

Tom McClintock
Ranking Member
Subcommittee on Immigration and Citizenship

Tom Tiffany
Member of Congress

Chip Roy
Member of Congress

Michelle Fischbach
Member of Congress

Matt Gaetz
Member of Congress

Andy Biggs
Ranking Member
Subcommittee on Crime, Terrorism and Homeland Security

W. Gregory Steube
Member of Congress

Thomas Massie
Member of Congress

Dan Bishop
Member of Congress

Victoria Spartz
Member of Congress

Scott Fitzgerald
Member of Congress

Cliff Bentz
Member of Congress

Burgess Owens
Member of Congress

JERROLD NADLER, New York
CHAIRMAN

JIM JORDAN, Ohio
RANKING MEMBER

ONE HUNDRED SEVENTEENTH CONGRESS

Congress of the United States

House of Representatives

COMMITTEE ON THE JUDICIARY

2138 RAYBURN HOUSE OFFICE BUILDING

WASHINGTON, DC 20515–6216

(202) 225–3951
judiciary.house.gov

April 6, 2022

Mr. David Priess
via e-mail

Dear Mr. Priess:

On October 14, 2020, the *New York Post* published a report detailing how Hunter Biden used the position and influence of his father, now-President Joe Biden, for personal gain with the apparent awareness of President Biden.[1] This article raised doubts about President Biden's earlier denial of ever speaking to his son about his international business dealings.[2] The *Post* reported on an email in which a Ukrainian businessman urged Hunter Biden to "use [his] influence to convey a message / signal, etc. to stop what we consider to be politically motivated actions."[3] In another email, the same businessman thanked Hunter Biden for arranging a meeting with his father, calling it "an honor and pleasure."[4] The *Post* reported that these emails came from a laptop belonging to Hunter Biden that he had abandoned in a Delaware computer shop.[5]

On October 19, 2020, you signed a public statement attempting to discredit the contents of the *New York Post*'s reporting about Hunter Biden.[6] This statement emphasized the national security credentials of you and the other signatories, implying that the assertions and conclusions in the statement were grounded in information unavailable to other Americans. Referencing this unique experience, you wrote:

> It is for all these reasons that we write to say that the arrival on the US political scene of emails purportedly belonging to Vice President Biden's son Hunter, much of it related to his time serving on the Board of the Ukrainian gas company Burisma, has all the classic earmarks of a Russian information operation.[7]

---

[1] Emma-Jo Morris & Gabrielle Fonrouge, *Smoking-gun email reveals how Hunter Biden introduced Ukrainian businessman to VP dad*, N.Y. Post, Oct. 14, 2020.
[2] *E.g.* Nick Givas, *Joe Biden again denies speaking to son about Ukrainian business dealings*, Fox News, Oct. 10, 2019.
[3] Morris & Fonrouge, *supra* note 1.
[4] *Id.*
[5] *Id.*
[6] Jim Clapper et al., Public Statement on the Hunter Biden Emails (Oct. 19, 2020).
[7] *Id.*

Although this statement acknowledged that you had seen no actual "evidence" of Russian involvement with respect to the publication of Hunter Biden's emails, you nonetheless conveyed a "deep[] suspicio[n] that the Russian government played a significant role in the case."[8] Later in the statement, you went further to state a "view"—not merely a suspicion anymore—"that the Russians are involved in the Hunter Biden email issue . . . ."[9]

Your public statement served as a basis for Democrat operatives to try to delegitimize the scandalous allegations about Hunter Biden and the Biden family. On the same day as your statement, *Politico* published a story about the statement, with the conclusive headline, "Hunter Biden story is Russian disinfo, dozens of former intel officials say."[10] Departing from the statement's careful wording, the *Politico* story quoted one signatory to the letter as being confident that "once again the Russians are interfering" in our elections.[11] Fifteen minutes after *Politico* published its story, Jen Psaki, who now serves as Press Secretary to the President, tweeted a link to the *Politico* story.[12] The Biden campaign repeatedly cited your statement to dismiss the allegations against Hunter Biden.[13] During the final presidential debate, Vice President Biden also dismissed concerns about Hunter Biden's international business dealings as part of a "Russian plan."[14]

Your public statement was consistent with a broader effort to minimize and censor the *New York Post*'s reporting about Hunter Biden and the Biden family. National news organizations called the allegations about Hunter Biden "dubious" and a "non-scandal"; CBS News reporter Leslie Stahl said the allegations "can't be verified"; and NPR called it a "waste . . . of time" and a "pure distraction."[15] Separately, Twitter and Facebook restricted access to the *New York Post*'s reporting about Hunter Biden, with Twitter locking the *Post*'s account and Facebook deferring to a so-called independent fact-check that never occurred.[16] These efforts likely affected public awareness of the serious allegations surrounding the Biden family in the crucial weeks before the 2020 election.

We now know from subsequent reporting that the *New York Post*'s article about Hunter Biden was not, as you and your co-signatories alleged, part of a "Russian information

---

[8] *Id.*
[9] *Id.*
[10] Natasha Bertrand, *Hunter Biden story is Russian disinfo, dozens of former intel officials say*, Politico, Oct. 19, 2020.
[11] *Id.*
[12] Tweet by Jen Psaki, Twitter.com (Oct. 19, 2020, 10:45 p.m.), https://twitter.com/jrpsaki/status/1318382779659411458.
[13] *E.g.* Houston Keene, *Flashback: Biden officials pushed angle that Hunter laptop was 'Russian disinfo,'* Fox News, Mar. 17, 2022.
[14] Deirdre Shesgreen, *"Nothing was unethical": Joe Biden defends Hunter Biden under pressure from Trump in debate*, USA Today, Oct. 22, 2020.
[15] Joe Concha, *Media's pre-election burial of Hunter Biden story proves dereliction of duty*, The Hill, Dec. 11, 2020.
[16] *E.g.* Elizabeth Dwoskin, *Facebook and Twitter take unusual steps to limit spread of New York Post story*, Wash. Post, Oct. 15, 2020.

operation."[17] This belated verification of the *Post*'s reporting raises fresh questions about the public statement you signed in October 2020. At best, the public statement was a reckless attempt by you and your co-signatories to erroneously opine about purported election interference. At worse—and more likely—the public statement was a deliberate and coordinated effort to mislead the American people about information relevant to the 2020 presidential election by invoking your national security experience to falsely suggest that the allegations about Hunter Biden were not based in fact.

The concerted effort to suppress public dissemination of the serious allegations about Hunter Biden and the Biden family, as first reported in October 2020 by the *New York Post*, was a grave disservice to American citizens' informed participation in our democracy. We are investigating the role that the public statement played in this effort. Accordingly, please provide the following material:

1. Identify all people with whom you communicated about the inception, drafting, editing, signing, publishing, or promotion of the "Public Statement on the Hunter Biden Emails" dated October 19, 2020; and

2. Produce all documents and communications referring or relating to the "Public Statement on the Hunter Biden Emails" dated October 19, 2020.

Please produce this material as soon as possible but no later than 5:00 p.m. on April 20, 2022. In addition, we request that you take all reasonable steps to preserve records that may be potentially responsive to this inquiry.

Thank you for your attention to this matter.

Sincerely,

Jim Jordan
Ranking Member

Steve Chabot
Member of Congress

Louie Gohmert
Member of Congress

Darrell Issa
Ranking Member
Subcommittee on Courts, Intellectual Property, and the Internet

---

[17] *E.g.* Katie Brenner et al., *Hunter Biden paid tax bill, but broad federal investigation continues*, N.Y. Times, Mar. 16, 2022; Matt Viser et al., *Inside Hunter Biden's multimillion-dollar deals with a Chinese energy company*, Wash. Post, Mar. 30, 2022.

Ken Buck
Ranking Member
Subcommittee on Antitrust, Commercial and Administrative Law

Matt Gaetz
Member of Congress

Mike Johnson
Ranking Member
Subcommittee on the Constitution, Civil Rights and Civil Liberties

Andy Biggs
Ranking Member
Subcommittee on Crime, Terrorism and Homeland Security

Tom McClintock
Ranking Member
Subcommittee on Immigration and Citizenship

W. Gregory Steube
Member of Congress

Tom Tiffany
Member of Congress

Thomas Massie
Member of Congress

Chip Roy
Member of Congress

Dan Bishop
Member of Congress

Michelle Fischbach
Member of Congress

Victoria Spartz
Member of Congress

Scott Fitzgerald
Member of Congress

Cliff Bentz
Member of Congress

Burgess Owens
Member of Congress

JERROLD NADLER, New York
CHAIRMAN

JIM JORDAN, Ohio
RANKING MEMBER

ONE HUNDRED SEVENTEENTH CONGRESS

Congress of the United States

House of Representatives

COMMITTEE ON THE JUDICIARY

2138 RAYBURN HOUSE OFFICE BUILDING

WASHINGTON, DC 20515-6216

(202) 225-3951
judiciary.house.gov

April 6, 2022

Ms. Pamela Purcilly
c/o Central Intelligence Agency
via e-mail

Dear Ms. Purcilly:

On October 14, 2020, the *New York Post* published a report detailing how Hunter Biden used the position and influence of his father, now-President Joe Biden, for personal gain with the apparent awareness of President Biden.[1] This article raised doubts about President Biden's earlier denial of ever speaking to his son about his international business dealings.[2] The *Post* reported on an email in which a Ukrainian businessman urged Hunter Biden to "use [his] influence to convey a message / signal, etc. to stop what we consider to be politically motivated actions."[3] In another email, the same businessman thanked Hunter Biden for arranging a meeting with his father, calling it "an honor and pleasure."[4] The *Post* reported that these emails came from a laptop belonging to Hunter Biden that he had abandoned in a Delaware computer shop.[5]

On October 19, 2020, you signed a public statement attempting to discredit the contents of the *New York Post*'s reporting about Hunter Biden.[6] This statement emphasized the national security credentials of you and the other signatories, implying that the assertions and conclusions in the statement were grounded in information unavailable to other Americans. Referencing this unique experience, you wrote:

> It is for all these reasons that we write to say that the arrival on the US political scene of emails purportedly belonging to Vice President Biden's son Hunter, much of it related to his time serving on the Board of the Ukrainian gas company Burisma, has all the classic earmarks of a Russian information operation.[7]

---

[1] Emma-Jo Morris & Gabrielle Fonrouge, *Smoking-gun email reveals how Hunter Biden introduced Ukrainian businessman to VP dad*, N.Y. Post, Oct. 14, 2020.
[2] *E.g.* Nick Givas, *Joe Biden again denies speaking to son about Ukrainian business dealings*, Fox News, Oct. 10, 2019.
[3] Morris & Fonrouge, *supra* note 1.
[4] *Id.*
[5] *Id.*
[6] Jim Clapper et al., Public Statement on the Hunter Biden Emails (Oct. 19, 2020).
[7] *Id.*

Although this statement acknowledged that you had seen no actual "evidence" of Russian involvement with respect to the publication of Hunter Biden's emails, you nonetheless conveyed a "deep[] suspicio[n] that the Russian government played a significant role in the case."[8] Later in the statement, you went further to state a "view"—not merely a suspicion anymore—"that the Russians are involved in the Hunter Biden email issue . . . ."[9]

Your public statement served as a basis for Democrat operatives to try to delegitimize the scandalous allegations about Hunter Biden and the Biden family. On the same day as your statement, *Politico* published a story about the statement, with the conclusive headline, "Hunter Biden story is Russian disinfo, dozens of former intel officials say."[10] Departing from the statement's careful wording, the *Politico* story quoted one signatory to the letter as being confident that "once again the Russians are interfering" in our elections.[11] Fifteen minutes after *Politico* published its story, Jen Psaki, who now serves as Press Secretary to the President, tweeted a link to the *Politico* story.[12] The Biden campaign repeatedly cited your statement to dismiss the allegations against Hunter Biden.[13] During the final presidential debate, Vice President Biden also dismissed concerns about Hunter Biden's international business dealings as part of a "Russian plan."[14]

Your public statement was consistent with a broader effort to minimize and censor the *New York Post*'s reporting about Hunter Biden and the Biden family. National news organizations called the allegations about Hunter Biden "dubious" and a "non-scandal"; CBS News reporter Leslie Stahl said the allegations "can't be verified"; and NPR called it a "waste . . . of time" and a "pure distraction."[15] Separately, Twitter and Facebook restricted access to the *New York Post*'s reporting about Hunter Biden, with Twitter locking the *Post*'s account and Facebook deferring to a so-called independent fact-check that never occurred.[16] These efforts likely affected public awareness of the serious allegations surrounding the Biden family in the crucial weeks before the 2020 election.

We now know from subsequent reporting that the *New York Post*'s article about Hunter Biden was not, as you and your co-signatories alleged, part of a "Russian information

---

[8] *Id.*
[9] *Id.*
[10] Natasha Bertrand, *Hunter Biden story is Russian disinfo, dozens of former intel officials say*, Politico, Oct. 19, 2020.
[11] *Id.*
[12] Tweet by Jen Psaki, Twitter.com (Oct. 19, 2020, 10:45 p.m.), https://twitter.com/jrpsaki/status/1318382779659411458.
[13] *E.g.* Houston Keene, *Flashback: Biden officials pushed angle that Hunter laptop was 'Russian disinfo,'* Fox News, Mar. 17, 2022.
[14] Deirdre Shesgreen, *"Nothing was unethical": Joe Biden defends Hunter Biden under pressure from Trump in debate*, USA Today, Oct. 22, 2020.
[15] Joe Concha, *Media's pre-election burial of Hunter Biden story proves dereliction of duty*, The Hill, Dec. 11, 2020.
[16] *E.g.* Elizabeth Dwoskin, *Facebook and Twitter take unusual steps to limit spread of New York Post story*, Wash. Post, Oct. 15, 2020.

operation."[17] This belated verification of the *Post*'s reporting raises fresh questions about the public statement you signed in October 2020. At best, the public statement was a reckless attempt by you and your co-signatories to erroneously opine about purported election interference. At worse—and more likely—the public statement was a deliberate and coordinated effort to mislead the American people about information relevant to the 2020 presidential election by invoking your national security experience to falsely suggest that the allegations about Hunter Biden were not based in fact.

The concerted effort to suppress public dissemination of the serious allegations about Hunter Biden and the Biden family, as first reported in October 2020 by the *New York Post*, was a grave disservice to American citizens' informed participation in our democracy. We are investigating the role that the public statement played in this effort. Accordingly, please provide the following material:

1. Identify all people with whom you communicated about the inception, drafting, editing, signing, publishing, or promotion of the "Public Statement on the Hunter Biden Emails" dated October 19, 2020; and

2. Produce all documents and communications referring or relating to the "Public Statement on the Hunter Biden Emails" dated October 19, 2020.

Please produce this material as soon as possible but no later than 5:00 p.m. on April 20, 2022. In addition, we request that you take all reasonable steps to preserve records that may be potentially responsive to this inquiry.

Thank you for your attention to this matter.

Sincerely,

Jim Jordan
Ranking Member

Steve Chabot
Member of Congress

Louie Gohmert
Member of Congress

Darrell Issa
Ranking Member
Subcommittee on Courts, Intellectual Property, and the Internet

[17] *E.g.* Katie Brenner et al., *Hunter Biden paid tax bill, but broad federal investigation continues*, N.Y. Times, Mar. 16, 2022; Matt Viser et al., *Inside Hunter Biden's multimillion-dollar deals with a Chinese energy company*, Wash. Post, Mar. 30, 2022.

Ms. Pamela Purcilly
April 6, 2022
Page 4

Ken Buck
Ranking Member
Subcommittee on Antitrust, Commercial and Administrative Law

Matt Gaetz
Member of Congress

Mike Johnson
Ranking Member
Subcommittee on the Constitution, Civil Rights and Civil Liberties

Andy Biggs
Ranking Member
Subcommittee on Crime, Terrorism and Homeland Security

Tom McClintock
Ranking Member
Subcommittee on Immigration and Citizenship

W. Gregory Steube
Member of Congress

Tom Tiffany
Member of Congress

Thomas Massie
Member of Congress

Chip Roy
Member of Congress

Dan Bishop
Member of Congress

Michelle Fischbach
Member of Congress

Victoria Spartz
Member of Congress

Scott Fitzgerald
Member of Congress

Cliff Bentz
Member of Congress

Burgess Owens
Member of Congress

JERROLD NADLER, New York
CHAIRMAN

JIM JORDAN, Ohio
RANKING MEMBER

ONE HUNDRED SEVENTEENTH CONGRESS

Congress of the United States

House of Representatives

COMMITTEE ON THE JUDICIARY

2138 RAYBURN HOUSE OFFICE BUILDING

WASHINGTON, DC 20515-6216

(202) 225-3951
judiciary.house.gov

April 6, 2022

The Honorable Nicholas Rasmussen
via e-mail

Dear Mr. Rasmussen:

On October 14, 2020, the *New York Post* published a report detailing how Hunter Biden used the position and influence of his father, now-President Joe Biden, for personal gain with the apparent awareness of President Biden.[1] This article raised doubts about President Biden's earlier denial of ever speaking to his son about his international business dealings.[2] The *Post* reported on an email in which a Ukrainian businessman urged Hunter Biden to "use [his] influence to convey a message / signal, etc. to stop what we consider to be politically motivated actions."[3] In another email, the same businessman thanked Hunter Biden for arranging a meeting with his father, calling it "an honor and pleasure."[4] The *Post* reported that these emails came from a laptop belonging to Hunter Biden that he had abandoned in a Delaware computer shop.[5]

On October 19, 2020, you signed a public statement attempting to discredit the contents of the *New York Post*'s reporting about Hunter Biden.[6] This statement emphasized the national security credentials of you and the other signatories, implying that the assertions and conclusions in the statement were grounded in information unavailable to other Americans. Referencing this unique experience, you wrote:

> It is for all these reasons that we write to say that the arrival on the US political scene of emails purportedly belonging to Vice President Biden's son Hunter, much of it related to his time serving on the Board of the Ukrainian gas company Burisma, has all the classic earmarks of a Russian information operation.[7]

---

[1] Emma-Jo Morris & Gabrielle Fonrouge, *Smoking-gun email reveals how Hunter Biden introduced Ukrainian businessman to VP dad*, N.Y. Post, Oct. 14, 2020.
[2] *E.g.* Nick Givas, *Joe Biden again denies speaking to son about Ukrainian business dealings*, Fox News, Oct. 10, 2019.
[3] Morris & Fonrouge, *supra* note 1.
[4] *Id.*
[5] *Id.*
[6] Jim Clapper et al., Public Statement on the Hunter Biden Emails (Oct. 19, 2020).
[7] *Id.*

Although this statement acknowledged that you had seen no actual "evidence" of Russian involvement with respect to the publication of Hunter Biden's emails, you nonetheless conveyed a "deep[] suspicio[n] that the Russian government played a significant role in the case."[8] Later in the statement, you went further to state a "view"—not merely a suspicion anymore—"that the Russians are involved in the Hunter Biden email issue . . . ."[9]

Your public statement served as a basis for Democrat operatives to try to delegitimize the scandalous allegations about Hunter Biden and the Biden family. On the same day as your statement, *Politico* published a story about the statement, with the conclusive headline, "Hunter Biden story is Russian disinfo, dozens of former intel officials say."[10] Departing from the statement's careful wording, the *Politico* story quoted one signatory to the letter as being confident that "once again the Russians are interfering" in our elections.[11] Fifteen minutes after *Politico* published its story, Jen Psaki, who now serves as Press Secretary to the President, tweeted a link to the *Politico* story.[12] The Biden campaign repeatedly cited your statement to dismiss the allegations against Hunter Biden.[13] During the final presidential debate, Vice President Biden also dismissed concerns about Hunter Biden's international business dealings as part of a "Russian plan."[14]

Your public statement was consistent with a broader effort to minimize and censor the *New York Post*'s reporting about Hunter Biden and the Biden family. National news organizations called the allegations about Hunter Biden "dubious" and a "non-scandal"; CBS News reporter Leslie Stahl said the allegations "can't be verified"; and NPR called it a "waste . . . of time" and a "pure distraction."[15] Separately, Twitter and Facebook restricted access to the *New York Post*'s reporting about Hunter Biden, with Twitter locking the *Post*'s account and Facebook deferring to a so-called independent fact-check that never occurred.[16] These efforts likely affected public awareness of the serious allegations surrounding the Biden family in the crucial weeks before the 2020 election.

We now know from subsequent reporting that the *New York Post*'s article about Hunter Biden was not, as you and your co-signatories alleged, part of a "Russian information

---

[8] *Id.*
[9] *Id.*
[10] Natasha Bertrand, *Hunter Biden story is Russian disinfo, dozens of former intel officials say*, Politico, Oct. 19, 2020.
[11] *Id.*
[12] Tweet by Jen Psaki, Twitter.com (Oct. 19, 2020, 10:45 p.m.), https://twitter.com/jrpsaki/status/1318382779659411458.
[13] *E.g.* Houston Keene, *Flashback: Biden officials pushed angle that Hunter laptop was 'Russian disinfo,'* Fox News, Mar. 17, 2022.
[14] Deirdre Shesgreen, *"Nothing was unethical": Joe Biden defends Hunter Biden under pressure from Trump in debate*, USA Today, Oct. 22, 2020.
[15] Joe Concha, *Media's pre-election burial of Hunter Biden story proves dereliction of duty*, The Hill, Dec. 11, 2020.
[16] *E.g.* Elizabeth Dwoskin, *Facebook and Twitter take unusual steps to limit spread of New York Post story*, Wash. Post, Oct. 15, 2020.

operation."[17] This belated verification of the *Post*'s reporting raises fresh questions about the public statement you signed in October 2020. At best, the public statement was a reckless attempt by you and your co-signatories to erroneously opine about purported election interference. At worse—and more likely—the public statement was a deliberate and coordinated effort to mislead the American people about information relevant to the 2020 presidential election by invoking your national security experience to falsely suggest that the allegations about Hunter Biden were not based in fact.

The concerted effort to suppress public dissemination of the serious allegations about Hunter Biden and the Biden family, as first reported in October 2020 by the *New York Post*, was a grave disservice to American citizens' informed participation in our democracy. We are investigating the role that the public statement played in this effort. Accordingly, please provide the following material:

1. Identify all people with whom you communicated about the inception, drafting, editing, signing, publishing, or promotion of the "Public Statement on the Hunter Biden Emails" dated October 19, 2020; and

2. Produce all documents and communications referring or relating to the "Public Statement on the Hunter Biden Emails" dated October 19, 2020.

Please produce this material as soon as possible but no later than 5:00 p.m. on April 20, 2022. In addition, we request that you take all reasonable steps to preserve records that may be potentially responsive to this inquiry.

Thank you for your attention to this matter.

Sincerely,

Jim Jordan
Ranking Member

Steve Chabot
Member of Congress

Louie Gohmert
Member of Congress

Darrell Issa
Ranking Member
Subcommittee on Courts, Intellectual Property, and the Internet

---

[17] *E.g.* Katie Brenner et al., *Hunter Biden paid tax bill, but broad federal investigation continues*, N.Y. Times, Mar. 16, 2022; Matt Viser et al., *Inside Hunter Biden's multimillion-dollar deals with a Chinese energy company*, Wash. Post, Mar. 30, 2022.

Ken Buck
Ranking Member
Subcommittee on Antitrust, Commercial and Administrative Law

Matt Gaetz
Member of Congress

Mike Johnson
Ranking Member
Subcommittee on the Constitution, Civil Rights and Civil Liberties

Andy Biggs
Ranking Member
Subcommittee on Crime, Terrorism and Homeland Security

Tom McClintock
Ranking Member
Subcommittee on Immigration and Citizenship

W. Gregory Steube
Member of Congress

Tom Tiffany
Member of Congress

Thomas Massie
Member of Congress

Chip Roy
Member of Congress

Dan Bishop
Member of Congress

Michelle Fischbach
Member of Congress

Victoria Spartz
Member of Congress

Scott Fitzgerald
Member of Congress

Cliff Bentz
Member of Congress

Burgess Owens
Member of Congress

JERROLD NADLER, New York
CHAIRMAN

JIM JORDAN, Ohio
RANKING MEMBER

ONE HUNDRED SEVENTEENTH CONGRESS

Congress of the United States
House of Representatives
COMMITTEE ON THE JUDICIARY

2138 RAYBURN HOUSE OFFICE BUILDING
WASHINGTON, DC 20515-6216
(202) 225-3951
judiciary.house.gov

April 6, 2022

Mr. Chris Savos
c/o Central Intelligence Agency
via e-mail

Dear Mr. Savos:

On October 14, 2020, the *New York Post* published a report detailing how Hunter Biden used the position and influence of his father, now-President Joe Biden, for personal gain with the apparent awareness of President Biden.[1] This article raised doubts about President Biden's earlier denial of ever speaking to his son about his international business dealings.[2] The *Post* reported on an email in which a Ukrainian businessman urged Hunter Biden to "use [his] influence to convey a message / signal, etc. to stop what we consider to be politically motivated actions."[3] In another email, the same businessman thanked Hunter Biden for arranging a meeting with his father, calling it "an honor and pleasure."[4] The *Post* reported that these emails came from a laptop belonging to Hunter Biden that he had abandoned in a Delaware computer shop.[5]

On October 19, 2020, you signed a public statement attempting to discredit the contents of the *New York Post*'s reporting about Hunter Biden.[6] This statement emphasized the national security credentials of you and the other signatories, implying that the assertions and conclusions in the statement were grounded in information unavailable to other Americans. Referencing this unique experience, you wrote:

> It is for all these reasons that we write to say that the arrival on the US political scene of emails purportedly belonging to Vice President Biden's son Hunter, much of it related to his time serving on the Board of the Ukrainian gas company Burisma, has all the classic earmarks of a Russian information operation.[7]

---

[1] Emma-Jo Morris & Gabrielle Fonrouge, *Smoking-gun email reveals how Hunter Biden introduced Ukrainian businessman to VP dad*, N.Y. Post, Oct. 14, 2020.
[2] *E.g.* Nick Givas, *Joe Biden again denies speaking to son about Ukrainian business dealings*, Fox News, Oct. 10, 2019.
[3] Morris & Fonrouge, *supra* note 1.
[4] *Id.*
[5] *Id.*
[6] Jim Clapper et al., Public Statement on the Hunter Biden Emails (Oct. 19, 2020).
[7] *Id.*

Although this statement acknowledged that you had seen no actual "evidence" of Russian involvement with respect to the publication of Hunter Biden's emails, you nonetheless conveyed a "deep[] suspicio[n] that the Russian government played a significant role in the case."[8] Later in the statement, you went further to state a "view"—not merely a suspicion anymore—"that the Russians are involved in the Hunter Biden email issue . . . ."[9]

Your public statement served as a basis for Democrat operatives to try to delegitimize the scandalous allegations about Hunter Biden and the Biden family. On the same day as your statement, *Politico* published a story about the statement, with the conclusive headline, "Hunter Biden story is Russian disinfo, dozens of former intel officials say."[10] Departing from the statement's careful wording, the *Politico* story quoted one signatory to the letter as being confident that "once again the Russians are interfering" in our elections.[11] Fifteen minutes after *Politico* published its story, Jen Psaki, who now serves as Press Secretary to the President, tweeted a link to the *Politico* story.[12] The Biden campaign repeatedly cited your statement to dismiss the allegations against Hunter Biden.[13] During the final presidential debate, Vice President Biden also dismissed concerns about Hunter Biden's international business dealings as part of a "Russian plan."[14]

Your public statement was consistent with a broader effort to minimize and censor the *New York Post*'s reporting about Hunter Biden and the Biden family. National news organizations called the allegations about Hunter Biden "dubious" and a "non-scandal"; CBS News reporter Leslie Stahl said the allegations "can't be verified"; and NPR called it a "waste . . . of time" and a "pure distraction."[15] Separately, Twitter and Facebook restricted access to the *New York Post*'s reporting about Hunter Biden, with Twitter locking the *Post*'s account and Facebook deferring to a so-called independent fact-check that never occurred.[16] These efforts likely affected public awareness of the serious allegations surrounding the Biden family in the crucial weeks before the 2020 election.

We now know from subsequent reporting that the *New York Post*'s article about Hunter Biden was not, as you and your co-signatories alleged, part of a "Russian information

---

[8] *Id.*
[9] *Id.*
[10] Natasha Bertrand, *Hunter Biden story is Russian disinfo, dozens of former intel officials say*, Politico, Oct. 19, 2020.
[11] *Id.*
[12] Tweet by Jen Psaki, Twitter.com (Oct. 19, 2020, 10:45 p.m.), https://twitter.com/jrpsaki/status/1318382779659411458.
[13] *E.g.* Houston Keene, *Flashback: Biden officials pushed angle that Hunter laptop was 'Russian disinfo,'* Fox News, Mar. 17, 2022.
[14] Deirdre Shesgreen, *"Nothing was unethical": Joe Biden defends Hunter Biden under pressure from Trump in debate*, USA Today, Oct. 22, 2020.
[15] Joe Concha, *Media's pre-election burial of Hunter Biden story proves dereliction of duty*, The Hill, Dec. 11, 2020.
[16] *E.g.* Elizabeth Dwoskin, *Facebook and Twitter take unusual steps to limit spread of New York Post story*, Wash. Post, Oct. 15, 2020.

operation."[17] This belated verification of the *Post*'s reporting raises fresh questions about the public statement you signed in October 2020. At best, the public statement was a reckless attempt by you and your co-signatories to erroneously opine about purported election interference. At worse—and more likely—the public statement was a deliberate and coordinated effort to mislead the American people about information relevant to the 2020 presidential election by invoking your national security experience to falsely suggest that the allegations about Hunter Biden were not based in fact.

The concerted effort to suppress public dissemination of the serious allegations about Hunter Biden and the Biden family, as first reported in October 2020 by the *New York Post*, was a grave disservice to American citizens' informed participation in our democracy. We are investigating the role that the public statement played in this effort. Accordingly, please provide the following material:

1. Identify all people with whom you communicated about the inception, drafting, editing, signing, publishing, or promotion of the "Public Statement on the Hunter Biden Emails" dated October 19, 2020; and

2. Produce all documents and communications referring or relating to the "Public Statement on the Hunter Biden Emails" dated October 19, 2020.

Please produce this material as soon as possible but no later than 5:00 p.m. on April 20, 2022. In addition, we request that you take all reasonable steps to preserve records that may be potentially responsive to this inquiry.

Thank you for your attention to this matter.

Sincerely,

Jim Jordan
Ranking Member

Steve Chabot
Member of Congress

Louie Gohmert
Member of Congress

Darrell Issa
Ranking Member
Subcommittee on Courts, Intellectual Property, and the Internet

[17] *E.g.* Katie Brenner et al., *Hunter Biden paid tax bill, but broad federal investigation continues*, N.Y. Times, Mar. 16, 2022; Matt Viser et al., *Inside Hunter Biden's multimillion-dollar deals with a Chinese energy company*, Wash. Post, Mar. 30, 2022.

Ken Buck
Ranking Member
Subcommittee on Antitrust, Commercial and Administrative Law

Matt Gaetz
Member of Congress

Mike Johnson
Ranking Member
Subcommittee on the Constitution, Civil Rights and Civil Liberties

Andy Biggs
Ranking Member
Subcommittee on Crime, Terrorism and Homeland Security

Tom McClintock
Ranking Member
Subcommittee on Immigration and Citizenship

W. Gregory Steube
Member of Congress

Tom Tiffany
Member of Congress

Thomas Massie
Member of Congress

Chip Roy
Member of Congress

Dan Bishop
Member of Congress

Michelle Fischbach
Member of Congress

Victoria Spartz
Member of Congress

Scott Fitzgerald
Member of Congress

Cliff Bentz
Member of Congress

Burgess Owens
Member of Congress

JERROLD NADLER, New York
CHAIRMAN

JIM JORDAN, Ohio
RANKING MEMBER

ONE HUNDRED SEVENTEENTH CONGRESS

Congress of the United States

House of Representatives

COMMITTEE ON THE JUDICIARY

2138 RAYBURN HOUSE OFFICE BUILDING

WASHINGTON, DC 20515-6216

(202) 225-3951
judiciary.house.gov

April 6, 2022

Mr. Nick Shapiro
via e-mail

Dear Mr. Shapiro:

On October 14, 2020, the *New York Post* published a report detailing how Hunter Biden used the position and influence of his father, now-President Joe Biden, for personal gain with the apparent awareness of President Biden.[1] This article raised doubts about President Biden's earlier denial of ever speaking to his son about his international business dealings.[2] The *Post* reported on an email in which a Ukrainian businessman urged Hunter Biden to "use [his] influence to convey a message / signal, etc. to stop what we consider to be politically motivated actions."[3] In another email, the same businessman thanked Hunter Biden for arranging a meeting with his father, calling it "an honor and pleasure."[4] The *Post* reported that these emails came from a laptop belonging to Hunter Biden that he had abandoned in a Delaware computer shop.[5]

On October 19, 2020, you signed a public statement attempting to discredit the contents of the *New York Post*'s reporting about Hunter Biden.[6] This statement emphasized the national security credentials of you and the other signatories, implying that the assertions and conclusions in the statement were grounded in information unavailable to other Americans. Referencing this unique experience, you wrote:

> It is for all these reasons that we write to say that the arrival on the US political scene of emails purportedly belonging to Vice President Biden's son Hunter, much of it related to his time serving on the Board of the Ukrainian gas company Burisma, has all the classic earmarks of a Russian information operation.[7]

---

[1] Emma-Jo Morris & Gabrielle Fonrouge, *Smoking-gun email reveals how Hunter Biden introduced Ukrainian businessman to VP dad*, N.Y. Post, Oct. 14, 2020.
[2] *E.g.* Nick Givas, *Joe Biden again denies speaking to son about Ukrainian business dealings*, Fox News, Oct. 10, 2019.
[3] Morris & Fonrouge, *supra* note 1.
[4] *Id.*
[5] *Id.*
[6] Jim Clapper et al., Public Statement on the Hunter Biden Emails (Oct. 19, 2020).
[7] *Id.*

Although this statement acknowledged that you had seen no actual "evidence" of Russian involvement with respect to the publication of Hunter Biden's emails, you nonetheless conveyed a "deep[] suspicio[n] that the Russian government played a significant role in the case."[8] Later in the statement, you went further to state a "view"—not merely a suspicion anymore—"that the Russians are involved in the Hunter Biden email issue . . . ."[9]

Your public statement served as a basis for Democrat operatives to try to delegitimize the scandalous allegations about Hunter Biden and the Biden family. On the same day as your statement, *Politico* published a story about the statement, with the conclusive headline, "Hunter Biden story is Russian disinfo, dozens of former intel officials say."[10] Departing from the statement's careful wording, the *Politico* story quoted one signatory to the letter as being confident that "once again the Russians are interfering" in our elections.[11] Fifteen minutes after *Politico* published its story, Jen Psaki, who now serves as Press Secretary to the President, tweeted a link to the *Politico* story.[12] The Biden campaign repeatedly cited your statement to dismiss the allegations against Hunter Biden.[13] During the final presidential debate, Vice President Biden also dismissed concerns about Hunter Biden's international business dealings as part of a "Russian plan."[14]

Your public statement was consistent with a broader effort to minimize and censor the *New York Post*'s reporting about Hunter Biden and the Biden family. National news organizations called the allegations about Hunter Biden "dubious" and a "non-scandal"; CBS News reporter Leslie Stahl said the allegations "can't be verified"; and NPR called it a "waste . . . of time" and a "pure distraction."[15] Separately, Twitter and Facebook restricted access to the *New York Post*'s reporting about Hunter Biden, with Twitter locking the *Post*'s account and Facebook deferring to a so-called independent fact-check that never occurred.[16] These efforts likely affected public awareness of the serious allegations surrounding the Biden family in the crucial weeks before the 2020 election.

We now know from subsequent reporting that the *New York Post*'s article about Hunter Biden was not, as you and your co-signatories alleged, part of a "Russian information

---

[8] *Id.*
[9] *Id.*
[10] Natasha Bertrand, *Hunter Biden story is Russian disinfo, dozens of former intel officials say*, Politico, Oct. 19, 2020.
[11] *Id.*
[12] Tweet by Jen Psaki, Twitter.com (Oct. 19, 2020, 10:45 p.m.), https://twitter.com/jrpsaki/status/1318382779659411458.
[13] *E.g.* Houston Keene, *Flashback: Biden officials pushed angle that Hunter laptop was 'Russian disinfo,'* Fox News, Mar. 17, 2022.
[14] Deirdre Shesgreen, *"Nothing was unethical": Joe Biden defends Hunter Biden under pressure from Trump in debate*, USA Today, Oct. 22, 2020.
[15] Joe Concha, *Media's pre-election burial of Hunter Biden story proves dereliction of duty*, The Hill, Dec. 11, 2020.
[16] *E.g.* Elizabeth Dwoskin, *Facebook and Twitter take unusual steps to limit spread of New York Post story*, Wash. Post, Oct. 15, 2020.

operation."[17] This belated verification of the *Post*'s reporting raises fresh questions about the public statement you signed in October 2020. At best, the public statement was a reckless attempt by you and your co-signatories to erroneously opine about purported election interference. At worse—and more likely—the public statement was a deliberate and coordinated effort to mislead the American people about information relevant to the 2020 presidential election by invoking your national security experience to falsely suggest that the allegations about Hunter Biden were not based in fact.

The concerted effort to suppress public dissemination of the serious allegations about Hunter Biden and the Biden family, as first reported in October 2020 by the *New York Post*, was a grave disservice to American citizens' informed participation in our democracy. We are investigating the role that the public statement played in this effort. Accordingly, please provide the following material:

1. Identify all people with whom you communicated about the inception, drafting, editing, signing, publishing, or promotion of the "Public Statement on the Hunter Biden Emails" dated October 19, 2020; and

2. Produce all documents and communications referring or relating to the "Public Statement on the Hunter Biden Emails" dated October 19, 2020.

Please produce this material as soon as possible but no later than 5:00 p.m. on April 20, 2022. In addition, we request that you take all reasonable steps to preserve records that may be potentially responsive to this inquiry.

Thank you for your attention to this matter.

Sincerely,

Jim Jordan
Ranking Member

Steve Chabot
Member of Congress

Louie Gohmert
Member of Congress

Darrell Issa
Ranking Member
Subcommittee on Courts, Intellectual Property, and the Internet

---

[17] *E.g.* Katie Brenner et al., *Hunter Biden paid tax bill, but broad federal investigation continues*, N.Y. Times, Mar. 16, 2022; Matt Viser et al., *Inside Hunter Biden's multimillion-dollar deals with a Chinese energy company*, Wash. Post, Mar. 30, 2022.

Ken Buck
Ranking Member
Subcommittee on Antitrust, Commercial
and Administrative Law

Mike Johnson
Ranking Member
Subcommittee on the Constitution,
Civil Rights and Civil Liberties

Tom McClintock
Ranking Member
Subcommittee on Immigration
and Citizenship

Tom Tiffany
Member of Congress

Chip Roy
Member of Congress

Michelle Fischbach
Member of Congress

Matt Gaetz
Member of Congress

Andy Biggs
Ranking Member
Subcommittee on Crime, Terrorism
and Homeland Security

W. Gregory Steube
Member of Congress

Thomas Massie
Member of Congress

Dan Bishop
Member of Congress

Victoria Spartz
Member of Congress

Scott Fitzgerald
Member of Congress

Cliff Bentz
Member of Congress

Burgess Owens
Member of Congress

JERROLD NADLER, New York
CHAIRMAN

JIM JORDAN, Ohio
RANKING MEMBER

ONE HUNDRED SEVENTEENTH CONGRESS

Congress of the United States

House of Representatives

COMMITTEE ON THE JUDICIARY

2138 RAYBURN HOUSE OFFICE BUILDING

WASHINGTON, DC 20515–6216

(202) 225–3951
judiciary.house.gov

April 6, 2022

Mr. John Sipher
via e-mail

Dear Mr. Sipher:

On October 14, 2020, the *New York Post* published a report detailing how Hunter Biden used the position and influence of his father, now-President Joe Biden, for personal gain with the apparent awareness of President Biden.[1] This article raised doubts about President Biden's earlier denial of ever speaking to his son about his international business dealings.[2] The *Post* reported on an email in which a Ukrainian businessman urged Hunter Biden to "use [his] influence to convey a message / signal, etc. to stop what we consider to be politically motivated actions."[3] In another email, the same businessman thanked Hunter Biden for arranging a meeting with his father, calling it "an honor and pleasure."[4] The *Post* reported that these emails came from a laptop belonging to Hunter Biden that he had abandoned in a Delaware computer shop.[5]

On October 19, 2020, you signed a public statement attempting to discredit the contents of the *New York Post*'s reporting about Hunter Biden.[6] This statement emphasized the national security credentials of you and the other signatories, implying that the assertions and conclusions in the statement were grounded in information unavailable to other Americans. Referencing this unique experience, you wrote:

> It is for all these reasons that we write to say that the arrival on the US political scene of emails purportedly belonging to Vice President Biden's son Hunter, much of it related to his time serving on the Board of the Ukrainian gas company Burisma, has all the classic earmarks of a Russian information operation.[7]

---

[1] Emma-Jo Morris & Gabrielle Fonrouge, *Smoking-gun email reveals how Hunter Biden introduced Ukrainian businessman to VP dad*, N.Y. Post, Oct. 14, 2020.
[2] *E.g.* Nick Givas, *Joe Biden again denies speaking to son about Ukrainian business dealings*, Fox News, Oct. 10, 2019.
[3] Morris & Fonrouge, *supra* note 1.
[4] *Id.*
[5] *Id.*
[6] Jim Clapper et al., Public Statement on the Hunter Biden Emails (Oct. 19, 2020).
[7] *Id.*

Although this statement acknowledged that you had seen no actual "evidence" of Russian involvement with respect to the publication of Hunter Biden's emails, you nonetheless conveyed a "deep[] suspicio[n] that the Russian government played a significant role in the case."[8] Later in the statement, you went further to state a "view"—not merely a suspicion anymore—"that the Russians are involved in the Hunter Biden email issue . . . ."[9]

Your public statement served as a basis for Democrat operatives to try to delegitimize the scandalous allegations about Hunter Biden and the Biden family. On the same day as your statement, *Politico* published a story about the statement, with the conclusive headline, "Hunter Biden story is Russian disinfo, dozens of former intel officials say."[10] Departing from the statement's careful wording, the *Politico* story quoted one signatory to the letter as being confident that "once again the Russians are interfering" in our elections.[11] Fifteen minutes after *Politico* published its story, Jen Psaki, who now serves as Press Secretary to the President, tweeted a link to the *Politico* story.[12] The Biden campaign repeatedly cited your statement to dismiss the allegations against Hunter Biden.[13] During the final presidential debate, Vice President Biden also dismissed concerns about Hunter Biden's international business dealings as part of a "Russian plan."[14]

Your public statement was consistent with a broader effort to minimize and censor the *New York Post*'s reporting about Hunter Biden and the Biden family. National news organizations called the allegations about Hunter Biden "dubious" and a "non-scandal"; CBS News reporter Leslie Stahl said the allegations "can't be verified"; and NPR called it a "waste . . . of time" and a "pure distraction."[15] Separately, Twitter and Facebook restricted access to the *New York Post*'s reporting about Hunter Biden, with Twitter locking the *Post*'s account and Facebook deferring to a so-called independent fact-check that never occurred.[16] These efforts likely affected public awareness of the serious allegations surrounding the Biden family in the crucial weeks before the 2020 election.

We now know from subsequent reporting that the *New York Post*'s article about Hunter Biden was not, as you and your co-signatories alleged, part of a "Russian information

---

[8] *Id.*
[9] *Id.*
[10] Natasha Bertrand, *Hunter Biden story is Russian disinfo, dozens of former intel officials say*, Politico, Oct. 19, 2020.
[11] *Id.*
[12] Tweet by Jen Psaki, Twitter.com (Oct. 19, 2020, 10:45 p.m.), https://twitter.com/jrpsaki/status/1318382779659411458.
[13] *E.g.* Houston Keene, *Flashback: Biden officials pushed angle that Hunter laptop was 'Russian disinfo,'* Fox News, Mar. 17, 2022.
[14] Deirdre Shesgreen, *"Nothing was unethical": Joe Biden defends Hunter Biden under pressure from Trump in debate*, USA Today, Oct. 22, 2020.
[15] Joe Concha, *Media's pre-election burial of Hunter Biden story proves dereliction of duty*, The Hill, Dec. 11, 2020.
[16] *E.g.* Elizabeth Dwoskin, *Facebook and Twitter take unusual steps to limit spread of New York Post story*, Wash. Post, Oct. 15, 2020.

operation."[17] This belated verification of the *Post*'s reporting raises fresh questions about the public statement you signed in October 2020. At best, the public statement was a reckless attempt by you and your co-signatories to erroneously opine about purported election interference. At worse—and more likely—the public statement was a deliberate and coordinated effort to mislead the American people about information relevant to the 2020 presidential election by invoking your national security experience to falsely suggest that the allegations about Hunter Biden were not based in fact.

The concerted effort to suppress public dissemination of the serious allegations about Hunter Biden and the Biden family, as first reported in October 2020 by the *New York Post*, was a grave disservice to American citizens' informed participation in our democracy. We are investigating the role that the public statement played in this effort. Accordingly, please provide the following material:

1. Identify all people with whom you communicated about the inception, drafting, editing, signing, publishing, or promotion of the "Public Statement on the Hunter Biden Emails" dated October 19, 2020; and

2. Produce all documents and communications referring or relating to the "Public Statement on the Hunter Biden Emails" dated October 19, 2020.

Please produce this material as soon as possible but no later than 5:00 p.m. on April 20, 2022. In addition, we request that you take all reasonable steps to preserve records that may be potentially responsive to this inquiry.

Thank you for your attention to this matter.

Sincerely,

Jim Jordan
Ranking Member

Steve Chabot
Member of Congress

Louie Gohmert
Member of Congress

Darrell Issa
Ranking Member
Subcommittee on Courts, Intellectual Property, and the Internet

[17] *E.g.* Katie Brenner et al., *Hunter Biden paid tax bill, but broad federal investigation continues*, N.Y. Times, Mar. 16, 2022; Matt Viser et al., *Inside Hunter Biden's multimillion-dollar deals with a Chinese energy company*, Wash. Post, Mar. 30, 2022.

Ken Buck
Ranking Member
Subcommittee on Antitrust, Commercial and Administrative Law

Matt Gaetz
Member of Congress

Mike Johnson
Ranking Member
Subcommittee on the Constitution, Civil Rights and Civil Liberties

Andy Biggs
Ranking Member
Subcommittee on Crime, Terrorism and Homeland Security

Tom McClintock
Ranking Member
Subcommittee on Immigration and Citizenship

W. Gregory Steube
Member of Congress

Tom Tiffany
Member of Congress

Thomas Massie
Member of Congress

Chip Roy
Member of Congress

Dan Bishop
Member of Congress

Michelle Fischbach
Member of Congress

Victoria Spartz
Member of Congress

Scott Fitzgerald
Member of Congress

Cliff Bentz
Member of Congress

Burgess Owens
Member of Congress

JERROLD NADLER, New York
CHAIRMAN

JIM JORDAN, Ohio
RANKING MEMBER

ONE HUNDRED SEVENTEENTH CONGRESS
Congress of the United States
House of Representatives
COMMITTEE ON THE JUDICIARY
2138 RAYBURN HOUSE OFFICE BUILDING
WASHINGTON, DC 20515-6216
(202) 225-3951
judiciary.house.gov

April 6, 2022

Mr. Stephen Slick
via e-mail

Dear Mr. Slick:

On October 14, 2020, the *New York Post* published a report detailing how Hunter Biden used the position and influence of his father, now-President Joe Biden, for personal gain with the apparent awareness of President Biden.[1] This article raised doubts about President Biden's earlier denial of ever speaking to his son about his international business dealings.[2] The *Post* reported on an email in which a Ukrainian businessman urged Hunter Biden to "use [his] influence to convey a message / signal, etc. to stop what we consider to be politically motivated actions."[3] In another email, the same businessman thanked Hunter Biden for arranging a meeting with his father, calling it "an honor and pleasure."[4] The *Post* reported that these emails came from a laptop belonging to Hunter Biden that he had abandoned in a Delaware computer shop.[5]

On October 19, 2020, you signed a public statement attempting to discredit the contents of the *New York Post*'s reporting about Hunter Biden.[6] This statement emphasized the national security credentials of you and the other signatories, implying that the assertions and conclusions in the statement were grounded in information unavailable to other Americans. Referencing this unique experience, you wrote:

> It is for all these reasons that we write to say that the arrival on the US political scene of emails purportedly belonging to Vice President Biden's son Hunter, much of it related to his time serving on the Board of the Ukrainian gas company Burisma, has all the classic earmarks of a Russian information operation.[7]

---

[1] Emma-Jo Morris & Gabrielle Fonrouge, *Smoking-gun email reveals how Hunter Biden introduced Ukrainian businessman to VP dad*, N.Y. Post, Oct. 14, 2020.
[2] *E.g.* Nick Givas, *Joe Biden again denies speaking to son about Ukrainian business dealings*, Fox News, Oct. 10, 2019.
[3] Morris & Fonrouge, *supra* note 1.
[4] *Id.*
[5] *Id.*
[6] Jim Clapper et al., Public Statement on the Hunter Biden Emails (Oct. 19, 2020).
[7] *Id.*

Although this statement acknowledged that you had seen no actual "evidence" of Russian involvement with respect to the publication of Hunter Biden's emails, you nonetheless conveyed a "deep[] suspicio[n] that the Russian government played a significant role in the case."[8] Later in the statement, you went further to state a "view"—not merely a suspicion anymore—"that the Russians are involved in the Hunter Biden email issue . . . ."[9]

Your public statement served as a basis for Democrat operatives to try to delegitimize the scandalous allegations about Hunter Biden and the Biden family. On the same day as your statement, *Politico* published a story about the statement, with the conclusive headline, "Hunter Biden story is Russian disinfo, dozens of former intel officials say."[10] Departing from the statement's careful wording, the *Politico* story quoted one signatory to the letter as being confident that "once again the Russians are interfering" in our elections.[11] Fifteen minutes after *Politico* published its story, Jen Psaki, who now serves as Press Secretary to the President, tweeted a link to the *Politico* story.[12] The Biden campaign repeatedly cited your statement to dismiss the allegations against Hunter Biden.[13] During the final presidential debate, Vice President Biden also dismissed concerns about Hunter Biden's international business dealings as part of a "Russian plan."[14]

Your public statement was consistent with a broader effort to minimize and censor the *New York Post*'s reporting about Hunter Biden and the Biden family. National news organizations called the allegations about Hunter Biden "dubious" and a "non-scandal"; CBS News reporter Leslie Stahl said the allegations "can't be verified"; and NPR called it a "waste . . . of time" and a "pure distraction."[15] Separately, Twitter and Facebook restricted access to the *New York Post*'s reporting about Hunter Biden, with Twitter locking the *Post*'s account and Facebook deferring to a so-called independent fact-check that never occurred.[16] These efforts likely affected public awareness of the serious allegations surrounding the Biden family in the crucial weeks before the 2020 election.

We now know from subsequent reporting that the *New York Post*'s article about Hunter Biden was not, as you and your co-signatories alleged, part of a "Russian information

---

[8] *Id.*
[9] *Id.*
[10] Natasha Bertrand, *Hunter Biden story is Russian disinfo, dozens of former intel officials say*, Politico, Oct. 19, 2020.
[11] *Id.*
[12] Tweet by Jen Psaki, Twitter.com (Oct. 19, 2020, 10:45 p.m.), https://twitter.com/jrpsaki/status/1318382779659411458.
[13] *E.g.* Houston Keene, *Flashback: Biden officials pushed angle that Hunter laptop was 'Russian disinfo,'* Fox News, Mar. 17, 2022.
[14] Deirdre Shesgreen, *"Nothing was unethical": Joe Biden defends Hunter Biden under pressure from Trump in debate*, USA Today, Oct. 22, 2020.
[15] Joe Concha, *Media's pre-election burial of Hunter Biden story proves dereliction of duty*, The Hill, Dec. 11, 2020.
[16] *E.g.* Elizabeth Dwoskin, *Facebook and Twitter take unusual steps to limit spread of New York Post story*, Wash. Post, Oct. 15, 2020.

operation."[17] This belated verification of the *Post*'s reporting raises fresh questions about the public statement you signed in October 2020. At best, the public statement was a reckless attempt by you and your co-signatories to erroneously opine about purported election interference. At worse—and more likely—the public statement was a deliberate and coordinated effort to mislead the American people about information relevant to the 2020 presidential election by invoking your national security experience to falsely suggest that the allegations about Hunter Biden were not based in fact.

The concerted effort to suppress public dissemination of the serious allegations about Hunter Biden and the Biden family, as first reported in October 2020 by the *New York Post*, was a grave disservice to American citizens' informed participation in our democracy. We are investigating the role that the public statement played in this effort. Accordingly, please provide the following material:

1. Identify all people with whom you communicated about the inception, drafting, editing, signing, publishing, or promotion of the "Public Statement on the Hunter Biden Emails" dated October 19, 2020; and

2. Produce all documents and communications referring or relating to the "Public Statement on the Hunter Biden Emails" dated October 19, 2020.

Please produce this material as soon as possible but no later than 5:00 p.m. on April 20, 2022. In addition, we request that you take all reasonable steps to preserve records that may be potentially responsive to this inquiry.

Thank you for your attention to this matter.

Sincerely,

Jim Jordan
Ranking Member

Steve Chabot
Member of Congress

Louie Gohmert
Member of Congress

Darrell Issa
Ranking Member
Subcommittee on Courts, Intellectual Property, and the Internet

---

[17] *E.g.* Katie Brenner et al., *Hunter Biden paid tax bill, but broad federal investigation continues*, N.Y. Times, Mar. 16, 2022; Matt Viser et al., *Inside Hunter Biden's multimillion-dollar deals with a Chinese energy company*, Wash. Post, Mar. 30, 2022.

Ken Buck
Ranking Member
Subcommittee on Antitrust, Commercial and Administrative Law

Matt Gaetz
Member of Congress

Mike Johnson
Ranking Member
Subcommittee on the Constitution, Civil Rights and Civil Liberties

Andy Biggs
Ranking Member
Subcommittee on Crime, Terrorism and Homeland Security

Tom McClintock
Ranking Member
Subcommittee on Immigration and Citizenship

W. Gregory Steube
Member of Congress

Tom Tiffany
Member of Congress

Thomas Massie
Member of Congress

Chip Roy
Member of Congress

Dan Bishop
Member of Congress

Michelle Fischbach
Member of Congress

Victoria Spartz
Member of Congress

Scott Fitzgerald
Member of Congress

Cliff Bentz
Member of Congress

Burgess Owens
Member of Congress

JERROLD NADLER, New York
CHAIRMAN

JIM JORDAN, Ohio
RANKING MEMBER

ONE HUNDRED SEVENTEENTH CONGRESS

Congress of the United States
House of Representatives
COMMITTEE ON THE JUDICIARY

2138 Rayburn House Office Building

Washington, DC 20515-6216

(202) 225-3951
judiciary.house.gov

April 6, 2022

Mr. Rodney Snyder
via e-mail

Dear Mr. Snyder:

On October 14, 2020, the *New York Post* published a report detailing how Hunter Biden used the position and influence of his father, now-President Joe Biden, for personal gain with the apparent awareness of President Biden.[1] This article raised doubts about President Biden's earlier denial of ever speaking to his son about his international business dealings.[2] The *Post* reported on an email in which a Ukrainian businessman urged Hunter Biden to "use [his] influence to convey a message / signal, etc. to stop what we consider to be politically motivated actions."[3] In another email, the same businessman thanked Hunter Biden for arranging a meeting with his father, calling it "an honor and pleasure."[4] The *Post* reported that these emails came from a laptop belonging to Hunter Biden that he had abandoned in a Delaware computer shop.[5]

On October 19, 2020, you signed a public statement attempting to discredit the contents of the *New York Post*'s reporting about Hunter Biden.[6] This statement emphasized the national security credentials of you and the other signatories, implying that the assertions and conclusions in the statement were grounded in information unavailable to other Americans. Referencing this unique experience, you wrote:

> It is for all these reasons that we write to say that the arrival on the US political scene of emails purportedly belonging to Vice President Biden's son Hunter, much of it related to his time serving on the Board of the Ukrainian gas company Burisma, has all the classic earmarks of a Russian information operation.[7]

---

[1] Emma-Jo Morris & Gabrielle Fonrouge, *Smoking-gun email reveals how Hunter Biden introduced Ukrainian businessman to VP dad*, N.Y. Post, Oct. 14, 2020.
[2] *E.g.* Nick Givas, *Joe Biden again denies speaking to son about Ukrainian business dealings*, Fox News, Oct. 10, 2019.
[3] Morris & Fonrouge, *supra* note 1.
[4] *Id.*
[5] *Id.*
[6] Jim Clapper et al., Public Statement on the Hunter Biden Emails (Oct. 19, 2020).
[7] *Id.*

Although this statement acknowledged that you had seen no actual "evidence" of Russian involvement with respect to the publication of Hunter Biden's emails, you nonetheless conveyed a "deep[] suspicio[n] that the Russian government played a significant role in the case."[8] Later in the statement, you went further to state a "view"—not merely a suspicion anymore—"that the Russians are involved in the Hunter Biden email issue . . . ."[9]

Your public statement served as a basis for Democrat operatives to try to delegitimize the scandalous allegations about Hunter Biden and the Biden family. On the same day as your statement, *Politico* published a story about the statement, with the conclusive headline, "Hunter Biden story is Russian disinfo, dozens of former intel officials say."[10] Departing from the statement's careful wording, the *Politico* story quoted one signatory to the letter as being confident that "once again the Russians are interfering" in our elections.[11] Fifteen minutes after *Politico* published its story, Jen Psaki, who now serves as Press Secretary to the President, tweeted a link to the *Politico* story.[12] The Biden campaign repeatedly cited your statement to dismiss the allegations against Hunter Biden.[13] During the final presidential debate, Vice President Biden also dismissed concerns about Hunter Biden's international business dealings as part of a "Russian plan."[14]

Your public statement was consistent with a broader effort to minimize and censor the *New York Post*'s reporting about Hunter Biden and the Biden family. National news organizations called the allegations about Hunter Biden "dubious" and a "non-scandal"; CBS News reporter Leslie Stahl said the allegations "can't be verified"; and NPR called it a "waste . . . of time" and a "pure distraction."[15] Separately, Twitter and Facebook restricted access to the *New York Post*'s reporting about Hunter Biden, with Twitter locking the *Post*'s account and Facebook deferring to a so-called independent fact-check that never occurred.[16] These efforts likely affected public awareness of the serious allegations surrounding the Biden family in the crucial weeks before the 2020 election.

We now know from subsequent reporting that the *New York Post*'s article about Hunter Biden was not, as you and your co-signatories alleged, part of a "Russian information

---

[8] *Id.*
[9] *Id.*
[10] Natasha Bertrand, *Hunter Biden story is Russian disinfo, dozens of former intel officials say*, Politico, Oct. 19, 2020.
[11] *Id.*
[12] Tweet by Jen Psaki, Twitter.com (Oct. 19, 2020, 10:45 p.m.), https://twitter.com/jrpsaki/status/1318382779659411458.
[13] *E.g.* Houston Keene, *Flashback: Biden officials pushed angle that Hunter laptop was 'Russian disinfo,'* Fox News, Mar. 17, 2022.
[14] Deirdre Shesgreen, *"Nothing was unethical": Joe Biden defends Hunter Biden under pressure from Trump in debate*, USA Today, Oct. 22, 2020.
[15] Joe Concha, *Media's pre-election burial of Hunter Biden story proves dereliction of duty*, The Hill, Dec. 11, 2020.
[16] *E.g.* Elizabeth Dwoskin, *Facebook and Twitter take unusual steps to limit spread of New York Post story*, Wash. Post, Oct. 15, 2020.

operation."[17] This belated verification of the *Post*'s reporting raises fresh questions about the public statement you signed in October 2020. At best, the public statement was a reckless attempt by you and your co-signatories to erroneously opine about purported election interference. At worse—and more likely—the public statement was a deliberate and coordinated effort to mislead the American people about information relevant to the 2020 presidential election by invoking your national security experience to falsely suggest that the allegations about Hunter Biden were not based in fact.

The concerted effort to suppress public dissemination of the serious allegations about Hunter Biden and the Biden family, as first reported in October 2020 by the *New York Post*, was a grave disservice to American citizens' informed participation in our democracy. We are investigating the role that the public statement played in this effort. Accordingly, please provide the following material:

1. Identify all people with whom you communicated about the inception, drafting, editing, signing, publishing, or promotion of the "Public Statement on the Hunter Biden Emails" dated October 19, 2020; and

2. Produce all documents and communications referring or relating to the "Public Statement on the Hunter Biden Emails" dated October 19, 2020.

Please produce this material as soon as possible but no later than 5:00 p.m. on April 20, 2022. In addition, we request that you take all reasonable steps to preserve records that may be potentially responsive to this inquiry.

Thank you for your attention to this matter.

Sincerely,

Jim Jordan
Ranking Member

Steve Chabot
Member of Congress

Louie Gohmert
Member of Congress

Darrell Issa
Ranking Member
Subcommittee on Courts, Intellectual Property, and the Internet

---

[17] *E.g.* Katie Brenner et al., *Hunter Biden paid tax bill, but broad federal investigation continues*, N.Y. Times, Mar. 16, 2022; Matt Viser et al., *Inside Hunter Biden's multimillion-dollar deals with a Chinese energy company*, Wash. Post, Mar. 30, 2022.

Ken Buck
Ranking Member
Subcommittee on Antitrust, Commercial and Administrative Law

Matt Gaetz
Member of Congress

Mike Johnson
Ranking Member
Subcommittee on the Constitution, Civil Rights and Civil Liberties

Andy Biggs
Ranking Member
Subcommittee on Crime, Terrorism and Homeland Security

Tom McClintock
Ranking Member
Subcommittee on Immigration and Citizenship

W. Gregory Steube
Member of Congress

Tom Tiffany
Member of Congress

Thomas Massie
Member of Congress

Chip Roy
Member of Congress

Dan Bishop
Member of Congress

Michelle Fischbach
Member of Congress

Victoria Spartz
Member of Congress

Scott Fitzgerald
Member of Congress

Cliff Bentz
Member of Congress

Burgess Owens
Member of Congress

JERROLD NADLER, New York
CHAIRMAN

JIM JORDAN, Ohio
RANKING MEMBER

ONE HUNDRED SEVENTEENTH CONGRESS

Congress of the United States

House of Representatives

COMMITTEE ON THE JUDICIARY

2138 RAYBURN HOUSE OFFICE BUILDING

WASHINGTON, DC 20515-6216

(202) 225-3951
judiciary.house.gov

April 6, 2022

Ms. Cynthia Strand
via e-mail

Dear Ms. Strand:

On October 14, 2020, the *New York Post* published a report detailing how Hunter Biden used the position and influence of his father, now-President Joe Biden, for personal gain with the apparent awareness of President Biden.[1] This article raised doubts about President Biden's earlier denial of ever speaking to his son about his international business dealings.[2] The *Post* reported on an email in which a Ukrainian businessman urged Hunter Biden to "use [his] influence to convey a message / signal, etc. to stop what we consider to be politically motivated actions."[3] In another email, the same businessman thanked Hunter Biden for arranging a meeting with his father, calling it "an honor and pleasure."[4] The *Post* reported that these emails came from a laptop belonging to Hunter Biden that he had abandoned in a Delaware computer shop.[5]

On October 19, 2020, you signed a public statement attempting to discredit the contents of the *New York Post*'s reporting about Hunter Biden.[6] This statement emphasized the national security credentials of you and the other signatories, implying that the assertions and conclusions in the statement were grounded in information unavailable to other Americans. Referencing this unique experience, you wrote:

> It is for all these reasons that we write to say that the arrival on the US political scene of emails purportedly belonging to Vice President Biden's son Hunter, much of it related to his time serving on the Board of the Ukrainian gas company Burisma, has all the classic earmarks of a Russian information operation.[7]

---

[1] Emma-Jo Morris & Gabrielle Fonrouge, *Smoking-gun email reveals how Hunter Biden introduced Ukrainian businessman to VP dad*, N.Y. Post, Oct. 14, 2020.
[2] *E.g.* Nick Givas, *Joe Biden again denies speaking to son about Ukrainian business dealings*, Fox News, Oct. 10, 2019.
[3] Morris & Fonrouge, *supra* note 1.
[4] *Id.*
[5] *Id.*
[6] Jim Clapper et al., Public Statement on the Hunter Biden Emails (Oct. 19, 2020).
[7] *Id.*

Although this statement acknowledged that you had seen no actual "evidence" of Russian involvement with respect to the publication of Hunter Biden's emails, you nonetheless conveyed a "deep[] suspicio[n] that the Russian government played a significant role in the case."[8] Later in the statement, you went further to state a "view"—not merely a suspicion anymore—"that the Russians are involved in the Hunter Biden email issue . . . ."[9]

Your public statement served as a basis for Democrat operatives to try to delegitimize the scandalous allegations about Hunter Biden and the Biden family. On the same day as your statement, *Politico* published a story about the statement, with the conclusive headline, "Hunter Biden story is Russian disinfo, dozens of former intel officials say."[10] Departing from the statement's careful wording, the *Politico* story quoted one signatory to the letter as being confident that "once again the Russians are interfering" in our elections.[11] Fifteen minutes after *Politico* published its story, Jen Psaki, who now serves as Press Secretary to the President, tweeted a link to the *Politico* story.[12] The Biden campaign repeatedly cited your statement to dismiss the allegations against Hunter Biden.[13] During the final presidential debate, Vice President Biden also dismissed concerns about Hunter Biden's international business dealings as part of a "Russian plan."[14]

Your public statement was consistent with a broader effort to minimize and censor the *New York Post*'s reporting about Hunter Biden and the Biden family. National news organizations called the allegations about Hunter Biden "dubious" and a "non-scandal"; CBS News reporter Leslie Stahl said the allegations "can't be verified"; and NPR called it a "waste . . . of time" and a "pure distraction."[15] Separately, Twitter and Facebook restricted access to the *New York Post*'s reporting about Hunter Biden, with Twitter locking the *Post*'s account and Facebook deferring to a so-called independent fact-check that never occurred.[16] These efforts likely affected public awareness of the serious allegations surrounding the Biden family in the crucial weeks before the 2020 election.

We now know from subsequent reporting that the *New York Post*'s article about Hunter Biden was not, as you and your co-signatories alleged, part of a "Russian information

---

[8] *Id.*
[9] *Id.*
[10] Natasha Bertrand, *Hunter Biden story is Russian disinfo, dozens of former intel officials say*, Politico, Oct. 19, 2020.
[11] *Id.*
[12] Tweet by Jen Psaki, Twitter.com (Oct. 19, 2020, 10:45 p.m.), https://twitter.com/jrpsaki/status/1318382779659411458.
[13] *E.g.* Houston Keene, *Flashback: Biden officials pushed angle that Hunter laptop was 'Russian disinfo,'* Fox News, Mar. 17, 2022.
[14] Deirdre Shesgreen, *"Nothing was unethical": Joe Biden defends Hunter Biden under pressure from Trump in debate*, USA Today, Oct. 22, 2020.
[15] Joe Concha, *Media's pre-election burial of Hunter Biden story proves dereliction of duty*, The Hill, Dec. 11, 2020.
[16] *E.g.* Elizabeth Dwoskin, *Facebook and Twitter take unusual steps to limit spread of New York Post story*, Wash. Post, Oct. 15, 2020.

operation."[17] This belated verification of the *Post*'s reporting raises fresh questions about the public statement you signed in October 2020. At best, the public statement was a reckless attempt by you and your co-signatories to erroneously opine about purported election interference. At worse—and more likely—the public statement was a deliberate and coordinated effort to mislead the American people about information relevant to the 2020 presidential election by invoking your national security experience to falsely suggest that the allegations about Hunter Biden were not based in fact.

The concerted effort to suppress public dissemination of the serious allegations about Hunter Biden and the Biden family, as first reported in October 2020 by the *New York Post*, was a grave disservice to American citizens' informed participation in our democracy. We are investigating the role that the public statement played in this effort. Accordingly, please provide the following material:

1. Identify all people with whom you communicated about the inception, drafting, editing, signing, publishing, or promotion of the "Public Statement on the Hunter Biden Emails" dated October 19, 2020; and

2. Produce all documents and communications referring or relating to the "Public Statement on the Hunter Biden Emails" dated October 19, 2020.

Please produce this material as soon as possible but no later than 5:00 p.m. on April 20, 2022. In addition, we request that you take all reasonable steps to preserve records that may be potentially responsive to this inquiry.

Thank you for your attention to this matter.

Sincerely,

Jim Jordan
Ranking Member

Steve Chabot
Member of Congress

Louie Gohmert
Member of Congress

Darrell Issa
Ranking Member
Subcommittee on Courts, Intellectual Property, and the Internet

---

[17] *E.g.* Katie Brenner et al., *Hunter Biden paid tax bill, but broad federal investigation continues*, N.Y. Times, Mar. 16, 2022; Matt Viser et al., *Inside Hunter Biden's multimillion-dollar deals with a Chinese energy company*, Wash. Post, Mar. 30, 2022.

Ken Buck
Ranking Member
Subcommittee on Antitrust, Commercial and Administrative Law

Matt Gaetz
Member of Congress

Mike Johnson
Ranking Member
Subcommittee on the Constitution, Civil Rights and Civil Liberties

Andy Biggs
Ranking Member
Subcommittee on Crime, Terrorism and Homeland Security

Tom McClintock
Ranking Member
Subcommittee on Immigration and Citizenship

W. Gregory Steube
Member of Congress

Tom Tiffany
Member of Congress

Thomas Massie
Member of Congress

Chip Roy
Member of Congress

Dan Bishop
Member of Congress

Michelle Fischbach
Member of Congress

Victoria Spartz
Member of Congress

Scott Fitzgerald
Member of Congress

Cliff Bentz
Member of Congress

Burgess Owens
Member of Congress

JERROLD NADLER, New York
CHAIRMAN

JIM JORDAN, Ohio
RANKING MEMBER

ONE HUNDRED SEVENTEENTH CONGRESS

Congress of the United States
House of Representatives
COMMITTEE ON THE JUDICIARY

2138 RAYBURN HOUSE OFFICE BUILDING

WASHINGTON, DC 20515–6216

(202) 225–3951
judiciary.house.gov

April 6, 2022

Mr. Greg Tarbell
c/o Central Intelligence Agency
via e-mail

Dear Mr. Tarbell:

On October 14, 2020, the *New York Post* published a report detailing how Hunter Biden used the position and influence of his father, now-President Joe Biden, for personal gain with the apparent awareness of President Biden.[1] This article raised doubts about President Biden's earlier denial of ever speaking to his son about his international business dealings.[2] The *Post* reported on an email in which a Ukrainian businessman urged Hunter Biden to "use [his] influence to convey a message / signal, etc. to stop what we consider to be politically motivated actions."[3] In another email, the same businessman thanked Hunter Biden for arranging a meeting with his father, calling it "an honor and pleasure."[4] The *Post* reported that these emails came from a laptop belonging to Hunter Biden that he had abandoned in a Delaware computer shop.[5]

On October 19, 2020, you signed a public statement attempting to discredit the contents of the *New York Post*'s reporting about Hunter Biden.[6] This statement emphasized the national security credentials of you and the other signatories, implying that the assertions and conclusions in the statement were grounded in information unavailable to other Americans. Referencing this unique experience, you wrote:

> It is for all these reasons that we write to say that the arrival on the US political scene of emails purportedly belonging to Vice President Biden's son Hunter, much of it related to his time serving on the Board of the Ukrainian gas company Burisma, has all the classic earmarks of a Russian information operation.[7]

---

[1] Emma-Jo Morris & Gabrielle Fonrouge, *Smoking-gun email reveals how Hunter Biden introduced Ukrainian businessman to VP dad*, N.Y. Post, Oct. 14, 2020.
[2] *E.g.* Nick Givas, *Joe Biden again denies speaking to son about Ukrainian business dealings*, Fox News, Oct. 10, 2019.
[3] Morris & Fonrouge, *supra* note 1.
[4] *Id.*
[5] *Id.*
[6] Jim Clapper et al., Public Statement on the Hunter Biden Emails (Oct. 19, 2020).
[7] *Id.*

Although this statement acknowledged that you had seen no actual "evidence" of Russian involvement with respect to the publication of Hunter Biden's emails, you nonetheless conveyed a "deep[] suspicio[n] that the Russian government played a significant role in the case."[8] Later in the statement, you went further to state a "view"—not merely a suspicion anymore—"that the Russians are involved in the Hunter Biden email issue . . . ."[9]

Your public statement served as a basis for Democrat operatives to try to delegitimize the scandalous allegations about Hunter Biden and the Biden family. On the same day as your statement, *Politico* published a story about the statement, with the conclusive headline, "Hunter Biden story is Russian disinfo, dozens of former intel officials say."[10] Departing from the statement's careful wording, the *Politico* story quoted one signatory to the letter as being confident that "once again the Russians are interfering" in our elections.[11] Fifteen minutes after *Politico* published its story, Jen Psaki, who now serves as Press Secretary to the President, tweeted a link to the *Politico* story.[12] The Biden campaign repeatedly cited your statement to dismiss the allegations against Hunter Biden.[13] During the final presidential debate, Vice President Biden also dismissed concerns about Hunter Biden's international business dealings as part of a "Russian plan."[14]

Your public statement was consistent with a broader effort to minimize and censor the *New York Post*'s reporting about Hunter Biden and the Biden family. National news organizations called the allegations about Hunter Biden "dubious" and a "non-scandal"; CBS News reporter Leslie Stahl said the allegations "can't be verified"; and NPR called it a "waste . . . of time" and a "pure distraction."[15] Separately, Twitter and Facebook restricted access to the *New York Post*'s reporting about Hunter Biden, with Twitter locking the *Post*'s account and Facebook deferring to a so-called independent fact-check that never occurred.[16] These efforts likely affected public awareness of the serious allegations surrounding the Biden family in the crucial weeks before the 2020 election.

We now know from subsequent reporting that the *New York Post*'s article about Hunter Biden was not, as you and your co-signatories alleged, part of a "Russian information

---

[8] *Id.*
[9] *Id.*
[10] Natasha Bertrand, *Hunter Biden story is Russian disinfo, dozens of former intel officials say*, Politico, Oct. 19, 2020.
[11] *Id.*
[12] Tweet by Jen Psaki, Twitter.com (Oct. 19, 2020, 10:45 p.m.), https://twitter.com/jrpsaki/status/1318382779659411458.
[13] *E.g.* Houston Keene, *Flashback: Biden officials pushed angle that Hunter laptop was 'Russian disinfo,'* Fox News, Mar. 17, 2022.
[14] Deirdre Shesgreen, *"Nothing was unethical": Joe Biden defends Hunter Biden under pressure from Trump in debate*, USA Today, Oct. 22, 2020.
[15] Joe Concha, *Media's pre-election burial of Hunter Biden story proves dereliction of duty*, The Hill, Dec. 11, 2020.
[16] *E.g.* Elizabeth Dwoskin, *Facebook and Twitter take unusual steps to limit spread of New York Post story*, Wash. Post, Oct. 15, 2020.

operation."[17] This belated verification of the *Post*'s reporting raises fresh questions about the public statement you signed in October 2020. At best, the public statement was a reckless attempt by you and your co-signatories to erroneously opine about purported election interference. At worse—and more likely—the public statement was a deliberate and coordinated effort to mislead the American people about information relevant to the 2020 presidential election by invoking your national security experience to falsely suggest that the allegations about Hunter Biden were not based in fact.

The concerted effort to suppress public dissemination of the serious allegations about Hunter Biden and the Biden family, as first reported in October 2020 by the *New York Post*, was a grave disservice to American citizens' informed participation in our democracy. We are investigating the role that the public statement played in this effort. Accordingly, please provide the following material:

1. Identify all people with whom you communicated about the inception, drafting, editing, signing, publishing, or promotion of the "Public Statement on the Hunter Biden Emails" dated October 19, 2020; and

2. Produce all documents and communications referring or relating to the "Public Statement on the Hunter Biden Emails" dated October 19, 2020.

Please produce this material as soon as possible but no later than 5:00 p.m. on April 20, 2022. In addition, we request that you take all reasonable steps to preserve records that may be potentially responsive to this inquiry.

Thank you for your attention to this matter.

Sincerely,

Jim Jordan
Ranking Member

Steve Chabot
Member of Congress

Louie Gohmert
Member of Congress

Darrell Issa
Ranking Member
Subcommittee on Courts, Intellectual Property, and the Internet

---

[17] *E.g.* Katie Brenner et al., *Hunter Biden paid tax bill, but broad federal investigation continues*, N.Y. Times, Mar. 16, 2022; Matt Viser et al., *Inside Hunter Biden's multimillion-dollar deals with a Chinese energy company*, Wash. Post, Mar. 30, 2022.

Ken Buck
Ranking Member
Subcommittee on Antitrust, Commercial and Administrative Law

Matt Gaetz
Member of Congress

Mike Johnson
Ranking Member
Subcommittee on the Constitution, Civil Rights and Civil Liberties

Andy Biggs
Ranking Member
Subcommittee on Crime, Terrorism and Homeland Security

Tom McClintock
Ranking Member
Subcommittee on Immigration and Citizenship

W. Gregory Steube
Member of Congress

Tom Tiffany
Member of Congress

Thomas Massie
Member of Congress

Chip Roy
Member of Congress

Dan Bishop
Member of Congress

Michelle Fischbach
Member of Congress

Victoria Spartz
Member of Congress

Scott Fitzgerald
Member of Congress

Cliff Bentz
Member of Congress

Burgess Owens
Member of Congress

JERROLD NADLER, New York
CHAIRMAN

JIM JORDAN, Ohio
RANKING MEMBER

ONE HUNDRED SEVENTEENTH CONGRESS
Congress of the United States
House of Representatives
COMMITTEE ON THE JUDICIARY
2138 RAYBURN HOUSE OFFICE BUILDING
WASHINGTON, DC 20515–6216
(202) 225–3951
judiciary.house.gov

April 6, 2022

Mr. David Terry
c/o Central Intelligence Agency
via e-mail

Dear Mr. Terry:

On October 14, 2020, the *New York Post* published a report detailing how Hunter Biden used the position and influence of his father, now-President Joe Biden, for personal gain with the apparent awareness of President Biden.[1] This article raised doubts about President Biden's earlier denial of ever speaking to his son about his international business dealings.[2] The *Post* reported on an email in which a Ukrainian businessman urged Hunter Biden to "use [his] influence to convey a message / signal, etc. to stop what we consider to be politically motivated actions."[3] In another email, the same businessman thanked Hunter Biden for arranging a meeting with his father, calling it "an honor and pleasure."[4] The *Post* reported that these emails came from a laptop belonging to Hunter Biden that he had abandoned in a Delaware computer shop.[5]

On October 19, 2020, you signed a public statement attempting to discredit the contents of the *New York Post*'s reporting about Hunter Biden.[6] This statement emphasized the national security credentials of you and the other signatories, implying that the assertions and conclusions in the statement were grounded in information unavailable to other Americans. Referencing this unique experience, you wrote:

> It is for all these reasons that we write to say that the arrival on the US political scene of emails purportedly belonging to Vice President Biden's son Hunter, much of it related to his time serving on the Board of the Ukrainian gas company Burisma, has all the classic earmarks of a Russian information operation.[7]

---

[1] Emma-Jo Morris & Gabrielle Fonrouge, *Smoking-gun email reveals how Hunter Biden introduced Ukrainian businessman to VP dad*, N.Y. Post, Oct. 14, 2020.
[2] *E.g.* Nick Givas, *Joe Biden again denies speaking to son about Ukrainian business dealings*, Fox News, Oct. 10, 2019.
[3] Morris & Fonrouge, *supra* note 1.
[4] *Id.*
[5] *Id.*
[6] Jim Clapper et al., Public Statement on the Hunter Biden Emails (Oct. 19, 2020).
[7] *Id.*

Although this statement acknowledged that you had seen no actual "evidence" of Russian involvement with respect to the publication of Hunter Biden's emails, you nonetheless conveyed a "deep[] suspicio[n] that the Russian government played a significant role in the case."[8] Later in the statement, you went further to state a "view"—not merely a suspicion anymore—"that the Russians are involved in the Hunter Biden email issue . . . ."[9]

Your public statement served as a basis for Democrat operatives to try to delegitimize the scandalous allegations about Hunter Biden and the Biden family. On the same day as your statement, *Politico* published a story about the statement, with the conclusive headline, "Hunter Biden story is Russian disinfo, dozens of former intel officials say."[10] Departing from the statement's careful wording, the *Politico* story quoted one signatory to the letter as being confident that "once again the Russians are interfering" in our elections.[11] Fifteen minutes after *Politico* published its story, Jen Psaki, who now serves as Press Secretary to the President, tweeted a link to the *Politico* story.[12] The Biden campaign repeatedly cited your statement to dismiss the allegations against Hunter Biden.[13] During the final presidential debate, Vice President Biden also dismissed concerns about Hunter Biden's international business dealings as part of a "Russian plan."[14]

Your public statement was consistent with a broader effort to minimize and censor the *New York Post*'s reporting about Hunter Biden and the Biden family. National news organizations called the allegations about Hunter Biden "dubious" and a "non-scandal"; CBS News reporter Leslie Stahl said the allegations "can't be verified"; and NPR called it a "waste . . . of time" and a "pure distraction."[15] Separately, Twitter and Facebook restricted access to the *New York Post*'s reporting about Hunter Biden, with Twitter locking the *Post*'s account and Facebook deferring to a so-called independent fact-check that never occurred.[16] These efforts likely affected public awareness of the serious allegations surrounding the Biden family in the crucial weeks before the 2020 election.

We now know from subsequent reporting that the *New York Post*'s article about Hunter Biden was not, as you and your co-signatories alleged, part of a "Russian information

---

[8] *Id.*
[9] *Id.*
[10] Natasha Bertrand, *Hunter Biden story is Russian disinfo, dozens of former intel officials say*, Politico, Oct. 19, 2020.
[11] *Id.*
[12] Tweet by Jen Psaki, Twitter.com (Oct. 19, 2020, 10:45 p.m.), https://twitter.com/jrpsaki/status/1318382779659411458.
[13] *E.g.* Houston Keene, *Flashback: Biden officials pushed angle that Hunter laptop was 'Russian disinfo,'* Fox News, Mar. 17, 2022.
[14] Deirdre Shesgreen, *"Nothing was unethical": Joe Biden defends Hunter Biden under pressure from Trump in debate*, USA Today, Oct. 22, 2020.
[15] Joe Concha, *Media's pre-election burial of Hunter Biden story proves dereliction of duty*, The Hill, Dec. 11, 2020.
[16] *E.g.* Elizabeth Dwoskin, *Facebook and Twitter take unusual steps to limit spread of New York Post story*, Wash. Post, Oct. 15, 2020.

operation."[17] This belated verification of the *Post*'s reporting raises fresh questions about the public statement you signed in October 2020. At best, the public statement was a reckless attempt by you and your co-signatories to erroneously opine about purported election interference. At worse—and more likely—the public statement was a deliberate and coordinated effort to mislead the American people about information relevant to the 2020 presidential election by invoking your national security experience to falsely suggest that the allegations about Hunter Biden were not based in fact.

The concerted effort to suppress public dissemination of the serious allegations about Hunter Biden and the Biden family, as first reported in October 2020 by the *New York Post*, was a grave disservice to American citizens' informed participation in our democracy. We are investigating the role that the public statement played in this effort. Accordingly, please provide the following material:

1. Identify all people with whom you communicated about the inception, drafting, editing, signing, publishing, or promotion of the "Public Statement on the Hunter Biden Emails" dated October 19, 2020; and

2. Produce all documents and communications referring or relating to the "Public Statement on the Hunter Biden Emails" dated October 19, 2020.

Please produce this material as soon as possible but no later than 5:00 p.m. on April 20, 2022. In addition, we request that you take all reasonable steps to preserve records that may be potentially responsive to this inquiry.

Thank you for your attention to this matter.

Sincerely,

Jim Jordan
Ranking Member

Steve Chabot
Member of Congress

Louie Gohmert
Member of Congress

Darrell Issa
Ranking Member
Subcommittee on Courts, Intellectual Property, and the Internet

---

[17] *E.g.* Katie Brenner et al., *Hunter Biden paid tax bill, but broad federal investigation continues*, N.Y. Times, Mar. 16, 2022; Matt Viser et al., *Inside Hunter Biden's multimillion-dollar deals with a Chinese energy company*, Wash. Post, Mar. 30, 2022.

Ken Buck
Ranking Member
Subcommittee on Antitrust, Commercial
and Administrative Law

Mike Johnson
Ranking Member
Subcommittee on the Constitution,
Civil Rights and Civil Liberties

Tom McClintock
Ranking Member
Subcommittee on Immigration
and Citizenship

Tom Tiffany
Member of Congress

Chip Roy
Member of Congress

Michelle Fischbach
Member of Congress

Matt Gaetz
Member of Congress

Andy Biggs
Ranking Member
Subcommittee on Crime, Terrorism
and Homeland Security

W. Gregory Steube
Member of Congress

Thomas Massie
Member of Congress

Dan Bishop
Member of Congress

Victoria Spartz
Member of Congress

Scott Fitzgerald
Member of Congress

Cliff Bentz
Member of Congress

Burgess Owens
Member of Congress

JERROLD NADLER, New York
CHAIRMAN

JIM JORDAN, Ohio
RANKING MEMBER

ONE HUNDRED SEVENTEENTH CONGRESS
Congress of the United States
House of Representatives
COMMITTEE ON THE JUDICIARY
2138 RAYBURN HOUSE OFFICE BUILDING
WASHINGTON, DC 20515-6216
(202) 225-3951
judiciary.house.gov

April 6, 2022

Mr. Russell Travers
c/o National Counterterrorism Center
via e-mail

Dear Mr. Travers:

On October 14, 2020, the *New York Post* published a report detailing how Hunter Biden used the position and influence of his father, now-President Joe Biden, for personal gain with the apparent awareness of President Biden.[1] This article raised doubts about President Biden's earlier denial of ever speaking to his son about his international business dealings.[2] The *Post* reported on an email in which a Ukrainian businessman urged Hunter Biden to "use [his] influence to convey a message / signal, etc. to stop what we consider to be politically motivated actions."[3] In another email, the same businessman thanked Hunter Biden for arranging a meeting with his father, calling it "an honor and pleasure."[4] The *Post* reported that these emails came from a laptop belonging to Hunter Biden that he had abandoned in a Delaware computer shop.[5]

On October 19, 2020, you signed a public statement attempting to discredit the contents of the *New York Post*'s reporting about Hunter Biden.[6] This statement emphasized the national security credentials of you and the other signatories, implying that the assertions and conclusions in the statement were grounded in information unavailable to other Americans. Referencing this unique experience, you wrote:

> It is for all these reasons that we write to say that the arrival on the US political scene of emails purportedly belonging to Vice President Biden's son Hunter, much of it related to his time serving on the Board of the Ukrainian gas company Burisma, has all the classic earmarks of a Russian information operation.[7]

---

[1] Emma-Jo Morris & Gabrielle Fonrouge, *Smoking-gun email reveals how Hunter Biden introduced Ukrainian businessman to VP dad*, N.Y. Post, Oct. 14, 2020.
[2] *E.g.* Nick Givas, *Joe Biden again denies speaking to son about Ukrainian business dealings*, Fox News, Oct. 10, 2019.
[3] Morris & Fonrouge, *supra* note 1.
[4] *Id.*
[5] *Id.*
[6] Jim Clapper et al., Public Statement on the Hunter Biden Emails (Oct. 19, 2020).
[7] *Id.*

Although this statement acknowledged that you had seen no actual "evidence" of Russian involvement with respect to the publication of Hunter Biden's emails, you nonetheless conveyed a "deep[] suspicio[n] that the Russian government played a significant role in the case."[8] Later in the statement, you went further to state a "view"—not merely a suspicion anymore—"that the Russians are involved in the Hunter Biden email issue . . . ."[9]

Your public statement served as a basis for Democrat operatives to try to delegitimize the scandalous allegations about Hunter Biden and the Biden family. On the same day as your statement, *Politico* published a story about the statement, with the conclusive headline, "Hunter Biden story is Russian disinfo, dozens of former intel officials say."[10] Departing from the statement's careful wording, the *Politico* story quoted one signatory to the letter as being confident that "once again the Russians are interfering" in our elections.[11] Fifteen minutes after *Politico* published its story, Jen Psaki, who now serves as Press Secretary to the President, tweeted a link to the *Politico* story.[12] The Biden campaign repeatedly cited your statement to dismiss the allegations against Hunter Biden.[13] During the final presidential debate, Vice President Biden also dismissed concerns about Hunter Biden's international business dealings as part of a "Russian plan."[14]

Your public statement was consistent with a broader effort to minimize and censor the *New York Post*'s reporting about Hunter Biden and the Biden family. National news organizations called the allegations about Hunter Biden "dubious" and a "non-scandal"; CBS News reporter Leslie Stahl said the allegations "can't be verified"; and NPR called it a "waste . . . of time" and a "pure distraction."[15] Separately, Twitter and Facebook restricted access to the *New York Post*'s reporting about Hunter Biden, with Twitter locking the *Post*'s account and Facebook deferring to a so-called independent fact-check that never occurred.[16] These efforts likely affected public awareness of the serious allegations surrounding the Biden family in the crucial weeks before the 2020 election.

We now know from subsequent reporting that the *New York Post*'s article about Hunter Biden was not, as you and your co-signatories alleged, part of a "Russian information

---

[8] *Id.*
[9] *Id.*
[10] Natasha Bertrand, *Hunter Biden story is Russian disinfo, dozens of former intel officials say*, Politico, Oct. 19, 2020.
[11] *Id.*
[12] Tweet by Jen Psaki, Twitter.com (Oct. 19, 2020, 10:45 p.m.), https://twitter.com/jrpsaki/status/1318382779659411458.
[13] *E.g.* Houston Keene, *Flashback: Biden officials pushed angle that Hunter laptop was 'Russian disinfo,'* Fox News, Mar. 17, 2022.
[14] Deirdre Shesgreen, *"Nothing was unethical": Joe Biden defends Hunter Biden under pressure from Trump in debate*, USA Today, Oct. 22, 2020.
[15] Joe Concha, *Media's pre-election burial of Hunter Biden story proves dereliction of duty*, The Hill, Dec. 11, 2020.
[16] *E.g.* Elizabeth Dwoskin, *Facebook and Twitter take unusual steps to limit spread of New York Post story*, Wash. Post, Oct. 15, 2020.

operation."[17] This belated verification of the *Post*'s reporting raises fresh questions about the public statement you signed in October 2020. At best, the public statement was a reckless attempt by you and your co-signatories to erroneously opine about purported election interference. At worse—and more likely—the public statement was a deliberate and coordinated effort to mislead the American people about information relevant to the 2020 presidential election by invoking your national security experience to falsely suggest that the allegations about Hunter Biden were not based in fact.

The concerted effort to suppress public dissemination of the serious allegations about Hunter Biden and the Biden family, as first reported in October 2020 by the *New York Post*, was a grave disservice to American citizens' informed participation in our democracy. We are investigating the role that the public statement played in this effort. Accordingly, please provide the following material:

1. Identify all people with whom you communicated about the inception, drafting, editing, signing, publishing, or promotion of the "Public Statement on the Hunter Biden Emails" dated October 19, 2020; and

2. Produce all documents and communications referring or relating to the "Public Statement on the Hunter Biden Emails" dated October 19, 2020.

Please produce this material as soon as possible but no later than 5:00 p.m. on April 20, 2022. In addition, we request that you take all reasonable steps to preserve records that may be potentially responsive to this inquiry.

Thank you for your attention to this matter.

Sincerely,

Jim Jordan
Ranking Member

Steve Chabot
Member of Congress

Louie Gohmert
Member of Congress

Darrell Issa
Ranking Member
Subcommittee on Courts, Intellectual Property, and the Internet

[17] *E.g.* Katie Brenner et al., *Hunter Biden paid tax bill, but broad federal investigation continues*, N.Y. Times, Mar. 16, 2022; Matt Viser et al., *Inside Hunter Biden's multimillion-dollar deals with a Chinese energy company*, Wash. Post, Mar. 30, 2022.

Ken Buck
Ranking Member
Subcommittee on Antitrust, Commercial and Administrative Law

Matt Gaetz
Member of Congress

Mike Johnson
Ranking Member
Subcommittee on the Constitution, Civil Rights and Civil Liberties

Andy Biggs
Ranking Member
Subcommittee on Crime, Terrorism and Homeland Security

Tom McClintock
Ranking Member
Subcommittee on Immigration and Citizenship

W. Gregory Steube
Member of Congress

Tom Tiffany
Member of Congress

Thomas Massie
Member of Congress

Chip Roy
Member of Congress

Dan Bishop
Member of Congress

Michelle Fischbach
Member of Congress

Victoria Spartz
Member of Congress

Scott Fitzgerald
Member of Congress

Cliff Bentz
Member of Congress

Burgess Owens
Member of Congress

JERROLD NADLER, New York
CHAIRMAN

JIM JORDAN, Ohio
RANKING MEMBER

ONE HUNDRED SEVENTEENTH CONGRESS

Congress of the United States

House of Representatives

COMMITTEE ON THE JUDICIARY

2138 RAYBURN HOUSE OFFICE BUILDING

WASHINGTON, DC 20515–6216

(202) 225–3951
judiciary.house.gov

April 6, 2022

Mr. Gregory Treverton
via e-mail

Dear Mr. Treverton:

On October 14, 2020, the *New York Post* published a report detailing how Hunter Biden used the position and influence of his father, now-President Joe Biden, for personal gain with the apparent awareness of President Biden.[1] This article raised doubts about President Biden's earlier denial of ever speaking to his son about his international business dealings.[2] The *Post* reported on an email in which a Ukrainian businessman urged Hunter Biden to "use [his] influence to convey a message / signal, etc. to stop what we consider to be politically motivated actions."[3] In another email, the same businessman thanked Hunter Biden for arranging a meeting with his father, calling it "an honor and pleasure."[4] The *Post* reported that these emails came from a laptop belonging to Hunter Biden that he had abandoned in a Delaware computer shop.[5]

On October 19, 2020, you signed a public statement attempting to discredit the contents of the *New York Post*'s reporting about Hunter Biden.[6] This statement emphasized the national security credentials of you and the other signatories, implying that the assertions and conclusions in the statement were grounded in information unavailable to other Americans. Referencing this unique experience, you wrote:

> It is for all these reasons that we write to say that the arrival on the US political scene of emails purportedly belonging to Vice President Biden's son Hunter, much of it related to his time serving on the Board of the Ukrainian gas company Burisma, has all the classic earmarks of a Russian information operation.[7]

---

[1] Emma-Jo Morris & Gabrielle Fonrouge, *Smoking-gun email reveals how Hunter Biden introduced Ukrainian businessman to VP dad*, N.Y. Post, Oct. 14, 2020.
[2] *E.g.* Nick Givas, *Joe Biden again denies speaking to son about Ukrainian business dealings*, Fox News, Oct. 10, 2019.
[3] Morris & Fonrouge, *supra* note 1.
[4] *Id.*
[5] *Id.*
[6] Jim Clapper et al., Public Statement on the Hunter Biden Emails (Oct. 19, 2020).
[7] *Id.*

Although this statement acknowledged that you had seen no actual "evidence" of Russian involvement with respect to the publication of Hunter Biden's emails, you nonetheless conveyed a "deep[] suspicio[n] that the Russian government played a significant role in the case."[8] Later in the statement, you went further to state a "view"—not merely a suspicion anymore—"that the Russians are involved in the Hunter Biden email issue . . . ."[9]

Your public statement served as a basis for Democrat operatives to try to delegitimize the scandalous allegations about Hunter Biden and the Biden family. On the same day as your statement, *Politico* published a story about the statement, with the conclusive headline, "Hunter Biden story is Russian disinfo, dozens of former intel officials say."[10] Departing from the statement's careful wording, the *Politico* story quoted one signatory to the letter as being confident that "once again the Russians are interfering" in our elections.[11] Fifteen minutes after *Politico* published its story, Jen Psaki, who now serves as Press Secretary to the President, tweeted a link to the *Politico* story.[12] The Biden campaign repeatedly cited your statement to dismiss the allegations against Hunter Biden.[13] During the final presidential debate, Vice President Biden also dismissed concerns about Hunter Biden's international business dealings as part of a "Russian plan."[14]

Your public statement was consistent with a broader effort to minimize and censor the *New York Post*'s reporting about Hunter Biden and the Biden family. National news organizations called the allegations about Hunter Biden "dubious" and a "non-scandal"; CBS News reporter Leslie Stahl said the allegations "can't be verified"; and NPR called it a "waste . . . of time" and a "pure distraction."[15] Separately, Twitter and Facebook restricted access to the *New York Post*'s reporting about Hunter Biden, with Twitter locking the *Post*'s account and Facebook deferring to a so-called independent fact-check that never occurred.[16] These efforts likely affected public awareness of the serious allegations surrounding the Biden family in the crucial weeks before the 2020 election.

We now know from subsequent reporting that the *New York Post*'s article about Hunter Biden was not, as you and your co-signatories alleged, part of a "Russian information

---

[8] *Id.*
[9] *Id.*
[10] Natasha Bertrand, *Hunter Biden story is Russian disinfo, dozens of former intel officials say*, Politico, Oct. 19, 2020.
[11] *Id.*
[12] Tweet by Jen Psaki, Twitter.com (Oct. 19, 2020, 10:45 p.m.), https://twitter.com/jrpsaki/status/1318382779659411458.
[13] *E.g.* Houston Keene, *Flashback: Biden officials pushed angle that Hunter laptop was 'Russian disinfo,'* Fox News, Mar. 17, 2022.
[14] Deirdre Shesgreen, *"Nothing was unethical": Joe Biden defends Hunter Biden under pressure from Trump in debate*, USA Today, Oct. 22, 2020.
[15] Joe Concha, *Media's pre-election burial of Hunter Biden story proves dereliction of duty*, The Hill, Dec. 11, 2020.
[16] *E.g.* Elizabeth Dwoskin, *Facebook and Twitter take unusual steps to limit spread of New York Post story*, Wash. Post, Oct. 15, 2020.

operation."[17] This belated verification of the *Post*'s reporting raises fresh questions about the public statement you signed in October 2020. At best, the public statement was a reckless attempt by you and your co-signatories to erroneously opine about purported election interference. At worse—and more likely—the public statement was a deliberate and coordinated effort to mislead the American people about information relevant to the 2020 presidential election by invoking your national security experience to falsely suggest that the allegations about Hunter Biden were not based in fact.

The concerted effort to suppress public dissemination of the serious allegations about Hunter Biden and the Biden family, as first reported in October 2020 by the *New York Post*, was a grave disservice to American citizens' informed participation in our democracy. We are investigating the role that the public statement played in this effort. Accordingly, please provide the following material:

1. Identify all people with whom you communicated about the inception, drafting, editing, signing, publishing, or promotion of the "Public Statement on the Hunter Biden Emails" dated October 19, 2020; and

2. Produce all documents and communications referring or relating to the "Public Statement on the Hunter Biden Emails" dated October 19, 2020.

Please produce this material as soon as possible but no later than 5:00 p.m. on April 20, 2022. In addition, we request that you take all reasonable steps to preserve records that may be potentially responsive to this inquiry.

Thank you for your attention to this matter.

Sincerely,

Jim Jordan
Ranking Member

Steve Chabot
Member of Congress

Louie Gohmert
Member of Congress

Darrell Issa
Ranking Member
Subcommittee on Courts, Intellectual Property, and the Internet

---

[17] *E.g.* Katie Brenner et al., *Hunter Biden paid tax bill, but broad federal investigation continues*, N.Y. Times, Mar. 16, 2022; Matt Viser et al., *Inside Hunter Biden's multimillion-dollar deals with a Chinese energy company*, Wash. Post, Mar. 30, 2022.

Ken Buck
Ranking Member
Subcommittee on Antitrust, Commercial
and Administrative Law

Matt Gaetz
Member of Congress

Mike Johnson
Ranking Member
Subcommittee on the Constitution,
Civil Rights and Civil Liberties

Andy Biggs
Ranking Member
Subcommittee on Crime, Terrorism
and Homeland Security

Tom McClintock
Ranking Member
Subcommittee on Immigration
and Citizenship

W. Gregory Steube
Member of Congress

Tom Tiffany
Member of Congress

Thomas Massie
Member of Congress

Chip Roy
Member of Congress

Dan Bishop
Member of Congress

Michelle Fischbach
Member of Congress

Victoria Spartz
Member of Congress

Scott Fitzgerald
Member of Congress

Cliff Bentz
Member of Congress

Burgess Owens
Member of Congress

JERROLD NADLER, New York
CHAIRMAN

JIM JORDAN, Ohio
RANKING MEMBER

ONE HUNDRED SEVENTEENTH CONGRESS

Congress of the United States

House of Representatives

COMMITTEE ON THE JUDICIARY

2138 RAYBURN HOUSE OFFICE BUILDING
WASHINGTON, DC 20515–6216
(202) 225–3951
judiciary.house.gov

April 6, 2022

Mr. John D. Tullius
c/o Central Intelligence Agency
via e-mail

Dear Mr. Tullius:

On October 14, 2020, the *New York Post* published a report detailing how Hunter Biden used the position and influence of his father, now-President Joe Biden, for personal gain with the apparent awareness of President Biden.[1] This article raised doubts about President Biden's earlier denial of ever speaking to his son about his international business dealings.[2] The *Post* reported on an email in which a Ukrainian businessman urged Hunter Biden to "use [his] influence to convey a message / signal, etc. to stop what we consider to be politically motivated actions."[3] In another email, the same businessman thanked Hunter Biden for arranging a meeting with his father, calling it "an honor and pleasure."[4] The *Post* reported that these emails came from a laptop belonging to Hunter Biden that he had abandoned in a Delaware computer shop.[5]

On October 19, 2020, you signed a public statement attempting to discredit the contents of the *New York Post*'s reporting about Hunter Biden.[6] This statement emphasized the national security credentials of you and the other signatories, implying that the assertions and conclusions in the statement were grounded in information unavailable to other Americans. Referencing this unique experience, you wrote:

> It is for all these reasons that we write to say that the arrival on the US political scene of emails purportedly belonging to Vice President Biden's son Hunter, much of it related to his time serving on the Board of the Ukrainian gas company Burisma, has all the classic earmarks of a Russian information operation.[7]

---

[1] Emma-Jo Morris & Gabrielle Fonrouge, *Smoking-gun email reveals how Hunter Biden introduced Ukrainian businessman to VP dad*, N.Y. Post, Oct. 14, 2020.
[2] *E.g.* Nick Givas, *Joe Biden again denies speaking to son about Ukrainian business dealings*, Fox News, Oct. 10, 2019.
[3] Morris & Fonrouge, *supra* note 1.
[4] *Id.*
[5] *Id.*
[6] Jim Clapper et al., Public Statement on the Hunter Biden Emails (Oct. 19, 2020).
[7] *Id.*

Although this statement acknowledged that you had seen no actual "evidence" of Russian involvement with respect to the publication of Hunter Biden's emails, you nonetheless conveyed a "deep[] suspicio[n] that the Russian government played a significant role in the case."[8] Later in the statement, you went further to state a "view"—not merely a suspicion anymore—"that the Russians are involved in the Hunter Biden email issue . . . ."[9]

Your public statement served as a basis for Democrat operatives to try to delegitimize the scandalous allegations about Hunter Biden and the Biden family. On the same day as your statement, *Politico* published a story about the statement, with the conclusive headline, "Hunter Biden story is Russian disinfo, dozens of former intel officials say."[10] Departing from the statement's careful wording, the *Politico* story quoted one signatory to the letter as being confident that "once again the Russians are interfering" in our elections.[11] Fifteen minutes after *Politico* published its story, Jen Psaki, who now serves as Press Secretary to the President, tweeted a link to the *Politico* story.[12] The Biden campaign repeatedly cited your statement to dismiss the allegations against Hunter Biden.[13] During the final presidential debate, Vice President Biden also dismissed concerns about Hunter Biden's international business dealings as part of a "Russian plan."[14]

Your public statement was consistent with a broader effort to minimize and censor the *New York Post*'s reporting about Hunter Biden and the Biden family. National news organizations called the allegations about Hunter Biden "dubious" and a "non-scandal"; CBS News reporter Leslie Stahl said the allegations "can't be verified"; and NPR called it a "waste . . . of time" and a "pure distraction."[15] Separately, Twitter and Facebook restricted access to the *New York Post*'s reporting about Hunter Biden, with Twitter locking the *Post*'s account and Facebook deferring to a so-called independent fact-check that never occurred.[16] These efforts likely affected public awareness of the serious allegations surrounding the Biden family in the crucial weeks before the 2020 election.

We now know from subsequent reporting that the *New York Post*'s article about Hunter Biden was not, as you and your co-signatories alleged, part of a "Russian information

---

[8] *Id.*
[9] *Id.*
[10] Natasha Bertrand, *Hunter Biden story is Russian disinfo, dozens of former intel officials say*, Politico, Oct. 19, 2020.
[11] *Id.*
[12] Tweet by Jen Psaki, Twitter.com (Oct. 19, 2020, 10:45 p.m.), https://twitter.com/jrpsaki/status/1318382779659411458.
[13] *E.g.* Houston Keene, *Flashback: Biden officials pushed angle that Hunter laptop was 'Russian disinfo,'* Fox News, Mar. 17, 2022.
[14] Deirdre Shesgreen, *"Nothing was unethical": Joe Biden defends Hunter Biden under pressure from Trump in debate*, USA Today, Oct. 22, 2020.
[15] Joe Concha, *Media's pre-election burial of Hunter Biden story proves dereliction of duty*, The Hill, Dec. 11, 2020.
[16] *E.g.* Elizabeth Dwoskin, *Facebook and Twitter take unusual steps to limit spread of New York Post story*, Wash. Post, Oct. 15, 2020.

operation."[17] This belated verification of the *Post*'s reporting raises fresh questions about the public statement you signed in October 2020. At best, the public statement was a reckless attempt by you and your co-signatories to erroneously opine about purported election interference. At worse—and more likely—the public statement was a deliberate and coordinated effort to mislead the American people about information relevant to the 2020 presidential election by invoking your national security experience to falsely suggest that the allegations about Hunter Biden were not based in fact.

The concerted effort to suppress public dissemination of the serious allegations about Hunter Biden and the Biden family, as first reported in October 2020 by the *New York Post*, was a grave disservice to American citizens' informed participation in our democracy. We are investigating the role that the public statement played in this effort. Accordingly, please provide the following material:

1. Identify all people with whom you communicated about the inception, drafting, editing, signing, publishing, or promotion of the "Public Statement on the Hunter Biden Emails" dated October 19, 2020; and

2. Produce all documents and communications referring or relating to the "Public Statement on the Hunter Biden Emails" dated October 19, 2020.

Please produce this material as soon as possible but no later than 5:00 p.m. on April 20, 2022. In addition, we request that you take all reasonable steps to preserve records that may be potentially responsive to this inquiry.

Thank you for your attention to this matter.

Sincerely,

Jim Jordan
Ranking Member

Steve Chabot
Member of Congress

Louie Gohmert
Member of Congress

Darrell Issa
Ranking Member
Subcommittee on Courts, Intellectual Property, and the Internet

---

[17] *E.g.* Katie Brenner et al., *Hunter Biden paid tax bill, but broad federal investigation continues*, N.Y. Times, Mar. 16, 2022; Matt Viser et al., *Inside Hunter Biden's multimillion-dollar deals with a Chinese energy company*, Wash. Post, Mar. 30, 2022.

Ken Buck
Ranking Member
Subcommittee on Antitrust, Commercial and Administrative Law

Mike Johnson
Ranking Member
Subcommittee on the Constitution, Civil Rights and Civil Liberties

Tom McClintock
Ranking Member
Subcommittee on Immigration and Citizenship

Tom Tiffany
Member of Congress

Chip Roy
Member of Congress

Michelle Fischbach
Member of Congress

Matt Gaetz
Member of Congress

Andy Biggs
Ranking Member
Subcommittee on Crime, Terrorism and Homeland Security

W. Gregory Steube
Member of Congress

Thomas Massie
Member of Congress

Dan Bishop
Member of Congress

Victoria Spartz
Member of Congress

Scott Fitzgerald
Member of Congress

Cliff Bentz
Member of Congress

Burgess Owens
Member of Congress

JERROLD NADLER, New York
CHAIRMAN

JIM JORDAN, Ohio
RANKING MEMBER

ONE HUNDRED SEVENTEENTH CONGRESS

Congress of the United States
House of Representatives
COMMITTEE ON THE JUDICIARY

2138 RAYBURN HOUSE OFFICE BUILDING
WASHINGTON, DC 20515–6216
(202) 225–3951
judiciary.house.gov

April 6, 2022

Mr. David A. Vanell
via e-mail

Dear Mr. Vanell:

On October 14, 2020, the *New York Post* published a report detailing how Hunter Biden used the position and influence of his father, now-President Joe Biden, for personal gain with the apparent awareness of President Biden.[1] This article raised doubts about President Biden's earlier denial of ever speaking to his son about his international business dealings.[2] The *Post* reported on an email in which a Ukrainian businessman urged Hunter Biden to "use [his] influence to convey a message / signal, etc. to stop what we consider to be politically motivated actions."[3] In another email, the same businessman thanked Hunter Biden for arranging a meeting with his father, calling it "an honor and pleasure."[4] The *Post* reported that these emails came from a laptop belonging to Hunter Biden that he had abandoned in a Delaware computer shop.[5]

On October 19, 2020, you signed a public statement attempting to discredit the contents of the *New York Post*'s reporting about Hunter Biden.[6] This statement emphasized the national security credentials of you and the other signatories, implying that the assertions and conclusions in the statement were grounded in information unavailable to other Americans. Referencing this unique experience, you wrote:

> It is for all these reasons that we write to say that the arrival on the US political scene of emails purportedly belonging to Vice President Biden's son Hunter, much of it related to his time serving on the Board of the Ukrainian gas company Burisma, has all the classic earmarks of a Russian information operation.[7]

---

[1] Emma-Jo Morris & Gabrielle Fonrouge, *Smoking-gun email reveals how Hunter Biden introduced Ukrainian businessman to VP dad*, N.Y. Post, Oct. 14, 2020.
[2] *E.g.* Nick Givas, *Joe Biden again denies speaking to son about Ukrainian business dealings*, Fox News, Oct. 10, 2019.
[3] Morris & Fonrouge, *supra* note 1.
[4] *Id.*
[5] *Id.*
[6] Jim Clapper et al., Public Statement on the Hunter Biden Emails (Oct. 19, 2020).
[7] *Id.*

Although this statement acknowledged that you had seen no actual "evidence" of Russian involvement with respect to the publication of Hunter Biden's emails, you nonetheless conveyed a "deep[] suspicio[n] that the Russian government played a significant role in the case."[8] Later in the statement, you went further to state a "view"—not merely a suspicion anymore—"that the Russians are involved in the Hunter Biden email issue . . . ."[9]

Your public statement served as a basis for Democrat operatives to try to delegitimize the scandalous allegations about Hunter Biden and the Biden family. On the same day as your statement, *Politico* published a story about the statement, with the conclusive headline, "Hunter Biden story is Russian disinfo, dozens of former intel officials say."[10] Departing from the statement's careful wording, the *Politico* story quoted one signatory to the letter as being confident that "once again the Russians are interfering" in our elections.[11] Fifteen minutes after *Politico* published its story, Jen Psaki, who now serves as Press Secretary to the President, tweeted a link to the *Politico* story.[12] The Biden campaign repeatedly cited your statement to dismiss the allegations against Hunter Biden.[13] During the final presidential debate, Vice President Biden also dismissed concerns about Hunter Biden's international business dealings as part of a "Russian plan."[14]

Your public statement was consistent with a broader effort to minimize and censor the *New York Post*'s reporting about Hunter Biden and the Biden family. National news organizations called the allegations about Hunter Biden "dubious" and a "non-scandal"; CBS News reporter Leslie Stahl said the allegations "can't be verified"; and NPR called it a "waste . . . of time" and a "pure distraction."[15] Separately, Twitter and Facebook restricted access to the *New York Post*'s reporting about Hunter Biden, with Twitter locking the *Post*'s account and Facebook deferring to a so-called independent fact-check that never occurred.[16] These efforts likely affected public awareness of the serious allegations surrounding the Biden family in the crucial weeks before the 2020 election.

We now know from subsequent reporting that the *New York Post*'s article about Hunter Biden was not, as you and your co-signatories alleged, part of a "Russian information

---

[8] *Id.*
[9] *Id.*
[10] Natasha Bertrand, *Hunter Biden story is Russian disinfo, dozens of former intel officials say*, Politico, Oct. 19, 2020.
[11] *Id.*
[12] Tweet by Jen Psaki, Twitter.com (Oct. 19, 2020, 10:45 p.m.), https://twitter.com/jrpsaki/status/1318382779659411458.
[13] *E.g.* Houston Keene, *Flashback: Biden officials pushed angle that Hunter laptop was 'Russian disinfo,'* Fox News, Mar. 17, 2022.
[14] Deirdre Shesgreen, *"Nothing was unethical": Joe Biden defends Hunter Biden under pressure from Trump in debate*, USA Today, Oct. 22, 2020.
[15] Joe Concha, *Media's pre-election burial of Hunter Biden story proves dereliction of duty*, The Hill, Dec. 11, 2020.
[16] *E.g.* Elizabeth Dwoskin, *Facebook and Twitter take unusual steps to limit spread of New York Post story*, Wash. Post, Oct. 15, 2020.

operation."[17] This belated verification of the *Post*'s reporting raises fresh questions about the public statement you signed in October 2020. At best, the public statement was a reckless attempt by you and your co-signatories to erroneously opine about purported election interference. At worse—and more likely—the public statement was a deliberate and coordinated effort to mislead the American people about information relevant to the 2020 presidential election by invoking your national security experience to falsely suggest that the allegations about Hunter Biden were not based in fact.

The concerted effort to suppress public dissemination of the serious allegations about Hunter Biden and the Biden family, as first reported in October 2020 by the *New York Post*, was a grave disservice to American citizens' informed participation in our democracy. We are investigating the role that the public statement played in this effort. Accordingly, please provide the following material:

1. Identify all people with whom you communicated about the inception, drafting, editing, signing, publishing, or promotion of the "Public Statement on the Hunter Biden Emails" dated October 19, 2020; and

2. Produce all documents and communications referring or relating to the "Public Statement on the Hunter Biden Emails" dated October 19, 2020.

Please produce this material as soon as possible but no later than 5:00 p.m. on April 20, 2022. In addition, we request that you take all reasonable steps to preserve records that may be potentially responsive to this inquiry.

Thank you for your attention to this matter.

Sincerely,

Jim Jordan
Ranking Member

Steve Chabot
Member of Congress

Louie Gohmert
Member of Congress

Darrell Issa
Ranking Member
Subcommittee on Courts, Intellectual Property, and the Internet

---

[17] *E.g.* Katie Brenner et al., *Hunter Biden paid tax bill, but broad federal investigation continues*, N.Y. Times, Mar. 16, 2022; Matt Viser et al., *Inside Hunter Biden's multimillion-dollar deals with a Chinese energy company*, Wash. Post, Mar. 30, 2022.

Ken Buck
Ranking Member
Subcommittee on Antitrust, Commercial
and Administrative Law

Matt Gaetz
Member of Congress

Mike Johnson
Ranking Member
Subcommittee on the Constitution,
Civil Rights and Civil Liberties

Andy Biggs
Ranking Member
Subcommittee on Crime, Terrorism
and Homeland Security

Tom McClintock
Ranking Member
Subcommittee on Immigration
and Citizenship

W. Gregory Steube
Member of Congress

Tom Tiffany
Member of Congress

Thomas Massie
Member of Congress

Chip Roy
Member of Congress

Dan Bishop
Member of Congress

Michelle Fischbach
Member of Congress

Victoria Spartz
Member of Congress

Scott Fitzgerald
Member of Congress

Cliff Bentz
Member of Congress

Burgess Owens
Member of Congress

JERROLD NADLER, New York
CHAIRMAN

JIM JORDAN, Ohio
RANKING MEMBER

ONE HUNDRED SEVENTEENTH CONGRESS
Congress of the United States
House of Representatives
COMMITTEE ON THE JUDICIARY
2138 RAYBURN HOUSE OFFICE BUILDING
WASHINGTON, DC 20515-6216
(202) 225-3951
judiciary.house.gov

April 6, 2022

The Honorable Michael G. Vickers
2001 Jefferson Davis Hwy
Suite 400
Arlington, VA 22202

Dear Mr. Vickers:

On October 14, 2020, the *New York Post* published a report detailing how Hunter Biden used the position and influence of his father, now-President Joe Biden, for personal gain with the apparent awareness of President Biden.[1] This article raised doubts about President Biden's earlier denial of ever speaking to his son about his international business dealings.[2] The *Post* reported on an email in which a Ukrainian businessman urged Hunter Biden to "use [his] influence to convey a message / signal, etc. to stop what we consider to be politically motivated actions."[3] In another email, the same businessman thanked Hunter Biden for arranging a meeting with his father, calling it "an honor and pleasure."[4] The *Post* reported that these emails came from a laptop belonging to Hunter Biden that he had abandoned in a Delaware computer shop.[5]

On October 19, 2020, you signed a public statement attempting to discredit the contents of the *New York Post*'s reporting about Hunter Biden.[6] This statement emphasized the national security credentials of you and the other signatories, implying that the assertions and conclusions in the statement were grounded in information unavailable to other Americans. Referencing this unique experience, you wrote:

> It is for all these reasons that we write to say that the arrival on the US political scene of emails purportedly belonging to Vice President Biden's son Hunter, much of it related to his time serving on the Board of the Ukrainian gas company Burisma, has all the classic earmarks of a Russian information operation.[7]

[1] Emma-Jo Morris & Gabrielle Fonrouge, *Smoking-gun email reveals how Hunter Biden introduced Ukrainian businessman to VP dad*, N.Y. Post, Oct. 14, 2020.
[2] *E.g.* Nick Givas, *Joe Biden again denies speaking to son about Ukrainian business dealings*, Fox News, Oct. 10, 2019.
[3] Morris & Fonrouge, *supra* note 1.
[4] *Id.*
[5] *Id.*
[6] Jim Clapper et al., Public Statement on the Hunter Biden Emails (Oct. 19, 2020).
[7] *Id.*

Although this statement acknowledged that you had seen no actual "evidence" of Russian involvement with respect to the publication of Hunter Biden's emails, you nonetheless conveyed a "deep[] suspicio[n] that the Russian government played a significant role in the case."[8] Later in the statement, you went further to state a "view"—not merely a suspicion anymore—"that the Russians are involved in the Hunter Biden email issue . . . ."[9]

Your public statement served as a basis for Democrat operatives to try to delegitimize the scandalous allegations about Hunter Biden and the Biden family. On the same day as your statement, *Politico* published a story about the statement, with the conclusive headline, "Hunter Biden story is Russian disinfo, dozens of former intel officials say."[10] Departing from the statement's careful wording, the *Politico* story quoted one signatory to the letter as being confident that "once again the Russians are interfering" in our elections.[11] Fifteen minutes after *Politico* published its story, Jen Psaki, who now serves as Press Secretary to the President, tweeted a link to the *Politico* story.[12] The Biden campaign repeatedly cited your statement to dismiss the allegations against Hunter Biden.[13] During the final presidential debate, Vice President Biden also dismissed concerns about Hunter Biden's international business dealings as part of a "Russian plan."[14]

Your public statement was consistent with a broader effort to minimize and censor the *New York Post*'s reporting about Hunter Biden and the Biden family. National news organizations called the allegations about Hunter Biden "dubious" and a "non-scandal"; CBS News reporter Leslie Stahl said the allegations "can't be verified"; and NPR called it a "waste . . . of time" and a "pure distraction."[15] Separately, Twitter and Facebook restricted access to the *New York Post*'s reporting about Hunter Biden, with Twitter locking the *Post*'s account and Facebook deferring to a so-called independent fact-check that never occurred.[16] These efforts likely affected public awareness of the serious allegations surrounding the Biden family in the crucial weeks before the 2020 election.

We now know from subsequent reporting that the *New York Post*'s article about Hunter Biden was not, as you and your co-signatories alleged, part of a "Russian information

---

[8] *Id.*
[9] *Id.*
[10] Natasha Bertrand, *Hunter Biden story is Russian disinfo, dozens of former intel officials say*, Politico, Oct. 19, 2020.
[11] *Id.*
[12] Tweet by Jen Psaki, Twitter.com (Oct. 19, 2020, 10:45 p.m.), https://twitter.com/jrpsaki/status/1318382779659411458.
[13] *E.g.* Houston Keene, *Flashback: Biden officials pushed angle that Hunter laptop was 'Russian disinfo,'* Fox News, Mar. 17, 2022.
[14] Deirdre Shesgreen, *"Nothing was unethical": Joe Biden defends Hunter Biden under pressure from Trump in debate*, USA Today, Oct. 22, 2020.
[15] Joe Concha, *Media's pre-election burial of Hunter Biden story proves dereliction of duty*, The Hill, Dec. 11, 2020.
[16] *E.g.* Elizabeth Dwoskin, *Facebook and Twitter take unusual steps to limit spread of New York Post story*, Wash. Post, Oct. 15, 2020.

operation."[17] This belated verification of the *Post*'s reporting raises fresh questions about the public statement you signed in October 2020. At best, the public statement was a reckless attempt by you and your co-signatories to erroneously opine about purported election interference. At worse—and more likely—the public statement was a deliberate and coordinated effort to mislead the American people about information relevant to the 2020 presidential election by invoking your national security experience to falsely suggest that the allegations about Hunter Biden were not based in fact.

The concerted effort to suppress public dissemination of the serious allegations about Hunter Biden and the Biden family, as first reported in October 2020 by the *New York Post*, was a grave disservice to American citizens' informed participation in our democracy. We are investigating the role that the public statement played in this effort. Accordingly, please provide the following material:

1. Identify all people with whom you communicated about the inception, drafting, editing, signing, publishing, or promotion of the "Public Statement on the Hunter Biden Emails" dated October 19, 2020; and

2. Produce all documents and communications referring or relating to the "Public Statement on the Hunter Biden Emails" dated October 19, 2020.

Please produce this material as soon as possible but no later than 5:00 p.m. on April 20, 2022. In addition, we request that you take all reasonable steps to preserve records that may be potentially responsive to this inquiry.

Thank you for your attention to this matter.

Sincerely,

Jim Jordan
Ranking Member

Steve Chabot
Member of Congress

Louie Gohmert
Member of Congress

Darrell Issa
Ranking Member
Subcommittee on Courts, Intellectual Property, and the Internet

[17] *E.g.* Katie Brenner et al., *Hunter Biden paid tax bill, but broad federal investigation continues*, N.Y. Times, Mar. 16, 2022; Matt Viser et al., *Inside Hunter Biden's multimillion-dollar deals with a Chinese energy company*, Wash. Post, Mar. 30, 2022.

Ken Buck
Ranking Member
Subcommittee on Antitrust, Commercial and Administrative Law

Matt Gaetz
Member of Congress

Mike Johnson
Ranking Member
Subcommittee on the Constitution, Civil Rights and Civil Liberties

Andy Biggs
Ranking Member
Subcommittee on Crime, Terrorism and Homeland Security

Tom McClintock
Ranking Member
Subcommittee on Immigration and Citizenship

W. Gregory Steube
Member of Congress

Tom Tiffany
Member of Congress

Thomas Massie
Member of Congress

Chip Roy
Member of Congress

Dan Bishop
Member of Congress

Michelle Fischbach
Member of Congress

Victoria Spartz
Member of Congress

Scott Fitzgerald
Member of Congress

Cliff Bentz
Member of Congress

Burgess Owens
Member of Congress

JERROLD NADLER, New York
CHAIRMAN

JIM JORDAN, Ohio
RANKING MEMBER

ONE HUNDRED SEVENTEENTH CONGRESS

Congress of the United States
House of Representatives
COMMITTEE ON THE JUDICIARY
2138 RAYBURN HOUSE OFFICE BUILDING
WASHINGTON, DC 20515–6216
(202) 225–3951
judiciary.house.gov

April 6, 2022

Mr. Winston Wiley
c/o Central Intelligence Agency
via e-mail

Dear Mr. Wiley:

On October 14, 2020, the *New York Post* published a report detailing how Hunter Biden used the position and influence of his father, now-President Joe Biden, for personal gain with the apparent awareness of President Biden.[1] This article raised doubts about President Biden's earlier denial of ever speaking to his son about his international business dealings.[2] The *Post* reported on an email in which a Ukrainian businessman urged Hunter Biden to "use [his] influence to convey a message / signal, etc. to stop what we consider to be politically motivated actions."[3] In another email, the same businessman thanked Hunter Biden for arranging a meeting with his father, calling it "an honor and pleasure."[4] The *Post* reported that these emails came from a laptop belonging to Hunter Biden that he had abandoned in a Delaware computer shop.[5]

On October 19, 2020, you signed a public statement attempting to discredit the contents of the *New York Post*'s reporting about Hunter Biden.[6] This statement emphasized the national security credentials of you and the other signatories, implying that the assertions and conclusions in the statement were grounded in information unavailable to other Americans. Referencing this unique experience, you wrote:

> It is for all these reasons that we write to say that the arrival on the US political scene of emails purportedly belonging to Vice President Biden's son Hunter, much of it related to his time serving on the Board of the Ukrainian gas company Burisma, has all the classic earmarks of a Russian information operation.[7]

---

[1] Emma-Jo Morris & Gabrielle Fonrouge, *Smoking-gun email reveals how Hunter Biden introduced Ukrainian businessman to VP dad*, N.Y. Post, Oct. 14, 2020.
[2] *E.g.* Nick Givas, *Joe Biden again denies speaking to son about Ukrainian business dealings*, Fox News, Oct. 10, 2019.
[3] Morris & Fonrouge, *supra* note 1.
[4] *Id.*
[5] *Id.*
[6] Jim Clapper et al., Public Statement on the Hunter Biden Emails (Oct. 19, 2020).
[7] *Id.*

Although this statement acknowledged that you had seen no actual "evidence" of Russian involvement with respect to the publication of Hunter Biden's emails, you nonetheless conveyed a "deep[] suspicio[n] that the Russian government played a significant role in the case."[8] Later in the statement, you went further to state a "view"—not merely a suspicion anymore—"that the Russians are involved in the Hunter Biden email issue . . . ."[9]

Your public statement served as a basis for Democrat operatives to try to delegitimize the scandalous allegations about Hunter Biden and the Biden family. On the same day as your statement, *Politico* published a story about the statement, with the conclusive headline, "Hunter Biden story is Russian disinfo, dozens of former intel officials say."[10] Departing from the statement's careful wording, the *Politico* story quoted one signatory to the letter as being confident that "once again the Russians are interfering" in our elections.[11] Fifteen minutes after *Politico* published its story, Jen Psaki, who now serves as Press Secretary to the President, tweeted a link to the *Politico* story.[12] The Biden campaign repeatedly cited your statement to dismiss the allegations against Hunter Biden.[13] During the final presidential debate, Vice President Biden also dismissed concerns about Hunter Biden's international business dealings as part of a "Russian plan."[14]

Your public statement was consistent with a broader effort to minimize and censor the *New York Post*'s reporting about Hunter Biden and the Biden family. National news organizations called the allegations about Hunter Biden "dubious" and a "non-scandal"; CBS News reporter Leslie Stahl said the allegations "can't be verified"; and NPR called it a "waste . . . of time" and a "pure distraction."[15] Separately, Twitter and Facebook restricted access to the *New York Post*'s reporting about Hunter Biden, with Twitter locking the *Post*'s account and Facebook deferring to a so-called independent fact-check that never occurred.[16] These efforts likely affected public awareness of the serious allegations surrounding the Biden family in the crucial weeks before the 2020 election.

We now know from subsequent reporting that the *New York Post*'s article about Hunter Biden was not, as you and your co-signatories alleged, part of a "Russian information

---

[8] *Id.*
[9] *Id.*
[10] Natasha Bertrand, *Hunter Biden story is Russian disinfo, dozens of former intel officials say*, Politico, Oct. 19, 2020.
[11] *Id.*
[12] Tweet by Jen Psaki, Twitter.com (Oct. 19, 2020, 10:45 p.m.), https://twitter.com/jrpsaki/status/1318382779659411458.
[13] *E.g.* Houston Keene, *Flashback: Biden officials pushed angle that Hunter laptop was 'Russian disinfo,'* Fox News, Mar. 17, 2022.
[14] Deirdre Shesgreen, *"Nothing was unethical": Joe Biden defends Hunter Biden under pressure from Trump in debate*, USA Today, Oct. 22, 2020.
[15] Joe Concha, *Media's pre-election burial of Hunter Biden story proves dereliction of duty*, The Hill, Dec. 11, 2020.
[16] *E.g.* Elizabeth Dwoskin, *Facebook and Twitter take unusual steps to limit spread of New York Post story*, Wash. Post, Oct. 15, 2020.

operation."[17] This belated verification of the *Post*'s reporting raises fresh questions about the public statement you signed in October 2020. At best, the public statement was a reckless attempt by you and your co-signatories to erroneously opine about purported election interference. At worse—and more likely—the public statement was a deliberate and coordinated effort to mislead the American people about information relevant to the 2020 presidential election by invoking your national security experience to falsely suggest that the allegations about Hunter Biden were not based in fact.

The concerted effort to suppress public dissemination of the serious allegations about Hunter Biden and the Biden family, as first reported in October 2020 by the *New York Post*, was a grave disservice to American citizens' informed participation in our democracy. We are investigating the role that the public statement played in this effort. Accordingly, please provide the following material:

1. Identify all people with whom you communicated about the inception, drafting, editing, signing, publishing, or promotion of the "Public Statement on the Hunter Biden Emails" dated October 19, 2020; and

2. Produce all documents and communications referring or relating to the "Public Statement on the Hunter Biden Emails" dated October 19, 2020.

Please produce this material as soon as possible but no later than 5:00 p.m. on April 20, 2022. In addition, we request that you take all reasonable steps to preserve records that may be potentially responsive to this inquiry.

Thank you for your attention to this matter.

Sincerely,

Jim Jordan
Ranking Member

Steve Chabot
Member of Congress

Louie Gohmert
Member of Congress

Darrell Issa
Ranking Member
Subcommittee on Courts, Intellectual Property, and the Internet

---

[17] *E.g.* Katie Brenner et al., *Hunter Biden paid tax bill, but broad federal investigation continues*, N.Y. Times, Mar. 16, 2022; Matt Viser et al., *Inside Hunter Biden's multimillion-dollar deals with a Chinese energy company*, Wash. Post, Mar. 30, 2022.

Ken Buck
Ranking Member
Subcommittee on Antitrust, Commercial and Administrative Law

Matt Gaetz
Member of Congress

Mike Johnson
Ranking Member
Subcommittee on the Constitution, Civil Rights and Civil Liberties

Andy Biggs
Ranking Member
Subcommittee on Crime, Terrorism and Homeland Security

Tom McClintock
Ranking Member
Subcommittee on Immigration and Citizenship

W. Gregory Steube
Member of Congress

Tom Tiffany
Member of Congress

Thomas Massie
Member of Congress

Chip Roy
Member of Congress

Dan Bishop
Member of Congress

Michelle Fischbach
Member of Congress

Victoria Spartz
Member of Congress

Scott Fitzgerald
Member of Congress

Cliff Bentz
Member of Congress

Burgess Owens
Member of Congress

JERROLD NADLER, New York
CHAIRMAN

JIM JORDAN, Ohio
RANKING MEMBER

ONE HUNDRED SEVENTEENTH CONGRESS

Congress of the United States

House of Representatives

COMMITTEE ON THE JUDICIARY

2138 RAYBURN HOUSE OFFICE BUILDING

WASHINGTON, DC 20515-6216

(202) 225-3951
judiciary.house.gov

April 6, 2022

Mr. Douglas Wise
via e-mail

Dear Mr. Wise:

On October 14, 2020, the *New York Post* published a report detailing how Hunter Biden used the position and influence of his father, now-President Joe Biden, for personal gain with the apparent awareness of President Biden.[1] This article raised doubts about President Biden's earlier denial of ever speaking to his son about his international business dealings.[2] The *Post* reported on an email in which a Ukrainian businessman urged Hunter Biden to "use [his] influence to convey a message / signal, etc. to stop what we consider to be politically motivated actions."[3] In another email, the same businessman thanked Hunter Biden for arranging a meeting with his father, calling it "an honor and pleasure."[4] The *Post* reported that these emails came from a laptop belonging to Hunter Biden that he had abandoned in a Delaware computer shop.[5]

On October 19, 2020, you signed a public statement attempting to discredit the contents of the *New York Post*'s reporting about Hunter Biden.[6] This statement emphasized the national security credentials of you and the other signatories, implying that the assertions and conclusions in the statement were grounded in information unavailable to other Americans. Referencing this unique experience, you wrote:

> It is for all these reasons that we write to say that the arrival on the US political scene of emails purportedly belonging to Vice President Biden's son Hunter, much of it related to his time serving on the Board of the Ukrainian gas company Burisma, has all the classic earmarks of a Russian information operation.[7]

---

[1] Emma-Jo Morris & Gabrielle Fonrouge, *Smoking-gun email reveals how Hunter Biden introduced Ukrainian businessman to VP dad*, N.Y. Post, Oct. 14, 2020.
[2] *E.g.* Nick Givas, *Joe Biden again denies speaking to son about Ukrainian business dealings*, Fox News, Oct. 10, 2019.
[3] Morris & Fonrouge, *supra* note 1.
[4] *Id.*
[5] *Id.*
[6] Jim Clapper et al., Public Statement on the Hunter Biden Emails (Oct. 19, 2020).
[7] *Id.*

Although this statement acknowledged that you had seen no actual "evidence" of Russian involvement with respect to the publication of Hunter Biden's emails, you nonetheless conveyed a "deep[] suspicio[n] that the Russian government played a significant role in the case."[8] Later in the statement, you went further to state a "view"—not merely a suspicion anymore—"that the Russians are involved in the Hunter Biden email issue . . . ."[9]

Your public statement served as a basis for Democrat operatives to try to delegitimize the scandalous allegations about Hunter Biden and the Biden family. On the same day as your statement, *Politico* published a story about the statement, with the conclusive headline, "Hunter Biden story is Russian disinfo, dozens of former intel officials say."[10] Departing from the statement's careful wording, the *Politico* story quoted one signatory to the letter as being confident that "once again the Russians are interfering" in our elections.[11] Fifteen minutes after *Politico* published its story, Jen Psaki, who now serves as Press Secretary to the President, tweeted a link to the *Politico* story.[12] The Biden campaign repeatedly cited your statement to dismiss the allegations against Hunter Biden.[13] During the final presidential debate, Vice President Biden also dismissed concerns about Hunter Biden's international business dealings as part of a "Russian plan."[14]

Your public statement was consistent with a broader effort to minimize and censor the *New York Post*'s reporting about Hunter Biden and the Biden family. National news organizations called the allegations about Hunter Biden "dubious" and a "non-scandal"; CBS News reporter Leslie Stahl said the allegations "can't be verified"; and NPR called it a "waste . . . of time" and a "pure distraction."[15] Separately, Twitter and Facebook restricted access to the *New York Post*'s reporting about Hunter Biden, with Twitter locking the *Post*'s account and Facebook deferring to a so-called independent fact-check that never occurred.[16] These efforts likely affected public awareness of the serious allegations surrounding the Biden family in the crucial weeks before the 2020 election.

We now know from subsequent reporting that the *New York Post*'s article about Hunter Biden was not, as you and your co-signatories alleged, part of a "Russian information

---

[8] *Id.*
[9] *Id.*
[10] Natasha Bertrand, *Hunter Biden story is Russian disinfo, dozens of former intel officials say*, Politico, Oct. 19, 2020.
[11] *Id.*
[12] Tweet by Jen Psaki, Twitter.com (Oct. 19, 2020, 10:45 p.m.), https://twitter.com/jrpsaki/status/1318382779659411458.
[13] *E.g.* Houston Keene, *Flashback: Biden officials pushed angle that Hunter laptop was 'Russian disinfo,'* Fox News, Mar. 17, 2022.
[14] Deirdre Shesgreen, *"Nothing was unethical": Joe Biden defends Hunter Biden under pressure from Trump in debate*, USA Today, Oct. 22, 2020.
[15] Joe Concha, *Media's pre-election burial of Hunter Biden story proves dereliction of duty*, The Hill, Dec. 11, 2020.
[16] *E.g.* Elizabeth Dwoskin, *Facebook and Twitter take unusual steps to limit spread of New York Post story*, Wash. Post, Oct. 15, 2020.

operation."[17] This belated verification of the *Post*'s reporting raises fresh questions about the public statement you signed in October 2020. At best, the public statement was a reckless attempt by you and your co-signatories to erroneously opine about purported election interference. At worse—and more likely—the public statement was a deliberate and coordinated effort to mislead the American people about information relevant to the 2020 presidential election by invoking your national security experience to falsely suggest that the allegations about Hunter Biden were not based in fact.

The concerted effort to suppress public dissemination of the serious allegations about Hunter Biden and the Biden family, as first reported in October 2020 by the *New York Post*, was a grave disservice to American citizens' informed participation in our democracy. We are investigating the role that the public statement played in this effort. Accordingly, please provide the following material:

1. Identify all people with whom you communicated about the inception, drafting, editing, signing, publishing, or promotion of the "Public Statement on the Hunter Biden Emails" dated October 19, 2020; and

2. Produce all documents and communications referring or relating to the "Public Statement on the Hunter Biden Emails" dated October 19, 2020.

Please produce this material as soon as possible but no later than 5:00 p.m. on April 20, 2022. In addition, we request that you take all reasonable steps to preserve records that may be potentially responsive to this inquiry.

Thank you for your attention to this matter.

Sincerely,

Jim Jordan
Ranking Member

Steve Chabot
Member of Congress

Louie Gohmert
Member of Congress

Darrell Issa
Ranking Member
Subcommittee on Courts, Intellectual Property, and the Internet

[17] *E.g.* Katie Brenner et al., *Hunter Biden paid tax bill, but broad federal investigation continues*, N.Y. Times, Mar. 16, 2022; Matt Viser et al., *Inside Hunter Biden's multimillion-dollar deals with a Chinese energy company*, Wash. Post, Mar. 30, 2022.

Ken Buck
Ranking Member
Subcommittee on Antitrust, Commercial and Administrative Law

Matt Gaetz
Member of Congress

Mike Johnson
Ranking Member
Subcommittee on the Constitution, Civil Rights and Civil Liberties

Andy Biggs
Ranking Member
Subcommittee on Crime, Terrorism and Homeland Security

Tom McClintock
Ranking Member
Subcommittee on Immigration and Citizenship

W. Gregory Steube
Member of Congress

Tom Tiffany
Member of Congress

Thomas Massie
Member of Congress

Chip Roy
Member of Congress

Dan Bishop
Member of Congress

Michelle Fischbach
Member of Congress

Victoria Spartz
Member of Congress

Scott Fitzgerald
Member of Congress

Cliff Bentz
Member of Congress

Burgess Owens
Member of Congress

JERROLD NADLER, New York
CHAIRMAN

JIM JORDAN, Ohio
RANKING MEMBER

ONE HUNDRED SEVENTEENTH CONGRESS

Congress of the United States

House of Representatives

COMMITTEE ON THE JUDICIARY

2138 RAYBURN HOUSE OFFICE BUILDING

WASHINGTON, DC 20515-6216

(202) 225-3951
judiciary.house.gov

April 6, 2022

Ms. Kristin Wood
c/o Central Intelligence Agency
via e-mail

Dear Ms. Wood:

On October 14, 2020, the *New York Post* published a report detailing how Hunter Biden used the position and influence of his father, now-President Joe Biden, for personal gain with the apparent awareness of President Biden.[1] This article raised doubts about President Biden's earlier denial of ever speaking to his son about his international business dealings.[2] The *Post* reported on an email in which a Ukrainian businessman urged Hunter Biden to "use [his] influence to convey a message / signal, etc. to stop what we consider to be politically motivated actions."[3] In another email, the same businessman thanked Hunter Biden for arranging a meeting with his father, calling it "an honor and pleasure."[4] The *Post* reported that these emails came from a laptop belonging to Hunter Biden that he had abandoned in a Delaware computer shop.[5]

On October 19, 2020, you signed a public statement attempting to discredit the contents of the *New York Post*'s reporting about Hunter Biden.[6] This statement emphasized the national security credentials of you and the other signatories, implying that the assertions and conclusions in the statement were grounded in information unavailable to other Americans. Referencing this unique experience, you wrote:

> It is for all these reasons that we write to say that the arrival on the US political scene of emails purportedly belonging to Vice President Biden's son Hunter, much of it related to his time serving on the Board of the Ukrainian gas company Burisma, has all the classic earmarks of a Russian information operation.[7]

---

[1] Emma-Jo Morris & Gabrielle Fonrouge, *Smoking-gun email reveals how Hunter Biden introduced Ukrainian businessman to VP dad*, N.Y. Post, Oct. 14, 2020.
[2] *E.g.* Nick Givas, *Joe Biden again denies speaking to son about Ukrainian business dealings*, Fox News, Oct. 10, 2019.
[3] Morris & Fonrouge, *supra* note 1.
[4] *Id.*
[5] *Id.*
[6] Jim Clapper et al., Public Statement on the Hunter Biden Emails (Oct. 19, 2020).
[7] *Id.*

Although this statement acknowledged that you had seen no actual "evidence" of Russian involvement with respect to the publication of Hunter Biden's emails, you nonetheless conveyed a "deep[] suspicio[n] that the Russian government played a significant role in the case."[8] Later in the statement, you went further to state a "view"—not merely a suspicion anymore—"that the Russians are involved in the Hunter Biden email issue . . . ."[9]

Your public statement served as a basis for Democrat operatives to try to delegitimize the scandalous allegations about Hunter Biden and the Biden family. On the same day as your statement, *Politico* published a story about the statement, with the conclusive headline, "Hunter Biden story is Russian disinfo, dozens of former intel officials say."[10] Departing from the statement's careful wording, the *Politico* story quoted one signatory to the letter as being confident that "once again the Russians are interfering" in our elections.[11] Fifteen minutes after *Politico* published its story, Jen Psaki, who now serves as Press Secretary to the President, tweeted a link to the *Politico* story.[12] The Biden campaign repeatedly cited your statement to dismiss the allegations against Hunter Biden.[13] During the final presidential debate, Vice President Biden also dismissed concerns about Hunter Biden's international business dealings as part of a "Russian plan."[14]

Your public statement was consistent with a broader effort to minimize and censor the *New York Post*'s reporting about Hunter Biden and the Biden family. National news organizations called the allegations about Hunter Biden "dubious" and a "non-scandal"; CBS News reporter Leslie Stahl said the allegations "can't be verified"; and NPR called it a "waste . . . of time" and a "pure distraction."[15] Separately, Twitter and Facebook restricted access to the *New York Post*'s reporting about Hunter Biden, with Twitter locking the *Post*'s account and Facebook deferring to a so-called independent fact-check that never occurred.[16] These efforts likely affected public awareness of the serious allegations surrounding the Biden family in the crucial weeks before the 2020 election.

We now know from subsequent reporting that the *New York Post*'s article about Hunter Biden was not, as you and your co-signatories alleged, part of a "Russian information

---

[8] *Id.*
[9] *Id.*
[10] Natasha Bertrand, *Hunter Biden story is Russian disinfo, dozens of former intel officials say*, Politico, Oct. 19, 2020.
[11] *Id.*
[12] Tweet by Jen Psaki, Twitter.com (Oct. 19, 2020, 10:45 p.m.), https://twitter.com/jrpsaki/status/1318382779659411458.
[13] *E.g.* Houston Keene, *Flashback: Biden officials pushed angle that Hunter laptop was 'Russian disinfo,'* Fox News, Mar. 17, 2022.
[14] Deirdre Shesgreen, *"Nothing was unethical": Joe Biden defends Hunter Biden under pressure from Trump in debate*, USA Today, Oct. 22, 2020.
[15] Joe Concha, *Media's pre-election burial of Hunter Biden story proves dereliction of duty*, The Hill, Dec. 11, 2020.
[16] *E.g.* Elizabeth Dwoskin, *Facebook and Twitter take unusual steps to limit spread of New York Post story*, Wash. Post, Oct. 15, 2020.

operation."[17] This belated verification of the *Post*'s reporting raises fresh questions about the public statement you signed in October 2020. At best, the public statement was a reckless attempt by you and your co-signatories to erroneously opine about purported election interference. At worse—and more likely—the public statement was a deliberate and coordinated effort to mislead the American people about information relevant to the 2020 presidential election by invoking your national security experience to falsely suggest that the allegations about Hunter Biden were not based in fact.

The concerted effort to suppress public dissemination of the serious allegations about Hunter Biden and the Biden family, as first reported in October 2020 by the *New York Post*, was a grave disservice to American citizens' informed participation in our democracy. We are investigating the role that the public statement played in this effort. Accordingly, please provide the following material:

1. Identify all people with whom you communicated about the inception, drafting, editing, signing, publishing, or promotion of the "Public Statement on the Hunter Biden Emails" dated October 19, 2020; and

2. Produce all documents and communications referring or relating to the "Public Statement on the Hunter Biden Emails" dated October 19, 2020.

Please produce this material as soon as possible but no later than 5:00 p.m. on April 20, 2022. In addition, we request that you take all reasonable steps to preserve records that may be potentially responsive to this inquiry.

Thank you for your attention to this matter.

Sincerely,

Jim Jordan
Ranking Member

Steve Chabot
Member of Congress

Louie Gohmert
Member of Congress

Darrell Issa
Ranking Member
Subcommittee on Courts, Intellectual Property, and the Internet

---

[17] *E.g.* Katie Brenner et al., *Hunter Biden paid tax bill, but broad federal investigation continues*, N.Y. Times, Mar. 16, 2022; Matt Viser et al., *Inside Hunter Biden's multimillion-dollar deals with a Chinese energy company*, Wash. Post, Mar. 30, 2022.

Ken Buck
Ranking Member
Subcommittee on Antitrust, Commercial and Administrative Law

Matt Gaetz
Member of Congress

Mike Johnson
Ranking Member
Subcommittee on the Constitution, Civil Rights and Civil Liberties

Andy Biggs
Ranking Member
Subcommittee on Crime, Terrorism and Homeland Security

Tom McClintock
Ranking Member
Subcommittee on Immigration and Citizenship

W. Gregory Steube
Member of Congress

Tom Tiffany
Member of Congress

Thomas Massie
Member of Congress

Chip Roy
Member of Congress

Dan Bishop
Member of Congress

Michelle Fischbach
Member of Congress

Victoria Spartz
Member of Congress

Scott Fitzgerald
Member of Congress

Cliff Bentz
Member of Congress

Burgess Owens
Member of Congress

JERROLD NADLER, New York
CHAIRMAN

JIM JORDAN, Ohio
RANKING MEMBER

ONE HUNDRED SEVENTEENTH CONGRESS

Congress of the United States

House of Representatives

COMMITTEE ON THE JUDICIARY

2138 RAYBURN HOUSE OFFICE BUILDING

WASHINGTON, DC 20515-6216

(202) 225-3951
judiciary.house.gov

April 5, 2022

Mr. Hunter Biden
c/o Christopher J. Clark
Latham & Watkins
1271 Avenue of the Americas
New York, NY 10020

Re: Record Preservation

Dear Mr. Biden:

We write to request that you immediately preserve all records and materials relating to your international business dealings during the Obama-Biden Administration, your abandoned laptop and its contents, and media inquiries and communications related to these topics.

On October 14, 2020, the *New York Post* published a report detailing how you used the position and influence of your father, now-President Joe Biden, for personal gain, with his apparent awareness.[1] This article raised doubts about President Biden's denial of ever speaking to you about your international business dealings.[2] The *Post* reported on an email in which a Ukrainian businessman urged you to "use your influence to convey a message / signal, etc. to stop what we consider to be politically motivated actions."[3] In another email, the same businessman thanked you for arranging a meeting with your father, then-Vice President Biden, calling it "an honor and pleasure."[4] The *Post* reported that these emails came from a laptop belonging to you that you abandoned in a Delaware computer shop.[5]

At the time of the *New York Post* story, the Biden campaign and prominent Washington insiders falsely dismissed the contents of the story as the product of Russian intelligence. On October 19, 2020, Jen Psaki, now Press Secretary to the President, tweeted a *Politico* article about an open letter from former intelligence officials that falsely categorized the *Post* story as

[1] Emma-Jo Morris & Gabrielle Fonrouge, *Smoking-gun email reveals how Hunter Biden introduced Ukranian businessman to VP dad*, N.Y. Post, Oct. 14, 2020.
[2] *E.g.* Nick Givas, *Joe Biden again denies speaking to son about Ukrainian business dealings*, Fox News, Oct. 10, 2019.
[3] Morris & Fonrouge, *supra* note 1.
[4] *Id.*
[5] *Id.*

Russian disinformation.[6] Three days later, before the final presidential debate, Kate Bedingfield, deputy campaign manager for the Biden campaign, said that questions about your abandoned laptop would "amplify[] Russian misinformation."[7] During the debate, Vice President Biden similarly dismissed concerns about your international business dealings, calling scrutiny on the arrangement part of a "Russian plan."[8] You likewise suggested the *New York Post*'s reporting could be Russian disinformation as recently as April 2021. In an interview with CBS Sunday Morning about the authenticity of the abandoned laptop, you stated: "Of course, there could be a laptop stolen from me. There could be that I was hacked. It could be that it was Russian intelligence."[9]

Contrary to the assertions of the Biden campaign and prominent Democrats, the contents of the *New York Post*'s reporting have never been refuted. Contrariwise, eighteen months after the *Post*'s story, other news outlets are finally confirming the *Post*'s reporting. On March 16, 2022, the *New York Times* reported on the contents of records from your abandoned laptop, explaining the emails were obtained "from a cache of files that appears to have come from a laptop abandoned by Mr. Biden in a Delaware repair shop" and that the documents "were authenticated by people familiar with them."[10] The *Times* reported on one email in which you invited foreign business associates to "dinner at a Washington restaurant where Vice President Biden would stop by."[11] On March 30, 2022, the *Washington Post* published a similar article that also confirmed the *New York Post*'s original reporting.[12]

Congress has an obligation to examine these facts to understand the sufficiency of existing federal statutes and to assess the Executive Branch's execution of these statutes. Material preservation is essential for us to conduct a comprehensive review of these matters. You should construe this preservation notice as an instruction to preserve all documents, communications, and other information, including electronic information and metadata, that is or may be potentially responsive to this congressional inquiry. This instruction includes all electronic messages sent using official and personal accounts or devices, including records created using text messages, phone-based message applications, or encryption software. For purposes of this request, "preserve" includes taking reasonable steps to prevent the partial or full destruction, alteration, testing, deletion, shredding, incineration, wiping, relocation, migration, theft, mutation, or negligent or reckless handling that could render the information incomplete or inaccessible. These steps include preserving all compilations of documents that have already

---

[6] Tweet by Jen Psaki, Twitter.com (Oct. 19, 2020, 10:45 p.m.), https://twitter.com/jrpsaki/status/1318382779659411458; Natasha Bertrand, *Hunter Biden story is Russian disinfo, dozens of former intel officials say*, Politico, Oct. 19, 2020.

[7] Jonathan Easley, *Trump expected to bring Hunter Biden's former business partner to debate*, The Hill, Oct. 22, 2020.

[8] Deirdre Shesgreen, *"Nothing was unethical": Joe Biden defends Hunter Biden under pressure from Trump in debate*, USA Today, Oct. 22, 2020.

[9] CBS Sunday Morning (CBS television broadcast Apr. 4, 2021).

[10] Katie Brenner et al., *Hunter Biden paid tax bill, but broad federal investigation continues*, N.Y. Times, Mar. 16, 2022.

[11] *Id.*

[12] Matt Viser et al., *Inside Hunter Biden's multimillion-dollar deals with a Chinese energy company*, Wash. Post, Mar. 30, 2022.

been gathered in response to other government or litigation requests, even if copies of individual documents or materials may still exist elsewhere in the organization.

Thank you for your cooperation in this critical oversight matter.

Sincerely,

Darrell Issa
Ranking Member
Subcommittee on Courts, Intellectual Property, and the Internet

Jim Jordan
Ranking Member

Louie Gohmert
Member of Congress

Ken Buck
Ranking Member
Subcommittee on Antitrust, Commercial and Administrative Law

Matt Gaetz
Member of Congress

Mike Johnson
Ranking Member
Subcommittee on the Constitution, Civil Rights and Civil Liberties

Andy Biggs
Ranking Member
Subcommittee on Crime, Terrorism, and Homeland Security

Tom McClintock
Ranking Member
Subcommittee on Immigration and Citizenship

Tom Tiffany
Member of Congress

Dan Bishop
Member of Congress

Victoria Spartz
Member of Congress

Cliff Bentz
Member of Congress

Burgess Owens
Member of Congress

cc: The Honorable Jerrold L. Nadler
Chairman

JERROLD NADLER, New York
CHAIRMAN

JIM JORDAN, Ohio
RANKING MEMBER

ONE HUNDRED SEVENTEENTH CONGRESS

Congress of the United States
House of Representatives

COMMITTEE ON THE JUDICIARY
2138 RAYBURN HOUSE OFFICE BUILDING
WASHINGTON, DC 20515-6216
(202) 225-3951
judiciary.house.gov

March 31, 2022

Mr. Parag Agrawal
Chief Executive Officer
Twitter, Inc.
1335 Market Street, Suite 900
San Franscisco, CA 94103

Dear Mr. Agrawal:

Shortly before the 2020 election, Twitter suppressed an explosive *New York Post* article detailing how Hunter Biden used the position and influence of his father, now-President Biden, for personal gain, with the apparent awareness of President Biden. We wrote to Twitter at the time with important questions about Twitter's knowing suppression of First-Amendment-protected activity.[1] Twitter ignored our letter and, in the months since, has avoided any meaningful accountability for its actions. Now, with even the *New York Times* confirming the accuracy of the *Post*'s reporting,[2] we are investigating Twitter's actions to interfere in free and fair election-related public discourse on its platform to the benefit of President Biden and the detriment of former President Trump.

Although the *Post* article concerned a topic of importance to many voters in the run-up to the election,[3] Twitter still censored it.[4] Twitter locked the *Post*'s account, blocked users from

[1] Letter from Rep. Jim Jordan, Ranking Member, H. Comm. on the Judiciary, to Mr. Jack Dorsey, CEO, Twitter, Inc. (Oct. 15, 2020).

[2] Katie Benner et al., *Hunter Biden Paid Tax Bill, but Broad Federal Investigation Continues*, N.Y. TIMES, Mar. 16, 2022; Emma-Jo Morris & Gabrielle Fonrouge, *Smoking-gun email reveals how Hunter Biden introduced Ukrainian businessman to VP dad*, N.Y. POST, Oct. 14, 2020.

[3] James Anthony, *FLASHBACK: 16% of Biden voters would have voted differently if Hunter Biden laptop story was not suppressed by media, big tech*, POST MILLENNIAL, Mar. 17, 2022 ("After the *New York Post*'s reporting on Hunter Biden's laptop was suppressed, a poll was released showing that 16 percent of voters who were unaware of the laptop scandal would have not voted for Biden had they known about it at the time."); Timothy P. Carney, *Yes, they lied about Hunter Biden's laptop. So what are they lying about now?*, WASH. EXAMINER, Mar. 17, 2022 ("This story was highly relevant to the presidential election going on that year. It showed how Joe Biden's family used his power to gain riches, and how Biden thought there was nothing wrong with it."); Gerard Baker, Opinion, *Hunter Biden's Laptop and America's Crisis of Accountability*, WALL ST. J., Mar. 21, 2022 ("[E]nough influential people in and out of government . . . were so alarmed that it [the *Post*'s reporting] would affect the outcome that they pulled off one of the greatest disappearing tricks since Harry Houdini made that elephant vanish from a New York stage.").

[4] Jessica Bursztynsky, *Twitter CEO Jack Dorsey says blocking New York Post story was 'wrong,'* CNBC, Oct. 16, 2020.

sharing the link to the article, and even labeled the material "unsafe" for users.[5] Twitter also censored the official House Judiciary Committee website, where we reposted the article so the public could access it without Twitter's interfence. Although Twitter's former CEO admitted that Twitter's censorship actions were "wrong,"[6] Twitter continues to censor political speech in a manner that suppresses conservative voices.

The *Post* article was likely to have significant implications for the presidential election. It detailed how Hunter Biden leveraged his father's influence as then-Vice President for personal gain. When Hunter Biden served on the board of Burisma, a Ukrainian company, a company executive asked him to "use [his] influence" to stop a domestic Ukrainian investigation into Burisma.[7] Another time, the same executive thanked Hunter Biden for arranging a meeting with then-Vice President Biden.[8] Eight months after that, Vice President Biden pressured the Ukrainian government to fire a prosecutor who was investigating Burisma,[9] a firing about which Vice President Biden later bragged.[10] The *Post* article challenged President Biden's claim that he had "never spoken to [his] son about his overseas business dealings."[11]

Although the *Post* explained exactly how it obtained the emails on which it reported,[12] Twitter still suppressed the article—going so far as to lock the *Post*'s account and the account of any user who tried sharing the article—because the article supposedly violated Twitter's "Hacked Materials Policy."[13] The mainsteam media followed Twitter's lead, wrongly claiming the *Post* story was "disinfo" and unverified.[14] Twitter also claimed that it censored the article because it included images of "personal and private information."[15] But when we posted the article on our website without personal or private information, Twitter censored us too.

It appears that Twitter knowingly and deliberately used its platform to control election-related information accessible to the American people shortly before the 2020 election, and that Twitter did so to the primary benefit of then-Vice President Biden. Twitter's actions helped shield Vice President Biden from increased scrutiny about the impropriety detailed in the *Post* article. In addition, Twitter's actions gave rise to other news outlets, tech platforms, and even

---

[5] Noah Manskar, *Twitter, Facebook censor Post over Hunter Biden expose*, N.Y. POST, Oct. 14, 2020; Joe Concha, Opinion, *Media's pre-election burial of Hunter Biden story proves dereliction of duty*, THE HILL, Dec. 11, 2020 ("Twitter went through the Orwellian exercise of locking the New York Post's Twitter account while initially demanding that the country's oldest newspaper delete its original tweet or stay in social-media lockdown for the foreseeable future. The locked accounts also extended to those who shared the Post's reporting . . . .").
[6] Bursztynsky, *supra* note 4.
[7] Morris & Fonrouge, *supra* note 2.
[8] *Id.*
[9] *Id.*
[10] *Id.*; *see also* Council on Foreign Relations, Foreign Affairs Issue Launch with Former Vice President Joe Biden (Jan. 23, 2018).
[11] Morris & Fonrouge, *supra* note 2.
[12] *Id.*
[13] Manskar, *supra* note 5.
[14] Concha, *supra* note 5 (listing news sources that downplayed or tried to cast doubt on the *Post* story); *see also* Nikolas Lanum, *FLASHBACK: MSNBC, CNN, CBS told viewers Hunter Biden laptop story was Russian disinformation*, FOX NEWS, Mar. 21, 2022.
[15] Manskar, *supra* note 5.

Biden himself dismissing the *Post* story as disinformation or untrue—when, in fact, it had never been rebutted. This irresponsible conduct demands a thorough investigation so that we may understand how Big Tech wields its enormous power over the free flow of information to the detriment of free and fair elections.

Big Tech is out to get conservatives. Twitter's suppression of the *Post* article detailing Biden family wrongdoing only underscores that point. Given the importance of these issues, we request the following documents and information:

1. All documents and communications between October 1, 2020, and the present referring or relating to Twitter's decision to reduce the dissemination of the *New York Post* article on its platform and what factors Twitter considered in this decision.

2. All documents and communications between October 1, 2020, and the present referring or relating to Twitter's determination that the *New York Post* article violated its "Hacked Materials Policy."

3. All documents and communications between October 1, 2020, and the present referring or relating to Twitter's decision to censor the House Judiciary Committee's website for reposting the *New York Post* article.

4. All documents and communications between October 1, 2020, and the present between or among any employee or contractor of Twitter and any individual affiliated with the Biden campaign or the Democrat National Committee referring or relating to Twitter's decision to reduce the dissemination of the *New York Post* article on its platform.

5. All documents and communications between October 1, 2020, and the present between or among any employee or contractor of Twitter and any employee or contractor of any other social media company referring or relating to Twitter's decision to reduce the dissemination of the *New York Post* article on its platform.

6. All documents and communications between October 1, 2020, and the present between or among any employee or contractor of Twitter and any employee or contractor of any media organization referring or relating to Twitter's decision to reduce the dissemination of the *New York Post* article on its platform.

7. All documents and communications between October 1, 2020, and the present referring or relating to Twitter's decision to report, or not report, its actions to the Federal Election Commission as an in-kind contribution to the Biden campaign.

8. Identify which employee(s) of Twitter made the decision to reduce the dissemination of the *New York Post* article on its platform.

9. Explain how Twitter's actions in reducing the dissemination of the *New York Post* article on its platform is not a publisher function for purposes of section 230 of the Communications Decency Act.

Please produce these documents and information as soon as possible but no later than 5:00 p.m. on April 14, 2022. Thank you for your prompt attention to this matter.

Sincerely,

Jim Jordan
Ranking Member

Steve Chabot
Member of Congress

Louie Gohmert
Member of Congress

Darrell Issa
Ranking Member
Subcommittee on Courts, Intellectual Property, and the Internet

Ken Buck
Ranking Member
Subcommittee on Antitrust, Commercial and Administrative Law

Matt Gaetz
Member of Congress

Mike Johnson
Ranking Member
Subcommittee on the Constitution, Civil Rights and Civil Liberties

Andy Biggs
Ranking Member
Subcommittee on Crime, Terrorism and Homeland Security

Tom McClintock
Ranking Member
Subcommittee on Immigration and Citizenship

W. Gregory Steube
Member of Congress

Tom Tiffany
Member of Congress

Thomas Massie
Member of Congress

Chip Roy
Member of Congress

Dan Bishop
Member of Congress

Michelle Fischbach
Member of Congress

Victoria Spartz
Member of Congress

Scott Fitzgerald
Member of Congress

Cliff Bentz
Member of Congress

Burgess Owens
Member of Congress

cc: The Honorable Jerrold L. Nadler, Chairman

JERROLD NADLER, New York
CHAIRMAN

JIM JORDAN, Ohio
RANKING MEMBER

ONE HUNDRED SEVENTEENTH CONGRESS

Congress of the United States
House of Representatives

COMMITTEE ON THE JUDICIARY

2138 RAYBURN HOUSE OFFICE BUILDING

WASHINGTON, DC 20515-6216

(202) 225-3951
judiciary.house.gov

March 31, 2022

Mr. Mark Zuckerberg
Chief Executive Officer
Facebook, Inc.
1 Hacker Way
Menlo Park, CA 94025

Dear Mr. Zuckerberg:

Shortly before the 2020 election, Facebook suppressed an explosive *New York Post* article detailing how Hunter Biden used the position and influence of his father, now-President Biden, for personal gain, with the apparent awareness of President Biden. We wrote to Facebook at the time with important questions about Facebook's knowing suppression of First Amendment-protected activity.[1] Facebook ignored our letter and, in the months since, has avoided any meaningful accountability for its actions. Now, with even the *New York Times* confirming the accuracy of the *Post*'s reporting,[2] we are investigating Facebook 's actions to interfere in free and fair election-related public discourse on its platform to the benefit of President Biden and the detriment of former President Trump.

Although the *Post* article concerned a topic of importance to many voters in the run-up to the election,[3] Facebook still censored it. Soon after the *Post* published its article, Facebook's Policy Communications Director, a former staffer for Democrat elected officials, announced that

---

[1] Letter from Rep. Jim Jordan, Ranking Member, H. Comm. on the Judiciary, to Mr. Mark Zuckerberg, CEO, Facebook, Inc. (Oct. 14, 2020).

[2] Katie Benner et al., *Hunter Biden Paid Tax Bill, but Broad Federal Investigation Continues*, N.Y. Times, Mar. 16, 2022; Emma-Jo Morris & Gabrielle Fonrouge, *Smoking-gun email reveals how Hunter Biden introduced Ukrainian businessman to VP dad*, N.Y. Post, Oct. 14, 2020.

[3] James Anthony, *FLASHBACK: 16% of Biden voters would have voted differently if Hunter Biden laptop story was not suppressed by media, big tech*, POST MILLENNIAL, Mar. 17, 2022 ("After the *New York Post*'s reporting on Hunter Biden's laptop was suppressed, a poll was released showing that 16 percent of voters who were unaware of the laptop scandal would have not voted for Biden had they known about it at the time."); Timothy P. Carney, *Yes, they lied about Hunter Biden's laptop. So what are they lying about now?*, WASH. EXAMINER, Mar. 17, 2022 ("This story was highly relevant to the presidential election going on that year. It showed how Joe Biden's family used his power to gain riches, and how Biden thought there was nothing wrong with it."); Gerard Baker, Opinion, *Hunter Biden's Laptop and America's Crisis of Accountability*, WALL ST. J., Mar. 21, 2022 ("[E]nough influential people in and out of government . . . were so alarmed that it [the *Post*'s reporting] would affect the outcome that they pulled off one of the greatest disappearing tricks since Harry Houdini made that elephant vanish from a New York stage.").

Facebook was "reducing its distribution on our platform."[4] Facebook presumably did this because "it s[aw] 'signals'" that the *Post* story was "false."[5] As far as we know, Facebook has never identified or explained these "signals." Instead, Facebook announced that the article would be "eligible to be fact checked by [the company's] third-party fact checking partners";[6] however, Facebook has never revealed the results of this fact-check, or even whether it occurred.

The *Post* article was likely to have significant implications for the presidential election. It detailed how Hunter Biden leveraged his father's influence as then-Vice President for personal gain. When Hunter Biden served on the board of Burisma, a Ukrainian company, a company executive asked him to "use [his] influence" to stop a domestic Ukrainian investigation into Burisma.[7] Another time, the same executive thanked Hunter Biden for arranging a meeting with then-Vice President Biden.[8] Eight months after that, Vice President Biden pressured the Ukrainian government to fire a prosecutor who was investigating Burisma,[9] a firing about which Vice President Biden later bragged.[10] The *Post* article challenged President Biden's claim that he had "never spoken to [his] son about his overseas business dealings."[11]

Although the *Post* explained exactly how it obtained the emails on which it reported and included pictures of certain emails,[12] Facebook still suppressed the article. The mainsteam media followed Facebook's lead, wrongly claiming the *Post* story was "disinfo" and unverified.[13]

It appears that Facebook knowingly and deliberately used its platform to control election-related information accessible to the American people shortly before the 2020 election, and that Facebook did so to the primary benefit of then-Vice President Biden. Facebook's actions helped shield Vice President Biden from increased scrutiny about the impropriety detailed in the *Post* article. In addition, Facebook's actions gave rise to other news outlets, tech platforms, and even Biden himself dismissing the *Post* story as disinformation or untrue—when, in fact, it had never been rebutted. This irresponsible conduct demands a thorough investigation so that we may understand how Big Tech wields its enormous power over the free flow of information to the detriment of free and fair elections.

---

[4] Tweet by Andy Stone, Policy Communications Director, Facebook, Twitter.com (Oct. 14, 2020, 11:10 a.m.), https://twitter.com/andymstone/status/1316395902479872000 [hereinafter "Stone Tweet"].

[5] Shannon Bond, *Facebook And Twitter Limit Sharing 'New York Post' Story About Joe Biden*, NPR, Oct. 14, 2020 ("Stone said Facebook sometimes takes this step [of limiting distribution] if it sees 'signals' that something gaining traction is false, to give fact-checkers time to evaluate the story before it spreads widely. He did not give more detail on what signals Facebook uses or how often it takes this approach.").

[6] Stone Tweet, *supra* note 4.

[7] Morris & Fonrouge, *supra* note 2.

[8] *Id.*

[9] *Id.*

[10] *Id.*; *see also* Council on Foreign Relations, Foreign Affairs Issue Launch with Former Vice President Joe Biden (Jan. 23, 2018), https://www.cfr.org/event/foreign-affairs-issue-launch-former-vice-president-joe-biden.

[11] Morris & Fonrouge, *supra* note 2.

[12] *Id.*

[13] Joe Concha, Opinion, *Media's pre-election burial of Hunter Biden story proves dereliction of duty*, THE HILL, Dec. 11, 2020 (listing news sources that downplayed or tried to cast doubt on the *Post* story); *see also* Nikolas Lanum, *FLASHBACK: MSNBC, CNN, CBS told viewers Hunter Biden laptop story was Russian disinformation*, FOX NEWS, Mar. 21, 2022.

Big Tech is out to get conservatives. Facebook's suppression of the *Post* article detailing Biden family wrongdoing only underscores that point. Given the importance of these issues, we request the following documents and information:

1. All documents and communications between October 1, 2020, and the present referring or relating to Facebook's decision to reduce the dissemination of the *New York Post* article on its platform and what factors, including any "signals," Facebook considered in this decision.

2. All documents and communications between October 1, 2020, and the present referring or relating to Facebook's or its third-party partners' efforts to fact check the *New York Post* article.

3. All documents and communications between October 1, 2020, and the present between or among any employee or contractor of Facebook and any individual affiliated with the Biden campaign or the Democrat National Committee referring or relating to Facebook's decision to reduce the dissemination of the *New York Post* article on its platform.

4. All documents and communications between October 1, 2020, and the present between or among any employee or contractor of Facebook and any employee or contractor of any other social media company referring or relating to Facebook's decision to reduce the dissemination of the *New York Post* article on its platform.

5. All documents and communications between October 1, 2020, and the present between or among any employee or contractor of Facebook and any employee or contractor of any media organization referring or relating to Facebook's decision to reduce the dissemination of the *New York Post* article on its platform.

6. All documents and communications between October 1, 2020, and the present referring or relating to Facebook's decision to report, or not report, its actions to the Federal Election Commission as an in-kind contribution to the Biden campaign.

7. Identify which employee(s) of Facebook made the decision to reduce the dissemination of the *New York Post* article on its platform.

8. Explain how Facebook's actions in reducing the dissemination of the *New York Post* article on its platform is not a publisher function for purposes of section 230 of the Communications Decency Act.

Please produce these documents and information as soon as possible but no later than 5:00 p.m. on April 14, 2022. Thank you for your prompt attention to this matter.

Sincerely,

Jim Jordan
Ranking Member

Steve Chabot
Member of Congress

Louie Gohmert
Member of Congress

Darrell Issa
Ranking Member
Subcommittee on Courts, Intellectual Property, and the Internet

Ken Buck
Ranking Member
Subcommittee on Antitrust, Commercial and Administrative Law

Matt Gaetz
Member of Congress

Mike Johnson
Ranking Member
Subcommittee on the Constitution, Civil Rights and Civil Liberties

Andy Biggs
Ranking Member
Subcommittee on Crime, Terrorism and Homeland Security

Tom McClintock
Ranking Member
Subcommittee on Immigration and Citizenship

W. Gregory Steube
Member of Congress

Tom Tiffany
Member of Congress

Thomas Massie
Member of Congress

Chip Roy
Member of Congress

Dan Bishop
Member of Congress

Michelle Fischbach
Member of Congress

Victoria Spartz
Member of Congress

Scott Fitzgerald
Member of Congress

Cliff Bentz
Member of Congress

Burgess Owens
Member of Congress

cc: The Honorable Jerrold L. Nadler, Chairman

Congress of the United States
House of Representatives
Washington, DC 20515

March 29, 2022

The Honorable Christopher Wray
Director
Federal Bureau of Investigation
935 Pennsylvania Avenue, NW
Washington, DC 20535

Dear Director Wray,

As you are aware, the 2018 Schoharie limousine crash was this country's worst transportation disaster in decades. This senseless tragedy cost the lives of 18 people from Upstate New York and was wholly preventable. Subsequent developments since that tragic day have further proved that this crash should never have happened.

Statewide reporting has brought to the public's attention serious concerns surrounding the owner of the limousine company, Shahed Hussein, a longtime informant of the FBI for prominent antiterrorism cases, and his multiple run-ins with the law and shady business dealings while working with the FBI.[1] During his time as an informant, Hussein is said to have lied on tax returns and immigration papers, committed bankruptcy fraud, refused to pay property taxes, and falsified safety inspection reports at Prestige Limousine that would have prevented this tragedy.[2] Further, his son, who himself operated a number of the day-to-day operations of the limousine business, may have referenced Hussein's work for the FBI to intimidate regulators and law enforcement.[3]

The Schoharie limo tragedy could have been avoided had a blind eye not been turned on this FBI informant, his associates, and their history of breaking the law. If these circumstances weren't troubling enough, following the tragedy, the National Transportation Safety Board (NTSB) was denied access to evidence and the crash site, and Hussein's son—whose prior disregard for the law led to this tragedy—was offered a plea agreement that included no jail time.[4]

The families of the 18 people killed in this tragedy deserve answers to questions surrounding the deaths of their loved ones and the FBI informant at the center of this tragedy. Furthermore,

---

[1] *See, e.g.*, Larry Rulison, "Tonko asks FBI for details about informant who owned limo in Schoharie disaster," Albany Times Union, Feb. 1, 2022, *available at* https://www.timesunion.com/business/article/Tonko-asks-FBI-for-details-about-informant-who-16822345.php?IPID=Times-Union-limo-crash-spotlight.
[2] Ben Ryder Howe, "13,000 Pounds at 118 Miles Per Hour," Intelligencer, Jan. 19, 2022, *available at* https://nymag.com/intelligencer/article/limo-crash-ny-fbi-informant.html.
[3] Larry Rulison, "Records reveal mysterious life of FBI informant Shahed Hussain," Albany Times Union, Oct. 31, 2018, *available at* https://www.timesunion.com/news/article/Who-is-FBI-informant-Shahed-Hussain-13351511.php.
[4] Howe, *supra* note 2.

Congress is constitutionally entitled to information regarding the FBI's relationship with Shahed Hussein and its knowledge of Hussein's criminal activities. As such, we request an official response to the following questions:

1. Was the FBI aware of Shahed Hussein's violation of numerous laws while engaged in activities unrelated to any case or investigation he was informing on?
2. Did the FBI ever intervene to protect Shahed Hussein from prosecution for any unrelated violations of the law?
3. Was the FBI aware that Shahed Hussein's associates would reference his work for the FBI to intimidate regulators and law enforcement? If so, how did the FBI respond?
4. Was the FBI aware that Shahed Hussein's businesses, and Prestige Limousine in particular, were in repeated violation of New York State laws and regulations?
5. When Prestige Limousine was involved the 2018 crash, was the FBI informed? If so, when, and by whom?
6. Did the FBI, in any way, involve itself in the investigation of the 2018 crash?
7. Was the FBI involved, in any way, in the trial of Shahed Hussein's son, to include securing his plea deal?

In addition to your prompt response to these questions, we also demand the FBI turn over all documents related to Shahed Hussein, including any documents and correspondence related to the investigation and trial of the 2018 accident involving Shahed Hussein's son and Prestige Limousine.

Please provide this information as soon as possible, but no later than April 12, 2022. We appreciate your prompt compliance and look forward to receiving the requested information and documentation.

Sincerely,

Elise M. Stefanik
Member of Congress
House Permanent Select
Committee on Intelligence

Michael. R. Turner
Ranking Member
House Permanent Select
Committee on Intelligence

Jim Jordan
Ranking Member
House Committee on the Judiciary

JERROLD NADLER, New York
CHAIRMAN

JIM JORDAN, Ohio
RANKING MEMBER

ONE HUNDRED SEVENTEENTH CONGRESS

Congress of the United States

House of Representatives

COMMITTEE ON THE JUDICIARY

2138 RAYBURN HOUSE OFFICE BUILDING

WASHINGTON, DC 20515-6216

(202) 225-3951
judiciary.house.gov

March 21, 2022

The Honorable Christopher A. Wray
Director
Federal Bureau of Investigation
935 Pennsylvania Avenue, N.W.
Washington, DC 20535

Dear Director Wray:

On March 11, 2022, a news report revealed the existence of a secret Federal Bureau of Investigation audit detailing rampant violations of internal policies governing FBI investigations concerning "politicians, candidates, religious groups, news media and others."[1] The FBI conducted this internal review in 2019 to gauge compliance with FBI rules for handling high-profile and delicate cases—known as sensitive investigative matters (SIMs)—that generally involve the activities of a domestic public official, political candidate, or religious organization.[2] The FBI's audit of 353 cases found a total of 747 compliance errors in violation of internal FBI rules.[3] This internal audit and the staggering number of errors it found suggest a pattern of misconduct and mismanagement within the FBI in failing to uphold internal rules for its most sensitive cases.

This internal review documented systemic FBI failures to follow its own rules and procedures. In particular, the audit found that FBI officials failed to receive approval from supervisors to open an investigation, failed to ensure that appropriate FBI attorneys review a SIM prior to opening an investigation, and did not notify the appropriate United States Attorney's Office in writing within a month of starting an investigation—all in violation of FBI policy.[4] Of the 353 SIMs examined, the audit noted that more than half concerned a "domestic public official."[5] The audit found 74 cases "had a lack of investigative activity for periods of 90 days or longer," suggesting that these cases lingered for longer than necessary.[6] It also noted 33

---

[1] Ryan Lovelace, *Exclusive: Audit Reveals FBI rule-breaking in probes involving politicians, religious groups, media*, WASH. TIMES (Mar. 11, 2022), https://www.washingtontimes.com/news/2022/mar/11/fbi-audit-reveals-agents-rule-breaking-investigati/.
[2] Fed. Bureau of Investigation, Inspections Division, External Audit and Compliance Section, 2019 Domestic Investigations and Operations Guide Audit at 2, (Jan. 10, 2020), https://media.washtimes.com/media/misc/2022/03/11/audit.pdf.
[3] *Id.* at 3.
[4] *Id.* at 4-6.
[5] *Id.* at 7.
[6] *Id.* at 6.

cases in which the FBI headquarters failed to notify the Justice Department about "all known SIMs."[7] Portions of the internal audit, including sections concerning search warrants and investigative methods, are redacted in the publicly available version, suggesting there could be additional misconduct that the FBI continues to shield from public scrutiny.

This secret audit adds to the list of troubling FBI misconduct when investigating sensitive matters. In 2015, when the FBI investigated former Secretary of State Hillary Clinton's mishandling of classified information, it ran a so-called "headquarters special" that ultimately excused Secretary Clinton's actions.[8] Meanwhile, the FBI abused its authority to illegally spy on the Trump campaign.[9] Two FBI agents assigned to the case boasted about their anti-Trump bias in official communications, and an FBI attorney even doctored evidence to spy on a Trump campaign official.[10] The FBI has also abused its authorities under the Foreign Intelligence Surveillance Act to conduct warrantless surveillance on American citizens.[11] Most recently, the FBI's Counterterrorism Division created a "threat tag" for FBI agents to use in tracking and monitoring the protected First Amendment activity of concerned parents at school board meetings.[12]

Last year, during your testimony before the Judiciary Committee, you claimed that the FBI "investigate[s] individuals with proper predication" and does not "investigate First Amendment groups . . . [or] people for speech, association, for assembly, [or] for membership in domestic First Amendment groups."[13] However, this internal review—which you never disclosed and which shows fundamental errors with FBI investigations touching on sensitive political and constitutional matters—calls into question the reliability of your statements. The Committee must examine whether the FBI is taking seriously its compliance with its own rules intended to protect American civil liberties.

---

[7] *Id.* at 4.

[8] *See* S. Comm. on Homeland Sec. & Governmental Aff., The Clinton Email Scandal and the FBI's Investigation of It (Feb. 7, 2018); Thomas J. Baker, *How to Restore the FBI's Culture*, Wall St. J., Aug. 27, 2018; Transcribed Interview of Andrew McCabe, in Wash., D.C. (Dec. 21, 2017); Transcribed Interview of Peter Strzok, in Wash., D.C. (June 27, 2018); Transcribed Interview of John Giacalone, in Wash., D.C. (June 21, 2018).

[9] Dep't of Justice Off. of Inspector Gen., *Review of Four FISA Applications and Other Aspects of the FBI's Crossfire Hurricane Investigation* (Dec. 2019).

[10] *Id.* at xi; Dep't of Justice Off. of Inspector Gen., *A Review of Various Actions by the Federal Bureau of Investigation and Department of Justice in Advance of the 2016 Election* at 395-400 (2018).

[11] Dep't of Justice Off. of Inspector Gen., *Review of Four FISA Applications and Other Aspects of the FBI's Crossfire Hurricane Investigation* (Dec. 2019); Dep't of Justice Off. of Inspector Gen., *Management Advisory Memorandum for Director of the Federal Bureau of Investigation Regarding the Execution of Woods Procedures for Applications Filed with the Foreign Intelligence Surveillance Court Relating to U.S. Persons* (Mar. 2020); Dep't of Justice Off. of Inspector Gen., *Audit of the Federal Bureau of Investigation's Execution of Its Woods Procedures for the Applications Filed with the Foreign Intelligence Surveillance Court Relating to U.S. Persons* (Sept. 2021); Memorandum Opinion and Order, *Document re Section 702 Certification* (FISA Ct. Nov. 18, 2020); Ellen Nakashima, *Federal court approved FBI's continued use of warrantless surveillance power despite repeated violations of privacy rules*, WASH. POST (Apr. 26, 2021).

[12] Email from Carlton Peeples, Deputy Assistant Dir., Criminal Investigative Div., Fed. Bureau of Investigation, to FBI_SACS (Oct. 20, 2021).

[13] *Oversight of the Federal Bureau of Investigation: Hearing before the H. Comm. on the Judiciary*, 117th Cong. (2021).

In light of this troubling internal review and to assist the Committee's investigative and oversight work, please provide the following documents and information:

1. An unredacted copy of the FBI Inspection Division's audit titled "2019 Domestic Investigations and Operations Guide Audit" dated January 10, 2020;

2. All documents and communications referring or relating to the FBI Inspection Division's 2019 Domestic Investigations and Operations Guide Audit dated January 10, 2020;

3. A description of the FBI's predicate to open sensitive investigative matters of politicians, candidates, religious groups, and others, as documented in the FBI Inspection Division's 2019 Domestic Investigations and Operations Guide Audit dated January 10, 2020;

4. An explanation of whether the FBI has resolved compliance issues related to sensitive investigative matters identified in the secret audit; and

5. Unredacted copies of all internal reviews conducted by the FBI's Inspection Division between November 1, 2019, and the present.

Please provide this information and briefing as soon as possible but not later than 5:00 p.m. on April 4, 2022. After you have provided this information in writing, we ask that your staff provide a staff-level briefing on this topic. If you have any questions about this request, please contact Committee staff at (202) 225-6906.

Thank you for your prompt attention to this matter.

Sincerely,

Jim Jordan
Ranking Member

Andy Biggs
Ranking Member
Subcommittee on Crime, Terrorism, and Homeland Security

Mike Johnson
Ranking Member
Subcommittee on the Constitution, Civil Rights and Civil Liberties

cc: The Honorable Jerrold L. Nadler, Chairman
The Honorable Sheila Jackson Lee, Chair, Subcommittee on Crime, Terrorism, and Homeland Security
The Honorable Steve Cohen, Chairman, Subcommittee on the Constitution, Civil Rights and Civil Liberties
The Honorable Michael E. Horowitz, Inspector General, U.S. Department of Justice

Congress of the United States
Washington, DC 20515

March 14, 2022

Mr. Jacob Sullivan
National Security Advisor
The White House
Washington, D.C. 20500

Dear Mr. Sullivan:

In August 2021, the Biden Administration released Aleksei Burkov, a notorious Russian cybercriminal, early from federal custody.[1] Burkov has been described as an "asset of supreme importance" and possibly "one of the most connected and skilled malicious hackers ever apprehended by U.S. authorities."[2] In light of the danger posed by Burkov's activities and President Biden's statement that Russian cyberattacks against U.S. interests would face "consequences,"[3] we have questions about the Biden Administration's decision to allow Burkov to return to Russia.[4] We request your cooperation with our investigation into this matter.

The decision to prematurely release Burkov is curious given the lengths to which the U.S. government went to secure Burkov's arrest. U.S. authorities pursued Burkov for years on hacking-related charges, including identity theft, wire fraud, computer intrusion, and money laundering.[5] One of the two illegal websites he ran, named "Cardplanet," sold credit and debit card information, many of which belonged to U.S. citizens and resulted in over $20 million in fraudulent purchases on U.S. cards.[6] Burkov operated another website that served as an exclusive "invite-only club" where some of the world's most dangerous cybercriminals could advertise stolen goods and criminal services.[7]

In December 2015, at the U.S. government's request, Israeli authorities arrested Burkov.[8] Russia aggressively fought Burkov's extradition to the U.S. and even attempted to bait Israel in a

---

[1] *See* Dustin Volz & Aruna Viswanatha, *U.S. Deports High-Profile Hacker to Russia Before End of Prison Sentence*, WALL STREET JOURNAL (Sept. 29, 2021), https://www.wsj.com/articles/u-s-deports-high-profile-hacker-to-russia-before-end-of-prison-sentence-11632871404; Shannon Vavra, *Why the Hell Did America Just Send This Master Cybercriminal Back to Russia?*, THE DAILY BEAST (Oct. 1, 2021), https://www.thedailybeast.com/why-the-hell-did-america-just-send-russian-cybercriminal-aleksei-burkov-back-to-moscow.

[2] Brian Krebs, *Russian Cybercrime Boss Burkov Pleads Guilty*, KREBS ON SECURITY (Jan. 27, 2020), https://krebsonsecurity.com/2020/01/russian-cybercrime-boss-burkov-pleads-guilty.

[3] Zeke Miller & Eric Tucker, *Biden Tells Putin Russia Must Crack Down on Cybercriminals*, ASSOCIATED PRESS (July 10, 2021), https://apnews.com/article/joe-biden-europe-technology-government-and-politics-russia-594b22105c93a4cb2962fea6a4763da0.

[4] Federal Bureau of Prisons, Inmate Locator: Aleksei Burkov, https://www.bop.gov/inmateloc (last accessed on Mar. 9, 2022).

[5] Press Release, U.S. DEP'T OF JUSTICE, U.S. ATTORNEY G. ZACHARY TERWILLIGER, E.D. VA, *Russian National Pleads Guilty to Running Online Criminal Marketplace* (Jan. 23, 2020), https://www.justice.gov/usao-edva/page/file/1238961/download.

[6] *Id.*

[7] *Id.*

[8] *Id.*

prisoner-swap by imprisoning a young Israeli woman on exaggerated drug charges during a layover in Russia.[9] Despite Russia's best efforts to prevent his transferal to U.S. custody, the Trump Administration secured Burkov's extradition to the U.S. in November 2019.[10] Burkov pleaded guilty and a federal judge sentenced him to nine years in prison in June 2020.[11] At the time of his sentence, he was given credit for time served while incarcerated in both Israel and the United States.[12]

The Biden Administration released Burkov at least a year early on August 25, 2021, when U.S. Immigration and Customs Enforcement (ICE) officials escorted him onto a plane destined for Moscow.[13] An ICE spokesperson stated that "Burkov is wanted by Russian authorities,"[14] and a DOJ spokesperson denied that a prisoner exchange took place.[15]

Although a Kremlin spokesperson applauded Burkov's premature release, calling it "rather a positive development," current and former U.S. officials have been described as "befuddled" and "surprised."[16] The U.S. does not have an extradition treaty with Russia, which commentators have cited as a reason why the Biden Administration's actions are especially peculiar.[17] The Russian government has a history of using cybercriminals as assets for Russian intelligence services.[18] Some former officials have suggested that Burkov may now be working for Russia, against U.S. interests.[19]

In light of the Biden Administration's sudden reversal on Burkov's case, the potential that he may now be working against U.S. interests, and to better understand the Administration's efforts to address the pervasive threats posed by Russian cybercriminals, we respectfully request the following information:

1. An explanation as to why the Biden Administration granted Burkov early release from U.S. custody;

---

[9] Josh Breiner, Bar Peleg, & Liza Rozovsky, *Washington Wants Him – and So Does Putin. Who Is the Russian Hacker Jailed in Israel?*, HAARETZ (Oct. 15, 2019), https://www.haaretz.com/israel-news/.premium-the-russian-hacker-who-just-became-one-of-israel-s-most-famous-prisoners-1.7972490; Brian Krebs, *supra* note 2.
[10] U.S. DEP'T OF JUSTICE, U.S. ATTORNEY G. ZACHARY TERWILLIGER, E.D. VA, *supra* note 5.
[11] Press Release, U.S. DEP'T OF JUSTICE, OFFICE OF PUBLIC AFFAIRS, *Russian National Sentenced to Prison for Operating Websites Devoted to Fraud and Malicious Cyber Activities* (June 26, 2020), https://www.justice.gov/opa/pr/russian-national-sentenced-prison-operating-websites-devoted-fraud-and-malicious-cyber.
[12] *United States of America v. Aleksei Yurievich Burkov*, 1:15-cr-00245-TSE-1 (E.D. VA. 2020), *available at* https://krebsonsecurity.com/wp-content/uploads/2020/06/burkov-judgment.pdf.
[13] Federal Bureau of Prisons, Inmate Locator: Aleksei Burkov, https://www.bop.gov/inmateloc (last accessed on Mar. 9, 2022); Dustin Volz & Aruna Viswanatha, *supra* note 1.
[14] Shannon Vavra, *supra* note 1.
[15] Sean Lyngaas, *US Deports Convicted Russian Hacker Amid Cyber Tensions with Moscow*, CNN (Sept. 28, 2021), https://www.cnn.com/2021/09/28/politics/us-deport-russian-hacker/index.html.
[16] Dustin Volz & Aruna Viswanatha, *supra* note 1; Shannon Vavra, *supra* note 1.
[17] *Id.*
[18] *Id.*
[19] *Id.*

2. An assessment of where Burkov is now and whether the Biden Administration believes he is appropriately being held accountable for his crimes in Russia;

3. An explanation of what, if anything, the U.S. received in return for his release to Russia; and

4. A list of Russian nationals in U.S. federal custody pursuant to criminal charges or convictions at any point since January 21, 2021, who the Biden Administration released prior to the end of the individual's criminal sentence, including the charge(s) for which the individual was in custody or convicted.

Please provide this information as soon as possible, but no later than 5:00 p.m. on March 28, 2022. If a full response requires the disclosure of classified information, please provide such information under separate cover. After you have provided this information in writing, we ask that you arrange for the DOJ to provide a staff-level briefing. Thank you for your prompt attention to this matter.

Sincerely,

Jim Jordan
Ranking Member
House Committee on the Judiciary

Michael R. Turner
Ranking Member
House Permanent Select Committee on Intelligence

John Katko
Ranking Member
House Committee on Homeland Security

Michael T. McCaul
Ranking Member
House Committee on Foreign Affairs

cc: The Honorable Jerrold Nadler
Chairman, House Committee on the Judiciary

The Honorable Adam Schiff
Chairman, House Permanent Select Committee on Intelligence

The Honorable Bennie Thompson
Chairman, House Committee on Homeland Security

The Honorable Gregory Meeks
Chairman, House Committee on Foreign Affairs

JERROLD NADLER, New York
CHAIRMAN

JIM JORDAN, Ohio
RANKING MEMBER

ONE HUNDRED SEVENTEENTH CONGRESS

Congress of the United States

House of Representatives

COMMITTEE ON THE JUDICIARY

2138 RAYBURN HOUSE OFFICE BUILDING

WASHINGTON, DC 20515–6216

(202) 225–3951
judiciary.house.gov

March 9, 2022

The Honorable Christopher A. Wray
Director
Federal Bureau of Investigation
935 Pennsylvania Avenue, N.W.
Washington, DC 20535

Dear Director Wray:

We have received a whistleblower disclosure from a senior FBI special agent concerning the investigation into the pipe bombs placed near the headquarters of the Democratic National Committee and Republican National Committee on January 5, 2021.[1] According to the special agent, on February 7, 2022—over a year after the placement of the bombs—the FBI's Washington Field Office asked FBI field offices to canvass all confidential human sources nationwide for information about the individual and the crime.[2] In part, the message asked that the canvass "include sources reporting on all [types of] threats" because the suspect's "motive and ideology remain unknown."[3] The special agent explained that the WFO request was "unusual" because it was transmitted more than a year after the FBI had begun the investigation, and it raises questions about the progress and extent of the FBI's investigation.

In addition to this whistleblower disclosure, we have learned that the FBI has failed to sufficiently answer questions posed by Rep. Bill Posey about the status of the investigation. On September 2, 2021, Rep. Posey wrote to you requesting a briefing on the status of the pipe bomb investigation, citing concerns for his office's safety, for the residences of many Members of Congress, and for the public at large.[4] The FBI, however, has not fully responded to Rep. Posey's request, explaining that it was exclusively providing information to the partisan Democrat-led Select Committee investigating the events of January 6, 2021.[5]

The FBI's decision to provide information on a partisan basis is antithetical to the FBI's purported impartiality and it further erodes public confidence in the FBI's senior leadership. The

---

[1] Press Release, *FBI Washington Field Office Releases Video and Additional Information Regarding the Pipe Bomb Investigation,* Fed. Bureau of Investigation (Sept. 8, 2021).
[2] Fed. Bureau of Investigation e-mail (Feb. 7, 2022).
[3] *Id.*
[4] Letter from Bill Posey, Member of Congress, to Christopher A. Wray, Director, Fed. Bureau of Investigation (Sept. 2, 2021).
[5] Letter from Jill C. Tyson, Assistant Director, Fed. Bureau of Investigation, to Bill Posey, Member of Congress (Sept. 17, 2021).

Committee on the Judiciary is the FBI's authorizing committee, responsible for conducting oversight of the FBI's activities. To support Rep. Posey's request, and in light of the whistleblower disclosure we have received, we ask that you direct your staff to provide a briefing to the Committee and Rep. Posey about the status and extent of the pipe bomb investigation.

Please provide this briefing as soon as possible, but no later than March 23, 2022. In addition, we remind you that whistleblower disclosures to Congress are protected by law and that we will not tolerate any effort to retaliate against whistleblowers for their disclosures. Thank you for your attention to this important matter.

Sincerely,

Jim Jordan
Ranking Member

cc: The Honorable Jerrold L. Nadler
Chairman

JERROLD NADLER, New York
CHAIRMAN

JIM JORDAN, Ohio
RANKING MEMBER

ONE HUNDRED SEVENTEENTH CONGRESS
Congress of the United States
House of Representatives
COMMITTEE ON THE JUDICIARY
2138 RAYBURN HOUSE OFFICE BUILDING
WASHINGTON, DC 20515-6216
(202) 225-3951
judiciary.house.gov

March 9, 2022

Dr. John Heim, Executive Director and CEO
Dr. Viola M. Garcia, President
National School Boards Association
1680 Duke St., Second Floor
Alexandria, VA 22314-3493

Dear Drs. Heim and Garcia:

It has been over four months since we first requested documents and information about the National School Boards Association's (NSBA) letter to President Biden in which the NSBA equated parents with domestic terrorists and urged federal intervention—including use of the Patriot Act—to silence parents at school board meetings.[1] We received absolutely no response, despite several follow-up emails and phone calls, until early February 2022. Despite new CEO John Heim's effort to rehabilitate the NSBA's image and "restore trust" in the association,[2] you have still failed to produce a single document responsive to our requests.

The NSBA's letter to President Biden initiated a rapid and stunning response from the Biden Administration that culminated in a directive from the Attorney General for federal law enforcement entities to monitor local school board matters.[3] We know from a brave whistleblower that the Federal Bureau of Investigation operationalized the Attorney General's directive, with the head of the FBI's Counterterrorism Division directing FBI agents to use a new "threat tag"—EDUOFFICIAL—to track school board-related investigations.[4] In other words, because of the NSBA's letter to President Biden, the FBI is using federal counterterrorism tools to track and categorize an unknown number of American parents simply for standing up at school board meetings to advocate for their children's future.

---

[1] Letter from Rep. Jim Jordan et al., Ranking Member, H. Comm. on the Judiciary, to Dr. Viola M. Garcia et al, President, Nat'l School Boards Assoc. (Oct. 27, 2021).

[2] Patrick Reilly, *NSBA head knew about AG's controversial school board memo, emails show*, N.Y. POST (Feb. 14, 2022); Laura Meckler, *National School Boards Association stumbles into politics and is blasted apart*, WASH. POST (Jan. 13, 2022).

[3] *See generally* Memorandum from Atty Gen. Merrick Garland, U.S. Dep't of Justice, Partnership Among Federal, State, Local, Tribal, And Territorial Law Enforcement to Address Threats Against School Administrators, Board Members, Teachers, and Staff (Oct. 4, 2021); *Oversight of the United States Department of Justice: Hearing Before the H. comm. on the Judiciary,* 117th Cong. at 68 (2021) (testimony from Hon. Merrick Garland, Atty Gen., U.S. Dep't of Justice).

[4] Email from Carlton Peeples, Deputy Assistant Dir., Criminal Investigative Div., Fed. Bureau of Investigation, to FBI_SACS (Oct. 20, 2021).

The NSBA has expressed regret and apologized for its letter to President Biden,[5] and has announced an internal review of the circumstances leading to the letter. However, former CEO Chip Slaven has defended the NSBA's letter, and another former senior NSBA officer, Charlie Wilson, has maintained that outrage about the letter was "distorted" and "cherry-picked."[6] Mr. Wilson, a former NSBA President, was only forced to leave the board after his state withdrew from the association.[7] In light of the stubborn defense of the letter by these former senior NSBA officials, as well as the NSBA's failure to date to produce any documents responsive to our investigation, we still have concerns about the NSBA's collusion with the Biden Administration to develop a pretext for invoking federal law enforcement to intimidate and silence parents.

Parents have an undisputed right to direct the upbringing and education of their children, including expressing concerns about the inclusion of controversial curricula in their child's education.[8] We know from publicly available information that the NSBA has information that is relevant and necessary to our investigation. We are committed to fully examining the Biden Administration's use of counterterrorism resources in relation to school board meetings at the urging of the NSBA. We reiterate our outstanding document requests from our October 27 letter and request that you produce this material immediately.

Sincerely,

Jim Jordan
Ranking Member

cc: The Honorable Jerrold L. Nadler
Chairman

[5] Memorandum from NSBA Board of Directors, Message to NSBA Members (Oct. 22, 2021).
[6] Meckler, *supra* note 2.
[7] *Id.*
[8] *Troxel v. Granville,* 530 U.S. 57, 65 (2000) (citing *Meyer v. Nebraska,* 262 U.S. 390, 399 (1923)).

JERROLD NADLER, New York
CHAIRMAN

JIM JORDAN, Ohio
RANKING MEMBER

ONE HUNDRED SEVENTEENTH CONGRESS

Congress of the United States
House of Representatives
COMMITTEE ON THE JUDICIARY

2138 RAYBURN HOUSE OFFICE BUILDING
WASHINGTON, DC 20515-6216
(202) 225-3951
judiciary.house.gov

March 3, 2022

The Honorable Christopher A. Wray
Director
Federal Bureau of Investigation
935 Pennsylvania Avenue, N.W.
Washington, DC 20535

Dear Director Wray:

The NSO Group, an Israeli software company, gained widespread notoriety in 2021 after several media organizations published allegations that one of its products—named "Pegasus"—had been used by foreign governments to surveil dissidents, journalists, U.S. officials, and others.[1] Pegasus is a spyware tool that allows an operator to compromise a target's mobile device without requiring any input from the target.[2] After compromising a device, the operator can retrieve data on the device, track the device's location, and commandeer the device's camera and microphone.[3] The Federal Bureau of Investigation has reportedly investigated whether Pegasus has been used against targets within the U.S. in recent years.[4]

As part of the allegations in 2021, media outlets reported that Pegasus was incapable of compromising mobile devices with U.S. phone numbers.[5] However, on January 28, 2022, the *New York Times* reported that the NSO Group has made a version of Pegasus capable of targeting U.S. mobile devices, called "Phantom."[6] This same report alleged that the FBI had acquired access to NSO Group spyware in 2019, tested it, and retains the hardware necessary to use it.[7] The FBI has since acknowledged that it acquired and tested NSO Group spyware.[8]

Although the FBI has stated that it "procured a limited license for product testing and evaluation only" and that "[t]here was no operational use in support of any investigation," the FBI reportedly had an active software license for NSO's spyware for approximately two years

[1] *See, e.g.*, Drew Harwell and Craig Timberg, *NSO Group vows to investigate potential spyware abuse following Pegasus Project investigation*, WASH. POST (Jul. 20, 2021); *see also* Craig Timberg et al., *Pegasus spyware used to hack U.S. diplomats working abroad*, WASH. POST (Dec. 3, 2021).
[2] Timberg et al., *supra* note 1.
[3] *Id.*
[4] *See* Joseph Menn and Jack Stubbs, *Exclusive: FBI proves use of Israeli firm's spyware in personal and government hacks – sources*, REUTERS (Jan. 30, 2020).
[5] *See* Timberg et al., *supra* note 1.
[6] Ronen Bergman and Mark Mazzetti, *The Battle for the World's Most Powerful Cyberweapon*, N.Y. TIMES (Jan. 28, 2022).
[7] *Id.*
[8] Ellen Nakashima, *FBI acknowledges it tested NSO Group's spyware*, WASH. POST (Feb. 2, 2022).

and paid the NSO Group approximately $5 million.[9] During this period, lawyers at the FBI and Department of Justice debated the legality of using Phantom on domestic targets and "NSO engineers were in frequent contact with F.B.I. employees, asking about the various technological details that could change the legal implications of an attack."[10]

In light of the FBI's repeated failure to adhere to safeguards on its use of Foreign Intelligence Surveillance Act authorities,[11] and the FBI's spying on protected First Amendment activities during the campaign of President Donald Trump, the FBI acquiring yet another tool to spy on Americans is deeply troubling and presents significant risks to the civil liberties of U.S. persons. To assist the Committee in conducting oversight of the FBI's acquisition, testing, and use of NSO Group spyware, please provide the following documents and information:

1. All documents and communications between or among the FBI and the NSO Group, Westbridge Technologies, or any other NSO Group affiliate or subsidiary referring or relating to the FBI's acquisition, testing, or use of NSO Group spyware;

2. All documents and communications referring or relating to the FBI's decision to acquire NSO Group spyware; and

3. All documents and communications referring or relating to the FBI's or Justice Department's assessment of the legality of using Phantom against domestic targets.

Please provide this information as soon as possible but not later than 5:00 p.m. on March 17, 2022. To the extent a complete response to this inquiry requires the provision of classified information, please do so under separate cover.

If you have any questions about this request, please contact Judiciary Committee staff at (202) 225-6906. Thank you for your prompt attention to this matter.

Sincerely,

Jim Jordan
Ranking Member

Mike Johnson
Ranking Member
Subcommittee on the Constitution,
Civil Rights, and Civil Liberties

cc: The Honorable Jerrold Nadler, Chairman
The Honorable Steve Cohen, Chairman, Subcommittee on the Constitution, Civil Rights and Civil Liberties

---

[9] *Id.*; Bergman and Mazzetti, *supra* note 5.
[10] Bergman and Mazzetti, *supra* note 6.
[11] *See, e.g.*, Letter from Jim Jordan, Ranking Member, H. Comm. on the Judiciary, and Mike Johnson, Ranking Member, Subcommittee on the Constitution, Civil Rights, and Civil Liberties of the H. Comm. on the Judiciary, to The Honorable Christopher A. Wray, Director, Federal Bureau of Investigation (Jan. 27, 2022).

JERROLD NADLER, New York
CHAIRMAN

JIM JORDAN, Ohio
RANKING MEMBER

ONE HUNDRED SEVENTEENTH CONGRESS
Congress of the United States
House of Representatives
COMMITTEE ON THE JUDICIARY
2138 RAYBURN HOUSE OFFICE BUILDING
WASHINGTON, DC 20515-6216
(202) 225-3951
judiciary.house.gov

March 3, 2022

Mr. Tim Cook
Chief Executive Officer
Apple Inc.
1 Infinite Loop
Cupertino, CA 94025

Dear Mr. Cook:

The NSO Group, an Israeli software company, gained widespread notoriety in 2021 after several media organizations published allegations that one of its products—named "Pegasus"—had been used by foreign governments to surveil dissidents, journalists, U.S. officials, and others.[1] Pegasus is a spyware tool that allows an operator to compromise a target's mobile device without requiring any input from the target.[2] After compromising a device, the operator can retrieve data on the device, track the device's location, and commandeer the device's camera and microphone.[3]

As part of the allegations in 2021, media outlets reported that Pegasus was incapable of compromising mobile devices with U.S. phone numbers.[4] However, on January 28, 2022, the *New York Times* reported that the NSO Group has made a version of Pegasus capable of targeting U.S. mobile devices, called "Phantom."[5] This same report alleged that the Federal Bureau of Investigation had acquired access to NSO Group spyware in 2019, tested it, and retains the hardware necessary to use it.[6] The FBI has since acknowledged that it acquired and tested NSO Group spyware.[7]

Reporting by media outlets and Apple's own public statements indicate that Apple is able to ascertain when the user of an Apple device has been targeted by Pegasus.[8] The Committee is

[1] *See, e.g.*, Drew Harwell and Craig Timberg, *NSO Group vows to investigate potential spyware abuse following Pegasus Project investigation*, WASH. POST (Jul. 20, 2021); *see also* Craig Timberg et al., *Pegasus spyware used to hack U.S. diplomats working abroad*, WASH. POST (Dec. 3, 2021).
[2] Timberg et al., *supra* note 1.
[3] *Id.*
[4] *See Id.*
[5] Ronen Bergman and Mark Mazzetti, *The Battle for the World's Most Powerful Cyberweapon*, N.Y. TIMES (Jan. 28, 2022).
[6] *Id.*
[7] Ellen Nakashima, *FBI acknowledges it tested NSO Group's spyware*, WASH. POST (Feb. 2, 2022).
[8] *See, e.g.*, Press Release, Apple Inc., Apple sues NSO Group to curb the abuse of state-sponsored spyware (Nov. 23, 2021) ("Apple is notifying the small number of users that it discovered may have been targeted by

examining the FBI's acquisition, testing, and use of NSO's spyware, and potential civil liberty implications of the use of Pegasus or Phantom against U.S. persons. To assist the Committee in conducting this investigation, please provide the following information:

1. Apple's ability to detect when a user of an Apple device has been targeted by Pegasus or Phantom;

2. The number of attacks using Pegasus or Phantom that Apple has detected, the dates of those attacks, the geographical regions in which Apple detected those attacks, and any other relevant information about those attacks; and

3. A staff level briefing about Apple's communications, if any, with representatives of the Justice Department, Federal Bureau of Investigation, or any other U.S. Government entity about Pegasus or Phantom.

Please arrange to provide this briefing as soon as possible but not later than 5:00 p.m. on March 17, 2022. If you have any questions about this request, please contact Judiciary Committee staff at (202) 225-6906.

Thank you for your prompt attention to this matter.

Sincerely,

Jim Jordan
Ranking Member

Mike Johnson
Ranking Member
Subcommittee on the Constitution,
Civil Rights, and Civil Liberties

cc: The Honorable Jerrold Nadler, Chairman

The Honorable Steve Cohen, Chairman
Subcommittee on the Constitution, Civil Rights, and Civil Liberties

---

FORCEDENTRY.:); *see also* Timberg et al., *supra* note 1 (noting that "Apple has alerted 11 U.S. Embassy employees that their iPhones have been hacked in recent months with Pegasus spyware from NSO Group . . . .").

JERROLD NADLER, New York
CHAIRMAN

JIM JORDAN, Ohio
RANKING MEMBER

ONE HUNDRED SEVENTEENTH CONGRESS
Congress of the United States
House of Representatives
COMMITTEE ON THE JUDICIARY
2138 RAYBURN HOUSE OFFICE BUILDING
WASHINGTON, DC 20515-6216
(202) 225-3951
judiciary.house.gov

February 28, 2022

The Honorable Merrick B. Garland
Attorney General
U.S. Department of Justice
950 Pennsylvania Avenue, N.W.
Washington, DC 20530

Dear Attorney General Garland:

We are investigating the troubling attempts by the Department of Justice and the White House to use the heavy hand of federal law enforcement—including federal counterterrorism tools—to target concerned parents at local school board meetings and chill their protected First Amendment activity. Since October 2021, House Judiciary Committee Republicans have sent nearly 100 letters to Department components requesting documents and information related to this investigation.[1] To date, we have received only a single half-page response from the Federal Bureau of Investigation, and none of the requested documents or substantive information.

We know from public reporting that the National School Boards Association (NSBA) coordinated with the White House prior to sending a letter dated September 29, 2021, to President Biden urging the Justice Department to use federal antiterrorism tools—including the Patriot Act—to target parents.[2] Just five days later, on October 4, you issued a memorandum directing the FBI and other Departmental components to address a purported "disturbing spike in harassment, intimidation, and threats of violence" at school board meetings.[3] A protected whistleblower disclosure shows that the FBI's Counterterrorism Division quickly effectuated

[1] *See* Letter from Rep. Mike Johnson et al, to Hon. Merrick Garland, Atty Gen., U.S. Dep't of Justice (Oct. 13, 2021); Letter from Rep. Jim Jordan et al, Ranking Member, H. Comm. on the Judiciary, to Hon. Merrick Garland, Atty Gen., U.S. Dep't of Justice (Oct. 25, 2021); Letter from Rep. Jim Jordan et al, Ranking Member, H. Comm. on the Judiciary, to Mr. E. Bryan Wilson et al, Acting U.S. Atty, District of Alaska (Nov. 1, 2021); Letter from Rep. Jim Jordan et al, Ranking Member, H. Comm. on the Judiciary, to Mr. Mark Lesko, Acting Assistant Atty Gen., Nat'l Sec. Division, U.S. Dep't of Justice (Nov. 2, 2021); Letter from Rep. Jim Jordan et al, Ranking Member, H. Comm. on the Judiciary, to Hon. Christopher Wray, Dir., Fed. Bureau of Investigation (Nov. 3, 2021); Letter from Rep. Jim Jordan, Ranking Member, H. Comm. on the Judiciary, to Hon. Merrick Garland, Atty Gen., U.S. Dep't of Justice (Nov. 16, 2021); Letter from Rep. Jim Jordan, Ranking Member, H. Comm. on the Judiciary, to Hon. Christopher Wray, Dir., Fed. Bureau of Investigation (Nov. 18, 2021).

[2] Callie Patteson, *WH 'actively engaged' with NSBA before 'domestic terror' letter: memo* N.Y. Post, Nov. 11, 2021.

[3] Memorandum from Atty Gen. Merrick Garland, U.S. Dep't of Justice, Partnership Among Federal, State, Local, Tribal, And Territorial Law Enforcement to Address Threats Against School Administrators, Board Members, Teachers, and Staff (Oct. 4, 2021).

your directive by compiling and categorizing threat assessments related to parents.[4] Timothy Langan, the FBI's Assistant Director of the Counterterrorism Division, later testified to the House Intelligence Committee that the FBI discussed your directive with Justice Department officials prior to its issuance.[5]

The NSBA Board of Directors has apologized for its letter to President Biden, writing: "On behalf of NSBA, we regret and apologize for the letter."[6] (emphasis in original). You, however, have refused to rescind your directive, even though you testified that the NSBA letter was the basis for your October 4 memorandum.[7] Your anti-parent directive remains in effect and, as a result, the FBI continues to "tag" American parents as potential counterterrorism threats.

Our Committee has a constitutional responsibility to conduct oversight of the Department of Justice.[8] During your confirmation hearing to become Attorney General, you promised "the Department I lead [would] be as responsive as possible" to congressional oversight.[9] You explained that the "oversight responsibility" of Congress is a "duty imposed by the Constitution" that you "greatly respect."[10] By your obstruction during these past four months, you have failed to live up to your promise. Committee Republicans will not let this matter rest. We are committed to fully examining the Biden Administration's use of counterterrorism resources in relation to school board meetings. We reiterate our outstanding document requests to the various Departmental components and ask that you produce this material immediately.

Sincerely,

Jim Jordan
Ranking Member

Steve Chabot
Member of Congress

Louie Gohmert
Member of Congress

Darrell Issa
Ranking Member
Subcommittee on Courts, Intellectual Property, and the Internet

---

[4] Email from Carlton Peeples to FBI_SACS (Oct. 20, 2021).
[5] *Open C3 Subcommittee Hearing on Countering Domestic Terrorism, Hearing Before the H. Permanent Select Comm. on Intelligence,* 117th Cong. (Nov. 3, 2021) (testimony of Mr. Timothy Langan Jr., Assistant Dir., Counterterrorism Division, Fed. Bureau of Investigation).
[6] Memorandum from NSBA Board of Directors, Message to NSBA Members (Oct. 22, 2021).
[7] *Oversight of the United States Department of Justice: Hearing Before the H. comm. on the Judiciary,* 117th Cong. (2021) (testimony from Hon. Merrick Garland, Atty Gen., U.S. Dep't of Justice).
[8] *See McGrain v. Daugherty,* 273 U.S. 135, 174-175 (1926).
[9] *The Nomination of the Honorable Merrick Brian Garland to be Attorney General of the United States: Hearing Before the S. Comm. on the Judiciary*, 117fh Cong. (Feb. 22, 2021) (statement of Hon. Merrick B. Garland).
[10] *Id.*

Ken Buck
Ranking Member
Subcommittee on Antitrust, Commercial and Administrative Law

Matt Gaetz
Member of Congress

Mike Johnson
Ranking Member
Subcommittee on the Constitution, Civil Rights and Civil Liberties

Andy Biggs
Ranking Member
Subcommittee on Crime, Terrorism and Homeland Security

Tom McClintock
Ranking Member
Subcommittee on Immigration and Citizenship

W. Gregory Steube
Member of Congress

Tom Tiffany
Member of Congress

Thomas Massie
Member of Congress

Chip Roy
Member of Congress

Dan Bishop
Member of Congress

Michelle Fischbach
Member of Congress

Victoria Spartz
Member of Congress

Scott Fitzgerald
Member of Congress

Cliff Bentz
Member of Congress

Burgess Owens
Member of Congress

cc: The Honorable Jerrold L. Nadler
Chairman

JERROLD NADLER, New York
CHAIRMAN

JIM JORDAN, Ohio
RANKING MEMBER

ONE HUNDRED SEVENTEENTH CONGRESS

Congress of the United States
House of Representatives

COMMITTEE ON THE JUDICIARY
2138 RAYBURN HOUSE OFFICE BUILDING
WASHINGTON, DC 20515–6216
(202) 225–3951
judiciary.house.gov

February 17, 2022

The Honorable Matthew G. Olsen
Assistant Attorney General
National Security Division
U.S. Department of Justice
950 Pennsylvania Avenue, NW
Washington, DC 20530

Dear Assistant Attorney General Olsen:

We write to request information about the newly-formed domestic terrorism office within the Counterterrorism Section (CTS) of the Justice Department's National Security Division (NSD). The creation of a new domestic terrorism office has reportedly raised serious concerns from "longtime dedicated career lawyers" at the Department that it is unnecessary and potentially harmful.[1] Especially in light of the Justice Department's recent misuse of its counterterrorism resources to target concerned parents at school board meetings—concerns that the Attorney General has refused to acknowledge or address—the Committee must fully assess the Department's creation of a new office that could be misused to target American citizens.

Career Department employees have voiced concern over the creation of a new domestic terrorism office within NSD.[2] On January 19, 2021, the Department provided feedback about potential legislation in the Senate that would create a new Department unit to address domestic terrorism.[3] In this document, the career Department attorneys warned that it "is unnecessary and potentially harmful to establish a dedicated domestic terrorism office in CTS."[4] The career attorneys also warned that "[a]rtificially splitting CTS into separate domestic and international terrorism offices would weaken the broad expertise currently housed in CTS, reduce synergy in our counterterrorism efforts, and deny our attorneys the benefits of cross-pollination."[5]

The Department must combat legitimate threats of terrorism while respecting American civil liberties and ensuring fair and impartial justice. Under the Biden Administration, however, the Department and the White House have used the heavy hand of federal law enforcement—

---

[1] Betsy Woodruff Swan, *Memo reveals DOJ pushback on domestic terrorism bill*, POLITICO (Apr. 7, 2021).
[2] *Id.*; Informal, Not-Officially Cleared Comments of the Department of Justice on H.R. 5602, the "Domestic Terrorism Prevention Act of 2020."
[3] Informal, Not-Officially Cleared Comments of the Department of Justice on H.R. 5602, the "Domestic Terrorism Prevention Act of 2020."
[4] *Id.*
[5] *Id.*

including counterterrorism resources—to target concerned parents at local school board meetings and chill their protected First Amendment activity. The Department's documented misuse of existing counterterrorism resources to target American parents raises serious concerns that NSD could similarly misuse the new domestic terrorism office. In fact, just days ago, the Biden Administration asserted that "undermining public trust in U.S. government institutions" through so-called "mis- dis- and mal-information" can be a form of domestic terrorism.[6] It is not a stretch to imagine how the NSD's new domestic terrorism office could abuse this definition to target Americans engaged in protected First Amendment activities.

To advance the Committee's oversight of the Department, we request that you produce the following documents and information:

1. All documents and communications referring or relating to the creation of the Department of Justice's new domestic terrorism unit within the Counterterrorism Section of the National Security Division;

2. All documents and communications between or among officials or employees of the Executive Office of the President and the Department or National Security Division about the creation of the new domestic terrorism office within the Counterterrorism Section of the National Security Division;

3. An explanation as to why you decided to establish a new domestic terrorism office within the Counterterrorism Section of the National Security Division, in contravention of prior advice of career Department of Justice officials;

4. An explanation as to whether you or your staff consulted with the Department's career lawyers in the Counterterrorism Section or elsewhere in the Department prior to the establishment of this new office. If so, provide all recommendations and advice, both formal and informal, that was made to the National Security Division about the newly-formed office;

5. An explanation whether the resources and personnel of this new domestic terrorism office is being used or will be used to target concerned parents at local school board meetings;

6. Quantify the number of personnel assigned to the newly-formed domestic terrorism office within the Counterterrorism Section of the National Security Division; and

7. Quantify the number of active domestic terrorism investigations, including by type of case, for the period of January 1, 2021, to the present.

Please provide this information as soon as possible but no later than March 3, 2022. After you have provided this information in writing, we ask that the Department provide a staff-level

[6] U.S. Dep't of Homeland Security, National Terrorism Advisory System Bulletin (Feb. 7, 2022).

briefing on this topic. To the extent a complete response requires the provision of classified information, please provide this information under separate cover.

The House Committee on the Judiciary has jurisdiction pursuant to Rule X of the Rules of the House of Representatives to conduct oversight of matters concerning "subversive activities affecting the internal security of the United States" as well as "criminal law enforcement and criminalization."[7]

If you have any questions about this request, please ask your staff to contact Judiciary Committee staff at (202) 225-6906. Thank you for your prompt attention to this serious matter.

Sincerely,

Jim Jordan
Ranking Member

Mike Johnson
Ranking Member
Subcommittee on the Constitution, Civil Rights and Civil Liberties

Andy Biggs
Ranking Member
Subcommittee on Crime, Terrorism, and Homeland Security

cc: The Honorable Jerrold L. Nadler, Chairman
The Honorable Steve Cohen, Chairman, Subcommittee on the Constitution, Civil Rights and Civil Liberties
The Honorable Sheila Jackson Lee, Chair, Subcommittee on Crime, Terrorism, and Homeland Security

[7] Rules of the House of Representatives, R. X, 117th Cong. (2021).

JERROLD NADLER, New York
CHAIRMAN

JIM JORDAN, Ohio
RANKING MEMBER

ONE HUNDRED SEVENTEENTH CONGRESS

Congress of the United States
House of Representatives

COMMITTEE ON THE JUDICIARY

2138 RAYBURN HOUSE OFFICE BUILDING

WASHINGTON, DC 20515-6216

(202) 225-3951
judiciary.house.gov

February 10, 2022

The Honorable Christopher A. Wray
Director
Federal Bureau of Investigation
935 Pennsylvania Avenue, N.W.
Washington, DC 20535

Dear Director Wray:

We received the Federal Bureau of Investigation's half-page response to our serious concerns about the FBI's use of counterterrorism resources—as evidenced by documents provided to us by a whistleblower—to target concerned parents at local school board meetings.[1] Your response declined to answer in detail any questions we posed or to provide any documents we sought. Your response regrettably highlights the FBI's pattern of refusing to accept accountability for its actions and explains why public trust in the FBI's senior leadership has eroded so significantly.

We know from publicly available information that the Biden Administration coordinated with a special interest group, the National School Boards Association, to develop a pretext for the Attorney General to direct federal law enforcement resources, including the FBI, to investigate concerned parents at school board meetings.[2] On October 20, 2021, the FBI operationalized the Attorney General's directive in an email sent on behalf of Counterterrorism Division Assistant Director Timothy Langan directing all FBI personnel to apply a new "threat tag" to all "investigations and assessments of threats specifically directed against school board administrators, board members, teachers, and staff."[3] Mr. Langan later testified to the House

---

[1] Letter from Jill C. Tyson, Assistant Director, Office of Congressional Affairs, Federal Bureau of Investigation, to Ranking Member Jim Jordan, U.S. House Committee on the Judiciary (Jan. 28, 2022); *see* Email from Carlton Peeples, Deputy Assistant Dir., Criminal Investigative Div., Fed. Bureau of Investigation, to FBI_SACS (Oct. 20, 2021).

[2] Memorandum from Atty Gen. Merrick Garland, U.S. Dep't of Justice, Partnership Among Federal, State, Local, Tribal, And Territorial Law Enforcement to Address Threats Against School Administrators, Board Members, Teachers, and Staff (Oct. 4, 2021).

[3] Email from Carlton Peeples, Deputy Assistant Dir., Criminal Investigative Div., Fed. Bureau of Investigation, to FBI_SACS (Oct. 20, 2021).

Intelligence Committee that the FBI also discussed the Attorney General's directive with the Justice Department prior to its issuance.[4]

Although the FBI claims that it "is fully committed to preserving and protecting" Americans' constitutional rights,[5] these assurances ring hollow in light of how the FBI spied on protected First Amendment activities during the campaign of President Trump and how the FBI continues to misuse its warrantless surveillance authorities under the Foreign Intelligence Surveillance Act. In light of these abuses and the FBI's unfortunate history of civil liberty violations, we cannot trust the FBI's assurances at face value. Committee Republicans are committed to fully examining the FBI's use of counterterrorism resources in relation to school board meetings. Your half-page response does not alleviate our concerns, and therefore we reiterate our requests once more. Please provide the following documents and information:

1. All documents and communications referring or relating to convening meeting(s) with U.S. Attorneys' Offices in accordance with the Attorney General's October 4, 2021, memorandum, the establishment of the Department's task force, or the FBI's role as a member of the task force;

2. All agendas, minutes, and notes created or relied upon by FBI employees referring or relating to meeting(s) in each judicial district in accordance with the Attorney General's October 4, 2021, memorandum or the FBI's role as a member of the task force;

3. Please explain whether you consider the Attorney General's October 4, 2021, memorandum to be lawful and whether you intend to direct FBI agents and employees to enforce the Attorney General's directives;

4. Please explain whether you have issued any internal guidance to FBI field offices or special agents in charge referring or relating to the Attorney General's October 4, 2021, memorandum;

5. Please explain the FBI's role in convening meetings as directed by the Attorney General's October 4, 2021, memorandum;

6. Please explain the FBI's role in the Department's task force, including what federal statutes the FBI intends to use in investigating concerned parents at school board meetings;

7. Please identify by name, title, and field office each FBI employee involved in the meeting(s) and task force referenced in the Attorney General's October 4, 2021, memorandum;

---

[4] *Open C3 Subcommittee Hearing on Countering Domestic Terrorism, Hearing Before the H. Permanent Select Comm. on Intelligence,* 117th Cong. (Nov. 3, 2021) (testimony of Mr. Timothy Langan Jr., Assistant Dir., Counterterrorism Division, Fed. Bureau of Investigation).

[5] Letter from Jill C. Tyson, Assistant Director, Office of Congressional Affairs, Federal Bureau of Investigation, to Ranking Member Jim Jordan, U.S. House Committee on the Judiciary (Jan. 28, 2022).

8. Please identify all federal, state, local, Tribal, and territorial organizations invited to or that have attended the meetings convened in accordance with the October 4, 2021, memorandum;

9. Please provide all recommendations, both formal and informal, and any meeting minutes produced at the meeting(s) in accordance with the Attorney General's October 4, 2021, memorandum;

10. Please provide all recommendations, both formal and informal, that the FBI has made to the Department's task force;

11. Provide the number of parents who have been tagged by FBI with the EDUOFFICIALS threat tag;

12. All documents and communications referring or relating to the EDUOFFICIALS threat tag;

13. All documents and communications referring or relating to investigations identified and labeled with the EDUOFFICIALS threat tag; and

14. All documents and communications referring or relating to FBI investigations of school board threats sent or received by the following individuals:

    a. Carlton L. Peeples, Deputy Assistant Director, Criminal Investigative Division;

    b. Jay Greenberg, Deputy Assistant Director, Criminal Investigative Division;

    c. Calvin A. Shivers, Assistant Director, Criminal Division;

    d. Brian M. Cohen, Criminal Division;

    e. Timothy R. Langan Jr., Assistant Director, Counterterrorism Division; and

    f. Kevin Vorndran, Deputy Assistant Director, Counterterrorism Division.

In addition, we reiterate the request for interviews with Timothy Langan and Kevin Vorndran, which FBI staff initially offered to arrange in email correspondence with Committee staff, but has since ignored. We ask that you arrange for these meetings to occur promptly.

Thank you for your attention to this important matter.

Sincerely,

Jim Jordan
Ranking Member

Steve Chabot
Member of Congress

Louie Gohmert
Member of Congress

Darrell Issa
Ranking Member
Subcommittee on Courts, Intellectual Property, and the Internet

Matt Gaetz
Member of Congress

Mike Johnson
Ranking Member
Subcommittee on the Constitution, Civil Rights and Civil Liberties

Andy Biggs
Ranking Member
Subcommittee on Crime, Terrorism and Homeland Security

Tom McClintock
Ranking Member
Subcommittee on Immigration and Citizenship

W. Gregory Steube
Member of Congress

Tom Tiffany
Member of Congress

Thomas Massie
Member of Congress

Chip Roy
Member of Congress

Dan Bishop
Member of Congress

Michelle Fischbach
Member of Congress

Victoria Spartz
Member of Congress

Scott Fitzgerald
Member of Congress

Cliff Bentz
Member of Congress

Burgess Owens
Member of Congress

cc: The Honorable Jerrold L. Nadler
Chairman

JERROLD NADLER, New York
CHAIRMAN

JIM JORDAN, Ohio
RANKING MEMBER

ONE HUNDRED SEVENTEENTH CONGRESS

Congress of the United States
House of Representatives
COMMITTEE ON THE JUDICIARY

2138 RAYBURN HOUSE OFFICE BUILDING
WASHINGTON, DC 20515-6216
(202) 225-3951
judiciary.house.gov

January 27, 2022

The Honorable Christopher A. Wray
Director
Federal Bureau of Investigation
935 Pennsylvania Avenue, N.W.
Washington, DC 20535

Dear Director Wray:

We continue to conduct oversight of the Federal Bureau of Investigation's use of Foreign Intelligence Surveillance Act (FISA) authorities. On December 2, 2021, the Committee received both unclassified and classified briefings from FBI officials about its FISA authorities.[1] The FBI subsequently provided additional information about section 702 of FISA via a letter dated December 23, 2021.[2] We write to follow up on a number of matters raised during the December 2 briefings and the December 23 letter.[3]

Section 702 authorizes the Attorney General and the Director of National Intelligence, subject to limitations, to jointly authorize warrantless surveillance of non-U.S. persons reasonably believed to be located outside the United States.[4] In November 2020, the Foreign Intelligence Surveillance Court (FISC) issued a memorandum opinion and order finding that the FBI had committed "apparent widespread violations" of privacy rules in conducting surveillance under section 702 of FISA.[5]

In addition to those documented concerns raised by the FISC, the DOJ's Office of Inspector General (OIG) has issued troubling reports over the last several years suggesting a

---

[1] Briefing of H. Comm. on the Judic. (Dec. 2, 2021).
[2] Letter from Jill C. Tyson, Assistant Director, Federal Bureau of Investigation, to the Rep. Jim Jordan, Ranking Member, H. Comm. on the Judic. (Dec. 23, 2021) (on file with committee).
[3] During the December 2 unclassified briefing, we also raised several questions with respect to the FBI's use of federal counterterrorism resources to target concerned parents at school board meetings. The FBI officials at the briefing could not answer the questions at the time but promised to answer those questions promptly. As of today, almost two months after the briefing—and three months since my letters to you on this topic—the FBI still has ignored fundamental questions and refused to produce any documents about its use of counterterrorism resources at school board meetings.
[4] 50 U.S.C § 1881(a)-(b).
[5] Memorandum Opinion and Order, *Document re Section 702 Certification* (FISA Ct. Nov. 18, 2020); Ellen Nakashima, *Federal court approved FBI's continued use of warrantless surveillance power despite repeated violations of privacy rules*, WASH. POST (Apr. 26, 2021).

pattern of abuses and deficiencies in the FBI's internal FISA processes.[6] Most recently, in September 2021, the OIG issued a detailed report—confirming its March 2020 initial findings—of widespread non-compliance with Woods Procedures, which are an internal FBI process to minimize factual inaccuracies in FISA applications by requiring the FBI to maintain supporting documentation for each factual assertion in the application.[7] The September 2021 report documented over 400 instances of non-compliance with the Woods Procedures in connection with 29 FISA applications.[8] The OIG also found that out of over 7,000 FISA applications approved between January 2015 and March 2020, there were 183 FISA applications for which the Woods File was missing in whole or in part.[9] This lack of documentation suggests, at best, the FBI maintains sloppy oversight of its use of warrantless spying authorities. At worst, it suggests the FBI holds a cavalier disregard for the fundamental protections enshrined in the Bill of Rights.

It is imperative that Congress is fully informed about the FBI's steps to improve its respect for the constitutional and statutory parameters of FISA—including section 702, which will be up for reauthorization in 2023. Therefore, to assist the Committee's oversight of the FBI's use of FISA and its related provisions, we ask that you please provide the following documents and information:

1. Quantify the number of FBI employees who have access to section 702 FISA-acquired data;

2. Identify the frequency of batch queries of FISA-acquired data for 99 or fewer queries, and explain why users must only obtain attorney approval before conducting a batch search of 100 or more queries;

3. Explain the processes developed by the FBI's new Office of Internal Auditing relating to FISA, including section 702 compliance measures;

4. Explain whether the FBI has located all of the missing Woods Files identified in the OIG's September 2021 report, and provide the reason(s) why the FBI cannot locate all missing Woods Files;

5. Provide an update on the FBI's implementation of the five recommendations from the OIG's September 2021 report that the FBI has not yet implemented; and

---

[6] Dep't of Justice Off. of Inspector Gen., Review of Four FISA Applications and Other Aspects of the FBI's Crossfire Hurricane Investigation (Dec. 2019); Dep't of Justice Off. of Inspector Gen., Management Advisory Memorandum for Director of the Federal Bureau of Investigation Regarding the Execution of Woods Procedures for Applications Filed with the Foreign Intelligence Surveillance Court Relating to U.S. Persons (Mar. 2020); Dep't of Justice Off. of Inspector Gen., *Audit of the Federal Bureau of Investigation's Execution of Its Woods Procedures for the Applications Filed with the Foreign Intelligence Surveillance Court Relating to U.S. Persons* (Sept. 2021).
[7] Dep't of Justice Off. of Inspector Gen., *Audit of the Federal Bureau of Investigation's Execution of Its Woods Procedures for the Applications Filed with the Foreign Intelligence Surveillance Court Relating to U.S. Persons* (Sept. 2021).
[8] *Id.* at 7, 19.
[9] *Id.* at ii, 28.

6. Produce all guidance documents or training materials issued to FBI personnel with access to FISA-acquired data.

Please provide this information as soon as possible, but no later than 5:00 p.m. on February 10, 2022. In addition, we ask that your staff provide a staff-level in-person review of the FBI's FISA processes, which the FBI offered during its December 2, 2021, briefing.

If you have any questions about this request, please ask your staff to contact Committee staff at (202) 225-6909. Thank you for your prompt attention to this important matter.

Sincerely,

Jim Jordan
Ranking Member

Mike Johnson
Ranking Member
Subcommittee on the Constitution, Civil Rights, and Civil Liberties

cc: The Honorable Jerrold Nadler, Chairman

The Honorable Steve Cohen, Chairman, Subcommittee on the Constitution, Civil Rights, and Civil Liberties

JERROLD NADLER, New York
CHAIRMAN

JIM JORDAN, Ohio
RANKING MEMBER

ONE HUNDRED SEVENTEENTH CONGRESS

Congress of the United States

House of Representatives

COMMITTEE ON THE JUDICIARY

2138 Rayburn House Office Building

Washington, DC 20515-6216

(202) 225-3951
judiciary.house.gov

December 2, 2021

The Honorable Jerrold L. Nadler
Chairman
Committee on the Judiciary
U.S. House of Representatives
Washington, DC 20515

Dear Chairman Nadler:

We are investigating the troubling attempts by the Department of Justice and the White House to use the heavy hand of federal law enforcement—including federal counterterrorism tools—to target concerned parents at local school board meetings and chill their protected First Amendment activity. Since October, we have sent several letters to the Biden Administration and the National School Boards Association (NSBA) requesting documents and information necessary for our investigation.[1] To date, we have received no responsive material. Therefore, pursuant to Committee rules, we ask that you notice consideration of subpoenas for these documents at the next business meeting.

The information in the public realm and already available to the Committee shows how the Biden Administration colluded with a special interest group to orchestrate a letter urging for federal law enforcement intervention against a set of citizens who opposed the far-left policies favored by the Biden Administration. That letter served as the basis for the Attorney General to weaponize federal law enforcement and counterterrorism tools against those same citizens for exercising their right to direct the upbringing and education of their children.[2]

[1] Letter from Rep. Jim Jordan et al., Ranking Member, H. Comm. on the Judiciary, to Merrick B. Garland, Att'y Gen., Dep't of Justice (Oct. 25, 2021); Letter from Rep. Jim Jordan et al., Ranking Member, H. Comm. on the Judiciary, to Dr. Viola M. Garcia et al, President, Nat'l School Boards Assoc. (Oct. 27, 2021); Letter from Rep. Jim Jordan et al., Ranking Member, H. Comm. on the Judiciary, to Mark Lesko, Acting Ass't Att'y Gen., Nat'l Sec. Division, Dep't of Justice (Nov. 2, 2021); Letter from Rep. Jim Jordan et al., Ranking Member, H. Comm. on the Judiciary, to Christopher A. Wray, Director, Fed. Bureau of Investigation (Nov. 3, 2021); Letter from Rep. Jim Jordan, Ranking Member, H. Comm. on the Judiciary, to Dr. Viola M. Garcia, President, Nat'l School Boards Assoc. (Nov. 12, 2021); Letter from Rep. Jim Jordan, Ranking Member, H. Comm. on the Judiciary, to Chip Slaven, Interim Executive Director and CEO, Nat'l School Boards Assoc. (Nov. 12, 2021); Letter from Rep. Jim Jordan, Ranking Member, H. Comm. on the Judiciary, to Merrick B. Garland, Att'y Gen., Dep't of Justice (Nov. 16, 2021); Letter from Rep. Jim Jordan, Ranking Member, H. Comm. on the Judiciary, & Virginia Foxx, Ranking Member, H. Comm. on Education & Labor, to Miguel A. Cardona, EdD, Secretary, Dep't of Ed. (Nov. 16, 2021); Letter from Rep. Jim Jordan, Ranking Member, H. Comm. on the Judiciary, to Christopher A. Wray, Director, Fed. Bureau of Investigation (Nov. 18, 2021).

[2] *Troxel v. Granville,* 530 U.S. 57, 65 (2000) (citing *Meyer v. Nebraska,* 262 U.S. 390, 399 (1923)).

On September 29, 2021, the NSBA sent a letter to President Joe Biden requesting help from the federal government with concerned parents voicing their opinions at school board meetings.[3] With minimal evidence, the NSBA letter asserted that "malice, violence, and threats" made at school board meetings could be "the equivalent of a form of domestic terrorism or hate crime."[4] The NSBA even cited the Patriot Act, the anti-terrorism law passed in the wake of the September 11th attacks, as a potential vehicle to pursue parents.[5]

Contemporaneous emails obtained and released by a grassroots group called Parents Defending Education reveal that the NSBA coordinated its letter in advance with the Biden Administration. In one email dated September 29—the same date as the NSBA letter—the NSBA Interim Executive Director & CEO Chip Slaven wrote:

> [I]n talks over the last several weeks with White House staff, they requested additional information on some of the specific threats, so the letter also details many of the incidents that have been occurring.[6]

Similarly, on October 2, the NSBA's President, Dr. Viola Garcia, wrote that the NSBA had "been engaged with the White House and Department of Education . . . for several weeks now."[7] On October 13, less than a month after the NSBA letter to President Biden, the Biden Administration announced that it had appointed Dr. Garcia to be one of five members of a federal education advisory board.[8]

On October 4, 2021, a mere five days after the NSBA sent its letter to President Biden, Attorney General Merrick Garland issued a memorandum that directed the Federal Bureau of Investigation and U.S. Attorneys' Offices to address the "disturbing spike in harassment, intimidation, and threats of violence" at school board meetings.[9] In an accompanying press release, the Justice Department indicated it would "open dedicated lines of communication for threat reporting, assessment and response by law enforcement"—in other words, snitch lines for complaints about concerned parents.[10] The press release noted that the Department's National

---

[3] Letter from Dr. Viola M. Garcia, President, Nat'l School Board Assoc. & Mr. Chip Slaven, Chief Exec. Officer, Nat'l School Board Assoc., to President Joseph R. Biden, White House (Sept. 29, 2021)
[4] *Id.*
[5] *Id.*
[6] Email from Chip Slaven (Sept. 29, 2021, 8:18 p.m.), *available at* https://defendinged.org/wp-content/uploads/2021/10/Email-Correspondence_NSBA-Letter-to-President-Biden_Redacted.pdf.
[7] Email from Viola Garcia (Oct. 2, 2021, 6:59 a.m.), *available at* https://defendinged.org/wp-content/uploads/2021/10/Email-Correspondence_NSBA-Letter-to-President-Biden_Redacted.pdf.
[8] Press Release, Dep't of Education, Five Board Members Appointed to Board Overseeing the Nation's Report Card (Oct. 13, 2021).
[9] Memorandum from Atty Gen. Merrick Garland, U.S. Dep't of Justice, Partnership Among Federal, State, Local, Tribal, And Territorial Law Enforcement to Address Threats Against School Administrators, Board Members, Teachers, and Staff (Oct. 4, 2021).
[10] Press Release, U.S. Dep't of Justice, Justice Department Addresses Violent Threats Against School Officials and Teachers (Oct. 4, 2021).

Security Division, which is responsible for prosecuting terrorism cases, would be part of a task force "to determine how federal enforcement tools can be used to prosecute these crimes."[11]

On October 20, 2021, the Deputy Assistant Director of the FBI's Criminal Investigative Division sent an email to an "FBI_SACS" listserv "on behalf of" the FBI's Assistant Director for the Counterterrorism Division, Timothy Langan, and the Assistant Director for the Criminal Division, Calvin Shivers.[12] The email referenced the Attorney General's October 4 memorandum and notified FBI personnel about a new "threat tag" created by the Counterterrorism and Criminal Divisions.[13] The email directed FBI personnel to apply this new threat tag to all "investigations and assessments of threats" relating to school boards.[14]

The following day, October 21, 2021, Attorney General Garland testified before our Committee.[15] During his testimony, Attorney General Garland stated that the Department and its components were not using counterterrorism statutes and resources to target concerned parents at school board meetings.[16] Specifically, he testified that he could not "imagine any circumstance in which the Patriot Act would be used in the circumstances of parents complaining about their children, nor . . . a circumstance where they would be labeled as domestic terrorists."[17] He also testified: "I do not think that parents getting angry at school boards for whatever reason constitute domestic terrorism. It's not even a close question."[18] The Attorney General also acknowledged that the NSBA letter was the basis his memorandum.[19]

On October 22, 2021, following Attorney General Garland's testimony to our Committee, the NSBA effectively withdrew its letter to the President, writing: "On behalf of NSBA, <u>we regret and apologize for the letter</u>."[20] (emphasis in original). Attorney General Garland, however, has stubbornly refused to rescind his memorandum, and his directive to use the heavy hand of federal law enforcement and federal counterterrorism tools against parents remains in effect.

This information is scandalous and we have good reason to believe that the Biden Administration and the NSBA possess additional material that is necessary and important for our investigation. To date, we have requested documents and information from the Justice Department and its components, the Education Department, the FBI, and the NSBA. None of these entities have cooperated with our requests or have engaged with us in any constructive

---

[11] *Id.*
[12] Email from Carlton Peeples, Deputy Assistant Dir., Criminal Investigative Div., Fed. Bureau of Investigation, to FBI_SACS (Oct. 20, 2021).
[13] *Id.*
[14] *Id.*
[15] *Oversight of the United States Department of Justice: Hearing Before the H. comm. on the Judiciary,* 117th Cong. at 68 (2021) (testimony from Hon. Merrick Garland, Atty Gen., U.S. Dep't of Justice).
[16] *Id.*
[17] *Id.*
[18] *Id.*
[19] *Id.*
[20] Memorandum from NSBA Board of Directors, Message to NSBA Members (Oct. 22, 2021).

manner toward fulfilling our requests. We have also repeatedly asked that you convene hearings on the Biden Administration's targeting of parents,[21] but you have failed to act.

Last Congress, when you aggressively pursued politicized and debunked allegations against President Trump, you promised that the Committee would "not rest" until it obtained the material it sought.[22] We ask that you remain consistent in applying this standard. Accordingly, consistent with Committee Rule IV, we request that you notice Committee consideration at our next business meeting of subpoenas to the Biden Administration and the NSBA for the documents we have requested and they have failed to produce. For your convenience, draft schedules of documents to be subpoenaed are attached to this letter.

Thank you for your attention to this important matter.

Sincerely,

Jim Jordan
Ranking Member

Attachment

---

[21] *See, e.g.*, Letter from Rep. Jim Jordan et al., Ranking Member, H. Comm. on the Judiciary, to Jerrold L. Nadler, Chairman, H. Comm. on the Judiciary (Oct. 28, 2021).

[22] Andre Desiderio & Kyle Cheney, *House Judiciary approves subpoenas for 12 key witnesses, including Jared Kushner,* POLITICO (Jul. 11, 2019).

Attachment
Draft Schedules of Documents to be Subpoenaed

To Dr. Viola Garcia, President, National School Boards Association

1. All documents and communications for the period January 20, 2021, to the present referring or relating to the NSBA's September 29, 2021 letter to President Biden;

2. All documents and communications for the period January 20, 2021, to the present referring or relating to the NSBA's October 22, 2021 memorandum;

3. All documents and communications for the period January 20, 2021, to the present between or among Executive Office of the President employees or staff and any NSBA officer, Board member, delegate, or staff referring or relating to the September 29, 2021 letter or October 22, 2021 memorandum;

4. All documents and communications for the period January 20, 2021, to the present between or among Department of Justice officials or employees, including those at the FBI, and any of NSBA officer, Board members, delegate, or staff referring or relating to the September 29, 2021 letter or October 22, 2021 memorandum;

5. All documents and communications for the period January 20, 2021, to the present referring or relating to the Biden Administration's selection of Dr. Viola Garcia to the National Assessment Governing Board; and

6. Any guidance issued by the NSBA regarding parental engagement at school board meetings.

To Merrick B. Garland, Attorney General, Department of Justice

1. All documents and communications referring or relating to the establishment of the Department's task force and the National Security Division's role as a member of the task force;

2. All documents and communications between employees of the Department of Justice and U.S. intelligence agencies referring or relating to alleged threats posed by concerned parents at local school board meetings, the NSBA's letter dated September 29, 2021, or the Attorney General's memo dated October 4, 2021;

3. All agendas, minutes, and notes created by or relied upon by National Security Division employees referring or relating to the Department's task force;

4. All documents and communications referring or relating to convening meeting(s) in the respective judicial districts in accordance with the Attorney General's October 4, 2021 memorandum; and

5. All agendas, minutes, and notes created or relied upon by U.S. Attorney's Office employees referring or relating to meeting(s) in the respective judicial district in accordance with the Attorney General's October 4, 2021 memorandum.

To Christopher Wray, Director, Federal Bureau of Investigation

1. All documents and communications referring or relating to convening meeting(s) with U.S. Attorneys' Offices in accordance with the Attorney General's October 4, 2021 memorandum, the establishment of the Department's task force, or the FBI's role as a member of the task force;

2. All agendas, minutes, and notes created or relied upon by FBI employees referring or relating to meeting(s) in each judicial district in accordance with the Attorney General's October 4, 2021 memorandum or the FBI's role as a member of the task force;

3. All documents and communications referring or relating to the EDUOFFICIALS threat tag;

4. All documents and communications referring or relating to investigations identified and labeled with the EDUOFFICIALS threat tag; and

5. All documents and communications referring or relating to FBI investigations of school board threats sent or received by the following individuals:

    a. Carlton L. Peeples, Deputy Assistant Director, Criminal Investigative Division;

    b. Jay Greenberg, Deputy Assistant Director, Criminal Investigative Division;

    c. Calvin A. Shivers, Assistant Director, Criminal Division;

    d. Brian M. Cohen, Criminal Division;

    e. Timothy R. Langan Jr., Assistant Director, Counterterrorism Division; and

    f. Kevin Vorndran, Deputy Assistant Director, Counterterrorism Division.

To Miguel A. Cardona, Secretary, Department of Education

1. All documents and communications for the period January 20, 2021, to the present referring or relating to the NSBA;

2. All documents and communications for the period January 20, 2021, to the present between or among Department of Education employees or staff and any NSBA officer,

Board member, delegate, or staff referring or relating to the September 29, 2021 letter to President Biden or the October 4, 2021, memorandum from Attorney General Garland;

3. All documents and communications for the period January 20, 2021, to the present between or among Department of Education employees or staff and Executive Office of the President employees or staff referring or relating to the September 29, 2021 letter to President Biden or the October 4, 2021, memorandum from Attorney General Garland;

4. All documents and communications for the period January 20, 2021, to the present between or among Department of Education employees or staff and Department of Justice employees or staff referring or relating to the September 29, 2021 letter to President Biden or the October 4, 2021, memorandum from Attorney General Garland;

5. All documents and communications for the period January 20, 2021, to the present regarding Viola Garcia's appointment to the National Assessment Governing Board; and

6. All documents and communications for the period January 20, 2021, to the present between or among Department of Education employees or staff and Executive Office of the President employees or staff regarding Viola Garcia's appointment to the National Assessment Governing Board.

Congress of the United States
House of Representatives
Washington, DC 20515

November 24, 2021

Mr. Timothy Langan
Assistant Director
Counterterrorism Division
Federal Bureau of Investigation
Washington, DC 20535

Dear Assistant Director Langan:

We write to follow up on the November 3, 2021 exchange you had with Congresswoman Elise Stefanik during the House Permanent Select Committee on Intelligence open hearing on domestic terrorism.

As you know, Members of Congress and the public have expressed strong concern about the October 4, 2021, memo issued by the Attorney General directing the Federal Bureau of Investigation (FBI) and U.S. Attorneys across the country to examine threats of violence against school officials. We remain concerned about the way this directive was created and the chilling effect it is having on free speech and parental rights.

During the hearing, Congresswoman Stefanik asked you if "the FBI held any of [the] meetings directed by Attorney General Garland," and you responded, "We will get you that number."[1] Additionally, she requested you provide Congress with "the emails relating to the issuing of the Garland memo, as well as any planning for messaging," and you responded, "Whatever I can provide you legally, I will."[2] During the hearing, you also agreed to inform the Committee as to which FBI field personnel participated in such meetings and the analytical resources utilized.[3]

We appreciate your willingness to share documentation, emails, and additional background information with Congress on this important matter. Consistent with your testimony, we ask that you provide the following:

---

[1] Countering Domestic Terrorism, Subcommittee on Counterterrorism, Counterintelligence and Counterproliferation of the House Permanent Select Committee on Intelligence, 117th Cong. 1st Session, November 3, 2021.
[2] *Id.*
[3] *Id.*

1. The date and location of each meeting held pursuant to the Attorney General's memo.
2. An overview of FBI field office programs represented by FBI participants in each meeting, to include whether FBI personnel assigned to Joint Terrorism Task Forces (JTTFs) participated.
3. The number of FBI Intelligence Analysts and other analytic resources assigned to activities associated with or following up on the Attorney General's memo; and
4. All documents and communications, including but not limited to your emails and emails of other FBI employees, referring, or related to the issuance of the Attorney General's memo, as well as any planned messaging in response to the memo.

Thank you for your prompt attention to this request. Please provide this information as soon as possible, but no later than December 7, 2021.

Sincerely,

ELISE STEFANIK Member of Congress	DEVIN NUNES Ranking Member Select Committee on Intelligence
JIM JORDAN Ranking Member Committee on the Judiciary	JAMES COMER Ranking Member Committee on Oversight and Reform

JERROLD NADLER, New York
CHAIRMAN

JIM JORDAN, Ohio
RANKING MEMBER

ONE HUNDRED SEVENTEENTH CONGRESS

Congress of the United States

House of Representatives

COMMITTEE ON THE JUDICIARY

2138 RAYBURN HOUSE OFFICE BUILDING

WASHINGTON, DC 20515-6216

(202) 225-3951
judiciary.house.gov

November 18, 2021

The Honorable Christopher A. Wray
Director
Federal Bureau of Investigation
935 Pennsylvania Avenue, N.W.
Washington, DC 20535

Dear Director Wray:

We are investigating the troubling attempts by the Department of Justice and the White House to use the heavy hand of federal law enforcement to target concerned parents at local school board meetings and chill their protected First Amendment activity. On November 3, 2021, Committee Republicans wrote to you requesting documents and information relating to the Federal Bureau of Investigation's role in investigating and prosecuting concerned parents.[1] You have not responded to our request. Since then, we have received a protected whistleblower disclosure showing the FBI used counterterrorism resources to compile and categorize threat assessments related to parents. We therefore write again to reiterate and expand our request.

On October 20, 2021, the Deputy Assistant Director of the FBI's Criminal Investigative Division sent an email to an "FBI_SACS" listserv "on behalf of" the FBI's Assistant Director for the Counterterrorism Division, Timothy Langan and the Assistant Director for the Criminal Division, Calvin Shivers.[2] The email, which is enclosed, referenced the Attorney General's October 4 directive to the FBI to address school board threats and notified FBI personnel about a new "threat tag" created by the Counterterrorism and Criminal Divisions.[3] The email directed FBI personnel to apply this new threat tag to all "investigations and assessments of threats specifically directed against school board administrators, board members, teachers, and staff."[4] The email articulated the purpose as "scop[ing] this threat on a national level and provid[ing] an opportunity for comprehensive analysis of the threat picture for effective engagement with law enforcement partners at all levels."[5]

---

[1] Letter from House Judiciary Committee Republicans to Christopher A. Wray, Director, Fed. Bureau of Investigation (Nov. 3, 2021).
[2] Email from Carlton Peeples, Deputy Assistant Dir., Criminal Investigative Div., Fed. Bureau of Investigation, to FBI_SACS (Oct. 20, 2021).
[3] *Id.*
[4] *Id.*
[5] *Id.*

This disclosure provides specific evidence that federal law enforcement operationalized counterterrorism tools at the behest of a left-wing special interest group against concerned parents. News reports indicate that the National School Boards Association (NSBA) coordinated with the White House prior to sending a letter dated September 29 to President Biden labeling parents as domestic terrorists and urging the Department to use federal tools—including the Patriot Act—to target parents.[6] Just five days later, on October 4, Attorney General Garland issued a memorandum directing the FBI and other Departmental components to address a purported "disturbing spike in harassment, intimidation, and threats of violence" at school board meetings.[7] As the whistleblower's disclosure shows, the FBI's Counterterrorism Division quickly effectuated the Attorney General's directive.[8]

The NSBA Board of Directors has apologized for its letter to President Biden, writing: "On behalf of NSBA, <u>we regret and apologize for the letter</u>."[9] (emphasis in original). Attorney General Garland, however, has refused to rescind his directive, despite testifying that the NSBA letter was the basis for his October 4 memorandum.[10] His directive to the FBI therefore remains in effect.

The whistleblower disclosure only amplifies our need to investigate how the Biden Administration is using federal law enforcement resources, including counterterrorism tools, to target concerned parents at school board meetings. In addition, during testimony before the House Permanent Select Committee on Intelligence on November 3, Assistant Director Langan acknowledged that the Department and FBI conducted a "discussion" the "weekend before" the issuance of the memorandum—presumably the weekend of October 2 and 3—concerning the letter and that the "Department was looking to put out some messaging."[11] The whistleblower disclosure and Assistant Director Langan's testimony confirm that the FBI possesses documents responsive to our initial request. We therefore reiterate the requests made in our November 3 letter to you and ask that you produce this material immediately. In addition, in light of the whistleblower disclosure, we request that you provide the following additional documents and information:

1. Provide the number of parents who have been tagged by FBI with the EDUOFFICIALS threat tag;

---

[6] Callie Patteson, *WH 'actively engaged' with NSBA before 'domestic terror' letter: memo,* N.Y. POST (Nov. 11, 2021).
[7] Memorandum from Atty Gen. Merrick Garland, U.S. Dep't of Justice, Partnership Among Federal, State, Local, Tribal, And Territorial Law Enforcement to Address Threats Against School Administrators, Board Members, Teachers, and Staff (Oct. 4, 2021).
[8] Email from Carlton Peeples, Deputy Assistant Dir., Criminal Investigative Div., Fed. Bureau of Investigation, to FBI_SACS (Oct. 20, 2021).
[9] Memorandum from NSBA Board of Directors, Message to NSBA Members (Oct. 22, 2021).
[10] *Oversight of the United States Department of Justice: Hearing Before the H. Comm. on the Judiciary,* 117th Cong. (2021) (testimony from Hon. Merrick Garland, Atty Gen., U.S. Dep't of Justice).
[11] *Open C3 Subcommittee Hearing on Countering Domestic Terrorism, Hearing Before the H. Permanent Select Comm. on Intelligence,* 117th Cong. (Nov. 3, 2021) (testimony of Mr. Timothy Langan Jr., Assistant Dir., Counterterrorism Division, Fed. Bureau of Investigation).

2. All documents and communications referring or relating to the EDUOFFICIALS threat tag;

3. All documents and communications referring or relating to investigations identified and labeled with the EDUOFFICIALS threat tag; and

4. All documents and communications referring or relating to FBI investigations of school board threats sent or received by the following individuals:

    a. Carlton L. Peeples, Deputy Assistant Director, Criminal Investigative Division;

    b. Jay Greenberg, Deputy Assistant Director, Criminal Investigative Division;

    c. Calvin A. Shivers, Assistant Director, Criminal Division;

    d. Brian M. Cohen, Criminal Division;

    e. Timothy R. Langan Jr., Assistant Director, Counterterrorism Division; and

    f. Kevin Vorndran, Deputy Assistant Director, Counterterrorism Division.

Please provide this material as soon as possible but no later than 5:00 p.m. on December 2, 2021. In addition, we remind you that whistleblower disclosures to Congress are protected by law and that we will not tolerate any effort to retaliate against whistleblowers for their disclosures.

Thank you for your attention to this important matter.

Sincerely,

Jim Jordan
Ranking Member

cc: The Honorable Jerrold L. Nadler
Chairman

Enclosure

From: Peeples, Carlton L. (INSD) (FBI) < >
Sent: Wednesday, October 20, 2021 10:02 AM
To: FBI_SACS < >
Cc: Greenberg, Jay (CID) (FBI) < >; Shivers, Calvin A. (CID) (FBI) < >; Cohen, Brian M. (CID) (FBI) < >; Langan, Timothy R. Jr. (CTD) (FBI) < >; Vorndran, Kevin (CTD) (FBI) < >
Subject: Guidance: Threat to violence against School Administrators --- UNCLASSIFIED

Classification: UNCLASSIFIED
===

A JOINT MESSAGE FROM CRIMINAL INVESTIGATIVE DIVISION & COUNTERTERRORISM DIVISION

FEDERAL BUREAU OF INVESTIGATION

All,

On October 04, 2021, the Attorney General forwarded a memorandum addressing a spike in harassment, intimidation, and threats of violence against school administrators, board members, teachers, and staff. The memorandum directed each United States Attorney, in coordination with the FBI, to convene meetings with federal, state, local, Tribal, and territorial leaders in each federal judicial district within 30 days of the issuance of the memorandum.

We share an obligation to ensure all individuals are able to do their jobs without threats of violence or fear for their safety. This can only be accomplished with effective coordination internally between relevant Divisions and through effective coordination and engagement with our law enforcement partners and United States Attorney Offices.

As a result, the Counterterrorism and Criminal Divisions created a threat tag, EDUOFFICIALS, to track instances of related threats. We ask that your offices apply the threat tag to investigations and assessments of threats specifically directed against school board administrators, board members, teachers, and staff. The purpose of the threat tag is to help scope this threat on a national level and provide an opportunity for comprehensive analysis of the threat picture for effective engagement with law enforcement partners at all levels. When evaluating potential threats, we ask that you attempt to identify the following:

a) Is there a federal nexus?

b) Are there potential federal violations that can be investigated and charged?

c) What's the motivation behind the criminal activity?

We appreciate your attention to this matter and welcome any engagement to identify trends, strategies, and best practices to accomplish discouraging, identifying, and prosecuting those who use violence, threats of violence, and other forms of intimidation and harassment pertaining to this threat.

On behalf of,

AD Timothy R. Langan Jr.
Counterterrorism Division

AD Calvin A. Shivers
Criminal Division

Respectfully,
Carlton Peeples
A/Deputy Assistant Director
Criminal Investigative Division

==
Classification: UNCLASSIFIED

==
Classification: UNCLASSIFIED

==
Classification: UNCLASSIFIED

==
Classification: UNCLASSIFIED

Congress of the United States
Washington, DC 20515

November 18, 2021

The Honorable Merrick B. Garland
Attorney General
U.S. Department of Justice
950 Pennsylvania Avenue, N.W.
Washington, DC 20530

Dear Attorney General Garland:

We write to request information about the Federal Bureau of Investigation's (FBI) early-morning raid of a residence belonging to James O'Keefe, the founder of Project Veritas, a non-profit media organization.[1] The FBI also reportedly conducted similar raids on residences of other former Project Veritas journalists and employees.[2] According to reports, the FBI conducted these raids in connection with an investigation relating to a diary purportedly belonging to President Biden's daughter.[3] The FBI's actions raise questions about whether you are enforcing the prohibition you announced in July—and President Biden endorsed—against federal law enforcement seizing records from journalists.[4]

According to reports, during Project Veritas' news-gathering activities in late 2020, the organization obtained a diary purported to belong to President Biden's daughter.[5] Project Veritas could not determine the legitimacy of the diary and chose not to publish its contents.[6] Instead, the organization reportedly handed over the diary to law enforcement.[7] Then, on November 6, 2021, FBI agents reportedly executed a search of O'Keefe's residence in connection with an investigation relating to the diary.[8] Two days prior to the raid of O'Keefe's residence, the FBI reportedly also searched the homes of two former Project Veritas associates in connection with

---

[1] Michael S. Schmidt, et al., *F.B.I. Searches James O'Keefe's Home in Ashley Biden Diary Theft Inquiry*, N.Y. TIMES (Nov. 6, 2021).
[2] *Id.*
[3] *Id;* Amy B. Wang and Devlin Barrett, *FBI searches Project Veritas associates in probe over diary purportedly belonging to Biden's daughter*, WASH. POST (Nov. 5, 2021).
[4] Memorandum from Atty Gen. Merrick Garland, U.S. Dep't of Justice, Use of Compulsory Process to Obtain Information From, or Records of, Members of the News Media (July 19, 2021); Eric Tucker, *Justice Dept. says it'll no longer seize reporters' records*, AP NEWS (June 5, 2021); Alexandra Jaffe, *Biden won't allow Justice Dept. to seize reporters' records*, AP NEWS (May 21, 2021).
[5] James O'Keefe, *FBI and Southern District of New York Raid Project Veritas Journalists' Homes*, PROJECT VERITAS (Nov. 5, 2021).
[6] *Id.*
[7] *Id.*
[8] Michael S. Schmidt, et al., *F.B.I. Searches James O'Keefe's Home in Ashley Biden Diary Theft Inquiry*, N.Y. TIMES (Nov. 6, 2021).

an investigation relating to the diary.[9] According to O'Keefe, the Department of Justice requested that the Project Veritas journalists not disclose the existence of the warrant.[10] Yet, within an hour of the FBI's raid, the *New York Times* published a story about the search, even though the search warrant and the subject matter of the search warrant were apparently part of a grand jury investigation and should have been nonpublic.[11] The *Times* later published information from confidential and sensitive documents belonging to Project Veritas, including legal advice obtained relating to its news gathering activities.[12] On the same day, a federal judge in New York ordered the Department to stop extracting and reviewing the contents of Project Veritas materials that the FBI seized.[13] The court's order and the *Times*' publishing of nonpublic Project Veritas information raise questions about whether any Department employee leaked, or contributed to the leak of, any nonpublic information as part of this investigation.

The FBI's actions raise concerns about the enforcement of the policy you implemented just months ago concerning searching and seizing records from journalists and media organizations. On July 19, 2021, you issued a memorandum announcing a new policy broadly banning the Department's use of compulsory means for obtaining information from journalists.[14] Your policy extends to all subpoenas, warrants, court orders, and civil investigative demands, which would appear to include the search warrants executed against Project Veritas journalists.[15] President Biden has endorsed your prohibition, saying that it is "simply, simply wrong" to confiscate journalists' records and that he would not allow the Department to do so.[16] Similarly, House Judiciary Committee Chairman Jerrold Nadler said he was "genuinely encouraged" by your new policy and that he "look[s] forward to working with" you "to make certain that these changes are codified [in law] and remain the policy of the Department for years to come."[17]

The Department and the FBI must not be used for political purposes to target the Administration's political rivals. During your confirmation hearing to be Attorney General, you vowed not to weaponize the Department, promising the Department "will be under my protection for the purpose of preventing any kind of partisan or other improper motive in making any kind of investigation or prosecution. That's my vow. That's the only reason I'm willing to do this

---

[9] Amy B. Wang and Devlin Barrett, *FBI searches Project Veritas associates in probe over diary purportedly belonging to Biden's daughter*, WASH. POST (Nov. 5, 2021); Michael S. Schmidt and Adam Goldman, *Project Veritas Tells Judge It Was Assured Biden Diary Was Legally Obtained*, N.Y. TIMES (Nov. 12, 2021).
[10] James O'Keefe, *FBI and Southern District of New York Raid Project Veritas Journalists' Homes*, PROJECT VERITAS (Nov. 5, 2021).
[11] *Id.*
[12] Adam Goldman and Mark Mazzetti, *Project Veritas and the Line Between Journalism and Political Spying*, N.Y. TIMES (Nov. 11, 2021).
[13] Order, In re Search Warrant dated November 5, 2021, 21 MAG 10685 (S.D.N.Y. Nov. 11, 2021).
[14] Memorandum from Atty Gen. Merrick Garland, U.S. Dep't of Justice, Use of Compulsory Process to Obtain Information From, or Records of, Members of the News Media (July 19, 2021).
[15] *Id.* at 1.
[16] Eric Tucker, *Justice Dept. says it'll no longer seize reporters' records*, AP NEWS (June 5, 2021); Alexandra Jaffe, *Biden won't allow Justice Dept. to seize reporters' records*, AP NEWS (May 21, 2021).
[17] Press Release, H. Comm. on the Judiciary, *Chairman Nadler Statement on DOJ Policy Restricting Use of Compulsory Process to Obtain Journalists' Records*, (July 19, 2021).

job."[18] Unfortunately, as you have failed to live up to your promises on other important matters facing the Department—including by mobilizing federal law enforcement to silence concerned parents at school board meetings—we question whether the Department's actions in this matter are consistent with your commitment.

Accordingly, to assist our oversight of the Department, we respectfully request the following documents and information:

1. Explain when and how the FBI became aware of the diary purportedly belonging to President Biden's daughter and describe when and why it opened an investigation into the matter;

2. Provide copies of the search warrants, affidavits, and all other supporting documents related to the FBI's search of residences of James O'Keefe and other current or former journalists or employees of Project Veritas;

3. Explain the factual and legal predicate for the FBI to conduct raids at the homes of James O'Keefe and other current or former journalists or employees of Project Veritas;

4. Describe the process the Department followed when obtaining subpoenas for the FBI to obtain information from, or records of, James O'Keefe and other current or former journalists or employees of Project Veritas, including whether you and/or any other Department officials approved the decision to obtain such subpoenas;

5. Explain what steps, if any, the Department has taken or will take to investigate the leaking of Project Veritas' information to the *New York Times*; and

6. Explain whether any official or employee of the Executive Office of the President communicated with the Department and/or the FBI about investigating or searching the residences of James O'Keefe and other current or former employees of Project Veritas.

Please provide this information as soon as possible but no later than 5:00 p.m. on December 2, 2021. If you have any questions about this request, please contact House Judiciary Committee staff at (202) 225-6906, House Oversight Committee staff at (202) 225-5074, or Senate Permanent Subcommittee on Investigations staff at (202) 224-3721.

---

[18] Jeremy Herb, *Garland vows at confirmation hearing to keep politics out of DOJ while drawing bipartisan praise*, CNN (Feb. 22, 2021).

Thank you for your attention to this matter.

Sincerely,

Jim Jordan
Ranking Member
House Committee on the Judiciary

James Comer
Ranking Member
House Committee on
Oversight and Reform

Ron Johnson
Ranking Member
Senate Permanent Subcommittee on Investigations

cc: The Honorable Jerrold L. Nadler
Chairman
U.S. House Committee on the Judiciary

The Honorable Carolyn B. Maloney
Chairwoman
U.S. House Committee on Oversight and Reform

The Honorable Christopher Wray
Director
Federal Bureau of Investigation

The Honorable Michael E. Horowitz
Inspector General
U.S. Department of Justice

Congress of the United States

Washington, DC 20515

November 16, 2021

The Honorable Miguel A. Cardona, EdD
Secretary
U.S. Department of Education
400 Maryland Avenue, S.W.
Washington, DC 20202

Dear Secretary Cardona:

We are continuing to investigate the troubling attempts by the Biden Administration to use the heavy hand of federal law enforcement to target concerned parents at local school board meetings and chill their protected First Amendment activity. On October 1, 2021, you testified in a Senate hearing that parents should not be the "primary stakeholder" in their children's education.[1] At the time of your statement, the Biden Administration, including the Education Department, was colluding with the National School Boards Association (NSBA) to orchestrate federal law enforcement action against concerned parents.[2] Accordingly, we respectfully request your assistance with our investigation.

On September 29, 2021, the NSBA sent a letter to President Joe Biden requesting federal intervention to address concerned parents voicing their opinions at school board meetings.[3] The NSBA letter asserted that "malice, violence, and threats" against school officials "could be the equivalent of a form of domestic terrorism or hate crimes."[4] The letter cited a number of interactions at school board meetings, none of which rose to the level of domestic terrorism. In fact, the vast majority of incidents cited by the NSBA did not involve threats or violence.[5] Most notably, as an example of domestic terrorism, the NSBA cited an incident in which a father angrily confronted members at a school board meeting in Loudoun County, Virginia, about the heinous sexual assault of his daughter.[6]

---

[1] *School Reopening During COVID-19: Supporting Students, Educators, and Families: Hearing Before the S. Comm. on Health, Education, Labor, & Pensions*, 117th Cong. (2021) (testimony from Hon. Dr. Miguel Cardona); *see also* Tyler Stone, *Biden Education Sec. Cardona: Parents shouldn't be "primary stakeholder" in their kids' education*, POLITICO (Oct. 1, 2021).
[2] Letter from Viola M. Garcia, EdD, President, Nat'l School Board Assoc. & Mr. Chip Slaven, Esq., Chief Exec. Officer, Nat'l School Board Assoc., to President Joseph R. Biden, White House (Sept. 29, 2021); Email from Viola Garcia (Oct. 2, 2021, 6:59 AM), *available at* https://defendinged.org/wp-content/uploads/2021/10/Email-Correspondence_NSBA-Letter-to-President-Biden_Redacted.pdf.
[3] Letter from Garcia & Slaven, *supra* note 2.
[4] *Id.*
[5] *See* Caroline Downey, *Vast majority of incidents cited by school-board group to justify federal intervention didn't involve threats,* NAT'L REV. (Oct. 2, 2021).
[6] *Id.*; *see also* Jessica Chasmar, *Loudoun County father arrested at school board events says school tried to cover up daughter's bathroom assault*, FOX NEWS (Oct. 12, 2021).

On October 4, 2021, a mere five days after the NSBA sent its letter to President Biden, Attorney General Merrick Garland issued an unusual memorandum directing the Federal Bureau of Investigation (FBI) and U.S. Attorneys' Offices to address the "disturbing spike in harassment, intimidation, and threats of violence" at school board meetings.[7] In a press release publicizing the memorandum, the Justice Department indicated its directive would "open dedicated lines of communication for threat reporting, assessment and response by law enforcement"—in other words, a snitch line for complaints about concerned parents.[8] The press release noted that the Department's National Security Division, the Department component responsible for prosecuting terrorism cases, would be part of a task force "to determine how federal enforcement tools can be used to prosecute these crimes."[9]

Publicly available information shows that the Education Department interacted with the NSBA before the group urged President Biden to target concerned parents in local school board meetings. The NSBA's September 29 letter, signed by the group's President Viola M. Garcia and Interim Executive Director and CEO Chip Slaven, noted that the group had been in discussions with the Biden White House and the Education Department.[10] In addition, in an October 2 email to NSBA board members, released pursuant to open-records laws, NSBA President Garcia wrote that the NSBA had "been engaged with the White House and Department of Education . . . for several weeks now."[11] On October 13, shortly after the NSBA's letter and the Attorney General's memorandum, you appointed Dr. Garcia to the National Assessment Governing Board.[12]

On October 21, 2021, Attorney General Garland testified before our Committee. During his testimony, Attorney General Garland acknowledged that he relied upon the NSBA letter as the basis for issuing his memorandum.[13] He claimed, however, not to know whether the Justice Department had communicated with the NSBA about its letter to President Biden.[14]

On October 22, 2021, a day after the Attorney General's testimony, the NSBA Board of Directors, apparently recognizing the consequences of its ill-conceived letter and the resulting Justice Department action, issued a new memorandum to its members apologizing for the letter, stating: "On behalf of NSBA, <u>we regret and apologize for the letter</u>."[15] (emphasis in original). Despite this apology, the Attorney General has yet to rescind his memorandum.

---

[7] Memorandum from Atty Gen. Merrick Garland, U.S. Dep't of Justice, Partnership Among Federal, State, Local, Tribal, And Territorial Law Enforcement to Address Threats Against School Administrators, Board Members, Teachers, and Staff (Oct. 4, 2021).
[8] Press Release, U.S. Dep't of Justice, Justice Department Addresses Violent Threats Against School Officials and Teachers (Oct. 4, 2021).
[9] *Id.*
[10] Letter from Garcia & Slaven, *supra* note 2.
[11] Email from Viola Garcia, *supra* note 2.
[12] Press Release, U.S. Dep't of Education, Five Board Members Appointed to Board Overseeing the Nation's Report Card (Oct. 13, 2021).
[13] *Oversight of the United States Department of Justice: Hearing Before the H. comm. on the Judiciary,* 117th Cong. at 68 (2021) (testimony from Hon. Merrick Garland, Atty Gen., U.S. Dep't of Justice).
[14] *Id.* at 65.
[15] Memorandum from NSBA Board of Directors, Message to NSBA Members (Oct. 22, 2021).

Concerned parents voicing their strong opposition to controversial curricula at local schools are not domestic terrorists. Parents have an undisputed right to direct the upbringing and education of their children.[16] When parents cross the line to commit a violent act or issue a criminal threat,[17] state and local authorities are best-equipped to handle these violations of state law. We must not tolerate the Biden Administration's collusion with a special interest group to use the federal law enforcement apparatus to intimidate and silence parents. The Education Department's role in this ill-conceived effort to target concerned parents requires immediate congressional attention.

To assist our investigation, we request that you provide the following documents and information:

1. All documents and communications for the period January 20, 2021, to the present referring or relating to the NSBA;

2. All documents and communications for the period January 20, 2021, to the present between or among Department of Education employees or staff and any NSBA officer, Board member, delegate, or staff referring or relating to the September 29, 2021 letter to President Biden or the October 4, 2021, memorandum from Attorney General Garland;

3. All documents and communications for the period January 20, 2021, to the present between or among Department of Education employees or staff and Executive Office of the President employees or staff referring or relating to the September 29, 2021 letter to President Biden or the October 4, 2021, memorandum from Attorney General Garland;

4. All documents and communications for the period January 20, 2021, to the present between or among Department of Education employees or staff and Department of Justice employees or staff referring or relating to the September 29, 2021 letter to President Biden or the October 4, 2021, memorandum from Attorney General Garland;

5. All documents and communications for the period January 20, 2021, to the present regarding Viola Garcia's appointment to the National Assessment Governing Board; and

6. All documents and communications for the period January 20, 2021, to the present between or among Department of Education employees or staff and White House employees or staff regarding Viola Garcia's appointment to the National Assessment Governing Board.

Please provide this material as soon as possible but no later than 5:00 p.m. on November 30, 2021.

---

[16] *Troxel v. Granville,* 530 U.S. 57, 65 (2000) (citing *Meyer v. Nebraska,* 262 U.S. 390, 399 (1923)).
[17] *Merrick Garland's federal offense,* WALL ST. J. (Oct. 6, 2021).

If you have any questions about this request, please contact Judiciary Committee staff at (202) 225-6906, or Education and Labor Committee staff at (202) 225-6558. Thank you for your attention to this important matter.

Sincerely,

Jim Jordan
Ranking Member
Committee on the Judiciary

Virginia Foxx
Ranking Member
Committee on Education and Labor

cc: The Honorable Jerrold L. Nadler
Chairman, Committee on the Judiciary

The Honorable Bobby Scott
Chairman, Committee on Education and Labor

JERROLD NADLER, New York
CHAIRMAN

JIM JORDAN, Ohio
RANKING MEMBER

ONE HUNDRED SEVENTEENTH CONGRESS
Congress of the United States
House of Representatives
COMMITTEE ON THE JUDICIARY
2138 RAYBURN HOUSE OFFICE BUILDING
WASHINGTON, DC 20515-6216
(202) 225-3951
judiciary.house.gov

November 16, 2021

The Honorable Merrick B. Garland
Attorney General
U.S. Department of Justice
950 Pennsylvania Avenue, N.W.
Washington, DC 20530

Dear Attorney General Garland:

Last month, during your testimony before the Judiciary Committee, you testified that the Department of Justice and Federal Bureau of Investigation were not using federal counterterrorism tools to target concerned parents at local school board meetings.[1] We are now in receipt of a protected disclosure from a Department whistleblower showing that the FBI's Counterterrorism Division is compiling and categorizing threat assessments related to parents, including a document directing FBI personnel to use a specific "threat tag" to track potential investigations. This new information calls into question the accuracy and completeness of your sworn testimony.

On October 21, 2021, you testified that the Department and its components were not using counterterrorism statutes and resources to target concerned parents at school board meetings.[2] Specifically, you testified that you could not "imagine any circumstance in which the Patriot Act would be used in the circumstances of parents complaining about their children, nor . . . a circumstance where they would be labeled as domestic terrorists."[3] You also testified: "I do not think that parents getting angry at school boards for whatever reason constitute domestic terrorism. It's not even a close question."[4]

Later in the hearing, however, you were questioned about the Department's press release touting the inclusion of the National Security Division—the Departmental component responsible for enforcing federal terrorism laws, including the Patriot Act[5]—in a task force you

[1] *Oversight of the United States Department of Justice: Hearing Before the H. comm. on the Judiciary,* 117th Cong. (2021) (testimony from Hon. Merrick Garland, Atty Gen., U.S. Dep't of Justice) [hereinafter "AG Garland testimony"].
[2] *Id.*
[3] *Id.*
[4] *Id.*
[5] *National Security Division: About the Division*, U.S. Dep't of Justice (last updated Apr. 12, 2019), https://www.justice.gov/nsd/about-division.

created to "address the rising criminal conduct directed toward school personnel."[6] You appeared surprised to learn about the National Security Division's involvement in the task force, but you avoided a direct answer to the question and offered no clarification or explanation for the National Security Division's role in the task force.[7]

We have now received a disclosure from a Department whistleblower calling into question the accuracy and completeness of your testimony. The whistleblower provided an FBI email dated October 20—the day before your testimony—and sent "on behalf of" the FBI's Assistant Director for the Counterterrorism Division and the Assistant Director for the Criminal Division.[8] The email, which is enclosed, referenced your October 4 directive to the FBI to address school board threats and notified FBI personnel about a new "threat tag" created by the Counterterrorism and Criminal Divisions.[9] The email directed FBI personnel to apply this new threat tag to all "investigations and assessments of threats specifically directed against school board administrators, board members, teachers, and staff."[10] The email articulated the purpose as "scop[ing] this threat on a national level and provid[ing] an opportunity for comprehensive analysis of the threat picture for effective engagement with law enforcement partners at all levels."[11]

This disclosure provides specific evidence that federal law enforcement operationalized counterterrorism tools at the behest of a left-wing special interest group against concerned parents. We know from public reporting that the National School Boards Association coordinated with the White House prior to sending a letter dated September 29 to President Biden labeling parents as domestic terrorists and urging the Justice Department to use federal tools—including the Patriot Act—to target parents.[12] Just five days later, on October 4, you issued a memorandum directing the FBI and other Departmental components to address a purported "disturbing spike in harassment, intimidation, and threats of violence" at school board meetings.[13] As the whistleblower's disclosure shows, the FBI's Counterterrorism Division quickly effectuated your directive.[14] The FBI's actions were an entirely foreseeable—and perhaps intended—result of your October 4 memorandum.

The NSBA Board of Directors later apologized for its letter to President Biden, writing: "On behalf of NSBA, <u>we regret and apologize for the letter</u>."[15] (emphasis in original). You,

---

[6] Press Release, U.S. Dep't of Justice, Justice Department Addresses Violent Threats Against School Officials and Teachers (Oct. 4, 2021).
[7] AG Garland testimony, *supra* note 1.
[8] Email from Carlton Peeples to FBI_SACS (Oct. 20, 2021).
[9] *Id.*
[10] *Id.*
[11] *Id.*
[12] Callie Patteson, *WH 'actively engaged' with NSBA before 'domestic terror' letter: memo* N.Y. Post, Nov. 11, 2021.
[13] Memorandum from Atty Gen. Merrick Garland, U.S. Dep't of Justice, Partnership Among Federal, State, Local, Tribal, And Territorial Law Enforcement to Address Threats Against School Administrators, Board Members, Teachers, and Staff (Oct. 4, 2021).
[14] Email from Carlton Peeples to FBI_SACS (Oct. 20, 2021).
[15] Memorandum from NSBA Board of Directors, Message to NSBA Members (Oct. 22, 2021).

however, have stubbornly refused to rescind your directive, even though you testified that the NSBA letter was the basis for your October 4 memorandum.[16] Your directive to the FBI therefore remains in effect.

This whistleblower disclosure calls into question the accuracy and completeness of your testimony before the Committee. At best, if we assume that you were ignorant of the FBI's actions in response to your October 4 memorandum at the time of your testimony, this new evidence suggests that your testimony to the Committee was incomplete and requires additional explanation. If, however, you were aware of the FBI's actions at the time of your testimony, this evidence shows that you willfully misled the Committee about the nature and extent of the Department's use of federal counterterrorism tools to target concerned parents at school board meetings.

To allow us to assess the accuracy and completeness of your sworn testimony, we invite you to amend your testimony as to whether the Department or any of its components has used or is using counterterrorism resources or tools for the purpose of investigating, tracking, or prosecuting threats relating to school board meetings. In addition, to independently verify the truthfulness of your testimony and to investigate this matter further, we reiterate our outstanding document requests to the various Departmental components and ask that you produce this material immediately. Finally, we remind you that whistleblower disclosures to Congress are protected by law and that we will not tolerate any effort to retaliate against whistleblowers for their disclosures.

Sincerely,

Jim Jordan
Ranking Member

cc: The Honorable Jerrold L. Nadler
Chairman

Enclosure

[16] AG Garland testimony, *supra* note 1.

From: Peeples, Carlton L. (INSD) (FBI) <>
Sent: Wednesday, October 20, 2021 10:02 AM
To: FBI_SACS <>
Cc: Greenberg, Jay (CID) (FBI) <>; Shivers, Calvin A. (CID) (FBI) <>; Cohen, Brian M. (CID) (FBI) <>; Langan, Timothy R. Jr. (CTD) (FBI) <>; Vorndran, Kevin (CTD) (FBI) <>
Subject: Guidance: Threat to violence against School Administrators --- UNCLASSIFIED

Classification: UNCLASSIFIED
==

A JOINT MESSAGE FROM CRIMINAL INVESTIGATIVE DIVISION & COUNTERTERRORISM DIVISION
FEDERAL BUREAU OF INVESTIGATION

All,

On October 04, 2021, the Attorney General forwarded a memorandum addressing a spike in harassment, intimidation, and threats of violence against school administrators, board members, teachers, and staff. The memorandum directed each United States Attorney, in coordination with the FBI, to convene meetings with federal, state, local, Tribal, and territorial leaders in each federal judicial district within 30 days of the issuance of the memorandum.

We share an obligation to ensure all individuals are able to do their jobs without threats of violence or fear for their safety. This can only be accomplished with effective coordination internally between relevant Divisions and through effective coordination and engagement with our law enforcement partners and United States Attorney Offices.

As a result, the Counterterrorism and Criminal Divisions created a threat tag, EDUOFFICIALS, to track instances of related threats. We ask that your offices apply the threat tag to investigations and assessments of threats specifically directed against school board administrators, board members, teachers, and staff. The purpose of the threat tag is to help scope this threat on a national level and provide an opportunity for comprehensive analysis of the threat picture for effective engagement with law enforcement partners at all levels. When evaluating potential threats, we ask that you attempt to identify the following:

a) Is there a federal nexus?

b) Are there potential federal violations that can be investigated and charged?

c) What's the motivation behind the criminal activity?

We appreciate your attention to this matter and welcome any engagement to identify trends, strategies, and best practices to accomplish discouraging, identifying, and prosecuting those who use violence, threats of violence, and other forms of intimidation and harassment pertaining to this threat.

On behalf of,

AD Timothy R. Langan Jr.
Counterterrorism Division

AD Calvin A. Shivers
Criminal Division

Respectfully,
Carlton Peeples
A/Deputy Assistant Director
Criminal Investigative Division

==
Classification: UNCLASSIFIED

==
Classification: UNCLASSIFIED

==
Classification: UNCLASSIFIED

==
Classification: UNCLASSIFIED

JERROLD NADLER, New York
CHAIRMAN

JIM JORDAN, Ohio
RANKING MEMBER

ONE HUNDRED SEVENTEENTH CONGRESS

Congress of the United States

House of Representatives

COMMITTEE ON THE JUDICIARY

2138 RAYBURN HOUSE OFFICE BUILDING

WASHINGTON, DC 20515–6216

(202) 225–3951
judiciary.house.gov

November 12, 2021

Mr. Chip Slaven
Interim Executive Director & CEO
National School Boards Association
1680 Duke St., Floor 2
Alexandria, VA 22314-3493

Dear Mr. Slaven:

We are investigating the troubling attempts by the Department of Justice and the White House to use the heavy hand of federal law enforcement to target concerned parents at local school board meetings and chill their protected First Amendment activity.[1] Publicly available documents suggest that you, as the Interim Executive Director & CEO of the National School Boards Association (NSBA), have information that is relevant and necessary to our investigation. Accordingly, we ask that you make yourself available for a transcribed interview with Committee staff.

On September 29, 2021, on behalf of the NSBA, you and Dr. Viola Garcia sent a letter to President Joe Biden requesting help from the federal government with concerned parents voicing their opinions at school board meetings.[2] Your letter stated that "malice, violence, and threats" against school officials "could be the equivalent of a form of domestic terrorism or hate crimes."[3] Your letter also cited the Patriot Act as a potential federal statute that the Biden Administration could use to prosecute parents.[4]

In an email that same day, you shared your letter with the NSBA board of directors, explaining how the letter was the product of "several weeks" of discussions with the Biden White House. You wrote:

> We co-signed the letter which lays out the current issues local school board members are facing and askes [*sic*] for federal cooperation with state and local law enforcement as well as public schools to address these serious issues. . . .

---

[1] Letter from Rep. Jim Jordan et al., Ranking Member, H. Comm. on the Judiciary, to Dr. Viola M. Garcia et al, President, Nat'l School Boards Assoc. (Oct. 27, 2021).
[2] Letter from Dr. Viola M. Garcia, President, Nat'l School Board Assoc. & Mr. Chip Slaven, Chief Exec. Officer, Nat'l School Board Assoc., to President Joseph R. Biden, White House (Sept. 29, 2021).
[3] *Id.*
[4] *Id.*

> Additionally, in talks over the last several weeks with White House staff, they requested additional information on some of these specific threats, so the letter also details many of the incidents that have been occurring.[5]

Five days after your letter to the President, Attorney General Merrick Garland directed the Federal Bureau of Investigation and U.S. Attorneys' Offices to address the "disturbing spike in harassment, intimidation, and threats of violence" at school board meetings.[6] In a press release publicizing the memorandum, the Justice Department noted that the Department's National Security Division—the Department component responsible for prosecuting terrorism cases—would be part of a task force "to determine how federal enforcement tools can be used to prosecute these crimes."[7] In testimony to our Committee, Attorney General Garland confirmed that your letter was the basis for his unusual directive to target parents.[8]

On October 22, 2021, following Attorney General Garland's testimony, the NSBA Board of Directors issued a new memorandum to its members apologizing for your letter, stating: "On behalf of NSBA, <u>we regret and apologize for the letter</u>."[9] (emphasis in original). The Attorney General, however, has refused to withdraw his directive to target parents.

Parents have an undisputed right to direct the upbringing and education of their children, including expressing concerns about the inclusion of controversial curricula in their child's education.[10] However, your letter to President Biden never once mentioned "parents" or parents' right with respect to their children's education, although the NSBA's subsequent apology purported to value the "voices of parents."[11] Concerned parents are absolutely not domestic terrorists and, to the extent actual threats exist, local law enforcement—and not the FBI—are the appropriate authorities to address those situations.

Parents cannot tolerate this collusion between the NSBA and the Biden Administration to construct a justification for invoking federal law enforcement to intimidate and silence parents using their Constitutional rights to advocate for their child's future. Therefore, to assist our investigation, we request that you make yourself available for a transcribed interview with the Committee as soon as possible.

---

[5] Email from Chip Slaven (Sept. 29, 2021, 8:18 p.m.), *available at* https://defendinged.org/wp-content/uploads/2021/10/Email-Correspondence_NSBA-Letter-to-President-Biden_Redacted.pdf.
[6] Memorandum from Atty Gen. Merrick Garland, U.S. Dep't of Justice, Partnership Among Federal, State, Local, Tribal, And Territorial Law Enforcement to Address Threats Against School Administrators, Board Members, Teachers, and Staff (Oct. 4, 2021).
[7] Press Release, U.S. Dep't of Justice, Justice Department Addresses Violent Threats Against School Officials and Teachers (Oct. 4, 2021).
[8] *Oversight of the United States Department of Justice: Hearing Before the H. comm. on the Judiciary,* 117th Cong. at 68 (2021) (testimony from Hon. Merrick Garland, Atty Gen., U.S. Dep't of Justice).
[9] Memorandum from NSBA Board of Directors, Message to NSBA Members (Oct. 22, 2021).
[10] *Troxel v. Granville,* 530 U.S. 57, 65 (2000) (citing *Meyer v. Nebraska,* 262 U.S. 390, 399 (1923)).
[11] *Compare* Letter from Dr. Viola M. Garcia, *supra* note 2, *with* Memorandum from NSBA Board of Directors, *supra* note 9.

If you have any questions and to schedule the interview, please contact Committee staff at (202) 225-6906. If you are represented by counsel, please ask your attorney to contact Committee staff on your behalf.

Thank you for your attention to this important matter.

Sincerely,

Jim Jordan
Ranking Member

cc: The Honorable Jerrold L. Nadler
Chairman

JERROLD NADLER, New York
CHAIRMAN

JIM JORDAN, Ohio
RANKING MEMBER

ONE HUNDRED SEVENTEENTH CONGRESS

Congress of the United States
House of Representatives
COMMITTEE ON THE JUDICIARY

2138 RAYBURN HOUSE OFFICE BUILDING
WASHINGTON, DC 20515–6216
(202) 225–3951
judiciary.house.gov

November 12, 2021

Dr. Viola M. Garcia
President
National School Boards Association
1680 Duke St., Floor 2
Alexandria, VA 22314-3493

Dear Dr. Garcia:

We are investigating the troubling attempts by the Department of Justice and the White House to use the heavy hand of federal law enforcement to target concerned parents at local school board meetings and chill their protected First Amendment activity.[1] Publicly available documents suggest that you, as the President of the National School Boards Association (NSBA), have information that is relevant and necessary to our investigation. Accordingly, we ask that you make yourself available for a transcribed interview with Committee staff.

On September 29, 2021, on behalf of the NSBA, you and Chip Slaven sent a letter to President Joe Biden requesting help from the federal government with concerned parents voicing their opinions at school board meetings.[2] Your letter stated that "malice, violence, and threats" against school officials "could be the equivalent of a form of domestic terrorism or hate crimes."[3] Your letter also cited the Patriot Act as a potential federal statute that the Biden Administration could use to prosecute parents.[4]

On October 2, 2021, in an email to NSBA board members, you explained the NSBA had "been engaged with the White House and Department of Education . . . for several weeks now" prior to the NSBA's letter to the President.[5] On October 13, 2021, the Biden Administration announced that it had appointed you to be one of five members of the National Assessment Governing Board.[6]

---

[1] Letter from Rep. Jim Jordan et al., Ranking Member, H. Comm. on the Judiciary, to Dr. Viola M. Garcia et al, President, Nat'l School Boards Assoc. (Oct. 27, 2021).
[2] Letter from Dr. Viola M. Garcia, President, Nat'l School Board Assoc. & Mr. Chip Slaven, Chief Exec. Officer, Nat'l School Board Assoc., to President Joseph R. Biden, White House (Sept. 29, 2021).
[3] *Id.*
[4] *Id.*
[5] Email from Viola Garcia (Oct. 2, 2021, 6:59 a.m.), *available at* https://defendinged.org/wp-content/uploads/2021/10/Email-Correspondence_NSBA-Letter-to-President-Biden_Redacted.pdf.
[6] Dep't of Ed., Five Board Members Appointed to Board Overseeing the Nation's Report Card (Oct. 13, 2021).

Five days after your letter to the President, Attorney General Merrick Garland directed the Federal Bureau of Investigation and U.S. Attorneys' Offices to address the "disturbing spike in harassment, intimidation, and threats of violence" at school board meetings.[7] In a press release publicizing the memorandum, the Justice Department noted that the Department's National Security Division—the Department component responsible for prosecuting terrorism cases—would be part of a task force "to determine how federal enforcement tools can be used to prosecute these crimes."[8] In testimony to our Committee, Attorney General Garland confirmed that your letter was the basis for his unusual directive to target parents.[9]

On October 22, 2021, following Attorney General Garland's testimony, the NSBA Board of Directors issued a new memorandum to its members apologizing for your letter, stating: "On behalf of NSBA, we regret and apologize for the letter."[10] (emphasis in original). The Attorney General, however, has refused to withdraw his directive to target parents.

Parents have an undisputed right to direct the upbringing and education of their children, including expressing concerns about the inclusion of controversial curricula in their child's education.[11] However, your letter to President Biden never once mentioned "parents" or parents' right with respect to their children's education, although the NSBA's subsequent apology purported to value the "voices of parents."[12] Concerned parents are absolutely not domestic terrorists and, to the extent actual threats exist, local law enforcement—and not the FBI—are the appropriate authorities to address those situations.

Parents cannot tolerate this collusion between the NSBA and the Biden Administration to construct a justification for invoking federal law enforcement to intimidate and silence parents using their Constitutional rights to advocate for their child's future. Therefore, to assist our investigation, we request that you make yourself available for a transcribed interview with the Committee as soon as possible.

If you have any questions and to schedule the interview, please contact Committee staff at (202) 225-6906. If you are represented by counsel, please ask your attorney to contact Committee staff on your behalf.

---

[7] Memorandum from Atty Gen. Merrick Garland, U.S. Dep't of Justice, Partnership Among Federal, State, Local, Tribal, And Territorial Law Enforcement to Address Threats Against School Administrators, Board Members, Teachers, and Staff (Oct. 4, 2021).
[8] Press Release, U.S. Dep't of Justice, Justice Department Addresses Violent Threats Against School Officials and Teachers (Oct. 4, 2021).
[9] *Oversight of the United States Department of Justice: Hearing Before the H. comm. on the Judiciary,* 117th Cong. at 68 (2021) (testimony from Hon. Merrick Garland, Atty Gen., U.S. Dep't of Justice).
[10] Memorandum from NSBA Board of Directors, Message to NSBA Members (Oct. 22, 2021).
[11] *Troxel v. Granville,* 530 U.S. 57, 65 (2000) (citing *Meyer v. Nebraska,* 262 U.S. 390, 399 (1923)).
[12] *Compare* Letter from Dr. Viola M. Garcia, *supra* note 2, *with* Memorandum from NSBA Board of Directors, *supra* note 10.

Thank you for your attention to this important matter.

Sincerely,

Jim Jordan
Ranking Member

cc: The Honorable Jerrold L. Nadler
Chairman

JERROLD NADLER, New York
CHAIRMAN

JIM JORDAN, Ohio
RANKING MEMBER

ONE HUNDRED SEVENTEENTH CONGRESS

Congress of the United States

House of Representatives

COMMITTEE ON THE JUDICIARY

2138 RAYBURN HOUSE OFFICE BUILDING

WASHINGTON, DC 20515–6216

(202) 225–3951
judiciary.house.gov

November 3, 2021

The Honorable Christopher A. Wray
Director
Federal Bureau of Investigation
935 Pennsylvania Avenue, N.W.
Washington, DC 20535

Dear Director Wray:

We are continuing to investigate the troubling attempts by the Department of Justice and the White House to use the heavy hand of federal law enforcement to target concerned parents at local school board meetings and chill their protected First Amendment activity. The Attorney General directed you and all U.S. Attorneys' Offices to take action to address parents attending school board meetings.[1] This unusual directive is particularly worrisome as it applies to the Federal Bureau of Investigation (FBI) given the FBI's illegal spying on the Trump campaign and its scandalous history of misconduct and politicization.

On September 29, 2021, the National School Boards Association (NSBA) sent a letter to President Joe Biden requesting help from the federal government with concerned parents voicing their opinions at school board meetings.[2] The NSBA letter stated that "malice, violence, and threats" against school officials "could be the equivalent of a form of domestic terrorism or hate crimes."[3] The letter cited a number of interactions at school board meetings, none of which rose to the level of domestic terrorism. In fact, the vast majority of incidents cited by the NSBA did not involve threats or violence.[4] Most notably, as an example of domestic terrorism, the NSBA cited an incident in which a father angrily confronted members at a school board meeting in Loudoun County, Virginia, about the heinous sexual assault of his daughter.[5]

---

[1] Memorandum from Atty Gen. Merrick Garland, U.S. Dep't of Justice, Partnership Among Federal, State, Local, Tribal, And Territorial Law Enforcement to Address Threats Against School Administrators, Board Members, Teachers, and Staff (Oct. 4, 2021).
[2] Letter from Dr. Viola M. Garcia, President, Nat'l School Board Assoc. & Mr. Chip Slaven, Chief Exec. Officer, Nat'l School Board Assoc., to President Joseph R. Biden, White House (Sept. 29, 2021).
[3] *Id.*
[4] *See* Caroline Downey, *Vast majority of incidents cited by school-board group to justify federal intervention didn't involve threats,* NAT'L REV. (Oct. 2, 2021).
[5] *Id.*; *see also* Jessica Chasmar, *Loudoun County father arrested at school board events says school tried to cover up daughter's bathroom assault*, FOX NEWS (Oct. 12, 2021).

A mere five days after the NSBA sent its letter to President Biden, on October 4, 2021, Attorney General Merrick Garland issued a shocking memorandum that directed the FBI and U.S. Attorneys' Offices to "convene meetings" in each judicial district "with federal, state, local, Tribal, and territorial leaders" within 30 days.[6] The Justice Department simultaneously issued a press release indicating that the Attorney General's directive would "open dedicated lines of communication for threat reporting, assessment and response by law enforcement"—in other words, create a snitch line for complaints about concerned parents.[7] The release also announced that the FBI would be part of a Department-wide task force "to determine how federal enforcement can be used to prosecute these crimes."[8]

During Attorney General Garland's testimony before our Committee on October 21, he appeared to have no idea whether the meetings he ordered were actually taking place. He stated: "I don't know whether [the meetings] are ongoing, but I expect and hope that they are going . . . because I did ask that they take place."[9] Attorney General Garland testified that he doubted "there have been meetings in every jurisdiction," but reiterated his belief that it is important for federal law enforcement authorities to conduct these meetings in every judicial district.[10] However, Attorney General Garland testified that FBI agents "will not be attending local school board meetings."[11] According to the Attorney General's directives, meetings are to be convened in all 94 judicial districts by November 3, 2021, at the latest.

Following the Attorney General's testimony, the NSBA Board of Directors, apparently recognizing the ill-conceived consequences of its letter and the resulting Justice Department action, issued a new memorandum to its members apologizing for the letter, stating: "On behalf of NSBA, <u>we regret and apologize for the letter</u>."[12] (emphasis in original). Although Attorney General Garland testified that the NSBA letter to President Biden was the basis for his October 4 directive to insert federal law enforcement into local school board matters, the Attorney General has yet to rescind his memorandum. His directives to you and all U.S. Attorneys remain in effect.

Concerned parents voicing their strong opposition to controversial curricula at local schools are not domestic terrorists. Parents have an undisputed right to direct the upbringing and education of their children.[13] When parents, however, cross the line to commit a violent act or issue a criminal threat,[14] state and local authorities are best-equipped to handle these violations of state law. But we must not tolerate the use of the federal law enforcement apparatus to

---

[6] Memorandum from Atty Gen. Merrick Garland, U.S. Dep't of Justice, Partnership Among Federal, State, Local, Tribal, And Territorial Law Enforcement to Address Threats Against School Administrators, Board Members, Teachers, and Staff (Oct. 4, 2021).
[7] Press Release, U.S. Dep't of Justice, Justice Department Addresses Violent Threats Against School Officials and Teachers (Oct. 4, 2021).
[8] *Id.*
[9] *Oversight of the United States Department of Justice: Hearing Before the H. comm. on the Judiciary,* 117th Cong. at 94 (2021) (testimony from Hon. Merrick Garland, Atty Gen., U.S. Dep't of Justice).
[10] *Id.* at 95.
[11] *Id.* at 62.
[12] Memorandum from NSBA Board of Directors, Message to NSBA Members (Oct. 22, 2021).
[13] *Troxel v. Granville,* 530 U.S. 57, 65 (2000) (citing *Meyer v. Nebraska,* 262 U.S. 390, 399 (1923)).
[14] *Merrick Garland's federal offense,* WALL ST. J. (Oct. 6, 2021).

intimidate and silence parents using their Constitutional rights to advocate for their child's future.

To assist our investigation and determine whether these meetings are ongoing, we request that you provide the following documents and information:

1. All documents and communications referring or relating to convening meeting(s) with U.S. Attorneys' Offices in accordance with the Attorney General's October 4, 2021 memorandum, the establishment of the Department's task force, or the FBI's role as a member of the task force;

2. All agendas, minutes, and notes created or relied upon by FBI employees referring or relating to meeting(s) in each judicial district in accordance with the Attorney General's October 4, 2021 memorandum or the FBI's role as a member of the task force;

3. Please explain whether you consider the Attorney General's October 4, 2021 memorandum to be lawful and whether you intend to direct FBI agents and employees to enforce the Attorney General's directives;

4. Please explain whether you have issued any internal guidance to FBI field offices or special agents in charge referring or relating to the Attorney General's October 4, 2021 memorandum;

5. Please explain the FBI's role in convening meetings as directed by the Attorney General's October 4, 2021 memorandum;

6. Please explain the FBI's role in the Department's task force, including what federal statutes the FBI intends to use in investigating concerned parents at school board meetings;

7. Please identify by name, title, and field office each FBI employee involved in the meeting(s) and task force referenced in the Attorney General's October 4, 2021 memorandum;

8. Please identify all federal, state, local, Tribal, and territorial organizations invited to or that have attended the meetings convened in accordance with the October 4, 2021 memorandum;

9. Please provide all recommendations, both formal and informal, and any meeting minutes produced at the meeting(s) in accordance with the Attorney General's October 4, 2021 memorandum; and

10. Please provide all recommendations, both formal and informal, that the FBI has made to the Department's task force.

Please provide this material as soon as possible but no later than 5:00 p.m. on November 17, 2021.

If you have any questions about this request, please contact Committee staff at (202) 225-6906. Thank you for your attention to this important matter.

Sincerely,

Jim Jordan
Ranking Member

Steve Chabot
Member of Congress

Louie Gohmert
Member of Congress

Darrell Issa
Ranking Member
Subcommittee on Courts, Intellectual Property, and the Internet

Ken Buck
Ranking Member
Subcommittee on Antitrust, Commercial and Administrative Law

Matt Gaetz
Member of Congress

Mike Johnson
Ranking Member
Subcommittee on the Constitution, Civil Rights and Civil Liberties

Andy Biggs
Ranking Member
Subcommittee on Crime, Terrorism and Homeland Security

Tom McClintock
Ranking Member
Subcommittee on Immigration and Citizenship

W. Gregory Steube
Member of Congress

Tom Tiffany
Member of Congress

Thomas Massie
Member of Congress

Chip Roy
Member of Congress

Dan Bishop
Member of Congress

Michelle Fischbach
Member of Congress

Victoria Spartz
Member of Congress

Scott Fitzgerald
Member of Congress

Cliff Bentz
Member of Congress

Burgess Owens
Member of Congress

cc: The Honorable Jerrold L. Nadler
Chairman

JERROLD NADLER, New York
CHAIRMAN

JIM JORDAN, Ohio
RANKING MEMBER

ONE HUNDRED SEVENTEENTH CONGRESS

Congress of the United States

House of Representatives

COMMITTEE ON THE JUDICIARY

2138 RAYBURN HOUSE OFFICE BUILDING

WASHINGTON, DC 20515-6216

(202) 225-3951
judiciary.house.gov

November 2, 2021

Mr. Mark Lesko
Acting Assistant Attorney General
National Security Division
U.S. Department of Justice
950 Pennsylvania Avenue, NW
Washington, DC 20530

Dear Mr. Lesko:

We are continuing to investigate the troubling attempts by the Department of Justice and the White House to use the heavy hand of federal law enforcement to target concerned parents at local school board meetings and chill their protected First Amendment activity. The Department's actions, including the involvement of the National Security Division, came days after the Biden Administration received a letter from the National School Boards Association (NSBA) equating parents as domestic terrorists and urging the Department to exercise its authorities under the Patriot Act.

The National Security Division was created by the Patriot Act, and its mission is to "protect the United States from threats to our national security."[1] It is organized to "ensure greater coordination and unity of purpose between prosecutors and law enforcement agencies, on the one hand, and intelligence attorneys and the Intelligence Community, on the other."[2] It is unclear what threat the Department believes American parents pose to our national security, nor why the Department could view any threat posed by parents as requiring coordination with our foreign intelligence agencies. Unfortunately, in testimony before the Committee, Attorney General Garland was unable or unwilling to explain why he directed the National Security Division to participate in this ill-conceived endeavor.[3] Thus, we write to request additional information about the Division's role in the Biden Administration's efforts to target concerned parents.

On September 29, 2021, the NSBA sent a letter to President Joe Biden requesting help from the federal government with concerned parents voicing their opinions at school board

---

[1] *National Security Division: About the Division*, U.S. Dep't of Justice (last updated Apr. 12, 2019), https://www.justice.gov/nsd/about-division.
[2] *Id.*
[3] *Oversight of the United States Department of Justice: Hearing Before the H. comm. on the Judiciary,* 117th Cong. at 67 (2021) (testimony from Hon. Merrick Garland, Atty Gen., U.S. Dep't of Justice).

meetings.[4] The NSBA letter stated that "malice, violence, and threats" against school officials "could be the equivalent of a form of domestic terrorism or hate crimes."[5] The NSBA letter cited a number of interactions at school board meetings, including one "example" of alleged domestic terrorism in Loudoun County, Virginia, where a father angrily confronted members at a school board meeting about the heinous sexual assault of his daughter.[6]

On October 4, 2021, just five days after the NSBA letter, Attorney General Merrick Garland issued a shocking memorandum that directed the Federal Bureau of Investigation and U.S. Attorneys' Offices to address a purported "disturbing spike in harassment, intimidation, and threats of violence" at school board meetings.[7] The memorandum explained that the Department would be "using its authority and resources to discourage these threats, identify them when they occur, and prosecute them when appropriate."[8] In a press release announcing the Attorney General's memorandum, the Justice Department announced that the National Security Division would be part of a Department-wide task force "to determine how federal enforcement tools can be used to prosecute these crimes."[9]

Following the Attorney General's testimony, the NSBA Board of Directors, apparently recognizing the ill-conceived consequences of its letter and the resulting Justice Department action, issued a new memorandum to its members apologizing for the letter, stating: "On behalf of NSBA, <u>we regret and apologize for the letter</u>."[10] (emphasis in original). Although Attorney General Garland testified that the NSBA letter to President Biden was the basis for his October 4 directive to insert federal law enforcement into local school board matters, the Attorney General has yet to rescind his memorandum. His directives to the National Security Division remain in effect.

Concerned parents voicing their strong opposition to controversial curricula at local schools are not domestic terrorists. Parents have an undisputed right to direct the upbringing and education of their children.[11] When parents, however, cross the line to commit a violent act or issue a criminal threat,[12] state and local authorities are best-equipped to handle these violations of state law. But we must not tolerate the use of the federal law enforcement apparatus to intimidate and silence parents using their Constitutional rights to advocate for their child's future.

---

[4] Letter from Dr. Viola M. Garcia, President, Nat'l School Board Assoc. & Mr. Chip Slaven, Chief Exec. Officer, Nat'l School Board Assoc., to President Joseph R. Biden, White House (Sept. 29, 2021).
[5] *Id.*
[6] *Id.*; *see also* Jessica Chasmar, *Loudoun County father arrested at school board events says school tried to cover up daughter's bathroom assault*, FOX NEWS (Oct. 12, 2021); Caroline Downey, *Vast majority of incidents cited by school-board group to justify federal intervention didn't involve threats,* NAT'L REV. (Oct. 2, 2021).
[7] Memorandum from Atty Gen. Merrick Garland, U.S. Dep't of Justice, Partnership Among Federal, State, Local, Tribal, And Territorial Law Enforcement to Address Threats Against School Administrators, Board Members, Teachers, and Staff (Oct. 4, 2021).
[8] *Id.*
[9] Press Release, U.S. Dep't of Justice, Justice Department Addresses Violent Threats Against School Officials and Teachers (Oct. 4, 2021).
[10] Memorandum from NSBA Board of Directors, Message to NSBA Members (Oct. 22, 2021).
[11] *Troxel v. Granville,* 530 U.S. 57, 65 (2000) (citing *Meyer v. Nebraska,* 262 U.S. 390, 399 (1923)).
[12] *Merrick Garland's federal offense,* WALL ST. J. (Oct. 6, 2021).

To assist our investigation, we request that you produce the following documents and information:

1. All documents and communications referring or relating to the establishment of the Department's task force and the National Security Division's role as a member of the task force;

2. All documents and communications between employees of the Department of Justice and U.S. intelligence agencies referring or relating to alleged threats posed by concerned parents at local school board meetings, the NSBA's letter dated September 29, 2021, or the Attorney General's memo dated October 4, 2021;

3. All agendas, minutes, and notes created by or relied upon by National Security Division employees referring or relating to the Department's task force;

4. Please explain the National Security Division's role in the Department's task force, including what federal statutes within the Division's jurisdiction it intends to use in investigating concerned parents at school board meetings;

5. Please identity by name and title all National Security Division employees involved in the Department's task force; and

6. Please provide all recommendations, both formal and informal, that the National Security Division has made to the Department's task force.

Please provide this material as soon as possible but no later than 5:00 p.m. on November 16, 2021.

If you have any questions about this request, please contact Committee staff at (202) 225-6906. Thank you for your attention to this matter.

Sincerely,

Jim Jordan
Ranking Member

Steve Chabot
Member of Congress

Louie Gohmert
Member of Congress

Darrell Issa
Ranking Member
Subcommittee on Courts, Intellectual Property, and the Internet

Ken Buck
Ranking Member
Subcommittee on Antitrust, Commercial and Administrative Law

Matt Gaetz
Member of Congress

Mike Johnson
Ranking Member
Subcommittee on the Constitution, Civil Rights and Civil Liberties

Andy Biggs
Ranking Member
Subcommittee on Crime, Terrorism and Homeland Security

Tom McClintock
Ranking Member
Subcommittee on Immigration and Citizenship

W. Gregory Steube
Member of Congress

Tom Tiffany
Member of Congress

Thomas Massie
Member of Congress

Chip Roy
Member of Congress

Dan Bishop
Member of Congress

Michelle Fischbach
Member of Congress

Victoria Spartz
Member of Congress

Scott Fitzgerald
Member of Congress

Cliff Bentz
Member of Congress

Burgess Owens
Member of Congress

cc: The Honorable Jerrold L. Nadler
Chairman

JERROLD NADLER, New York
CHAIRMAN

JIM JORDAN, Ohio
RANKING MEMBER

ONE HUNDRED SEVENTEENTH CONGRESS

Congress of the United States
House of Representatives
COMMITTEE ON THE JUDICIARY

2138 RAYBURN HOUSE OFFICE BUILDING
WASHINGTON, DC 20515-6216
(202) 225-3951
judiciary.house.gov

November 1, 2021

Mr. E. Bryan Wilson
Acting U.S. Attorney
District of Alaska
222 West 7th Avenue, Room 253, #9
Anchorage, AK 99513

Dear Mr. Wilson:

We are continuing to investigate the troubling attempts by the Department of Justice and the White House to use the heavy hand of federal law enforcement to target concerned parents at local school board meetings and chill their protected First Amendment activity. Because the Department directed you, along with all other U.S. Attorneys, and the Federal Bureau of Investigation (FBI) to take action to address parents attending school board meetings,[1] we respectfully request your assistance with our investigation.

On September 29, 2021, the National School Boards Association (NSBA) sent a letter to President Joe Biden requesting help from the federal government with concerned parents voicing their opinions at school board meetings.[2] The NSBA letter stated that "malice, violence, and threats" against school officials "could be the equivalent of a form of domestic terrorism or hate crimes."[3] The letter cited a number of interactions at school board meetings, none of which rose to the level of domestic terrorism. In fact, the vast majority of incidents cited by the NSBA did not involve threats or violence.[4] Most notably, as an example of domestic terrorism, the NSBA cited an incident in which a father angrily confronted members at a school board meeting in Loudoun County, Virginia about the heinous sexual assault of his daughter.[5]

A mere five days after the NSBA sent its letter to President Biden, on October 4, 2021, Attorney General Merrick Garland issued a shocking memorandum that directed the FBI and

---

[1] Memorandum from Atty Gen. Merrick Garland, U.S. Dep't of Justice, Partnership Among Federal, State, Local, Tribal, And Territorial Law Enforcement to Address Threats Against School Administrators, Board Members, Teachers, and Staff (Oct. 4, 2021).

[2] Letter from Dr. Viola M. Garcia, President, Nat'l School Board Assoc. & Mr. Chip Slaven, Chief Exec. Officer, Nat'l School Board Assoc., to President Joseph R. Biden, White House (Sept. 29, 2021).

[3] *Id.*

[4] *See* Caroline Downey, *Vast majority of incidents cited by school-board group to justify federal intervention didn't involve threats,* NAT'L REV. (Oct. 2, 2021).

[5] *Id.*; *see also* Jessica Chasmar, *Loudoun County father arrested at school board events says school tried to cover up daughter's bathroom assault*, FOX NEWS (Oct. 12, 2021).

U.S. Attorneys' Offices to "convene meetings" in your judicial district "with federal, state, local, Tribal, and territorial leaders" within 30 days.[6] The Justice Department simultaneously issued a press release indicating that the Attorney General's directive would "open dedicated lines of communication for threat reporting, assessment and response by law enforcement"—in other words, create a snitch line for complaints about concerned parents.[7]

During Attorney General Garland's testimony before our Committee on October 21, he appeared to have no idea whether the U.S. Attorney meetings he ordered were actually taking place. He stated: "I don't know whether [the meetings] are ongoing, but I expect and hope that they are going . . . because I did ask that they take place."[8] Attorney General Garland testified that he doubted "there have been meetings in every jurisdiction," but reiterated his belief that it is important for federal law enforcement authorities to conduct these meetings in every judicial district.[9] According to the Attorney General's directives, meetings are to be convened in all 94 judicial districts by November 3, 2021, at the latest.

Following the Attorney General's testimony, the NSBA Board of Directors, apparently recognizing the ill-conceived consequences of its letter and the resulting Justice Department action, issued a new memorandum to its members apologizing for the letter, stating: "On behalf of NSBA, <u>we regret and apologize for the letter</u>."[10] (emphasis in original). Although Attorney General Garland testified that the NSBA letter to President Biden was the basis for his October 4 directive to insert federal law enforcement into local school board matters, the Attorney General has yet to rescind his memorandum. His directives to you and other U.S. Attorneys remain in effect.

Concerned parents voicing their strong opposition to controversial curricula at local schools are not domestic terrorists. Parents have an undisputed right to direct the upbringing and education of their children.[11] When parents, however, cross the line to commit a violent act or issue a criminal threat,[12] state and local authorities are best-equipped to handle these violations of state law. But we must not tolerate the use of the federal law enforcement apparatus to intimidate and silence parents using their Constitutional rights to advocate for their child's future.

To assist our investigation and determine whether these meetings are ongoing, we request that you provide the following documents and information:

---

[6] Memorandum from Atty Gen. Merrick Garland, U.S. Dep't of Justice, Partnership Among Federal, State, Local, Tribal, And Territorial Law Enforcement to Address Threats Against School Administrators, Board Members, Teachers, and Staff (Oct. 4, 2021).
[7] Press Release, U.S. Dep't of Justice, Justice Department Addresses Violent Threats Against School Officials and Teachers (Oct. 4, 2021).
[8] *Oversight of the United States Department of Justice: Hearing Before the H. comm. on the Judiciary,* 117th Cong. at 94 (2021) (testimony from Hon. Merrick Garland, Atty Gen., U.S. Dep't of Justice).
[9] *Id.* at 95.
[10] Memorandum from NSBA Board of Directors, Message to NSBA Members (Oct. 22, 2021).
[11] *Troxel v. Granville,* 530 U.S. 57, 65 (2000) (citing *Meyer v. Nebraska,* 262 U.S. 390, 399 (1923)).
[12] *Merrick Garland's federal offense,* WALL ST. J. (Oct. 6, 2021).

1. All documents and communications referring or relating to convening meeting(s) in your judicial district in accordance with the Attorney General's October 4, 2021 memorandum;

2. All agendas, minutes, and notes created or relied upon by U.S. Attorney's Office employees referring or relating to meeting(s) in your judicial district in accordance with the Attorney General's October 4, 2021 memorandum;

3. Please explain when meeting(s) in your judicial district in accordance with the Attorney General's October 4, 2021 memorandum have occurred or will occur;

4. Please identify by name and title of all U.S. Attorney's Office employees involved in the meeting(s) in your judicial district in accordance with the Attorney General's October 4, 2021 memorandum ;

5. Please identify all federal, state, local, Tribal, and territorial organizations invited to or that have attended the meetings convened in your judicial district in accordance with the October 4, 2021 memorandum; and

6. Please provide all recommendations, both formal and informal, and any meeting minutes produced at the meeting(s) in your judicial district in accordance with the Attorney General's October 4, 2021 memorandum.

Please provide this material as soon as possible but no later than 5:00 p.m. on November 15, 2021.

If you have any questions about this request, please contact Committee staff at (202) 225-6906. Thank you for your attention to this important matter.

Sincerely,

Jim Jordan
Ranking Member

Steve Chabot
Member of Congress

Louie Gohmert
Member of Congress

Darrell Issa
Ranking Member
Subcommittee on Courts, Intellectual Property, and the Internet

Ken Buck
Ranking Member
Subcommittee on Antitrust, Commercial and Administrative Law

Matt Gaetz
Member of Congress

Mike Johnson
Ranking Member
Subcommittee on the Constitution, Civil Rights and Civil Liberties

Andy Biggs
Ranking Member
Subcommittee on Crime, Terrorism and Homeland Security

Tom McClintock
Ranking Member
Subcommittee on Immigration and Citizenship

W. Gregory Steube
Member of Congress

Tom Tiffany
Member of Congress

Thomas Massie
Member of Congress

Chip Roy
Member of Congress

Dan Bishop
Member of Congress

Michelle Fischbach
Member of Congress

Victoria Spartz
Member of Congress

Scott Fitzgerald
Member of Congress

Cliff Bentz
Member of Congress

Burgess Owens
Member of Congress

cc: The Honorable Jerrold L. Nadler
Chairman

Mr. Monty Wilkinson
Director, Executive Office for U.S. Attorneys

JERROLD NADLER, New York
CHAIRMAN

JIM JORDAN, Ohio
RANKING MEMBER

ONE HUNDRED SEVENTEENTH CONGRESS

Congress of the United States

House of Representatives

COMMITTEE ON THE JUDICIARY

2138 RAYBURN HOUSE OFFICE BUILDING

WASHINGTON, DC 20515-6216

(202) 225-3951
judiciary.house.gov

November 1, 2021

Mr. Sean P. Costello
U.S. Attorney
Southern District of Alabama
63 South Royal Street, Suite 600
Mobile, AL 36602

Dear Mr. Costello:

We are continuing to investigate the troubling attempts by the Department of Justice and the White House to use the heavy hand of federal law enforcement to target concerned parents at local school board meetings and chill their protected First Amendment activity. Because the Department directed you, along with all other U.S. Attorneys, and the Federal Bureau of Investigation (FBI) to take action to address parents attending school board meetings,[1] we respectfully request your assistance with our investigation.

On September 29, 2021, the National School Boards Association (NSBA) sent a letter to President Joe Biden requesting help from the federal government with concerned parents voicing their opinions at school board meetings.[2] The NSBA letter stated that "malice, violence, and threats" against school officials "could be the equivalent of a form of domestic terrorism or hate crimes."[3] The letter cited a number of interactions at school board meetings, none of which rose to the level of domestic terrorism. In fact, the vast majority of incidents cited by the NSBA did not involve threats or violence.[4] Most notably, as an example of domestic terrorism, the NSBA cited an incident in which a father angrily confronted members at a school board meeting in Loudoun County, Virginia about the heinous sexual assault of his daughter.[5]

A mere five days after the NSBA sent its letter to President Biden, on October 4, 2021, Attorney General Merrick Garland issued a shocking memorandum that directed the FBI and

---

[1] Memorandum from Atty Gen. Merrick Garland, U.S. Dep't of Justice, Partnership Among Federal, State, Local, Tribal, And Territorial Law Enforcement to Address Threats Against School Administrators, Board Members, Teachers, and Staff (Oct. 4, 2021).
[2] Letter from Dr. Viola M. Garcia, President, Nat'l School Board Assoc. & Mr. Chip Slaven, Chief Exec. Officer, Nat'l School Board Assoc., to President Joseph R. Biden, White House (Sept. 29, 2021).
[3] *Id.*
[4] *See* Caroline Downey, *Vast majority of incidents cited by school-board group to justify federal intervention didn't involve threats,* NAT'L REV. (Oct. 2, 2021).
[5] *Id.*; *see also* Jessica Chasmar, *Loudoun County father arrested at school board events says school tried to cover up daughter's bathroom assault*, FOX NEWS (Oct. 12, 2021).

U.S. Attorneys' Offices to "convene meetings" in your judicial district "with federal, state, local, Tribal, and territorial leaders" within 30 days.[6] The Justice Department simultaneously issued a press release indicating that the Attorney General's directive would "open dedicated lines of communication for threat reporting, assessment and response by law enforcement"—in other words, create a snitch line for complaints about concerned parents.[7]

During Attorney General Garland's testimony before our Committee on October 21, he appeared to have no idea whether the U.S. Attorney meetings he ordered were actually taking place. He stated: "I don't know whether [the meetings] are ongoing, but I expect and hope that they are going . . . because I did ask that they take place."[8] Attorney General Garland testified that he doubted "there have been meetings in every jurisdiction," but reiterated his belief that it is important for federal law enforcement authorities to conduct these meetings in every judicial district.[9] According to the Attorney General's directives, meetings are to be convened in all 94 judicial districts by November 3, 2021, at the latest.

Following the Attorney General's testimony, the NSBA Board of Directors, apparently recognizing the ill-conceived consequences of its letter and the resulting Justice Department action, issued a new memorandum to its members apologizing for the letter, stating: "On behalf of NSBA, <u>we regret and apologize for the letter</u>."[10] (emphasis in original). Although Attorney General Garland testified that the NSBA letter to President Biden was the basis for his October 4 directive to insert federal law enforcement into local school board matters, the Attorney General has yet to rescind his memorandum. His directives to you and other U.S. Attorneys remain in effect.

Concerned parents voicing their strong opposition to controversial curricula at local schools are not domestic terrorists. Parents have an undisputed right to direct the upbringing and education of their children.[11] When parents, however, cross the line to commit a violent act or issue a criminal threat,[12] state and local authorities are best-equipped to handle these violations of state law. But we must not tolerate the use of the federal law enforcement apparatus to intimidate and silence parents using their Constitutional rights to advocate for their child's future.

To assist our investigation and determine whether these meetings are ongoing, we request that you provide the following documents and information:

---

[6] Memorandum from Atty Gen. Merrick Garland, U.S. Dep't of Justice, Partnership Among Federal, State, Local, Tribal, And Territorial Law Enforcement to Address Threats Against School Administrators, Board Members, Teachers, and Staff (Oct. 4, 2021).

[7] Press Release, U.S. Dep't of Justice, Justice Department Addresses Violent Threats Against School Officials and Teachers (Oct. 4, 2021).

[8] *Oversight of the United States Department of Justice: Hearing Before the H. comm. on the Judiciary,* 117th Cong. at 94 (2021) (testimony from Hon. Merrick Garland, Atty Gen., U.S. Dep't of Justice).

[9] *Id.* at 95.

[10] Memorandum from NSBA Board of Directors, Message to NSBA Members (Oct. 22, 2021).

[11] *Troxel v. Granville,* 530 U.S. 57, 65 (2000) (citing *Meyer v. Nebraska,* 262 U.S. 390, 399 (1923)).

[12] *Merrick Garland's federal offense,* WALL ST. J. (Oct. 6, 2021).

1. All documents and communications referring or relating to convening meeting(s) in your judicial district in accordance with the Attorney General's October 4, 2021 memorandum;

2. All agendas, minutes, and notes created or relied upon by U.S. Attorney's Office employees referring or relating to meeting(s) in your judicial district in accordance with the Attorney General's October 4, 2021 memorandum;

3. Please explain when meeting(s) in your judicial district in accordance with the Attorney General's October 4, 2021 memorandum have occurred or will occur;

4. Please identify by name and title of all U.S. Attorney's Office employees involved in the meeting(s) in your judicial district in accordance with the Attorney General's October 4, 2021 memorandum ;

5. Please identify all federal, state, local, Tribal, and territorial organizations invited to or that have attended the meetings convened in your judicial district in accordance with the October 4, 2021 memorandum; and

6. Please provide all recommendations, both formal and informal, and any meeting minutes produced at the meeting(s) in your judicial district in accordance with the Attorney General's October 4, 2021 memorandum.

Please provide this material as soon as possible but no later than 5:00 p.m. on November 15, 2021.

If you have any questions about this request, please contact Committee staff at (202) 225-6906. Thank you for your attention to this important matter.

Sincerely,

Jim Jordan
Ranking Member

Steve Chabot
Member of Congress

Louie Gohmert
Member of Congress

Darrell Issa
Ranking Member
Subcommittee on Courts, Intellectual Property, and the Internet

Ken Buck
Ranking Member
Subcommittee on Antitrust, Commercial and Administrative Law

Matt Gaetz
Member of Congress

Mike Johnson
Ranking Member
Subcommittee on the Constitution, Civil Rights and Civil Liberties

Andy Biggs
Ranking Member
Subcommittee on Crime, Terrorism and Homeland Security

Tom McClintock
Ranking Member
Subcommittee on Immigration and Citizenship

W. Gregory Steube
Member of Congress

Tom Tiffany
Member of Congress

Thomas Massie
Member of Congress

Chip Roy
Member of Congress

Dan Bishop
Member of Congress

Michelle Fischbach
Member of Congress

Victoria Spartz
Member of Congress

Scott Fitzgerald
Member of Congress

Cliff Bentz
Member of Congress

Burgess Owens
Member of Congress

cc: The Honorable Jerrold L. Nadler
Chairman

Mr. Monty Wilkinson
Director, Executive Office for U.S. Attorneys

JERROLD NADLER, New York
CHAIRMAN

JIM JORDAN, Ohio
RANKING MEMBER

ONE HUNDRED SEVENTEENTH CONGRESS

Congress of the United States

House of Representatives

COMMITTEE ON THE JUDICIARY

2138 RAYBURN HOUSE OFFICE BUILDING

WASHINGTON, DC 20515-6216

(202) 225-3951
judiciary.house.gov

November 1, 2021

Ms. Prim F. Escalona
U.S. Attorney
Northern District of Alabama
1801 4th Avenue North
Birmingham, AL 35203

Dear Ms. Escalona:

We are continuing to investigate the troubling attempts by the Department of Justice and the White House to use the heavy hand of federal law enforcement to target concerned parents at local school board meetings and chill their protected First Amendment activity. Because the Department directed you, along with all other U.S. Attorneys, and the Federal Bureau of Investigation (FBI) to take action to address parents attending school board meetings,[1] we respectfully request your assistance with our investigation.

On September 29, 2021, the National School Boards Association (NSBA) sent a letter to President Joe Biden requesting help from the federal government with concerned parents voicing their opinions at school board meetings.[2] The NSBA letter stated that "malice, violence, and threats" against school officials "could be the equivalent of a form of domestic terrorism or hate crimes."[3] The letter cited a number of interactions at school board meetings, none of which rose to the level of domestic terrorism. In fact, the vast majority of incidents cited by the NSBA did not involve threats or violence.[4] Most notably, as an example of domestic terrorism, the NSBA cited an incident in which a father angrily confronted members at a school board meeting in Loudoun County, Virginia about the heinous sexual assault of his daughter.[5]

A mere five days after the NSBA sent its letter to President Biden, on October 4, 2021, Attorney General Merrick Garland issued a shocking memorandum that directed the FBI and

---

[1] Memorandum from Atty Gen. Merrick Garland, U.S. Dep't of Justice, Partnership Among Federal, State, Local, Tribal, And Territorial Law Enforcement to Address Threats Against School Administrators, Board Members, Teachers, and Staff (Oct. 4, 2021).
[2] Letter from Dr. Viola M. Garcia, President, Nat'l School Board Assoc. & Mr. Chip Slaven, Chief Exec. Officer, Nat'l School Board Assoc., to President Joseph R. Biden, White House (Sept. 29, 2021).
[3] *Id.*
[4] *See* Caroline Downey, *Vast majority of incidents cited by school-board group to justify federal intervention didn't involve threats,* NAT'L REV. (Oct. 2, 2021).
[5] *Id.*; *see also* Jessica Chasmar, *Loudoun County father arrested at school board events says school tried to cover up daughter's bathroom assault*, FOX NEWS (Oct. 12, 2021).

U.S. Attorneys' Offices to "convene meetings" in your judicial district "with federal, state, local, Tribal, and territorial leaders" within 30 days.[6] The Justice Department simultaneously issued a press release indicating that the Attorney General's directive would "open dedicated lines of communication for threat reporting, assessment and response by law enforcement"—in other words, create a snitch line for complaints about concerned parents.[7]

During Attorney General Garland's testimony before our Committee on October 21, he appeared to have no idea whether the U.S. Attorney meetings he ordered were actually taking place. He stated: "I don't know whether [the meetings] are ongoing, but I expect and hope that they are going . . . because I did ask that they take place."[8] Attorney General Garland testified that he doubted "there have been meetings in every jurisdiction," but reiterated his belief that it is important for federal law enforcement authorities to conduct these meetings in every judicial district.[9] According to the Attorney General's directives, meetings are to be convened in all 94 judicial districts by November 3, 2021, at the latest.

Following the Attorney General's testimony, the NSBA Board of Directors, apparently recognizing the ill-conceived consequences of its letter and the resulting Justice Department action, issued a new memorandum to its members apologizing for the letter, stating: "On behalf of NSBA, we regret and apologize for the letter."[10] (emphasis in original). Although Attorney General Garland testified that the NSBA letter to President Biden was the basis for his October 4 directive to insert federal law enforcement into local school board matters, the Attorney General has yet to rescind his memorandum. His directives to you and other U.S. Attorneys remain in effect.

Concerned parents voicing their strong opposition to controversial curricula at local schools are not domestic terrorists. Parents have an undisputed right to direct the upbringing and education of their children.[11] When parents, however, cross the line to commit a violent act or issue a criminal threat,[12] state and local authorities are best-equipped to handle these violations of state law. But we must not tolerate the use of the federal law enforcement apparatus to intimidate and silence parents using their Constitutional rights to advocate for their child's future.

To assist our investigation and determine whether these meetings are ongoing, we request that you provide the following documents and information:

---

[6] Memorandum from Atty Gen. Merrick Garland, U.S. Dep't of Justice, Partnership Among Federal, State, Local, Tribal, And Territorial Law Enforcement to Address Threats Against School Administrators, Board Members, Teachers, and Staff (Oct. 4, 2021).
[7] Press Release, U.S. Dep't of Justice, Justice Department Addresses Violent Threats Against School Officials and Teachers (Oct. 4, 2021).
[8] *Oversight of the United States Department of Justice: Hearing Before the H. comm. on the Judiciary,* 117th Cong. at 94 (2021) (testimony from Hon. Merrick Garland, Atty Gen., U.S. Dep't of Justice).
[9] *Id.* at 95.
[10] Memorandum from NSBA Board of Directors, Message to NSBA Members (Oct. 22, 2021).
[11] *Troxel v. Granville,* 530 U.S. 57, 65 (2000) (citing *Meyer v. Nebraska,* 262 U.S. 390, 399 (1923)).
[12] *Merrick Garland's federal offense,* WALL ST. J. (Oct. 6, 2021).

1. All documents and communications referring or relating to convening meeting(s) in your judicial district in accordance with the Attorney General's October 4, 2021 memorandum;

2. All agendas, minutes, and notes created or relied upon by U.S. Attorney's Office employees referring or relating to meeting(s) in your judicial district in accordance with the Attorney General's October 4, 2021 memorandum;

3. Please explain when meeting(s) in your judicial district in accordance with the Attorney General's October 4, 2021 memorandum have occurred or will occur;

4. Please identify by name and title of all U.S. Attorney's Office employees involved in the meeting(s) in your judicial district in accordance with the Attorney General's October 4, 2021 memorandum ;

5. Please identify all federal, state, local, Tribal, and territorial organizations invited to or that have attended the meetings convened in your judicial district in accordance with the October 4, 2021 memorandum; and

6. Please provide all recommendations, both formal and informal, and any meeting minutes produced at the meeting(s) in your judicial district in accordance with the Attorney General's October 4, 2021 memorandum.

Please provide this material as soon as possible but no later than 5:00 p.m. on November 15, 2021.

If you have any questions about this request, please contact Committee staff at (202) 225-6906. Thank you for your attention to this important matter.

Sincerely,

Jim Jordan
Ranking Member

Steve Chabot
Member of Congress

Louie Gohmert
Member of Congress

Darrell Issa
Ranking Member
Subcommittee on Courts, Intellectual Property, and the Internet

Ken Buck
Ranking Member
Subcommittee on Antitrust, Commercial and Administrative Law

Matt Gaetz
Member of Congress

Mike Johnson
Ranking Member
Subcommittee on the Constitution, Civil Rights and Civil Liberties

Andy Biggs
Ranking Member
Subcommittee on Crime, Terrorism and Homeland Security

Tom McClintock
Ranking Member
Subcommittee on Immigration and Citizenship

W. Gregory Steube
Member of Congress

Tom Tiffany
Member of Congress

Thomas Massie
Member of Congress

Chip Roy
Member of Congress

Dan Bishop
Member of Congress

Michelle Fischbach
Member of Congress

Victoria Spartz
Member of Congress

Scott Fitzgerald
Member of Congress

Cliff Bentz
Member of Congress

Burgess Owens
Member of Congress

cc: The Honorable Jerrold L. Nadler
Chairman

Mr. Monty Wilkinson
Director, Executive Office for U.S. Attorneys

JERROLD NADLER, New York
CHAIRMAN

JIM JORDAN, Ohio
RANKING MEMBER

ONE HUNDRED SEVENTEENTH CONGRESS

Congress of the United States
House of Representatives
COMMITTEE ON THE JUDICIARY
2138 RAYBURN HOUSE OFFICE BUILDING
WASHINGTON, DC 20515-6216
(202) 225-3951
judiciary.house.gov

November 1, 2021

Ms. Sandra Stewart
Acting U.S. Attorney
Middle District of Alabama
131 Clayton Street
Montgomery, AL 36104

Dear Ms. Stewart:

We are continuing to investigate the troubling attempts by the Department of Justice and the White House to use the heavy hand of federal law enforcement to target concerned parents at local school board meetings and chill their protected First Amendment activity. Because the Department directed you, along with all other U.S. Attorneys, and the Federal Bureau of Investigation (FBI) to take action to address parents attending school board meetings,[1] we respectfully request your assistance with our investigation.

On September 29, 2021, the National School Boards Association (NSBA) sent a letter to President Joe Biden requesting help from the federal government with concerned parents voicing their opinions at school board meetings.[2] The NSBA letter stated that "malice, violence, and threats" against school officials "could be the equivalent of a form of domestic terrorism or hate crimes."[3] The letter cited a number of interactions at school board meetings, none of which rose to the level of domestic terrorism. In fact, the vast majority of incidents cited by the NSBA did not involve threats or violence.[4] Most notably, as an example of domestic terrorism, the NSBA cited an incident in which a father angrily confronted members at a school board meeting in Loudoun County, Virginia about the heinous sexual assault of his daughter.[5]

A mere five days after the NSBA sent its letter to President Biden, on October 4, 2021, Attorney General Merrick Garland issued a shocking memorandum that directed the FBI and

---

[1] Memorandum from Atty Gen. Merrick Garland, U.S. Dep't of Justice, Partnership Among Federal, State, Local, Tribal, And Territorial Law Enforcement to Address Threats Against School Administrators, Board Members, Teachers, and Staff (Oct. 4, 2021).
[2] Letter from Dr. Viola M. Garcia, President, Nat'l School Board Assoc. & Mr. Chip Slaven, Chief Exec. Officer, Nat'l School Board Assoc., to President Joseph R. Biden, White House (Sept. 29, 2021).
[3] *Id.*
[4] *See* Caroline Downey, *Vast majority of incidents cited by school-board group to justify federal intervention didn't involve threats,* NAT'L REV. (Oct. 2, 2021).
[5] *Id.*; *see also* Jessica Chasmar, *Loudoun County father arrested at school board events says school tried to cover up daughter's bathroom assault*, FOX NEWS (Oct. 12, 2021).

U.S. Attorneys' Offices to "convene meetings" in your judicial district "with federal, state, local, Tribal, and territorial leaders" within 30 days.[6] The Justice Department simultaneously issued a press release indicating that the Attorney General's directive would "open dedicated lines of communication for threat reporting, assessment and response by law enforcement"—in other words, create a snitch line for complaints about concerned parents.[7]

During Attorney General Garland's testimony before our Committee on October 21, he appeared to have no idea whether the U.S. Attorney meetings he ordered were actually taking place. He stated: "I don't know whether [the meetings] are ongoing, but I expect and hope that they are going . . . because I did ask that they take place."[8] Attorney General Garland testified that he doubted "there have been meetings in every jurisdiction," but reiterated his belief that it is important for federal law enforcement authorities to conduct these meetings in every judicial district.[9] According to the Attorney General's directives, meetings are to be convened in all 94 judicial districts by November 3, 2021, at the latest.

Following the Attorney General's testimony, the NSBA Board of Directors, apparently recognizing the ill-conceived consequences of its letter and the resulting Justice Department action, issued a new memorandum to its members apologizing for the letter, stating: "On behalf of NSBA, <u>we regret and apologize for the letter</u>."[10] (emphasis in original). Although Attorney General Garland testified that the NSBA letter to President Biden was the basis for his October 4 directive to insert federal law enforcement into local school board matters, the Attorney General has yet to rescind his memorandum. His directives to you and other U.S. Attorneys remain in effect.

Concerned parents voicing their strong opposition to controversial curricula at local schools are not domestic terrorists. Parents have an undisputed right to direct the upbringing and education of their children.[11] When parents, however, cross the line to commit a violent act or issue a criminal threat,[12] state and local authorities are best-equipped to handle these violations of state law. But we must not tolerate the use of the federal law enforcement apparatus to intimidate and silence parents using their Constitutional rights to advocate for their child's future.

To assist our investigation and determine whether these meetings are ongoing, we request that you provide the following documents and information:

---

[6] Memorandum from Atty Gen. Merrick Garland, U.S. Dep't of Justice, Partnership Among Federal, State, Local, Tribal, And Territorial Law Enforcement to Address Threats Against School Administrators, Board Members, Teachers, and Staff (Oct. 4, 2021).

[7] Press Release, U.S. Dep't of Justice, Justice Department Addresses Violent Threats Against School Officials and Teachers (Oct. 4, 2021).

[8] *Oversight of the United States Department of Justice: Hearing Before the H. comm. on the Judiciary,* 117th Cong. at 94 (2021) (testimony from Hon. Merrick Garland, Atty Gen., U.S. Dep't of Justice).

[9] *Id.* at 95.

[10] Memorandum from NSBA Board of Directors, Message to NSBA Members (Oct. 22, 2021).

[11] *Troxel v. Granville,* 530 U.S. 57, 65 (2000) (citing *Meyer v. Nebraska,* 262 U.S. 390, 399 (1923)).

[12] *Merrick Garland's federal offense,* WALL ST. J. (Oct. 6, 2021).

1. All documents and communications referring or relating to convening meeting(s) in your judicial district in accordance with the Attorney General's October 4, 2021 memorandum;

2. All agendas, minutes, and notes created or relied upon by U.S. Attorney's Office employees referring or relating to meeting(s) in your judicial district in accordance with the Attorney General's October 4, 2021 memorandum;

3. Please explain when meeting(s) in your judicial district in accordance with the Attorney General's October 4, 2021 memorandum have occurred or will occur;

4. Please identify by name and title of all U.S. Attorney's Office employees involved in the meeting(s) in your judicial district in accordance with the Attorney General's October 4, 2021 memorandum ;

5. Please identify all federal, state, local, Tribal, and territorial organizations invited to or that have attended the meetings convened in your judicial district in accordance with the October 4, 2021 memorandum; and

6. Please provide all recommendations, both formal and informal, and any meeting minutes produced at the meeting(s) in your judicial district in accordance with the Attorney General's October 4, 2021 memorandum.

Please provide this material as soon as possible but no later than 5:00 p.m. on November 15, 2021.

If you have any questions about this request, please contact Committee staff at (202) 225-6906. Thank you for your attention to this important matter.

Sincerely,

Jim Jordan
Ranking Member

Steve Chabot
Member of Congress

Louie Gohmert
Member of Congress

Darrell Issa
Ranking Member
Subcommittee on Courts, Intellectual Property, and the Internet

Ms. Sandra Stewart
November 1, 2021
Page 4

Ken Buck
Ranking Member
Subcommittee on Antitrust, Commercial and Administrative Law

Matt Gaetz
Member of Congress

Mike Johnson
Ranking Member
Subcommittee on the Constitution, Civil Rights and Civil Liberties

Andy Biggs
Ranking Member
Subcommittee on Crime, Terrorism and Homeland Security

Tom McClintock
Ranking Member
Subcommittee on Immigration and Citizenship

W. Gregory Steube
Member of Congress

Tom Tiffany
Member of Congress

Thomas Massie
Member of Congress

Chip Roy
Member of Congress

Dan Bishop
Member of Congress

Michelle Fischbach
Member of Congress

Victoria Spartz
Member of Congress

Scott Fitzgerald
Member of Congress

Cliff Bentz
Member of Congress

Burgess Owens
Member of Congress

cc: The Honorable Jerrold L. Nadler
Chairman

Mr. Monty Wilkinson
Director, Executive Office for U.S. Attorneys

JERROLD NADLER, New York
CHAIRMAN

JIM JORDAN, Ohio
RANKING MEMBER

ONE HUNDRED SEVENTEENTH CONGRESS

Congress of the United States

House of Representatives

COMMITTEE ON THE JUDICIARY

2138 RAYBURN HOUSE OFFICE BUILDING

WASHINGTON, DC 20515-6216

(202) 225-3951
judiciary.house.gov

November 1, 2021

Mr. David Clay Fowlkes
Acting U.S. Attorney
Western District of Arkansas
414 Parker Avenue
Fort Smith, AR 72901

Dear Mr. Fowlkes:

We are continuing to investigate the troubling attempts by the Department of Justice and the White House to use the heavy hand of federal law enforcement to target concerned parents at local school board meetings and chill their protected First Amendment activity. Because the Department directed you, along with all other U.S. Attorneys, and the Federal Bureau of Investigation (FBI) to take action to address parents attending school board meetings,[1] we respectfully request your assistance with our investigation.

On September 29, 2021, the National School Boards Association (NSBA) sent a letter to President Joe Biden requesting help from the federal government with concerned parents voicing their opinions at school board meetings.[2] The NSBA letter stated that "malice, violence, and threats" against school officials "could be the equivalent of a form of domestic terrorism or hate crimes."[3] The letter cited a number of interactions at school board meetings, none of which rose to the level of domestic terrorism. In fact, the vast majority of incidents cited by the NSBA did not involve threats or violence.[4] Most notably, as an example of domestic terrorism, the NSBA cited an incident in which a father angrily confronted members at a school board meeting in Loudoun County, Virginia about the heinous sexual assault of his daughter.[5]

A mere five days after the NSBA sent its letter to President Biden, on October 4, 2021, Attorney General Merrick Garland issued a shocking memorandum that directed the FBI and

---

[1] Memorandum from Atty Gen. Merrick Garland, U.S. Dep't of Justice, Partnership Among Federal, State, Local, Tribal, And Territorial Law Enforcement to Address Threats Against School Administrators, Board Members, Teachers, and Staff (Oct. 4, 2021).
[2] Letter from Dr. Viola M. Garcia, President, Nat'l School Board Assoc. & Mr. Chip Slaven, Chief Exec. Officer, Nat'l School Board Assoc., to President Joseph R. Biden, White House (Sept. 29, 2021).
[3] *Id.*
[4] *See* Caroline Downey, *Vast majority of incidents cited by school-board group to justify federal intervention didn't involve threats,* NAT'L REV. (Oct. 2, 2021).
[5] *Id.*; *see also* Jessica Chasmar, *Loudoun County father arrested at school board events says school tried to cover up daughter's bathroom assault*, FOX NEWS (Oct. 12, 2021).

U.S. Attorneys' Offices to "convene meetings" in your judicial district "with federal, state, local, Tribal, and territorial leaders" within 30 days.[6] The Justice Department simultaneously issued a press release indicating that the Attorney General's directive would "open dedicated lines of communication for threat reporting, assessment and response by law enforcement"—in other words, create a snitch line for complaints about concerned parents.[7]

During Attorney General Garland's testimony before our Committee on October 21, he appeared to have no idea whether the U.S. Attorney meetings he ordered were actually taking place. He stated: "I don't know whether [the meetings] are ongoing, but I expect and hope that they are going . . . because I did ask that they take place."[8] Attorney General Garland testified that he doubted "there have been meetings in every jurisdiction," but reiterated his belief that it is important for federal law enforcement authorities to conduct these meetings in every judicial district.[9] According to the Attorney General's directives, meetings are to be convened in all 94 judicial districts by November 3, 2021, at the latest.

Following the Attorney General's testimony, the NSBA Board of Directors, apparently recognizing the ill-conceived consequences of its letter and the resulting Justice Department action, issued a new memorandum to its members apologizing for the letter, stating: "On behalf of NSBA, <u>we regret and apologize for the letter</u>."[10] (emphasis in original). Although Attorney General Garland testified that the NSBA letter to President Biden was the basis for his October 4 directive to insert federal law enforcement into local school board matters, the Attorney General has yet to rescind his memorandum. His directives to you and other U.S. Attorneys remain in effect.

Concerned parents voicing their strong opposition to controversial curricula at local schools are not domestic terrorists. Parents have an undisputed right to direct the upbringing and education of their children.[11] When parents, however, cross the line to commit a violent act or issue a criminal threat,[12] state and local authorities are best-equipped to handle these violations of state law. But we must not tolerate the use of the federal law enforcement apparatus to intimidate and silence parents using their Constitutional rights to advocate for their child's future.

To assist our investigation and determine whether these meetings are ongoing, we request that you provide the following documents and information:

---

[6] Memorandum from Atty Gen. Merrick Garland, U.S. Dep't of Justice, Partnership Among Federal, State, Local, Tribal, And Territorial Law Enforcement to Address Threats Against School Administrators, Board Members, Teachers, and Staff (Oct. 4, 2021).
[7] Press Release, U.S. Dep't of Justice, Justice Department Addresses Violent Threats Against School Officials and Teachers (Oct. 4, 2021).
[8] *Oversight of the United States Department of Justice: Hearing Before the H. comm. on the Judiciary,* 117th Cong. at 94 (2021) (testimony from Hon. Merrick Garland, Atty Gen., U.S. Dep't of Justice).
[9] *Id.* at 95.
[10] Memorandum from NSBA Board of Directors, Message to NSBA Members (Oct. 22, 2021).
[11] *Troxel v. Granville,* 530 U.S. 57, 65 (2000) (citing *Meyer v. Nebraska,* 262 U.S. 390, 399 (1923)).
[12] *Merrick Garland's federal offense,* WALL ST. J. (Oct. 6, 2021).

1. All documents and communications referring or relating to convening meeting(s) in your judicial district in accordance with the Attorney General's October 4, 2021 memorandum;

2. All agendas, minutes, and notes created or relied upon by U.S. Attorney's Office employees referring or relating to meeting(s) in your judicial district in accordance with the Attorney General's October 4, 2021 memorandum;

3. Please explain when meeting(s) in your judicial district in accordance with the Attorney General's October 4, 2021 memorandum have occurred or will occur;

4. Please identify by name and title of all U.S. Attorney's Office employees involved in the meeting(s) in your judicial district in accordance with the Attorney General's October 4, 2021 memorandum ;

5. Please identify all federal, state, local, Tribal, and territorial organizations invited to or that have attended the meetings convened in your judicial district in accordance with the October 4, 2021 memorandum; and

6. Please provide all recommendations, both formal and informal, and any meeting minutes produced at the meeting(s) in your judicial district in accordance with the Attorney General's October 4, 2021 memorandum.

Please provide this material as soon as possible but no later than 5:00 p.m. on November 15, 2021.

If you have any questions about this request, please contact Committee staff at (202) 225-6906. Thank you for your attention to this important matter.

Sincerely,

Jim Jordan
Ranking Member

Steve Chabot
Member of Congress

Louie Gohmert
Member of Congress

Darrell Issa
Ranking Member
Subcommittee on Courts, Intellectual Property, and the Internet

Ken Buck
Ranking Member
Subcommittee on Antitrust, Commercial and Administrative Law

Matt Gaetz
Member of Congress

Mike Johnson
Ranking Member
Subcommittee on the Constitution, Civil Rights and Civil Liberties

Andy Biggs
Ranking Member
Subcommittee on Crime, Terrorism and Homeland Security

Tom McClintock
Ranking Member
Subcommittee on Immigration and Citizenship

W. Gregory Steube
Member of Congress

Tom Tiffany
Member of Congress

Thomas Massie
Member of Congress

Chip Roy
Member of Congress

Dan Bishop
Member of Congress

Michelle Fischbach
Member of Congress

Victoria Spartz
Member of Congress

Scott Fitzgerald
Member of Congress

Cliff Bentz
Member of Congress

Burgess Owens
Member of Congress

cc: The Honorable Jerrold L. Nadler
Chairman

Mr. Monty Wilkinson
Director, Executive Office for U.S. Attorneys

JERROLD NADLER, New York
CHAIRMAN

JIM JORDAN, Ohio
RANKING MEMBER

ONE HUNDRED SEVENTEENTH CONGRESS
Congress of the United States
House of Representatives
COMMITTEE ON THE JUDICIARY
2138 RAYBURN HOUSE OFFICE BUILDING
WASHINGTON, DC 20515-6216
(202) 225-3951
judiciary.house.gov

November 1, 2021

Mr. Jonathan D. Ross
Acting U.S. Attorney
Eastern District of Arkansas
425 West Capitol Avenue, Suite 500
Little Rock, AR 72201

Dear Mr. Ross:

We are continuing to investigate the troubling attempts by the Department of Justice and the White House to use the heavy hand of federal law enforcement to target concerned parents at local school board meetings and chill their protected First Amendment activity. Because the Department directed you, along with all other U.S. Attorneys, and the Federal Bureau of Investigation (FBI) to take action to address parents attending school board meetings,[1] we respectfully request your assistance with our investigation.

On September 29, 2021, the National School Boards Association (NSBA) sent a letter to President Joe Biden requesting help from the federal government with concerned parents voicing their opinions at school board meetings.[2] The NSBA letter stated that "malice, violence, and threats" against school officials "could be the equivalent of a form of domestic terrorism or hate crimes."[3] The letter cited a number of interactions at school board meetings, none of which rose to the level of domestic terrorism. In fact, the vast majority of incidents cited by the NSBA did not involve threats or violence.[4] Most notably, as an example of domestic terrorism, the NSBA cited an incident in which a father angrily confronted members at a school board meeting in Loudoun County, Virginia about the heinous sexual assault of his daughter.[5]

A mere five days after the NSBA sent its letter to President Biden, on October 4, 2021, Attorney General Merrick Garland issued a shocking memorandum that directed the FBI and

---

[1] Memorandum from Atty Gen. Merrick Garland, U.S. Dep't of Justice, Partnership Among Federal, State, Local, Tribal, And Territorial Law Enforcement to Address Threats Against School Administrators, Board Members, Teachers, and Staff (Oct. 4, 2021).
[2] Letter from Dr. Viola M. Garcia, President, Nat'l School Board Assoc. & Mr. Chip Slaven, Chief Exec. Officer, Nat'l School Board Assoc., to President Joseph R. Biden, White House (Sept. 29, 2021).
[3] *Id.*
[4] *See* Caroline Downey, *Vast majority of incidents cited by school-board group to justify federal intervention didn't involve threats,* NAT'L REV. (Oct. 2, 2021).
[5] *Id.*; *see also* Jessica Chasmar, *Loudoun County father arrested at school board events says school tried to cover up daughter's bathroom assault*, FOX NEWS (Oct. 12, 2021).

U.S. Attorneys' Offices to "convene meetings" in your judicial district "with federal, state, local, Tribal, and territorial leaders" within 30 days.[6] The Justice Department simultaneously issued a press release indicating that the Attorney General's directive would "open dedicated lines of communication for threat reporting, assessment and response by law enforcement"—in other words, create a snitch line for complaints about concerned parents.[7]

During Attorney General Garland's testimony before our Committee on October 21, he appeared to have no idea whether the U.S. Attorney meetings he ordered were actually taking place. He stated: "I don't know whether [the meetings] are ongoing, but I expect and hope that they are going . . . because I did ask that they take place."[8] Attorney General Garland testified that he doubted "there have been meetings in every jurisdiction," but reiterated his belief that it is important for federal law enforcement authorities to conduct these meetings in every judicial district.[9] According to the Attorney General's directives, meetings are to be convened in all 94 judicial districts by November 3, 2021, at the latest.

Following the Attorney General's testimony, the NSBA Board of Directors, apparently recognizing the ill-conceived consequences of its letter and the resulting Justice Department action, issued a new memorandum to its members apologizing for the letter, stating: "On behalf of NSBA, <u>we regret and apologize for the letter</u>."[10] (emphasis in original). Although Attorney General Garland testified that the NSBA letter to President Biden was the basis for his October 4 directive to insert federal law enforcement into local school board matters, the Attorney General has yet to rescind his memorandum. His directives to you and other U.S. Attorneys remain in effect.

Concerned parents voicing their strong opposition to controversial curricula at local schools are not domestic terrorists. Parents have an undisputed right to direct the upbringing and education of their children.[11] When parents, however, cross the line to commit a violent act or issue a criminal threat,[12] state and local authorities are best-equipped to handle these violations of state law. But we must not tolerate the use of the federal law enforcement apparatus to intimidate and silence parents using their Constitutional rights to advocate for their child's future.

To assist our investigation and determine whether these meetings are ongoing, we request that you provide the following documents and information:

---

[6] Memorandum from Atty Gen. Merrick Garland, U.S. Dep't of Justice, Partnership Among Federal, State, Local, Tribal, And Territorial Law Enforcement to Address Threats Against School Administrators, Board Members, Teachers, and Staff (Oct. 4, 2021).
[7] Press Release, U.S. Dep't of Justice, Justice Department Addresses Violent Threats Against School Officials and Teachers (Oct. 4, 2021).
[8] *Oversight of the United States Department of Justice: Hearing Before the H. comm. on the Judiciary,* 117th Cong. at 94 (2021) (testimony from Hon. Merrick Garland, Atty Gen., U.S. Dep't of Justice).
[9] *Id.* at 95.
[10] Memorandum from NSBA Board of Directors, Message to NSBA Members (Oct. 22, 2021).
[11] *Troxel v. Granville,* 530 U.S. 57, 65 (2000) (citing *Meyer v. Nebraska,* 262 U.S. 390, 399 (1923)).
[12] *Merrick Garland's federal offense,* WALL ST. J. (Oct. 6, 2021).

1. All documents and communications referring or relating to convening meeting(s) in your judicial district in accordance with the Attorney General's October 4, 2021 memorandum;

2. All agendas, minutes, and notes created or relied upon by U.S. Attorney's Office employees referring or relating to meeting(s) in your judicial district in accordance with the Attorney General's October 4, 2021 memorandum;

3. Please explain when meeting(s) in your judicial district in accordance with the Attorney General's October 4, 2021 memorandum have occurred or will occur;

4. Please identify by name and title of all U.S. Attorney's Office employees involved in the meeting(s) in your judicial district in accordance with the Attorney General's October 4, 2021 memorandum ;

5. Please identify all federal, state, local, Tribal, and territorial organizations invited to or that have attended the meetings convened in your judicial district in accordance with the October 4, 2021 memorandum; and

6. Please provide all recommendations, both formal and informal, and any meeting minutes produced at the meeting(s) in your judicial district in accordance with the Attorney General's October 4, 2021 memorandum.

Please provide this material as soon as possible but no later than 5:00 p.m. on November 15, 2021.

If you have any questions about this request, please contact Committee staff at (202) 225-6906. Thank you for your attention to this important matter.

Sincerely,

Jim Jordan
Ranking Member

Steve Chabot
Member of Congress

Louie Gohmert
Member of Congress

Darrell Issa
Ranking Member
Subcommittee on Courts, Intellectual Property, and the Internet

Ken Buck
Ranking Member
Subcommittee on Antitrust, Commercial and Administrative Law

Matt Gaetz
Member of Congress

Mike Johnson
Ranking Member
Subcommittee on the Constitution, Civil Rights and Civil Liberties

Andy Biggs
Ranking Member
Subcommittee on Crime, Terrorism and Homeland Security

Tom McClintock
Ranking Member
Subcommittee on Immigration and Citizenship

W. Gregory Steube
Member of Congress

Tom Tiffany
Member of Congress

Thomas Massie
Member of Congress

Chip Roy
Member of Congress

Dan Bishop
Member of Congress

Michelle Fischbach
Member of Congress

Victoria Spartz
Member of Congress

Scott Fitzgerald
Member of Congress

Cliff Bentz
Member of Congress

Burgess Owens
Member of Congress

cc: The Honorable Jerrold L. Nadler
Chairman

Mr. Monty Wilkinson
Director, Executive Office for U.S. Attorneys

JERROLD NADLER, New York
CHAIRMAN

JIM JORDAN, Ohio
RANKING MEMBER

ONE HUNDRED SEVENTEENTH CONGRESS

Congress of the United States
House of Representatives
COMMITTEE ON THE JUDICIARY

2138 RAYBURN HOUSE OFFICE BUILDING
WASHINGTON, DC 20515–6216
(202) 225–3951
judiciary.house.gov

November 1, 2021

Mr. Glenn B. McCormick
Acting U.S. Attorney
District of Arizona
Two Renaissance Square 40 N. Central Avenue, Suite 1800
Phoenix, AZ 85004

Dear Mr. McCormick:

We are continuing to investigate the troubling attempts by the Department of Justice and the White House to use the heavy hand of federal law enforcement to target concerned parents at local school board meetings and chill their protected First Amendment activity. Because the Department directed you, along with all other U.S. Attorneys, and the Federal Bureau of Investigation (FBI) to take action to address parents attending school board meetings,[1] we respectfully request your assistance with our investigation.

On September 29, 2021, the National School Boards Association (NSBA) sent a letter to President Joe Biden requesting help from the federal government with concerned parents voicing their opinions at school board meetings.[2] The NSBA letter stated that "malice, violence, and threats" against school officials "could be the equivalent of a form of domestic terrorism or hate crimes."[3] The letter cited a number of interactions at school board meetings, none of which rose to the level of domestic terrorism. In fact, the vast majority of incidents cited by the NSBA did not involve threats or violence.[4] Most notably, as an example of domestic terrorism, the NSBA cited an incident in which a father angrily confronted members at a school board meeting in Loudoun County, Virginia about the heinous sexual assault of his daughter.[5]

A mere five days after the NSBA sent its letter to President Biden, on October 4, 2021, Attorney General Merrick Garland issued a shocking memorandum that directed the FBI and

---

[1] Memorandum from Atty Gen. Merrick Garland, U.S. Dep't of Justice, Partnership Among Federal, State, Local, Tribal, And Territorial Law Enforcement to Address Threats Against School Administrators, Board Members, Teachers, and Staff (Oct. 4, 2021).
[2] Letter from Dr. Viola M. Garcia, President, Nat'l School Board Assoc. & Mr. Chip Slaven, Chief Exec. Officer, Nat'l School Board Assoc., to President Joseph R. Biden, White House (Sept. 29, 2021).
[3] *Id.*
[4] *See* Caroline Downey, *Vast majority of incidents cited by school-board group to justify federal intervention didn't involve threats,* NAT'L REV. (Oct. 2, 2021).
[5] *Id.*; *see also* Jessica Chasmar, *Loudoun County father arrested at school board events says school tried to cover up daughter's bathroom assault*, FOX NEWS (Oct. 12, 2021).

U.S. Attorneys' Offices to "convene meetings" in your judicial district "with federal, state, local, Tribal, and territorial leaders" within 30 days.[6] The Justice Department simultaneously issued a press release indicating that the Attorney General's directive would "open dedicated lines of communication for threat reporting, assessment and response by law enforcement"—in other words, create a snitch line for complaints about concerned parents.[7]

During Attorney General Garland's testimony before our Committee on October 21, he appeared to have no idea whether the U.S. Attorney meetings he ordered were actually taking place. He stated: "I don't know whether [the meetings] are ongoing, but I expect and hope that they are going . . . because I did ask that they take place."[8] Attorney General Garland testified that he doubted "there have been meetings in every jurisdiction," but reiterated his belief that it is important for federal law enforcement authorities to conduct these meetings in every judicial district.[9] According to the Attorney General's directives, meetings are to be convened in all 94 judicial districts by November 3, 2021, at the latest.

Following the Attorney General's testimony, the NSBA Board of Directors, apparently recognizing the ill-conceived consequences of its letter and the resulting Justice Department action, issued a new memorandum to its members apologizing for the letter, stating: "On behalf of NSBA, <u>we regret and apologize for the letter</u>."[10] (emphasis in original). Although Attorney General Garland testified that the NSBA letter to President Biden was the basis for his October 4 directive to insert federal law enforcement into local school board matters, the Attorney General has yet to rescind his memorandum. His directives to you and other U.S. Attorneys remain in effect.

Concerned parents voicing their strong opposition to controversial curricula at local schools are not domestic terrorists. Parents have an undisputed right to direct the upbringing and education of their children.[11] When parents, however, cross the line to commit a violent act or issue a criminal threat,[12] state and local authorities are best-equipped to handle these violations of state law. But we must not tolerate the use of the federal law enforcement apparatus to intimidate and silence parents using their Constitutional rights to advocate for their child's future.

To assist our investigation and determine whether these meetings are ongoing, we request that you provide the following documents and information:

---

[6] Memorandum from Atty Gen. Merrick Garland, U.S. Dep't of Justice, Partnership Among Federal, State, Local, Tribal, And Territorial Law Enforcement to Address Threats Against School Administrators, Board Members, Teachers, and Staff (Oct. 4, 2021).
[7] Press Release, U.S. Dep't of Justice, Justice Department Addresses Violent Threats Against School Officials and Teachers (Oct. 4, 2021).
[8] *Oversight of the United States Department of Justice: Hearing Before the H. comm. on the Judiciary,* 117th Cong. at 94 (2021) (testimony from Hon. Merrick Garland, Atty Gen., U.S. Dep't of Justice).
[9] *Id.* at 95.
[10] Memorandum from NSBA Board of Directors, Message to NSBA Members (Oct. 22, 2021).
[11] *Troxel v. Granville,* 530 U.S. 57, 65 (2000) (citing *Meyer v. Nebraska,* 262 U.S. 390, 399 (1923)).
[12] *Merrick Garland's federal offense,* WALL ST. J. (Oct. 6, 2021).

1. All documents and communications referring or relating to convening meeting(s) in your judicial district in accordance with the Attorney General's October 4, 2021 memorandum;

2. All agendas, minutes, and notes created or relied upon by U.S. Attorney's Office employees referring or relating to meeting(s) in your judicial district in accordance with the Attorney General's October 4, 2021 memorandum;

3. Please explain when meeting(s) in your judicial district in accordance with the Attorney General's October 4, 2021 memorandum have occurred or will occur;

4. Please identify by name and title of all U.S. Attorney's Office employees involved in the meeting(s) in your judicial district in accordance with the Attorney General's October 4, 2021 memorandum ;

5. Please identify all federal, state, local, Tribal, and territorial organizations invited to or that have attended the meetings convened in your judicial district in accordance with the October 4, 2021 memorandum; and

6. Please provide all recommendations, both formal and informal, and any meeting minutes produced at the meeting(s) in your judicial district in accordance with the Attorney General's October 4, 2021 memorandum.

Please provide this material as soon as possible but no later than 5:00 p.m. on November 15, 2021.

If you have any questions about this request, please contact Committee staff at (202) 225-6906. Thank you for your attention to this important matter.

Sincerely,

Jim Jordan
Ranking Member

Steve Chabot
Member of Congress

Louie Gohmert
Member of Congress

Darrell Issa
Ranking Member
Subcommittee on Courts, Intellectual Property, and the Internet

Ken Buck
Ranking Member
Subcommittee on Antitrust, Commercial and Administrative Law

Matt Gaetz
Member of Congress

Mike Johnson
Ranking Member
Subcommittee on the Constitution, Civil Rights and Civil Liberties

Andy Biggs
Ranking Member
Subcommittee on Crime, Terrorism and Homeland Security

Tom McClintock
Ranking Member
Subcommittee on Immigration and Citizenship

W. Gregory Steube
Member of Congress

Tom Tiffany
Member of Congress

Thomas Massie
Member of Congress

Chip Roy
Member of Congress

Dan Bishop
Member of Congress

Michelle Fischbach
Member of Congress

Victoria Spartz
Member of Congress

Scott Fitzgerald
Member of Congress

Cliff Bentz
Member of Congress

Burgess Owens
Member of Congress

cc: The Honorable Jerrold L. Nadler
Chairman

Mr. Monty Wilkinson
Director, Executive Office for U.S. Attorneys

JERROLD NADLER, New York
CHAIRMAN

JIM JORDAN, Ohio
RANKING MEMBER

ONE HUNDRED SEVENTEENTH CONGRESS
Congress of the United States
House of Representatives
COMMITTEE ON THE JUDICIARY
2138 Rayburn House Office Building
Washington, DC 20515-6216
(202) 225-3951
judiciary.house.gov

November 1, 2021

Mr. Randy S. Grossman
Acting U.S. Attorney
Southern District of California
880 Front Street, Room 6293
San Diego, CA 92101

Dear Mr. Grossman:

We are continuing to investigate the troubling attempts by the Department of Justice and the White House to use the heavy hand of federal law enforcement to target concerned parents at local school board meetings and chill their protected First Amendment activity. Because the Department directed you, along with all other U.S. Attorneys, and the Federal Bureau of Investigation (FBI) to take action to address parents attending school board meetings,[1] we respectfully request your assistance with our investigation.

On September 29, 2021, the National School Boards Association (NSBA) sent a letter to President Joe Biden requesting help from the federal government with concerned parents voicing their opinions at school board meetings.[2] The NSBA letter stated that "malice, violence, and threats" against school officials "could be the equivalent of a form of domestic terrorism or hate crimes."[3] The letter cited a number of interactions at school board meetings, none of which rose to the level of domestic terrorism. In fact, the vast majority of incidents cited by the NSBA did not involve threats or violence.[4] Most notably, as an example of domestic terrorism, the NSBA cited an incident in which a father angrily confronted members at a school board meeting in Loudoun County, Virginia about the heinous sexual assault of his daughter.[5]

A mere five days after the NSBA sent its letter to President Biden, on October 4, 2021, Attorney General Merrick Garland issued a shocking memorandum that directed the FBI and

---

[1] Memorandum from Atty Gen. Merrick Garland, U.S. Dep't of Justice, Partnership Among Federal, State, Local, Tribal, And Territorial Law Enforcement to Address Threats Against School Administrators, Board Members, Teachers, and Staff (Oct. 4, 2021).
[2] Letter from Dr. Viola M. Garcia, President, Nat'l School Board Assoc. & Mr. Chip Slaven, Chief Exec. Officer, Nat'l School Board Assoc., to President Joseph R. Biden, White House (Sept. 29, 2021).
[3] *Id.*
[4] *See* Caroline Downey, *Vast majority of incidents cited by school-board group to justify federal intervention didn't involve threats,* NAT'L REV. (Oct. 2, 2021).
[5] *Id.*; *see also* Jessica Chasmar, *Loudoun County father arrested at school board events says school tried to cover up daughter's bathroom assault*, FOX NEWS (Oct. 12, 2021).

U.S. Attorneys' Offices to "convene meetings" in your judicial district "with federal, state, local, Tribal, and territorial leaders" within 30 days.[6] The Justice Department simultaneously issued a press release indicating that the Attorney General's directive would "open dedicated lines of communication for threat reporting, assessment and response by law enforcement"—in other words, create a snitch line for complaints about concerned parents.[7]

During Attorney General Garland's testimony before our Committee on October 21, he appeared to have no idea whether the U.S. Attorney meetings he ordered were actually taking place. He stated: "I don't know whether [the meetings] are ongoing, but I expect and hope that they are going . . . because I did ask that they take place."[8] Attorney General Garland testified that he doubted "there have been meetings in every jurisdiction," but reiterated his belief that it is important for federal law enforcement authorities to conduct these meetings in every judicial district.[9] According to the Attorney General's directives, meetings are to be convened in all 94 judicial districts by November 3, 2021, at the latest.

Following the Attorney General's testimony, the NSBA Board of Directors, apparently recognizing the ill-conceived consequences of its letter and the resulting Justice Department action, issued a new memorandum to its members apologizing for the letter, stating: "On behalf of NSBA, <u>we regret and apologize for the letter</u>."[10] (emphasis in original). Although Attorney General Garland testified that the NSBA letter to President Biden was the basis for his October 4 directive to insert federal law enforcement into local school board matters, the Attorney General has yet to rescind his memorandum. His directives to you and other U.S. Attorneys remain in effect.

Concerned parents voicing their strong opposition to controversial curricula at local schools are not domestic terrorists. Parents have an undisputed right to direct the upbringing and education of their children.[11] When parents, however, cross the line to commit a violent act or issue a criminal threat,[12] state and local authorities are best-equipped to handle these violations of state law. But we must not tolerate the use of the federal law enforcement apparatus to intimidate and silence parents using their Constitutional rights to advocate for their child's future.

To assist our investigation and determine whether these meetings are ongoing, we request that you provide the following documents and information:

---

[6] Memorandum from Atty Gen. Merrick Garland, U.S. Dep't of Justice, Partnership Among Federal, State, Local, Tribal, And Territorial Law Enforcement to Address Threats Against School Administrators, Board Members, Teachers, and Staff (Oct. 4, 2021).
[7] Press Release, U.S. Dep't of Justice, Justice Department Addresses Violent Threats Against School Officials and Teachers (Oct. 4, 2021).
[8] *Oversight of the United States Department of Justice: Hearing Before the H. comm. on the Judiciary,* 117th Cong. at 94 (2021) (testimony from Hon. Merrick Garland, Atty Gen., U.S. Dep't of Justice).
[9] *Id.* at 95.
[10] Memorandum from NSBA Board of Directors, Message to NSBA Members (Oct. 22, 2021).
[11] *Troxel v. Granville,* 530 U.S. 57, 65 (2000) (citing *Meyer v. Nebraska,* 262 U.S. 390, 399 (1923)).
[12] *Merrick Garland's federal offense,* WALL ST. J. (Oct. 6, 2021).

1. All documents and communications referring or relating to convening meeting(s) in your judicial district in accordance with the Attorney General's October 4, 2021 memorandum;

2. All agendas, minutes, and notes created or relied upon by U.S. Attorney's Office employees referring or relating to meeting(s) in your judicial district in accordance with the Attorney General's October 4, 2021 memorandum;

3. Please explain when meeting(s) in your judicial district in accordance with the Attorney General's October 4, 2021 memorandum have occurred or will occur;

4. Please identify by name and title of all U.S. Attorney's Office employees involved in the meeting(s) in your judicial district in accordance with the Attorney General's October 4, 2021 memorandum ;

5. Please identify all federal, state, local, Tribal, and territorial organizations invited to or that have attended the meetings convened in your judicial district in accordance with the October 4, 2021 memorandum; and

6. Please provide all recommendations, both formal and informal, and any meeting minutes produced at the meeting(s) in your judicial district in accordance with the Attorney General's October 4, 2021 memorandum.

Please provide this material as soon as possible but no later than 5:00 p.m. on November 15, 2021.

If you have any questions about this request, please contact Committee staff at (202) 225-6906. Thank you for your attention to this important matter.

Sincerely,

Jim Jordan
Ranking Member

Steve Chabot
Member of Congress

Louie Gohmert
Member of Congress

Darrell Issa
Ranking Member
Subcommittee on Courts, Intellectual Property, and the Internet

Ken Buck
Ranking Member
Subcommittee on Antitrust, Commercial and Administrative Law

Matt Gaetz
Member of Congress

Mike Johnson
Ranking Member
Subcommittee on the Constitution, Civil Rights and Civil Liberties

Andy Biggs
Ranking Member
Subcommittee on Crime, Terrorism and Homeland Security

Tom McClintock
Ranking Member
Subcommittee on Immigration and Citizenship

W. Gregory Steube
Member of Congress

Tom Tiffany
Member of Congress

Thomas Massie
Member of Congress

Chip Roy
Member of Congress

Dan Bishop
Member of Congress

Michelle Fischbach
Member of Congress

Victoria Spartz
Member of Congress

Scott Fitzgerald
Member of Congress

Cliff Bentz
Member of Congress

Burgess Owens
Member of Congress

cc: The Honorable Jerrold L. Nadler
Chairman

Mr. Monty Wilkinson
Director, Executive Office for U.S. Attorneys

JERROLD NADLER, New York
CHAIRMAN

JIM JORDAN, Ohio
RANKING MEMBER

ONE HUNDRED SEVENTEENTH CONGRESS
Congress of the United States
House of Representatives
COMMITTEE ON THE JUDICIARY
2138 RAYBURN HOUSE OFFICE BUILDING
WASHINGTON, DC 20515-6216
(202) 225-3951
judiciary.house.gov

November 1, 2021

Ms. Stephanie Hinds
Acting U.S. Attorney
Northern District of California
450 Golden Gate Avenue
San Francisco, CA 94102

Dear Ms. Hinds:

We are continuing to investigate the troubling attempts by the Department of Justice and the White House to use the heavy hand of federal law enforcement to target concerned parents at local school board meetings and chill their protected First Amendment activity. Because the Department directed you, along with all other U.S. Attorneys, and the Federal Bureau of Investigation (FBI) to take action to address parents attending school board meetings,[1] we respectfully request your assistance with our investigation.

On September 29, 2021, the National School Boards Association (NSBA) sent a letter to President Joe Biden requesting help from the federal government with concerned parents voicing their opinions at school board meetings.[2] The NSBA letter stated that "malice, violence, and threats" against school officials "could be the equivalent of a form of domestic terrorism or hate crimes."[3] The letter cited a number of interactions at school board meetings, none of which rose to the level of domestic terrorism. In fact, the vast majority of incidents cited by the NSBA did not involve threats or violence.[4] Most notably, as an example of domestic terrorism, the NSBA cited an incident in which a father angrily confronted members at a school board meeting in Loudoun County, Virginia about the heinous sexual assault of his daughter.[5]

A mere five days after the NSBA sent its letter to President Biden, on October 4, 2021, Attorney General Merrick Garland issued a shocking memorandum that directed the FBI and

---

[1] Memorandum from Atty Gen. Merrick Garland, U.S. Dep't of Justice, Partnership Among Federal, State, Local, Tribal, And Territorial Law Enforcement to Address Threats Against School Administrators, Board Members, Teachers, and Staff (Oct. 4, 2021).
[2] Letter from Dr. Viola M. Garcia, President, Nat'l School Board Assoc. & Mr. Chip Slaven, Chief Exec. Officer, Nat'l School Board Assoc., to President Joseph R. Biden, White House (Sept. 29, 2021).
[3] *Id.*
[4] *See* Caroline Downey, *Vast majority of incidents cited by school-board group to justify federal intervention didn't involve threats,* NAT'L REV. (Oct. 2, 2021).
[5] *Id.*; *see also* Jessica Chasmar, *Loudoun County father arrested at school board events says school tried to cover up daughter's bathroom assault*, FOX NEWS (Oct. 12, 2021).

U.S. Attorneys' Offices to "convene meetings" in your judicial district "with federal, state, local, Tribal, and territorial leaders" within 30 days.[6] The Justice Department simultaneously issued a press release indicating that the Attorney General's directive would "open dedicated lines of communication for threat reporting, assessment and response by law enforcement"—in other words, create a snitch line for complaints about concerned parents.[7]

During Attorney General Garland's testimony before our Committee on October 21, he appeared to have no idea whether the U.S. Attorney meetings he ordered were actually taking place. He stated: "I don't know whether [the meetings] are ongoing, but I expect and hope that they are going . . . because I did ask that they take place."[8] Attorney General Garland testified that he doubted "there have been meetings in every jurisdiction," but reiterated his belief that it is important for federal law enforcement authorities to conduct these meetings in every judicial district.[9] According to the Attorney General's directives, meetings are to be convened in all 94 judicial districts by November 3, 2021, at the latest.

Following the Attorney General's testimony, the NSBA Board of Directors, apparently recognizing the ill-conceived consequences of its letter and the resulting Justice Department action, issued a new memorandum to its members apologizing for the letter, stating: "On behalf of NSBA, <u>we regret and apologize for the letter</u>."[10] (emphasis in original). Although Attorney General Garland testified that the NSBA letter to President Biden was the basis for his October 4 directive to insert federal law enforcement into local school board matters, the Attorney General has yet to rescind his memorandum. His directives to you and other U.S. Attorneys remain in effect.

Concerned parents voicing their strong opposition to controversial curricula at local schools are not domestic terrorists. Parents have an undisputed right to direct the upbringing and education of their children.[11] When parents, however, cross the line to commit a violent act or issue a criminal threat,[12] state and local authorities are best-equipped to handle these violations of state law. But we must not tolerate the use of the federal law enforcement apparatus to intimidate and silence parents using their Constitutional rights to advocate for their child's future.

To assist our investigation and determine whether these meetings are ongoing, we request that you provide the following documents and information:

---

[6] Memorandum from Atty Gen. Merrick Garland, U.S. Dep't of Justice, Partnership Among Federal, State, Local, Tribal, And Territorial Law Enforcement to Address Threats Against School Administrators, Board Members, Teachers, and Staff (Oct. 4, 2021).
[7] Press Release, U.S. Dep't of Justice, Justice Department Addresses Violent Threats Against School Officials and Teachers (Oct. 4, 2021).
[8] *Oversight of the United States Department of Justice: Hearing Before the H. comm. on the Judiciary,* 117th Cong. at 94 (2021) (testimony from Hon. Merrick Garland, Atty Gen., U.S. Dep't of Justice).
[9] *Id.* at 95.
[10] Memorandum from NSBA Board of Directors, Message to NSBA Members (Oct. 22, 2021).
[11] *Troxel v. Granville,* 530 U.S. 57, 65 (2000) (citing *Meyer v. Nebraska,* 262 U.S. 390, 399 (1923)).
[12] *Merrick Garland's federal offense,* WALL ST. J. (Oct. 6, 2021).

1. All documents and communications referring or relating to convening meeting(s) in your judicial district in accordance with the Attorney General's October 4, 2021 memorandum;

2. All agendas, minutes, and notes created or relied upon by U.S. Attorney's Office employees referring or relating to meeting(s) in your judicial district in accordance with the Attorney General's October 4, 2021 memorandum;

3. Please explain when meeting(s) in your judicial district in accordance with the Attorney General's October 4, 2021 memorandum have occurred or will occur;

4. Please identify by name and title of all U.S. Attorney's Office employees involved in the meeting(s) in your judicial district in accordance with the Attorney General's October 4, 2021 memorandum ;

5. Please identify all federal, state, local, Tribal, and territorial organizations invited to or that have attended the meetings convened in your judicial district in accordance with the October 4, 2021 memorandum; and

6. Please provide all recommendations, both formal and informal, and any meeting minutes produced at the meeting(s) in your judicial district in accordance with the Attorney General's October 4, 2021 memorandum.

Please provide this material as soon as possible but no later than 5:00 p.m. on November 15, 2021.

If you have any questions about this request, please contact Committee staff at (202) 225-6906. Thank you for your attention to this important matter.

Sincerely,

Jim Jordan
Ranking Member

Steve Chabot
Member of Congress

Louie Gohmert
Member of Congress

Darrell Issa
Ranking Member
Subcommittee on Courts, Intellectual Property, and the Internet

Ken Buck
Ranking Member
Subcommittee on Antitrust, Commercial and Administrative Law

Matt Gaetz
Member of Congress

Mike Johnson
Ranking Member
Subcommittee on the Constitution, Civil Rights and Civil Liberties

Andy Biggs
Ranking Member
Subcommittee on Crime, Terrorism and Homeland Security

Tom McClintock
Ranking Member
Subcommittee on Immigration and Citizenship

W. Gregory Steube
Member of Congress

Tom Tiffany
Member of Congress

Thomas Massie
Member of Congress

Chip Roy
Member of Congress

Dan Bishop
Member of Congress

Michelle Fischbach
Member of Congress

Victoria Spartz
Member of Congress

Scott Fitzgerald
Member of Congress

Cliff Bentz
Member of Congress

Burgess Owens
Member of Congress

cc: The Honorable Jerrold L. Nadler
Chairman

Mr. Monty Wilkinson
Director, Executive Office for U.S. Attorneys

JERROLD NADLER, New York
CHAIRMAN

JIM JORDAN, Ohio
RANKING MEMBER

ONE HUNDRED SEVENTEENTH CONGRESS

Congress of the United States
House of Representatives
COMMITTEE ON THE JUDICIARY

2138 RAYBURN HOUSE OFFICE BUILDING
WASHINGTON, DC 20515-6216
(202) 225-3951
judiciary.house.gov

November 1, 2021

Mr. Phillip A. Talbert
Acting U.S. Attorney
Eastern District of California
501 I Street, Suite 10-100
Sacramento, CA 95814

Dear Mr. Talbert:

We are continuing to investigate the troubling attempts by the Department of Justice and the White House to use the heavy hand of federal law enforcement to target concerned parents at local school board meetings and chill their protected First Amendment activity. Because the Department directed you, along with all other U.S. Attorneys, and the Federal Bureau of Investigation (FBI) to take action to address parents attending school board meetings,[1] we respectfully request your assistance with our investigation.

On September 29, 2021, the National School Boards Association (NSBA) sent a letter to President Joe Biden requesting help from the federal government with concerned parents voicing their opinions at school board meetings.[2] The NSBA letter stated that "malice, violence, and threats" against school officials "could be the equivalent of a form of domestic terrorism or hate crimes."[3] The letter cited a number of interactions at school board meetings, none of which rose to the level of domestic terrorism. In fact, the vast majority of incidents cited by the NSBA did not involve threats or violence.[4] Most notably, as an example of domestic terrorism, the NSBA cited an incident in which a father angrily confronted members at a school board meeting in Loudoun County, Virginia about the heinous sexual assault of his daughter.[5]

A mere five days after the NSBA sent its letter to President Biden, on October 4, 2021, Attorney General Merrick Garland issued a shocking memorandum that directed the FBI and

---

[1] Memorandum from Atty Gen. Merrick Garland, U.S. Dep't of Justice, Partnership Among Federal, State, Local, Tribal, And Territorial Law Enforcement to Address Threats Against School Administrators, Board Members, Teachers, and Staff (Oct. 4, 2021).
[2] Letter from Dr. Viola M. Garcia, President, Nat'l School Board Assoc. & Mr. Chip Slaven, Chief Exec. Officer, Nat'l School Board Assoc., to President Joseph R. Biden, White House (Sept. 29, 2021).
[3] *Id.*
[4] *See* Caroline Downey, *Vast majority of incidents cited by school-board group to justify federal intervention didn't involve threats,* NAT'L REV. (Oct. 2, 2021).
[5] *Id.*; *see also* Jessica Chasmar, *Loudoun County father arrested at school board events says school tried to cover up daughter's bathroom assault*, FOX NEWS (Oct. 12, 2021).

U.S. Attorneys' Offices to "convene meetings" in your judicial district "with federal, state, local, Tribal, and territorial leaders" within 30 days.[6] The Justice Department simultaneously issued a press release indicating that the Attorney General's directive would "open dedicated lines of communication for threat reporting, assessment and response by law enforcement"—in other words, create a snitch line for complaints about concerned parents.[7]

During Attorney General Garland's testimony before our Committee on October 21, he appeared to have no idea whether the U.S. Attorney meetings he ordered were actually taking place. He stated: "I don't know whether [the meetings] are ongoing, but I expect and hope that they are going . . . because I did ask that they take place."[8] Attorney General Garland testified that he doubted "there have been meetings in every jurisdiction," but reiterated his belief that it is important for federal law enforcement authorities to conduct these meetings in every judicial district.[9] According to the Attorney General's directives, meetings are to be convened in all 94 judicial districts by November 3, 2021, at the latest.

Following the Attorney General's testimony, the NSBA Board of Directors, apparently recognizing the ill-conceived consequences of its letter and the resulting Justice Department action, issued a new memorandum to its members apologizing for the letter, stating: "On behalf of NSBA, <u>we regret and apologize for the letter</u>."[10] (emphasis in original). Although Attorney General Garland testified that the NSBA letter to President Biden was the basis for his October 4 directive to insert federal law enforcement into local school board matters, the Attorney General has yet to rescind his memorandum. His directives to you and other U.S. Attorneys remain in effect.

Concerned parents voicing their strong opposition to controversial curricula at local schools are not domestic terrorists. Parents have an undisputed right to direct the upbringing and education of their children.[11] When parents, however, cross the line to commit a violent act or issue a criminal threat,[12] state and local authorities are best-equipped to handle these violations of state law. But we must not tolerate the use of the federal law enforcement apparatus to intimidate and silence parents using their Constitutional rights to advocate for their child's future.

To assist our investigation and determine whether these meetings are ongoing, we request that you provide the following documents and information:

---

[6] Memorandum from Atty Gen. Merrick Garland, U.S. Dep't of Justice, Partnership Among Federal, State, Local, Tribal, And Territorial Law Enforcement to Address Threats Against School Administrators, Board Members, Teachers, and Staff (Oct. 4, 2021).

[7] Press Release, U.S. Dep't of Justice, Justice Department Addresses Violent Threats Against School Officials and Teachers (Oct. 4, 2021).

[8] *Oversight of the United States Department of Justice: Hearing Before the H. comm. on the Judiciary,* 117th Cong. at 94 (2021) (testimony from Hon. Merrick Garland, Atty Gen., U.S. Dep't of Justice).

[9] *Id.* at 95.

[10] Memorandum from NSBA Board of Directors, Message to NSBA Members (Oct. 22, 2021).

[11] *Troxel v. Granville,* 530 U.S. 57, 65 (2000) (citing *Meyer v. Nebraska,* 262 U.S. 390, 399 (1923)).

[12] *Merrick Garland's federal offense,* WALL ST. J. (Oct. 6, 2021).

1. All documents and communications referring or relating to convening meeting(s) in your judicial district in accordance with the Attorney General's October 4, 2021 memorandum;

2. All agendas, minutes, and notes created or relied upon by U.S. Attorney's Office employees referring or relating to meeting(s) in your judicial district in accordance with the Attorney General's October 4, 2021 memorandum;

3. Please explain when meeting(s) in your judicial district in accordance with the Attorney General's October 4, 2021 memorandum have occurred or will occur;

4. Please identify by name and title of all U.S. Attorney's Office employees involved in the meeting(s) in your judicial district in accordance with the Attorney General's October 4, 2021 memorandum ;

5. Please identify all federal, state, local, Tribal, and territorial organizations invited to or that have attended the meetings convened in your judicial district in accordance with the October 4, 2021 memorandum; and

6. Please provide all recommendations, both formal and informal, and any meeting minutes produced at the meeting(s) in your judicial district in accordance with the Attorney General's October 4, 2021 memorandum.

Please provide this material as soon as possible but no later than 5:00 p.m. on November 15, 2021.

If you have any questions about this request, please contact Committee staff at (202) 225-6906. Thank you for your attention to this important matter.

Sincerely,

Jim Jordan
Ranking Member

Steve Chabot
Member of Congress

Louie Gohmert
Member of Congress

Darrell Issa
Ranking Member
Subcommittee on Courts, Intellectual Property, and the Internet

Ken Buck
Ranking Member
Subcommittee on Antitrust, Commercial and Administrative Law

Matt Gaetz
Member of Congress

Mike Johnson
Ranking Member
Subcommittee on the Constitution, Civil Rights and Civil Liberties

Andy Biggs
Ranking Member
Subcommittee on Crime, Terrorism and Homeland Security

Tom McClintock
Ranking Member
Subcommittee on Immigration and Citizenship

W. Gregory Steube
Member of Congress

Tom Tiffany
Member of Congress

Thomas Massie
Member of Congress

Chip Roy
Member of Congress

Dan Bishop
Member of Congress

Michelle Fischbach
Member of Congress

Victoria Spartz
Member of Congress

Scott Fitzgerald
Member of Congress

Cliff Bentz
Member of Congress

Burgess Owens
Member of Congress

cc: The Honorable Jerrold L. Nadler
Chairman

Mr. Monty Wilkinson
Director, Executive Office for U.S. Attorneys

JERROLD NADLER, New York
CHAIRMAN

JIM JORDAN, Ohio
RANKING MEMBER

ONE HUNDRED SEVENTEENTH CONGRESS

Congress of the United States

House of Representatives

COMMITTEE ON THE JUDICIARY

2138 RAYBURN HOUSE OFFICE BUILDING

WASHINGTON, DC 20515–6216

(202) 225–3951
judiciary.house.gov

November 1, 2021

Ms. Tracy Wilkison
Acting U.S. Attorney
Central District of California
312 North Spring Street, Suite 1200
Los Angeles, CA 90012

Dear Ms. Tracy Wilkison:

We are continuing to investigate the troubling attempts by the Department of Justice and the White House to use the heavy hand of federal law enforcement to target concerned parents at local school board meetings and chill their protected First Amendment activity. Because the Department directed you, along with all other U.S. Attorneys, and the Federal Bureau of Investigation (FBI) to take action to address parents attending school board meetings,[1] we respectfully request your assistance with our investigation.

On September 29, 2021, the National School Boards Association (NSBA) sent a letter to President Joe Biden requesting help from the federal government with concerned parents voicing their opinions at school board meetings.[2] The NSBA letter stated that "malice, violence, and threats" against school officials "could be the equivalent of a form of domestic terrorism or hate crimes."[3] The letter cited a number of interactions at school board meetings, none of which rose to the level of domestic terrorism. In fact, the vast majority of incidents cited by the NSBA did not involve threats or violence.[4] Most notably, as an example of domestic terrorism, the NSBA cited an incident in which a father angrily confronted members at a school board meeting in Loudoun County, Virginia about the heinous sexual assault of his daughter.[5]

A mere five days after the NSBA sent its letter to President Biden, on October 4, 2021, Attorney General Merrick Garland issued a shocking memorandum that directed the FBI and

---

[1] Memorandum from Atty Gen. Merrick Garland, U.S. Dep't of Justice, Partnership Among Federal, State, Local, Tribal, And Territorial Law Enforcement to Address Threats Against School Administrators, Board Members, Teachers, and Staff (Oct. 4, 2021).
[2] Letter from Dr. Viola M. Garcia, President, Nat'l School Board Assoc. & Mr. Chip Slaven, Chief Exec. Officer, Nat'l School Board Assoc., to President Joseph R. Biden, White House (Sept. 29, 2021).
[3] *Id.*
[4] *See* Caroline Downey, *Vast majority of incidents cited by school-board group to justify federal intervention didn't involve threats,* NAT'L REV. (Oct. 2, 2021).
[5] *Id.*; *see also* Jessica Chasmar, *Loudoun County father arrested at school board events says school tried to cover up daughter's bathroom assault*, FOX NEWS (Oct. 12, 2021).

U.S. Attorneys' Offices to "convene meetings" in your judicial district "with federal, state, local, Tribal, and territorial leaders" within 30 days.[6] The Justice Department simultaneously issued a press release indicating that the Attorney General's directive would "open dedicated lines of communication for threat reporting, assessment and response by law enforcement"—in other words, create a snitch line for complaints about concerned parents.[7]

During Attorney General Garland's testimony before our Committee on October 21, he appeared to have no idea whether the U.S. Attorney meetings he ordered were actually taking place. He stated: "I don't know whether [the meetings] are ongoing, but I expect and hope that they are going . . . because I did ask that they take place."[8] Attorney General Garland testified that he doubted "there have been meetings in every jurisdiction," but reiterated his belief that it is important for federal law enforcement authorities to conduct these meetings in every judicial district.[9] According to the Attorney General's directives, meetings are to be convened in all 94 judicial districts by November 3, 2021, at the latest.

Following the Attorney General's testimony, the NSBA Board of Directors, apparently recognizing the ill-conceived consequences of its letter and the resulting Justice Department action, issued a new memorandum to its members apologizing for the letter, stating: "On behalf of NSBA, <u>we regret and apologize for the letter</u>."[10] (emphasis in original). Although Attorney General Garland testified that the NSBA letter to President Biden was the basis for his October 4 directive to insert federal law enforcement into local school board matters, the Attorney General has yet to rescind his memorandum. His directives to you and other U.S. Attorneys remain in effect.

Concerned parents voicing their strong opposition to controversial curricula at local schools are not domestic terrorists. Parents have an undisputed right to direct the upbringing and education of their children.[11] When parents, however, cross the line to commit a violent act or issue a criminal threat,[12] state and local authorities are best-equipped to handle these violations of state law. But we must not tolerate the use of the federal law enforcement apparatus to intimidate and silence parents using their Constitutional rights to advocate for their child's future.

To assist our investigation and determine whether these meetings are ongoing, we request that you provide the following documents and information:

---

[6] Memorandum from Atty Gen. Merrick Garland, U.S. Dep't of Justice, Partnership Among Federal, State, Local, Tribal, And Territorial Law Enforcement to Address Threats Against School Administrators, Board Members, Teachers, and Staff (Oct. 4, 2021).
[7] Press Release, U.S. Dep't of Justice, Justice Department Addresses Violent Threats Against School Officials and Teachers (Oct. 4, 2021).
[8] *Oversight of the United States Department of Justice: Hearing Before the H. comm. on the Judiciary,* 117th Cong. at 94 (2021) (testimony from Hon. Merrick Garland, Atty Gen., U.S. Dep't of Justice).
[9] *Id.* at 95.
[10] Memorandum from NSBA Board of Directors, Message to NSBA Members (Oct. 22, 2021).
[11] *Troxel v. Granville,* 530 U.S. 57, 65 (2000) (citing *Meyer v. Nebraska,* 262 U.S. 390, 399 (1923)).
[12] *Merrick Garland's federal offense,* WALL ST. J. (Oct. 6, 2021).

1. All documents and communications referring or relating to convening meeting(s) in your judicial district in accordance with the Attorney General's October 4, 2021 memorandum;

2. All agendas, minutes, and notes created or relied upon by U.S. Attorney's Office employees referring or relating to meeting(s) in your judicial district in accordance with the Attorney General's October 4, 2021 memorandum;

3. Please explain when meeting(s) in your judicial district in accordance with the Attorney General's October 4, 2021 memorandum have occurred or will occur;

4. Please identify by name and title of all U.S. Attorney's Office employees involved in the meeting(s) in your judicial district in accordance with the Attorney General's October 4, 2021 memorandum ;

5. Please identify all federal, state, local, Tribal, and territorial organizations invited to or that have attended the meetings convened in your judicial district in accordance with the October 4, 2021 memorandum; and

6. Please provide all recommendations, both formal and informal, and any meeting minutes produced at the meeting(s) in your judicial district in accordance with the Attorney General's October 4, 2021 memorandum.

Please provide this material as soon as possible but no later than 5:00 p.m. on November 15, 2021.

If you have any questions about this request, please contact Committee staff at (202) 225-6906. Thank you for your attention to this important matter.

Sincerely,

Jim Jordan
Ranking Member

Steve Chabot
Member of Congress

Louie Gohmert
Member of Congress

Darrell Issa
Ranking Member
Subcommittee on Courts, Intellectual Property, and the Internet

Ken Buck
Ranking Member
Subcommittee on Antitrust, Commercial and Administrative Law

Matt Gaetz
Member of Congress

Mike Johnson
Ranking Member
Subcommittee on the Constitution, Civil Rights and Civil Liberties

Andy Biggs
Ranking Member
Subcommittee on Crime, Terrorism and Homeland Security

Tom McClintock
Ranking Member
Subcommittee on Immigration and Citizenship

W. Gregory Steube
Member of Congress

Tom Tiffany
Member of Congress

Thomas Massie
Member of Congress

Chip Roy
Member of Congress

Dan Bishop
Member of Congress

Michelle Fischbach
Member of Congress

Victoria Spartz
Member of Congress

Scott Fitzgerald
Member of Congress

Cliff Bentz
Member of Congress

Burgess Owens
Member of Congress

cc: The Honorable Jerrold L. Nadler
Chairman

Mr. Monty Wilkinson
Director, Executive Office for U.S. Attorneys

JERROLD NADLER, New York
CHAIRMAN

JIM JORDAN, Ohio
RANKING MEMBER

ONE HUNDRED SEVENTEENTH CONGRESS

Congress of the United States

House of Representatives

COMMITTEE ON THE JUDICIARY

2138 RAYBURN HOUSE OFFICE BUILDING
WASHINGTON, DC 20515–6216
(202) 225–3951
judiciary.house.gov

November 1, 2021

Mr. Matthew T. Kirsch
Acting U.S. Attorney
District of Colorado
1801 California Street, Suite 1600
Denver, CO 80202

Dear Mr. Kirsch:

We are continuing to investigate the troubling attempts by the Department of Justice and the White House to use the heavy hand of federal law enforcement to target concerned parents at local school board meetings and chill their protected First Amendment activity. Because the Department directed you, along with all other U.S. Attorneys, and the Federal Bureau of Investigation (FBI) to take action to address parents attending school board meetings,[1] we respectfully request your assistance with our investigation.

On September 29, 2021, the National School Boards Association (NSBA) sent a letter to President Joe Biden requesting help from the federal government with concerned parents voicing their opinions at school board meetings.[2] The NSBA letter stated that "malice, violence, and threats" against school officials "could be the equivalent of a form of domestic terrorism or hate crimes."[3] The letter cited a number of interactions at school board meetings, none of which rose to the level of domestic terrorism. In fact, the vast majority of incidents cited by the NSBA did not involve threats or violence.[4] Most notably, as an example of domestic terrorism, the NSBA cited an incident in which a father angrily confronted members at a school board meeting in Loudoun County, Virginia about the heinous sexual assault of his daughter.[5]

A mere five days after the NSBA sent its letter to President Biden, on October 4, 2021, Attorney General Merrick Garland issued a shocking memorandum that directed the FBI and

---

[1] Memorandum from Atty Gen. Merrick Garland, U.S. Dep't of Justice, Partnership Among Federal, State, Local, Tribal, And Territorial Law Enforcement to Address Threats Against School Administrators, Board Members, Teachers, and Staff (Oct. 4, 2021).
[2] Letter from Dr. Viola M. Garcia, President, Nat'l School Board Assoc. & Mr. Chip Slaven, Chief Exec. Officer, Nat'l School Board Assoc., to President Joseph R. Biden, White House (Sept. 29, 2021).
[3] *Id.*
[4] *See* Caroline Downey, *Vast majority of incidents cited by school-board group to justify federal intervention didn't involve threats,* NAT'L REV. (Oct. 2, 2021).
[5] *Id.*; *see also* Jessica Chasmar, *Loudoun County father arrested at school board events says school tried to cover up daughter's bathroom assault*, FOX NEWS (Oct. 12, 2021).

U.S. Attorneys' Offices to "convene meetings" in your judicial district "with federal, state, local, Tribal, and territorial leaders" within 30 days.[6] The Justice Department simultaneously issued a press release indicating that the Attorney General's directive would "open dedicated lines of communication for threat reporting, assessment and response by law enforcement"—in other words, create a snitch line for complaints about concerned parents.[7]

During Attorney General Garland's testimony before our Committee on October 21, he appeared to have no idea whether the U.S. Attorney meetings he ordered were actually taking place. He stated: "I don't know whether [the meetings] are ongoing, but I expect and hope that they are going . . . because I did ask that they take place."[8] Attorney General Garland testified that he doubted "there have been meetings in every jurisdiction," but reiterated his belief that it is important for federal law enforcement authorities to conduct these meetings in every judicial district.[9] According to the Attorney General's directives, meetings are to be convened in all 94 judicial districts by November 3, 2021, at the latest.

Following the Attorney General's testimony, the NSBA Board of Directors, apparently recognizing the ill-conceived consequences of its letter and the resulting Justice Department action, issued a new memorandum to its members apologizing for the letter, stating: "On behalf of NSBA, <u>we regret and apologize for the letter</u>."[10] (emphasis in original). Although Attorney General Garland testified that the NSBA letter to President Biden was the basis for his October 4 directive to insert federal law enforcement into local school board matters, the Attorney General has yet to rescind his memorandum. His directives to you and other U.S. Attorneys remain in effect.

Concerned parents voicing their strong opposition to controversial curricula at local schools are not domestic terrorists. Parents have an undisputed right to direct the upbringing and education of their children.[11] When parents, however, cross the line to commit a violent act or issue a criminal threat,[12] state and local authorities are best-equipped to handle these violations of state law. But we must not tolerate the use of the federal law enforcement apparatus to intimidate and silence parents using their Constitutional rights to advocate for their child's future.

To assist our investigation and determine whether these meetings are ongoing, we request that you provide the following documents and information:

---

[6] Memorandum from Atty Gen. Merrick Garland, U.S. Dep't of Justice, Partnership Among Federal, State, Local, Tribal, And Territorial Law Enforcement to Address Threats Against School Administrators, Board Members, Teachers, and Staff (Oct. 4, 2021).
[7] Press Release, U.S. Dep't of Justice, Justice Department Addresses Violent Threats Against School Officials and Teachers (Oct. 4, 2021).
[8] *Oversight of the United States Department of Justice: Hearing Before the H. comm. on the Judiciary,* 117th Cong. at 94 (2021) (testimony from Hon. Merrick Garland, Atty Gen., U.S. Dep't of Justice).
[9] *Id.* at 95.
[10] Memorandum from NSBA Board of Directors, Message to NSBA Members (Oct. 22, 2021).
[11] *Troxel v. Granville,* 530 U.S. 57, 65 (2000) (citing *Meyer v. Nebraska,* 262 U.S. 390, 399 (1923)).
[12] *Merrick Garland's federal offense,* WALL ST. J. (Oct. 6, 2021).

1. All documents and communications referring or relating to convening meeting(s) in your judicial district in accordance with the Attorney General's October 4, 2021 memorandum;

2. All agendas, minutes, and notes created or relied upon by U.S. Attorney's Office employees referring or relating to meeting(s) in your judicial district in accordance with the Attorney General's October 4, 2021 memorandum;

3. Please explain when meeting(s) in your judicial district in accordance with the Attorney General's October 4, 2021 memorandum have occurred or will occur;

4. Please identify by name and title of all U.S. Attorney's Office employees involved in the meeting(s) in your judicial district in accordance with the Attorney General's October 4, 2021 memorandum ;

5. Please identify all federal, state, local, Tribal, and territorial organizations invited to or that have attended the meetings convened in your judicial district in accordance with the October 4, 2021 memorandum; and

6. Please provide all recommendations, both formal and informal, and any meeting minutes produced at the meeting(s) in your judicial district in accordance with the Attorney General's October 4, 2021 memorandum.

Please provide this material as soon as possible but no later than 5:00 p.m. on November 15, 2021.

If you have any questions about this request, please contact Committee staff at (202) 225-6906. Thank you for your attention to this important matter.

Sincerely,

Jim Jordan
Ranking Member

Steve Chabot
Member of Congress

Louie Gohmert
Member of Congress

Darrell Issa
Ranking Member
Subcommittee on Courts, Intellectual Property, and the Internet

Ken Buck
Ranking Member
Subcommittee on Antitrust, Commercial and Administrative Law

Matt Gaetz
Member of Congress

Mike Johnson
Ranking Member
Subcommittee on the Constitution, Civil Rights and Civil Liberties

Andy Biggs
Ranking Member
Subcommittee on Crime, Terrorism and Homeland Security

Tom McClintock
Ranking Member
Subcommittee on Immigration and Citizenship

W. Gregory Steube
Member of Congress

Tom Tiffany
Member of Congress

Thomas Massie
Member of Congress

Chip Roy
Member of Congress

Dan Bishop
Member of Congress

Michelle Fischbach
Member of Congress

Victoria Spartz
Member of Congress

Scott Fitzgerald
Member of Congress

Cliff Bentz
Member of Congress

Burgess Owens
Member of Congress

cc: The Honorable Jerrold L. Nadler
Chairman

Mr. Monty Wilkinson
Director, Executive Office for U.S. Attorneys

JERROLD NADLER, New York
CHAIRMAN

JIM JORDAN, Ohio
RANKING MEMBER

ONE HUNDRED SEVENTEENTH CONGRESS

Congress of the United States
House of Representatives
COMMITTEE ON THE JUDICIARY

2138 RAYBURN HOUSE OFFICE BUILDING
WASHINGTON, DC 20515-6216
(202) 225-3951
judiciary.house.gov

November 1, 2021

Mr. Leonard C. Boyle
Acting U.S. Attorney
District of Connecticut
1000 Lafayette Blvd., 10th Floor
Bridgeport, CT 06604

Dear Mr. Boyle:

We are continuing to investigate the troubling attempts by the Department of Justice and the White House to use the heavy hand of federal law enforcement to target concerned parents at local school board meetings and chill their protected First Amendment activity. Because the Department directed you, along with all other U.S. Attorneys, and the Federal Bureau of Investigation (FBI) to take action to address parents attending school board meetings,[1] we respectfully request your assistance with our investigation.

On September 29, 2021, the National School Boards Association (NSBA) sent a letter to President Joe Biden requesting help from the federal government with concerned parents voicing their opinions at school board meetings.[2] The NSBA letter stated that "malice, violence, and threats" against school officials "could be the equivalent of a form of domestic terrorism or hate crimes."[3] The letter cited a number of interactions at school board meetings, none of which rose to the level of domestic terrorism. In fact, the vast majority of incidents cited by the NSBA did not involve threats or violence.[4] Most notably, as an example of domestic terrorism, the NSBA cited an incident in which a father angrily confronted members at a school board meeting in Loudoun County, Virginia about the heinous sexual assault of his daughter.[5]

A mere five days after the NSBA sent its letter to President Biden, on October 4, 2021, Attorney General Merrick Garland issued a shocking memorandum that directed the FBI and

---

[1] Memorandum from Atty Gen. Merrick Garland, U.S. Dep't of Justice, Partnership Among Federal, State, Local, Tribal, And Territorial Law Enforcement to Address Threats Against School Administrators, Board Members, Teachers, and Staff (Oct. 4, 2021).
[2] Letter from Dr. Viola M. Garcia, President, Nat'l School Board Assoc. & Mr. Chip Slaven, Chief Exec. Officer, Nat'l School Board Assoc., to President Joseph R. Biden, White House (Sept. 29, 2021).
[3] *Id.*
[4] *See* Caroline Downey, *Vast majority of incidents cited by school-board group to justify federal intervention didn't involve threats,* NAT'L REV. (Oct. 2, 2021).
[5] *Id.*; *see also* Jessica Chasmar, *Loudoun County father arrested at school board events says school tried to cover up daughter's bathroom assault*, FOX NEWS (Oct. 12, 2021).

U.S. Attorneys' Offices to "convene meetings" in your judicial district "with federal, state, local, Tribal, and territorial leaders" within 30 days.[6] The Justice Department simultaneously issued a press release indicating that the Attorney General's directive would "open dedicated lines of communication for threat reporting, assessment and response by law enforcement"—in other words, create a snitch line for complaints about concerned parents.[7]

During Attorney General Garland's testimony before our Committee on October 21, he appeared to have no idea whether the U.S. Attorney meetings he ordered were actually taking place. He stated: "I don't know whether [the meetings] are ongoing, but I expect and hope that they are going . . . because I did ask that they take place."[8] Attorney General Garland testified that he doubted "there have been meetings in every jurisdiction," but reiterated his belief that it is important for federal law enforcement authorities to conduct these meetings in every judicial district.[9] According to the Attorney General's directives, meetings are to be convened in all 94 judicial districts by November 3, 2021, at the latest.

Following the Attorney General's testimony, the NSBA Board of Directors, apparently recognizing the ill-conceived consequences of its letter and the resulting Justice Department action, issued a new memorandum to its members apologizing for the letter, stating: "On behalf of NSBA, <u>we regret and apologize for the letter</u>."[10] (emphasis in original). Although Attorney General Garland testified that the NSBA letter to President Biden was the basis for his October 4 directive to insert federal law enforcement into local school board matters, the Attorney General has yet to rescind his memorandum. His directives to you and other U.S. Attorneys remain in effect.

Concerned parents voicing their strong opposition to controversial curricula at local schools are not domestic terrorists. Parents have an undisputed right to direct the upbringing and education of their children.[11] When parents, however, cross the line to commit a violent act or issue a criminal threat,[12] state and local authorities are best-equipped to handle these violations of state law. But we must not tolerate the use of the federal law enforcement apparatus to intimidate and silence parents using their Constitutional rights to advocate for their child's future.

To assist our investigation and determine whether these meetings are ongoing, we request that you provide the following documents and information:

---

[6] Memorandum from Atty Gen. Merrick Garland, U.S. Dep't of Justice, Partnership Among Federal, State, Local, Tribal, And Territorial Law Enforcement to Address Threats Against School Administrators, Board Members, Teachers, and Staff (Oct. 4, 2021).
[7] Press Release, U.S. Dep't of Justice, Justice Department Addresses Violent Threats Against School Officials and Teachers (Oct. 4, 2021).
[8] *Oversight of the United States Department of Justice: Hearing Before the H. comm. on the Judiciary,* 117th Cong. at 94 (2021) (testimony from Hon. Merrick Garland, Atty Gen., U.S. Dep't of Justice).
[9] *Id.* at 95.
[10] Memorandum from NSBA Board of Directors, Message to NSBA Members (Oct. 22, 2021).
[11] *Troxel v. Granville,* 530 U.S. 57, 65 (2000) (citing *Meyer v. Nebraska,* 262 U.S. 390, 399 (1923)).
[12] *Merrick Garland's federal offense,* WALL ST. J. (Oct. 6, 2021).

1. All documents and communications referring or relating to convening meeting(s) in your judicial district in accordance with the Attorney General's October 4, 2021 memorandum;

2. All agendas, minutes, and notes created or relied upon by U.S. Attorney's Office employees referring or relating to meeting(s) in your judicial district in accordance with the Attorney General's October 4, 2021 memorandum;

3. Please explain when meeting(s) in your judicial district in accordance with the Attorney General's October 4, 2021 memorandum have occurred or will occur;

4. Please identify by name and title of all U.S. Attorney's Office employees involved in the meeting(s) in your judicial district in accordance with the Attorney General's October 4, 2021 memorandum ;

5. Please identify all federal, state, local, Tribal, and territorial organizations invited to or that have attended the meetings convened in your judicial district in accordance with the October 4, 2021 memorandum; and

6. Please provide all recommendations, both formal and informal, and any meeting minutes produced at the meeting(s) in your judicial district in accordance with the Attorney General's October 4, 2021 memorandum.

Please provide this material as soon as possible but no later than 5:00 p.m. on November 15, 2021.

If you have any questions about this request, please contact Committee staff at (202) 225-6906. Thank you for your attention to this important matter.

Sincerely,

Jim Jordan
Ranking Member

Steve Chabot
Member of Congress

Louie Gohmert
Member of Congress

Darrell Issa
Ranking Member
Subcommittee on Courts, Intellectual Property, and the Internet

Ken Buck
Ranking Member
Subcommittee on Antitrust, Commercial and Administrative Law

Matt Gaetz
Member of Congress

Mike Johnson
Ranking Member
Subcommittee on the Constitution, Civil Rights and Civil Liberties

Andy Biggs
Ranking Member
Subcommittee on Crime, Terrorism and Homeland Security

Tom McClintock
Ranking Member
Subcommittee on Immigration and Citizenship

W. Gregory Steube
Member of Congress

Tom Tiffany
Member of Congress

Thomas Massie
Member of Congress

Chip Roy
Member of Congress

Dan Bishop
Member of Congress

Michelle Fischbach
Member of Congress

Victoria Spartz
Member of Congress

Scott Fitzgerald
Member of Congress

Cliff Bentz
Member of Congress

Burgess Owens
Member of Congress

cc: The Honorable Jerrold L. Nadler
Chairman

Mr. Monty Wilkinson
Director, Executive Office for U.S. Attorneys

JERROLD NADLER, New York
CHAIRMAN

JIM JORDAN, Ohio
RANKING MEMBER

ONE HUNDRED SEVENTEENTH CONGRESS

Congress of the United States

House of Representatives

COMMITTEE ON THE JUDICIARY

2138 RAYBURN HOUSE OFFICE BUILDING

WASHINGTON, DC 20515-6216

(202) 225-3951
judiciary.house.gov

November 1, 2021

Mr. Channing D. Phillips
Acting U.S. Attorney
District of Columbia
555 4th Street, NW
Washington, D.C. 20001

Dear Mr. Phillips:

We are continuing to investigate the troubling attempts by the Department of Justice and the White House to use the heavy hand of federal law enforcement to target concerned parents at local school board meetings and chill their protected First Amendment activity. Because the Department directed you, along with all other U.S. Attorneys, and the Federal Bureau of Investigation (FBI) to take action to address parents attending school board meetings,[1] we respectfully request your assistance with our investigation.

On September 29, 2021, the National School Boards Association (NSBA) sent a letter to President Joe Biden requesting help from the federal government with concerned parents voicing their opinions at school board meetings.[2] The NSBA letter stated that "malice, violence, and threats" against school officials "could be the equivalent of a form of domestic terrorism or hate crimes."[3] The letter cited a number of interactions at school board meetings, none of which rose to the level of domestic terrorism. In fact, the vast majority of incidents cited by the NSBA did not involve threats or violence.[4] Most notably, as an example of domestic terrorism, the NSBA cited an incident in which a father angrily confronted members at a school board meeting in Loudoun County, Virginia about the heinous sexual assault of his daughter.[5]

A mere five days after the NSBA sent its letter to President Biden, on October 4, 2021, Attorney General Merrick Garland issued a shocking memorandum that directed the FBI and

[1] Memorandum from Atty Gen. Merrick Garland, U.S. Dep't of Justice, Partnership Among Federal, State, Local, Tribal, And Territorial Law Enforcement to Address Threats Against School Administrators, Board Members, Teachers, and Staff (Oct. 4, 2021).

[2] Letter from Dr. Viola M. Garcia, President, Nat'l School Board Assoc. & Mr. Chip Slaven, Chief Exec. Officer, Nat'l School Board Assoc., to President Joseph R. Biden, White House (Sept. 29, 2021).

[3] *Id.*

[4] *See* Caroline Downey, *Vast majority of incidents cited by school-board group to justify federal intervention didn't involve threats,* NAT'L REV. (Oct. 2, 2021).

[5] *Id.*; *see also* Jessica Chasmar, *Loudoun County father arrested at school board events says school tried to cover up daughter's bathroom assault*, FOX NEWS (Oct. 12, 2021).

U.S. Attorneys' Offices to "convene meetings" in your judicial district "with federal, state, local, Tribal, and territorial leaders" within 30 days.[6] The Justice Department simultaneously issued a press release indicating that the Attorney General's directive would "open dedicated lines of communication for threat reporting, assessment and response by law enforcement"—in other words, create a snitch line for complaints about concerned parents.[7]

During Attorney General Garland's testimony before our Committee on October 21, he appeared to have no idea whether the U.S. Attorney meetings he ordered were actually taking place. He stated: "I don't know whether [the meetings] are ongoing, but I expect and hope that they are going . . . because I did ask that they take place."[8] Attorney General Garland testified that he doubted "there have been meetings in every jurisdiction," but reiterated his belief that it is important for federal law enforcement authorities to conduct these meetings in every judicial district.[9] According to the Attorney General's directives, meetings are to be convened in all 94 judicial districts by November 3, 2021, at the latest.

Following the Attorney General's testimony, the NSBA Board of Directors, apparently recognizing the ill-conceived consequences of its letter and the resulting Justice Department action, issued a new memorandum to its members apologizing for the letter, stating: "On behalf of NSBA, <u>we regret and apologize for the letter</u>."[10] (emphasis in original). Although Attorney General Garland testified that the NSBA letter to President Biden was the basis for his October 4 directive to insert federal law enforcement into local school board matters, the Attorney General has yet to rescind his memorandum. His directives to you and other U.S. Attorneys remain in effect.

Concerned parents voicing their strong opposition to controversial curricula at local schools are not domestic terrorists. Parents have an undisputed right to direct the upbringing and education of their children.[11] When parents, however, cross the line to commit a violent act or issue a criminal threat,[12] state and local authorities are best-equipped to handle these violations of state law. But we must not tolerate the use of the federal law enforcement apparatus to intimidate and silence parents using their Constitutional rights to advocate for their child's future.

To assist our investigation and determine whether these meetings are ongoing, we request that you provide the following documents and information:

---

[6] Memorandum from Atty Gen. Merrick Garland, U.S. Dep't of Justice, Partnership Among Federal, State, Local, Tribal, And Territorial Law Enforcement to Address Threats Against School Administrators, Board Members, Teachers, and Staff (Oct. 4, 2021).
[7] Press Release, U.S. Dep't of Justice, Justice Department Addresses Violent Threats Against School Officials and Teachers (Oct. 4, 2021).
[8] *Oversight of the United States Department of Justice: Hearing Before the H. comm. on the Judiciary,* 117th Cong. at 94 (2021) (testimony from Hon. Merrick Garland, Atty Gen., U.S. Dep't of Justice).
[9] *Id.* at 95.
[10] Memorandum from NSBA Board of Directors, Message to NSBA Members (Oct. 22, 2021).
[11] *Troxel v. Granville,* 530 U.S. 57, 65 (2000) (citing *Meyer v. Nebraska,* 262 U.S. 390, 399 (1923)).
[12] *Merrick Garland's federal offense,* WALL ST. J. (Oct. 6, 2021).

1. All documents and communications referring or relating to convening meeting(s) in your judicial district in accordance with the Attorney General's October 4, 2021 memorandum;

2. All agendas, minutes, and notes created or relied upon by U.S. Attorney's Office employees referring or relating to meeting(s) in your judicial district in accordance with the Attorney General's October 4, 2021 memorandum;

3. Please explain when meeting(s) in your judicial district in accordance with the Attorney General's October 4, 2021 memorandum have occurred or will occur;

4. Please identify by name and title of all U.S. Attorney's Office employees involved in the meeting(s) in your judicial district in accordance with the Attorney General's October 4, 2021 memorandum ;

5. Please identify all federal, state, local, Tribal, and territorial organizations invited to or that have attended the meetings convened in your judicial district in accordance with the October 4, 2021 memorandum; and

6. Please provide all recommendations, both formal and informal, and any meeting minutes produced at the meeting(s) in your judicial district in accordance with the Attorney General's October 4, 2021 memorandum.

Please provide this material as soon as possible but no later than 5:00 p.m. on November 15, 2021.

If you have any questions about this request, please contact Committee staff at (202) 225-6906. Thank you for your attention to this important matter.

Sincerely,

Jim Jordan
Ranking Member

Steve Chabot
Member of Congress

Louie Gohmert
Member of Congress

Darrell Issa
Ranking Member
Subcommittee on Courts, Intellectual Property, and the Internet

Ken Buck
Ranking Member
Subcommittee on Antitrust, Commercial and Administrative Law

Matt Gaetz
Member of Congress

Mike Johnson
Ranking Member
Subcommittee on the Constitution, Civil Rights and Civil Liberties

Andy Biggs
Ranking Member
Subcommittee on Crime, Terrorism and Homeland Security

Tom McClintock
Ranking Member
Subcommittee on Immigration and Citizenship

W. Gregory Steube
Member of Congress

Tom Tiffany
Member of Congress

Thomas Massie
Member of Congress

Chip Roy
Member of Congress

Dan Bishop
Member of Congress

Michelle Fischbach
Member of Congress

Victoria Spartz
Member of Congress

Scott Fitzgerald
Member of Congress

Cliff Bentz
Member of Congress

Burgess Owens
Member of Congress

cc: The Honorable Jerrold L. Nadler
Chairman

Mr. Monty Wilkinson
Director, Executive Office for U.S. Attorneys

JERROLD NADLER, New York
CHAIRMAN

JIM JORDAN, Ohio
RANKING MEMBER

ONE HUNDRED SEVENTEENTH CONGRESS

Congress of the United States
House of Representatives

COMMITTEE ON THE JUDICIARY
2138 RAYBURN HOUSE OFFICE BUILDING
WASHINGTON, DC 20515-6216
(202) 225-3951
judiciary.house.gov

November 1, 2021

The Honorable David C. Weiss
U.S. Attorney
District of Delaware
1313 North Market Street
Wilmington, DE 19801

Dear Mr. Weiss:

We are continuing to investigate the troubling attempts by the Department of Justice and the White House to use the heavy hand of federal law enforcement to target concerned parents at local school board meetings and chill their protected First Amendment activity. Because the Department directed you, along with all other U.S. Attorneys, and the Federal Bureau of Investigation (FBI) to take action to address parents attending school board meetings,[1] we respectfully request your assistance with our investigation.

On September 29, 2021, the National School Boards Association (NSBA) sent a letter to President Joe Biden requesting help from the federal government with concerned parents voicing their opinions at school board meetings.[2] The NSBA letter stated that "malice, violence, and threats" against school officials "could be the equivalent of a form of domestic terrorism or hate crimes."[3] The letter cited a number of interactions at school board meetings, none of which rose to the level of domestic terrorism. In fact, the vast majority of incidents cited by the NSBA did not involve threats or violence.[4] Most notably, as an example of domestic terrorism, the NSBA cited an incident in which a father angrily confronted members at a school board meeting in Loudoun County, Virginia about the heinous sexual assault of his daughter.[5]

A mere five days after the NSBA sent its letter to President Biden, on October 4, 2021, Attorney General Merrick Garland issued a shocking memorandum that directed the FBI and

---

[1] Memorandum from Atty Gen. Merrick Garland, U.S. Dep't of Justice, Partnership Among Federal, State, Local, Tribal, And Territorial Law Enforcement to Address Threats Against School Administrators, Board Members, Teachers, and Staff (Oct. 4, 2021).
[2] Letter from Dr. Viola M. Garcia, President, Nat'l School Board Assoc. & Mr. Chip Slaven, Chief Exec. Officer, Nat'l School Board Assoc., to President Joseph R. Biden, White House (Sept. 29, 2021).
[3] *Id.*
[4] *See* Caroline Downey, *Vast majority of incidents cited by school-board group to justify federal intervention didn't involve threats,* NAT'L REV. (Oct. 2, 2021).
[5] *Id.*; *see also* Jessica Chasmar, *Loudoun County father arrested at school board events says school tried to cover up daughter's bathroom assault*, FOX NEWS (Oct. 12, 2021).

U.S. Attorneys' Offices to "convene meetings" in your judicial district "with federal, state, local, Tribal, and territorial leaders" within 30 days.[6] The Justice Department simultaneously issued a press release indicating that the Attorney General's directive would "open dedicated lines of communication for threat reporting, assessment and response by law enforcement"—in other words, create a snitch line for complaints about concerned parents.[7]

During Attorney General Garland's testimony before our Committee on October 21, he appeared to have no idea whether the U.S. Attorney meetings he ordered were actually taking place. He stated: "I don't know whether [the meetings] are ongoing, but I expect and hope that they are going . . . because I did ask that they take place."[8] Attorney General Garland testified that he doubted "there have been meetings in every jurisdiction," but reiterated his belief that it is important for federal law enforcement authorities to conduct these meetings in every judicial district.[9] According to the Attorney General's directives, meetings are to be convened in all 94 judicial districts by November 3, 2021, at the latest.

Following the Attorney General's testimony, the NSBA Board of Directors, apparently recognizing the ill-conceived consequences of its letter and the resulting Justice Department action, issued a new memorandum to its members apologizing for the letter, stating: "On behalf of NSBA, <u>we regret and apologize for the letter</u>."[10] (emphasis in original). Although Attorney General Garland testified that the NSBA letter to President Biden was the basis for his October 4 directive to insert federal law enforcement into local school board matters, the Attorney General has yet to rescind his memorandum. His directives to you and other U.S. Attorneys remain in effect.

Concerned parents voicing their strong opposition to controversial curricula at local schools are not domestic terrorists. Parents have an undisputed right to direct the upbringing and education of their children.[11] When parents, however, cross the line to commit a violent act or issue a criminal threat,[12] state and local authorities are best-equipped to handle these violations of state law. But we must not tolerate the use of the federal law enforcement apparatus to intimidate and silence parents using their Constitutional rights to advocate for their child's future.

To assist our investigation and determine whether these meetings are ongoing, we request that you provide the following documents and information:

---

[6] Memorandum from Atty Gen. Merrick Garland, U.S. Dep't of Justice, Partnership Among Federal, State, Local, Tribal, And Territorial Law Enforcement to Address Threats Against School Administrators, Board Members, Teachers, and Staff (Oct. 4, 2021).
[7] Press Release, U.S. Dep't of Justice, Justice Department Addresses Violent Threats Against School Officials and Teachers (Oct. 4, 2021).
[8] *Oversight of the United States Department of Justice: Hearing Before the H. comm. on the Judiciary,* 117th Cong. at 94 (2021) (testimony from Hon. Merrick Garland, Atty Gen., U.S. Dep't of Justice).
[9] *Id.* at 95.
[10] Memorandum from NSBA Board of Directors, Message to NSBA Members (Oct. 22, 2021).
[11] *Troxel v. Granville,* 530 U.S. 57, 65 (2000) (citing *Meyer v. Nebraska,* 262 U.S. 390, 399 (1923)).
[12] *Merrick Garland's federal offense,* WALL ST. J. (Oct. 6, 2021).

1. All documents and communications referring or relating to convening meeting(s) in your judicial district in accordance with the Attorney General's October 4, 2021 memorandum;

2. All agendas, minutes, and notes created or relied upon by U.S. Attorney's Office employees referring or relating to meeting(s) in your judicial district in accordance with the Attorney General's October 4, 2021 memorandum;

3. Please explain when meeting(s) in your judicial district in accordance with the Attorney General's October 4, 2021 memorandum have occurred or will occur;

4. Please identify by name and title of all U.S. Attorney's Office employees involved in the meeting(s) in your judicial district in accordance with the Attorney General's October 4, 2021 memorandum ;

5. Please identify all federal, state, local, Tribal, and territorial organizations invited to or that have attended the meetings convened in your judicial district in accordance with the October 4, 2021 memorandum; and

6. Please provide all recommendations, both formal and informal, and any meeting minutes produced at the meeting(s) in your judicial district in accordance with the Attorney General's October 4, 2021 memorandum.

Please provide this material as soon as possible but no later than 5:00 p.m. on November 15, 2021.

If you have any questions about this request, please contact Committee staff at (202) 225-6906. Thank you for your attention to this important matter.

Sincerely,

Jim Jordan
Ranking Member

Steve Chabot
Member of Congress

Louie Gohmert
Member of Congress

Darrell Issa
Ranking Member
Subcommittee on Courts, Intellectual Property, and the Internet

Ken Buck
Ranking Member
Subcommittee on Antitrust, Commercial and Administrative Law

Matt Gaetz
Member of Congress

Mike Johnson
Ranking Member
Subcommittee on the Constitution, Civil Rights and Civil Liberties

Andy Biggs
Ranking Member
Subcommittee on Crime, Terrorism and Homeland Security

Tom McClintock
Ranking Member
Subcommittee on Immigration and Citizenship

W. Gregory Steube
Member of Congress

Tom Tiffany
Member of Congress

Thomas Massie
Member of Congress

Chip Roy
Member of Congress

Dan Bishop
Member of Congress

Michelle Fischbach
Member of Congress

Victoria Spartz
Member of Congress

Scott Fitzgerald
Member of Congress

Cliff Bentz
Member of Congress

Burgess Owens
Member of Congress

cc: The Honorable Jerrold L. Nadler
Chairman

Mr. Monty Wilkinson
Director, Executive Office for U.S. Attorneys

JERROLD NADLER, New York
CHAIRMAN

JIM JORDAN, Ohio
RANKING MEMBER

ONE HUNDRED SEVENTEENTH CONGRESS

Congress of the United States
House of Representatives
COMMITTEE ON THE JUDICIARY

2138 RAYBURN HOUSE OFFICE BUILDING
WASHINGTON, DC 20515–6216
(202) 225–3951
judiciary.house.gov

November 1, 2021

Mr. Jason R. Coody
Acting U.S. Attorney
Northern District of Florida
111 North Adams Street, 4th Floor U.S. Courthouse
Tallahassee, FL 32301

Dear Mr. Coody:

We are continuing to investigate the troubling attempts by the Department of Justice and the White House to use the heavy hand of federal law enforcement to target concerned parents at local school board meetings and chill their protected First Amendment activity. Because the Department directed you, along with all other U.S. Attorneys, and the Federal Bureau of Investigation (FBI) to take action to address parents attending school board meetings,[1] we respectfully request your assistance with our investigation.

On September 29, 2021, the National School Boards Association (NSBA) sent a letter to President Joe Biden requesting help from the federal government with concerned parents voicing their opinions at school board meetings.[2] The NSBA letter stated that "malice, violence, and threats" against school officials "could be the equivalent of a form of domestic terrorism or hate crimes."[3] The letter cited a number of interactions at school board meetings, none of which rose to the level of domestic terrorism. In fact, the vast majority of incidents cited by the NSBA did not involve threats or violence.[4] Most notably, as an example of domestic terrorism, the NSBA cited an incident in which a father angrily confronted members at a school board meeting in Loudoun County, Virginia about the heinous sexual assault of his daughter.[5]

A mere five days after the NSBA sent its letter to President Biden, on October 4, 2021, Attorney General Merrick Garland issued a shocking memorandum that directed the FBI and

---

[1] Memorandum from Atty Gen. Merrick Garland, U.S. Dep't of Justice, Partnership Among Federal, State, Local, Tribal, And Territorial Law Enforcement to Address Threats Against School Administrators, Board Members, Teachers, and Staff (Oct. 4, 2021).
[2] Letter from Dr. Viola M. Garcia, President, Nat'l School Board Assoc. & Mr. Chip Slaven, Chief Exec. Officer, Nat'l School Board Assoc., to President Joseph R. Biden, White House (Sept. 29, 2021).
[3] *Id.*
[4] *See* Caroline Downey, *Vast majority of incidents cited by school-board group to justify federal intervention didn't involve threats,* NAT'L REV. (Oct. 2, 2021).
[5] *Id.*; *see also* Jessica Chasmar, *Loudoun County father arrested at school board events says school tried to cover up daughter's bathroom assault*, FOX NEWS (Oct. 12, 2021).

U.S. Attorneys' Offices to "convene meetings" in your judicial district "with federal, state, local, Tribal, and territorial leaders" within 30 days.[6] The Justice Department simultaneously issued a press release indicating that the Attorney General's directive would "open dedicated lines of communication for threat reporting, assessment and response by law enforcement"—in other words, create a snitch line for complaints about concerned parents.[7]

During Attorney General Garland's testimony before our Committee on October 21, he appeared to have no idea whether the U.S. Attorney meetings he ordered were actually taking place. He stated: "I don't know whether [the meetings] are ongoing, but I expect and hope that they are going . . . because I did ask that they take place."[8] Attorney General Garland testified that he doubted "there have been meetings in every jurisdiction," but reiterated his belief that it is important for federal law enforcement authorities to conduct these meetings in every judicial district.[9] According to the Attorney General's directives, meetings are to be convened in all 94 judicial districts by November 3, 2021, at the latest.

Following the Attorney General's testimony, the NSBA Board of Directors, apparently recognizing the ill-conceived consequences of its letter and the resulting Justice Department action, issued a new memorandum to its members apologizing for the letter, stating: "On behalf of NSBA, <u>we regret and apologize for the letter</u>."[10] (emphasis in original). Although Attorney General Garland testified that the NSBA letter to President Biden was the basis for his October 4 directive to insert federal law enforcement into local school board matters, the Attorney General has yet to rescind his memorandum. His directives to you and other U.S. Attorneys remain in effect.

Concerned parents voicing their strong opposition to controversial curricula at local schools are not domestic terrorists. Parents have an undisputed right to direct the upbringing and education of their children.[11] When parents, however, cross the line to commit a violent act or issue a criminal threat,[12] state and local authorities are best-equipped to handle these violations of state law. But we must not tolerate the use of the federal law enforcement apparatus to intimidate and silence parents using their Constitutional rights to advocate for their child's future.

To assist our investigation and determine whether these meetings are ongoing, we request that you provide the following documents and information:

---

[6] Memorandum from Atty Gen. Merrick Garland, U.S. Dep't of Justice, Partnership Among Federal, State, Local, Tribal, And Territorial Law Enforcement to Address Threats Against School Administrators, Board Members, Teachers, and Staff (Oct. 4, 2021).
[7] Press Release, U.S. Dep't of Justice, Justice Department Addresses Violent Threats Against School Officials and Teachers (Oct. 4, 2021).
[8] *Oversight of the United States Department of Justice: Hearing Before the H. comm. on the Judiciary,* 117th Cong. at 94 (2021) (testimony from Hon. Merrick Garland, Atty Gen., U.S. Dep't of Justice).
[9] *Id.* at 95.
[10] Memorandum from NSBA Board of Directors, Message to NSBA Members (Oct. 22, 2021).
[11] *Troxel v. Granville,* 530 U.S. 57, 65 (2000) (citing *Meyer v. Nebraska,* 262 U.S. 390, 399 (1923)).
[12] *Merrick Garland's federal offense,* WALL ST. J. (Oct. 6, 2021).

1. All documents and communications referring or relating to convening meeting(s) in your judicial district in accordance with the Attorney General's October 4, 2021 memorandum;

2. All agendas, minutes, and notes created or relied upon by U.S. Attorney's Office employees referring or relating to meeting(s) in your judicial district in accordance with the Attorney General's October 4, 2021 memorandum;

3. Please explain when meeting(s) in your judicial district in accordance with the Attorney General's October 4, 2021 memorandum have occurred or will occur;

4. Please identify by name and title of all U.S. Attorney's Office employees involved in the meeting(s) in your judicial district in accordance with the Attorney General's October 4, 2021 memorandum ;

5. Please identify all federal, state, local, Tribal, and territorial organizations invited to or that have attended the meetings convened in your judicial district in accordance with the October 4, 2021 memorandum; and

6. Please provide all recommendations, both formal and informal, and any meeting minutes produced at the meeting(s) in your judicial district in accordance with the Attorney General's October 4, 2021 memorandum.

Please provide this material as soon as possible but no later than 5:00 p.m. on November 15, 2021.

If you have any questions about this request, please contact Committee staff at (202) 225-6906. Thank you for your attention to this important matter.

Sincerely,

Jim Jordan
Ranking Member

Steve Chabot
Member of Congress

Louie Gohmert
Member of Congress

Darrell Issa
Ranking Member
Subcommittee on Courts, Intellectual Property, and the Internet

Ken Buck
Ranking Member
Subcommittee on Antitrust, Commercial and Administrative Law

Matt Gaetz
Member of Congress

Mike Johnson
Ranking Member
Subcommittee on the Constitution, Civil Rights and Civil Liberties

Andy Biggs
Ranking Member
Subcommittee on Crime, Terrorism and Homeland Security

Tom McClintock
Ranking Member
Subcommittee on Immigration and Citizenship

W. Gregory Steube
Member of Congress

Tom Tiffany
Member of Congress

Thomas Massie
Member of Congress

Chip Roy
Member of Congress

Dan Bishop
Member of Congress

Michelle Fischbach
Member of Congress

Victoria Spartz
Member of Congress

Scott Fitzgerald
Member of Congress

Cliff Bentz
Member of Congress

Burgess Owens
Member of Congress

cc: The Honorable Jerrold L. Nadler
Chairman

Mr. Monty Wilkinson
Director, Executive Office for U.S. Attorneys

JERROLD NADLER, New York
CHAIRMAN

JIM JORDAN, Ohio
RANKING MEMBER

ONE HUNDRED SEVENTEENTH CONGRESS

Congress of the United States

House of Representatives

COMMITTEE ON THE JUDICIARY

2138 RAYBURN HOUSE OFFICE BUILDING

WASHINGTON, DC 20515–6216

(202) 225–3951
judiciary.house.gov

November 1, 2021

Mr. Juan A. Gonzalez
U.S. Attorney
Southern District of Florida
99 N.E. 4th Street
Miami, FL 33132

Dear Mr. Gonzalez:

We are continuing to investigate the troubling attempts by the Department of Justice and the White House to use the heavy hand of federal law enforcement to target concerned parents at local school board meetings and chill their protected First Amendment activity. Because the Department directed you, along with all other U.S. Attorneys, and the Federal Bureau of Investigation (FBI) to take action to address parents attending school board meetings,[1] we respectfully request your assistance with our investigation.

On September 29, 2021, the National School Boards Association (NSBA) sent a letter to President Joe Biden requesting help from the federal government with concerned parents voicing their opinions at school board meetings.[2] The NSBA letter stated that "malice, violence, and threats" against school officials "could be the equivalent of a form of domestic terrorism or hate crimes."[3] The letter cited a number of interactions at school board meetings, none of which rose to the level of domestic terrorism. In fact, the vast majority of incidents cited by the NSBA did not involve threats or violence.[4] Most notably, as an example of domestic terrorism, the NSBA cited an incident in which a father angrily confronted members at a school board meeting in Loudoun County, Virginia about the heinous sexual assault of his daughter.[5]

A mere five days after the NSBA sent its letter to President Biden, on October 4, 2021, Attorney General Merrick Garland issued a shocking memorandum that directed the FBI and

---

[1] Memorandum from Atty Gen. Merrick Garland, U.S. Dep't of Justice, Partnership Among Federal, State, Local, Tribal, And Territorial Law Enforcement to Address Threats Against School Administrators, Board Members, Teachers, and Staff (Oct. 4, 2021).

[2] Letter from Dr. Viola M. Garcia, President, Nat'l School Board Assoc. & Mr. Chip Slaven, Chief Exec. Officer, Nat'l School Board Assoc., to President Joseph R. Biden, White House (Sept. 29, 2021).

[3] *Id.*

[4] *See* Caroline Downey, *Vast majority of incidents cited by school-board group to justify federal intervention didn't involve threats,* NAT'L REV. (Oct. 2, 2021).

[5] *Id.*; *see also* Jessica Chasmar, *Loudoun County father arrested at school board events says school tried to cover up daughter's bathroom assault*, FOX NEWS (Oct. 12, 2021).

U.S. Attorneys' Offices to "convene meetings" in your judicial district "with federal, state, local, Tribal, and territorial leaders" within 30 days.[6] The Justice Department simultaneously issued a press release indicating that the Attorney General's directive would "open dedicated lines of communication for threat reporting, assessment and response by law enforcement"—in other words, create a snitch line for complaints about concerned parents.[7]

During Attorney General Garland's testimony before our Committee on October 21, he appeared to have no idea whether the U.S. Attorney meetings he ordered were actually taking place. He stated: "I don't know whether [the meetings] are ongoing, but I expect and hope that they are going . . . because I did ask that they take place."[8] Attorney General Garland testified that he doubted "there have been meetings in every jurisdiction," but reiterated his belief that it is important for federal law enforcement authorities to conduct these meetings in every judicial district.[9] According to the Attorney General's directives, meetings are to be convened in all 94 judicial districts by November 3, 2021, at the latest.

Following the Attorney General's testimony, the NSBA Board of Directors, apparently recognizing the ill-conceived consequences of its letter and the resulting Justice Department action, issued a new memorandum to its members apologizing for the letter, stating: "On behalf of NSBA, <u>we regret and apologize for the letter</u>."[10] (emphasis in original). Although Attorney General Garland testified that the NSBA letter to President Biden was the basis for his October 4 directive to insert federal law enforcement into local school board matters, the Attorney General has yet to rescind his memorandum. His directives to you and other U.S. Attorneys remain in effect.

Concerned parents voicing their strong opposition to controversial curricula at local schools are not domestic terrorists. Parents have an undisputed right to direct the upbringing and education of their children.[11] When parents, however, cross the line to commit a violent act or issue a criminal threat,[12] state and local authorities are best-equipped to handle these violations of state law. But we must not tolerate the use of the federal law enforcement apparatus to intimidate and silence parents using their Constitutional rights to advocate for their child's future.

To assist our investigation and determine whether these meetings are ongoing, we request that you provide the following documents and information:

---

[6] Memorandum from Atty Gen. Merrick Garland, U.S. Dep't of Justice, Partnership Among Federal, State, Local, Tribal, And Territorial Law Enforcement to Address Threats Against School Administrators, Board Members, Teachers, and Staff (Oct. 4, 2021).
[7] Press Release, U.S. Dep't of Justice, Justice Department Addresses Violent Threats Against School Officials and Teachers (Oct. 4, 2021).
[8] *Oversight of the United States Department of Justice: Hearing Before the H. comm. on the Judiciary,* 117th Cong. at 94 (2021) (testimony from Hon. Merrick Garland, Atty Gen., U.S. Dep't of Justice).
[9] *Id.* at 95.
[10] Memorandum from NSBA Board of Directors, Message to NSBA Members (Oct. 22, 2021).
[11] *Troxel v. Granville,* 530 U.S. 57, 65 (2000) (citing *Meyer v. Nebraska,* 262 U.S. 390, 399 (1923)).
[12] *Merrick Garland's federal offense,* WALL ST. J. (Oct. 6, 2021).

1. All documents and communications referring or relating to convening meeting(s) in your judicial district in accordance with the Attorney General's October 4, 2021 memorandum;

2. All agendas, minutes, and notes created or relied upon by U.S. Attorney's Office employees referring or relating to meeting(s) in your judicial district in accordance with the Attorney General's October 4, 2021 memorandum;

3. Please explain when meeting(s) in your judicial district in accordance with the Attorney General's October 4, 2021 memorandum have occurred or will occur;

4. Please identify by name and title of all U.S. Attorney's Office employees involved in the meeting(s) in your judicial district in accordance with the Attorney General's October 4, 2021 memorandum ;

5. Please identify all federal, state, local, Tribal, and territorial organizations invited to or that have attended the meetings convened in your judicial district in accordance with the October 4, 2021 memorandum; and

6. Please provide all recommendations, both formal and informal, and any meeting minutes produced at the meeting(s) in your judicial district in accordance with the Attorney General's October 4, 2021 memorandum.

Please provide this material as soon as possible but no later than 5:00 p.m. on November 15, 2021.

If you have any questions about this request, please contact Committee staff at (202) 225-6906. Thank you for your attention to this important matter.

Sincerely,

Jim Jordan
Ranking Member

Steve Chabot
Member of Congress

Louie Gohmert
Member of Congress

Darrell Issa
Ranking Member
Subcommittee on Courts, Intellectual Property, and the Internet

Ken Buck
Ranking Member
Subcommittee on Antitrust, Commercial and Administrative Law

Matt Gaetz
Member of Congress

Mike Johnson
Ranking Member
Subcommittee on the Constitution, Civil Rights and Civil Liberties

Andy Biggs
Ranking Member
Subcommittee on Crime, Terrorism and Homeland Security

Tom McClintock
Ranking Member
Subcommittee on Immigration and Citizenship

W. Gregory Steube
Member of Congress

Tom Tiffany
Member of Congress

Thomas Massie
Member of Congress

Chip Roy
Member of Congress

Dan Bishop
Member of Congress

Michelle Fischbach
Member of Congress

Victoria Spartz
Member of Congress

Scott Fitzgerald
Member of Congress

Cliff Bentz
Member of Congress

Burgess Owens
Member of Congress

cc: The Honorable Jerrold L. Nadler
Chairman

Mr. Monty Wilkinson
Director, Executive Office for U.S. Attorneys

JERROLD NADLER, New York
CHAIRMAN

JIM JORDAN, Ohio
RANKING MEMBER

ONE HUNDRED SEVENTEENTH CONGRESS

Congress of the United States
House of Representatives

COMMITTEE ON THE JUDICIARY
2138 RAYBURN HOUSE OFFICE BUILDING
WASHINGTON, DC 20515–6216
(202) 225–3951
judiciary.house.gov

November 1, 2021

Ms. Karin Hoppmann
Acting U.S. Attorney
Middle District of Florida
400 North Tampa Street, Suite 3200
Tampa, FL 33602

Dear Ms. Hoppmann:

We are continuing to investigate the troubling attempts by the Department of Justice and the White House to use the heavy hand of federal law enforcement to target concerned parents at local school board meetings and chill their protected First Amendment activity. Because the Department directed you, along with all other U.S. Attorneys, and the Federal Bureau of Investigation (FBI) to take action to address parents attending school board meetings,[1] we respectfully request your assistance with our investigation.

On September 29, 2021, the National School Boards Association (NSBA) sent a letter to President Joe Biden requesting help from the federal government with concerned parents voicing their opinions at school board meetings.[2] The NSBA letter stated that "malice, violence, and threats" against school officials "could be the equivalent of a form of domestic terrorism or hate crimes."[3] The letter cited a number of interactions at school board meetings, none of which rose to the level of domestic terrorism. In fact, the vast majority of incidents cited by the NSBA did not involve threats or violence.[4] Most notably, as an example of domestic terrorism, the NSBA cited an incident in which a father angrily confronted members at a school board meeting in Loudoun County, Virginia about the heinous sexual assault of his daughter.[5]

A mere five days after the NSBA sent its letter to President Biden, on October 4, 2021, Attorney General Merrick Garland issued a shocking memorandum that directed the FBI and

---

[1] Memorandum from Atty Gen. Merrick Garland, U.S. Dep't of Justice, Partnership Among Federal, State, Local, Tribal, And Territorial Law Enforcement to Address Threats Against School Administrators, Board Members, Teachers, and Staff (Oct. 4, 2021).

[2] Letter from Dr. Viola M. Garcia, President, Nat'l School Board Assoc. & Mr. Chip Slaven, Chief Exec. Officer, Nat'l School Board Assoc., to President Joseph R. Biden, White House (Sept. 29, 2021).

[3] *Id.*

[4] *See* Caroline Downey, *Vast majority of incidents cited by school-board group to justify federal intervention didn't involve threats,* NAT'L REV. (Oct. 2, 2021).

[5] *Id.*; *see also* Jessica Chasmar, *Loudoun County father arrested at school board events says school tried to cover up daughter's bathroom assault*, FOX NEWS (Oct. 12, 2021).

U.S. Attorneys' Offices to "convene meetings" in your judicial district "with federal, state, local, Tribal, and territorial leaders" within 30 days.[6] The Justice Department simultaneously issued a press release indicating that the Attorney General's directive would "open dedicated lines of communication for threat reporting, assessment and response by law enforcement"—in other words, create a snitch line for complaints about concerned parents.[7]

During Attorney General Garland's testimony before our Committee on October 21, he appeared to have no idea whether the U.S. Attorney meetings he ordered were actually taking place. He stated: "I don't know whether [the meetings] are ongoing, but I expect and hope that they are going . . . because I did ask that they take place."[8] Attorney General Garland testified that he doubted "there have been meetings in every jurisdiction," but reiterated his belief that it is important for federal law enforcement authorities to conduct these meetings in every judicial district.[9] According to the Attorney General's directives, meetings are to be convened in all 94 judicial districts by November 3, 2021, at the latest.

Following the Attorney General's testimony, the NSBA Board of Directors, apparently recognizing the ill-conceived consequences of its letter and the resulting Justice Department action, issued a new memorandum to its members apologizing for the letter, stating: "On behalf of NSBA, <u>we regret and apologize for the letter</u>."[10] (emphasis in original). Although Attorney General Garland testified that the NSBA letter to President Biden was the basis for his October 4 directive to insert federal law enforcement into local school board matters, the Attorney General has yet to rescind his memorandum. His directives to you and other U.S. Attorneys remain in effect.

Concerned parents voicing their strong opposition to controversial curricula at local schools are not domestic terrorists. Parents have an undisputed right to direct the upbringing and education of their children.[11] When parents, however, cross the line to commit a violent act or issue a criminal threat,[12] state and local authorities are best-equipped to handle these violations of state law. But we must not tolerate the use of the federal law enforcement apparatus to intimidate and silence parents using their Constitutional rights to advocate for their child's future.

To assist our investigation and determine whether these meetings are ongoing, we request that you provide the following documents and information:

---

[6] Memorandum from Atty Gen. Merrick Garland, U.S. Dep't of Justice, Partnership Among Federal, State, Local, Tribal, And Territorial Law Enforcement to Address Threats Against School Administrators, Board Members, Teachers, and Staff (Oct. 4, 2021).
[7] Press Release, U.S. Dep't of Justice, Justice Department Addresses Violent Threats Against School Officials and Teachers (Oct. 4, 2021).
[8] *Oversight of the United States Department of Justice: Hearing Before the H. comm. on the Judiciary,* 117th Cong. at 94 (2021) (testimony from Hon. Merrick Garland, Atty Gen., U.S. Dep't of Justice).
[9] *Id.* at 95.
[10] Memorandum from NSBA Board of Directors, Message to NSBA Members (Oct. 22, 2021).
[11] *Troxel v. Granville,* 530 U.S. 57, 65 (2000) (citing *Meyer v. Nebraska,* 262 U.S. 390, 399 (1923)).
[12] *Merrick Garland's federal offense,* WALL ST. J. (Oct. 6, 2021).

1. All documents and communications referring or relating to convening meeting(s) in your judicial district in accordance with the Attorney General's October 4, 2021 memorandum;

2. All agendas, minutes, and notes created or relied upon by U.S. Attorney's Office employees referring or relating to meeting(s) in your judicial district in accordance with the Attorney General's October 4, 2021 memorandum;

3. Please explain when meeting(s) in your judicial district in accordance with the Attorney General's October 4, 2021 memorandum have occurred or will occur;

4. Please identify by name and title of all U.S. Attorney's Office employees involved in the meeting(s) in your judicial district in accordance with the Attorney General's October 4, 2021 memorandum ;

5. Please identify all federal, state, local, Tribal, and territorial organizations invited to or that have attended the meetings convened in your judicial district in accordance with the October 4, 2021 memorandum; and

6. Please provide all recommendations, both formal and informal, and any meeting minutes produced at the meeting(s) in your judicial district in accordance with the Attorney General's October 4, 2021 memorandum.

Please provide this material as soon as possible but no later than 5:00 p.m. on November 15, 2021.

If you have any questions about this request, please contact Committee staff at (202) 225-6906. Thank you for your attention to this important matter.

Sincerely,

Jim Jordan
Ranking Member

Steve Chabot
Member of Congress

Louie Gohmert
Member of Congress

Darrell Issa
Ranking Member
Subcommittee on Courts, Intellectual Property, and the Internet

Ken Buck
Ranking Member
Subcommittee on Antitrust, Commercial and Administrative Law

Matt Gaetz
Member of Congress

Mike Johnson
Ranking Member
Subcommittee on the Constitution, Civil Rights and Civil Liberties

Andy Biggs
Ranking Member
Subcommittee on Crime, Terrorism and Homeland Security

Tom McClintock
Ranking Member
Subcommittee on Immigration and Citizenship

W. Gregory Steube
Member of Congress

Tom Tiffany
Member of Congress

Thomas Massie
Member of Congress

Chip Roy
Member of Congress

Dan Bishop
Member of Congress

Michelle Fischbach
Member of Congress

Victoria Spartz
Member of Congress

Scott Fitzgerald
Member of Congress

Cliff Bentz
Member of Congress

Burgess Owens
Member of Congress

cc: The Honorable Jerrold L. Nadler
Chairman

Mr. Monty Wilkinson
Director, Executive Office for U.S. Attorneys

JERROLD NADLER, New York
CHAIRMAN

JIM JORDAN, Ohio
RANKING MEMBER

ONE HUNDRED SEVENTEENTH CONGRESS

Congress of the United States
House of Representatives

COMMITTEE ON THE JUDICIARY

2138 RAYBURN HOUSE OFFICE BUILDING
WASHINGTON, DC 20515–6216
(202) 225–3951
judiciary.house.gov

November 1, 2021

Mr. Kurt R. Erskine
Acting U.S. Attorney
Northern District of Georgia
75 Ted Turner Drive SW, Suite 600
Atlanta, GA 30303

Dear Mr. Erskine:

We are continuing to investigate the troubling attempts by the Department of Justice and the White House to use the heavy hand of federal law enforcement to target concerned parents at local school board meetings and chill their protected First Amendment activity. Because the Department directed you, along with all other U.S. Attorneys, and the Federal Bureau of Investigation (FBI) to take action to address parents attending school board meetings,[1] we respectfully request your assistance with our investigation.

On September 29, 2021, the National School Boards Association (NSBA) sent a letter to President Joe Biden requesting help from the federal government with concerned parents voicing their opinions at school board meetings.[2] The NSBA letter stated that "malice, violence, and threats" against school officials "could be the equivalent of a form of domestic terrorism or hate crimes."[3] The letter cited a number of interactions at school board meetings, none of which rose to the level of domestic terrorism. In fact, the vast majority of incidents cited by the NSBA did not involve threats or violence.[4] Most notably, as an example of domestic terrorism, the NSBA cited an incident in which a father angrily confronted members at a school board meeting in Loudoun County, Virginia about the heinous sexual assault of his daughter.[5]

A mere five days after the NSBA sent its letter to President Biden, on October 4, 2021, Attorney General Merrick Garland issued a shocking memorandum that directed the FBI and

[1] Memorandum from Atty Gen. Merrick Garland, U.S. Dep't of Justice, Partnership Among Federal, State, Local, Tribal, And Territorial Law Enforcement to Address Threats Against School Administrators, Board Members, Teachers, and Staff (Oct. 4, 2021).
[2] Letter from Dr. Viola M. Garcia, President, Nat'l School Board Assoc. & Mr. Chip Slaven, Chief Exec. Officer, Nat'l School Board Assoc., to President Joseph R. Biden, White House (Sept. 29, 2021).
[3] *Id.*
[4] *See* Caroline Downey, *Vast majority of incidents cited by school-board group to justify federal intervention didn't involve threats,* NAT'L REV. (Oct. 2, 2021).
[5] *Id.*; *see also* Jessica Chasmar, *Loudoun County father arrested at school board events says school tried to cover up daughter's bathroom assault*, FOX NEWS (Oct. 12, 2021).

U.S. Attorneys' Offices to "convene meetings" in your judicial district "with federal, state, local, Tribal, and territorial leaders" within 30 days.[6] The Justice Department simultaneously issued a press release indicating that the Attorney General's directive would "open dedicated lines of communication for threat reporting, assessment and response by law enforcement"—in other words, create a snitch line for complaints about concerned parents.[7]

During Attorney General Garland's testimony before our Committee on October 21, he appeared to have no idea whether the U.S. Attorney meetings he ordered were actually taking place. He stated: "I don't know whether [the meetings] are ongoing, but I expect and hope that they are going . . . because I did ask that they take place."[8] Attorney General Garland testified that he doubted "there have been meetings in every jurisdiction," but reiterated his belief that it is important for federal law enforcement authorities to conduct these meetings in every judicial district.[9] According to the Attorney General's directives, meetings are to be convened in all 94 judicial districts by November 3, 2021, at the latest.

Following the Attorney General's testimony, the NSBA Board of Directors, apparently recognizing the ill-conceived consequences of its letter and the resulting Justice Department action, issued a new memorandum to its members apologizing for the letter, stating: "On behalf of NSBA, <u>we regret and apologize for the letter</u>."[10] (emphasis in original). Although Attorney General Garland testified that the NSBA letter to President Biden was the basis for his October 4 directive to insert federal law enforcement into local school board matters, the Attorney General has yet to rescind his memorandum. His directives to you and other U.S. Attorneys remain in effect.

Concerned parents voicing their strong opposition to controversial curricula at local schools are not domestic terrorists. Parents have an undisputed right to direct the upbringing and education of their children.[11] When parents, however, cross the line to commit a violent act or issue a criminal threat,[12] state and local authorities are best-equipped to handle these violations of state law. But we must not tolerate the use of the federal law enforcement apparatus to intimidate and silence parents using their Constitutional rights to advocate for their child's future.

To assist our investigation and determine whether these meetings are ongoing, we request that you provide the following documents and information:

---

[6] Memorandum from Atty Gen. Merrick Garland, U.S. Dep't of Justice, Partnership Among Federal, State, Local, Tribal, And Territorial Law Enforcement to Address Threats Against School Administrators, Board Members, Teachers, and Staff (Oct. 4, 2021).
[7] Press Release, U.S. Dep't of Justice, Justice Department Addresses Violent Threats Against School Officials and Teachers (Oct. 4, 2021).
[8] *Oversight of the United States Department of Justice: Hearing Before the H. comm. on the Judiciary,* 117th Cong. at 94 (2021) (testimony from Hon. Merrick Garland, Atty Gen., U.S. Dep't of Justice).
[9] *Id.* at 95.
[10] Memorandum from NSBA Board of Directors, Message to NSBA Members (Oct. 22, 2021).
[11] *Troxel v. Granville,* 530 U.S. 57, 65 (2000) (citing *Meyer v. Nebraska,* 262 U.S. 390, 399 (1923)).
[12] *Merrick Garland's federal offense,* WALL ST. J. (Oct. 6, 2021).

1. All documents and communications referring or relating to convening meeting(s) in your judicial district in accordance with the Attorney General's October 4, 2021 memorandum;

2. All agendas, minutes, and notes created or relied upon by U.S. Attorney's Office employees referring or relating to meeting(s) in your judicial district in accordance with the Attorney General's October 4, 2021 memorandum;

3. Please explain when meeting(s) in your judicial district in accordance with the Attorney General's October 4, 2021 memorandum have occurred or will occur;

4. Please identify by name and title of all U.S. Attorney's Office employees involved in the meeting(s) in your judicial district in accordance with the Attorney General's October 4, 2021 memorandum ;

5. Please identify all federal, state, local, Tribal, and territorial organizations invited to or that have attended the meetings convened in your judicial district in accordance with the October 4, 2021 memorandum; and

6. Please provide all recommendations, both formal and informal, and any meeting minutes produced at the meeting(s) in your judicial district in accordance with the Attorney General's October 4, 2021 memorandum.

Please provide this material as soon as possible but no later than 5:00 p.m. on November 15, 2021.

If you have any questions about this request, please contact Committee staff at (202) 225-6906. Thank you for your attention to this important matter.

Sincerely,

Jim Jordan
Ranking Member

Steve Chabot
Member of Congress

Louie Gohmert
Member of Congress

Darrell Issa
Ranking Member
Subcommittee on Courts, Intellectual Property, and the Internet

Ken Buck
Ranking Member
Subcommittee on Antitrust, Commercial and Administrative Law

Matt Gaetz
Member of Congress

Mike Johnson
Ranking Member
Subcommittee on the Constitution, Civil Rights and Civil Liberties

Andy Biggs
Ranking Member
Subcommittee on Crime, Terrorism and Homeland Security

Tom McClintock
Ranking Member
Subcommittee on Immigration and Citizenship

W. Gregory Steube
Member of Congress

Tom Tiffany
Member of Congress

Thomas Massie
Member of Congress

Chip Roy
Member of Congress

Dan Bishop
Member of Congress

Michelle Fischbach
Member of Congress

Victoria Spartz
Member of Congress

Scott Fitzgerald
Member of Congress

Cliff Bentz
Member of Congress

Burgess Owens
Member of Congress

cc: The Honorable Jerrold L. Nadler
Chairman

Mr. Monty Wilkinson
Director, Executive Office for U.S. Attorneys

JERROLD NADLER, New York
CHAIRMAN

JIM JORDAN, Ohio
RANKING MEMBER

ONE HUNDRED SEVENTEENTH CONGRESS

Congress of the United States

House of Representatives

COMMITTEE ON THE JUDICIARY

2138 RAYBURN HOUSE OFFICE BUILDING

WASHINGTON, DC 20515–6216

(202) 225–3951
judiciary.house.gov

November 1, 2021

Mr. David H. Estes
Acting U.S. Attorney
Southern District of Georgia
600 James Brown Blvd, Suite 200
Augusta, Georgia 30901

Dear Mr. Estes:

We are continuing to investigate the troubling attempts by the Department of Justice and the White House to use the heavy hand of federal law enforcement to target concerned parents at local school board meetings and chill their protected First Amendment activity. Because the Department directed you, along with all other U.S. Attorneys, and the Federal Bureau of Investigation (FBI) to take action to address parents attending school board meetings,[1] we respectfully request your assistance with our investigation.

On September 29, 2021, the National School Boards Association (NSBA) sent a letter to President Joe Biden requesting help from the federal government with concerned parents voicing their opinions at school board meetings.[2] The NSBA letter stated that "malice, violence, and threats" against school officials "could be the equivalent of a form of domestic terrorism or hate crimes."[3] The letter cited a number of interactions at school board meetings, none of which rose to the level of domestic terrorism. In fact, the vast majority of incidents cited by the NSBA did not involve threats or violence.[4] Most notably, as an example of domestic terrorism, the NSBA cited an incident in which a father angrily confronted members at a school board meeting in Loudoun County, Virginia about the heinous sexual assault of his daughter.[5]

A mere five days after the NSBA sent its letter to President Biden, on October 4, 2021, Attorney General Merrick Garland issued a shocking memorandum that directed the FBI and

---

[1] Memorandum from Atty Gen. Merrick Garland, U.S. Dep't of Justice, Partnership Among Federal, State, Local, Tribal, And Territorial Law Enforcement to Address Threats Against School Administrators, Board Members, Teachers, and Staff (Oct. 4, 2021).

[2] Letter from Dr. Viola M. Garcia, President, Nat'l School Board Assoc. & Mr. Chip Slaven, Chief Exec. Officer, Nat'l School Board Assoc., to President Joseph R. Biden, White House (Sept. 29, 2021).

[3] *Id.*

[4] *See* Caroline Downey, *Vast majority of incidents cited by school-board group to justify federal intervention didn't involve threats,* NAT'L REV. (Oct. 2, 2021).

[5] *Id.*; *see also* Jessica Chasmar, *Loudoun County father arrested at school board events says school tried to cover up daughter's bathroom assault*, FOX NEWS (Oct. 12, 2021).

U.S. Attorneys' Offices to "convene meetings" in your judicial district "with federal, state, local, Tribal, and territorial leaders" within 30 days.[6] The Justice Department simultaneously issued a press release indicating that the Attorney General's directive would "open dedicated lines of communication for threat reporting, assessment and response by law enforcement"—in other words, create a snitch line for complaints about concerned parents.[7]

During Attorney General Garland's testimony before our Committee on October 21, he appeared to have no idea whether the U.S. Attorney meetings he ordered were actually taking place. He stated: "I don't know whether [the meetings] are ongoing, but I expect and hope that they are going . . . because I did ask that they take place."[8] Attorney General Garland testified that he doubted "there have been meetings in every jurisdiction," but reiterated his belief that it is important for federal law enforcement authorities to conduct these meetings in every judicial district.[9] According to the Attorney General's directives, meetings are to be convened in all 94 judicial districts by November 3, 2021, at the latest.

Following the Attorney General's testimony, the NSBA Board of Directors, apparently recognizing the ill-conceived consequences of its letter and the resulting Justice Department action, issued a new memorandum to its members apologizing for the letter, stating: "On behalf of NSBA, <u>we regret and apologize for the letter</u>."[10] (emphasis in original). Although Attorney General Garland testified that the NSBA letter to President Biden was the basis for his October 4 directive to insert federal law enforcement into local school board matters, the Attorney General has yet to rescind his memorandum. His directives to you and other U.S. Attorneys remain in effect.

Concerned parents voicing their strong opposition to controversial curricula at local schools are not domestic terrorists. Parents have an undisputed right to direct the upbringing and education of their children.[11] When parents, however, cross the line to commit a violent act or issue a criminal threat,[12] state and local authorities are best-equipped to handle these violations of state law. But we must not tolerate the use of the federal law enforcement apparatus to intimidate and silence parents using their Constitutional rights to advocate for their child's future.

To assist our investigation and determine whether these meetings are ongoing, we request that you provide the following documents and information:

---

[6] Memorandum from Atty Gen. Merrick Garland, U.S. Dep't of Justice, Partnership Among Federal, State, Local, Tribal, And Territorial Law Enforcement to Address Threats Against School Administrators, Board Members, Teachers, and Staff (Oct. 4, 2021).
[7] Press Release, U.S. Dep't of Justice, Justice Department Addresses Violent Threats Against School Officials and Teachers (Oct. 4, 2021).
[8] *Oversight of the United States Department of Justice: Hearing Before the H. comm. on the Judiciary,* 117th Cong. at 94 (2021) (testimony from Hon. Merrick Garland, Atty Gen., U.S. Dep't of Justice).
[9] *Id.* at 95.
[10] Memorandum from NSBA Board of Directors, Message to NSBA Members (Oct. 22, 2021).
[11] *Troxel v. Granville,* 530 U.S. 57, 65 (2000) (citing *Meyer v. Nebraska,* 262 U.S. 390, 399 (1923)).
[12] *Merrick Garland's federal offense,* WALL ST. J. (Oct. 6, 2021).

1. All documents and communications referring or relating to convening meeting(s) in your judicial district in accordance with the Attorney General's October 4, 2021 memorandum;

2. All agendas, minutes, and notes created or relied upon by U.S. Attorney's Office employees referring or relating to meeting(s) in your judicial district in accordance with the Attorney General's October 4, 2021 memorandum;

3. Please explain when meeting(s) in your judicial district in accordance with the Attorney General's October 4, 2021 memorandum have occurred or will occur;

4. Please identify by name and title of all U.S. Attorney's Office employees involved in the meeting(s) in your judicial district in accordance with the Attorney General's October 4, 2021 memorandum ;

5. Please identify all federal, state, local, Tribal, and territorial organizations invited to or that have attended the meetings convened in your judicial district in accordance with the October 4, 2021 memorandum; and

6. Please provide all recommendations, both formal and informal, and any meeting minutes produced at the meeting(s) in your judicial district in accordance with the Attorney General's October 4, 2021 memorandum.

Please provide this material as soon as possible but no later than 5:00 p.m. on November 15, 2021.

If you have any questions about this request, please contact Committee staff at (202) 225-6906. Thank you for your attention to this important matter.

Sincerely,

Jim Jordan
Ranking Member

Steve Chabot
Member of Congress

Louie Gohmert
Member of Congress

Darrell Issa
Ranking Member
Subcommittee on Courts, Intellectual Property, and the Internet

Ken Buck
Ranking Member
Subcommittee on Antitrust, Commercial and Administrative Law

Mike Johnson
Ranking Member
Subcommittee on the Constitution, Civil Rights and Civil Liberties

Tom McClintock
Ranking Member
Subcommittee on Immigration and Citizenship

Tom Tiffany
Member of Congress

Chip Roy
Member of Congress

Michelle Fischbach
Member of Congress

Matt Gaetz
Member of Congress

Andy Biggs
Ranking Member
Subcommittee on Crime, Terrorism and Homeland Security

W. Gregory Steube
Member of Congress

Thomas Massie
Member of Congress

Dan Bishop
Member of Congress

Victoria Spartz
Member of Congress

Scott Fitzgerald
Member of Congress

Cliff Bentz
Member of Congress

Burgess Owens
Member of Congress

cc: The Honorable Jerrold L. Nadler
Chairman

Mr. Monty Wilkinson
Director, Executive Office for U.S. Attorneys

JERROLD NADLER, New York
CHAIRMAN

JIM JORDAN, Ohio
RANKING MEMBER

ONE HUNDRED SEVENTEENTH CONGRESS

Congress of the United States

House of Representatives

COMMITTEE ON THE JUDICIARY

2138 RAYBURN HOUSE OFFICE BUILDING

WASHINGTON, DC 20515-6216

(202) 225-3951
judiciary.house.gov

November 1, 2021

Mr. Peter D. Leary
Acting U.S. Attorney
Middle District of Georgia
P.O. Box 2568
Columbus, GA 31902

Dear Mr. Leary:

We are continuing to investigate the troubling attempts by the Department of Justice and the White House to use the heavy hand of federal law enforcement to target concerned parents at local school board meetings and chill their protected First Amendment activity. Because the Department directed you, along with all other U.S. Attorneys, and the Federal Bureau of Investigation (FBI) to take action to address parents attending school board meetings,[1] we respectfully request your assistance with our investigation.

On September 29, 2021, the National School Boards Association (NSBA) sent a letter to President Joe Biden requesting help from the federal government with concerned parents voicing their opinions at school board meetings.[2] The NSBA letter stated that "malice, violence, and threats" against school officials "could be the equivalent of a form of domestic terrorism or hate crimes."[3] The letter cited a number of interactions at school board meetings, none of which rose to the level of domestic terrorism. In fact, the vast majority of incidents cited by the NSBA did not involve threats or violence.[4] Most notably, as an example of domestic terrorism, the NSBA cited an incident in which a father angrily confronted members at a school board meeting in Loudoun County, Virginia about the heinous sexual assault of his daughter.[5]

A mere five days after the NSBA sent its letter to President Biden, on October 4, 2021, Attorney General Merrick Garland issued a shocking memorandum that directed the FBI and

---

[1] Memorandum from Atty Gen. Merrick Garland, U.S. Dep't of Justice, Partnership Among Federal, State, Local, Tribal, And Territorial Law Enforcement to Address Threats Against School Administrators, Board Members, Teachers, and Staff (Oct. 4, 2021).
[2] Letter from Dr. Viola M. Garcia, President, Nat'l School Board Assoc. & Mr. Chip Slaven, Chief Exec. Officer, Nat'l School Board Assoc., to President Joseph R. Biden, White House (Sept. 29, 2021).
[3] *Id.*
[4] *See* Caroline Downey, *Vast majority of incidents cited by school-board group to justify federal intervention didn't involve threats,* NAT'L REV. (Oct. 2, 2021).
[5] *Id.*; *see also* Jessica Chasmar, *Loudoun County father arrested at school board events says school tried to cover up daughter's bathroom assault*, FOX NEWS (Oct. 12, 2021).

U.S. Attorneys' Offices to "convene meetings" in your judicial district "with federal, state, local, Tribal, and territorial leaders" within 30 days.[6] The Justice Department simultaneously issued a press release indicating that the Attorney General's directive would "open dedicated lines of communication for threat reporting, assessment and response by law enforcement"—in other words, create a snitch line for complaints about concerned parents.[7]

During Attorney General Garland's testimony before our Committee on October 21, he appeared to have no idea whether the U.S. Attorney meetings he ordered were actually taking place. He stated: "I don't know whether [the meetings] are ongoing, but I expect and hope that they are going . . . because I did ask that they take place."[8] Attorney General Garland testified that he doubted "there have been meetings in every jurisdiction," but reiterated his belief that it is important for federal law enforcement authorities to conduct these meetings in every judicial district.[9] According to the Attorney General's directives, meetings are to be convened in all 94 judicial districts by November 3, 2021, at the latest.

Following the Attorney General's testimony, the NSBA Board of Directors, apparently recognizing the ill-conceived consequences of its letter and the resulting Justice Department action, issued a new memorandum to its members apologizing for the letter, stating: "On behalf of NSBA, <u>we regret and apologize for the letter</u>."[10] (emphasis in original). Although Attorney General Garland testified that the NSBA letter to President Biden was the basis for his October 4 directive to insert federal law enforcement into local school board matters, the Attorney General has yet to rescind his memorandum. His directives to you and other U.S. Attorneys remain in effect.

Concerned parents voicing their strong opposition to controversial curricula at local schools are not domestic terrorists. Parents have an undisputed right to direct the upbringing and education of their children.[11] When parents, however, cross the line to commit a violent act or issue a criminal threat,[12] state and local authorities are best-equipped to handle these violations of state law. But we must not tolerate the use of the federal law enforcement apparatus to intimidate and silence parents using their Constitutional rights to advocate for their child's future.

To assist our investigation and determine whether these meetings are ongoing, we request that you provide the following documents and information:

---

[6] Memorandum from Atty Gen. Merrick Garland, U.S. Dep't of Justice, Partnership Among Federal, State, Local, Tribal, And Territorial Law Enforcement to Address Threats Against School Administrators, Board Members, Teachers, and Staff (Oct. 4, 2021).
[7] Press Release, U.S. Dep't of Justice, Justice Department Addresses Violent Threats Against School Officials and Teachers (Oct. 4, 2021).
[8] *Oversight of the United States Department of Justice: Hearing Before the H. comm. on the Judiciary,* 117th Cong. at 94 (2021) (testimony from Hon. Merrick Garland, Atty Gen., U.S. Dep't of Justice).
[9] *Id.* at 95.
[10] Memorandum from NSBA Board of Directors, Message to NSBA Members (Oct. 22, 2021).
[11] *Troxel v. Granville,* 530 U.S. 57, 65 (2000) (citing *Meyer v. Nebraska,* 262 U.S. 390, 399 (1923)).
[12] *Merrick Garland's federal offense,* WALL ST. J. (Oct. 6, 2021).

1. All documents and communications referring or relating to convening meeting(s) in your judicial district in accordance with the Attorney General's October 4, 2021 memorandum;

2. All agendas, minutes, and notes created or relied upon by U.S. Attorney's Office employees referring or relating to meeting(s) in your judicial district in accordance with the Attorney General's October 4, 2021 memorandum;

3. Please explain when meeting(s) in your judicial district in accordance with the Attorney General's October 4, 2021 memorandum have occurred or will occur;

4. Please identify by name and title of all U.S. Attorney's Office employees involved in the meeting(s) in your judicial district in accordance with the Attorney General's October 4, 2021 memorandum ;

5. Please identify all federal, state, local, Tribal, and territorial organizations invited to or that have attended the meetings convened in your judicial district in accordance with the October 4, 2021 memorandum; and

6. Please provide all recommendations, both formal and informal, and any meeting minutes produced at the meeting(s) in your judicial district in accordance with the Attorney General's October 4, 2021 memorandum.

Please provide this material as soon as possible but no later than 5:00 p.m. on November 15, 2021.

If you have any questions about this request, please contact Committee staff at (202) 225-6906. Thank you for your attention to this important matter.

Sincerely,

Jim Jordan
Ranking Member

Steve Chabot
Member of Congress

Louie Gohmert
Member of Congress

Darrell Issa
Ranking Member
Subcommittee on Courts, Intellectual Property, and the Internet

Ken Buck
Ranking Member
Subcommittee on Antitrust, Commercial and Administrative Law

Matt Gaetz
Member of Congress

Mike Johnson
Ranking Member
Subcommittee on the Constitution, Civil Rights and Civil Liberties

Andy Biggs
Ranking Member
Subcommittee on Crime, Terrorism and Homeland Security

Tom McClintock
Ranking Member
Subcommittee on Immigration and Citizenship

W. Gregory Steube
Member of Congress

Tom Tiffany
Member of Congress

Thomas Massie
Member of Congress

Chip Roy
Member of Congress

Dan Bishop
Member of Congress

Michelle Fischbach
Member of Congress

Victoria Spartz
Member of Congress

Scott Fitzgerald
Member of Congress

Cliff Bentz
Member of Congress

Burgess Owens
Member of Congress

cc: The Honorable Jerrold L. Nadler
Chairman

Mr. Monty Wilkinson
Director, Executive Office for U.S. Attorneys

JERROLD NADLER, New York
CHAIRMAN

JIM JORDAN, Ohio
RANKING MEMBER

ONE HUNDRED SEVENTEENTH CONGRESS

Congress of the United States

House of Representatives

COMMITTEE ON THE JUDICIARY

2138 RAYBURN HOUSE OFFICE BUILDING

WASHINGTON, DC 20515-6216

(202) 225-3951
judiciary.house.gov

November 1, 2021

Mr. Shawn N. Anderson
U.S. Attorney
Districts of Guam & Northern Mariana Islands
108 Hernan Cortez, Suite 500
Hagåtña, GU 96910

Dear Mr. Anderson:

We are continuing to investigate the troubling attempts by the Department of Justice and the White House to use the heavy hand of federal law enforcement to target concerned parents at local school board meetings and chill their protected First Amendment activity. Because the Department directed you, along with all other U.S. Attorneys, and the Federal Bureau of Investigation (FBI) to take action to address parents attending school board meetings,[1] we respectfully request your assistance with our investigation.

On September 29, 2021, the National School Boards Association (NSBA) sent a letter to President Joe Biden requesting help from the federal government with concerned parents voicing their opinions at school board meetings.[2] The NSBA letter stated that "malice, violence, and threats" against school officials "could be the equivalent of a form of domestic terrorism or hate crimes."[3] The letter cited a number of interactions at school board meetings, none of which rose to the level of domestic terrorism. In fact, the vast majority of incidents cited by the NSBA did not involve threats or violence.[4] Most notably, as an example of domestic terrorism, the NSBA cited an incident in which a father angrily confronted members at a school board meeting in Loudoun County, Virginia about the heinous sexual assault of his daughter.[5]

A mere five days after the NSBA sent its letter to President Biden, on October 4, 2021, Attorney General Merrick Garland issued a shocking memorandum that directed the FBI and

---

[1] Memorandum from Atty Gen. Merrick Garland, U.S. Dep't of Justice, Partnership Among Federal, State, Local, Tribal, And Territorial Law Enforcement to Address Threats Against School Administrators, Board Members, Teachers, and Staff (Oct. 4, 2021).
[2] Letter from Dr. Viola M. Garcia, President, Nat'l School Board Assoc. & Mr. Chip Slaven, Chief Exec. Officer, Nat'l School Board Assoc., to President Joseph R. Biden, White House (Sept. 29, 2021).
[3] *Id.*
[4] *See* Caroline Downey, *Vast majority of incidents cited by school-board group to justify federal intervention didn't involve threats,* NAT'L REV. (Oct. 2, 2021).
[5] *Id.*; *see also* Jessica Chasmar, *Loudoun County father arrested at school board events says school tried to cover up daughter's bathroom assault*, FOX NEWS (Oct. 12, 2021).

U.S. Attorneys' Offices to "convene meetings" in your judicial district "with federal, state, local, Tribal, and territorial leaders" within 30 days.[6] The Justice Department simultaneously issued a press release indicating that the Attorney General's directive would "open dedicated lines of communication for threat reporting, assessment and response by law enforcement"—in other words, create a snitch line for complaints about concerned parents.[7]

During Attorney General Garland's testimony before our Committee on October 21, he appeared to have no idea whether the U.S. Attorney meetings he ordered were actually taking place. He stated: "I don't know whether [the meetings] are ongoing, but I expect and hope that they are going . . . because I did ask that they take place."[8] Attorney General Garland testified that he doubted "there have been meetings in every jurisdiction," but reiterated his belief that it is important for federal law enforcement authorities to conduct these meetings in every judicial district.[9] According to the Attorney General's directives, meetings are to be convened in all 94 judicial districts by November 3, 2021, at the latest.

Following the Attorney General's testimony, the NSBA Board of Directors, apparently recognizing the ill-conceived consequences of its letter and the resulting Justice Department action, issued a new memorandum to its members apologizing for the letter, stating: "On behalf of NSBA, <u>we regret and apologize for the letter</u>."[10] (emphasis in original). Although Attorney General Garland testified that the NSBA letter to President Biden was the basis for his October 4 directive to insert federal law enforcement into local school board matters, the Attorney General has yet to rescind his memorandum. His directives to you and other U.S. Attorneys remain in effect.

Concerned parents voicing their strong opposition to controversial curricula at local schools are not domestic terrorists. Parents have an undisputed right to direct the upbringing and education of their children.[11] When parents, however, cross the line to commit a violent act or issue a criminal threat,[12] state and local authorities are best-equipped to handle these violations of state law. But we must not tolerate the use of the federal law enforcement apparatus to intimidate and silence parents using their Constitutional rights to advocate for their child's future.

To assist our investigation and determine whether these meetings are ongoing, we request that you provide the following documents and information:

---

[6] Memorandum from Atty Gen. Merrick Garland, U.S. Dep't of Justice, Partnership Among Federal, State, Local, Tribal, And Territorial Law Enforcement to Address Threats Against School Administrators, Board Members, Teachers, and Staff (Oct. 4, 2021).

[7] Press Release, U.S. Dep't of Justice, Justice Department Addresses Violent Threats Against School Officials and Teachers (Oct. 4, 2021).

[8] *Oversight of the United States Department of Justice: Hearing Before the H. comm. on the Judiciary,* 117th Cong. at 94 (2021) (testimony from Hon. Merrick Garland, Atty Gen., U.S. Dep't of Justice).

[9] *Id.* at 95.

[10] Memorandum from NSBA Board of Directors, Message to NSBA Members (Oct. 22, 2021).

[11] *Troxel v. Granville,* 530 U.S. 57, 65 (2000) (citing *Meyer v. Nebraska,* 262 U.S. 390, 399 (1923)).

[12] *Merrick Garland's federal offense,* WALL ST. J. (Oct. 6, 2021).

1. All documents and communications referring or relating to convening meeting(s) in your judicial district in accordance with the Attorney General's October 4, 2021 memorandum;

2. All agendas, minutes, and notes created or relied upon by U.S. Attorney's Office employees referring or relating to meeting(s) in your judicial district in accordance with the Attorney General's October 4, 2021 memorandum;

3. Please explain when meeting(s) in your judicial district in accordance with the Attorney General's October 4, 2021 memorandum have occurred or will occur;

4. Please identify by name and title of all U.S. Attorney's Office employees involved in the meeting(s) in your judicial district in accordance with the Attorney General's October 4, 2021 memorandum ;

5. Please identify all federal, state, local, Tribal, and territorial organizations invited to or that have attended the meetings convened in your judicial district in accordance with the October 4, 2021 memorandum; and

6. Please provide all recommendations, both formal and informal, and any meeting minutes produced at the meeting(s) in your judicial district in accordance with the Attorney General's October 4, 2021 memorandum.

Please provide this material as soon as possible but no later than 5:00 p.m. on November 15, 2021.

If you have any questions about this request, please contact Committee staff at (202) 225-6906. Thank you for your attention to this important matter.

Sincerely,

Jim Jordan
Ranking Member

Steve Chabot
Member of Congress

Louie Gohmert
Member of Congress

Darrell Issa
Ranking Member
Subcommittee on Courts, Intellectual Property, and the Internet

Ken Buck
Ranking Member
Subcommittee on Antitrust, Commercial and Administrative Law

Matt Gaetz
Member of Congress

Mike Johnson
Ranking Member
Subcommittee on the Constitution, Civil Rights and Civil Liberties

Andy Biggs
Ranking Member
Subcommittee on Crime, Terrorism and Homeland Security

Tom McClintock
Ranking Member
Subcommittee on Immigration and Citizenship

W. Gregory Steube
Member of Congress

Tom Tiffany
Member of Congress

Thomas Massie
Member of Congress

Chip Roy
Member of Congress

Dan Bishop
Member of Congress

Michelle Fischbach
Member of Congress

Victoria Spartz
Member of Congress

Scott Fitzgerald
Member of Congress

Cliff Bentz
Member of Congress

Burgess Owens
Member of Congress

cc: The Honorable Jerrold L. Nadler
Chairman

Mr. Monty Wilkinson
Director, Executive Office for U.S. Attorneys

JERROLD NADLER, New York
CHAIRMAN

JIM JORDAN, Ohio
RANKING MEMBER

ONE HUNDRED SEVENTEENTH CONGRESS

Congress of the United States
House of Representatives
COMMITTEE ON THE JUDICIARY
2138 RAYBURN HOUSE OFFICE BUILDING
WASHINGTON, DC 20515-6216
(202) 225-3951
judiciary.house.gov

November 1, 2021

Ms. Judith A. Philips
Acting U.S. Attorney
District of Hawaii
300 Ala Moana Blvd., #6-100
Honolulu, HI 96850

Dear Ms. Philips:

We are continuing to investigate the troubling attempts by the Department of Justice and the White House to use the heavy hand of federal law enforcement to target concerned parents at local school board meetings and chill their protected First Amendment activity. Because the Department directed you, along with all other U.S. Attorneys, and the Federal Bureau of Investigation (FBI) to take action to address parents attending school board meetings,[1] we respectfully request your assistance with our investigation.

On September 29, 2021, the National School Boards Association (NSBA) sent a letter to President Joe Biden requesting help from the federal government with concerned parents voicing their opinions at school board meetings.[2] The NSBA letter stated that "malice, violence, and threats" against school officials "could be the equivalent of a form of domestic terrorism or hate crimes."[3] The letter cited a number of interactions at school board meetings, none of which rose to the level of domestic terrorism. In fact, the vast majority of incidents cited by the NSBA did not involve threats or violence.[4] Most notably, as an example of domestic terrorism, the NSBA cited an incident in which a father angrily confronted members at a school board meeting in Loudoun County, Virginia about the heinous sexual assault of his daughter.[5]

A mere five days after the NSBA sent its letter to President Biden, on October 4, 2021, Attorney General Merrick Garland issued a shocking memorandum that directed the FBI and

---

[1] Memorandum from Atty Gen. Merrick Garland, U.S. Dep't of Justice, Partnership Among Federal, State, Local, Tribal, And Territorial Law Enforcement to Address Threats Against School Administrators, Board Members, Teachers, and Staff (Oct. 4, 2021).
[2] Letter from Dr. Viola M. Garcia, President, Nat'l School Board Assoc. & Mr. Chip Slaven, Chief Exec. Officer, Nat'l School Board Assoc., to President Joseph R. Biden, White House (Sept. 29, 2021).
[3] *Id.*
[4] *See* Caroline Downey, *Vast majority of incidents cited by school-board group to justify federal intervention didn't involve threats,* NAT'L REV. (Oct. 2, 2021).
[5] *Id.*; *see also* Jessica Chasmar, *Loudoun County father arrested at school board events says school tried to cover up daughter's bathroom assault*, FOX NEWS (Oct. 12, 2021).

U.S. Attorneys' Offices to "convene meetings" in your judicial district "with federal, state, local, Tribal, and territorial leaders" within 30 days.[6] The Justice Department simultaneously issued a press release indicating that the Attorney General's directive would "open dedicated lines of communication for threat reporting, assessment and response by law enforcement"—in other words, create a snitch line for complaints about concerned parents.[7]

During Attorney General Garland's testimony before our Committee on October 21, he appeared to have no idea whether the U.S. Attorney meetings he ordered were actually taking place. He stated: "I don't know whether [the meetings] are ongoing, but I expect and hope that they are going . . . because I did ask that they take place."[8] Attorney General Garland testified that he doubted "there have been meetings in every jurisdiction," but reiterated his belief that it is important for federal law enforcement authorities to conduct these meetings in every judicial district.[9] According to the Attorney General's directives, meetings are to be convened in all 94 judicial districts by November 3, 2021, at the latest.

Following the Attorney General's testimony, the NSBA Board of Directors, apparently recognizing the ill-conceived consequences of its letter and the resulting Justice Department action, issued a new memorandum to its members apologizing for the letter, stating: "On behalf of NSBA, <u>we regret and apologize for the letter</u>."[10] (emphasis in original). Although Attorney General Garland testified that the NSBA letter to President Biden was the basis for his October 4 directive to insert federal law enforcement into local school board matters, the Attorney General has yet to rescind his memorandum. His directives to you and other U.S. Attorneys remain in effect.

Concerned parents voicing their strong opposition to controversial curricula at local schools are not domestic terrorists. Parents have an undisputed right to direct the upbringing and education of their children.[11] When parents, however, cross the line to commit a violent act or issue a criminal threat,[12] state and local authorities are best-equipped to handle these violations of state law. But we must not tolerate the use of the federal law enforcement apparatus to intimidate and silence parents using their Constitutional rights to advocate for their child's future.

To assist our investigation and determine whether these meetings are ongoing, we request that you provide the following documents and information:

---

[6] Memorandum from Atty Gen. Merrick Garland, U.S. Dep't of Justice, Partnership Among Federal, State, Local, Tribal, And Territorial Law Enforcement to Address Threats Against School Administrators, Board Members, Teachers, and Staff (Oct. 4, 2021).
[7] Press Release, U.S. Dep't of Justice, Justice Department Addresses Violent Threats Against School Officials and Teachers (Oct. 4, 2021).
[8] *Oversight of the United States Department of Justice: Hearing Before the H. comm. on the Judiciary,* 117th Cong. at 94 (2021) (testimony from Hon. Merrick Garland, Atty Gen., U.S. Dep't of Justice).
[9] *Id.* at 95.
[10] Memorandum from NSBA Board of Directors, Message to NSBA Members (Oct. 22, 2021).
[11] *Troxel v. Granville,* 530 U.S. 57, 65 (2000) (citing *Meyer v. Nebraska,* 262 U.S. 390, 399 (1923)).
[12] *Merrick Garland's federal offense,* WALL ST. J. (Oct. 6, 2021).

1. All documents and communications referring or relating to convening meeting(s) in your judicial district in accordance with the Attorney General's October 4, 2021 memorandum;

2. All agendas, minutes, and notes created or relied upon by U.S. Attorney's Office employees referring or relating to meeting(s) in your judicial district in accordance with the Attorney General's October 4, 2021 memorandum;

3. Please explain when meeting(s) in your judicial district in accordance with the Attorney General's October 4, 2021 memorandum have occurred or will occur;

4. Please identify by name and title of all U.S. Attorney's Office employees involved in the meeting(s) in your judicial district in accordance with the Attorney General's October 4, 2021 memorandum ;

5. Please identify all federal, state, local, Tribal, and territorial organizations invited to or that have attended the meetings convened in your judicial district in accordance with the October 4, 2021 memorandum; and

6. Please provide all recommendations, both formal and informal, and any meeting minutes produced at the meeting(s) in your judicial district in accordance with the Attorney General's October 4, 2021 memorandum.

Please provide this material as soon as possible but no later than 5:00 p.m. on November 15, 2021.

If you have any questions about this request, please contact Committee staff at (202) 225-6906. Thank you for your attention to this important matter.

Sincerely,

Jim Jordan
Ranking Member

Steve Chabot
Member of Congress

Louie Gohmert
Member of Congress

Darrell Issa
Ranking Member
Subcommittee on Courts, Intellectual Property, and the Internet

Ken Buck
Ranking Member
Subcommittee on Antitrust, Commercial and Administrative Law

Matt Gaetz
Member of Congress

Mike Johnson
Ranking Member
Subcommittee on the Constitution, Civil Rights and Civil Liberties

Andy Biggs
Ranking Member
Subcommittee on Crime, Terrorism and Homeland Security

Tom McClintock
Ranking Member
Subcommittee on Immigration and Citizenship

W. Gregory Steube
Member of Congress

Tom Tiffany
Member of Congress

Thomas Massie
Member of Congress

Chip Roy
Member of Congress

Dan Bishop
Member of Congress

Michelle Fischbach
Member of Congress

Victoria Spartz
Member of Congress

Scott Fitzgerald
Member of Congress

Cliff Bentz
Member of Congress

Burgess Owens
Member of Congress

cc: The Honorable Jerrold L. Nadler
Chairman

Mr. Monty Wilkinson
Director, Executive Office for U.S. Attorneys

JERROLD NADLER, New York
CHAIRMAN

JIM JORDAN, Ohio
RANKING MEMBER

ONE HUNDRED SEVENTEENTH CONGRESS
Congress of the United States
House of Representatives
COMMITTEE ON THE JUDICIARY
2138 RAYBURN HOUSE OFFICE BUILDING
WASHINGTON, DC 20515–6216
(202) 225–3951
judiciary.house.gov

November 1, 2021

Mr. Sean R. Berry
Acting U.S. Attorney
Northern District of Iowa
111 7th Avenue, SE, Box #1
Cedar Rapids, IA 52401

Dear Mr. Berry:

We are continuing to investigate the troubling attempts by the Department of Justice and the White House to use the heavy hand of federal law enforcement to target concerned parents at local school board meetings and chill their protected First Amendment activity. Because the Department directed you, along with all other U.S. Attorneys, and the Federal Bureau of Investigation (FBI) to take action to address parents attending school board meetings,[1] we respectfully request your assistance with our investigation.

On September 29, 2021, the National School Boards Association (NSBA) sent a letter to President Joe Biden requesting help from the federal government with concerned parents voicing their opinions at school board meetings.[2] The NSBA letter stated that "malice, violence, and threats" against school officials "could be the equivalent of a form of domestic terrorism or hate crimes."[3] The letter cited a number of interactions at school board meetings, none of which rose to the level of domestic terrorism. In fact, the vast majority of incidents cited by the NSBA did not involve threats or violence.[4] Most notably, as an example of domestic terrorism, the NSBA cited an incident in which a father angrily confronted members at a school board meeting in Loudoun County, Virginia about the heinous sexual assault of his daughter.[5]

A mere five days after the NSBA sent its letter to President Biden, on October 4, 2021, Attorney General Merrick Garland issued a shocking memorandum that directed the FBI and

---

[1] Memorandum from Atty Gen. Merrick Garland, U.S. Dep't of Justice, Partnership Among Federal, State, Local, Tribal, And Territorial Law Enforcement to Address Threats Against School Administrators, Board Members, Teachers, and Staff (Oct. 4, 2021).
[2] Letter from Dr. Viola M. Garcia, President, Nat'l School Board Assoc. & Mr. Chip Slaven, Chief Exec. Officer, Nat'l School Board Assoc., to President Joseph R. Biden, White House (Sept. 29, 2021).
[3] *Id.*
[4] *See* Caroline Downey, *Vast majority of incidents cited by school-board group to justify federal intervention didn't involve threats,* NAT'L REV. (Oct. 2, 2021).
[5] *Id.*; *see also* Jessica Chasmar, *Loudoun County father arrested at school board events says school tried to cover up daughter's bathroom assault*, FOX NEWS (Oct. 12, 2021).

U.S. Attorneys' Offices to "convene meetings" in your judicial district "with federal, state, local, Tribal, and territorial leaders" within 30 days.[6] The Justice Department simultaneously issued a press release indicating that the Attorney General's directive would "open dedicated lines of communication for threat reporting, assessment and response by law enforcement"—in other words, create a snitch line for complaints about concerned parents.[7]

During Attorney General Garland's testimony before our Committee on October 21, he appeared to have no idea whether the U.S. Attorney meetings he ordered were actually taking place. He stated: "I don't know whether [the meetings] are ongoing, but I expect and hope that they are going . . . because I did ask that they take place."[8] Attorney General Garland testified that he doubted "there have been meetings in every jurisdiction," but reiterated his belief that it is important for federal law enforcement authorities to conduct these meetings in every judicial district.[9] According to the Attorney General's directives, meetings are to be convened in all 94 judicial districts by November 3, 2021, at the latest.

Following the Attorney General's testimony, the NSBA Board of Directors, apparently recognizing the ill-conceived consequences of its letter and the resulting Justice Department action, issued a new memorandum to its members apologizing for the letter, stating: "On behalf of NSBA, <u>we regret and apologize for the letter</u>."[10] (emphasis in original). Although Attorney General Garland testified that the NSBA letter to President Biden was the basis for his October 4 directive to insert federal law enforcement into local school board matters, the Attorney General has yet to rescind his memorandum. His directives to you and other U.S. Attorneys remain in effect.

Concerned parents voicing their strong opposition to controversial curricula at local schools are not domestic terrorists. Parents have an undisputed right to direct the upbringing and education of their children.[11] When parents, however, cross the line to commit a violent act or issue a criminal threat,[12] state and local authorities are best-equipped to handle these violations of state law. But we must not tolerate the use of the federal law enforcement apparatus to intimidate and silence parents using their Constitutional rights to advocate for their child's future.

To assist our investigation and determine whether these meetings are ongoing, we request that you provide the following documents and information:

---

[6] Memorandum from Atty Gen. Merrick Garland, U.S. Dep't of Justice, Partnership Among Federal, State, Local, Tribal, And Territorial Law Enforcement to Address Threats Against School Administrators, Board Members, Teachers, and Staff (Oct. 4, 2021).

[7] Press Release, U.S. Dep't of Justice, Justice Department Addresses Violent Threats Against School Officials and Teachers (Oct. 4, 2021).

[8] *Oversight of the United States Department of Justice: Hearing Before the H. comm. on the Judiciary,* 117th Cong. at 94 (2021) (testimony from Hon. Merrick Garland, Atty Gen., U.S. Dep't of Justice).

[9] *Id.* at 95.

[10] Memorandum from NSBA Board of Directors, Message to NSBA Members (Oct. 22, 2021).

[11] *Troxel v. Granville,* 530 U.S. 57, 65 (2000) (citing *Meyer v. Nebraska,* 262 U.S. 390, 399 (1923)).

[12] *Merrick Garland's federal offense,* WALL ST. J. (Oct. 6, 2021).

1. All documents and communications referring or relating to convening meeting(s) in your judicial district in accordance with the Attorney General's October 4, 2021 memorandum;

2. All agendas, minutes, and notes created or relied upon by U.S. Attorney's Office employees referring or relating to meeting(s) in your judicial district in accordance with the Attorney General's October 4, 2021 memorandum;

3. Please explain when meeting(s) in your judicial district in accordance with the Attorney General's October 4, 2021 memorandum have occurred or will occur;

4. Please identify by name and title of all U.S. Attorney's Office employees involved in the meeting(s) in your judicial district in accordance with the Attorney General's October 4, 2021 memorandum ;

5. Please identify all federal, state, local, Tribal, and territorial organizations invited to or that have attended the meetings convened in your judicial district in accordance with the October 4, 2021 memorandum; and

6. Please provide all recommendations, both formal and informal, and any meeting minutes produced at the meeting(s) in your judicial district in accordance with the Attorney General's October 4, 2021 memorandum.

Please provide this material as soon as possible but no later than 5:00 p.m. on November 15, 2021.

If you have any questions about this request, please contact Committee staff at (202) 225-6906. Thank you for your attention to this important matter.

Sincerely,

Jim Jordan
Ranking Member

Steve Chabot
Member of Congress

Louie Gohmert
Member of Congress

Darrell Issa
Ranking Member
Subcommittee on Courts, Intellectual Property, and the Internet

Ken Buck
Ranking Member
Subcommittee on Antitrust, Commercial and Administrative Law

Matt Gaetz
Member of Congress

Mike Johnson
Ranking Member
Subcommittee on the Constitution, Civil Rights and Civil Liberties

Andy Biggs
Ranking Member
Subcommittee on Crime, Terrorism and Homeland Security

Tom McClintock
Ranking Member
Subcommittee on Immigration and Citizenship

W. Gregory Steube
Member of Congress

Tom Tiffany
Member of Congress

Thomas Massie
Member of Congress

Chip Roy
Member of Congress

Dan Bishop
Member of Congress

Michelle Fischbach
Member of Congress

Victoria Spartz
Member of Congress

Scott Fitzgerald
Member of Congress

Cliff Bentz
Member of Congress

Burgess Owens
Member of Congress

cc: The Honorable Jerrold L. Nadler
Chairman

Mr. Monty Wilkinson
Director, Executive Office for U.S. Attorneys

JERROLD NADLER, New York
CHAIRMAN

JIM JORDAN, Ohio
RANKING MEMBER

ONE HUNDRED SEVENTEENTH CONGRESS
Congress of the United States
House of Representatives
COMMITTEE ON THE JUDICIARY
2138 RAYBURN HOUSE OFFICE BUILDING
WASHINGTON, DC 20515–6216
(202) 225–3951
judiciary.house.gov

November 1, 2021

Mr. Richard D. Westphal
Acting U.S. Attorney
Southern District of Iowa
110 East Court Avenue, Suite 286
Des Moines, IA 50309

Dear Mr. Westphal:

We are continuing to investigate the troubling attempts by the Department of Justice and the White House to use the heavy hand of federal law enforcement to target concerned parents at local school board meetings and chill their protected First Amendment activity. Because the Department directed you, along with all other U.S. Attorneys, and the Federal Bureau of Investigation (FBI) to take action to address parents attending school board meetings,[1] we respectfully request your assistance with our investigation.

On September 29, 2021, the National School Boards Association (NSBA) sent a letter to President Joe Biden requesting help from the federal government with concerned parents voicing their opinions at school board meetings.[2] The NSBA letter stated that "malice, violence, and threats" against school officials "could be the equivalent of a form of domestic terrorism or hate crimes."[3] The letter cited a number of interactions at school board meetings, none of which rose to the level of domestic terrorism. In fact, the vast majority of incidents cited by the NSBA did not involve threats or violence.[4] Most notably, as an example of domestic terrorism, the NSBA cited an incident in which a father angrily confronted members at a school board meeting in Loudoun County, Virginia about the heinous sexual assault of his daughter.[5]

A mere five days after the NSBA sent its letter to President Biden, on October 4, 2021, Attorney General Merrick Garland issued a shocking memorandum that directed the FBI and

---

[1] Memorandum from Atty Gen. Merrick Garland, U.S. Dep't of Justice, Partnership Among Federal, State, Local, Tribal, And Territorial Law Enforcement to Address Threats Against School Administrators, Board Members, Teachers, and Staff (Oct. 4, 2021).
[2] Letter from Dr. Viola M. Garcia, President, Nat'l School Board Assoc. & Mr. Chip Slaven, Chief Exec. Officer, Nat'l School Board Assoc., to President Joseph R. Biden, White House (Sept. 29, 2021).
[3] *Id.*
[4] *See* Caroline Downey, *Vast majority of incidents cited by school-board group to justify federal intervention didn't involve threats,* NAT'L REV. (Oct. 2, 2021).
[5] *Id.*; *see also* Jessica Chasmar, *Loudoun County father arrested at school board events says school tried to cover up daughter's bathroom assault*, FOX NEWS (Oct. 12, 2021).

U.S. Attorneys' Offices to "convene meetings" in your judicial district "with federal, state, local, Tribal, and territorial leaders" within 30 days.[6] The Justice Department simultaneously issued a press release indicating that the Attorney General's directive would "open dedicated lines of communication for threat reporting, assessment and response by law enforcement"—in other words, create a snitch line for complaints about concerned parents.[7]

During Attorney General Garland's testimony before our Committee on October 21, he appeared to have no idea whether the U.S. Attorney meetings he ordered were actually taking place. He stated: "I don't know whether [the meetings] are ongoing, but I expect and hope that they are going . . . because I did ask that they take place."[8] Attorney General Garland testified that he doubted "there have been meetings in every jurisdiction," but reiterated his belief that it is important for federal law enforcement authorities to conduct these meetings in every judicial district.[9] According to the Attorney General's directives, meetings are to be convened in all 94 judicial districts by November 3, 2021, at the latest.

Following the Attorney General's testimony, the NSBA Board of Directors, apparently recognizing the ill-conceived consequences of its letter and the resulting Justice Department action, issued a new memorandum to its members apologizing for the letter, stating: "On behalf of NSBA, <u>we regret and apologize for the letter</u>."[10] (emphasis in original). Although Attorney General Garland testified that the NSBA letter to President Biden was the basis for his October 4 directive to insert federal law enforcement into local school board matters, the Attorney General has yet to rescind his memorandum. His directives to you and other U.S. Attorneys remain in effect.

Concerned parents voicing their strong opposition to controversial curricula at local schools are not domestic terrorists. Parents have an undisputed right to direct the upbringing and education of their children.[11] When parents, however, cross the line to commit a violent act or issue a criminal threat,[12] state and local authorities are best-equipped to handle these violations of state law. But we must not tolerate the use of the federal law enforcement apparatus to intimidate and silence parents using their Constitutional rights to advocate for their child's future.

To assist our investigation and determine whether these meetings are ongoing, we request that you provide the following documents and information:

---

[6] Memorandum from Atty Gen. Merrick Garland, U.S. Dep't of Justice, Partnership Among Federal, State, Local, Tribal, And Territorial Law Enforcement to Address Threats Against School Administrators, Board Members, Teachers, and Staff (Oct. 4, 2021).
[7] Press Release, U.S. Dep't of Justice, Justice Department Addresses Violent Threats Against School Officials and Teachers (Oct. 4, 2021).
[8] *Oversight of the United States Department of Justice: Hearing Before the H. comm. on the Judiciary,* 117th Cong. at 94 (2021) (testimony from Hon. Merrick Garland, Atty Gen., U.S. Dep't of Justice).
[9] *Id.* at 95.
[10] Memorandum from NSBA Board of Directors, Message to NSBA Members (Oct. 22, 2021).
[11] *Troxel v. Granville,* 530 U.S. 57, 65 (2000) (citing *Meyer v. Nebraska,* 262 U.S. 390, 399 (1923)).
[12] *Merrick Garland's federal offense,* WALL ST. J. (Oct. 6, 2021).

1. All documents and communications referring or relating to convening meeting(s) in your judicial district in accordance with the Attorney General's October 4, 2021 memorandum;

2. All agendas, minutes, and notes created or relied upon by U.S. Attorney's Office employees referring or relating to meeting(s) in your judicial district in accordance with the Attorney General's October 4, 2021 memorandum;

3. Please explain when meeting(s) in your judicial district in accordance with the Attorney General's October 4, 2021 memorandum have occurred or will occur;

4. Please identify by name and title of all U.S. Attorney's Office employees involved in the meeting(s) in your judicial district in accordance with the Attorney General's October 4, 2021 memorandum ;

5. Please identify all federal, state, local, Tribal, and territorial organizations invited to or that have attended the meetings convened in your judicial district in accordance with the October 4, 2021 memorandum; and

6. Please provide all recommendations, both formal and informal, and any meeting minutes produced at the meeting(s) in your judicial district in accordance with the Attorney General's October 4, 2021 memorandum.

Please provide this material as soon as possible but no later than 5:00 p.m. on November 15, 2021.

If you have any questions about this request, please contact Committee staff at (202) 225-6906. Thank you for your attention to this important matter.

Sincerely,

Jim Jordan
Ranking Member

Steve Chabot
Member of Congress

Louie Gohmert
Member of Congress

Darrell Issa
Ranking Member
Subcommittee on Courts, Intellectual Property, and the Internet

Ken Buck
Ranking Member
Subcommittee on Antitrust, Commercial and Administrative Law

Matt Gaetz
Member of Congress

Mike Johnson
Ranking Member
Subcommittee on the Constitution, Civil Rights and Civil Liberties

Andy Biggs
Ranking Member
Subcommittee on Crime, Terrorism and Homeland Security

Tom McClintock
Ranking Member
Subcommittee on Immigration and Citizenship

W. Gregory Steube
Member of Congress

Tom Tiffany
Member of Congress

Thomas Massie
Member of Congress

Chip Roy
Member of Congress

Dan Bishop
Member of Congress

Michelle Fischbach
Member of Congress

Victoria Spartz
Member of Congress

Scott Fitzgerald
Member of Congress

Cliff Bentz
Member of Congress

Burgess Owens
Member of Congress

cc: The Honorable Jerrold L. Nadler
Chairman

Mr. Monty Wilkinson
Director, Executive Office for U.S. Attorneys

JERROLD NADLER, New York
CHAIRMAN

JIM JORDAN, Ohio
RANKING MEMBER

ONE HUNDRED SEVENTEENTH CONGRESS

Congress of the United States
House of Representatives

COMMITTEE ON THE JUDICIARY

2138 RAYBURN HOUSE OFFICE BUILDING

WASHINGTON, DC 20515–6216

(202) 225–3951
judiciary.house.gov

November 1, 2021

Mr. Rafael M. Gonzalez Jr.
Acting U.S. Attorney
District of Idaho
1290 West Myrtle Street, Suite 500
Boise, ID 83702

Dear Mr. Gonzalez:

We are continuing to investigate the troubling attempts by the Department of Justice and the White House to use the heavy hand of federal law enforcement to target concerned parents at local school board meetings and chill their protected First Amendment activity. Because the Department directed you, along with all other U.S. Attorneys, and the Federal Bureau of Investigation (FBI) to take action to address parents attending school board meetings,[1] we respectfully request your assistance with our investigation.

On September 29, 2021, the National School Boards Association (NSBA) sent a letter to President Joe Biden requesting help from the federal government with concerned parents voicing their opinions at school board meetings.[2] The NSBA letter stated that "malice, violence, and threats" against school officials "could be the equivalent of a form of domestic terrorism or hate crimes."[3] The letter cited a number of interactions at school board meetings, none of which rose to the level of domestic terrorism. In fact, the vast majority of incidents cited by the NSBA did not involve threats or violence.[4] Most notably, as an example of domestic terrorism, the NSBA cited an incident in which a father angrily confronted members at a school board meeting in Loudoun County, Virginia about the heinous sexual assault of his daughter.[5]

A mere five days after the NSBA sent its letter to President Biden, on October 4, 2021, Attorney General Merrick Garland issued a shocking memorandum that directed the FBI and

---

[1] Memorandum from Atty Gen. Merrick Garland, U.S. Dep't of Justice, Partnership Among Federal, State, Local, Tribal, And Territorial Law Enforcement to Address Threats Against School Administrators, Board Members, Teachers, and Staff (Oct. 4, 2021).
[2] Letter from Dr. Viola M. Garcia, President, Nat'l School Board Assoc. & Mr. Chip Slaven, Chief Exec. Officer, Nat'l School Board Assoc., to President Joseph R. Biden, White House (Sept. 29, 2021).
[3] *Id.*
[4] *See* Caroline Downey, *Vast majority of incidents cited by school-board group to justify federal intervention didn't involve threats,* NAT'L REV. (Oct. 2, 2021).
[5] *Id.*; *see also* Jessica Chasmar, *Loudoun County father arrested at school board events says school tried to cover up daughter's bathroom assault*, FOX NEWS (Oct. 12, 2021).

U.S. Attorneys' Offices to "convene meetings" in your judicial district "with federal, state, local, Tribal, and territorial leaders" within 30 days.[6] The Justice Department simultaneously issued a press release indicating that the Attorney General's directive would "open dedicated lines of communication for threat reporting, assessment and response by law enforcement"—in other words, create a snitch line for complaints about concerned parents.[7]

During Attorney General Garland's testimony before our Committee on October 21, he appeared to have no idea whether the U.S. Attorney meetings he ordered were actually taking place. He stated: "I don't know whether [the meetings] are ongoing, but I expect and hope that they are going . . . because I did ask that they take place."[8] Attorney General Garland testified that he doubted "there have been meetings in every jurisdiction," but reiterated his belief that it is important for federal law enforcement authorities to conduct these meetings in every judicial district.[9] According to the Attorney General's directives, meetings are to be convened in all 94 judicial districts by November 3, 2021, at the latest.

Following the Attorney General's testimony, the NSBA Board of Directors, apparently recognizing the ill-conceived consequences of its letter and the resulting Justice Department action, issued a new memorandum to its members apologizing for the letter, stating: "On behalf of NSBA, <u>we regret and apologize for the letter</u>."[10] (emphasis in original). Although Attorney General Garland testified that the NSBA letter to President Biden was the basis for his October 4 directive to insert federal law enforcement into local school board matters, the Attorney General has yet to rescind his memorandum. His directives to you and other U.S. Attorneys remain in effect.

Concerned parents voicing their strong opposition to controversial curricula at local schools are not domestic terrorists. Parents have an undisputed right to direct the upbringing and education of their children.[11] When parents, however, cross the line to commit a violent act or issue a criminal threat,[12] state and local authorities are best-equipped to handle these violations of state law. But we must not tolerate the use of the federal law enforcement apparatus to intimidate and silence parents using their Constitutional rights to advocate for their child's future.

To assist our investigation and determine whether these meetings are ongoing, we request that you provide the following documents and information:

---

[6] Memorandum from Atty Gen. Merrick Garland, U.S. Dep't of Justice, Partnership Among Federal, State, Local, Tribal, And Territorial Law Enforcement to Address Threats Against School Administrators, Board Members, Teachers, and Staff (Oct. 4, 2021).
[7] Press Release, U.S. Dep't of Justice, Justice Department Addresses Violent Threats Against School Officials and Teachers (Oct. 4, 2021).
[8] *Oversight of the United States Department of Justice: Hearing Before the H. comm. on the Judiciary,* 117th Cong. at 94 (2021) (testimony from Hon. Merrick Garland, Atty Gen., U.S. Dep't of Justice).
[9] *Id.* at 95.
[10] Memorandum from NSBA Board of Directors, Message to NSBA Members (Oct. 22, 2021).
[11] *Troxel v. Granville,* 530 U.S. 57, 65 (2000) (citing *Meyer v. Nebraska,* 262 U.S. 390, 399 (1923)).
[12] *Merrick Garland's federal offense,* WALL ST. J. (Oct. 6, 2021).

1. All documents and communications referring or relating to convening meeting(s) in your judicial district in accordance with the Attorney General's October 4, 2021 memorandum;

2. All agendas, minutes, and notes created or relied upon by U.S. Attorney's Office employees referring or relating to meeting(s) in your judicial district in accordance with the Attorney General's October 4, 2021 memorandum;

3. Please explain when meeting(s) in your judicial district in accordance with the Attorney General's October 4, 2021 memorandum have occurred or will occur;

4. Please identify by name and title of all U.S. Attorney's Office employees involved in the meeting(s) in your judicial district in accordance with the Attorney General's October 4, 2021 memorandum ;

5. Please identify all federal, state, local, Tribal, and territorial organizations invited to or that have attended the meetings convened in your judicial district in accordance with the October 4, 2021 memorandum; and

6. Please provide all recommendations, both formal and informal, and any meeting minutes produced at the meeting(s) in your judicial district in accordance with the Attorney General's October 4, 2021 memorandum.

Please provide this material as soon as possible but no later than 5:00 p.m. on November 15, 2021.

If you have any questions about this request, please contact Committee staff at (202) 225-6906. Thank you for your attention to this important matter.

Sincerely,

Jim Jordan
Ranking Member

Steve Chabot
Member of Congress

Louie Gohmert
Member of Congress

Darrell Issa
Ranking Member
Subcommittee on Courts, Intellectual Property, and the Internet

Ken Buck
Ranking Member
Subcommittee on Antitrust, Commercial and Administrative Law

Matt Gaetz
Member of Congress

Mike Johnson
Ranking Member
Subcommittee on the Constitution, Civil Rights and Civil Liberties

Andy Biggs
Ranking Member
Subcommittee on Crime, Terrorism and Homeland Security

Tom McClintock
Ranking Member
Subcommittee on Immigration and Citizenship

W. Gregory Steube
Member of Congress

Tom Tiffany
Member of Congress

Thomas Massie
Member of Congress

Chip Roy
Member of Congress

Dan Bishop
Member of Congress

Michelle Fischbach
Member of Congress

Victoria Spartz
Member of Congress

Scott Fitzgerald
Member of Congress

Cliff Bentz
Member of Congress

Burgess Owens
Member of Congress

cc: The Honorable Jerrold L. Nadler
Chairman

Mr. Monty Wilkinson
Director, Executive Office for U.S. Attorneys

JERROLD NADLER, New York
CHAIRMAN

JIM JORDAN, Ohio
RANKING MEMBER

ONE HUNDRED SEVENTEENTH CONGRESS
Congress of the United States
House of Representatives
COMMITTEE ON THE JUDICIARY
2138 RAYBURN HOUSE OFFICE BUILDING
WASHINGTON, DC 20515–6216
(202) 225–3951
judiciary.house.gov

November 1, 2021

The Honorable John R. Lausch, Jr.
U.S. Attorney
Northern District of Illinois
219 South Dearborn Street, 5th Floor
Chicago, IL 60604

Dear Mr. Lausch:

We are continuing to investigate the troubling attempts by the Department of Justice and the White House to use the heavy hand of federal law enforcement to target concerned parents at local school board meetings and chill their protected First Amendment activity. Because the Department directed you, along with all other U.S. Attorneys, and the Federal Bureau of Investigation (FBI) to take action to address parents attending school board meetings,[1] we respectfully request your assistance with our investigation.

On September 29, 2021, the National School Boards Association (NSBA) sent a letter to President Joe Biden requesting help from the federal government with concerned parents voicing their opinions at school board meetings.[2] The NSBA letter stated that "malice, violence, and threats" against school officials "could be the equivalent of a form of domestic terrorism or hate crimes."[3] The letter cited a number of interactions at school board meetings, none of which rose to the level of domestic terrorism. In fact, the vast majority of incidents cited by the NSBA did not involve threats or violence.[4] Most notably, as an example of domestic terrorism, the NSBA cited an incident in which a father angrily confronted members at a school board meeting in Loudoun County, Virginia about the heinous sexual assault of his daughter.[5]

A mere five days after the NSBA sent its letter to President Biden, on October 4, 2021, Attorney General Merrick Garland issued a shocking memorandum that directed the FBI and

---

[1] Memorandum from Atty Gen. Merrick Garland, U.S. Dep't of Justice, Partnership Among Federal, State, Local, Tribal, And Territorial Law Enforcement to Address Threats Against School Administrators, Board Members, Teachers, and Staff (Oct. 4, 2021).
[2] Letter from Dr. Viola M. Garcia, President, Nat'l School Board Assoc. & Mr. Chip Slaven, Chief Exec. Officer, Nat'l School Board Assoc., to President Joseph R. Biden, White House (Sept. 29, 2021).
[3] *Id.*
[4] *See* Caroline Downey, *Vast majority of incidents cited by school-board group to justify federal intervention didn't involve threats,* NAT'L REV. (Oct. 2, 2021).
[5] *Id.*; *see also* Jessica Chasmar, *Loudoun County father arrested at school board events says school tried to cover up daughter's bathroom assault*, FOX NEWS (Oct. 12, 2021).

U.S. Attorneys' Offices to "convene meetings" in your judicial district "with federal, state, local, Tribal, and territorial leaders" within 30 days.[6] The Justice Department simultaneously issued a press release indicating that the Attorney General's directive would "open dedicated lines of communication for threat reporting, assessment and response by law enforcement"—in other words, create a snitch line for complaints about concerned parents.[7]

During Attorney General Garland's testimony before our Committee on October 21, he appeared to have no idea whether the U.S. Attorney meetings he ordered were actually taking place. He stated: "I don't know whether [the meetings] are ongoing, but I expect and hope that they are going . . . because I did ask that they take place."[8] Attorney General Garland testified that he doubted "there have been meetings in every jurisdiction," but reiterated his belief that it is important for federal law enforcement authorities to conduct these meetings in every judicial district.[9] According to the Attorney General's directives, meetings are to be convened in all 94 judicial districts by November 3, 2021, at the latest.

Following the Attorney General's testimony, the NSBA Board of Directors, apparently recognizing the ill-conceived consequences of its letter and the resulting Justice Department action, issued a new memorandum to its members apologizing for the letter, stating: "On behalf of NSBA, we regret and apologize for the letter."[10] (emphasis in original). Although Attorney General Garland testified that the NSBA letter to President Biden was the basis for his October 4 directive to insert federal law enforcement into local school board matters, the Attorney General has yet to rescind his memorandum. His directives to you and other U.S. Attorneys remain in effect.

Concerned parents voicing their strong opposition to controversial curricula at local schools are not domestic terrorists. Parents have an undisputed right to direct the upbringing and education of their children.[11] When parents, however, cross the line to commit a violent act or issue a criminal threat,[12] state and local authorities are best-equipped to handle these violations of state law. But we must not tolerate the use of the federal law enforcement apparatus to intimidate and silence parents using their Constitutional rights to advocate for their child's future.

To assist our investigation and determine whether these meetings are ongoing, we request that you provide the following documents and information:

---

[6] Memorandum from Atty Gen. Merrick Garland, U.S. Dep't of Justice, Partnership Among Federal, State, Local, Tribal, And Territorial Law Enforcement to Address Threats Against School Administrators, Board Members, Teachers, and Staff (Oct. 4, 2021).
[7] Press Release, U.S. Dep't of Justice, Justice Department Addresses Violent Threats Against School Officials and Teachers (Oct. 4, 2021).
[8] *Oversight of the United States Department of Justice: Hearing Before the H. comm. on the Judiciary,* 117th Cong. at 94 (2021) (testimony from Hon. Merrick Garland, Atty Gen., U.S. Dep't of Justice).
[9] *Id.* at 95.
[10] Memorandum from NSBA Board of Directors, Message to NSBA Members (Oct. 22, 2021).
[11] *Troxel v. Granville,* 530 U.S. 57, 65 (2000) (citing *Meyer v. Nebraska,* 262 U.S. 390, 399 (1923)).
[12] *Merrick Garland's federal offense,* WALL ST. J. (Oct. 6, 2021).

1. All documents and communications referring or relating to convening meeting(s) in your judicial district in accordance with the Attorney General's October 4, 2021 memorandum;

2. All agendas, minutes, and notes created or relied upon by U.S. Attorney's Office employees referring or relating to meeting(s) in your judicial district in accordance with the Attorney General's October 4, 2021 memorandum;

3. Please explain when meeting(s) in your judicial district in accordance with the Attorney General's October 4, 2021 memorandum have occurred or will occur;

4. Please identify by name and title of all U.S. Attorney's Office employees involved in the meeting(s) in your judicial district in accordance with the Attorney General's October 4, 2021 memorandum ;

5. Please identify all federal, state, local, Tribal, and territorial organizations invited to or that have attended the meetings convened in your judicial district in accordance with the October 4, 2021 memorandum; and

6. Please provide all recommendations, both formal and informal, and any meeting minutes produced at the meeting(s) in your judicial district in accordance with the Attorney General's October 4, 2021 memorandum.

Please provide this material as soon as possible but no later than 5:00 p.m. on November 15, 2021.

If you have any questions about this request, please contact Committee staff at (202) 225-6906. Thank you for your attention to this important matter.

Sincerely,

Jim Jordan
Ranking Member

Steve Chabot
Member of Congress

Louie Gohmert
Member of Congress

Darrell Issa
Ranking Member
Subcommittee on Courts, Intellectual Property, and the Internet

Ken Buck
Ranking Member
Subcommittee on Antitrust, Commercial and Administrative Law

Matt Gaetz
Member of Congress

Mike Johnson
Ranking Member
Subcommittee on the Constitution, Civil Rights and Civil Liberties

Andy Biggs
Ranking Member
Subcommittee on Crime, Terrorism and Homeland Security

Tom McClintock
Ranking Member
Subcommittee on Immigration and Citizenship

W. Gregory Steube
Member of Congress

Tom Tiffany
Member of Congress

Thomas Massie
Member of Congress

Chip Roy
Member of Congress

Dan Bishop
Member of Congress

Michelle Fischbach
Member of Congress

Victoria Spartz
Member of Congress

Scott Fitzgerald
Member of Congress

Cliff Bentz
Member of Congress

Burgess Owens
Member of Congress

cc: The Honorable Jerrold L. Nadler
Chairman

Mr. Monty Wilkinson
Director, Executive Office for U.S. Attorneys

JERROLD NADLER, New York
CHAIRMAN

JIM JORDAN, Ohio
RANKING MEMBER

ONE HUNDRED SEVENTEENTH CONGRESS

Congress of the United States

House of Representatives

COMMITTEE ON THE JUDICIARY

2138 RAYBURN HOUSE OFFICE BUILDING
WASHINGTON, DC 20515-6216
(202) 225-3951
judiciary.house.gov

November 1, 2021

Mr. Douglas J. Quivey
Acting U.S. Attorney
Central District of Illinois
318 South Sixth Street
Springfield, IL 62701

Dear Mr. Quivey:

We are continuing to investigate the troubling attempts by the Department of Justice and the White House to use the heavy hand of federal law enforcement to target concerned parents at local school board meetings and chill their protected First Amendment activity. Because the Department directed you, along with all other U.S. Attorneys, and the Federal Bureau of Investigation (FBI) to take action to address parents attending school board meetings,[1] we respectfully request your assistance with our investigation.

On September 29, 2021, the National School Boards Association (NSBA) sent a letter to President Joe Biden requesting help from the federal government with concerned parents voicing their opinions at school board meetings.[2] The NSBA letter stated that "malice, violence, and threats" against school officials "could be the equivalent of a form of domestic terrorism or hate crimes."[3] The letter cited a number of interactions at school board meetings, none of which rose to the level of domestic terrorism. In fact, the vast majority of incidents cited by the NSBA did not involve threats or violence.[4] Most notably, as an example of domestic terrorism, the NSBA cited an incident in which a father angrily confronted members at a school board meeting in Loudoun County, Virginia about the heinous sexual assault of his daughter.[5]

A mere five days after the NSBA sent its letter to President Biden, on October 4, 2021, Attorney General Merrick Garland issued a shocking memorandum that directed the FBI and

---

[1] Memorandum from Atty Gen. Merrick Garland, U.S. Dep't of Justice, Partnership Among Federal, State, Local, Tribal, And Territorial Law Enforcement to Address Threats Against School Administrators, Board Members, Teachers, and Staff (Oct. 4, 2021).
[2] Letter from Dr. Viola M. Garcia, President, Nat'l School Board Assoc. & Mr. Chip Slaven, Chief Exec. Officer, Nat'l School Board Assoc., to President Joseph R. Biden, White House (Sept. 29, 2021).
[3] *Id.*
[4] *See* Caroline Downey, *Vast majority of incidents cited by school-board group to justify federal intervention didn't involve threats,* NAT'L REV. (Oct. 2, 2021).
[5] *Id.*; *see also* Jessica Chasmar, *Loudoun County father arrested at school board events says school tried to cover up daughter's bathroom assault*, FOX NEWS (Oct. 12, 2021).

U.S. Attorneys' Offices to "convene meetings" in your judicial district "with federal, state, local, Tribal, and territorial leaders" within 30 days.[6] The Justice Department simultaneously issued a press release indicating that the Attorney General's directive would "open dedicated lines of communication for threat reporting, assessment and response by law enforcement"—in other words, create a snitch line for complaints about concerned parents.[7]

During Attorney General Garland's testimony before our Committee on October 21, he appeared to have no idea whether the U.S. Attorney meetings he ordered were actually taking place. He stated: "I don't know whether [the meetings] are ongoing, but I expect and hope that they are going . . . because I did ask that they take place."[8] Attorney General Garland testified that he doubted "there have been meetings in every jurisdiction," but reiterated his belief that it is important for federal law enforcement authorities to conduct these meetings in every judicial district.[9] According to the Attorney General's directives, meetings are to be convened in all 94 judicial districts by November 3, 2021, at the latest.

Following the Attorney General's testimony, the NSBA Board of Directors, apparently recognizing the ill-conceived consequences of its letter and the resulting Justice Department action, issued a new memorandum to its members apologizing for the letter, stating: "On behalf of NSBA, <u>we regret and apologize for the letter</u>."[10] (emphasis in original). Although Attorney General Garland testified that the NSBA letter to President Biden was the basis for his October 4 directive to insert federal law enforcement into local school board matters, the Attorney General has yet to rescind his memorandum. His directives to you and other U.S. Attorneys remain in effect.

Concerned parents voicing their strong opposition to controversial curricula at local schools are not domestic terrorists. Parents have an undisputed right to direct the upbringing and education of their children.[11] When parents, however, cross the line to commit a violent act or issue a criminal threat,[12] state and local authorities are best-equipped to handle these violations of state law. But we must not tolerate the use of the federal law enforcement apparatus to intimidate and silence parents using their Constitutional rights to advocate for their child's future.

To assist our investigation and determine whether these meetings are ongoing, we request that you provide the following documents and information:

---

[6] Memorandum from Atty Gen. Merrick Garland, U.S. Dep't of Justice, Partnership Among Federal, State, Local, Tribal, And Territorial Law Enforcement to Address Threats Against School Administrators, Board Members, Teachers, and Staff (Oct. 4, 2021).
[7] Press Release, U.S. Dep't of Justice, Justice Department Addresses Violent Threats Against School Officials and Teachers (Oct. 4, 2021).
[8] *Oversight of the United States Department of Justice: Hearing Before the H. comm. on the Judiciary,* 117th Cong. at 94 (2021) (testimony from Hon. Merrick Garland, Atty Gen., U.S. Dep't of Justice).
[9] *Id.* at 95.
[10] Memorandum from NSBA Board of Directors, Message to NSBA Members (Oct. 22, 2021).
[11] *Troxel v. Granville,* 530 U.S. 57, 65 (2000) (citing *Meyer v. Nebraska,* 262 U.S. 390, 399 (1923)).
[12] *Merrick Garland's federal offense,* WALL ST. J. (Oct. 6, 2021).

1. All documents and communications referring or relating to convening meeting(s) in your judicial district in accordance with the Attorney General's October 4, 2021 memorandum;

2. All agendas, minutes, and notes created or relied upon by U.S. Attorney's Office employees referring or relating to meeting(s) in your judicial district in accordance with the Attorney General's October 4, 2021 memorandum;

3. Please explain when meeting(s) in your judicial district in accordance with the Attorney General's October 4, 2021 memorandum have occurred or will occur;

4. Please identify by name and title of all U.S. Attorney's Office employees involved in the meeting(s) in your judicial district in accordance with the Attorney General's October 4, 2021 memorandum ;

5. Please identify all federal, state, local, Tribal, and territorial organizations invited to or that have attended the meetings convened in your judicial district in accordance with the October 4, 2021 memorandum; and

6. Please provide all recommendations, both formal and informal, and any meeting minutes produced at the meeting(s) in your judicial district in accordance with the Attorney General's October 4, 2021 memorandum.

Please provide this material as soon as possible but no later than 5:00 p.m. on November 15, 2021.

If you have any questions about this request, please contact Committee staff at (202) 225-6906. Thank you for your attention to this important matter.

Sincerely,

Jim Jordan
Ranking Member

Steve Chabot
Member of Congress

Louie Gohmert
Member of Congress

Darrell Issa
Ranking Member
Subcommittee on Courts, Intellectual Property, and the Internet

Ken Buck
Ranking Member
Subcommittee on Antitrust, Commercial and Administrative Law

Mike Johnson
Ranking Member
Subcommittee on the Constitution, Civil Rights and Civil Liberties

Tom McClintock
Ranking Member
Subcommittee on Immigration and Citizenship

Tom Tiffany
Member of Congress

Chip Roy
Member of Congress

Michelle Fischbach
Member of Congress

Matt Gaetz
Member of Congress

Andy Biggs
Ranking Member
Subcommittee on Crime, Terrorism and Homeland Security

W. Gregory Steube
Member of Congress

Thomas Massie
Member of Congress

Dan Bishop
Member of Congress

Victoria Spartz
Member of Congress

Scott Fitzgerald
Member of Congress

Cliff Bentz
Member of Congress

Burgess Owens
Member of Congress

cc: The Honorable Jerrold L. Nadler
Chairman

Mr. Monty Wilkinson
Director, Executive Office for U.S. Attorneys

JERROLD NADLER, New York
CHAIRMAN

JIM JORDAN, Ohio
RANKING MEMBER

ONE HUNDRED SEVENTEENTH CONGRESS

Congress of the United States

House of Representatives

COMMITTEE ON THE JUDICIARY

2138 RAYBURN HOUSE OFFICE BUILDING

WASHINGTON, DC 20515-6216

(202) 225-3951
judiciary.house.gov

November 1, 2021

Mr. Steven D. Weinhoeft
U.S. Attorney
Southern District of Illinois
9 Executive Drive
Fairview Heights, IL 62208

Dear Mr. Weinhoeft:

We are continuing to investigate the troubling attempts by the Department of Justice and the White House to use the heavy hand of federal law enforcement to target concerned parents at local school board meetings and chill their protected First Amendment activity. Because the Department directed you, along with all other U.S. Attorneys, and the Federal Bureau of Investigation (FBI) to take action to address parents attending school board meetings,[1] we respectfully request your assistance with our investigation.

On September 29, 2021, the National School Boards Association (NSBA) sent a letter to President Joe Biden requesting help from the federal government with concerned parents voicing their opinions at school board meetings.[2] The NSBA letter stated that "malice, violence, and threats" against school officials "could be the equivalent of a form of domestic terrorism or hate crimes."[3] The letter cited a number of interactions at school board meetings, none of which rose to the level of domestic terrorism. In fact, the vast majority of incidents cited by the NSBA did not involve threats or violence.[4] Most notably, as an example of domestic terrorism, the NSBA cited an incident in which a father angrily confronted members at a school board meeting in Loudoun County, Virginia about the heinous sexual assault of his daughter.[5]

A mere five days after the NSBA sent its letter to President Biden, on October 4, 2021, Attorney General Merrick Garland issued a shocking memorandum that directed the FBI and

---

[1] Memorandum from Atty Gen. Merrick Garland, U.S. Dep't of Justice, Partnership Among Federal, State, Local, Tribal, And Territorial Law Enforcement to Address Threats Against School Administrators, Board Members, Teachers, and Staff (Oct. 4, 2021).

[2] Letter from Dr. Viola M. Garcia, President, Nat'l School Board Assoc. & Mr. Chip Slaven, Chief Exec. Officer, Nat'l School Board Assoc., to President Joseph R. Biden, White House (Sept. 29, 2021).

[3] *Id.*

[4] *See* Caroline Downey, *Vast majority of incidents cited by school-board group to justify federal intervention didn't involve threats,* NAT'L REV. (Oct. 2, 2021).

[5] *Id.*; *see also* Jessica Chasmar, *Loudoun County father arrested at school board events says school tried to cover up daughter's bathroom assault*, FOX NEWS (Oct. 12, 2021).

U.S. Attorneys' Offices to "convene meetings" in your judicial district "with federal, state, local, Tribal, and territorial leaders" within 30 days.[6] The Justice Department simultaneously issued a press release indicating that the Attorney General's directive would "open dedicated lines of communication for threat reporting, assessment and response by law enforcement"—in other words, create a snitch line for complaints about concerned parents.[7]

During Attorney General Garland's testimony before our Committee on October 21, he appeared to have no idea whether the U.S. Attorney meetings he ordered were actually taking place. He stated: "I don't know whether [the meetings] are ongoing, but I expect and hope that they are going . . . because I did ask that they take place."[8] Attorney General Garland testified that he doubted "there have been meetings in every jurisdiction," but reiterated his belief that it is important for federal law enforcement authorities to conduct these meetings in every judicial district.[9] According to the Attorney General's directives, meetings are to be convened in all 94 judicial districts by November 3, 2021, at the latest.

Following the Attorney General's testimony, the NSBA Board of Directors, apparently recognizing the ill-conceived consequences of its letter and the resulting Justice Department action, issued a new memorandum to its members apologizing for the letter, stating: "On behalf of NSBA, <u>we regret and apologize for the letter</u>."[10] (emphasis in original). Although Attorney General Garland testified that the NSBA letter to President Biden was the basis for his October 4 directive to insert federal law enforcement into local school board matters, the Attorney General has yet to rescind his memorandum. His directives to you and other U.S. Attorneys remain in effect.

Concerned parents voicing their strong opposition to controversial curricula at local schools are not domestic terrorists. Parents have an undisputed right to direct the upbringing and education of their children.[11] When parents, however, cross the line to commit a violent act or issue a criminal threat,[12] state and local authorities are best-equipped to handle these violations of state law. But we must not tolerate the use of the federal law enforcement apparatus to intimidate and silence parents using their Constitutional rights to advocate for their child's future.

To assist our investigation and determine whether these meetings are ongoing, we request that you provide the following documents and information:

---

[6] Memorandum from Atty Gen. Merrick Garland, U.S. Dep't of Justice, Partnership Among Federal, State, Local, Tribal, And Territorial Law Enforcement to Address Threats Against School Administrators, Board Members, Teachers, and Staff (Oct. 4, 2021).

[7] Press Release, U.S. Dep't of Justice, Justice Department Addresses Violent Threats Against School Officials and Teachers (Oct. 4, 2021).

[8] *Oversight of the United States Department of Justice: Hearing Before the H. comm. on the Judiciary,* 117th Cong. at 94 (2021) (testimony from Hon. Merrick Garland, Atty Gen., U.S. Dep't of Justice).

[9] *Id.* at 95.

[10] Memorandum from NSBA Board of Directors, Message to NSBA Members (Oct. 22, 2021).

[11] *Troxel v. Granville,* 530 U.S. 57, 65 (2000) (citing *Meyer v. Nebraska,* 262 U.S. 390, 399 (1923)).

[12] *Merrick Garland's federal offense,* WALL ST. J. (Oct. 6, 2021).

1. All documents and communications referring or relating to convening meeting(s) in your judicial district in accordance with the Attorney General's October 4, 2021 memorandum;

2. All agendas, minutes, and notes created or relied upon by U.S. Attorney's Office employees referring or relating to meeting(s) in your judicial district in accordance with the Attorney General's October 4, 2021 memorandum;

3. Please explain when meeting(s) in your judicial district in accordance with the Attorney General's October 4, 2021 memorandum have occurred or will occur;

4. Please identify by name and title of all U.S. Attorney's Office employees involved in the meeting(s) in your judicial district in accordance with the Attorney General's October 4, 2021 memorandum ;

5. Please identify all federal, state, local, Tribal, and territorial organizations invited to or that have attended the meetings convened in your judicial district in accordance with the October 4, 2021 memorandum; and

6. Please provide all recommendations, both formal and informal, and any meeting minutes produced at the meeting(s) in your judicial district in accordance with the Attorney General's October 4, 2021 memorandum.

Please provide this material as soon as possible but no later than 5:00 p.m. on November 15, 2021.

If you have any questions about this request, please contact Committee staff at (202) 225-6906. Thank you for your attention to this important matter.

Sincerely,

Jim Jordan
Ranking Member

Steve Chabot
Member of Congress

Louie Gohmert
Member of Congress

Darrell Issa
Ranking Member
Subcommittee on Courts, Intellectual Property, and the Internet

Ken Buck
Ranking Member
Subcommittee on Antitrust, Commercial and Administrative Law

Matt Gaetz
Member of Congress

Mike Johnson
Ranking Member
Subcommittee on the Constitution, Civil Rights and Civil Liberties

Andy Biggs
Ranking Member
Subcommittee on Crime, Terrorism and Homeland Security

Tom McClintock
Ranking Member
Subcommittee on Immigration and Citizenship

W. Gregory Steube
Member of Congress

Tom Tiffany
Member of Congress

Thomas Massie
Member of Congress

Chip Roy
Member of Congress

Dan Bishop
Member of Congress

Michelle Fischbach
Member of Congress

Victoria Spartz
Member of Congress

Scott Fitzgerald
Member of Congress

Cliff Bentz
Member of Congress

Burgess Owens
Member of Congress

cc: The Honorable Jerrold L. Nadler
Chairman

Mr. Monty Wilkinson
Director, Executive Office for U.S. Attorneys

JERROLD NADLER, New York
CHAIRMAN

JIM JORDAN, Ohio
RANKING MEMBER

ONE HUNDRED SEVENTEENTH CONGRESS

Congress of the United States

House of Representatives

COMMITTEE ON THE JUDICIARY

2138 RAYBURN HOUSE OFFICE BUILDING

WASHINGTON, DC 20515-6216

(202) 225-3951
judiciary.house.gov

November 1, 2021

Mr. John E. Childress
Acting U.S. Attorney
Southern District of Indiana
10 West Market Street, Suite 2100
Indianapolis, IN 46204

Dear Mr. Childress:

We are continuing to investigate the troubling attempts by the Department of Justice and the White House to use the heavy hand of federal law enforcement to target concerned parents at local school board meetings and chill their protected First Amendment activity. Because the Department directed you, along with all other U.S. Attorneys, and the Federal Bureau of Investigation (FBI) to take action to address parents attending school board meetings,[1] we respectfully request your assistance with our investigation.

On September 29, 2021, the National School Boards Association (NSBA) sent a letter to President Joe Biden requesting help from the federal government with concerned parents voicing their opinions at school board meetings.[2] The NSBA letter stated that "malice, violence, and threats" against school officials "could be the equivalent of a form of domestic terrorism or hate crimes."[3] The letter cited a number of interactions at school board meetings, none of which rose to the level of domestic terrorism. In fact, the vast majority of incidents cited by the NSBA did not involve threats or violence.[4] Most notably, as an example of domestic terrorism, the NSBA cited an incident in which a father angrily confronted members at a school board meeting in Loudoun County, Virginia about the heinous sexual assault of his daughter.[5]

A mere five days after the NSBA sent its letter to President Biden, on October 4, 2021, Attorney General Merrick Garland issued a shocking memorandum that directed the FBI and

---

[1] Memorandum from Atty Gen. Merrick Garland, U.S. Dep't of Justice, Partnership Among Federal, State, Local, Tribal, And Territorial Law Enforcement to Address Threats Against School Administrators, Board Members, Teachers, and Staff (Oct. 4, 2021).
[2] Letter from Dr. Viola M. Garcia, President, Nat'l School Board Assoc. & Mr. Chip Slaven, Chief Exec. Officer, Nat'l School Board Assoc., to President Joseph R. Biden, White House (Sept. 29, 2021).
[3] *Id.*
[4] *See* Caroline Downey, *Vast majority of incidents cited by school-board group to justify federal intervention didn't involve threats,* NAT'L REV. (Oct. 2, 2021).
[5] *Id.*; *see also* Jessica Chasmar, *Loudoun County father arrested at school board events says school tried to cover up daughter's bathroom assault*, FOX NEWS (Oct. 12, 2021).

U.S. Attorneys' Offices to "convene meetings" in your judicial district "with federal, state, local, Tribal, and territorial leaders" within 30 days.[6] The Justice Department simultaneously issued a press release indicating that the Attorney General's directive would "open dedicated lines of communication for threat reporting, assessment and response by law enforcement"—in other words, create a snitch line for complaints about concerned parents.[7]

During Attorney General Garland's testimony before our Committee on October 21, he appeared to have no idea whether the U.S. Attorney meetings he ordered were actually taking place. He stated: "I don't know whether [the meetings] are ongoing, but I expect and hope that they are going . . . because I did ask that they take place."[8] Attorney General Garland testified that he doubted "there have been meetings in every jurisdiction," but reiterated his belief that it is important for federal law enforcement authorities to conduct these meetings in every judicial district.[9] According to the Attorney General's directives, meetings are to be convened in all 94 judicial districts by November 3, 2021, at the latest.

Following the Attorney General's testimony, the NSBA Board of Directors, apparently recognizing the ill-conceived consequences of its letter and the resulting Justice Department action, issued a new memorandum to its members apologizing for the letter, stating: "On behalf of NSBA, we regret and apologize for the letter."[10] (emphasis in original). Although Attorney General Garland testified that the NSBA letter to President Biden was the basis for his October 4 directive to insert federal law enforcement into local school board matters, the Attorney General has yet to rescind his memorandum. His directives to you and other U.S. Attorneys remain in effect.

Concerned parents voicing their strong opposition to controversial curricula at local schools are not domestic terrorists. Parents have an undisputed right to direct the upbringing and education of their children.[11] When parents, however, cross the line to commit a violent act or issue a criminal threat,[12] state and local authorities are best-equipped to handle these violations of state law. But we must not tolerate the use of the federal law enforcement apparatus to intimidate and silence parents using their Constitutional rights to advocate for their child's future.

To assist our investigation and determine whether these meetings are ongoing, we request that you provide the following documents and information:

---

[6] Memorandum from Atty Gen. Merrick Garland, U.S. Dep't of Justice, Partnership Among Federal, State, Local, Tribal, And Territorial Law Enforcement to Address Threats Against School Administrators, Board Members, Teachers, and Staff (Oct. 4, 2021).
[7] Press Release, U.S. Dep't of Justice, Justice Department Addresses Violent Threats Against School Officials and Teachers (Oct. 4, 2021).
[8] *Oversight of the United States Department of Justice: Hearing Before the H. comm. on the Judiciary,* 117th Cong. at 94 (2021) (testimony from Hon. Merrick Garland, Atty Gen., U.S. Dep't of Justice).
[9] *Id.* at 95.
[10] Memorandum from NSBA Board of Directors, Message to NSBA Members (Oct. 22, 2021).
[11] *Troxel v. Granville,* 530 U.S. 57, 65 (2000) (citing *Meyer v. Nebraska,* 262 U.S. 390, 399 (1923)).
[12] *Merrick Garland's federal offense,* WALL ST. J. (Oct. 6, 2021).

1. All documents and communications referring or relating to convening meeting(s) in your judicial district in accordance with the Attorney General's October 4, 2021 memorandum;

2. All agendas, minutes, and notes created or relied upon by U.S. Attorney's Office employees referring or relating to meeting(s) in your judicial district in accordance with the Attorney General's October 4, 2021 memorandum;

3. Please explain when meeting(s) in your judicial district in accordance with the Attorney General's October 4, 2021 memorandum have occurred or will occur;

4. Please identify by name and title of all U.S. Attorney's Office employees involved in the meeting(s) in your judicial district in accordance with the Attorney General's October 4, 2021 memorandum ;

5. Please identify all federal, state, local, Tribal, and territorial organizations invited to or that have attended the meetings convened in your judicial district in accordance with the October 4, 2021 memorandum; and

6. Please provide all recommendations, both formal and informal, and any meeting minutes produced at the meeting(s) in your judicial district in accordance with the Attorney General's October 4, 2021 memorandum.

Please provide this material as soon as possible but no later than 5:00 p.m. on November 15, 2021.

If you have any questions about this request, please contact Committee staff at (202) 225-6906. Thank you for your attention to this important matter.

Sincerely,

Jim Jordan
Ranking Member

Steve Chabot
Member of Congress

Louie Gohmert
Member of Congress

Darrell Issa
Ranking Member
Subcommittee on Courts, Intellectual Property, and the Internet

Ken Buck
Ranking Member
Subcommittee on Antitrust, Commercial
and Administrative Law

Mike Johnson
Ranking Member
Subcommittee on the Constitution,
Civil Rights and Civil Liberties

Tom McClintock
Ranking Member
Subcommittee on Immigration
and Citizenship

Tom Tiffany
Member of Congress

Chip Roy
Member of Congress

Michelle Fischbach
Member of Congress

Matt Gaetz
Member of Congress

Andy Biggs
Ranking Member
Subcommittee on Crime, Terrorism
and Homeland Security

W. Gregory Steube
Member of Congress

Thomas Massie
Member of Congress

Dan Bishop
Member of Congress

Victoria Spartz
Member of Congress

Scott Fitzgerald
Member of Congress

Cliff Bentz
Member of Congress

Burgess Owens
Member of Congress

cc: The Honorable Jerrold L. Nadler
Chairman

Mr. Monty Wilkinson
Director, Executive Office for U.S. Attorneys

JERROLD NADLER, New York
CHAIRMAN

JIM JORDAN, Ohio
RANKING MEMBER

ONE HUNDRED SEVENTEENTH CONGRESS
Congress of the United States
House of Representatives
COMMITTEE ON THE JUDICIARY
2138 RAYBURN HOUSE OFFICE BUILDING
WASHINGTON, DC 20515-6216
(202) 225-3951
judiciary.house.gov

November 1, 2021

The Honorable Clifford D. Johnson
U.S. Attorney
Northern District of Indiana
5400 Federal Plaza, Suite 1500
Hammond, IN 46320

Dear Mr. Johnson:

We are continuing to investigate the troubling attempts by the Department of Justice and the White House to use the heavy hand of federal law enforcement to target concerned parents at local school board meetings and chill their protected First Amendment activity. Because the Department directed you, along with all other U.S. Attorneys, and the Federal Bureau of Investigation (FBI) to take action to address parents attending school board meetings,[1] we respectfully request your assistance with our investigation.

On September 29, 2021, the National School Boards Association (NSBA) sent a letter to President Joe Biden requesting help from the federal government with concerned parents voicing their opinions at school board meetings.[2] The NSBA letter stated that "malice, violence, and threats" against school officials "could be the equivalent of a form of domestic terrorism or hate crimes."[3] The letter cited a number of interactions at school board meetings, none of which rose to the level of domestic terrorism. In fact, the vast majority of incidents cited by the NSBA did not involve threats or violence.[4] Most notably, as an example of domestic terrorism, the NSBA cited an incident in which a father angrily confronted members at a school board meeting in Loudoun County, Virginia about the heinous sexual assault of his daughter.[5]

A mere five days after the NSBA sent its letter to President Biden, on October 4, 2021, Attorney General Merrick Garland issued a shocking memorandum that directed the FBI and

---

[1] Memorandum from Atty Gen. Merrick Garland, U.S. Dep't of Justice, Partnership Among Federal, State, Local, Tribal, And Territorial Law Enforcement to Address Threats Against School Administrators, Board Members, Teachers, and Staff (Oct. 4, 2021).
[2] Letter from Dr. Viola M. Garcia, President, Nat'l School Board Assoc. & Mr. Chip Slaven, Chief Exec. Officer, Nat'l School Board Assoc., to President Joseph R. Biden, White House (Sept. 29, 2021).
[3] *Id.*
[4] *See* Caroline Downey, *Vast majority of incidents cited by school-board group to justify federal intervention didn't involve threats,* NAT'L REV. (Oct. 2, 2021).
[5] *Id.*; *see also* Jessica Chasmar, *Loudoun County father arrested at school board events says school tried to cover up daughter's bathroom assault*, FOX NEWS (Oct. 12, 2021).

U.S. Attorneys' Offices to "convene meetings" in your judicial district "with federal, state, local, Tribal, and territorial leaders" within 30 days.[6] The Justice Department simultaneously issued a press release indicating that the Attorney General's directive would "open dedicated lines of communication for threat reporting, assessment and response by law enforcement"—in other words, create a snitch line for complaints about concerned parents.[7]

During Attorney General Garland's testimony before our Committee on October 21, he appeared to have no idea whether the U.S. Attorney meetings he ordered were actually taking place. He stated: "I don't know whether [the meetings] are ongoing, but I expect and hope that they are going . . . because I did ask that they take place."[8] Attorney General Garland testified that he doubted "there have been meetings in every jurisdiction," but reiterated his belief that it is important for federal law enforcement authorities to conduct these meetings in every judicial district.[9] According to the Attorney General's directives, meetings are to be convened in all 94 judicial districts by November 3, 2021, at the latest.

Following the Attorney General's testimony, the NSBA Board of Directors, apparently recognizing the ill-conceived consequences of its letter and the resulting Justice Department action, issued a new memorandum to its members apologizing for the letter, stating: "On behalf of NSBA, <u>we regret and apologize for the letter</u>."[10] (emphasis in original). Although Attorney General Garland testified that the NSBA letter to President Biden was the basis for his October 4 directive to insert federal law enforcement into local school board matters, the Attorney General has yet to rescind his memorandum. His directives to you and other U.S. Attorneys remain in effect.

Concerned parents voicing their strong opposition to controversial curricula at local schools are not domestic terrorists. Parents have an undisputed right to direct the upbringing and education of their children.[11] When parents, however, cross the line to commit a violent act or issue a criminal threat,[12] state and local authorities are best-equipped to handle these violations of state law. But we must not tolerate the use of the federal law enforcement apparatus to intimidate and silence parents using their Constitutional rights to advocate for their child's future.

To assist our investigation and determine whether these meetings are ongoing, we request that you provide the following documents and information:

---

[6] Memorandum from Atty Gen. Merrick Garland, U.S. Dep't of Justice, Partnership Among Federal, State, Local, Tribal, And Territorial Law Enforcement to Address Threats Against School Administrators, Board Members, Teachers, and Staff (Oct. 4, 2021).
[7] Press Release, U.S. Dep't of Justice, Justice Department Addresses Violent Threats Against School Officials and Teachers (Oct. 4, 2021).
[8] *Oversight of the United States Department of Justice: Hearing Before the H. comm. on the Judiciary,* 117th Cong. at 94 (2021) (testimony from Hon. Merrick Garland, Atty Gen., U.S. Dep't of Justice).
[9] *Id.* at 95.
[10] Memorandum from NSBA Board of Directors, Message to NSBA Members (Oct. 22, 2021).
[11] *Troxel v. Granville,* 530 U.S. 57, 65 (2000) (citing *Meyer v. Nebraska,* 262 U.S. 390, 399 (1923)).
[12] *Merrick Garland's federal offense,* WALL ST. J. (Oct. 6, 2021).

1. All documents and communications referring or relating to convening meeting(s) in your judicial district in accordance with the Attorney General's October 4, 2021 memorandum;

2. All agendas, minutes, and notes created or relied upon by U.S. Attorney's Office employees referring or relating to meeting(s) in your judicial district in accordance with the Attorney General's October 4, 2021 memorandum;

3. Please explain when meeting(s) in your judicial district in accordance with the Attorney General's October 4, 2021 memorandum have occurred or will occur;

4. Please identify by name and title of all U.S. Attorney's Office employees involved in the meeting(s) in your judicial district in accordance with the Attorney General's October 4, 2021 memorandum ;

5. Please identify all federal, state, local, Tribal, and territorial organizations invited to or that have attended the meetings convened in your judicial district in accordance with the October 4, 2021 memorandum; and

6. Please provide all recommendations, both formal and informal, and any meeting minutes produced at the meeting(s) in your judicial district in accordance with the Attorney General's October 4, 2021 memorandum.

Please provide this material as soon as possible but no later than 5:00 p.m. on November 15, 2021.

If you have any questions about this request, please contact Committee staff at (202) 225-6906. Thank you for your attention to this important matter.

Sincerely,

Jim Jordan
Ranking Member

Steve Chabot
Member of Congress

Louie Gohmert
Member of Congress

Darrell Issa
Ranking Member
Subcommittee on Courts, Intellectual Property, and the Internet

The Honorable Clifford D. Johnson
November 1, 2021
Page 4

Ken Buck
Ranking Member
Subcommittee on Antitrust, Commercial and Administrative Law

Matt Gaetz
Member of Congress

Mike Johnson
Ranking Member
Subcommittee on the Constitution, Civil Rights and Civil Liberties

Andy Biggs
Ranking Member
Subcommittee on Crime, Terrorism and Homeland Security

Tom McClintock
Ranking Member
Subcommittee on Immigration and Citizenship

W. Gregory Steube
Member of Congress

Tom Tiffany
Member of Congress

Thomas Massie
Member of Congress

Chip Roy
Member of Congress

Dan Bishop
Member of Congress

Michelle Fischbach
Member of Congress

Victoria Spartz
Member of Congress

Scott Fitzgerald
Member of Congress

Cliff Bentz
Member of Congress

Burgess Owens
Member of Congress

cc: The Honorable Jerrold L. Nadler
Chairman

Mr. Monty Wilkinson
Director, Executive Office for U.S. Attorneys

JERROLD NADLER, New York
CHAIRMAN

JIM JORDAN, Ohio
RANKING MEMBER

ONE HUNDRED SEVENTEENTH CONGRESS

Congress of the United States

House of Representatives

COMMITTEE ON THE JUDICIARY

2138 RAYBURN HOUSE OFFICE BUILDING
WASHINGTON, DC 20515-6216
(202) 225-3951
judiciary.house.gov

November 1, 2021

Mr. Duston J. Slinkard
Acting U.S. Attorney
District of Kansas
444 SE Quincy Street, Suite 290
Topeka, KS

Dear Mr. Slinkard:

We are continuing to investigate the troubling attempts by the Department of Justice and the White House to use the heavy hand of federal law enforcement to target concerned parents at local school board meetings and chill their protected First Amendment activity. Because the Department directed you, along with all other U.S. Attorneys, and the Federal Bureau of Investigation (FBI) to take action to address parents attending school board meetings,[1] we respectfully request your assistance with our investigation.

On September 29, 2021, the National School Boards Association (NSBA) sent a letter to President Joe Biden requesting help from the federal government with concerned parents voicing their opinions at school board meetings.[2] The NSBA letter stated that "malice, violence, and threats" against school officials "could be the equivalent of a form of domestic terrorism or hate crimes."[3] The letter cited a number of interactions at school board meetings, none of which rose to the level of domestic terrorism. In fact, the vast majority of incidents cited by the NSBA did not involve threats or violence.[4] Most notably, as an example of domestic terrorism, the NSBA cited an incident in which a father angrily confronted members at a school board meeting in Loudoun County, Virginia about the heinous sexual assault of his daughter.[5]

A mere five days after the NSBA sent its letter to President Biden, on October 4, 2021, Attorney General Merrick Garland issued a shocking memorandum that directed the FBI and

---

[1] Memorandum from Atty Gen. Merrick Garland, U.S. Dep't of Justice, Partnership Among Federal, State, Local, Tribal, And Territorial Law Enforcement to Address Threats Against School Administrators, Board Members, Teachers, and Staff (Oct. 4, 2021).
[2] Letter from Dr. Viola M. Garcia, President, Nat'l School Board Assoc. & Mr. Chip Slaven, Chief Exec. Officer, Nat'l School Board Assoc., to President Joseph R. Biden, White House (Sept. 29, 2021).
[3] *Id.*
[4] *See* Caroline Downey, *Vast majority of incidents cited by school-board group to justify federal intervention didn't involve threats,* NAT'L REV. (Oct. 2, 2021).
[5] *Id.*; *see also* Jessica Chasmar, *Loudoun County father arrested at school board events says school tried to cover up daughter's bathroom assault*, FOX NEWS (Oct. 12, 2021).

U.S. Attorneys' Offices to "convene meetings" in your judicial district "with federal, state, local, Tribal, and territorial leaders" within 30 days.[6] The Justice Department simultaneously issued a press release indicating that the Attorney General's directive would "open dedicated lines of communication for threat reporting, assessment and response by law enforcement"—in other words, create a snitch line for complaints about concerned parents.[7]

During Attorney General Garland's testimony before our Committee on October 21, he appeared to have no idea whether the U.S. Attorney meetings he ordered were actually taking place. He stated: "I don't know whether [the meetings] are ongoing, but I expect and hope that they are going . . . because I did ask that they take place."[8] Attorney General Garland testified that he doubted "there have been meetings in every jurisdiction," but reiterated his belief that it is important for federal law enforcement authorities to conduct these meetings in every judicial district.[9] According to the Attorney General's directives, meetings are to be convened in all 94 judicial districts by November 3, 2021, at the latest.

Following the Attorney General's testimony, the NSBA Board of Directors, apparently recognizing the ill-conceived consequences of its letter and the resulting Justice Department action, issued a new memorandum to its members apologizing for the letter, stating: "On behalf of NSBA, <u>we regret and apologize for the letter</u>."[10] (emphasis in original). Although Attorney General Garland testified that the NSBA letter to President Biden was the basis for his October 4 directive to insert federal law enforcement into local school board matters, the Attorney General has yet to rescind his memorandum. His directives to you and other U.S. Attorneys remain in effect.

Concerned parents voicing their strong opposition to controversial curricula at local schools are not domestic terrorists. Parents have an undisputed right to direct the upbringing and education of their children.[11] When parents, however, cross the line to commit a violent act or issue a criminal threat,[12] state and local authorities are best-equipped to handle these violations of state law. But we must not tolerate the use of the federal law enforcement apparatus to intimidate and silence parents using their Constitutional rights to advocate for their child's future.

To assist our investigation and determine whether these meetings are ongoing, we request that you provide the following documents and information:

---

[6] Memorandum from Atty Gen. Merrick Garland, U.S. Dep't of Justice, Partnership Among Federal, State, Local, Tribal, And Territorial Law Enforcement to Address Threats Against School Administrators, Board Members, Teachers, and Staff (Oct. 4, 2021).

[7] Press Release, U.S. Dep't of Justice, Justice Department Addresses Violent Threats Against School Officials and Teachers (Oct. 4, 2021).

[8] *Oversight of the United States Department of Justice: Hearing Before the H. comm. on the Judiciary,* 117th Cong. at 94 (2021) (testimony from Hon. Merrick Garland, Atty Gen., U.S. Dep't of Justice).

[9] *Id.* at 95.

[10] Memorandum from NSBA Board of Directors, Message to NSBA Members (Oct. 22, 2021).

[11] *Troxel v. Granville,* 530 U.S. 57, 65 (2000) (citing *Meyer v. Nebraska,* 262 U.S. 390, 399 (1923)).

[12] *Merrick Garland's federal offense,* WALL ST. J. (Oct. 6, 2021).

1. All documents and communications referring or relating to convening meeting(s) in your judicial district in accordance with the Attorney General's October 4, 2021 memorandum;

2. All agendas, minutes, and notes created or relied upon by U.S. Attorney's Office employees referring or relating to meeting(s) in your judicial district in accordance with the Attorney General's October 4, 2021 memorandum;

3. Please explain when meeting(s) in your judicial district in accordance with the Attorney General's October 4, 2021 memorandum have occurred or will occur;

4. Please identify by name and title of all U.S. Attorney's Office employees involved in the meeting(s) in your judicial district in accordance with the Attorney General's October 4, 2021 memorandum ;

5. Please identify all federal, state, local, Tribal, and territorial organizations invited to or that have attended the meetings convened in your judicial district in accordance with the October 4, 2021 memorandum; and

6. Please provide all recommendations, both formal and informal, and any meeting minutes produced at the meeting(s) in your judicial district in accordance with the Attorney General's October 4, 2021 memorandum.

Please provide this material as soon as possible but no later than 5:00 p.m. on November 15, 2021.

If you have any questions about this request, please contact Committee staff at (202) 225-6906. Thank you for your attention to this important matter.

Sincerely,

Jim Jordan
Ranking Member

Steve Chabot
Member of Congress

Louie Gohmert
Member of Congress

Darrell Issa
Ranking Member
Subcommittee on Courts, Intellectual Property, and the Internet

Ken Buck
Ranking Member
Subcommittee on Antitrust, Commercial and Administrative Law

Matt Gaetz
Member of Congress

Mike Johnson
Ranking Member
Subcommittee on the Constitution, Civil Rights and Civil Liberties

Andy Biggs
Ranking Member
Subcommittee on Crime, Terrorism and Homeland Security

Tom McClintock
Ranking Member
Subcommittee on Immigration and Citizenship

W. Gregory Steube
Member of Congress

Tom Tiffany
Member of Congress

Thomas Massie
Member of Congress

Chip Roy
Member of Congress

Dan Bishop
Member of Congress

Michelle Fischbach
Member of Congress

Victoria Spartz
Member of Congress

Scott Fitzgerald
Member of Congress

Cliff Bentz
Member of Congress

Burgess Owens
Member of Congress

cc: The Honorable Jerrold L. Nadler
Chairman

Mr. Monty Wilkinson
Director, Executive Office for U.S. Attorneys

JERROLD NADLER, New York
CHAIRMAN

JIM JORDAN, Ohio
RANKING MEMBER

ONE HUNDRED SEVENTEENTH CONGRESS

Congress of the United States

House of Representatives

COMMITTEE ON THE JUDICIARY

2138 RAYBURN HOUSE OFFICE BUILDING

WASHINGTON, DC 20515-6216

(202) 225-3951
judiciary.house.gov

November 1, 2021

Mr. Michael A. Bennett
Acting U.S. Attorney
Western District of Kentucky
717 West Broadway
Louisville, KY 40202

Dear Mr. Bennett:

We are continuing to investigate the troubling attempts by the Department of Justice and the White House to use the heavy hand of federal law enforcement to target concerned parents at local school board meetings and chill their protected First Amendment activity. Because the Department directed you, along with all other U.S. Attorneys, and the Federal Bureau of Investigation (FBI) to take action to address parents attending school board meetings,[1] we respectfully request your assistance with our investigation.

On September 29, 2021, the National School Boards Association (NSBA) sent a letter to President Joe Biden requesting help from the federal government with concerned parents voicing their opinions at school board meetings.[2] The NSBA letter stated that "malice, violence, and threats" against school officials "could be the equivalent of a form of domestic terrorism or hate crimes."[3] The letter cited a number of interactions at school board meetings, none of which rose to the level of domestic terrorism. In fact, the vast majority of incidents cited by the NSBA did not involve threats or violence.[4] Most notably, as an example of domestic terrorism, the NSBA cited an incident in which a father angrily confronted members at a school board meeting in Loudoun County, Virginia about the heinous sexual assault of his daughter.[5]

A mere five days after the NSBA sent its letter to President Biden, on October 4, 2021, Attorney General Merrick Garland issued a shocking memorandum that directed the FBI and

---

[1] Memorandum from Atty Gen. Merrick Garland, U.S. Dep't of Justice, Partnership Among Federal, State, Local, Tribal, And Territorial Law Enforcement to Address Threats Against School Administrators, Board Members, Teachers, and Staff (Oct. 4, 2021).

[2] Letter from Dr. Viola M. Garcia, President, Nat'l School Board Assoc. & Mr. Chip Slaven, Chief Exec. Officer, Nat'l School Board Assoc., to President Joseph R. Biden, White House (Sept. 29, 2021).

[3] *Id.*

[4] *See* Caroline Downey, *Vast majority of incidents cited by school-board group to justify federal intervention didn't involve threats,* NAT'L REV. (Oct. 2, 2021).

[5] *Id.*; *see also* Jessica Chasmar, *Loudoun County father arrested at school board events says school tried to cover up daughter's bathroom assault*, FOX NEWS (Oct. 12, 2021).

U.S. Attorneys' Offices to "convene meetings" in your judicial district "with federal, state, local, Tribal, and territorial leaders" within 30 days.[6] The Justice Department simultaneously issued a press release indicating that the Attorney General's directive would "open dedicated lines of communication for threat reporting, assessment and response by law enforcement"—in other words, create a snitch line for complaints about concerned parents.[7]

During Attorney General Garland's testimony before our Committee on October 21, he appeared to have no idea whether the U.S. Attorney meetings he ordered were actually taking place. He stated: "I don't know whether [the meetings] are ongoing, but I expect and hope that they are going . . . because I did ask that they take place."[8] Attorney General Garland testified that he doubted "there have been meetings in every jurisdiction," but reiterated his belief that it is important for federal law enforcement authorities to conduct these meetings in every judicial district.[9] According to the Attorney General's directives, meetings are to be convened in all 94 judicial districts by November 3, 2021, at the latest.

Following the Attorney General's testimony, the NSBA Board of Directors, apparently recognizing the ill-conceived consequences of its letter and the resulting Justice Department action, issued a new memorandum to its members apologizing for the letter, stating: "On behalf of NSBA, <u>we regret and apologize for the letter</u>."[10] (emphasis in original). Although Attorney General Garland testified that the NSBA letter to President Biden was the basis for his October 4 directive to insert federal law enforcement into local school board matters, the Attorney General has yet to rescind his memorandum. His directives to you and other U.S. Attorneys remain in effect.

Concerned parents voicing their strong opposition to controversial curricula at local schools are not domestic terrorists. Parents have an undisputed right to direct the upbringing and education of their children.[11] When parents, however, cross the line to commit a violent act or issue a criminal threat,[12] state and local authorities are best-equipped to handle these violations of state law. But we must not tolerate the use of the federal law enforcement apparatus to intimidate and silence parents using their Constitutional rights to advocate for their child's future.

To assist our investigation and determine whether these meetings are ongoing, we request that you provide the following documents and information:

---

[6] Memorandum from Atty Gen. Merrick Garland, U.S. Dep't of Justice, Partnership Among Federal, State, Local, Tribal, And Territorial Law Enforcement to Address Threats Against School Administrators, Board Members, Teachers, and Staff (Oct. 4, 2021).
[7] Press Release, U.S. Dep't of Justice, Justice Department Addresses Violent Threats Against School Officials and Teachers (Oct. 4, 2021).
[8] *Oversight of the United States Department of Justice: Hearing Before the H. comm. on the Judiciary,* 117th Cong. at 94 (2021) (testimony from Hon. Merrick Garland, Atty Gen., U.S. Dep't of Justice).
[9] *Id.* at 95.
[10] Memorandum from NSBA Board of Directors, Message to NSBA Members (Oct. 22, 2021).
[11] *Troxel v. Granville,* 530 U.S. 57, 65 (2000) (citing *Meyer v. Nebraska,* 262 U.S. 390, 399 (1923)).
[12] *Merrick Garland's federal offense,* WALL ST. J. (Oct. 6, 2021).

1. All documents and communications referring or relating to convening meeting(s) in your judicial district in accordance with the Attorney General's October 4, 2021 memorandum;

2. All agendas, minutes, and notes created or relied upon by U.S. Attorney's Office employees referring or relating to meeting(s) in your judicial district in accordance with the Attorney General's October 4, 2021 memorandum;

3. Please explain when meeting(s) in your judicial district in accordance with the Attorney General's October 4, 2021 memorandum have occurred or will occur;

4. Please identify by name and title of all U.S. Attorney's Office employees involved in the meeting(s) in your judicial district in accordance with the Attorney General's October 4, 2021 memorandum ;

5. Please identify all federal, state, local, Tribal, and territorial organizations invited to or that have attended the meetings convened in your judicial district in accordance with the October 4, 2021 memorandum; and

6. Please provide all recommendations, both formal and informal, and any meeting minutes produced at the meeting(s) in your judicial district in accordance with the Attorney General's October 4, 2021 memorandum.

Please provide this material as soon as possible but no later than 5:00 p.m. on November 15, 2021.

If you have any questions about this request, please contact Committee staff at (202) 225-6906. Thank you for your attention to this important matter.

Sincerely,

Jim Jordan
Ranking Member

Steve Chabot
Member of Congress

Louie Gohmert
Member of Congress

Darrell Issa
Ranking Member
Subcommittee on Courts, Intellectual Property, and the Internet

Ken Buck
Ranking Member
Subcommittee on Antitrust, Commercial and Administrative Law

Matt Gaetz
Member of Congress

Mike Johnson
Ranking Member
Subcommittee on the Constitution, Civil Rights and Civil Liberties

Andy Biggs
Ranking Member
Subcommittee on Crime, Terrorism and Homeland Security

Tom McClintock
Ranking Member
Subcommittee on Immigration and Citizenship

W. Gregory Steube
Member of Congress

Tom Tiffany
Member of Congress

Thomas Massie
Member of Congress

Chip Roy
Member of Congress

Dan Bishop
Member of Congress

Michelle Fischbach
Member of Congress

Victoria Spartz
Member of Congress

Scott Fitzgerald
Member of Congress

Cliff Bentz
Member of Congress

Burgess Owens
Member of Congress

cc: The Honorable Jerrold L. Nadler
Chairman

Mr. Monty Wilkinson
Director, Executive Office for U.S. Attorneys

JERROLD NADLER, New York
CHAIRMAN

JIM JORDAN, Ohio
RANKING MEMBER

ONE HUNDRED SEVENTEENTH CONGRESS

Congress of the United States
House of Representatives
COMMITTEE ON THE JUDICIARY
2138 RAYBURN HOUSE OFFICE BUILDING
WASHINGTON, DC 20515–6216
(202) 225–3951
judiciary.house.gov

November 1, 2021

Mr. Carlton S. Shier, IV
Acting U.S. Attorney
Eastern District of Kentucky
260 West Vine Street, Suite 300
Lexington, KY 40507

Dear Mr. Shier:

We are continuing to investigate the troubling attempts by the Department of Justice and the White House to use the heavy hand of federal law enforcement to target concerned parents at local school board meetings and chill their protected First Amendment activity. Because the Department directed you, along with all other U.S. Attorneys, and the Federal Bureau of Investigation (FBI) to take action to address parents attending school board meetings,[1] we respectfully request your assistance with our investigation.

On September 29, 2021, the National School Boards Association (NSBA) sent a letter to President Joe Biden requesting help from the federal government with concerned parents voicing their opinions at school board meetings.[2] The NSBA letter stated that "malice, violence, and threats" against school officials "could be the equivalent of a form of domestic terrorism or hate crimes."[3] The letter cited a number of interactions at school board meetings, none of which rose to the level of domestic terrorism. In fact, the vast majority of incidents cited by the NSBA did not involve threats or violence.[4] Most notably, as an example of domestic terrorism, the NSBA cited an incident in which a father angrily confronted members at a school board meeting in Loudoun County, Virginia about the heinous sexual assault of his daughter.[5]

A mere five days after the NSBA sent its letter to President Biden, on October 4, 2021, Attorney General Merrick Garland issued a shocking memorandum that directed the FBI and

---

[1] Memorandum from Atty Gen. Merrick Garland, U.S. Dep't of Justice, Partnership Among Federal, State, Local, Tribal, And Territorial Law Enforcement to Address Threats Against School Administrators, Board Members, Teachers, and Staff (Oct. 4, 2021).
[2] Letter from Dr. Viola M. Garcia, President, Nat'l School Board Assoc. & Mr. Chip Slaven, Chief Exec. Officer, Nat'l School Board Assoc., to President Joseph R. Biden, White House (Sept. 29, 2021).
[3] *Id.*
[4] *See* Caroline Downey, *Vast majority of incidents cited by school-board group to justify federal intervention didn't involve threats,* NAT'L REV. (Oct. 2, 2021).
[5] *Id.*; *see also* Jessica Chasmar, *Loudoun County father arrested at school board events says school tried to cover up daughter's bathroom assault*, FOX NEWS (Oct. 12, 2021).

U.S. Attorneys' Offices to "convene meetings" in your judicial district "with federal, state, local, Tribal, and territorial leaders" within 30 days.[6] The Justice Department simultaneously issued a press release indicating that the Attorney General's directive would "open dedicated lines of communication for threat reporting, assessment and response by law enforcement"—in other words, create a snitch line for complaints about concerned parents.[7]

During Attorney General Garland's testimony before our Committee on October 21, he appeared to have no idea whether the U.S. Attorney meetings he ordered were actually taking place. He stated: "I don't know whether [the meetings] are ongoing, but I expect and hope that they are going . . . because I did ask that they take place."[8] Attorney General Garland testified that he doubted "there have been meetings in every jurisdiction," but reiterated his belief that it is important for federal law enforcement authorities to conduct these meetings in every judicial district.[9] According to the Attorney General's directives, meetings are to be convened in all 94 judicial districts by November 3, 2021, at the latest.

Following the Attorney General's testimony, the NSBA Board of Directors, apparently recognizing the ill-conceived consequences of its letter and the resulting Justice Department action, issued a new memorandum to its members apologizing for the letter, stating: "On behalf of NSBA, we regret and apologize for the letter."[10] (emphasis in original). Although Attorney General Garland testified that the NSBA letter to President Biden was the basis for his October 4 directive to insert federal law enforcement into local school board matters, the Attorney General has yet to rescind his memorandum. His directives to you and other U.S. Attorneys remain in effect.

Concerned parents voicing their strong opposition to controversial curricula at local schools are not domestic terrorists. Parents have an undisputed right to direct the upbringing and education of their children.[11] When parents, however, cross the line to commit a violent act or issue a criminal threat,[12] state and local authorities are best-equipped to handle these violations of state law. But we must not tolerate the use of the federal law enforcement apparatus to intimidate and silence parents using their Constitutional rights to advocate for their child's future.

To assist our investigation and determine whether these meetings are ongoing, we request that you provide the following documents and information:

---

[6] Memorandum from Atty Gen. Merrick Garland, U.S. Dep't of Justice, Partnership Among Federal, State, Local, Tribal, And Territorial Law Enforcement to Address Threats Against School Administrators, Board Members, Teachers, and Staff (Oct. 4, 2021).

[7] Press Release, U.S. Dep't of Justice, Justice Department Addresses Violent Threats Against School Officials and Teachers (Oct. 4, 2021).

[8] *Oversight of the United States Department of Justice: Hearing Before the H. comm. on the Judiciary,* 117th Cong. at 94 (2021) (testimony from Hon. Merrick Garland, Atty Gen., U.S. Dep't of Justice).

[9] *Id.* at 95.

[10] Memorandum from NSBA Board of Directors, Message to NSBA Members (Oct. 22, 2021).

[11] *Troxel v. Granville,* 530 U.S. 57, 65 (2000) (citing *Meyer v. Nebraska,* 262 U.S. 390, 399 (1923)).

[12] *Merrick Garland's federal offense,* WALL ST. J. (Oct. 6, 2021).

1. All documents and communications referring or relating to convening meeting(s) in your judicial district in accordance with the Attorney General's October 4, 2021 memorandum;

2. All agendas, minutes, and notes created or relied upon by U.S. Attorney's Office employees referring or relating to meeting(s) in your judicial district in accordance with the Attorney General's October 4, 2021 memorandum;

3. Please explain when meeting(s) in your judicial district in accordance with the Attorney General's October 4, 2021 memorandum have occurred or will occur;

4. Please identify by name and title of all U.S. Attorney's Office employees involved in the meeting(s) in your judicial district in accordance with the Attorney General's October 4, 2021 memorandum ;

5. Please identify all federal, state, local, Tribal, and territorial organizations invited to or that have attended the meetings convened in your judicial district in accordance with the October 4, 2021 memorandum; and

6. Please provide all recommendations, both formal and informal, and any meeting minutes produced at the meeting(s) in your judicial district in accordance with the Attorney General's October 4, 2021 memorandum.

Please provide this material as soon as possible but no later than 5:00 p.m. on November 15, 2021.

If you have any questions about this request, please contact Committee staff at (202) 225-6906. Thank you for your attention to this important matter.

Sincerely,

Jim Jordan
Ranking Member

Steve Chabot
Member of Congress

Louie Gohmert
Member of Congress

Darrell Issa
Ranking Member
Subcommittee on Courts, Intellectual Property, and the Internet

Ken Buck
Ranking Member
Subcommittee on Antitrust, Commercial and Administrative Law

Matt Gaetz
Member of Congress

Mike Johnson
Ranking Member
Subcommittee on the Constitution, Civil Rights and Civil Liberties

Andy Biggs
Ranking Member
Subcommittee on Crime, Terrorism and Homeland Security

Tom McClintock
Ranking Member
Subcommittee on Immigration and Citizenship

W. Gregory Steube
Member of Congress

Tom Tiffany
Member of Congress

Thomas Massie
Member of Congress

Chip Roy
Member of Congress

Dan Bishop
Member of Congress

Michelle Fischbach
Member of Congress

Victoria Spartz
Member of Congress

Scott Fitzgerald
Member of Congress

Cliff Bentz
Member of Congress

Burgess Owens
Member of Congress

cc: The Honorable Jerrold L. Nadler
Chairman

Mr. Monty Wilkinson
Director, Executive Office for U.S. Attorneys

JERROLD NADLER, New York
CHAIRMAN

JIM JORDAN, Ohio
RANKING MEMBER

ONE HUNDRED SEVENTEENTH CONGRESS

Congress of the United States
House of Representatives
COMMITTEE ON THE JUDICIARY

2138 RAYBURN HOUSE OFFICE BUILDING

WASHINGTON, DC 20515-6216

(202) 225-3951
judiciary.house.gov

November 1, 2021

Mr. Duane A. Evans
U.S. Attorney
Eastern District of Louisiana
650 Poydras Street, Suite 1600
New Orleans, LA 70130

Dear Mr. Evans:

We are continuing to investigate the troubling attempts by the Department of Justice and the White House to use the heavy hand of federal law enforcement to target concerned parents at local school board meetings and chill their protected First Amendment activity. Because the Department directed you, along with all other U.S. Attorneys, and the Federal Bureau of Investigation (FBI) to take action to address parents attending school board meetings,[1] we respectfully request your assistance with our investigation.

On September 29, 2021, the National School Boards Association (NSBA) sent a letter to President Joe Biden requesting help from the federal government with concerned parents voicing their opinions at school board meetings.[2] The NSBA letter stated that "malice, violence, and threats" against school officials "could be the equivalent of a form of domestic terrorism or hate crimes."[3] The letter cited a number of interactions at school board meetings, none of which rose to the level of domestic terrorism. In fact, the vast majority of incidents cited by the NSBA did not involve threats or violence.[4] Most notably, as an example of domestic terrorism, the NSBA cited an incident in which a father angrily confronted members at a school board meeting in Loudoun County, Virginia about the heinous sexual assault of his daughter.[5]

A mere five days after the NSBA sent its letter to President Biden, on October 4, 2021, Attorney General Merrick Garland issued a shocking memorandum that directed the FBI and

---

[1] Memorandum from Atty Gen. Merrick Garland, U.S. Dep't of Justice, Partnership Among Federal, State, Local, Tribal, And Territorial Law Enforcement to Address Threats Against School Administrators, Board Members, Teachers, and Staff (Oct. 4, 2021).
[2] Letter from Dr. Viola M. Garcia, President, Nat'l School Board Assoc. & Mr. Chip Slaven, Chief Exec. Officer, Nat'l School Board Assoc., to President Joseph R. Biden, White House (Sept. 29, 2021).
[3] *Id.*
[4] *See* Caroline Downey, *Vast majority of incidents cited by school-board group to justify federal intervention didn't involve threats,* NAT'L REV. (Oct. 2, 2021).
[5] *Id.*; *see also* Jessica Chasmar, *Loudoun County father arrested at school board events says school tried to cover up daughter's bathroom assault*, FOX NEWS (Oct. 12, 2021).

U.S. Attorneys' Offices to "convene meetings" in your judicial district "with federal, state, local, Tribal, and territorial leaders" within 30 days.[6] The Justice Department simultaneously issued a press release indicating that the Attorney General's directive would "open dedicated lines of communication for threat reporting, assessment and response by law enforcement"—in other words, create a snitch line for complaints about concerned parents.[7]

During Attorney General Garland's testimony before our Committee on October 21, he appeared to have no idea whether the U.S. Attorney meetings he ordered were actually taking place. He stated: "I don't know whether [the meetings] are ongoing, but I expect and hope that they are going . . . because I did ask that they take place."[8] Attorney General Garland testified that he doubted "there have been meetings in every jurisdiction," but reiterated his belief that it is important for federal law enforcement authorities to conduct these meetings in every judicial district.[9] According to the Attorney General's directives, meetings are to be convened in all 94 judicial districts by November 3, 2021, at the latest.

Following the Attorney General's testimony, the NSBA Board of Directors, apparently recognizing the ill-conceived consequences of its letter and the resulting Justice Department action, issued a new memorandum to its members apologizing for the letter, stating: "On behalf of NSBA, <u>we regret and apologize for the letter</u>."[10] (emphasis in original). Although Attorney General Garland testified that the NSBA letter to President Biden was the basis for his October 4 directive to insert federal law enforcement into local school board matters, the Attorney General has yet to rescind his memorandum. His directives to you and other U.S. Attorneys remain in effect.

Concerned parents voicing their strong opposition to controversial curricula at local schools are not domestic terrorists. Parents have an undisputed right to direct the upbringing and education of their children.[11] When parents, however, cross the line to commit a violent act or issue a criminal threat,[12] state and local authorities are best-equipped to handle these violations of state law. But we must not tolerate the use of the federal law enforcement apparatus to intimidate and silence parents using their Constitutional rights to advocate for their child's future.

To assist our investigation and determine whether these meetings are ongoing, we request that you provide the following documents and information:

---

[6] Memorandum from Atty Gen. Merrick Garland, U.S. Dep't of Justice, Partnership Among Federal, State, Local, Tribal, And Territorial Law Enforcement to Address Threats Against School Administrators, Board Members, Teachers, and Staff (Oct. 4, 2021).
[7] Press Release, U.S. Dep't of Justice, Justice Department Addresses Violent Threats Against School Officials and Teachers (Oct. 4, 2021).
[8] *Oversight of the United States Department of Justice: Hearing Before the H. comm. on the Judiciary,* 117th Cong. at 94 (2021) (testimony from Hon. Merrick Garland, Atty Gen., U.S. Dep't of Justice).
[9] *Id.* at 95.
[10] Memorandum from NSBA Board of Directors, Message to NSBA Members (Oct. 22, 2021).
[11] *Troxel v. Granville,* 530 U.S. 57, 65 (2000) (citing *Meyer v. Nebraska,* 262 U.S. 390, 399 (1923)).
[12] *Merrick Garland's federal offense,* WALL ST. J. (Oct. 6, 2021).

1. All documents and communications referring or relating to convening meeting(s) in your judicial district in accordance with the Attorney General's October 4, 2021 memorandum;

2. All agendas, minutes, and notes created or relied upon by U.S. Attorney's Office employees referring or relating to meeting(s) in your judicial district in accordance with the Attorney General's October 4, 2021 memorandum;

3. Please explain when meeting(s) in your judicial district in accordance with the Attorney General's October 4, 2021 memorandum have occurred or will occur;

4. Please identify by name and title of all U.S. Attorney's Office employees involved in the meeting(s) in your judicial district in accordance with the Attorney General's October 4, 2021 memorandum ;

5. Please identify all federal, state, local, Tribal, and territorial organizations invited to or that have attended the meetings convened in your judicial district in accordance with the October 4, 2021 memorandum; and

6. Please provide all recommendations, both formal and informal, and any meeting minutes produced at the meeting(s) in your judicial district in accordance with the Attorney General's October 4, 2021 memorandum.

Please provide this material as soon as possible but no later than 5:00 p.m. on November 15, 2021.

If you have any questions about this request, please contact Committee staff at (202) 225-6906. Thank you for your attention to this important matter.

Sincerely,

Jim Jordan
Ranking Member

Steve Chabot
Member of Congress

Louie Gohmert
Member of Congress

Darrell Issa
Ranking Member
Subcommittee on Courts, Intellectual Property, and the Internet

Ken Buck
Ranking Member
Subcommittee on Antitrust, Commercial and Administrative Law

Matt Gaetz
Member of Congress

Mike Johnson
Ranking Member
Subcommittee on the Constitution, Civil Rights and Civil Liberties

Andy Biggs
Ranking Member
Subcommittee on Crime, Terrorism and Homeland Security

Tom McClintock
Ranking Member
Subcommittee on Immigration and Citizenship

W. Gregory Steube
Member of Congress

Tom Tiffany
Member of Congress

Thomas Massie
Member of Congress

Chip Roy
Member of Congress

Dan Bishop
Member of Congress

Michelle Fischbach
Member of Congress

Victoria Spartz
Member of Congress

Scott Fitzgerald
Member of Congress

Cliff Bentz
Member of Congress

Burgess Owens
Member of Congress

cc: The Honorable Jerrold L. Nadler
Chairman

Mr. Monty Wilkinson
Director, Executive Office for U.S. Attorneys

JERROLD NADLER, New York
CHAIRMAN

JIM JORDAN, Ohio
RANKING MEMBER

ONE HUNDRED SEVENTEENTH CONGRESS

Congress of the United States
House of Representatives
COMMITTEE ON THE JUDICIARY

2138 RAYBURN HOUSE OFFICE BUILDING
WASHINGTON, DC 20515–6216
(202) 225–3951
judiciary.house.gov

November 1, 2021

Mr. Ellison C. Travis
Acting U.S. Attorney
Middle District of Louisiana
777 Florida Street, Suite 208
Baton Rouge, LA 70801

Dear Mr. Travis:

We are continuing to investigate the troubling attempts by the Department of Justice and the White House to use the heavy hand of federal law enforcement to target concerned parents at local school board meetings and chill their protected First Amendment activity. Because the Department directed you, along with all other U.S. Attorneys, and the Federal Bureau of Investigation (FBI) to take action to address parents attending school board meetings,[1] we respectfully request your assistance with our investigation.

On September 29, 2021, the National School Boards Association (NSBA) sent a letter to President Joe Biden requesting help from the federal government with concerned parents voicing their opinions at school board meetings.[2] The NSBA letter stated that "malice, violence, and threats" against school officials "could be the equivalent of a form of domestic terrorism or hate crimes."[3] The letter cited a number of interactions at school board meetings, none of which rose to the level of domestic terrorism. In fact, the vast majority of incidents cited by the NSBA did not involve threats or violence.[4] Most notably, as an example of domestic terrorism, the NSBA cited an incident in which a father angrily confronted members at a school board meeting in Loudoun County, Virginia about the heinous sexual assault of his daughter.[5]

A mere five days after the NSBA sent its letter to President Biden, on October 4, 2021, Attorney General Merrick Garland issued a shocking memorandum that directed the FBI and

---

[1] Memorandum from Atty Gen. Merrick Garland, U.S. Dep't of Justice, Partnership Among Federal, State, Local, Tribal, And Territorial Law Enforcement to Address Threats Against School Administrators, Board Members, Teachers, and Staff (Oct. 4, 2021).

[2] Letter from Dr. Viola M. Garcia, President, Nat'l School Board Assoc. & Mr. Chip Slaven, Chief Exec. Officer, Nat'l School Board Assoc., to President Joseph R. Biden, White House (Sept. 29, 2021).

[3] *Id.*

[4] *See* Caroline Downey, *Vast majority of incidents cited by school-board group to justify federal intervention didn't involve threats,* NAT'L REV. (Oct. 2, 2021).

[5] *Id.*; *see also* Jessica Chasmar, *Loudoun County father arrested at school board events says school tried to cover up daughter's bathroom assault*, FOX NEWS (Oct. 12, 2021).

U.S. Attorneys' Offices to "convene meetings" in your judicial district "with federal, state, local, Tribal, and territorial leaders" within 30 days.[6] The Justice Department simultaneously issued a press release indicating that the Attorney General's directive would "open dedicated lines of communication for threat reporting, assessment and response by law enforcement"—in other words, create a snitch line for complaints about concerned parents.[7]

During Attorney General Garland's testimony before our Committee on October 21, he appeared to have no idea whether the U.S. Attorney meetings he ordered were actually taking place. He stated: "I don't know whether [the meetings] are ongoing, but I expect and hope that they are going . . . because I did ask that they take place."[8] Attorney General Garland testified that he doubted "there have been meetings in every jurisdiction," but reiterated his belief that it is important for federal law enforcement authorities to conduct these meetings in every judicial district.[9] According to the Attorney General's directives, meetings are to be convened in all 94 judicial districts by November 3, 2021, at the latest.

Following the Attorney General's testimony, the NSBA Board of Directors, apparently recognizing the ill-conceived consequences of its letter and the resulting Justice Department action, issued a new memorandum to its members apologizing for the letter, stating: "On behalf of NSBA, <u>we regret and apologize for the letter</u>."[10] (emphasis in original). Although Attorney General Garland testified that the NSBA letter to President Biden was the basis for his October 4 directive to insert federal law enforcement into local school board matters, the Attorney General has yet to rescind his memorandum. His directives to you and other U.S. Attorneys remain in effect.

Concerned parents voicing their strong opposition to controversial curricula at local schools are not domestic terrorists. Parents have an undisputed right to direct the upbringing and education of their children.[11] When parents, however, cross the line to commit a violent act or issue a criminal threat,[12] state and local authorities are best-equipped to handle these violations of state law. But we must not tolerate the use of the federal law enforcement apparatus to intimidate and silence parents using their Constitutional rights to advocate for their child's future.

To assist our investigation and determine whether these meetings are ongoing, we request that you provide the following documents and information:

---

[6] Memorandum from Atty Gen. Merrick Garland, U.S. Dep't of Justice, Partnership Among Federal, State, Local, Tribal, And Territorial Law Enforcement to Address Threats Against School Administrators, Board Members, Teachers, and Staff (Oct. 4, 2021).
[7] Press Release, U.S. Dep't of Justice, Justice Department Addresses Violent Threats Against School Officials and Teachers (Oct. 4, 2021).
[8] *Oversight of the United States Department of Justice: Hearing Before the H. comm. on the Judiciary,* 117th Cong. at 94 (2021) (testimony from Hon. Merrick Garland, Atty Gen., U.S. Dep't of Justice).
[9] *Id.* at 95.
[10] Memorandum from NSBA Board of Directors, Message to NSBA Members (Oct. 22, 2021).
[11] *Troxel v. Granville,* 530 U.S. 57, 65 (2000) (citing *Meyer v. Nebraska,* 262 U.S. 390, 399 (1923)).
[12] *Merrick Garland's federal offense,* WALL ST. J. (Oct. 6, 2021).

1. All documents and communications referring or relating to convening meeting(s) in your judicial district in accordance with the Attorney General's October 4, 2021 memorandum;

2. All agendas, minutes, and notes created or relied upon by U.S. Attorney's Office employees referring or relating to meeting(s) in your judicial district in accordance with the Attorney General's October 4, 2021 memorandum;

3. Please explain when meeting(s) in your judicial district in accordance with the Attorney General's October 4, 2021 memorandum have occurred or will occur;

4. Please identify by name and title of all U.S. Attorney's Office employees involved in the meeting(s) in your judicial district in accordance with the Attorney General's October 4, 2021 memorandum ;

5. Please identify all federal, state, local, Tribal, and territorial organizations invited to or that have attended the meetings convened in your judicial district in accordance with the October 4, 2021 memorandum; and

6. Please provide all recommendations, both formal and informal, and any meeting minutes produced at the meeting(s) in your judicial district in accordance with the Attorney General's October 4, 2021 memorandum.

Please provide this material as soon as possible but no later than 5:00 p.m. on November 15, 2021.

If you have any questions about this request, please contact Committee staff at (202) 225-6906. Thank you for your attention to this important matter.

Sincerely,

Jim Jordan
Ranking Member

Steve Chabot
Member of Congress

Louie Gohmert
Member of Congress

Darrell Issa
Ranking Member
Subcommittee on Courts, Intellectual Property, and the Internet

Ken Buck
Ranking Member
Subcommittee on Antitrust, Commercial and Administrative Law

Matt Gaetz
Member of Congress

Mike Johnson
Ranking Member
Subcommittee on the Constitution, Civil Rights and Civil Liberties

Andy Biggs
Ranking Member
Subcommittee on Crime, Terrorism and Homeland Security

Tom McClintock
Ranking Member
Subcommittee on Immigration and Citizenship

W. Gregory Steube
Member of Congress

Tom Tiffany
Member of Congress

Thomas Massie
Member of Congress

Chip Roy
Member of Congress

Dan Bishop
Member of Congress

Michelle Fischbach
Member of Congress

Victoria Spartz
Member of Congress

Scott Fitzgerald
Member of Congress

Cliff Bentz
Member of Congress

Burgess Owens
Member of Congress

cc: The Honorable Jerrold L. Nadler
Chairman

Mr. Monty Wilkinson
Director, Executive Office for U.S. Attorneys

JERROLD NADLER, New York
CHAIRMAN

JIM JORDAN, Ohio
RANKING MEMBER

ONE HUNDRED SEVENTEENTH CONGRESS
Congress of the United States
House of Representatives
COMMITTEE ON THE JUDICIARY
2138 RAYBURN HOUSE OFFICE BUILDING
WASHINGTON, DC 20515-6216
(202) 225-3951
judiciary.house.gov

November 1, 2021

Mr. Alexander C. Van Hook
Acting U.S. Attorney
Western District of Louisiana
300 Fannin Street, Suite 3201
Shreveport, LA 71101

Dear Mr. Van Hook:

We are continuing to investigate the troubling attempts by the Department of Justice and the White House to use the heavy hand of federal law enforcement to target concerned parents at local school board meetings and chill their protected First Amendment activity. Because the Department directed you, along with all other U.S. Attorneys, and the Federal Bureau of Investigation (FBI) to take action to address parents attending school board meetings,[1] we respectfully request your assistance with our investigation.

On September 29, 2021, the National School Boards Association (NSBA) sent a letter to President Joe Biden requesting help from the federal government with concerned parents voicing their opinions at school board meetings.[2] The NSBA letter stated that "malice, violence, and threats" against school officials "could be the equivalent of a form of domestic terrorism or hate crimes."[3] The letter cited a number of interactions at school board meetings, none of which rose to the level of domestic terrorism. In fact, the vast majority of incidents cited by the NSBA did not involve threats or violence.[4] Most notably, as an example of domestic terrorism, the NSBA cited an incident in which a father angrily confronted members at a school board meeting in Loudoun County, Virginia about the heinous sexual assault of his daughter.[5]

A mere five days after the NSBA sent its letter to President Biden, on October 4, 2021, Attorney General Merrick Garland issued a shocking memorandum that directed the FBI and

---

[1] Memorandum from Atty Gen. Merrick Garland, U.S. Dep't of Justice, Partnership Among Federal, State, Local, Tribal, And Territorial Law Enforcement to Address Threats Against School Administrators, Board Members, Teachers, and Staff (Oct. 4, 2021).
[2] Letter from Dr. Viola M. Garcia, President, Nat'l School Board Assoc. & Mr. Chip Slaven, Chief Exec. Officer, Nat'l School Board Assoc., to President Joseph R. Biden, White House (Sept. 29, 2021).
[3] *Id.*
[4] *See* Caroline Downey, *Vast majority of incidents cited by school-board group to justify federal intervention didn't involve threats,* NAT'L REV. (Oct. 2, 2021).
[5] *Id.*; *see also* Jessica Chasmar, *Loudoun County father arrested at school board events says school tried to cover up daughter's bathroom assault*, FOX NEWS (Oct. 12, 2021).

U.S. Attorneys' Offices to "convene meetings" in your judicial district "with federal, state, local, Tribal, and territorial leaders" within 30 days.[6] The Justice Department simultaneously issued a press release indicating that the Attorney General's directive would "open dedicated lines of communication for threat reporting, assessment and response by law enforcement"—in other words, create a snitch line for complaints about concerned parents.[7]

During Attorney General Garland's testimony before our Committee on October 21, he appeared to have no idea whether the U.S. Attorney meetings he ordered were actually taking place. He stated: "I don't know whether [the meetings] are ongoing, but I expect and hope that they are going . . . because I did ask that they take place."[8] Attorney General Garland testified that he doubted "there have been meetings in every jurisdiction," but reiterated his belief that it is important for federal law enforcement authorities to conduct these meetings in every judicial district.[9] According to the Attorney General's directives, meetings are to be convened in all 94 judicial districts by November 3, 2021, at the latest.

Following the Attorney General's testimony, the NSBA Board of Directors, apparently recognizing the ill-conceived consequences of its letter and the resulting Justice Department action, issued a new memorandum to its members apologizing for the letter, stating: "On behalf of NSBA, <u>we regret and apologize for the letter</u>."[10] (emphasis in original). Although Attorney General Garland testified that the NSBA letter to President Biden was the basis for his October 4 directive to insert federal law enforcement into local school board matters, the Attorney General has yet to rescind his memorandum. His directives to you and other U.S. Attorneys remain in effect.

Concerned parents voicing their strong opposition to controversial curricula at local schools are not domestic terrorists. Parents have an undisputed right to direct the upbringing and education of their children.[11] When parents, however, cross the line to commit a violent act or issue a criminal threat,[12] state and local authorities are best-equipped to handle these violations of state law. But we must not tolerate the use of the federal law enforcement apparatus to intimidate and silence parents using their Constitutional rights to advocate for their child's future.

To assist our investigation and determine whether these meetings are ongoing, we request that you provide the following documents and information:

---

[6] Memorandum from Atty Gen. Merrick Garland, U.S. Dep't of Justice, Partnership Among Federal, State, Local, Tribal, And Territorial Law Enforcement to Address Threats Against School Administrators, Board Members, Teachers, and Staff (Oct. 4, 2021).
[7] Press Release, U.S. Dep't of Justice, Justice Department Addresses Violent Threats Against School Officials and Teachers (Oct. 4, 2021).
[8] *Oversight of the United States Department of Justice: Hearing Before the H. comm. on the Judiciary,* 117th Cong. at 94 (2021) (testimony from Hon. Merrick Garland, Atty Gen., U.S. Dep't of Justice).
[9] *Id.* at 95.
[10] Memorandum from NSBA Board of Directors, Message to NSBA Members (Oct. 22, 2021).
[11] *Troxel v. Granville,* 530 U.S. 57, 65 (2000) (citing *Meyer v. Nebraska,* 262 U.S. 390, 399 (1923)).
[12] *Merrick Garland's federal offense,* WALL ST. J. (Oct. 6, 2021).

1. All documents and communications referring or relating to convening meeting(s) in your judicial district in accordance with the Attorney General's October 4, 2021 memorandum;

2. All agendas, minutes, and notes created or relied upon by U.S. Attorney's Office employees referring or relating to meeting(s) in your judicial district in accordance with the Attorney General's October 4, 2021 memorandum;

3. Please explain when meeting(s) in your judicial district in accordance with the Attorney General's October 4, 2021 memorandum have occurred or will occur;

4. Please identify by name and title of all U.S. Attorney's Office employees involved in the meeting(s) in your judicial district in accordance with the Attorney General's October 4, 2021 memorandum ;

5. Please identify all federal, state, local, Tribal, and territorial organizations invited to or that have attended the meetings convened in your judicial district in accordance with the October 4, 2021 memorandum; and

6. Please provide all recommendations, both formal and informal, and any meeting minutes produced at the meeting(s) in your judicial district in accordance with the Attorney General's October 4, 2021 memorandum.

Please provide this material as soon as possible but no later than 5:00 p.m. on November 15, 2021.

If you have any questions about this request, please contact Committee staff at (202) 225-6906. Thank you for your attention to this important matter.

Sincerely,

Jim Jordan
Ranking Member

Steve Chabot
Member of Congress

Louie Gohmert
Member of Congress

Darrell Issa
Ranking Member
Subcommittee on Courts, Intellectual Property, and the Internet

Ken Buck
Ranking Member
Subcommittee on Antitrust, Commercial and Administrative Law

Matt Gaetz
Member of Congress

Mike Johnson
Ranking Member
Subcommittee on the Constitution, Civil Rights and Civil Liberties

Andy Biggs
Ranking Member
Subcommittee on Crime, Terrorism and Homeland Security

Tom McClintock
Ranking Member
Subcommittee on Immigration and Citizenship

W. Gregory Steube
Member of Congress

Tom Tiffany
Member of Congress

Thomas Massie
Member of Congress

Chip Roy
Member of Congress

Dan Bishop
Member of Congress

Michelle Fischbach
Member of Congress

Victoria Spartz
Member of Congress

Scott Fitzgerald
Member of Congress

Cliff Bentz
Member of Congress

Burgess Owens
Member of Congress

cc: The Honorable Jerrold L. Nadler
Chairman

Mr. Monty Wilkinson
Director, Executive Office for U.S. Attorneys

JERROLD NADLER, New York
CHAIRMAN

JIM JORDAN, Ohio
RANKING MEMBER

ONE HUNDRED SEVENTEENTH CONGRESS

Congress of the United States

House of Representatives

COMMITTEE ON THE JUDICIARY

2138 RAYBURN HOUSE OFFICE BUILDING

WASHINGTON, DC 20515–6216

(202) 225–3951
judiciary.house.gov

November 1, 2021

Mr. Nathaniel R. Mendell
Acting U.S. Attorney
District of Massachusetts
1 Courthouse Way, Suite 9200
Boston, MA 02210

Dear Mr. Mendell:

We are continuing to investigate the troubling attempts by the Department of Justice and the White House to use the heavy hand of federal law enforcement to target concerned parents at local school board meetings and chill their protected First Amendment activity. Because the Department directed you, along with all other U.S. Attorneys, and the Federal Bureau of Investigation (FBI) to take action to address parents attending school board meetings,[1] we respectfully request your assistance with our investigation.

On September 29, 2021, the National School Boards Association (NSBA) sent a letter to President Joe Biden requesting help from the federal government with concerned parents voicing their opinions at school board meetings.[2] The NSBA letter stated that "malice, violence, and threats" against school officials "could be the equivalent of a form of domestic terrorism or hate crimes."[3] The letter cited a number of interactions at school board meetings, none of which rose to the level of domestic terrorism. In fact, the vast majority of incidents cited by the NSBA did not involve threats or violence.[4] Most notably, as an example of domestic terrorism, the NSBA cited an incident in which a father angrily confronted members at a school board meeting in Loudoun County, Virginia about the heinous sexual assault of his daughter.[5]

A mere five days after the NSBA sent its letter to President Biden, on October 4, 2021, Attorney General Merrick Garland issued a shocking memorandum that directed the FBI and

---

[1] Memorandum from Atty Gen. Merrick Garland, U.S. Dep't of Justice, Partnership Among Federal, State, Local, Tribal, And Territorial Law Enforcement to Address Threats Against School Administrators, Board Members, Teachers, and Staff (Oct. 4, 2021).
[2] Letter from Dr. Viola M. Garcia, President, Nat'l School Board Assoc. & Mr. Chip Slaven, Chief Exec. Officer, Nat'l School Board Assoc., to President Joseph R. Biden, White House (Sept. 29, 2021).
[3] *Id.*
[4] *See* Caroline Downey, *Vast majority of incidents cited by school-board group to justify federal intervention didn't involve threats,* NAT'L REV. (Oct. 2, 2021).
[5] *Id.*; *see also* Jessica Chasmar, *Loudoun County father arrested at school board events says school tried to cover up daughter's bathroom assault*, FOX NEWS (Oct. 12, 2021).

U.S. Attorneys' Offices to "convene meetings" in your judicial district "with federal, state, local, Tribal, and territorial leaders" within 30 days.[6] The Justice Department simultaneously issued a press release indicating that the Attorney General's directive would "open dedicated lines of communication for threat reporting, assessment and response by law enforcement"—in other words, create a snitch line for complaints about concerned parents.[7]

During Attorney General Garland's testimony before our Committee on October 21, he appeared to have no idea whether the U.S. Attorney meetings he ordered were actually taking place. He stated: "I don't know whether [the meetings] are ongoing, but I expect and hope that they are going . . . because I did ask that they take place."[8] Attorney General Garland testified that he doubted "there have been meetings in every jurisdiction," but reiterated his belief that it is important for federal law enforcement authorities to conduct these meetings in every judicial district.[9] According to the Attorney General's directives, meetings are to be convened in all 94 judicial districts by November 3, 2021, at the latest.

Following the Attorney General's testimony, the NSBA Board of Directors, apparently recognizing the ill-conceived consequences of its letter and the resulting Justice Department action, issued a new memorandum to its members apologizing for the letter, stating: "On behalf of NSBA, <u>we regret and apologize for the letter</u>."[10] (emphasis in original). Although Attorney General Garland testified that the NSBA letter to President Biden was the basis for his October 4 directive to insert federal law enforcement into local school board matters, the Attorney General has yet to rescind his memorandum. His directives to you and other U.S. Attorneys remain in effect.

Concerned parents voicing their strong opposition to controversial curricula at local schools are not domestic terrorists. Parents have an undisputed right to direct the upbringing and education of their children.[11] When parents, however, cross the line to commit a violent act or issue a criminal threat,[12] state and local authorities are best-equipped to handle these violations of state law. But we must not tolerate the use of the federal law enforcement apparatus to intimidate and silence parents using their Constitutional rights to advocate for their child's future.

To assist our investigation and determine whether these meetings are ongoing, we request that you provide the following documents and information:

---

[6] Memorandum from Atty Gen. Merrick Garland, U.S. Dep't of Justice, Partnership Among Federal, State, Local, Tribal, And Territorial Law Enforcement to Address Threats Against School Administrators, Board Members, Teachers, and Staff (Oct. 4, 2021).

[7] Press Release, U.S. Dep't of Justice, Justice Department Addresses Violent Threats Against School Officials and Teachers (Oct. 4, 2021).

[8] *Oversight of the United States Department of Justice: Hearing Before the H. comm. on the Judiciary,* 117th Cong. at 94 (2021) (testimony from Hon. Merrick Garland, Atty Gen., U.S. Dep't of Justice).

[9] *Id.* at 95.

[10] Memorandum from NSBA Board of Directors, Message to NSBA Members (Oct. 22, 2021).

[11] *Troxel v. Granville,* 530 U.S. 57, 65 (2000) (citing *Meyer v. Nebraska,* 262 U.S. 390, 399 (1923)).

[12] *Merrick Garland's federal offense,* WALL ST. J. (Oct. 6, 2021).

1. All documents and communications referring or relating to convening meeting(s) in your judicial district in accordance with the Attorney General's October 4, 2021 memorandum;

2. All agendas, minutes, and notes created or relied upon by U.S. Attorney's Office employees referring or relating to meeting(s) in your judicial district in accordance with the Attorney General's October 4, 2021 memorandum;

3. Please explain when meeting(s) in your judicial district in accordance with the Attorney General's October 4, 2021 memorandum have occurred or will occur;

4. Please identify by name and title of all U.S. Attorney's Office employees involved in the meeting(s) in your judicial district in accordance with the Attorney General's October 4, 2021 memorandum ;

5. Please identify all federal, state, local, Tribal, and territorial organizations invited to or that have attended the meetings convened in your judicial district in accordance with the October 4, 2021 memorandum; and

6. Please provide all recommendations, both formal and informal, and any meeting minutes produced at the meeting(s) in your judicial district in accordance with the Attorney General's October 4, 2021 memorandum.

Please provide this material as soon as possible but no later than 5:00 p.m. on November 15, 2021.

If you have any questions about this request, please contact Committee staff at (202) 225-6906. Thank you for your attention to this important matter.

Sincerely,

Jim Jordan
Ranking Member

Steve Chabot
Member of Congress

Louie Gohmert
Member of Congress

Darrell Issa
Ranking Member
Subcommittee on Courts, Intellectual Property, and the Internet

Ken Buck
Ranking Member
Subcommittee on Antitrust, Commercial and Administrative Law

Matt Gaetz
Member of Congress

Mike Johnson
Ranking Member
Subcommittee on the Constitution, Civil Rights and Civil Liberties

Andy Biggs
Ranking Member
Subcommittee on Crime, Terrorism and Homeland Security

Tom McClintock
Ranking Member
Subcommittee on Immigration and Citizenship

W. Gregory Steube
Member of Congress

Tom Tiffany
Member of Congress

Thomas Massie
Member of Congress

Chip Roy
Member of Congress

Dan Bishop
Member of Congress

Michelle Fischbach
Member of Congress

Victoria Spartz
Member of Congress

Scott Fitzgerald
Member of Congress

Cliff Bentz
Member of Congress

Burgess Owens
Member of Congress

cc: The Honorable Jerrold L. Nadler
Chairman

Mr. Monty Wilkinson
Director, Executive Office for U.S. Attorneys

JERROLD NADLER, New York
CHAIRMAN

JIM JORDAN, Ohio
RANKING MEMBER

ONE HUNDRED SEVENTEENTH CONGRESS

Congress of the United States

House of Representatives

COMMITTEE ON THE JUDICIARY

2138 RAYBURN HOUSE OFFICE BUILDING

WASHINGTON, DC 20515–6216

(202) 225–3951
judiciary.house.gov

November 1, 2021

The Honorable Erek L. Barron
U.S. Attorney
District of Maryland
36 South Charles Street, 4th Floor
Baltimore, MD 21201

Dear Mr. Barron:

We are continuing to investigate the troubling attempts by the Department of Justice and the White House to use the heavy hand of federal law enforcement to target concerned parents at local school board meetings and chill their protected First Amendment activity. Because the Department directed you, along with all other U.S. Attorneys, and the Federal Bureau of Investigation (FBI) to take action to address parents attending school board meetings,[1] we respectfully request your assistance with our investigation.

On September 29, 2021, the National School Boards Association (NSBA) sent a letter to President Joe Biden requesting help from the federal government with concerned parents voicing their opinions at school board meetings.[2] The NSBA letter stated that "malice, violence, and threats" against school officials "could be the equivalent of a form of domestic terrorism or hate crimes."[3] The letter cited a number of interactions at school board meetings, none of which rose to the level of domestic terrorism. In fact, the vast majority of incidents cited by the NSBA did not involve threats or violence.[4] Most notably, as an example of domestic terrorism, the NSBA cited an incident in which a father angrily confronted members at a school board meeting in Loudoun County, Virginia about the heinous sexual assault of his daughter.[5]

A mere five days after the NSBA sent its letter to President Biden, on October 4, 2021, Attorney General Merrick Garland issued a shocking memorandum that directed the FBI and

---

[1] Memorandum from Atty Gen. Merrick Garland, U.S. Dep't of Justice, Partnership Among Federal, State, Local, Tribal, And Territorial Law Enforcement to Address Threats Against School Administrators, Board Members, Teachers, and Staff (Oct. 4, 2021).
[2] Letter from Dr. Viola M. Garcia, President, Nat'l School Board Assoc. & Mr. Chip Slaven, Chief Exec. Officer, Nat'l School Board Assoc., to President Joseph R. Biden, White House (Sept. 29, 2021).
[3] *Id.*
[4] *See* Caroline Downey, *Vast majority of incidents cited by school-board group to justify federal intervention didn't involve threats,* NAT'L REV. (Oct. 2, 2021).
[5] *Id.*; *see also* Jessica Chasmar, *Loudoun County father arrested at school board events says school tried to cover up daughter's bathroom assault*, FOX NEWS (Oct. 12, 2021).

U.S. Attorneys' Offices to "convene meetings" in your judicial district "with federal, state, local, Tribal, and territorial leaders" within 30 days.[6] The Justice Department simultaneously issued a press release indicating that the Attorney General's directive would "open dedicated lines of communication for threat reporting, assessment and response by law enforcement"—in other words, create a snitch line for complaints about concerned parents.[7]

During Attorney General Garland's testimony before our Committee on October 21, he appeared to have no idea whether the U.S. Attorney meetings he ordered were actually taking place. He stated: "I don't know whether [the meetings] are ongoing, but I expect and hope that they are going . . . because I did ask that they take place."[8] Attorney General Garland testified that he doubted "there have been meetings in every jurisdiction," but reiterated his belief that it is important for federal law enforcement authorities to conduct these meetings in every judicial district.[9] According to the Attorney General's directives, meetings are to be convened in all 94 judicial districts by November 3, 2021, at the latest.

Following the Attorney General's testimony, the NSBA Board of Directors, apparently recognizing the ill-conceived consequences of its letter and the resulting Justice Department action, issued a new memorandum to its members apologizing for the letter, stating: "On behalf of NSBA, <u>we regret and apologize for the letter</u>."[10] (emphasis in original). Although Attorney General Garland testified that the NSBA letter to President Biden was the basis for his October 4 directive to insert federal law enforcement into local school board matters, the Attorney General has yet to rescind his memorandum. His directives to you and other U.S. Attorneys remain in effect.

Concerned parents voicing their strong opposition to controversial curricula at local schools are not domestic terrorists. Parents have an undisputed right to direct the upbringing and education of their children.[11] When parents, however, cross the line to commit a violent act or issue a criminal threat,[12] state and local authorities are best-equipped to handle these violations of state law. But we must not tolerate the use of the federal law enforcement apparatus to intimidate and silence parents using their Constitutional rights to advocate for their child's future.

To assist our investigation and determine whether these meetings are ongoing, we request that you provide the following documents and information:

---

[6] Memorandum from Atty Gen. Merrick Garland, U.S. Dep't of Justice, Partnership Among Federal, State, Local, Tribal, And Territorial Law Enforcement to Address Threats Against School Administrators, Board Members, Teachers, and Staff (Oct. 4, 2021).
[7] Press Release, U.S. Dep't of Justice, Justice Department Addresses Violent Threats Against School Officials and Teachers (Oct. 4, 2021).
[8] *Oversight of the United States Department of Justice: Hearing Before the H. comm. on the Judiciary,* 117th Cong. at 94 (2021) (testimony from Hon. Merrick Garland, Atty Gen., U.S. Dep't of Justice).
[9] *Id.* at 95.
[10] Memorandum from NSBA Board of Directors, Message to NSBA Members (Oct. 22, 2021).
[11] *Troxel v. Granville,* 530 U.S. 57, 65 (2000) (citing *Meyer v. Nebraska,* 262 U.S. 390, 399 (1923)).
[12] *Merrick Garland's federal offense,* WALL ST. J. (Oct. 6, 2021).

1. All documents and communications referring or relating to convening meeting(s) in your judicial district in accordance with the Attorney General's October 4, 2021 memorandum;

2. All agendas, minutes, and notes created or relied upon by U.S. Attorney's Office employees referring or relating to meeting(s) in your judicial district in accordance with the Attorney General's October 4, 2021 memorandum;

3. Please explain when meeting(s) in your judicial district in accordance with the Attorney General's October 4, 2021 memorandum have occurred or will occur;

4. Please identify by name and title of all U.S. Attorney's Office employees involved in the meeting(s) in your judicial district in accordance with the Attorney General's October 4, 2021 memorandum ;

5. Please identify all federal, state, local, Tribal, and territorial organizations invited to or that have attended the meetings convened in your judicial district in accordance with the October 4, 2021 memorandum; and

6. Please provide all recommendations, both formal and informal, and any meeting minutes produced at the meeting(s) in your judicial district in accordance with the Attorney General's October 4, 2021 memorandum.

Please provide this material as soon as possible but no later than 5:00 p.m. on November 15, 2021.

If you have any questions about this request, please contact Committee staff at (202) 225-6906. Thank you for your attention to this important matter.

Sincerely,

Jim Jordan
Ranking Member

Steve Chabot
Member of Congress

Louie Gohmert
Member of Congress

Darrell Issa
Ranking Member
Subcommittee on Courts, Intellectual Property, and the Internet

Ken Buck
Ranking Member
Subcommittee on Antitrust, Commercial and Administrative Law

Matt Gaetz
Member of Congress

Mike Johnson
Ranking Member
Subcommittee on the Constitution, Civil Rights and Civil Liberties

Andy Biggs
Ranking Member
Subcommittee on Crime, Terrorism and Homeland Security

Tom McClintock
Ranking Member
Subcommittee on Immigration and Citizenship

W. Gregory Steube
Member of Congress

Tom Tiffany
Member of Congress

Thomas Massie
Member of Congress

Chip Roy
Member of Congress

Dan Bishop
Member of Congress

Michelle Fischbach
Member of Congress

Victoria Spartz
Member of Congress

Scott Fitzgerald
Member of Congress

Cliff Bentz
Member of Congress

Burgess Owens
Member of Congress

cc: The Honorable Jerrold L. Nadler
Chairman

Mr. Monty Wilkinson
Director, Executive Office for U.S. Attorneys

JERROLD NADLER, New York
CHAIRMAN

JIM JORDAN, Ohio
RANKING MEMBER

ONE HUNDRED SEVENTEENTH CONGRESS

Congress of the United States

House of Representatives

COMMITTEE ON THE JUDICIARY

2138 RAYBURN HOUSE OFFICE BUILDING

WASHINGTON, DC 20515-6216

(202) 225-3951
judiciary.house.gov

November 1, 2021

The Honorable Darcie N. McElwee
U.S. Attorney
District of Maine
100 Middle Street, East Tower, 6th Floor
Portland, ME 04101

Dear Ms. McElwee:

We are continuing to investigate the troubling attempts by the Department of Justice and the White House to use the heavy hand of federal law enforcement to target concerned parents at local school board meetings and chill their protected First Amendment activity. Because the Department directed you, along with all other U.S. Attorneys, and the Federal Bureau of Investigation (FBI) to take action to address parents attending school board meetings,[1] we respectfully request your assistance with our investigation.

On September 29, 2021, the National School Boards Association (NSBA) sent a letter to President Joe Biden requesting help from the federal government with concerned parents voicing their opinions at school board meetings.[2] The NSBA letter stated that "malice, violence, and threats" against school officials "could be the equivalent of a form of domestic terrorism or hate crimes."[3] The letter cited a number of interactions at school board meetings, none of which rose to the level of domestic terrorism. In fact, the vast majority of incidents cited by the NSBA did not involve threats or violence.[4] Most notably, as an example of domestic terrorism, the NSBA cited an incident in which a father angrily confronted members at a school board meeting in Loudoun County, Virginia about the heinous sexual assault of his daughter.[5]

A mere five days after the NSBA sent its letter to President Biden, on October 4, 2021, Attorney General Merrick Garland issued a shocking memorandum that directed the FBI and

---

[1] Memorandum from Atty Gen. Merrick Garland, U.S. Dep't of Justice, Partnership Among Federal, State, Local, Tribal, And Territorial Law Enforcement to Address Threats Against School Administrators, Board Members, Teachers, and Staff (Oct. 4, 2021).
[2] Letter from Dr. Viola M. Garcia, President, Nat'l School Board Assoc. & Mr. Chip Slaven, Chief Exec. Officer, Nat'l School Board Assoc., to President Joseph R. Biden, White House (Sept. 29, 2021).
[3] *Id.*
[4] *See* Caroline Downey, *Vast majority of incidents cited by school-board group to justify federal intervention didn't involve threats,* NAT'L REV. (Oct. 2, 2021).
[5] *Id.*; *see also* Jessica Chasmar, *Loudoun County father arrested at school board events says school tried to cover up daughter's bathroom assault*, FOX NEWS (Oct. 12, 2021).

U.S. Attorneys' Offices to "convene meetings" in your judicial district "with federal, state, local, Tribal, and territorial leaders" within 30 days.[6] The Justice Department simultaneously issued a press release indicating that the Attorney General's directive would "open dedicated lines of communication for threat reporting, assessment and response by law enforcement"—in other words, create a snitch line for complaints about concerned parents.[7]

During Attorney General Garland's testimony before our Committee on October 21, he appeared to have no idea whether the U.S. Attorney meetings he ordered were actually taking place. He stated: "I don't know whether [the meetings] are ongoing, but I expect and hope that they are going . . . because I did ask that they take place."[8] Attorney General Garland testified that he doubted "there have been meetings in every jurisdiction," but reiterated his belief that it is important for federal law enforcement authorities to conduct these meetings in every judicial district.[9] According to the Attorney General's directives, meetings are to be convened in all 94 judicial districts by November 3, 2021, at the latest.

Following the Attorney General's testimony, the NSBA Board of Directors, apparently recognizing the ill-conceived consequences of its letter and the resulting Justice Department action, issued a new memorandum to its members apologizing for the letter, stating: "On behalf of NSBA, we regret and apologize for the letter."[10] (emphasis in original). Although Attorney General Garland testified that the NSBA letter to President Biden was the basis for his October 4 directive to insert federal law enforcement into local school board matters, the Attorney General has yet to rescind his memorandum. His directives to you and other U.S. Attorneys remain in effect.

Concerned parents voicing their strong opposition to controversial curricula at local schools are not domestic terrorists. Parents have an undisputed right to direct the upbringing and education of their children.[11] When parents, however, cross the line to commit a violent act or issue a criminal threat,[12] state and local authorities are best-equipped to handle these violations of state law. But we must not tolerate the use of the federal law enforcement apparatus to intimidate and silence parents using their Constitutional rights to advocate for their child's future.

To assist our investigation and determine whether these meetings are ongoing, we request that you provide the following documents and information:

---

[6] Memorandum from Atty Gen. Merrick Garland, U.S. Dep't of Justice, Partnership Among Federal, State, Local, Tribal, And Territorial Law Enforcement to Address Threats Against School Administrators, Board Members, Teachers, and Staff (Oct. 4, 2021).
[7] Press Release, U.S. Dep't of Justice, Justice Department Addresses Violent Threats Against School Officials and Teachers (Oct. 4, 2021).
[8] *Oversight of the United States Department of Justice: Hearing Before the H. comm. on the Judiciary,* 117th Cong. at 94 (2021) (testimony from Hon. Merrick Garland, Atty Gen., U.S. Dep't of Justice).
[9] *Id.* at 95.
[10] Memorandum from NSBA Board of Directors, Message to NSBA Members (Oct. 22, 2021).
[11] *Troxel v. Granville,* 530 U.S. 57, 65 (2000) (citing *Meyer v. Nebraska,* 262 U.S. 390, 399 (1923)).
[12] *Merrick Garland's federal offense,* WALL ST. J. (Oct. 6, 2021).

1. All documents and communications referring or relating to convening meeting(s) in your judicial district in accordance with the Attorney General's October 4, 2021 memorandum;

2. All agendas, minutes, and notes created or relied upon by U.S. Attorney's Office employees referring or relating to meeting(s) in your judicial district in accordance with the Attorney General's October 4, 2021 memorandum;

3. Please explain when meeting(s) in your judicial district in accordance with the Attorney General's October 4, 2021 memorandum have occurred or will occur;

4. Please identify by name and title of all U.S. Attorney's Office employees involved in the meeting(s) in your judicial district in accordance with the Attorney General's October 4, 2021 memorandum ;

5. Please identify all federal, state, local, Tribal, and territorial organizations invited to or that have attended the meetings convened in your judicial district in accordance with the October 4, 2021 memorandum; and

6. Please provide all recommendations, both formal and informal, and any meeting minutes produced at the meeting(s) in your judicial district in accordance with the Attorney General's October 4, 2021 memorandum.

Please provide this material as soon as possible but no later than 5:00 p.m. on November 15, 2021.

If you have any questions about this request, please contact Committee staff at (202) 225-6906. Thank you for your attention to this important matter.

Sincerely,

Jim Jordan
Ranking Member

Steve Chabot
Member of Congress

Louie Gohmert
Member of Congress

Darrell Issa
Ranking Member
Subcommittee on Courts, Intellectual Property, and the Internet

The Honorable Darcie N. McElwee
November 1, 2021
Page 4

Ken Buck
Ranking Member
Subcommittee on Antitrust, Commercial and Administrative Law

Matt Gaetz
Member of Congress

Mike Johnson
Ranking Member
Subcommittee on the Constitution, Civil Rights and Civil Liberties

Andy Biggs
Ranking Member
Subcommittee on Crime, Terrorism and Homeland Security

Tom McClintock
Ranking Member
Subcommittee on Immigration and Citizenship

W. Gregory Steube
Member of Congress

Tom Tiffany
Member of Congress

Thomas Massie
Member of Congress

Chip Roy
Member of Congress

Dan Bishop
Member of Congress

Michelle Fischbach
Member of Congress

Victoria Spartz
Member of Congress

Scott Fitzgerald
Member of Congress

Cliff Bentz
Member of Congress

Burgess Owens
Member of Congress

cc: The Honorable Jerrold L. Nadler
Chairman

Mr. Monty Wilkinson
Director, Executive Office for U.S. Attorneys

JERROLD NADLER, New York
CHAIRMAN

JIM JORDAN, Ohio
RANKING MEMBER

ONE HUNDRED SEVENTEENTH CONGRESS
Congress of the United States
House of Representatives
COMMITTEE ON THE JUDICIARY
2138 RAYBURN HOUSE OFFICE BUILDING
WASHINGTON, DC 20515-6216
(202) 225-3951
judiciary.house.gov

November 1, 2021

Mr. Andrew B. Birge
U.S. Attorney
Western District of Michigan
315 West Allegan, Room 209
Lansing, MI 48933

Dear Mr. Birge:

We are continuing to investigate the troubling attempts by the Department of Justice and the White House to use the heavy hand of federal law enforcement to target concerned parents at local school board meetings and chill their protected First Amendment activity. Because the Department directed you, along with all other U.S. Attorneys, and the Federal Bureau of Investigation (FBI) to take action to address parents attending school board meetings,[1] we respectfully request your assistance with our investigation.

On September 29, 2021, the National School Boards Association (NSBA) sent a letter to President Joe Biden requesting help from the federal government with concerned parents voicing their opinions at school board meetings.[2] The NSBA letter stated that "malice, violence, and threats" against school officials "could be the equivalent of a form of domestic terrorism or hate crimes."[3] The letter cited a number of interactions at school board meetings, none of which rose to the level of domestic terrorism. In fact, the vast majority of incidents cited by the NSBA did not involve threats or violence.[4] Most notably, as an example of domestic terrorism, the NSBA cited an incident in which a father angrily confronted members at a school board meeting in Loudoun County, Virginia about the heinous sexual assault of his daughter.[5]

A mere five days after the NSBA sent its letter to President Biden, on October 4, 2021, Attorney General Merrick Garland issued a shocking memorandum that directed the FBI and

---

[1] Memorandum from Atty Gen. Merrick Garland, U.S. Dep't of Justice, Partnership Among Federal, State, Local, Tribal, And Territorial Law Enforcement to Address Threats Against School Administrators, Board Members, Teachers, and Staff (Oct. 4, 2021).
[2] Letter from Dr. Viola M. Garcia, President, Nat'l School Board Assoc. & Mr. Chip Slaven, Chief Exec. Officer, Nat'l School Board Assoc., to President Joseph R. Biden, White House (Sept. 29, 2021).
[3] *Id.*
[4] *See* Caroline Downey, *Vast majority of incidents cited by school-board group to justify federal intervention didn't involve threats,* NAT'L REV. (Oct. 2, 2021).
[5] *Id.*; *see also* Jessica Chasmar, *Loudoun County father arrested at school board events says school tried to cover up daughter's bathroom assault*, FOX NEWS (Oct. 12, 2021).

U.S. Attorneys' Offices to "convene meetings" in your judicial district "with federal, state, local, Tribal, and territorial leaders" within 30 days.[6] The Justice Department simultaneously issued a press release indicating that the Attorney General's directive would "open dedicated lines of communication for threat reporting, assessment and response by law enforcement"—in other words, create a snitch line for complaints about concerned parents.[7]

During Attorney General Garland's testimony before our Committee on October 21, he appeared to have no idea whether the U.S. Attorney meetings he ordered were actually taking place. He stated: "I don't know whether [the meetings] are ongoing, but I expect and hope that they are going . . . because I did ask that they take place."[8] Attorney General Garland testified that he doubted "there have been meetings in every jurisdiction," but reiterated his belief that it is important for federal law enforcement authorities to conduct these meetings in every judicial district.[9] According to the Attorney General's directives, meetings are to be convened in all 94 judicial districts by November 3, 2021, at the latest.

Following the Attorney General's testimony, the NSBA Board of Directors, apparently recognizing the ill-conceived consequences of its letter and the resulting Justice Department action, issued a new memorandum to its members apologizing for the letter, stating: "On behalf of NSBA, <u>we regret and apologize for the letter</u>."[10] (emphasis in original). Although Attorney General Garland testified that the NSBA letter to President Biden was the basis for his October 4 directive to insert federal law enforcement into local school board matters, the Attorney General has yet to rescind his memorandum. His directives to you and other U.S. Attorneys remain in effect.

Concerned parents voicing their strong opposition to controversial curricula at local schools are not domestic terrorists. Parents have an undisputed right to direct the upbringing and education of their children.[11] When parents, however, cross the line to commit a violent act or issue a criminal threat,[12] state and local authorities are best-equipped to handle these violations of state law. But we must not tolerate the use of the federal law enforcement apparatus to intimidate and silence parents using their Constitutional rights to advocate for their child's future.

To assist our investigation and determine whether these meetings are ongoing, we request that you provide the following documents and information:

---

[6] Memorandum from Atty Gen. Merrick Garland, U.S. Dep't of Justice, Partnership Among Federal, State, Local, Tribal, And Territorial Law Enforcement to Address Threats Against School Administrators, Board Members, Teachers, and Staff (Oct. 4, 2021).

[7] Press Release, U.S. Dep't of Justice, Justice Department Addresses Violent Threats Against School Officials and Teachers (Oct. 4, 2021).

[8] *Oversight of the United States Department of Justice: Hearing Before the H. comm. on the Judiciary,* 117th Cong. at 94 (2021) (testimony from Hon. Merrick Garland, Atty Gen., U.S. Dep't of Justice).

[9] *Id.* at 95.

[10] Memorandum from NSBA Board of Directors, Message to NSBA Members (Oct. 22, 2021).

[11] *Troxel v. Granville,* 530 U.S. 57, 65 (2000) (citing *Meyer v. Nebraska,* 262 U.S. 390, 399 (1923)).

[12] *Merrick Garland's federal offense,* WALL ST. J. (Oct. 6, 2021).

1. All documents and communications referring or relating to convening meeting(s) in your judicial district in accordance with the Attorney General's October 4, 2021 memorandum;

2. All agendas, minutes, and notes created or relied upon by U.S. Attorney's Office employees referring or relating to meeting(s) in your judicial district in accordance with the Attorney General's October 4, 2021 memorandum;

3. Please explain when meeting(s) in your judicial district in accordance with the Attorney General's October 4, 2021 memorandum have occurred or will occur;

4. Please identify by name and title of all U.S. Attorney's Office employees involved in the meeting(s) in your judicial district in accordance with the Attorney General's October 4, 2021 memorandum ;

5. Please identify all federal, state, local, Tribal, and territorial organizations invited to or that have attended the meetings convened in your judicial district in accordance with the October 4, 2021 memorandum; and

6. Please provide all recommendations, both formal and informal, and any meeting minutes produced at the meeting(s) in your judicial district in accordance with the Attorney General's October 4, 2021 memorandum.

Please provide this material as soon as possible but no later than 5:00 p.m. on November 15, 2021.

If you have any questions about this request, please contact Committee staff at (202) 225-6906. Thank you for your attention to this important matter.

Sincerely,

Jim Jordan
Ranking Member

Steve Chabot
Member of Congress

Louie Gohmert
Member of Congress

Darrell Issa
Ranking Member
Subcommittee on Courts, Intellectual Property, and the Internet

Ken Buck
Ranking Member
Subcommittee on Antitrust, Commercial and Administrative Law

Matt Gaetz
Member of Congress

Mike Johnson
Ranking Member
Subcommittee on the Constitution, Civil Rights and Civil Liberties

Andy Biggs
Ranking Member
Subcommittee on Crime, Terrorism and Homeland Security

Tom McClintock
Ranking Member
Subcommittee on Immigration and Citizenship

W. Gregory Steube
Member of Congress

Tom Tiffany
Member of Congress

Thomas Massie
Member of Congress

Chip Roy
Member of Congress

Dan Bishop
Member of Congress

Michelle Fischbach
Member of Congress

Victoria Spartz
Member of Congress

Scott Fitzgerald
Member of Congress

Cliff Bentz
Member of Congress

Burgess Owens
Member of Congress

cc: The Honorable Jerrold L. Nadler
Chairman

Mr. Monty Wilkinson
Director, Executive Office for U.S. Attorneys

JERROLD NADLER, New York
CHAIRMAN

JIM JORDAN, Ohio
RANKING MEMBER

ONE HUNDRED SEVENTEENTH CONGRESS

Congress of the United States

House of Representatives

COMMITTEE ON THE JUDICIARY

2138 RAYBURN HOUSE OFFICE BUILDING

WASHINGTON, DC 20515-6216

(202) 225-3951
judiciary.house.gov

November 1, 2021

Ms. Saima S. Mohsin
Acting U.S. Attorney
Eastern District of Michigan
211 West Fort Street, Suite 2001
Detroit, MI 48226

Dear Ms. Mohsin:

We are continuing to investigate the troubling attempts by the Department of Justice and the White House to use the heavy hand of federal law enforcement to target concerned parents at local school board meetings and chill their protected First Amendment activity. Because the Department directed you, along with all other U.S. Attorneys, and the Federal Bureau of Investigation (FBI) to take action to address parents attending school board meetings,[1] we respectfully request your assistance with our investigation.

On September 29, 2021, the National School Boards Association (NSBA) sent a letter to President Joe Biden requesting help from the federal government with concerned parents voicing their opinions at school board meetings.[2] The NSBA letter stated that "malice, violence, and threats" against school officials "could be the equivalent of a form of domestic terrorism or hate crimes."[3] The letter cited a number of interactions at school board meetings, none of which rose to the level of domestic terrorism. In fact, the vast majority of incidents cited by the NSBA did not involve threats or violence.[4] Most notably, as an example of domestic terrorism, the NSBA cited an incident in which a father angrily confronted members at a school board meeting in Loudoun County, Virginia about the heinous sexual assault of his daughter.[5]

A mere five days after the NSBA sent its letter to President Biden, on October 4, 2021, Attorney General Merrick Garland issued a shocking memorandum that directed the FBI and

---

[1] Memorandum from Atty Gen. Merrick Garland, U.S. Dep't of Justice, Partnership Among Federal, State, Local, Tribal, And Territorial Law Enforcement to Address Threats Against School Administrators, Board Members, Teachers, and Staff (Oct. 4, 2021).
[2] Letter from Dr. Viola M. Garcia, President, Nat'l School Board Assoc. & Mr. Chip Slaven, Chief Exec. Officer, Nat'l School Board Assoc., to President Joseph R. Biden, White House (Sept. 29, 2021).
[3] *Id.*
[4] *See* Caroline Downey, *Vast majority of incidents cited by school-board group to justify federal intervention didn't involve threats,* NAT'L REV. (Oct. 2, 2021).
[5] *Id.*; *see also* Jessica Chasmar, *Loudoun County father arrested at school board events says school tried to cover up daughter's bathroom assault*, FOX NEWS (Oct. 12, 2021).

U.S. Attorneys' Offices to "convene meetings" in your judicial district "with federal, state, local, Tribal, and territorial leaders" within 30 days.[6] The Justice Department simultaneously issued a press release indicating that the Attorney General's directive would "open dedicated lines of communication for threat reporting, assessment and response by law enforcement"—in other words, create a snitch line for complaints about concerned parents.[7]

During Attorney General Garland's testimony before our Committee on October 21, he appeared to have no idea whether the U.S. Attorney meetings he ordered were actually taking place. He stated: "I don't know whether [the meetings] are ongoing, but I expect and hope that they are going . . . because I did ask that they take place."[8] Attorney General Garland testified that he doubted "there have been meetings in every jurisdiction," but reiterated his belief that it is important for federal law enforcement authorities to conduct these meetings in every judicial district.[9] According to the Attorney General's directives, meetings are to be convened in all 94 judicial districts by November 3, 2021, at the latest.

Following the Attorney General's testimony, the NSBA Board of Directors, apparently recognizing the ill-conceived consequences of its letter and the resulting Justice Department action, issued a new memorandum to its members apologizing for the letter, stating: "On behalf of NSBA, <u>we regret and apologize for the letter</u>."[10] (emphasis in original). Although Attorney General Garland testified that the NSBA letter to President Biden was the basis for his October 4 directive to insert federal law enforcement into local school board matters, the Attorney General has yet to rescind his memorandum. His directives to you and other U.S. Attorneys remain in effect.

Concerned parents voicing their strong opposition to controversial curricula at local schools are not domestic terrorists. Parents have an undisputed right to direct the upbringing and education of their children.[11] When parents, however, cross the line to commit a violent act or issue a criminal threat,[12] state and local authorities are best-equipped to handle these violations of state law. But we must not tolerate the use of the federal law enforcement apparatus to intimidate and silence parents using their Constitutional rights to advocate for their child's future.

To assist our investigation and determine whether these meetings are ongoing, we request that you provide the following documents and information:

---

[6] Memorandum from Atty Gen. Merrick Garland, U.S. Dep't of Justice, Partnership Among Federal, State, Local, Tribal, And Territorial Law Enforcement to Address Threats Against School Administrators, Board Members, Teachers, and Staff (Oct. 4, 2021).
[7] Press Release, U.S. Dep't of Justice, Justice Department Addresses Violent Threats Against School Officials and Teachers (Oct. 4, 2021).
[8] *Oversight of the United States Department of Justice: Hearing Before the H. comm. on the Judiciary,* 117th Cong. at 94 (2021) (testimony from Hon. Merrick Garland, Atty Gen., U.S. Dep't of Justice).
[9] *Id.* at 95.
[10] Memorandum from NSBA Board of Directors, Message to NSBA Members (Oct. 22, 2021).
[11] *Troxel v. Granville,* 530 U.S. 57, 65 (2000) (citing *Meyer v. Nebraska,* 262 U.S. 390, 399 (1923)).
[12] *Merrick Garland's federal offense,* WALL ST. J. (Oct. 6, 2021).

1. All documents and communications referring or relating to convening meeting(s) in your judicial district in accordance with the Attorney General's October 4, 2021 memorandum;

2. All agendas, minutes, and notes created or relied upon by U.S. Attorney's Office employees referring or relating to meeting(s) in your judicial district in accordance with the Attorney General's October 4, 2021 memorandum;

3. Please explain when meeting(s) in your judicial district in accordance with the Attorney General's October 4, 2021 memorandum have occurred or will occur;

4. Please identify by name and title of all U.S. Attorney's Office employees involved in the meeting(s) in your judicial district in accordance with the Attorney General's October 4, 2021 memorandum ;

5. Please identify all federal, state, local, Tribal, and territorial organizations invited to or that have attended the meetings convened in your judicial district in accordance with the October 4, 2021 memorandum; and

6. Please provide all recommendations, both formal and informal, and any meeting minutes produced at the meeting(s) in your judicial district in accordance with the Attorney General's October 4, 2021 memorandum.

Please provide this material as soon as possible but no later than 5:00 p.m. on November 15, 2021.

If you have any questions about this request, please contact Committee staff at (202) 225-6906. Thank you for your attention to this important matter.

Sincerely,

Jim Jordan
Ranking Member

Steve Chabot
Member of Congress

Louie Gohmert
Member of Congress

Darrell Issa
Ranking Member
Subcommittee on Courts, Intellectual Property, and the Internet

Ken Buck
Ranking Member
Subcommittee on Antitrust, Commercial and Administrative Law

Matt Gaetz
Member of Congress

Mike Johnson
Ranking Member
Subcommittee on the Constitution, Civil Rights and Civil Liberties

Andy Biggs
Ranking Member
Subcommittee on Crime, Terrorism and Homeland Security

Tom McClintock
Ranking Member
Subcommittee on Immigration and Citizenship

W. Gregory Steube
Member of Congress

Tom Tiffany
Member of Congress

Thomas Massie
Member of Congress

Chip Roy
Member of Congress

Dan Bishop
Member of Congress

Michelle Fischbach
Member of Congress

Victoria Spartz
Member of Congress

Scott Fitzgerald
Member of Congress

Cliff Bentz
Member of Congress

Burgess Owens
Member of Congress

cc: The Honorable Jerrold L. Nadler
Chairman

Mr. Monty Wilkinson
Director, Executive Office for U.S. Attorneys

JERROLD NADLER, New York
CHAIRMAN

JIM JORDAN, Ohio
RANKING MEMBER

ONE HUNDRED SEVENTEENTH CONGRESS
Congress of the United States
House of Representatives
COMMITTEE ON THE JUDICIARY
2138 RAYBURN HOUSE OFFICE BUILDING
WASHINGTON, DC 20515–6216
(202) 225–3951
judiciary.house.gov

November 1, 2021

Mr. W. Anders Folk
Acting U.S. Attorney
District of Minnesota
300 South 4th Street, Suite 600
Minneapolis, MN 55415

Dear Mr. Folk:

We are continuing to investigate the troubling attempts by the Department of Justice and the White House to use the heavy hand of federal law enforcement to target concerned parents at local school board meetings and chill their protected First Amendment activity. Because the Department directed you, along with all other U.S. Attorneys, and the Federal Bureau of Investigation (FBI) to take action to address parents attending school board meetings,[1] we respectfully request your assistance with our investigation.

On September 29, 2021, the National School Boards Association (NSBA) sent a letter to President Joe Biden requesting help from the federal government with concerned parents voicing their opinions at school board meetings.[2] The NSBA letter stated that "malice, violence, and threats" against school officials "could be the equivalent of a form of domestic terrorism or hate crimes."[3] The letter cited a number of interactions at school board meetings, none of which rose to the level of domestic terrorism. In fact, the vast majority of incidents cited by the NSBA did not involve threats or violence.[4] Most notably, as an example of domestic terrorism, the NSBA cited an incident in which a father angrily confronted members at a school board meeting in Loudoun County, Virginia about the heinous sexual assault of his daughter.[5]

A mere five days after the NSBA sent its letter to President Biden, on October 4, 2021, Attorney General Merrick Garland issued a shocking memorandum that directed the FBI and

---

[1] Memorandum from Atty Gen. Merrick Garland, U.S. Dep't of Justice, Partnership Among Federal, State, Local, Tribal, And Territorial Law Enforcement to Address Threats Against School Administrators, Board Members, Teachers, and Staff (Oct. 4, 2021).
[2] Letter from Dr. Viola M. Garcia, President, Nat'l School Board Assoc. & Mr. Chip Slaven, Chief Exec. Officer, Nat'l School Board Assoc., to President Joseph R. Biden, White House (Sept. 29, 2021).
[3] *Id.*
[4] *See* Caroline Downey, *Vast majority of incidents cited by school-board group to justify federal intervention didn't involve threats,* NAT'L REV. (Oct. 2, 2021).
[5] *Id.*; *see also* Jessica Chasmar, *Loudoun County father arrested at school board events says school tried to cover up daughter's bathroom assault*, FOX NEWS (Oct. 12, 2021).

U.S. Attorneys' Offices to "convene meetings" in your judicial district "with federal, state, local, Tribal, and territorial leaders" within 30 days.[6] The Justice Department simultaneously issued a press release indicating that the Attorney General's directive would "open dedicated lines of communication for threat reporting, assessment and response by law enforcement"—in other words, create a snitch line for complaints about concerned parents.[7]

During Attorney General Garland's testimony before our Committee on October 21, he appeared to have no idea whether the U.S. Attorney meetings he ordered were actually taking place. He stated: "I don't know whether [the meetings] are ongoing, but I expect and hope that they are going . . . because I did ask that they take place."[8] Attorney General Garland testified that he doubted "there have been meetings in every jurisdiction," but reiterated his belief that it is important for federal law enforcement authorities to conduct these meetings in every judicial district.[9] According to the Attorney General's directives, meetings are to be convened in all 94 judicial districts by November 3, 2021, at the latest.

Following the Attorney General's testimony, the NSBA Board of Directors, apparently recognizing the ill-conceived consequences of its letter and the resulting Justice Department action, issued a new memorandum to its members apologizing for the letter, stating: "On behalf of NSBA, <u>we regret and apologize for the letter</u>."[10] (emphasis in original). Although Attorney General Garland testified that the NSBA letter to President Biden was the basis for his October 4 directive to insert federal law enforcement into local school board matters, the Attorney General has yet to rescind his memorandum. His directives to you and other U.S. Attorneys remain in effect.

Concerned parents voicing their strong opposition to controversial curricula at local schools are not domestic terrorists. Parents have an undisputed right to direct the upbringing and education of their children.[11] When parents, however, cross the line to commit a violent act or issue a criminal threat,[12] state and local authorities are best-equipped to handle these violations of state law. But we must not tolerate the use of the federal law enforcement apparatus to intimidate and silence parents using their Constitutional rights to advocate for their child's future.

To assist our investigation and determine whether these meetings are ongoing, we request that you provide the following documents and information:

---

[6] Memorandum from Atty Gen. Merrick Garland, U.S. Dep't of Justice, Partnership Among Federal, State, Local, Tribal, And Territorial Law Enforcement to Address Threats Against School Administrators, Board Members, Teachers, and Staff (Oct. 4, 2021).

[7] Press Release, U.S. Dep't of Justice, Justice Department Addresses Violent Threats Against School Officials and Teachers (Oct. 4, 2021).

[8] *Oversight of the United States Department of Justice: Hearing Before the H. comm. on the Judiciary,* 117th Cong. at 94 (2021) (testimony from Hon. Merrick Garland, Atty Gen., U.S. Dep't of Justice).

[9] *Id.* at 95.

[10] Memorandum from NSBA Board of Directors, Message to NSBA Members (Oct. 22, 2021).

[11] *Troxel v. Granville,* 530 U.S. 57, 65 (2000) (citing *Meyer v. Nebraska,* 262 U.S. 390, 399 (1923)).

[12] *Merrick Garland's federal offense,* WALL ST. J. (Oct. 6, 2021).

1. All documents and communications referring or relating to convening meeting(s) in your judicial district in accordance with the Attorney General's October 4, 2021 memorandum;

2. All agendas, minutes, and notes created or relied upon by U.S. Attorney's Office employees referring or relating to meeting(s) in your judicial district in accordance with the Attorney General's October 4, 2021 memorandum;

3. Please explain when meeting(s) in your judicial district in accordance with the Attorney General's October 4, 2021 memorandum have occurred or will occur;

4. Please identify by name and title of all U.S. Attorney's Office employees involved in the meeting(s) in your judicial district in accordance with the Attorney General's October 4, 2021 memorandum ;

5. Please identify all federal, state, local, Tribal, and territorial organizations invited to or that have attended the meetings convened in your judicial district in accordance with the October 4, 2021 memorandum; and

6. Please provide all recommendations, both formal and informal, and any meeting minutes produced at the meeting(s) in your judicial district in accordance with the Attorney General's October 4, 2021 memorandum.

Please provide this material as soon as possible but no later than 5:00 p.m. on November 15, 2021.

If you have any questions about this request, please contact Committee staff at (202) 225-6906. Thank you for your attention to this important matter.

Sincerely,

Jim Jordan
Ranking Member

Steve Chabot
Member of Congress

Louie Gohmert
Member of Congress

Darrell Issa
Ranking Member
Subcommittee on Courts, Intellectual Property, and the Internet

Ken Buck
Ranking Member
Subcommittee on Antitrust, Commercial and Administrative Law

Matt Gaetz
Member of Congress

Mike Johnson
Ranking Member
Subcommittee on the Constitution, Civil Rights and Civil Liberties

Andy Biggs
Ranking Member
Subcommittee on Crime, Terrorism and Homeland Security

Tom McClintock
Ranking Member
Subcommittee on Immigration and Citizenship

W. Gregory Steube
Member of Congress

Tom Tiffany
Member of Congress

Thomas Massie
Member of Congress

Chip Roy
Member of Congress

Dan Bishop
Member of Congress

Michelle Fischbach
Member of Congress

Victoria Spartz
Member of Congress

Scott Fitzgerald
Member of Congress

Cliff Bentz
Member of Congress

Burgess Owens
Member of Congress

cc: The Honorable Jerrold L. Nadler
Chairman

Mr. Monty Wilkinson
Director, Executive Office for U.S. Attorneys

JERROLD NADLER, New York
CHAIRMAN

JIM JORDAN, Ohio
RANKING MEMBER

ONE HUNDRED SEVENTEENTH CONGRESS

Congress of the United States
House of Representatives

COMMITTEE ON THE JUDICIARY
2138 RAYBURN HOUSE OFFICE BUILDING
WASHINGTON, DC 20515–6216
(202) 225–3951
judiciary.house.gov

November 1, 2021

Ms. Sayler A. Fleming
U.S. Attorney
Eastern District of Missouri
111 South 10th Street, 20th Floor
St. Louis, MO 63102

Dear Ms. Fleming:

We are continuing to investigate the troubling attempts by the Department of Justice and the White House to use the heavy hand of federal law enforcement to target concerned parents at local school board meetings and chill their protected First Amendment activity. Because the Department directed you, along with all other U.S. Attorneys, and the Federal Bureau of Investigation (FBI) to take action to address parents attending school board meetings,[1] we respectfully request your assistance with our investigation.

On September 29, 2021, the National School Boards Association (NSBA) sent a letter to President Joe Biden requesting help from the federal government with concerned parents voicing their opinions at school board meetings.[2] The NSBA letter stated that "malice, violence, and threats" against school officials "could be the equivalent of a form of domestic terrorism or hate crimes."[3] The letter cited a number of interactions at school board meetings, none of which rose to the level of domestic terrorism. In fact, the vast majority of incidents cited by the NSBA did not involve threats or violence.[4] Most notably, as an example of domestic terrorism, the NSBA cited an incident in which a father angrily confronted members at a school board meeting in Loudoun County, Virginia about the heinous sexual assault of his daughter.[5]

A mere five days after the NSBA sent its letter to President Biden, on October 4, 2021, Attorney General Merrick Garland issued a shocking memorandum that directed the FBI and

---

[1] Memorandum from Atty Gen. Merrick Garland, U.S. Dep't of Justice, Partnership Among Federal, State, Local, Tribal, And Territorial Law Enforcement to Address Threats Against School Administrators, Board Members, Teachers, and Staff (Oct. 4, 2021).
[2] Letter from Dr. Viola M. Garcia, President, Nat'l School Board Assoc. & Mr. Chip Slaven, Chief Exec. Officer, Nat'l School Board Assoc., to President Joseph R. Biden, White House (Sept. 29, 2021).
[3] *Id.*
[4] *See* Caroline Downey, *Vast majority of incidents cited by school-board group to justify federal intervention didn't involve threats,* NAT'L REV. (Oct. 2, 2021).
[5] *Id.*; *see also* Jessica Chasmar, *Loudoun County father arrested at school board events says school tried to cover up daughter's bathroom assault*, FOX NEWS (Oct. 12, 2021).

U.S. Attorneys' Offices to "convene meetings" in your judicial district "with federal, state, local, Tribal, and territorial leaders" within 30 days.[6] The Justice Department simultaneously issued a press release indicating that the Attorney General's directive would "open dedicated lines of communication for threat reporting, assessment and response by law enforcement"—in other words, create a snitch line for complaints about concerned parents.[7]

During Attorney General Garland's testimony before our Committee on October 21, he appeared to have no idea whether the U.S. Attorney meetings he ordered were actually taking place. He stated: "I don't know whether [the meetings] are ongoing, but I expect and hope that they are going . . . because I did ask that they take place."[8] Attorney General Garland testified that he doubted "there have been meetings in every jurisdiction," but reiterated his belief that it is important for federal law enforcement authorities to conduct these meetings in every judicial district.[9] According to the Attorney General's directives, meetings are to be convened in all 94 judicial districts by November 3, 2021, at the latest.

Following the Attorney General's testimony, the NSBA Board of Directors, apparently recognizing the ill-conceived consequences of its letter and the resulting Justice Department action, issued a new memorandum to its members apologizing for the letter, stating: "On behalf of NSBA, we regret and apologize for the letter."[10] (emphasis in original). Although Attorney General Garland testified that the NSBA letter to President Biden was the basis for his October 4 directive to insert federal law enforcement into local school board matters, the Attorney General has yet to rescind his memorandum. His directives to you and other U.S. Attorneys remain in effect.

Concerned parents voicing their strong opposition to controversial curricula at local schools are not domestic terrorists. Parents have an undisputed right to direct the upbringing and education of their children.[11] When parents, however, cross the line to commit a violent act or issue a criminal threat,[12] state and local authorities are best-equipped to handle these violations of state law. But we must not tolerate the use of the federal law enforcement apparatus to intimidate and silence parents using their Constitutional rights to advocate for their child's future.

To assist our investigation and determine whether these meetings are ongoing, we request that you provide the following documents and information:

---

[6] Memorandum from Atty Gen. Merrick Garland, U.S. Dep't of Justice, Partnership Among Federal, State, Local, Tribal, And Territorial Law Enforcement to Address Threats Against School Administrators, Board Members, Teachers, and Staff (Oct. 4, 2021).
[7] Press Release, U.S. Dep't of Justice, Justice Department Addresses Violent Threats Against School Officials and Teachers (Oct. 4, 2021).
[8] *Oversight of the United States Department of Justice: Hearing Before the H. comm. on the Judiciary,* 117th Cong. at 94 (2021) (testimony from Hon. Merrick Garland, Atty Gen., U.S. Dep't of Justice).
[9] *Id.* at 95.
[10] Memorandum from NSBA Board of Directors, Message to NSBA Members (Oct. 22, 2021).
[11] *Troxel v. Granville,* 530 U.S. 57, 65 (2000) (citing *Meyer v. Nebraska,* 262 U.S. 390, 399 (1923)).
[12] *Merrick Garland's federal offense,* WALL ST. J. (Oct. 6, 2021).

1. All documents and communications referring or relating to convening meeting(s) in your judicial district in accordance with the Attorney General's October 4, 2021 memorandum;

2. All agendas, minutes, and notes created or relied upon by U.S. Attorney's Office employees referring or relating to meeting(s) in your judicial district in accordance with the Attorney General's October 4, 2021 memorandum;

3. Please explain when meeting(s) in your judicial district in accordance with the Attorney General's October 4, 2021 memorandum have occurred or will occur;

4. Please identify by name and title of all U.S. Attorney's Office employees involved in the meeting(s) in your judicial district in accordance with the Attorney General's October 4, 2021 memorandum ;

5. Please identify all federal, state, local, Tribal, and territorial organizations invited to or that have attended the meetings convened in your judicial district in accordance with the October 4, 2021 memorandum; and

6. Please provide all recommendations, both formal and informal, and any meeting minutes produced at the meeting(s) in your judicial district in accordance with the Attorney General's October 4, 2021 memorandum.

Please provide this material as soon as possible but no later than 5:00 p.m. on November 15, 2021.

If you have any questions about this request, please contact Committee staff at (202) 225-6906. Thank you for your attention to this important matter.

Sincerely,

Jim Jordan
Ranking Member

Steve Chabot
Member of Congress

Louie Gohmert
Member of Congress

Darrell Issa
Ranking Member
Subcommittee on Courts, Intellectual Property, and the Internet

Ms. Sayler A. Fleming
November 1, 2021
Page 4

Ken Buck
Ranking Member
Subcommittee on Antitrust, Commercial
and Administrative Law

Matt Gaetz
Member of Congress

Mike Johnson
Ranking Member
Subcommittee on the Constitution,
Civil Rights and Civil Liberties

Andy Biggs
Ranking Member
Subcommittee on Crime, Terrorism
and Homeland Security

Tom McClintock
Ranking Member
Subcommittee on Immigration
and Citizenship

W. Gregory Steube
Member of Congress

Tom Tiffany
Member of Congress

Thomas Massie
Member of Congress

Chip Roy
Member of Congress

Dan Bishop
Member of Congress

Michelle Fischbach
Member of Congress

Victoria Spartz
Member of Congress

Scott Fitzgerald
Member of Congress

Cliff Bentz
Member of Congress

Burgess Owens
Member of Congress

cc: The Honorable Jerrold L. Nadler
Chairman

Mr. Monty Wilkinson
Director, Executive Office for U.S. Attorneys

JERROLD NADLER, New York
CHAIRMAN

JIM JORDAN, Ohio
RANKING MEMBER

ONE HUNDRED SEVENTEENTH CONGRESS
Congress of the United States
House of Representatives
COMMITTEE ON THE JUDICIARY
2138 RAYBURN HOUSE OFFICE BUILDING
WASHINGTON, DC 20515-6216
(202) 225-3951
judiciary.house.gov

November 1, 2021

Ms. Teresa A. Moore
Acting U.S. Attorney
Western District of Missouri
400 East 9th Street, Room 5510
Kansas City, MO 64106

Dear Ms. Moore:

We are continuing to investigate the troubling attempts by the Department of Justice and the White House to use the heavy hand of federal law enforcement to target concerned parents at local school board meetings and chill their protected First Amendment activity. Because the Department directed you, along with all other U.S. Attorneys, and the Federal Bureau of Investigation (FBI) to take action to address parents attending school board meetings,[1] we respectfully request your assistance with our investigation.

On September 29, 2021, the National School Boards Association (NSBA) sent a letter to President Joe Biden requesting help from the federal government with concerned parents voicing their opinions at school board meetings.[2] The NSBA letter stated that "malice, violence, and threats" against school officials "could be the equivalent of a form of domestic terrorism or hate crimes."[3] The letter cited a number of interactions at school board meetings, none of which rose to the level of domestic terrorism. In fact, the vast majority of incidents cited by the NSBA did not involve threats or violence.[4] Most notably, as an example of domestic terrorism, the NSBA cited an incident in which a father angrily confronted members at a school board meeting in Loudoun County, Virginia about the heinous sexual assault of his daughter.[5]

A mere five days after the NSBA sent its letter to President Biden, on October 4, 2021, Attorney General Merrick Garland issued a shocking memorandum that directed the FBI and

---

[1] Memorandum from Atty Gen. Merrick Garland, U.S. Dep't of Justice, Partnership Among Federal, State, Local, Tribal, And Territorial Law Enforcement to Address Threats Against School Administrators, Board Members, Teachers, and Staff (Oct. 4, 2021).
[2] Letter from Dr. Viola M. Garcia, President, Nat'l School Board Assoc. & Mr. Chip Slaven, Chief Exec. Officer, Nat'l School Board Assoc., to President Joseph R. Biden, White House (Sept. 29, 2021).
[3] *Id.*
[4] *See* Caroline Downey, *Vast majority of incidents cited by school-board group to justify federal intervention didn't involve threats,* NAT'L REV. (Oct. 2, 2021).
[5] *Id.*; *see also* Jessica Chasmar, *Loudoun County father arrested at school board events says school tried to cover up daughter's bathroom assault*, FOX NEWS (Oct. 12, 2021).

U.S. Attorneys' Offices to "convene meetings" in your judicial district "with federal, state, local, Tribal, and territorial leaders" within 30 days.[6] The Justice Department simultaneously issued a press release indicating that the Attorney General's directive would "open dedicated lines of communication for threat reporting, assessment and response by law enforcement"—in other words, create a snitch line for complaints about concerned parents.[7]

During Attorney General Garland's testimony before our Committee on October 21, he appeared to have no idea whether the U.S. Attorney meetings he ordered were actually taking place. He stated: "I don't know whether [the meetings] are ongoing, but I expect and hope that they are going . . . because I did ask that they take place."[8] Attorney General Garland testified that he doubted "there have been meetings in every jurisdiction," but reiterated his belief that it is important for federal law enforcement authorities to conduct these meetings in every judicial district.[9] According to the Attorney General's directives, meetings are to be convened in all 94 judicial districts by November 3, 2021, at the latest.

Following the Attorney General's testimony, the NSBA Board of Directors, apparently recognizing the ill-conceived consequences of its letter and the resulting Justice Department action, issued a new memorandum to its members apologizing for the letter, stating: "On behalf of NSBA, we regret and apologize for the letter."[10] (emphasis in original). Although Attorney General Garland testified that the NSBA letter to President Biden was the basis for his October 4 directive to insert federal law enforcement into local school board matters, the Attorney General has yet to rescind his memorandum. His directives to you and other U.S. Attorneys remain in effect.

Concerned parents voicing their strong opposition to controversial curricula at local schools are not domestic terrorists. Parents have an undisputed right to direct the upbringing and education of their children.[11] When parents, however, cross the line to commit a violent act or issue a criminal threat,[12] state and local authorities are best-equipped to handle these violations of state law. But we must not tolerate the use of the federal law enforcement apparatus to intimidate and silence parents using their Constitutional rights to advocate for their child's future.

To assist our investigation and determine whether these meetings are ongoing, we request that you provide the following documents and information:

---

[6] Memorandum from Atty Gen. Merrick Garland, U.S. Dep't of Justice, Partnership Among Federal, State, Local, Tribal, And Territorial Law Enforcement to Address Threats Against School Administrators, Board Members, Teachers, and Staff (Oct. 4, 2021).
[7] Press Release, U.S. Dep't of Justice, Justice Department Addresses Violent Threats Against School Officials and Teachers (Oct. 4, 2021).
[8] *Oversight of the United States Department of Justice: Hearing Before the H. comm. on the Judiciary,* 117th Cong. at 94 (2021) (testimony from Hon. Merrick Garland, Atty Gen., U.S. Dep't of Justice).
[9] *Id.* at 95.
[10] Memorandum from NSBA Board of Directors, Message to NSBA Members (Oct. 22, 2021).
[11] *Troxel v. Granville,* 530 U.S. 57, 65 (2000) (citing *Meyer v. Nebraska,* 262 U.S. 390, 399 (1923)).
[12] *Merrick Garland's federal offense,* WALL ST. J. (Oct. 6, 2021).

1. All documents and communications referring or relating to convening meeting(s) in your judicial district in accordance with the Attorney General's October 4, 2021 memorandum;

2. All agendas, minutes, and notes created or relied upon by U.S. Attorney's Office employees referring or relating to meeting(s) in your judicial district in accordance with the Attorney General's October 4, 2021 memorandum;

3. Please explain when meeting(s) in your judicial district in accordance with the Attorney General's October 4, 2021 memorandum have occurred or will occur;

4. Please identify by name and title of all U.S. Attorney's Office employees involved in the meeting(s) in your judicial district in accordance with the Attorney General's October 4, 2021 memorandum ;

5. Please identify all federal, state, local, Tribal, and territorial organizations invited to or that have attended the meetings convened in your judicial district in accordance with the October 4, 2021 memorandum; and

6. Please provide all recommendations, both formal and informal, and any meeting minutes produced at the meeting(s) in your judicial district in accordance with the Attorney General's October 4, 2021 memorandum.

Please provide this material as soon as possible but no later than 5:00 p.m. on November 15, 2021.

If you have any questions about this request, please contact Committee staff at (202) 225-6906. Thank you for your attention to this important matter.

Sincerely,

Jim Jordan
Ranking Member

Steve Chabot
Member of Congress

Louie Gohmert
Member of Congress

Darrell Issa
Ranking Member
Subcommittee on Courts, Intellectual Property, and the Internet

Ken Buck
Ranking Member
Subcommittee on Antitrust, Commercial and Administrative Law

Matt Gaetz
Member of Congress

Mike Johnson
Ranking Member
Subcommittee on the Constitution, Civil Rights and Civil Liberties

Andy Biggs
Ranking Member
Subcommittee on Crime, Terrorism and Homeland Security

Tom McClintock
Ranking Member
Subcommittee on Immigration and Citizenship

W. Gregory Steube
Member of Congress

Tom Tiffany
Member of Congress

Thomas Massie
Member of Congress

Chip Roy
Member of Congress

Dan Bishop
Member of Congress

Michelle Fischbach
Member of Congress

Victoria Spartz
Member of Congress

Scott Fitzgerald
Member of Congress

Cliff Bentz
Member of Congress

Burgess Owens
Member of Congress

cc: The Honorable Jerrold L. Nadler
Chairman

Mr. Monty Wilkinson
Director, Executive Office for U.S. Attorneys

JERROLD NADLER, New York
CHAIRMAN

JIM JORDAN, Ohio
RANKING MEMBER

ONE HUNDRED SEVENTEENTH CONGRESS

Congress of the United States

House of Representatives

COMMITTEE ON THE JUDICIARY

2138 RAYBURN HOUSE OFFICE BUILDING

WASHINGTON, DC 20515-6216

(202) 225-3951
judiciary.house.gov

November 1, 2021

Mr. James C. "Clay" Joyner
Acting U.S. Attorney
Northern District of Mississippi
900 Jefferson Avenue
Oxford, MS 38655

Dear Mr. Joyner:

We are continuing to investigate the troubling attempts by the Department of Justice and the White House to use the heavy hand of federal law enforcement to target concerned parents at local school board meetings and chill their protected First Amendment activity. Because the Department directed you, along with all other U.S. Attorneys, and the Federal Bureau of Investigation (FBI) to take action to address parents attending school board meetings,[1] we respectfully request your assistance with our investigation.

On September 29, 2021, the National School Boards Association (NSBA) sent a letter to President Joe Biden requesting help from the federal government with concerned parents voicing their opinions at school board meetings.[2] The NSBA letter stated that "malice, violence, and threats" against school officials "could be the equivalent of a form of domestic terrorism or hate crimes."[3] The letter cited a number of interactions at school board meetings, none of which rose to the level of domestic terrorism. In fact, the vast majority of incidents cited by the NSBA did not involve threats or violence.[4] Most notably, as an example of domestic terrorism, the NSBA cited an incident in which a father angrily confronted members at a school board meeting in Loudoun County, Virginia about the heinous sexual assault of his daughter.[5]

A mere five days after the NSBA sent its letter to President Biden, on October 4, 2021, Attorney General Merrick Garland issued a shocking memorandum that directed the FBI and

---

[1] Memorandum from Atty Gen. Merrick Garland, U.S. Dep't of Justice, Partnership Among Federal, State, Local, Tribal, And Territorial Law Enforcement to Address Threats Against School Administrators, Board Members, Teachers, and Staff (Oct. 4, 2021).
[2] Letter from Dr. Viola M. Garcia, President, Nat'l School Board Assoc. & Mr. Chip Slaven, Chief Exec. Officer, Nat'l School Board Assoc., to President Joseph R. Biden, White House (Sept. 29, 2021).
[3] *Id.*
[4] *See* Caroline Downey, *Vast majority of incidents cited by school-board group to justify federal intervention didn't involve threats,* NAT'L REV. (Oct. 2, 2021).
[5] *Id.*; *see also* Jessica Chasmar, *Loudoun County father arrested at school board events says school tried to cover up daughter's bathroom assault*, FOX NEWS (Oct. 12, 2021).

U.S. Attorneys' Offices to "convene meetings" in your judicial district "with federal, state, local, Tribal, and territorial leaders" within 30 days.[6] The Justice Department simultaneously issued a press release indicating that the Attorney General's directive would "open dedicated lines of communication for threat reporting, assessment and response by law enforcement"—in other words, create a snitch line for complaints about concerned parents.[7]

During Attorney General Garland's testimony before our Committee on October 21, he appeared to have no idea whether the U.S. Attorney meetings he ordered were actually taking place. He stated: "I don't know whether [the meetings] are ongoing, but I expect and hope that they are going . . . because I did ask that they take place."[8] Attorney General Garland testified that he doubted "there have been meetings in every jurisdiction," but reiterated his belief that it is important for federal law enforcement authorities to conduct these meetings in every judicial district.[9] According to the Attorney General's directives, meetings are to be convened in all 94 judicial districts by November 3, 2021, at the latest.

Following the Attorney General's testimony, the NSBA Board of Directors, apparently recognizing the ill-conceived consequences of its letter and the resulting Justice Department action, issued a new memorandum to its members apologizing for the letter, stating: "On behalf of NSBA, <u>we regret and apologize for the letter</u>."[10] (emphasis in original). Although Attorney General Garland testified that the NSBA letter to President Biden was the basis for his October 4 directive to insert federal law enforcement into local school board matters, the Attorney General has yet to rescind his memorandum. His directives to you and other U.S. Attorneys remain in effect.

Concerned parents voicing their strong opposition to controversial curricula at local schools are not domestic terrorists. Parents have an undisputed right to direct the upbringing and education of their children.[11] When parents, however, cross the line to commit a violent act or issue a criminal threat,[12] state and local authorities are best-equipped to handle these violations of state law. But we must not tolerate the use of the federal law enforcement apparatus to intimidate and silence parents using their Constitutional rights to advocate for their child's future.

To assist our investigation and determine whether these meetings are ongoing, we request that you provide the following documents and information:

---

[6] Memorandum from Atty Gen. Merrick Garland, U.S. Dep't of Justice, Partnership Among Federal, State, Local, Tribal, And Territorial Law Enforcement to Address Threats Against School Administrators, Board Members, Teachers, and Staff (Oct. 4, 2021).

[7] Press Release, U.S. Dep't of Justice, Justice Department Addresses Violent Threats Against School Officials and Teachers (Oct. 4, 2021).

[8] *Oversight of the United States Department of Justice: Hearing Before the H. comm. on the Judiciary,* 117th Cong. at 94 (2021) (testimony from Hon. Merrick Garland, Atty Gen., U.S. Dep't of Justice).

[9] *Id.* at 95.

[10] Memorandum from NSBA Board of Directors, Message to NSBA Members (Oct. 22, 2021).

[11] *Troxel v. Granville,* 530 U.S. 57, 65 (2000) (citing *Meyer v. Nebraska,* 262 U.S. 390, 399 (1923)).

[12] *Merrick Garland's federal offense,* WALL ST. J. (Oct. 6, 2021).

1. All documents and communications referring or relating to convening meeting(s) in your judicial district in accordance with the Attorney General's October 4, 2021 memorandum;

2. All agendas, minutes, and notes created or relied upon by U.S. Attorney's Office employees referring or relating to meeting(s) in your judicial district in accordance with the Attorney General's October 4, 2021 memorandum;

3. Please explain when meeting(s) in your judicial district in accordance with the Attorney General's October 4, 2021 memorandum have occurred or will occur;

4. Please identify by name and title of all U.S. Attorney's Office employees involved in the meeting(s) in your judicial district in accordance with the Attorney General's October 4, 2021 memorandum ;

5. Please identify all federal, state, local, Tribal, and territorial organizations invited to or that have attended the meetings convened in your judicial district in accordance with the October 4, 2021 memorandum; and

6. Please provide all recommendations, both formal and informal, and any meeting minutes produced at the meeting(s) in your judicial district in accordance with the Attorney General's October 4, 2021 memorandum.

Please provide this material as soon as possible but no later than 5:00 p.m. on November 15, 2021.

If you have any questions about this request, please contact Committee staff at (202) 225-6906. Thank you for your attention to this important matter.

Sincerely,

Jim Jordan
Ranking Member

Steve Chabot
Member of Congress

Louie Gohmert
Member of Congress

Darrell Issa
Ranking Member
Subcommittee on Courts, Intellectual Property, and the Internet

Ken Buck
Ranking Member
Subcommittee on Antitrust, Commercial and Administrative Law

Matt Gaetz
Member of Congress

Mike Johnson
Ranking Member
Subcommittee on the Constitution, Civil Rights and Civil Liberties

Andy Biggs
Ranking Member
Subcommittee on Crime, Terrorism and Homeland Security

Tom McClintock
Ranking Member
Subcommittee on Immigration and Citizenship

W. Gregory Steube
Member of Congress

Tom Tiffany
Member of Congress

Thomas Massie
Member of Congress

Chip Roy
Member of Congress

Dan Bishop
Member of Congress

Michelle Fischbach
Member of Congress

Victoria Spartz
Member of Congress

Scott Fitzgerald
Member of Congress

Cliff Bentz
Member of Congress

Burgess Owens
Member of Congress

cc: The Honorable Jerrold L. Nadler
Chairman

Mr. Monty Wilkinson
Director, Executive Office for U.S. Attorneys

JERROLD NADLER, New York
CHAIRMAN

JIM JORDAN, Ohio
RANKING MEMBER

ONE HUNDRED SEVENTEENTH CONGRESS

Congress of the United States
House of Representatives
COMMITTEE ON THE JUDICIARY
2138 RAYBURN HOUSE OFFICE BUILDING
WASHINGTON, DC 20515-6216
(202) 225-3951
judiciary.house.gov

November 1, 2021

Mr. Darren J. LaMarca
Acting U.S. Attorney
Southern District of Mississippi
501 East Court Street, Suite 4.430
Jackson, MS 39201

Dear Mr. LaMarca:

We are continuing to investigate the troubling attempts by the Department of Justice and the White House to use the heavy hand of federal law enforcement to target concerned parents at local school board meetings and chill their protected First Amendment activity. Because the Department directed you, along with all other U.S. Attorneys, and the Federal Bureau of Investigation (FBI) to take action to address parents attending school board meetings,[1] we respectfully request your assistance with our investigation.

On September 29, 2021, the National School Boards Association (NSBA) sent a letter to President Joe Biden requesting help from the federal government with concerned parents voicing their opinions at school board meetings.[2] The NSBA letter stated that "malice, violence, and threats" against school officials "could be the equivalent of a form of domestic terrorism or hate crimes."[3] The letter cited a number of interactions at school board meetings, none of which rose to the level of domestic terrorism. In fact, the vast majority of incidents cited by the NSBA did not involve threats or violence.[4] Most notably, as an example of domestic terrorism, the NSBA cited an incident in which a father angrily confronted members at a school board meeting in Loudoun County, Virginia about the heinous sexual assault of his daughter.[5]

A mere five days after the NSBA sent its letter to President Biden, on October 4, 2021, Attorney General Merrick Garland issued a shocking memorandum that directed the FBI and

---

[1] Memorandum from Atty Gen. Merrick Garland, U.S. Dep't of Justice, Partnership Among Federal, State, Local, Tribal, And Territorial Law Enforcement to Address Threats Against School Administrators, Board Members, Teachers, and Staff (Oct. 4, 2021).
[2] Letter from Dr. Viola M. Garcia, President, Nat'l School Board Assoc. & Mr. Chip Slaven, Chief Exec. Officer, Nat'l School Board Assoc., to President Joseph R. Biden, White House (Sept. 29, 2021).
[3] *Id.*
[4] *See* Caroline Downey, *Vast majority of incidents cited by school-board group to justify federal intervention didn't involve threats,* NAT'L REV. (Oct. 2, 2021).
[5] *Id.*; *see also* Jessica Chasmar, *Loudoun County father arrested at school board events says school tried to cover up daughter's bathroom assault*, FOX NEWS (Oct. 12, 2021).

U.S. Attorneys' Offices to "convene meetings" in your judicial district "with federal, state, local, Tribal, and territorial leaders" within 30 days.[6] The Justice Department simultaneously issued a press release indicating that the Attorney General's directive would "open dedicated lines of communication for threat reporting, assessment and response by law enforcement"—in other words, create a snitch line for complaints about concerned parents.[7]

During Attorney General Garland's testimony before our Committee on October 21, he appeared to have no idea whether the U.S. Attorney meetings he ordered were actually taking place. He stated: "I don't know whether [the meetings] are ongoing, but I expect and hope that they are going . . . because I did ask that they take place."[8] Attorney General Garland testified that he doubted "there have been meetings in every jurisdiction," but reiterated his belief that it is important for federal law enforcement authorities to conduct these meetings in every judicial district.[9] According to the Attorney General's directives, meetings are to be convened in all 94 judicial districts by November 3, 2021, at the latest.

Following the Attorney General's testimony, the NSBA Board of Directors, apparently recognizing the ill-conceived consequences of its letter and the resulting Justice Department action, issued a new memorandum to its members apologizing for the letter, stating: "On behalf of NSBA, <u>we regret and apologize for the letter</u>."[10] (emphasis in original). Although Attorney General Garland testified that the NSBA letter to President Biden was the basis for his October 4 directive to insert federal law enforcement into local school board matters, the Attorney General has yet to rescind his memorandum. His directives to you and other U.S. Attorneys remain in effect.

Concerned parents voicing their strong opposition to controversial curricula at local schools are not domestic terrorists. Parents have an undisputed right to direct the upbringing and education of their children.[11] When parents, however, cross the line to commit a violent act or issue a criminal threat,[12] state and local authorities are best-equipped to handle these violations of state law. But we must not tolerate the use of the federal law enforcement apparatus to intimidate and silence parents using their Constitutional rights to advocate for their child's future.

To assist our investigation and determine whether these meetings are ongoing, we request that you provide the following documents and information:

---

[6] Memorandum from Atty Gen. Merrick Garland, U.S. Dep't of Justice, Partnership Among Federal, State, Local, Tribal, And Territorial Law Enforcement to Address Threats Against School Administrators, Board Members, Teachers, and Staff (Oct. 4, 2021).
[7] Press Release, U.S. Dep't of Justice, Justice Department Addresses Violent Threats Against School Officials and Teachers (Oct. 4, 2021).
[8] *Oversight of the United States Department of Justice: Hearing Before the H. comm. on the Judiciary,* 117th Cong. at 94 (2021) (testimony from Hon. Merrick Garland, Atty Gen., U.S. Dep't of Justice).
[9] *Id.* at 95.
[10] Memorandum from NSBA Board of Directors, Message to NSBA Members (Oct. 22, 2021).
[11] *Troxel v. Granville,* 530 U.S. 57, 65 (2000) (citing *Meyer v. Nebraska,* 262 U.S. 390, 399 (1923)).
[12] *Merrick Garland's federal offense,* WALL ST. J. (Oct. 6, 2021).

1. All documents and communications referring or relating to convening meeting(s) in your judicial district in accordance with the Attorney General's October 4, 2021 memorandum;

2. All agendas, minutes, and notes created or relied upon by U.S. Attorney's Office employees referring or relating to meeting(s) in your judicial district in accordance with the Attorney General's October 4, 2021 memorandum;

3. Please explain when meeting(s) in your judicial district in accordance with the Attorney General's October 4, 2021 memorandum have occurred or will occur;

4. Please identify by name and title of all U.S. Attorney's Office employees involved in the meeting(s) in your judicial district in accordance with the Attorney General's October 4, 2021 memorandum ;

5. Please identify all federal, state, local, Tribal, and territorial organizations invited to or that have attended the meetings convened in your judicial district in accordance with the October 4, 2021 memorandum; and

6. Please provide all recommendations, both formal and informal, and any meeting minutes produced at the meeting(s) in your judicial district in accordance with the Attorney General's October 4, 2021 memorandum.

Please provide this material as soon as possible but no later than 5:00 p.m. on November 15, 2021.

If you have any questions about this request, please contact Committee staff at (202) 225-6906. Thank you for your attention to this important matter.

Sincerely,

Jim Jordan
Ranking Member

Steve Chabot
Member of Congress

Louie Gohmert
Member of Congress

Darrell Issa
Ranking Member
Subcommittee on Courts, Intellectual Property, and the Internet

Ken Buck
Ranking Member
Subcommittee on Antitrust, Commercial and Administrative Law

Matt Gaetz
Member of Congress

Mike Johnson
Ranking Member
Subcommittee on the Constitution, Civil Rights and Civil Liberties

Andy Biggs
Ranking Member
Subcommittee on Crime, Terrorism and Homeland Security

Tom McClintock
Ranking Member
Subcommittee on Immigration and Citizenship

W. Gregory Steube
Member of Congress

Tom Tiffany
Member of Congress

Thomas Massie
Member of Congress

Chip Roy
Member of Congress

Dan Bishop
Member of Congress

Michelle Fischbach
Member of Congress

Victoria Spartz
Member of Congress

Scott Fitzgerald
Member of Congress

Cliff Bentz
Member of Congress

Burgess Owens
Member of Congress

cc: The Honorable Jerrold L. Nadler
Chairman

Mr. Monty Wilkinson
Director, Executive Office for U.S. Attorneys

JERROLD NADLER, New York
CHAIRMAN

JIM JORDAN, Ohio
RANKING MEMBER

ONE HUNDRED SEVENTEENTH CONGRESS

Congress of the United States

House of Representatives

COMMITTEE ON THE JUDICIARY

2138 RAYBURN HOUSE OFFICE BUILDING

WASHINGTON, DC 20515–6216

(202) 225–3951

judiciary.house.gov

November 1, 2021

Mr. Leif M. Johnson
Acting U.S. Attorney
District of Montana
2601 2nd Ave N., Suite 3200
Billings, MT 59101

Dear Mr. Johnson:

We are continuing to investigate the troubling attempts by the Department of Justice and the White House to use the heavy hand of federal law enforcement to target concerned parents at local school board meetings and chill their protected First Amendment activity. Because the Department directed you, along with all other U.S. Attorneys, and the Federal Bureau of Investigation (FBI) to take action to address parents attending school board meetings,[1] we respectfully request your assistance with our investigation.

On September 29, 2021, the National School Boards Association (NSBA) sent a letter to President Joe Biden requesting help from the federal government with concerned parents voicing their opinions at school board meetings.[2] The NSBA letter stated that "malice, violence, and threats" against school officials "could be the equivalent of a form of domestic terrorism or hate crimes."[3] The letter cited a number of interactions at school board meetings, none of which rose to the level of domestic terrorism. In fact, the vast majority of incidents cited by the NSBA did not involve threats or violence.[4] Most notably, as an example of domestic terrorism, the NSBA cited an incident in which a father angrily confronted members at a school board meeting in Loudoun County, Virginia about the heinous sexual assault of his daughter.[5]

A mere five days after the NSBA sent its letter to President Biden, on October 4, 2021, Attorney General Merrick Garland issued a shocking memorandum that directed the FBI and

---

[1] Memorandum from Atty Gen. Merrick Garland, U.S. Dep't of Justice, Partnership Among Federal, State, Local, Tribal, And Territorial Law Enforcement to Address Threats Against School Administrators, Board Members, Teachers, and Staff (Oct. 4, 2021).
[2] Letter from Dr. Viola M. Garcia, President, Nat'l School Board Assoc. & Mr. Chip Slaven, Chief Exec. Officer, Nat'l School Board Assoc., to President Joseph R. Biden, White House (Sept. 29, 2021).
[3] *Id.*
[4] *See* Caroline Downey, *Vast majority of incidents cited by school-board group to justify federal intervention didn't involve threats,* NAT'L REV. (Oct. 2, 2021).
[5] *Id.*; *see also* Jessica Chasmar, *Loudoun County father arrested at school board events says school tried to cover up daughter's bathroom assault*, FOX NEWS (Oct. 12, 2021).

U.S. Attorneys' Offices to "convene meetings" in your judicial district "with federal, state, local, Tribal, and territorial leaders" within 30 days.[6] The Justice Department simultaneously issued a press release indicating that the Attorney General's directive would "open dedicated lines of communication for threat reporting, assessment and response by law enforcement"—in other words, create a snitch line for complaints about concerned parents.[7]

During Attorney General Garland's testimony before our Committee on October 21, he appeared to have no idea whether the U.S. Attorney meetings he ordered were actually taking place. He stated: "I don't know whether [the meetings] are ongoing, but I expect and hope that they are going . . . because I did ask that they take place."[8] Attorney General Garland testified that he doubted "there have been meetings in every jurisdiction," but reiterated his belief that it is important for federal law enforcement authorities to conduct these meetings in every judicial district.[9] According to the Attorney General's directives, meetings are to be convened in all 94 judicial districts by November 3, 2021, at the latest.

Following the Attorney General's testimony, the NSBA Board of Directors, apparently recognizing the ill-conceived consequences of its letter and the resulting Justice Department action, issued a new memorandum to its members apologizing for the letter, stating: "On behalf of NSBA, <u>we regret and apologize for the letter</u>."[10] (emphasis in original). Although Attorney General Garland testified that the NSBA letter to President Biden was the basis for his October 4 directive to insert federal law enforcement into local school board matters, the Attorney General has yet to rescind his memorandum. His directives to you and other U.S. Attorneys remain in effect.

Concerned parents voicing their strong opposition to controversial curricula at local schools are not domestic terrorists. Parents have an undisputed right to direct the upbringing and education of their children.[11] When parents, however, cross the line to commit a violent act or issue a criminal threat,[12] state and local authorities are best-equipped to handle these violations of state law. But we must not tolerate the use of the federal law enforcement apparatus to intimidate and silence parents using their Constitutional rights to advocate for their child's future.

To assist our investigation and determine whether these meetings are ongoing, we request that you provide the following documents and information:

---

[6] Memorandum from Atty Gen. Merrick Garland, U.S. Dep't of Justice, Partnership Among Federal, State, Local, Tribal, And Territorial Law Enforcement to Address Threats Against School Administrators, Board Members, Teachers, and Staff (Oct. 4, 2021).
[7] Press Release, U.S. Dep't of Justice, Justice Department Addresses Violent Threats Against School Officials and Teachers (Oct. 4, 2021).
[8] *Oversight of the United States Department of Justice: Hearing Before the H. comm. on the Judiciary,* 117th Cong. at 94 (2021) (testimony from Hon. Merrick Garland, Atty Gen., U.S. Dep't of Justice).
[9] *Id.* at 95.
[10] Memorandum from NSBA Board of Directors, Message to NSBA Members (Oct. 22, 2021).
[11] *Troxel v. Granville,* 530 U.S. 57, 65 (2000) (citing *Meyer v. Nebraska,* 262 U.S. 390, 399 (1923)).
[12] *Merrick Garland's federal offense,* WALL ST. J. (Oct. 6, 2021).

1. All documents and communications referring or relating to convening meeting(s) in your judicial district in accordance with the Attorney General's October 4, 2021 memorandum;

2. All agendas, minutes, and notes created or relied upon by U.S. Attorney's Office employees referring or relating to meeting(s) in your judicial district in accordance with the Attorney General's October 4, 2021 memorandum;

3. Please explain when meeting(s) in your judicial district in accordance with the Attorney General's October 4, 2021 memorandum have occurred or will occur;

4. Please identify by name and title of all U.S. Attorney's Office employees involved in the meeting(s) in your judicial district in accordance with the Attorney General's October 4, 2021 memorandum ;

5. Please identify all federal, state, local, Tribal, and territorial organizations invited to or that have attended the meetings convened in your judicial district in accordance with the October 4, 2021 memorandum; and

6. Please provide all recommendations, both formal and informal, and any meeting minutes produced at the meeting(s) in your judicial district in accordance with the Attorney General's October 4, 2021 memorandum.

Please provide this material as soon as possible but no later than 5:00 p.m. on November 15, 2021.

If you have any questions about this request, please contact Committee staff at (202) 225-6906. Thank you for your attention to this important matter.

Sincerely,

Jim Jordan
Ranking Member

Steve Chabot
Member of Congress

Louie Gohmert
Member of Congress

Darrell Issa
Ranking Member
Subcommittee on Courts, Intellectual Property, and the Internet

Ken Buck
Ranking Member
Subcommittee on Antitrust, Commercial and Administrative Law

Matt Gaetz
Member of Congress

Mike Johnson
Ranking Member
Subcommittee on the Constitution, Civil Rights and Civil Liberties

Andy Biggs
Ranking Member
Subcommittee on Crime, Terrorism and Homeland Security

Tom McClintock
Ranking Member
Subcommittee on Immigration and Citizenship

W. Gregory Steube
Member of Congress

Tom Tiffany
Member of Congress

Thomas Massie
Member of Congress

Chip Roy
Member of Congress

Dan Bishop
Member of Congress

Michelle Fischbach
Member of Congress

Victoria Spartz
Member of Congress

Scott Fitzgerald
Member of Congress

Cliff Bentz
Member of Congress

Burgess Owens
Member of Congress

cc: The Honorable Jerrold L. Nadler
Chairman

Mr. Monty Wilkinson
Director, Executive Office for U.S. Attorneys

JERROLD NADLER, New York
CHAIRMAN

JIM JORDAN, Ohio
RANKING MEMBER

ONE HUNDRED SEVENTEENTH CONGRESS

Congress of the United States

House of Representatives

COMMITTEE ON THE JUDICIARY

2138 RAYBURN HOUSE OFFICE BUILDING

WASHINGTON, DC 20515–6216

(202) 225–3951
judiciary.house.gov

November 1, 2021

Mr. G. Norman Acker, III
Acting U.S. Attorney
Eastern District of North Carolina
150 Fayetteville Street, Suite 2100
Raleigh, NC 27601

Dear Mr. Acker:

We are continuing to investigate the troubling attempts by the Department of Justice and the White House to use the heavy hand of federal law enforcement to target concerned parents at local school board meetings and chill their protected First Amendment activity. Because the Department directed you, along with all other U.S. Attorneys, and the Federal Bureau of Investigation (FBI) to take action to address parents attending school board meetings,[1] we respectfully request your assistance with our investigation.

On September 29, 2021, the National School Boards Association (NSBA) sent a letter to President Joe Biden requesting help from the federal government with concerned parents voicing their opinions at school board meetings.[2] The NSBA letter stated that "malice, violence, and threats" against school officials "could be the equivalent of a form of domestic terrorism or hate crimes."[3] The letter cited a number of interactions at school board meetings, none of which rose to the level of domestic terrorism. In fact, the vast majority of incidents cited by the NSBA did not involve threats or violence.[4] Most notably, as an example of domestic terrorism, the NSBA cited an incident in which a father angrily confronted members at a school board meeting in Loudoun County, Virginia about the heinous sexual assault of his daughter.[5]

A mere five days after the NSBA sent its letter to President Biden, on October 4, 2021, Attorney General Merrick Garland issued a shocking memorandum that directed the FBI and

---

[1] Memorandum from Atty Gen. Merrick Garland, U.S. Dep't of Justice, Partnership Among Federal, State, Local, Tribal, And Territorial Law Enforcement to Address Threats Against School Administrators, Board Members, Teachers, and Staff (Oct. 4, 2021).
[2] Letter from Dr. Viola M. Garcia, President, Nat'l School Board Assoc. & Mr. Chip Slaven, Chief Exec. Officer, Nat'l School Board Assoc., to President Joseph R. Biden, White House (Sept. 29, 2021).
[3] *Id.*
[4] *See* Caroline Downey, *Vast majority of incidents cited by school-board group to justify federal intervention didn't involve threats,* NAT'L REV. (Oct. 2, 2021).
[5] *Id.*; *see also* Jessica Chasmar, *Loudoun County father arrested at school board events says school tried to cover up daughter's bathroom assault*, FOX NEWS (Oct. 12, 2021).

U.S. Attorneys' Offices to "convene meetings" in your judicial district "with federal, state, local, Tribal, and territorial leaders" within 30 days.[6] The Justice Department simultaneously issued a press release indicating that the Attorney General's directive would "open dedicated lines of communication for threat reporting, assessment and response by law enforcement"—in other words, create a snitch line for complaints about concerned parents.[7]

During Attorney General Garland's testimony before our Committee on October 21, he appeared to have no idea whether the U.S. Attorney meetings he ordered were actually taking place. He stated: "I don't know whether [the meetings] are ongoing, but I expect and hope that they are going . . . because I did ask that they take place."[8] Attorney General Garland testified that he doubted "there have been meetings in every jurisdiction," but reiterated his belief that it is important for federal law enforcement authorities to conduct these meetings in every judicial district.[9] According to the Attorney General's directives, meetings are to be convened in all 94 judicial districts by November 3, 2021, at the latest.

Following the Attorney General's testimony, the NSBA Board of Directors, apparently recognizing the ill-conceived consequences of its letter and the resulting Justice Department action, issued a new memorandum to its members apologizing for the letter, stating: "On behalf of NSBA, <u>we regret and apologize for the letter</u>."[10] (emphasis in original). Although Attorney General Garland testified that the NSBA letter to President Biden was the basis for his October 4 directive to insert federal law enforcement into local school board matters, the Attorney General has yet to rescind his memorandum. His directives to you and other U.S. Attorneys remain in effect.

Concerned parents voicing their strong opposition to controversial curricula at local schools are not domestic terrorists. Parents have an undisputed right to direct the upbringing and education of their children.[11] When parents, however, cross the line to commit a violent act or issue a criminal threat,[12] state and local authorities are best-equipped to handle these violations of state law. But we must not tolerate the use of the federal law enforcement apparatus to intimidate and silence parents using their Constitutional rights to advocate for their child's future.

To assist our investigation and determine whether these meetings are ongoing, we request that you provide the following documents and information:

---

[6] Memorandum from Atty Gen. Merrick Garland, U.S. Dep't of Justice, Partnership Among Federal, State, Local, Tribal, And Territorial Law Enforcement to Address Threats Against School Administrators, Board Members, Teachers, and Staff (Oct. 4, 2021).

[7] Press Release, U.S. Dep't of Justice, Justice Department Addresses Violent Threats Against School Officials and Teachers (Oct. 4, 2021).

[8] *Oversight of the United States Department of Justice: Hearing Before the H. comm. on the Judiciary,* 117th Cong. at 94 (2021) (testimony from Hon. Merrick Garland, Atty Gen., U.S. Dep't of Justice).

[9] *Id.* at 95.

[10] Memorandum from NSBA Board of Directors, Message to NSBA Members (Oct. 22, 2021).

[11] *Troxel v. Granville,* 530 U.S. 57, 65 (2000) (citing *Meyer v. Nebraska,* 262 U.S. 390, 399 (1923)).

[12] *Merrick Garland's federal offense,* WALL ST. J. (Oct. 6, 2021).

1. All documents and communications referring or relating to convening meeting(s) in your judicial district in accordance with the Attorney General's October 4, 2021 memorandum;

2. All agendas, minutes, and notes created or relied upon by U.S. Attorney's Office employees referring or relating to meeting(s) in your judicial district in accordance with the Attorney General's October 4, 2021 memorandum;

3. Please explain when meeting(s) in your judicial district in accordance with the Attorney General's October 4, 2021 memorandum have occurred or will occur;

4. Please identify by name and title of all U.S. Attorney's Office employees involved in the meeting(s) in your judicial district in accordance with the Attorney General's October 4, 2021 memorandum ;

5. Please identify all federal, state, local, Tribal, and territorial organizations invited to or that have attended the meetings convened in your judicial district in accordance with the October 4, 2021 memorandum; and

6. Please provide all recommendations, both formal and informal, and any meeting minutes produced at the meeting(s) in your judicial district in accordance with the Attorney General's October 4, 2021 memorandum.

Please provide this material as soon as possible but no later than 5:00 p.m. on November 15, 2021.

If you have any questions about this request, please contact Committee staff at (202) 225-6906. Thank you for your attention to this important matter.

Sincerely,

Jim Jordan
Ranking Member

Steve Chabot
Member of Congress

Louie Gohmert
Member of Congress

Darrell Issa
Ranking Member
Subcommittee on Courts, Intellectual Property, and the Internet

Ken Buck
Ranking Member
Subcommittee on Antitrust, Commercial and Administrative Law

Matt Gaetz
Member of Congress

Mike Johnson
Ranking Member
Subcommittee on the Constitution, Civil Rights and Civil Liberties

Andy Biggs
Ranking Member
Subcommittee on Crime, Terrorism and Homeland Security

Tom McClintock
Ranking Member
Subcommittee on Immigration and Citizenship

W. Gregory Steube
Member of Congress

Tom Tiffany
Member of Congress

Thomas Massie
Member of Congress

Chip Roy
Member of Congress

Dan Bishop
Member of Congress

Michelle Fischbach
Member of Congress

Victoria Spartz
Member of Congress

Scott Fitzgerald
Member of Congress

Cliff Bentz
Member of Congress

Burgess Owens
Member of Congress

cc: The Honorable Jerrold L. Nadler
Chairman

Mr. Monty Wilkinson
Director, Executive Office for U.S. Attorneys

JERROLD NADLER, New York
CHAIRMAN

JIM JORDAN, Ohio
RANKING MEMBER

ONE HUNDRED SEVENTEENTH CONGRESS
Congress of the United States
House of Representatives
COMMITTEE ON THE JUDICIARY
2138 RAYBURN HOUSE OFFICE BUILDING
WASHINGTON, DC 20515-6216
(202) 225-3951
judiciary.house.gov

November 1, 2021

Ms. Sandra J. Hairston
Acting U.S. Attorney
Middle District of North Carolina
101 South Edgeworth Street, 4th Floor
Greensboro, NC 27401

Dear Ms. Hairston:

We are continuing to investigate the troubling attempts by the Department of Justice and the White House to use the heavy hand of federal law enforcement to target concerned parents at local school board meetings and chill their protected First Amendment activity. Because the Department directed you, along with all other U.S. Attorneys, and the Federal Bureau of Investigation (FBI) to take action to address parents attending school board meetings,[1] we respectfully request your assistance with our investigation.

On September 29, 2021, the National School Boards Association (NSBA) sent a letter to President Joe Biden requesting help from the federal government with concerned parents voicing their opinions at school board meetings.[2] The NSBA letter stated that "malice, violence, and threats" against school officials "could be the equivalent of a form of domestic terrorism or hate crimes."[3] The letter cited a number of interactions at school board meetings, none of which rose to the level of domestic terrorism. In fact, the vast majority of incidents cited by the NSBA did not involve threats or violence.[4] Most notably, as an example of domestic terrorism, the NSBA cited an incident in which a father angrily confronted members at a school board meeting in Loudoun County, Virginia about the heinous sexual assault of his daughter.[5]

A mere five days after the NSBA sent its letter to President Biden, on October 4, 2021, Attorney General Merrick Garland issued a shocking memorandum that directed the FBI and

[1] Memorandum from Atty Gen. Merrick Garland, U.S. Dep't of Justice, Partnership Among Federal, State, Local, Tribal, And Territorial Law Enforcement to Address Threats Against School Administrators, Board Members, Teachers, and Staff (Oct. 4, 2021).
[2] Letter from Dr. Viola M. Garcia, President, Nat'l School Board Assoc. & Mr. Chip Slaven, Chief Exec. Officer, Nat'l School Board Assoc., to President Joseph R. Biden, White House (Sept. 29, 2021).
[3] *Id.*
[4] *See* Caroline Downey, *Vast majority of incidents cited by school-board group to justify federal intervention didn't involve threats,* NAT'L REV. (Oct. 2, 2021).
[5] *Id.*; *see also* Jessica Chasmar, *Loudoun County father arrested at school board events says school tried to cover up daughter's bathroom assault*, FOX NEWS (Oct. 12, 2021).

U.S. Attorneys' Offices to "convene meetings" in your judicial district "with federal, state, local, Tribal, and territorial leaders" within 30 days.[6] The Justice Department simultaneously issued a press release indicating that the Attorney General's directive would "open dedicated lines of communication for threat reporting, assessment and response by law enforcement"—in other words, create a snitch line for complaints about concerned parents.[7]

During Attorney General Garland's testimony before our Committee on October 21, he appeared to have no idea whether the U.S. Attorney meetings he ordered were actually taking place. He stated: "I don't know whether [the meetings] are ongoing, but I expect and hope that they are going . . . because I did ask that they take place."[8] Attorney General Garland testified that he doubted "there have been meetings in every jurisdiction," but reiterated his belief that it is important for federal law enforcement authorities to conduct these meetings in every judicial district.[9] According to the Attorney General's directives, meetings are to be convened in all 94 judicial districts by November 3, 2021, at the latest.

Following the Attorney General's testimony, the NSBA Board of Directors, apparently recognizing the ill-conceived consequences of its letter and the resulting Justice Department action, issued a new memorandum to its members apologizing for the letter, stating: "On behalf of NSBA, <u>we regret and apologize for the letter</u>."[10] (emphasis in original). Although Attorney General Garland testified that the NSBA letter to President Biden was the basis for his October 4 directive to insert federal law enforcement into local school board matters, the Attorney General has yet to rescind his memorandum. His directives to you and other U.S. Attorneys remain in effect.

Concerned parents voicing their strong opposition to controversial curricula at local schools are not domestic terrorists. Parents have an undisputed right to direct the upbringing and education of their children.[11] When parents, however, cross the line to commit a violent act or issue a criminal threat,[12] state and local authorities are best-equipped to handle these violations of state law. But we must not tolerate the use of the federal law enforcement apparatus to intimidate and silence parents using their Constitutional rights to advocate for their child's future.

To assist our investigation and determine whether these meetings are ongoing, we request that you provide the following documents and information:

---

[6] Memorandum from Atty Gen. Merrick Garland, U.S. Dep't of Justice, Partnership Among Federal, State, Local, Tribal, And Territorial Law Enforcement to Address Threats Against School Administrators, Board Members, Teachers, and Staff (Oct. 4, 2021).

[7] Press Release, U.S. Dep't of Justice, Justice Department Addresses Violent Threats Against School Officials and Teachers (Oct. 4, 2021).

[8] *Oversight of the United States Department of Justice: Hearing Before the H. comm. on the Judiciary,* 117th Cong. at 94 (2021) (testimony from Hon. Merrick Garland, Atty Gen., U.S. Dep't of Justice).

[9] *Id.* at 95.

[10] Memorandum from NSBA Board of Directors, Message to NSBA Members (Oct. 22, 2021).

[11] *Troxel v. Granville,* 530 U.S. 57, 65 (2000) (citing *Meyer v. Nebraska,* 262 U.S. 390, 399 (1923)).

[12] *Merrick Garland's federal offense,* WALL ST. J. (Oct. 6, 2021).

1. All documents and communications referring or relating to convening meeting(s) in your judicial district in accordance with the Attorney General's October 4, 2021 memorandum;

2. All agendas, minutes, and notes created or relied upon by U.S. Attorney's Office employees referring or relating to meeting(s) in your judicial district in accordance with the Attorney General's October 4, 2021 memorandum;

3. Please explain when meeting(s) in your judicial district in accordance with the Attorney General's October 4, 2021 memorandum have occurred or will occur;

4. Please identify by name and title of all U.S. Attorney's Office employees involved in the meeting(s) in your judicial district in accordance with the Attorney General's October 4, 2021 memorandum ;

5. Please identify all federal, state, local, Tribal, and territorial organizations invited to or that have attended the meetings convened in your judicial district in accordance with the October 4, 2021 memorandum; and

6. Please provide all recommendations, both formal and informal, and any meeting minutes produced at the meeting(s) in your judicial district in accordance with the Attorney General's October 4, 2021 memorandum.

Please provide this material as soon as possible but no later than 5:00 p.m. on November 15, 2021.

If you have any questions about this request, please contact Committee staff at (202) 225-6906. Thank you for your attention to this important matter.

Sincerely,

Jim Jordan
Ranking Member

Steve Chabot
Member of Congress

Louie Gohmert
Member of Congress

Darrell Issa
Ranking Member
Subcommittee on Courts, Intellectual Property, and the Internet

Ken Buck
Ranking Member
Subcommittee on Antitrust, Commercial
and Administrative Law

Matt Gaetz
Member of Congress

Mike Johnson
Ranking Member
Subcommittee on the Constitution,
Civil Rights and Civil Liberties

Andy Biggs
Ranking Member
Subcommittee on Crime, Terrorism
and Homeland Security

Tom McClintock
Ranking Member
Subcommittee on Immigration
and Citizenship

W. Gregory Steube
Member of Congress

Tom Tiffany
Member of Congress

Thomas Massie
Member of Congress

Chip Roy
Member of Congress

Dan Bishop
Member of Congress

Michelle Fischbach
Member of Congress

Victoria Spartz
Member of Congress

Scott Fitzgerald
Member of Congress

Cliff Bentz
Member of Congress

Burgess Owens
Member of Congress

cc: The Honorable Jerrold L. Nadler
Chairman

Mr. Monty Wilkinson
Director, Executive Office for U.S. Attorneys

JERROLD NADLER, New York
CHAIRMAN

JIM JORDAN, Ohio
RANKING MEMBER

ONE HUNDRED SEVENTEENTH CONGRESS
Congress of the United States
House of Representatives
COMMITTEE ON THE JUDICIARY
2138 RAYBURN HOUSE OFFICE BUILDING
WASHINGTON, DC 20515–6216
(202) 225–3951
judiciary.house.gov

November 1, 2021

Mr. William T. Stetzer
Acting U.S. Attorney
Western District of North Carolina
227 West Trade St., Suite 1650
Charlotte, NC 28202

Dear Mr. Stetzer:

We are continuing to investigate the troubling attempts by the Department of Justice and the White House to use the heavy hand of federal law enforcement to target concerned parents at local school board meetings and chill their protected First Amendment activity. Because the Department directed you, along with all other U.S. Attorneys, and the Federal Bureau of Investigation (FBI) to take action to address parents attending school board meetings,[1] we respectfully request your assistance with our investigation.

On September 29, 2021, the National School Boards Association (NSBA) sent a letter to President Joe Biden requesting help from the federal government with concerned parents voicing their opinions at school board meetings.[2] The NSBA letter stated that "malice, violence, and threats" against school officials "could be the equivalent of a form of domestic terrorism or hate crimes."[3] The letter cited a number of interactions at school board meetings, none of which rose to the level of domestic terrorism. In fact, the vast majority of incidents cited by the NSBA did not involve threats or violence.[4] Most notably, as an example of domestic terrorism, the NSBA cited an incident in which a father angrily confronted members at a school board meeting in Loudoun County, Virginia about the heinous sexual assault of his daughter.[5]

A mere five days after the NSBA sent its letter to President Biden, on October 4, 2021, Attorney General Merrick Garland issued a shocking memorandum that directed the FBI and

---

[1] Memorandum from Atty Gen. Merrick Garland, U.S. Dep't of Justice, Partnership Among Federal, State, Local, Tribal, And Territorial Law Enforcement to Address Threats Against School Administrators, Board Members, Teachers, and Staff (Oct. 4, 2021).
[2] Letter from Dr. Viola M. Garcia, President, Nat'l School Board Assoc. & Mr. Chip Slaven, Chief Exec. Officer, Nat'l School Board Assoc., to President Joseph R. Biden, White House (Sept. 29, 2021).
[3] *Id.*
[4] *See* Caroline Downey, *Vast majority of incidents cited by school-board group to justify federal intervention didn't involve threats,* NAT'L REV. (Oct. 2, 2021).
[5] *Id.*; *see also* Jessica Chasmar, *Loudoun County father arrested at school board events says school tried to cover up daughter's bathroom assault*, FOX NEWS (Oct. 12, 2021).

U.S. Attorneys' Offices to "convene meetings" in your judicial district "with federal, state, local, Tribal, and territorial leaders" within 30 days.[6] The Justice Department simultaneously issued a press release indicating that the Attorney General's directive would "open dedicated lines of communication for threat reporting, assessment and response by law enforcement"—in other words, create a snitch line for complaints about concerned parents.[7]

During Attorney General Garland's testimony before our Committee on October 21, he appeared to have no idea whether the U.S. Attorney meetings he ordered were actually taking place. He stated: "I don't know whether [the meetings] are ongoing, but I expect and hope that they are going . . . because I did ask that they take place."[8] Attorney General Garland testified that he doubted "there have been meetings in every jurisdiction," but reiterated his belief that it is important for federal law enforcement authorities to conduct these meetings in every judicial district.[9] According to the Attorney General's directives, meetings are to be convened in all 94 judicial districts by November 3, 2021, at the latest.

Following the Attorney General's testimony, the NSBA Board of Directors, apparently recognizing the ill-conceived consequences of its letter and the resulting Justice Department action, issued a new memorandum to its members apologizing for the letter, stating: "On behalf of NSBA, <u>we regret and apologize for the letter</u>."[10] (emphasis in original). Although Attorney General Garland testified that the NSBA letter to President Biden was the basis for his October 4 directive to insert federal law enforcement into local school board matters, the Attorney General has yet to rescind his memorandum. His directives to you and other U.S. Attorneys remain in effect.

Concerned parents voicing their strong opposition to controversial curricula at local schools are not domestic terrorists. Parents have an undisputed right to direct the upbringing and education of their children.[11] When parents, however, cross the line to commit a violent act or issue a criminal threat,[12] state and local authorities are best-equipped to handle these violations of state law. But we must not tolerate the use of the federal law enforcement apparatus to intimidate and silence parents using their Constitutional rights to advocate for their child's future.

To assist our investigation and determine whether these meetings are ongoing, we request that you provide the following documents and information:

---

[6] Memorandum from Atty Gen. Merrick Garland, U.S. Dep't of Justice, Partnership Among Federal, State, Local, Tribal, And Territorial Law Enforcement to Address Threats Against School Administrators, Board Members, Teachers, and Staff (Oct. 4, 2021).
[7] Press Release, U.S. Dep't of Justice, Justice Department Addresses Violent Threats Against School Officials and Teachers (Oct. 4, 2021).
[8] *Oversight of the United States Department of Justice: Hearing Before the H. comm. on the Judiciary,* 117th Cong. at 94 (2021) (testimony from Hon. Merrick Garland, Atty Gen., U.S. Dep't of Justice).
[9] *Id.* at 95.
[10] Memorandum from NSBA Board of Directors, Message to NSBA Members (Oct. 22, 2021).
[11] *Troxel v. Granville,* 530 U.S. 57, 65 (2000) (citing *Meyer v. Nebraska,* 262 U.S. 390, 399 (1923)).
[12] *Merrick Garland's federal offense,* WALL ST. J. (Oct. 6, 2021).

1. All documents and communications referring or relating to convening meeting(s) in your judicial district in accordance with the Attorney General's October 4, 2021 memorandum;

2. All agendas, minutes, and notes created or relied upon by U.S. Attorney's Office employees referring or relating to meeting(s) in your judicial district in accordance with the Attorney General's October 4, 2021 memorandum;

3. Please explain when meeting(s) in your judicial district in accordance with the Attorney General's October 4, 2021 memorandum have occurred or will occur;

4. Please identify by name and title of all U.S. Attorney's Office employees involved in the meeting(s) in your judicial district in accordance with the Attorney General's October 4, 2021 memorandum ;

5. Please identify all federal, state, local, Tribal, and territorial organizations invited to or that have attended the meetings convened in your judicial district in accordance with the October 4, 2021 memorandum; and

6. Please provide all recommendations, both formal and informal, and any meeting minutes produced at the meeting(s) in your judicial district in accordance with the Attorney General's October 4, 2021 memorandum.

Please provide this material as soon as possible but no later than 5:00 p.m. on November 15, 2021.

If you have any questions about this request, please contact Committee staff at (202) 225-6906. Thank you for your attention to this important matter.

Sincerely,

Jim Jordan
Ranking Member

Steve Chabot
Member of Congress

Louie Gohmert
Member of Congress

Darrell Issa
Ranking Member
Subcommittee on Courts, Intellectual Property, and the Internet

Ken Buck
Ranking Member
Subcommittee on Antitrust, Commercial
and Administrative Law

Matt Gaetz
Member of Congress

Mike Johnson
Ranking Member
Subcommittee on the Constitution,
Civil Rights and Civil Liberties

Andy Biggs
Ranking Member
Subcommittee on Crime, Terrorism
and Homeland Security

Tom McClintock
Ranking Member
Subcommittee on Immigration
and Citizenship

W. Gregory Steube
Member of Congress

Tom Tiffany
Member of Congress

Thomas Massie
Member of Congress

Chip Roy
Member of Congress

Dan Bishop
Member of Congress

Michelle Fischbach
Member of Congress

Victoria Spartz
Member of Congress

Scott Fitzgerald
Member of Congress

Cliff Bentz
Member of Congress

Burgess Owens
Member of Congress

cc: The Honorable Jerrold L. Nadler
Chairman

Mr. Monty Wilkinson
Director, Executive Office for U.S. Attorneys

JERROLD NADLER, New York
CHAIRMAN

JIM JORDAN, Ohio
RANKING MEMBER

ONE HUNDRED SEVENTEENTH CONGRESS

Congress of the United States

House of Representatives

COMMITTEE ON THE JUDICIARY

2138 RAYBURN HOUSE OFFICE BUILDING

WASHINGTON, DC 20515–6216

(202) 225–3951
judiciary.house.gov

November 1, 2021

Mr. Nicholas W. Chase
Acting U.S. Attorney
District of North Dakota
655 First Avenue North, Suite 250
Fargo, ND 58102

Dear Mr. Chase:

We are continuing to investigate the troubling attempts by the Department of Justice and the White House to use the heavy hand of federal law enforcement to target concerned parents at local school board meetings and chill their protected First Amendment activity. Because the Department directed you, along with all other U.S. Attorneys, and the Federal Bureau of Investigation (FBI) to take action to address parents attending school board meetings,[1] we respectfully request your assistance with our investigation.

On September 29, 2021, the National School Boards Association (NSBA) sent a letter to President Joe Biden requesting help from the federal government with concerned parents voicing their opinions at school board meetings.[2] The NSBA letter stated that "malice, violence, and threats" against school officials "could be the equivalent of a form of domestic terrorism or hate crimes."[3] The letter cited a number of interactions at school board meetings, none of which rose to the level of domestic terrorism. In fact, the vast majority of incidents cited by the NSBA did not involve threats or violence.[4] Most notably, as an example of domestic terrorism, the NSBA cited an incident in which a father angrily confronted members at a school board meeting in Loudoun County, Virginia about the heinous sexual assault of his daughter.[5]

A mere five days after the NSBA sent its letter to President Biden, on October 4, 2021, Attorney General Merrick Garland issued a shocking memorandum that directed the FBI and

---

[1] Memorandum from Atty Gen. Merrick Garland, U.S. Dep't of Justice, Partnership Among Federal, State, Local, Tribal, And Territorial Law Enforcement to Address Threats Against School Administrators, Board Members, Teachers, and Staff (Oct. 4, 2021).
[2] Letter from Dr. Viola M. Garcia, President, Nat'l School Board Assoc. & Mr. Chip Slaven, Chief Exec. Officer, Nat'l School Board Assoc., to President Joseph R. Biden, White House (Sept. 29, 2021).
[3] *Id.*
[4] *See* Caroline Downey, *Vast majority of incidents cited by school-board group to justify federal intervention didn't involve threats,* NAT'L REV. (Oct. 2, 2021).
[5] *Id.*; *see also* Jessica Chasmar, *Loudoun County father arrested at school board events says school tried to cover up daughter's bathroom assault*, FOX NEWS (Oct. 12, 2021).

U.S. Attorneys' Offices to "convene meetings" in your judicial district "with federal, state, local, Tribal, and territorial leaders" within 30 days.[6] The Justice Department simultaneously issued a press release indicating that the Attorney General's directive would "open dedicated lines of communication for threat reporting, assessment and response by law enforcement"—in other words, create a snitch line for complaints about concerned parents.[7]

During Attorney General Garland's testimony before our Committee on October 21, he appeared to have no idea whether the U.S. Attorney meetings he ordered were actually taking place. He stated: "I don't know whether [the meetings] are ongoing, but I expect and hope that they are going . . . because I did ask that they take place."[8] Attorney General Garland testified that he doubted "there have been meetings in every jurisdiction," but reiterated his belief that it is important for federal law enforcement authorities to conduct these meetings in every judicial district.[9] According to the Attorney General's directives, meetings are to be convened in all 94 judicial districts by November 3, 2021, at the latest.

Following the Attorney General's testimony, the NSBA Board of Directors, apparently recognizing the ill-conceived consequences of its letter and the resulting Justice Department action, issued a new memorandum to its members apologizing for the letter, stating: "On behalf of NSBA, we regret and apologize for the letter."[10] (emphasis in original). Although Attorney General Garland testified that the NSBA letter to President Biden was the basis for his October 4 directive to insert federal law enforcement into local school board matters, the Attorney General has yet to rescind his memorandum. His directives to you and other U.S. Attorneys remain in effect.

Concerned parents voicing their strong opposition to controversial curricula at local schools are not domestic terrorists. Parents have an undisputed right to direct the upbringing and education of their children.[11] When parents, however, cross the line to commit a violent act or issue a criminal threat,[12] state and local authorities are best-equipped to handle these violations of state law. But we must not tolerate the use of the federal law enforcement apparatus to intimidate and silence parents using their Constitutional rights to advocate for their child's future.

To assist our investigation and determine whether these meetings are ongoing, we request that you provide the following documents and information:

---

[6] Memorandum from Atty Gen. Merrick Garland, U.S. Dep't of Justice, Partnership Among Federal, State, Local, Tribal, And Territorial Law Enforcement to Address Threats Against School Administrators, Board Members, Teachers, and Staff (Oct. 4, 2021).
[7] Press Release, U.S. Dep't of Justice, Justice Department Addresses Violent Threats Against School Officials and Teachers (Oct. 4, 2021).
[8] *Oversight of the United States Department of Justice: Hearing Before the H. comm. on the Judiciary,* 117th Cong. at 94 (2021) (testimony from Hon. Merrick Garland, Atty Gen., U.S. Dep't of Justice).
[9] *Id.* at 95.
[10] Memorandum from NSBA Board of Directors, Message to NSBA Members (Oct. 22, 2021).
[11] *Troxel v. Granville,* 530 U.S. 57, 65 (2000) (citing *Meyer v. Nebraska,* 262 U.S. 390, 399 (1923)).
[12] *Merrick Garland's federal offense,* WALL ST. J. (Oct. 6, 2021).

1. All documents and communications referring or relating to convening meeting(s) in your judicial district in accordance with the Attorney General's October 4, 2021 memorandum;

2. All agendas, minutes, and notes created or relied upon by U.S. Attorney's Office employees referring or relating to meeting(s) in your judicial district in accordance with the Attorney General's October 4, 2021 memorandum;

3. Please explain when meeting(s) in your judicial district in accordance with the Attorney General's October 4, 2021 memorandum have occurred or will occur;

4. Please identify by name and title of all U.S. Attorney's Office employees involved in the meeting(s) in your judicial district in accordance with the Attorney General's October 4, 2021 memorandum ;

5. Please identify all federal, state, local, Tribal, and territorial organizations invited to or that have attended the meetings convened in your judicial district in accordance with the October 4, 2021 memorandum; and

6. Please provide all recommendations, both formal and informal, and any meeting minutes produced at the meeting(s) in your judicial district in accordance with the Attorney General's October 4, 2021 memorandum.

Please provide this material as soon as possible but no later than 5:00 p.m. on November 15, 2021.

If you have any questions about this request, please contact Committee staff at (202) 225-6906. Thank you for your attention to this important matter.

Sincerely,

Jim Jordan
Ranking Member

Steve Chabot
Member of Congress

Louie Gohmert
Member of Congress

Darrell Issa
Ranking Member
Subcommittee on Courts, Intellectual Property, and the Internet

Ken Buck
Ranking Member
Subcommittee on Antitrust, Commercial and Administrative Law

Matt Gaetz
Member of Congress

Mike Johnson
Ranking Member
Subcommittee on the Constitution, Civil Rights and Civil Liberties

Andy Biggs
Ranking Member
Subcommittee on Crime, Terrorism and Homeland Security

Tom McClintock
Ranking Member
Subcommittee on Immigration and Citizenship

W. Gregory Steube
Member of Congress

Tom Tiffany
Member of Congress

Thomas Massie
Member of Congress

Chip Roy
Member of Congress

Dan Bishop
Member of Congress

Michelle Fischbach
Member of Congress

Victoria Spartz
Member of Congress

Scott Fitzgerald
Member of Congress

Cliff Bentz
Member of Congress

Burgess Owens
Member of Congress

cc: The Honorable Jerrold L. Nadler
Chairman

Mr. Monty Wilkinson
Director, Executive Office for U.S. Attorneys

JERROLD NADLER, New York
CHAIRMAN

JIM JORDAN, Ohio
RANKING MEMBER

ONE HUNDRED SEVENTEENTH CONGRESS

Congress of the United States

House of Representatives

COMMITTEE ON THE JUDICIARY

2138 RAYBURN HOUSE OFFICE BUILDING

WASHINGTON, DC 20515–6216

(202) 225–3951
judiciary.house.gov

November 1, 2021

Mr. Jan W. Sharp
Acting U.S. Attorney
District of Nebraska
1620 Dodge St, Suite 1400
Omaha, NE 68102

Dear Mr. Sharp:

We are continuing to investigate the troubling attempts by the Department of Justice and the White House to use the heavy hand of federal law enforcement to target concerned parents at local school board meetings and chill their protected First Amendment activity. Because the Department directed you, along with all other U.S. Attorneys, and the Federal Bureau of Investigation (FBI) to take action to address parents attending school board meetings,[1] we respectfully request your assistance with our investigation.

On September 29, 2021, the National School Boards Association (NSBA) sent a letter to President Joe Biden requesting help from the federal government with concerned parents voicing their opinions at school board meetings.[2] The NSBA letter stated that "malice, violence, and threats" against school officials "could be the equivalent of a form of domestic terrorism or hate crimes."[3] The letter cited a number of interactions at school board meetings, none of which rose to the level of domestic terrorism. In fact, the vast majority of incidents cited by the NSBA did not involve threats or violence.[4] Most notably, as an example of domestic terrorism, the NSBA cited an incident in which a father angrily confronted members at a school board meeting in Loudoun County, Virginia about the heinous sexual assault of his daughter.[5]

A mere five days after the NSBA sent its letter to President Biden, on October 4, 2021, Attorney General Merrick Garland issued a shocking memorandum that directed the FBI and

---

[1] Memorandum from Atty Gen. Merrick Garland, U.S. Dep't of Justice, Partnership Among Federal, State, Local, Tribal, And Territorial Law Enforcement to Address Threats Against School Administrators, Board Members, Teachers, and Staff (Oct. 4, 2021).
[2] Letter from Dr. Viola M. Garcia, President, Nat'l School Board Assoc. & Mr. Chip Slaven, Chief Exec. Officer, Nat'l School Board Assoc., to President Joseph R. Biden, White House (Sept. 29, 2021).
[3] *Id.*
[4] *See* Caroline Downey, *Vast majority of incidents cited by school-board group to justify federal intervention didn't involve threats,* NAT'L REV. (Oct. 2, 2021).
[5] *Id.*; *see also* Jessica Chasmar, *Loudoun County father arrested at school board events says school tried to cover up daughter's bathroom assault*, FOX NEWS (Oct. 12, 2021).

U.S. Attorneys' Offices to "convene meetings" in your judicial district "with federal, state, local, Tribal, and territorial leaders" within 30 days.[6] The Justice Department simultaneously issued a press release indicating that the Attorney General's directive would "open dedicated lines of communication for threat reporting, assessment and response by law enforcement"—in other words, create a snitch line for complaints about concerned parents.[7]

During Attorney General Garland's testimony before our Committee on October 21, he appeared to have no idea whether the U.S. Attorney meetings he ordered were actually taking place. He stated: "I don't know whether [the meetings] are ongoing, but I expect and hope that they are going . . . because I did ask that they take place."[8] Attorney General Garland testified that he doubted "there have been meetings in every jurisdiction," but reiterated his belief that it is important for federal law enforcement authorities to conduct these meetings in every judicial district.[9] According to the Attorney General's directives, meetings are to be convened in all 94 judicial districts by November 3, 2021, at the latest.

Following the Attorney General's testimony, the NSBA Board of Directors, apparently recognizing the ill-conceived consequences of its letter and the resulting Justice Department action, issued a new memorandum to its members apologizing for the letter, stating: "On behalf of NSBA, <u>we regret and apologize for the letter</u>."[10] (emphasis in original). Although Attorney General Garland testified that the NSBA letter to President Biden was the basis for his October 4 directive to insert federal law enforcement into local school board matters, the Attorney General has yet to rescind his memorandum. His directives to you and other U.S. Attorneys remain in effect.

Concerned parents voicing their strong opposition to controversial curricula at local schools are not domestic terrorists. Parents have an undisputed right to direct the upbringing and education of their children.[11] When parents, however, cross the line to commit a violent act or issue a criminal threat,[12] state and local authorities are best-equipped to handle these violations of state law. But we must not tolerate the use of the federal law enforcement apparatus to intimidate and silence parents using their Constitutional rights to advocate for their child's future.

To assist our investigation and determine whether these meetings are ongoing, we request that you provide the following documents and information:

---

[6] Memorandum from Atty Gen. Merrick Garland, U.S. Dep't of Justice, Partnership Among Federal, State, Local, Tribal, And Territorial Law Enforcement to Address Threats Against School Administrators, Board Members, Teachers, and Staff (Oct. 4, 2021).
[7] Press Release, U.S. Dep't of Justice, Justice Department Addresses Violent Threats Against School Officials and Teachers (Oct. 4, 2021).
[8] *Oversight of the United States Department of Justice: Hearing Before the H. comm. on the Judiciary,* 117th Cong. at 94 (2021) (testimony from Hon. Merrick Garland, Atty Gen., U.S. Dep't of Justice).
[9] *Id.* at 95.
[10] Memorandum from NSBA Board of Directors, Message to NSBA Members (Oct. 22, 2021).
[11] *Troxel v. Granville,* 530 U.S. 57, 65 (2000) (citing *Meyer v. Nebraska,* 262 U.S. 390, 399 (1923)).
[12] *Merrick Garland's federal offense,* WALL ST. J. (Oct. 6, 2021).

1. All documents and communications referring or relating to convening meeting(s) in your judicial district in accordance with the Attorney General's October 4, 2021 memorandum;

2. All agendas, minutes, and notes created or relied upon by U.S. Attorney's Office employees referring or relating to meeting(s) in your judicial district in accordance with the Attorney General's October 4, 2021 memorandum;

3. Please explain when meeting(s) in your judicial district in accordance with the Attorney General's October 4, 2021 memorandum have occurred or will occur;

4. Please identify by name and title of all U.S. Attorney's Office employees involved in the meeting(s) in your judicial district in accordance with the Attorney General's October 4, 2021 memorandum ;

5. Please identify all federal, state, local, Tribal, and territorial organizations invited to or that have attended the meetings convened in your judicial district in accordance with the October 4, 2021 memorandum; and

6. Please provide all recommendations, both formal and informal, and any meeting minutes produced at the meeting(s) in your judicial district in accordance with the Attorney General's October 4, 2021 memorandum.

Please provide this material as soon as possible but no later than 5:00 p.m. on November 15, 2021.

If you have any questions about this request, please contact Committee staff at (202) 225-6906. Thank you for your attention to this important matter.

Sincerely,

Jim Jordan
Ranking Member

Steve Chabot
Member of Congress

Louie Gohmert
Member of Congress

Darrell Issa
Ranking Member
Subcommittee on Courts, Intellectual Property, and the Internet

Ken Buck
Ranking Member
Subcommittee on Antitrust, Commercial and Administrative Law

Matt Gaetz
Member of Congress

Mike Johnson
Ranking Member
Subcommittee on the Constitution, Civil Rights and Civil Liberties

Andy Biggs
Ranking Member
Subcommittee on Crime, Terrorism and Homeland Security

Tom McClintock
Ranking Member
Subcommittee on Immigration and Citizenship

W. Gregory Steube
Member of Congress

Tom Tiffany
Member of Congress

Thomas Massie
Member of Congress

Chip Roy
Member of Congress

Dan Bishop
Member of Congress

Michelle Fischbach
Member of Congress

Victoria Spartz
Member of Congress

Scott Fitzgerald
Member of Congress

Cliff Bentz
Member of Congress

Burgess Owens
Member of Congress

cc: The Honorable Jerrold L. Nadler
Chairman

Mr. Monty Wilkinson
Director, Executive Office for U.S. Attorneys

JERROLD NADLER, New York
CHAIRMAN

JIM JORDAN, Ohio
RANKING MEMBER

ONE HUNDRED SEVENTEENTH CONGRESS

Congress of the United States

House of Representatives

COMMITTEE ON THE JUDICIARY

2138 RAYBURN HOUSE OFFICE BUILDING

WASHINGTON, DC 20515-6216

(202) 225-3951
judiciary.house.gov

November 1, 2021

Mr. John J. Farley
Acting U.S. Attorney
District of New Hampshire
53 Pleasant Street, 4th Floor
Concord, NH 03301

Dear Mr. Farley:

We are continuing to investigate the troubling attempts by the Department of Justice and the White House to use the heavy hand of federal law enforcement to target concerned parents at local school board meetings and chill their protected First Amendment activity. Because the Department directed you, along with all other U.S. Attorneys, and the Federal Bureau of Investigation (FBI) to take action to address parents attending school board meetings,[1] we respectfully request your assistance with our investigation.

On September 29, 2021, the National School Boards Association (NSBA) sent a letter to President Joe Biden requesting help from the federal government with concerned parents voicing their opinions at school board meetings.[2] The NSBA letter stated that "malice, violence, and threats" against school officials "could be the equivalent of a form of domestic terrorism or hate crimes."[3] The letter cited a number of interactions at school board meetings, none of which rose to the level of domestic terrorism. In fact, the vast majority of incidents cited by the NSBA did not involve threats or violence.[4] Most notably, as an example of domestic terrorism, the NSBA cited an incident in which a father angrily confronted members at a school board meeting in Loudoun County, Virginia about the heinous sexual assault of his daughter.[5]

A mere five days after the NSBA sent its letter to President Biden, on October 4, 2021, Attorney General Merrick Garland issued a shocking memorandum that directed the FBI and

[1] Memorandum from Atty Gen. Merrick Garland, U.S. Dep't of Justice, Partnership Among Federal, State, Local, Tribal, And Territorial Law Enforcement to Address Threats Against School Administrators, Board Members, Teachers, and Staff (Oct. 4, 2021).
[2] Letter from Dr. Viola M. Garcia, President, Nat'l School Board Assoc. & Mr. Chip Slaven, Chief Exec. Officer, Nat'l School Board Assoc., to President Joseph R. Biden, White House (Sept. 29, 2021).
[3] *Id.*
[4] *See* Caroline Downey, *Vast majority of incidents cited by school-board group to justify federal intervention didn't involve threats,* NAT'L REV. (Oct. 2, 2021).
[5] *Id.*; *see also* Jessica Chasmar, *Loudoun County father arrested at school board events says school tried to cover up daughter's bathroom assault*, FOX NEWS (Oct. 12, 2021).

U.S. Attorneys' Offices to "convene meetings" in your judicial district "with federal, state, local, Tribal, and territorial leaders" within 30 days.[6] The Justice Department simultaneously issued a press release indicating that the Attorney General's directive would "open dedicated lines of communication for threat reporting, assessment and response by law enforcement"—in other words, create a snitch line for complaints about concerned parents.[7]

During Attorney General Garland's testimony before our Committee on October 21, he appeared to have no idea whether the U.S. Attorney meetings he ordered were actually taking place. He stated: "I don't know whether [the meetings] are ongoing, but I expect and hope that they are going . . . because I did ask that they take place."[8] Attorney General Garland testified that he doubted "there have been meetings in every jurisdiction," but reiterated his belief that it is important for federal law enforcement authorities to conduct these meetings in every judicial district.[9] According to the Attorney General's directives, meetings are to be convened in all 94 judicial districts by November 3, 2021, at the latest.

Following the Attorney General's testimony, the NSBA Board of Directors, apparently recognizing the ill-conceived consequences of its letter and the resulting Justice Department action, issued a new memorandum to its members apologizing for the letter, stating: "On behalf of NSBA, <u>we regret and apologize for the letter</u>."[10] (emphasis in original). Although Attorney General Garland testified that the NSBA letter to President Biden was the basis for his October 4 directive to insert federal law enforcement into local school board matters, the Attorney General has yet to rescind his memorandum. His directives to you and other U.S. Attorneys remain in effect.

Concerned parents voicing their strong opposition to controversial curricula at local schools are not domestic terrorists. Parents have an undisputed right to direct the upbringing and education of their children.[11] When parents, however, cross the line to commit a violent act or issue a criminal threat,[12] state and local authorities are best-equipped to handle these violations of state law. But we must not tolerate the use of the federal law enforcement apparatus to intimidate and silence parents using their Constitutional rights to advocate for their child's future.

To assist our investigation and determine whether these meetings are ongoing, we request that you provide the following documents and information:

---

[6] Memorandum from Atty Gen. Merrick Garland, U.S. Dep't of Justice, Partnership Among Federal, State, Local, Tribal, And Territorial Law Enforcement to Address Threats Against School Administrators, Board Members, Teachers, and Staff (Oct. 4, 2021).
[7] Press Release, U.S. Dep't of Justice, Justice Department Addresses Violent Threats Against School Officials and Teachers (Oct. 4, 2021).
[8] *Oversight of the United States Department of Justice: Hearing Before the H. comm. on the Judiciary,* 117th Cong. at 94 (2021) (testimony from Hon. Merrick Garland, Atty Gen., U.S. Dep't of Justice).
[9] *Id.* at 95.
[10] Memorandum from NSBA Board of Directors, Message to NSBA Members (Oct. 22, 2021).
[11] *Troxel v. Granville,* 530 U.S. 57, 65 (2000) (citing *Meyer v. Nebraska,* 262 U.S. 390, 399 (1923)).
[12] *Merrick Garland's federal offense,* WALL ST. J. (Oct. 6, 2021).

1. All documents and communications referring or relating to convening meeting(s) in your judicial district in accordance with the Attorney General's October 4, 2021 memorandum;

2. All agendas, minutes, and notes created or relied upon by U.S. Attorney's Office employees referring or relating to meeting(s) in your judicial district in accordance with the Attorney General's October 4, 2021 memorandum;

3. Please explain when meeting(s) in your judicial district in accordance with the Attorney General's October 4, 2021 memorandum have occurred or will occur;

4. Please identify by name and title of all U.S. Attorney's Office employees involved in the meeting(s) in your judicial district in accordance with the Attorney General's October 4, 2021 memorandum ;

5. Please identify all federal, state, local, Tribal, and territorial organizations invited to or that have attended the meetings convened in your judicial district in accordance with the October 4, 2021 memorandum; and

6. Please provide all recommendations, both formal and informal, and any meeting minutes produced at the meeting(s) in your judicial district in accordance with the Attorney General's October 4, 2021 memorandum.

Please provide this material as soon as possible but no later than 5:00 p.m. on November 15, 2021.

If you have any questions about this request, please contact Committee staff at (202) 225-6906. Thank you for your attention to this important matter.

Sincerely,

Jim Jordan
Ranking Member

Steve Chabot
Member of Congress

Louie Gohmert
Member of Congress

Darrell Issa
Ranking Member
Subcommittee on Courts, Intellectual Property, and the Internet

Mr. John J. Farley
November 1, 2021
Page 4

Ken Buck
Ranking Member
Subcommittee on Antitrust, Commercial and Administrative Law

Matt Gaetz
Member of Congress

Mike Johnson
Ranking Member
Subcommittee on the Constitution, Civil Rights and Civil Liberties

Andy Biggs
Ranking Member
Subcommittee on Crime, Terrorism and Homeland Security

Tom McClintock
Ranking Member
Subcommittee on Immigration and Citizenship

W. Gregory Steube
Member of Congress

Tom Tiffany
Member of Congress

Thomas Massie
Member of Congress

Chip Roy
Member of Congress

Dan Bishop
Member of Congress

Michelle Fischbach
Member of Congress

Victoria Spartz
Member of Congress

Scott Fitzgerald
Member of Congress

Cliff Bentz
Member of Congress

Burgess Owens
Member of Congress

cc: The Honorable Jerrold L. Nadler
Chairman

Mr. Monty Wilkinson
Director, Executive Office for U.S. Attorneys

JERROLD NADLER, New York
CHAIRMAN

JIM JORDAN, Ohio
RANKING MEMBER

ONE HUNDRED SEVENTEENTH CONGRESS

Congress of the United States

House of Representatives

COMMITTEE ON THE JUDICIARY

2138 RAYBURN HOUSE OFFICE BUILDING

WASHINGTON, DC 20515-6216

(202) 225-3951
judiciary.house.gov

November 1, 2021

Ms. Rachael A. Honig
Acting U.S. Attorney
District of New Jersey
970 Broad Street, 7th Floor
Newark, NJ 07102

Dear Ms. Honig:

We are continuing to investigate the troubling attempts by the Department of Justice and the White House to use the heavy hand of federal law enforcement to target concerned parents at local school board meetings and chill their protected First Amendment activity. Because the Department directed you, along with all other U.S. Attorneys, and the Federal Bureau of Investigation (FBI) to take action to address parents attending school board meetings,[1] we respectfully request your assistance with our investigation.

On September 29, 2021, the National School Boards Association (NSBA) sent a letter to President Joe Biden requesting help from the federal government with concerned parents voicing their opinions at school board meetings.[2] The NSBA letter stated that "malice, violence, and threats" against school officials "could be the equivalent of a form of domestic terrorism or hate crimes."[3] The letter cited a number of interactions at school board meetings, none of which rose to the level of domestic terrorism. In fact, the vast majority of incidents cited by the NSBA did not involve threats or violence.[4] Most notably, as an example of domestic terrorism, the NSBA cited an incident in which a father angrily confronted members at a school board meeting in Loudoun County, Virginia about the heinous sexual assault of his daughter.[5]

A mere five days after the NSBA sent its letter to President Biden, on October 4, 2021, Attorney General Merrick Garland issued a shocking memorandum that directed the FBI and

---

[1] Memorandum from Atty Gen. Merrick Garland, U.S. Dep't of Justice, Partnership Among Federal, State, Local, Tribal, And Territorial Law Enforcement to Address Threats Against School Administrators, Board Members, Teachers, and Staff (Oct. 4, 2021).
[2] Letter from Dr. Viola M. Garcia, President, Nat'l School Board Assoc. & Mr. Chip Slaven, Chief Exec. Officer, Nat'l School Board Assoc., to President Joseph R. Biden, White House (Sept. 29, 2021).
[3] *Id.*
[4] *See* Caroline Downey, *Vast majority of incidents cited by school-board group to justify federal intervention didn't involve threats,* NAT'L REV. (Oct. 2, 2021).
[5] *Id.*; *see also* Jessica Chasmar, *Loudoun County father arrested at school board events says school tried to cover up daughter's bathroom assault*, FOX NEWS (Oct. 12, 2021).

U.S. Attorneys' Offices to "convene meetings" in your judicial district "with federal, state, local, Tribal, and territorial leaders" within 30 days.[6] The Justice Department simultaneously issued a press release indicating that the Attorney General's directive would "open dedicated lines of communication for threat reporting, assessment and response by law enforcement"—in other words, create a snitch line for complaints about concerned parents.[7]

During Attorney General Garland's testimony before our Committee on October 21, he appeared to have no idea whether the U.S. Attorney meetings he ordered were actually taking place. He stated: "I don't know whether [the meetings] are ongoing, but I expect and hope that they are going . . . because I did ask that they take place."[8] Attorney General Garland testified that he doubted "there have been meetings in every jurisdiction," but reiterated his belief that it is important for federal law enforcement authorities to conduct these meetings in every judicial district.[9] According to the Attorney General's directives, meetings are to be convened in all 94 judicial districts by November 3, 2021, at the latest.

Following the Attorney General's testimony, the NSBA Board of Directors, apparently recognizing the ill-conceived consequences of its letter and the resulting Justice Department action, issued a new memorandum to its members apologizing for the letter, stating: "On behalf of NSBA, <u>we regret and apologize for the letter</u>."[10] (emphasis in original). Although Attorney General Garland testified that the NSBA letter to President Biden was the basis for his October 4 directive to insert federal law enforcement into local school board matters, the Attorney General has yet to rescind his memorandum. His directives to you and other U.S. Attorneys remain in effect.

Concerned parents voicing their strong opposition to controversial curricula at local schools are not domestic terrorists. Parents have an undisputed right to direct the upbringing and education of their children.[11] When parents, however, cross the line to commit a violent act or issue a criminal threat,[12] state and local authorities are best-equipped to handle these violations of state law. But we must not tolerate the use of the federal law enforcement apparatus to intimidate and silence parents using their Constitutional rights to advocate for their child's future.

To assist our investigation and determine whether these meetings are ongoing, we request that you provide the following documents and information:

---

[6] Memorandum from Atty Gen. Merrick Garland, U.S. Dep't of Justice, Partnership Among Federal, State, Local, Tribal, And Territorial Law Enforcement to Address Threats Against School Administrators, Board Members, Teachers, and Staff (Oct. 4, 2021).
[7] Press Release, U.S. Dep't of Justice, Justice Department Addresses Violent Threats Against School Officials and Teachers (Oct. 4, 2021).
[8] *Oversight of the United States Department of Justice: Hearing Before the H. comm. on the Judiciary,* 117th Cong. at 94 (2021) (testimony from Hon. Merrick Garland, Atty Gen., U.S. Dep't of Justice).
[9] *Id.* at 95.
[10] Memorandum from NSBA Board of Directors, Message to NSBA Members (Oct. 22, 2021).
[11] *Troxel v. Granville,* 530 U.S. 57, 65 (2000) (citing *Meyer v. Nebraska,* 262 U.S. 390, 399 (1923)).
[12] *Merrick Garland's federal offense,* WALL ST. J. (Oct. 6, 2021).

1. All documents and communications referring or relating to convening meeting(s) in your judicial district in accordance with the Attorney General's October 4, 2021 memorandum;

2. All agendas, minutes, and notes created or relied upon by U.S. Attorney's Office employees referring or relating to meeting(s) in your judicial district in accordance with the Attorney General's October 4, 2021 memorandum;

3. Please explain when meeting(s) in your judicial district in accordance with the Attorney General's October 4, 2021 memorandum have occurred or will occur;

4. Please identify by name and title of all U.S. Attorney's Office employees involved in the meeting(s) in your judicial district in accordance with the Attorney General's October 4, 2021 memorandum ;

5. Please identify all federal, state, local, Tribal, and territorial organizations invited to or that have attended the meetings convened in your judicial district in accordance with the October 4, 2021 memorandum; and

6. Please provide all recommendations, both formal and informal, and any meeting minutes produced at the meeting(s) in your judicial district in accordance with the Attorney General's October 4, 2021 memorandum.

Please provide this material as soon as possible but no later than 5:00 p.m. on November 15, 2021.

If you have any questions about this request, please contact Committee staff at (202) 225-6906. Thank you for your attention to this important matter.

Sincerely,

Jim Jordan
Ranking Member

Steve Chabot
Member of Congress

Louie Gohmert
Member of Congress

Darrell Issa
Ranking Member
Subcommittee on Courts, Intellectual Property, and the Internet

Ken Buck
Ranking Member
Subcommittee on Antitrust, Commercial and Administrative Law

Mike Johnson
Ranking Member
Subcommittee on the Constitution, Civil Rights and Civil Liberties

Tom McClintock
Ranking Member
Subcommittee on Immigration and Citizenship

Tom Tiffany
Member of Congress

Chip Roy
Member of Congress

Michelle Fischbach
Member of Congress

Matt Gaetz
Member of Congress

Andy Biggs
Ranking Member
Subcommittee on Crime, Terrorism and Homeland Security

W. Gregory Steube
Member of Congress

Thomas Massie
Member of Congress

Dan Bishop
Member of Congress

Victoria Spartz
Member of Congress

Scott Fitzgerald
Member of Congress

Cliff Bentz
Member of Congress

Burgess Owens
Member of Congress

cc: The Honorable Jerrold L. Nadler
Chairman

Mr. Monty Wilkinson
Director, Executive Office for U.S. Attorneys

JERROLD NADLER, New York
CHAIRMAN

JIM JORDAN, Ohio
RANKING MEMBER

ONE HUNDRED SEVENTEENTH CONGRESS
Congress of the United States
House of Representatives
COMMITTEE ON THE JUDICIARY
2138 RAYBURN HOUSE OFFICE BUILDING
WASHINGTON, DC 20515–6216
(202) 225–3951
judiciary.house.gov

November 1, 2021

Mr. Fred J. Federici
Acting U.S. Attorney
District of New Mexico
P.O. Box 607
Albuquerque, New Mexico 87103

Dear Mr. Federici:

We are continuing to investigate the troubling attempts by the Department of Justice and the White House to use the heavy hand of federal law enforcement to target concerned parents at local school board meetings and chill their protected First Amendment activity. Because the Department directed you, along with all other U.S. Attorneys, and the Federal Bureau of Investigation (FBI) to take action to address parents attending school board meetings,[1] we respectfully request your assistance with our investigation.

On September 29, 2021, the National School Boards Association (NSBA) sent a letter to President Joe Biden requesting help from the federal government with concerned parents voicing their opinions at school board meetings.[2] The NSBA letter stated that "malice, violence, and threats" against school officials "could be the equivalent of a form of domestic terrorism or hate crimes."[3] The letter cited a number of interactions at school board meetings, none of which rose to the level of domestic terrorism. In fact, the vast majority of incidents cited by the NSBA did not involve threats or violence.[4] Most notably, as an example of domestic terrorism, the NSBA cited an incident in which a father angrily confronted members at a school board meeting in Loudoun County, Virginia about the heinous sexual assault of his daughter.[5]

A mere five days after the NSBA sent its letter to President Biden, on October 4, 2021, Attorney General Merrick Garland issued a shocking memorandum that directed the FBI and

---

[1] Memorandum from Atty Gen. Merrick Garland, U.S. Dep't of Justice, Partnership Among Federal, State, Local, Tribal, And Territorial Law Enforcement to Address Threats Against School Administrators, Board Members, Teachers, and Staff (Oct. 4, 2021).
[2] Letter from Dr. Viola M. Garcia, President, Nat'l School Board Assoc. & Mr. Chip Slaven, Chief Exec. Officer, Nat'l School Board Assoc., to President Joseph R. Biden, White House (Sept. 29, 2021).
[3] *Id.*
[4] *See* Caroline Downey, *Vast majority of incidents cited by school-board group to justify federal intervention didn't involve threats,* NAT'L REV. (Oct. 2, 2021).
[5] *Id.*; *see also* Jessica Chasmar, *Loudoun County father arrested at school board events says school tried to cover up daughter's bathroom assault*, FOX NEWS (Oct. 12, 2021).

U.S. Attorneys' Offices to "convene meetings" in your judicial district "with federal, state, local, Tribal, and territorial leaders" within 30 days.[6] The Justice Department simultaneously issued a press release indicating that the Attorney General's directive would "open dedicated lines of communication for threat reporting, assessment and response by law enforcement"—in other words, create a snitch line for complaints about concerned parents.[7]

During Attorney General Garland's testimony before our Committee on October 21, he appeared to have no idea whether the U.S. Attorney meetings he ordered were actually taking place. He stated: "I don't know whether [the meetings] are ongoing, but I expect and hope that they are going . . . because I did ask that they take place."[8] Attorney General Garland testified that he doubted "there have been meetings in every jurisdiction," but reiterated his belief that it is important for federal law enforcement authorities to conduct these meetings in every judicial district.[9] According to the Attorney General's directives, meetings are to be convened in all 94 judicial districts by November 3, 2021, at the latest.

Following the Attorney General's testimony, the NSBA Board of Directors, apparently recognizing the ill-conceived consequences of its letter and the resulting Justice Department action, issued a new memorandum to its members apologizing for the letter, stating: "On behalf of NSBA, <u>we regret and apologize for the letter</u>."[10] (emphasis in original). Although Attorney General Garland testified that the NSBA letter to President Biden was the basis for his October 4 directive to insert federal law enforcement into local school board matters, the Attorney General has yet to rescind his memorandum. His directives to you and other U.S. Attorneys remain in effect.

Concerned parents voicing their strong opposition to controversial curricula at local schools are not domestic terrorists. Parents have an undisputed right to direct the upbringing and education of their children.[11] When parents, however, cross the line to commit a violent act or issue a criminal threat,[12] state and local authorities are best-equipped to handle these violations of state law. But we must not tolerate the use of the federal law enforcement apparatus to intimidate and silence parents using their Constitutional rights to advocate for their child's future.

To assist our investigation and determine whether these meetings are ongoing, we request that you provide the following documents and information:

---

[6] Memorandum from Atty Gen. Merrick Garland, U.S. Dep't of Justice, Partnership Among Federal, State, Local, Tribal, And Territorial Law Enforcement to Address Threats Against School Administrators, Board Members, Teachers, and Staff (Oct. 4, 2021).
[7] Press Release, U.S. Dep't of Justice, Justice Department Addresses Violent Threats Against School Officials and Teachers (Oct. 4, 2021).
[8] *Oversight of the United States Department of Justice: Hearing Before the H. comm. on the Judiciary,* 117th Cong. at 94 (2021) (testimony from Hon. Merrick Garland, Atty Gen., U.S. Dep't of Justice).
[9] *Id.* at 95.
[10] Memorandum from NSBA Board of Directors, Message to NSBA Members (Oct. 22, 2021).
[11] *Troxel v. Granville,* 530 U.S. 57, 65 (2000) (citing *Meyer v. Nebraska,* 262 U.S. 390, 399 (1923)).
[12] *Merrick Garland's federal offense,* WALL ST. J. (Oct. 6, 2021).

1. All documents and communications referring or relating to convening meeting(s) in your judicial district in accordance with the Attorney General's October 4, 2021 memorandum;

2. All agendas, minutes, and notes created or relied upon by U.S. Attorney's Office employees referring or relating to meeting(s) in your judicial district in accordance with the Attorney General's October 4, 2021 memorandum;

3. Please explain when meeting(s) in your judicial district in accordance with the Attorney General's October 4, 2021 memorandum have occurred or will occur;

4. Please identify by name and title of all U.S. Attorney's Office employees involved in the meeting(s) in your judicial district in accordance with the Attorney General's October 4, 2021 memorandum ;

5. Please identify all federal, state, local, Tribal, and territorial organizations invited to or that have attended the meetings convened in your judicial district in accordance with the October 4, 2021 memorandum; and

6. Please provide all recommendations, both formal and informal, and any meeting minutes produced at the meeting(s) in your judicial district in accordance with the Attorney General's October 4, 2021 memorandum.

Please provide this material as soon as possible but no later than 5:00 p.m. on November 15, 2021.

If you have any questions about this request, please contact Committee staff at (202) 225-6906. Thank you for your attention to this important matter.

Sincerely,

Jim Jordan
Ranking Member

Steve Chabot
Member of Congress

Louie Gohmert
Member of Congress

Darrell Issa
Ranking Member
Subcommittee on Courts, Intellectual Property, and the Internet

Ken Buck
Ranking Member
Subcommittee on Antitrust, Commercial and Administrative Law

Matt Gaetz
Member of Congress

Mike Johnson
Ranking Member
Subcommittee on the Constitution, Civil Rights and Civil Liberties

Andy Biggs
Ranking Member
Subcommittee on Crime, Terrorism and Homeland Security

Tom McClintock
Ranking Member
Subcommittee on Immigration and Citizenship

W. Gregory Steube
Member of Congress

Tom Tiffany
Member of Congress

Thomas Massie
Member of Congress

Chip Roy
Member of Congress

Dan Bishop
Member of Congress

Michelle Fischbach
Member of Congress

Victoria Spartz
Member of Congress

Scott Fitzgerald
Member of Congress

Cliff Bentz
Member of Congress

Burgess Owens
Member of Congress

cc: The Honorable Jerrold L. Nadler
Chairman

Mr. Monty Wilkinson
Director, Executive Office for U.S. Attorneys

JERROLD NADLER, New York
CHAIRMAN

JIM JORDAN, Ohio
RANKING MEMBER

ONE HUNDRED SEVENTEENTH CONGRESS

Congress of the United States

House of Representatives

COMMITTEE ON THE JUDICIARY

2138 RAYBURN HOUSE OFFICE BUILDING

WASHINGTON, DC 20515-6216

(202) 225-3951
judiciary.house.gov

November 1, 2021

Mr. Christopher Chiou
Acting U.S. Attorney
District of Nevada
501 Las Vegas Boulevard South, Suite 1100
Las Vegas, NV 89101

Dear Mr. Chiou:

We are continuing to investigate the troubling attempts by the Department of Justice and the White House to use the heavy hand of federal law enforcement to target concerned parents at local school board meetings and chill their protected First Amendment activity. Because the Department directed you, along with all other U.S. Attorneys, and the Federal Bureau of Investigation (FBI) to take action to address parents attending school board meetings,[1] we respectfully request your assistance with our investigation.

On September 29, 2021, the National School Boards Association (NSBA) sent a letter to President Joe Biden requesting help from the federal government with concerned parents voicing their opinions at school board meetings.[2] The NSBA letter stated that "malice, violence, and threats" against school officials "could be the equivalent of a form of domestic terrorism or hate crimes."[3] The letter cited a number of interactions at school board meetings, none of which rose to the level of domestic terrorism. In fact, the vast majority of incidents cited by the NSBA did not involve threats or violence.[4] Most notably, as an example of domestic terrorism, the NSBA cited an incident in which a father angrily confronted members at a school board meeting in Loudoun County, Virginia about the heinous sexual assault of his daughter.[5]

A mere five days after the NSBA sent its letter to President Biden, on October 4, 2021, Attorney General Merrick Garland issued a shocking memorandum that directed the FBI and

---

[1] Memorandum from Atty Gen. Merrick Garland, U.S. Dep't of Justice, Partnership Among Federal, State, Local, Tribal, And Territorial Law Enforcement to Address Threats Against School Administrators, Board Members, Teachers, and Staff (Oct. 4, 2021).
[2] Letter from Dr. Viola M. Garcia, President, Nat'l School Board Assoc. & Mr. Chip Slaven, Chief Exec. Officer, Nat'l School Board Assoc., to President Joseph R. Biden, White House (Sept. 29, 2021).
[3] *Id.*
[4] *See* Caroline Downey, *Vast majority of incidents cited by school-board group to justify federal intervention didn't involve threats,* NAT'L REV. (Oct. 2, 2021).
[5] *Id.*; *see also* Jessica Chasmar, *Loudoun County father arrested at school board events says school tried to cover up daughter's bathroom assault*, FOX NEWS (Oct. 12, 2021).

U.S. Attorneys' Offices to "convene meetings" in your judicial district "with federal, state, local, Tribal, and territorial leaders" within 30 days.[6] The Justice Department simultaneously issued a press release indicating that the Attorney General's directive would "open dedicated lines of communication for threat reporting, assessment and response by law enforcement"—in other words, create a snitch line for complaints about concerned parents.[7]

During Attorney General Garland's testimony before our Committee on October 21, he appeared to have no idea whether the U.S. Attorney meetings he ordered were actually taking place. He stated: "I don't know whether [the meetings] are ongoing, but I expect and hope that they are going . . . because I did ask that they take place."[8] Attorney General Garland testified that he doubted "there have been meetings in every jurisdiction," but reiterated his belief that it is important for federal law enforcement authorities to conduct these meetings in every judicial district.[9] According to the Attorney General's directives, meetings are to be convened in all 94 judicial districts by November 3, 2021, at the latest.

Following the Attorney General's testimony, the NSBA Board of Directors, apparently recognizing the ill-conceived consequences of its letter and the resulting Justice Department action, issued a new memorandum to its members apologizing for the letter, stating: "On behalf of NSBA, <u>we regret and apologize for the letter</u>."[10] (emphasis in original). Although Attorney General Garland testified that the NSBA letter to President Biden was the basis for his October 4 directive to insert federal law enforcement into local school board matters, the Attorney General has yet to rescind his memorandum. His directives to you and other U.S. Attorneys remain in effect.

Concerned parents voicing their strong opposition to controversial curricula at local schools are not domestic terrorists. Parents have an undisputed right to direct the upbringing and education of their children.[11] When parents, however, cross the line to commit a violent act or issue a criminal threat,[12] state and local authorities are best-equipped to handle these violations of state law. But we must not tolerate the use of the federal law enforcement apparatus to intimidate and silence parents using their Constitutional rights to advocate for their child's future.

To assist our investigation and determine whether these meetings are ongoing, we request that you provide the following documents and information:

---

[6] Memorandum from Atty Gen. Merrick Garland, U.S. Dep't of Justice, Partnership Among Federal, State, Local, Tribal, And Territorial Law Enforcement to Address Threats Against School Administrators, Board Members, Teachers, and Staff (Oct. 4, 2021).
[7] Press Release, U.S. Dep't of Justice, Justice Department Addresses Violent Threats Against School Officials and Teachers (Oct. 4, 2021).
[8] *Oversight of the United States Department of Justice: Hearing Before the H. comm. on the Judiciary,* 117th Cong. at 94 (2021) (testimony from Hon. Merrick Garland, Atty Gen., U.S. Dep't of Justice).
[9] *Id.* at 95.
[10] Memorandum from NSBA Board of Directors, Message to NSBA Members (Oct. 22, 2021).
[11] *Troxel v. Granville,* 530 U.S. 57, 65 (2000) (citing *Meyer v. Nebraska,* 262 U.S. 390, 399 (1923)).
[12] *Merrick Garland's federal offense,* WALL ST. J. (Oct. 6, 2021).

1. All documents and communications referring or relating to convening meeting(s) in your judicial district in accordance with the Attorney General's October 4, 2021 memorandum;

2. All agendas, minutes, and notes created or relied upon by U.S. Attorney's Office employees referring or relating to meeting(s) in your judicial district in accordance with the Attorney General's October 4, 2021 memorandum;

3. Please explain when meeting(s) in your judicial district in accordance with the Attorney General's October 4, 2021 memorandum have occurred or will occur;

4. Please identify by name and title of all U.S. Attorney's Office employees involved in the meeting(s) in your judicial district in accordance with the Attorney General's October 4, 2021 memorandum ;

5. Please identify all federal, state, local, Tribal, and territorial organizations invited to or that have attended the meetings convened in your judicial district in accordance with the October 4, 2021 memorandum; and

6. Please provide all recommendations, both formal and informal, and any meeting minutes produced at the meeting(s) in your judicial district in accordance with the Attorney General's October 4, 2021 memorandum.

Please provide this material as soon as possible but no later than 5:00 p.m. on November 15, 2021.

If you have any questions about this request, please contact Committee staff at (202) 225-6906. Thank you for your attention to this important matter.

Sincerely,

Jim Jordan
Ranking Member

Steve Chabot
Member of Congress

Louie Gohmert
Member of Congress

Darrell Issa
Ranking Member
Subcommittee on Courts, Intellectual Property, and the Internet

Ken Buck
Ranking Member
Subcommittee on Antitrust, Commercial and Administrative Law

Matt Gaetz
Member of Congress

Mike Johnson
Ranking Member
Subcommittee on the Constitution, Civil Rights and Civil Liberties

Andy Biggs
Ranking Member
Subcommittee on Crime, Terrorism and Homeland Security

Tom McClintock
Ranking Member
Subcommittee on Immigration and Citizenship

W. Gregory Steube
Member of Congress

Tom Tiffany
Member of Congress

Thomas Massie
Member of Congress

Chip Roy
Member of Congress

Dan Bishop
Member of Congress

Michelle Fischbach
Member of Congress

Victoria Spartz
Member of Congress

Scott Fitzgerald
Member of Congress

Cliff Bentz
Member of Congress

Burgess Owens
Member of Congress

cc: The Honorable Jerrold L. Nadler
Chairman

Mr. Monty Wilkinson
Director, Executive Office for U.S. Attorneys

JERROLD NADLER, New York
CHAIRMAN

JIM JORDAN, Ohio
RANKING MEMBER

ONE HUNDRED SEVENTEENTH CONGRESS

Congress of the United States

House of Representatives

COMMITTEE ON THE JUDICIARY

2138 RAYBURN HOUSE OFFICE BUILDING

WASHINGTON, DC 20515-6216

(202) 225-3951
judiciary.house.gov

November 1, 2021

The Honorable Carla B. Freedman
U.S. Attorney
Northern District of New York
100 South Clinton Street, P.O. Box 7198
Syracuse, NY 13261

Dear Ms. Freedman:

We are continuing to investigate the troubling attempts by the Department of Justice and the White House to use the heavy hand of federal law enforcement to target concerned parents at local school board meetings and chill their protected First Amendment activity. Because the Department directed you, along with all other U.S. Attorneys, and the Federal Bureau of Investigation (FBI) to take action to address parents attending school board meetings,[1] we respectfully request your assistance with our investigation.

On September 29, 2021, the National School Boards Association (NSBA) sent a letter to President Joe Biden requesting help from the federal government with concerned parents voicing their opinions at school board meetings.[2] The NSBA letter stated that "malice, violence, and threats" against school officials "could be the equivalent of a form of domestic terrorism or hate crimes."[3] The letter cited a number of interactions at school board meetings, none of which rose to the level of domestic terrorism. In fact, the vast majority of incidents cited by the NSBA did not involve threats or violence.[4] Most notably, as an example of domestic terrorism, the NSBA cited an incident in which a father angrily confronted members at a school board meeting in Loudoun County, Virginia about the heinous sexual assault of his daughter.[5]

A mere five days after the NSBA sent its letter to President Biden, on October 4, 2021, Attorney General Merrick Garland issued a shocking memorandum that directed the FBI and

---

[1] Memorandum from Atty Gen. Merrick Garland, U.S. Dep't of Justice, Partnership Among Federal, State, Local, Tribal, And Territorial Law Enforcement to Address Threats Against School Administrators, Board Members, Teachers, and Staff (Oct. 4, 2021).

[2] Letter from Dr. Viola M. Garcia, President, Nat'l School Board Assoc. & Mr. Chip Slaven, Chief Exec. Officer, Nat'l School Board Assoc., to President Joseph R. Biden, White House (Sept. 29, 2021).

[3] *Id.*

[4] *See* Caroline Downey, *Vast majority of incidents cited by school-board group to justify federal intervention didn't involve threats,* NAT'L REV. (Oct. 2, 2021).

[5] *Id.*; *see also* Jessica Chasmar, *Loudoun County father arrested at school board events says school tried to cover up daughter's bathroom assault*, FOX NEWS (Oct. 12, 2021).

U.S. Attorneys' Offices to "convene meetings" in your judicial district "with federal, state, local, Tribal, and territorial leaders" within 30 days.[6] The Justice Department simultaneously issued a press release indicating that the Attorney General's directive would "open dedicated lines of communication for threat reporting, assessment and response by law enforcement"—in other words, create a snitch line for complaints about concerned parents.[7]

During Attorney General Garland's testimony before our Committee on October 21, he appeared to have no idea whether the U.S. Attorney meetings he ordered were actually taking place. He stated: "I don't know whether [the meetings] are ongoing, but I expect and hope that they are going . . . because I did ask that they take place."[8] Attorney General Garland testified that he doubted "there have been meetings in every jurisdiction," but reiterated his belief that it is important for federal law enforcement authorities to conduct these meetings in every judicial district.[9] According to the Attorney General's directives, meetings are to be convened in all 94 judicial districts by November 3, 2021, at the latest.

Following the Attorney General's testimony, the NSBA Board of Directors, apparently recognizing the ill-conceived consequences of its letter and the resulting Justice Department action, issued a new memorandum to its members apologizing for the letter, stating: "On behalf of NSBA, <u>we regret and apologize for the letter</u>."[10] (emphasis in original). Although Attorney General Garland testified that the NSBA letter to President Biden was the basis for his October 4 directive to insert federal law enforcement into local school board matters, the Attorney General has yet to rescind his memorandum. His directives to you and other U.S. Attorneys remain in effect.

Concerned parents voicing their strong opposition to controversial curricula at local schools are not domestic terrorists. Parents have an undisputed right to direct the upbringing and education of their children.[11] When parents, however, cross the line to commit a violent act or issue a criminal threat,[12] state and local authorities are best-equipped to handle these violations of state law. But we must not tolerate the use of the federal law enforcement apparatus to intimidate and silence parents using their Constitutional rights to advocate for their child's future.

To assist our investigation and determine whether these meetings are ongoing, we request that you provide the following documents and information:

---

[6] Memorandum from Atty Gen. Merrick Garland, U.S. Dep't of Justice, Partnership Among Federal, State, Local, Tribal, And Territorial Law Enforcement to Address Threats Against School Administrators, Board Members, Teachers, and Staff (Oct. 4, 2021).
[7] Press Release, U.S. Dep't of Justice, Justice Department Addresses Violent Threats Against School Officials and Teachers (Oct. 4, 2021).
[8] *Oversight of the United States Department of Justice: Hearing Before the H. comm. on the Judiciary,* 117th Cong. at 94 (2021) (testimony from Hon. Merrick Garland, Atty Gen., U.S. Dep't of Justice).
[9] *Id.* at 95.
[10] Memorandum from NSBA Board of Directors, Message to NSBA Members (Oct. 22, 2021).
[11] *Troxel v. Granville,* 530 U.S. 57, 65 (2000) (citing *Meyer v. Nebraska,* 262 U.S. 390, 399 (1923)).
[12] *Merrick Garland's federal offense,* WALL ST. J. (Oct. 6, 2021).

1. All documents and communications referring or relating to convening meeting(s) in your judicial district in accordance with the Attorney General's October 4, 2021 memorandum;

2. All agendas, minutes, and notes created or relied upon by U.S. Attorney's Office employees referring or relating to meeting(s) in your judicial district in accordance with the Attorney General's October 4, 2021 memorandum;

3. Please explain when meeting(s) in your judicial district in accordance with the Attorney General's October 4, 2021 memorandum have occurred or will occur;

4. Please identify by name and title of all U.S. Attorney's Office employees involved in the meeting(s) in your judicial district in accordance with the Attorney General's October 4, 2021 memorandum ;

5. Please identify all federal, state, local, Tribal, and territorial organizations invited to or that have attended the meetings convened in your judicial district in accordance with the October 4, 2021 memorandum; and

6. Please provide all recommendations, both formal and informal, and any meeting minutes produced at the meeting(s) in your judicial district in accordance with the Attorney General's October 4, 2021 memorandum.

Please provide this material as soon as possible but no later than 5:00 p.m. on November 15, 2021.

If you have any questions about this request, please contact Committee staff at (202) 225-6906. Thank you for your attention to this important matter.

Sincerely,

Jim Jordan
Ranking Member

Steve Chabot
Member of Congress

Louie Gohmert
Member of Congress

Darrell Issa
Ranking Member
Subcommittee on Courts, Intellectual Property, and the Internet

Ken Buck
Ranking Member
Subcommittee on Antitrust, Commercial and Administrative Law

Matt Gaetz
Member of Congress

Mike Johnson
Ranking Member
Subcommittee on the Constitution, Civil Rights and Civil Liberties

Andy Biggs
Ranking Member
Subcommittee on Crime, Terrorism and Homeland Security

Tom McClintock
Ranking Member
Subcommittee on Immigration and Citizenship

W. Gregory Steube
Member of Congress

Tom Tiffany
Member of Congress

Thomas Massie
Member of Congress

Chip Roy
Member of Congress

Dan Bishop
Member of Congress

Michelle Fischbach
Member of Congress

Victoria Spartz
Member of Congress

Scott Fitzgerald
Member of Congress

Cliff Bentz
Member of Congress

Burgess Owens
Member of Congress

cc: The Honorable Jerrold L. Nadler
Chairman

Mr. Monty Wilkinson
Director, Executive Office for U.S. Attorneys

JERROLD NADLER, New York
CHAIRMAN

JIM JORDAN, Ohio
RANKING MEMBER

ONE HUNDRED SEVENTEENTH CONGRESS

Congress of the United States
House of Representatives
COMMITTEE ON THE JUDICIARY

2138 RAYBURN HOUSE OFFICE BUILDING
WASHINGTON, DC 20515-6216
(202) 225-3951
judiciary.house.gov

November 1, 2021

The Honorable Breon Peace
U.S. Attorney
Eastern District of New York
271 Cadman Plaza East
Brooklyn, NY 11201

Dear Mr. Peace:

We are continuing to investigate the troubling attempts by the Department of Justice and the White House to use the heavy hand of federal law enforcement to target concerned parents at local school board meetings and chill their protected First Amendment activity. Because the Department directed you, along with all other U.S. Attorneys, and the Federal Bureau of Investigation (FBI) to take action to address parents attending school board meetings,[1] we respectfully request your assistance with our investigation.

On September 29, 2021, the National School Boards Association (NSBA) sent a letter to President Joe Biden requesting help from the federal government with concerned parents voicing their opinions at school board meetings.[2] The NSBA letter stated that "malice, violence, and threats" against school officials "could be the equivalent of a form of domestic terrorism or hate crimes."[3] The letter cited a number of interactions at school board meetings, none of which rose to the level of domestic terrorism. In fact, the vast majority of incidents cited by the NSBA did not involve threats or violence.[4] Most notably, as an example of domestic terrorism, the NSBA cited an incident in which a father angrily confronted members at a school board meeting in Loudoun County, Virginia about the heinous sexual assault of his daughter.[5]

A mere five days after the NSBA sent its letter to President Biden, on October 4, 2021, Attorney General Merrick Garland issued a shocking memorandum that directed the FBI and

---

[1] Memorandum from Atty Gen. Merrick Garland, U.S. Dep't of Justice, Partnership Among Federal, State, Local, Tribal, And Territorial Law Enforcement to Address Threats Against School Administrators, Board Members, Teachers, and Staff (Oct. 4, 2021).
[2] Letter from Dr. Viola M. Garcia, President, Nat'l School Board Assoc. & Mr. Chip Slaven, Chief Exec. Officer, Nat'l School Board Assoc., to President Joseph R. Biden, White House (Sept. 29, 2021).
[3] *Id.*
[4] *See* Caroline Downey, *Vast majority of incidents cited by school-board group to justify federal intervention didn't involve threats,* NAT'L REV. (Oct. 2, 2021).
[5] *Id.*; *see also* Jessica Chasmar, *Loudoun County father arrested at school board events says school tried to cover up daughter's bathroom assault*, FOX NEWS (Oct. 12, 2021).

U.S. Attorneys' Offices to "convene meetings" in your judicial district "with federal, state, local, Tribal, and territorial leaders" within 30 days.[6] The Justice Department simultaneously issued a press release indicating that the Attorney General's directive would "open dedicated lines of communication for threat reporting, assessment and response by law enforcement"—in other words, create a snitch line for complaints about concerned parents.[7]

During Attorney General Garland's testimony before our Committee on October 21, he appeared to have no idea whether the U.S. Attorney meetings he ordered were actually taking place. He stated: "I don't know whether [the meetings] are ongoing, but I expect and hope that they are going . . . because I did ask that they take place."[8] Attorney General Garland testified that he doubted "there have been meetings in every jurisdiction," but reiterated his belief that it is important for federal law enforcement authorities to conduct these meetings in every judicial district.[9] According to the Attorney General's directives, meetings are to be convened in all 94 judicial districts by November 3, 2021, at the latest.

Following the Attorney General's testimony, the NSBA Board of Directors, apparently recognizing the ill-conceived consequences of its letter and the resulting Justice Department action, issued a new memorandum to its members apologizing for the letter, stating: "On behalf of NSBA, <u>we regret and apologize for the letter</u>."[10] (emphasis in original). Although Attorney General Garland testified that the NSBA letter to President Biden was the basis for his October 4 directive to insert federal law enforcement into local school board matters, the Attorney General has yet to rescind his memorandum. His directives to you and other U.S. Attorneys remain in effect.

Concerned parents voicing their strong opposition to controversial curricula at local schools are not domestic terrorists. Parents have an undisputed right to direct the upbringing and education of their children.[11] When parents, however, cross the line to commit a violent act or issue a criminal threat,[12] state and local authorities are best-equipped to handle these violations of state law. But we must not tolerate the use of the federal law enforcement apparatus to intimidate and silence parents using their Constitutional rights to advocate for their child's future.

To assist our investigation and determine whether these meetings are ongoing, we request that you provide the following documents and information:

---

[6] Memorandum from Atty Gen. Merrick Garland, U.S. Dep't of Justice, Partnership Among Federal, State, Local, Tribal, And Territorial Law Enforcement to Address Threats Against School Administrators, Board Members, Teachers, and Staff (Oct. 4, 2021).

[7] Press Release, U.S. Dep't of Justice, Justice Department Addresses Violent Threats Against School Officials and Teachers (Oct. 4, 2021).

[8] *Oversight of the United States Department of Justice: Hearing Before the H. comm. on the Judiciary,* 117th Cong. at 94 (2021) (testimony from Hon. Merrick Garland, Atty Gen., U.S. Dep't of Justice).

[9] *Id.* at 95.

[10] Memorandum from NSBA Board of Directors, Message to NSBA Members (Oct. 22, 2021).

[11] *Troxel v. Granville,* 530 U.S. 57, 65 (2000) (citing *Meyer v. Nebraska,* 262 U.S. 390, 399 (1923)).

[12] *Merrick Garland's federal offense,* WALL ST. J. (Oct. 6, 2021).

1. All documents and communications referring or relating to convening meeting(s) in your judicial district in accordance with the Attorney General's October 4, 2021 memorandum;

2. All agendas, minutes, and notes created or relied upon by U.S. Attorney's Office employees referring or relating to meeting(s) in your judicial district in accordance with the Attorney General's October 4, 2021 memorandum;

3. Please explain when meeting(s) in your judicial district in accordance with the Attorney General's October 4, 2021 memorandum have occurred or will occur;

4. Please identify by name and title of all U.S. Attorney's Office employees involved in the meeting(s) in your judicial district in accordance with the Attorney General's October 4, 2021 memorandum ;

5. Please identify all federal, state, local, Tribal, and territorial organizations invited to or that have attended the meetings convened in your judicial district in accordance with the October 4, 2021 memorandum; and

6. Please provide all recommendations, both formal and informal, and any meeting minutes produced at the meeting(s) in your judicial district in accordance with the Attorney General's October 4, 2021 memorandum.

Please provide this material as soon as possible but no later than 5:00 p.m. on November 15, 2021.

If you have any questions about this request, please contact Committee staff at (202) 225-6906. Thank you for your attention to this important matter.

Sincerely,

Jim Jordan
Ranking Member

Steve Chabot
Member of Congress

Louie Gohmert
Member of Congress

Darrell Issa
Ranking Member
Subcommittee on Courts, Intellectual Property, and the Internet

Ken Buck
Ranking Member
Subcommittee on Antitrust, Commercial
and Administrative Law

Matt Gaetz
Member of Congress

Mike Johnson
Ranking Member
Subcommittee on the Constitution,
Civil Rights and Civil Liberties

Andy Biggs
Ranking Member
Subcommittee on Crime, Terrorism
and Homeland Security

Tom McClintock
Ranking Member
Subcommittee on Immigration
and Citizenship

W. Gregory Steube
Member of Congress

Tom Tiffany
Member of Congress

Thomas Massie
Member of Congress

Chip Roy
Member of Congress

Dan Bishop
Member of Congress

Michelle Fischbach
Member of Congress

Victoria Spartz
Member of Congress

Scott Fitzgerald
Member of Congress

Cliff Bentz
Member of Congress

Burgess Owens
Member of Congress

cc: The Honorable Jerrold L. Nadler
Chairman

Mr. Monty Wilkinson
Director, Executive Office for U.S. Attorneys

JERROLD NADLER, New York
CHAIRMAN

JIM JORDAN, Ohio
RANKING MEMBER

ONE HUNDRED SEVENTEENTH CONGRESS

Congress of the United States
House of Representatives

COMMITTEE ON THE JUDICIARY
2138 RAYBURN HOUSE OFFICE BUILDING
WASHINGTON, DC 20515–6216
(202) 225–3951
judiciary.house.gov

November 1, 2021

The Honorable Trini E. Ross
U.S. Attorney
Western District of New York
138 Delaware Avenue
Buffalo, NY 14202

Dear Ms. Ross:

We are continuing to investigate the troubling attempts by the Department of Justice and the White House to use the heavy hand of federal law enforcement to target concerned parents at local school board meetings and chill their protected First Amendment activity. Because the Department directed you, along with all other U.S. Attorneys, and the Federal Bureau of Investigation (FBI) to take action to address parents attending school board meetings,[1] we respectfully request your assistance with our investigation.

On September 29, 2021, the National School Boards Association (NSBA) sent a letter to President Joe Biden requesting help from the federal government with concerned parents voicing their opinions at school board meetings.[2] The NSBA letter stated that "malice, violence, and threats" against school officials "could be the equivalent of a form of domestic terrorism or hate crimes."[3] The letter cited a number of interactions at school board meetings, none of which rose to the level of domestic terrorism. In fact, the vast majority of incidents cited by the NSBA did not involve threats or violence.[4] Most notably, as an example of domestic terrorism, the NSBA cited an incident in which a father angrily confronted members at a school board meeting in Loudoun County, Virginia about the heinous sexual assault of his daughter.[5]

A mere five days after the NSBA sent its letter to President Biden, on October 4, 2021, Attorney General Merrick Garland issued a shocking memorandum that directed the FBI and

---

[1] Memorandum from Atty Gen. Merrick Garland, U.S. Dep't of Justice, Partnership Among Federal, State, Local, Tribal, And Territorial Law Enforcement to Address Threats Against School Administrators, Board Members, Teachers, and Staff (Oct. 4, 2021).

[2] Letter from Dr. Viola M. Garcia, President, Nat'l School Board Assoc. & Mr. Chip Slaven, Chief Exec. Officer, Nat'l School Board Assoc., to President Joseph R. Biden, White House (Sept. 29, 2021).

[3] *Id.*

[4] *See* Caroline Downey, *Vast majority of incidents cited by school-board group to justify federal intervention didn't involve threats,* NAT'L REV. (Oct. 2, 2021).

[5] *Id.*; *see also* Jessica Chasmar, *Loudoun County father arrested at school board events says school tried to cover up daughter's bathroom assault*, FOX NEWS (Oct. 12, 2021).

U.S. Attorneys' Offices to "convene meetings" in your judicial district "with federal, state, local, Tribal, and territorial leaders" within 30 days.[6] The Justice Department simultaneously issued a press release indicating that the Attorney General's directive would "open dedicated lines of communication for threat reporting, assessment and response by law enforcement"—in other words, create a snitch line for complaints about concerned parents.[7]

During Attorney General Garland's testimony before our Committee on October 21, he appeared to have no idea whether the U.S. Attorney meetings he ordered were actually taking place. He stated: "I don't know whether [the meetings] are ongoing, but I expect and hope that they are going . . . because I did ask that they take place."[8] Attorney General Garland testified that he doubted "there have been meetings in every jurisdiction," but reiterated his belief that it is important for federal law enforcement authorities to conduct these meetings in every judicial district.[9] According to the Attorney General's directives, meetings are to be convened in all 94 judicial districts by November 3, 2021, at the latest.

Following the Attorney General's testimony, the NSBA Board of Directors, apparently recognizing the ill-conceived consequences of its letter and the resulting Justice Department action, issued a new memorandum to its members apologizing for the letter, stating: "On behalf of NSBA, <u>we regret and apologize for the letter</u>."[10] (emphasis in original). Although Attorney General Garland testified that the NSBA letter to President Biden was the basis for his October 4 directive to insert federal law enforcement into local school board matters, the Attorney General has yet to rescind his memorandum. His directives to you and other U.S. Attorneys remain in effect.

Concerned parents voicing their strong opposition to controversial curricula at local schools are not domestic terrorists. Parents have an undisputed right to direct the upbringing and education of their children.[11] When parents, however, cross the line to commit a violent act or issue a criminal threat,[12] state and local authorities are best-equipped to handle these violations of state law. But we must not tolerate the use of the federal law enforcement apparatus to intimidate and silence parents using their Constitutional rights to advocate for their child's future.

To assist our investigation and determine whether these meetings are ongoing, we request that you provide the following documents and information:

---

[6] Memorandum from Atty Gen. Merrick Garland, U.S. Dep't of Justice, Partnership Among Federal, State, Local, Tribal, And Territorial Law Enforcement to Address Threats Against School Administrators, Board Members, Teachers, and Staff (Oct. 4, 2021).
[7] Press Release, U.S. Dep't of Justice, Justice Department Addresses Violent Threats Against School Officials and Teachers (Oct. 4, 2021).
[8] *Oversight of the United States Department of Justice: Hearing Before the H. comm. on the Judiciary,* 117th Cong. at 94 (2021) (testimony from Hon. Merrick Garland, Atty Gen., U.S. Dep't of Justice).
[9] *Id.* at 95.
[10] Memorandum from NSBA Board of Directors, Message to NSBA Members (Oct. 22, 2021).
[11] *Troxel v. Granville,* 530 U.S. 57, 65 (2000) (citing *Meyer v. Nebraska,* 262 U.S. 390, 399 (1923)).
[12] *Merrick Garland's federal offense,* WALL ST. J. (Oct. 6, 2021).

1. All documents and communications referring or relating to convening meeting(s) in your judicial district in accordance with the Attorney General's October 4, 2021 memorandum;

2. All agendas, minutes, and notes created or relied upon by U.S. Attorney's Office employees referring or relating to meeting(s) in your judicial district in accordance with the Attorney General's October 4, 2021 memorandum;

3. Please explain when meeting(s) in your judicial district in accordance with the Attorney General's October 4, 2021 memorandum have occurred or will occur;

4. Please identify by name and title of all U.S. Attorney's Office employees involved in the meeting(s) in your judicial district in accordance with the Attorney General's October 4, 2021 memorandum ;

5. Please identify all federal, state, local, Tribal, and territorial organizations invited to or that have attended the meetings convened in your judicial district in accordance with the October 4, 2021 memorandum; and

6. Please provide all recommendations, both formal and informal, and any meeting minutes produced at the meeting(s) in your judicial district in accordance with the Attorney General's October 4, 2021 memorandum.

Please provide this material as soon as possible but no later than 5:00 p.m. on November 15, 2021.

If you have any questions about this request, please contact Committee staff at (202) 225-6906. Thank you for your attention to this important matter.

Sincerely,

Jim Jordan
Ranking Member

Steve Chabot
Member of Congress

Louie Gohmert
Member of Congress

Darrell Issa
Ranking Member
Subcommittee on Courts, Intellectual Property, and the Internet

Ken Buck
Ranking Member
Subcommittee on Antitrust, Commercial and Administrative Law

Matt Gaetz
Member of Congress

Mike Johnson
Ranking Member
Subcommittee on the Constitution, Civil Rights and Civil Liberties

Andy Biggs
Ranking Member
Subcommittee on Crime, Terrorism and Homeland Security

Tom McClintock
Ranking Member
Subcommittee on Immigration and Citizenship

W. Gregory Steube
Member of Congress

Tom Tiffany
Member of Congress

Thomas Massie
Member of Congress

Chip Roy
Member of Congress

Dan Bishop
Member of Congress

Michelle Fischbach
Member of Congress

Victoria Spartz
Member of Congress

Scott Fitzgerald
Member of Congress

Cliff Bentz
Member of Congress

Burgess Owens
Member of Congress

cc: The Honorable Jerrold L. Nadler
Chairman

Mr. Monty Wilkinson
Director, Executive Office for U.S. Attorneys

JERROLD NADLER, New York
CHAIRMAN

JIM JORDAN, Ohio
RANKING MEMBER

ONE HUNDRED SEVENTEENTH CONGRESS

Congress of the United States

House of Representatives

COMMITTEE ON THE JUDICIARY

2138 RAYBURN HOUSE OFFICE BUILDING

WASHINGTON, DC 20515–6216

(202) 225–3951
judiciary.house.gov

November 1, 2021

The Honorable Damian Williams
U.S. Attorney
Southern District of New York
1 St. Andrew's Plaza
New York City, NY 10007

Dear Mr. Williams:

We are continuing to investigate the troubling attempts by the Department of Justice and the White House to use the heavy hand of federal law enforcement to target concerned parents at local school board meetings and chill their protected First Amendment activity. Because the Department directed you, along with all other U.S. Attorneys, and the Federal Bureau of Investigation (FBI) to take action to address parents attending school board meetings,[1] we respectfully request your assistance with our investigation.

On September 29, 2021, the National School Boards Association (NSBA) sent a letter to President Joe Biden requesting help from the federal government with concerned parents voicing their opinions at school board meetings.[2] The NSBA letter stated that "malice, violence, and threats" against school officials "could be the equivalent of a form of domestic terrorism or hate crimes."[3] The letter cited a number of interactions at school board meetings, none of which rose to the level of domestic terrorism. In fact, the vast majority of incidents cited by the NSBA did not involve threats or violence.[4] Most notably, as an example of domestic terrorism, the NSBA cited an incident in which a father angrily confronted members at a school board meeting in Loudoun County, Virginia about the heinous sexual assault of his daughter.[5]

A mere five days after the NSBA sent its letter to President Biden, on October 4, 2021, Attorney General Merrick Garland issued a shocking memorandum that directed the FBI and

---

[1] Memorandum from Atty Gen. Merrick Garland, U.S. Dep't of Justice, Partnership Among Federal, State, Local, Tribal, And Territorial Law Enforcement to Address Threats Against School Administrators, Board Members, Teachers, and Staff (Oct. 4, 2021).

[2] Letter from Dr. Viola M. Garcia, President, Nat'l School Board Assoc. & Mr. Chip Slaven, Chief Exec. Officer, Nat'l School Board Assoc., to President Joseph R. Biden, White House (Sept. 29, 2021).

[3] *Id.*

[4] *See* Caroline Downey, *Vast majority of incidents cited by school-board group to justify federal intervention didn't involve threats,* NAT'L REV. (Oct. 2, 2021).

[5] *Id.*; *see also* Jessica Chasmar, *Loudoun County father arrested at school board events says school tried to cover up daughter's bathroom assault*, FOX NEWS (Oct. 12, 2021).

U.S. Attorneys' Offices to "convene meetings" in your judicial district "with federal, state, local, Tribal, and territorial leaders" within 30 days.[6] The Justice Department simultaneously issued a press release indicating that the Attorney General's directive would "open dedicated lines of communication for threat reporting, assessment and response by law enforcement"—in other words, create a snitch line for complaints about concerned parents.[7]

During Attorney General Garland's testimony before our Committee on October 21, he appeared to have no idea whether the U.S. Attorney meetings he ordered were actually taking place. He stated: "I don't know whether [the meetings] are ongoing, but I expect and hope that they are going . . . because I did ask that they take place."[8] Attorney General Garland testified that he doubted "there have been meetings in every jurisdiction," but reiterated his belief that it is important for federal law enforcement authorities to conduct these meetings in every judicial district.[9] According to the Attorney General's directives, meetings are to be convened in all 94 judicial districts by November 3, 2021, at the latest.

Following the Attorney General's testimony, the NSBA Board of Directors, apparently recognizing the ill-conceived consequences of its letter and the resulting Justice Department action, issued a new memorandum to its members apologizing for the letter, stating: "On behalf of NSBA, <u>we regret and apologize for the letter</u>."[10] (emphasis in original). Although Attorney General Garland testified that the NSBA letter to President Biden was the basis for his October 4 directive to insert federal law enforcement into local school board matters, the Attorney General has yet to rescind his memorandum. His directives to you and other U.S. Attorneys remain in effect.

Concerned parents voicing their strong opposition to controversial curricula at local schools are not domestic terrorists. Parents have an undisputed right to direct the upbringing and education of their children.[11] When parents, however, cross the line to commit a violent act or issue a criminal threat,[12] state and local authorities are best-equipped to handle these violations of state law. But we must not tolerate the use of the federal law enforcement apparatus to intimidate and silence parents using their Constitutional rights to advocate for their child's future.

To assist our investigation and determine whether these meetings are ongoing, we request that you provide the following documents and information:

---

[6] Memorandum from Atty Gen. Merrick Garland, U.S. Dep't of Justice, Partnership Among Federal, State, Local, Tribal, And Territorial Law Enforcement to Address Threats Against School Administrators, Board Members, Teachers, and Staff (Oct. 4, 2021).
[7] Press Release, U.S. Dep't of Justice, Justice Department Addresses Violent Threats Against School Officials and Teachers (Oct. 4, 2021).
[8] *Oversight of the United States Department of Justice: Hearing Before the H. comm. on the Judiciary,* 117th Cong. at 94 (2021) (testimony from Hon. Merrick Garland, Atty Gen., U.S. Dep't of Justice).
[9] *Id.* at 95.
[10] Memorandum from NSBA Board of Directors, Message to NSBA Members (Oct. 22, 2021).
[11] *Troxel v. Granville,* 530 U.S. 57, 65 (2000) (citing *Meyer v. Nebraska,* 262 U.S. 390, 399 (1923)).
[12] *Merrick Garland's federal offense,* WALL ST. J. (Oct. 6, 2021).

1. All documents and communications referring or relating to convening meeting(s) in your judicial district in accordance with the Attorney General's October 4, 2021 memorandum;

2. All agendas, minutes, and notes created or relied upon by U.S. Attorney's Office employees referring or relating to meeting(s) in your judicial district in accordance with the Attorney General's October 4, 2021 memorandum;

3. Please explain when meeting(s) in your judicial district in accordance with the Attorney General's October 4, 2021 memorandum have occurred or will occur;

4. Please identify by name and title of all U.S. Attorney's Office employees involved in the meeting(s) in your judicial district in accordance with the Attorney General's October 4, 2021 memorandum ;

5. Please identify all federal, state, local, Tribal, and territorial organizations invited to or that have attended the meetings convened in your judicial district in accordance with the October 4, 2021 memorandum; and

6. Please provide all recommendations, both formal and informal, and any meeting minutes produced at the meeting(s) in your judicial district in accordance with the Attorney General's October 4, 2021 memorandum.

Please provide this material as soon as possible but no later than 5:00 p.m. on November 15, 2021.

If you have any questions about this request, please contact Committee staff at (202) 225-6906. Thank you for your attention to this important matter.

Sincerely,

Jim Jordan
Ranking Member

Steve Chabot
Member of Congress

Louie Gohmert
Member of Congress

Darrell Issa
Ranking Member
Subcommittee on Courts, Intellectual Property, and the Internet

Ken Buck
Ranking Member
Subcommittee on Antitrust, Commercial and Administrative Law

Matt Gaetz
Member of Congress

Mike Johnson
Ranking Member
Subcommittee on the Constitution, Civil Rights and Civil Liberties

Andy Biggs
Ranking Member
Subcommittee on Crime, Terrorism and Homeland Security

Tom McClintock
Ranking Member
Subcommittee on Immigration and Citizenship

W. Gregory Steube
Member of Congress

Tom Tiffany
Member of Congress

Thomas Massie
Member of Congress

Chip Roy
Member of Congress

Dan Bishop
Member of Congress

Michelle Fischbach
Member of Congress

Victoria Spartz
Member of Congress

Scott Fitzgerald
Member of Congress

Cliff Bentz
Member of Congress

Burgess Owens
Member of Congress

cc: The Honorable Jerrold L. Nadler
Chairman

Mr. Monty Wilkinson
Director, Executive Office for U.S. Attorneys

JERROLD NADLER, New York
CHAIRMAN

JIM JORDAN, Ohio
RANKING MEMBER

ONE HUNDRED SEVENTEENTH CONGRESS

Congress of the United States

House of Representatives

COMMITTEE ON THE JUDICIARY

2138 RAYBURN HOUSE OFFICE BUILDING

WASHINGTON, DC 20515–6216

(202) 225–3951
judiciary.house.gov

November 1, 2021

Ms. Bridget M. Brennan
Acting U.S. Attorney
Northern District of Ohio
801 West Superior Avenue, Suite 400
Cleveland, Ohio 44113

Dear Ms. Brennan:

We are continuing to investigate the troubling attempts by the Department of Justice and the White House to use the heavy hand of federal law enforcement to target concerned parents at local school board meetings and chill their protected First Amendment activity. Because the Department directed you, along with all other U.S. Attorneys, and the Federal Bureau of Investigation (FBI) to take action to address parents attending school board meetings,[1] we respectfully request your assistance with our investigation.

On September 29, 2021, the National School Boards Association (NSBA) sent a letter to President Joe Biden requesting help from the federal government with concerned parents voicing their opinions at school board meetings.[2] The NSBA letter stated that "malice, violence, and threats" against school officials "could be the equivalent of a form of domestic terrorism or hate crimes."[3] The letter cited a number of interactions at school board meetings, none of which rose to the level of domestic terrorism. In fact, the vast majority of incidents cited by the NSBA did not involve threats or violence.[4] Most notably, as an example of domestic terrorism, the NSBA cited an incident in which a father angrily confronted members at a school board meeting in Loudoun County, Virginia about the heinous sexual assault of his daughter.[5]

A mere five days after the NSBA sent its letter to President Biden, on October 4, 2021, Attorney General Merrick Garland issued a shocking memorandum that directed the FBI and

---

[1] Memorandum from Atty Gen. Merrick Garland, U.S. Dep't of Justice, Partnership Among Federal, State, Local, Tribal, And Territorial Law Enforcement to Address Threats Against School Administrators, Board Members, Teachers, and Staff (Oct. 4, 2021).
[2] Letter from Dr. Viola M. Garcia, President, Nat'l School Board Assoc. & Mr. Chip Slaven, Chief Exec. Officer, Nat'l School Board Assoc., to President Joseph R. Biden, White House (Sept. 29, 2021).
[3] *Id.*
[4] *See* Caroline Downey, *Vast majority of incidents cited by school-board group to justify federal intervention didn't involve threats,* NAT'L REV. (Oct. 2, 2021).
[5] *Id.*; *see also* Jessica Chasmar, *Loudoun County father arrested at school board events says school tried to cover up daughter's bathroom assault*, FOX NEWS (Oct. 12, 2021).

U.S. Attorneys' Offices to "convene meetings" in your judicial district "with federal, state, local, Tribal, and territorial leaders" within 30 days.[6] The Justice Department simultaneously issued a press release indicating that the Attorney General's directive would "open dedicated lines of communication for threat reporting, assessment and response by law enforcement"—in other words, create a snitch line for complaints about concerned parents.[7]

During Attorney General Garland's testimony before our Committee on October 21, he appeared to have no idea whether the U.S. Attorney meetings he ordered were actually taking place. He stated: "I don't know whether [the meetings] are ongoing, but I expect and hope that they are going . . . because I did ask that they take place."[8] Attorney General Garland testified that he doubted "there have been meetings in every jurisdiction," but reiterated his belief that it is important for federal law enforcement authorities to conduct these meetings in every judicial district.[9] According to the Attorney General's directives, meetings are to be convened in all 94 judicial districts by November 3, 2021, at the latest.

Following the Attorney General's testimony, the NSBA Board of Directors, apparently recognizing the ill-conceived consequences of its letter and the resulting Justice Department action, issued a new memorandum to its members apologizing for the letter, stating: "On behalf of NSBA, <u>we regret and apologize for the letter</u>."[10] (emphasis in original). Although Attorney General Garland testified that the NSBA letter to President Biden was the basis for his October 4 directive to insert federal law enforcement into local school board matters, the Attorney General has yet to rescind his memorandum. His directives to you and other U.S. Attorneys remain in effect.

Concerned parents voicing their strong opposition to controversial curricula at local schools are not domestic terrorists. Parents have an undisputed right to direct the upbringing and education of their children.[11] When parents, however, cross the line to commit a violent act or issue a criminal threat,[12] state and local authorities are best-equipped to handle these violations of state law. But we must not tolerate the use of the federal law enforcement apparatus to intimidate and silence parents using their Constitutional rights to advocate for their child's future.

To assist our investigation and determine whether these meetings are ongoing, we request that you provide the following documents and information:

---

[6] Memorandum from Atty Gen. Merrick Garland, U.S. Dep't of Justice, Partnership Among Federal, State, Local, Tribal, And Territorial Law Enforcement to Address Threats Against School Administrators, Board Members, Teachers, and Staff (Oct. 4, 2021).
[7] Press Release, U.S. Dep't of Justice, Justice Department Addresses Violent Threats Against School Officials and Teachers (Oct. 4, 2021).
[8] *Oversight of the United States Department of Justice: Hearing Before the H. comm. on the Judiciary,* 117th Cong. at 94 (2021) (testimony from Hon. Merrick Garland, Atty Gen., U.S. Dep't of Justice).
[9] *Id.* at 95.
[10] Memorandum from NSBA Board of Directors, Message to NSBA Members (Oct. 22, 2021).
[11] *Troxel v. Granville,* 530 U.S. 57, 65 (2000) (citing *Meyer v. Nebraska,* 262 U.S. 390, 399 (1923)).
[12] *Merrick Garland's federal offense,* WALL ST. J. (Oct. 6, 2021).

1. All documents and communications referring or relating to convening meeting(s) in your judicial district in accordance with the Attorney General's October 4, 2021 memorandum;

2. All agendas, minutes, and notes created or relied upon by U.S. Attorney's Office employees referring or relating to meeting(s) in your judicial district in accordance with the Attorney General's October 4, 2021 memorandum;

3. Please explain when meeting(s) in your judicial district in accordance with the Attorney General's October 4, 2021 memorandum have occurred or will occur;

4. Please identify by name and title of all U.S. Attorney's Office employees involved in the meeting(s) in your judicial district in accordance with the Attorney General's October 4, 2021 memorandum ;

5. Please identify all federal, state, local, Tribal, and territorial organizations invited to or that have attended the meetings convened in your judicial district in accordance with the October 4, 2021 memorandum; and

6. Please provide all recommendations, both formal and informal, and any meeting minutes produced at the meeting(s) in your judicial district in accordance with the Attorney General's October 4, 2021 memorandum.

Please provide this material as soon as possible but no later than 5:00 p.m. on November 15, 2021.

If you have any questions about this request, please contact Committee staff at (202) 225-6906. Thank you for your attention to this important matter.

Sincerely,

Jim Jordan
Ranking Member

Steve Chabot
Member of Congress

Louie Gohmert
Member of Congress

Darrell Issa
Ranking Member
Subcommittee on Courts, Intellectual Property, and the Internet

Ken Buck
Ranking Member
Subcommittee on Antitrust, Commercial and Administrative Law

Matt Gaetz
Member of Congress

Mike Johnson
Ranking Member
Subcommittee on the Constitution, Civil Rights and Civil Liberties

Andy Biggs
Ranking Member
Subcommittee on Crime, Terrorism and Homeland Security

Tom McClintock
Ranking Member
Subcommittee on Immigration and Citizenship

W. Gregory Steube
Member of Congress

Tom Tiffany
Member of Congress

Thomas Massie
Member of Congress

Chip Roy
Member of Congress

Dan Bishop
Member of Congress

Michelle Fischbach
Member of Congress

Victoria Spartz
Member of Congress

Scott Fitzgerald
Member of Congress

Cliff Bentz
Member of Congress

Burgess Owens
Member of Congress

cc: The Honorable Jerrold L. Nadler
Chairman

Mr. Monty Wilkinson
Director, Executive Office for U.S. Attorneys

JERROLD NADLER, New York
CHAIRMAN

JIM JORDAN, Ohio
RANKING MEMBER

ONE HUNDRED SEVENTEENTH CONGRESS
Congress of the United States
House of Representatives
COMMITTEE ON THE JUDICIARY
2138 RAYBURN HOUSE OFFICE BUILDING
WASHINGTON, DC 20515–6216
(202) 225–3951
judiciary.house.gov

November 1, 2021

Mr. Vipal J. Patel
Acting U.S. Attorney
Southern District of Ohio
303 Marconi Boulevard, Suite 200
Columbus, OH 43215

Dear Mr. Patel:

We are continuing to investigate the troubling attempts by the Department of Justice and the White House to use the heavy hand of federal law enforcement to target concerned parents at local school board meetings and chill their protected First Amendment activity. Because the Department directed you, along with all other U.S. Attorneys, and the Federal Bureau of Investigation (FBI) to take action to address parents attending school board meetings,[1] we respectfully request your assistance with our investigation.

On September 29, 2021, the National School Boards Association (NSBA) sent a letter to President Joe Biden requesting help from the federal government with concerned parents voicing their opinions at school board meetings.[2] The NSBA letter stated that "malice, violence, and threats" against school officials "could be the equivalent of a form of domestic terrorism or hate crimes."[3] The letter cited a number of interactions at school board meetings, none of which rose to the level of domestic terrorism. In fact, the vast majority of incidents cited by the NSBA did not involve threats or violence.[4] Most notably, as an example of domestic terrorism, the NSBA cited an incident in which a father angrily confronted members at a school board meeting in Loudoun County, Virginia about the heinous sexual assault of his daughter.[5]

A mere five days after the NSBA sent its letter to President Biden, on October 4, 2021, Attorney General Merrick Garland issued a shocking memorandum that directed the FBI and

---

[1] Memorandum from Atty Gen. Merrick Garland, U.S. Dep't of Justice, Partnership Among Federal, State, Local, Tribal, And Territorial Law Enforcement to Address Threats Against School Administrators, Board Members, Teachers, and Staff (Oct. 4, 2021).
[2] Letter from Dr. Viola M. Garcia, President, Nat'l School Board Assoc. & Mr. Chip Slaven, Chief Exec. Officer, Nat'l School Board Assoc., to President Joseph R. Biden, White House (Sept. 29, 2021).
[3] *Id.*
[4] *See* Caroline Downey, *Vast majority of incidents cited by school-board group to justify federal intervention didn't involve threats,* NAT'L REV. (Oct. 2, 2021).
[5] *Id.*; *see also* Jessica Chasmar, *Loudoun County father arrested at school board events says school tried to cover up daughter's bathroom assault*, FOX NEWS (Oct. 12, 2021).

U.S. Attorneys' Offices to "convene meetings" in your judicial district "with federal, state, local, Tribal, and territorial leaders" within 30 days.[6] The Justice Department simultaneously issued a press release indicating that the Attorney General's directive would "open dedicated lines of communication for threat reporting, assessment and response by law enforcement"—in other words, create a snitch line for complaints about concerned parents.[7]

During Attorney General Garland's testimony before our Committee on October 21, he appeared to have no idea whether the U.S. Attorney meetings he ordered were actually taking place. He stated: "I don't know whether [the meetings] are ongoing, but I expect and hope that they are going . . . because I did ask that they take place."[8] Attorney General Garland testified that he doubted "there have been meetings in every jurisdiction," but reiterated his belief that it is important for federal law enforcement authorities to conduct these meetings in every judicial district.[9] According to the Attorney General's directives, meetings are to be convened in all 94 judicial districts by November 3, 2021, at the latest.

Following the Attorney General's testimony, the NSBA Board of Directors, apparently recognizing the ill-conceived consequences of its letter and the resulting Justice Department action, issued a new memorandum to its members apologizing for the letter, stating: "On behalf of NSBA, <u>we regret and apologize for the letter</u>."[10] (emphasis in original). Although Attorney General Garland testified that the NSBA letter to President Biden was the basis for his October 4 directive to insert federal law enforcement into local school board matters, the Attorney General has yet to rescind his memorandum. His directives to you and other U.S. Attorneys remain in effect.

Concerned parents voicing their strong opposition to controversial curricula at local schools are not domestic terrorists. Parents have an undisputed right to direct the upbringing and education of their children.[11] When parents, however, cross the line to commit a violent act or issue a criminal threat,[12] state and local authorities are best-equipped to handle these violations of state law. But we must not tolerate the use of the federal law enforcement apparatus to intimidate and silence parents using their Constitutional rights to advocate for their child's future.

To assist our investigation and determine whether these meetings are ongoing, we request that you provide the following documents and information:

---

[6] Memorandum from Atty Gen. Merrick Garland, U.S. Dep't of Justice, Partnership Among Federal, State, Local, Tribal, And Territorial Law Enforcement to Address Threats Against School Administrators, Board Members, Teachers, and Staff (Oct. 4, 2021).
[7] Press Release, U.S. Dep't of Justice, Justice Department Addresses Violent Threats Against School Officials and Teachers (Oct. 4, 2021).
[8] *Oversight of the United States Department of Justice: Hearing Before the H. comm. on the Judiciary,* 117th Cong. at 94 (2021) (testimony from Hon. Merrick Garland, Atty Gen., U.S. Dep't of Justice).
[9] *Id.* at 95.
[10] Memorandum from NSBA Board of Directors, Message to NSBA Members (Oct. 22, 2021).
[11] *Troxel v. Granville,* 530 U.S. 57, 65 (2000) (citing *Meyer v. Nebraska,* 262 U.S. 390, 399 (1923)).
[12] *Merrick Garland's federal offense,* WALL ST. J. (Oct. 6, 2021).

1. All documents and communications referring or relating to convening meeting(s) in your judicial district in accordance with the Attorney General's October 4, 2021 memorandum;

2. All agendas, minutes, and notes created or relied upon by U.S. Attorney's Office employees referring or relating to meeting(s) in your judicial district in accordance with the Attorney General's October 4, 2021 memorandum;

3. Please explain when meeting(s) in your judicial district in accordance with the Attorney General's October 4, 2021 memorandum have occurred or will occur;

4. Please identify by name and title of all U.S. Attorney's Office employees involved in the meeting(s) in your judicial district in accordance with the Attorney General's October 4, 2021 memorandum ;

5. Please identify all federal, state, local, Tribal, and territorial organizations invited to or that have attended the meetings convened in your judicial district in accordance with the October 4, 2021 memorandum; and

6. Please provide all recommendations, both formal and informal, and any meeting minutes produced at the meeting(s) in your judicial district in accordance with the Attorney General's October 4, 2021 memorandum.

Please provide this material as soon as possible but no later than 5:00 p.m. on November 15, 2021.

If you have any questions about this request, please contact Committee staff at (202) 225-6906. Thank you for your attention to this important matter.

Sincerely,

Jim Jordan
Ranking Member

Steve Chabot
Member of Congress

Louie Gohmert
Member of Congress

Darrell Issa
Ranking Member
Subcommittee on Courts, Intellectual Property, and the Internet

Ken Buck
Ranking Member
Subcommittee on Antitrust, Commercial and Administrative Law

Matt Gaetz
Member of Congress

Mike Johnson
Ranking Member
Subcommittee on the Constitution, Civil Rights and Civil Liberties

Andy Biggs
Ranking Member
Subcommittee on Crime, Terrorism and Homeland Security

Tom McClintock
Ranking Member
Subcommittee on Immigration and Citizenship

W. Gregory Steube
Member of Congress

Tom Tiffany
Member of Congress

Thomas Massie
Member of Congress

Chip Roy
Member of Congress

Dan Bishop
Member of Congress

Michelle Fischbach
Member of Congress

Victoria Spartz
Member of Congress

Scott Fitzgerald
Member of Congress

Cliff Bentz
Member of Congress

Burgess Owens
Member of Congress

cc: The Honorable Jerrold L. Nadler
Chairman

Mr. Monty Wilkinson
Director, Executive Office for U.S. Attorneys

JERROLD NADLER, New York
CHAIRMAN

JIM JORDAN, Ohio
RANKING MEMBER

ONE HUNDRED SEVENTEENTH CONGRESS

Congress of the United States

House of Representatives

COMMITTEE ON THE JUDICIARY

2138 RAYBURN HOUSE OFFICE BUILDING

WASHINGTON, DC 20515-6216

(202) 225-3951
judiciary.house.gov

November 1, 2021

Mr. Clinton J. Johnson
Acting U.S. Attorney
Northern District of Oklahoma
110 W. 7th Street, Suite 300
Tulsa, OK 74119

Dear Mr. Johnson:

We are continuing to investigate the troubling attempts by the Department of Justice and the White House to use the heavy hand of federal law enforcement to target concerned parents at local school board meetings and chill their protected First Amendment activity. Because the Department directed you, along with all other U.S. Attorneys, and the Federal Bureau of Investigation (FBI) to take action to address parents attending school board meetings,[1] we respectfully request your assistance with our investigation.

On September 29, 2021, the National School Boards Association (NSBA) sent a letter to President Joe Biden requesting help from the federal government with concerned parents voicing their opinions at school board meetings.[2] The NSBA letter stated that "malice, violence, and threats" against school officials "could be the equivalent of a form of domestic terrorism or hate crimes."[3] The letter cited a number of interactions at school board meetings, none of which rose to the level of domestic terrorism. In fact, the vast majority of incidents cited by the NSBA did not involve threats or violence.[4] Most notably, as an example of domestic terrorism, the NSBA cited an incident in which a father angrily confronted members at a school board meeting in Loudoun County, Virginia about the heinous sexual assault of his daughter.[5]

A mere five days after the NSBA sent its letter to President Biden, on October 4, 2021, Attorney General Merrick Garland issued a shocking memorandum that directed the FBI and

---

[1] Memorandum from Atty Gen. Merrick Garland, U.S. Dep't of Justice, Partnership Among Federal, State, Local, Tribal, And Territorial Law Enforcement to Address Threats Against School Administrators, Board Members, Teachers, and Staff (Oct. 4, 2021).
[2] Letter from Dr. Viola M. Garcia, President, Nat'l School Board Assoc. & Mr. Chip Slaven, Chief Exec. Officer, Nat'l School Board Assoc., to President Joseph R. Biden, White House (Sept. 29, 2021).
[3] *Id.*
[4] *See* Caroline Downey, *Vast majority of incidents cited by school-board group to justify federal intervention didn't involve threats,* NAT'L REV. (Oct. 2, 2021).
[5] *Id.*; *see also* Jessica Chasmar, *Loudoun County father arrested at school board events says school tried to cover up daughter's bathroom assault*, FOX NEWS (Oct. 12, 2021).

U.S. Attorneys' Offices to "convene meetings" in your judicial district "with federal, state, local, Tribal, and territorial leaders" within 30 days.[6] The Justice Department simultaneously issued a press release indicating that the Attorney General's directive would "open dedicated lines of communication for threat reporting, assessment and response by law enforcement"—in other words, create a snitch line for complaints about concerned parents.[7]

During Attorney General Garland's testimony before our Committee on October 21, he appeared to have no idea whether the U.S. Attorney meetings he ordered were actually taking place. He stated: "I don't know whether [the meetings] are ongoing, but I expect and hope that they are going . . . because I did ask that they take place."[8] Attorney General Garland testified that he doubted "there have been meetings in every jurisdiction," but reiterated his belief that it is important for federal law enforcement authorities to conduct these meetings in every judicial district.[9] According to the Attorney General's directives, meetings are to be convened in all 94 judicial districts by November 3, 2021, at the latest.

Following the Attorney General's testimony, the NSBA Board of Directors, apparently recognizing the ill-conceived consequences of its letter and the resulting Justice Department action, issued a new memorandum to its members apologizing for the letter, stating: "On behalf of NSBA, <u>we regret and apologize for the letter</u>."[10] (emphasis in original). Although Attorney General Garland testified that the NSBA letter to President Biden was the basis for his October 4 directive to insert federal law enforcement into local school board matters, the Attorney General has yet to rescind his memorandum. His directives to you and other U.S. Attorneys remain in effect.

Concerned parents voicing their strong opposition to controversial curricula at local schools are not domestic terrorists. Parents have an undisputed right to direct the upbringing and education of their children.[11] When parents, however, cross the line to commit a violent act or issue a criminal threat,[12] state and local authorities are best-equipped to handle these violations of state law. But we must not tolerate the use of the federal law enforcement apparatus to intimidate and silence parents using their Constitutional rights to advocate for their child's future.

To assist our investigation and determine whether these meetings are ongoing, we request that you provide the following documents and information:

---

[6] Memorandum from Atty Gen. Merrick Garland, U.S. Dep't of Justice, Partnership Among Federal, State, Local, Tribal, And Territorial Law Enforcement to Address Threats Against School Administrators, Board Members, Teachers, and Staff (Oct. 4, 2021).
[7] Press Release, U.S. Dep't of Justice, Justice Department Addresses Violent Threats Against School Officials and Teachers (Oct. 4, 2021).
[8] *Oversight of the United States Department of Justice: Hearing Before the H. comm. on the Judiciary,* 117th Cong. at 94 (2021) (testimony from Hon. Merrick Garland, Atty Gen., U.S. Dep't of Justice).
[9] *Id.* at 95.
[10] Memorandum from NSBA Board of Directors, Message to NSBA Members (Oct. 22, 2021).
[11] *Troxel v. Granville,* 530 U.S. 57, 65 (2000) (citing *Meyer v. Nebraska,* 262 U.S. 390, 399 (1923)).
[12] *Merrick Garland's federal offense,* WALL ST. J. (Oct. 6, 2021).

1. All documents and communications referring or relating to convening meeting(s) in your judicial district in accordance with the Attorney General's October 4, 2021 memorandum;

2. All agendas, minutes, and notes created or relied upon by U.S. Attorney's Office employees referring or relating to meeting(s) in your judicial district in accordance with the Attorney General's October 4, 2021 memorandum;

3. Please explain when meeting(s) in your judicial district in accordance with the Attorney General's October 4, 2021 memorandum have occurred or will occur;

4. Please identify by name and title of all U.S. Attorney's Office employees involved in the meeting(s) in your judicial district in accordance with the Attorney General's October 4, 2021 memorandum ;

5. Please identify all federal, state, local, Tribal, and territorial organizations invited to or that have attended the meetings convened in your judicial district in accordance with the October 4, 2021 memorandum; and

6. Please provide all recommendations, both formal and informal, and any meeting minutes produced at the meeting(s) in your judicial district in accordance with the Attorney General's October 4, 2021 memorandum.

Please provide this material as soon as possible but no later than 5:00 p.m. on November 15, 2021.

If you have any questions about this request, please contact Committee staff at (202) 225-6906. Thank you for your attention to this important matter.

Sincerely,

Jim Jordan
Ranking Member

Steve Chabot
Member of Congress

Louie Gohmert
Member of Congress

Darrell Issa
Ranking Member
Subcommittee on Courts, Intellectual Property, and the Internet

Ken Buck
Ranking Member
Subcommittee on Antitrust, Commercial and Administrative Law

Matt Gaetz
Member of Congress

Mike Johnson
Ranking Member
Subcommittee on the Constitution, Civil Rights and Civil Liberties

Andy Biggs
Ranking Member
Subcommittee on Crime, Terrorism and Homeland Security

Tom McClintock
Ranking Member
Subcommittee on Immigration and Citizenship

W. Gregory Steube
Member of Congress

Tom Tiffany
Member of Congress

Thomas Massie
Member of Congress

Chip Roy
Member of Congress

Dan Bishop
Member of Congress

Michelle Fischbach
Member of Congress

Victoria Spartz
Member of Congress

Scott Fitzgerald
Member of Congress

Cliff Bentz
Member of Congress

Burgess Owens
Member of Congress

cc: The Honorable Jerrold L. Nadler
Chairman

Mr. Monty Wilkinson
Director, Executive Office for U.S. Attorneys

JERROLD NADLER, New York
CHAIRMAN

JIM JORDAN, Ohio
RANKING MEMBER

ONE HUNDRED SEVENTEENTH CONGRESS
Congress of the United States
House of Representatives
COMMITTEE ON THE JUDICIARY
2138 RAYBURN HOUSE OFFICE BUILDING
WASHINGTON, DC 20515–6216
(202) 225–3951
judiciary.house.gov

November 1, 2021

Mr. Robert J. "Bob" Troester
Acting U.S. Attorney
Western District of Oklahoma
210 West Park Avenue, Suite 400
Oklahoma City, OK 73102

Dear Mr. Troester:

We are continuing to investigate the troubling attempts by the Department of Justice and the White House to use the heavy hand of federal law enforcement to target concerned parents at local school board meetings and chill their protected First Amendment activity. Because the Department directed you, along with all other U.S. Attorneys, and the Federal Bureau of Investigation (FBI) to take action to address parents attending school board meetings,[1] we respectfully request your assistance with our investigation.

On September 29, 2021, the National School Boards Association (NSBA) sent a letter to President Joe Biden requesting help from the federal government with concerned parents voicing their opinions at school board meetings.[2] The NSBA letter stated that "malice, violence, and threats" against school officials "could be the equivalent of a form of domestic terrorism or hate crimes."[3] The letter cited a number of interactions at school board meetings, none of which rose to the level of domestic terrorism. In fact, the vast majority of incidents cited by the NSBA did not involve threats or violence.[4] Most notably, as an example of domestic terrorism, the NSBA cited an incident in which a father angrily confronted members at a school board meeting in Loudoun County, Virginia about the heinous sexual assault of his daughter.[5]

A mere five days after the NSBA sent its letter to President Biden, on October 4, 2021, Attorney General Merrick Garland issued a shocking memorandum that directed the FBI and

---

[1] Memorandum from Atty Gen. Merrick Garland, U.S. Dep't of Justice, Partnership Among Federal, State, Local, Tribal, And Territorial Law Enforcement to Address Threats Against School Administrators, Board Members, Teachers, and Staff (Oct. 4, 2021).

[2] Letter from Dr. Viola M. Garcia, President, Nat'l School Board Assoc. & Mr. Chip Slaven, Chief Exec. Officer, Nat'l School Board Assoc., to President Joseph R. Biden, White House (Sept. 29, 2021).

[3] *Id.*

[4] *See* Caroline Downey, *Vast majority of incidents cited by school-board group to justify federal intervention didn't involve threats,* NAT'L REV. (Oct. 2, 2021).

[5] *Id.*; *see also* Jessica Chasmar, *Loudoun County father arrested at school board events says school tried to cover up daughter's bathroom assault*, FOX NEWS (Oct. 12, 2021).

U.S. Attorneys' Offices to "convene meetings" in your judicial district "with federal, state, local, Tribal, and territorial leaders" within 30 days.[6] The Justice Department simultaneously issued a press release indicating that the Attorney General's directive would "open dedicated lines of communication for threat reporting, assessment and response by law enforcement"—in other words, create a snitch line for complaints about concerned parents.[7]

During Attorney General Garland's testimony before our Committee on October 21, he appeared to have no idea whether the U.S. Attorney meetings he ordered were actually taking place. He stated: "I don't know whether [the meetings] are ongoing, but I expect and hope that they are going . . . because I did ask that they take place."[8] Attorney General Garland testified that he doubted "there have been meetings in every jurisdiction," but reiterated his belief that it is important for federal law enforcement authorities to conduct these meetings in every judicial district.[9] According to the Attorney General's directives, meetings are to be convened in all 94 judicial districts by November 3, 2021, at the latest.

Following the Attorney General's testimony, the NSBA Board of Directors, apparently recognizing the ill-conceived consequences of its letter and the resulting Justice Department action, issued a new memorandum to its members apologizing for the letter, stating: "On behalf of NSBA, we regret and apologize for the letter."[10] (emphasis in original). Although Attorney General Garland testified that the NSBA letter to President Biden was the basis for his October 4 directive to insert federal law enforcement into local school board matters, the Attorney General has yet to rescind his memorandum. His directives to you and other U.S. Attorneys remain in effect.

Concerned parents voicing their strong opposition to controversial curricula at local schools are not domestic terrorists. Parents have an undisputed right to direct the upbringing and education of their children.[11] When parents, however, cross the line to commit a violent act or issue a criminal threat,[12] state and local authorities are best-equipped to handle these violations of state law. But we must not tolerate the use of the federal law enforcement apparatus to intimidate and silence parents using their Constitutional rights to advocate for their child's future.

To assist our investigation and determine whether these meetings are ongoing, we request that you provide the following documents and information:

---

[6] Memorandum from Atty Gen. Merrick Garland, U.S. Dep't of Justice, Partnership Among Federal, State, Local, Tribal, And Territorial Law Enforcement to Address Threats Against School Administrators, Board Members, Teachers, and Staff (Oct. 4, 2021).

[7] Press Release, U.S. Dep't of Justice, Justice Department Addresses Violent Threats Against School Officials and Teachers (Oct. 4, 2021).

[8] *Oversight of the United States Department of Justice: Hearing Before the H. comm. on the Judiciary,* 117th Cong. at 94 (2021) (testimony from Hon. Merrick Garland, Atty Gen., U.S. Dep't of Justice).

[9] *Id.* at 95.

[10] Memorandum from NSBA Board of Directors, Message to NSBA Members (Oct. 22, 2021).

[11] *Troxel v. Granville,* 530 U.S. 57, 65 (2000) (citing *Meyer v. Nebraska,* 262 U.S. 390, 399 (1923)).

[12] *Merrick Garland's federal offense,* WALL ST. J. (Oct. 6, 2021).

1. All documents and communications referring or relating to convening meeting(s) in your judicial district in accordance with the Attorney General's October 4, 2021 memorandum;

2. All agendas, minutes, and notes created or relied upon by U.S. Attorney's Office employees referring or relating to meeting(s) in your judicial district in accordance with the Attorney General's October 4, 2021 memorandum;

3. Please explain when meeting(s) in your judicial district in accordance with the Attorney General's October 4, 2021 memorandum have occurred or will occur;

4. Please identify by name and title of all U.S. Attorney's Office employees involved in the meeting(s) in your judicial district in accordance with the Attorney General's October 4, 2021 memorandum ;

5. Please identify all federal, state, local, Tribal, and territorial organizations invited to or that have attended the meetings convened in your judicial district in accordance with the October 4, 2021 memorandum; and

6. Please provide all recommendations, both formal and informal, and any meeting minutes produced at the meeting(s) in your judicial district in accordance with the Attorney General's October 4, 2021 memorandum.

Please provide this material as soon as possible but no later than 5:00 p.m. on November 15, 2021.

If you have any questions about this request, please contact Committee staff at (202) 225-6906. Thank you for your attention to this important matter.

Sincerely,

Jim Jordan
Ranking Member

Steve Chabot
Member of Congress

Louie Gohmert
Member of Congress

Darrell Issa
Ranking Member
Subcommittee on Courts, Intellectual Property, and the Internet

Ken Buck
Ranking Member
Subcommittee on Antitrust, Commercial and Administrative Law

Matt Gaetz
Member of Congress

Mike Johnson
Ranking Member
Subcommittee on the Constitution, Civil Rights and Civil Liberties

Andy Biggs
Ranking Member
Subcommittee on Crime, Terrorism and Homeland Security

Tom McClintock
Ranking Member
Subcommittee on Immigration and Citizenship

W. Gregory Steube
Member of Congress

Tom Tiffany
Member of Congress

Thomas Massie
Member of Congress

Chip Roy
Member of Congress

Dan Bishop
Member of Congress

Michelle Fischbach
Member of Congress

Victoria Spartz
Member of Congress

Scott Fitzgerald
Member of Congress

Cliff Bentz
Member of Congress

Burgess Owens
Member of Congress

cc: The Honorable Jerrold L. Nadler
Chairman

Mr. Monty Wilkinson
Director, Executive Office for U.S. Attorneys

JERROLD NADLER, New York
CHAIRMAN

JIM JORDAN, Ohio
RANKING MEMBER

ONE HUNDRED SEVENTEENTH CONGRESS

Congress of the United States

House of Representatives

COMMITTEE ON THE JUDICIARY

2138 RAYBURN HOUSE OFFICE BUILDING

WASHINGTON, DC 20515–6216

(202) 225–3951
judiciary.house.gov

November 1, 2021

Mr. Christopher J. Wilson
Acting U.S. Attorney
Eastern District of Oklahoma
520 Denison Ave
Muskogee, OK 74401

Dear Mr. Wilson:

We are continuing to investigate the troubling attempts by the Department of Justice and the White House to use the heavy hand of federal law enforcement to target concerned parents at local school board meetings and chill their protected First Amendment activity. Because the Department directed you, along with all other U.S. Attorneys, and the Federal Bureau of Investigation (FBI) to take action to address parents attending school board meetings,[1] we respectfully request your assistance with our investigation.

On September 29, 2021, the National School Boards Association (NSBA) sent a letter to President Joe Biden requesting help from the federal government with concerned parents voicing their opinions at school board meetings.[2] The NSBA letter stated that "malice, violence, and threats" against school officials "could be the equivalent of a form of domestic terrorism or hate crimes."[3] The letter cited a number of interactions at school board meetings, none of which rose to the level of domestic terrorism. In fact, the vast majority of incidents cited by the NSBA did not involve threats or violence.[4] Most notably, as an example of domestic terrorism, the NSBA cited an incident in which a father angrily confronted members at a school board meeting in Loudoun County, Virginia about the heinous sexual assault of his daughter.[5]

A mere five days after the NSBA sent its letter to President Biden, on October 4, 2021, Attorney General Merrick Garland issued a shocking memorandum that directed the FBI and

---

[1] Memorandum from Atty Gen. Merrick Garland, U.S. Dep't of Justice, Partnership Among Federal, State, Local, Tribal, And Territorial Law Enforcement to Address Threats Against School Administrators, Board Members, Teachers, and Staff (Oct. 4, 2021).
[2] Letter from Dr. Viola M. Garcia, President, Nat'l School Board Assoc. & Mr. Chip Slaven, Chief Exec. Officer, Nat'l School Board Assoc., to President Joseph R. Biden, White House (Sept. 29, 2021).
[3] *Id.*
[4] *See* Caroline Downey, *Vast majority of incidents cited by school-board group to justify federal intervention didn't involve threats,* NAT'L REV. (Oct. 2, 2021).
[5] *Id.*; *see also* Jessica Chasmar, *Loudoun County father arrested at school board events says school tried to cover up daughter's bathroom assault*, FOX NEWS (Oct. 12, 2021).

U.S. Attorneys' Offices to "convene meetings" in your judicial district "with federal, state, local, Tribal, and territorial leaders" within 30 days.[6] The Justice Department simultaneously issued a press release indicating that the Attorney General's directive would "open dedicated lines of communication for threat reporting, assessment and response by law enforcement"—in other words, create a snitch line for complaints about concerned parents.[7]

During Attorney General Garland's testimony before our Committee on October 21, he appeared to have no idea whether the U.S. Attorney meetings he ordered were actually taking place. He stated: "I don't know whether [the meetings] are ongoing, but I expect and hope that they are going . . . because I did ask that they take place."[8] Attorney General Garland testified that he doubted "there have been meetings in every jurisdiction," but reiterated his belief that it is important for federal law enforcement authorities to conduct these meetings in every judicial district.[9] According to the Attorney General's directives, meetings are to be convened in all 94 judicial districts by November 3, 2021, at the latest.

Following the Attorney General's testimony, the NSBA Board of Directors, apparently recognizing the ill-conceived consequences of its letter and the resulting Justice Department action, issued a new memorandum to its members apologizing for the letter, stating: "On behalf of NSBA, <u>we regret and apologize for the letter</u>."[10] (emphasis in original). Although Attorney General Garland testified that the NSBA letter to President Biden was the basis for his October 4 directive to insert federal law enforcement into local school board matters, the Attorney General has yet to rescind his memorandum. His directives to you and other U.S. Attorneys remain in effect.

Concerned parents voicing their strong opposition to controversial curricula at local schools are not domestic terrorists. Parents have an undisputed right to direct the upbringing and education of their children.[11] When parents, however, cross the line to commit a violent act or issue a criminal threat,[12] state and local authorities are best-equipped to handle these violations of state law. But we must not tolerate the use of the federal law enforcement apparatus to intimidate and silence parents using their Constitutional rights to advocate for their child's future.

To assist our investigation and determine whether these meetings are ongoing, we request that you provide the following documents and information:

---

[6] Memorandum from Atty Gen. Merrick Garland, U.S. Dep't of Justice, Partnership Among Federal, State, Local, Tribal, And Territorial Law Enforcement to Address Threats Against School Administrators, Board Members, Teachers, and Staff (Oct. 4, 2021).

[7] Press Release, U.S. Dep't of Justice, Justice Department Addresses Violent Threats Against School Officials and Teachers (Oct. 4, 2021).

[8] *Oversight of the United States Department of Justice: Hearing Before the H. comm. on the Judiciary,* 117th Cong. at 94 (2021) (testimony from Hon. Merrick Garland, Atty Gen., U.S. Dep't of Justice).

[9] *Id.* at 95.

[10] Memorandum from NSBA Board of Directors, Message to NSBA Members (Oct. 22, 2021).

[11] *Troxel v. Granville,* 530 U.S. 57, 65 (2000) (citing *Meyer v. Nebraska,* 262 U.S. 390, 399 (1923)).

[12] *Merrick Garland's federal offense,* WALL ST. J. (Oct. 6, 2021).

1. All documents and communications referring or relating to convening meeting(s) in your judicial district in accordance with the Attorney General's October 4, 2021 memorandum;

2. All agendas, minutes, and notes created or relied upon by U.S. Attorney's Office employees referring or relating to meeting(s) in your judicial district in accordance with the Attorney General's October 4, 2021 memorandum;

3. Please explain when meeting(s) in your judicial district in accordance with the Attorney General's October 4, 2021 memorandum have occurred or will occur;

4. Please identify by name and title of all U.S. Attorney's Office employees involved in the meeting(s) in your judicial district in accordance with the Attorney General's October 4, 2021 memorandum ;

5. Please identify all federal, state, local, Tribal, and territorial organizations invited to or that have attended the meetings convened in your judicial district in accordance with the October 4, 2021 memorandum; and

6. Please provide all recommendations, both formal and informal, and any meeting minutes produced at the meeting(s) in your judicial district in accordance with the Attorney General's October 4, 2021 memorandum.

Please provide this material as soon as possible but no later than 5:00 p.m. on November 15, 2021.

If you have any questions about this request, please contact Committee staff at (202) 225-6906. Thank you for your attention to this important matter.

Sincerely,

Jim Jordan
Ranking Member

Steve Chabot
Member of Congress

Louie Gohmert
Member of Congress

Darrell Issa
Ranking Member
Subcommittee on Courts, Intellectual Property, and the Internet

Ken Buck
Ranking Member
Subcommittee on Antitrust, Commercial and Administrative Law

Matt Gaetz
Member of Congress

Mike Johnson
Ranking Member
Subcommittee on the Constitution, Civil Rights and Civil Liberties

Andy Biggs
Ranking Member
Subcommittee on Crime, Terrorism and Homeland Security

Tom McClintock
Ranking Member
Subcommittee on Immigration and Citizenship

W. Gregory Steube
Member of Congress

Tom Tiffany
Member of Congress

Thomas Massie
Member of Congress

Chip Roy
Member of Congress

Dan Bishop
Member of Congress

Michelle Fischbach
Member of Congress

Victoria Spartz
Member of Congress

Scott Fitzgerald
Member of Congress

Cliff Bentz
Member of Congress

Burgess Owens
Member of Congress

cc: The Honorable Jerrold L. Nadler
Chairman

Mr. Monty Wilkinson
Director, Executive Office for U.S. Attorneys

JERROLD NADLER, New York
CHAIRMAN

JIM JORDAN, Ohio
RANKING MEMBER

ONE HUNDRED SEVENTEENTH CONGRESS

Congress of the United States

House of Representatives

COMMITTEE ON THE JUDICIARY

2138 RAYBURN HOUSE OFFICE BUILDING

WASHINGTON, DC 20515-6216

(202) 225-3951
judiciary.house.gov

November 1, 2021

Mr. Scott E. Asphaug
Acting U.S. Attorney
District of Oregon
1000 SW Third Ave, Suite 600
Portland, OR 97204

Dear Mr. Asphaug:

We are continuing to investigate the troubling attempts by the Department of Justice and the White House to use the heavy hand of federal law enforcement to target concerned parents at local school board meetings and chill their protected First Amendment activity. Because the Department directed you, along with all other U.S. Attorneys, and the Federal Bureau of Investigation (FBI) to take action to address parents attending school board meetings,[1] we respectfully request your assistance with our investigation.

On September 29, 2021, the National School Boards Association (NSBA) sent a letter to President Joe Biden requesting help from the federal government with concerned parents voicing their opinions at school board meetings.[2] The NSBA letter stated that "malice, violence, and threats" against school officials "could be the equivalent of a form of domestic terrorism or hate crimes."[3] The letter cited a number of interactions at school board meetings, none of which rose to the level of domestic terrorism. In fact, the vast majority of incidents cited by the NSBA did not involve threats or violence.[4] Most notably, as an example of domestic terrorism, the NSBA cited an incident in which a father angrily confronted members at a school board meeting in Loudoun County, Virginia about the heinous sexual assault of his daughter.[5]

A mere five days after the NSBA sent its letter to President Biden, on October 4, 2021, Attorney General Merrick Garland issued a shocking memorandum that directed the FBI and

---

[1] Memorandum from Atty Gen. Merrick Garland, U.S. Dep't of Justice, Partnership Among Federal, State, Local, Tribal, And Territorial Law Enforcement to Address Threats Against School Administrators, Board Members, Teachers, and Staff (Oct. 4, 2021).
[2] Letter from Dr. Viola M. Garcia, President, Nat'l School Board Assoc. & Mr. Chip Slaven, Chief Exec. Officer, Nat'l School Board Assoc., to President Joseph R. Biden, White House (Sept. 29, 2021).
[3] *Id.*
[4] *See* Caroline Downey, *Vast majority of incidents cited by school-board group to justify federal intervention didn't involve threats,* NAT'L REV. (Oct. 2, 2021).
[5] *Id.*; *see also* Jessica Chasmar, *Loudoun County father arrested at school board events says school tried to cover up daughter's bathroom assault*, FOX NEWS (Oct. 12, 2021).

U.S. Attorneys' Offices to "convene meetings" in your judicial district "with federal, state, local, Tribal, and territorial leaders" within 30 days.[6] The Justice Department simultaneously issued a press release indicating that the Attorney General's directive would "open dedicated lines of communication for threat reporting, assessment and response by law enforcement"—in other words, create a snitch line for complaints about concerned parents.[7]

During Attorney General Garland's testimony before our Committee on October 21, he appeared to have no idea whether the U.S. Attorney meetings he ordered were actually taking place. He stated: "I don't know whether [the meetings] are ongoing, but I expect and hope that they are going . . . because I did ask that they take place."[8] Attorney General Garland testified that he doubted "there have been meetings in every jurisdiction," but reiterated his belief that it is important for federal law enforcement authorities to conduct these meetings in every judicial district.[9] According to the Attorney General's directives, meetings are to be convened in all 94 judicial districts by November 3, 2021, at the latest.

Following the Attorney General's testimony, the NSBA Board of Directors, apparently recognizing the ill-conceived consequences of its letter and the resulting Justice Department action, issued a new memorandum to its members apologizing for the letter, stating: "On behalf of NSBA, we regret and apologize for the letter."[10] (emphasis in original). Although Attorney General Garland testified that the NSBA letter to President Biden was the basis for his October 4 directive to insert federal law enforcement into local school board matters, the Attorney General has yet to rescind his memorandum. His directives to you and other U.S. Attorneys remain in effect.

Concerned parents voicing their strong opposition to controversial curricula at local schools are not domestic terrorists. Parents have an undisputed right to direct the upbringing and education of their children.[11] When parents, however, cross the line to commit a violent act or issue a criminal threat,[12] state and local authorities are best-equipped to handle these violations of state law. But we must not tolerate the use of the federal law enforcement apparatus to intimidate and silence parents using their Constitutional rights to advocate for their child's future.

To assist our investigation and determine whether these meetings are ongoing, we request that you provide the following documents and information:

---

[6] Memorandum from Atty Gen. Merrick Garland, U.S. Dep't of Justice, Partnership Among Federal, State, Local, Tribal, And Territorial Law Enforcement to Address Threats Against School Administrators, Board Members, Teachers, and Staff (Oct. 4, 2021).

[7] Press Release, U.S. Dep't of Justice, Justice Department Addresses Violent Threats Against School Officials and Teachers (Oct. 4, 2021).

[8] *Oversight of the United States Department of Justice: Hearing Before the H. comm. on the Judiciary,* 117th Cong. at 94 (2021) (testimony from Hon. Merrick Garland, Atty Gen., U.S. Dep't of Justice).

[9] *Id.* at 95.

[10] Memorandum from NSBA Board of Directors, Message to NSBA Members (Oct. 22, 2021).

[11] *Troxel v. Granville,* 530 U.S. 57, 65 (2000) (citing *Meyer v. Nebraska,* 262 U.S. 390, 399 (1923)).

[12] *Merrick Garland's federal offense,* WALL ST. J. (Oct. 6, 2021).

1. All documents and communications referring or relating to convening meeting(s) in your judicial district in accordance with the Attorney General's October 4, 2021 memorandum;

2. All agendas, minutes, and notes created or relied upon by U.S. Attorney's Office employees referring or relating to meeting(s) in your judicial district in accordance with the Attorney General's October 4, 2021 memorandum;

3. Please explain when meeting(s) in your judicial district in accordance with the Attorney General's October 4, 2021 memorandum have occurred or will occur;

4. Please identify by name and title of all U.S. Attorney's Office employees involved in the meeting(s) in your judicial district in accordance with the Attorney General's October 4, 2021 memorandum ;

5. Please identify all federal, state, local, Tribal, and territorial organizations invited to or that have attended the meetings convened in your judicial district in accordance with the October 4, 2021 memorandum; and

6. Please provide all recommendations, both formal and informal, and any meeting minutes produced at the meeting(s) in your judicial district in accordance with the Attorney General's October 4, 2021 memorandum.

Please provide this material as soon as possible but no later than 5:00 p.m. on November 15, 2021.

If you have any questions about this request, please contact Committee staff at (202) 225-6906. Thank you for your attention to this important matter.

Sincerely,

Jim Jordan
Ranking Member

Steve Chabot
Member of Congress

Louie Gohmert
Member of Congress

Darrell Issa
Ranking Member
Subcommittee on Courts, Intellectual Property, and the Internet

Ken Buck
Ranking Member
Subcommittee on Antitrust, Commercial and Administrative Law

Matt Gaetz
Member of Congress

Mike Johnson
Ranking Member
Subcommittee on the Constitution, Civil Rights and Civil Liberties

Andy Biggs
Ranking Member
Subcommittee on Crime, Terrorism and Homeland Security

Tom McClintock
Ranking Member
Subcommittee on Immigration and Citizenship

W. Gregory Steube
Member of Congress

Tom Tiffany
Member of Congress

Thomas Massie
Member of Congress

Chip Roy
Member of Congress

Dan Bishop
Member of Congress

Michelle Fischbach
Member of Congress

Victoria Spartz
Member of Congress

Scott Fitzgerald
Member of Congress

Cliff Bentz
Member of Congress

Burgess Owens
Member of Congress

cc: The Honorable Jerrold L. Nadler
Chairman

Mr. Monty Wilkinson
Director, Executive Office for U.S. Attorneys

JERROLD NADLER, New York
CHAIRMAN

JIM JORDAN, Ohio
RANKING MEMBER

ONE HUNDRED SEVENTEENTH CONGRESS
Congress of the United States
House of Representatives
COMMITTEE ON THE JUDICIARY
2138 RAYBURN HOUSE OFFICE BUILDING
WASHINGTON, DC 20515–6216
(202) 225–3951
judiciary.house.gov

November 1, 2021

Mr. Bruce D. Brandler
Acting U.S. Attorney
Middle District of Pennsylvania
235 N. Washington Ave, Suite 311
Scranton, PA 18503

Dear Mr. Brandler:

We are continuing to investigate the troubling attempts by the Department of Justice and the White House to use the heavy hand of federal law enforcement to target concerned parents at local school board meetings and chill their protected First Amendment activity. Because the Department directed you, along with all other U.S. Attorneys, and the Federal Bureau of Investigation (FBI) to take action to address parents attending school board meetings,[1] we respectfully request your assistance with our investigation.

On September 29, 2021, the National School Boards Association (NSBA) sent a letter to President Joe Biden requesting help from the federal government with concerned parents voicing their opinions at school board meetings.[2] The NSBA letter stated that "malice, violence, and threats" against school officials "could be the equivalent of a form of domestic terrorism or hate crimes."[3] The letter cited a number of interactions at school board meetings, none of which rose to the level of domestic terrorism. In fact, the vast majority of incidents cited by the NSBA did not involve threats or violence.[4] Most notably, as an example of domestic terrorism, the NSBA cited an incident in which a father angrily confronted members at a school board meeting in Loudoun County, Virginia about the heinous sexual assault of his daughter.[5]

A mere five days after the NSBA sent its letter to President Biden, on October 4, 2021, Attorney General Merrick Garland issued a shocking memorandum that directed the FBI and

[1] Memorandum from Atty Gen. Merrick Garland, U.S. Dep't of Justice, Partnership Among Federal, State, Local, Tribal, And Territorial Law Enforcement to Address Threats Against School Administrators, Board Members, Teachers, and Staff (Oct. 4, 2021).
[2] Letter from Dr. Viola M. Garcia, President, Nat'l School Board Assoc. & Mr. Chip Slaven, Chief Exec. Officer, Nat'l School Board Assoc., to President Joseph R. Biden, White House (Sept. 29, 2021).
[3] *Id.*
[4] *See* Caroline Downey, *Vast majority of incidents cited by school-board group to justify federal intervention didn't involve threats,* NAT'L REV. (Oct. 2, 2021).
[5] *Id.*; *see also* Jessica Chasmar, *Loudoun County father arrested at school board events says school tried to cover up daughter's bathroom assault*, FOX NEWS (Oct. 12, 2021).

U.S. Attorneys' Offices to "convene meetings" in your judicial district "with federal, state, local, Tribal, and territorial leaders" within 30 days.[6] The Justice Department simultaneously issued a press release indicating that the Attorney General's directive would "open dedicated lines of communication for threat reporting, assessment and response by law enforcement"—in other words, create a snitch line for complaints about concerned parents.[7]

During Attorney General Garland's testimony before our Committee on October 21, he appeared to have no idea whether the U.S. Attorney meetings he ordered were actually taking place. He stated: "I don't know whether [the meetings] are ongoing, but I expect and hope that they are going . . . because I did ask that they take place."[8] Attorney General Garland testified that he doubted "there have been meetings in every jurisdiction," but reiterated his belief that it is important for federal law enforcement authorities to conduct these meetings in every judicial district.[9] According to the Attorney General's directives, meetings are to be convened in all 94 judicial districts by November 3, 2021, at the latest.

Following the Attorney General's testimony, the NSBA Board of Directors, apparently recognizing the ill-conceived consequences of its letter and the resulting Justice Department action, issued a new memorandum to its members apologizing for the letter, stating: "On behalf of NSBA, <u>we regret and apologize for the letter</u>."[10] (emphasis in original). Although Attorney General Garland testified that the NSBA letter to President Biden was the basis for his October 4 directive to insert federal law enforcement into local school board matters, the Attorney General has yet to rescind his memorandum. His directives to you and other U.S. Attorneys remain in effect.

Concerned parents voicing their strong opposition to controversial curricula at local schools are not domestic terrorists. Parents have an undisputed right to direct the upbringing and education of their children.[11] When parents, however, cross the line to commit a violent act or issue a criminal threat,[12] state and local authorities are best-equipped to handle these violations of state law. But we must not tolerate the use of the federal law enforcement apparatus to intimidate and silence parents using their Constitutional rights to advocate for their child's future.

To assist our investigation and determine whether these meetings are ongoing, we request that you provide the following documents and information:

---

[6] Memorandum from Atty Gen. Merrick Garland, U.S. Dep't of Justice, Partnership Among Federal, State, Local, Tribal, And Territorial Law Enforcement to Address Threats Against School Administrators, Board Members, Teachers, and Staff (Oct. 4, 2021).
[7] Press Release, U.S. Dep't of Justice, Justice Department Addresses Violent Threats Against School Officials and Teachers (Oct. 4, 2021).
[8] *Oversight of the United States Department of Justice: Hearing Before the H. comm. on the Judiciary,* 117th Cong. at 94 (2021) (testimony from Hon. Merrick Garland, Atty Gen., U.S. Dep't of Justice).
[9] *Id.* at 95.
[10] Memorandum from NSBA Board of Directors, Message to NSBA Members (Oct. 22, 2021).
[11] *Troxel v. Granville,* 530 U.S. 57, 65 (2000) (citing *Meyer v. Nebraska,* 262 U.S. 390, 399 (1923)).
[12] *Merrick Garland's federal offense,* WALL ST. J. (Oct. 6, 2021).

1. All documents and communications referring or relating to convening meeting(s) in your judicial district in accordance with the Attorney General's October 4, 2021 memorandum;

2. All agendas, minutes, and notes created or relied upon by U.S. Attorney's Office employees referring or relating to meeting(s) in your judicial district in accordance with the Attorney General's October 4, 2021 memorandum;

3. Please explain when meeting(s) in your judicial district in accordance with the Attorney General's October 4, 2021 memorandum have occurred or will occur;

4. Please identify by name and title of all U.S. Attorney's Office employees involved in the meeting(s) in your judicial district in accordance with the Attorney General's October 4, 2021 memorandum ;

5. Please identify all federal, state, local, Tribal, and territorial organizations invited to or that have attended the meetings convened in your judicial district in accordance with the October 4, 2021 memorandum; and

6. Please provide all recommendations, both formal and informal, and any meeting minutes produced at the meeting(s) in your judicial district in accordance with the Attorney General's October 4, 2021 memorandum.

Please provide this material as soon as possible but no later than 5:00 p.m. on November 15, 2021.

If you have any questions about this request, please contact Committee staff at (202) 225-6906. Thank you for your attention to this important matter.

Sincerely,

Jim Jordan
Ranking Member

Steve Chabot
Member of Congress

Louie Gohmert
Member of Congress

Darrell Issa
Ranking Member
Subcommittee on Courts, Intellectual Property, and the Internet

Ken Buck
Ranking Member
Subcommittee on Antitrust, Commercial and Administrative Law

Matt Gaetz
Member of Congress

Mike Johnson
Ranking Member
Subcommittee on the Constitution, Civil Rights and Civil Liberties

Andy Biggs
Ranking Member
Subcommittee on Crime, Terrorism and Homeland Security

Tom McClintock
Ranking Member
Subcommittee on Immigration and Citizenship

W. Gregory Steube
Member of Congress

Tom Tiffany
Member of Congress

Thomas Massie
Member of Congress

Chip Roy
Member of Congress

Dan Bishop
Member of Congress

Michelle Fischbach
Member of Congress

Victoria Spartz
Member of Congress

Scott Fitzgerald
Member of Congress

Cliff Bentz
Member of Congress

Burgess Owens
Member of Congress

cc: The Honorable Jerrold L. Nadler
Chairman

Mr. Monty Wilkinson
Director, Executive Office for U.S. Attorneys

JERROLD NADLER, New York
CHAIRMAN

JIM JORDAN, Ohio
RANKING MEMBER

ONE HUNDRED SEVENTEENTH CONGRESS

Congress of the United States

House of Representatives

COMMITTEE ON THE JUDICIARY

2138 RAYBURN HOUSE OFFICE BUILDING

WASHINGTON, DC 20515-6216

(202) 225-3951
judiciary.house.gov

November 1, 2021

Mr. Stephen R. Kaufman
Acting U.S. Attorney
Western District of Pennsylvania
700 Grant Street, Suite 400
Pittsburgh, PA 15219

Dear Mr. Kaufman:

We are continuing to investigate the troubling attempts by the Department of Justice and the White House to use the heavy hand of federal law enforcement to target concerned parents at local school board meetings and chill their protected First Amendment activity. Because the Department directed you, along with all other U.S. Attorneys, and the Federal Bureau of Investigation (FBI) to take action to address parents attending school board meetings,[1] we respectfully request your assistance with our investigation.

On September 29, 2021, the National School Boards Association (NSBA) sent a letter to President Joe Biden requesting help from the federal government with concerned parents voicing their opinions at school board meetings.[2] The NSBA letter stated that "malice, violence, and threats" against school officials "could be the equivalent of a form of domestic terrorism or hate crimes."[3] The letter cited a number of interactions at school board meetings, none of which rose to the level of domestic terrorism. In fact, the vast majority of incidents cited by the NSBA did not involve threats or violence.[4] Most notably, as an example of domestic terrorism, the NSBA cited an incident in which a father angrily confronted members at a school board meeting in Loudoun County, Virginia about the heinous sexual assault of his daughter.[5]

A mere five days after the NSBA sent its letter to President Biden, on October 4, 2021, Attorney General Merrick Garland issued a shocking memorandum that directed the FBI and

---

[1] Memorandum from Atty Gen. Merrick Garland, U.S. Dep't of Justice, Partnership Among Federal, State, Local, Tribal, And Territorial Law Enforcement to Address Threats Against School Administrators, Board Members, Teachers, and Staff (Oct. 4, 2021).
[2] Letter from Dr. Viola M. Garcia, President, Nat'l School Board Assoc. & Mr. Chip Slaven, Chief Exec. Officer, Nat'l School Board Assoc., to President Joseph R. Biden, White House (Sept. 29, 2021).
[3] *Id.*
[4] *See* Caroline Downey, *Vast majority of incidents cited by school-board group to justify federal intervention didn't involve threats,* NAT'L REV. (Oct. 2, 2021).
[5] *Id.*; *see also* Jessica Chasmar, *Loudoun County father arrested at school board events says school tried to cover up daughter's bathroom assault*, FOX NEWS (Oct. 12, 2021).

U.S. Attorneys' Offices to "convene meetings" in your judicial district "with federal, state, local, Tribal, and territorial leaders" within 30 days.[6] The Justice Department simultaneously issued a press release indicating that the Attorney General's directive would "open dedicated lines of communication for threat reporting, assessment and response by law enforcement"—in other words, create a snitch line for complaints about concerned parents.[7]

During Attorney General Garland's testimony before our Committee on October 21, he appeared to have no idea whether the U.S. Attorney meetings he ordered were actually taking place. He stated: "I don't know whether [the meetings] are ongoing, but I expect and hope that they are going . . . because I did ask that they take place."[8] Attorney General Garland testified that he doubted "there have been meetings in every jurisdiction," but reiterated his belief that it is important for federal law enforcement authorities to conduct these meetings in every judicial district.[9] According to the Attorney General's directives, meetings are to be convened in all 94 judicial districts by November 3, 2021, at the latest.

Following the Attorney General's testimony, the NSBA Board of Directors, apparently recognizing the ill-conceived consequences of its letter and the resulting Justice Department action, issued a new memorandum to its members apologizing for the letter, stating: "On behalf of NSBA, <u>we regret and apologize for the letter</u>."[10] (emphasis in original). Although Attorney General Garland testified that the NSBA letter to President Biden was the basis for his October 4 directive to insert federal law enforcement into local school board matters, the Attorney General has yet to rescind his memorandum. His directives to you and other U.S. Attorneys remain in effect.

Concerned parents voicing their strong opposition to controversial curricula at local schools are not domestic terrorists. Parents have an undisputed right to direct the upbringing and education of their children.[11] When parents, however, cross the line to commit a violent act or issue a criminal threat,[12] state and local authorities are best-equipped to handle these violations of state law. But we must not tolerate the use of the federal law enforcement apparatus to intimidate and silence parents using their Constitutional rights to advocate for their child's future.

To assist our investigation and determine whether these meetings are ongoing, we request that you provide the following documents and information:

---

[6] Memorandum from Atty Gen. Merrick Garland, U.S. Dep't of Justice, Partnership Among Federal, State, Local, Tribal, And Territorial Law Enforcement to Address Threats Against School Administrators, Board Members, Teachers, and Staff (Oct. 4, 2021).

[7] Press Release, U.S. Dep't of Justice, Justice Department Addresses Violent Threats Against School Officials and Teachers (Oct. 4, 2021).

[8] *Oversight of the United States Department of Justice: Hearing Before the H. comm. on the Judiciary,* 117th Cong. at 94 (2021) (testimony from Hon. Merrick Garland, Atty Gen., U.S. Dep't of Justice).

[9] *Id.* at 95.

[10] Memorandum from NSBA Board of Directors, Message to NSBA Members (Oct. 22, 2021).

[11] *Troxel v. Granville,* 530 U.S. 57, 65 (2000) (citing *Meyer v. Nebraska,* 262 U.S. 390, 399 (1923)).

[12] *Merrick Garland's federal offense,* WALL ST. J. (Oct. 6, 2021).

1. All documents and communications referring or relating to convening meeting(s) in your judicial district in accordance with the Attorney General's October 4, 2021 memorandum;

2. All agendas, minutes, and notes created or relied upon by U.S. Attorney's Office employees referring or relating to meeting(s) in your judicial district in accordance with the Attorney General's October 4, 2021 memorandum;

3. Please explain when meeting(s) in your judicial district in accordance with the Attorney General's October 4, 2021 memorandum have occurred or will occur;

4. Please identify by name and title of all U.S. Attorney's Office employees involved in the meeting(s) in your judicial district in accordance with the Attorney General's October 4, 2021 memorandum ;

5. Please identify all federal, state, local, Tribal, and territorial organizations invited to or that have attended the meetings convened in your judicial district in accordance with the October 4, 2021 memorandum; and

6. Please provide all recommendations, both formal and informal, and any meeting minutes produced at the meeting(s) in your judicial district in accordance with the Attorney General's October 4, 2021 memorandum.

Please provide this material as soon as possible but no later than 5:00 p.m. on November 15, 2021.

If you have any questions about this request, please contact Committee staff at (202) 225-6906. Thank you for your attention to this important matter.

Sincerely,

Jim Jordan
Ranking Member

Steve Chabot
Member of Congress

Louie Gohmert
Member of Congress

Darrell Issa
Ranking Member
Subcommittee on Courts, Intellectual Property, and the Internet

Ken Buck
Ranking Member
Subcommittee on Antitrust, Commercial and Administrative Law

Matt Gaetz
Member of Congress

Mike Johnson
Ranking Member
Subcommittee on the Constitution, Civil Rights and Civil Liberties

Andy Biggs
Ranking Member
Subcommittee on Crime, Terrorism and Homeland Security

Tom McClintock
Ranking Member
Subcommittee on Immigration and Citizenship

W. Gregory Steube
Member of Congress

Tom Tiffany
Member of Congress

Thomas Massie
Member of Congress

Chip Roy
Member of Congress

Dan Bishop
Member of Congress

Michelle Fischbach
Member of Congress

Victoria Spartz
Member of Congress

Scott Fitzgerald
Member of Congress

Cliff Bentz
Member of Congress

Burgess Owens
Member of Congress

cc: The Honorable Jerrold L. Nadler
Chairman

Mr. Monty Wilkinson
Director, Executive Office for U.S. Attorneys

JERROLD NADLER, New York
CHAIRMAN

JIM JORDAN, Ohio
RANKING MEMBER

ONE HUNDRED SEVENTEENTH CONGRESS

Congress of the United States

House of Representatives

COMMITTEE ON THE JUDICIARY

2138 RAYBURN HOUSE OFFICE BUILDING

WASHINGTON, DC 20515-6216

(202) 225-3951
judiciary.house.gov

November 1, 2021

Ms. Jennifer A. Williams
Acting U.S. Attorney
Eastern District of Pennsylvania
615 Chestnut Street, Suite 1250
Philadelphia, PA 19106

Dear Ms. Williams:

We are continuing to investigate the troubling attempts by the Department of Justice and the White House to use the heavy hand of federal law enforcement to target concerned parents at local school board meetings and chill their protected First Amendment activity. Because the Department directed you, along with all other U.S. Attorneys, and the Federal Bureau of Investigation (FBI) to take action to address parents attending school board meetings,[1] we respectfully request your assistance with our investigation.

On September 29, 2021, the National School Boards Association (NSBA) sent a letter to President Joe Biden requesting help from the federal government with concerned parents voicing their opinions at school board meetings.[2] The NSBA letter stated that "malice, violence, and threats" against school officials "could be the equivalent of a form of domestic terrorism or hate crimes."[3] The letter cited a number of interactions at school board meetings, none of which rose to the level of domestic terrorism. In fact, the vast majority of incidents cited by the NSBA did not involve threats or violence.[4] Most notably, as an example of domestic terrorism, the NSBA cited an incident in which a father angrily confronted members at a school board meeting in Loudoun County, Virginia about the heinous sexual assault of his daughter.[5]

A mere five days after the NSBA sent its letter to President Biden, on October 4, 2021, Attorney General Merrick Garland issued a shocking memorandum that directed the FBI and

---

[1] Memorandum from Atty Gen. Merrick Garland, U.S. Dep't of Justice, Partnership Among Federal, State, Local, Tribal, And Territorial Law Enforcement to Address Threats Against School Administrators, Board Members, Teachers, and Staff (Oct. 4, 2021).
[2] Letter from Dr. Viola M. Garcia, President, Nat'l School Board Assoc. & Mr. Chip Slaven, Chief Exec. Officer, Nat'l School Board Assoc., to President Joseph R. Biden, White House (Sept. 29, 2021).
[3] *Id.*
[4] *See* Caroline Downey, *Vast majority of incidents cited by school-board group to justify federal intervention didn't involve threats,* NAT'L REV. (Oct. 2, 2021).
[5] *Id.*; *see also* Jessica Chasmar, *Loudoun County father arrested at school board events says school tried to cover up daughter's bathroom assault*, FOX NEWS (Oct. 12, 2021).

U.S. Attorneys' Offices to "convene meetings" in your judicial district "with federal, state, local, Tribal, and territorial leaders" within 30 days.[6] The Justice Department simultaneously issued a press release indicating that the Attorney General's directive would "open dedicated lines of communication for threat reporting, assessment and response by law enforcement"—in other words, create a snitch line for complaints about concerned parents.[7]

During Attorney General Garland's testimony before our Committee on October 21, he appeared to have no idea whether the U.S. Attorney meetings he ordered were actually taking place. He stated: "I don't know whether [the meetings] are ongoing, but I expect and hope that they are going . . . because I did ask that they take place."[8] Attorney General Garland testified that he doubted "there have been meetings in every jurisdiction," but reiterated his belief that it is important for federal law enforcement authorities to conduct these meetings in every judicial district.[9] According to the Attorney General's directives, meetings are to be convened in all 94 judicial districts by November 3, 2021, at the latest.

Following the Attorney General's testimony, the NSBA Board of Directors, apparently recognizing the ill-conceived consequences of its letter and the resulting Justice Department action, issued a new memorandum to its members apologizing for the letter, stating: "On behalf of NSBA, <u>we regret and apologize for the letter</u>."[10] (emphasis in original). Although Attorney General Garland testified that the NSBA letter to President Biden was the basis for his October 4 directive to insert federal law enforcement into local school board matters, the Attorney General has yet to rescind his memorandum. His directives to you and other U.S. Attorneys remain in effect.

Concerned parents voicing their strong opposition to controversial curricula at local schools are not domestic terrorists. Parents have an undisputed right to direct the upbringing and education of their children.[11] When parents, however, cross the line to commit a violent act or issue a criminal threat,[12] state and local authorities are best-equipped to handle these violations of state law. But we must not tolerate the use of the federal law enforcement apparatus to intimidate and silence parents using their Constitutional rights to advocate for their child's future.

To assist our investigation and determine whether these meetings are ongoing, we request that you provide the following documents and information:

---

[6] Memorandum from Atty Gen. Merrick Garland, U.S. Dep't of Justice, Partnership Among Federal, State, Local, Tribal, And Territorial Law Enforcement to Address Threats Against School Administrators, Board Members, Teachers, and Staff (Oct. 4, 2021).
[7] Press Release, U.S. Dep't of Justice, Justice Department Addresses Violent Threats Against School Officials and Teachers (Oct. 4, 2021).
[8] *Oversight of the United States Department of Justice: Hearing Before the H. comm. on the Judiciary,* 117th Cong. at 94 (2021) (testimony from Hon. Merrick Garland, Atty Gen., U.S. Dep't of Justice).
[9] *Id.* at 95.
[10] Memorandum from NSBA Board of Directors, Message to NSBA Members (Oct. 22, 2021).
[11] *Troxel v. Granville,* 530 U.S. 57, 65 (2000) (citing *Meyer v. Nebraska,* 262 U.S. 390, 399 (1923)).
[12] *Merrick Garland's federal offense,* WALL ST. J. (Oct. 6, 2021).

Ms. Jennifer A. Williams
November 1, 2021
Page 3

1. All documents and communications referring or relating to convening meeting(s) in your judicial district in accordance with the Attorney General's October 4, 2021 memorandum;

2. All agendas, minutes, and notes created or relied upon by U.S. Attorney's Office employees referring or relating to meeting(s) in your judicial district in accordance with the Attorney General's October 4, 2021 memorandum;

3. Please explain when meeting(s) in your judicial district in accordance with the Attorney General's October 4, 2021 memorandum have occurred or will occur;

4. Please identify by name and title of all U.S. Attorney's Office employees involved in the meeting(s) in your judicial district in accordance with the Attorney General's October 4, 2021 memorandum ;

5. Please identify all federal, state, local, Tribal, and territorial organizations invited to or that have attended the meetings convened in your judicial district in accordance with the October 4, 2021 memorandum; and

6. Please provide all recommendations, both formal and informal, and any meeting minutes produced at the meeting(s) in your judicial district in accordance with the Attorney General's October 4, 2021 memorandum.

Please provide this material as soon as possible but no later than 5:00 p.m. on November 15, 2021.

If you have any questions about this request, please contact Committee staff at (202) 225-6906. Thank you for your attention to this important matter.

Sincerely,

Jim Jordan
Ranking Member

Steve Chabot
Member of Congress

Louie Gohmert
Member of Congress

Darrell Issa
Ranking Member
Subcommittee on Courts, Intellectual Property, and the Internet

Ken Buck
Ranking Member
Subcommittee on Antitrust, Commercial and Administrative Law

Matt Gaetz
Member of Congress

Mike Johnson
Ranking Member
Subcommittee on the Constitution, Civil Rights and Civil Liberties

Andy Biggs
Ranking Member
Subcommittee on Crime, Terrorism and Homeland Security

Tom McClintock
Ranking Member
Subcommittee on Immigration and Citizenship

W. Gregory Steube
Member of Congress

Tom Tiffany
Member of Congress

Thomas Massie
Member of Congress

Chip Roy
Member of Congress

Dan Bishop
Member of Congress

Michelle Fischbach
Member of Congress

Victoria Spartz
Member of Congress

Scott Fitzgerald
Member of Congress

Cliff Bentz
Member of Congress

Burgess Owens
Member of Congress

cc: The Honorable Jerrold L. Nadler
Chairman

Mr. Monty Wilkinson
Director, Executive Office for U.S. Attorneys

JERROLD NADLER, New York
CHAIRMAN

JIM JORDAN, Ohio
RANKING MEMBER

ONE HUNDRED SEVENTEENTH CONGRESS

Congress of the United States
House of Representatives

COMMITTEE ON THE JUDICIARY

2138 RAYBURN HOUSE OFFICE BUILDING

WASHINGTON, DC 20515-6216

(202) 225-3951
judiciary.house.gov

November 1, 2021

The Honorable W. Stephen Muldrow
U.S. Attorney
District of Puerto Rico
350 Carlos Chardón Street
San Juan, PR 00918

Dear Mr. Muldrow:

We are continuing to investigate the troubling attempts by the Department of Justice and the White House to use the heavy hand of federal law enforcement to target concerned parents at local school board meetings and chill their protected First Amendment activity. Because the Department directed you, along with all other U.S. Attorneys, and the Federal Bureau of Investigation (FBI) to take action to address parents attending school board meetings,[1] we respectfully request your assistance with our investigation.

On September 29, 2021, the National School Boards Association (NSBA) sent a letter to President Joe Biden requesting help from the federal government with concerned parents voicing their opinions at school board meetings.[2] The NSBA letter stated that "malice, violence, and threats" against school officials "could be the equivalent of a form of domestic terrorism or hate crimes."[3] The letter cited a number of interactions at school board meetings, none of which rose to the level of domestic terrorism. In fact, the vast majority of incidents cited by the NSBA did not involve threats or violence.[4] Most notably, as an example of domestic terrorism, the NSBA cited an incident in which a father angrily confronted members at a school board meeting in Loudoun County, Virginia about the heinous sexual assault of his daughter.[5]

A mere five days after the NSBA sent its letter to President Biden, on October 4, 2021, Attorney General Merrick Garland issued a shocking memorandum that directed the FBI and

---

[1] Memorandum from Atty Gen. Merrick Garland, U.S. Dep't of Justice, Partnership Among Federal, State, Local, Tribal, And Territorial Law Enforcement to Address Threats Against School Administrators, Board Members, Teachers, and Staff (Oct. 4, 2021).
[2] Letter from Dr. Viola M. Garcia, President, Nat'l School Board Assoc. & Mr. Chip Slaven, Chief Exec. Officer, Nat'l School Board Assoc., to President Joseph R. Biden, White House (Sept. 29, 2021).
[3] *Id.*
[4] *See* Caroline Downey, *Vast majority of incidents cited by school-board group to justify federal intervention didn't involve threats,* NAT'L REV. (Oct. 2, 2021).
[5] *Id.*; *see also* Jessica Chasmar, *Loudoun County father arrested at school board events says school tried to cover up daughter's bathroom assault*, FOX NEWS (Oct. 12, 2021).

U.S. Attorneys' Offices to "convene meetings" in your judicial district "with federal, state, local, Tribal, and territorial leaders" within 30 days.[6] The Justice Department simultaneously issued a press release indicating that the Attorney General's directive would "open dedicated lines of communication for threat reporting, assessment and response by law enforcement"—in other words, create a snitch line for complaints about concerned parents.[7]

During Attorney General Garland's testimony before our Committee on October 21, he appeared to have no idea whether the U.S. Attorney meetings he ordered were actually taking place. He stated: "I don't know whether [the meetings] are ongoing, but I expect and hope that they are going . . . because I did ask that they take place."[8] Attorney General Garland testified that he doubted "there have been meetings in every jurisdiction," but reiterated his belief that it is important for federal law enforcement authorities to conduct these meetings in every judicial district.[9] According to the Attorney General's directives, meetings are to be convened in all 94 judicial districts by November 3, 2021, at the latest.

Following the Attorney General's testimony, the NSBA Board of Directors, apparently recognizing the ill-conceived consequences of its letter and the resulting Justice Department action, issued a new memorandum to its members apologizing for the letter, stating: "On behalf of NSBA, <u>we regret and apologize for the letter</u>."[10] (emphasis in original). Although Attorney General Garland testified that the NSBA letter to President Biden was the basis for his October 4 directive to insert federal law enforcement into local school board matters, the Attorney General has yet to rescind his memorandum. His directives to you and other U.S. Attorneys remain in effect.

Concerned parents voicing their strong opposition to controversial curricula at local schools are not domestic terrorists. Parents have an undisputed right to direct the upbringing and education of their children.[11] When parents, however, cross the line to commit a violent act or issue a criminal threat,[12] state and local authorities are best-equipped to handle these violations of state law. But we must not tolerate the use of the federal law enforcement apparatus to intimidate and silence parents using their Constitutional rights to advocate for their child's future.

To assist our investigation and determine whether these meetings are ongoing, we request that you provide the following documents and information:

---

[6] Memorandum from Atty Gen. Merrick Garland, U.S. Dep't of Justice, Partnership Among Federal, State, Local, Tribal, And Territorial Law Enforcement to Address Threats Against School Administrators, Board Members, Teachers, and Staff (Oct. 4, 2021).
[7] Press Release, U.S. Dep't of Justice, Justice Department Addresses Violent Threats Against School Officials and Teachers (Oct. 4, 2021).
[8] *Oversight of the United States Department of Justice: Hearing Before the H. comm. on the Judiciary,* 117th Cong. at 94 (2021) (testimony from Hon. Merrick Garland, Atty Gen., U.S. Dep't of Justice).
[9] *Id.* at 95.
[10] Memorandum from NSBA Board of Directors, Message to NSBA Members (Oct. 22, 2021).
[11] *Troxel v. Granville,* 530 U.S. 57, 65 (2000) (citing *Meyer v. Nebraska,* 262 U.S. 390, 399 (1923)).
[12] *Merrick Garland's federal offense,* WALL ST. J. (Oct. 6, 2021).

1. All documents and communications referring or relating to convening meeting(s) in your judicial district in accordance with the Attorney General's October 4, 2021 memorandum;

2. All agendas, minutes, and notes created or relied upon by U.S. Attorney's Office employees referring or relating to meeting(s) in your judicial district in accordance with the Attorney General's October 4, 2021 memorandum;

3. Please explain when meeting(s) in your judicial district in accordance with the Attorney General's October 4, 2021 memorandum have occurred or will occur;

4. Please identify by name and title of all U.S. Attorney's Office employees involved in the meeting(s) in your judicial district in accordance with the Attorney General's October 4, 2021 memorandum ;

5. Please identify all federal, state, local, Tribal, and territorial organizations invited to or that have attended the meetings convened in your judicial district in accordance with the October 4, 2021 memorandum; and

6. Please provide all recommendations, both formal and informal, and any meeting minutes produced at the meeting(s) in your judicial district in accordance with the Attorney General's October 4, 2021 memorandum.

Please provide this material as soon as possible but no later than 5:00 p.m. on November 15, 2021.

If you have any questions about this request, please contact Committee staff at (202) 225-6906. Thank you for your attention to this important matter.

Sincerely,

Jim Jordan
Ranking Member

Steve Chabot
Member of Congress

Louie Gohmert
Member of Congress

Darrell Issa
Ranking Member
Subcommittee on Courts, Intellectual Property, and the Internet

The Honorable W. Stephen Muldrow
November 1, 2021
Page 4

Ken Buck
Ranking Member
Subcommittee on Antitrust, Commercial and Administrative Law

Matt Gaetz
Member of Congress

Mike Johnson
Ranking Member
Subcommittee on the Constitution, Civil Rights and Civil Liberties

Andy Biggs
Ranking Member
Subcommittee on Crime, Terrorism and Homeland Security

Tom McClintock
Ranking Member
Subcommittee on Immigration and Citizenship

W. Gregory Steube
Member of Congress

Tom Tiffany
Member of Congress

Thomas Massie
Member of Congress

Chip Roy
Member of Congress

Dan Bishop
Member of Congress

Michelle Fischbach
Member of Congress

Victoria Spartz
Member of Congress

Scott Fitzgerald
Member of Congress

Cliff Bentz
Member of Congress

Burgess Owens
Member of Congress

cc: The Honorable Jerrold L. Nadler
Chairman

Mr. Monty Wilkinson
Director, Executive Office for U.S. Attorneys

JERROLD NADLER, New York
CHAIRMAN

JIM JORDAN, Ohio
RANKING MEMBER

ONE HUNDRED SEVENTEENTH CONGRESS

Congress of the United States

House of Representatives

COMMITTEE ON THE JUDICIARY

2138 RAYBURN HOUSE OFFICE BUILDING
WASHINGTON, DC 20515-6216
(202) 225-3951
judiciary.house.gov

November 1, 2021

Mr. Richard B. Myrus
Acting U.S. Attorney
District of Rhode Island
50 Kennedy Plaza, 8th Floor
Providence, RI 02903

Dear Mr. Myrus:

We are continuing to investigate the troubling attempts by the Department of Justice and the White House to use the heavy hand of federal law enforcement to target concerned parents at local school board meetings and chill their protected First Amendment activity. Because the Department directed you, along with all other U.S. Attorneys, and the Federal Bureau of Investigation (FBI) to take action to address parents attending school board meetings,[1] we respectfully request your assistance with our investigation.

On September 29, 2021, the National School Boards Association (NSBA) sent a letter to President Joe Biden requesting help from the federal government with concerned parents voicing their opinions at school board meetings.[2] The NSBA letter stated that "malice, violence, and threats" against school officials "could be the equivalent of a form of domestic terrorism or hate crimes."[3] The letter cited a number of interactions at school board meetings, none of which rose to the level of domestic terrorism. In fact, the vast majority of incidents cited by the NSBA did not involve threats or violence.[4] Most notably, as an example of domestic terrorism, the NSBA cited an incident in which a father angrily confronted members at a school board meeting in Loudoun County, Virginia about the heinous sexual assault of his daughter.[5]

A mere five days after the NSBA sent its letter to President Biden, on October 4, 2021, Attorney General Merrick Garland issued a shocking memorandum that directed the FBI and

[1] Memorandum from Atty Gen. Merrick Garland, U.S. Dep't of Justice, Partnership Among Federal, State, Local, Tribal, And Territorial Law Enforcement to Address Threats Against School Administrators, Board Members, Teachers, and Staff (Oct. 4, 2021).
[2] Letter from Dr. Viola M. Garcia, President, Nat'l School Board Assoc. & Mr. Chip Slaven, Chief Exec. Officer, Nat'l School Board Assoc., to President Joseph R. Biden, White House (Sept. 29, 2021).
[3] *Id.*
[4] *See* Caroline Downey, *Vast majority of incidents cited by school-board group to justify federal intervention didn't involve threats,* NAT'L REV. (Oct. 2, 2021).
[5] *Id.*; *see also* Jessica Chasmar, *Loudoun County father arrested at school board events says school tried to cover up daughter's bathroom assault*, FOX NEWS (Oct. 12, 2021).

U.S. Attorneys' Offices to "convene meetings" in your judicial district "with federal, state, local, Tribal, and territorial leaders" within 30 days.[6] The Justice Department simultaneously issued a press release indicating that the Attorney General's directive would "open dedicated lines of communication for threat reporting, assessment and response by law enforcement"—in other words, create a snitch line for complaints about concerned parents.[7]

During Attorney General Garland's testimony before our Committee on October 21, he appeared to have no idea whether the U.S. Attorney meetings he ordered were actually taking place. He stated: "I don't know whether [the meetings] are ongoing, but I expect and hope that they are going . . . because I did ask that they take place."[8] Attorney General Garland testified that he doubted "there have been meetings in every jurisdiction," but reiterated his belief that it is important for federal law enforcement authorities to conduct these meetings in every judicial district.[9] According to the Attorney General's directives, meetings are to be convened in all 94 judicial districts by November 3, 2021, at the latest.

Following the Attorney General's testimony, the NSBA Board of Directors, apparently recognizing the ill-conceived consequences of its letter and the resulting Justice Department action, issued a new memorandum to its members apologizing for the letter, stating: "On behalf of NSBA, <u>we regret and apologize for the letter</u>."[10] (emphasis in original). Although Attorney General Garland testified that the NSBA letter to President Biden was the basis for his October 4 directive to insert federal law enforcement into local school board matters, the Attorney General has yet to rescind his memorandum. His directives to you and other U.S. Attorneys remain in effect.

Concerned parents voicing their strong opposition to controversial curricula at local schools are not domestic terrorists. Parents have an undisputed right to direct the upbringing and education of their children.[11] When parents, however, cross the line to commit a violent act or issue a criminal threat,[12] state and local authorities are best-equipped to handle these violations of state law. But we must not tolerate the use of the federal law enforcement apparatus to intimidate and silence parents using their Constitutional rights to advocate for their child's future.

To assist our investigation and determine whether these meetings are ongoing, we request that you provide the following documents and information:

---

[6] Memorandum from Atty Gen. Merrick Garland, U.S. Dep't of Justice, Partnership Among Federal, State, Local, Tribal, And Territorial Law Enforcement to Address Threats Against School Administrators, Board Members, Teachers, and Staff (Oct. 4, 2021).

[7] Press Release, U.S. Dep't of Justice, Justice Department Addresses Violent Threats Against School Officials and Teachers (Oct. 4, 2021).

[8] *Oversight of the United States Department of Justice: Hearing Before the H. comm. on the Judiciary,* 117th Cong. at 94 (2021) (testimony from Hon. Merrick Garland, Atty Gen., U.S. Dep't of Justice).

[9] *Id.* at 95.

[10] Memorandum from NSBA Board of Directors, Message to NSBA Members (Oct. 22, 2021).

[11] *Troxel v. Granville,* 530 U.S. 57, 65 (2000) (citing *Meyer v. Nebraska,* 262 U.S. 390, 399 (1923)).

[12] *Merrick Garland's federal offense,* WALL ST. J. (Oct. 6, 2021).

1. All documents and communications referring or relating to convening meeting(s) in your judicial district in accordance with the Attorney General's October 4, 2021 memorandum;

2. All agendas, minutes, and notes created or relied upon by U.S. Attorney's Office employees referring or relating to meeting(s) in your judicial district in accordance with the Attorney General's October 4, 2021 memorandum;

3. Please explain when meeting(s) in your judicial district in accordance with the Attorney General's October 4, 2021 memorandum have occurred or will occur;

4. Please identify by name and title of all U.S. Attorney's Office employees involved in the meeting(s) in your judicial district in accordance with the Attorney General's October 4, 2021 memorandum ;

5. Please identify all federal, state, local, Tribal, and territorial organizations invited to or that have attended the meetings convened in your judicial district in accordance with the October 4, 2021 memorandum; and

6. Please provide all recommendations, both formal and informal, and any meeting minutes produced at the meeting(s) in your judicial district in accordance with the Attorney General's October 4, 2021 memorandum.

Please provide this material as soon as possible but no later than 5:00 p.m. on November 15, 2021.

If you have any questions about this request, please contact Committee staff at (202) 225-6906. Thank you for your attention to this important matter.

Sincerely,

Jim Jordan
Ranking Member

Steve Chabot
Member of Congress

Louie Gohmert
Member of Congress

Darrell Issa
Ranking Member
Subcommittee on Courts, Intellectual Property, and the Internet

Ken Buck
Ranking Member
Subcommittee on Antitrust, Commercial and Administrative Law

Matt Gaetz
Member of Congress

Mike Johnson
Ranking Member
Subcommittee on the Constitution, Civil Rights and Civil Liberties

Andy Biggs
Ranking Member
Subcommittee on Crime, Terrorism and Homeland Security

Tom McClintock
Ranking Member
Subcommittee on Immigration and Citizenship

W. Gregory Steube
Member of Congress

Tom Tiffany
Member of Congress

Thomas Massie
Member of Congress

Chip Roy
Member of Congress

Dan Bishop
Member of Congress

Michelle Fischbach
Member of Congress

Victoria Spartz
Member of Congress

Scott Fitzgerald
Member of Congress

Cliff Bentz
Member of Congress

Burgess Owens
Member of Congress

cc: The Honorable Jerrold L. Nadler
Chairman

Mr. Monty Wilkinson
Director, Executive Office for U.S. Attorneys

JERROLD NADLER, New York
CHAIRMAN

JIM JORDAN, Ohio
RANKING MEMBER

ONE HUNDRED SEVENTEENTH CONGRESS

Congress of the United States

House of Representatives

COMMITTEE ON THE JUDICIARY

2138 RAYBURN HOUSE OFFICE BUILDING

WASHINGTON, DC 20515–6216

(202) 225–3951
judiciary.house.gov

November 1, 2021

Mr. M. Rhett DeHart
Acting U.S. Attorney
District of South Carolina
1441 Main Street, Suite 500
Columbia, SC 29201

Dear Mr. DeHart:

We are continuing to investigate the troubling attempts by the Department of Justice and the White House to use the heavy hand of federal law enforcement to target concerned parents at local school board meetings and chill their protected First Amendment activity. Because the Department directed you, along with all other U.S. Attorneys, and the Federal Bureau of Investigation (FBI) to take action to address parents attending school board meetings,[1] we respectfully request your assistance with our investigation.

On September 29, 2021, the National School Boards Association (NSBA) sent a letter to President Joe Biden requesting help from the federal government with concerned parents voicing their opinions at school board meetings.[2] The NSBA letter stated that "malice, violence, and threats" against school officials "could be the equivalent of a form of domestic terrorism or hate crimes."[3] The letter cited a number of interactions at school board meetings, none of which rose to the level of domestic terrorism. In fact, the vast majority of incidents cited by the NSBA did not involve threats or violence.[4] Most notably, as an example of domestic terrorism, the NSBA cited an incident in which a father angrily confronted members at a school board meeting in Loudoun County, Virginia about the heinous sexual assault of his daughter.[5]

A mere five days after the NSBA sent its letter to President Biden, on October 4, 2021, Attorney General Merrick Garland issued a shocking memorandum that directed the FBI and

---

[1] Memorandum from Atty Gen. Merrick Garland, U.S. Dep't of Justice, Partnership Among Federal, State, Local, Tribal, And Territorial Law Enforcement to Address Threats Against School Administrators, Board Members, Teachers, and Staff (Oct. 4, 2021).
[2] Letter from Dr. Viola M. Garcia, President, Nat'l School Board Assoc. & Mr. Chip Slaven, Chief Exec. Officer, Nat'l School Board Assoc., to President Joseph R. Biden, White House (Sept. 29, 2021).
[3] *Id.*
[4] *See* Caroline Downey, *Vast majority of incidents cited by school-board group to justify federal intervention didn't involve threats,* NAT'L REV. (Oct. 2, 2021).
[5] *Id.*; *see also* Jessica Chasmar, *Loudoun County father arrested at school board events says school tried to cover up daughter's bathroom assault*, FOX NEWS (Oct. 12, 2021).

U.S. Attorneys' Offices to "convene meetings" in your judicial district "with federal, state, local, Tribal, and territorial leaders" within 30 days.[6] The Justice Department simultaneously issued a press release indicating that the Attorney General's directive would "open dedicated lines of communication for threat reporting, assessment and response by law enforcement"—in other words, create a snitch line for complaints about concerned parents.[7]

During Attorney General Garland's testimony before our Committee on October 21, he appeared to have no idea whether the U.S. Attorney meetings he ordered were actually taking place. He stated: "I don't know whether [the meetings] are ongoing, but I expect and hope that they are going . . . because I did ask that they take place."[8] Attorney General Garland testified that he doubted "there have been meetings in every jurisdiction," but reiterated his belief that it is important for federal law enforcement authorities to conduct these meetings in every judicial district.[9] According to the Attorney General's directives, meetings are to be convened in all 94 judicial districts by November 3, 2021, at the latest.

Following the Attorney General's testimony, the NSBA Board of Directors, apparently recognizing the ill-conceived consequences of its letter and the resulting Justice Department action, issued a new memorandum to its members apologizing for the letter, stating: "On behalf of NSBA, <u>we regret and apologize for the letter</u>."[10] (emphasis in original). Although Attorney General Garland testified that the NSBA letter to President Biden was the basis for his October 4 directive to insert federal law enforcement into local school board matters, the Attorney General has yet to rescind his memorandum. His directives to you and other U.S. Attorneys remain in effect.

Concerned parents voicing their strong opposition to controversial curricula at local schools are not domestic terrorists. Parents have an undisputed right to direct the upbringing and education of their children.[11] When parents, however, cross the line to commit a violent act or issue a criminal threat,[12] state and local authorities are best-equipped to handle these violations of state law. But we must not tolerate the use of the federal law enforcement apparatus to intimidate and silence parents using their Constitutional rights to advocate for their child's future.

To assist our investigation and determine whether these meetings are ongoing, we request that you provide the following documents and information:

---

[6] Memorandum from Atty Gen. Merrick Garland, U.S. Dep't of Justice, Partnership Among Federal, State, Local, Tribal, And Territorial Law Enforcement to Address Threats Against School Administrators, Board Members, Teachers, and Staff (Oct. 4, 2021).
[7] Press Release, U.S. Dep't of Justice, Justice Department Addresses Violent Threats Against School Officials and Teachers (Oct. 4, 2021).
[8] *Oversight of the United States Department of Justice: Hearing Before the H. comm. on the Judiciary,* 117th Cong. at 94 (2021) (testimony from Hon. Merrick Garland, Atty Gen., U.S. Dep't of Justice).
[9] *Id.* at 95.
[10] Memorandum from NSBA Board of Directors, Message to NSBA Members (Oct. 22, 2021).
[11] *Troxel v. Granville,* 530 U.S. 57, 65 (2000) (citing *Meyer v. Nebraska,* 262 U.S. 390, 399 (1923)).
[12] *Merrick Garland's federal offense,* WALL ST. J. (Oct. 6, 2021).

1. All documents and communications referring or relating to convening meeting(s) in your judicial district in accordance with the Attorney General's October 4, 2021 memorandum;

2. All agendas, minutes, and notes created or relied upon by U.S. Attorney's Office employees referring or relating to meeting(s) in your judicial district in accordance with the Attorney General's October 4, 2021 memorandum;

3. Please explain when meeting(s) in your judicial district in accordance with the Attorney General's October 4, 2021 memorandum have occurred or will occur;

4. Please identify by name and title of all U.S. Attorney's Office employees involved in the meeting(s) in your judicial district in accordance with the Attorney General's October 4, 2021 memorandum ;

5. Please identify all federal, state, local, Tribal, and territorial organizations invited to or that have attended the meetings convened in your judicial district in accordance with the October 4, 2021 memorandum; and

6. Please provide all recommendations, both formal and informal, and any meeting minutes produced at the meeting(s) in your judicial district in accordance with the Attorney General's October 4, 2021 memorandum.

Please provide this material as soon as possible but no later than 5:00 p.m. on November 15, 2021.

If you have any questions about this request, please contact Committee staff at (202) 225-6906. Thank you for your attention to this important matter.

Sincerely,

Jim Jordan
Ranking Member

Steve Chabot
Member of Congress

Louie Gohmert
Member of Congress

Darrell Issa
Ranking Member
Subcommittee on Courts, Intellectual Property, and the Internet

Ken Buck
Ranking Member
Subcommittee on Antitrust, Commercial and Administrative Law

Matt Gaetz
Member of Congress

Mike Johnson
Ranking Member
Subcommittee on the Constitution, Civil Rights and Civil Liberties

Andy Biggs
Ranking Member
Subcommittee on Crime, Terrorism and Homeland Security

Tom McClintock
Ranking Member
Subcommittee on Immigration and Citizenship

W. Gregory Steube
Member of Congress

Tom Tiffany
Member of Congress

Thomas Massie
Member of Congress

Chip Roy
Member of Congress

Dan Bishop
Member of Congress

Michelle Fischbach
Member of Congress

Victoria Spartz
Member of Congress

Scott Fitzgerald
Member of Congress

Cliff Bentz
Member of Congress

Burgess Owens
Member of Congress

cc: The Honorable Jerrold L. Nadler
Chairman

Mr. Monty Wilkinson
Director, Executive Office for U.S. Attorneys

JERROLD NADLER, New York
CHAIRMAN

JIM JORDAN, Ohio
RANKING MEMBER

ONE HUNDRED SEVENTEENTH CONGRESS
Congress of the United States
House of Representatives
COMMITTEE ON THE JUDICIARY
2138 RAYBURN HOUSE OFFICE BUILDING
WASHINGTON, DC 20515-6216
(202) 225-3951
judiciary.house.gov

November 1, 2021

Mr. Dennis R. Holmes
Acting U.S. Attorney
District of South Dakota
P.O. Box 2638
Sioux Falls, SD 57101

Dear Mr. Holmes:

We are continuing to investigate the troubling attempts by the Department of Justice and the White House to use the heavy hand of federal law enforcement to target concerned parents at local school board meetings and chill their protected First Amendment activity. Because the Department directed you, along with all other U.S. Attorneys, and the Federal Bureau of Investigation (FBI) to take action to address parents attending school board meetings,[1] we respectfully request your assistance with our investigation.

On September 29, 2021, the National School Boards Association (NSBA) sent a letter to President Joe Biden requesting help from the federal government with concerned parents voicing their opinions at school board meetings.[2] The NSBA letter stated that "malice, violence, and threats" against school officials "could be the equivalent of a form of domestic terrorism or hate crimes."[3] The letter cited a number of interactions at school board meetings, none of which rose to the level of domestic terrorism. In fact, the vast majority of incidents cited by the NSBA did not involve threats or violence.[4] Most notably, as an example of domestic terrorism, the NSBA cited an incident in which a father angrily confronted members at a school board meeting in Loudoun County, Virginia about the heinous sexual assault of his daughter.[5]

A mere five days after the NSBA sent its letter to President Biden, on October 4, 2021, Attorney General Merrick Garland issued a shocking memorandum that directed the FBI and

---

[1] Memorandum from Atty Gen. Merrick Garland, U.S. Dep't of Justice, Partnership Among Federal, State, Local, Tribal, And Territorial Law Enforcement to Address Threats Against School Administrators, Board Members, Teachers, and Staff (Oct. 4, 2021).
[2] Letter from Dr. Viola M. Garcia, President, Nat'l School Board Assoc. & Mr. Chip Slaven, Chief Exec. Officer, Nat'l School Board Assoc., to President Joseph R. Biden, White House (Sept. 29, 2021).
[3] *Id.*
[4] *See* Caroline Downey, *Vast majority of incidents cited by school-board group to justify federal intervention didn't involve threats,* NAT'L REV. (Oct. 2, 2021).
[5] *Id.*; *see also* Jessica Chasmar, *Loudoun County father arrested at school board events says school tried to cover up daughter's bathroom assault*, FOX NEWS (Oct. 12, 2021).

U.S. Attorneys' Offices to "convene meetings" in your judicial district "with federal, state, local, Tribal, and territorial leaders" within 30 days.[6] The Justice Department simultaneously issued a press release indicating that the Attorney General's directive would "open dedicated lines of communication for threat reporting, assessment and response by law enforcement"—in other words, create a snitch line for complaints about concerned parents.[7]

During Attorney General Garland's testimony before our Committee on October 21, he appeared to have no idea whether the U.S. Attorney meetings he ordered were actually taking place. He stated: "I don't know whether [the meetings] are ongoing, but I expect and hope that they are going . . . because I did ask that they take place."[8] Attorney General Garland testified that he doubted "there have been meetings in every jurisdiction," but reiterated his belief that it is important for federal law enforcement authorities to conduct these meetings in every judicial district.[9] According to the Attorney General's directives, meetings are to be convened in all 94 judicial districts by November 3, 2021, at the latest.

Following the Attorney General's testimony, the NSBA Board of Directors, apparently recognizing the ill-conceived consequences of its letter and the resulting Justice Department action, issued a new memorandum to its members apologizing for the letter, stating: "On behalf of NSBA, <u>we regret and apologize for the letter</u>."[10] (emphasis in original). Although Attorney General Garland testified that the NSBA letter to President Biden was the basis for his October 4 directive to insert federal law enforcement into local school board matters, the Attorney General has yet to rescind his memorandum. His directives to you and other U.S. Attorneys remain in effect.

Concerned parents voicing their strong opposition to controversial curricula at local schools are not domestic terrorists. Parents have an undisputed right to direct the upbringing and education of their children.[11] When parents, however, cross the line to commit a violent act or issue a criminal threat,[12] state and local authorities are best-equipped to handle these violations of state law. But we must not tolerate the use of the federal law enforcement apparatus to intimidate and silence parents using their Constitutional rights to advocate for their child's future.

To assist our investigation and determine whether these meetings are ongoing, we request that you provide the following documents and information:

---

[6] Memorandum from Atty Gen. Merrick Garland, U.S. Dep't of Justice, Partnership Among Federal, State, Local, Tribal, And Territorial Law Enforcement to Address Threats Against School Administrators, Board Members, Teachers, and Staff (Oct. 4, 2021).

[7] Press Release, U.S. Dep't of Justice, Justice Department Addresses Violent Threats Against School Officials and Teachers (Oct. 4, 2021).

[8] *Oversight of the United States Department of Justice: Hearing Before the H. comm. on the Judiciary,* 117th Cong. at 94 (2021) (testimony from Hon. Merrick Garland, Atty Gen., U.S. Dep't of Justice).

[9] *Id.* at 95.

[10] Memorandum from NSBA Board of Directors, Message to NSBA Members (Oct. 22, 2021).

[11] *Troxel v. Granville,* 530 U.S. 57, 65 (2000) (citing *Meyer v. Nebraska,* 262 U.S. 390, 399 (1923)).

[12] *Merrick Garland's federal offense,* WALL ST. J. (Oct. 6, 2021).

1. All documents and communications referring or relating to convening meeting(s) in your judicial district in accordance with the Attorney General's October 4, 2021 memorandum;

2. All agendas, minutes, and notes created or relied upon by U.S. Attorney's Office employees referring or relating to meeting(s) in your judicial district in accordance with the Attorney General's October 4, 2021 memorandum;

3. Please explain when meeting(s) in your judicial district in accordance with the Attorney General's October 4, 2021 memorandum have occurred or will occur;

4. Please identify by name and title of all U.S. Attorney's Office employees involved in the meeting(s) in your judicial district in accordance with the Attorney General's October 4, 2021 memorandum ;

5. Please identify all federal, state, local, Tribal, and territorial organizations invited to or that have attended the meetings convened in your judicial district in accordance with the October 4, 2021 memorandum; and

6. Please provide all recommendations, both formal and informal, and any meeting minutes produced at the meeting(s) in your judicial district in accordance with the Attorney General's October 4, 2021 memorandum.

Please provide this material as soon as possible but no later than 5:00 p.m. on November 15, 2021.

If you have any questions about this request, please contact Committee staff at (202) 225-6906. Thank you for your attention to this important matter.

Sincerely,

Jim Jordan
Ranking Member

Steve Chabot
Member of Congress

Louie Gohmert
Member of Congress

Darrell Issa
Ranking Member
Subcommittee on Courts, Intellectual Property, and the Internet

Ken Buck
Ranking Member
Subcommittee on Antitrust, Commercial and Administrative Law

Matt Gaetz
Member of Congress

Mike Johnson
Ranking Member
Subcommittee on the Constitution, Civil Rights and Civil Liberties

Andy Biggs
Ranking Member
Subcommittee on Crime, Terrorism and Homeland Security

Tom McClintock
Ranking Member
Subcommittee on Immigration and Citizenship

W. Gregory Steube
Member of Congress

Tom Tiffany
Member of Congress

Thomas Massie
Member of Congress

Chip Roy
Member of Congress

Dan Bishop
Member of Congress

Michelle Fischbach
Member of Congress

Victoria Spartz
Member of Congress

Scott Fitzgerald
Member of Congress

Cliff Bentz
Member of Congress

Burgess Owens
Member of Congress

cc: The Honorable Jerrold L. Nadler
Chairman

Mr. Monty Wilkinson
Director, Executive Office for U.S. Attorneys

JERROLD NADLER, New York
CHAIRMAN

JIM JORDAN, Ohio
RANKING MEMBER

ONE HUNDRED SEVENTEENTH CONGRESS

Congress of the United States
House of Representatives
COMMITTEE ON THE JUDICIARY
2138 RAYBURN HOUSE OFFICE BUILDING
WASHINGTON, DC 20515–6216
(202) 225–3951
judiciary.house.gov

November 1, 2021

Mr. Francis M. (Trey) Hamilton III
Acting U.S. Attorney
Eastern District of Tennessee
800 Market Street, Suite 211
Knoxville, TN 37902

Dear Mr. Hamilton:

We are continuing to investigate the troubling attempts by the Department of Justice and the White House to use the heavy hand of federal law enforcement to target concerned parents at local school board meetings and chill their protected First Amendment activity. Because the Department directed you, along with all other U.S. Attorneys, and the Federal Bureau of Investigation (FBI) to take action to address parents attending school board meetings,[1] we respectfully request your assistance with our investigation.

On September 29, 2021, the National School Boards Association (NSBA) sent a letter to President Joe Biden requesting help from the federal government with concerned parents voicing their opinions at school board meetings.[2] The NSBA letter stated that "malice, violence, and threats" against school officials "could be the equivalent of a form of domestic terrorism or hate crimes."[3] The letter cited a number of interactions at school board meetings, none of which rose to the level of domestic terrorism. In fact, the vast majority of incidents cited by the NSBA did not involve threats or violence.[4] Most notably, as an example of domestic terrorism, the NSBA cited an incident in which a father angrily confronted members at a school board meeting in Loudoun County, Virginia about the heinous sexual assault of his daughter.[5]

A mere five days after the NSBA sent its letter to President Biden, on October 4, 2021, Attorney General Merrick Garland issued a shocking memorandum that directed the FBI and

---

[1] Memorandum from Atty Gen. Merrick Garland, U.S. Dep't of Justice, Partnership Among Federal, State, Local, Tribal, And Territorial Law Enforcement to Address Threats Against School Administrators, Board Members, Teachers, and Staff (Oct. 4, 2021).
[2] Letter from Dr. Viola M. Garcia, President, Nat'l School Board Assoc. & Mr. Chip Slaven, Chief Exec. Officer, Nat'l School Board Assoc., to President Joseph R. Biden, White House (Sept. 29, 2021).
[3] *Id.*
[4] *See* Caroline Downey, *Vast majority of incidents cited by school-board group to justify federal intervention didn't involve threats,* NAT'L REV. (Oct. 2, 2021).
[5] *Id.*; *see also* Jessica Chasmar, *Loudoun County father arrested at school board events says school tried to cover up daughter's bathroom assault*, FOX NEWS (Oct. 12, 2021).

U.S. Attorneys' Offices to "convene meetings" in your judicial district "with federal, state, local, Tribal, and territorial leaders" within 30 days.[6] The Justice Department simultaneously issued a press release indicating that the Attorney General's directive would "open dedicated lines of communication for threat reporting, assessment and response by law enforcement"—in other words, create a snitch line for complaints about concerned parents.[7]

During Attorney General Garland's testimony before our Committee on October 21, he appeared to have no idea whether the U.S. Attorney meetings he ordered were actually taking place. He stated: "I don't know whether [the meetings] are ongoing, but I expect and hope that they are going . . . because I did ask that they take place."[8] Attorney General Garland testified that he doubted "there have been meetings in every jurisdiction," but reiterated his belief that it is important for federal law enforcement authorities to conduct these meetings in every judicial district.[9] According to the Attorney General's directives, meetings are to be convened in all 94 judicial districts by November 3, 2021, at the latest.

Following the Attorney General's testimony, the NSBA Board of Directors, apparently recognizing the ill-conceived consequences of its letter and the resulting Justice Department action, issued a new memorandum to its members apologizing for the letter, stating: "On behalf of NSBA, <u>we regret and apologize for the letter</u>."[10] (emphasis in original). Although Attorney General Garland testified that the NSBA letter to President Biden was the basis for his October 4 directive to insert federal law enforcement into local school board matters, the Attorney General has yet to rescind his memorandum. His directives to you and other U.S. Attorneys remain in effect.

Concerned parents voicing their strong opposition to controversial curricula at local schools are not domestic terrorists. Parents have an undisputed right to direct the upbringing and education of their children.[11] When parents, however, cross the line to commit a violent act or issue a criminal threat,[12] state and local authorities are best-equipped to handle these violations of state law. But we must not tolerate the use of the federal law enforcement apparatus to intimidate and silence parents using their Constitutional rights to advocate for their child's future.

To assist our investigation and determine whether these meetings are ongoing, we request that you provide the following documents and information:

---

[6] Memorandum from Atty Gen. Merrick Garland, U.S. Dep't of Justice, Partnership Among Federal, State, Local, Tribal, And Territorial Law Enforcement to Address Threats Against School Administrators, Board Members, Teachers, and Staff (Oct. 4, 2021).

[7] Press Release, U.S. Dep't of Justice, Justice Department Addresses Violent Threats Against School Officials and Teachers (Oct. 4, 2021).

[8] *Oversight of the United States Department of Justice: Hearing Before the H. comm. on the Judiciary,* 117th Cong. at 94 (2021) (testimony from Hon. Merrick Garland, Atty Gen., U.S. Dep't of Justice).

[9] *Id.* at 95.

[10] Memorandum from NSBA Board of Directors, Message to NSBA Members (Oct. 22, 2021).

[11] *Troxel v. Granville,* 530 U.S. 57, 65 (2000) (citing *Meyer v. Nebraska,* 262 U.S. 390, 399 (1923)).

[12] *Merrick Garland's federal offense,* WALL ST. J. (Oct. 6, 2021).

1. All documents and communications referring or relating to convening meeting(s) in your judicial district in accordance with the Attorney General's October 4, 2021 memorandum;

2. All agendas, minutes, and notes created or relied upon by U.S. Attorney's Office employees referring or relating to meeting(s) in your judicial district in accordance with the Attorney General's October 4, 2021 memorandum;

3. Please explain when meeting(s) in your judicial district in accordance with the Attorney General's October 4, 2021 memorandum have occurred or will occur;

4. Please identify by name and title of all U.S. Attorney's Office employees involved in the meeting(s) in your judicial district in accordance with the Attorney General's October 4, 2021 memorandum ;

5. Please identify all federal, state, local, Tribal, and territorial organizations invited to or that have attended the meetings convened in your judicial district in accordance with the October 4, 2021 memorandum; and

6. Please provide all recommendations, both formal and informal, and any meeting minutes produced at the meeting(s) in your judicial district in accordance with the Attorney General's October 4, 2021 memorandum.

Please provide this material as soon as possible but no later than 5:00 p.m. on November 15, 2021.

If you have any questions about this request, please contact Committee staff at (202) 225-6906. Thank you for your attention to this important matter.

Sincerely,

Jim Jordan
Ranking Member

Steve Chabot
Member of Congress

Louie Gohmert
Member of Congress

Darrell Issa
Ranking Member
Subcommittee on Courts, Intellectual Property, and the Internet

Ken Buck
Ranking Member
Subcommittee on Antitrust, Commercial
and Administrative Law

Matt Gaetz
Member of Congress

Mike Johnson
Ranking Member
Subcommittee on the Constitution,
Civil Rights and Civil Liberties

Andy Biggs
Ranking Member
Subcommittee on Crime, Terrorism
and Homeland Security

Tom McClintock
Ranking Member
Subcommittee on Immigration
and Citizenship

W. Gregory Steube
Member of Congress

Tom Tiffany
Member of Congress

Thomas Massie
Member of Congress

Chip Roy
Member of Congress

Dan Bishop
Member of Congress

Michelle Fischbach
Member of Congress

Victoria Spartz
Member of Congress

Scott Fitzgerald
Member of Congress

Cliff Bentz
Member of Congress

Burgess Owens
Member of Congress

cc: The Honorable Jerrold L. Nadler
Chairman

Mr. Monty Wilkinson
Director, Executive Office for U.S. Attorneys

JERROLD NADLER, New York
CHAIRMAN

JIM JORDAN, Ohio
RANKING MEMBER

ONE HUNDRED SEVENTEENTH CONGRESS

Congress of the United States
House of Representatives

COMMITTEE ON THE JUDICIARY

2138 RAYBURN HOUSE OFFICE BUILDING

WASHINGTON, DC 20515–6216

(202) 225–3951
judiciary.house.gov

November 1, 2021

Mr. Joseph C. Murphy, Jr.
Acting U.S. Attorney
Western District of Tennessee
167 North Main Street, Suite 800
Memphis, TN 38103

Dear Mr. Murphy:

We are continuing to investigate the troubling attempts by the Department of Justice and the White House to use the heavy hand of federal law enforcement to target concerned parents at local school board meetings and chill their protected First Amendment activity. Because the Department directed you, along with all other U.S. Attorneys, and the Federal Bureau of Investigation (FBI) to take action to address parents attending school board meetings,[1] we respectfully request your assistance with our investigation.

On September 29, 2021, the National School Boards Association (NSBA) sent a letter to President Joe Biden requesting help from the federal government with concerned parents voicing their opinions at school board meetings.[2] The NSBA letter stated that "malice, violence, and threats" against school officials "could be the equivalent of a form of domestic terrorism or hate crimes."[3] The letter cited a number of interactions at school board meetings, none of which rose to the level of domestic terrorism. In fact, the vast majority of incidents cited by the NSBA did not involve threats or violence.[4] Most notably, as an example of domestic terrorism, the NSBA cited an incident in which a father angrily confronted members at a school board meeting in Loudoun County, Virginia about the heinous sexual assault of his daughter.[5]

A mere five days after the NSBA sent its letter to President Biden, on October 4, 2021, Attorney General Merrick Garland issued a shocking memorandum that directed the FBI and

---

[1] Memorandum from Atty Gen. Merrick Garland, U.S. Dep't of Justice, Partnership Among Federal, State, Local, Tribal, And Territorial Law Enforcement to Address Threats Against School Administrators, Board Members, Teachers, and Staff (Oct. 4, 2021).
[2] Letter from Dr. Viola M. Garcia, President, Nat'l School Board Assoc. & Mr. Chip Slaven, Chief Exec. Officer, Nat'l School Board Assoc., to President Joseph R. Biden, White House (Sept. 29, 2021).
[3] *Id.*
[4] *See* Caroline Downey, *Vast majority of incidents cited by school-board group to justify federal intervention didn't involve threats,* NAT'L REV. (Oct. 2, 2021).
[5] *Id.*; *see also* Jessica Chasmar, *Loudoun County father arrested at school board events says school tried to cover up daughter's bathroom assault*, FOX NEWS (Oct. 12, 2021).

U.S. Attorneys' Offices to "convene meetings" in your judicial district "with federal, state, local, Tribal, and territorial leaders" within 30 days.[6] The Justice Department simultaneously issued a press release indicating that the Attorney General's directive would "open dedicated lines of communication for threat reporting, assessment and response by law enforcement"—in other words, create a snitch line for complaints about concerned parents.[7]

During Attorney General Garland's testimony before our Committee on October 21, he appeared to have no idea whether the U.S. Attorney meetings he ordered were actually taking place. He stated: "I don't know whether [the meetings] are ongoing, but I expect and hope that they are going . . . because I did ask that they take place."[8] Attorney General Garland testified that he doubted "there have been meetings in every jurisdiction," but reiterated his belief that it is important for federal law enforcement authorities to conduct these meetings in every judicial district.[9] According to the Attorney General's directives, meetings are to be convened in all 94 judicial districts by November 3, 2021, at the latest.

Following the Attorney General's testimony, the NSBA Board of Directors, apparently recognizing the ill-conceived consequences of its letter and the resulting Justice Department action, issued a new memorandum to its members apologizing for the letter, stating: "On behalf of NSBA, we regret and apologize for the letter."[10] (emphasis in original). Although Attorney General Garland testified that the NSBA letter to President Biden was the basis for his October 4 directive to insert federal law enforcement into local school board matters, the Attorney General has yet to rescind his memorandum. His directives to you and other U.S. Attorneys remain in effect.

Concerned parents voicing their strong opposition to controversial curricula at local schools are not domestic terrorists. Parents have an undisputed right to direct the upbringing and education of their children.[11] When parents, however, cross the line to commit a violent act or issue a criminal threat,[12] state and local authorities are best-equipped to handle these violations of state law. But we must not tolerate the use of the federal law enforcement apparatus to intimidate and silence parents using their Constitutional rights to advocate for their child's future.

To assist our investigation and determine whether these meetings are ongoing, we request that you provide the following documents and information:

---

[6] Memorandum from Atty Gen. Merrick Garland, U.S. Dep't of Justice, Partnership Among Federal, State, Local, Tribal, And Territorial Law Enforcement to Address Threats Against School Administrators, Board Members, Teachers, and Staff (Oct. 4, 2021).
[7] Press Release, U.S. Dep't of Justice, Justice Department Addresses Violent Threats Against School Officials and Teachers (Oct. 4, 2021).
[8] *Oversight of the United States Department of Justice: Hearing Before the H. comm. on the Judiciary,* 117th Cong. at 94 (2021) (testimony from Hon. Merrick Garland, Atty Gen., U.S. Dep't of Justice).
[9] *Id.* at 95.
[10] Memorandum from NSBA Board of Directors, Message to NSBA Members (Oct. 22, 2021).
[11] *Troxel v. Granville,* 530 U.S. 57, 65 (2000) (citing *Meyer v. Nebraska,* 262 U.S. 390, 399 (1923)).
[12] *Merrick Garland's federal offense,* WALL ST. J. (Oct. 6, 2021).

1. All documents and communications referring or relating to convening meeting(s) in your judicial district in accordance with the Attorney General's October 4, 2021 memorandum;

2. All agendas, minutes, and notes created or relied upon by U.S. Attorney's Office employees referring or relating to meeting(s) in your judicial district in accordance with the Attorney General's October 4, 2021 memorandum;

3. Please explain when meeting(s) in your judicial district in accordance with the Attorney General's October 4, 2021 memorandum have occurred or will occur;

4. Please identify by name and title of all U.S. Attorney's Office employees involved in the meeting(s) in your judicial district in accordance with the Attorney General's October 4, 2021 memorandum ;

5. Please identify all federal, state, local, Tribal, and territorial organizations invited to or that have attended the meetings convened in your judicial district in accordance with the October 4, 2021 memorandum; and

6. Please provide all recommendations, both formal and informal, and any meeting minutes produced at the meeting(s) in your judicial district in accordance with the Attorney General's October 4, 2021 memorandum.

Please provide this material as soon as possible but no later than 5:00 p.m. on November 15, 2021.

If you have any questions about this request, please contact Committee staff at (202) 225-6906. Thank you for your attention to this important matter.

Sincerely,

Jim Jordan
Ranking Member

Steve Chabot
Member of Congress

Louie Gohmert
Member of Congress

Darrell Issa
Ranking Member
Subcommittee on Courts, Intellectual Property, and the Internet

Ken Buck
Ranking Member
Subcommittee on Antitrust, Commercial and Administrative Law

Matt Gaetz
Member of Congress

Mike Johnson
Ranking Member
Subcommittee on the Constitution, Civil Rights and Civil Liberties

Andy Biggs
Ranking Member
Subcommittee on Crime, Terrorism and Homeland Security

Tom McClintock
Ranking Member
Subcommittee on Immigration and Citizenship

W. Gregory Steube
Member of Congress

Tom Tiffany
Member of Congress

Thomas Massie
Member of Congress

Chip Roy
Member of Congress

Dan Bishop
Member of Congress

Michelle Fischbach
Member of Congress

Victoria Spartz
Member of Congress

Scott Fitzgerald
Member of Congress

Cliff Bentz
Member of Congress

Burgess Owens
Member of Congress

cc: The Honorable Jerrold L. Nadler
Chairman

Mr. Monty Wilkinson
Director, Executive Office for U.S. Attorneys

JERROLD NADLER, New York
CHAIRMAN

JIM JORDAN, Ohio
RANKING MEMBER

ONE HUNDRED SEVENTEENTH CONGRESS

Congress of the United States

House of Representatives

COMMITTEE ON THE JUDICIARY

2138 RAYBURN HOUSE OFFICE BUILDING

WASHINGTON, DC 20515-6216

(202) 225-3951
judiciary.house.gov

November 1, 2021

Ms. Mary Jane Stewart
Acting U.S. Attorney
Middle District of Tennessee
110 9th Avenue South, Suite A-961
Nashville, TN 37203

Dear Ms. Stewart:

We are continuing to investigate the troubling attempts by the Department of Justice and the White House to use the heavy hand of federal law enforcement to target concerned parents at local school board meetings and chill their protected First Amendment activity. Because the Department directed you, along with all other U.S. Attorneys, and the Federal Bureau of Investigation (FBI) to take action to address parents attending school board meetings,[1] we respectfully request your assistance with our investigation.

On September 29, 2021, the National School Boards Association (NSBA) sent a letter to President Joe Biden requesting help from the federal government with concerned parents voicing their opinions at school board meetings.[2] The NSBA letter stated that "malice, violence, and threats" against school officials "could be the equivalent of a form of domestic terrorism or hate crimes."[3] The letter cited a number of interactions at school board meetings, none of which rose to the level of domestic terrorism. In fact, the vast majority of incidents cited by the NSBA did not involve threats or violence.[4] Most notably, as an example of domestic terrorism, the NSBA cited an incident in which a father angrily confronted members at a school board meeting in Loudoun County, Virginia about the heinous sexual assault of his daughter.[5]

A mere five days after the NSBA sent its letter to President Biden, on October 4, 2021, Attorney General Merrick Garland issued a shocking memorandum that directed the FBI and

---

[1] Memorandum from Atty Gen. Merrick Garland, U.S. Dep't of Justice, Partnership Among Federal, State, Local, Tribal, And Territorial Law Enforcement to Address Threats Against School Administrators, Board Members, Teachers, and Staff (Oct. 4, 2021).
[2] Letter from Dr. Viola M. Garcia, President, Nat'l School Board Assoc. & Mr. Chip Slaven, Chief Exec. Officer, Nat'l School Board Assoc., to President Joseph R. Biden, White House (Sept. 29, 2021).
[3] *Id.*
[4] *See* Caroline Downey, *Vast majority of incidents cited by school-board group to justify federal intervention didn't involve threats,* NAT'L REV. (Oct. 2, 2021).
[5] *Id.*; *see also* Jessica Chasmar, *Loudoun County father arrested at school board events says school tried to cover up daughter's bathroom assault*, FOX NEWS (Oct. 12, 2021).

U.S. Attorneys' Offices to "convene meetings" in your judicial district "with federal, state, local, Tribal, and territorial leaders" within 30 days.[6] The Justice Department simultaneously issued a press release indicating that the Attorney General's directive would "open dedicated lines of communication for threat reporting, assessment and response by law enforcement"—in other words, create a snitch line for complaints about concerned parents.[7]

During Attorney General Garland's testimony before our Committee on October 21, he appeared to have no idea whether the U.S. Attorney meetings he ordered were actually taking place. He stated: "I don't know whether [the meetings] are ongoing, but I expect and hope that they are going . . . because I did ask that they take place."[8] Attorney General Garland testified that he doubted "there have been meetings in every jurisdiction," but reiterated his belief that it is important for federal law enforcement authorities to conduct these meetings in every judicial district.[9] According to the Attorney General's directives, meetings are to be convened in all 94 judicial districts by November 3, 2021, at the latest.

Following the Attorney General's testimony, the NSBA Board of Directors, apparently recognizing the ill-conceived consequences of its letter and the resulting Justice Department action, issued a new memorandum to its members apologizing for the letter, stating: "On behalf of NSBA, <u>we regret and apologize for the letter</u>."[10] (emphasis in original). Although Attorney General Garland testified that the NSBA letter to President Biden was the basis for his October 4 directive to insert federal law enforcement into local school board matters, the Attorney General has yet to rescind his memorandum. His directives to you and other U.S. Attorneys remain in effect.

Concerned parents voicing their strong opposition to controversial curricula at local schools are not domestic terrorists. Parents have an undisputed right to direct the upbringing and education of their children.[11] When parents, however, cross the line to commit a violent act or issue a criminal threat,[12] state and local authorities are best-equipped to handle these violations of state law. But we must not tolerate the use of the federal law enforcement apparatus to intimidate and silence parents using their Constitutional rights to advocate for their child's future.

To assist our investigation and determine whether these meetings are ongoing, we request that you provide the following documents and information:

---

[6] Memorandum from Atty Gen. Merrick Garland, U.S. Dep't of Justice, Partnership Among Federal, State, Local, Tribal, And Territorial Law Enforcement to Address Threats Against School Administrators, Board Members, Teachers, and Staff (Oct. 4, 2021).

[7] Press Release, U.S. Dep't of Justice, Justice Department Addresses Violent Threats Against School Officials and Teachers (Oct. 4, 2021).

[8] *Oversight of the United States Department of Justice: Hearing Before the H. comm. on the Judiciary,* 117th Cong. at 94 (2021) (testimony from Hon. Merrick Garland, Atty Gen., U.S. Dep't of Justice).

[9] *Id.* at 95.

[10] Memorandum from NSBA Board of Directors, Message to NSBA Members (Oct. 22, 2021).

[11] *Troxel v. Granville,* 530 U.S. 57, 65 (2000) (citing *Meyer v. Nebraska,* 262 U.S. 390, 399 (1923)).

[12] *Merrick Garland's federal offense,* WALL ST. J. (Oct. 6, 2021).

1. All documents and communications referring or relating to convening meeting(s) in your judicial district in accordance with the Attorney General's October 4, 2021 memorandum;

2. All agendas, minutes, and notes created or relied upon by U.S. Attorney's Office employees referring or relating to meeting(s) in your judicial district in accordance with the Attorney General's October 4, 2021 memorandum;

3. Please explain when meeting(s) in your judicial district in accordance with the Attorney General's October 4, 2021 memorandum have occurred or will occur;

4. Please identify by name and title of all U.S. Attorney's Office employees involved in the meeting(s) in your judicial district in accordance with the Attorney General's October 4, 2021 memorandum ;

5. Please identify all federal, state, local, Tribal, and territorial organizations invited to or that have attended the meetings convened in your judicial district in accordance with the October 4, 2021 memorandum; and

6. Please provide all recommendations, both formal and informal, and any meeting minutes produced at the meeting(s) in your judicial district in accordance with the Attorney General's October 4, 2021 memorandum.

Please provide this material as soon as possible but no later than 5:00 p.m. on November 15, 2021.

If you have any questions about this request, please contact Committee staff at (202) 225-6906. Thank you for your attention to this important matter.

Sincerely,

Jim Jordan
Ranking Member

Steve Chabot
Member of Congress

Louie Gohmert
Member of Congress

Darrell Issa
Ranking Member
Subcommittee on Courts, Intellectual Property, and the Internet

Ken Buck
Ranking Member
Subcommittee on Antitrust, Commercial and Administrative Law

Matt Gaetz
Member of Congress

Mike Johnson
Ranking Member
Subcommittee on the Constitution, Civil Rights and Civil Liberties

Andy Biggs
Ranking Member
Subcommittee on Crime, Terrorism and Homeland Security

Tom McClintock
Ranking Member
Subcommittee on Immigration and Citizenship

W. Gregory Steube
Member of Congress

Tom Tiffany
Member of Congress

Thomas Massie
Member of Congress

Chip Roy
Member of Congress

Dan Bishop
Member of Congress

Michelle Fischbach
Member of Congress

Victoria Spartz
Member of Congress

Scott Fitzgerald
Member of Congress

Cliff Bentz
Member of Congress

Burgess Owens
Member of Congress

cc: The Honorable Jerrold L. Nadler
Chairman

Mr. Monty Wilkinson
Director, Executive Office for U.S. Attorneys

JERROLD NADLER, New York
CHAIRMAN

JIM JORDAN, Ohio
RANKING MEMBER

ONE HUNDRED SEVENTEENTH CONGRESS

Congress of the United States

House of Representatives

COMMITTEE ON THE JUDICIARY

2138 RAYBURN HOUSE OFFICE BUILDING
WASHINGTON, DC 20515–6216
(202) 225–3951
judiciary.house.gov

November 1, 2021

Mr. Nicholas J. Ganjei
Acting U.S. Attorney
Eastern District of Texas
101 E. Park Boulevard, Suite 500
Plano, TX 75074

Dear Mr. Ganjei:

We are continuing to investigate the troubling attempts by the Department of Justice and the White House to use the heavy hand of federal law enforcement to target concerned parents at local school board meetings and chill their protected First Amendment activity. Because the Department directed you, along with all other U.S. Attorneys, and the Federal Bureau of Investigation (FBI) to take action to address parents attending school board meetings,[1] we respectfully request your assistance with our investigation.

On September 29, 2021, the National School Boards Association (NSBA) sent a letter to President Joe Biden requesting help from the federal government with concerned parents voicing their opinions at school board meetings.[2] The NSBA letter stated that "malice, violence, and threats" against school officials "could be the equivalent of a form of domestic terrorism or hate crimes."[3] The letter cited a number of interactions at school board meetings, none of which rose to the level of domestic terrorism. In fact, the vast majority of incidents cited by the NSBA did not involve threats or violence.[4] Most notably, as an example of domestic terrorism, the NSBA cited an incident in which a father angrily confronted members at a school board meeting in Loudoun County, Virginia about the heinous sexual assault of his daughter.[5]

A mere five days after the NSBA sent its letter to President Biden, on October 4, 2021, Attorney General Merrick Garland issued a shocking memorandum that directed the FBI and

---

[1] Memorandum from Atty Gen. Merrick Garland, U.S. Dep't of Justice, Partnership Among Federal, State, Local, Tribal, And Territorial Law Enforcement to Address Threats Against School Administrators, Board Members, Teachers, and Staff (Oct. 4, 2021).
[2] Letter from Dr. Viola M. Garcia, President, Nat'l School Board Assoc. & Mr. Chip Slaven, Chief Exec. Officer, Nat'l School Board Assoc., to President Joseph R. Biden, White House (Sept. 29, 2021).
[3] *Id.*
[4] *See* Caroline Downey, *Vast majority of incidents cited by school-board group to justify federal intervention didn't involve threats,* NAT'L REV. (Oct. 2, 2021).
[5] *Id.*; *see also* Jessica Chasmar, *Loudoun County father arrested at school board events says school tried to cover up daughter's bathroom assault*, FOX NEWS (Oct. 12, 2021).

U.S. Attorneys' Offices to "convene meetings" in your judicial district "with federal, state, local, Tribal, and territorial leaders" within 30 days.[6] The Justice Department simultaneously issued a press release indicating that the Attorney General's directive would "open dedicated lines of communication for threat reporting, assessment and response by law enforcement"—in other words, create a snitch line for complaints about concerned parents.[7]

During Attorney General Garland's testimony before our Committee on October 21, he appeared to have no idea whether the U.S. Attorney meetings he ordered were actually taking place. He stated: "I don't know whether [the meetings] are ongoing, but I expect and hope that they are going . . . because I did ask that they take place."[8] Attorney General Garland testified that he doubted "there have been meetings in every jurisdiction," but reiterated his belief that it is important for federal law enforcement authorities to conduct these meetings in every judicial district.[9] According to the Attorney General's directives, meetings are to be convened in all 94 judicial districts by November 3, 2021, at the latest.

Following the Attorney General's testimony, the NSBA Board of Directors, apparently recognizing the ill-conceived consequences of its letter and the resulting Justice Department action, issued a new memorandum to its members apologizing for the letter, stating: "On behalf of NSBA, we regret and apologize for the letter."[10] (emphasis in original). Although Attorney General Garland testified that the NSBA letter to President Biden was the basis for his October 4 directive to insert federal law enforcement into local school board matters, the Attorney General has yet to rescind his memorandum. His directives to you and other U.S. Attorneys remain in effect.

Concerned parents voicing their strong opposition to controversial curricula at local schools are not domestic terrorists. Parents have an undisputed right to direct the upbringing and education of their children.[11] When parents, however, cross the line to commit a violent act or issue a criminal threat,[12] state and local authorities are best-equipped to handle these violations of state law. But we must not tolerate the use of the federal law enforcement apparatus to intimidate and silence parents using their Constitutional rights to advocate for their child's future.

To assist our investigation and determine whether these meetings are ongoing, we request that you provide the following documents and information:

---

[6] Memorandum from Atty Gen. Merrick Garland, U.S. Dep't of Justice, Partnership Among Federal, State, Local, Tribal, And Territorial Law Enforcement to Address Threats Against School Administrators, Board Members, Teachers, and Staff (Oct. 4, 2021).
[7] Press Release, U.S. Dep't of Justice, Justice Department Addresses Violent Threats Against School Officials and Teachers (Oct. 4, 2021).
[8] *Oversight of the United States Department of Justice: Hearing Before the H. comm. on the Judiciary,* 117th Cong. at 94 (2021) (testimony from Hon. Merrick Garland, Atty Gen., U.S. Dep't of Justice).
[9] *Id.* at 95.
[10] Memorandum from NSBA Board of Directors, Message to NSBA Members (Oct. 22, 2021).
[11] *Troxel v. Granville,* 530 U.S. 57, 65 (2000) (citing *Meyer v. Nebraska,* 262 U.S. 390, 399 (1923)).
[12] *Merrick Garland's federal offense,* WALL ST. J. (Oct. 6, 2021).

1. All documents and communications referring or relating to convening meeting(s) in your judicial district in accordance with the Attorney General's October 4, 2021 memorandum;

2. All agendas, minutes, and notes created or relied upon by U.S. Attorney's Office employees referring or relating to meeting(s) in your judicial district in accordance with the Attorney General's October 4, 2021 memorandum;

3. Please explain when meeting(s) in your judicial district in accordance with the Attorney General's October 4, 2021 memorandum have occurred or will occur;

4. Please identify by name and title of all U.S. Attorney's Office employees involved in the meeting(s) in your judicial district in accordance with the Attorney General's October 4, 2021 memorandum ;

5. Please identify all federal, state, local, Tribal, and territorial organizations invited to or that have attended the meetings convened in your judicial district in accordance with the October 4, 2021 memorandum; and

6. Please provide all recommendations, both formal and informal, and any meeting minutes produced at the meeting(s) in your judicial district in accordance with the Attorney General's October 4, 2021 memorandum.

Please provide this material as soon as possible but no later than 5:00 p.m. on November 15, 2021.

If you have any questions about this request, please contact Committee staff at (202) 225-6906. Thank you for your attention to this important matter.

Sincerely,

Jim Jordan
Ranking Member

Steve Chabot
Member of Congress

Louie Gohmert
Member of Congress

Darrell Issa
Ranking Member
Subcommittee on Courts, Intellectual Property, and the Internet

Ken Buck
Ranking Member
Subcommittee on Antitrust, Commercial and Administrative Law

Matt Gaetz
Member of Congress

Mike Johnson
Ranking Member
Subcommittee on the Constitution, Civil Rights and Civil Liberties

Andy Biggs
Ranking Member
Subcommittee on Crime, Terrorism and Homeland Security

Tom McClintock
Ranking Member
Subcommittee on Immigration and Citizenship

W. Gregory Steube
Member of Congress

Tom Tiffany
Member of Congress

Thomas Massie
Member of Congress

Chip Roy
Member of Congress

Dan Bishop
Member of Congress

Michelle Fischbach
Member of Congress

Victoria Spartz
Member of Congress

Scott Fitzgerald
Member of Congress

Cliff Bentz
Member of Congress

Burgess Owens
Member of Congress

cc: The Honorable Jerrold L. Nadler
Chairman

Mr. Monty Wilkinson
Director, Executive Office for U.S. Attorneys

JERROLD NADLER, New York
CHAIRMAN

JIM JORDAN, Ohio
RANKING MEMBER

ONE HUNDRED SEVENTEENTH CONGRESS

Congress of the United States
House of Representatives

COMMITTEE ON THE JUDICIARY
2138 RAYBURN HOUSE OFFICE BUILDING
WASHINGTON, DC 20515–6216
(202) 225–3951
judiciary.house.gov

November 1, 2021

Ms. Ashley C. Hoff
U.S. Attorney
Western District of Texas
601 NW Loop 410, Suite 600
San Antonio, TX 78216

Dear Ms. Hoff:

We are continuing to investigate the troubling attempts by the Department of Justice and the White House to use the heavy hand of federal law enforcement to target concerned parents at local school board meetings and chill their protected First Amendment activity. Because the Department directed you, along with all other U.S. Attorneys, and the Federal Bureau of Investigation (FBI) to take action to address parents attending school board meetings,[1] we respectfully request your assistance with our investigation.

On September 29, 2021, the National School Boards Association (NSBA) sent a letter to President Joe Biden requesting help from the federal government with concerned parents voicing their opinions at school board meetings.[2] The NSBA letter stated that "malice, violence, and threats" against school officials "could be the equivalent of a form of domestic terrorism or hate crimes."[3] The letter cited a number of interactions at school board meetings, none of which rose to the level of domestic terrorism. In fact, the vast majority of incidents cited by the NSBA did not involve threats or violence.[4] Most notably, as an example of domestic terrorism, the NSBA cited an incident in which a father angrily confronted members at a school board meeting in Loudoun County, Virginia about the heinous sexual assault of his daughter.[5]

A mere five days after the NSBA sent its letter to President Biden, on October 4, 2021, Attorney General Merrick Garland issued a shocking memorandum that directed the FBI and

---

[1] Memorandum from Atty Gen. Merrick Garland, U.S. Dep't of Justice, Partnership Among Federal, State, Local, Tribal, And Territorial Law Enforcement to Address Threats Against School Administrators, Board Members, Teachers, and Staff (Oct. 4, 2021).
[2] Letter from Dr. Viola M. Garcia, President, Nat'l School Board Assoc. & Mr. Chip Slaven, Chief Exec. Officer, Nat'l School Board Assoc., to President Joseph R. Biden, White House (Sept. 29, 2021).
[3] *Id.*
[4] *See* Caroline Downey, *Vast majority of incidents cited by school-board group to justify federal intervention didn't involve threats,* NAT'L REV. (Oct. 2, 2021).
[5] *Id.*; *see also* Jessica Chasmar, *Loudoun County father arrested at school board events says school tried to cover up daughter's bathroom assault*, FOX NEWS (Oct. 12, 2021).

U.S. Attorneys' Offices to "convene meetings" in your judicial district "with federal, state, local, Tribal, and territorial leaders" within 30 days.[6] The Justice Department simultaneously issued a press release indicating that the Attorney General's directive would "open dedicated lines of communication for threat reporting, assessment and response by law enforcement"—in other words, create a snitch line for complaints about concerned parents.[7]

During Attorney General Garland's testimony before our Committee on October 21, he appeared to have no idea whether the U.S. Attorney meetings he ordered were actually taking place. He stated: "I don't know whether [the meetings] are ongoing, but I expect and hope that they are going . . . because I did ask that they take place."[8] Attorney General Garland testified that he doubted "there have been meetings in every jurisdiction," but reiterated his belief that it is important for federal law enforcement authorities to conduct these meetings in every judicial district.[9] According to the Attorney General's directives, meetings are to be convened in all 94 judicial districts by November 3, 2021, at the latest.

Following the Attorney General's testimony, the NSBA Board of Directors, apparently recognizing the ill-conceived consequences of its letter and the resulting Justice Department action, issued a new memorandum to its members apologizing for the letter, stating: "On behalf of NSBA, <u>we regret and apologize for the letter</u>."[10] (emphasis in original). Although Attorney General Garland testified that the NSBA letter to President Biden was the basis for his October 4 directive to insert federal law enforcement into local school board matters, the Attorney General has yet to rescind his memorandum. His directives to you and other U.S. Attorneys remain in effect.

Concerned parents voicing their strong opposition to controversial curricula at local schools are not domestic terrorists. Parents have an undisputed right to direct the upbringing and education of their children.[11] When parents, however, cross the line to commit a violent act or issue a criminal threat,[12] state and local authorities are best-equipped to handle these violations of state law. But we must not tolerate the use of the federal law enforcement apparatus to intimidate and silence parents using their Constitutional rights to advocate for their child's future.

To assist our investigation and determine whether these meetings are ongoing, we request that you provide the following documents and information:

---

[6] Memorandum from Atty Gen. Merrick Garland, U.S. Dep't of Justice, Partnership Among Federal, State, Local, Tribal, And Territorial Law Enforcement to Address Threats Against School Administrators, Board Members, Teachers, and Staff (Oct. 4, 2021).
[7] Press Release, U.S. Dep't of Justice, Justice Department Addresses Violent Threats Against School Officials and Teachers (Oct. 4, 2021).
[8] *Oversight of the United States Department of Justice: Hearing Before the H. comm. on the Judiciary,* 117th Cong. at 94 (2021) (testimony from Hon. Merrick Garland, Atty Gen., U.S. Dep't of Justice).
[9] *Id.* at 95.
[10] Memorandum from NSBA Board of Directors, Message to NSBA Members (Oct. 22, 2021).
[11] *Troxel v. Granville,* 530 U.S. 57, 65 (2000) (citing *Meyer v. Nebraska,* 262 U.S. 390, 399 (1923)).
[12] *Merrick Garland's federal offense,* WALL ST. J. (Oct. 6, 2021).

1. All documents and communications referring or relating to convening meeting(s) in your judicial district in accordance with the Attorney General's October 4, 2021 memorandum;

2. All agendas, minutes, and notes created or relied upon by U.S. Attorney's Office employees referring or relating to meeting(s) in your judicial district in accordance with the Attorney General's October 4, 2021 memorandum;

3. Please explain when meeting(s) in your judicial district in accordance with the Attorney General's October 4, 2021 memorandum have occurred or will occur;

4. Please identify by name and title of all U.S. Attorney's Office employees involved in the meeting(s) in your judicial district in accordance with the Attorney General's October 4, 2021 memorandum ;

5. Please identify all federal, state, local, Tribal, and territorial organizations invited to or that have attended the meetings convened in your judicial district in accordance with the October 4, 2021 memorandum; and

6. Please provide all recommendations, both formal and informal, and any meeting minutes produced at the meeting(s) in your judicial district in accordance with the Attorney General's October 4, 2021 memorandum.

Please provide this material as soon as possible but no later than 5:00 p.m. on November 15, 2021.

If you have any questions about this request, please contact Committee staff at (202) 225-6906. Thank you for your attention to this important matter.

Sincerely,

Jim Jordan
Ranking Member

Steve Chabot
Member of Congress

Louie Gohmert
Member of Congress

Darrell Issa
Ranking Member
Subcommittee on Courts, Intellectual Property, and the Internet

Ken Buck
Ranking Member
Subcommittee on Antitrust, Commercial and Administrative Law

Matt Gaetz
Member of Congress

Mike Johnson
Ranking Member
Subcommittee on the Constitution, Civil Rights and Civil Liberties

Andy Biggs
Ranking Member
Subcommittee on Crime, Terrorism and Homeland Security

Tom McClintock
Ranking Member
Subcommittee on Immigration and Citizenship

W. Gregory Steube
Member of Congress

Tom Tiffany
Member of Congress

Thomas Massie
Member of Congress

Chip Roy
Member of Congress

Dan Bishop
Member of Congress

Michelle Fischbach
Member of Congress

Victoria Spartz
Member of Congress

Scott Fitzgerald
Member of Congress

Cliff Bentz
Member of Congress

Burgess Owens
Member of Congress

cc: The Honorable Jerrold L. Nadler
Chairman

Mr. Monty Wilkinson
Director, Executive Office for U.S. Attorneys

JERROLD NADLER, New York
CHAIRMAN

JIM JORDAN, Ohio
RANKING MEMBER

ONE HUNDRED SEVENTEENTH CONGRESS

Congress of the United States

House of Representatives

COMMITTEE ON THE JUDICIARY

2138 RAYBURN HOUSE OFFICE BUILDING

WASHINGTON, DC 20515-6216

(202) 225-3951
judiciary.house.gov

November 1, 2021

Ms. Jennifer Lowery
Acting U.S. Attorney
Southern District of Texas
1000 Louisiana, Suite 2300
Houston, TX 77002

Dear Ms. Lowery:

We are continuing to investigate the troubling attempts by the Department of Justice and the White House to use the heavy hand of federal law enforcement to target concerned parents at local school board meetings and chill their protected First Amendment activity. Because the Department directed you, along with all other U.S. Attorneys, and the Federal Bureau of Investigation (FBI) to take action to address parents attending school board meetings,[1] we respectfully request your assistance with our investigation.

On September 29, 2021, the National School Boards Association (NSBA) sent a letter to President Joe Biden requesting help from the federal government with concerned parents voicing their opinions at school board meetings.[2] The NSBA letter stated that "malice, violence, and threats" against school officials "could be the equivalent of a form of domestic terrorism or hate crimes."[3] The letter cited a number of interactions at school board meetings, none of which rose to the level of domestic terrorism. In fact, the vast majority of incidents cited by the NSBA did not involve threats or violence.[4] Most notably, as an example of domestic terrorism, the NSBA cited an incident in which a father angrily confronted members at a school board meeting in Loudoun County, Virginia about the heinous sexual assault of his daughter.[5]

A mere five days after the NSBA sent its letter to President Biden, on October 4, 2021, Attorney General Merrick Garland issued a shocking memorandum that directed the FBI and

---

[1] Memorandum from Atty Gen. Merrick Garland, U.S. Dep't of Justice, Partnership Among Federal, State, Local, Tribal, And Territorial Law Enforcement to Address Threats Against School Administrators, Board Members, Teachers, and Staff (Oct. 4, 2021).
[2] Letter from Dr. Viola M. Garcia, President, Nat'l School Board Assoc. & Mr. Chip Slaven, Chief Exec. Officer, Nat'l School Board Assoc., to President Joseph R. Biden, White House (Sept. 29, 2021).
[3] *Id.*
[4] *See* Caroline Downey, *Vast majority of incidents cited by school-board group to justify federal intervention didn't involve threats,* NAT'L REV. (Oct. 2, 2021).
[5] *Id.*; *see also* Jessica Chasmar, *Loudoun County father arrested at school board events says school tried to cover up daughter's bathroom assault*, FOX NEWS (Oct. 12, 2021).

U.S. Attorneys' Offices to "convene meetings" in your judicial district "with federal, state, local, Tribal, and territorial leaders" within 30 days.[6] The Justice Department simultaneously issued a press release indicating that the Attorney General's directive would "open dedicated lines of communication for threat reporting, assessment and response by law enforcement"—in other words, create a snitch line for complaints about concerned parents.[7]

During Attorney General Garland's testimony before our Committee on October 21, he appeared to have no idea whether the U.S. Attorney meetings he ordered were actually taking place. He stated: "I don't know whether [the meetings] are ongoing, but I expect and hope that they are going . . . because I did ask that they take place."[8] Attorney General Garland testified that he doubted "there have been meetings in every jurisdiction," but reiterated his belief that it is important for federal law enforcement authorities to conduct these meetings in every judicial district.[9] According to the Attorney General's directives, meetings are to be convened in all 94 judicial districts by November 3, 2021, at the latest.

Following the Attorney General's testimony, the NSBA Board of Directors, apparently recognizing the ill-conceived consequences of its letter and the resulting Justice Department action, issued a new memorandum to its members apologizing for the letter, stating: "On behalf of NSBA, <u>we regret and apologize for the letter</u>."[10] (emphasis in original). Although Attorney General Garland testified that the NSBA letter to President Biden was the basis for his October 4 directive to insert federal law enforcement into local school board matters, the Attorney General has yet to rescind his memorandum. His directives to you and other U.S. Attorneys remain in effect.

Concerned parents voicing their strong opposition to controversial curricula at local schools are not domestic terrorists. Parents have an undisputed right to direct the upbringing and education of their children.[11] When parents, however, cross the line to commit a violent act or issue a criminal threat,[12] state and local authorities are best-equipped to handle these violations of state law. But we must not tolerate the use of the federal law enforcement apparatus to intimidate and silence parents using their Constitutional rights to advocate for their child's future.

To assist our investigation and determine whether these meetings are ongoing, we request that you provide the following documents and information:

---

[6] Memorandum from Atty Gen. Merrick Garland, U.S. Dep't of Justice, Partnership Among Federal, State, Local, Tribal, And Territorial Law Enforcement to Address Threats Against School Administrators, Board Members, Teachers, and Staff (Oct. 4, 2021).
[7] Press Release, U.S. Dep't of Justice, Justice Department Addresses Violent Threats Against School Officials and Teachers (Oct. 4, 2021).
[8] *Oversight of the United States Department of Justice: Hearing Before the H. comm. on the Judiciary,* 117th Cong. at 94 (2021) (testimony from Hon. Merrick Garland, Atty Gen., U.S. Dep't of Justice).
[9] *Id.* at 95.
[10] Memorandum from NSBA Board of Directors, Message to NSBA Members (Oct. 22, 2021).
[11] *Troxel v. Granville,* 530 U.S. 57, 65 (2000) (citing *Meyer v. Nebraska,* 262 U.S. 390, 399 (1923)).
[12] *Merrick Garland's federal offense,* WALL ST. J. (Oct. 6, 2021).

1. All documents and communications referring or relating to convening meeting(s) in your judicial district in accordance with the Attorney General's October 4, 2021 memorandum;

2. All agendas, minutes, and notes created or relied upon by U.S. Attorney's Office employees referring or relating to meeting(s) in your judicial district in accordance with the Attorney General's October 4, 2021 memorandum;

3. Please explain when meeting(s) in your judicial district in accordance with the Attorney General's October 4, 2021 memorandum have occurred or will occur;

4. Please identify by name and title of all U.S. Attorney's Office employees involved in the meeting(s) in your judicial district in accordance with the Attorney General's October 4, 2021 memorandum ;

5. Please identify all federal, state, local, Tribal, and territorial organizations invited to or that have attended the meetings convened in your judicial district in accordance with the October 4, 2021 memorandum; and

6. Please provide all recommendations, both formal and informal, and any meeting minutes produced at the meeting(s) in your judicial district in accordance with the Attorney General's October 4, 2021 memorandum.

Please provide this material as soon as possible but no later than 5:00 p.m. on November 15, 2021.

If you have any questions about this request, please contact Committee staff at (202) 225-6906. Thank you for your attention to this important matter.

Sincerely,

Jim Jordan
Ranking Member

Steve Chabot
Member of Congress

Louie Gohmert
Member of Congress

Darrell Issa
Ranking Member
Subcommittee on Courts, Intellectual Property, and the Internet

Ken Buck
Ranking Member
Subcommittee on Antitrust, Commercial and Administrative Law

Matt Gaetz
Member of Congress

Mike Johnson
Ranking Member
Subcommittee on the Constitution, Civil Rights and Civil Liberties

Andy Biggs
Ranking Member
Subcommittee on Crime, Terrorism and Homeland Security

Tom McClintock
Ranking Member
Subcommittee on Immigration and Citizenship

W. Gregory Steube
Member of Congress

Tom Tiffany
Member of Congress

Thomas Massie
Member of Congress

Chip Roy
Member of Congress

Dan Bishop
Member of Congress

Michelle Fischbach
Member of Congress

Victoria Spartz
Member of Congress

Scott Fitzgerald
Member of Congress

Cliff Bentz
Member of Congress

Burgess Owens
Member of Congress

cc: The Honorable Jerrold L. Nadler
Chairman

Mr. Monty Wilkinson
Director, Executive Office for U.S. Attorneys

JERROLD NADLER, New York
CHAIRMAN

JIM JORDAN, Ohio
RANKING MEMBER

ONE HUNDRED SEVENTEENTH CONGRESS

Congress of the United States

House of Representatives

COMMITTEE ON THE JUDICIARY

2138 RAYBURN HOUSE OFFICE BUILDING

WASHINGTON, DC 20515–6216

(202) 225–3951
judiciary.house.gov

November 1, 2021

Mr. Chad E. Meacham
Acting U.S. Attorney
Northern District of Texas
1100 Commerce Street, Third Floor
Dallas, TX 75242

Dear Mr. Meacham:

We are continuing to investigate the troubling attempts by the Department of Justice and the White House to use the heavy hand of federal law enforcement to target concerned parents at local school board meetings and chill their protected First Amendment activity. Because the Department directed you, along with all other U.S. Attorneys, and the Federal Bureau of Investigation (FBI) to take action to address parents attending school board meetings,[1] we respectfully request your assistance with our investigation.

On September 29, 2021, the National School Boards Association (NSBA) sent a letter to President Joe Biden requesting help from the federal government with concerned parents voicing their opinions at school board meetings.[2] The NSBA letter stated that "malice, violence, and threats" against school officials "could be the equivalent of a form of domestic terrorism or hate crimes."[3] The letter cited a number of interactions at school board meetings, none of which rose to the level of domestic terrorism. In fact, the vast majority of incidents cited by the NSBA did not involve threats or violence.[4] Most notably, as an example of domestic terrorism, the NSBA cited an incident in which a father angrily confronted members at a school board meeting in Loudoun County, Virginia about the heinous sexual assault of his daughter.[5]

A mere five days after the NSBA sent its letter to President Biden, on October 4, 2021, Attorney General Merrick Garland issued a shocking memorandum that directed the FBI and

---

[1] Memorandum from Atty Gen. Merrick Garland, U.S. Dep't of Justice, Partnership Among Federal, State, Local, Tribal, And Territorial Law Enforcement to Address Threats Against School Administrators, Board Members, Teachers, and Staff (Oct. 4, 2021).
[2] Letter from Dr. Viola M. Garcia, President, Nat'l School Board Assoc. & Mr. Chip Slaven, Chief Exec. Officer, Nat'l School Board Assoc., to President Joseph R. Biden, White House (Sept. 29, 2021).
[3] *Id.*
[4] *See* Caroline Downey, *Vast majority of incidents cited by school-board group to justify federal intervention didn't involve threats,* NAT'L REV. (Oct. 2, 2021).
[5] *Id.*; *see also* Jessica Chasmar, *Loudoun County father arrested at school board events says school tried to cover up daughter's bathroom assault*, FOX NEWS (Oct. 12, 2021).

U.S. Attorneys' Offices to "convene meetings" in your judicial district "with federal, state, local, Tribal, and territorial leaders" within 30 days.[6] The Justice Department simultaneously issued a press release indicating that the Attorney General's directive would "open dedicated lines of communication for threat reporting, assessment and response by law enforcement"—in other words, create a snitch line for complaints about concerned parents.[7]

During Attorney General Garland's testimony before our Committee on October 21, he appeared to have no idea whether the U.S. Attorney meetings he ordered were actually taking place. He stated: "I don't know whether [the meetings] are ongoing, but I expect and hope that they are going . . . because I did ask that they take place."[8] Attorney General Garland testified that he doubted "there have been meetings in every jurisdiction," but reiterated his belief that it is important for federal law enforcement authorities to conduct these meetings in every judicial district.[9] According to the Attorney General's directives, meetings are to be convened in all 94 judicial districts by November 3, 2021, at the latest.

Following the Attorney General's testimony, the NSBA Board of Directors, apparently recognizing the ill-conceived consequences of its letter and the resulting Justice Department action, issued a new memorandum to its members apologizing for the letter, stating: "On behalf of NSBA, we regret and apologize for the letter."[10] (emphasis in original). Although Attorney General Garland testified that the NSBA letter to President Biden was the basis for his October 4 directive to insert federal law enforcement into local school board matters, the Attorney General has yet to rescind his memorandum. His directives to you and other U.S. Attorneys remain in effect.

Concerned parents voicing their strong opposition to controversial curricula at local schools are not domestic terrorists. Parents have an undisputed right to direct the upbringing and education of their children.[11] When parents, however, cross the line to commit a violent act or issue a criminal threat,[12] state and local authorities are best-equipped to handle these violations of state law. But we must not tolerate the use of the federal law enforcement apparatus to intimidate and silence parents using their Constitutional rights to advocate for their child's future.

To assist our investigation and determine whether these meetings are ongoing, we request that you provide the following documents and information:

---

[6] Memorandum from Atty Gen. Merrick Garland, U.S. Dep't of Justice, Partnership Among Federal, State, Local, Tribal, And Territorial Law Enforcement to Address Threats Against School Administrators, Board Members, Teachers, and Staff (Oct. 4, 2021).
[7] Press Release, U.S. Dep't of Justice, Justice Department Addresses Violent Threats Against School Officials and Teachers (Oct. 4, 2021).
[8] *Oversight of the United States Department of Justice: Hearing Before the H. comm. on the Judiciary,* 117th Cong. at 94 (2021) (testimony from Hon. Merrick Garland, Atty Gen., U.S. Dep't of Justice).
[9] *Id.* at 95.
[10] Memorandum from NSBA Board of Directors, Message to NSBA Members (Oct. 22, 2021).
[11] *Troxel v. Granville,* 530 U.S. 57, 65 (2000) (citing *Meyer v. Nebraska,* 262 U.S. 390, 399 (1923)).
[12] *Merrick Garland's federal offense,* WALL ST. J. (Oct. 6, 2021).

1. All documents and communications referring or relating to convening meeting(s) in your judicial district in accordance with the Attorney General's October 4, 2021 memorandum;

2. All agendas, minutes, and notes created or relied upon by U.S. Attorney's Office employees referring or relating to meeting(s) in your judicial district in accordance with the Attorney General's October 4, 2021 memorandum;

3. Please explain when meeting(s) in your judicial district in accordance with the Attorney General's October 4, 2021 memorandum have occurred or will occur;

4. Please identify by name and title of all U.S. Attorney's Office employees involved in the meeting(s) in your judicial district in accordance with the Attorney General's October 4, 2021 memorandum ;

5. Please identify all federal, state, local, Tribal, and territorial organizations invited to or that have attended the meetings convened in your judicial district in accordance with the October 4, 2021 memorandum; and

6. Please provide all recommendations, both formal and informal, and any meeting minutes produced at the meeting(s) in your judicial district in accordance with the Attorney General's October 4, 2021 memorandum.

Please provide this material as soon as possible but no later than 5:00 p.m. on November 15, 2021.

If you have any questions about this request, please contact Committee staff at (202) 225-6906. Thank you for your attention to this important matter.

Sincerely,

Jim Jordan
Ranking Member

Steve Chabot
Member of Congress

Louie Gohmert
Member of Congress

Darrell Issa
Ranking Member
Subcommittee on Courts, Intellectual Property, and the Internet

Ken Buck
Ranking Member
Subcommittee on Antitrust, Commercial
and Administrative Law

Matt Gaetz
Member of Congress

Mike Johnson
Ranking Member
Subcommittee on the Constitution,
Civil Rights and Civil Liberties

Andy Biggs
Ranking Member
Subcommittee on Crime, Terrorism
and Homeland Security

Tom McClintock
Ranking Member
Subcommittee on Immigration
and Citizenship

W. Gregory Steube
Member of Congress

Tom Tiffany
Member of Congress

Thomas Massie
Member of Congress

Chip Roy
Member of Congress

Dan Bishop
Member of Congress

Michelle Fischbach
Member of Congress

Victoria Spartz
Member of Congress

Scott Fitzgerald
Member of Congress

Cliff Bentz
Member of Congress

Burgess Owens
Member of Congress

cc: The Honorable Jerrold L. Nadler
Chairman

Mr. Monty Wilkinson
Director, Executive Office for U.S. Attorneys

JERROLD NADLER, New York
CHAIRMAN

JIM JORDAN, Ohio
RANKING MEMBER

ONE HUNDRED SEVENTEENTH CONGRESS

Congress of the United States

House of Representatives

COMMITTEE ON THE JUDICIARY

2138 RAYBURN HOUSE OFFICE BUILDING
WASHINGTON, DC 20515–6216
(202) 225–3951
judiciary.house.gov

November 1, 2021

Ms. Andrea T. Martinez
Acting U.S. Attorney
District of Utah
111 South Main Street
Salt Lake City, UT 84111

Dear Ms. Martinez:

We are continuing to investigate the troubling attempts by the Department of Justice and the White House to use the heavy hand of federal law enforcement to target concerned parents at local school board meetings and chill their protected First Amendment activity. Because the Department directed you, along with all other U.S. Attorneys, and the Federal Bureau of Investigation (FBI) to take action to address parents attending school board meetings,[1] we respectfully request your assistance with our investigation.

On September 29, 2021, the National School Boards Association (NSBA) sent a letter to President Joe Biden requesting help from the federal government with concerned parents voicing their opinions at school board meetings.[2] The NSBA letter stated that "malice, violence, and threats" against school officials "could be the equivalent of a form of domestic terrorism or hate crimes."[3] The letter cited a number of interactions at school board meetings, none of which rose to the level of domestic terrorism. In fact, the vast majority of incidents cited by the NSBA did not involve threats or violence.[4] Most notably, as an example of domestic terrorism, the NSBA cited an incident in which a father angrily confronted members at a school board meeting in Loudoun County, Virginia about the heinous sexual assault of his daughter.[5]

A mere five days after the NSBA sent its letter to President Biden, on October 4, 2021, Attorney General Merrick Garland issued a shocking memorandum that directed the FBI and

---

[1] Memorandum from Atty Gen. Merrick Garland, U.S. Dep't of Justice, Partnership Among Federal, State, Local, Tribal, And Territorial Law Enforcement to Address Threats Against School Administrators, Board Members, Teachers, and Staff (Oct. 4, 2021).

[2] Letter from Dr. Viola M. Garcia, President, Nat'l School Board Assoc. & Mr. Chip Slaven, Chief Exec. Officer, Nat'l School Board Assoc., to President Joseph R. Biden, White House (Sept. 29, 2021).

[3] *Id.*

[4] *See* Caroline Downey, *Vast majority of incidents cited by school-board group to justify federal intervention didn't involve threats,* NAT'L REV. (Oct. 2, 2021).

[5] *Id.*; *see also* Jessica Chasmar, *Loudoun County father arrested at school board events says school tried to cover up daughter's bathroom assault*, FOX NEWS (Oct. 12, 2021).

U.S. Attorneys' Offices to "convene meetings" in your judicial district "with federal, state, local, Tribal, and territorial leaders" within 30 days.[6] The Justice Department simultaneously issued a press release indicating that the Attorney General's directive would "open dedicated lines of communication for threat reporting, assessment and response by law enforcement"—in other words, create a snitch line for complaints about concerned parents.[7]

During Attorney General Garland's testimony before our Committee on October 21, he appeared to have no idea whether the U.S. Attorney meetings he ordered were actually taking place. He stated: "I don't know whether [the meetings] are ongoing, but I expect and hope that they are going . . . because I did ask that they take place."[8] Attorney General Garland testified that he doubted "there have been meetings in every jurisdiction," but reiterated his belief that it is important for federal law enforcement authorities to conduct these meetings in every judicial district.[9] According to the Attorney General's directives, meetings are to be convened in all 94 judicial districts by November 3, 2021, at the latest.

Following the Attorney General's testimony, the NSBA Board of Directors, apparently recognizing the ill-conceived consequences of its letter and the resulting Justice Department action, issued a new memorandum to its members apologizing for the letter, stating: "On behalf of NSBA, <u>we regret and apologize for the letter</u>."[10] (emphasis in original). Although Attorney General Garland testified that the NSBA letter to President Biden was the basis for his October 4 directive to insert federal law enforcement into local school board matters, the Attorney General has yet to rescind his memorandum. His directives to you and other U.S. Attorneys remain in effect.

Concerned parents voicing their strong opposition to controversial curricula at local schools are not domestic terrorists. Parents have an undisputed right to direct the upbringing and education of their children.[11] When parents, however, cross the line to commit a violent act or issue a criminal threat,[12] state and local authorities are best-equipped to handle these violations of state law. But we must not tolerate the use of the federal law enforcement apparatus to intimidate and silence parents using their Constitutional rights to advocate for their child's future.

To assist our investigation and determine whether these meetings are ongoing, we request that you provide the following documents and information:

---

[6] Memorandum from Atty Gen. Merrick Garland, U.S. Dep't of Justice, Partnership Among Federal, State, Local, Tribal, And Territorial Law Enforcement to Address Threats Against School Administrators, Board Members, Teachers, and Staff (Oct. 4, 2021).

[7] Press Release, U.S. Dep't of Justice, Justice Department Addresses Violent Threats Against School Officials and Teachers (Oct. 4, 2021).

[8] *Oversight of the United States Department of Justice: Hearing Before the H. comm. on the Judiciary,* 117th Cong. at 94 (2021) (testimony from Hon. Merrick Garland, Atty Gen., U.S. Dep't of Justice).

[9] *Id.* at 95.

[10] Memorandum from NSBA Board of Directors, Message to NSBA Members (Oct. 22, 2021).

[11] *Troxel v. Granville,* 530 U.S. 57, 65 (2000) (citing *Meyer v. Nebraska,* 262 U.S. 390, 399 (1923)).

[12] *Merrick Garland's federal offense,* WALL ST. J. (Oct. 6, 2021).

1. All documents and communications referring or relating to convening meeting(s) in your judicial district in accordance with the Attorney General's October 4, 2021 memorandum;

2. All agendas, minutes, and notes created or relied upon by U.S. Attorney's Office employees referring or relating to meeting(s) in your judicial district in accordance with the Attorney General's October 4, 2021 memorandum;

3. Please explain when meeting(s) in your judicial district in accordance with the Attorney General's October 4, 2021 memorandum have occurred or will occur;

4. Please identify by name and title of all U.S. Attorney's Office employees involved in the meeting(s) in your judicial district in accordance with the Attorney General's October 4, 2021 memorandum ;

5. Please identify all federal, state, local, Tribal, and territorial organizations invited to or that have attended the meetings convened in your judicial district in accordance with the October 4, 2021 memorandum; and

6. Please provide all recommendations, both formal and informal, and any meeting minutes produced at the meeting(s) in your judicial district in accordance with the Attorney General's October 4, 2021 memorandum.

Please provide this material as soon as possible but no later than 5:00 p.m. on November 15, 2021.

If you have any questions about this request, please contact Committee staff at (202) 225-6906. Thank you for your attention to this important matter.

Sincerely,

Jim Jordan
Ranking Member

Steve Chabot
Member of Congress

Louie Gohmert
Member of Congress

Darrell Issa
Ranking Member
Subcommittee on Courts, Intellectual Property, and the Internet

Ken Buck
Ranking Member
Subcommittee on Antitrust, Commercial and Administrative Law

Matt Gaetz
Member of Congress

Mike Johnson
Ranking Member
Subcommittee on the Constitution, Civil Rights and Civil Liberties

Andy Biggs
Ranking Member
Subcommittee on Crime, Terrorism and Homeland Security

Tom McClintock
Ranking Member
Subcommittee on Immigration and Citizenship

W. Gregory Steube
Member of Congress

Tom Tiffany
Member of Congress

Thomas Massie
Member of Congress

Chip Roy
Member of Congress

Dan Bishop
Member of Congress

Michelle Fischbach
Member of Congress

Victoria Spartz
Member of Congress

Scott Fitzgerald
Member of Congress

Cliff Bentz
Member of Congress

Burgess Owens
Member of Congress

cc: The Honorable Jerrold L. Nadler
Chairman

Mr. Monty Wilkinson
Director, Executive Office for U.S. Attorneys

JERROLD NADLER, New York
CHAIRMAN

JIM JORDAN, Ohio
RANKING MEMBER

ONE HUNDRED SEVENTEENTH CONGRESS

Congress of the United States

House of Representatives

COMMITTEE ON THE JUDICIARY

2138 RAYBURN HOUSE OFFICE BUILDING

WASHINGTON, DC 20515–6216

(202) 225–3951
judiciary.house.gov

November 1, 2021

The Honorable Jessica D. Aber
U.S. Attorney
Eastern District of Virginia
101 W. Main Street, Suite 8000
Norfolk, VA 23510

Dear Ms. Aber:

We are continuing to investigate the troubling attempts by the Department of Justice and the White House to use the heavy hand of federal law enforcement to target concerned parents at local school board meetings and chill their protected First Amendment activity. Because the Department directed you, along with all other U.S. Attorneys, and the Federal Bureau of Investigation (FBI) to take action to address parents attending school board meetings,[1] we respectfully request your assistance with our investigation.

On September 29, 2021, the National School Boards Association (NSBA) sent a letter to President Joe Biden requesting help from the federal government with concerned parents voicing their opinions at school board meetings.[2] The NSBA letter stated that "malice, violence, and threats" against school officials "could be the equivalent of a form of domestic terrorism or hate crimes."[3] The letter cited a number of interactions at school board meetings, none of which rose to the level of domestic terrorism. In fact, the vast majority of incidents cited by the NSBA did not involve threats or violence.[4] Most notably, as an example of domestic terrorism, the NSBA cited an incident in which a father angrily confronted members at a school board meeting in Loudoun County, Virginia about the heinous sexual assault of his daughter.[5]

A mere five days after the NSBA sent its letter to President Biden, on October 4, 2021, Attorney General Merrick Garland issued a shocking memorandum that directed the FBI and

---

[1] Memorandum from Atty Gen. Merrick Garland, U.S. Dep't of Justice, Partnership Among Federal, State, Local, Tribal, And Territorial Law Enforcement to Address Threats Against School Administrators, Board Members, Teachers, and Staff (Oct. 4, 2021).

[2] Letter from Dr. Viola M. Garcia, President, Nat'l School Board Assoc. & Mr. Chip Slaven, Chief Exec. Officer, Nat'l School Board Assoc., to President Joseph R. Biden, White House (Sept. 29, 2021).

[3] *Id.*

[4] *See* Caroline Downey, *Vast majority of incidents cited by school-board group to justify federal intervention didn't involve threats,* NAT'L REV. (Oct. 2, 2021).

[5] *Id.*; *see also* Jessica Chasmar, *Loudoun County father arrested at school board events says school tried to cover up daughter's bathroom assault*, FOX NEWS (Oct. 12, 2021).

U.S. Attorneys' Offices to "convene meetings" in your judicial district "with federal, state, local, Tribal, and territorial leaders" within 30 days.[6] The Justice Department simultaneously issued a press release indicating that the Attorney General's directive would "open dedicated lines of communication for threat reporting, assessment and response by law enforcement"—in other words, create a snitch line for complaints about concerned parents.[7]

During Attorney General Garland's testimony before our Committee on October 21, he appeared to have no idea whether the U.S. Attorney meetings he ordered were actually taking place. He stated: "I don't know whether [the meetings] are ongoing, but I expect and hope that they are going . . . because I did ask that they take place."[8] Attorney General Garland testified that he doubted "there have been meetings in every jurisdiction," but reiterated his belief that it is important for federal law enforcement authorities to conduct these meetings in every judicial district.[9] According to the Attorney General's directives, meetings are to be convened in all 94 judicial districts by November 3, 2021, at the latest.

Following the Attorney General's testimony, the NSBA Board of Directors, apparently recognizing the ill-conceived consequences of its letter and the resulting Justice Department action, issued a new memorandum to its members apologizing for the letter, stating: "On behalf of NSBA, <u>we regret and apologize for the letter</u>."[10] (emphasis in original). Although Attorney General Garland testified that the NSBA letter to President Biden was the basis for his October 4 directive to insert federal law enforcement into local school board matters, the Attorney General has yet to rescind his memorandum. His directives to you and other U.S. Attorneys remain in effect.

Concerned parents voicing their strong opposition to controversial curricula at local schools are not domestic terrorists. Parents have an undisputed right to direct the upbringing and education of their children.[11] When parents, however, cross the line to commit a violent act or issue a criminal threat,[12] state and local authorities are best-equipped to handle these violations of state law. But we must not tolerate the use of the federal law enforcement apparatus to intimidate and silence parents using their Constitutional rights to advocate for their child's future.

To assist our investigation and determine whether these meetings are ongoing, we request that you provide the following documents and information:

---

[6] Memorandum from Atty Gen. Merrick Garland, U.S. Dep't of Justice, Partnership Among Federal, State, Local, Tribal, And Territorial Law Enforcement to Address Threats Against School Administrators, Board Members, Teachers, and Staff (Oct. 4, 2021).
[7] Press Release, U.S. Dep't of Justice, Justice Department Addresses Violent Threats Against School Officials and Teachers (Oct. 4, 2021).
[8] *Oversight of the United States Department of Justice: Hearing Before the H. comm. on the Judiciary,* 117th Cong. at 94 (2021) (testimony from Hon. Merrick Garland, Atty Gen., U.S. Dep't of Justice).
[9] *Id.* at 95.
[10] Memorandum from NSBA Board of Directors, Message to NSBA Members (Oct. 22, 2021).
[11] *Troxel v. Granville,* 530 U.S. 57, 65 (2000) (citing *Meyer v. Nebraska,* 262 U.S. 390, 399 (1923)).
[12] *Merrick Garland's federal offense,* WALL ST. J. (Oct. 6, 2021).

1. All documents and communications referring or relating to convening meeting(s) in your judicial district in accordance with the Attorney General's October 4, 2021 memorandum;

2. All agendas, minutes, and notes created or relied upon by U.S. Attorney's Office employees referring or relating to meeting(s) in your judicial district in accordance with the Attorney General's October 4, 2021 memorandum;

3. Please explain when meeting(s) in your judicial district in accordance with the Attorney General's October 4, 2021 memorandum have occurred or will occur;

4. Please identify by name and title of all U.S. Attorney's Office employees involved in the meeting(s) in your judicial district in accordance with the Attorney General's October 4, 2021 memorandum ;

5. Please identify all federal, state, local, Tribal, and territorial organizations invited to or that have attended the meetings convened in your judicial district in accordance with the October 4, 2021 memorandum; and

6. Please provide all recommendations, both formal and informal, and any meeting minutes produced at the meeting(s) in your judicial district in accordance with the Attorney General's October 4, 2021 memorandum.

Please provide this material as soon as possible but no later than 5:00 p.m. on November 15, 2021.

If you have any questions about this request, please contact Committee staff at (202) 225-6906. Thank you for your attention to this important matter.

Sincerely,

Jim Jordan
Ranking Member

Steve Chabot
Member of Congress

Louie Gohmert
Member of Congress

Darrell Issa
Ranking Member
Subcommittee on Courts, Intellectual Property, and the Internet

Ken Buck
Ranking Member
Subcommittee on Antitrust, Commercial and Administrative Law

Matt Gaetz
Member of Congress

Mike Johnson
Ranking Member
Subcommittee on the Constitution, Civil Rights and Civil Liberties

Andy Biggs
Ranking Member
Subcommittee on Crime, Terrorism and Homeland Security

Tom McClintock
Ranking Member
Subcommittee on Immigration and Citizenship

W. Gregory Steube
Member of Congress

Tom Tiffany
Member of Congress

Thomas Massie
Member of Congress

Chip Roy
Member of Congress

Dan Bishop
Member of Congress

Michelle Fischbach
Member of Congress

Victoria Spartz
Member of Congress

Scott Fitzgerald
Member of Congress

Cliff Bentz
Member of Congress

Burgess Owens
Member of Congress

cc: The Honorable Jerrold L. Nadler
Chairman

Mr. Monty Wilkinson
Director, Executive Office for U.S. Attorneys

JERROLD NADLER, New York
CHAIRMAN

JIM JORDAN, Ohio
RANKING MEMBER

ONE HUNDRED SEVENTEENTH CONGRESS

Congress of the United States

House of Representatives

COMMITTEE ON THE JUDICIARY

2138 RAYBURN HOUSE OFFICE BUILDING

WASHINGTON, DC 20515-6216

(202) 225-3951
judiciary.house.gov

November 1, 2021

The Honorable Christopher R. Kavanaugh
U.S. Attorney
Western District of Virginia
P.O. Box 1709
Roanoke, VA 24008

Dear Mr. Kavanaugh:

We are continuing to investigate the troubling attempts by the Department of Justice and the White House to use the heavy hand of federal law enforcement to target concerned parents at local school board meetings and chill their protected First Amendment activity. Because the Department directed you, along with all other U.S. Attorneys, and the Federal Bureau of Investigation (FBI) to take action to address parents attending school board meetings,[1] we respectfully request your assistance with our investigation.

On September 29, 2021, the National School Boards Association (NSBA) sent a letter to President Joe Biden requesting help from the federal government with concerned parents voicing their opinions at school board meetings.[2] The NSBA letter stated that "malice, violence, and threats" against school officials "could be the equivalent of a form of domestic terrorism or hate crimes."[3] The letter cited a number of interactions at school board meetings, none of which rose to the level of domestic terrorism. In fact, the vast majority of incidents cited by the NSBA did not involve threats or violence.[4] Most notably, as an example of domestic terrorism, the NSBA cited an incident in which a father angrily confronted members at a school board meeting in Loudoun County, Virginia about the heinous sexual assault of his daughter.[5]

A mere five days after the NSBA sent its letter to President Biden, on October 4, 2021, Attorney General Merrick Garland issued a shocking memorandum that directed the FBI and

---

[1] Memorandum from Atty Gen. Merrick Garland, U.S. Dep't of Justice, Partnership Among Federal, State, Local, Tribal, And Territorial Law Enforcement to Address Threats Against School Administrators, Board Members, Teachers, and Staff (Oct. 4, 2021).
[2] Letter from Dr. Viola M. Garcia, President, Nat'l School Board Assoc. & Mr. Chip Slaven, Chief Exec. Officer, Nat'l School Board Assoc., to President Joseph R. Biden, White House (Sept. 29, 2021).
[3] *Id.*
[4] *See* Caroline Downey, *Vast majority of incidents cited by school-board group to justify federal intervention didn't involve threats,* NAT'L REV. (Oct. 2, 2021).
[5] *Id.*; *see also* Jessica Chasmar, *Loudoun County father arrested at school board events says school tried to cover up daughter's bathroom assault*, FOX NEWS (Oct. 12, 2021).

U.S. Attorneys' Offices to "convene meetings" in your judicial district "with federal, state, local, Tribal, and territorial leaders" within 30 days.[6] The Justice Department simultaneously issued a press release indicating that the Attorney General's directive would "open dedicated lines of communication for threat reporting, assessment and response by law enforcement"—in other words, create a snitch line for complaints about concerned parents.[7]

During Attorney General Garland's testimony before our Committee on October 21, he appeared to have no idea whether the U.S. Attorney meetings he ordered were actually taking place. He stated: "I don't know whether [the meetings] are ongoing, but I expect and hope that they are going . . . because I did ask that they take place."[8] Attorney General Garland testified that he doubted "there have been meetings in every jurisdiction," but reiterated his belief that it is important for federal law enforcement authorities to conduct these meetings in every judicial district.[9] According to the Attorney General's directives, meetings are to be convened in all 94 judicial districts by November 3, 2021, at the latest.

Following the Attorney General's testimony, the NSBA Board of Directors, apparently recognizing the ill-conceived consequences of its letter and the resulting Justice Department action, issued a new memorandum to its members apologizing for the letter, stating: "On behalf of NSBA, <u>we regret and apologize for the letter</u>."[10] (emphasis in original). Although Attorney General Garland testified that the NSBA letter to President Biden was the basis for his October 4 directive to insert federal law enforcement into local school board matters, the Attorney General has yet to rescind his memorandum. His directives to you and other U.S. Attorneys remain in effect.

Concerned parents voicing their strong opposition to controversial curricula at local schools are not domestic terrorists. Parents have an undisputed right to direct the upbringing and education of their children.[11] When parents, however, cross the line to commit a violent act or issue a criminal threat,[12] state and local authorities are best-equipped to handle these violations of state law. But we must not tolerate the use of the federal law enforcement apparatus to intimidate and silence parents using their Constitutional rights to advocate for their child's future.

To assist our investigation and determine whether these meetings are ongoing, we request that you provide the following documents and information:

---

[6] Memorandum from Atty Gen. Merrick Garland, U.S. Dep't of Justice, Partnership Among Federal, State, Local, Tribal, And Territorial Law Enforcement to Address Threats Against School Administrators, Board Members, Teachers, and Staff (Oct. 4, 2021).
[7] Press Release, U.S. Dep't of Justice, Justice Department Addresses Violent Threats Against School Officials and Teachers (Oct. 4, 2021).
[8] *Oversight of the United States Department of Justice: Hearing Before the H. comm. on the Judiciary,* 117th Cong. at 94 (2021) (testimony from Hon. Merrick Garland, Atty Gen., U.S. Dep't of Justice).
[9] *Id.* at 95.
[10] Memorandum from NSBA Board of Directors, Message to NSBA Members (Oct. 22, 2021).
[11] *Troxel v. Granville,* 530 U.S. 57, 65 (2000) (citing *Meyer v. Nebraska,* 262 U.S. 390, 399 (1923)).
[12] *Merrick Garland's federal offense,* WALL ST. J. (Oct. 6, 2021).

1. All documents and communications referring or relating to convening meeting(s) in your judicial district in accordance with the Attorney General's October 4, 2021 memorandum;

2. All agendas, minutes, and notes created or relied upon by U.S. Attorney's Office employees referring or relating to meeting(s) in your judicial district in accordance with the Attorney General's October 4, 2021 memorandum;

3. Please explain when meeting(s) in your judicial district in accordance with the Attorney General's October 4, 2021 memorandum have occurred or will occur;

4. Please identify by name and title of all U.S. Attorney's Office employees involved in the meeting(s) in your judicial district in accordance with the Attorney General's October 4, 2021 memorandum ;

5. Please identify all federal, state, local, Tribal, and territorial organizations invited to or that have attended the meetings convened in your judicial district in accordance with the October 4, 2021 memorandum; and

6. Please provide all recommendations, both formal and informal, and any meeting minutes produced at the meeting(s) in your judicial district in accordance with the Attorney General's October 4, 2021 memorandum.

Please provide this material as soon as possible but no later than 5:00 p.m. on November 15, 2021.

If you have any questions about this request, please contact Committee staff at (202) 225-6906. Thank you for your attention to this important matter.

Sincerely,

Jim Jordan
Ranking Member

Steve Chabot
Member of Congress

Louie Gohmert
Member of Congress

Darrell Issa
Ranking Member
Subcommittee on Courts, Intellectual Property, and the Internet

Ken Buck
Ranking Member
Subcommittee on Antitrust, Commercial and Administrative Law

Matt Gaetz
Member of Congress

Mike Johnson
Ranking Member
Subcommittee on the Constitution, Civil Rights and Civil Liberties

Andy Biggs
Ranking Member
Subcommittee on Crime, Terrorism and Homeland Security

Tom McClintock
Ranking Member
Subcommittee on Immigration and Citizenship

W. Gregory Steube
Member of Congress

Tom Tiffany
Member of Congress

Thomas Massie
Member of Congress

Chip Roy
Member of Congress

Dan Bishop
Member of Congress

Michelle Fischbach
Member of Congress

Victoria Spartz
Member of Congress

Scott Fitzgerald
Member of Congress

Cliff Bentz
Member of Congress

Burgess Owens
Member of Congress

cc: The Honorable Jerrold L. Nadler
Chairman

Mr. Monty Wilkinson
Director, Executive Office for U.S. Attorneys

JERROLD NADLER, New York
CHAIRMAN

JIM JORDAN, Ohio
RANKING MEMBER

ONE HUNDRED SEVENTEENTH CONGRESS

Congress of the United States

House of Representatives

COMMITTEE ON THE JUDICIARY

2138 RAYBURN HOUSE OFFICE BUILDING

WASHINGTON, DC 20515-6216

(202) 225-3951
judiciary.house.gov

November 1, 2021

Ms. Gretchen C.F. Shappert
U.S. Attorney
District of The Virgin Islands
5500 Veterans Drive, Room 260
St. Thomas, VI 00802

Dear Ms. Shappert:

We are continuing to investigate the troubling attempts by the Department of Justice and the White House to use the heavy hand of federal law enforcement to target concerned parents at local school board meetings and chill their protected First Amendment activity. Because the Department directed you, along with all other U.S. Attorneys, and the Federal Bureau of Investigation (FBI) to take action to address parents attending school board meetings,[1] we respectfully request your assistance with our investigation.

On September 29, 2021, the National School Boards Association (NSBA) sent a letter to President Joe Biden requesting help from the federal government with concerned parents voicing their opinions at school board meetings.[2] The NSBA letter stated that "malice, violence, and threats" against school officials "could be the equivalent of a form of domestic terrorism or hate crimes."[3] The letter cited a number of interactions at school board meetings, none of which rose to the level of domestic terrorism. In fact, the vast majority of incidents cited by the NSBA did not involve threats or violence.[4] Most notably, as an example of domestic terrorism, the NSBA cited an incident in which a father angrily confronted members at a school board meeting in Loudoun County, Virginia about the heinous sexual assault of his daughter.[5]

A mere five days after the NSBA sent its letter to President Biden, on October 4, 2021, Attorney General Merrick Garland issued a shocking memorandum that directed the FBI and

---

[1] Memorandum from Atty Gen. Merrick Garland, U.S. Dep't of Justice, Partnership Among Federal, State, Local, Tribal, And Territorial Law Enforcement to Address Threats Against School Administrators, Board Members, Teachers, and Staff (Oct. 4, 2021).
[2] Letter from Dr. Viola M. Garcia, President, Nat'l School Board Assoc. & Mr. Chip Slaven, Chief Exec. Officer, Nat'l School Board Assoc., to President Joseph R. Biden, White House (Sept. 29, 2021).
[3] *Id.*
[4] *See* Caroline Downey, *Vast majority of incidents cited by school-board group to justify federal intervention didn't involve threats,* NAT'L REV. (Oct. 2, 2021).
[5] *Id.*; *see also* Jessica Chasmar, *Loudoun County father arrested at school board events says school tried to cover up daughter's bathroom assault*, FOX NEWS (Oct. 12, 2021).

U.S. Attorneys' Offices to "convene meetings" in your judicial district "with federal, state, local, Tribal, and territorial leaders" within 30 days.[6] The Justice Department simultaneously issued a press release indicating that the Attorney General's directive would "open dedicated lines of communication for threat reporting, assessment and response by law enforcement"—in other words, create a snitch line for complaints about concerned parents.[7]

During Attorney General Garland's testimony before our Committee on October 21, he appeared to have no idea whether the U.S. Attorney meetings he ordered were actually taking place. He stated: "I don't know whether [the meetings] are ongoing, but I expect and hope that they are going . . . because I did ask that they take place."[8] Attorney General Garland testified that he doubted "there have been meetings in every jurisdiction," but reiterated his belief that it is important for federal law enforcement authorities to conduct these meetings in every judicial district.[9] According to the Attorney General's directives, meetings are to be convened in all 94 judicial districts by November 3, 2021, at the latest.

Following the Attorney General's testimony, the NSBA Board of Directors, apparently recognizing the ill-conceived consequences of its letter and the resulting Justice Department action, issued a new memorandum to its members apologizing for the letter, stating: "On behalf of NSBA, <u>we regret and apologize for the letter</u>."[10] (emphasis in original). Although Attorney General Garland testified that the NSBA letter to President Biden was the basis for his October 4 directive to insert federal law enforcement into local school board matters, the Attorney General has yet to rescind his memorandum. His directives to you and other U.S. Attorneys remain in effect.

Concerned parents voicing their strong opposition to controversial curricula at local schools are not domestic terrorists. Parents have an undisputed right to direct the upbringing and education of their children.[11] When parents, however, cross the line to commit a violent act or issue a criminal threat,[12] state and local authorities are best-equipped to handle these violations of state law. But we must not tolerate the use of the federal law enforcement apparatus to intimidate and silence parents using their Constitutional rights to advocate for their child's future.

To assist our investigation and determine whether these meetings are ongoing, we request that you provide the following documents and information:

---

[6] Memorandum from Atty Gen. Merrick Garland, U.S. Dep't of Justice, Partnership Among Federal, State, Local, Tribal, And Territorial Law Enforcement to Address Threats Against School Administrators, Board Members, Teachers, and Staff (Oct. 4, 2021).
[7] Press Release, U.S. Dep't of Justice, Justice Department Addresses Violent Threats Against School Officials and Teachers (Oct. 4, 2021).
[8] *Oversight of the United States Department of Justice: Hearing Before the H. comm. on the Judiciary,* 117th Cong. at 94 (2021) (testimony from Hon. Merrick Garland, Atty Gen., U.S. Dep't of Justice).
[9] *Id.* at 95.
[10] Memorandum from NSBA Board of Directors, Message to NSBA Members (Oct. 22, 2021).
[11] *Troxel v. Granville,* 530 U.S. 57, 65 (2000) (citing *Meyer v. Nebraska,* 262 U.S. 390, 399 (1923)).
[12] *Merrick Garland's federal offense,* WALL ST. J. (Oct. 6, 2021).

1. All documents and communications referring or relating to convening meeting(s) in your judicial district in accordance with the Attorney General's October 4, 2021 memorandum;

2. All agendas, minutes, and notes created or relied upon by U.S. Attorney's Office employees referring or relating to meeting(s) in your judicial district in accordance with the Attorney General's October 4, 2021 memorandum;

3. Please explain when meeting(s) in your judicial district in accordance with the Attorney General's October 4, 2021 memorandum have occurred or will occur;

4. Please identify by name and title of all U.S. Attorney's Office employees involved in the meeting(s) in your judicial district in accordance with the Attorney General's October 4, 2021 memorandum ;

5. Please identify all federal, state, local, Tribal, and territorial organizations invited to or that have attended the meetings convened in your judicial district in accordance with the October 4, 2021 memorandum; and

6. Please provide all recommendations, both formal and informal, and any meeting minutes produced at the meeting(s) in your judicial district in accordance with the Attorney General's October 4, 2021 memorandum.

Please provide this material as soon as possible but no later than 5:00 p.m. on November 15, 2021.

If you have any questions about this request, please contact Committee staff at (202) 225-6906. Thank you for your attention to this important matter.

Sincerely,

Jim Jordan
Ranking Member

Steve Chabot
Member of Congress

Louie Gohmert
Member of Congress

Darrell Issa
Ranking Member
Subcommittee on Courts, Intellectual Property, and the Internet

Ken Buck
Ranking Member
Subcommittee on Antitrust, Commercial and Administrative Law

Matt Gaetz
Member of Congress

Mike Johnson
Ranking Member
Subcommittee on the Constitution, Civil Rights and Civil Liberties

Andy Biggs
Ranking Member
Subcommittee on Crime, Terrorism and Homeland Security

Tom McClintock
Ranking Member
Subcommittee on Immigration and Citizenship

W. Gregory Steube
Member of Congress

Tom Tiffany
Member of Congress

Thomas Massie
Member of Congress

Chip Roy
Member of Congress

Dan Bishop
Member of Congress

Michelle Fischbach
Member of Congress

Victoria Spartz
Member of Congress

Scott Fitzgerald
Member of Congress

Cliff Bentz
Member of Congress

Burgess Owens
Member of Congress

cc: The Honorable Jerrold L. Nadler
Chairman

Mr. Monty Wilkinson
Director, Executive Office for U.S. Attorneys

JERROLD NADLER, New York
CHAIRMAN

JIM JORDAN, Ohio
RANKING MEMBER

ONE HUNDRED SEVENTEENTH CONGRESS

Congress of the United States

House of Representatives

COMMITTEE ON THE JUDICIARY

2138 RAYBURN HOUSE OFFICE BUILDING

WASHINGTON, DC 20515–6216

(202) 225–3951
judiciary.house.gov

November 1, 2021

Mr. Jonathan A. Ophardt
Acting U.S. Attorney
District of Vermont
11 Elmwood Avenue, 3rd Floor, P.O. Box 570
Burlington, VT 05402

Dear Mr. Ophardt:

We are continuing to investigate the troubling attempts by the Department of Justice and the White House to use the heavy hand of federal law enforcement to target concerned parents at local school board meetings and chill their protected First Amendment activity. Because the Department directed you, along with all other U.S. Attorneys, and the Federal Bureau of Investigation (FBI) to take action to address parents attending school board meetings,[1] we respectfully request your assistance with our investigation.

On September 29, 2021, the National School Boards Association (NSBA) sent a letter to President Joe Biden requesting help from the federal government with concerned parents voicing their opinions at school board meetings.[2] The NSBA letter stated that "malice, violence, and threats" against school officials "could be the equivalent of a form of domestic terrorism or hate crimes."[3] The letter cited a number of interactions at school board meetings, none of which rose to the level of domestic terrorism. In fact, the vast majority of incidents cited by the NSBA did not involve threats or violence.[4] Most notably, as an example of domestic terrorism, the NSBA cited an incident in which a father angrily confronted members at a school board meeting in Loudoun County, Virginia about the heinous sexual assault of his daughter.[5]

A mere five days after the NSBA sent its letter to President Biden, on October 4, 2021, Attorney General Merrick Garland issued a shocking memorandum that directed the FBI and

---

[1] Memorandum from Atty Gen. Merrick Garland, U.S. Dep't of Justice, Partnership Among Federal, State, Local, Tribal, And Territorial Law Enforcement to Address Threats Against School Administrators, Board Members, Teachers, and Staff (Oct. 4, 2021).
[2] Letter from Dr. Viola M. Garcia, President, Nat'l School Board Assoc. & Mr. Chip Slaven, Chief Exec. Officer, Nat'l School Board Assoc., to President Joseph R. Biden, White House (Sept. 29, 2021).
[3] *Id.*
[4] *See* Caroline Downey, *Vast majority of incidents cited by school-board group to justify federal intervention didn't involve threats,* NAT'L REV. (Oct. 2, 2021).
[5] *Id.*; *see also* Jessica Chasmar, *Loudoun County father arrested at school board events says school tried to cover up daughter's bathroom assault*, FOX NEWS (Oct. 12, 2021).

U.S. Attorneys' Offices to "convene meetings" in your judicial district "with federal, state, local, Tribal, and territorial leaders" within 30 days.[6] The Justice Department simultaneously issued a press release indicating that the Attorney General's directive would "open dedicated lines of communication for threat reporting, assessment and response by law enforcement"—in other words, create a snitch line for complaints about concerned parents.[7]

During Attorney General Garland's testimony before our Committee on October 21, he appeared to have no idea whether the U.S. Attorney meetings he ordered were actually taking place. He stated: "I don't know whether [the meetings] are ongoing, but I expect and hope that they are going . . . because I did ask that they take place."[8] Attorney General Garland testified that he doubted "there have been meetings in every jurisdiction," but reiterated his belief that it is important for federal law enforcement authorities to conduct these meetings in every judicial district.[9] According to the Attorney General's directives, meetings are to be convened in all 94 judicial districts by November 3, 2021, at the latest.

Following the Attorney General's testimony, the NSBA Board of Directors, apparently recognizing the ill-conceived consequences of its letter and the resulting Justice Department action, issued a new memorandum to its members apologizing for the letter, stating: "On behalf of NSBA, <u>we regret and apologize for the letter</u>."[10] (emphasis in original). Although Attorney General Garland testified that the NSBA letter to President Biden was the basis for his October 4 directive to insert federal law enforcement into local school board matters, the Attorney General has yet to rescind his memorandum. His directives to you and other U.S. Attorneys remain in effect.

Concerned parents voicing their strong opposition to controversial curricula at local schools are not domestic terrorists. Parents have an undisputed right to direct the upbringing and education of their children.[11] When parents, however, cross the line to commit a violent act or issue a criminal threat,[12] state and local authorities are best-equipped to handle these violations of state law. But we must not tolerate the use of the federal law enforcement apparatus to intimidate and silence parents using their Constitutional rights to advocate for their child's future.

To assist our investigation and determine whether these meetings are ongoing, we request that you provide the following documents and information:

---

[6] Memorandum from Atty Gen. Merrick Garland, U.S. Dep't of Justice, Partnership Among Federal, State, Local, Tribal, And Territorial Law Enforcement to Address Threats Against School Administrators, Board Members, Teachers, and Staff (Oct. 4, 2021).

[7] Press Release, U.S. Dep't of Justice, Justice Department Addresses Violent Threats Against School Officials and Teachers (Oct. 4, 2021).

[8] *Oversight of the United States Department of Justice: Hearing Before the H. comm. on the Judiciary,* 117th Cong. at 94 (2021) (testimony from Hon. Merrick Garland, Atty Gen., U.S. Dep't of Justice).

[9] *Id.* at 95.

[10] Memorandum from NSBA Board of Directors, Message to NSBA Members (Oct. 22, 2021).

[11] *Troxel v. Granville,* 530 U.S. 57, 65 (2000) (citing *Meyer v. Nebraska,* 262 U.S. 390, 399 (1923)).

[12] *Merrick Garland's federal offense,* WALL ST. J. (Oct. 6, 2021).

1. All documents and communications referring or relating to convening meeting(s) in your judicial district in accordance with the Attorney General's October 4, 2021 memorandum;

2. All agendas, minutes, and notes created or relied upon by U.S. Attorney's Office employees referring or relating to meeting(s) in your judicial district in accordance with the Attorney General's October 4, 2021 memorandum;

3. Please explain when meeting(s) in your judicial district in accordance with the Attorney General's October 4, 2021 memorandum have occurred or will occur;

4. Please identify by name and title of all U.S. Attorney's Office employees involved in the meeting(s) in your judicial district in accordance with the Attorney General's October 4, 2021 memorandum ;

5. Please identify all federal, state, local, Tribal, and territorial organizations invited to or that have attended the meetings convened in your judicial district in accordance with the October 4, 2021 memorandum; and

6. Please provide all recommendations, both formal and informal, and any meeting minutes produced at the meeting(s) in your judicial district in accordance with the Attorney General's October 4, 2021 memorandum.

Please provide this material as soon as possible but no later than 5:00 p.m. on November 15, 2021.

If you have any questions about this request, please contact Committee staff at (202) 225-6906. Thank you for your attention to this important matter.

Sincerely,

Jim Jordan
Ranking Member

Steve Chabot
Member of Congress

Louie Gohmert
Member of Congress

Darrell Issa
Ranking Member
Subcommittee on Courts, Intellectual Property, and the Internet

Ken Buck
Ranking Member
Subcommittee on Antitrust, Commercial and Administrative Law

Matt Gaetz
Member of Congress

Mike Johnson
Ranking Member
Subcommittee on the Constitution, Civil Rights and Civil Liberties

Andy Biggs
Ranking Member
Subcommittee on Crime, Terrorism and Homeland Security

Tom McClintock
Ranking Member
Subcommittee on Immigration and Citizenship

W. Gregory Steube
Member of Congress

Tom Tiffany
Member of Congress

Thomas Massie
Member of Congress

Chip Roy
Member of Congress

Dan Bishop
Member of Congress

Michelle Fischbach
Member of Congress

Victoria Spartz
Member of Congress

Scott Fitzgerald
Member of Congress

Cliff Bentz
Member of Congress

Burgess Owens
Member of Congress

cc: The Honorable Jerrold L. Nadler
Chairman

Mr. Monty Wilkinson
Director, Executive Office for U.S. Attorneys

JERROLD NADLER, New York
CHAIRMAN

JIM JORDAN, Ohio
RANKING MEMBER

ONE HUNDRED SEVENTEENTH CONGRESS

Congress of the United States
House of Representatives

COMMITTEE ON THE JUDICIARY
2138 RAYBURN HOUSE OFFICE BUILDING
WASHINGTON, DC 20515–6216
(202) 225–3951
judiciary.house.gov

November 1, 2021

The Honorable Nicholas W. Brown
U.S. Attorney
Western District of Washington
700 Stewart Street, Suite 5220
Seattle, WA 98101

Dear Mr. Brown:

We are continuing to investigate the troubling attempts by the Department of Justice and the White House to use the heavy hand of federal law enforcement to target concerned parents at local school board meetings and chill their protected First Amendment activity. Because the Department directed you, along with all other U.S. Attorneys, and the Federal Bureau of Investigation (FBI) to take action to address parents attending school board meetings,[1] we respectfully request your assistance with our investigation.

On September 29, 2021, the National School Boards Association (NSBA) sent a letter to President Joe Biden requesting help from the federal government with concerned parents voicing their opinions at school board meetings.[2] The NSBA letter stated that "malice, violence, and threats" against school officials "could be the equivalent of a form of domestic terrorism or hate crimes."[3] The letter cited a number of interactions at school board meetings, none of which rose to the level of domestic terrorism. In fact, the vast majority of incidents cited by the NSBA did not involve threats or violence.[4] Most notably, as an example of domestic terrorism, the NSBA cited an incident in which a father angrily confronted members at a school board meeting in Loudoun County, Virginia about the heinous sexual assault of his daughter.[5]

A mere five days after the NSBA sent its letter to President Biden, on October 4, 2021, Attorney General Merrick Garland issued a shocking memorandum that directed the FBI and

---

[1] Memorandum from Atty Gen. Merrick Garland, U.S. Dep't of Justice, Partnership Among Federal, State, Local, Tribal, And Territorial Law Enforcement to Address Threats Against School Administrators, Board Members, Teachers, and Staff (Oct. 4, 2021).
[2] Letter from Dr. Viola M. Garcia, President, Nat'l School Board Assoc. & Mr. Chip Slaven, Chief Exec. Officer, Nat'l School Board Assoc., to President Joseph R. Biden, White House (Sept. 29, 2021).
[3] *Id.*
[4] *See* Caroline Downey, *Vast majority of incidents cited by school-board group to justify federal intervention didn't involve threats,* NAT'L REV. (Oct. 2, 2021).
[5] *Id.*; *see also* Jessica Chasmar, *Loudoun County father arrested at school board events says school tried to cover up daughter's bathroom assault*, FOX NEWS (Oct. 12, 2021).

U.S. Attorneys' Offices to "convene meetings" in your judicial district "with federal, state, local, Tribal, and territorial leaders" within 30 days.[6] The Justice Department simultaneously issued a press release indicating that the Attorney General's directive would "open dedicated lines of communication for threat reporting, assessment and response by law enforcement"—in other words, create a snitch line for complaints about concerned parents.[7]

During Attorney General Garland's testimony before our Committee on October 21, he appeared to have no idea whether the U.S. Attorney meetings he ordered were actually taking place. He stated: "I don't know whether [the meetings] are ongoing, but I expect and hope that they are going . . . because I did ask that they take place."[8] Attorney General Garland testified that he doubted "there have been meetings in every jurisdiction," but reiterated his belief that it is important for federal law enforcement authorities to conduct these meetings in every judicial district.[9] According to the Attorney General's directives, meetings are to be convened in all 94 judicial districts by November 3, 2021, at the latest.

Following the Attorney General's testimony, the NSBA Board of Directors, apparently recognizing the ill-conceived consequences of its letter and the resulting Justice Department action, issued a new memorandum to its members apologizing for the letter, stating: "On behalf of NSBA, <u>we regret and apologize for the letter</u>."[10] (emphasis in original). Although Attorney General Garland testified that the NSBA letter to President Biden was the basis for his October 4 directive to insert federal law enforcement into local school board matters, the Attorney General has yet to rescind his memorandum. His directives to you and other U.S. Attorneys remain in effect.

Concerned parents voicing their strong opposition to controversial curricula at local schools are not domestic terrorists. Parents have an undisputed right to direct the upbringing and education of their children.[11] When parents, however, cross the line to commit a violent act or issue a criminal threat,[12] state and local authorities are best-equipped to handle these violations of state law. But we must not tolerate the use of the federal law enforcement apparatus to intimidate and silence parents using their Constitutional rights to advocate for their child's future.

To assist our investigation and determine whether these meetings are ongoing, we request that you provide the following documents and information:

---

[6] Memorandum from Atty Gen. Merrick Garland, U.S. Dep't of Justice, Partnership Among Federal, State, Local, Tribal, And Territorial Law Enforcement to Address Threats Against School Administrators, Board Members, Teachers, and Staff (Oct. 4, 2021).

[7] Press Release, U.S. Dep't of Justice, Justice Department Addresses Violent Threats Against School Officials and Teachers (Oct. 4, 2021).

[8] *Oversight of the United States Department of Justice: Hearing Before the H. comm. on the Judiciary,* 117th Cong. at 94 (2021) (testimony from Hon. Merrick Garland, Atty Gen., U.S. Dep't of Justice).

[9] *Id.* at 95.

[10] Memorandum from NSBA Board of Directors, Message to NSBA Members (Oct. 22, 2021).

[11] *Troxel v. Granville,* 530 U.S. 57, 65 (2000) (citing *Meyer v. Nebraska,* 262 U.S. 390, 399 (1923)).

[12] *Merrick Garland's federal offense,* WALL ST. J. (Oct. 6, 2021).

1. All documents and communications referring or relating to convening meeting(s) in your judicial district in accordance with the Attorney General's October 4, 2021 memorandum;

2. All agendas, minutes, and notes created or relied upon by U.S. Attorney's Office employees referring or relating to meeting(s) in your judicial district in accordance with the Attorney General's October 4, 2021 memorandum;

3. Please explain when meeting(s) in your judicial district in accordance with the Attorney General's October 4, 2021 memorandum have occurred or will occur;

4. Please identify by name and title of all U.S. Attorney's Office employees involved in the meeting(s) in your judicial district in accordance with the Attorney General's October 4, 2021 memorandum ;

5. Please identify all federal, state, local, Tribal, and territorial organizations invited to or that have attended the meetings convened in your judicial district in accordance with the October 4, 2021 memorandum; and

6. Please provide all recommendations, both formal and informal, and any meeting minutes produced at the meeting(s) in your judicial district in accordance with the Attorney General's October 4, 2021 memorandum.

Please provide this material as soon as possible but no later than 5:00 p.m. on November 15, 2021.

If you have any questions about this request, please contact Committee staff at (202) 225-6906. Thank you for your attention to this important matter.

Sincerely,

Jim Jordan
Ranking Member

Steve Chabot
Member of Congress

Louie Gohmert
Member of Congress

Darrell Issa
Ranking Member
Subcommittee on Courts, Intellectual Property, and the Internet

Ken Buck
Ranking Member
Subcommittee on Antitrust, Commercial and Administrative Law

Matt Gaetz
Member of Congress

Mike Johnson
Ranking Member
Subcommittee on the Constitution, Civil Rights and Civil Liberties

Andy Biggs
Ranking Member
Subcommittee on Crime, Terrorism and Homeland Security

Tom McClintock
Ranking Member
Subcommittee on Immigration and Citizenship

W. Gregory Steube
Member of Congress

Tom Tiffany
Member of Congress

Thomas Massie
Member of Congress

Chip Roy
Member of Congress

Dan Bishop
Member of Congress

Michelle Fischbach
Member of Congress

Victoria Spartz
Member of Congress

Scott Fitzgerald
Member of Congress

Cliff Bentz
Member of Congress

Burgess Owens
Member of Congress

cc: The Honorable Jerrold L. Nadler
Chairman

Mr. Monty Wilkinson
Director, Executive Office for U.S. Attorneys

JERROLD NADLER, New York
CHAIRMAN

JIM JORDAN, Ohio
RANKING MEMBER

ONE HUNDRED SEVENTEENTH CONGRESS

Congress of the United States
House of Representatives
COMMITTEE ON THE JUDICIARY

2138 RAYBURN HOUSE OFFICE BUILDING
WASHINGTON, DC 20515-6216
(202) 225-3951
judiciary.house.gov

November 1, 2021

The Honorable Vanessa R. Waldref
U.S. Attorney
Eastern District of Washington
P.O. Box 1494
Spokane, WA 99210

Dear Ms. Waldref:

We are continuing to investigate the troubling attempts by the Department of Justice and the White House to use the heavy hand of federal law enforcement to target concerned parents at local school board meetings and chill their protected First Amendment activity. Because the Department directed you, along with all other U.S. Attorneys, and the Federal Bureau of Investigation (FBI) to take action to address parents attending school board meetings,[1] we respectfully request your assistance with our investigation.

On September 29, 2021, the National School Boards Association (NSBA) sent a letter to President Joe Biden requesting help from the federal government with concerned parents voicing their opinions at school board meetings.[2] The NSBA letter stated that "malice, violence, and threats" against school officials "could be the equivalent of a form of domestic terrorism or hate crimes."[3] The letter cited a number of interactions at school board meetings, none of which rose to the level of domestic terrorism. In fact, the vast majority of incidents cited by the NSBA did not involve threats or violence.[4] Most notably, as an example of domestic terrorism, the NSBA cited an incident in which a father angrily confronted members at a school board meeting in Loudoun County, Virginia about the heinous sexual assault of his daughter.[5]

A mere five days after the NSBA sent its letter to President Biden, on October 4, 2021, Attorney General Merrick Garland issued a shocking memorandum that directed the FBI and

---

[1] Memorandum from Atty Gen. Merrick Garland, U.S. Dep't of Justice, Partnership Among Federal, State, Local, Tribal, And Territorial Law Enforcement to Address Threats Against School Administrators, Board Members, Teachers, and Staff (Oct. 4, 2021).
[2] Letter from Dr. Viola M. Garcia, President, Nat'l School Board Assoc. & Mr. Chip Slaven, Chief Exec. Officer, Nat'l School Board Assoc., to President Joseph R. Biden, White House (Sept. 29, 2021).
[3] *Id.*
[4] *See* Caroline Downey, *Vast majority of incidents cited by school-board group to justify federal intervention didn't involve threats,* NAT'L REV. (Oct. 2, 2021).
[5] *Id.*; *see also* Jessica Chasmar, *Loudoun County father arrested at school board events says school tried to cover up daughter's bathroom assault*, FOX NEWS (Oct. 12, 2021).

U.S. Attorneys' Offices to "convene meetings" in your judicial district "with federal, state, local, Tribal, and territorial leaders" within 30 days.[6] The Justice Department simultaneously issued a press release indicating that the Attorney General's directive would "open dedicated lines of communication for threat reporting, assessment and response by law enforcement"—in other words, create a snitch line for complaints about concerned parents.[7]

During Attorney General Garland's testimony before our Committee on October 21, he appeared to have no idea whether the U.S. Attorney meetings he ordered were actually taking place. He stated: "I don't know whether [the meetings] are ongoing, but I expect and hope that they are going . . . because I did ask that they take place."[8] Attorney General Garland testified that he doubted "there have been meetings in every jurisdiction," but reiterated his belief that it is important for federal law enforcement authorities to conduct these meetings in every judicial district.[9] According to the Attorney General's directives, meetings are to be convened in all 94 judicial districts by November 3, 2021, at the latest.

Following the Attorney General's testimony, the NSBA Board of Directors, apparently recognizing the ill-conceived consequences of its letter and the resulting Justice Department action, issued a new memorandum to its members apologizing for the letter, stating: "On behalf of NSBA, <u>we regret and apologize for the letter</u>."[10] (emphasis in original). Although Attorney General Garland testified that the NSBA letter to President Biden was the basis for his October 4 directive to insert federal law enforcement into local school board matters, the Attorney General has yet to rescind his memorandum. His directives to you and other U.S. Attorneys remain in effect.

Concerned parents voicing their strong opposition to controversial curricula at local schools are not domestic terrorists. Parents have an undisputed right to direct the upbringing and education of their children.[11] When parents, however, cross the line to commit a violent act or issue a criminal threat,[12] state and local authorities are best-equipped to handle these violations of state law. But we must not tolerate the use of the federal law enforcement apparatus to intimidate and silence parents using their Constitutional rights to advocate for their child's future.

To assist our investigation and determine whether these meetings are ongoing, we request that you provide the following documents and information:

---

[6] Memorandum from Atty Gen. Merrick Garland, U.S. Dep't of Justice, Partnership Among Federal, State, Local, Tribal, And Territorial Law Enforcement to Address Threats Against School Administrators, Board Members, Teachers, and Staff (Oct. 4, 2021).

[7] Press Release, U.S. Dep't of Justice, Justice Department Addresses Violent Threats Against School Officials and Teachers (Oct. 4, 2021).

[8] *Oversight of the United States Department of Justice: Hearing Before the H. comm. on the Judiciary,* 117th Cong. at 94 (2021) (testimony from Hon. Merrick Garland, Atty Gen., U.S. Dep't of Justice).

[9] *Id.* at 95.

[10] Memorandum from NSBA Board of Directors, Message to NSBA Members (Oct. 22, 2021).

[11] *Troxel v. Granville,* 530 U.S. 57, 65 (2000) (citing *Meyer v. Nebraska,* 262 U.S. 390, 399 (1923)).

[12] *Merrick Garland's federal offense,* WALL ST. J. (Oct. 6, 2021).

1. All documents and communications referring or relating to convening meeting(s) in your judicial district in accordance with the Attorney General's October 4, 2021 memorandum;

2. All agendas, minutes, and notes created or relied upon by U.S. Attorney's Office employees referring or relating to meeting(s) in your judicial district in accordance with the Attorney General's October 4, 2021 memorandum;

3. Please explain when meeting(s) in your judicial district in accordance with the Attorney General's October 4, 2021 memorandum have occurred or will occur;

4. Please identify by name and title of all U.S. Attorney's Office employees involved in the meeting(s) in your judicial district in accordance with the Attorney General's October 4, 2021 memorandum ;

5. Please identify all federal, state, local, Tribal, and territorial organizations invited to or that have attended the meetings convened in your judicial district in accordance with the October 4, 2021 memorandum; and

6. Please provide all recommendations, both formal and informal, and any meeting minutes produced at the meeting(s) in your judicial district in accordance with the Attorney General's October 4, 2021 memorandum.

Please provide this material as soon as possible but no later than 5:00 p.m. on November 15, 2021.

If you have any questions about this request, please contact Committee staff at (202) 225-6906. Thank you for your attention to this important matter.

Sincerely,

Jim Jordan
Ranking Member

Steve Chabot
Member of Congress

Louie Gohmert
Member of Congress

Darrell Issa
Ranking Member
Subcommittee on Courts, Intellectual Property, and the Internet

Ken Buck
Ranking Member
Subcommittee on Antitrust, Commercial and Administrative Law

Matt Gaetz
Member of Congress

Mike Johnson
Ranking Member
Subcommittee on the Constitution, Civil Rights and Civil Liberties

Andy Biggs
Ranking Member
Subcommittee on Crime, Terrorism and Homeland Security

Tom McClintock
Ranking Member
Subcommittee on Immigration and Citizenship

W. Gregory Steube
Member of Congress

Tom Tiffany
Member of Congress

Thomas Massie
Member of Congress

Chip Roy
Member of Congress

Dan Bishop
Member of Congress

Michelle Fischbach
Member of Congress

Victoria Spartz
Member of Congress

Scott Fitzgerald
Member of Congress

Cliff Bentz
Member of Congress

Burgess Owens
Member of Congress

cc: The Honorable Jerrold L. Nadler
Chairman

Mr. Monty Wilkinson
Director, Executive Office for U.S. Attorneys

JERROLD NADLER, New York
CHAIRMAN

JIM JORDAN, Ohio
RANKING MEMBER

ONE HUNDRED SEVENTEENTH CONGRESS

Congress of the United States
House of Representatives
COMMITTEE ON THE JUDICIARY
2138 RAYBURN HOUSE OFFICE BUILDING
WASHINGTON, DC 20515-6216
(202) 225-3951
judiciary.house.gov

November 1, 2021

Mr. Richard G. Frohling
Acting U.S. Attorney
Eastern District of Wisconsin
517 E. Wisconsin Ave, Suite 530
Milwaukee, WI 53202

Dear Mr. Frohling:

We are continuing to investigate the troubling attempts by the Department of Justice and the White House to use the heavy hand of federal law enforcement to target concerned parents at local school board meetings and chill their protected First Amendment activity. Because the Department directed you, along with all other U.S. Attorneys, and the Federal Bureau of Investigation (FBI) to take action to address parents attending school board meetings,[1] we respectfully request your assistance with our investigation.

On September 29, 2021, the National School Boards Association (NSBA) sent a letter to President Joe Biden requesting help from the federal government with concerned parents voicing their opinions at school board meetings.[2] The NSBA letter stated that "malice, violence, and threats" against school officials "could be the equivalent of a form of domestic terrorism or hate crimes."[3] The letter cited a number of interactions at school board meetings, none of which rose to the level of domestic terrorism. In fact, the vast majority of incidents cited by the NSBA did not involve threats or violence.[4] Most notably, as an example of domestic terrorism, the NSBA cited an incident in which a father angrily confronted members at a school board meeting in Loudoun County, Virginia about the heinous sexual assault of his daughter.[5]

A mere five days after the NSBA sent its letter to President Biden, on October 4, 2021, Attorney General Merrick Garland issued a shocking memorandum that directed the FBI and

---

[1] Memorandum from Atty Gen. Merrick Garland, U.S. Dep't of Justice, Partnership Among Federal, State, Local, Tribal, And Territorial Law Enforcement to Address Threats Against School Administrators, Board Members, Teachers, and Staff (Oct. 4, 2021).
[2] Letter from Dr. Viola M. Garcia, President, Nat'l School Board Assoc. & Mr. Chip Slaven, Chief Exec. Officer, Nat'l School Board Assoc., to President Joseph R. Biden, White House (Sept. 29, 2021).
[3] *Id.*
[4] *See* Caroline Downey, *Vast majority of incidents cited by school-board group to justify federal intervention didn't involve threats,* NAT'L REV. (Oct. 2, 2021).
[5] *Id.*; *see also* Jessica Chasmar, *Loudoun County father arrested at school board events says school tried to cover up daughter's bathroom assault*, FOX NEWS (Oct. 12, 2021).

U.S. Attorneys' Offices to "convene meetings" in your judicial district "with federal, state, local, Tribal, and territorial leaders" within 30 days.[6] The Justice Department simultaneously issued a press release indicating that the Attorney General's directive would "open dedicated lines of communication for threat reporting, assessment and response by law enforcement"—in other words, create a snitch line for complaints about concerned parents.[7]

During Attorney General Garland's testimony before our Committee on October 21, he appeared to have no idea whether the U.S. Attorney meetings he ordered were actually taking place. He stated: "I don't know whether [the meetings] are ongoing, but I expect and hope that they are going . . . because I did ask that they take place."[8] Attorney General Garland testified that he doubted "there have been meetings in every jurisdiction," but reiterated his belief that it is important for federal law enforcement authorities to conduct these meetings in every judicial district.[9] According to the Attorney General's directives, meetings are to be convened in all 94 judicial districts by November 3, 2021, at the latest.

Following the Attorney General's testimony, the NSBA Board of Directors, apparently recognizing the ill-conceived consequences of its letter and the resulting Justice Department action, issued a new memorandum to its members apologizing for the letter, stating: "On behalf of NSBA, <u>we regret and apologize for the letter</u>."[10] (emphasis in original). Although Attorney General Garland testified that the NSBA letter to President Biden was the basis for his October 4 directive to insert federal law enforcement into local school board matters, the Attorney General has yet to rescind his memorandum. His directives to you and other U.S. Attorneys remain in effect.

Concerned parents voicing their strong opposition to controversial curricula at local schools are not domestic terrorists. Parents have an undisputed right to direct the upbringing and education of their children.[11] When parents, however, cross the line to commit a violent act or issue a criminal threat,[12] state and local authorities are best-equipped to handle these violations of state law. But we must not tolerate the use of the federal law enforcement apparatus to intimidate and silence parents using their Constitutional rights to advocate for their child's future.

To assist our investigation and determine whether these meetings are ongoing, we request that you provide the following documents and information:

---

[6] Memorandum from Atty Gen. Merrick Garland, U.S. Dep't of Justice, Partnership Among Federal, State, Local, Tribal, And Territorial Law Enforcement to Address Threats Against School Administrators, Board Members, Teachers, and Staff (Oct. 4, 2021).
[7] Press Release, U.S. Dep't of Justice, Justice Department Addresses Violent Threats Against School Officials and Teachers (Oct. 4, 2021).
[8] *Oversight of the United States Department of Justice: Hearing Before the H. comm. on the Judiciary,* 117th Cong. at 94 (2021) (testimony from Hon. Merrick Garland, Atty Gen., U.S. Dep't of Justice).
[9] *Id.* at 95.
[10] Memorandum from NSBA Board of Directors, Message to NSBA Members (Oct. 22, 2021).
[11] *Troxel v. Granville,* 530 U.S. 57, 65 (2000) (citing *Meyer v. Nebraska,* 262 U.S. 390, 399 (1923)).
[12] *Merrick Garland's federal offense,* WALL ST. J. (Oct. 6, 2021).

1. All documents and communications referring or relating to convening meeting(s) in your judicial district in accordance with the Attorney General's October 4, 2021 memorandum;

2. All agendas, minutes, and notes created or relied upon by U.S. Attorney's Office employees referring or relating to meeting(s) in your judicial district in accordance with the Attorney General's October 4, 2021 memorandum;

3. Please explain when meeting(s) in your judicial district in accordance with the Attorney General's October 4, 2021 memorandum have occurred or will occur;

4. Please identify by name and title of all U.S. Attorney's Office employees involved in the meeting(s) in your judicial district in accordance with the Attorney General's October 4, 2021 memorandum ;

5. Please identify all federal, state, local, Tribal, and territorial organizations invited to or that have attended the meetings convened in your judicial district in accordance with the October 4, 2021 memorandum; and

6. Please provide all recommendations, both formal and informal, and any meeting minutes produced at the meeting(s) in your judicial district in accordance with the Attorney General's October 4, 2021 memorandum.

Please provide this material as soon as possible but no later than 5:00 p.m. on November 15, 2021.

If you have any questions about this request, please contact Committee staff at (202) 225-6906. Thank you for your attention to this important matter.

Sincerely,

Jim Jordan
Ranking Member

Steve Chabot
Member of Congress

Louie Gohmert
Member of Congress

Darrell Issa
Ranking Member
Subcommittee on Courts, Intellectual Property, and the Internet

Ken Buck
Ranking Member
Subcommittee on Antitrust, Commercial
and Administrative Law

Mike Johnson
Ranking Member
Subcommittee on the Constitution,
Civil Rights and Civil Liberties

Tom McClintock
Ranking Member
Subcommittee on Immigration
and Citizenship

Tom Tiffany
Member of Congress

Chip Roy
Member of Congress

Michelle Fischbach
Member of Congress

Matt Gaetz
Member of Congress

Andy Biggs
Ranking Member
Subcommittee on Crime, Terrorism
and Homeland Security

W. Gregory Steube
Member of Congress

Thomas Massie
Member of Congress

Dan Bishop
Member of Congress

Victoria Spartz
Member of Congress

Scott Fitzgerald
Member of Congress

Cliff Bentz
Member of Congress

Burgess Owens
Member of Congress

cc: The Honorable Jerrold L. Nadler
Chairman

Mr. Monty Wilkinson
Director, Executive Office for U.S. Attorneys

JERROLD NADLER, New York
CHAIRMAN

JIM JORDAN, Ohio
RANKING MEMBER

ONE HUNDRED SEVENTEENTH CONGRESS

Congress of the United States

House of Representatives

COMMITTEE ON THE JUDICIARY

2138 RAYBURN HOUSE OFFICE BUILDING

WASHINGTON, DC 20515–6216

(202) 225–3951
judiciary.house.gov

November 1, 2021

Mr. Timothy M. O'Shea
Acting U.S. Attorney
Western District of Wisconsin
222 West Washington Avenue, Suite 700
Madison, WI 53703

Dear Mr. O'Shea:

We are continuing to investigate the troubling attempts by the Department of Justice and the White House to use the heavy hand of federal law enforcement to target concerned parents at local school board meetings and chill their protected First Amendment activity. Because the Department directed you, along with all other U.S. Attorneys, and the Federal Bureau of Investigation (FBI) to take action to address parents attending school board meetings,[1] we respectfully request your assistance with our investigation.

On September 29, 2021, the National School Boards Association (NSBA) sent a letter to President Joe Biden requesting help from the federal government with concerned parents voicing their opinions at school board meetings.[2] The NSBA letter stated that "malice, violence, and threats" against school officials "could be the equivalent of a form of domestic terrorism or hate crimes."[3] The letter cited a number of interactions at school board meetings, none of which rose to the level of domestic terrorism. In fact, the vast majority of incidents cited by the NSBA did not involve threats or violence.[4] Most notably, as an example of domestic terrorism, the NSBA cited an incident in which a father angrily confronted members at a school board meeting in Loudoun County, Virginia about the heinous sexual assault of his daughter.[5]

A mere five days after the NSBA sent its letter to President Biden, on October 4, 2021, Attorney General Merrick Garland issued a shocking memorandum that directed the FBI and

---

[1] Memorandum from Atty Gen. Merrick Garland, U.S. Dep't of Justice, Partnership Among Federal, State, Local, Tribal, And Territorial Law Enforcement to Address Threats Against School Administrators, Board Members, Teachers, and Staff (Oct. 4, 2021).
[2] Letter from Dr. Viola M. Garcia, President, Nat'l School Board Assoc. & Mr. Chip Slaven, Chief Exec. Officer, Nat'l School Board Assoc., to President Joseph R. Biden, White House (Sept. 29, 2021).
[3] *Id.*
[4] *See* Caroline Downey, *Vast majority of incidents cited by school-board group to justify federal intervention didn't involve threats,* NAT'L REV. (Oct. 2, 2021).
[5] *Id.*; *see also* Jessica Chasmar, *Loudoun County father arrested at school board events says school tried to cover up daughter's bathroom assault*, FOX NEWS (Oct. 12, 2021).

U.S. Attorneys' Offices to "convene meetings" in your judicial district "with federal, state, local, Tribal, and territorial leaders" within 30 days.[6] The Justice Department simultaneously issued a press release indicating that the Attorney General's directive would "open dedicated lines of communication for threat reporting, assessment and response by law enforcement"—in other words, create a snitch line for complaints about concerned parents.[7]

During Attorney General Garland's testimony before our Committee on October 21, he appeared to have no idea whether the U.S. Attorney meetings he ordered were actually taking place. He stated: "I don't know whether [the meetings] are ongoing, but I expect and hope that they are going . . . because I did ask that they take place."[8] Attorney General Garland testified that he doubted "there have been meetings in every jurisdiction," but reiterated his belief that it is important for federal law enforcement authorities to conduct these meetings in every judicial district.[9] According to the Attorney General's directives, meetings are to be convened in all 94 judicial districts by November 3, 2021, at the latest.

Following the Attorney General's testimony, the NSBA Board of Directors, apparently recognizing the ill-conceived consequences of its letter and the resulting Justice Department action, issued a new memorandum to its members apologizing for the letter, stating: "On behalf of NSBA, <u>we regret and apologize for the letter</u>."[10] (emphasis in original). Although Attorney General Garland testified that the NSBA letter to President Biden was the basis for his October 4 directive to insert federal law enforcement into local school board matters, the Attorney General has yet to rescind his memorandum. His directives to you and other U.S. Attorneys remain in effect.

Concerned parents voicing their strong opposition to controversial curricula at local schools are not domestic terrorists. Parents have an undisputed right to direct the upbringing and education of their children.[11] When parents, however, cross the line to commit a violent act or issue a criminal threat,[12] state and local authorities are best-equipped to handle these violations of state law. But we must not tolerate the use of the federal law enforcement apparatus to intimidate and silence parents using their Constitutional rights to advocate for their child's future.

To assist our investigation and determine whether these meetings are ongoing, we request that you provide the following documents and information:

---

[6] Memorandum from Atty Gen. Merrick Garland, U.S. Dep't of Justice, Partnership Among Federal, State, Local, Tribal, And Territorial Law Enforcement to Address Threats Against School Administrators, Board Members, Teachers, and Staff (Oct. 4, 2021).
[7] Press Release, U.S. Dep't of Justice, Justice Department Addresses Violent Threats Against School Officials and Teachers (Oct. 4, 2021).
[8] *Oversight of the United States Department of Justice: Hearing Before the H. comm. on the Judiciary,* 117th Cong. at 94 (2021) (testimony from Hon. Merrick Garland, Atty Gen., U.S. Dep't of Justice).
[9] *Id.* at 95.
[10] Memorandum from NSBA Board of Directors, Message to NSBA Members (Oct. 22, 2021).
[11] *Troxel v. Granville,* 530 U.S. 57, 65 (2000) (citing *Meyer v. Nebraska,* 262 U.S. 390, 399 (1923)).
[12] *Merrick Garland's federal offense,* WALL ST. J. (Oct. 6, 2021).

1. All documents and communications referring or relating to convening meeting(s) in your judicial district in accordance with the Attorney General's October 4, 2021 memorandum;

2. All agendas, minutes, and notes created or relied upon by U.S. Attorney's Office employees referring or relating to meeting(s) in your judicial district in accordance with the Attorney General's October 4, 2021 memorandum;

3. Please explain when meeting(s) in your judicial district in accordance with the Attorney General's October 4, 2021 memorandum have occurred or will occur;

4. Please identify by name and title of all U.S. Attorney's Office employees involved in the meeting(s) in your judicial district in accordance with the Attorney General's October 4, 2021 memorandum ;

5. Please identify all federal, state, local, Tribal, and territorial organizations invited to or that have attended the meetings convened in your judicial district in accordance with the October 4, 2021 memorandum; and

6. Please provide all recommendations, both formal and informal, and any meeting minutes produced at the meeting(s) in your judicial district in accordance with the Attorney General's October 4, 2021 memorandum.

Please provide this material as soon as possible but no later than 5:00 p.m. on November 15, 2021.

If you have any questions about this request, please contact Committee staff at (202) 225-6906. Thank you for your attention to this important matter.

Sincerely,

Jim Jordan
Ranking Member

Steve Chabot
Member of Congress

Louie Gohmert
Member of Congress

Darrell Issa
Ranking Member
Subcommittee on Courts, Intellectual Property, and the Internet

Ken Buck
Ranking Member
Subcommittee on Antitrust, Commercial and Administrative Law

Matt Gaetz
Member of Congress

Mike Johnson
Ranking Member
Subcommittee on the Constitution, Civil Rights and Civil Liberties

Andy Biggs
Ranking Member
Subcommittee on Crime, Terrorism and Homeland Security

Tom McClintock
Ranking Member
Subcommittee on Immigration and Citizenship

W. Gregory Steube
Member of Congress

Tom Tiffany
Member of Congress

Thomas Massie
Member of Congress

Chip Roy
Member of Congress

Dan Bishop
Member of Congress

Michelle Fischbach
Member of Congress

Victoria Spartz
Member of Congress

Scott Fitzgerald
Member of Congress

Cliff Bentz
Member of Congress

Burgess Owens
Member of Congress

cc: The Honorable Jerrold L. Nadler
Chairman

Mr. Monty Wilkinson
Director, Executive Office for U.S. Attorneys

JERROLD NADLER, New York
CHAIRMAN

JIM JORDAN, Ohio
RANKING MEMBER

ONE HUNDRED SEVENTEENTH CONGRESS

Congress of the United States
House of Representatives

COMMITTEE ON THE JUDICIARY

2138 RAYBURN HOUSE OFFICE BUILDING

WASHINGTON, DC 20515-6216

(202) 225-3951
judiciary.house.gov

November 1, 2021

The Honorable William J. Ihlenfeld, II
U.S. Attorney
Northern District of West Virginia
1125 Chapline Street, Suite 3000
Wheeling, WV 26003

Dear Mr. Ihlenfeld:

We are continuing to investigate the troubling attempts by the Department of Justice and the White House to use the heavy hand of federal law enforcement to target concerned parents at local school board meetings and chill their protected First Amendment activity. Because the Department directed you, along with all other U.S. Attorneys, and the Federal Bureau of Investigation (FBI) to take action to address parents attending school board meetings,[1] we respectfully request your assistance with our investigation.

On September 29, 2021, the National School Boards Association (NSBA) sent a letter to President Joe Biden requesting help from the federal government with concerned parents voicing their opinions at school board meetings.[2] The NSBA letter stated that "malice, violence, and threats" against school officials "could be the equivalent of a form of domestic terrorism or hate crimes."[3] The letter cited a number of interactions at school board meetings, none of which rose to the level of domestic terrorism. In fact, the vast majority of incidents cited by the NSBA did not involve threats or violence.[4] Most notably, as an example of domestic terrorism, the NSBA cited an incident in which a father angrily confronted members at a school board meeting in Loudoun County, Virginia about the heinous sexual assault of his daughter.[5]

A mere five days after the NSBA sent its letter to President Biden, on October 4, 2021, Attorney General Merrick Garland issued a shocking memorandum that directed the FBI and

---

[1] Memorandum from Atty Gen. Merrick Garland, U.S. Dep't of Justice, Partnership Among Federal, State, Local, Tribal, And Territorial Law Enforcement to Address Threats Against School Administrators, Board Members, Teachers, and Staff (Oct. 4, 2021).
[2] Letter from Dr. Viola M. Garcia, President, Nat'l School Board Assoc. & Mr. Chip Slaven, Chief Exec. Officer, Nat'l School Board Assoc., to President Joseph R. Biden, White House (Sept. 29, 2021).
[3] *Id.*
[4] *See* Caroline Downey, *Vast majority of incidents cited by school-board group to justify federal intervention didn't involve threats,* NAT'L REV. (Oct. 2, 2021).
[5] *Id.*; *see also* Jessica Chasmar, *Loudoun County father arrested at school board events says school tried to cover up daughter's bathroom assault*, FOX NEWS (Oct. 12, 2021).

U.S. Attorneys' Offices to "convene meetings" in your judicial district "with federal, state, local, Tribal, and territorial leaders" within 30 days.[6] The Justice Department simultaneously issued a press release indicating that the Attorney General's directive would "open dedicated lines of communication for threat reporting, assessment and response by law enforcement"—in other words, create a snitch line for complaints about concerned parents.[7]

During Attorney General Garland's testimony before our Committee on October 21, he appeared to have no idea whether the U.S. Attorney meetings he ordered were actually taking place. He stated: "I don't know whether [the meetings] are ongoing, but I expect and hope that they are going . . . because I did ask that they take place."[8] Attorney General Garland testified that he doubted "there have been meetings in every jurisdiction," but reiterated his belief that it is important for federal law enforcement authorities to conduct these meetings in every judicial district.[9] According to the Attorney General's directives, meetings are to be convened in all 94 judicial districts by November 3, 2021, at the latest.

Following the Attorney General's testimony, the NSBA Board of Directors, apparently recognizing the ill-conceived consequences of its letter and the resulting Justice Department action, issued a new memorandum to its members apologizing for the letter, stating: "On behalf of NSBA, <u>we regret and apologize for the letter</u>."[10] (emphasis in original). Although Attorney General Garland testified that the NSBA letter to President Biden was the basis for his October 4 directive to insert federal law enforcement into local school board matters, the Attorney General has yet to rescind his memorandum. His directives to you and other U.S. Attorneys remain in effect.

Concerned parents voicing their strong opposition to controversial curricula at local schools are not domestic terrorists. Parents have an undisputed right to direct the upbringing and education of their children.[11] When parents, however, cross the line to commit a violent act or issue a criminal threat,[12] state and local authorities are best-equipped to handle these violations of state law. But we must not tolerate the use of the federal law enforcement apparatus to intimidate and silence parents using their Constitutional rights to advocate for their child's future.

To assist our investigation and determine whether these meetings are ongoing, we request that you provide the following documents and information:

---

[6] Memorandum from Atty Gen. Merrick Garland, U.S. Dep't of Justice, Partnership Among Federal, State, Local, Tribal, And Territorial Law Enforcement to Address Threats Against School Administrators, Board Members, Teachers, and Staff (Oct. 4, 2021).
[7] Press Release, U.S. Dep't of Justice, Justice Department Addresses Violent Threats Against School Officials and Teachers (Oct. 4, 2021).
[8] *Oversight of the United States Department of Justice: Hearing Before the H. comm. on the Judiciary,* 117th Cong. at 94 (2021) (testimony from Hon. Merrick Garland, Atty Gen., U.S. Dep't of Justice).
[9] *Id.* at 95.
[10] Memorandum from NSBA Board of Directors, Message to NSBA Members (Oct. 22, 2021).
[11] *Troxel v. Granville,* 530 U.S. 57, 65 (2000) (citing *Meyer v. Nebraska,* 262 U.S. 390, 399 (1923)).
[12] *Merrick Garland's federal offense,* WALL ST. J. (Oct. 6, 2021).

1. All documents and communications referring or relating to convening meeting(s) in your judicial district in accordance with the Attorney General's October 4, 2021 memorandum;

2. All agendas, minutes, and notes created or relied upon by U.S. Attorney's Office employees referring or relating to meeting(s) in your judicial district in accordance with the Attorney General's October 4, 2021 memorandum;

3. Please explain when meeting(s) in your judicial district in accordance with the Attorney General's October 4, 2021 memorandum have occurred or will occur;

4. Please identify by name and title of all U.S. Attorney's Office employees involved in the meeting(s) in your judicial district in accordance with the Attorney General's October 4, 2021 memorandum ;

5. Please identify all federal, state, local, Tribal, and territorial organizations invited to or that have attended the meetings convened in your judicial district in accordance with the October 4, 2021 memorandum; and

6. Please provide all recommendations, both formal and informal, and any meeting minutes produced at the meeting(s) in your judicial district in accordance with the Attorney General's October 4, 2021 memorandum.

Please provide this material as soon as possible but no later than 5:00 p.m. on November 15, 2021.

If you have any questions about this request, please contact Committee staff at (202) 225-6906. Thank you for your attention to this important matter.

Sincerely,

Jim Jordan
Ranking Member

Steve Chabot
Member of Congress

Louie Gohmert
Member of Congress

Darrell Issa
Ranking Member
Subcommittee on Courts, Intellectual Property, and the Internet

Ken Buck
Ranking Member
Subcommittee on Antitrust, Commercial
and Administrative Law

Mike Johnson
Ranking Member
Subcommittee on the Constitution,
Civil Rights and Civil Liberties

Tom McClintock
Ranking Member
Subcommittee on Immigration
and Citizenship

Tom Tiffany
Member of Congress

Chip Roy
Member of Congress

Michelle Fischbach
Member of Congress

Matt Gaetz
Member of Congress

Andy Biggs
Ranking Member
Subcommittee on Crime, Terrorism
and Homeland Security

W. Gregory Steube
Member of Congress

Thomas Massie
Member of Congress

Dan Bishop
Member of Congress

Victoria Spartz
Member of Congress

Scott Fitzgerald
Member of Congress

Cliff Bentz
Member of Congress

Burgess Owens
Member of Congress

cc: The Honorable Jerrold L. Nadler
Chairman

Mr. Monty Wilkinson
Director, Executive Office for U.S. Attorneys

JERROLD NADLER, New York
CHAIRMAN

JIM JORDAN, Ohio
RANKING MEMBER

ONE HUNDRED SEVENTEENTH CONGRESS

Congress of the United States

House of Representatives

COMMITTEE ON THE JUDICIARY

2138 RAYBURN HOUSE OFFICE BUILDING

WASHINGTON, DC 20515–6216

(202) 225–3951
judiciary.house.gov

November 1, 2021

The Honorable William S. Thompson
U.S. Attorney
Southern District of West Virginia
300 Virginia Street, Suite 4000
Charleston, WV 25301

Dear Mr. Thompson:

We are continuing to investigate the troubling attempts by the Department of Justice and the White House to use the heavy hand of federal law enforcement to target concerned parents at local school board meetings and chill their protected First Amendment activity. Because the Department directed you, along with all other U.S. Attorneys, and the Federal Bureau of Investigation (FBI) to take action to address parents attending school board meetings,[1] we respectfully request your assistance with our investigation.

On September 29, 2021, the National School Boards Association (NSBA) sent a letter to President Joe Biden requesting help from the federal government with concerned parents voicing their opinions at school board meetings.[2] The NSBA letter stated that "malice, violence, and threats" against school officials "could be the equivalent of a form of domestic terrorism or hate crimes."[3] The letter cited a number of interactions at school board meetings, none of which rose to the level of domestic terrorism. In fact, the vast majority of incidents cited by the NSBA did not involve threats or violence.[4] Most notably, as an example of domestic terrorism, the NSBA cited an incident in which a father angrily confronted members at a school board meeting in Loudoun County, Virginia about the heinous sexual assault of his daughter.[5]

A mere five days after the NSBA sent its letter to President Biden, on October 4, 2021, Attorney General Merrick Garland issued a shocking memorandum that directed the FBI and

---

[1] Memorandum from Atty Gen. Merrick Garland, U.S. Dep't of Justice, Partnership Among Federal, State, Local, Tribal, And Territorial Law Enforcement to Address Threats Against School Administrators, Board Members, Teachers, and Staff (Oct. 4, 2021).
[2] Letter from Dr. Viola M. Garcia, President, Nat'l School Board Assoc. & Mr. Chip Slaven, Chief Exec. Officer, Nat'l School Board Assoc., to President Joseph R. Biden, White House (Sept. 29, 2021).
[3] *Id.*
[4] *See* Caroline Downey, *Vast majority of incidents cited by school-board group to justify federal intervention didn't involve threats,* NAT'L REV. (Oct. 2, 2021).
[5] *Id.*; *see also* Jessica Chasmar, *Loudoun County father arrested at school board events says school tried to cover up daughter's bathroom assault*, FOX NEWS (Oct. 12, 2021).

U.S. Attorneys' Offices to "convene meetings" in your judicial district "with federal, state, local, Tribal, and territorial leaders" within 30 days.[6] The Justice Department simultaneously issued a press release indicating that the Attorney General's directive would "open dedicated lines of communication for threat reporting, assessment and response by law enforcement"—in other words, create a snitch line for complaints about concerned parents.[7]

During Attorney General Garland's testimony before our Committee on October 21, he appeared to have no idea whether the U.S. Attorney meetings he ordered were actually taking place. He stated: "I don't know whether [the meetings] are ongoing, but I expect and hope that they are going . . . because I did ask that they take place."[8] Attorney General Garland testified that he doubted "there have been meetings in every jurisdiction," but reiterated his belief that it is important for federal law enforcement authorities to conduct these meetings in every judicial district.[9] According to the Attorney General's directives, meetings are to be convened in all 94 judicial districts by November 3, 2021, at the latest.

Following the Attorney General's testimony, the NSBA Board of Directors, apparently recognizing the ill-conceived consequences of its letter and the resulting Justice Department action, issued a new memorandum to its members apologizing for the letter, stating: "On behalf of NSBA, <u>we regret and apologize for the letter</u>."[10] (emphasis in original). Although Attorney General Garland testified that the NSBA letter to President Biden was the basis for his October 4 directive to insert federal law enforcement into local school board matters, the Attorney General has yet to rescind his memorandum. His directives to you and other U.S. Attorneys remain in effect.

Concerned parents voicing their strong opposition to controversial curricula at local schools are not domestic terrorists. Parents have an undisputed right to direct the upbringing and education of their children.[11] When parents, however, cross the line to commit a violent act or issue a criminal threat,[12] state and local authorities are best-equipped to handle these violations of state law. But we must not tolerate the use of the federal law enforcement apparatus to intimidate and silence parents using their Constitutional rights to advocate for their child's future.

To assist our investigation and determine whether these meetings are ongoing, we request that you provide the following documents and information:

---

[6] Memorandum from Atty Gen. Merrick Garland, U.S. Dep't of Justice, Partnership Among Federal, State, Local, Tribal, And Territorial Law Enforcement to Address Threats Against School Administrators, Board Members, Teachers, and Staff (Oct. 4, 2021).
[7] Press Release, U.S. Dep't of Justice, Justice Department Addresses Violent Threats Against School Officials and Teachers (Oct. 4, 2021).
[8] *Oversight of the United States Department of Justice: Hearing Before the H. comm. on the Judiciary,* 117th Cong. at 94 (2021) (testimony from Hon. Merrick Garland, Atty Gen., U.S. Dep't of Justice).
[9] *Id.* at 95.
[10] Memorandum from NSBA Board of Directors, Message to NSBA Members (Oct. 22, 2021).
[11] *Troxel v. Granville,* 530 U.S. 57, 65 (2000) (citing *Meyer v. Nebraska,* 262 U.S. 390, 399 (1923)).
[12] *Merrick Garland's federal offense,* WALL ST. J. (Oct. 6, 2021).

1. All documents and communications referring or relating to convening meeting(s) in your judicial district in accordance with the Attorney General's October 4, 2021 memorandum;

2. All agendas, minutes, and notes created or relied upon by U.S. Attorney's Office employees referring or relating to meeting(s) in your judicial district in accordance with the Attorney General's October 4, 2021 memorandum;

3. Please explain when meeting(s) in your judicial district in accordance with the Attorney General's October 4, 2021 memorandum have occurred or will occur;

4. Please identify by name and title of all U.S. Attorney's Office employees involved in the meeting(s) in your judicial district in accordance with the Attorney General's October 4, 2021 memorandum ;

5. Please identify all federal, state, local, Tribal, and territorial organizations invited to or that have attended the meetings convened in your judicial district in accordance with the October 4, 2021 memorandum; and

6. Please provide all recommendations, both formal and informal, and any meeting minutes produced at the meeting(s) in your judicial district in accordance with the Attorney General's October 4, 2021 memorandum.

Please provide this material as soon as possible but no later than 5:00 p.m. on November 15, 2021.

If you have any questions about this request, please contact Committee staff at (202) 225-6906. Thank you for your attention to this important matter.

Sincerely,

Jim Jordan
Ranking Member

Steve Chabot
Member of Congress

Louie Gohmert
Member of Congress

Darrell Issa
Ranking Member
Subcommittee on Courts, Intellectual Property, and the Internet

Ken Buck
Ranking Member
Subcommittee on Antitrust, Commercial and Administrative Law

Matt Gaetz
Member of Congress

Mike Johnson
Ranking Member
Subcommittee on the Constitution, Civil Rights and Civil Liberties

Andy Biggs
Ranking Member
Subcommittee on Crime, Terrorism and Homeland Security

Tom McClintock
Ranking Member
Subcommittee on Immigration and Citizenship

W. Gregory Steube
Member of Congress

Tom Tiffany
Member of Congress

Thomas Massie
Member of Congress

Chip Roy
Member of Congress

Dan Bishop
Member of Congress

Michelle Fischbach
Member of Congress

Victoria Spartz
Member of Congress

Scott Fitzgerald
Member of Congress

Cliff Bentz
Member of Congress

Burgess Owens
Member of Congress

cc: The Honorable Jerrold L. Nadler
Chairman

Mr. Monty Wilkinson
Director, Executive Office for U.S. Attorneys

JERROLD NADLER, New York
CHAIRMAN

JIM JORDAN, Ohio
RANKING MEMBER

ONE HUNDRED SEVENTEENTH CONGRESS

Congress of the United States

House of Representatives

COMMITTEE ON THE JUDICIARY

2138 RAYBURN HOUSE OFFICE BUILDING
WASHINGTON, DC 20515-6216
(202) 225-3951
judiciary.house.gov

November 1, 2021

Mr. L. Robert Murray
Acting U.S. Attorney
District of Wyoming
2120 Capitol Avenue, Suite 4000
Cheyenne, WY 82001

Dear Mr. Murray:

We are continuing to investigate the troubling attempts by the Department of Justice and the White House to use the heavy hand of federal law enforcement to target concerned parents at local school board meetings and chill their protected First Amendment activity. Because the Department directed you, along with all other U.S. Attorneys, and the Federal Bureau of Investigation (FBI) to take action to address parents attending school board meetings,[1] we respectfully request your assistance with our investigation.

On September 29, 2021, the National School Boards Association (NSBA) sent a letter to President Joe Biden requesting help from the federal government with concerned parents voicing their opinions at school board meetings.[2] The NSBA letter stated that "malice, violence, and threats" against school officials "could be the equivalent of a form of domestic terrorism or hate crimes."[3] The letter cited a number of interactions at school board meetings, none of which rose to the level of domestic terrorism. In fact, the vast majority of incidents cited by the NSBA did not involve threats or violence.[4] Most notably, as an example of domestic terrorism, the NSBA cited an incident in which a father angrily confronted members at a school board meeting in Loudoun County, Virginia about the heinous sexual assault of his daughter.[5]

A mere five days after the NSBA sent its letter to President Biden, on October 4, 2021, Attorney General Merrick Garland issued a shocking memorandum that directed the FBI and

---

[1] Memorandum from Atty Gen. Merrick Garland, U.S. Dep't of Justice, Partnership Among Federal, State, Local, Tribal, And Territorial Law Enforcement to Address Threats Against School Administrators, Board Members, Teachers, and Staff (Oct. 4, 2021).
[2] Letter from Dr. Viola M. Garcia, President, Nat'l School Board Assoc. & Mr. Chip Slaven, Chief Exec. Officer, Nat'l School Board Assoc., to President Joseph R. Biden, White House (Sept. 29, 2021).
[3] *Id.*
[4] *See* Caroline Downey, *Vast majority of incidents cited by school-board group to justify federal intervention didn't involve threats,* NAT'L REV. (Oct. 2, 2021).
[5] *Id.*; *see also* Jessica Chasmar, *Loudoun County father arrested at school board events says school tried to cover up daughter's bathroom assault*, FOX NEWS (Oct. 12, 2021).

U.S. Attorneys' Offices to "convene meetings" in your judicial district "with federal, state, local, Tribal, and territorial leaders" within 30 days.[6] The Justice Department simultaneously issued a press release indicating that the Attorney General's directive would "open dedicated lines of communication for threat reporting, assessment and response by law enforcement"—in other words, create a snitch line for complaints about concerned parents.[7]

During Attorney General Garland's testimony before our Committee on October 21, he appeared to have no idea whether the U.S. Attorney meetings he ordered were actually taking place. He stated: "I don't know whether [the meetings] are ongoing, but I expect and hope that they are going . . . because I did ask that they take place."[8] Attorney General Garland testified that he doubted "there have been meetings in every jurisdiction," but reiterated his belief that it is important for federal law enforcement authorities to conduct these meetings in every judicial district.[9] According to the Attorney General's directives, meetings are to be convened in all 94 judicial districts by November 3, 2021, at the latest.

Following the Attorney General's testimony, the NSBA Board of Directors, apparently recognizing the ill-conceived consequences of its letter and the resulting Justice Department action, issued a new memorandum to its members apologizing for the letter, stating: "On behalf of NSBA, <u>we regret and apologize for the letter</u>."[10] (emphasis in original). Although Attorney General Garland testified that the NSBA letter to President Biden was the basis for his October 4 directive to insert federal law enforcement into local school board matters, the Attorney General has yet to rescind his memorandum. His directives to you and other U.S. Attorneys remain in effect.

Concerned parents voicing their strong opposition to controversial curricula at local schools are not domestic terrorists. Parents have an undisputed right to direct the upbringing and education of their children.[11] When parents, however, cross the line to commit a violent act or issue a criminal threat,[12] state and local authorities are best-equipped to handle these violations of state law. But we must not tolerate the use of the federal law enforcement apparatus to intimidate and silence parents using their Constitutional rights to advocate for their child's future.

To assist our investigation and determine whether these meetings are ongoing, we request that you provide the following documents and information:

---

[6] Memorandum from Atty Gen. Merrick Garland, U.S. Dep't of Justice, Partnership Among Federal, State, Local, Tribal, And Territorial Law Enforcement to Address Threats Against School Administrators, Board Members, Teachers, and Staff (Oct. 4, 2021).
[7] Press Release, U.S. Dep't of Justice, Justice Department Addresses Violent Threats Against School Officials and Teachers (Oct. 4, 2021).
[8] *Oversight of the United States Department of Justice: Hearing Before the H. comm. on the Judiciary,* 117th Cong. at 94 (2021) (testimony from Hon. Merrick Garland, Atty Gen., U.S. Dep't of Justice).
[9] *Id.* at 95.
[10] Memorandum from NSBA Board of Directors, Message to NSBA Members (Oct. 22, 2021).
[11] *Troxel v. Granville,* 530 U.S. 57, 65 (2000) (citing *Meyer v. Nebraska,* 262 U.S. 390, 399 (1923)).
[12] *Merrick Garland's federal offense,* WALL ST. J. (Oct. 6, 2021).

1. All documents and communications referring or relating to convening meeting(s) in your judicial district in accordance with the Attorney General's October 4, 2021 memorandum;

2. All agendas, minutes, and notes created or relied upon by U.S. Attorney's Office employees referring or relating to meeting(s) in your judicial district in accordance with the Attorney General's October 4, 2021 memorandum;

3. Please explain when meeting(s) in your judicial district in accordance with the Attorney General's October 4, 2021 memorandum have occurred or will occur;

4. Please identify by name and title of all U.S. Attorney's Office employees involved in the meeting(s) in your judicial district in accordance with the Attorney General's October 4, 2021 memorandum ;

5. Please identify all federal, state, local, Tribal, and territorial organizations invited to or that have attended the meetings convened in your judicial district in accordance with the October 4, 2021 memorandum; and

6. Please provide all recommendations, both formal and informal, and any meeting minutes produced at the meeting(s) in your judicial district in accordance with the Attorney General's October 4, 2021 memorandum.

Please provide this material as soon as possible but no later than 5:00 p.m. on November 15, 2021.

If you have any questions about this request, please contact Committee staff at (202) 225-6906. Thank you for your attention to this important matter.

Sincerely,

Jim Jordan
Ranking Member

Steve Chabot
Member of Congress

Louie Gohmert
Member of Congress

Darrell Issa
Ranking Member
Subcommittee on Courts, Intellectual Property, and the Internet

Ken Buck
Ranking Member
Subcommittee on Antitrust, Commercial and Administrative Law

Matt Gaetz
Member of Congress

Mike Johnson
Ranking Member
Subcommittee on the Constitution, Civil Rights and Civil Liberties

Andy Biggs
Ranking Member
Subcommittee on Crime, Terrorism and Homeland Security

Tom McClintock
Ranking Member
Subcommittee on Immigration and Citizenship

W. Gregory Steube
Member of Congress

Tom Tiffany
Member of Congress

Thomas Massie
Member of Congress

Chip Roy
Member of Congress

Dan Bishop
Member of Congress

Michelle Fischbach
Member of Congress

Victoria Spartz
Member of Congress

Scott Fitzgerald
Member of Congress

Cliff Bentz
Member of Congress

Burgess Owens
Member of Congress

cc: The Honorable Jerrold L. Nadler
Chairman

Mr. Monty Wilkinson
Director, Executive Office for U.S. Attorneys

JERROLD NADLER, New York
CHAIRMAN

JIM JORDAN, Ohio
RANKING MEMBER

ONE HUNDRED SEVENTEENTH CONGRESS

Congress of the United States
House of Representatives

COMMITTEE ON THE JUDICIARY
2138 RAYBURN HOUSE OFFICE BUILDING
WASHINGTON, DC 20515–6216
(202) 225–3951
judiciary.house.gov

October 28, 2021

The Honorable Jerrold L. Nadler
Chairman
Committee on the Judiciary
U.S. House of Representatives
Washington, DC 20515

Dear Chairman Nadler:

The Department of Justice and the Biden White House attempted to use the heavy hand of federal law enforcement to target concerned parents at local school board meetings and chill their protected First Amendment activity. The Department's actions, including the involvement of the National Security Division, came days after the Biden Administration received a letter from the National School Boards Association (NSBA) equating parents as domestic terrorists and urging the Department to exercise its authorities under the Patriot Act. This collusion demands the Committee's attention.

The National Security Division was created by the Patriot Act, and its mission is to "protect the United States from threats to our national security."[1] It is organized to "ensure greater coordination and unity of purpose between prosecutors and law enforcement agencies, on the one hand, and intelligence attorneys and the Intelligence Community, on the other."[2] It is unclear what threat the Department believes American parents pose to our national security, nor why the Department could view any threat posed by parents as requiring coordination with our foreign intelligence agencies. Unfortunately, in testimony before the Committee, Attorney General Garland was unable or unwilling to explain why he directed the National Security Division to participate in this ill-conceived endeavor.[3] Thus, we request that you convene a hearing promptly with Deputy Attorney General Lisa Monaco and Acting Assistant Attorney General Mark Lesko, head of the National Security Division, so we can get to the bottom of the Biden Administration's attack on concerned parents.

On September 29, 2021, the NSBA sent a letter to President Joe Biden requesting help from the federal government with concerned parents voicing their opinions at school board

---

[1] *National Security Division: About the Division*, U.S. Dep't of Justice (last updated Apr. 12, 2019), https://www.justice.gov/nsd/about-division.
[2] *Id.*
[3] *Oversight of the United States Department of Justice: Hearing Before the H. comm. on the Judiciary,* 117th Cong. at 67 (2021) (testimony from Hon. Merrick Garland, Atty Gen., U.S. Dep't of Justice).

meetings.[4] The NSBA letter stated that "malice, violence, and threats" against school officials "could be the equivalent of a form of domestic terrorism or hate crimes."[5] The NSBA letter cited a number of interactions at school board meetings, including one "example" of alleged domestic terrorism in Loudoun County, Virginia, where a father angrily confronted members at a school board meeting about the heinous sexual assault of his daughter.[6]

On October 4, 2021, just five days after the NSBA letter, Attorney General Merrick Garland issued a shocking memorandum that directed the Federal Bureau of Investigation and U.S. Attorneys' Offices to address a purported "disturbing spike in harassment, intimidation, and threats of violence" at school board meetings.[7] The memorandum explained that the Department would be "using its authority and resources to discourage these threats, identify them when they occur, and prosecute them when appropriate."[8] In a press release announcing the Attorney General's memorandum, the Justice Department announced that the National Security Division would be part of a Department-wide task force "to determine how federal enforcement tools can be used to prosecute these crimes."[9]

Following the Attorney General's testimony, the NSBA Board of Directors, apparently recognizing the ill-conceived consequences of its letter and the resulting Justice Department action, issued a new memorandum to its members apologizing for the letter, stating: "On behalf of NSBA, <u>we regret and apologize for the letter</u>."[10] (emphasis in original). Although Attorney General Garland testified that the NSBA letter to President Biden was the basis for his October 4 directive to insert federal law enforcement into local school board matters, the Attorney General has yet to rescind his memorandum. His directives to the National Security Division remain in effect.

Concerned parents voicing their strong opposition to controversial curricula at local schools are not domestic terrorists. Parents have an undisputed right to direct the upbringing and education of their children.[11] When parents, however, cross the line to commit a violent act or issue a criminal threat,[12] state and local authorities are best-equipped to handle these violations of state law. But we must not tolerate the use of the federal law enforcement apparatus to intimidate and silence parents using their Constitutional rights to advocate for their child's future.

---

[4] Letter from Dr. Viola M. Garcia, President, Nat'l School Board Assoc. & Mr. Chip Slaven, Chief Exec. Officer, Nat'l School Board Assoc., to President Joseph R. Biden, White House (Sept. 29, 2021).
[5] *Id.*
[6] *Id.*; *see also* Jessica Chasmar, *Loudoun County father arrested at school board events says school tried to cover up daughter's bathroom assault*, FOX NEWS (Oct. 12, 2021); Caroline Downey, *Vast majority of incidents cited by school-board group to justify federal intervention didn't involve threats,* NAT'L REV. (Oct. 2, 2021).
[7] Memorandum from Atty Gen. Merrick Garland, U.S. Dep't of Justice, Partnership Among Federal, State, Local, Tribal, And Territorial Law Enforcement to Address Threats Against School Administrators, Board Members, Teachers, and Staff (Oct. 4, 2021).
[8] *Id.*
[9] Press Release, U.S. Dep't of Justice, Justice Department Addresses Violent Threats Against School Officials and Teachers (Oct. 4, 2021).
[10] Memorandum from NSBA Board of Directors, Message to NSBA Members (Oct. 22, 2021).
[11] *Troxel v. Granville,* 530 U.S. 57, 65 (2000) (citing *Meyer v. Nebraska,* 262 U.S. 390, 399 (1923)).
[12] *Merrick Garland's federal offense,* WALL ST. J. (Oct. 6, 2021).

We therefore request that you immediately convene a hearing with Deputy Attorney General Lisa Monaco and Acting Assistant Attorney General Mark Lesko so the Committee may examine the troubling role of the National Security Division in targeting concerned parents at school board meetings. Thank you for your attention to this matter.

Sincerely,

Jim Jordan
Ranking Member

Steve Chabot
Member of Congress

Louie Gohmert
Member of Congress

Darrell Issa
Ranking Member
Subcommittee on Courts, Intellectual Property, and the Internet

Ken Buck
Ranking Member
Subcommittee on Antitrust, Commercial and Administrative Law

Matt Gaetz
Member of Congress

Mike Johnson
Ranking Member
Subcommittee on the Constitution, Civil Rights and Civil Liberties

Andy Biggs
Ranking Member
Subcommittee on Crime, Terrorism and Homeland Security

Tom McClintock
Ranking Member
Subcommittee on Immigration and Citizenship

W. Gregory Steube
Member of Congress

Tom Tiffany
Member of Congress

Thomas Massie
Member of Congress

Chip Roy
Member of Congress

Dan Bishop
Member of Congress

Michelle Fischbach
Member of Congress

Victoria Spartz
Member of Congress

Scott Fitzgerald
Member of Congress

Cliff Bentz
Member of Congress

Burgess Owens
Member of Congress

Congress of the United States

Washington, DC 20515

October 27, 2021

The Honorable Merrick B. Garland
Attorney General
U.S. Department of Justice
950 Pennsylvania Avenue, NW
Washington, D.C. 20530

Dear Attorney General Garland:

We have been investigating whether U.S. taxpayer dollars funded dangerous research into deadly pathogens in Wuhan, China. For more than a year, the National Institutes of Health (NIH) and Dr. Anthony Fauci, director of the NIH's National Institute of Allergy and Infectious Diseases (NIAID), have denied using taxpayer money to fund this type of research. However, a recent admission from the NIH reveals that EcoHealth Alliance, Inc. (EcoHealth), a NIAID grant recipient, may have violated federal law in its taxpayer-funded work on deadly pathogens.[1] We accordingly refer this matter to the Justice Department for investigation.

On June 1, 2014, EcoHealth received a $3.7 million dollar grant from NIAID, entitled "Understanding the Risk of Bat Coronavirus Emergence."[2] Through this grant, EcoHealth sent more than $600,000 to the Wuhan Institute of Virology (WIV) in Wuhan, China. Further, pursuant to this grant, EcoHealth was required to report to NIH and "immediately stop all experiments" if it created a virus that showed evidence of viral growth 1,000 percent that of the original virus.[3] Even if EcoHealth did not immediately report an experiment that met these parameters as required by the grant, EcoHealth would have to submit its annual progress report by September 30, 2019. EcoHealth failed on both counts.

On October 20, 2021, we received a letter from Dr. Lawrence Tabak, Principal Deputy Director of the NIH. According to Dr. Tabak, EcoHealth "failed" to properly and promptly report an experiment that violated the terms of the grant.[4] The grant required EcoHealth to report any experiment that creates, intentionally or otherwise, a new virus that is 1,000 percent more virulent than its progenitor.[5] In one experiment, EcoHealth did just that but subsequently failed to report it. EcoHealth subsequently failed to file an annual report until August 3, 2021, almost two years after it was required to do so.[6]

---

[1] Letter from Lawrence A. Tabak, Principal Deputy Director, U.S. Nat'l Inst. Of Health, to Hon. James Comer, Ranking Member, H. Comm. on Oversight & Reform (Oct. 20, 2021).
[2] Project Grant, Understanding the Risk of Bat Coronavirus Research, EcoHealth Alliance, Inc. (June 1, 2014).
[3] Letter from Hon. Francis Collins, Dir., Nat'l Insts. Of Health, to Hon. James Comer, Ranking Member, H. Comm. on Oversight & Reform (July 28, 2021).
[4] Letter from Lawrence A. Tabak, *supra* note 1.
[5] *Id.*
[6] Understanding the Risk of Bat Coronavirus Emergence, 5RO1AI110964-05 (June 6, 2018 – May 31, 2019).

The revelation in Dr. Tabak's letter raises the prospect about whether EcoHealth violated 18 U.S.C. § 1031 and committed a major fraud against the United States. Section 1031 states, in relevant part, "[w]hoever knowingly executes, or attempts to execute, any scheme or artifice with the intent to defraud the United States; or to obtain money or property by means of false or fraudulent pretenses, representations, or promises, in any grant . . . if the value of such grant . . . is $1,000,000 or more shall . . . be fined not more than $1,000,000, or imprisoned not more than 10 years, or both."[7] The section's prohibition includes "misrepresenting a project's status to continue receiving funds."[8]

Between September 30, 2019 and August 3, 2021, EcoHealth received $21,648,574 in grant funds from U.S. taxpayers that the company may not have received if it had timely disclosed to NIH that it had created a virus that would trigger the cessation of its experiments.[9] The fact that EcoHealth received more than $21 million during this period shows that the company had a clear financial incentive to violate the terms of its grant by failing to stop its experiments. In addition, EcoHealth's failure to provide the required reporting to NIH for nearly two years—despite a requirement in the grant to do so annually—suggests that EcoHealth knowingly withheld information from NIH in an effort to misrepresent the project's status.

Based on the information available to us, we respectfully request that the Department of Justice investigate whether EcoHealth violated federal law by misrepresenting the status of its project to NIAID or NIH. Please respond by November 3, 2021 to inform us whether the Department intends to investigate this matter. Thank you for your attention to this matter.

Sincerely,

James Comer
Ranking Member
Committee on Oversight and Reform

Jim Jordan
Ranking Member
Committee on the Judiciary

cc: The Honorable Carolyn B. Maloney, Chairwoman
Committee on Oversight and Reform

The Honorable Jerrold Nadler, Chairman
Committee on the Judiciary

---

[7] 18 U.S.C. § 1031.
[8] *Grant Fraud Responsibilities,* Grants.gov (last accessed Oct. 21, 2021).
[9] USASpending.gov (last accessed Oct. 21, 2021), https://www.usaspending.gov/search/?hash=d664bf197193e61d56504abf646e5410.

JERROLD NADLER, New York
CHAIRMAN

JIM JORDAN, Ohio
RANKING MEMBER

ONE HUNDRED SEVENTEENTH CONGRESS

Congress of the United States
House of Representatives
COMMITTEE ON THE JUDICIARY

2138 RAYBURN HOUSE OFFICE BUILDING
WASHINGTON, DC 20515-6216
(202) 225-3951
judiciary.house.gov

October 27, 2021

Dr. Viola M. Garcia, President
Mr. Frank S. Henderson, Jr., President-elect
Ms. Kristi Sweet, Secretary-Treasurer
Mr. Charlie Wilson, Immediate Past President
National School Boards Association
1680 Duke St., Second Floor
Alexandria, VA 22314-3493

Dear Dr. Garcia, Mr. Henderson, Ms. Sweet, and Mr. Wilson:

We are investigating the troubling attempts by the Department of Justice and the White House to use the heavy hand of federal law enforcement to target concerned parents at local school board meetings and chill their protected First Amendment activity. Because you are the officers of the National School Boards Association's (NSBA) board of directors, which exercises "supervision, control and direction of the affairs of the Association,"[1] we respectfully request your assistance with our investigation.

On September 29, 2021, the NSBA sent a letter to President Joe Biden requesting help from the federal government with concerned parents voicing their opinions at school board meetings.[2] The NSBA letter stated that "malice, violence, and threats" against school officials "could be the equivalent of a form of domestic terrorism or hate crimes."[3] The letter cited a number of interactions at school board meetings, the vast majority of which did not involve violence or threats.[4] Notably, as one "example" of alleged domestic terrorism, the NSBA cited an instance in Loudoun County, Virginia, where a father angrily confronted members at a school board meeting about the heinous sexual assault of his daughter.[5]

---

[1] Nat'l School Board Assn., Constitution and Bylaws of the National School Board Association, Art. VI, sec. 1 (as amended Aug. 13, 2021), https://www.nsba.org/-/media/NSBA/File/nsba-constitution-and-bylaws-8-13-21.pdf?la=en&hash=2AD2BB0EDE213D8D4BE90ADC3B833FE73EE78B95.
[2] Letter from Dr. Viola M. Garcia, President, Nat'l School Board Assoc. & Mr. Chip Slaven, Chief Exec. Officer, Nat'l School Board Assoc., to President Joseph R. Biden, White House (Sept. 29, 2021)
[3] *Id.*
[4] *Id.*; *see also* Caroline Downey, *Vast majority of incidents cited by school-board group to justify federal intervention didn't involve threats,* NAT'L REV. (Oct. 2, 2021).
[5] *Id.*; *see also* Jessica Chasmar, *Loudoun County father arrested at school board events says school tried to cover up daughter's bathroom assault*, FOX NEWS (Oct. 12, 2021).

On October 4, 2021, a mere five days after the NSBA sent its letter to President Biden, Attorney General Merrick Garland issued an unusual memorandum that directed the Federal Bureau of Investigation (FBI) and U.S. Attorneys' Offices to address the "disturbing spike in harassment, intimidation, and threats of violence" at school board meetings.[6] In a press release publicizing the memorandum, the Justice Department indicated its directive would "open dedicated lines of communication for threat reporting, assessment and response by law enforcement"—in other words, a snitch line for complaints about concerned parents.[7] The press release noted that the Department's National Security Division—the Department component responsible for prosecuting terrorism cases—would be part of a task force "to determine how federal enforcement tools can be used to prosecute these crimes."[8]

On October 21, 2021, Attorney General Garland testified before our Committee. During his testimony, Attorney General Garland acknowledged that he relied upon the NSBA letter as the basis for issuing his memorandum.[9] In addition, a news report published the same day revealed that the NSBA communicated with the White House about the September 29 letter *prior* to its transmission.[10] In one email dated September 29—the same date as the NSBA letter—the NSBA Interim Executive Director & CEO, Chip Slaven, wrote:

> [I]n talks over the last several weeks with White House staff, they requested additional information on some of the specific threats, so the letter also details many of the incidents that have been occurring.[11]

Similarly, on October 2, the NSBA's President, Dr. Viola Garcia, separately wrote that the NSBA had "been engaged with the White House and Department of Education . . . for several weeks now."[12] On October 13, less than a month after the NSBA letter to President Biden, the Biden Administration announced that it had appointed Dr. Garcia to be one of five members of a federal education advisory board.[13]

The Biden Administration seemingly relied upon the NSBA letter—which it coordinated in advance with the NSBA—as justification to unleash the full weight of the federal law enforcement apparatus upon America's parents. During his testimony, Attorney General Garland

---

[6] Memorandum from Atty Gen. Merrick Garland, U.S. Dep't of Justice, Partnership Among Federal, State, Local, Tribal, And Territorial Law Enforcement to Address Threats Against School Administrators, Board Members, Teachers, and Staff (Oct. 4, 2021).
[7] Press Release, U.S. Dep't of Justice, Justice Department Addresses Violent Threats Against School Officials and Teachers (Oct. 4, 2021).
[8] *Id.*
[9] *Oversight of the United States Department of Justice: Hearing Before the H. comm. on the Judiciary,* 117th Cong. at 68 (2021) (testimony from Hon. Merrick Garland, Atty Gen., U.S. Dep't of Justice).
[10] Caroline Downey, *National school board group communicated with White House while crafting letter likening parents to terrorists,* NAT'L REV. (Oct. 21, 2021).
[11] Email from Chip Slaven (Sept. 29, 2021, 8:18 p.m.), *available at* https://defendinged.org/wp-content/uploads/2021/10/Email-Correspondence_NSBA-Letter-to-President-Biden_Redacted.pdf.
[12] Email from Viola Garcia (Oct. 2, 2021, 6:59 a.m.), *available at* https://defendinged.org/wp-content/uploads/2021/10/Email-Correspondence_NSBA-Letter-to-President-Biden_Redacted.pdf.
[13] Press Release, Dep't of Education, Five Board Members Appointed to Board Overseeing the Nation's Report Card (Oct. 13, 2021).

denied that the intent of his memorandum was to threaten parents or chill their protected First Amendment activity. However, on October 22, 2021, following Attorney General Garland's testimony, the NSBA Board of Directors, apparently recognizing the ill-conceived consequences of its letter and the resulting Justice Department action, issued a new memorandum to its members apologizing for the letter, stating: "On behalf of NSBA, we regret and apologize for the letter."[14] (emphasis in original).

Parents have an undisputed right to direct the upbringing and education of their children, including expressing concerns about the inclusion of controversial curricula in their child's education.[15] Unsurprisingly, the NSBA's September 29 letter to President Biden never once mentioned "parents" or parents' role in their children's education—although its subsequent apology memorandum purported to value the "voices of parents."[16] Concerned parents are absolutely not domestic terrorists and, to the extent actual threats exist, local law enforcement—and not the FBI—are the appropriate authorities to address those situations. Parents cannot tolerate this collusion between the NSBA and the Biden Administration to construct a justification for invoking federal law enforcement to intimidate and silence parents using their Constitutional rights to advocate for their child's future.

To assist our investigation, we request that you produce the following documents concerning the NSBA's September 29 letter and its October 22 memorandum:

1. All documents and communications for the period January 20, 2021, to the present referring or relating to the NSBA's September 29, 2021 letter to President Biden;

2. All documents and communications for the period January 20, 2021, to the present referring or related to the NSBA's October 22, 2021 memorandum;

3. All documents and communications for the period January 20, 2021, to the present between or among Executive Office of the President employees or staff and any NSBA officer, Board member, delegate, or staff referring or relating to the September 29, 2021 letter or October 22, 2021 memorandum;

4. All documents and communications for the period January 20, 2021, to the present between or among Department of Justice officials or employees, including those at the FBI, and any of NSBA officer, Board members, delegate, or staff referring or relating to the September 29, 2021 letter or October 22, 2021 memorandum;

5. All documents and communications for the period January 20, 2021, to the present referring or relating to the Biden Administration's selection of Dr. Viola Garcia to the National Assessment Governing Board; and

---

[14] Memorandum from NSBA Board of Directors, Message to NSBA Members (Oct. 22, 2021).
[15] *Troxel v. Granville,* 530 U.S. 57, 65 (2000) (citing *Meyer v. Nebraska,* 262 U.S. 390, 399 (1923)).
[16] *Compare* Letter from Dr. Viola M. Garcia, *supra* note 2, *with* Memorandum from NSBA Board of Directors, *supra* note 14.

6. Any guidance issued by the NSBA regarding parental engagement at school board meetings.

In addition, please provide the following information:

7. Please explain whether the NSBA will urge Attorney General Garland to withdraw or rescind his October 4 memorandum.

8. Please detail all NSBA interactions with officials from the Justice Department or FBI following the Attorney General's October 4 memorandum. Please include the date(s), participant(s), and topic(s) of these interactions.

9. Please describe in detail the "formal review" that the NSBA will conduct of its internal processes and procedures. When does the NSBA expect to announce the results? Will the NSBA commit to being transparent about its review?

Please produce this material and schedule the briefing as soon as possible but no later than 5:00 p.m. on November 10, 2021. In addition, we ask that you arrange for a staff briefing on this matter.

If you have any questions about this request, please contact Committee staff at (202) 225-6906. Thank you for your attention to this important matter.

Sincerely,

Jim Jordan
Ranking Member

Steve Chabot
Member of Congress

Louie Gohmert
Member of Congress

Darrell Issa
Ranking Member
Subcommittee on Courts, Intellectual Property, and the Internet

Ken Buck
Ranking Member
Subcommittee on Antitrust, Commercial and Administrative Law

Matt Gaetz
Member of Congress

Mike Johnson
Ranking Member
Subcommittee on the Constitution,
Civil Rights and Civil Liberties

Andy Biggs
Ranking Member
Subcommittee on Crime, Terrorism
and Homeland Security

Tom McClintock
Ranking Member
Subcommittee on Immigration
and Citizenship

W. Gregory Steube
Member of Congress

Tom Tiffany
Member of Congress

Thomas Massie
Member of Congress

Chip Roy
Member of Congress

Dan Bishop
Member of Congress

Michelle Fischbach
Member of Congress

Victoria Spartz
Member of Congress

Scott Fitzgerald
Member of Congress

Cliff Bentz
Member of Congress

Burgess Owens
Member of Congress

cc: The Honorable Jerrold L. Nadler
Chairman

JERROLD NADLER, New York
CHAIRMAN

JIM JORDAN, Ohio
RANKING MEMBER

ONE HUNDRED SEVENTEENTH CONGRESS

Congress of the United States

House of Representatives

COMMITTEE ON THE JUDICIARY

2138 RAYBURN HOUSE OFFICE BUILDING
WASHINGTON, DC 20515-6216
(202) 225-3951
judiciary.house.gov

October 25, 2021

The Honorable Merrick B. Garland
Attorney General
U.S. Department of Justice
950 Pennsylvania Avenue, N.W.
Washington, DC 20530

Dear Attorney General Garland:

Your testimony before the Judiciary Committee last week concerning your October 4, 2021, memorandum targeting concerned parents at school board meetings was troubling. You acknowledged that you issued the unusual directive soon after reading about the thinly sourced letter sent by the National School Boards Association (NSBA) to President Biden and not because of any specific request from state or local law enforcement.[1] You appeared to be surprised that the Department's press release publicizing your memorandum noted the involvement of the National Security Division, the Departmental component responsible for prosecuting terrorism cases—despite testifying that concerned parents expressing themselves is protected First Amendment activity.[2] You admitted to being completely unaware of a widely reported, high-profile case in Loudoun County, Virginia, cited in the NSBA's letter as an example of domestic terrorism, in which a father angrily confronted the local school board about the heinous sexual assault of his daughter.[3]

During your testimony, you sidestepped the obvious effect of your ill-conceived memorandum and the chilling effect that invoking the full weight of the federal law enforcement apparatus would have on parents' protected First Amendment speech. Parents have an undisputed right to direct the upbringing and education of their children,[4] especially as school boards attempt to install controversial curricula. Local law enforcement—and not the FBI—are the appropriate authorities to address any local threats or violence.

---

[1] *Oversight of the United States Department of Justice: Hearing Before the H. comm. on the Judiciary,* 117th Cong. (2021) (testimony from Hon. Merrick Garland, Atty Gen., U.S. Dep't of Justice).
[2] *Id.*
[3] *See Id.*; Letter from Ms. Viola M. Garcia, President, Nat'l School Board Assoc. & Mr. Chip Slaven, Chief Exec. Officer, Nat'l School Board Assoc., to President Joseph R. Biden, White House (Sept. 29, 2021); Jessica Chasmar, *Loudoun County father arrested at school board events says school tried to cover up daughter's bathroom assault,* FOX NEWS (Oct. 12, 2021)
[4] *Troxel v. Granville,* 530 U.S. 57, 65 (2000) (citing *Meyer v. Nebraska,* 262 U.S. 390, 399 (1923)).

On October 22, 2021, the NSBA expressed regret about and formally apologized for its letter to President Biden.[5] Because the NSBA letter was the basis for your memorandum and given that your memorandum has been and will continue to be read as threatening parents and chilling their protected First Amendment rights, the only responsible course of action is for you to fully and unequivocally withdraw your memorandum immediately.

Sincerely,

Jim Jordan
Ranking Member

Steve Chabot
Member of Congress

Louie Gohmert
Member of Congress

Darrell Issa
Ranking Member
Subcommittee on Courts, Intellectual Property, and the Internet

Ken Buck
Ranking Member
Subcommittee on Antitrust, Commercial and Administrative Law

Matt Gaetz
Member of Congress

Mike Johnson
Ranking Member
Subcommittee on the Constitution, Civil Rights and Civil Liberties

Andy Biggs
Ranking Member
Subcommittee on Crime, Terrorism and Homeland Security

---

[5] Memorandum from NSBA Board of Directors, Message to NSBA Members (Oct. 22, 2021).

Tom McClintock
Ranking Member
Subcommittee on Immigration
and Citizenship

W. Gregory Steube
Member of Congress

Tom Tiffany
Member of Congress

Thomas Massie
Member of Congress

Chip Roy
Member of Congress

Dan Bishop
Member of Congress

Michelle Fischbach
Member of Congress

Victoria Spartz
Member of Congress

Scott Fitzgerald
Member of Congress

Cliff Bentz
Member of Congress

Burgess Owens
Member of Congress

cc: The Honorable Jerrold L. Nadler
Chairman

JERROLD NADLER, New York
CHAIRMAN

JIM JORDAN, Ohio
RANKING MEMBER

ONE HUNDRED SEVENTEENTH CONGRESS

Congress of the United States

House of Representatives

COMMITTEE ON THE JUDICIARY

2138 RAYBURN HOUSE OFFICE BUILDING

WASHINGTON, DC 20515-6216

(202) 225-3951

judiciary.house.gov

October 13, 2021

The Honorable Merrick B. Garland
Attorney General
U.S. Department of Justice
950 Pennsylvania Avenue, N.W.
Washington, DC 20530

Dear Attorney General Garland:

This letter is to express our serious concerns about your recent decision to involve federal law enforcement entities in local school board debates and to stifle First Amendment-protected political speech. Your actions are not just inappropriate, but also appear to have been improperly influenced by politics and by your family's interest in the matter. As members of the House Committee on the Judiciary, we have a responsibility to conduct oversight of the U.S. Department of Justice (DOJ) and we trust that you will fully cooperate with our inquiry.

On October 4, 2021, you issued a memorandum directing the Federal Bureau of Investigation and U.S. Attorneys' offices to strategize with state and local leaders in response to perceived threats against public school officials.[1] Local law enforcement should properly address and prevent legitimate threats and any actual violence against school board officials. But there is little—if any—basis to interject the immense powers of the federal government into these local matters. Your directive to do so will only serve to discourage parents from voicing concerns or disagreement about the important issues of education policy in their communities.

Your memorandum appears to be motivated by politics more than by any pressing federal law enforcement need. You issued your directive just days after President Biden received a letter from the National School Board Association (NSBA) that equated concerned parents with domestic terrorists and perpetrators of hate crimes.[2] This letter referred to what are legitimate parental concerns about far-left curricula such as Critical Race Theory, radical gender identity ideology, and oppressive coronavirus-related mandates in their local schools.[3] The NSBA urged

---

[1] Memorandum from Atty Gen. Merrick Garland, U.S. Dep't of Justice, Partnership Among Federal, State, Local, Tribal, And Territorial Law Enforcement to Address Threats Against School Administrators, Board Members, Teachers, and Staff (Oct. 4, 2021).
[2] Letter from Ms. Viola M. Garcia, President, Nat'l School Board Assoc. & Mr. Chip Slaven, Chief Exec. Officer, Nat'l School Board Assoc., to President Joseph R. Biden, White House (Sept. 29, 2021).
[3] *Id.*

"the federal government's intervention against individuals or hate groups who are targeting our schools and educators."[4]

Even more concerning is the appearance that a member of your family has a financial stake in local school boards adopting a far-left educational curriculum. Reports allege that your son-in-law is the co-founder of Panorama Education, Inc., a company that publishes and sells Critical Race Theory and "anti-racism" materials and works with school districts nationwide to obtain and analyze data on students.[5] The company's surveys reportedly include intrusive questions such as whether a student feels "gender fluid."[6] To avoid student privacy laws and collect student data without parental consent, Panorama Education staff members are classified as "school officials."[7] The company has reportedly surveyed more than 13 million students in 21,000 schools in all 50 states to date[8] and has received funding from liberal activists such as Mark Zuckerberg.[9]

Your actions appear to run afoul of relevant rules of federal ethics. According to the Code of Federal Regulations, an employee of the Executive Branch is discouraged from engaging in conduct that is likely to affect the financial interests of "a person with whom he has a covered relationship."[10] A covered relationship includes "a relative with whom the employee has a close personal relationship."[11] You and your daughter and son-in-law may meet this criterion, and it is unclear whether you consulted with the Department's designated agency ethics official on this matter prior to issuing your memorandum.[12]

As our nation's top law enforcement official, your most fundamental responsibility is to uphold the standards of equal justice under the law and to protect the constitutional rights and liberties of all Americans. The circumstances around the issues of your memorandum jeopardize these standards and call into question the propriety of your actions. More fundamentally, your directive to insert the might of the federal government into legitimate debates about local education policies shows a serious misunderstanding of the duties of your office.

---

[4] *Id.*

[5] Mark Moore, *Parents group: AG Garland has conflict of interest with Facebook, critical race theory*, N. Y. Post (Oct. 6, 2021, 3:54 PM), https://nypost.com/2021/10/06/parents-group-garland-has-conflict-of-interest-with-facebook/.

[6] Elizabeth Elkind, *Daugter of Attorney General who ordered DOJ to probe angry parents for domestic terrorism is married to founder of education group that promotes Critical Race Theory: Merrick Garland accused of a conflict of interest*, Daily Mail (Oct. 8, 2021, 12:37 PM), https://www.dailymail.co.uk/news/article-10069425/Garland-accused-conflict-ties-education-group-promoting-Critical-Race-Theory.html.

[7] Fairfax County increases five-year contract to \$2.4 million to Panorama Education, a government contractor cofounded by son-in-law of U.S. Attorney General, Parents Defending Education, https://defendinged.org/incidents/panorama-education-datamining/ (last visited Oct. 8, 2021).

[8] Panorama, Our Story, https://www.panoramaed.com/about (last visited Oct. 7, 2021).

[9] Press Release, Newswire, Serving 5 Million Students, Panorama Education Raises \$16M to Expand Reach of Social-Emotional Learning and Increase College Readiness in Schools (Nov. 7, 2017).

[10] Impartiality in Performing Official Duties, 5 C.F.R. §§ 2635.501(a) & 2635.502(b)(1)(ii) (1997).

[11] *Id.*

[12] U.S. Dep't of Justice, Dep't Ethics Office, Conflicts, https://www.justice.gov/jmd/conflicts (last visited Oct. 8, 2021).

Thus, we request you promptly consult with the designated agency ethics official to determine if your actions in this matter have resulted in an ethics violation for a breach of impartiality. The results of this inquiry must be made public and reported to the House and Senate Committees on the Judiciary in order to protect the integrity of the office of Attorney General. Furthermore, depending on the result, your recusal from this issue may be warranted, and the rescission of the memorandum required.

Thank you for your prompt attention to this matter. We await your response.

Sincerely,

Mike Johnson
Ranking Member
Subcommittee on the Constitution
Civil Rights and Civil Liberties

Jim Jordan
Ranking Member

Dan Bishop
Member of Congress

Steve Chabot
Member of Congress

Louie Gohmert
Member of Congress

Darrell Issa
Ranking Member
Subcommittee on Courts, Intellectual
Property and the Internet

Ken Buck
Ranking Member
Subcommittee on Antitrust,
Commercial and Administrative Law

Matt Gaetz
Member of Congress

Andy Biggs
Ranking Member
Subcommittee on Crime, Terrorism and Homeland Security

Tom McClintock
Ranking Member
Subcommittee on Immigration and Citizenship

W. Gregory Steube
Member of Congress

Tom Tiffany
Member of Congress

Thomas Massie
Member of Congress

Chip Roy
Member of Congress

Michelle Fischbach
Member of Congress

Victoria Spartz
Member of Congress

Scott Fitzgerald
Member of Congress

Cliff Bentz
Member of Congress

Burgess Owens
Member of Congress

JERROLD NADLER, New York
CHAIRMAN

JIM JORDAN, Ohio
RANKING MEMBER

ONE HUNDRED SEVENTEENTH CONGRESS

Congress of the United States
House of Representatives
COMMITTEE ON THE JUDICIARY
2138 RAYBURN HOUSE OFFICE BUILDING
WASHINGTON, DC 20515-6216
(202) 225-3951
judiciary.house.gov

September 27, 2021

The Honorable Merrick B. Garland
Attorney General
U.S. Department of Justice
950 Pennsylvania Avenue, NW
Washington, DC 20530

Dear Attorney General Garland:

Earlier this year, the Department of Justice moved to dismiss charges against six suspected Chinese spies, including some who openly admitted to conducting espionage for the Chinese military. It is not clear whether the Department dismissed these changes due to reported misconduct by the Federal Bureau of Investigation (FBI) or because the Department under your leadership is more invested in pursuing the far-left political goals of the Biden-Harris Administration than in protecting American national security interests. These actions by the Department raise serious concerns about its commitment to confronting the national security threats posed by the People's Republic of China (PRC).

Unlike the current Administration, President Trump and his Administration understood the threat posed by China. In November 2018, the Trump Administration launched the China Initiative to address some of the most critical threats to national security posed by the Chinese regime.[1] The Trump Administration's China Initiative sought to identify and prosecute Chinese trade secret theft and economic espionage and to protect American critical infrastructure and supply chains from covert influence.[2]

The threat from China is real and growing. Then-Attorney General William Barr explained last year that "[a]bout 80 percent of all federal economic espionage prosecutions have alleged conduct that would benefit the Chinese state, and about 60 percent of all U.S. trade secret theft cases have had a nexus to China."[3] The FBI similarly warned that "[t]he greatest long-term threat to our nation's information and intellectual property, and to our economic vitality, is the

---

[1] Press Release, U.S. DEP'T OF JUSTICE, The China Initiative: Year-in-Review (2019-20) (Nov. 16, 2020), https://www.justice.gov/opa/pr/china-initiative-year-review-2019-20.
[2] *Information About the Department of Justice's China Initiative and a Compilation of China-Related Prosecutions Since 2018*, U.S. DEP'T OF JUSTICE, https://www.justice.gov/nsd/information-about-department-justice-s-china-initiative-and-compilation-china-related (last updated June 14, 2021).
[3] Attorney General William Barr, Remarks on China Policy, Address at Gerald R. Ford Presidential Museum (July 16, 2020), https://www.justice.gov/opa/speech/attorney-general-william-p-barr-delivers-remarks-china-policy-gerald-r-ford-presidential.

counterintelligence and economic espionage threat from China."[4] In particular, the serious threat posed by "non-traditional collectors"—such as academic researchers—is well-documented.[5] In August 2021, former Director of the U.S. National Counterintelligence and Security Center William Evanina testified that "China utilizes non-traditional collectors to conduct a plurality of their nefarious efforts here in the U.S. due to their successful ability to hide in plain sight," describing these non-traditional collectors as "shrouded in legitimate work and research."[6]

In July 2021, the Department filed motions to dismiss charges against six Chinese researchers who allegedly lied about and concealed their affiliations with the Chinese Communist Party (CCP) and the Chinese People's Liberation Army (PLA).[7] One of these researchers lied about holding a rank in the PLA and acknowledged to U.S. officials that he "had been instructed by his supervisor, the director of his military university lab in the PRC, to observe the layout of the UCSF [University of California San Francisco] lab and bring back information on how to replicate it in China."[8] Another spy reportedly attempted to destroy evidence of her PLA affiliations, including an image of her PLA credentials, a photo of her in military uniform, and her true resume.[9] In another case, a "researcher" with PLA connections hid out in the Chinese consulate in San Francisco after being interviewed by investigators, prompting officials to accuse the Chinese government of harboring a known fugitive.[10]

The Department justified dismissing these Chinese espionage cases, claiming that "[r]ecent developments in a handful of cases involving defendants with alleged, undisclosed ties to the People's Liberation Army of the People's Republic of China have prompted the

---

[4] FBI Director Christopher Wray, The Threat Posed by the Chinese Government and the Chinese Communist Party to the Economic and National Security of the United States, Address at the Hudson Institute, (July 7, 2020), https://www.fbi.gov/news/speeches/the-threat-posed-by-the-chinese-government-and-the-chinese-communist-party-to-the-economic-and-national-security-of-the-united-states.

[5] *See* FBI Director Christopher Wray, Responding Effectively to the Chinese Economic Espionage Threat, Address at Department of Justice China Initiative Conference, Center for Strategic and International Studies (Feb. 6, 2020), https://www.fbi.gov/news/speeches/responding-effectively-to-the-chinese-economic-espionage-threat ("[T]he Chinese government doesn't play by the same rules of academic integrity and freedom that the U.S. does. . . . We know that through their 'Thousand Talents Plan' and similar programs, they try to entice scientists at our universities to bring their knowledge to China—even if that means stealing proprietary information or violating export controls or conflict-of-interest policies to do so."); *see also* Press Release, U.S. DEP'T OF JUSTICE, The China Initiative: Year-in-Review (2019-20) (Nov. 16, 2020), https://www.justice.gov/opa/pr/china-initiative-year-review-2019-20 ("At the outset, the Department identified academia as one of our most vulnerable sectors, because its traditions of openness, and the importance of international exchanges to the free flow of ideas, leave it vulnerable to PRC exploitation.").

[6] *Beijing's Long Arm: Threats to U.S. National Security: Hearing Before the S. Select Comm. on Intelligence*, 117th Cong. (Aug. 4, 2021) (testimony of William Evanina,, former Director of the U.S. National Counterintelligence and Security Center), https://www.intelligence.senate.gov/sites/default/files/documents/os-bevanina-080421.pdf.

[7] George P. Varghese, Benjamin Conery, Hyun-Soo Lim, Christina Luo, *DOJ's "China Initiative" Falters*, WILMERHALE (Aug. 5, 2021), https://www.wilmerhale.com/en/insights/client-alerts/20210805-dojs-china-initiative-falters.

[8] Press Release, U.S. DEP'T OF JUSTICE, Researchers Charged with Visa Fraud After Lying About Their Work for China's People's Liberation Army (July 23, 2020), https://www.justice.gov/opa/pr/researchers-charged-visa-fraud-after-lying-about-their-work-china-s-people-s-liberation-army.

[9] *Id.*

[10] *Id.*

department to re-evaluate these prosecutions."[11] The Department said that dismissing the cases was "in the interest of justice."[12] However, other reports suggest the Department dismissed the cases for other reasons, including the FBI supposedly failing to Mirandize and FBI questions about the value of bringing these cases.[13] Others suggest that the timing of the dismissals—mere days before the Deputy Secretary of the State Wendy Sherman's first trip to China—is dubious.[14]

Especially at a time when President Biden's disastrous foreign policy in Afghanistan has alienated allies and alarmed Americans, our country cannot afford the threat to the United States posed by Chinese espionage. We have sought information about the dismissals, but the Department's Office of Legislative Affairs has stonewalled our requests, citing a reluctance to discuss "prosecutorial decisions."[15] These dismissals—including the allegations of misconduct that may have contributed to the decisions—go well beyond mere "prosecutorial decisions." They include potential misconduct and broader Administration policy matters that demand robust congressional oversight. The Department cannot avoid these serious questions.

In light of the Department's sudden reversal on these cases, a lack of details behind those reversals, and to better understand the Department's overall efforts to address the pervasive threats posed by the CCP to U.S. national and economic security, we respectfully request the following information:

1. Please explain why it is "in the interest of justice" to drop the charges against the six alleged Chinese spies.

2. Please explain the "recent developments" that led to the charges being dropped and whether the Deputy Secretary of State's July 2021 trip to China was a factor in the decision.

3. Please explain whether the Justice Department supports the Trump Administration's China Initiative and whether it has any plans to reform, prioritize, or reinforce its duties and responsibilities.

4. Please explain whether the Justice Department believes the DS-160 or any other immigration benefit application or petition filed by these individuals needs clarification with regards to an individual's connections to a foreign military like the PLA. If so, what individual changes need to be made to each application or petition?

---

[11] Katie Benner, *U.S. Moves to Drop Cases Against Chinese Researchers Accused of Hiding Military Ties*, N.Y. TIMES (July 26, 2021), https://www.nytimes.com/2021/07/24/us/politics/chinese-researchers-justice-dept.html.
[12] *Id.*
[13] *Id.*; Aruna Viswanatha, *U.S. Drops Visa Fraud Cases Against Five Chinese Researchers*, WALL STREET JOURNAL (July 23, 2021), https://www.wsj.com/articles/u-s-drops-visa-fraud-cases-against-5-chinese-researchers-11627074870.
[14] *See* K. Lloyd Billingsley, *DOJ Dropping Case Against Chinese Researcher Will Encourage Spying*, THE INDEPENDENT INSTITUTE (July 29, 2021), https://www.independent.org/news/article.asp?id=13692.
[15] Emails between U.S. House Comm. on the Judiciary staff and U.S. Dep't of Justice Office of Legislative Affairs staff (Aug. 2021) (on file with Committee staff).

5. Please explain whether the Justice Department agrees with the Director of the Federal Bureau of Investigation that "[t]he greatest long-term threat to our nation's information and intellectual property, and to our economic vitality, is the counterintelligence and economic espionage threat from China."[16]

6. Please provide the number of active China-related counterintelligence cases the FBI is investigating.

7. Please provide the number of attorneys, support staff, and other resources assigned to the China Initiative.

Please provide this information as soon as possible, but no later than 5:00 p.m. on October 11, 2021. If a full response requires the disclosure of classified information, please provide such information under separate cover. After you have provided this information in writing, we ask that you arrange for the Department to provide a staff-level briefing.

The House Committee on the Judiciary has jurisdiction pursuant to Rule X of the Rules of the House of Representatives to conduct oversight of matters concerning "subversive activities affecting the internal security of the United States" as well as "criminal law enforcement and criminalization." [17]

To schedule the briefing or if you have any questions about this request, please ask your staff to contact Judiciary Committee staff at (202) 225-6906. Thank you for your prompt attention to this matter.

Sincerely,

Jim Jordan
Ranking Member

Andy Biggs
Ranking Member
Subcommittee on Crime, Terrorism, and Homeland Security

cc: The Honorable Jerrold L. Nadler, Chairman, Committee on the Judiciary

The Honorable Sheila Jackson Lee, Chair, Subcommittee on Crime, Terrorism, and Homeland Security

The Honorable Michael E. Horowitz, Inspector General, U.S. Department of Justice

---

[16] FBI Director Christopher Wray, The Threat Posed by the Chinese Government and the Chinese Communist Party to the Economic and National Security of the United States, Address at the Hudson Institute (July 7, 2020), https://www.fbi.gov/news/speeches/the-threat-posed-by-the-chinese-government-and-the-chinese-communist-party-to-the-economic-and-national-security-of-the-united-states.

[17] Rules of the House of Representatives, R. X, 117th Cong. (2021).

JERROLD NADLER, New York
CHAIRMAN

JIM JORDAN, Ohio
RANKING MEMBER

ONE HUNDRED SEVENTEENTH CONGRESS
Congress of the United States
House of Representatives
COMMITTEE ON THE JUDICIARY
2138 RAYBURN HOUSE OFFICE BUILDING
WASHINGTON, DC 20515-6216
(202) 225-3951
judiciary.house.gov

August 12, 2021

The Honorable Merrick B. Garland
Attorney General
U.S. Department of Justice
950 Pennsylvania Avenue, NW
Washington, DC 20530

Dear Attorney General Garland:

On July 28, 2021, on behalf of the Department of Justice (DOJ), you issued new guidance regarding state efforts to remove temporary, emergency voting procedures implemented last year during the unprecedented COVID-19 pandemic.[1] The Biden Administration's new guidance bizarrely suggests that states may not return to voting laws and procedures that existed prior to the pandemic, saying those laws and procedures may not be "presumptively lawful."[2] We have serious concerns about the Department's radical attempt to politicize enforcement of the Voting Rights Act of 1965 (VRA).

The Election Clause of the U.S. Constitution gives state legislatures the authority to prescribe "[t]he Times, Places and Manner of holding Elections" within their jurisdictions.[3] Article II of the U.S. Constitution grants state legislatures the power to determine the manner of appointing presidential electors.[4] Thus, in our system of government, state legislatures "bear primary responsibility for setting election rules,"[5] and this responsibility extends to federal elections.[6]

In 2020, state and local governments were tasked with administering elections in a safe manner during a once-in-a-lifetime pandemic. Many states adopted temporary voting procedures to reduce public health risks, despite prominent public health officials saying that in-person voting was safe.[7] Recognizing the temporary nature of these voting procedure changes, Attorney General William Barr directed the Civil Rights Division to adopt an enforcement policy that

---

[1] Press Release, U.S. Dep't of Justice, Justice Department Issues Guidance on Federal Statutes Regarding Voting Methods and Post-election "Audits" (Jul. 28, 2021).
[2] U.S. DEP'T OF JUSTICE, GUIDANCE CONCERNING FEDERAL STATUTES AFFECTING METHODS OF VOTING 1 (2021).
[3] U.S. CONST. art I § 4, cl. 1.
[4] U.S. CONST. art. II, § 1, cl. 2.
[5] *Democratic Nat'l Comm. v. Wisconsin State Legislature,* 141 U.S. 28, 29 (2020) (Gorsuch, J., concurring).
[6] *See* U.S. CONST. art I § 4, cl. 1; U.S. CONST. art. II, § 1, cl. 2.
[7] Nsikan Akpan, *What Fauci says the U.S. really needs to reopen safely*, NAT'L GEOGRAPHIC (Aug. 13, 2020).

would "presume[] lawful" a state's re-adoption of prior election laws or procedures.[8] Attorney General Barr explained:

> Both the Constitution and federal statutory law recognize that state and local jurisdictions can and will address changing circumstances, sometimes-unique local issues, and different policy preferences related to voting, and that their voting-related laws and processes will change from time to time.
>
> * * *
>
> This care [to respect state and local authority] is particularly important when a state or local jurisdiction maintains a voting-related procedure that is lawful, then changes to another lawful procedure, then changes back to the original procedure. The Department of Justice will presume that enactment of a state or local voting-related procedure that reverts back to or adopts a state or local jurisdiction's prior lawful voting procedures complies with federal law.[9]

On February 3, 2021, then-Acting Attorney General Monty Wilkinson abruptly rescinded Attorney General Barr's guidance.[10] Then, on July 28, you issued a new guidance that upended the constitutional balance between state and federal governments with respect to voting-related laws. You wrote:

> The Department's enforcement policy does not consider a jurisdiction's re-adoption of prior voting laws or procedures to be presumptively lawful; instead, the Department will review a jurisdiction's changes in voting laws or procedures for compliance with all federal laws regarding elections, as the facts and circumstances warrant.[11]

The new guidance is misguided and contrary to Congressional intent. Many of the changes that state and local governments made to voting procedures in 2020 were temporary, emergency changes to "promote both the safety of their citizens and robust democratic participation" during the pandemic.[12] These jurisdictions should be allowed to evaluate the changing circumstances and their experiences in 2020 and make appropriate lawful changes, without the threat of litigation from the federal government. With your new guidance, the Department instead takes the position that these temporary, emergency measures are the new

---

[8] Memorandum from Hon. William P. Barr, Atty Gen., U.S. Dep't of Justice to Assistant Atty Gen. of the Civil Rights Division (Dec. 22, 2020).

[9] *Id.* at 2-3.

[10] Memorandum from Hon. Monty Wilkinson, Acting Atty Gen., U.S. Dep't of Justice, to U.S. Attys (Feb. 3, 2021).

[11] U.S. DEP'T OF JUSTICE, GUIDANCE CONCERNING FEDERAL STATUTES AFFECTING METHODS OF VOTING 1 (2021).

[12] *Id.*

baseline from which to judge compliance with the VRA—contrary to Congress's intention in passing the legislation.[13]

Whether wittingly or not, your new guidance makes you complicit in a broader effort by elected Democrats to politicize federal voting rights laws. Democrats allege that recent lawful state voter integrity measures, such as Georgia's S.B. 202 and proposed Texas legislation, constitutes "Jim Crow 2.0" and "voter suppression."[14] In reality, these states are enacting commonsense voter integrity measures, many of which *increase* voting access beyond what is available in Democrat-run states. For example, Georgia's new law provides 17 days of early voting while President Biden's home state of Delaware will only have ten days beginning in 2022.[15] New York only provides ten days of early voting.[16] In addition, the pending Texas legislation would prohibit drive-through and 24-hour voting, which local jurisdictions implemented temporarily due to the pandemic and the practices were not implemented by the whole state.[17] Both Delaware and New York currently do not allow drive-through or 24-hour voting.[18]

Although it is easier to vote in Georgia than some Democrat-run states, the Department filed suit against the state to enjoin several provisions of S.B. 202.[19] Notably, the Department did not file suit against Delaware or New York. These facts make it appear that you are attempting to enforce the VRA based on partisan considerations rather than blindly applying the facts to the law. One commentator rightly noted that your complaint against Georgia read "more like a press release from the Democratic National Committee than a serious lawsuit by an apolitical Justice Department."[20]

You and the Justice Department are sadly playing into the hands of the baseless and partisan Democrat opposition to state voting reform efforts by politicizing VRA enforcement and making it the policy that any change from temporary, emergency COVID-19 voting methods is presumed to be evidence of voter suppression.[21] At a time when Congressional Democrats are considering unprecedented and brazen attempts to federalize our nation's election processes, we strongly urge you to rescind the July 28, 2021 guidance and to reimplement Attorney General Barr's thoughtful guidance. In addition, we request that you provide the following information:

---

[13] *See generally* S. REP. NO. 109-295, at 2 (2006).

[14] *See* Karl Rove, *Biden's election-reform deception,* WALL ST. J. (Mar. 31, 2021); Chandelis Duster, *Abrams on GOP efforts to target voting: "It is a redux of Jim Crow in a suit and tie',* CNN (Mar. 14, 2021); Kathryn Watson, *Biden denounces "21st century Jim Crow assault" on voting access*, CBS NEWS (Jul. 13, 2021).

[15] S.B. 202, 2021 Gen. Assemb., Reg. Sess. (Ga. 2021). *See also* Nat'l Conference of State Legislatures, State Laws Governing Early Voting, https://www.ncsl.org/research/elections-and-campaigns/early-voting-in-state-elections.aspx (last visited Jul. 29, 2021).

[16] *Id.*

[17] *'No constitutional right to have 24-hour voting,' Gov. Abbott speaks to KHOU II about voting rights, results of 2020 election*, KHOU-11 (Jul. 14, 2021).

[18] Karl Rove, *Texas Democrats Suppress the Vote*, WALL ST. J. (Jul. 14, 2021).

[19] Erin Doherty, *Justice Department sues Georgia over GOP voting restrictions,* AXIOS (Jun. 25, 2021).

[20] Hans A. von Spakovsky & Zack Smith, *In the feds versus Georgia's voting law, bet on Georgia,* Heritage Found. (Jul. 6, 2021).

[21] *See generally* Editorial Board, *Biden Justice Plays Election Politics*, WALL ST. J. (Jun. 27, 2021).

1. All documents and communications referring or relating to the memorandum entitled "Guidance Concerning Federal Statutes Affecting Methods of Voting" and dated July 28, 2021;

2. All documents and communications referring or relating to the complaint filed by the Department of Justice against the State of Georgia in the Northern District of Georgia on June 25, 2021; and

3. All documents and communications between or among the Department of Justice and the Executive Office of the President referring or relating to state reforms to voting laws.

Please provide this information immediately but no later than 5:00 p.m. on August 23, 2021.

Americans deserve free, fair, and accurate elections—and ones in which all Americans have confidence in the results. To achieve this ideal, enforcement of the VRA and other federal statutes protecting the right to vote must be apolitical. Thank you for your attention to this serious matter.

Sincerely,

Jim Jordan
Ranking Member

Mike Johnson
Ranking Member Subcommittee on Constitution, Civil Rights, and Civil Liberties

cc: The Honorable Jerrold Nadler, Chairman

The Honorable Steve Cohen, Chairman, Subcommittee on Constitution, Civil Rights, and Civil Liberties

JERROLD NADLER, New York
CHAIRMAN

JIM JORDAN, Ohio
RANKING MEMBER

ONE HUNDRED SEVENTEENTH CONGRESS

Congress of the United States

House of Representatives

COMMITTEE ON THE JUDICIARY
2138 RAYBURN HOUSE OFFICE BUILDING
WASHINGTON, DC 20515–6216
(202) 225–3951
judiciary.house.gov

August 11, 2021

The Honorable Christopher A. Wray
Director
Federal Bureau of Investigation
935 Pennsylvania Avenue, N.W.
Washington, DC 20535

Dear Director Wray:

On July 14, 2021, the Cato Institute reported that it had obtained a Federal Bureau of Investigation (FBI) document detailing a "Charity Assessment" of Concerned Women for America (CWA) conducted by the FBI's Washington Field Office.[1] Significant portions of the document are redacted, but it shows that the FBI examined CWA in July 2016 for potential financial crimes merely because third-party charity rating services deemed the charity to be "underperform[ing]."[2] While CWA is a domestic organization that advocates for certain policies at the federal, state, and local levels, the document also notes that there was an "Intelligence" component to the FBI's assessment.[3] The assessment ultimately recommended against opening an investigation into CWA.

This document raises serious questions about the FBI's targeting of domestic civil society organizations on the basis of a third-party opinion, and not any credible allegation of a crime. During your recent appearance before our Committee, you testified that the FBI "investigate[s] individuals with proper predication" and does not "investigate First Amendment groups . . . [or] people for speech, association, for assembly, [or] for membership in domestic First Amendment groups."[4] The existence of this assessment, however, raises a question of whether the policy you described at the hearing was in place at the FBI in July 2016 under then-Director Comey and whether these "charity assessments" continue in some form today.

To assist the Committee in conducting oversight of the FBI's assessment of CWA and its use of such assessments more broadly, please provide the following information:

---

[1] *See* Patrick G. Eddington, *The FBI's Unjustified Targeting of Concerned Women for America*, CATO INSTITUTE (Jul. 14, 2021). The document was obtained through a Freedom of Information Act request. *See Id.*
[2] *See* Charity Assessment: Concerned Women for America, Federal Bureau of Investigation (Jul. 5, 2016) (on file with the Committee).
[3] *Id.*; *see also What We Do*, CONCERNED WOMEN FOR AMERICA, https://concernedwomen.org/what-we-do-2/.
[4] *Oversight of the Federal Bureau of Investigation: Hearing before the H. Comm. on the Judiciary*, 117th Cong. (2021).

1. An unredacted copy of the FBI electronic communication titled "Charity Assessment: Concerned Women for America" dated July 5, 2016;

2. All documents and communications referring or relating to the FBI's assessment of CWA;

3. A staff-level briefing on the FBI's assessment of CWA, including when it began, when it concluded, the basis for conducting the assessment, and what methods were used to conduct the assessment;

4. An accounting of all assessments conducted by the FBI since January 1, 2016, including the identity of the target, the predicate for undertaking the assessment, and whether the assessment led to the opening of a formal investigation; and

5. Unredacted copies of all "Charity Assessments" conducted by the FBI between January 1, 2016, and the present.

Please provide this information and briefing as soon as possible but not later than 5:00 p.m. on August 24, 2021. If you have any questions about this request, please contact Committee staff at (202) 225-6906.

Thank you for your prompt attention to this matter.

Sincerely,

Jim Jordan
Ranking Member

cc: The Honorable Jerrold L. Nadler, Chairman

JERROLD NADLER, New York
CHAIRMAN

JIM JORDAN, Ohio
RANKING MEMBER

ONE HUNDRED SEVENTEENTH CONGRESS

Congress of the United States

House of Representatives

COMMITTEE ON THE JUDICIARY

2138 RAYBURN HOUSE OFFICE BUILDING
WASHINGTON, DC 20515-6216
(202) 225-3951
judiciary.house.gov

July 26, 2021

The Honorable Christopher A. Wray
Director
Federal Bureau of Investigation
935 Pennsylvania Avenue, N.W.
Washington, DC 20535

Dear Director Wray:

On June 10, 2021, you testified before the Committee during our annual oversight hearing of the Federal Bureau of Investigation (FBI).[1] During that hearing, you committed to follow up with information and responses to a number of questions. Over a month has passed, and the FBI has not yet complied with many of these outstanding requests. We write to ask that you provide the requested information immediately.

Of notable concern, both Republicans and Democrats questioned you about the serious and systematic problems with the FBI's use of its warrantless electronic surveillance powers under section 702 of the Foreign Intelligence Surveillance Act. Members requested a briefing on the matter, which you agreed to provide. The FBI has not yet provided this briefing, let alone begin to schedule the briefing.

In addition, the FBI has not yet provided responses to questions for the record posed following your testimony at the Committee's 2020 oversight hearing. For instance, on February 12, 2020, Representative Mike Johnson posed a number of questions for the record pertaining to the FBI's Crossfire Hurricane investigation. It is our understanding that you have not answered Representative Johnson's questions. We therefore ask that you provide a copy of your response to the questions for the record from the 2020 hearing.

The FBI must be forthcoming and transparent to Congress and the American people. Both a table of our outstanding requests from your June 2021 testimony and a copy of the February 2020 questions for the record are attached for your convenience. Please provide full responses and information to the Committee as soon as possible but no later than 5:00 p.m. on August 9, 2021.

---

[1] *Oversight of the Federal Bureau of Investigation, Hearing before the H. Comm. on the Judiciary*, 117th Cong. (2021).

Thank you for your attention to this matter.

Sincerely,

Jim Jordan
Ranking Member

cc: The Honorable Jerrold Nadler, Chairman

June 10, 2021 Full Committee Hearing

Member	Member Ask	Wray Response
Rep. Tom McClintock	• Specific number of terrorists, criminals, and gang members apprehended at the southern border • Number of agents and money spent by FBI on border operations • Requested briefing about terrorist border-crossings	"Congressman, I'm not sure that I have that number, but it may be that we can provide the specifics separately."[2] "Again, I'd be happy to see if I can provide specific numbers and information to be helpful to your request separately. So I'm happy to follow up with your staff on that."[3] "Again, I'm happy to see what information we can provide to be helpful."[4]
Rep. Matt Gaetz	• Requested any scientific analysis that the FBI has done regarding Dr. Li-Meng Yan's COVID-19 origin claims	"I am happy to see what information we can provide. I will have my staff follow up with yours and see what information we can share on the subject."[5] "Let me commit to you that I will go back with my folks and see what information can be provided and what form it would have to take if we can provide any."[6]
Rep. Victoria Spartz	• Re-requested same section 702 briefing as Lofgren as well as FBI's internal	"Sure, we'd be happy to provide a briefing, but certainly before the end of –"[7]

[2] *Id.* at 22.
[3] *Id.* at 23.
[4] *Id.* at 24.
[5] *Id.* at 53.
[6] *Id.* at 54.
[7] *Id.* at 71.

	FISA audit initiatives by end of fiscal year	
Rep. Chip Roy	• Briefing on Jan. 6 prosecutions/investigations • Requested additional information about FBI's role in assisting CBP to combat drug trafficking at the southern border	"I am happy to see what kind of briefing we could provide to the committee."[8] "I'll provide a brief answer, and then maybe we can supply some more information after the fact."[9]
Rep. Tom Tiffany	• Requested information on FBI's handling of Bernell Trammell murder case in Milwaukee, Wisconsin	"Certainly, I am happy to follow up with our Milwaukee office to see what the status of that particular issue is."[10]
Rep. Thomas Massie	• Asked FBI to work with DNI to look at JASTA families • Requested investigation whether there is racial disparity in the NICS system background checks	"Well, I will make sure that our folks are doing everything they possibly can consistent with our responsibilities."[11] "I am happy to take a look with the DNI and others to see if there's more information that can be declassified."[12] "I am happy to look further into the issue. I might have my staff follow up with yours to see -- make sure that we have the same information that you are referring to. But certainly, you've raised issues that would -- that I'd want to look into further."[13]

[8] *Id.* at 87.
[9] *Id.* at 89.
[10] *Id.* at 109.
[11] *Id.* at 113.
[12] *Id.* at 114.
[13] *Id.* at 115.

Rep. Andy Biggs	• Requested responses and information to questions one and two in his and Ranking Member Jordan's May 4, 2021 letter about reported FISA abuses	"I can look and see if there's more information we can provide you, perhaps in a classified setting."[14] "I'd have to check. I know that we deal with the FISC fairly regularly and provide all sorts of reports to them."[15] "I am happy to see what information we can provide you. The court, though, does not speak in terms of improprieties, and I think the court knows how to use that term when that's what it thinks it's found."[16]

[14] *Id.* at 95.
[15] *Id.*
[16] *Id.* at 96.

U.S. Congressman Mike Johnson
U.S. House Committee on the Judiciary
Questions for the Record
February 12, 2020

Hearing – "Oversight of the Federal Bureau of Investigation"

Director Wray, as you are aware Former Special Counsel Mueller brought on members of the FBI onto the Special Counsel's team when Crossfire Hurricane was transferred from the FBI to the Special Counsel. In Mr. Mueller's subsequent appearance before this Committee he refused to answer any questions related to the Steele Dossier. With that in mind, I would like to ask you a few questions regarding this phase of the investigation:

1. To your knowledge did Former Special Counsel Mueller ever question any of the Steele Dossier origins after or during the transition of Crossfire Hurricane from the FBI to the Special Counsel's team?

2. Are you aware of any FBI personnel that were not part of the Mueller team being asked by Former Director Mueller to carry out tasks during his tenure as Special Counsel?

3. In addition to addressing the relevant deficiencies found in the IG report, are you internally examining FBI protocols surrounding the transfer of investigations to a Special Counsel, particularly in instances where FBI staff are used by the Special Counsel?

4. Have you considered updating any sections of relevant Policy Implementation Guides or the Domestic Investigations Operations Guide (DIOG) regarding FBI interactions, or the transfer of investigations, to a Special Counsel?

JERROLD NADLER, New York
CHAIRMAN

JIM JORDAN, Ohio
RANKING MEMBER

ONE HUNDRED SEVENTEENTH CONGRESS

Congress of the United States

House of Representatives

COMMITTEE ON THE JUDICIARY

2138 RAYBURN HOUSE OFFICE BUILDING

WASHINGTON, DC 20515–6216

(202) 225–3951
judiciary.house.gov

July 21, 2021

The Honorable Michael E. Horowitz
Inspector General
U.S. Department of Justice
950 Pennsylvania Avenue NW, Suite 4706
Washington, D.C. 20530

Dear Inspector General Horowitz:

On July 20, 2021, the Justice Department Office of Inspector General (OIG) released an "investigative summary" with findings of misconduct by a former senior Federal Bureau of Investigation (FBI) official.[1] The investigative summary states, in relevant part:

> The OIG investigation substantiated the allegation that the Senior FBI Official had numerous unauthorized contacts with the media from 2014 through 2016, in violation of FBI policy. In addition to substantive communications with reporters, this media contact included unauthorized social engagements outside of FBI Headquarters involving drinks, lunches, and dinners. The OIG also found that the Senior FBI Official violated federal regulations and FBI policy when the Senior FBI Official accepted tickets from members of the media to two black tie dinner events, one valued at $225 and the other valued at $300, and received transportation to one event from a reporter, all without prior authorization.[2]

The investigative summary explains that the unnamed senior official retired from the FBI before an OIG interview could occur.[3] When asked to sit for a voluntary interview, the senior official declined.[4] The OIG also noted in the investigative summary that this investigation grew

---

[1] INSPECTOR GEN., DEP'T OF JUSTICE, *Findings of Misconduct by a Then-Senior FBI Official for Having Numerous Unauthorized Contacts with the Media, and for Accepting Unauthorized Gifts from Members of the Media* (July 2021) [hereinafter OIG Investigative Summary].
[2] OIG Investigative Summary.
[3] *Id.*
[4] *Id.*

out of OIG's investigation of misconduct by the FBI and Department of Justice in advance of the 2016 election.[5]

To allow the Committee to better understand the OIG's findings, determine the extent of this serious misconduct, and evaluate the FBI's handling of the matter, I ask that you please provide the complete unredacted case file for Investigative Summary 21-096, to include all documents, communications, and other evidence related to the report.

Please provide this information as soon as possible but no later than 5:00 p.m. on August 4, 2021. Thank you for your attention to this important matter.

Sincerely,

Jim Jordan
Ranking Member

cc: The Honorable Jerrold Nadler, Chairman

[5] INSPECTOR GEN., DEP'T OF JUSTICE, *A Review of Various Actions by the Federal Bureau of Investigation and Department of Justice in Advance of the 2016 Election* (June 2018).

KEVIN McCARTHY
23RD DISTRICT, CALIFORNIA

REPUBLICAN LEADER

H-204, U.S. CAPITOL
WASHINGTON, DC 20515
(202) 225-4000

www.republicanleader.gov

Congress of the United States
House of Representatives
Washington, DC 20515-6538

June 11, 2021

The Honorable Merrick B. Garland
Attorney General
U.S. Department of Justice
950 Pennsylvania Avenue, N.W.
Washington, DC 20530-0001

Dear Mr. Attorney General:

As you begin your tenure as our nation's 86th Attorney General, one issue that demands your immediate attention is the alarming rise in crime rates across the United States. Crime has increased in American cities over the past year—dramatically in some cases—as cities have moved to defund their police forces. Now, as many police departments are bracing for what experts predict will be a violent summer,[1] we are concerned about whether the Biden Administration is prepared to address the surge of violent crime in American cities.[2]

The radical and reckless decisions by some jurisdictions to defund their police forces have had a real and devastating effect on American communities. Crime is on the rise in nearly every category, but perhaps most disturbing is the increase in homicides in major American cities. The murder rate in major cities increased 33 percent overall in 2020, making it the worst year since the mid-1990s.[3] Austin, Texas, saw a 50 percent spike in homicides in 2020,[4] and Los Angeles experienced an increase of 11.6 percent in homicides.[5] In Minneapolis, the homicide rate increased 72 percent,[6] while Portland, Oregon, witnessed the most murders in a year in 27

---

[1] Bryan Walsh, *It's set to be a hot, violent summer*, Axios (May 1,2021), https://www.axios.com/murder-rates-rise-2021-coronavirus-pandemic-0b9855ad-4b54-4639-ad1f-871e8aa03063.html

[2] *See* Sadie Gurman, *Police Overhauls Help Fight Crime, Biden Administration Official Says*, Wall St. J. (May 26, 2021), https://www.wsj.com/article/police-overhauls-help-fight-crime-biden-administration-official-says-11622031515.

[3] Emma Tucker and Peter Nickeas, *The US saw significant crime rise across major cities in 2020. And it's not letting up*, CNN (April 3, 2021) https://www.cnn.com/2021/04/03/us/us-crime-rate-rise-2020/index.html.

[4] Jon Hilsenrath, *Homicide Spike Hits Most Large U.S. Cities,* Wall St. J. (Aug 2, 2020), https://www.wsj.com/articles/homicide-spike-cities-chicago-newyork-detroit-us-crime-police-lockdown-coronavirus-protests-11596395181.

[5] Julie Wernau and Joe Barnett, *Police Wrestle with Surge in Crime in U.S. Cities Amid Defunding Efforts*, Wall St. J. (July 11, 2020) https://www.wsj.com/articles/police-wrestle-with-surge-in-crime-in-u-s-cities-amid-defunding-efforts-11594472400?mod=article_ inline.

[6] Stephanie Pagones, *Crime Wave 2020: These cities smashed homicide records amid nationwide crime spike*, Fox News (Dec. 30, 2020), https://www.foxnews.com/us/crime-wave-2020-homicide-records-nationwide-crime-spike

years.[7] In Chicago, 18 people were murdered in a single day in 2020—the city's most violent day in six decades.[8]

The early data shows no improvement in crime rates for 2021. According to recent data, several major American cities have reported increased homicide rates in the first quarter of 2021 compared to the same period in 2020.[9] For example, Chicago has experienced a 36 percent increase in homicides in 2021.[10] Philadelphia reported a 25 percent increase in homicides so far in 2021, and Los Angeles reported a 41 percent increase.[11]

In the face of deteriorating public safety in American communities, it confounds us, and we hope you, that cities across the country even entertain the idea of defunding their police departments. Yet, over the past year, we have seen several major cities pursue these radical and reckless policies. Last year, Los Angeles defunded its police department to the tune of $150 million, reducing its police force to its lowest levels in a decade.[12] San Francisco cut its police budget by $120 million,[13] even as the city reported significant increases in homicides, burglaries, arsons, and thefts.[14] Seattle cut its police budget by $69 million as homicides in the city hit the highest levels in over a decade.[15] Most shockingly, after slashing its police budget by nearly $1 billion, New York City saw a 97 percent rise in shootings and almost a 45 percent increase in homicides.[16] And, notably, the Congressional Budget Office confirmed that H.R. 1280, the "George Floyd Justice in Policing Act of 2021," passed on a party line vote in the House of Representatives in March, would place an unfunded mandate on state and local police departments, costing them "several hundred million of dollars annually."[17]

---

[7] Pat Dooris, *Portland has had 52 homicides so far this year, the most in 27 years*, KGW8 (Dec. 18, 2020), https://www.kgw.com/article/news/crime/most-homicides-in-portland-in-27-years/283-b530bef4-5e02-4722-a418-8f50bf03e3fe

[8] Tommy Beer, *18 People Were Murdered In Chicago On May 31, Making It The City's Single Deadliest Day In 60 Years*, Forbes (Jun. 8, 2020), https://www.forbes.com/sites/tommybeer/2020/06/08/18-people-were-murdered-in-chicago-on-may-31-making-it-the-citys-single-deadliest-day-in-60-years/?sh=10c2613f7fb7

[9] *VIOLENT CRIME SURVEY – NATIONAL TOTALS First Quarter Comparison January 1 to March 31, 2021 and 2020*, Report, Major City Chiefs of Police, (May 14, 2021), https://majorcitieschiefs.com/wp-content/uploads/2021/05/MCCA-Violent-Crime-Report-2021-and-2020-First-Quarter.pdf

[10] *Id.*

[11] *Id.*

[12] Erin Myers and Rick Chambers, *L.A. cuts LAPD spending by $150 million, taking police staffing to lowest level in more than a decade*, Associated Press, (Jul. 1, 2020), available at https://ktla.com/news/local-news/l-a-cuts-lapd-spending-by-150-million-taking-police-staffing-to-its-lowest-level-in-12-years/

[13] Alix Martichoux, *San Francisco Mayor London Breed Announces Cuts to Police in New City Budget*, ABC 7 News (July 31, 2020).

[14] Ella Sogomonian, *Criminals Are Shifting their Behavior amid the Pandemic: San Francisco Police*, KRON 4 News (Dec. 15, 2020).

[15] Mairead McArdle, *Seattle to Slash Police Budget as Homicides Hit Highest Level in over a Decade*, Nat'l Review (Dec. 1, 2020).

[16] Ben Chapman, *New York City Homicides and Shootings Rose Dramatically in 2020*, Wall St. J. (Jan. 7, 2021), https://www.wsj.com/articles/new-york-city-homicides-and-shootings-rose-dramatically-in-2020-11610055243.

[17] Swagel, Philip L. "H.R. 1280, the George Floyd Justice in Policing Act of 2021." Received by The Honorable Jason Smith, 9 Mar. 2021, www.cbo.gov/system/files/2021-03/Hon_Jason_Smith_Response_Letter_0.pdf.

The mission of the Department of Justice is, in part, to ensure public safety and to provide federal leadership in preventing crime.[18] Now, more than ever, the men and women of American law-enforcement agencies across the country need strong and vocal federal support. As local law enforcement agencies brace for a difficult summer, we ask that you reject the radical demands of those who wish to weaken law enforcement by defunding the police and other tactics. We must support law enforcement and the vital work they do each day to serve our communities and keep us safe. Of primary importance is the strong support that you and the U.S. Department of Justice can provide by rejecting radical and reckless proposals to defund the police.

Thank you for your prompt attention to this matter.

Sincerely,

Kevin McCarthy
Republican Leader

Jim Jordan
Ranking Member
Committee on the Judiciary

[18] Dep't of Justice, About DOJ, Our Mission Statement, https://www.justice.gov/about.

Congress of the United States
Washington, DC 20515

June 10, 2021

The Honorable Merrick Garland
Attorney General of the United States
U.S. Department of Justice
950 Pennsylvania Avenue, NW
Washington, DC 20530

Dear Attorney General Garland:

We write to inquire into the Department of Justice's (DOJ) efforts to investigate a massive leak of the sensitive tax information of thousands of Americans from the Internal Revenue Service (IRS). Leaks of tax information, particularly by government officials entrusted with caring for that sensitive information, are completely unacceptable. Those responsible must be pursued to the fullest extent of the law.

On June 8, 2021, ProPublica published an article relying on "a vast cache of IRS information."[1] In a gross breach of public trust, it appears someone illegally leaked this sensitive and non-public information. The article contains details of federal tax filings going back more than a decade, involving individuals from across the business and political spectrum, including Jeff Bezos, Elon Musk, Bill Gates, Warren Buffett, Rupert Murdoch, Michael Bloomberg, and George Soros.[2] In fact, ProPublica alleges it obtained data "on the tax returns of thousands of the nation's wealthiest people, covering more than 15 years."[3]

Tax returns are filled with personal, private, and sensitive information including social security numbers and intimate details of one's financial situation. As you are aware, federal law requires that "[r]eturns and return information shall be confidential"[4] except as otherwise authorized by limited exceptions in federal law. "No officer or employee of the United States . . . shall disclose any return or return information obtained by him in any manner in connection with his service . . . ."[5] Furthermore, it is a felony for a federal officer or employee to unlawfully disclose tax return information.[6] Given the nature of this data, it appears very likely that a Federal officer or employee leaked that protected information to ProPublica.

Whether it is George Soros or Rupert Murdoch, every American should have confidence that their personal tax information is secure and safe from privacy violations. Especially as the

---

[1] *See* Eisinger, Jesse et. al., *The Secret IRS Files: Trove of Never-Before-Seen Records Reveal How the Wealthiest Avoid Income Tax*, PROPUBLICA (Jun. 8, 2021), *available at* https://www.propublica.org/article/the-secret-irs-files-trove-of-never-before-seen-records-reveal-how-the-wealthiest-avoid-income-tax.
[2] *Id.*
[3] *Id.*
[4] 26 U.S.C. § 6103(a).
[5] *Id.*
[6] 26 U.S.C. § 7213(a)(1).

Biden Administration's proposed budget would vastly increase the size and staffing of the IRS,[7] we are concerned about the potential for future leaks of sensitive tax information, particularly if such leaks are politically motivated or targeted against those who may take unpopular positions. Such leaks will continue to deteriorate the American people's trust in the IRS, and our federal government.

To assist the Committees in conducting oversight over this egregious and potentially criminal leak of personal tax information, we request a staff-level briefing no later than June 17, 2021 on efforts by the DOJ to investigate and bring those responsible to justice, as well as the following:

1. All documents and communications regarding efforts to enforce federal tax confidentiality law within the Department of Justice, particularly as those efforts relate to preventing Internal Revenue Service officials from misusing their positions to disclose confidential tax information; and

2. All documents and communications regarding efforts to investigate the leak of tax records which form the basis of the ProPublica article referenced above, including whether any criminal inquiry has been opened.

To make arrangements for the briefing, document delivery, or to ask any related follow-up questions, please contact Committee on Oversight and Reform Republican Staff at (202) 225-5074.

The Committee on Oversight and Reform is the principal oversight committee of the U.S. House of Representatives and has broad authority to investigate "any matter" at "any time" under House Rule X. Thank you for your cooperation with this inquiry.

Sincerely,

James Comer
Ranking Member
Committee on Oversight and Reform

Jim Jordan
Ranking Member
Committee on the Judiciary

Rodney Davis
Ranking Member
Committee on House Administration

[7] *See* The White House, Office of Management and Budget, *Budget of the U.S. Government, FY 2022, available at* https://www.whitehouse.gov/wp-content/uploads/2021/05/budget_fy22.pdf.

cc: The Honorable Carolyn Maloney, Chairwoman, Committee on Oversight and Reform
The Honorable Jerrold Nadler, Chairman, Committee on the Judiciary
The Honorable Zoe Lofgren, Chairwoman, Committee on House Administration

JERROLD NADLER, New York
CHAIRMAN

JIM JORDAN, Ohio
RANKING MEMBER

ONE HUNDRED SEVENTEENTH CONGRESS

Congress of the United States
House of Representatives

COMMITTEE ON THE JUDICIARY
2138 RAYBURN HOUSE OFFICE BUILDING
WASHINGTON, DC 20515–6216
(202) 225–3951
judiciary.house.gov

June 8, 2021

The Honorable Merrick B. Garland
Attorney General
U.S. Department of Justice
950 Pennsylvania Avenue, N.W.
Washington, DC 20530

Dear Attorney General Garland:

On May 28, 2021, journalist Andy Ngo was attacked and severely beaten by Antifa and other left-wing extremists while reporting on the ongoing violence in Portland, Oregon.[1] Mr. Ngo was able to barely escape the extremists after seeking refuge in a nearby hotel and receiving an escort by a Portland Fire and Rescue first responder to an ambulance, which transported him to a nearby emergency room.[2] We have repeatedly urged the Biden Administration to address the left-wing violence in Portland. Your refusal to do so has only emboldened these radical agitators to the degree that they feel comfortable targeting and viciously attacking a member of the press.

On February 24, 2021, Mr. Ngo provided testimony to our Committee about how the actions of Antifa and left-wing anarchists in Portland, Oregon have "resulted in a murder, hundreds of arson attacks, mass injuries, and mass property destruction."[3] In his testimony, Mr. Ngo stressed to the Congress the importance of not "downplaying Antifa's violent extremism."[4] Following his near-death experience at the hands of Antifa, Mr. Ngo called on "Portland Police and federal authorities to act on this before Antifa operatives hiding behind their masks succeed in murdering an American journalist on their watch."[5]

After the Committee received Mr. Ngo's testimony, Ranking Member Jordan wrote to you with questions about how the Justice Department would enforce federal law and protect federal property from left-wing violence in Portland, Oregon.[6] You ignored this inquiry. When

---

[1] Andy Ngo (@MrAndyNgo), Twitter, (Jun. 2, 2021, 9:42 PM), https://twitter.com/MrAndyNgo/status/1400266501601513475; Lee Brown, *Author Andy Ngo, who exposed Antifa, says he was beaten by 'masked mob,'* N.Y. POST (Jun. 3, 2021).
[2] *Id.*
[3] *Rise of Domestic Terrorism in America: Hearing Before the H. Subcomm. On Crime, Terrorism and Homeland Security of the H. Comm. On the Judiciary*, 117th Cong. (2021) (statement of Andy Ngo).
[4] *Id.*
[5] Andy Ngo (@MrAndyNgo), Twitter, (Jun. 2, 2021, 9:42), https://twitter.com/MrAndyNgo/status/1400266593377165313.
[6] Letter from Jim Jordan, Ranking Member, H. Comm. on Judiciary, to Merrick B. Garland, Attorney General, U.S. Dep't of Justice (Mar. 29, 2021) (on file with Committee).

Ranking Member Jordan wrote to you again to emphasize the seriousness of the issue, you again failed to respond.[7] The Biden Administration's tacit acceptance of left-wing political violence in Portland and the accompanying attacks on journalists is unacceptable and dangerous. Your acceptance of left-wing political violence in Portland will only incentivize further violence and attacks.

The Biden Administration has an obligation to protect Mr. Ngo and other journalists from Antifa's orchestrated campaign of violence and intimidation.[8] To better understand the Department of Justice's efforts to protect the civil rights of Mr. Ngo and other journalists reporting on left-wing political violence in Portland, we respectfully request the following information:

1. Please explain the Justice Department's current efforts to identify and prosecute individuals involved in the assaults of Mr. Ngo and other journalists in violation of federal statutes securing their civil rights.

2. Please explain how the Justice Department, in coordination with other relevant federal and state law enforcement agencies, is working to prevent individuals from engaging in violence and intimidation designed to impair the free exercise and enjoyment of rights and privileges that Mr. Ngo and other journalists possess under the Constitution and laws of the United States.

Please provide this information as soon as possible, but no later than 5:00 p.m. on June 22, 2021. After you have provided this information in writing, we ask that you provide an unclassified staff-level briefing.

The House Committee on the Judiciary has jurisdiction over matters concerning "subversive activities affecting the internal security of the United States" as well as "criminal law enforcement and criminalization" under House Rule X.[9]

To schedule the briefing or if you have any questions about this request, please have your staff contact Judiciary Committee staff at (202) 225-6906. Thank you for your prompt attention to this matter.

Sincerely,

Dan Bishop
Member of Congress

Jim Jordan
Ranking Member

---

[7] Letter from Jim Jordan, Ranking Member, H. Comm. on Judiciary, to Merrick B. Garland, Attorney General, U.S. Dep't of Justice (Apr. 27, 2021) (on file with Committee).
[8] *See, e.g.*, 18 U.S.C. § 241; *see also* 42 U.S.C. § 1986.
[9] House Rule X(1)(l), 117th Cong. (2021).

Andy Biggs
Ranking Member
Subcommittee on Crime, Terrorism
and Homeland Security

Mike Johnson
Ranking Member
Subcommittee on the Constitution,
Civil Rights and Civil Liberties

Cliff Bentz
Member of Congress

cc: The Honorable Jerrold L. Nadler, Chairman
The Honorable Sheila Jackson Lee, Chairwoman, Subcommittee on Crime, Terrorism and Homeland Security
The Honorable Steve Cohen, Chairman, Subcommittee on the Constitution, Civil Rights and Civil Liberties

JERROLD NADLER, New York
CHAIRMAN

JIM JORDAN, Ohio
RANKING MEMBER

ONE HUNDRED SEVENTEENTH CONGRESS

Congress of the United States

House of Representatives

COMMITTEE ON THE JUDICIARY

2138 RAYBURN HOUSE OFFICE BUILDING

WASHINGTON, DC 20515-6216

(202) 225-3951
judiciary.house.gov

June 3, 2021

The Honorable Merrick B. Garland
Attorney General
U.S. Department of Justice
950 Pennsylvania Avenue, NW
Washington, DC 20530

Dear Attorney General Garland:

We write to request information about the recent appointment of Susan Hennessey to a senior position in the Justice Department's National Security Division (NSD). Ms. Hennessey's appointment raises serious concerns about potential political bias and perceived conflicts of interest due to her previous statements about high-profile NSD matters.[1] Prior to her appointment, Ms. Hennessey also deleted tens of thousands of public statements from her Twitter account in an apparent effort to conceal her partisan bias.[2] The Justice Department must ensure all NSD employees—and especially those in senior positions—demonstrate objectivity, impartiality, and fairness in all national security matters. Ms. Hennessey's prejudiced statements and her effort to erase her past comments show that she cannot meet this important standard.

In several recent Justice Department investigations involving national security matters, Ms. Hennessey has been an outspoken and partisan critic of Republicans. For example, Ms. Hennessey extensively commented about the Federal Bureau of Investigation's (FBI) investigation into baseless allegations that the Trump campaign colluded with Russia, during which she relentlessly "hyp[ed] Russian collusion allegations."[3] She vouched that Christopher Steele, author of the so-called dossier filled with political opposition research and Russian disinformation, was a "person whose work intelligence professionals take seriously."[4] Although the Mueller investigation and declassified transcripts from the House Permanent Select Committee on Intelligence's investigation showed no evidence of collusion—even the Obama-

---

[1] The Editorial Board, *A Dangerous Pick at Justice,* WALL ST. J., (May 12, 2021); Susan Hennessey, (@Susan_Hennessey), Twitter, (May 10, 2021, 7:36 AM), https://twitter.com/Susan_Hennessey/status/1391718717093040128;

[2] Houston Keene, *New Biden DOJ staffer deleted over 39K tweets, including Russia collusion accusations*, FOX NEWS (May 10, 2021); Tobias Hoonhout and Isaac Schoor, *DOJ Pick Susan Hennessey's Long, Sordid History of Partisan Conspiracy-Mongering*, NAT'L REV. (May 10, 2021); Dan McLaughlin, *Susan Hennessey Brings Resistance Twitter to the Biden DOJ*, NAT'L REV., (May 10, 2021).

[3] The Editorial Board, *A Dangerous Pick at Justice,* WALL ST. J., (May 12, 2021); Susan Hennessey and Benjamin Wittes, *Why Are the Trump Allegations Hanging Around When They Haven't Been Substantiated?*, LAWFARE, (Jan. 17, 2017).

[4] Kimberley Strassel, *The Justice Department's Resident Conspiracy Theorist*, WALL ST. J., (May 13, 2021).

Biden Director of National Intelligence, James Clapper, testified that he saw no such evidence[5]—Ms. Hennessey prejudiced the public narrative and continually peddled a malicious fiction.

Ms. Hennessey was also a vocal critic of U.S. Attorney John Durham's investigation into the targeting of the Trump campaign and transition team, even calling the investigation "partisan silliness."[6] Because this investigation is ongoing and in her new role, Ms. Hennessey may exert supervisory functions over this investigation, her previous statement seriously undercuts any perception of her impartiality. But Ms. Hennessey's statement also suggests her willfulness to disregard serious allegations of misconduct, including findings by the Justice Department Office of Inspector General (OIG) that an FBI attorney altered evidence to support an application to surveil former Trump campaign adviser Carter Page.[7] The OIG also found that this same attorney expressed anti-conservative and anti-Trump bias.[8]

Ms. Hennessey also spoke critically about former National Security Advisor Lieutenant General (LTG) Michael T. Flynn's phone call with Russian Ambassador Sergey Kislyak, saying the conversation "posed a countervailing set of extraordinary circumstances."[9] In reality, Justice Department officials did not find the conversation troubling, and in fact considered it to be "pretty common."[10] However, the FBI used the conversation—which the Obama-Biden Administration leaked to a *Washington Post* columnist—as a pretext to set up LTG Flynn.[11] In an Oval Office meeting, it appears that then-Vice President Biden personally suggested to Justice Department officials that they use the Logan Act to target LTG Flynn, according to handwritten FBI notes.[12] Then-FBI Director James Comey later sent two FBI agents to interview LTG Flynn with the goal "to get him [Flynn] to lie, so we can prosecute or get him [Flynn] fired."[13] Even

---

[5] Transcribed Interview of James Clapper, in Wash. D.C. (July 17, 2017).

[6] Susan Hennessey, (@Susan_Hennessey), Twitter, (Dec. 1, 2020, 12:21 PM), https://twitter.com/ChuckRossDC/status/1391817359174799373/photo/1; The Editorial Board, *A Dangerous Pick at Justice,* WALL ST. J., (May 12, 2021).

[7] INSPECTOR GEN., DEP'T OF JUSTICE, *Review of Four FISA Applications and Other Aspects of the FBI's Crossfire Hurricane Investigation*, xi (2019).

[8] The lawyer texted his FBI colleagues these anti-Trump messages: "the crazies won finally"; "This is the tea party on steroids"; "I just can't imagine the systematic disassembly of the progress we made over the last 8 years;" "Pence is stupid" ; and "vive le resistance." *Id.* at 256.

[9] The Editorial Board, *A Dangerous Pick at Justice,* WALL ST. J., (May 12, 2021).

[10] Mary McCord Transcribed Interview 77, Nov. 1, 2017 ("And, you know, we had some discussions about how we -- you know, this is a statute that hadn't been used ever, you know, in 200 years on the books, and that we imagined that in many incoming administrations, its probably pretty common for incoming officials to reach out to who their counterparts are in advance of the transition to just sort of say we want to start developing a relationship.").

[11] Text Messages, Document 189-1, United States v. Flynn, No. 17-000232 (D.D.C. Apr. 30, 2020). (Documents shows that on January 4, 2017 at 2:22PM Strzok sent a series of text messages including one that stated, "7th floor involved" referencing FBI case Crossfire Razor—the code name for the FBI's case against LTG Flynn—and another text that stated, "Hey don't close RAZOR.").

[12] Handwritten Notes, Document 231-1, United States v. Flynn, No. 17-000232 (D.D.C. June 24, 2020).

[13] Government's Mot. to Dismiss the Criminal Information Against the Defendant Michael T. Flynn, Document 198, United States v. Flynn, No. 17-000232 (D.D.C. May 7, 2020); Josh Gerstein et al., *Documents show FBI debated how to handle investigation of Michael Flynn*, POLITICO (April 29, 2020).

after the Justice Department rightly decided to drop its charges against LTG Flynn in light of this misconduct, Ms. Hennessey called the decision "an astonishing assault on the rule of law."[14]

In addition to her controversial comments about high-profile NSD matters, Ms. Hennessey deleted tens of thousands of statements on her Twitter account prior to announcing her new position.[15] From the timing and volume of deletions, we can only conclude that Ms. Hennessey took such drastic steps to erase her past controversial statements about national security matters and hide her political bias. Ms. Hennessey's political bias is very concerning, but it is equally problematic for a Justice Department employee to exhibit a knowing and concerted effort to conceal inconvenient information. Ms. Hennessey's deletion of these tweets raises serious questions about her commitment to transparency and accountability as a Justice Department employee.

The Obama-Biden Justice Department weaponized the NSD and our intelligence community to target the Trump campaign. Ms. Hennessey played a large role in promoting and legitimizing these attacks. Your decision to hire Ms. Hennessey to a senior position within the NSD suggests that rather than execute the law impartially and without fear or favor, you intend to continue the Obama-Biden Administration's politicization and weaponization of our national security laws. Accordingly, we respectfully write to request that you provide the following information:

1. Explain Ms. Hennessey's role and responsibilities within the Justice Department's NSD;

2. Explain whether Ms. Hennessey was hired as a Schedule C political appointee of the excepted service or under another federal employment category; and

3. Explain whether the Justice Department or any component of the Biden-Harris Administration requested, directed, or suggested that Ms. Hennessey delete her tweets.

Please provide this information as soon as possible but no later than June 17, 2021. Thank you for your prompt attention to this serious matter.

Sincerely,

Jim Jordan
Ranking Member

Andy Biggs
Ranking Member
Subcommittee on Crime, Terrorism
and Homeland Security

---

[14] The Editorial Board, *A Dangerous Pick at Justice,* WALL ST. J., (May 12, 2021); William Davis, *CNN Legal Analyst Decries 'Astonishing Assault On The Rule Of Law' After Flynn Charges Dropped*, DAILY CALLER (May 7, 2020).

[15] Houston Keene, *New Biden DOJ staffer deleted over 39K tweets, including Russian collusion accusations*, Fox News (May 10, 2021).

Mike Johnson
Ranking Member
Subcommittee on the Constitution,
Civil Rights and Civil Liberties

cc: The Honorable Jerrold Nadler, Chairman
The Honorable Sheila Jackson Lee, Chairwoman, Subcommittee on Crime, Terrorism, and Homeland Security
The Honorable Steve Cohen, Chairman, Subcommittee on the Constitution, Civil Rights and Civil Liberties

JERROLD NADLER, New York
CHAIRMAN

JIM JORDAN, Ohio
RANKING MEMBER

ONE HUNDRED SEVENTEENTH CONGRESS

Congress of the United States

House of Representatives

COMMITTEE ON THE JUDICIARY

2138 RAYBURN HOUSE OFFICE BUILDING

WASHINGTON, DC 20515–6216

(202) 225–3951
judiciary.house.gov

May 4, 2021

The Honorable Christopher A. Wray
Director
Federal Bureau of Investigation
935 Pennsylvania Avenue, N.W.
Washington, DC 20535

Dear Director Wray:

According to a recently released opinion from the Foreign Intelligence Surveillance Court (FISC), the Federal Bureau of Investigation (FBI) has been seriously and systemically abusing its warrantless electronic surveillance authority. On April 26, 2021, the Office of the Director of National Intelligence declassified a 67-page FISC memorandum opinion and order from November 2020 detailing the FBI's "apparent widespread violations" of privacy rules in conducting surveillance under section 702 of the Foreign Intelligence Surveillance Act (FISA).[1] We write to request information about the FBI's illegal spying activities.

Section 702 authorizes the Attorney General and the Director of National Intelligence to jointly authorize warrantless surveillance of non-U.S. persons reasonably believed to be located outside the United States, subject to limitations.[2] For example, section 702 requires the adoption of "targeting procedures" to ensure that section 702-acquired information is limited to non-U.S. persons and to prevent the "intentional acquisition" of U.S. domestic communications.[3] Section 702 also requires the use of minimization and querying procedures, specifically requiring that the government obtain a FISC order for any review of section 702 query results in criminal investigations unrelated to national security.[4]

In its November 2020 opinion, the FISC reported the FBI violated the querying standard following a Department of Justice (DOJ) audit of the government's compliance with section 702 querying safeguards.[5] The FISC determined that the FBI had misused its section 702 surveillance powers, finding that "the FBI's failure to properly apply its querying standard when searching

---

[1] Memorandum Opinion and Order, *Document re Section 702 Certification* (FISA Ct. Nov. 18, 2020); Ellen Nakashima, *Federal court approved FBI's continued use of warrantless surveillance power despite repeated violations of privacy rules*, WASH. POST (Apr. 26, 2021).
[2] 50 U.S.C § 1881(a)-(b).
[3] 50 U.S.C. § 1881(d).
[4] 50 U.S.C. § 1881(e)-(f)(2).
[5] Memorandum Opinion and Order at 38-43, *Document re Section 702 Certification* (FISA Ct. Nov. 18, 2020).

section 702-acquired information was more pervasive than was previously believed."[6] The FISC noted that an FBI official responsible for "limited background investigations" conducted over 120 queries of section 702-acquired data using the names and other identifiers of individuals who had requested to participate in the FBI's "Citizens Academy"—a community outreach program.[7] The FBI also queried the names and other identifiers of individuals who needed access to an FBI field office for office repairs, and others who sought to report tips or were victims of a crime.[8] Other violations involved FBI personnel who failed to opt out of querying raw FISA-acquired information for reasons that did not meet its intent, such as an FBI analyst who conducted more than 100 "queries for analytic paper."[9]

The FISC further documented that "the government has reported numerous incidents" regarding searches of section 702 FISA information without first obtaining court permission.[10] For example, the FISC noted the discovery of 40 queries in which the FBI accessed information for investigations involving "healthcare fraud, transnational organized crime, violent gangs, domestic terrorism involving racially motivated violent extremists, as well as investigations relating to public corruption and bribery," all of which were unrelated to foreign surveillance.[11] According to the FISC, "[n]one of these queries was related to national security, and they returned numerous Section 702-acquired products in response."[12] Judge James E. Boasberg, the chief judge of the FISC, concluded that "the Court is concerned about the apparent widespread violations."[13]

These concerns are particularly disturbing in light of prior FBI misconduct thoroughly detailed by the DOJ Office of Inspector General (OIG), suggesting a pattern of abuses and deficiencies in the FBI's FISA processes. In December 2019, the OIG issued a report finding the FBI had abused the FISA process to illegally surveil an American citizen associated with President Trump's campaign.[14] That report discovered 17 significant "errors or omissions" and 51 incorrect or unsupported factual assertions in the FBI's application to conduct warrantless surveillance.[15] Similarly, in March 2020, the OIG warned you of extensive noncompliance with Woods Procedures, which act as a safeguard and are designed to minimize factual inaccuracies in FISA applications by maintaining supporting documentation for each factual assertion in the application.[16] The OIG alerted you to unsupported, uncorroborated, or inconsistent information in the Woods Files of all 25 surveillance applications on U.S. Persons that the OIG examined.[17]

---

[6] *Id.* at 39.
[7] *Id.* at 39-40.
[8] *Id.* at 40.
[9] *Id.*
[10] *Id.* at 42.
[11] *Id.*
[12] *Id.*
[13] *Id.* at 44.
[14] Dep't of Justice Off. of Inspector Gen., Review of Four FISA Applications and Other Aspects of the FBI's Crossfire Hurricane Investigation (Dec. 2019).
[15] *Id.*
[16] Dep't of Justice Off. of Inspector Gen., Management Advisory Memorandum for Director of the Federal Bureau of Investigation Regarding the Execution of Woods Procedures for Applications Filed with the Foreign Intelligence Surveillance Court Relating to U.S. Persons (Mar. 2020).
[17] *Id.* at 6.

The recently released FISC opinion only raises more questions about the FBI's respect for the constitutional and statutory parameters of FISA. Given the seriousness of this matter for civil liberties, please provide the following information immediately:

1. Please explain why almost a year after the OIG's report about FISA abuses, the FISC found the FBI to still be abusing its warrantless surveillance authority under section 702.

2. Please provide a detailed accounting of every instance since December 2019 in which the FBI has queried, accessed, otherwise used information obtained pursuant to section 702 for purposes unrelated to national security.

3. Please explain what actions you have taken in the wake of the FISC's November 2020 memorandum opinion and order to prevent the FBI from using its section 702 authorities to surveil, investigate, or otherwise examine U.S. citizens.

Thank you for your prompt attention to this serious matter.

Sincerely,

Jim Jordan
Ranking Member

Andy Biggs
Ranking Member
Subcommittee on Crime, Terrorism, and Homeland Security

cc: The Honorable Jerrold Nadler, Chairman

The Honorable Sheila Jackson Lee, Chair, Subcommittee on Crime, Terrorism, and Homeland Security

JERROLD NADLER, New York
CHAIRMAN

JIM JORDAN, Ohio
RANKING MEMBER

ONE HUNDRED SEVENTEENTH CONGRESS

Congress of the United States

House of Representatives

COMMITTEE ON THE JUDICIARY

2138 RAYBURN HOUSE OFFICE BUILDING

WASHINGTON, DC 20515-6216

(202) 225-3951
judiciary.house.gov

April 27, 2021

The Honorable Merrick B. Garland
Attorney General
U.S. Department of Justice
950 Pennsylvania Avenue, NW
Washington, DC 20530

Dear Attorney General Garland:

On March 29, 2021, we requested information from you about how the Biden Administration plans to enforce federal law and protect federal property from violent left-wing extremists in Portland, Oregon. We requested that you provide this information by April 12. You have ignored this request.

Since our request, left-wing agitators have continued to vandalize and destroy federal property in Portland, Oregon. On April 11, 2021, rioters set fire to a U.S. Immigration and Customs Enforcement (ICE) building.[1] After the building was set on fire, federal agents and local police officers arrived and attempted to disperse the crowd.[2] On April 12, 2021, over two-hundred individuals gathered outside the Penumbra Kelly Building, which provides an office for the Multnomah County Sheriff and Portland police, and began throwing rocks, frozen water bottles, glass bottles, and fireworks at law-enforcement officers.[3] On April 16, rioters vandalized multiple businesses, museums and places of worship, including the First Christian Church.[4]

---

[1] Michael Lee, *Rioters set Portland ICE facility on fire as federal agents shoot barrage of pepper bullets in an attempt to disperse crowd*, WASH. EXAMINER (April 11, 2021), https://www.washingtonexaminer.com/news/rioters-portland-ice-fire-agents-pepper-bullets.

[2] *Id.*

[3] Associated Press, *Portland police declares riot after vigil for Duante Wright*, WASH. TIMES (Apr. 13, 2021), https://www.washingtontimes.com/news/2021/apr/13/portland-police-declares-riot-after-vigil-for-daun/.

[4] Shane Dixon Kavanaugh, *Portland church, park, historical society damaged in downtown riot: 'The destruction is pretty gnarly'*, THE OREGONIAN (Apr. 17, 2021), https://www.oregonlive.com/news/2021/04/portland-church-park-historical-society-damaged-in-downtown-riot-the-destruction-is-pretty-gnarly.html.

The Biden Administration must not condone continued left-wing violence against federal property in Portland. We reiterate the requests made in our March 29 letter and ask that you provide a full response immediately. Thank you for your attention to this matter.

Sincerely,

Jim Jordan
Ranking Member

cc: The Honorable Jerrold L. Nadler
Chairman

JERROLD NADLER, New York
CHAIRMAN

JIM JORDAN, Ohio
RANKING MEMBER

ONE HUNDRED SEVENTEENTH CONGRESS

Congress of the United States

House of Representatives

COMMITTEE ON THE JUDICIARY

2138 RAYBURN HOUSE OFFICE BUILDING

WASHINGTON, DC 20515–6216

(202) 225–3951
judiciary.house.gov

March 29, 2021

The Honorable Merrick B. Garland
Attorney General
U.S. Department of Justice
950 Pennsylvania Avenue, NW
Washington, DC 20530

Dear Attorney General Garland:

Anarchists and violent left-wing extremists continue to vandalize and destroy federal property in Portland, Oregon. Following riots that erupted in May 2020, Portland experienced over 100 consecutive nights of violence as anarchists attacked federal courthouses, small businesses, and even police precincts.[1] In August 2020, amid the chaos and civil unrest, Portland Mayor Ted Wheeler rejected the Trump Administration's offer to assist in bringing law and order back to the city.[2] Shortly thereafter, the Department of Justice (DOJ) designated Portland as a jurisdiction that has "permitted violence and destruction of property to persist" and one that has "refused to undertake reasonable measures to counteract criminal activities."[3] We write to request information about DOJ's recent efforts to prosecute crimes against federal property in Portland.

The vandalism and destruction of federal and private property that began last summer in Portland has not stopped. On March 10, 2021, the Department of Homeland Security (DHS) removed protective fencing around the Mark O. Hatfield United States Courthouse "as part of a broader effort to help the city return to normalcy."[4] However, on March 11, 2021, just hours after the fencing was removed, left-wing agitators attempted to force their way into the courthouse

---

[1] David Shipley, *What Happened to Portland?*, BLOOMBERG OPINION (Sep. 17, 2020), https://www.bloomberg.com/opinion/articles/2020-09-17/u-s-protests-stopped-in-portland-oregon-they-continued-why.

[2] Letter from Ted Wheeler, Mayor of Portland, to Donald J. Trump, former President of the United States (Aug. 28, 2020), https://www.portland.gov/sites/default/files/2020-08/8.28.20-letter-to-president-trump.pdf.

[3] Press Release, U.S. Dep't of Justice, Department of Justice Identifies New York City, Portland and Seattle As Jurisdictions Permitting Violence And Destruction of Property (Sep. 21, 2020), https://www.justice.gov/opa/pr/department-justice-identifies-new-york-city-portland-and-seattle-jurisdictions-permitting.

[4] Lucas Manfredi, *Portland courthouse turns back into fortress after riots spike again*, FOX NEWS (Mar. 15, 2021), https://www.foxnews.com/us/portland-courthouse-turns-back-into-fortress-after-violent-antifa-riots-spike-again.

and set fire to the building.[5] Some individuals also burned American flags, smashed windows of local businesses, and attempted to storm a local bank.[6]

Since last summer, several federal courthouses and government properties in Portland have been damaged or vandalized. In addition to the Mark O. Hatfield United States Courthouse, left-wing agitators have attacked the Edith Green-Wendall Wyatt Federal Building, the Gus J. Solomon U.S. Courthouse, the Pioneer Courthouse, and the U.S. Immigration and Customs Enforcement building.[7] Although repairs to these federal properties are ongoing, the current cost of repairs has reached at least $2.3 million.[8] This figure will inevitably rise as repairs continue.

The situation in Portland has been exacerbated by the recent budget cuts to the Portland Police Bureau. On June 17, 2020, amid the chaos and violence, the Portland City Council voted to approve $16 million in cuts to the Portland Police Bureau, which dissolved its Gun Violence Reduction Team, School Resource Officers, and the Transit Police Division.[9] Between May 29, 2020, and August 27, 2020, federal law enforcement officers arrested over 100 individuals in Portland for crimes including, arson, assault, and damaging federal government property.[10]

On February 24, 2021, the Subcommittee on Crime, Terrorism, and Homeland Security held a hearing at which journalist Andy Ngo testified that Antifa and left-wing anarchists in Portland have "developed a riot apparatus that included streams of funding for accommodation, travel, riot gear, and weapons, which resulted in a murder, hundreds of arson attacks, mass injuries, and mass property destruction."[11] Mr. Ngo stressed to the Congress the importance of not "downplaying antifa's violent extremism."[12] Former Attorney General William P. Barr testified last summer that the DOJ considered attacks on federal property in Portland to be "federal crimes under statutes enacted by this Congress."[13]

---

[5] Zachary Evans, *Rioters Set Fire to Federal Courthouse in Portland One Day after Fencing Removed*, NATIONAL REVIEW (Mar. 12, 2021), https://www.nationalreview.com/news/rioters-set-fire-to-federal-courthouse-in-portland-one-day-after-fencing-removed/.

[6] Andrew Mark Miller, *Antifa rioters burn US flags, storm courthouse, and clash with police in Portland, Oregon*, WASH. EXAMINER (Mar. 12, 2021), https://www.washingtonexaminer.com/news/antifa-burn-american-flags-storm-courthouse-portland.

[7] Noelle Crombie, *Price tag so far for protest-related damage to federal buildings in Portland: $2.3 million*, OREGON LIVE (Feb. 2, 2021), https://www.oregonlive.com/crime/2021/02/price-tag-so-far-for-protest-related-damage-to-federal-buildings-in-portland-23-million.html.

[8] *Id.*

[9] *Portland, Ore., cuts police budget by $16 million, dissolves programs*, OANN (Nov. 6, 2020), https://www.oann.com/portland-votes-against-18m-police-funding-cut/.

[10] Press Release, U.S. Dep't of Justice, 74 People Facing Federal Charges for Crimes Committed During Portland Demonstrations (Aug. 27, 2020), https://www.justice.gov/usao-or/pr/74-people-facing-federal-charges-crimes-committed-during-portland-demonstrations.

[11] *The Rise of Domestic Terrorism in America: Hearing Before the H. Subcomm. On Crime, Terrorism and Homeland Security of the H. Comm. On the Judiciary*, 117th Cong. (2021) (statement of Andy Ngo).

[12] *Id.*

[13] *Oversight of the Department of Justice Part II: Attorney General William P. Barr, Hearing Before the H. Comm. on the Judiciary*, 116th Cong. (2020) (statement of Attorney General William P. Barr).

The Biden Administration has a duty to ensure that the federal law is enforced and that individuals who seek to destroy and vandalize federal property in Portland are prosecuted to the fullest extent of the law. In light of Mr. Ngo's testimony to the Committee and to better understand the Department of Justice's efforts to enforce federal law and protect federal property in Portland, we respectfully request the following information:

1. Please explain the Justice Department's current efforts to identify and prosecute individuals who are attacking federal law enforcement and damaging and vandalizing federal property in Portland, Oregon.

2. Please explain how the Justice Department, in coordination with other relevant federal law enforcement agencies, is working to prevent individuals from damaging and vandalizing federal property in Portland, Oregon.

3. Please explain whether the Justice Department still believes Portland, Oregon, has "permitted violence and destruction of property to persist" and has "refused to undertake reasonable measures to counteract criminal activities."[14]

4. Please explain whether the Justice Department still believes that "peaceful protestors do not throw explosives into federal courthouses, tear down plywood with crowbars, or launch fecal matter at federal officers. Such acts are in fact federal crimes under statutes enacted by this Congress."[15]

Please provide this information as soon as possible, but no later than 5:00 p.m. on April 12, 2021. After you have provided this information in writing, we ask that you provide a staff-level briefing. This briefing may be conducted remotely for convenience and safety issues.

The House Committee on the Judiciary has jurisdiction pursuant to Rule X of the Rules of the House of Representatives to conduct oversight of matters concerning "subversive activities affecting the internal security of the United States" as well as "criminal law enforcement and criminalization." [16]

---

[14] Press Release, Dep't of Justice, Department of Justice Identifies New York City, Portland and Seattle As Jurisdictions Permitting Violence And Destruction of Property (Sep. 21, 2020), https://www.justice.gov/opa/pr/department-justice-identifies-new-york-city-portland-and-seattle-jurisdictions-permitting.

[15] *Oversight of the Department of Justice Part II: Attorney General William P. Barr, Hearing Before the H. Comm. on the Judiciary*, 116th Cong. (2020) (statement of Attorney General William P. Barr).

[16] Rules of the House of Representatives, R. X, 117th Cong. (2021).

To schedule the briefing or if you have any questions about this request, please ask your staff to contact Judiciary Committee staff at (202) 225-6906. Thank you for your prompt attention to this matter.

Sincerely,

Jim Jordan
Ranking Member

cc: The Honorable Jerrold L. Nadler
Chairman

www.ingramcontent.com/pod-product-compliance
Lightning Source LLC
LaVergne TN
LVHW081947200926
848484LV00009B/2521